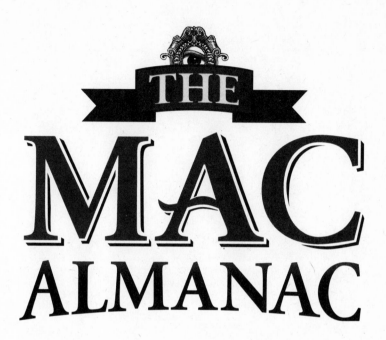

# THE MAC ALMANAC

# The Mac Almanac

## SHARON ZARDETTO AKER

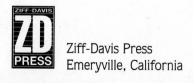

Ziff-Davis Press
Emeryville, California

| | |
|---|---|
| Copy Editor | Kayla Sussell |
| Technical Editor | Rich Wolfson |
| Technical Reviewer | Joe Holmes |
| Project Coordinator | Ami Knox |
| Proofreaders | Kayla Sussell and Ami Knox |
| Cover Illustration | "Eyeball" from Carol Aiton (Parallax Design) |
| Cover Design | Regan Honda |
| Book Design | Carol Aiton (Parallax Design) and Sharon Aker |
| Illustrations | Andy Baird, Carol Aiton, and Sharon Aker |
| Word Processing | Howard Blechman |
| Page Layout | Jerry Szubin, Rich Wolfson, and Sharon Aker |
| Indexer | Sharon Aker |

Ziff-Davis Press books are produced on a Macintosh computer system with the following applications: FrameMaker®, Microsoft® Word, QuarkXPress®, Adobe Illustrator®, Adobe Photoshop®, Adobe Streamline™, MacLink®Plus, Aldus® FreeHand™, Collage Plus™.

If you have comments or questions or would like to receive a free catalog, call or write:

Ziff-Davis Press
5903 Christie Avenue
Emeryville, CA 94608
1-800-688-0448

Illustrations/photographs on pages 230, 366, and 891 courtesy Apple Computer, reprinted with permission.

"Kitchen Metaphor" material in Chapter 2 reprinted with permission from *MacUser* magazine.

ISBN 1-56276-143-9

Manufactured in the United States of America
10 9 8 7 6 5 4 3 2

# Dedication

for

**Ilyse & Jonathan Blazar**

... whose Daddy will apparently do just about *anything* for another book dedication.

*with love from Auntie Sharon*

# PART ONE
## ✈ MAC SYSTEM BASICS ✈

# PART TWO
## ✦ MORE SYSTEM FEATURES ✦

# PART THREE
## ✦ FONTS & PRINTING ✦

# PART FOUR
## ⇥ HARDWARE ⇤

# PART FIVE
## ⇚ USING THE MAC ⇛

# ❧ REFERENCE & INDEX ❧

# Preface

**I always feel a little silly writing a preface** to a book. After all, what is there to say? The marketing people tell me that it's a way to grab potential buyers in the bookstore: I should synopsize the book so you don't have to thumb through it to see what it's like. But have you *ever* bought a how-to book without thumbing through it, even a little? So, take a look. Then come back and read the rest of this.

Okay, you're back. (Well, maybe you never left.) As you can see, there's quite a collection of information in here. Most of it is hands-on, try-this, do-it-this-way stuff to make working on the Mac even easier, or more understandable. Then there's the strictly fun stuff—some just for giggles, like the scattering of light bulb jokes ("How many software developers does it take to screw in a light bulb?"), and some just as points of interest (like how System and Finder version numbers used to be paired).

**All the information is organized** in quick-to-read entries so you don't have to wade through pages of prose to get to the point. Each entry starts with boldface type so you can quickly scan for the information you want within any topic heading. You don't even have to read the book in any particular order.

**You're using some version of System 7** by now, aren't you? That's what this book assumes. Whether it's 7.0.1, 7.1, or 7.5, we've got you covered. (And that's for standard Macs *or* the special Performa system software.)

**What you *won't* find in this book is** a collection of hints and tips for specific applications, no matter how popular they are; this book concentrates on the Mac itself, and the functions that are universal to all Mac systems. So, you'll find pointers on text entry and editing, and on character and paragraph formatting, but no tricks for Microsoft Word. You won't find a lot of product reviews, either. But third-party software isn't ignored; when it's time to recommend applications or utilities for specific purposes, I provide a list of possibilities and some recommendations without devoting pages to praise or insults of the products.

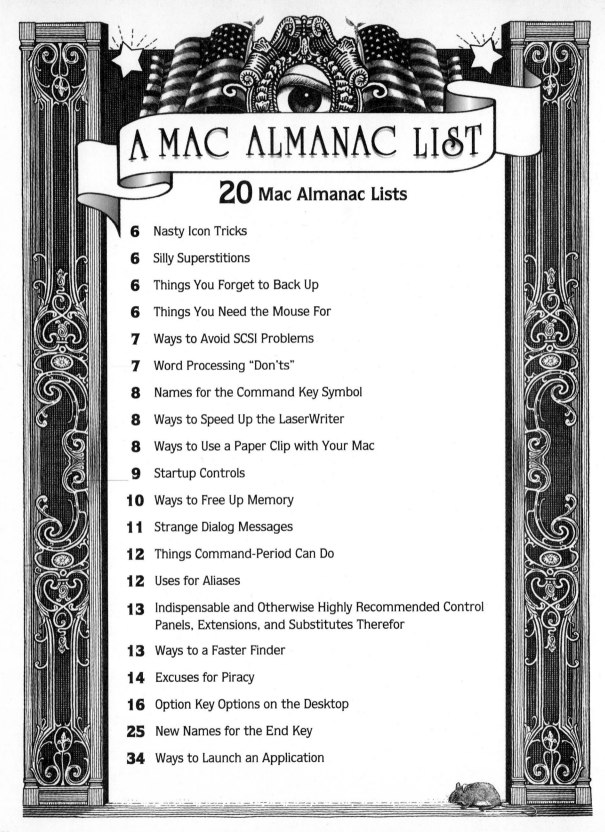

# A MAC ALMANAC LIST

## 20 Mac Almanac Lists

# ᐧ᙮᙮ᐨ **ACKNOWLEDGMENTS** ᐧ᙮᙮ᐨ

## Thanks to ...

**Cindy Hudson** for convincing me to once again do a large book after I had sworn I would never again do more than a 400-page project. And for letting me do it my way.

**Eric Stone** for taking over Cindy's thankless job (wait... didn't I just thank her?) towards the end of the project when she was promoted to President of Ziff-Davis Press.

**Joe Holmes,** whom I first met online and later in person, was an absolutely terrific tech reviewer. He's going to wake up one day and realize he's a terrific writer, too, and then we'll see if he stays in lawyerhood or not.

**The artists**—graphic and otherwise—who contributed to the book. My friend Carol Aiton did the book design, turning my ideas and "how abouts" into reality. Those nifty part-opener graphics are hers, as are the full-page graphics for Mac Almanac Lists and Charts—I think they should have been used on the cover of the book! My friend Andy Baird, whom I first met at the Princeton User Group, wrote the Mac People biographies and contributed artwork every time I yelled for help—usually at the last minute. Another good friend, Jerry Szubin, did the bulk of the layout; he practiced piano during the printouts and even vacuumed the pool a couple of times.

**Companies** who provided products and information made an overwhelming job a little easier. I'm especially grateful to Cliff Joyce at Dubl-Click for the use of his terrific WetPaint graphics and Paul McGraw at APS Technologies for lending me hardware to play with. And though not a "company," as such, BMUG's Tim Holmes was more than helpful, and the BMUG PD-ROM collection of shareware and freeware was invaluable.

**My family and friends**, many of whom pitched in any time they could, and all of whom accepted a year's worth of apologies (*Sorry, I can't, I'm busy*) with patience and grace. A special thanks to my sons, Nathaniel and Nicholas, for their patience and their help; Nick is older, but Nat's tired of seeing his name second all the time. They tested games, proofread copies, compiled statistics of laid-out chapters, and processed artwork through PhotoShop. Nat's friend, Joe Adelman, was also roped into working a few afternoons. I almost didn't let them leave for summer camp because the book wasn't finished! Claudia Wolfson worked on the printouts that I somewhat rudely but necessarily brought to her house on Father's Day, and she also spent a sunny weekend at my house immersed in PageMaker instead of out at the pool.

**Last but not least,** Rich Wolfson, for a layer of tech editing before the material even went to Joe Holmes, and for background research, and for lots of work on the layout. (Oh, and for that terrific diamond ring and romantic marriage proposal, too.)

# ❧ COLOPHON ❧

**Colophon?** That's a nifty word that means facts pertinent to the production of a book.

BENJAMIN DISRAELI

I hate definitions.

**All the writing** was done in that program that's either a boon or the bane for heavy-duty writing, Microsoft Word. The screen shots, originally captured with Capture, were polished up in SuperPaint. Illustrator, Freehand, and PhotoShop were all used for various other illustrations. Backups were tracked and made with PowerMerge. Online research and file transfers were done through CompuServe with CompuServe Navigator and CompuServe Information Manager ZMac edition, and on America Online and AppleLink.

**The layout** was done in QuarkXpress, against my better judgement but at the publisher's insistence. As a result, the index was done by using PageMaker, since Quark has no indexing function. Yes, there is an extension that does indexing, but for only one file at a time; it was helpfully suggested that I just cut and paste the individual chapter indexes together to make a book index. Right. We first exported the text as Word files, and imported them into PageMaker. But since Quark more often than not created Word files with garbage in the middle, we then exported each chapter as text files for PageMaker. Then, we manually inserted page breaks in the PageMaker files at appropriate spots to make the page numbers match the Quark layout. Of course, we had to export the PageMaker index to lay out in Quark … there, that's off my chest.

**Behind it all, Tempo macros** were taking the drudgery out of many operations, including some frustrating lacks of command keys in Quark. (There I go again …)

**The main fonts** in this book are the Goudy family for the body text and the Quorum family for tables and anecdotal material. The font used for the "see also" notes in the margin is actually still Quorum, stretched and otherwise manipulated in Quark; headings, headers, and footers are also Quorum. The rest of the fonts are freeware and shareware fonts: Caraway Bold, by Peter Jensen, is in the quote balloons; Shelldon, whose author's AOL address is NSIS, is the fancy one used in the part openers and chapter title pages; Garton, by David Rakowski, is used in the little memos in the page margins; Ornaments, by Nigel Yeoh, decorate section titles, headers and footers, and the ends of chapters. The nifty little arrows used in front of all the entries come from a special font that we made up; we called it, of course, the Almanac font.

°°➜ **The "real" information in this book is** a mixture of straight-out facts ("The zoom box toggles a window's size …") and hints and tips ("To make a Finder window scroll diagonally …"). They're organized in quick-to-read entries that start with boldface type so you can quickly scan for the information you want within any topic heading. And, they're prefaced by one of three arrows ( °➜ °°➜ °°°➜ ) to indicate the level of importance or complexity. (See those little dots in the arrow's shaft? One dot is first-level, two is second-level … )

°°⟜ **A hollow arrow like this one** indicates the entry is about a product rather than being a point of information or a trick or shortcut. The best products get awards: Very good ones get the Mac Almanac Seal of Approval, while outstanding ones get the Mac Almanac Blue Ribbon Award for Excellence. Both were awarded sparingly, so you can be sure a product deserves special recognition if you see either award.

When a product is mentioned in an entry, its publisher is noted in brackets at the end of the entry. You won't find a list of products at the end of the book, but you will find a vendor listing. If the software is shareware or freeware, that's noted, too. (That reminds me: Sometimes you'll see the notation *free from ZMac* and then the author's name as the credit for some piece of freeware. That means that it originated on the ZMac online service and while it can be freely distributed among Mac users and through users groups, you won't find it on any other online service, as you would for almost any other piece of freeware or shareware.)

°°➜ **When it comes to identifying keys on the keyboard,** I avoided sticking key symbols in the text because, as a reader, I find this disrupts the flow of the words. I do use key symbols in charts, although I opted for the easy-to-read [SHIFT] and [OPT] instead of the Mac's conventions of ⇧ and ⌥ for those key symbols. But when it comes to the arrow, or cursor, keys, I often use only the direction of the arrow as the name of the key ("press Command-Shift-Up"), despite some editors' questioning of the practice as hard to interpret. What else could Up be?

°°°➜ **There are lots of Lists** in the book: some helpful, some just for fun, and at least one—6 Nasty Icon Tricks—that could go either way. But in addition, there are several Charts (like those Zapf Dingbat symbols, and Desktop Keyboard Shortcuts) that are meant to be ripped out of the book and tacked up on the wall near your computer. (Or, for neatniks, carefully cut out, laminated, and mounted in an appropriate spot with decorative hardware.) But of course you won't want to rip a page out of the middle of a book, taking the information that's on the back of the Chart with it. So, each Chart is repeated at the end of the book, with nothing printed on its back, so you can remove it if you want to, without ruining the book.

°°°➜ **You'll find Pop Quiz answers** at the back of the book. Sort of.

# Mac System Basics

# CHAPTER 1
# THE BASICS

> To err is human but to really foul things up requires a computer.

Just some of the burning questions answered in this chapter:

- ➤ What is the Mac smiling about at startup? And how can you replace that polite but boring "Welcome" message?

- ➤ How do you turn on your Mac if it has umpteen external devices and some of those are partitioned into multiple startup volumes? (And just what *is* a "volume"?)

- ➤ Why are there so many "extra" keys on the keyboard?

- ➤ Is there really any difference between a pointer and a cursor?

- ➤ What in the world does 11001001 stand for, and why?

- ➤ What's the difference between a terabyte and a trilobite?

- ➤ How do quotations from Robert Frost and Snidely Whiplash fit in this chapter?

**BET YOU DIDN'T KNOW THAT...**

*The Mac didn't always have a Shut Down command.*

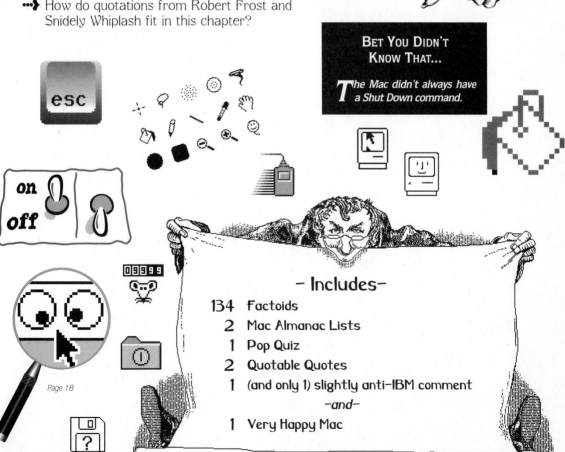

Page 18

## – Includes–

| | |
|---|---|
| 134 | Factoids |
| 2 | Mac Almanac Lists |
| 1 | Pop Quiz |
| 2 | Quotable Quotes |
| 1 | (and only 1) slightly anti-IBM comment |
| | –and– |
| 1 | Very Happy Mac |

# →I· STARTING UP & SHUTTING DOWN ·I←

## Turning On the Mac

∞•❯ **There's not much to turning on your Mac.** Depending on the model, you use either the switch on the back of the machine or the startup key on the keyboard. If you're using a modular Mac, you might have to turn the monitor on separately—again, it depends on the model.

∞•❯ **The Mac looks for a *startup disk*** when it's turned on—a disk with a System and Finder on it. If you want to be picky, any disk with a System and Finder on it is a *system disk;* if it's used to start the Mac, then it's called the *startup disk.* Your startup disk is almost always an internal hard drive. If there's no startup disk available, the Mac screen displays a disk icon with a blinking question mark in it—the visual equivalent of *So, where is it?*

∞•❯ **When the Mac finds a startup disk,** evidently it's quite pleased with itself, because it smiles and you'll see the Happy Mac icon, followed by the Welcome to Macintosh dialog.

 **A VERY HAPPY MAC (AND FRIEND)**

art: BMUG PD-ROM

∞•❯ **The icon parade at the bottom of the screen** during the startup procedure (after the Welcome dialog but before you see the desktop) shows which *inits* are being loaded into memory. (Inits are programs that load into memory at startup.) Most inits are extensions, but some are actually components of control panels; Chapter 8 discusses inits, extensions, and control panels.

∞•❯ **You can start your system from a floppy** even when there's an internal hard drive. This is a good thing, because sometimes the hard drive refuses to act as the startup (for instance, when some system files have been corrupted) and you have to get the Mac going somehow. On the other hand, it's not very easy to squeeze a system onto a floppy in the first place, but that's what minimal system installation is all about. Chapter 23 discusses this in detail.

## Turning On External Devices

◦•▸ **If you have an external hard drive,** turn it on before you turn on the Mac. Or, turn them on at the same time if they're both plugged into a power strip. The point is that the hard drive has to be on and spinning up to speed before the Mac looks around to see what's attached. If the Mac looks for the drive and it's not ready, the Mac won't know it's there. If the external drive is the startup, then the Mac won't start up; if the external drive is for extra storage, the Mac usually starts up anyway, but the drive won't appear on the desktop.

The timing isn't very tight. A hard drive may take as long as a full minute to get up to speed, but the Mac goes through its hardware check, which can take almost that long, and then politely waits for as much as half a minute before checking for the hard drive. I turn on all of my equipment—which includes two (and sometimes three) hard drives—at the same time, but in the time it takes the Mac to check out both itself and its 20 megs of RAM, the drives are up to speed.

✳ Well, that's what they had when I first wrote that sentence. Before this book was finished, they owned my IIci.

On the other hand, a slow hard drive and a Mac with a short hardware check can't be turned on at the same time. My kids have an LC II with 6 megs of memory that boots up faster than the old external hard drive that's attached to it, so they have to turn on the drive first, wait about 30 seconds, and then turn on the computer.✳

•••▸ **When an external hard drive doesn't "mount"**—that is, show up on the desktop— because it wasn't ready when the Mac looked for it, restarting the system will mount the hard drive. But you can also force the drive to show up on the desktop without restarting by using a special utility program like SCSI Probe. Chapter 18 covers this in detail.

As long as I mentioned "mount," I might as well mention its companion, *volume*, which is any disk, or anything that acts like a disk, on your desktop: a floppy disk, a hard drive, a CD-ROM disc, and so on.

•••▸ **You can turn on the monitor at any time**—before, during, or after the Mac's startup procedure. The Mac sends the information to the monitor and doesn't know or care whether it's on or off. For a lot of setups, this isn't an issue: In a compact Mac, the screen goes on automatically, and in many modular systems the monitor is powered on at the same time as the Mac itself.

•••▸ **Use a power strip** for convenience if you have several things to turn on. Leave the peripherals' switches on and use the power strip to turn everything else on and off at once.

I use two power strips together and I leave the first one on all the time. The Mac is plugged into it, and the 13-inch color monitor, which is plugged into the CPU, also gets its power from there. The computer is turned on from the keyboard and shut down from the Finder, and the monitor is controlled by the computer, so there's no need to turn them on and off from the power strip. I also keep a PowerBook AC adapter and a modem plugged into this strip. (Sometimes I leave the PowerBook charging overnight right next to the desk machine, so it needs a live power source even when the desk computer's shut down.) I keep the modem on that strip not because I want it on all the time, but because there's no room for it on the second strip and it doesn't hurt to leave it on. The PowerBook and modem adapters each cover two outlets on the strip, so that fills it—except for the sixth outlet, which the second strip is plugged into.

The second strip is command central for my peripherals: two external hard drives, a CD-ROM drive, a LaserWriter, and a two-page monitor. There's still one outlet left … I'll have to go shopping soon.

When I start up my system, I turn the peripheral power strip on and then press the startup key on the keyboard. By the time the Mac's fully awake and looking for external devices, the hard drives are spinning up to speed and the whole system's online.

Using two power strips for a large system.

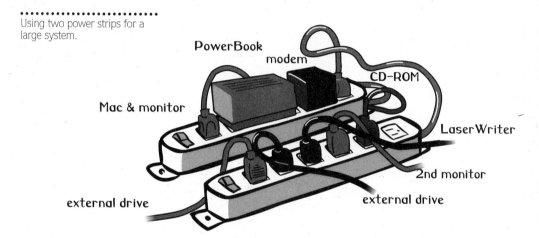

## Startup Procedures

●•❯ **Use the Startup Items folder** inside the System Folder if you want anything automatically opened at startup. For instance, if you always do word processing, you could put an alias of your word processor program in the folder. Documents can also go in the Startup Items folder, for example, a "To Do" list, or a desk accessory that you always use.

●•❯ **To prevent extensions from loading** during startup, hold down the Shift key.

●•❯ *Booting* or *booting up* is just another term for starting the computer. (*Rebooting*, logically enough, is restarting it.) The term comes from the phrase "Lifting yourself by your own bootstraps," which means to manage something on your own. Early computers used a series of "loader programs" to actually get going, because nothing at all was built in; you'd load one program that knew nothing except how to load the next one; that one would only be able to do some basics on the operating-system level and load the next program, and so on. (And, often the loading was done by feeding a punched paper tape into a reader.) This was referred to as *bootstrapping*, soon shortened to *booting*.

S ee Chapter 6 for more about the Startup Items folder.

There's another, lesser-known, meaning for the term *to boot*: giving the Mac a good swift kick when it's not behaving.

Don't forget, there are answers in the back of the book!

**POP QUIZ**                                              **[2 POINTS]**

So, what's a bootstrap?

**There's more to the startup procedure than meets the eye.** Once you wake up the Mac with a zap of electricity, the CPU (*central processing unit*) looks for its instructions. It finds them in a specific spot in ROM (*read-only memory*) which, not coincidentally, is the only place it looks. What it finds is a set of self-diagnostic procedures to run on its hardware to make sure that everything's okay—sort of like checking yourself in the mirror just before you leave for work. If everything checks out, the CPU searches for a startup disk. When it finds a startup, it reads through part of the System file and loads some of it into RAM (*random-access memory*). Interestingly enough, the first information the CPU puts into RAM is the part of the System that controls the CPU, thus putting itself out of business as the one in charge—at least until the next startup.*

> *Now, don't you think that's enough detail? You don't really want to know about things like initializing key memory variables and the Slot, SCSI, Sound, and Disk Managers, do you?

**The more memory you have,** the longer it takes to get to your desktop because part of the startup procedure includes checking out the installed memory. You probably won't notice this unless you upgrade your memory and, all of a sudden, the Welcome dialog takes longer to show up.

**If your desktop is taking longer** to show up than it used to, rebuilding the Desktop file might speed things up. To do this, hold down the Command and Option keys when you start the computer, until you get a dialog asking if you want rebuild the desktop. There's more about the Desktop file in Chapters 5, 17, and 18.

**What's the opposite of the Happy Mac?** A Sad Mac, and if something's terribly wrong during the startup process, that's what you'll see, on a black screen. It's accompanied by some ominous sounds, too, affectionately known as the *chimes of doom*. If you ever hear them, you'll understand why. The Sad Mac and the chimes of doom are covered in more detail in Chapter 24.

## HOW THE STARTUP PROCEDURE REALLY WORKS

Andy Baird

## Multiple Startup Devices

∞➔ **If you have more than one drive** connected to your Mac—an internal and an external hard drive, for instance—it's easy to tell which one is the startup. The startup disk always appears in the top-right corner of the screen.

The startup drive always appears on top.

∞➔ **If you have more than one startup disk** (a disk with a System Folder on it) attached to your Mac, you can specify which one will act as the startup by using the Startup Disk control panel.

•••➔ **If you want the internal hard drive ignored** at startup, hold down Command-Option-Shift-Delete when you start the Mac, releasing the keys as soon as you see the flashing question mark icon during the startup procedure. This works most of the time—and it assumes, of course, that there's another drive connected that has a System on it that the Mac can use. The internal drive won't show up on the desktop at all.

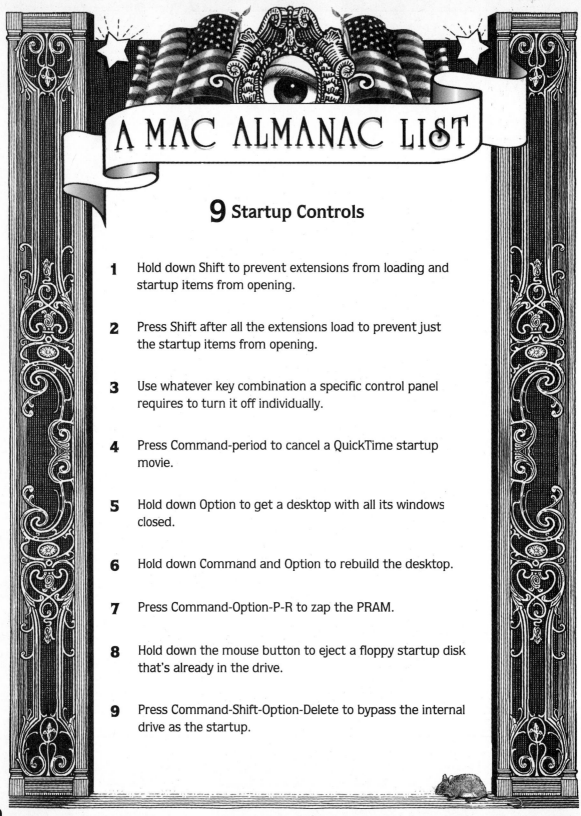

# A MAC ALMANAC LIST

## 9 Startup Controls

**1** Hold down Shift to prevent extensions from loading and startup items from opening.

**2** Press Shift after all the extensions load to prevent just the startup items from opening.

**3** Use whatever key combination a specific control panel requires to turn it off individually.

**4** Press Command-period to cancel a QuickTime startup movie.

**5** Hold down Option to get a desktop with all its windows closed.

**6** Hold down Command and Option to rebuild the desktop.

**7** Press Command-Option-P-R to zap the PRAM.

**8** Hold down the mouse button to eject a floppy startup disk that's already in the drive.

**9** Press Command-Shift-Option-Delete to bypass the internal drive as the startup.

••➤ **The Mac looks all over the place** for a startup disk when you turn it on. But it looks in the following very specific order:

1. Internal floppy drive
2. Second internal floppy drive
3. External floppy drive
4. Device identified in Startup Disk control panel
5. Internal hard drive
6. External SCSI devices, starting with the one with the highest ID number

If the Mac doesn't find a startup disk, it checks the internal hard drive once more, and then the internal floppy drive again. (Persistent little devil!) At that point, if it doesn't find a System Folder, it gives up, and you'll get a blinking question mark on a disk icon on the screen.

••➤ **The Startup Disk control panel doesn't work** on a Mac Plus. If you have two drives attached to a Plus, and they both have System Folders on them, you can control which is the startup by adjusting their SCSI ID numbers.

••➤ **If more than one partition** on a hard drive has a System on it, the Startup Disk control panel isn't much help. You'll see each partition as a separate drive in the control panel, and you can even select the partition you want, but it won't make any difference. When you select something in the Startup Disk control panel, the only thing that's really noted is the SCSI ID number of the hard drive, and that applies to the entire drive, not to any particular partition.

When a partitioned drive is set as the startup, the Mac looks through the partitions in alphabetical order. The first partition found with a System Folder becomes the startup disk.

There's more about multiple drives and systems in Chapter 23.

Using a CD-ROM as a startup is covered in Chapter 18.

## Startup Screens

••➤ **You see the *startup screen*** right after the Happy Mac icon. Usually, the startup screen is the Welcome to Macintosh* dialog, but you can make the Mac display almost any picture at startup. (Note that this is only a screen you see instead of the Welcome dialog, and it disappears immediately—it's not the same as a background picture for the desktop.)

Before defaulting to the Welcome dialog, the Mac looks in its System Folder for a file named *StartupScreen*. The file must be named exactly that: *StartupScreen*, with no space between the words, although the capitalization doesn't matter. It also has to be a PICT file—that's a basic graphics format that almost any Mac graphics program can produce. In fact, some graphics programs have an option that automatically creates a startup screen for you with just the right name.

So, all you have to do is get or create a PICT document, name it correctly, and put it in the System Folder. The next time you start up the Mac, you'll see the special picture instead of the Welcome dialog.

*When System 7 was in beta testing, the Mac used a special startup screen with a Welcome dialog that said: "Welcome to System 7. You're gonna love it." And I did.

The first custom startup screen I ever saw was done with two simple tools in MacPaint, the paint program that came bundled with the Macintosh. It used a filled rectangle with a brick pattern and the Spray Can to simulate graffiti painting, and it looked something like the picture here:

We're a lot more sophisticated now. (Aren't we?) Today, startup screens can be in full color, so you could go with red or brown brick.

▸ **If the startup screen picture is bigger** than the screen, it's displayed starting at the upper-left corner. It can be black and white or color, though, of course, you need a color monitor to see the color picture. This is the one used on the machines in the Mac Lab at Montclair State University, where I get to play with all the equipment in exchange for occasionally teaching there.

▸ **If you're not especially artistic,** or don't have a graphics program, startup screens are available online and through user groups.

▸ **Use a moving picture instead!** A QuickTime movie can serve as your startup screen as long as you:

QuickTime is covered in Chapter 21.

- Name it *Startup Movie*. Capitals and lowercase don't matter, but you do need to spell it correctly and leave the space between the words.
- Put it in the System Folder.
- Make sure Apple's QuickTime extension is in the Extensions folder.

If you don't want to watch the whole movie, press Command-period to stop it.

## Restarting the Mac

▸ **Restarting the computer** is not the same as shutting it down and then turning it on again. A restart is a separate procedure that uses the Restart command in the Special menu. Why would you want to do this? Well, many times you set a control panel to do something, or you install a new utility, but the settings register only during the startup sequence, when they're read into memory. So, you pick your options and then restart the computer to make them work.

⊶➤ **Restarting is also** sometimes referred to as a *reboot*, or any of several phrases containing the word "warm," implying that the machine's still warm from being used: *warm start, warm restart, warm boot, warm reboot.*

ROBERT FROST
*BIRCHES*

I'd like to get away ... and then come back to it and begin over.

## Shutting Down the Mac

⊶➤ **You can leave the Mac on** for long periods of time, even if you're gone for hours at a time. It doesn't use all that much electricity, and the general consensus of professional opinion is that leaving it on is less stressful to the components than turning it on and off several times a day.

I used to leave my Mac on for days at a time as long as I was using it every day. But that was back when I had a compact Mac and a single hard drive. Now my system gets powered up early in the morning and shut down late at night even if I'm gone for several hours in the middle of the day. This seems a reasonable compromise between stressing the components with too many on-off cycles and the waste of 12 hours of electricity for powering an average of eight components. My kids' Mac also gets shut off only at the end of the day rather than at the end of an activity.

*See Chapter 15 for details about leaving your monitor on for long periods of time.*

⊶➤ **Never shut off the computer without using the Shut Down** command in the Finder's Special menu.* The Mac does some important housekeeping before it shuts down. For one thing, it checks whether there are any unsaved documents and asks if you want to save them. That's pretty obvious, but don't think you can just save your documents and switch off the machine and be safe. There are things that you *think* you've done, because *you've* done them—but the Mac hasn't.

To speed things up on the interface front, there's stuff that looks to you as if it's done, but the Mac has merely stored the change in its memory so it can be done at a later, more convenient, time. This is like my son who is always so agreeable when I say "Take out the garbage" or "Clean your room." He says "Okay," makes some half-hearted attempts to get started, does part of the job, then wanders off into the sunset. The work gets done only when there's a firm deadline—like before the television goes on. If you shut off the computer without any warning, the Mac never transfers the information from memory to the disk. As a result, you may find, for instance, that the window you opened and reorganized is closed and still disorganized when you start the Mac again, or, worse, that the document you thought you saved wasn't completely written to the disk.

*The original Mac didn't have a Shut Down command! You just turned it off after saving your work, quitting a program, and returning to the Finder.*

⟶ **When you use the Shut Down command,** the Mac does its housekeeping and then shuts down. Some Mac models actually turn themselves off; others need to be turned off manually. You'll know when the Mac is ready to be switched off, because you'll get the shutdown dialog, which in System 7 was reworded to avoid previous grammatical errors.

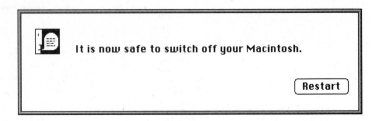

It is now safe to switch off your Macintosh.

Restart

There's another way to shut down the Mac in System 7.5. See the end of this chapter.

⟶ **Another reason that the Shut Down command** is so important is that some software and/or extensions run special routines at shutdown. If they don't know the computer is being shut down, they can't run. A shutdown routine might be as simple as one that empties the Trash, but it could be as important as one that takes care of disk security, file recovery, or backup information.

⟶ **Shutting down a PowerBook** can be an entirely different procedure because so often you don't shut it down—you just put it to sleep. See Chapter 22 for the details.

⟶ **The startup key on the keyboard shuts down** some models, like the Color Classic. If you press that key while the computer's running, you get a dialog asking if you really want to shut down the computer.

⟶ **A *soft shutdown*** is one where the Mac gets to do its housekeeping, and you're asked if you want to save your work if there are any unsaved documents hanging around. That's the kind you want. A *hard shutdown* is one where you just shut off the computer. That's the kind you don't want. These terms haven't been in general usage in the Mac world, but you'll be seeing them more often since we need the terminology because of the way the newer Macs behave. On a PowerBook 170, for instance, hitting the power button while the computer is on turns it off—with *no* warning. On a 180, when you hit the power button, you get the shutdown dialog, just as if you had used the Shut Down command in the Finder's Special menu. The words "hard" and "soft" come in handy to differentiate between the two situations.

## ⟶ USING THE MOUSE ⟵

### Mouse Moves

⟶ **There are five basic mouse moves.** *Pointing* means moving the cursor so it's touching something specific on the screen. *Clicking* is a press of the mouse button with an immediate release, while *pressing* means holding the mouse button down for a while. *Double-clicking* is clicking twice in a row—fast enough for the Mac to know you're double-clicking and not merely doing two single clicks. Finally, *dragging* is moving the mouse while the mouse button is down. (The expression doesn't refer to the fact that you're dragging the mouse around, but to the fact that usually you're dragging something around on the screen.)

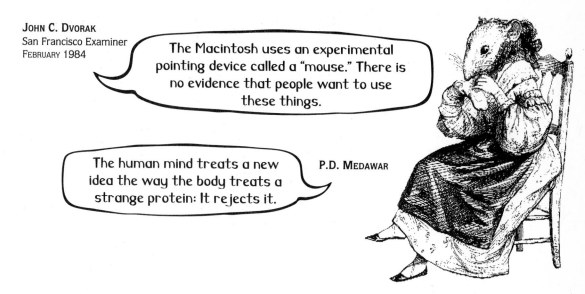

JOHN C. DVORAK
San Francisco Examiner
FEBRUARY 1984

The Macintosh uses an experimental pointing device called a "mouse." There is no evidence that people want to use these things.

The human mind treats a new idea the way the body treats a strange protein: It rejects it.

P.D. MEDAWAR

∞➔ **When the mouse reaches the edge** of its allotted space on your desk or mousepad, lift it, move it back to the center or opposite edge of the clear space, put it down, and continue rolling. The mouse cursor on the screen isn't going to move while the mouse is airborne, because it's the rolling ball on the bottom of the mouse that registers the motion.

This is so incredibly basic that it almost sounds silly when you read it (it sounded a little silly as I wrote it), but I've seen lots of beginners bewildered when they reach the edge of the rolling area. You don't have to be inept to feel awkward with a new piece of equipment, and though mouse use comes naturally after very little experience with it, in the beginning it can feel awkward.*

\* There are at least two people, though, who will probably never get the hang of it. One is a high school student who was working part time for a friend of mine and even after a week of Mac use tended to use two hands for the mouse: one to roll it around and one for clicking the mouse button. The other was a young man attending a course taught by my sister. After some basic instruction, she said "Okay, now point to the File menu with the mouse." He picked up the mouse and pointed to the File menu.

∞➔ **A double-click almost always "opens" something:** a folder on the desktop, or a file in a list. Usually, the double-click substitutes for a single click that selects something followed by an Open command from a menu or a button. The major exception to this is double-clicking on text, which selects a word.

Control panels are covered in Chapter 8.

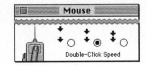

∘•➤ **What's the difference between a double-click** and two single clicks? It's a matter of speed. But *you* get to determine just how long the interval should be for two clicks to register as separate clicks instead of one double-click by using the Mouse control panel. You get three choices: slow, medium, and fast. The mouse button in the picture flashes twice when you make a choice so that you can see the speed.

∘•➤ **You can change the mouse tracking speed** in the Mouse control panel, too. So, if you're working on a big screen, you can make the mouse cursor move further in response to a roll of the mouse than if you're working on a standard or small screen.

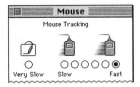

See Chapter 8 for more about the Mouse control panel and replacements for it.

If you select the *Very Slow* setting in the Mouse control panel, there's no difference between the mouse and the cursor "mileage" no matter what your speed: If you move the mouse two inches, the cursor moves two inches.

At any other setting, the cursor distance still matches the mouse distance when you're moving the mouse slowly. But if you move it more quickly while the tracking is set at one of the Slow buttons, the cursor travels about twice as far on the screen as the mouse moves on your desk. With the tracking set to one of the Fast buttons, the cursor can move up to five times the distance the mouse moves.

## Mouse Cursors

∘•➤ **That shape on the screen** that moves around when you move the mouse is referred to as the *pointer* in AppleSpeak (that's the language they use in the manual), and purists insist on calling it that no matter what. But when was the last time you pointed with your wristwatch?

That little moving shape is also called the *mouse cursor* (to differentiate it from a *blinking cursor*, which is usually called the *insertion point*, that marks your place while you're typing); I usually refer to it as simply the *cursor*. Unless, of course, it's an arrow, in which case I call it the *arrow*, or, sometimes, even, the *pointer*.

∘•➤ **The cursor changes shape** depending on what you're doing. There are four *system cursors* (the ones built into the Mac system), three of which you see all the time. The *arrow* shows up when you're using menus or manipulating windows or other objects on the screen. When the cursor is over editable text, it turns into the *text cursor*, or *I-beam*. The wristwatch appears when the Mac is busy doing something and you have to wait your turn. You don't see the fourth one quite as often unless you do a lot of work with spreadsheets: the *cross*.

### THE WAY WE WERE ...

The original Macs were so slow, especially at accessing disks (this was before they had hard drives!) that cynics often changed their wristwatch cursors to something more appropriate, like an hourglass.

**There are all sorts of cursors** used by different programs to show the options available at any given time. Art programs provide the widest variety of cursors, but spreadsheets and word processors aren't far behind any more. Here, for instance, are some basic paint program cursors:

**Each mouse cursor has a *hot spot*.** That's the one spot on the cursor, only one pixel in size, that really counts when you click on something. It's the tip of the arrow, for instance, that counts for the arrow cursor. The entire arrow doesn't have to be inside the object you're selecting; on the other hand, if everything except the tip is inside the object, it won't work at all.

Some enlarged cursors with their hot spots marked in black.

The tip of the arrow "counts" and has to be touching the disk icon if you want to select it.

**Sometimes you'll see the hands** on the wristwatch cursor spinning around. This tells you that the Mac is still working on a really time-consuming task; it hasn't frozen up and refused to work anymore. When you see this cursor, you're really looking at a series of cursors being displayed, one after the other. Any animated cursor (the "beachball" is another standard one) is actually a sequence of cursors—sort of like flip-book animation where you scribble something slightly different on each page and then flip the pages to animate the drawings. Here are some examples of the components used for cursor animation:

SNIDELY WHIPLASH

Cursors! Foiled again!

∞⟩ **There's no built-in way to change your cursors,** but there are lots of utilities around that let you do all sorts of things with them. For instance:

- When you can't keep an eye on your cursor, let Eyeballs do it for you. This little extension puts a set of eyes in the menu bar that follow the cursor around on the screen. When you put the cursor between them, the eyes cross (of course). [freeware, Ben Haller]

- Put some life into your arrow cursor with TailDragger, which simply makes the pointer wriggle around on the screen a bit. Several similes come to mind—one of them from a junior high film on human reproduction—but you get the right idea from the program's icon. [freeware, Dan Venola]

TailDragger

- They say a typist's fingers travel miles when all the little motions are added up. How far do you suppose your mouse travels even it's confined to its pad?* If your inquiring mind wants to know, Mouse Odometer can add it all up for you— even adjusting the mileage based on your screen resolution. [shareware, Sean P. Nolan]

Mouse Odometer

> *Apple engineers estimate that a mouse travels 25 to 30 miles in 5 years of use!

- When the cursor goes off the edge of the screen, it magically comes back at the opposite side if you use CursorWrap. [shareware, Paul Musselman]

CursorWrap

- PowerBook cursors tend to disappear when they're moving on passive-matrix displays, so most PowerBook utility packages include special cursors and a "cursor finder." There's more about this in Chapter 22.

- Bored with black-and-white cursors? There are two utilities (so far) that let you replace the basic system cursors with more interesting counterparts that are both colored and animated. How about a steaming, spinning coffee cup instead of the watch? Or, has it occurred to you how many different pointers you can use in place of the plain arrow: an arrow that shimmers through the colors of the rainbow, or a pulsing red wedge? And, if you don't like any of the cursors supplied with the package, each also has a cursor editor that lets you design your own.

  ClickChange provides more built-in choices and also provides a "find the cursor" function for PowerBooks and large screens. FunCursors lets you assign different cursors when the mouse button is up and when it's down. Either package gives you plenty to play with. Generally, I don't add little things like this to my system, but I have to admit that an ever-changing variety of replacements for that *!#@* wristwatch is nice. [ClickChange, DublClick Software; FunCursors-Now Fun!, Now Software]

The ClickChange cursor control module.

The FunCursors module from Now Fun!

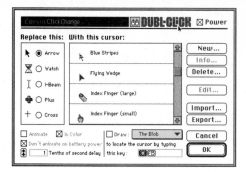

## ⇥ USING THE KEYBOARD ⇤

### The Basic Keyboard

∞•❥ **A computer is more than just an electronic typewriter,** and that's immediately apparent when you look at its keyboard. There are several different keyboards available for the Mac (see Chapter 14) but here's the layout of the largest—the *extended* keyboard—with the non-typewriter keys in darker gray:

∞•❥ **The Startup key** turns on some Macs, but on some models it's totally useless because you have to turn on the Mac with the switch at its back.

∞•❥ **The Delete key** moves the blinking text cursor backward one character at a time, erasing letters as it goes. It also erases selected text and graphics in a document. On older keyboards it was labeled "Backspace" (a carryover from typewriters), but *delete* describes its function much better.

∞•❥ **The arrow keys** move the text *insertion point*—the blinking vertical line that marks your place in text—left, right, up, and down. The keys are also called *cursor keys*

because they move that blinking cursor around. In some graphics programs, you can move a selection one pixel at a time on the screen (that's usually called *nudging*) with the arrow keys.

Arrow keys are in different locations on different keyboards. The most common, and most convenient (which is probably not a coincidence), is the inverted T.

● ● ● ● ● ● ● ● ● ● ● ● ● ● ● ● ● ● ● ● ● ● ● ● ● ● ● ● ● ● ● ● ● ● ● ● ● ● ●

### THE WAY WE WERE ...

The first two Macs (the 128K and 512K models) had no arrow keys on their keyboards because Steve Jobs was fanatically adamant that the mouse was what you should use to move and select things on the screen. When the Mac Plus was introduced in 1986, it had arrow keys on the keyboard—much to the relief of those of us who wanted to be able to move a blinking cursor just one letter or one line in text without having to reach for the mouse.

In retrospect, Job's initial insistence on mouse-only procedures was a blessing, because it forced programmers and designers to incorporate its use into their software. After all, it's much easier to drag across some spreadsheet cells instead of typing A12:G22; and, although the arrow keys are great for little movements, there's nothing like a mouse to make some sweeping changes in a word processor document. By the time arrow keys became available for Mac programs, the use of the mouse was imprinted in our psyches. Today most programs let you do almost everything with either the mouse or the keyboard, so now we have the best of both worlds.

●→ **The Caps Lock key,** for the most part, functions like its typewriter counterpart: It substitutes for holding down the Shift key. On desktop keyboards the key physically locks down, and on extended keyboards the Caps Lock light comes on.

On a typewriter, the key actually is a *shift* lock: It mechanically locks down the Shift key so you always get whatever you would get if you were holding the Shift key down— the "upper" character on the key. Your computer keyboard, though, has a *Caps* lock—it locks down just for capital letters. If you type a number key with Caps Lock down, you still get the number, not the character above it; typing a period or comma still gets you those punctuation symbols, not the < or > symbols.

●→ **A PowerBook has a Caps Lock key,** but it's "software-controlled"; that is, it doesn't physically lock down, but toggles a Caps Lock "mode" when you press it. There's a little symbol that appears in the menu bar when Caps Lock is active.

●→ *Modifiers* **are keys** that don't do anything by themselves, but are used in conjunction with another key. There are four modifier keys (although early keyboards had only three).

- Shift changes the character you're typing, usually from lowercase to upper, just as it does on a regular typewriter. (I didn't say the Mac didn't act at all like a typewriter; I said it does much more.)

- Option acts as another Shift key when you're typing, because it lets you get at an additional character for each key on the keyboard.

- Command (the cloverleaf symbol, sometimes paired with an outlined apple) is used to give commands from the keyboard instead of from menus.

- Control doesn't have a very specific function, because it wasn't on the early Mac keyboards. It often serves as an additional or alternative Command key. On some keyboards, the key is too small for the whole word to fit, so it's labeled *ctrl*.

### AT YOUR COMMAND

Where did that Command key shape come from? It's a Swedish campground trail marker that stands for "remarkable feature." Really!

The Mac's precursor, the Lisa, used an Apple symbol on the key and in its menus, but Steve Jobs decided that was not an "appropriate" use of the corporate logo. (Chris Espinosa likened that to the attitude of some British patriots who won't lick a postage stamp because it would be spitting on the back of the Queen's head.) In any case, Susan Kare and Barbara Koalkin found the symbol in a book and it translated beautifully to the Mac's bit-mapped screen.

For years, the pattern appeared alone on its special key, but now Mac keyboards have both the Command symbol *and* the Apple symbol on the same key. So sometimes it's even referred to as the "open Apple," a holdover from Apple II terminology.

●••❯ **Modifier keys are often used in combination.** In typing, for instance, Shift-8 is an asterisk, while Option-8 is a bullet; Shift-Option-8 is a degree symbol. In issuing keyboard commands, Command-W closes a window on the desktop, while Command-Option-W closes all windows. Programs with a plethora of commands will even assign three modifiers, like Command-Shift-Option plus a letter key.

I've never seen a program actually use all four modifiers, although I often assign them to a macro. (See Chapter 21 for more information about macros.) It's not as difficult as you might think to get all four keys down—after all, they're clustered together in the corner of the keyboard, so you can press them all down with just two, or maybe three, fingers, holding the fingers flat across several keys instead of pressing the keys with the fingertips.

❋Why can't they spell out "escape"? On my PowerBook, the Option key is the same size as the Esc key, but it gets spelled out—and they have the same number of letters.

●••❯ **The Esc key** (for *escape*) that's on later keyboards usually works as a Cancel command. As with the keys that are on some keyboards and not on others, there's no absolutely set function for the key. Some programs use it, some don't, and those that do also offer an alternative keyboard command.*

••◆ **The Enter key sometimes** is just an alternative for Return and sometimes it has its own function; this varies from one application to another. In general Mac use, Enter is the same as Return: either one selects a desktop icon's title, for instance, or "clicks" the default button in a dialog box.

Spreadsheets and databases, though, consistently see these as two different keys. When you press Enter, the number or text that you typed is entered into the spreadsheet's cell, or the database's field, but that cell or field remains selected. Using Return enters the information, too, but also moves you to the next cell or field.

## The Numeric Keypad

∞◆ **A numeric keypad** makes number entry more convenient. It includes standard math operators (* is for multiplication, / is for division), and a period for decimal points. The Clear key serves various functions in different programs.

• • • • • • • • • • • • • • • • • • • • • • • • • • • • • • • • • • • • • • • • • • • • • • • • • • •

**POP QUIZ**                                                      **[2 POINTS]**

Why are the numbers on the keypad—and on calculators—arranged from the bottom up (the numbers 1–3 are in the bottom row) while those on a telephone are top-down (the numbers 1–3 in the top row)?

••◆ **The Num Lock key** ("numeric lock") is the same as the Clear key. In programs where the keypad functions in two different ways (for both number entry and cursor control, for instance), the Num Lock key toggles the keypad between those two functions. When you're in numlock mode, pressing a key types a number.

•••◆ **There's a num lock light** on the keyboard that doesn't seem to be wired to anything consistently. It's never on in Word (which has a numlock mode), and it's almost always on when you're using Excel.

∞◇ **Do you want those keyboard lights**—num lock, caps lock, and scroll lock—to do *something ... anything?* Have I got a program for you. Actually, I've got two of them. WackyLights alternately lights each one, so they seem to chase each other on the keyboard; Key Lights lets you control the lighting pattern. [WackyLights, freeware, Andrew Welch; Key Lights, freeware, Rick Kaseguma]

num    caps    scroll
lock    lock    lock

## Extended Keyboards

⟶ The *function keys* along the top of some keyboards, labeled F1 through F15, do different things in different programs; more often than not, they don't do anything at all. Because not all keyboards have them, program designers can't afford to make them too important. But they are handy for those programs like Word, Excel, and PageMaker that use them for built-in shortcuts. Most of all, though, they're handy when you make your own keyboard shortcuts with a macro utility.

⟶ The keys F1 through F4 are supported at the system level as the Undo, Cut, Copy, and Paste commands.* That means they work that way on the desktop and in all programs that follow the rules (which is probably, maybe, *possibly*, a slight majority of the programs out there).

⟶ Function keys are not FKEYs. An FKEY is a different thing altogether—and is discussed in Chapter 8.

* I don't know why I like using the function keys so much. Is it really that much easier to press a single key, like F2 for Cut, instead of a two-key combination like Command-X? I don't think I'm that lazy. I've always thought pre-split English muffins were the epitome of laziness. I guess I'll have to start thinking of them as efficient.

⟶ The page control keys—Home, End, Page Up, and Page Down keys—function differently from one program to another. Home and End should move you to the beginning and end of a document, but sometimes they move you to the top and bottom of the screen instead, with some combination like Command-Home actually moving you "home."

Page Up and Page Down don't always function the way you might expect, either. Sometimes they move you (well, not *you*, but the text insertion point) to the top or bottom of a "page" that's actually a screenful of text; sometimes they move you according to what would be a printed page from the document.

These functional inconsistencies, which the Control, Esc, and function keys all share, stem from the same place: they weren't on the original Mac keyboards, so their uses weren't nailed down in Apple's initial programming guidelines.

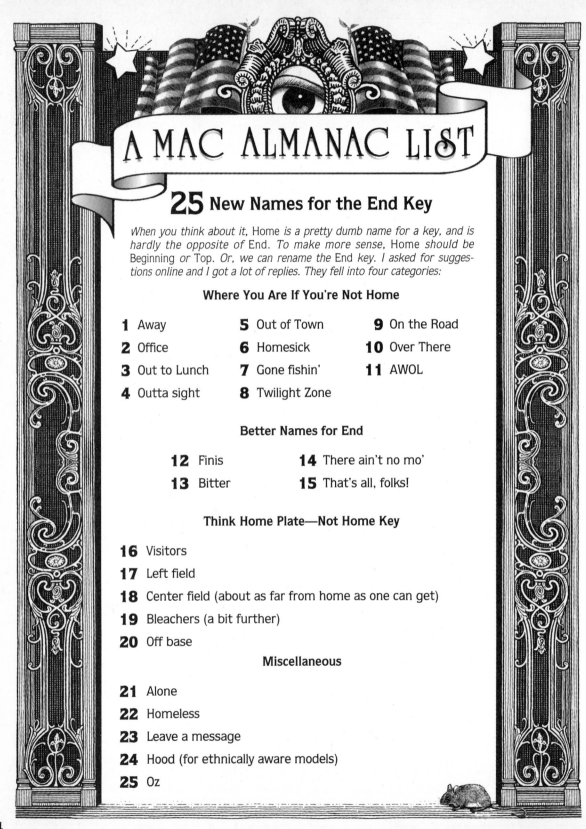

# A MAC ALMANAC LIST

## 25 New Names for the End Key

*When you think about it,* Home *is a pretty dumb name for a key, and is hardly the opposite of* End. *To make more sense,* Home *should be* Beginning *or* Top. *Or, we can rename the* End *key. I asked for suggestions online and I got a lot of replies. They fell into four categories:*

### Where You Are If You're Not Home

| | | |
|---|---|---|
| **1** Away | **5** Out of Town | **9** On the Road |
| **2** Office | **6** Homesick | **10** Over There |
| **3** Out to Lunch | **7** Gone fishin' | **11** AWOL |
| **4** Outta sight | **8** Twilight Zone | |

### Better Names for End

| | |
|---|---|
| **12** Finis | **14** There ain't no mo' |
| **13** Bitter | **15** That's all, folks! |

### Think Home Plate—Not Home Key

**16** Visitors

**17** Left field

**18** Center field (about as far from home as one can get)

**19** Bleachers (a bit further)

**20** Off base

### Miscellaneous

**21** Alone

**22** Homeless

**23** Leave a message

**24** Hood (for ethnically aware models)

**25** Oz

➤ **The Forward Delete key** erases the character to the right of the blinking text cursor. If you hold it down, it looks as if there's a vacuum cleaner sucking characters into the vertical line of the cursor. I'm not sure how I lived without it all those years before I had an extended keyboard. It's such a crutch that I had to make a macro to mimic its function on my PowerBook, which doesn't have a forward delete key of its own

➤ **The Help key is a good idea that fizzled.** In some programs that have built-in help systems, pressing the Help key opens the Help system. I'd like to see a system-level hook into this key so it would turn Balloon Help on and off. In fact, I've assigned a Help Balloon toggle macro to the Help button—more about that in Chapter 21.

## Keyboarding Tips

➤ **Adjust the key repeat rate** with the Keyboard control panel. The repeat rate governs how fast the letters appear while you're holding the key down. More importantly, the control panel lets you adjust the *delay* until the repeating starts. After all, if you don't give yourself time to get your finger off the key, you'll be typing lliikkee tthhiiss. For people with physical limitations that affect keyboarding, it's helpful to turn off the delay completely.

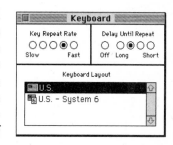

Using control panels is covered in Chapter 8.

➤ **If you, or someone you know, has trouble** with the keyboard because of physical limitations, Apple's Easy Access control panel makes it possible to type with a single finger, yet still keep any or all modifier keys pressed down at the same time. Details are in Chapter 8.

➤ **When Tab or Return** moves you around on a screen—in a dialog box, for instance, or in a database or spreadsheet—then Shift-Tab or Shift-Return almost always moves you back in the opposite direction.

➤ **Your keystrokes are remembered** even when the Mac is busy doing something else. Up to ten keystrokes go into a buffer that the Mac reads when it gets a chance. So, if you hit Command-S for Save, you don't have to wait for the dialog to appear to start typing the name of the document. Just type and the Mac catches up later.

This works for more than just typing characters, and in more places than just dialogs. You can, for instance, hit Command-S, type the name of the document and then hit Return before the dialog appears (assuming you're a fast typist and it's a short name). You'll never even see the complete dialog on the screen. Or, you can click in the window of a background application, hit Command-V for Paste, Command-S for Save, and Command-Q for Quit, and each operation will be carried out in turn as soon as the Mac has a chance to attend to them.

Typing ahead doesn't *always* work; there are times when the Mac is doing something important and then, when it comes back to you, one of the first things it does is to empty the keyboard buffer without paying any attention to what's in it. In many cases, this is an important feature because it keeps inappropriate keystrokes from being passed on to another program, say, or to the wrong part of the program you're working in.

**••} Why is teaching Driver's Ed easier than teaching the Mac?** Because they make cars with two sets of controls, one for the teacher and one for the student. But you can set up a Mac the same way: just hook up a second keyboard and mouse to the Mac. Some Mac models have an extra ADB port on the back that you can use for this purpose. If you're working on a model with a single ADB port, you can still hook up two keyboards (with the second one plugged into the first) and then share just the mouse, which will be at the end of the keyboard "chain." There are also Y and T connectors available for ADB cords that let you hook up two keyboard/mouse sets.*

> *My tech editor, Joe Holmes, pointed out when he read this that some monitors have extra ADB ports and so the Apple Portrait Monitor, for instance, can act as a very expensive Y-connector. Wouldn't you think a tech editor would be more, well, serious?

You won't be able to interrupt a mouse drag the same way you can slam on the brakes if the student driver is heading for a wall, but it's a convenient setup so you don't have to keep reaching across each other or changing seats.

**••} The lack of a numeric keypad** on some keyboards is most annoying when you're working with the Calculator or some other numeric entry, because the "+" symbol needs the Shift key to be accessed. You can use a macro program or a new keyboard layout to redefine a seldom-used key (like the "\") to act as the plus sign so you won't have to shift to get to it. Chapter 21 covers these tricks.

**••} The best keyboarding tip of all:** Learn to type! The time you have to put in learning will be saved hundreds of times over when you're working at the computer. You don't even have to learn to touch-type the top row of numbers—just get the alphabet and basic punctuation down pat. There are several typing programs available for the Mac, and they all include typing games.

## Keyboard Layouts

**••} A *keyboard layout* is** what "maps" the keys on your keyboard to a character in a font so that, for instance, when you press the Shift, Option, and 8 keys, you get a bullet character. When you open the Keyboard control panel, you'll see a list of keyboard layouts—but the list is really short. In System 7.0 there's only the U.S. layout; in System 7.1, there's the standard U.S. layout and the previous standard—the one from System 6. (Unless, of course, you're using one of Apple's foreign systems. In which case the U.S. is a foreign system, isn't it?)

There are, however, many keyboard layout variations that are useful even within a single language. For instance, you might want a Dvorak layout instead of the QWERTY standard, or you might want a layout that lets you type the period and comma while the Shift key is down, instead of the < and > symbols. When there's more than one keyboard layout in your system, you can choose among them through the Keyboard control panel.

Special keyboard layouts are available through user groups and online services.

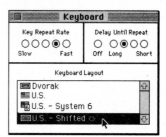

Selecting a layout from the keyboard control panel.

•→ **It's easy to install and remove keyboard layouts**—they're one of the resources you can drag in and out of your System File, just like fonts (in System 7.0) and sounds.

To put the keyboard layout into the system, drag it into the opened System file window, the closed System file icon, or the closed System Folder. If you put it in a closed System Folder, you'll get a dialog asking if you want it routed into the System file itself. (Click the OK button.)

To remove a keyboard layout, open the System file and drag the keyboard layout icon out of the window.

There's more about keyboard layouts in Chapters 6, 8, and 21.

Keyboard resources are in the System file, just like sounds and, in System 7.0, fonts.

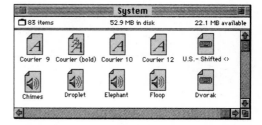

•→ **You won't find the U.S. layout**—or whatever your main, system-installed keyboard layout is—in the System file. This is to keep you from dragging it out and trashing it by mistake. (Read about "idiot-proofing" in the next chapter.)

•→ **The basic keyboard layout changed** from System 6 to System 7 in some subtle ways. To get the capital letter "A" topped by a circumflex accent, for instance, you used to type Option-Shift-R; now you must type Option-Shift-M. These changes are detailed in Chapter 20.

# ↦ THE BINARY MEASURING STICK ↤

## A Little Bit, More

∞➔ **Computers measure things** in bits, bytes, Ks, and megs. When you use your computer, you have to measure things that way, too. The size of your files, the capacity of disks and drives, the amount of memory the computer has, the size of its ROM ... they're all measured in things like Ks and megs, so it's important that you understand the basics of these units of measure.

∞➔ **A *bit* is the smallest unit of measure for information.** It's so small that usually we don't even talk about it. You can use your Mac for years and not run into the term *bit* except in books like this where we define it before going on to the more practical, larger units.

The word *bit* comes from the words *binary digit*. In the binary world, there are only two digits: zero and one. A computer's smarts come from its electronics, and there are only two states an electronic switch can possibly be in: on or off. So the world of computing is a world of binary counting. It doesn't really matter what the two states are: on and off, zero and one, black and white, yes and no; all that matters is that there are two, and only two, mutually exclusive possibilities.

Miraculously enough, the magnetic medium that's used for disks also exists in a binary state, since a magnetic particle can have one of only two possible charges: north or south.

∞➔ **Eight bits make up a byte.** A byte of information is enough to convey any one of 256 different items, because there are that many unique combinations when you string together eight numerals that can be either 1 or 0. 256? Yep. Think of it this way: you already know that a single bit can tell you one of two things. But two bits can tell you four different things: both bits could be 1, or both 0, or the first 1 while the second is 0, or the first 0 while the second is 1. This picture shows how one switch provides two possibilities, while two switches give four possibilities. Three switches would provide eight possibilities, four switches have sixteen combinations, and so on, so that eight switches give you 256 possibilities.

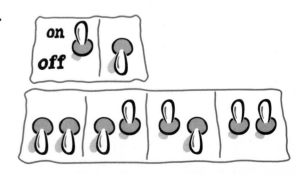

One switch provides two possibilities (top), while two switches give four different combinations (bottom).

You won't run into bytes too often, though, on the Mac. Occasionally you'll see a report of file size in bytes when you're compressing a file, or when you're transferring a file in a communications program, but bytes are still too small a unit of information to be very useful in day-to-day computing.

oo•> **A *kilobyte* is 1024 bytes.** Why such an odd number? (Well, such a *strange* number, since it's not odd, it's even.) *Kilo* normally indicates a jump of 1000, but in the binary world of computing that uses powers of 2 instead of powers of 10 (the way we do so we can count on our fingers), the nearest "round" number to 1000 is 1024.

Usually we just refer to a kilobyte as a K, and that's something you see on your Mac all the time. File size, for instance, is reported in kilobytes, as is memory—at least up to a certain point. When you have lots of something, it's easier to use a larger unit of measure. Otherwise, we'd be watching *360 Seconds* on Sunday nights, Eddie Murphy in *2880 Minutes*, Robert Redford in *72 Hours of the Condor*, and Dudley Moore in *144 Days*.

And that brings us to...

oo•> **A *megabyte* is 1024K.** (There's that number again.) In writing, megabyte is usually abbreviated as MB, but in speaking (and in the friendly conversational tone of books like this), it's referred to as a *meg*.

A *megabyte* is the measuring unit you'll use more than anything else while you're working on your Mac. In the early days, floppy disks had a capacity of 400K and there was 128K of memory; now, floppies hold 1.4 meg of information and the basic memory configuration is 4 megs.

Sometimes you'll see M as the abbreviation for megabyte, but watch out for M*b*. With the lowercase *b*, the abbreviation stands for mega*bits*, not mega*bytes*. (Or it's being used by someone who doesn't know the difference.)

### THE WAY WE WERE ...

The Mac system originally calculated a kilobyte as 1000 bytes, hoping to make it easier for beginner users. Bowing to the inevitable, it matched the rest of the computer world in 1986 with the release of System 3 and Finder 5 (more about *those* numbers elsewhere!) by measuring a K at 1024 bytes.

But pity the extra confusion of those caught in the transition: A then-standard 400K disk showed 400K available before the system update; the same disk showed 391K available afterwards. Where did the 9K go? They didn't go anywhere: 400 "old" K's equaled 400,000 bytes, (just under the true capacity of the disk) while 391 "new" K's equaled 400,384 bytes, the actual capacity of the disk.

↝ A *gigabyte,* or gig, is the next unit of measure. It's 1024 megs. (The amount of information on a CD-ROM is about half a gig.) So far, then, we've got this:

$$8 \text{ bits } = 1 \text{ byte}$$
$$1024 \text{ bytes } = 1 \text{ kilobyte}$$
$$1024\text{K} = 1 \text{ megabyte}$$
$$1024\text{MB} = 1 \text{ gigabyte}$$

What comes after a gigabyte? A *terabyte.* I've never seen anyone use a binary measurement larger than that. Maybe I can be the first to coin the terms. Based on the prefixes used in metric measurement (yes, after kilometer comes gigameter and terameter), the next unit would be a petabyte, and then an exabyte. What one-syllable nicknames would we use for them, à la *meg* and *gig* ? *Ter, Pet,* and *Ex?* No, we'll have to go back to the single-letter name, as with K for kilobyte: T, P, and E.

Then there's the trilobite (fossilized, of course) that I keep on my coffee table …

## Binary Numbering

↝ **You don't have to know anything about binary** numbers to use your computer—so skip this section if you want. But if you ever wondered why the Mac had 128K of memory, then 512K, then 1024K and so on, instead of, say, 130K and 600K and 1050K, read on.

↝ **We use a base 10 numbering system.** Each of the nine digits (0 through 9) can stand for many different values, depending on its *position* in a number. As you move to the left in a multiple-digit number, the value of the "place" increases by a factor of 10. Here's what the first four places are worth:

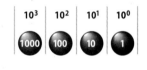

So, if you put a number in the third position from the right (the 100 place), it stands for that many hundreds: 4 stands for four hundreds. Put a 2 in the second place, and it means 2 tens; a 3 in the first place means 3 ones. Altogether, that's 4 hundreds, 2 tens, and 3 ones, or four hundred twenty-three:

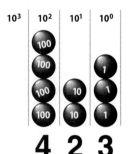

↝ **Binary numbering uses a base 2 system** but the rules are the same as base 10 rules. So, there are two different digits (0 and 1), but what they stand for depends on their position in a number. Again, moving to the left in a number increases the value of that "place"; in binary, the place value increases by a factor of 2 for every move. Here's what the first seven places are worth:

Putting a 1 in any place means 1 of that number: in the third place from the right, it stands for 1 four; in the fifth from the right, it's 1 sixteen; in the seventh position, it's 1 sixty-four. Together, that's a sixty-four, a sixteen, and a four: eighty-four, or 1010100 binary:

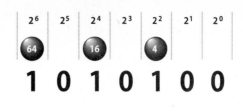

●••→ **Check out this short table** of the higher "round" numbers in binary. Do the decimal equivalents look familiar?

| Binary | | | Decimal |
|---|---|---|---|
| 10000000 | $(2^7)$ | = | 128 |
| 100000000 | $(2^8)$ | = | 256 |
| 1000000000 | $(2^9)$ | = | 512 |
| 10000000000 | $(2^{10})$ | = | 1024 |

●••→ **Computers use binary numbers but programmers** use hexadecimal (or "hex") numbers because it takes too long to write 10101010, and it's sure hard to take it in at a glance. Hexadecimal numbering is based on 16, where the first digit (at the right) stands for ones, the next digit for sixteens, and the next, two-hundred-fifty-sixes, and so on, up in powers of 16, as shown in the picture here.

Since you don't move to the second column until you have 16 of something, the problem arises: How do you indicate 10, or 11, or up to 15 units in a single digit? After 9, hexadecimal numbers use letters of the alphabet. So to count to fifteen, it's: 1, 2, 3, 4, 5, 6, 7, 8, 9, A, B, C, D, E, F. The letter F is the highest hex "number."

Why am I bothering you with all this? (This is where you politely mumble, "Oh, no, it's no bother at all; I like it.") Because if you dive into the Mac lifestyle, you'll run into hex numbering. The Sad Mac that indicates serious problems at startup is accompanied by a hex number that indicates the problem area.* You'll see hex numbers if you poke around with programs like ResEdit, too.

*I once received a call from a puzzled Mac Plus user asking me what it meant when the Mac asked for food. Now, I often use the phrase "feed in a disk," but I had no idea what she was referring to until she explained that her Mac had a black screen with a Sad Mac icon on it, with the word "food" under the icon. Aha! It was actually an error code in hex—which, if memory serves, was actually FOOOD.

## ⇥ SYSTEM 7.5 STUFF ⇤

### Shutting Down

∘∘→ **Choose the Shut Down desk accessory** from the Apple menu while you're in an application, instead of moving back to the desktop to use the command in the Special menu.

∘∘→ **An improper shutdown** can mean lost work or a desktop that's not the way you thought you left it; it can also mean that there's a *Rescued Items* folder sitting in the Trash (as described in Chapter 5). System 7.5 provides a Shut Down Warning checkbox in the General Controls control panel. If you keep it checked, you'll be warned at startup if the last shutdown was an "improper" one (usually because of a crash or power failure). The Mac displays the dialog shown here, but what it should mean to you is simple: Check the Trash for a Rescued Items folder. (Personally, I'm a little insulted that the dialog tells me how to shut down properly. I *know* how. I even do it—except when the Mac crashes on me. It's interesting—and a little misleading—that the dialog informs you the proper way is to use the Apple menu's Shut Down command, as if the one in the Finder's Special menu weren't the right way to do it.)

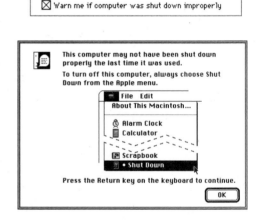

••→ **The Shutdown Items folder** is for scripts that you want executed automatically when the Mac shuts down—a script to empty the Trash, for instance, or to make backups. In the early version of System 7.5 that I'm using, its icon is exactly the same as the Startup Items folder's. I'm sure they won't leave it that way; maybe they'll at least turn the little switch on the folder to the horizontal position.

# CHAPTER 2
# THE INTERFACE

Technology is the science of arranging life so that one need not experience it.

ANON.

By the time you finish this chapter, you'll know all sorts of things, such as:

**⋯➔** The shortcut to a submenu.

**⋯➔** Why the Clipboard doesn't really exist, but how best to use it, anyway.

**⋯➔** How to shrink your windows down to their title bars, add color to the text and background of your menus, and how to generally ruin the elegant Macintosh interface.

**⋯➔** How to make your Mac sigh, scream, or sing instead of just beep.

**⋯➔** Why HAL sang about Daisy.

**⋯➔** Who Steve Jobs was. I mean is.

OK

## THE MOST TRIVIAL THING IN THIS CHAPTER

*If you let go of the mouse button while pointing to a gray line in a menu, the menu closes without any command being selected.*

—Including—

123 Factoids
  8 Quotable Quotes
  2 Quizzes
  1 Mac Almanac List
—and—
The first Mac Toon

*page 85*

## The Desktop Metaphor

## Menus

## Windows & Dialogs

## The Clipboard

## System Sounds

## System 7.5 Stuff

## ➤⊦ THE DESKTOP METAPHOR ⊦←

### The Mac Desktop

∞•➤ **The Mac's interface uses a desktop metaphor.**\* The desktop is the gray or colored background you see on the screen when you start your computer; it's the place where you manipulate the work you're doing by handling *icons*, little pictures that represent your files, folders, and disks.

As with most metaphors, the desktop one doesn't quite carry through. You probably don't keep a trash can on your desktop, for instance; it's more likely under your desk where you kick it over occasionally. And if you have *menus* on your real desktop, they're probably of the takeout variety, not ones that are filled with commands. But the basics of the desktop metaphor serve as a handy place to start as you shuffle your electronic documents around, storing them in electronic folders.

> \*I guess <u>interface</u> could use a definition, too. It's the thing between you and your computer—not what keeps you apart, but what lets you interact with each other.

∞•➤ **The Mac interface is not intuitive,** no matter what anyone tells you. There's nothing intuitive, or intrinsically sensible, about dragging little pictures around on the screen and putting them into other pictures, or rolling a mouse around, or using menus; and clicks and double-clicks are not instinctive actions for producing any predictable results.

What most people mistakenly call "intuitive" is actually an elegantly designed, *internally consistent* interface. Double-clicking on an icon opens a file; double-clicking on its name in a list also opens it. Shift-clicking on an icon adds it to or removes it from a selected group; shift-clicking in text adds to or subtracts from the selection. Once you learn the basics of using the Mac, you can figure out how most programs work. (Or, to put it another way, once you get into it, you can intuit.)

• • • • • • • • • • • • • • • • • • • • • • • • • • • • • • • • • • • • • • • • • •

### IF YOU CAN'T TAKE THE HEAT ...

*The "ownership" of a computer interface may be an odd concept, but it sure keeps lawyers busy. Apple has always aggressively protected the Mac interface (almost as if Apple had invented it!), and the GEM interface from Digital Research was an early target of Apple's interface police. Russ Coffman published a proposed solution for GEM in the Atlanta Mac User Group's newsletter "Fishwrap" and it was reprinted in MacUser Magazine in February of 1986. Here's what he said (presumably with tongue planted firmly in cheek):*

**66** ...Responding to Apple's threatened lawsuit, Digital Research, Inc. (DRI) has agreed to redesign GEM (a misnomer) to avoid similarity to Apple programs. An intense investigation discovered what the new GEM will look like. DRI has selected a metaphor perhaps even more familiar than the Mac's "desktop."

The computer itself is the Kitchen. GEM will now have Doors in place of Windows, Shelves and Refrigerators instead of Folders, a Garbage Disposal for the Trashcan, and Cupboards in place of disk icons. Shopping Lists replace the obvious but too-similar Menus. Up to four Cupboard Doors can be open at one time (double-density Cupboards counts as two Doors). Need I add it has Cuisinarts, Blenders, Toasters, etc. instead of desk accessories? The Countertop metaphor replaces Mac's desktop. The cursor is a Spatula or Hotpad. The mouse is now called a Roach, also a familiar item in the kitchen.

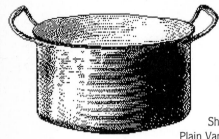

To Cook (launch) with an application (Dish), open the Oven Door and move the Dish from a Shelf or the Countertop with the Hotpad. To select an existing document (Food), open the Refrigerator Door and carry it to a Dish with the Spatula and double-flip. To begin a new application, don't return to the Countertop—just flip the Oven control to Clean, then select another Dish or Food from the Breakfast Counter (a kind of MiniFinder). To work on a new Food while in a Dish, save the Food to the Refrigerator or Freezer, Wash the Dish, and select Leftovers from the Shopping List. There is still only one font, but the user has the style choices of Plain Vanilla, Bowled, Italian, and Underscour.

Like the Mac, the document must match the application—text files (alphabet soup icon) fit snugly into the word processor (saucepan icon). Spreadsheets are cookie sheets, and its documents are, of course, cookies. This seems even clearer than the Mac. The Blender counter accessory permits the mixing of text and graphics. Tidy up the Countertop by selecting Paper Towel from the Shopping List. Food placed in the Garbage Disposal can be retrieved by the Plumber if the user has not used a Paper Towel on the Countertop. Food is locked by placing it in the Freezer Door and unlocked with Defrost. A Cupboard Door is locked by placing a Key in its Keyhole. While locked, you can Peek through its Keyhole, but can't place anything on the Shelves, even with Pork. To print, place Food on tables. Quality is determined by whether you place it on the Kitchen or Dining Room table.

You will be able to share Foods among several Kitchens when the Food Server network option becomes available this spring. Kitchens are connected by Halls. The network, called a House, can accommodate up to 32 Kitchens. One Kitchen is the Master and Food is transported around the House by Kitchen Maids. Food from other Houses can be brought in via the Intercom (modem), or by Butlers.

A Microwave option speeds processing, but doesn't work on large batch files. A degree of multitasking is possible by moving Pans (smaller than Dishes) from the Countertop to the Rangetop, or by using the Toaster or Crockpot counter accessories.

Graphics are much improved over earlier GEM releases. Pie charts, especially, look good enough to eat.

Error handling is similar to the Mac's Alert Box. For instance, if you forget to close the Refrigerator Door, Mom (the Kitchen Supervisor) forces you to stand in the Corner until you do. Here they have done a good job—in tests, any inappropriate command given to Mom resulted in the user being sent to Bed without Food.

DRI may still be in trouble. The debugger icon, a Raid can, bears a strong resemblance to MacPaint's spray can.

Other features: Editing has several Mac-like options including Gut, Baste, Slice, Dice, Chop, Grate, and Julienne Fries (now what would you pay?). When you use keyboard equivalents, the Roach scurries off into a Roach Motel icon. System shutdown is accomplished by closing the Kitchen Door. The Scrapbook equivalent is the Recipe File. The Note Pad equivalent is found under a little magnet icon shaped like a banana. It resides on the Refrigerator Door. 99

## ➔╞ MENUS ╞←

## Basic Menus & Commands

∘∘➤ **The *menu bar* at the top of the screen** displays *menu titles*. Each menu has a list of *commands*, often separated into related groups by gray lines (or dotted lines on a black-and-white system).

| Edit | |
|---|---|
| Undo | ⌘Z |
| | |
| Cut | ⌘H |
| Copy | ⌘C |
| Paste | ⌘U |
| Clear | |
| Select All | ⌘A |
| | |
| Show Clipboard | |

**S**ystem 7.5 puts a clock in the menu bar.

∘∘➤ ***System menus* have icons instead of names.** A system menu is one that is always present, since it "belongs" to the Mac system instead of to whatever application is running. (The File and Edit menus certainly seem to be omnipresent, but they're actually different menus, because each application has its own File and Edit menus.) So, the Apple menu at the left of the menu bar, and Balloon Help and the Application menu at its right, are icons instead of names. Lots of utilities put up their own system menus too, and many of them are icons or special single characters instead of words. This picture shows the main system menus, and the icon menus for two popular utilities: the spelling checker Thunder and the macro utility Tempo.

  🍎  File  Edit  View  Label  Special  ⚡  ⌘                    ❓  🖥

∘∘➤ **Some menu commands are *toggles,*** alternately turning something on and off. Text styles are usually toggles: you choose Italic, for instance, to make selected text italic, and choose it again to turn italic off. Many toggles have a checkmark in front of them to show when they're activated.

········································
Some toggle commands are checked in the menu when they're active.

| Style |
|---|
| Plain |
| ✓**Bold** |
| *Italic* |
| ✓<u>Underline</u> |
| Outline |
| Shadow |

But sometimes the name of a toggle command changes to suit the occasion—Show Ruler changes to Hide Ruler, for instance.

∘∘➤ **A dimmed item on a menu** can't be used. If there's nothing on the Clipboard, for instance, the Paste command is dimmed in the Edit menu. The Mac interface is filled with these kinds of elegant, subtle clues about what's going on. If you don't appreciate elegance and subtlety, you can at least appreciate the time it saves: you won't choose Paste—maybe repeatedly—and wonder why nothing's happening. (Of course, you might look at the dimmed Paste command and wonder why there's nothing on the Clipboard, but the Mac can't do *everything* for you.) In fact, if every command in a menu is unavailable, the menu title itself is dimmed.

········································
A dimmed item in a menu can't be used because it's inappropriate for the current situation.

| Edit | |
|---|---|
| Undo | ⌘Z |
| | |
| Cut | ⌘H |
| Copy | ⌘C |
| Paste | ⌘U |
| Clear | |
| Select All | ⌘A |
| | |
| Show Clipboard | |

The dimmed font is made from a checkered pattern on black-and-white screens. On grayscale and color screens, the dimmed font is actually a light gray, which is easier to read—although I suppose that reading the fine details of commands that you can't use anyway isn't an absolute necessity.

*Joe Holmes, tech editor extraordinaire, points out that as long as a menu command isn't highlighted, you can let go of the mouse button without invoking a command—that means that you can let go while you're pointing to one of the gray dividing lines in a menu. But then he thought perhaps that was too trivial to add to the text.

The way I see it, nothing's too trivial for this book!

**To get out of a menu without choosing anything,** you don't have to retrace your path all the way up to the menu bar. Just slide the pointer off the menu in any direction and let go of the mouse button. This works for both main menus and submenus.*

**A menu item blinks when you select it.** You can use the General Controls control panel to adjust how many times a menu item blinks, or if it blinks at all. It's amazing how much of a difference this little bit of feedback makes. Turning off the blink completely isn't a good idea; lots of times you'll wonder whether or not the command actually registered, or if the pointer just slid off the menu. Three blinks is a little frenetic, though—it reminds me of a flickering light bulb. Try one blink or two. (The Mac's designers wanted it permanently set at three blinks, but finally left it to the users.)

The blink setting in the General Controls control panel.

You'll find the General Controls control panel in the Control Panels folder in the System Folder.

**Some menu commands change** when you hold down Shift or Option while you open the menu. Close, for instance, might change to Close All. There are several things that work like this in the Finder (see Chapter 3), but don't forget to experiment in all your applications.

## Symbols in Menus

**A trailing ellipsis** (the three dots, like this ...) after a menu command means you're going to get a dialog box when you select the command. Choosing Open, for instance, gets you the Open dialog where you can select a file and then give the *real* Open command, which is actually a button.

Ellipses after commands?

Because English is such a wonderful language and ellipses is the plural of both ellipsis and ellipse, if we're not careful we could have a menu like this, with ellipses after some commands:

Just because the command is listed with an ellipsis after it doesn't mean I'm going to use the ellipsis every time I refer to the command. (I hope I'm not being too eliptical.) I can't stand reading those kind of references: "The File menu has the Open..., Save As..., and Print... commands." I bet you can figure out what commands I'm talking about even if I leave the dots out ....

**Keyboard equivalents for menu commands** are listed right in the menu. (Well, they're usually listed—some programs have all sorts of hidden treasures in them.) There are some keyboard commands that are standard across almost all applications:

| | | | |
|---|---|---|---|
| Command-Z | Undo | Command-N | New |
| Command-X | Cut | Command-O | Open |
| Command-C | Copy | Command-S | Save |
| Command-V | Paste | Command-P | Print |
| Command-A | Select All | Command-Q | Quit |

In the early days of the Mac (when menus were shorter and commands fewer), only the Undo, Cut, Copy, and Paste keyboard equivalents were standard. Apple's interface guidelines spelled out what other keyboard equivalents should be, but not all developers listened. Which, in some cases, was a good thing—because Command-P was originally reserved for Plain, the command that stripped all styles from text in one fell swoop (instead of, for instance, having to choose Bold and then Italic to remove both those formats). Of course, the programs that used P for Print then needed something for the Plain command, and many of them chose N (for No Style). That became confusing, because at the same time, many programs began using N for New.

∘∘•➤ **The letters in a menu are uppercase** for keyboard equivalents, but you don't press the Shift key to use them. (In fact, Command-P and Command-Shift-P can trigger entirely different commands.) The uppercase letters in the menu simply match the way the letters are printed on your keyboard's keys.

∘•➤ **The Mac is big on feedback.** (Or haven't you noticed?) Here's an example: If you use a keyboard equivalent for a menu command, the menu title blinks to acknowledge the command. If you're just using Command-I to italicize something, the fact that the selected letters switch to italic is certainly enough feedback, so the blink doesn't matter. But when you use something like Command-C for Copy, it's reassuring to know that you actually hit the right keys.

•➤ **The Command key isn't the only one used** for keyboard equivalents. There are only so many letters to go around (well, 26 to be exact, but even fewer when you try to logically match the letter to the command). So after a few years, some programs started using other modifier keys—Shift, Option, and later, Control—in the Command-key combination. This greatly expanded the possible combinations because the additional modifiers could be used singly or in combination. (Assuming use of only the 26 alphabetic characters, the possible combinations went from 26 with the Command key alone to 208 with the various permutations of modifying the Command key.)

These modifier keys don't have symbols printed on them on the keyboard, but they do have their own symbols when they're in menus. You can see what they look like in the picture here.

| Modifier Keys | |
|---|---|
| Command-Shift Letter | ⌘⇧ L |
| Command-Option | ⌘⌥ L |
| Control-Command Letter | ^⌘ L |
| Command-Shift-Option Letter | ⌘⇧⌥ L |
| Control-Command-Option Letter | ^⌘⌥ L |

The upward arrow for the Shift key is somewhat reasonable, given the ancestry of a Shift key for changing letters into uppercase; and the caret (^) also comes with a history, since it was the character for the Control key on those "other" machines. But there's no excuse for that symbol for the Option key!

➝ **Use one press of the Command key** for several commands in a row. If, for instance, you're changing selected text to italic, saving the edited document, then quitting the application, you can press Command-I, then, with the Command key still down, press S, and then (still keeping Command down) press Q. I use Command-S,Q all the time to save and quit.

➝ **Nonprinting keys are sometimes used** for a menu command in a combination like Command-Spacebar. The problem is: How do you represent a key that doesn't print anything? Each nonprinting key has its own special character, as shown in the following picture; there's even a special symbol (which sometimes varies from program to program) to indicate a number from the keypad as opposed to a number from the top row of the keyboard.

| Non-Printing Symbols | |
|---|---|
| **Command Spacebar** | ⌘ ␣ |
| **Command Enter** | ⌘ ⌅ |
| **Command Tab** | ⌘ ⇥ |
| **Command Return** | ⌘ ↵ |
| **Command Arrow Key** | ⌘ ← |
| **Command Forward Delete** | ⌘ ⌦ |
| **A Function Key** | F9 |
| **A Keypad Number** | ⌘⌨9 |

*C*hange the look of your menus. See (Inter) FaceLifts later in this chapter.

## Scrolling Menus

➝ **A scrolling menu** has too many items on it to fit on the screen; this is usually the case with the Apple and the Font menus. An arrow at the bottom of the menu indicates there are more choices down there somewhere. To make the menu scroll, hold the mouse pointer at the bottom of the menu, where the arrow is. Once the menu starts scrolling, some choices scroll off the top, so you'll see an arrow at the top showing there are choices in that direction, too.

Arrows inside a menu show there are more choices at the top or bottom of that menu.

| Fonts | Fonts |
|---|---|
| Athens | ▲ |
| Avant Garde | Futura Book |
| Benguiat | Geneva |
| Bookman | Helvetica |
| Cairo | Jott |
| Chicago | JottQuick |
| Courier | Korinna |
| Futura | London |
| Futura Book | Los Angeles |
| Geneva | Monaco |
| Helvetica | New York |
| Jott | Optima |
| JottQuick | Palatino |
| Korinna | Round |
| London | Sussex |
| Los Angeles | Symbol |
| Monaco | Times |
| New York | Thames |
| Optima | Utility City |
| Palatino | Venice |
| ▼ | Zapf Dingbats |

➝ **You don't need perfect aim** to get the menu to scroll—you don't have to land on the arrow. Hold the mouse cursor anywhere along the bottom of the menu and the menu scrolls. In fact, you can hold the cursor *below* the menu as long as you slide through the bottom of the menu and not off the side and then around to the bottom.

Positioning the cursor along the bottom of the menu, or even beneath it, still makes it scroll.

➝ **You don't have to catch an item as it slides by** in a scrolling menu, although it makes for an interesting game when there's nothing better to do. Once you see the item you want, move the pointer back up into the menu to point to it; as soon as you move away from the menu's up or down arrow, the menu stops scrolling.

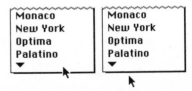

> It took a long time to get the first pull-down menus. At first they were across the top of each window as opposed to ... at the top of the screen. We ran into all kinds of problems [like] what happens when ... the menus are long and go off the bottom?*

BILL ATKINSON

*In fact, the menus were even at the bottom of each window for a while! By the time the Mac Plus was introduced (in 1986) they had figured out what to do when the menus are too long—that's when scrolling menus made it into system software.

➤ **You can control the scrolling speed of a menu.** This is another of those really tiny, practically hidden, beautifully elegant examples of the care that goes into the design of the Mac interface. The position of the mouse pointer controls the scrolling speed. When you hold it on the tip of the scrolling menu's arrow (left, in this picture), it scrolls faster than when you keep it in the body of the arrow (right).

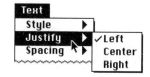

Control the speed of the scroll by where you position the cursor.

## Submenus & Popups

➤ A *hierarchical* **menu** is one that has submenus. Any item in the main menu that has an arrow after it has a submenu attached. When you pause on the main item, the submenu pops out. If the main menu is near the right edge of the screen, the submenu pops out to the left where there's more room for it, even though the arrow always points to the right.

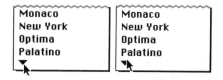

Hierarchical menus aren't limited to one level. Most programs use only one, but the Mac's system software allows for up to five levels of submenus. You'll find multiple levels where you need them the most—in hierarchical Apple menu utilities. (The utilities are covered in Chapter 6.)

➤ **You don't have to make a 90-degree turn** with the mouse when you move into a submenu. Instead of moving across from the main menu and then down through the submenu, you can drag at an angle if you do it just right. All you have to do is move from the main menu into the body of the submenu fast enough for the Mac to realize you're heading for the submenu and not just meandering down through the main menu.

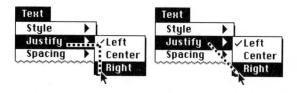

You don't have to move into the submenu and then down to your selection (left); you can head directly for the submenu choice (right) as long as you move quickly enough.

•◆ **Menus aren't always at the top of the screen.** You'll find *popup menus* in dialog boxes, tool palettes, and even in document windows of feature-laden programs. A word or phrase in a drop-shadowed rectangle is usually a popup menu (although I've seen programs that use that design for buttons).

There's no standard implementation for popup menus. Sometimes the word in the rectangle is the name of the menu; sometimes it's actually one of the menu choices. For most menus all you have to do is press right on them to pop them up, although some menus have little arrows next to them that you must use instead. Most of the popups with arrows give you the option of choosing something from the menu (a font size, for example) or typing in a box.

The two popup menus at the top of this picture should be very familiar even to new Mac users: at the left is the one in the standard Open/Save dialog, and at the right is the one built into Finder windows. The bottom row of popup samples are all from Microsoft Word: the first is from the "ribbon," lets you type in a font size or press the arrow to get to a list; the second is a simple popup from the Paragraph dialog; the third is from the Character dialog—you can't type in the box, although you can use the arrow to open the menu.

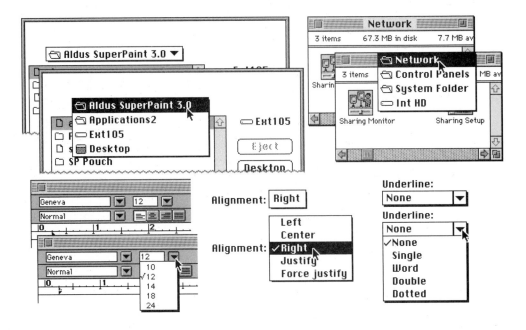

## ◆ WINDOWS & DIALOGS ◆

### Window Basics

◦◦◆ **A window** gives you a view of something: It lets you look into a document, or a folder, or a disk. Speaking more practically, a window is a bordered white area on the Mac screen that you can work in. The most common type of window on the Mac is the document window. It usually displays a document (hence its name), but it's also the type of window you use on the desktop. Its main components are shown in this picture.

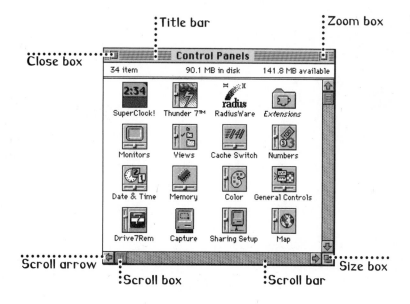

◦◦◆ **To move a window** on the screen, simply drag it around by its title bar.

◦◦◆ **Change a window's size** with the *size box* or the *zoom box*. Dragging the size box lets you choose any size for the window. Clicking the zoom box toggles between two different sizes.

The zoom box usually switches between a full-screen size and a "user-defined" one—whatever you've defined by dragging the size box. (When a window is switched to the user-defined size, its position changes, too, to wherever you last put it.) There's an awful lot (and I do mean *awful*, since it's terrible) of variety as to how this feature actually works. At first, some programs just toggled between the two most recent sizes that you created. Many times one of those would be a full-screen size (after all, the screen was only nine inches at the time). The full-screen/user-defined toggle seems pretty set now—but the definition of "full screen" isn't. And, if you're using an extra-large monitor, or a two-monitor setup, it's always an adventure to see what the zoom box does. On my 21-inch screen, for instance, "full screen" is sometimes the full screen; sometimes it's the full length but not the full width; sometimes it's only as much as is needed to

You can collapse a window down to its title bar in System 7.5. See the end of this chapter.

display the window contents; and sometimes the full size is constrained by memory considerations. (The Finder has a special way of handling zooming, which is covered in the next chapter.)

## THE WAY WE WERE ...

The Mac wasn't born with zoom boxes in its windows. They were added when the Mac Plus came out in 1986. (That's probably why there's some confusion as to how windows are supposed to "zoom"; it seems that anything that wasn't in the Mac's original interface specs is open to interpretation.)

> One of the problems ... was picking the names for things ... we used metaphoric names for lots of things—we used *window* because you look through it, *desktop* because it's what you do your work on, and *mouse* because it looks like one .... Those weren't the only names we tried. For a little while we were calling windows *viewers* and applications *skills*, because we thought those two words worked better together.

CHRIS ESPINOSA
(original Mac team)
*MacUser*, JANUARY 1989

∞❱ View **different parts** of a window's contents by using the scroll controls.

- Click in a scroll arrow to move the contents of the window a little bit at a time. What a "little bit" is depends on what's in the window. In a word processor, for instance, the window will scroll up or down a single line, and about an inch to the left or the right. In a spreadsheet, the window scrolls up or down a single row, and one column left or right. In the Finder, a window scrolls about a third of a full-size icon with each click.

- Hold down the mouse button on a scroll arrow for continuous, smooth scrolling. This is pretty handy for scanning through a word processed document until you find the spot you need.

- Drag the scroll box to a new position in the scroll bar to jump to the top, bottom, middle, or any other part of your document. The scroll box shows what part of the document you're viewing. For instance, if the box is in the middle of the vertical scroll bar, you're looking at the middle of your document; if it's at the top of the scroll bar, you're looking at the top of the document. (Apparently, the term *scroll box* is just too common for some people; you may hear it referred to as the *thumb* or the *elevator* sometimes, but I think that's pretty pretentious.)

- Click in the scroll bar on either side of the scroll box to move the contents a "windowful" at a time. There's always a little sliver of the previously displayed material left to keep you oriented—yet another elegant Mac touch. (Sometimes this is called "paging" but that gets confused with printed page equivalents; so we're left with no real word for this unit except "windowful," which also leaves something to be desired.)

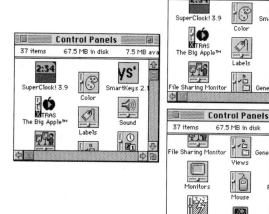

Using the scroll controls for a Finder window (left): the scroll arrow moves the contents a little (top), while clicking in the scroll box moves the contents in a larger increment (bottom).

◆ **When there's nothing to scroll around for**—that is, the window already is displaying everything there is to see—the scroll bar is blank instead of being filled with a dotted pattern, the scroll box is missing, and the scroll arrows are dimmed. This is a really useful visual clue; once you're used to it, you can tell at a glance in what direction a stray icon is hiding.

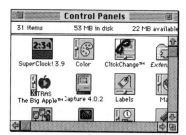

A window with active horizontal scroll bars (left); a window with nothing to scroll for horizontally (right).

◆ **Some windows can be *split*** by using the *split bar,* a thick black line at the top of the scroll arrow. By moving the split bar, you divide the window into two parts, each with its own scroll controls. The areas in a split window are sometimes referred to as *panes.*

Splitting a window lets you look at two different parts of your document at the same time. In a word processor, for instance, you can keep your introductory paragraph always in view while you work on the body of the document, making sure that you've covered all the points you introduced. In a spreadsheet, you can usually split a window both vertically and horizontally, giving you four independently scrolling areas on the screen.

⌐•➤ **Some utility programs** and desk accessories have windows; others, that don't handle documents as such, *are* windows. The Scrapbook, for instance, is a single window that displays many different pages. The Calculator is a window unto itself, too, even if it doesn't look like one. Its title bar is black, but there's still a close box in it.

The Calculator is a window.

⌐•➤ **A *floating window*,** also variously referred to as a *floating palette, tool palette,* or even *windoid* (my favorite, though it never made it into popular usage), defies the basic rule that the frontmost, or "top" window is the one that's affected by actions. You can still work in a document window while a floating window just, well, *floats* on top of it. I think HyperCard introduced the floating window approach, but today most graphics and layout programs provide this convenience.

Aside from the floating issue, these windows behave pretty much like standard windows. First of all, they have title bars of a sort—sometimes the title bar is checkered or gray instead of striped, sometimes it's at the side instead of on top, and many times it doesn't actually have a title in it. But you can use it to drag the window around, and it has a close box.

When you have more than one floating window around, they follow basic window rules. For instance, if you click on one, it comes to the top of the pile (the pile of floating windows, that is), and a click in its close box closes it.

A sampling of floating windows: the top three are from PageMaker; the "Shortcuts" palette is from ClarisWorks; the four at the right are from SuperPaint.

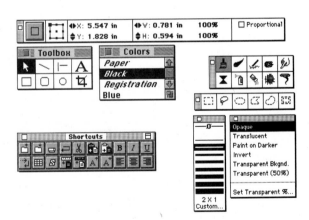

⌐•➤ **Use the Color control panel** to change your window color. Using any color except the Black & White choice gives you System 7's shaded frames and 3D-style controls on any color monitor or on a grayscale monitor set for 16 or more shades of gray. Applying a color doesn't change the background of the window, or its contents. It changes only the window "frame": the title bar and scroll controls.

Using the Color control panel to change the window color.

A black-and-white window (left) and a colored window (right).

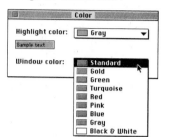
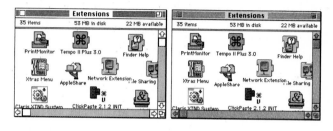

•••▶ **Your system runs faster** if you leave the windows set to black and white: the windows open, close, and scroll more quickly. Setting the windows to black and white won't affect the contents of the window.

•••▶ **Scroll controls seem to work backwards,** although maybe you haven't noticed. (From now on you will, and you'll probably think of me every time, too. Gosh!) You click on a down arrow and the contents of the window move *up*. You click on a right arrow and the window contents move *left*. That's because, conceptually, you're moving the window, not its contents. If the window moved to the right when you clicked the right arrow, your view of the contents would shift in that direction and it would look as if the contents moved left. You'll get used to it in no time.

Using a "down" control moves the window down, conceptually speaking, so the contents look as though they're moving up.

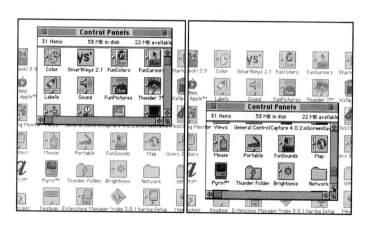

## Handling Multiple Windows

⟶ **There's only one *active* window** at any time. The active window is the one that you're working in, and it's affected by actions and commands. If you type or draw, the results appear in the active window; if you give a command, like Close, it's the active window that closes.

The active window is on top of any other windows on the screen. If windows aren't overlapping, you can identify the active window easily: It has a striped title bar and all its window controls are available. Inactive windows don't have any controls available—not even a close box—and, in color or grayscale systems, even their titles are dimmed.

To make a window active and move it to the top of the pile, you click in any exposed part of it.

An active window (left), and an inactive one (right).

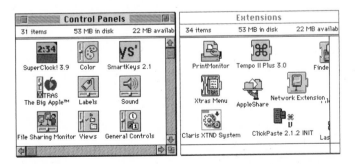

•••➤ **When you close the active window,** the last window you used in that same application is activated. If there aren't any other windows in the application, you'll just see whatever else is open in other applications and on the desktop—but no window will be active, because the application you're in is still running the show. (Although the only way you can tell is to check the menu bar.)

•••➤ **When you activate a window,** you also activate the application it belongs to. So, if you're at the desktop and click in the window that belongs to MacPaint, the Mac switches you into the MacPaint application while it activates the window.

When you move into an application by clicking on one of its windows, sometimes that's the window that's activated; sometimes, depending on the application, the window you were working in last is the one that's activated no matter which window you clicked on to get there.

•••➤ **In applications that have Window menus,** choosing a window's name from the menu activates it. Most of these menus, no matter what they're called, put a checkmark in front of the currently active window. Some applications even supply Command-key equivalents for selecting, and activating, windows.

Word's Window menu lists open documents (left). SuperPaint's View menu lists open documents with Command-key equivalents for their activation (right).

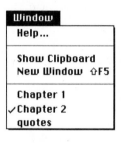

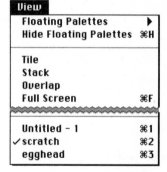

## MAC PEOPLE                                STEVE JOBS

In another life, Steven Jobs might have been a TV evangelist. Certainly when he teamed up with engineer Steve Wozniak in 1975, it was Jobs who supplied the inspiration. Woz would have been happy to give away the plans for his Apple I microcomputer boards to his fellow hackers at the Homebrew Computer Club; Jobs was the one who insisted that the things could be sold like kitchen appliances. His ability to inspire others with his visions was what got Apple going, and Apple, in turn, made Steve's visions real.

Ten years later, with the Apple II product line growing long in the tooth and the company starting to lose momentum, it was Jobs who commandeered a small in-house experimental group and brought forth the Macintosh. Applying both the carrot and the stick liberally, he lashed his crew into a fanatic frenzy of devotion to his dream: that the Mac would change everything about the way computers worked. Once again, Jobs succeeded in shaping the future to fit his vision. It was to be the last time Steve Jobs' dreams came true. His subsequent removal from the helm of Apple, in a 1986 palace coup engineered by newcomer John Sculley, left him a man without a company ... and his third computer, the NeXT machine, was his first flop.

—*Andy Baird*

•••❯ **When the screen is too cluttered** with background windows that belong to applications other than the one you're working in, use the Application menu's Hide Others command to make the other windows disappear. (There's more about the Application menu in Chapter 19.)

•••❯ **Many applications copy a desktop** capability that's very useful: You can move an inactive window without activating it, by holding down the Command key while you drag its title bar. This is handy when you're working in one window and need to refer to the contents of another window that's partially covered.

> The Macintosh "made it" because of a complex interweaving of people, places and events that I have come to refer to as the phenomenon of the Macintosh Community ... people began to form almost an electronic Woodstock .... Well, the love of a good computer system and of a good computer company was doing the same thing here. People ... were getting involved with more than just the Macintosh ... they were getting involved with other Macintosh *people*, other parts of the *community*.

**NEIL SHAPIRO**
*MACUSER*
MARCH 1988

GRACE SLICK

> I was appalled when the San Francisco ethic didn't mushroom and envelop the whole world into this loving community of acid freaks. I was very naive.

•••❯ **Juggling multiple windows** on a small screen can be difficult, especially when you have several open in an application that doesn't provide a Windows menu or any keyboard command to cycle around through open windows. Assuming that you don't need to see more than one window at a time, there are several ways you can always keep every window easily available for work.

My favorite method, before I graduated to a humongous screen and didn't have to worry about it any more, was the "tile and zoom" trick. Move and size your windows (let's assume there are four of them) so you can see them all completely—this is called *tiling*. Click in the zoom box of the one you want to work in, and it fills the screen. Click in its zoom box again and it moves back into its corner so you can see the other windows.

You can use this tiling method with fewer or more windows, of course—with three, for instance, you can make each occupy one-third of the screen horizontally. Five windows lend themselves to being long and skinny columns side by side with each other.

You can also work with multiple windows without zooming them in and out, if you don't mind using windows slightly smaller than screen size. Stack the windows so that one is all the way to the top and left of the screen; the next one should be slightly down and to the right; the next one a little further down and a little further to the right, and so on. When you're finished, and the last window is on the top, you'll be able to see the top and left edges of each of the windows in the pile. As soon as you activate one of the earlier windows, you won't be able to see the top edge of any of the later windows, but that doesn't matter: a piece of *every* window is always available in the upper-right corner of the screen.

With windows neatly stacked, as shown on the left, you can always see at least a corner of every other window no matter which window is on top.

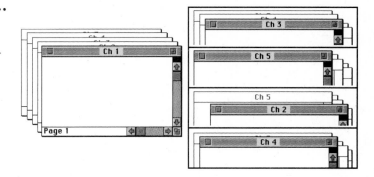

## Dialogs & Alerts

∞♦ A *dialog box*, or just *dialog*, is a special type of window where you're asked for certain information. Sometimes you only need to type a file name in it; sometimes you must choose options from a bewildering array of buttons, lists, and popup menus.

You might find any combination of the following elements in a dialog box:

- Text that describes what's going on.
- Text boxes that you can type in.
- Buttons—any of three basic kinds.
- Popup menus to select from.
- Icons that represent information or that you click on to choose an option.

The basic Page Setup dialog shown here combines most of the elements of a dialog.

Some dialogs are more like monologues, though not at all like Johnny's or Jay's or Arsenio's. An "About" box that gives information about the current program is a good example of this: You get some information but you don't have to supply any—and usually there's not even a button in it.

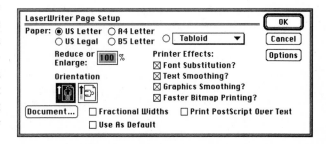

∘•▶ An *alert* is a dialog box that gives a warning which you acknowledge with an OK, or back out of with a Cancel button. It's almost always accompanied by a beep. In fact, sometimes you get only the beep, and not the dialog, until you've performed the same mistake several times in a row; at which point the Mac figures you *really* don't know what you're doing, and you'll finally get a dialog.

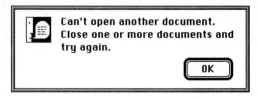

✳Speaking of "any key," my friend swears this is true: He was doing some training and instructed the new users to press the Tab key and type such-and-such; do so-and-so, and then press the Return key. When the screen appeared (this wasn't a Mac training session) that said: "Press any key to continue," one of the novices asked, "Where's the Any key?"

Apocryphal? Maybe. But I just picked up an Any key for my keyboard at a computer show. I'm going to Velcro it right next to the Panic button from the last show.

•▶ Some dialogs have no close controls—neither a close box nor any buttons. ("About" boxes that describe a program, or a program's opening screen, are often devoid of any close controls.) There are several ways you can get rid of these kinds of dialogs. Pressing Return, Enter, Esc, Command-period, or sometimes any key at all* might close the dialog. Sometimes you have to click on the dialog box itself; sometimes clicking anywhere on the screen works.

∘•▶ There are three standard icons used in alert boxes, for situations of varying intensity. *Note* is a talking head (not the official description), *Caution* is an exclamation point in a triangle that looks somewhat like a road sign, and *Stop* is a hand.

### MAC TRIVIA

Only one of the three basic alert icons in use today is from the original group of alert icons. The early Mac stuck much more to the idea of "dialog" and had a "talking head" for each of the three types of alerts. As you can see here, it was hard to figure out the hierarchy of problems: Which is more serious, an exclamation point or an asterisk?

∘•▶ Most dialog boxes are *modal*, meaning you can't do anything else until you've dealt with them—you're stuck in that mode, and you have to deal with the dialog before you can get back to a document, application, or the desktop. If you click outside the dialog, you'll just get a beep.

Modal dialog boxes used to be immovable windows with double frames around them, but that's not the case anymore. Sometimes a modal dialog will have a title bar that lets you drag it around on the screen.

A standard modal dialog (top) and a movable dialog (bottom).

The border for a modal dialog on grayscale and color systems, in keeping with System 7's general move toward 3-D styling, is shaded, but if you set your window color to black and white in the Color control panel, the dialogs revert to the plain double-line border.

**••➤** **You can continue working despite a modal dialog** when the dialog belongs to an application or function that can work in the background. A Finder copy operation, for instance, can run in the background while you continue working in your word processor. Most communications programs can work in the background while you do something else.

There's no indication that these dialogs aren't strictly modal, since they look exactly the same as other modal dialogs. You have to know that you can do something else in the application or that you can move to another application. If you're not sure whether something's a background operation, try clicking in another window or choosing an application from the Application menu.

## Text Boxes & Lists

**∞➤** **A *text box* in a dialog** (also referred to as a *text field*, or just as a *box* or *field*) is a place you type some information: the number of pages you want printed, for instance, or the name of the document you're saving. Text boxes accept most standard editing techniques like double-clicking to select a word; you can even use the arrow key to move through the text in the box.

The basic Print dialog has three text boxes.

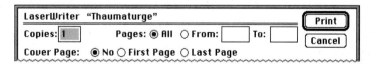

To move from one text box to another, you can click where you want to go or use Tab to cycle around the boxes. Clicking puts the insertion point in the text box at the spot you clicked; tabbing selects the entire contents of the box.

Clicking in a text box (top) and tabbing to it (bottom).

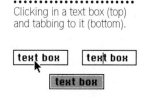

# A MAC ALMANAC LIST

## 11 Strange Dialog Messages

*Some of these messages were meant to be amusing; some were unintentionally so. (See if you can tell the difference.) The culprits are listed where possible, as are my comments where I couldn't restrain myself.*

**1** Make a LaunchKey of an FKEY? What planet are you from? Choose "OK" if you are very, very ashamed. [LaunchMaker]

**2** Due to an unfortunate disk duplication error, you have not received a working copy of SuperLaserSpool. Please contact SuperMac Software as soon as possible to receive a working copy of SuperLaserSpool. [SuperLaserSpool] *(Now, I ask you: If they could plan ahead to have that dialog appear when you double-click on the application's icon, couldn't they just as easily have planned to duplicate the correct disk?)*

**3** I must have amnesia. The date can't possibly be correct. We'd both be really happy if you'd fix it with the Control Panel. [MacServe]

**4** This disk is too full to save this document. Do you wish to cancel the "Quit"? [Ready, Set, Go! 4.0] *(This is no big deal unless you saw the dialog box itself, which offered a Cancel and an OK button. So, if you wanted to cancel the quit, as asked … would you use Cancel or OK?)*

**5** An unexplicably unexpected and therefore unexplainable ERROR has occurred extemporaneously and expunges the program integrity. Not to be an extenuator, but you should cycle the power and try again. [Softsync's Accountant]

**6** Real Mac users don't need Help! [RamDisk+] *(It showed up, of course, when you clicked on the Help button.)*

**7** Drat! An error occurred while reading or writing! [MassCopier] *(And the only button in the dialog was: Bummer.)*

**8** This one's a visual:

*Finally, three from System 7:*

**9** The command could not be completed, because it is in use. *(How do you suppose it could be completed if it* weren't *being used?)*

**10** Sorry, a Finder error occurred. Bad F-Line instruction. *(This occurs so frequently, it's often referred to as the F-word dialog.)*

**11** The alias [filename] could not be opened, because this item is really not an alias (oops!). The problem has now been corrected. Please try again.

∘•❯ **Tabbing cycles you through** text boxes, left to right and top to bottom, as you would read through the dialog. When you reach the last text box, another tab puts you back into the first box. When a dialog has text fields framed in a group, tabbing usually moves you through the group first and then to the next group.

Shift-Tab moves you in the opposite direction. So if you Tab too far or too quickly, you can Shift-Tab to move backwards instead of reaching for the mouse.

∘•❯ **Shift-Tab is a shortcut** to the last text box. When a dialog opens, the first text box is selected by default.* Since Shift-Tab moves you in the opposite direction from Tab, a Shift-Tab moves you backwards from the first text box to the end of the dialog, selecting the last box, then the next-to-the-last box, and so on.

> *Default is a word that's used repeatedly when it comes to things on your computer. The default is the choice that's going to be made unless you specify otherwise. When I take the kids to our favorite, oft-frequented, pizza place, the waitress brings me a Diet Coke unless I tell her otherwise; Diet Coke's my default.

∘•❯ **If text is highlighted** in a text box, you don't have to hit Delete to erase it before you type something new: Typing something always replaces selected text. That's why it's usually better to Tab to a text box than to click in it—with the contents automatically selected when you Tab, you can just go ahead and type the new words.

∘•❯ **When there's a scrolling list** in a dialog box, you can, of course, always scroll around until you find what you want and then click on it. But in many programs, you can type the first few letters of an item's name to select it; sometimes the up and down arrow keys will select things in the list. You won't necessarily find these functions spelled out in a program's manual, so always experiment in dialog boxes.

•••❯ **Pressing Tab selects** the contents of a text field even when it's the only text in the dialog. So what? So this: Say you have a Find dialog in your word processor and you search for the word *booklet*, but no occurrences are found. Then you remember you used the word *pamphlet*. The Find dialog is still open, with the cursor blinking after the "*t*" in *booklet*. Here are your choices: erase seven letters with the Delete key and then type the new word; reach for the mouse, double-click on the word to select it, and then go back to the keyboard to type over it; or, hit Tab to select the word and type the new one.

•••❯ **You can use Cut, Copy, and Paste** in the text boxes of some dialogs. Which ones? Sorry, you'll have to experiment to see which ones, because it depends on the application.

## Buttons

∘•❯ There are three basic button types.

• A push button is the most common type. Clicking in it is like selecting a command from a menu. In fact, some-

[ Cancel ]    [ OK ]    [ Open... ]

times you'll see a push button that has an ellipsis after it, indicating that it will open yet another dialog box—just like the ellipsis after a menu command.

- A radio button is used for a list of mutually exclusive options. When you select one, the previous one is deselected. They're called radio buttons after the selection buttons on old car radios, where, as you pushed one in to pick a station, the last one popped back out.

Radio buttons are for mutually exclusive choices; clicking on one deselects the previous one.

┌ Model ─────┐   ┌ Model ─────┐
│ ◉ Two doors │   │ ○ Two doors │
│ ○ Four doors│   │ ◉ Four doors│
│ ○ Hatchback │   │ ○ Hatchback │
└─────────────┘   └─────────────┘

- A checkbox is used when there's a list of options where you can choose as many as you want. Clicking in a checkbox selects the option and puts an X in the box; clicking in the checkbox again deselects the option and removes the X.

Checkboxes are for choices that are not mutually exclusive.

┌ Options ──────────────────────────────┐
│ ☐ Power windows      ☐ Air conditioning │
│ ☒ Leather seats      ☒ Stereo           │
│ ☒ Driver airbag      ☒ Sun roof         │
│ ☐ Passenger airbag   ☐ Anti-lock brakes │
└───────────────────────────────────────┘

•◂ **A dimmed button,** like a dimmed menu command, can't be used under the current circumstances.

•◂ **You don't have to click directly** in the circle of a radio button or the square of a checkbox—clicking anywhere on the title of the button works just as well. In fact, you can click inside any part of the rectangular area made by the button itself and its name.

•◂ **You can use the keyboard** to "click" buttons:

- The default button is a push button framed by a heavy line; it's the one the Mac assumes you want to use unless you tell it otherwise. Pressing Return or Enter is the same as clicking on a default button. (Sometimes it's also referred to as the *highlighted* button, since the frame calls attention to it, even though it's nothing like highlighted text.)

  [ **OK** ]

There are lots of shortcuts for Open and Save dialogs. See Chapter 19.

- Pressing Return or Enter usually works even if there's no button that's highlighted as the default (especially when there's only one button anyway).
- Command-period or Esc often works if there's a Cancel button in the dialog.
- Some applications provide keyboard shortcuts for their own dialog boxes so you can control everything from the keyboard. For example, in most Microsoft products, pressing the first letter of a button's name has the same effect as clicking the button; if there's a text box that would register the keypress, then pressing Command along with the letter activates the button. If you're not going to read your software manuals, don't forget to experiment a little in dialog boxes.

∞⟩ **Several utilities give you keyboard control** of dialog buttons and other elements.

- Click that OK button even when you're not there. If you've ever given a print command and then walked away from your computer only to come back an hour

Okey Dokey

later to find the Print dialog still on the screen, you'll appreciate a utility that clicks the OK button in a dialog that's been sitting on your screen for too long. Try OkayOkayOkay or Okey Dokey. (Don't you just love some of these names?) [OkayOkayOkay, freeware, author unknown; Okey Dokey, freeware, Dan Walkowski and Brent Pease]

- DialogKeys is a utility that comes with the QuicKeys macro program; it lets you control all dialog box elements from the keyboard. [QuicKeys, CE Software]
- Use a macro utility that lets you assign button clicks and even menu selections to certain keys. These are covered in Chapter 21.

➔ **The default button won't always** be the one you're most likely to use in a dialog box. Take, for instance, a dialog box that's confirming a "dangerous," and non-undoable command like, say, replacing an existing document named Novel with a new document named Novel.

If the program's designed correctly, the dialog's going to ask "Do you really want to do this?" and offer Yes and No buttons, with the No button highlighted. Now, if you've given the Replace command, it's very likely you really want that file replaced, and you'd like the Yes button highlighted so you can just hit Return to choose it. But what if, at the last second, you wonder if that other file has some purple passages in it that you just won't be able to re-create? And you hit the Return button anyway, out of habit? Well, with the Yes button highlighted, you'd have the new document saved over the other one, and there wouldn't be much you could do about it. Now, what happens when the situation is reversed: you really want to replace the document, the No button is highlighted, and you hit Return by mistake? No great loss—you've only cancelled the Replace command and you can choose it again; you've wasted only a few seconds.

This kind of protection against stupid and/or careless mistakes is referred to as *idiot-proofing,* and you shouldn't find that offensive; we're all part-time idiots. (Full-time idiots don't take offense because they don't think the term applies to them at all.)

JOHN C. DVORAK
*MacUser,* November 1990

> Use an idiot-oriented machine and you can feel like an idiot—and then become one.

➔ **Sometimes an icon is a button.** When HyperCard came out, it introduced this little problem; up until then, an icon was something you double-clicked on, while a button got a single click. Most "icon buttons" are inside square or rounded frames so they look a little more like buttons than plain icons.

➔ **A checkbox can be filled with gray**. This means that within the selection you've made, there are parts that the checkbox description applies to, but it doesn't apply to the whole selection. Clicking in a gray checkbox cycles it around from gray to checked to empty, and back to gray again. If you check the box, the option will apply to the entire selection; unchecked, the option is removed from the entire selection. Put it back to gray and the selection retains its mixed formats.

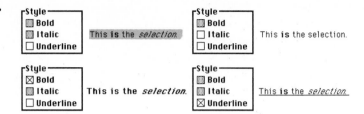

The original selection (top-left) and the results of cycling through some of the checkbox choices.

## (Inter) Facelifts

∞§ **The elegance of the Mac interface** took years of research and design. But you can ruin in it minutes. Color your menus, shrink your windows, change your button styles, make new window "frames" … the possibilities are endless.

There are many small utilities that let you tweak specific parts of the interface, like the way windows behave, or the way menus look, and I've sampled some of the best in this section for you. But two commercial collections stand out because of the wide variety of choices they provide.

**CLICKCHANGE**

• ClickChange's many options would be bewildering if they weren't so neatly combined into a simple control panel with an easy-to-use interface. Among its features are cursor-substitution (covered in the last chapter), sound-assignment (described at the end of this chapter), and desktop backgrounds (discussed in the next chapter). Apropos to this section is its ability to: change the style and color of window controls and title bars, including the pattern in scroll bars and the size of the scroll box; alter the look and color of all types of buttons; and, change menu titles to icons.

Some of the specific capabilities of ClickChange are described in the next few entries, under the appropriate category. But I'll say this: I've reviewed software for MacUser magazine since it started, and I've given its top five-mouse rating to only two products in eight years. ClickChange is one of them. (Unfortunately, the editors, in their infinite wisdom, bumped it back to 4.5 mice.) [Dubl-Click]

ClickChange's control panel.

- NowFun also lets you change the overall look of your Macintosh. It provides basically the same functions as ClickChange, but in a less elegant (lots of different control panels) and slightly smaller package. (It's missing, for instance, ClickChange's icon menu titles and double scroll arrows.) Its sound, cursor, and desktop pattern functions are covered elsewhere, but in the rest of this section, you'll find several mentions of the package's menu- and window-changing capabilities. [Now Software]

One of NowFun's control panels.

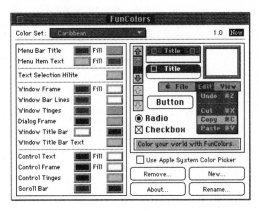

∞◊ **Access menus without** holding the mouse button down with AutoMenus. Just wander into the menu bar with the pointer and a menu will drop onto the screen—you don't have to press the mouse button to open the menu. Slide to the item you want and then click the mouse button to select the command. [shareware, Michael J. Conrad]

AutoMenus

∞◊ **Change your menu titles** when the menu bar is too crowded or boring. Change the long titles to short ones, change the words to icons, change the icons to animations … variety is the spice of life.

The Finder menu bar, before and after customization.

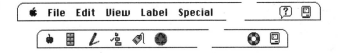

There are several utilities that let you alter your menu bar:

- ClickChange lets you replace any menu title in the Finder or any application with static or animated icons. [Dubl-Click]

- Menuette provides icons instead of names for menu titles and lets you switch between icon and text titles with a few clicks in the menu bar. You even get to choose what font the text titles should be in. [freeware, L Productions]

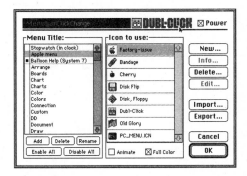

Menuette

- Zipple replaces any of the three system menus (Apple, Help, and Application) with an animated cursor of your choice—you can even create your own design. [shareware, Christopher Suley]

- MICN lets you replace any common menu title (File, Edit, Window, and so on) with an editable icon. [freeware, Mark Valance]

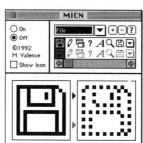

◦◦◊ **Color your menus** (which normally stay black and white no matter how you color your windows or desktop). Both ClickChange and NowFun! let you assign separate colors to the menu bar and its menu titles, the text in menus, and the background color of menus. NowFun! even lets you choose a highlight color for when you're selecting from a menu. (I think that, at least, should be a system-level option. Colors or grays for the text highlight are so much nicer than the inverted white-on-black highlight used in menus.) Greg's Buttons, despite its name, also lets you assign colors to the menu bar and menus.

Other menu utilities are discussed in Chapters 6 and 11.

◦◦◊ **Dragging a window** really drags just an outline of the window; when you let go of the mouse button, the window moves to where the outline was. With RealDrag, you can drag the window itself around on the screen. (I'm not sure why you'd want to, but, hey, the whole point of little utilities is that they make some of the people happy some of the time.) [freeware, James Osborne]

Real DRAG

◦◦◊ **It's much more convenient to have double scroll arrows** so you don't have to move from the top to the bottom of the window just to scroll back and forth.

This is one of those minor things that I always thought would be a good idea, but it took me years to get around to trying—now I refuse to live without it.* If you have a full-page screen, it's a long trip from the top of a window to the bottom just to scroll the document back a little bit; but double arrows are convenient even in a Save or Open dialog, and especially in something like the Scrapbook. And, if you use a PowerBook and have trouble with the trackball, it's a blessing. There are several utilities, listed on the next page, that add this feature to your system.

*Well, I say that I refuse to live without it, but it's one of the many things I have to do without while I'm working on this book. My friend and colleague, Bob LeVitus, was just bemoaning this fact with me in a recent conversation. We have to keep straight vanilla systems because when we take "screen shots" so you can see what we're talking about, there can't be any extraneous items like double scroll arrows in our windows—or you'll be looking through your control panels trying to find out how to activate that feature.
See what we sacrifice for our readers?

Double scroll arrows make even paging through the Scrapbook easier.

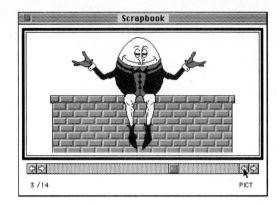

- ClickChange provides double scroll arrows in many styles.
- DoubleScroll is an extension that puts double arrows in your window controls. [shareware, Edward Voad, ISYS Development]

DoubleScroll 2.0

- Scroll2 provides double arrows as well as a choice of three different arrow styles and options for scroll bar patterns. [shareware, Mayson G. Lancaster]

Scroll2 v2.1

∘∘⬡ **Shrink windows down**—way down—with ClickChange, ZoomBar or WindowShade; all let you turn a window into nothing but its title bar with a few clicks. You can move the shrunken windows around on the screen (since it's the title bar that lets you move windows) and easily zoom them back to their former glory. It's a great way to handle multiple windows on a small screen. [ZoomBar, shareware, Brian Westley; WindowShade, shareware, Rob Johnston]

ZoomBar shrinks five windows into this neat stack of title bars.

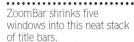
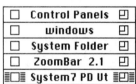

A Window-Shade control panel comes with System 7.5. It's described at the end of this Chapter

∘∘⬡ **WindowWizard** keeps track of all your windows at once—every open window for every application. You can configure it to pop up in the menu bar, in any window's title bar, or anywhere on the screen. WindowWizard's menu lists all the windows for the current application, as well as all the applications you have running—and every application in the list gets a submenu of its windows. Select a window and move directly to it. [shareware, Eric de la Musse]

WindowWizard's menu lists all the windows for all opened applications.

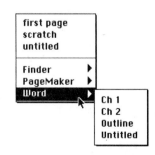

∘∘⬡ **Go wild with your windows** with ClickChange or NowFun, both of which go far beyond the Color control panel. Change the color of various window components: the title bar, the close and zoom boxes, even the window title itself. You can even change the pattern in the scroll bar.

ClickChange goes much further, though, since it allows you to change styles as well as colors: pick new title bars, scroll arrows, and scroll boxes. Choose a different font for the window title, and move it left or right instead of keeping it centered.

Some title bar and scroll bar options in ClickChange.

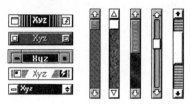

∞◊ **The only way you can resize** a window is by dragging from its lower-right corner, with the upper-left corner (where the close box is) pretty much anchored to its spot on the screen. But Stretch2 adds a frame around every window so you can stretch it in any direction: drag from the top and make the window taller or shorter without moving its bottom edge; drag it from any corner to resize it in two directions at once. As a bonus, Stretch2 also lets you multiple-click in a window's title bar to turn the window into an icon to save room on your screen. [shareware, Ross Tyler]

Stretch2's frame around a window lets you resize it in any direction.

∞◊ **You can't have plain buttons** once you've altered your windows and menus. Greg's Buttons lets you change the style of checkboxes and radio buttons. ClickChange, as usual, provides a wide variety of button styles and colors. [Greg's Buttons, shareware, Gregory D. Landweber]

Some of ClickChange's button styles.

∞◊ **Alert icons didn't change to 3D design** in System 7 even though windows did. If you want some better looking icons for your alert boxes, you can get them from the Red Alert module of the 7th Heaven utility collection; this picture shows some of the choices—although the real ones are in color. [7th Heaven, Logical Solutions]

## → THE CLIPBOARD ←

### Clipboard Basics

∞•➔ **The *Clipboard* is** a unique concept that was introduced by the Macintosh. You use it to transfer text, graphics, and even sound and animation, from one place to another. The "places" can be in the same document, in different documents in the same application, or even in documents that belong to different applications.

The three main facts to know about the Clipboard are:

- The Clipboard holds only one item at a time, although that item can be as large as an entire document.
- When you put a new item on the Clipboard, it erases the previous item.
- Clipboard contents are held in RAM—the part of the computer's memory that "forgets" everything when the computer's shut down or restarted.

The Clipboard doesn't actually *exist*. On one level, that's not as hard to absorb as the truth about Santa or the Tooth Fairy, but on another—since there seems to be a lot more evidence for the Clipboard's existence—it's more difficult. But it doesn't really exist the way other things do on the Mac, because it isn't, for instance, a desk accessory that you can take out, or a utility that you can run.

∞•➔ **The Edit menu** changes from one application to another, but it almost always contains the commands you need to work with the Clipboard.

- Cut removes selected material from a document and puts it on the Clipboard.
- Copy puts selected material on the Clipboard without removing the original from the document.
- Paste puts the material that's on the Clipboard into your document. Where the pasted material appears depends on the application you're using. In a text document, for instance, pasted text is placed at the insertion point or replaces a selection.

There's lots more about pasting text and graphics in Chapter 20.

- Clear deletes a selection from your document without putting it on the Clipboard; it's not available in all applications.

∞•➔ **The Clipboard isn't always entirely in RAM.** (Okay, so I lied before.) But it's important that you treat it as if it were, because the whole thing might as well be in memory—if you crash, or otherwise turn off your computer, you'll lose the material that's on it.

Sometimes, though, what you put on the Clipboard is really too large to fit in RAM, so the application in charge puts some of it on the disk and grabs it again later when you need it. So, you'll often find a Clipboard file in your System Folder.

••◆ **The keyboard equivalents** for Undo, Cut, Copy, and Paste are Command-Z, -X, -C, and -V, the first four letters on the bottom row of the keyboard. So what if C is the only letter that matches the word it stands for? You'll be using them so often that you'll start thinking that *Paste* begins with V and *Cut* begins with X. If you have trouble remembering the keyboard commands at first, it's helpful to think of the X as a pair of scissors. Any other mnemonics are pretty much a stretch; just force yourself to use the keyboard commands for a while, though, and they'll sink in.

### Mac Trivia

When the Clear command has a keyboard equivalent, it's usually Command-B. Why? Because C was already used for Copy? No. Because B was the only letter left after all the other commands got their letters? Nope. It's because the original Mac keyboards didn't have a Delete key—the key was the *Backspace* key, and hitting Backspace to delete a selection was the same as using the Clear command.

••◆ **When you use a Show Clipboard** command (like the one in the Finder's Edit menu), you get a "view-only" window that shows you what's on the Clipboard—you can't select it or edit it in any way.

••◆ **Double-clicking on the Clipboard icon** that's in the System Folder opens a window that displays the Clipboard contents. It's the same as using the Show Clipboard command.

••◆ **You can make a generic Show Clipboard** command that you can access from any application that doesn't provide one of its own:

Using a Show Clipboard command.

1. Make an alias of the Clipboard icon that's in the System Folder.
2. Rename the alias *Show Clipboard.*
3. Put the alias in the Apple Menu Items folder.

Any time you want to see the Clipboard, select the "command" from the Apple menu. You'll be switched to the desktop and the Clipboard window will open.

## Undo

••◆ **The Undo command is** an escape mechanism. If you have second thoughts about something you just changed in your document, selecting Undo "undoes" it. It's merely handy when you've made a phrase italic and then changed your mind. But it's a lifesaver when you've hit the Delete key by mistake and a selection has disappeared.

Some programs are very stingy when it comes to Undo. Aside from poorly designed programs that ignore the Mac interface and don't let you undo *anything*, there are perfectly wonderful programs, like PageMaker, that constantly surprise me as to how often Undo isn't available.

(The first sentence of the previous paragraph started out in life as: *Some programs are very niggardly when it comes to Undo.* It was suggested—I'm using the passive voice so no one in particular is blamed—that I find a substitute, as some readers might not be familiar with this utterly innocent, perfectly descriptive adjective, and it sounds like, well, such a *bad* word. Personally, I lump that criticism with the one that says *history* is sexist because it says "his story." Balderdash! (See, another great, soon-to-be-archaic word—it might offend the less hirsute among us.) I mention this only because this editing suggestion came just days after something was changed in the first draft of Chapter 1: the phrase "black humorists" was replaced with "cynics." Why? Because the editor had been misunderstood one too many times when he used the phrase—people thought he was talking about Richard Pryor. Come on. Political correctness is one thing, limited vocabularies another. May I suggest the *Reader's Digest* and its regular feature, *It Pays to Enrich Your Word Power™?*)

- - - - - - - - - - - - - - - - - - - - - - - - - - - - - - - - - - - - -

 **T-SHIRT SIGHTING**

*Front:* The problem with life …

*Back:* No Undo!

**What can Undo undo?** Undo basically undoes *editing* actions whether you're working with text, graphics, or sound. Did you type over a selection but now you want to return to the original material? Did you change your logo from puce to chartreuse but now you realize that the puce was *so* much classier? Those are both editing actions that can be undone. But you can't undo something like saving a document, or moving into a magnified view of your document, since those aren't editing actions. Sometimes the Undo command in the Edit menu is very explicit as in: Undo Formatting, or Undo Typing, or Undo Style Change.

**Undo undoes only** your *last* action. If you delete some selected text, Undo restores it. If you delete some text, then apply italic formatting to a phrase, Undo will remove the formatting, but it won't rescue the deleted text. (Some programs, like the word processor Nisus, provide multiple levels of Undo, but the Mac system itself provides only one.)

**You can undo your Undo,** and undo that Undo, moving back and forth between two states.* Sometimes the command in the Edit menu changes to Redo after an Undo; sometimes it's even more descriptive, like Redo Formatting, or Redo Typing, or Redo Style Change.

> *When the Mac was first released, bundled with MacWrite and MacPaint, we used the Undo command in MacPaint to provide Hanna-Barbera-like animation of, say, a penguin flapping its wing. (Hey, all we had was MacWrite and MacPaint!)

••➤ **When you use Undo after** cutting or copying something to the Clipboard, the Clipboard gets "undone," too—the item is removed, and the previous item is restored.

••➤ **Before you make any undoable** but really major change to your document, save it. That way, if you want to "undo" the change, all you have to do is close the document without saving it again and then reopen the previously saved version.

## Working with the Clipboard

••➤ **Pasting something doesn't take it off** the Clipboard; it puts a *copy* of what's on the Clipboard into the document. That means you can paste something from the Clipboard over and over again.

••➤ *Flush* **the Clipboard** to free up memory. If you've just copied 30 pages of text from one document to another, there's a lot of memory tied up and your application may start running more slowly. You can't actually empty the Clipboard, but you can put something smaller on it. Copy a single letter (or, if you're in a graphics program, a very small graphic item) to the Clipboard—*twice*. The first time you do it, the new item is on the Clipboard, but the old contents are being held in reserve in case you use the Undo command, which would undo the copy procedure and place the old contents back on the Clipboard.

••➤ **Some programs ask if you want to preserve** the Clipboard contents when you're quitting. If you don't need what's there, tell the program to get rid of it. If there's a lot on the Clipboard and you don't need it, but the program isn't smart enough to ask you, flush the Clipboard yourself.

••➤ **Not all programs know enough to** put large Clipboard contents on the disk. If you get any Out of Memory messages (*Can't complete operation—out of memory; Can't Undo— not enough memory; Running low on memory—save your document and quit the application*) it might be because the Clipboard contents are taking up so much room. Flushing the Clipboard sometimes alleviates the out of memory problem—at least for a while.

••➤ **If you "lose" what's on the Clipboard** as you transfer from one program to another it might be because the information just can't be transferred (see the next entry) or it might just be a minor glitch. There are lots of times I've copied, say, a graphic from a Word document, switched over to SuperPaint, and the Paste command either is dimmed because the Clipboard is blank or it pastes down the previous Clipboard item instead of the most recent. Looking at the Clipboard in SuperPaint shows the previous item; switching back to Word and looking at the Clipboard there shows that the most recent item *is* there. For some reason, the new Clipboard item is just not interpreted during the move from one application to another. (In my experience, Word is often a culprit in this area, but then I use Word more than anything else, so that's not exactly a statistically valid observation.) In any case, here are a few things you can try when your copied material doesn't seem to "stick" to the Clipboard between applications; they've all worked for me at sometime or another.

- Repeat the Copy command at the original location and try again.
- Hold Option while you choose the Copy command from the Edit menu.
- Paste the material inside the original application before switching to the other one.
- Go through the Finder: Move to the desktop, check the Clipboard with the Show Clipboard command, and if the material is there, move to the second application.
- Use the Scrapbook as a last result. From the original application, go to the Scrapbook and paste the material there. Then move to the second application—usually you can do a direct paste at this point, without having to copy the material out of the Scrapbook. But if the paste doesn't work, move back to the Scrapbook, Copy or Cut the material, and then paste it into the second application.

→ **The information that actually gets transferred** through the Clipboard sometimes depends on where you got it from and where you're putting it. When you're working within a single application, anything that you can select and copy can be pasted anywhere else, since that application "understands" everything you've put on the Clipboard.

But when you're copying and pasting between applications, you may lose some information—or not be able to paste at all. You can't, for instance, paste a sound into an icon you've selected on the desktop, even though you can copy a sound when you're in the Sound control panel. You can paste text into an icon's title, but you can't paste *formatted* text—icons on the desktop don't use bold, underline, and so on.

The "lost" information isn't really lost, as you'll see if you paste it back down in the application that it came from—it's still on the Clipboard. But when an application can't understand all the Clipboard information, it ignores what it doesn't understand and just interprets what it can—the plain text, for instance.

System 7.5's Clipboard should handle more formats and keep them consistent between applications.

Although the Macintosh ... was unarguably inspired by research done at Xerox PARC ... Apple deserves recognition for being the first to bring a graphic user interface to market in a personal computer.

FRED DAVIS
*MacUser*, NOVEMBER 1988

SIR WILLIAM OSLER
(1849–1919)

In science the credit goes to the man who convinces the world, not to the man to whom the idea first came.

⸱⸱➤ **There's no such thing as** a *system* Clipboard and an *application* Clipboard. There's only one Clipboard, but some people use these phrases to refer to the way the Clipboard can use internal formats within an application that might not transfer to another program.

⸱⸱➤ **There are three basic types of information** that the Clipboard is expected to handle, and each gets a four-letter resource label. (Resources are discussed in Chapter 21.) Plain, unformatted text is *TEXT*. Bit-mapped or object-oriented graphics that can be rendered with QuickDraw commands on the Mac's screen are *PICT* resources. Text with character formatting is a *styl* resource. But, in addition to these basic formats used by the Mac system, every program can also use any private format it wants; these internal formats are also special resource types with their own names.

The formats aren't entirely mutually exclusive—things are put on the Clipboard in both TEXT and styl formats, for instance. So, a program that can't interpret the styl information can still extract the TEXT.

And that's why, as explained in the last entry, internal copy and pastes always work but the Clipboard doesn't always transfer everything into another program. Unless that other program understands the special format, it won't know what to do with the information.

⸱⸱➤ **If you want to check the type** of information that's on the Clipboard (who am I to pass judgment on your eternal quest for knowledge?), paste it into the Scrapbook. You'll see a list of the data formats for each Scrapbook page.

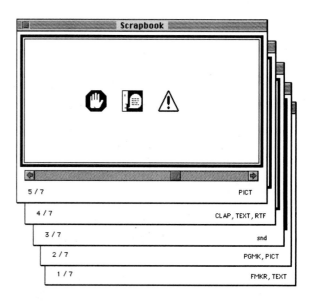

File types noted in the
Scrapbook window.

⸱⸱➤ **A full Clipboard slows you down** as you move from one program to another. The translation that a program does to interpret the contents of the Clipboard doesn't occur only when you use the Paste command—it happens whenever you move into an application, whether you're moving into it from another program that's running at the same time or you're just launching the program.

Having lots of stuff on the Clipboard can make the switch from one program to another take up to 30 seconds instead of, say, three. So, if you don't need what's on the Clipboard, flush it before you move to another program.

**A large Clipboard can interfere** with a program launch. When you open a program, it gets the amount of memory you've allocated to it. But sometimes the Mac puts a copy of the Clipboard into an application's memory partition when the application is first launched. If you have a really big Clipboard, you could have problems launching or later using that application. In all, it's a good idea to flush the Clipboard before opening any application.

**Most "Clipboard utilities" are** really Scrapbook replacements, and they're covered in Chapter 7. But there are products that really are Clipboard enhancers:

- MultiClip lets you use variations on the Cut, Copy, and Paste command-key equivalents (Command-Option-X, Command-Option-C, and Command-Option-V) to paste multiple items onto a special Clipboard. You can paste things from this Clipboard either in the order you copied them, or the reverse order. There's also a MultiClip command available from the Apple menu that lets you get at the items (they're called ClipFrames) on the Clipboard. You can do some minor editing, and you can even save them as separate files. [Olduvai]

- ClipClop is actually an application that runs in the background while you work. Every time you use the Cut or Copy command in any application, a new window is created in ClipClop to hold the "clip." When you use the Paste command, whatever's in the topmost ClipClop window is pasted. You can move into ClipClop itself any time you want to reorganize its windows or to close any of them. [Shareware, Pi Zero Software]

- The Clipper lets you resize or crop items on the Clipboard before they're pasted down in a document by using a transparent floating window with little stretch handles on it. [SmartScrap and The Clipper, Portfolio Systems]

## →I SYSTEM SOUNDS I←

## Basics

The *alert sound,* or *system beep,* is that, well, *beeping* sound you hear when an alert box shows up, or when you click outside of a dialog box where you can't do anything, or anytime the Mac wants to get your attention. Of course, the beep doesn't have to be a beep at all, but it's generally called that anyway.

**POP QUIZ**                  **[3 POINTS]**

What cartoon character's vocabulary consists of "Beep, Beep"? No, wait, that's too easy. Try this: Which Beatle song used "Beep, Beep" as a background refrain?

•→ **Use the Sound control panel** to change the beep to some other sound, or just to change its volume.

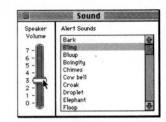

The standard Sound control panel (top) and the latest update (bottom).

An update to System 7.1 includes a new Sound control panel with an altered interface, but the basic functions are the same in both control panels. With the new one, you have to choose Alert Sounds from the popup menu to get to the list of installed sounds.

To change the sound, select another one from the list. (Four sounds come with your system.) When you click on a name, the sound plays. Be careful—if you double-click, it will play twice. That's no big deal for a simple chime, but if you have a longer sound, you'll have to listen to it twice—and there's no way to stop it once it starts.

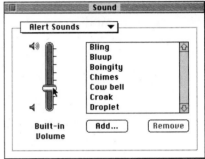

To change the volume, slide the bar up and down on the volume control. When you let go of the control, you'll hear the sound at that volume. If you set the sound to level 0, your menu bar will flash any time a sound would have played. (This is handy when you're using a PowerBook in a meeting, or on a plane, or in bed when your mate is already highly annoyed that it's there at all.)

•→ **The sounds listed in the Sound** control panel are the ones inside your System file, with one exception: the Simple Beep in the list isn't in the System file. That's so you won't drag all the sounds out and leave your Mac speechless. And the Mac won't let you delete it from the control panel's list, either.

The sounds listed in the Sound control panel are the ones in your System file.

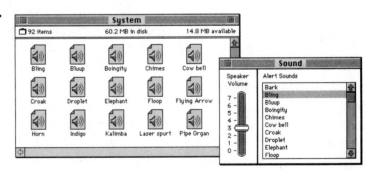

•→ **You can use the Cut or Copy** command on a selected sound in the list in the Sound control panel. You can't see a sound on the Clipboard, but you can hear it. Here's what the Clipboard window looks like when a sound is in it:

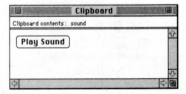

If you want to remove a sound without putting it on the Clipboard, you can use the Remove button that's in some Sound control panels, or the Clear command from the Edit menu.

You can paste a sound from the Clipboard into the Sound control panel. Just open the control panel and choose Paste. You get to name the sound before it's added to the list.

## HOW THE SOUND CONTROL PANEL *REALLY* WORKS

•••➤ **The Scrapbook can hold sounds,** and any page with a sound on it also gets a Play button. And that Play button is the only way you'll be able to figure out what the sound is, since all you'll see is the standard sound icon in the Scrapbook, and there's no way to name a Scrapbook page.

All sounds look alike in the Scrapbook, so the Play button comes in handy.

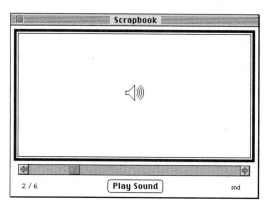

•••➤ **You can't simply rename a sound** in the Sound control panel. But here's the workaround: Select the sound you want to rename and cut it; then, paste it back in— you'll be asked to name it.

•••➤ **A sound loads *entirely* into memory** before it's played. For long sounds, you'll need lots of memory. You can't record too long a sound through the Sound control panel, because it limits you to ten seconds of recording. But if you collect sounds from elsewhere, you may be surprised at how much memory they can eat up. Basic system sounds take 3–20K of space on the disk. But a full minute of sound that's been recorded at 22kHz (better quality than the basic control panel sounds) takes more than a meg of disk space.

If you're running short on memory (well, not *you*, but your Mac), a sound may not play at all.

## Sound Files

∞✦ **Sounds are stored inside** the System file. If you double-click on the System file icon to open it, you'll see the sound files, each with its distinctive speaker icon.

∞✦ **To move a sound in or out** of the System file, just drag the file into or out of the System file icon or its window. You can also drag the sound file into the closed System Folder icon. You'll be asked if you want the sound stored inside the System file itself, where it belongs. But you can't add or remove a sound if there are any applications running.

∞✦ **Double-click on a sound file** to play the sound.

∞✦ **All sounds "look" the same** but you can use System 7's icon-editing capability (see Chapter 4) to change a sound's icon to something more appropriate. Unfortunately, a sound file loses its special icon if you put it in the System file.

Sound files in the System Folder.

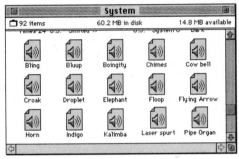

∘•➤ **There are two distinct ways** to handle system sounds. One is to manipulate the sound *files*, dragging them in and out of the System file. The other is to deal with the sound on the Clipboard, copying and pasting it from one place to another—in the Scrapbook, the Sound control panel, or an application that can handle sound.

But there's no *direct* way of connecting these two methods: You can't, for instance, select a sound icon on the desktop and copy the sound to the Clipboard. What gets copied is the *name* of the sound, not the sound itself. Nor can you just open the System file and paste in a sound from the Clipboard.

But you can use the Sound control panel as the intermediary between the Clipboard and the System file when it comes to sounds. If you have a sound on the Clipboard and you want it in the System file, paste the sound into the Sound control panel (you'll be asked to name it) and it will appear in the list. (If you're using the updated Sound control panel, you should choose Alert Sounds from the popup menu before using the Paste command.) It will also appear as a sound file in the System file. If you have a sound file and you want its sound on the Clipboard, install the sound in the System file, then open the Sound control panel. You'll see the sound in the list, where you can select it and cut or copy it to the Clipboard.

•••➤ **You can rename a sound** by editing it inside the System file. This is worth mentioning because it's the only type of file that can be renamed while inside the System file.

•••➤ **Get a special startup sound the easy way:** put a sound file in the Startup Items folder.

•••➤ **The Mac can play different types** of sounds—that is, sounds that are different *file types*. But the sounds that go in the System file (and therefore the control panel) are a special type of resource, called *snd*.

Since there were programs and hardware attachments that let you input and play sounds on the Mac before it supported anything besides its own basic beep, there are still lots of different *types* of sounds around, and many of them can't go into the System file. And, to make things even more confusing, the sounds that worked in System 6 aren't the same as the ones in System 7. And, HyperCard, which is sometimes an Apple product and sometimes not, sometimes system software and sometimes not, does lots of things with sounds, but not the kinds of sounds that you can put in your System file.

But it's not all that bad, really. First, you can easily tell a System 7 sound file: it has that distinctive speaker icon. Second, there are programs that convert different types of sounds into system sounds.

## Creating & Collecting Sounds

∘∘➤ **If your Mac can input sound,** it either has a built-in microphone or came with one that plugs into its own port. When you can input sound, the bottom of the standard Sound control panel has a microphone icon; clicking on it gives you the recording controls. In the updated control panel, first select Sound In from the popup menu, then click on the microphone icon.

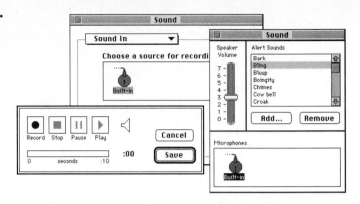

The Sound control panels for input-capable Macs, and the recording dialog.

When you click Add, you have up to 10 seconds of recording time. To stop the recording before 10 seconds, use the Stop button in the recording dialog. The Pause button stops the recording temporarily; to resume recording, click Pause again.

Play the recording back with the Play button; if it sounds right, use the Save button to save it. The name you give it will appear in the list with the other system sounds, and you can use it—your own voice, that of a loved one, your cat—instead of the built-in sounds.

## MAC TRIVIA

The Mac always had sound, even when it was only a simple beep and all you could do was change the volume. (But even that was more than "other" personal computers had; they needed special cards added in order to generate sounds.) When the Mac II was introduced, it had special controls for setting the system beep, which no longer had to be a beep; this capability became part of the system software in 1988, with System 6.0.

☞ **You can get sounds from** all sorts of places. For instance:

- Record your own if your Mac has input capability.
- There's an extra system sound in your Scrapbook when you install the System 7 system software.
- ClickTrax is a terrific, four-meg collection of sounds—mostly impersonations of famous people—that you can play with. The impersonations are of both identifiable celebrities (Elvis, Hepburn) and of "generic" people—there's a folder named "Oy Vey," for instance. It includes a control panel that lets you assign the sounds to various Mac "events." [DublClick]
- Star Trek Collection is two volumes of sounds from … well, you figure it out. [Sound Source Unlimited]
- Choose from the kazillion or more sounds on shareware disks and online. To give you an idea of the variety, here are the names of a few available through BMUG (Berkeley Mac User Group): Thunder; Look, up in the Sky; Echoes; Floyd Bells; Gong; F Troop; Yabba Dabba Doo; Harp-Arpeggio; Knock; Space Cookies; Vulcan Mind; Wow; Pipe Organ; Vacuum Cleaner; Mah Na Mah Na.
- Commercial utilities that let you assign sounds to different Mac operations include collections of sounds. (More about these in a minute.)

- Extract sounds from various programs with utilities that can take the sounds out and convert them to system-type sounds. (More about these, too, in a minute—or more, depending on your reading speed.)

**If you don't have sound input capability,** buy it! Macromedia's MacRecorder was around (as Farallon's Sound Recorder) before the Macs could do sound input by themselves, and it's still available. Its microphone hooks up to one of the Mac's serial ports.

But the MacRecorder isn't just for input-less Macs. You can record sounds at a higher quality, and for a longer time, than the Sound control panel allows. The Sound Edit program that comes with it lets you manipulate the sounds in any of your sound files, enhancing them, cutting them down, piecing them together, slicing off the beginning or end, and so on.

VoiceImpact is another product that provides basic recording and a microphone for your Mac; VoiceImpact Pro includes some editing software, too. [MacRecorder, Macromedia; VoiceImpact, Articulate Systems]

**For background sounds** while you work—sort of Mac Muzak—try Zounds. You select from sets of sounds (rain forest, farm, aviary) and appropriate sounds will play randomly at various intervals. You can even make your own sets of sound combinations. [Zounds, Digital Eclipse]

ZOUNDS

**POP QUIZ** [5 POINTS]

Where does the expression "Zounds" come from? (Hint: It was a medieval religious euphemism.)

**You can assign sounds to different "events"** with any of several sound utilities. Keeping in mind that almost everything is considered an event in Mac programming parlance, there are a lot of places you can assign sounds—if you want to: A click on the desktop; a click in a window's zoom box; launching a desk accessory; inserting a disk. The possibilities are endless (and sometimes annoying). Many utilities let you assign any sounds you have to any of these events; some even let you randomize the sounds for certain events.

What would you like at startup? Clint Eastwood's "Make my day"? A little Bach? Or just a simple trumpet fanfare to let you know that all your inits are loaded and the Mac is ready? How about shutdown—maybe a deep sigh of relief? And when the Trash is emptied—a flushing toilet is a popular, if trite, choice for that event.

- ClickChange, the ultimate in user-interface editors, includes a sound utility that lets you assign any sound or series of sounds to any of more than 50 events. [Dubl-Click.]

- Fun Sounds is more of the same—the same fun stuff: Assign sounds to events. (You know, I'm beginning to sound like a broken record. Wait! A broken record—you could assign that sound to a bad disk!) [Now Fun!, Now Software]

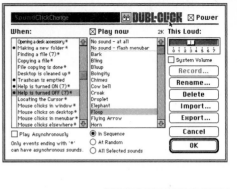

- SoundMaster is the original sound-control utility for the Mac. allowing you to set the sound to be played for a dozen different Mac events. [shareware, Bruce Tomlin]

- SndControl lets you assign any of the sounds you have in your system to any of several Mac events. [shareware, Riccardo Ettore]

SndControl

These event-dependent sounds are pretty neat the first few times you hear them, and I had a lot of fun listening through them while I compiled information for this chapter. But I can't use them for more than a day or two without their driving me nuts. A case in point: I restarted my Mac almost immediately after writing that comment. I still had a floop-boing sound (an arrow being shot and hitting a target) "attached" to the "event" of a disk being mounted. What was mounted on the restart? An internal drive. Two external drives. Another external drive with 5 partitions. A CD-ROM drive. *Nine* floop-boings later, I removed the sound utility.

**Kaboom!** started out as a commercial version of SoundMaster, but its latest version is much more. Not only do you get 150 sounds that you can assign to any event, you also get a sound editor, Kaboom! Factory, to let you twist and tweak any system sound until it's more annoying than the original. Add echoes; play things backwards; set up partial and complete loops; have fun and waste valuable work time, all in one easy, inexpensive package. More Kaboom is a package of—what else?—more sounds. [Kaboom! and More Kaboom!, Nova Development]

KABOOM!

Kaboom! Factory's sound editing window and Effects menu.

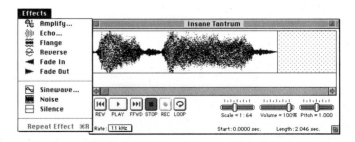

∞⟨⟩ **When you have sounds that** System 7 can't use, either because they're the wrong format or they're buried in some application or file, there's usually a utility that can come to the rescue. For instance:

- sndConverter converts sounds to System 7 format. [freeware, Joe Zobkiw]

sndConverter

- Overlay Sounds also does sound extraction and format conversion, using the Finder's drag and drop interface—you drag a file into the utility's icon and you get a window listing the sounds it contains. [shareware, Jim Moore]

- SoundExtractor lets you grab sounds from almost any file: a suitcase, an application, or a HyperCard stack; it also converts sounds to System 7 format. [shareware, Alberto Ricci]

SoundExtract

- Snd2SysBeep looks through any file you drop on it and extracts any sounds it finds, converting them to the right format for system sounds.

Snd2SysBeep

## ⤜┥ SYSTEM 7.5 STUFF ┝⤛

## The Menu Bar

∞➤ **The Help menu icon** has changed to a slightly less cartoonish, 3-D icon. Since System 7.5 includes the Apple Guide help system (covered in Chapter 5), and not just Balloon Help, they needed to get rid of the balloon icon. It also happens to be a terrific way to know at a glance just what system a Mac is running.

∞➤ **The Menubar Clock gives** a constant readout of the time and date in the right end of the menu bar. To alternate between the time and date, click on the readout. Or, just click once to see the date; in a few seconds, it will revert back to the time readout.

∞➤ **Turn the Menubar Clock on and off** with the Date & Time control panel; use the Clock Options button to set your preferences for the clock. You can adjust the readout in many ways, as you can see by the dialog of options shown on the next page.

Set your preferences in the Clock Options dialog.

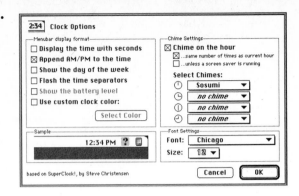

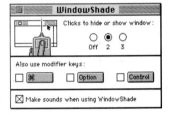

## Windows

∞•➤ **Shrink windows down to just their title bars** with any of the options provided by the WindowShade control panel. You can roll windows up and down as you please; it's a great way to control screen clutter. Use the control panel to specify what action triggers this terrific little feature: with one, two, or three clicks in the title bar; with or without a modifier key accompanying the click; and, with or without a cute little *pfft* sound.

The WindowShade capability extends to *all* windows on the Mac—not just the ones on the desktop.

## The Clipboard

∞•➤ **Skip the Clipboard**, the Copy and Paste commands, the Scrapbook, and every other utility you've ever used to send information from one place to another. (Oh, and forget publish and subscribe, too—which most people do anyway.) Under System 7.5, you can simply drag a selection from one document to another—even if they're in different applications. And if both applications aren't open, you can drag the selection to the desktop, where it stays as a "clipping" file until you need it. This is covered in more detail in Chapter 19.

•••➤ **The Clipboard** in System 7.5 will behave better than the one in previous systems. It's been beefed up to handle more formats, giving you more consistent results between applications. The catch is that you have to be using applications that know how to utilize the new Clipboard capabilities—applications that are "GX aware," GX being the new version of QuickDraw, the routines the Mac uses to create letters and shapes on the screen.

# CHAPTER 3
# ON THE
# DESKTOP

> Computers are useless. They can only give you answers.
>
> PABLO PICASSO

It's amazing what you can learn from this chapter. For instance:

➠ The desktop changed considerably from System 6 to System 7. Now it's a level in Open and Save dialogs, it's a folder, and it's more solid.

➠ You can open folders or you can expand them, but you can't do both at once. But you can do both from the keyboard.

➠ Your desktop background isn't limited to patterns of 8x8 pixels and eight colors.

➠ You don't need the View menu to sort the information in Finder windows.

➠ Apple bought a Cray; Cray bought a Mac.

➠ The Mac sorts numbers alphabetically.

—Including—

80 Factoids
5 Quotable Quotes
3 Memos
2 Quizzes
1 Mac Almanac Chart

—and—

Assorted desktop pattern examples

☒ Show size
☒ Show kind
☐ Show label
☒ Show date
☐ Show version
☐ Show comments

## THE MOST ASTOUNDING INFORMATION IN THIS CHAPTER

**1** Desktop windows can scroll diagonally.

**2** Desktop windows have variable-speed scrolling.

page 85

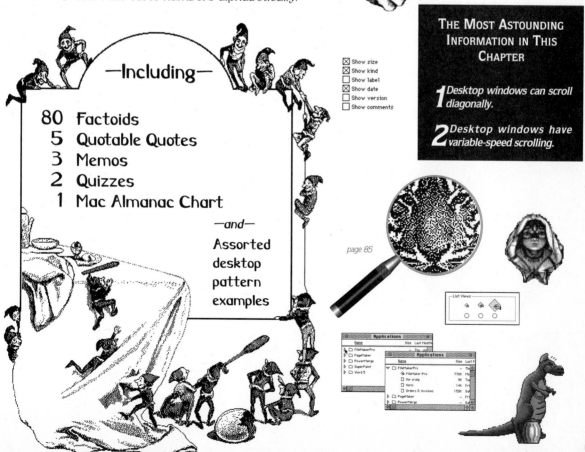

## ◄● THE FINDER ●►

## The Desktop

◦•❯ **Finder is more or less interchangeable with *desktop***, except for a few little expressions and nuances: You work *in* the Finder, but *on* the desktop, for instance. The Finder is actually the program that gives you your desktop; you'll find its icon in the System Folder.

The desktop is both a general place where you work ("go back to the desktop and open the System Folder") and also a specific physical thing—the background on the screen ("click on the desktop").

◦•❯ **The desktop changed in System 7** in several significant ways. It is, for instance, more "solid" than it used to be: If you're working in an application and can see the desktop in the background, clicking on the desktop itself moves you back to the Finder. (You used to have to click on a desktop window or icon to move there.) And it exists as a separate "level" inside Open and Save dialogs.

◦•❯ **The desktop itself can be active**, instead of any Finder window. This lets you use keyboard commands to select and manipulate icons on the desktop. (More about this later!)

If all the Finder windows are closed, the desktop is activated automatically, but you can also activate it in several ways without closing its windows:

- Click on any icon that's out on the desktop.
- Click anywhere on the desktop background.
- Press Command-Shift-Up.

When the desktop is activated while windows are still open, all the windows become inactive—none of them has a striped title bar.

### POP QUIZ                                          [2 POINTS]

When the millionth Mac rolled off the assembly line, who was it given to? Oh, okay, let's make this one multiple choice:

A. Steve Jobs

B. Bill Gates

C. Jef Raskin

D. Jerry Garcia

E. No one in particular—it was just boxed up like the one before and the one after it.

I'll take it!

····▶ **Rebuilding the desktop** has nothing to do with straightening out its loose icons or did-dling with its pattern. There are invisible files on your disk that keep track of where your windows are and what your icons look like; rebuilding the desktop forces the Mac to do some cleaning of these files.

See "Back to the Desktop" in Chapter 5 for some more advanced desktop information, including the invisible desktop files and Finder replacements.

## Items on the Desktop

····▶ **The desktop is shared** by every disk, hard drive, and any other volume (like a CD) that's mounted. Although the desktop is created and maintained by the system on your startup drive, not everything out on the desktop is stored on the startup drive.

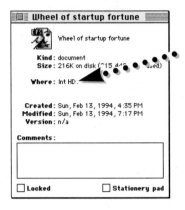

There's no way to tell just by looking at an icon whether it belongs to the hard drive that you're using as your startup, to another connected hard drive, or to an inserted disk. But if you use the Get Info command on an icon, you'll see what disk it belongs to.

····▶ **Dragging an icon onto the desktop** from a floppy or external hard drive doesn't put it on your internal drive. It's still stored on the disk you dragged it from. If you eject the disk, the item disappears from the desktop; when you put the disk back in, the item reappears on the desktop.

····▶ **When you want to drag a file from a floppy** onto your hard drive's desktop, hold down the Option key as you drag it. That will copy the file to the hard drive instead of leav-ing it on the floppy and merely displaying it on the desktop.

The Option-drag method for copying to the drive that's running your system works for dragging an item from any attached volume (a second hard drive, say) to the desktop.

····▶ **When you're on a network**—even a small one that's only two machines sharing a printer—file sharing lets each machine access the other's hard drive. But when a shared disk shows up on your desktop, it's not like inserting another disk whose desktop items spill out onto your desktop. On a shared volume, there's a special folder called, reason-ably enough, *Desktop Folder*, that holds all the items that are on the shared volume's desktop.

See Chapter 21 for more about file sharing.

····▶ **Dragging an item from a shared volume** on a network to your desktop is a little differ-ent from dragging it out of a volume that's actually attached to your system. If you drag an item from the shared volume to your desktop, you get the dialog shown on the next page.

You can use the Option-drag method to bypass this dialog, or you can just drag the item, get this dialog, and then hit Return or click the OK button.

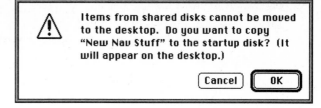

Items from shared disks cannot be moved to the desktop. Do you want to copy "New Nav Stuff" to the startup disk? (It will appear on the desktop.)

[ Cancel ]    [ OK ]

## The Desktop Pattern

∞♦ **Change the pattern or color** of your desktop background with the General Controls control panel. Flip through the preset patterns by clicking on the little arrows over the sample pattern. When you see one you like, just click on the pattern and the desktop background changes instantly.

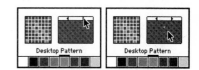

Flip through the preset patterns (left) and click on the one you want to use (right).

∞♦ **Customize the pattern** or color for your desktop through the General Controls control panel. The patterns you design in the control panel are limited to an 8x8-pixel grid and a combination of any eight colors.

First click in one of the squares underneath the displayed pattern. (If you're working in black and white, it doesn't matter which black or which white squares you use.) Clicking or dragging the mouse in the magnified view of the pattern puts squares of the selected color into the pattern.

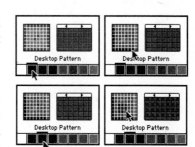

Selecting a color and editing the pattern.

In System 7.5, use the Desktop Patterns control panel, described at the end of this chapter

To change a color in the palette for the pattern, double-click on it. You'll get the standard Color Picker (detailed in Chapter 8).

∞♦ **The Performa system** has a different General Controls control panel that lets you use special desktop backgrounds simply by selecting one from a popup menu. (There's more information about Performa system software, and how it differs from standard system software, in Chapters 13 and 23.)

The Performa's General Controls control panel and its 12 desktop patterns.

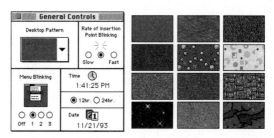

∞§⟩ **There are several programs** that let you design very fancy desktop backgrounds. You can create patterns that go beyond the standard 8x8 area—up to 128 dots square, for instance, and in as many colors as are available on your monitor. Other utilities even let you use a full-screen picture as your background.

Wallpaper was the first product to supply the fancy patterning capability, but the idea spread quickly. These background utilities not only come with patterns you can choose from (ranging from subtle to breathtaking to eyeball-bending), they also let you create your own; they can even randomize the desktop background either on startup or during your work session.

Some subdued backgrounds.

Eyeball benders.

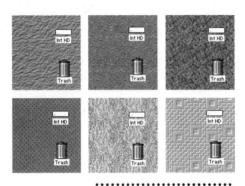

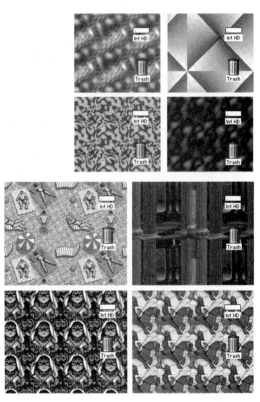

Slightly strange backgrounds.

I have to admit, of all the little add-ons that I admire for tweaking the Mac interface, this is one that I actually use. I can't deal with a busy pattern or picture in the background—I use a 21-inch grayscale monitor *and* a 14-inch color one, and that's lots of real estate. But I do like subtle marbles—they make my desktop so much more *solid* looking.

If you're working on a black and white system, don't despair—you're not forgotten. Black-and-white desktop patterns, when you're not limited to 8x8 repeating patterns, can be pretty amazing. There are samples from Wallpaper's Zebra edition on the next page.

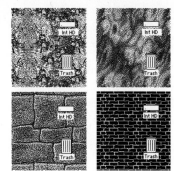

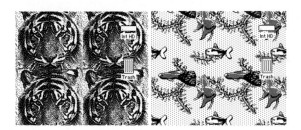

Standard black-and-white patterns (right) and fancy ones (below).

Here's a partial list of desktop background utilities:

- Wallpaper provides not only a plethora of patterns, but a terrific pattern editor that lets you create seamless backdrops for your work. If you can't draw, and if you think the supplied patterns don't have enough variety to choose from, you can subscribe to the special pattern services and receive disks of new patterns at regular intervals. There's also More Wallpaper, a collection of patterns; Wallpaper Zebra Edition, for black-and-white systems; and Wallpaper Light and Dark that includes a screen-saver module. [Thought I Could]

**WALLPAPER**

- Chameleon comes with its own patterns, licensed from a clip art company known for its selection of marble backgrounds. There's an editor so you can tweak any of the included patterns or create your own. Chameleon is a separate program that comes with lots of patterns, but it also comes, with a few patterns, as part of the 7th Heaven utilities package. [Logical Solutions]
- ClickChange seems to include everything, and one of the things is a desktop pattern module. You can use the supplied patterns or create your own with the editor. [Dubl-Click]
- NowFun gives you a pixel-by-pixel pattern editor if you want to make a desktop pattern, but the main approach of the FunPicture module is using pictures as backgrounds. You can use a screen-size picture, or create repeating tiles of smaller pictures to cover your desktop. [Now Software]
- Screen Gems includes a module that lets you use a picture as a desktop background. [Inline Design]

You don't have to buy background packages, though; as usual, there are shareware programs that fill the bill.

- BigPat is a replacement control panel that lets you create and work with patterns that are 32-pixels square. [shareware, Charles Dunn]
- BackSplash uses the picture that's in the BackSplash folder as the desktop background; it can also select at random from a collection of pictures. [free from ZMac, Mike Throckmorton]
- Before Dark is an inexpensive but terrific utility that lets you install various patterns as your desktop. The title is a play on words, since After Dark is a famous screen-saver utility (it's covered in Chapter 15). [shareware, Craig Marciniak]

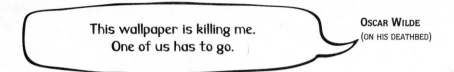

This wallpaper is killing me.
One of us has to go.

OSCAR WILDE
(ON HIS DEATHBED)

••▶ **If you can't change the desktop pattern**—the Mac beeps or gives an error dialog (along the misleading lines of *Cannot complete the operation. There may not be enough memory or the file may be damaged*)—your System file may have been accidentally locked. Use the Get Info command on the System file icon to check and unlock it.

••▶ **If the pattern editor** in the General Controls control panel starts misbehaving in subtle but annoying ways—perhaps you click on a pattern but a different one appears on the desktop—it might be caused by using a shareware or commercial desktop background utility. Some utilities alter the System file itself to do their tricks, and the General Controls control panel sort of loses its general control over the desktop background. Try removing the background utilities, performing an official de-install if the utility provides it. Or, if you're really stuck, you'll have to reinstall your system.

**UNDERWARE**

∞⟩ **Not exactly a desktop background.** Not exactly a screen-saver. Not *exactly* anything— except extremely clever. UnderWare—even the name is clever—gives you desktop backgrounds that do things. Like what? That depends. Choose the dragon, and he'll walk around the screen, burning holes in it with his fire breath; he'll even melt the Trash can icon. Choose the robber, and he'll climb out of a hole in the screen—or sometimes from beneath the hard drive icon—and make off with a folder or the Trash. He'll be chased by the cops, but when he ducks behind a window, the police car smashes into the window's edge. You can have pixies flying around, or a wizard making things happen. Even your folders sprout legs and walk off the screen.

UnderWare is unique not just for its animation—screen savers (covered in Chapter 15) are animated—but in the way its animated elements interact with the things already on the screen. A butterfly doesn't just flit across the desktop background: It can be behind or in front of desktop icons, and it might go behind, around, or even into an opened window. In addition to all this fun stuff, you also get a selection of desktop patterns and a pattern editor, as well as a screen saver. [Bit Jugglers]

## The About Command

∞➔ **The About this Macintosh** command under the Apple menu (which changes to *About* [*Whatever*], depending what application's running) gives some basic information about your Mac's hardware configuration and how its memory is being used. (There are details about the memory end of things in Chapter 9.)

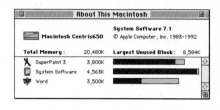

∞➔ **Hold Option while** you open the Apple menu and the About this Macintosh command changes to About the Finder—the wording used before System 7. You'll get a picture dialog (sometimes referred to as the Rocky Mountains) that harks back to the earliest days of the Macintosh; and, if you wait long enough, you'll see credits for various Finder incarnations scrolling along the bottom of the window.

Try holding both Command and Option when you choose About the Finder and see what happens to your cursor.

∞➔ **There are several utilities** that give variations on the information that's in the About This Macintosh box.

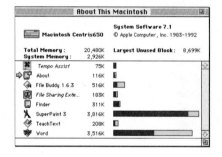

- About, a simply named freeware application, mimics the Finder's About box but gives more information and provides some functionality. You can, for instance, click on a program in the list and be switched to it; the current program has an arrow in front of it. You can list items by name, by size, or by launch order. You can even have the System Software partition broken down so you can see, for instance, how much memory the Finder is using. [freeware, Michael Hecht]

- DiskTools, a terrific file-management utility covered in more detail in Chapter 5, includes an About dialog for your Mac hardware and system software. [File Director, Fifth Generation Systems]

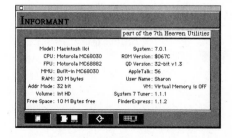

- Informant, part of the 7th Heaven utility package, also gives a more complete report on your hardware and system software setup. [Logical Solutions]

# HANDLING FINDER WINDOWS

## Basic Window Handling

⚬→ **The information in this section** is specific to Finder windows—the ones on the desktop. You'll find, however, that many of the techniques work on windows in various applications, too.

⚬→ **The terms *window* and *folder* are pretty much synonymous** on the desktop. Some desktop windows aren't folders—the main level of a disk, for instance, and the Trash—but most windows show you what's inside a folder.

*For general window information (scrolling, moving, resizing, and so on), see Chapter 2.*

> And then for a while we were kind of confused about the difference between a folder and window.
>
> **BILL ATKINSON**
> ORIGINAL LISA/MAC PROGRAMMER

⚬→ **Open a folder** the same way you open any icon—by double-clicking on it or by selecting it and using the File menu's Open command. You can also use Command-Down to open a selected folder or icon, a combination not quite as abstruse as it seems because of other keyboard commands that we'll get to later.

⚬→ **Use Option to close all** desktop windows at once:

- Option-click in a window's close box to close not only that window, but all the windows on the desktop.
- Hold Option while using the File menu, and the Close command changes to Close All.
- Command-Option-W closes all the desktop windows. Since Command-W is the Close command, adding Option to it closes all the windows. But, although the name of the command changes in the File menu when you hold down the Option key, the keyboard equivalent listed in the menu doesn't change.

*System 7.5's Window-Shade control panel lets you collapse windows down to their title bars.*

⚬→ **Hold down the Command key** to move a background window without activating it or bringing it to the top of the pile.

⚬→ **The zoom box** toggles a window's size (and position) between full size and one you define yourself. On the System 7 desktop, though, "full size" has some convenient definitions. First, the full-size zoom doesn't open the window any further than necessary; if there are only a few things in the window, it opens only large enough to display all the items. Second, no matter how many items are in a window, the largest it gets is the size of the screen *less* a strip along the right edge so disk icons and the Trash are still visible. This is a thoughtful touch—you can zoom open a large window but still drag things from it to the Trash, or onto another disk.

You can manually resize a window so that it's larger than its contents, or to the full size of the screen.

A desktop window zooms open only far enough to display its contents.

⚫➔ **To zoom a window to screen size** (less a strip along the right edge) regardless of its contents, hold Option while you click in the zoom box.

⚫➔ **On a multiple-monitor setup**, the Finder is very smart when you use a zoom box. First, if a window happens to be spanning two monitors and you click its zoom box, it zooms open to a single monitor—whichever monitor is displaying the larger portion of the window. And, a full-size zoom keeps the right edge of the screen clear only on the main monitor—the one with the menu bar (and the disk icons and Trash). On other monitors, full size really is the size of the full screen.

⚫➔ **A folder is still active when it's open,** until you select something inside that folder's window. The picture here shows a selected folder and its window, which is active. So? So that means that some commands you use in this situation will apply to the folder, while some apply to the window. Using Clean Up, or selecting a view from the Views menu, or using Select All, or typing a key to select an icon—all these things apply to the active window. That surely doesn't come as a surprise; you've worked like this all along. But what might come as a surprise is the fact that you can use a command like Get Info or Duplicate or Make Alias, and it's applied to the still-active folder in the background window.

(Interestingly enough, the Close command in a situation like this applies to both the window *and* the folder!)

## Folders & Paths

⚫➔ **To see a window's "path"**—which folder it's in and which folder that one's in, and so on, all the way back to the disk—hold down Command while you press on the active window's name. This works only on the active window, and you have to press on the name itself, not just anywhere on the title bar. This menu should look pretty familiar—it's basically the same one you use in Open and Save dialog boxes. There doesn't seem to be any official name for this menu, so I hereby dub it the Path menu.

The Path menu.

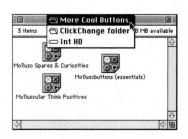

To move to any window listed in the menu, just choose it from the menu. The window will be opened (if necessary) and come to the top of whatever else is open on the desktop.

### POP QUIZ                                      [2 OR 10 POINTS]

When the Mac operating system moved from its original way of handling files to its much-ballyhooed HFS, or Hierarchical Filing System, how could you tell if a disk had been initialized as an HFS disk? Hint: something about Finder windows gave it away, if you knew what to look for. One of these windows is HFS, the other isn't.

*Why 2 or 10 points? If you were "there" when it happened—if you had a Mac before the Plus came out—you get 2 points. If you came in with the Plus, or later, and find the difference in the picture, you get 10 points.*

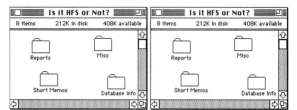

○•➔ **When there's no disk** or other volume listed in the Path menu, you're looking at a folder that's out on the desktop. This is *really* ridiculous because it's already hard enough to figure out which disk a desktop folder actually belongs to. It would great if desktop icons didn't have dead-end path menus.

•••➔ **Close the current window** when you choose another one from the Path menu by holding the Option key while you make your choice.

The dead-end Path menu of a desktop folder (top); and the way it should be (bottom).

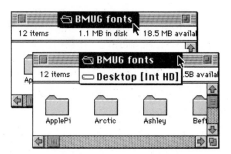

•••➔ **Open, close, and activate windows** entirely from the keyboard when you're dealing with nested folders. (Note that, once again, the Option key added to a keyboard action makes something close.)

- Command-Down opens a selected folder. (Of course, so does Command-O, but the down arrow option is also available in order to match the other keyboard options described here.)
- Command-Option-Down opens a selected folder while closing its "parent."

There's an illustration on the next page of the difference between those two options.

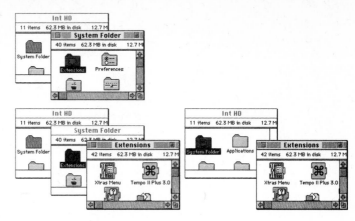

With the Extensions folder selected (top), Command-Down opens it (bottom, left); Command-Option-Down opens the folder and closes the window that it's in (bottom, right).

- Command-Up activates the "parent" of the current window, opening it if necessary.
- Command-Option-Up activates the "parent" while closing the current window.

Here's an illustration of these two options:

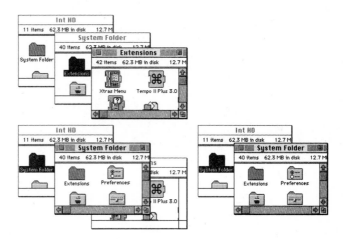

With the Extensions folder window active (top), Command-Up activates its parent (bottom, left); Command-Option-Up activates the parent and closes the current window (bottom,

## Special Scrolling Options

∞•➤ **If you drag against the edge of a window** while you're selecting icons with a rectangle, the window scrolls so you can get at whatever's past the edge. This is another so-minor-you-almost-miss-it System 7 enhancement. (Okay, I'm getting a little ahead of myself here, since icon selection comes later in the chapter, but I want to talk about scrolling in this window section.)

∞•➤ **The Home, End, Page Up and Page Down keys** on an extended keyboard control the vertical scrolling in a desktop window. Page Up and Page Down have the same effect as clicking in the scroll bar above or below the scroll box. Home and End are the equivalent of dragging the scroll box to the top or bottom of the scroll bar.

**···➔ You can make a window scroll** when you're dragging an icon as long as you know where to pause—otherwise, the Finder thinks you want to drag the icon right out of the window.

If you're dragging down or to the right, pause the mouse cursor on the scroll bars. If you're dragging up, pause the pointer in the header area beneath the title bar. Dragging to the left is a little different, since there's nothing but a single line between the window and whatever's behind it. But if you move the icon's outline so that the tip of pointer is within about a 20-pixel area (slightly wider than a scroll bar) along the left edge of the window, the window scrolls. In fact, the left edge seems to have a variable-speed scroll, unlike the other three sides of the window. The closer you move to the extreme left edge of the window, the faster the window scrolls.

Holding the mouse cursor in any of the areas shown in this picture makes the window scroll when you're dragging an icon.

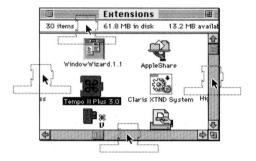

If you let go of the icon while it's on any scrolling edge of the window, it's moved to that general area of the window.

**MAC TOON**

# HACKER by Vadun

Note: By the act of reading this comic strip, you have entered into a licensing agreement with Chuck Vadun and are thereby required to mail him 62.5 percent of your wages for the remainder of your lifetime or 99 years.

—from BMUG PD-ROM

•••⟩ **Dragging an icon in a list view** scrolls the window, too. This is particularly convenient when you want to drag an item into a folder that's not currently displayed because the list is too long for the window. You grab the icon, hold it at the top or bottom of the window to make it scroll, and when the correct folder comes into view, you just drop the icon in.

If you let go of the icon while you're in the header or scroll bar, its position in the window isn't changed, since that's controlled by the sorting criterion you've chosen.

•••⟩ **Diagonal scrolling in Finder windows?** Sure, why not? There are "hot spots" in the window that make it scroll horizontally and vertically at the same time when you're dragging an icon.

To scroll contents up and left, for instance, drag the icon so that the mouse cursor is in the size box or in either of the scroll arrows in the lower-right corner of the window. There are similar hot areas in the other three corners of the window. In the upper left, it's a 16-pixel square in the corner of the window itself, as well as the area immediately above it, in the window's header. In the lower-left corner, it's the same size box within the corner of the window as well as the left scroll arrow. In the upper-right corner, it's the up scroll arrow and the area immediately above it in the header.

The hot spots for diagonal scrolling.

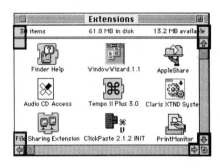

•••⟩ **You can scroll windows at variable speeds** by dragging the mouse but *not* dragging an icon. That is, draw a skinny rectangle—so skinny it can even be a single line—by starting in an empty spot in the window; keep the mouse button down and drag towards, into, and even *beyond* the edges of the window. As long as the mouse button is down, the window scrolls.

When you're at the inner edge of the scroll bars, header, or scrolling area at the left of the window, the window scrolls pretty slowly. Move to the center of the scrolling area (inside the scroll bar, inside the header) and the window scrolls faster. To make those icons really zip by, drag the mouse past the edge of the window: the farther you go, the faster you'll scroll. Any icon touched by the mouse as it whizzes by will be selected, but it's easy to deselect them with a click of the mouse when you're done scrolling.*

Use the rectangle technique to make the window scroll diagonally without moving any icons—and

✳This is probably pretty sick, but after playing around on the desktop all day to discover the fine points of scrolling, I called no fewer than four friends about the diagonal and variable-speed scrolling. That's not the sick part. What's really sick is that they each stopped what they were doing <u>immediately</u> to try it out; they were thrilled; they honed it further and got back to me. These people really do have lives. So do I. But the Macintosh influence is just so <u>insidious</u>!

if you drag beyond the window through the "hot spots" for diagonal scrolling, the scrolling speed increases.

Drag a skinny rectangle beyond the edge of the window for speedy scrolling.

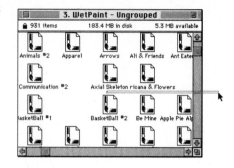

## ❧ WINDOW VIEWS ❧

## Setting Views

∞❥ **The way you see things** in Finder windows is very much under your control. The Views control panel lets you set separate options for all list view windows and all icon views.

The View menu lets you switch between icon and list views, and sort things in individual windows.

The Views control panel.

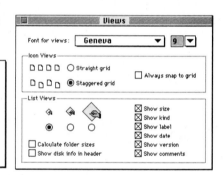

∞❥ **The by Small Icon, by Icon, and by Name** commands are always in the View menu, but you can add or remove the other items of information by using the checkboxes in the List Views area of the control panel.

The checkboxes in the Views control panel set the commands in the View menu.

The commands in the View menu really ought to be divided into two groups. The first two commands are which *icon view* you'd like—standard or small. (In fact, the commands ought to be "As Icon" and "As Small

Icon," since the "by" denotes some sort of order.)*
The other commands—and there can be up to seven
of them—are all *list views*, but they're not just a
type of view: The commands sort the contents of
the window according to the category you choose
in the menu.

> *I hate the fact that the items in the View
> menu start with lowercase letters. So, the word
> "by" isn't so important. But all the other
> commands in the Finder's menus begin with
> capitals. I mean, if you're giving a command—
> "By Name!"—it starts with a capital, the same
> way you say "Print!" If anything, it's the
> second word that should be lowercase.

∘•▶ **The font options** you set in the Views control panel are applied to icons in both types
of views, and are used for the headers in windows, too.

Font options apply to all windows, and to their headers.

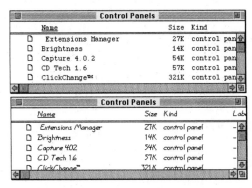

∘•▶ **Use a system font**—Chicago, Geneva, or Monaco—for your windows; other fonts can
slow things down on the desktop.

## Icon Views

∘•▶ **The Small Icon view** fits a lot more items into the window than the standard icon
view, although sometimes it's hard to figure out just what a small icon is supposed to be.
Small icons get their names to their right rather than beneath them.

Standard and small icon
views.

In general, when someone refers to *the* icon view, they mean the first command in the Views menu, by Icon, which uses the standard-size icons; *an* icon view is either size icon—it's just being differentiated from one of the list views.

**•••►** **There's an invisible grid** in desktop windows that's used to align icons neatly. You can define this grid as straight or staggered with the Views control panel. Staggered views are usually more practical (though less esthetically pleasing) because long file names won't run into each other as they sometimes do when you use the straight grid. A very long file name in the staggered view will still run into its neighbor (see the *High Sierra File Access* icon in the picture).

Using straight and staggered views from the Views control panel.

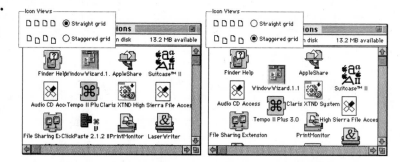

**•••►** **The Clean Up Window command** in the Special menu works for icon view windows. (You can't do much in the way of cleaning up a list view; those regimented columns are pretty clean already.) Using Clean Up aligns all the icons in the window to invisible grid points.

This can take a while in crowded windows, since there are little icon outlines moving around during the clean up operation just to show you how really *earnest* the Finder is when you give this command. In fact, if the window isn't displaying all its icons when you give the command, you'll see those little outlines moving around beyond the edge of the window, in the positions they'd be using if the window were open all the way.

The Clean Up command isn't all that fussy—it just moves icons to the nearest empty grid point, overlapping icon names where it has to, and often leaving plenty of empty spaces.

**•••►** **Change the Clean Up command** to Clean Up Selection by holding Shift down as you open the Special menu; it moves only selected items to their spots on the grid. I've never used this option, and I don't think I've ever met anyone who has. In fact, Clean Up Selection, in prior systems, was the default command if you had anything selected in the window. But so many people didn't use it that it's no longer the default.

**•••►** **Sort icons as you clean up** by holding Option when you open the Special menu. The Clean Up command changes to Clean Up by Name, or Clean Up by Kind, or whatever was the last list view used in that window. Icons are aligned to the grid and sorted at the same time.

Cleaning and sorting takes less time than just cleaning, because you get pretty instant results; you don't have to watch the icons move one at a time into position.

Some of the many faces of the Clean Up command.

•••**}** **There's a Clean Up Desktop command,** though most people never see it. In fact, I ran across it accidentally in the course of writing this book, and I have no idea how long it's been available in the Finder. The same grid that's in Finder windows is also on the desktop, and cleaning up the desktop moves all those "loose" icons onto the grid.

Oh, yes ... you get the Clean Up Desktop whenever the desktop itself is activated—when there are no windows open, or none of the open ones is active.

•••**}** **The most important thing** to know about an icon view is when to leave it. Icons help speed your work only to a certain point. If you have more than a dozen or so items in a window, it's hard to scan quickly for the one you want—especially if the icons all look the same because they're documents from a single application. At that point, you have to read their titles—so you might as well switch the window to a list view anyway. In addition, you can see more items in a list view than you can in an icon view window of the same size.

LAWRENCE J. PETER
*PETER'S QUOTATIONS*

If a cluttered desk is the sign of a cluttered mind, what is the significance of a clean desk?

## List Views

∞→ **There can be up to seven columns** of information in a list view window: Name, Size, Kind, Label, Date, Version, and Comments. The Name column is always present, but the other columns are turned on and off through the checkboxes in the Views control panel. Since these are the same controls that set up the View menu, the commands in the menu will always match the columns in your windows.

∞→ **The columns in a list view** are always in the same order no matter how you sort the window contents. The file name with its icon always comes first; next comes the file's size, then its kind, label, date, version, and comments. The columns are always the same width, too, and change only when you change the size of the font being used in the window. Most users find this really annoying, because either there's lots of space being wasted on the name of an icon if you tend to use short names, or there's not enough if you use long names.

∞→ **A list view window has a header** that's different from the one in an icon view window. In icon views, the header tells you the number of items in the window and the total space used and remaining on the disk. In list view windows, you get the names of the columns. To include the number of items and used/remaining disk space numbers in a list view window, check the *Show disk info in header* button in the Views control panel.

The basic icon view header (top); the standard list view header (middle); and the special header option for list view windows (bottom).

∞→ **You can use a 31-character** name for a file, but you probably won't be able to see it all in a list view. The width of the Name column is fixed—and depending on how you name your files, you might see as few as 22 characters. To add insult to injury, if the name is too long to fit in the column, the last two or three letters that should be able to be displayed are replaced by an ellipsis to indicate that the whole name isn't showing.

Top to bottom: Geneva-6, Geneva-9, FinderFont-9, Geneva-18.

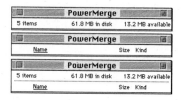

In any font except a mono-spaced one like Courier, you can squeeze more lowercase letters on a line than capitals, and more skinny letters like *i* than fat ones like *m*.

It hardly matters what font or size you use— the width of the name column grows and shrinks along with the font size. There's a shareware font, FinderFont, that has slightly narrower letters, but it makes only a little bit of a difference, and only if you use lots of capital letters.

➥ **List views usually use tiny,** generic icons for files, but you can choose two other sizes—the small and standard sizes invoked by the By Icon and By Small Icon commands; choose the size in the Views control panel. But you'll find, unless you need a large-size font, that using a standard icon in a list view wastes too much space.

List views using: tiny generic icons, small icons, large icons with a small font, and large icons with a large font.

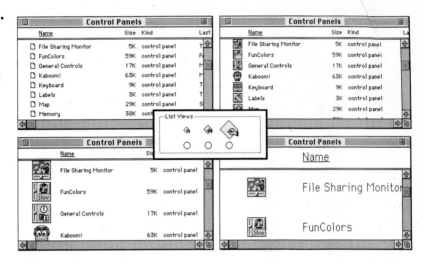

➥ **Folder sizes are not listed** in list view windows unless you specifically request it. Use the *Calculate folder sizes* checkbox in the Views control panel to turn this feature on and off.

Keeping this option on provides some convenient information, but you have to be patient since it takes a while for the Finder to calculate folder sizes (which includes the folders inside the folders). When I open my System Folder in a list view, with everything collapsed to show only the top level in the window, it takes about two seconds for the window to open. With the calculation function on, it still takes two seconds to open—but another 20 seconds before all the folder sizes are listed.

If you need only an occasional report on a folder size, it's much better to use the Get Info command on that folder.

A list window without and with folder sizes displayed.

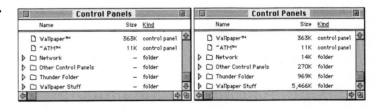

➥ **If you like long and narrow windows** to list your files so you see only their names, you don't have to shape each one of them manually. Use the Views control panel to turn off all the columns of information so that names are the only thing left in your list view. Then click in the zoom box of each of your desktop windows: They'll snap to long vertical windows to display only the name column. Then go back to the Views menu and turn on any of the other columns of information you want available.

From then on, any of the windows you set up while only the Name column was available can be toggled with the zoom box between the long, narrow, name-only version and one that displays all the columns of information that fit on the screen.

### MAC PEOPLE                                    BILL GATES

How does a cocky 20-year old parlay a talent for programming into control of the world's largest software company, a chokehold on the worldwide software market, and a personal worth valued in the billions? Are you listening, Horatio Alger? Yes, the answers have to do with luck and pluck—plus an ego as big as all outdoors.

Bill Gates started in 1975 by co-writing a simple BASIC interpreter for the pioneering (and long defunct) Altair home computer. It sold well, but "well" in those days meant that a couple of thousand hackers bought it. Bill's big break came in 1980 when IBM went shopping for a disk operating system for their newborn PC. Gates got "Quick and Dirty DOS" from a couple of Seattle hackers, renamed it MS-DOS—and an empire was born.

As the PC and its clones spread like a fungus, Gates raked in the cash—each and every machine required *his* operating system in order to work. As Microsoft branched out into application software, Gates' shrewd marketing ensured a dominant share for almost every Microsoft product. The company's profits snowballed.

Although an early supporter of the Macintosh, Gates was mostly interested in imitating its graphical interface on the ubiquitous PCs. After eight years of failures, he succeeded in producing Windows 3, which looked enough like a Mac to fool the uninitiated.

Brash, smart as a whip and very, very confident, Bill Gates continues to dominate the world of personal computer software. His products may lack originality, and his enemies are legion—you can count Apple, IBM, and the Federal Trade Commission among them—but nothing seems likely to slow him down in the foreseeable future.

—*Andy Baird*

> I swore off computers for about a year and a half, the end of the ninth grade and all of the tenth. I tried to be normal, the best I could.

**BILL GATES**

## Sorting in List Views

∞♦ **You can sort by any column** in a list view window. Here's how each criterion is sorted:

- by Name sorts alphabetically by the item's name.
- by Kind sorts alphabetically according the the item's type.
- by Size sorts the list so that the largest item is at the top.

- by Label sorts the items according to the order that the labels appear in the Label menu.
- by Version sorts by version numbers with the lowest on top. (Version numbers are used mainly for applications and system files like extensions and control panels.)
- by Comments sorts items alphabetically by the first few words in the Comments field of their Get Info windows.

*Chapter 4 discusses how the Mac handles alphabetic sorting.*

**You can tell how things are sorted** in a list view by checking the View menu, where the current sorting criterion is checked, or by looking at the column names in the window itself—the column name that's underlined is the one that the icons are sorted by.

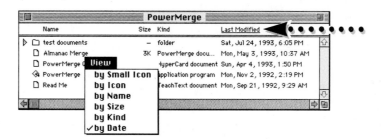

**Skip the Views menu for sorting:** Just click on the name of a column in the window header to sort by that column.

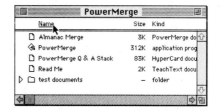

**Sorting by anything other than Name** actually groups items more than it sorts them, since an item's name is unique but many items can have the same Kind or Label. When items are grouped together by the criterion you used to sort them, they'll always be listed alphabetically within the group.

**When you sort by Size,** folders are clumped together at the bottom of the list unless their sizes are set to be displayed with the *Calculate folder size* checkbox in the Views control panel.

**Sorting by Date** should be easy and pretty handy, because it lets you find the newest or the oldest items so quickly, right? Theoretically, yes. But there are several problems that crop up:

- The modified date of a document sometimes gets altered by an application even if all you've done is *look* at a file and close it again without making any changes. This is especially true of databases.
- The Finder doesn't update open windows immediately. If you save a file, and the folder that it's in is open on the desktop, the new modified date/time often doesn't appear in the window right away—or, sometimes, at all. Even if you do a fresh

sort by date, the information isn't updated. This can be a nightmare and lead to such major errors as copying an older file over a newer one, since the Finder lies to you about the modified date of the file in the open window.

- A folder is considered modified if you put a new file in it, and it moves to the top of the list if you've sorted by date. But if you modify an *existing* file that's already in a folder, the folder itself hasn't been modified. So you may have a folder at the bottom of your window that, in fact, has your most recently altered files.

- Some applications create temporary files while you're working and then erase them when you quit. Whatever folder holds the temporary files is "modified" both when the files are created and when they're erased; when you get back to the Finder, you'll find that the folder has a new modified date/time even though its contents are the same as before.

•••✈ **Force the Finder to update** the modified time/date in a window by closing and reopening the window.

## Hierarchical Viewing

∞•✈ **List views provide a hierarchical outline** of your folders and files. You can *expand* a folder in the window to see a list of its contents and *collapse* it when you don't want to see the contents. It's important to use the right terminology here—there's a difference between *opening* a folder, which gives it a separate window, and *expanding* it, which lists its contents within the current window.

∞•✈ **Expand or collapse a folder** by clicking on the arrow in front of it. A single click is all you need, but double-clicking won't hurt—it won't expand and then immediately collapse a folder as you might expect. One of the many Finder interface niceties is that it just won't accept a second click on a folder arrow if it comes too soon after the first click—no matter how short an interval you've defined for a double-click in the Mouse control panel.

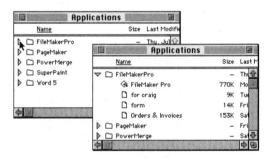
Expanding a folder.

∞•✈ **A folder's arrow** points downward when the folder is expanded. If the arrow's pointing down but nothing's listed, that means the folder's empty.

A folder that has no arrow in front of it is an alias of a folder. There's no arrow because the alias can't be expanded—the folder contents don't exist in the current window, they exist wherever the real folder is. (If you think about it, you'll realize you can't really *open* an alias, either: It's the original that opens when you double-click on a folder.)

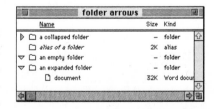
Folders and their arrows.

➤ **The hierarchical structure is easy to see** when there are only a few items in a window, or everything is neatly tucked into folders. But when you have a window that holds both folders and loose documents, it's more difficult to tell at a glance just where some things belong. In the following picture, for instance, in the window on the left, the only visual clue you have that the *Excel Toolbars* file is in the main level of the window, and not in the Excel folder above it, is that the folder's arrow indicates that the folder isn't expanded. It sure *looks* like that file is in the folder, since it's lined up right below it. But, as you can see in the File Sharing folder that's expanded right beneath it, things in folders are indented further to the right. But that can make it even worse: in that same window, for instance, where does the *Finder Preferences* file belong? It's on the main level of the window, although it looks like it's possibly part of the File Sharing folder because of the way the icons line up. Personally, I'd like to see items lined up beneath the folders they're in, and top-level files aligned to the left edge of the window.

The way it is (left); the way I wish it were (right).

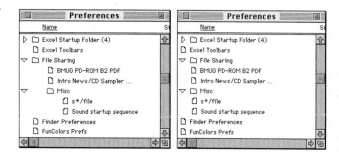

➤ **A folder can't be expanded and opened** at the same time. If you expand a folder by clicking its arrow in a list view window, and then double-click on the little folder icon to open it, the folder first collapses in the list view and then its window opens. The opposite is also true: if a folder's window is opened, clicking on the arrow to expand it closes its window.

### TIT FOR TAT

Apple bought a Cray supercomputer (a purple one) to help design the Mac. Seymour Cray, the Cray's designer, bought a Mac to help design the Cray III. That sounds like a joke, but it isn't: Seymour used the Mac for drawing pictures and typing descriptions, not for running simulations.

Now that he's no longer with Cray Computer, Seymour Cray isn't allowed to put his name on a computer. That sounds like a joke, too, but it's not. *Here's* the joke:

A Cray computer is so fast it can complete an infinite loop in under 5 seconds.*

> *I posted this little joke online, and Bob Seaver replied: "I'm not surprised, but I bet it's not running as many inits as I am."

➤ **The level of expansion** inside a folder is "remembered" when you collapse it. Say you expand your Applications folder, and inside that, expand only the PageMaker folder. Then you collapse the Applications folder. The next time you expand the Applications folder, the PageMaker folder will still be expanded within it.

# A MAC ALMANAC CHART

## Desktop Keyboard Shortcuts

**To** close all desktop windows

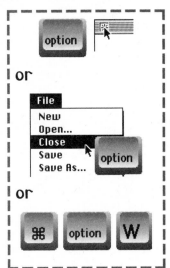

or

or

**To** open and close windows

Open selected folder [⌘] [↓]

Open selected folder and close its parent [⌘] [option] [↓]

Activate parent of current window [⌘] [↑]

Close current window and activate parent [⌘] [option] [↑]

**To** expand and collapse folders

Expand selected folder [⌘] [→]

Expand all levels of selected folder [⌘] [option] [→]

Collapse selected folder [⌘] [←]

Collapse all levels of selected folder [⌘] [option] [←]

**To** activate the desktop

[⌘] [shift] [↑]

**Expand everything at once** by holding Option when you click on an arrow to expand a folder; all the folders inside it (and the ones inside them, and the ones inside them, ad infinitum) will also be expanded. Of course, the reverse approach also works: Collapse everything at once by holding Option as you click on a folder's arrow. The next time you expand that folder, you'll see only its first level displayed—all the inside folders will be neatly collapsed.

**Sorting affects all the levels** in a hierarchical window view. But the column you sort by isn't "inherited" by a folder's window. So, an expanded folder is sorted by name if the window that it's in is sorted by name. But if you open that folder, its window will be sorted however it was the last time you opened it.

**You can expand and collapse** a selected folder in a list view with keyboard commands. (And, since you can *select* folders from the keyboard, too, that means you can navigate a Finder window completely from the keyboard. If you want to. If your mouse is broken.)

- Command-Right expands the first level of the selected folder.
- Command-Option Right expands all the levels of the selected folder.
- Command-Left collapses the selected folder; the level to which its inner folders were expanded will be remembered the next time you open it.
- Command-Option-Left collapses the selected folder, and also collapses all the folders within it.

Did you notice? Adding Option to the sequence affects the inner folders, just as it does when you click on a folder's arrow to expand or collapse it.

**Collapse all the folders** in a window by pressing Command-A and then pressing Command-Left. This invokes the Select All command to select all the folders in the window, then collapses them with the standard keyboard command for collapsing folders. Or, use Command-Option-Left after you select them all; that will collapse all the inner folders as well.

**Use the View menu to collapse** all the folders in a window: Switch to an icon view (with either the By Icon or By Small Icon command) and then switch back to a list view with any of the other View menu commands. No matter how you had folders expanded before the By Icon command, they'll all be collapsed when you switch back to the list view. This technique collapses only the top level of folders; if you expand a folder on the top level of the window, you'll see whatever levels of expansion you were using for that folder before you switched views.

**Keep things collapsed** in crowded folders to speed Finder operations. Opening my System Folder with everything collapsed takes about three seconds; with everything expanded, it takes 12 seconds to open.

## ⊰⊱ PRINTING ⊷

### Printing Windows

∘∘➤ **The Print Window command** prints the window with the current settings for view, font, font size, and so on. It prints the entire contents of the window—not the contents of unexpanded folders, but everything you would see if you scrolled through the window. You'll also get a page header that matches the window's header, and a page number at the bottom.

The Finder's Print command (as opposed to Print Window) is covered in Chapter 12.

∘∘➤ **The printout of a large window** is "tiled" to as many pages as necessary. So, for instance, if a list view window has too many columns to fit across a single piece of paper, two pages are printed—one for the left half of the window, and one for the right half.

∘∘➤ **Put more on a page** by using the Page Setup command. If you switch the orientation to landscape, you might fit a wide list view window on a single page instead of two pages. And using 50% reduction will get the equivalent of *four* pages (a large icon view window, for instance) on a single piece of paper.

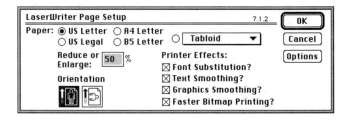

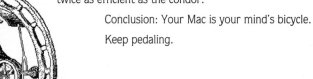

### NOT FOR THE BIRDS

The Apple University Consortium newsletter is named "Wheels for the Mind." The concept is one taken from one of Apple's early ad campaigns that featured a Steve Jobs "interview" wherein he talked about a study that compared the locomotion efficiency (distance traveled versus energy expended) of animals. The condor came in first, while humans barely made the top third of the list. But a man (or, one assumes, a woman) on a bicycle was twice as efficient as the condor.

Conclusion: Your Mac is your mind's bicycle.

Keep pedaling.

••➤ **There's no way to speed up** Finder window printing; since even list views include icons, you're printing graphics and not just text. Even switching to a LaserWriter font on a LaserWriter doesn't make any discernible speed difference.

••➤ **Print the window** of a floppy disk and store the printout with the disk as an easy reference when you're archiving files that you don't often use. If you print at 50% reduction and then trim the paper down to size, it's easy to file away with the disk.

## ⇥ SYSTEM 7.5 STUFF ⇤

### Desktop Patterns

∞➤ **The desktop pattern isn't limited** to 8x8, 8-color patterns in System 7.5. And it's not adjusted from the General Controls control panel anymore, either.

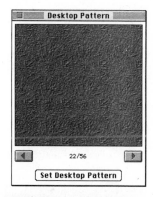

The Desktop Pattern control panel supplies 56 different patterns to choose from; some samples are shown here. To choose a pattern, just use the arrows in the control panel window and then click the Set Desktop pattern button.

∞➤ **Skip the Set Desktop Pattern button:** double-click on the pattern in the control panel instead to change your desktop.

∞➤ **Make your own pattern** in any graphics program and use it for your desktop. Just copy it to the Clipboard from the program where you created it, then open the Desktop Pattern control panel, and choose Paste.

∞➤ **Remove patterns you don't want** stored in the control panel by displaying them and then choosing Cut or Clear from the Edit menu.

### Desktop Windows

∞➤ **There's extra feedback from desktop windows** when you're dragging something into them: You'll see a thin gray frame just inside the viewing area of the window when you've dragged something into it but haven't yet let it go. This doesn't sound like much, but it's one of those minor tweaks that you really appreciate once you start using it.

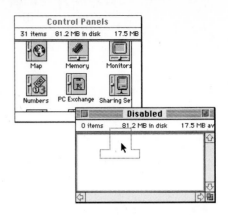

The window you're dragging
things to has a gray frame
surrounding the viewing area.

•→ **Don't forget you can collapse windows** into just their title bars by a setting in the WindowShade control panel.

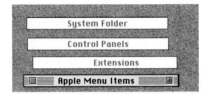

# CHAPTER 4
# DESKTOP ICONS

**ARTHUR NAIMAN**
*THE MACINTOSH BIBLE*

> This is the Mac. It's supposed to be fun.

This chapter includes answers to the eternal questions:

- ➻ How do you open an icon and close the window that it's in at the same time?
- ➻ What's a generic icon, and when does it mean trouble?
- ➻ What's a pathname?
- ➻ What's the difference between copying and duplicating?
- ➻ Why don't we use labels more?
- ➻ Why isn't a new folder named "Empty Folder" any more?
- ➻ How can icon editing help a practical joker?

*page 148*

Floppy    Hard Drive

Shared    CD ROM

### THE MOST INTELLECTUAL NOTE IN THIS CHAPTER

*The Finder is influenced by quantum physics, since you can see either how many files are in a folder, or how much space they take up, but not both at the same time.*

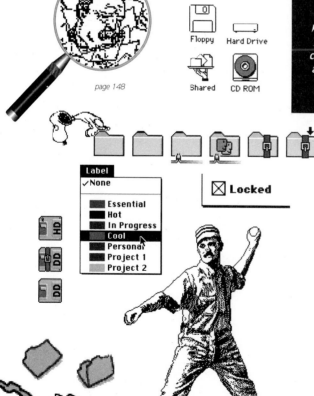

**Label**
- ✓None
- Essential
- Hot
- In Progress
- Cool
- Personal
- Project 1
- Project 2

☒ **Locked**

–Includes–

144  Factoids
4   Quotable Quotes
2   Quizzes
3   Mac Almanac Lists

## →ᵢ ICON BASICS ᵢ←

### In General

⚬•❯ **An icon is** a picture that represents something on your disk, or the disk itself. The icons on your desktop fall into four main groups:

- *File icons* for things like applications, documents, sounds, fonts—any discrete collection of information stored on a disk. (Generally, a *file* refers to any icon that is not a folder, disk, or the Trash.)
- *Folder icons* for storing and grouping other icons.
- *Disk icons*, and icons for other types of *volumes* like CD ROMs and file servers.
- *The Trash* icon, used for deleting files from disks.
- *Alias icons* that represent other icons on the disk.

Although *icon* sometimes refers only to the picture that you see (as when we talk about editing icons, or icon sizes), many times it also refers to the file that the icon represents. The meaning is usually pretty clear from the context. When you apply color to an icon, for instance, the icon changes but nothing happens to the file. When you drag an icon from one disk to another, it's the whole file that gets copied. (Except for alias icons, which are merely stand-ins for the real thing, anyway.)

⚬•❯ **The standard Finder icon is a specific size:** a square that's 32 dots on a side. An icon like the Trash can doesn't look square, but it's designed within a 32x32-pixel grid, as shown. Given the size constraint, it always amazes me just how many different *good-looking* icons there are.

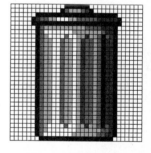

⚬•❯ **Most icons have several different versions** of themselves available for different occasions. A well-designed icon comes in a black-and-white, a 16-color, and a full-color version, as well as a mini version of each of these.

An icon designed only in black and white doesn't have anything wrong with it when it's on a color system—it's just not very interesting. But a color icon that doesn't have a black-and-white version available in it has significant problems on a black-and-white system. All the lighter shades turn white and the darker ones turn black, which can result in some strange looking icons. In the picture here, for instance, the left column shows icons in their color/grayscale version. The center column shows black-and-white icons derived from the color ones, while the right column shows true black-and-white icons.

The mini versions are used for small icon views in windows, for the Apple menu, and, in the case of applications, for the Application menu in the corner of the screen. When an icon doesn't have a special miniature version available, the Mac shrinks down the full-size one and all you get is a smudgy blur. In this picture, the small icons in the center were derived from the full-size versions at the left, while the ones at the right were designed specifically for a small view.

∞•▶ **Icons are always full size** on the desktop, no matter what they look like in the window you're dragging them from. In fact, when the desktop is active, the entire View menu is dimmed.

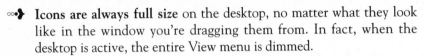

## THE WAY WE WERE ...

There were two basic icon types in the Mac's early days. A hand super-imposed on a diamond shape represented an application; a page-shaped rec-tangle with its corner turned down was for a document. Minor variations on the basic style helped identify the specific application or the type of docu-ment. Some current application icons reflect this design heritage—with either the diamond shape or the hand—but most don't worry about it at all:

ORIGINAL  AppleLink  Word  PageMaker  HyperCard

Illustrator  AOL  Excel  ClarisWorks  SuperPaint

Document icons are much more likely to stick to some variation of the original document icon:

ORIGINAL  AppleLink  Word  PageMaker  HyperCard

Illustrator  AOL  Excel  ClarisWorks  SuperPaint

∞•▶ **A *generic* icon** is one that doesn't have any special identifying features except for its general type. That is, there's a difference between a generic application icon and a generic document icon, but there's no difference between one application icon and another. The most "famous" of generic icons is the standard document icon, a vertical page with its upper-right corner turned down.

∞•▶ **Tiny generic icons** are used in dialog box lists (you'll see them in Open and Save dialogs) and in list views in Finder windows. Most generic icons are easy to identify at a glance, but note the subtle differences between: an application and a desk accessory;

a standard document and stationery; a standard document
and a System file (like a font
or sound).

| | | |
|---|---|---|
| ◈ application | ⬜ hard drive | ▯ stationery |
| ◈ desk accessory | 🖫 floppy disk | ▯ document |
| | ◻ folder | ▯ system file |

◦•▶ **Full-sized generic icons** sometimes show up on your disk, for one of several reasons:

- There's no "real" icon available: the programmer didn't take time to design a special icon for an application or its documents. This is no big deal; many public
  domain programs use generic icons. If you want to spruce them up, you can use
  the Finder's icon-editing capabilities. (Even some of the best designed programs
  use generic icons where you probably won't see them: for preferences files, for
  instance.)

- The application that created a document isn't available. If your friend has
  QuarkXpress and you don't, and you put one of her Quark documents on your
  drive, you won't see the special icon. That's because the icon itself isn't stored
  with the document. What's stored is the name of the document's creator, and the
  Finder looks up what kind of icon that creator uses. This is an efficient use of
  disk space because it takes a lot less room to store a code number than an icon.
  But if the application isn't around, the Finder won't know what to use. If you had
  Quark on your drive recently, though, and just erased it, you might get the correct icon, since the Finder stores that kind of information until you rebuild the
  desktop.

- You have a small problem with some documents somehow losing their "connection" to their applications. Rebuilding the desktop (detailed in Chapter 5)
  usually fixes this problem. Rebuilding the desktop also purges unused icon information, so if, as suggested a minute ago, you just erased Quark, then rebuilt the
  desktop, you won't get Quark document icons anymore.

- You have a large problem that may or may not be solved by rebuilding the desktop; you may have to reinstall your whole system.

Installing,
reinstalling,
and tuning up
your system is
covered in
Chapter 23.

•••▶ **If an icon disappears,** the reason might be as simple as one icon being on top of another in a window. Even using a Clean Up command doesn't usually fix this, if both icons
are on a grid point. This happened to me when I was reformatting a hard drive. I put all
the files from the drive into a folder on another hard drive, then I erased the first drive.
I went to copy back the folder with all the information in it and IT WASN'T THERE!!
*PANIC!!* But using the Find command found it—it was obscured by another icon.

Disappearing icons can also be a serious problem, indicative of a bug in your system
software—as it was in the original release of System 7.0, for instance. The interim solution is to use the Finder's Find command to find the invisible file; it becomes visible as
soon as it's selected. But the real solution is to "tune-up" the system, before the "invisible" files really disappear, forever.

•••▶ **Folder icons and the Trash** have a definite 3-D, shaded look to them in System 7 if
you're using a color or grayscale monitor. There are two reasons your icons might revert
to black and white even while your monitor is set to color or grayscale. (Okay, maybe
there are more than two reasons, but there are only two that I know of.)

First, some graphics programs, like PhotoShop and SuperPaint, alter what's known as the "color palette," the set of colors you're using in a document when you're restricted to displaying fewer than the 16 million or so that the Mac can produce. Switching back to the Finder sometimes means the Finder gets stuck with that palette (it shouldn't, but sometimes it gets confused) and won't use the standard palette for displaying icons.

If your black-and-white icons don't have anything to do with a graphics program you're using, you may have a "minimal system" installed for your computer instead of a full one; you'll have to reinstall a full system.

## Opening Icons

∞▶ To open an icon, you can:

- Double-click on it.
- Select it and choose Open from the File menu.
- Select it and press Command-O.
- Select it and press Command-Down.

∞▶ **You can open any desktop icon,** but what "open" means depends on what the icon is.* For instance, when you open:

> ✳️Tech reader Rich Wolfson points out that this double-click-on-anything capability of the Finder is even more elegant than you think, since it's almost clairvoyant. It's doing the most logical thing to the icon you're double-clicking. The first click selects the icon, and the second does the thing you're most likely to want done. It opens an application, document, or folder. But it plays a sound or shows samples of a font.

- A disk, folder, or the Trash, a window opens showing you what's inside.
- An application, the program launches.
- A document, the program that created it launches, and the document opens inside it.
- The System file, a window opens showing the resource files that are user-installable.
- A Suitcase file, a window opens showing the suitcase contents.
- A font file, a window opens showing font information and samples.
- A sound file, the sound is played.
- A control panel, a dialog opens that asks for and/or provides information.
- An extension, a dialog opens describing the general purpose of extensions.

∞▶ **It's easy to tell the "state" of an icon**—open or closed, selected or not—just by looking at it. On black-and-white systems, a selected icon is inverted to white on black; on color systems, a gray mask is applied on top of whatever colors the icon might have.

Not selected   Selected

Not selected   Selected

An opened icon—whether it's a folder, an application, or a document—is merely a silhouette of the icon filled with dots. If something's opened and selected, the dots and background are inverted (on black-and-white systems) or darkened with gray (on color systems).

**Just because an icon's open**, that doesn't mean you can't open it. Wait ... I know I can explain it better than that. If an icon—a document, application, folder, disk, anything—is already open, you can still double-click on its grayed silhouette. Double-clicking on the opened icon activates its window, whether it's a folder on the desktop or a document opened in an application. This can be a pretty handy shortcut when you can see the icon of what you want, but not its window. (If you double-click on an opened application that has no documents opened, you'll still be switched into it, although you'll see only its menu bar.)

**Hold Option while you double-click on** an icon, and the icon opens while its window closes. I already mentioned that in the last chapter, but that was specific to folder windows. The fact is, this works with any icon: Option-double-click on an application, and it launches while its window closes; option-double-click on a control panel and it opens while the Control Panels folder closes, and so on.

**When an icon opens,** you get visual feedback—a series of ever-enlarging rectangles that start at the icon and zoom over to wherever the icon's window is going to open. This happens not just for disks and folders opening their windows on the desktop, but for all icons—even control panels and applications.

But this feature—known as *ZoomRects*—slows the Finder down a little. This is noticeable on slower machines, but negligible on the faster ones. I admit to being a speed demon wherever possible, but there are some visual clues I don't like to give up—and ZoomRects is one of them. If you have two Get Info windows open, for instance, to compare two files with the same name because you want to know which is the most recent, when you click the close box, you can watch the window zoom down to its icon. This provides extra reinforcement so you know which Info box belonged to which icon. But, if you won't miss the feedback and you have a relatively slow machine, there are several utilities that can turn this feature off: The two that come to mind are both shareware utility collections. [SpeedyFinder7, Victor Tan; System 7 Pack, Adam Stein]

## Selecting Icons

**Select an icon by clicking on it.** In a list view, you can select an item by clicking on its icon or anywhere along the line where there's text—except on its name, since that selects the name for editing. In the picture here, the gray areas show where you can click to select ClickPaste in the list. To deselect an icon, you select something else or click in an empty spot in a window.

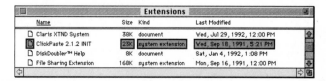

The only time clicking to select an icon is a problem is when you have an icon that just doesn't have much to click on. You have to click on a colored or enclosed area of an icon for the click to register unless the icon was specifically designed to let you click elsewhere in its 32x32 pixel area.

The two icons shown here are good examples. To select Set Clock, you have to click inside the little Macintosh, inside the tiny clock, or directly on one of those itsy-bitsy phone handsets. The selected version of the icon, as a matter of fact, shows pretty clearly just where clicking works. SCSI Evaluator could be even worse than Set Clock since you'd have to click directly on one of the black lines to catch it. But, in fact, you can click anywhere in its square design area, as its selected version shows.

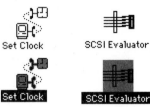

The whole concept and attitude towards icons and hieroglyphs is actually counterrevolutionary—it's a language that is hardly "user-friendly."

JOHN DVORAK
*SAN FRANCISCO EXAMINER*, 1984

**You can select more than one icon** at a time, which is useful when you want to move several icons from one place to another, or even to open more than one document at a time. There's more than one way to select more than one icon:

- Draw a rectangle with the mouse. You don't have to completely enclose an icon in the rectangle—catching just a piece of it will do. (A fine point: An icon is selected as soon as it's even partially included in the rectangle. In previous systems, the icons weren't highlighted until the rectangle was completed and your finger was off the mouse button.) Dragging a rectangle works in both icon and list views, as shown in the pictures here.

Selecting multiple icons
in icon and list views.

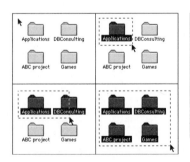

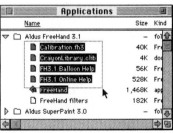

- Shift-click on icons to add items to what's already selected. This is handy when the icons you want aren't next to each other and you can't snare them in the same rectangle.
- Drag a second rectangle while holding the Shift key down to add more icons to the ones already selected.
- Combine the drag and click methods: Select a group with a rectangle and then shift-click on another one or two; or, select with clicks and shift-clicks, then shift-drag a rectangle around others.

◈▶ **The Shift key acts as a selection toggle.** Although we usually think of the Shift key as *extending* a selection, it actually toggles a selection on and off: If the icon you shift-click on isn't selected, it's added to the selection; if an icon's already selected, shift-clicking on it *deselects* it.

Shift-dragging a rectangle also either adds or deletes items from a selection. If you have some selected icons and shift-drag a rectangle around another group, the second group is added to the first. In fact, if you shift-drag a rectangle around a group of icons, some of which are already selected, the rectangle deselects them while selecting the others you catch.

◈▶ **Select icons from different folders** at the same time by working in an expanded list view. You couldn't do this before System 7's hierarchical views, because items in different folders were also always in different *windows*.

Items from different folders selected at the same time.

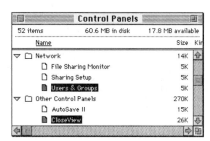

◈▶ **There are three ways to select icons** from the keyboard, no matter what view you're working in:

- Type an icon's name to select it. You have to type only enough letters to differentiate it from everything else in the window, so one or two letters is often enough to select the item you want.*
- Use the arrow keys to select an icon in any direction starting from the one that's currently selected. (Only the Up and Down keys work in list views.) If there's no icon selected yet, the Up and Left keys select the icon in the upper-left corner of the window; the Down and Right keys select the icon in the lower-right corner.
- Use Tab to select the next icon alphabetically; Shift-Tab selects icons in reverse alphabetical order. This works no matter what view you're in or how the icons are already arranged. It's an especially convenient approach when you've typed a character or two to select

> *This is just like selecting something in an Open dialog by typing part of its name, but I find that the similarity leads to a problem: When I use the keyboard to open a file from the Open dialog, I type part of its name and hit Return to activate the Open button. On the desktop, I type the icon's name and hit Return out of habit—and the icon's name is selected.

something and then realize you didn't type quite enough. If I go into my Control Panel's folder, for instance, and type the letter C to select the Color control panel, I get the Capture control panel instead. Instead of typing *co* to get the Color control panel, I simply hit Tab to move to it.

In the window in this figure, with the Labels icon selected, here's what using various keys would select:

Left....................The Big Apple
Right .................Sound
Down ...............Views
Up ....................Color
Tab ..................Map (next alphabetical)
Shift-Tab ..........Keyboard (previous alphabetical)
S ......................Sound (nearest alphabetic equivalent to letter typed)
St.....................Startup Disk (nearest alphabetic equivalent to letters typed)

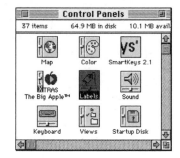

Selecting by typing letters or with Tab and Shift-Tab can be disconcerting in a list view, since the Finder looks at everything in the window and pays no attention to the hierarchical structure.

Don't forget, you can use the keyboard options to select "loose" items out on the desktop as long as the desktop itself is active instead of any of its windows.

••▶ **Organize your desktop** with keyboard selection techniques in mind. If you keep only a few folders on the root level of your hard drive, make sure each starts with a different letter: *Word Processing, Graphics, Communications, System Folder, Utilities, Fun.* Normally, you might name a folder *Games*, but that would clash with *Graphics* for the purposes of this technique. By starting every folder name with a unique letter, you have to press only one key to select the one you want. Once it's selected, you can open it to access its contents.

••▶ **The Select All command in the File menu** selects everything in a window. (Unless an icon's name is selected for editing, in which case the command highlights the entire name.) This means you can select everything in a window without scrolling around to see everything, and you can be sure you won't miss any files.

If you want everything *except* one item, it's easier to do a Select All and then shift-click to deselect that one item than to select all the items you want individually, avoiding the one you don't want.

If, for instance, you're working in a window and realize you want all of its current contents in a subfolder because you're going to create other subfolders, here's what you'd do:

1. Press Command-N for a new folder, and name it.
2. Press Command-A to select everything.
3. Shift-click on the new folder to deselect it.
4. Drag all the other selected files into the deselected folder.

It takes less time to do this than to read the description.

⇢ **Combine various keyboard shortcuts** to do almost anything without the mouse. For instance, eject a floppy disk even when there are several mounted disks and a couple of windows open:

1. Command-Shift-Up activates the desktop.
2. Typing the first letter, or the first few letters, of the disk's name selects it.
3. Command-Y ejects the disk.

Or, open your Fonts folder (in System 7.1) this way:

1. Command-Shift-Up activates the desktop.
2. Typing the first few letters of your hard disk's name selects it; or, if you keep an alias of the System Folder on the desktop, select it by typing a few letters, then skip to step 4.
3. Command-O opens the hard drive; type a few letters to select the System Folder.
4. Command-O opens the System folder (Command-Option-O closes the disk window at the same time.)
5. Typing a letter or two selects the Fonts folder.
6. Command-Option-O opens the Fonts folder while closing the System Folder window.

Here's another shortcut. Depending on how you organize your applications and name your folders, you can launch an application with a series of keystrokes. With the main disk window open, for instance (and folders and files named so you can take advantage of this technique):

1. Typing *W* selects the Word Processing folder.
2. Command-O opens the folder.
3. Typing *W* selects Microsoft Word's folder.
4. Command-Option-O opens Word's folder while closing its parent.
5. Typing *W* selects the Word application.
6. Command-Option-O launches Word while closing its folder.

Six steps to launch an application sounds like a lot, but if you can type without hunting and pecking, it takes only about five seconds to do the whole series of keystrokes—and you can "type ahead," completing the whole series before each window has opened and closed. And if your application folder is up on the root level of the drive instead of in a "category" folder, it's only four steps. Sometimes it's quicker than reaching for the mouse to open the Apple menu.

## Icon Names

∞♦ **Naming icons** involves only a few rules:

- The name can't be longer than 31 characters. A disk name has a limit of 27 characters.
- There's no difference between capitals and lowercase letters for file names: *My folder*, *My Folder*, and *MY FOLDER* are all the same name.
- You can't use a colon in the name.
- Two icons can't have the same name if they're in the same window (or loose on the desktop), although an icon *can* have the same name as the folder that it's in.

And you just can't break the rules. Go ahead and try. Type too long a name, and as you hit the 32nd character you'll get a dialog reminding you about the 31-character limit. Type a colon and it's automatically translated into a hyphen. Repeat a name and you'll be told there's already an item by that name and you should select another. The Mac is friendly, but very firm about some things.

### THE WAY WE WERE ...

You used to be able to use file names up to 256 characters long; the new 32-character limit was introduced in 1986 with the Mac Plus in HFS, the Hierarchical Filing System, that let the Mac deal with lots and lots of files—more than would fit, for instance, on a 400K floppy.

But those long file names used to make me feel so *superior* to DOS users. So what if we had less memory, fewer applications, and no hard drives? We could use file names like *supercalifragilistic-expialidocious* and *Chapter One—My First Few Minutes of Life, or, A World View from Upside Down* and still have room to spare.

∞♦ **You have to select an icon's name** to change it, and there's a difference between selecting an icon and selecting its *name*. To select an icon, you click on it; the icon is highlighted. To select the icon's name, you click on the name itself; the icon is highlighted *and* there's an editing rectangle around the name. If you're on a color system, the name is highlighted in whatever highlight color you're using instead of simply inverted white-on-black the way it is when the icon itself is selected. You can select icons and names in both icon and list views.

Selecting an icon and selecting its name in an icon view.

Selecting an icon and selecting its name in a list view.

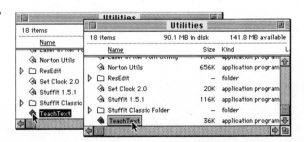

Setting highlight color is covered Chapter

◦•◆ **Basic editing techniques work** inside the icon's editing rectangle. You can type to replace selected text, click to put the insertion point anywhere on the line, double-click to select a word, and even use the left and right arrows to move the insertion point. And the Undo command works, too.

◦•◆ **Sometimes you can't select a name** by clicking on it. The reasons for this depend on the type of icon. If you can't select:

- A file's name, the file is locked to prevent changes—both to the contents and to the name. You can unlock a file icon with the Get Info command. (Folders, disks, and the Trash have no Lock option in Get Info.)
- A floppy disk's name, the disk itself is physically locked; eject the disk and unlock it.
- A hard disk's name, either File Sharing is activated or you've run into a famous (but harmless) System 7 bug. If File Sharing is the problem, just turn it off through the File menu's Sharing command. The bug can be avoided by updating your system, as discussed in Chapter 23.

> Names are not always what they seem. The common Welsh name Bzjxxllwcp is pronounced Jackson.
>
> MARK TWAIN

◦•◆ **If an icon's already selected,** you can activate its name by hitting Return or Enter. If you're selecting icons from the keyboard, this is the easiest and quickest way to get to the name, but it's not much of a time-saver if you're using the mouse to select icons.

◦•◆ **What's the Mac Minute?** It's the delay from the time you click on an icon's name to when the editing frame appears—sometimes as long as two full seconds. This rename delay can be really annoying, not just because two seconds can seem like a long time when you want something, but because you tend to click on the name a second time when it's not immediately selected with the first click—and you wind up opening the icon because the Mac thinks you double-clicked.*

✳The Mac Minute is a unit of measure that derives its name from the New York Minute: the time between the instant that a traffic light turns green and the cabbies start honking their horns. The New York Minute is considerably shorter than the Mac Minute.

◦•◆ **The length of the rename delay** is controlled by the double-click speed that's set in the Mouse control panel. (That makes so little sense that I had to go back and check it as soon as I wrote it. I *know* that's how it works, but I still find it hard to *believe*.) The longer you set the mouse double-click interval, the longer it takes for the name to be selected.

The mouse double-click speed controls the rename delay.

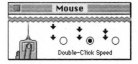

There's a Catch-22 here, did you notice? The longer the delay is, the more likely it is you'll click on the name a second time.

But the longer the delay, the longer the mouse double-click interval—which means you're almost sure to open that icon instead of just selecting it. It's a seemingly unavoidable problem, since you need to be able to double-click on any part of an icon—including its name—to open it. So, the edit box can't show up until after the double-click interval has safely passed.

⟋⟶ **To avoid the Mac Minute,** click on the icon's name and, as soon as you release the mouse button, move the mouse a little—about the length of two letters, or five pixels or so on the screen. The editing frame appears instantly.

The perfection of this move takes time and practice. Move the mouse too soon, and you'll drag the icon; wiggle it too little, and it won't register; move it too far and you might as well wait for the standard Mac Minute to pass. Here's the technique to cultivate: Click in the icon's name a few letters away from the spot you want to edit, then immediately move the mouse cursor to the spot you want and click there for the insertion point. The movement of the mouse activates the edit frame and it's ready when you are.

If you're serious about honing your Mac skills to perfection, try ten name-selects on the desktop every day when you start your Mac. Within a month, the proper reflexes will have developed, and the appropriate synapses will fire in your brain whenever you want to select an icon's name.

⟋⟶ **Disconnect the rename delay from** the mouse double-click speed with either SpeedName from Xtras for System 7 (for 7.0.1) or Set Rename Delay (for 7.1) from the 7 for Seven collection. [Xtras for System 7 (book/disk), Aker, Addison-Wesley; Set Rename Delay, shareware, Steve Kiene, also in 7 for Seven collection]

• • • • • • • • • • • • • • • • • • • • • • • • • • • • • • • • • • • • • • • • •

### By the Way ...

Speaking of icons ... Rock star Prince wants to be an icon. Talent issues aside, he's much too young to aspire to the title. Rock icons? Mick Jagger. Jimi Hendrix. Tina Turner. Grace Slick. Jim Morrison. Janis Joplin. Eric Clapton. John Lennon.

But Prince (that's his real name, by the way—Prince Rogers Nelson) is an icon of sorts now. He decided his name wasn't quite descriptive enough of his, well ... essential being, I suppose. So he renamed himself and has asked to be referred to simply by a nameless symbol. This is his new name here, although I may be mispronouncing it.

⟋⟶ **It's easy to edit the beginning or end** of an icon's name without using the mouse to place the insertion point at all. When you activate the icon's name, the entire name is selected. Just press the left or right arrow key to move to the beginning or end of the selection; the text is deselected in the process.

⟋⟶ **The Copy and Paste commands** work on icon names, but differ in one small but significant way. You can copy an icon's name to the Clipboard by simply selecting the icon—the name itself doesn't have to be activated. But to paste a new name, you have to select the icon's name first.

➔ **Every file has a** *path name* that consists of the disk that it's on, every folder that it's in, and, finally, the file name itself, with the names separated by colons. That's how the Mac keeps track of where things belong—and that's why you can't use a colon in a file's name. According to your Mac, the name of that item in your Fonts folder is actually something like *IntHD:System Folder:Fonts:Geneva.*

➔ **You can type a leading space** in front of any icon's name just as you'd type any other character. If you assumed that you could do this, you haven't been with the Mac long, or you never tried to type a space as the first character in a name in a previous system release. That used to be impossible without doing something tricky, like typing a "fake" first character followed by a space, and then deleting the first character.

As for *why* you'd want to use a space as the first "letter" of a file name … that mystery's solved a little later, in the "Mac Alphabet" section.

➔ **Alter the names of a group of icons** in a list by taking advantage of keyboard selection capabilities and basic editing techniques. For instance, I was working on the second edition of a book and wanted to rename all the first edition chapters by adding a bullet after their names (*Ch 1* versus *Ch 1•*). That way, I could tell at a glance if I was looking at an old chapter or a revised one, whether I was on the desktop or in the word processor. Working in a list view, I selected the first file; then all I had to do was:

1. Press Return to activate and select the file name.
2. Press Right Arrow to move the insertion point to the end of the selection—the end of the file name.
3. Type Option-8 for the bullet character.
4. Press Return to deactivate the file name.
5. Press Down Arrow to select the next file name.

The process takes a lot less time to do than it does to read, and I worked completely from the keyboard—I never had to move back and forth between the keyboard and the mouse. (Actually, I did it only once; I recorded it as a macro and played it back in a loop so all 18 chapters were renamed when I pressed one key.)

➔ **When a file name has a period followed** by three letters, like *icons.sit*, that's known as an *extension*. This isn't to be confused with *real* extensions, little programs that go in the Extensions folder in the System Folder. An extension to a name is a convention borrowed from the DOS* world, where file names are limited to eight letters plus a three-letter extension.

> *MS-DOS, Microsoft Disk Operating System, the basic way IBM-PCs and their clones work.

An extension on a file name is just a quick way to identify the type of file in a situation when you can't see its icon. Extensions in the Mac world are almost exclusively for files that have been compressed in some way—squeezed down to take less space and less transmission time from one computer to another. There's more about this in Chapter 21.

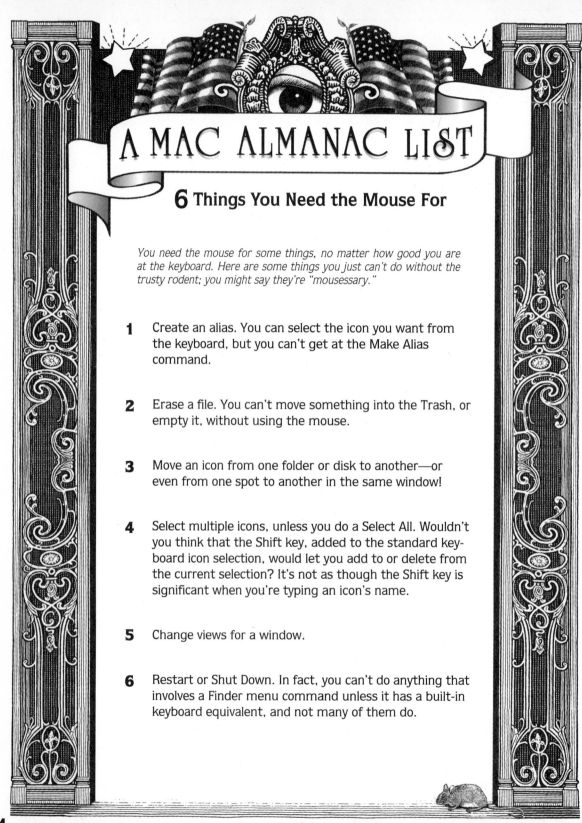

# A MAC ALMANAC LIST

## 6 Things You Need the Mouse For

*You need the mouse for some things, no matter how good you are at the keyboard. Here are some things you just can't do without the trusty rodent; you might say they're "mousessary."*

**1** Create an alias. You can select the icon you want from the keyboard, but you can't get at the Make Alias command.

**2** Erase a file. You can't move something into the Trash, or empty it, without using the mouse.

**3** Move an icon from one folder or disk to another—or even from one spot to another in the same window!

**4** Select multiple icons, unless you do a Select All. Wouldn't you think that the Shift key, added to the standard keyboard icon selection, would let you add to or delete from the current selection? It's not as though the Shift key is significant when you're typing an icon's name.

**5** Change views for a window.

**6** Restart or Shut Down. In fact, you can't do anything that involves a Finder menu command unless it has a built-in keyboard equivalent, and not many of them do.

## The Mac Alphabet

➜ **The Mac's rules for alphabetizing** are important to know because you deal with alphabetized lists in dialog boxes and in By Name views at the desktop. If you know the rules, you can keep certain files or folders together, or at the top or bottom of lists.

- Letters of the alphabet are sorted as you'd expect.
- There's no alphabetical difference between capitals and lowercase letters. (You probably assumed that, but from the computer's point of view, and in most programming environments, *a* comes way after *A* because all the capitals sort before the lowercase letters. So, I thought I'd mention it.)
- Numbers come before letters, so *16 candles* comes before *Sixteen candles*.
- Numbers are sorted alphabetically. Huh? That means they're treated as if they were letters: *B*, for instance, comes after *Aa*, and *2* comes after *11*—it's the first character that counts.
- Most basic punctuation characters come before both letters and numbers. With the exception of the carat (^) and the @ sign, all the symbols on your keyboard's number keys, as well as the plus and minus signs, come before both letters and numbers. Some punctuation—like the semicolon, greater-than and less-than signs, and the equals sign—sort between the numbers and letters. Other special symbols on your keyboard sort after the alphabetic characters. Here's how the characters that show on your keyboard sort in Finder windows:

  [space] ! " # $ % & ' ( ) * + , - . /
  0, 1, 2 ... 9
  ; < - > ? @
  A, B, C ... Z
  [ \ ] ^ _ ` { | } ~

- Option characters (the ones you get by typing Option or Shift-Option and another key) get sorted before, between, and after letters and numbers, depending on the specific characters. Most of the more "popular" option characters that get used in icon names (such as •, §, ∞, ™, ƒ, ®, and ©) are sorted at the end of the list, after both the letters and the keyboard characters that follow them. A few, like the international quotation marks (« ») get sorted even before the numbers.

Wouldn't you think that the Mac could at least alphabetize its symbols according to where they are on the keyboard? In fact, there's a reason for the ordering it uses—for the most part, the Mac adheres to the ASCII standard of character and symbol arrangement and sorts the characters according to their ASCII codes—an agreed-upon standard throughout the computer industry. (There's more about this in Chapter 20.)

➜ **To make numbers sort** numerically, you have to use a leader character on the lower numbers so that all the numbers have the same number of digits. So, if your highest number is going to have two digits, all the single-digit numbers need a single character in front of them; if the highest number is going to have three digits, then the two-digit numbers

| test | | test | | test | |
|------|---|------|---|------|---|
| Name | | Name | | Name | |
| ▷ 📁 1 | | ▷ 📁 1 | | ▷ 📁 -1 | |
| ▷ 📁 10 | | ▷ 📁 2 | | ▷ 📁 -2 | |
| ▷ 📁 11 | | ▷ 📁 3 | | ▷ 📁 -3 | |
| ▷ 📁 12 | | ▷ 📁 10 | | ▷ 📁 10 | |
| ▷ 📁 2 | | ▷ 📁 11 | | ▷ 📁 11 | |
| ▷ 📁 20 | | ▷ 📁 12 | | ▷ 📁 12 | |
| ▷ 📁 22 | | ▷ 📁 20 | | ▷ 📁 20 | |
| ▷ 📁 3 | | ▷ 📁 22 | | ▷ 📁 22 | |

need a single leader character and the single-digit numbers need two leading characters. And the leading character, of course, needs to be one that sorts before the numerals. A space is the best thing to use, not because it's the primary character for early sorting, but because you can't see it and the numbers look more natural that way. But any of the early-sorting characters will do. This picture shows a window sorted "naturally," with leading spaces for the low numbers, and with a hyphen as the leader character.

●●▶ **When you want a file or folder at the top** of a list, start its name with a special "leader character" that comes at the beginning of the Mac's alphabet: Starting the name with a space is the easiest and most elegant solution; the pound sign (#), asterisk, plus, and minus signs are also reasonably subdued.

To put a file or folder at the bottom of a list, using the tilde (~) isn't too intrusive; or if you don't mind the seeming emphasis, you can use any of the option characters that sort at the bottom, like • or §.

●●▶ **Why bother changing the basic alphabetical sorting** for files and folders? Because sometimes the files you use the most sift towards the bottom of windows and dialog boxes due to their names, and if you use the mouse instead of any available keyboard alternatives, you'll have to do a lot of scrolling to get to the item you want.

Forcing a special sort is also important for items in the Apple menu because you want the things you use the most to be near the top. (That's covered in Chapter 6.)

Finally, extensions load in alphabetical order and you can often solve conflicts by renaming them. (Chapter 8 deals with that.)

For instance: of the six basic folders that hold the material for this book while I'm working on it, there's one—*Chapters*—that I use more than any other; luckily, it sorts right to the top—but if it didn't, I'd have put a space in front of its name. I use four of the folders constantly, and the last two only occasionally, so I renamed those two to sink them to the bottom of the list. Here's what the window and my Apple submenu look like:

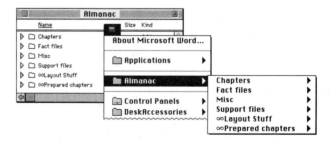

Here's another example: My Control Panels folder has a zillion (±10) control panels and some of them need their own folders full of support files. (A control panel with support files? Say it ain't so, Joe! But yes … the Thunder spell checker, the ClickPaste pop-up scrapbook, Wallpaper's background patterns, to name a few.) Anyway, these support folders can go anywhere, so I leave them together in a folder named ∞*Support Folders* that's inside the Control Panels folder. With the ∞ symbol in front of the name, the folder stays out of my way, at the bottom of the window and the Apple menu submenu.

**POP QUIZ**　　　　　　　**[10, 5, 15, AND 3 POINTS]**

That expression I just used—*Say it ain't so, Joe!*—which famous baseball player was it asked of? Why? And for extra credit: What was the name of the scandal? And what relatively recent movie featured his ghost?

••➔ **You can use special characters to group** things in windows and lists. Use the same initial character for all the items you want to keep together, like • or §. I was working on three different books at one point (sad, but true), and while I kept them in separate folders on the disk, I had all the chapters listed in my word processor's Work menu for easy access. To avoid the confusion of three "Chapter 1" titles in the menu, and to satisfy my innate urge to organize (despite anything you may have heard from my friends, or my housekeeper, to the contrary), I left the titles for one project "bare" while using leader characters for the other two projects. The menu looked something like this:

| Work |
|------|
| Ch 1 |
| Ch 2 |
| Ch 3 |
| § Ch 1 |
| § Ch 2 |
| § Ch 3 |
| • Ch 1 |
| • Ch 2 |
| • Ch 3 |

Using the Finder's label function on the desktop isn't quite as satisfactory, for several reasons—chiefly because labels get changed and they don't affect how items appear in dialog boxes or menus.

## ➔ MOVING & COPYING ➔

### Moving Icons

∞➔ **To move an icon,** just drag it from one place to another. The icon itself doesn't actually move as you drag it: An outline of the icon moves with the mouse pointer, and when you let it go, the icon moves to its new spot.

When you want to move an icon that's in a list view, grabbing it by the tiny icon that's in front of the name is the easiest, but anywhere along the line will do as long as you're touching some text—you can even drag it by its name without the name being activated for editing.

∞➔ **Moving an icon** within a window simply changes its position in that window. Moving it from one window to another—or from a window to the desktop—on the same disk changes its *location* so that it resides in the new folder, or on the desktop. But there's still only that one icon on the disk; you've only moved it from one spot to another.

Moving an icon from one disk to another, though, actually *copies* the file so that the original still exists in the first location, and an exact copy exists in the new location. There's more about this procedure in the next section, *Copying & Duplicating.*

∞❱ **When more than one icon is selected,** moving one of them moves them all—whether you're moving within or between windows, or even between disks. You'll see outlines of all the selected files moving as you drag the mouse.

When you're moving multiple icons, it's the position of the mouse cursor that counts. Don't worry if, as you move three items from one window to another, two of the icon outlines aren't in the destination window. They'll wind up in that window as long as that's where the mouse cursor is when you let go of the button.

Getting ready to move a multiple selection (top). All five selected folders will go into the destination folders even though their icon outlines are not in the folder (bottom).

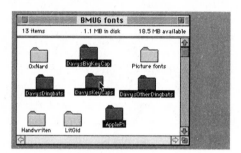 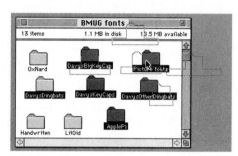

The "drag and drop" method of launching an application is another reason to put one icon into another. See Chapter 19.

∞❱ **To put one icon into another**—such as when you're putting something in a folder or into the Trash—you drag one right on top of the other. The "target" icon highlights when the mouse cursor is on it, and that's how you know you're in the right spot. I've seen beginners pile up garbage around the Trash icon

because they didn't watch for the highlight feedback that lets you know you're at the right spot. This picture shows, at the left, how an icon can look as though it's going in the Trash but, without the arrow in the right position, the Trash doesn't highlight. At the right, the cursor is touching the Trash icon, so it's highlighted and the dragged icon winds up inside the Trash.

You can also put an icon into something by dragging the icon into the other icon's open window.

> Although the Xerox Star had icons, the Lisa [Mac's predecessor] was the first product to let you drag them with the mouse, open them by double-clicking and watch them zoom into overlapping windows. ... It was the first to feature the menu bar, the one-button mouse, the Clipboard, and the Trash can.

LARRY TESLER
Lisa development team

➔ **Snap an icon into position** in a window's grid by holding down the Command key as you let go of the mouse button.

What the Command key actually does in this situation is reverse the *Always snap to grid* setting in the Views control panel. So, if you have the option off (my recommended setting), you drag icons anywhere you want and use the Command key to snap them to the grid occasionally. On the other hand, if you keep the option on, so the snap-to is the default, you can avoid the grid by holding Command when you drag an icon.

Some things slow down when you keep the snap-to option on. It doesn't matter much when you're moving a single icon, but if you're dragging a whole bunch, or you use the Clean Up command, the icons are moved into position one at a time.

➔ **When you move an icon into a folder** where something by that same name already exists, you'll get an alert, but the wording depends on whether you're about to copy over the older version or a newer version. Note the subtle difference in the wording of the two dialogs (*Do you want to/Are you sure*)—it can be disastrous if you copy an older file over its more recent version.

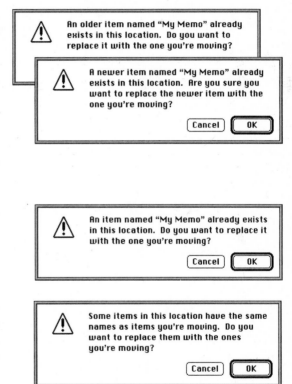

⚠ An older item named "My Memo" already exists in this location. Do you want to replace it with the one you're moving?

⚠ A newer item named "My Memo" already exists in this location. Are you sure you want to replace the newer item with the one you're moving?

[ Cancel ] [ OK ]

When there's an identical file in each location you get a more neutrally worded dialog:

⚠ An item named "My Memo" already exists in this location. Do you want to replace it with the one you're moving?

[ Cancel ] [ OK ]

When you're dragging multiple files from one place to another, you'll be warned of duplicate names, but you won't know which ones are more recent. Here's the dialog you get:

⚠ Some items in this location have the same names as items you're moving. Do you want to replace them with the ones you're moving?

[ Cancel ] [ OK ]

It's really annoying that the Finder won't go ahead and copy everything *except* the duplicates, or flag them somehow—you have to open both windows and figure out which files are the problem. Not only that, but all the items you selected for the move are deselected, and you have to select the right ones all over again.

➔ **Sometimes it takes a long time** for items to be copied into a folder: You select the items and drag them to the new location, but there's a delay of five or ten seconds, or even a full minute, before the items are moved or a copy dialog shows up. This is directly related to how many items you're moving. If you're dragging 100 font files from a CD onto your hard drive, for instance, the Mac has to look through the destination folder first to make sure that none of its files match any of the new files' names.

••▶ **When you copy or move a folder** from one place to another, be careful when the destination already has a folder of the same name. The Mac isn't smart enough (yet) to merge the files within folders that have the same names. If you move a folder named *Old Notes* to a place that already has a folder with that name, you'll get this dialog:

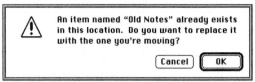

> ⚠ An item named "Old Notes" already exists in this location. Do you want to replace it with the one you're moving?
>
> [ Cancel ]  [ **OK** ]

A "Synching" program updates similar folders on different volumes; that's covered in Chapter 22.

If you click OK, the folder you're moving *and its contents* will replace the folder that's already there—and *its* contents, no matter what's newer or older or different. And if you copy an empty folder over a full one, well—tough luck.

If you're dealing with two folders that have the same name, it's *much* safer to open one of them, select all the items in it, and drag the items into the other folder.

••▶ **You can grab an icon from an inactive window** and drag it to a new location. Say your Control Panels window is active and another window, Control Panels (Disabled) is open but inactive. You want to drag one of the inactive control panels into the Control Panels window. In earlier systems, clicking on the icon you wanted from the inactive window would activate the window; then you could drag the icon into the destination window, but the window where the icon came from stayed active. You needed another click to activate the window where you were working when you began.

It's different in System 7 because now the Finder deals with icon dragging as a separate issue from window clicking. In fact, you can even drag an icon from one inactive window to another inactive window or to the desktop, leaving your current working window still on top and active.

••▶ **Dragging something back to the main level** of a window in a hierarchical list isn't easy. If you drag the item until it's touching something that's also stored on the main level, you can let go there—but you run the risk of accidentally dropping it into a folder that's on the window's main level, or letting it go while it's touching an application that will trigger the Finder's drag and drop launching. The easiest and surest method is to drag the item into the window's title bar or header and let go of it there. This picture shows two spots where you can drop an icon to get it back to the main level of the window.

Moving an item to the main level of a window: Let it go when it's touching a file that's on the main level (left) or when it's in the window's header or title bar (right).

**Moving things in hierarchical views** can be pretty tricky. If, for instance, you're moving something into an expanded folder, you can't just drag it into the area that lists the other things in that folder. You have to make sure the mouse pointer is touching one of the other items in the folder's list—either the icon or any text along the line; the white area between the columns of text doesn't work. You'll know you're in the right spot when the folder you're aiming for highlights. But if the folder icon is visible, the easiest thing to do anyway is to drag the item directly into the little folder icon. In this picture, if you're dragging the Portable icon into the Other Control Panels folder in the window, none of the positions at the left will work; all the spots at the right will.

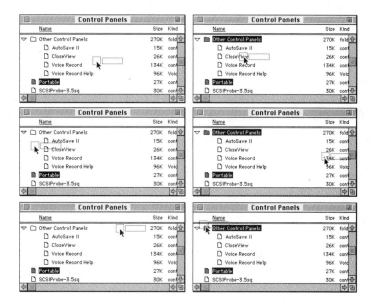

## Copying & Duplicating

**The Duplicate command** in the File menu duplicates files and folders; just select the icon and then choose the Duplicate command. (You can't use the Edit menu's Copy command, since that works only on an icon's name.) As the Finder "reads" the file's information into memory and then "writes" it back onto the disk, you'll get dialogs letting you know how far along it is in the process. The duplicate gets the same name as the original, with *copy* appended to the name; if you make another duplicate, its name is appended with *copy 2*, and so on. If the original file name is too long to accommodate the *copy* suffix, the Finder will drop a few letters from the end of the name and replace them with an ellipsis, so you'll wind up with a name something like *My Folder of Really Terri … Copy* and you won't know if its a folder of terrific or terrible stuff.

Interestingly enough (look out, here comes some *really* trivial information—but that's part of my job), whether you copy the original a second time or copy the duplicate a first time, the new file is named *copy 2*. This seems pretty magical, until you experiment a little and find out that a duplicate of *any* file whose name ends in *copy*—even it it's an original file and not a duplicate to start with—is named *copy 2*.

All in all, though, the Duplicate command is pretty lame. Say you want to have a copy of a file in two different places—the file itself, so an alias won't do. You duplicate the file, move the duplicate, and then have to rename it to get rid of the *copy* that's been appended to its name. Or, worse, you drag the duplicate to another disk. Now you have to not only change its name on the second disk, you also have to delete the duplicate file that's still on the first disk. There's nothing the Duplicate command can do that some mouse and keyboard tricks can't do better. Read on.

∞⤳ **Duplicating a folder** duplicates everything inside it—files and subfolders—but the names of the items inside the folder don't change.

### THE WAY WE WERE ...

In earlier Mac systems, the first duplicate file created by the Duplicate command was named *Copy of Filename*. The next was named *Copy of Copy of Filename*. And so on. If you needed a few duplicates, you ran into the file name length limit in a very short time (and you immediately lost any sorting advantage, because a copy of any file started with *c*).

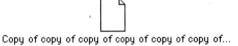

Copy of copy of copy of copy of copy of copy of...

This is somewhat analogous to the Martingale system of repeatedly betting red at roulette ... oh, wait—that's for a different book of tips.

∞⤳ **When you drag an item** from one disk to another, the file or folder is *copied*, not *moved* to the new location—the original is left behind. This automatic copying kicks in whenever you drag something from one "volume" to another, whether the volume is a floppy disk, a hard drive, a file server, a CD-ROM, and so on.

Utilities that really move a file from one disk to another, deleting the original, are covered in Chapter 5.

You get "reading" and "writing" dialogs during the copy process, just like the ones that the Duplicate command generates. If there's enough memory in the Finder, everything gets read in one pass from the source, and then written to the destination; if memory's tight, it reads a few at a time, writes them, and then goes back for some more.

But first you get a "Prepare" dialog while the Finder checks whether there's any file in the destination folder that has the same name as the item(s) you're dragging. (This is not an issue with the Duplicate command, which changes the name of the file.) The more items you're dragging, the longer this stage takes; if you're copying a single file into a folder with very few other items in it, the dialog may flash by too quickly to read. You'll get constant updates on what file's being read and what's being written, and how many files are left to read or write.

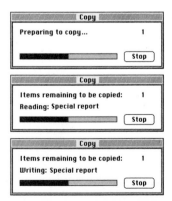

→ **A copied or duplicated file** is *exactly* the same as the original (except, in the case of a duplicate, for its name). The copy has the same creation and modified dates as the original; if you've applied a label to the original, the duplicate has the label, too; and, if you've given the original a special icon, that icon is used for the new file.

→ **You can stop the copy process** at any time. Stopping during the preparation or reading cycle just cancels the whole thing. If you stop during the write process, any files already completely written to the destination stay there. If you were copying a folder, it's likely that the folder itself will already be created at the destination, but it will be empty or have only a few files in it.

→ **Option-dragging a file or folder** icon makes a copy of it in the new location, leaving the original behind. If you've been paying attention, you may be thinking that this is the same as simply moving a file and letting the automatic copying process take over. Not quite—because with the Option key you can trigger a copy operation as you drag something from one place to another *on the same disk*—from one window to another, or from a window to the desktop.

→ **Increase the speed of desktop copying** within and between disks with a utility that cuts copying time in half—or better. These utilities install as inits that you never have to pay attention to again, but work swiftly and solidly in the background every time you use the Duplicate command or do a drag-copy on the desktop. Most of these utilities claim that copies across networks are also speeded up, but I haven't found that to be the case—at least in my small network when my PowerBook is attached to my desk machine. But it doesn't matter; the disk-to-disk copying acceleration is significant and enough of a bonus.

CopyDoubler provides copying speed and even includes a smart feature that doesn't bother copying identical files—it skips them and gets on with the important stuff. FinderExpress is also a commercial product, but speed-up utilities are also parts of the shareware packages SpeedyFinder and System7 Pack.

Note that some speeder-uppers get their speed from skipping the verification process that the Mac usually performs, making sure that it really copied every bit (literally) of a file perfectly. Make sure you don't mind living a mildly dangerous life if you're going to use one of those! [FinderExpress, 7th Heaven, Logical Solutions; System 7 Pack, shareware, Adam Stein; SpeedyFinder7, shareware, Victor Tan]

→ **You can copy files in the background**—drag them in the Finder to where they need to go, then move to any opened application and get on with your work. You'll see that your application slows down a little while the Mac is splitting its attention between the Finder and the application, but that's usually better than just twiddling your thumbs during a long copy procedure.

If the application you want to work in isn't already open when the copy procedure starts, you can't double-click on it to launch it while the Finder's copying. But if it's in your Apple menu, you can select it from there to open it even after the copying starts.

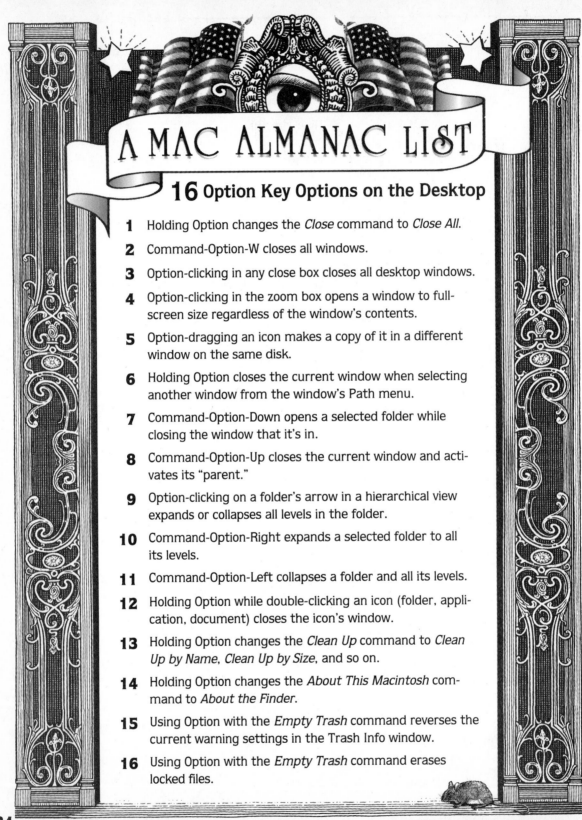

# A MAC ALMANAC LIST

## 16 Option Key Options on the Desktop

1. Holding Option changes the *Close* command to *Close All*.

2. Command-Option-W closes all windows.

3. Option-clicking in any close box closes all desktop windows.

4. Option-clicking in the zoom box opens a window to full-screen size regardless of the window's contents.

5. Option-dragging an icon makes a copy of it in a different window on the same disk.

6. Holding Option closes the current window when selecting another window from the window's Path menu.

7. Command-Option-Down opens a selected folder while closing the window that it's in.

8. Command-Option-Up closes the current window and activates its "parent."

9. Option-clicking on a folder's arrow in a hierarchical view expands or collapses all levels in the folder.

10. Command-Option-Right expands a selected folder to all its levels.

11. Command-Option-Left collapses a folder and all its levels.

12. Holding Option while double-clicking an icon (folder, application, document) closes the icon's window.

13. Holding Option changes the *Clean Up* command to *Clean Up by Name*, *Clean Up by Size*, and so on.

14. Holding Option changes the *About This Macintosh* command to *About the Finder*.

15. Using Option with the *Empty Trash* command reverses the current warning settings in the Trash Info window.

16. Using Option with the *Empty Trash* command erases locked files.

••➤ **You may run out of memory** when you're copying files on the desktop, but it's not likely. This used to be a frequent problem, but System 7 seems to use its Finder memory more efficiently for this procedure. Just before I wrote this chapter, I reformatted two hard drives, which completely erased their contents. First, I copied their contents over to a really big drive, and then I copied the stuff back onto the clean drives. In both cases, I copied more than 70 megs of information—well over a thousand individual files—in one fell swoop, with no memory problems. Previously, I'd run into polite messages that the Finder didn't have enough memory to complete the operation and would I please drag the files in smaller groups.

So, if you do run into a problem, drag those files in smaller groups. But if it happens often enough to drive you crazy—or you're copying a single, very large file that you can't split into two drag operations—you may have to allocate more memory to the Finder; this is covered in Chapter 5. It's also unlikely that you'll have problems dragging a single large file. I just checked with my friend Carol (all of my friends are on call—in fact, on auto-dial—for emergencies like these) who I know routinely works with giant files in her graphic design work. She says she has no trouble doing desktop copies of single files that are more than 60 megabytes! Which reminds me of another workaround—if you can't copy something from one place to another on the desktop, try opening the file in its application and using the Save As command to save it wherever you want.

••➤ **To copy an icon's name** to the Clipboard, you don't have to select the name as if you were going to edit it. Selecting the icon itself and then choosing the Copy command copies the name to the Clipboard.

In fact, if you select a bunch of icons and choose Copy, all the names get copied to the Clipboard, in a list. The picture shows selected icons in a window and what's copied to the Clipboard. There's a limit of 256 characters in the list, although you'll often get fewer because a partial name won't be copied; that's why there are fewer items in the list than are on the Clipboard.

The order of the items in the list seemed to defy explanation for a long time. When you're in a list view, they're in whatever order is used in the window. But when you select things in an icon view, there often seems to be no rhyme or reason to the Clipboard order. You wouldn't believe it if I told you how many man/woman-hours went into this thing. But I and my colleagues (Joe, Rich, Jerry, Andy) worked unceasingly until the pattern became clear: however you last sorted your icons in a list view,

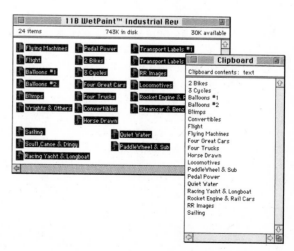

that's how they're listed in the Clipboard. If you want to know ahead of time how the list will turn out, hold the Option key and open the Special menu: The Clean Up command notes the last sorting criterion you used.

## ⇥ LABELS ⇤

### Assigning Labels

∞▸ **The Label menu provides a way to assign** a special tag to an icon. Every Mac icon has certain intrinsic attributes: it was created or modified on particular dates; it's a specific size; it's of a certain kind (an application, or a document, or a folder, for instance). But until the Label menu, there was no way to assign an attribute so you could, say, sort your files according to the project they're connected with. After all, you might have database files, a spreadsheet, some graphics, and lots of word processor documents all relating to the same project. Unless you kept them all in the same folder, there was no way to organize them or round them up.

By using one of the seven labels in the Label menu, you apply another attribute to any desktop icon and later use that criterion to sort things, or to search by.

∞▸ **Apply or change a label** by selecting the icon(s) and then choosing the label from the Label menu.

∞▸ **Remove a label** from an icon by selecting it and choosing None from the Label menu.

There's more about the Labels control panel in Chapter 8.

∞▸ **An icon's label appears in list views** if you've defined your windows (with the Views control panel) to include the labels. When you use icon views, you can't tell at a glance what label is assigned to an icon unless you have a color system and can remember what color means what.

∞▸ **To change the default label names** in the menu, use the Labels control panel and type in the new names that you want. The Label menu immediately reflects the changes. Oddly enough, there's nothing to prevent you from using the same label twice—or even seven times if you want to.

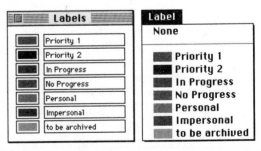

The Label menu reflects the entries in the Labels control panel.

## THE WAY WE WERE ...

Before there was a Label menu, there was a Color menu. The Color menu was added to System Set 5.0 (System 4.2 and Finder 6.0) specifically for the first color Mac, the Mac II.

But through all of System 6's versions, the Color menu showed up only on color machines, and it was far from intuitive: Were the red files more important than the blue ones? Did the green ones belong to the Building Committee research, or was that the brown ones? And did yellow sort before or after black?

**When you copy or duplicate** an icon on the desktop, the duplicate has the same label as the original.

**Using the Save As command** on a document within an application makes a brand new document; any label the original had is *not* applied to the new file.

**When you sort a window according to labels,** items are sorted according to their order in the Label menu. It's a good thing the labels aren't sorted alphabetically, because while *Priority 1* and *Priority 2* alphabetize correctly, *Most Important* and *Least Important* don't, and *Me First* and *Leave till Later* will come up in the opposite order of what you'd want. Of course, when you decide which labels you want, you have to make sure that they're in the correct order in the menu, or you might still have *Least Important* sorting on top of *Most Important*.

Sorting by label in a window is actually more of a "grouping" procedure than a sorting one, since items with the same label are bunched together, alphabetized by name.

**When "by Label" is missing** from your View menu, you haven't set the menu to show that option. Use the Views control panel to add the "by Label" option.

**The Label popup menu** in the full Find dialog matches the current settings for the Label menu.

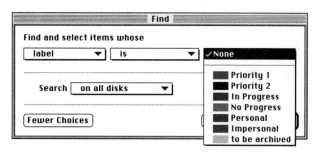

**Icons don't keep their labels** if you change the Label menu. It's not as though an icon is "stamped" with a label that it can keep. The Finder assigns and reads icon labels according to menu position, not the actual name. So, the Finder thinks (if it thinks at all) of an icon labeled *Essential* as one that's labeled with the first item in the Label menu.

As a result, if you change the name of a label, the change affects all the icons currently assigned that label. So, if you change the label *Personal* to *My Stuff* (which is more personal), the Personal icons change to My Stuff icons. This change-to-match-the-menu is going to be most evident if you label things according to current projects, which will eventually change. If you archive one project's files onto a floppy, and re-insert the disk after putting a new project name in that position in the Label menu, the older files will show up on the desktop with the new project's label.

**···❯** **Changing the position of labels in the Label menu** confuses things even more than changing the label names. Suppose you've changed your labels from the default so that the first label is *Personal Stuff* and the last is *Top Priority*. After a while, you realize that you're using the Top Priority label a lot more often than the Personal Stuff label. So, you decide to switch their positions, putting Top Priority at the top of the menu because it's faster to get at it there. Presto! All your Personal-labeled icons have just been re-labeled Top Priority, and vice versa. (Which might be of some use to those of us trying to re-prioritize our lives.)

You can swap label positions in the menu and keep icons labeled correctly with a little work and two unused labels for interim labeling. Let's say you want to swap the labels in the first two positions in the menu, which are currently in the order Personal and then Priority. Here's how you can do it, assuming you've got two unused labels elsewhere in the menu.

1. Rename the unused labels *Temp1* and *Temp2*.
2. Use the full Find command with its *all at once* option to select all the icons currently labeled Personal. You can set the search for a single window, or for the whole disk. When the search is finished, all the Personal icons are selected.
3. Choose Temp1 from the Label menu to apply that label to all the Personal icons.
4. Use the Find command to find and select all the Priority icons.
5. Choose Temp2 from the Label menu to re-label all the Priority icons.
6. In the Labels control panel, reassign Priority to the first spot and put Personal in the second.
7. Do another Find, this time for the Temp1 icons.
8. Choose Personal from the Labels menu.
9. Find and select all the Temp2 icons.
10. Choose Priority from the Labels menu.

When this is finished, your Personal icons are still Personal icons, and the Priority icons are once again Priority icons, even though you've switched the position of those labels in the menu.

**···❯** **The label for a selected icon is checked** in the Label menu, but if you select multiple icons with a mixture of labels, the labels involved are marked in the menu with a hyphen.

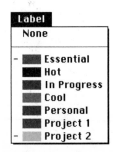

## Labels & Colors

✏ **On a color system,** colors appear next to each item in the Label menu. The color is assigned to the icon along with the label.

Since most icons are already in color on a color system, what happens when you assign a Label color depends on what the icon looked like originally. Generally, a color icon looks as though it had a wash of watercolor applied to it, with formerly white areas filled by a pastel shade of the label color, and other light colors or grays colored over with darker shades; sometimes the black areas are replaced by the label color.

In all, color as an identifying feature is useful only in a very general way—although it's particularly effective on folders.

✏ **To change the color assigned to a Label,** start with the Labels control panel. Click on the color you want to change. The Color Picker opens, and you can edit the color any way you want. (See the Color control panel in Chapter 8 for details on using the Color Picker.) When you click OK, the new color goes into the Labels control panel and the Label menu.

There's a new Color Picker in System 7.5. See Chapter 8.

Changing a color in the menu has the same effect as changing a name: Any icon assigned the previous color changes to the new color.

Use the Color Picker to change the colors in the Label menu.

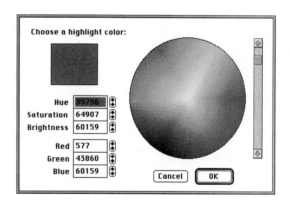

✏ **Avoid light colors for labels.** They make full-size folders attractive because the folders are filled with a light color to start with. But the tiny icons used in list views and dialog boxes are merely outlines, and light colors make them almost invisible.

✏ **If you don't want to change an icon's color** because you already like how your colored icons look, using black as a color for the label actually affects fewer icons than using white—and will keep your folder icons from disappearing entirely in list views. Just drag the scroll box in the Color Picker down to the bottom to set the brightness to zero to turn any color black

**BY THE WAY ...**

The UNIVAC computer was the first used to predict an election outcome, in 1952—Eisenhower versus Adlai Stevenson. By election night, with initial results in, UNIVAC's computations predicted 438 electoral votes for Eisenhower, a veritable landslide. But the polls had predicted a close race, and the television announcer (well, okay, maybe the producers) decided the computer must be wrong. The programmers hurriedly altered the programming—*twice* during the course of the evening—to bring the numbers closer to what was expected by even the most experienced political analysts. As a result, UNIVAC's final prediction was off by hundreds of votes. Eisenhower got 442 electoral votes.

Another by the way: UNIVAC stands for Universal Automatic Computer. But science fiction writer Isaac Asimov, in his early days, thought the "uni" part stood for "one." So, when he needed a name for the global computer in one of his early stories, he named it Multivac. One of science fiction's most famous computers (other writers adopted the concept and the name) was a misnomer because one of its most famous writers jumped to the wrong conclusion.

···❯ **On a grayscale monitor,** the colors in the Label menu are, of course, shades of gray. Although you can edit the colors so the differences are distinguishable in the menu, you can't tell the difference between even the lightest and darkest shades of gray once they're applied to an icon. So, unless you're working on a color system, forget color as an identifying feature for labels.

## Label Strategies

···❯ **The most logical** use for labeling is for priorities and by projects, since icons can be searched for and sorted by their labels. Don't worry about choosing the seven perfect labels for your Label menu, ones that will cover every eventuality and that you'll use always and forever. Instead, think in smaller groups—perhaps two labels for priorities, two for projects, two for desktop manipulation, and a spare. And think about how you'd use labels within specific folders instead of as disk-wide stamps.*

> ✳Did you notice that I didn't include too many tips for using labels? That's not because there aren't nifty things you can do with labels. But they're just so inconvenient to apply. You save a document, you'd like to label it—but you have to go back to the desktop and sift through umpteen folders to get to the document you just finished saving. Don't you think you should be able to apply a label through the Save dialog?

···❯ **Use a project label** to help archive items when a project is completed. ("Archive" here means to get them off your hard disk and stored on floppies in case you need them again.) When a project is completed, do a Find on the desktop to find all the items connected with the project and copy them to floppies. Do another Find procedure to select them again so you can drag them to the Trash. (Unfortunately, when you drag files from a window to a floppy, the copying is done and the files are de-selected in the window, so you have to select them again to throw them away.)

If you're working with a large number of files scattered around the hard drive, the easiest way to do the "archive and trash" procedure is to search through only a few folders, or even one folder at a time, and use an interim label, like this: Find items with the project label using the *all at once* option; while they're selected, change the label to something like *Archived*; (plan ahead and put something like that in your Label menu). While they're still selected, drag them to the floppy. Then find the next group of files labeled with the project's name; rename them and drag them to the floppy, and so on.

When everything's on floppies, use the Find command to find all the icons labeled *Archive* and drag them to the Trash.

➔ **If you like the idea of using labels**, but seven of them aren't enough, or you don't like the fact that previously labeled items change when you change the Label menu, try using Comments instead, for icons that have the Comments field in their Info boxes. (Details coming right up …)

## ➔ THE INFO WINDOW ➔

## The Get Info Command

➔ **You can use the Get Info command** on any icon you select on the desktop. The basic information includes:

- *Kind:* Whether it's a document, an application, a disk, a folder, and so on.
- *Size:* In megs or in K, whichever makes more sense, as well as a parenthetical note as to the size in bytes.
- *Where* the file is—in which folders on what disk.
- *Created* and *Modified* dates.
- A Comments box you can type notes in.

Because the information in an Info window depends on what kind of icon you've selected, the specifics of each one are covered elsewhere. Info windows for disks and folders are later in this chapter, for instance, while the ones for aliases and the Trash are in the next chapter. But here are the various forms of the Info window.

The Info window for an application (left) and a document (right).

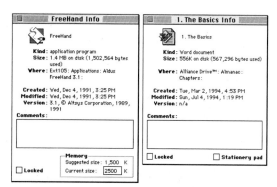

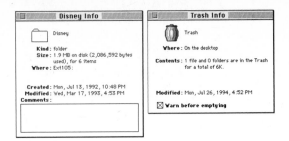

The Info window for a folder (left) and the Trash (right).

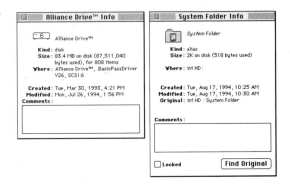

The Info window for a hard drive (left) and an alias (right).

•→ **Most of the Info window** information is also available by looking at a window in list view.

•→ **The Comments box** that's in most Info windows can be very handy, since you can both search and sort according to the comments you make. (The search is throughout the entire comment; the sort is according to the beginning characters.)

The text of the comments is limited to about 200 characters, most of which show in the box all at once. If you type beyond the last line, the text shifts up even though there's no scroll bar on the box. The text is always 9-point Geneva, even if you change the font you're using on the desktop.

∘∘∘⟩ **File Buddy** is an absolutely terrific little utility that will make you forget all about the Get Info command. It gives you more info and it's easier to use—all you do is drag and drop an item onto File Buddy's icon. And it does all sorts of tricks, like getting the info on the application that created the document you're dropping onto it. [shareware, Laurence Harris]

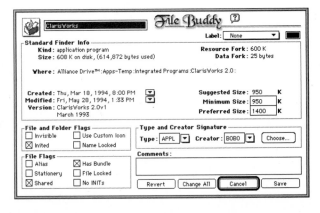

••➤ **The comments in an Info window are erased** when you rebuild the desktop. Since this is something you should be doing on a regular basis (see Chapter 5), there's not much incentive for using the Comments box at all. And that's *really* stupid, because when System 7 was developed, comments were made more important: now they're included in list view windows and are a criterion used by the Find command. Why'd they bother? At least now there's a warning about what's going to happen—in previous systems, the desktop rebuild dialog didn't include a comment on the comments.

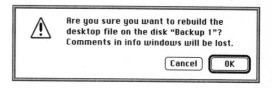

Are you sure you want to rebuild the desktop file on the disk "Backup 1"? Comments in info windows will be lost.

[ Cancel ]  [ OK ]

I think, though, that one of the reasons this warning was included in System 7 when it didn't exist previously is that preserving comments was *supposed* to be a feature of System 7—and it wasn't until the final release of the product that the plans fell through. I know I was writing a book about System 7 when it (System 7, that is) was still being tested, and I wrote that the Comments would be preserved during a desktop rebuild—because that's what was *supposed* to happen.

∞➢ **If you use the Comments box** regularly, there are utilities that can preserve the comments. They grab the comments from the Desktop File, before it's re-created from scratch during the rebuild process, then insert the comments back into the new file. CommentKeeper is a shareware utility; Norton Utilities includes a comment preserver. [CommentKeeper, shareware, Maurice Volaski; Norton Utilities, Symantec]

••➤ **The size reported** in a Get Info window for any icon is given in both bytes and also in either K or megs, depending on how big the file is. Now, as you might remember from Chapter 1 (if you've been paying attention, and if you're reading the chapters in order), 1024 bytes make a K, and 1024K makes a megabyte—and therefore 1,048,576 bytes make a meg. But when you look at the sizes in the Get Info window, they just don't work out. That's because the number of K is the space allocated for the file on the disk. The number of bytes is the actual size of the file.

In fact, the same file on two different drives can be reported as two different sizes. The picture here shows the Info windows for an alias that was copied to a second drive. In both cases, the size is parenthetically noted as 547 bytes, but on one disk that's 2K and on the other, 3K. This little anomaly is due to one drive's being an 80-meg model and the other a 100-meg partition. Files take up more room on larger drives because the minimum space given to a file varies with the drive size. (More about that in Chapter 17.) But you can trust the byte count, which is the actual size of the file, as opposed to the room allocated for it on the disk.

| Rizzo's Menu Info | Rizzo's Menu Info |
|---|---|
| Rizzo's Menu | Rizzo's Menu |
| **Kind:** alias | **Kind:** alias |
| **Size:** 2K on disk (547 bytes used) | **Size:** 3K on disk (547 bytes used) |
| **Where:** Int HD: | **Where:** Ext 230: |

## Locking Icons

∞➧ **You can lock file icons**—applications and documents—by using the Get Info command and checking the Locked button. (Unlocking, of course, is a matter of unchecking the button.) There are two main reasons for locking a file:

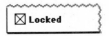

- You can't trash a locked file by mistake. You can put it in the Trash, but you'll be warned it's in there when you use the Empty Trash command. (More about that in Chapter 5.)
- You can't alter a locked file—you can't change its name, its icon, or its contents. You can open a locked document, view it, and even print it, but you can't edit it.

∞➧ **You can tell if a file is locked** without opening the Info window. If you can't select an icon's name, it's locked. And if you open a list view window wide enough, you'll see a lock icon at the far right for every locked file. When there's a lock icon in the window header for a floppy disk or a CD, that means the *disk* is locked, so you can't make any changes to it. But it doesn't mean the files themselves are locked (although they might be, on an individual basis); you can drag the files to your hard drive and work on them from there. This picture shows locked files (left) and a locked disk (right).

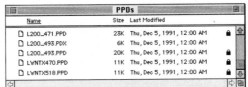

∞➧ *Locked* and *Not Locked* are criteria that you can use with the Find command as described in the next chapter.

∞➧ **Using Get Info for locking** and unlocking files is a real pain, so try Lock It! or Padlock. Each lets you just drag an icon and drop it into the application's icon to lock and unlock files. [Lock It!, shareware, Steve Smith; Padlock, shareware, John A. Schlack]

Lock It!    Padlock 1.0

∞➧ **Make a template** out of anything by locking a document. You can open the locked document, edit it, save it under a different name, and edit the newly created document, leaving the original unchanged for the next time you need it. This is a handy way to save time because you won't have to, for instance, set margins, paste in a logo, type a return address, select a font, or whatever else you might find yourself doing over and over for certain types of documents. This is the whole idea behind the concept of "Stationery," which is covered in Chapter 19. But not many applications picked up on the System 7 feature (although some provide their own version of it anyway).

When you open a locked document from the Finder, you get a dialog box:

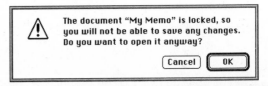

If you go ahead and open the document, you'll be able to edit it. But when you choose the Save command, you'll be presented with a Save dialog with no document title in it, as if the document were brand new.

Theoretically, at least, a locked document should behave like stationery. But a quick check shows that with Microsoft Word, while it behaves as expected at first, it lets you open, edit, and save the changes to a locked document if you open it from within Word itself instead of from the Finder.

## ✥ FOLDERS & DISKS ✥

## Folders

°°✥ **To create a folder,** use the New Folder command from the File menu. You get a new folder in the active window, with its temporary name—*Untitled Folder*—selected and ready to be renamed.* If you know the name you want for the folder, all you have to do is press Command-N and then type its name.

Most Save dialogs provide a New Folder button so you can create a new folder from within the application you're working in.

*In previous systems, a new folder was automatically titled <u>Empty Folder</u> and lots of beginners put stuff in a folder without changing its name; then, they'd trash the folder because it said it was empty. In the Third Edition of The Macintosh Bible, I complained about this and said, "Apple should change the default name of new folders to something less misleading, like <u>Untitled folder</u>."
Now, it's unlikely Apple fixed this little problem just because I suggested it. But I like to think so.

### THE WAY WE WERE ...

There wasn't always a New Folder command. In the earliest Mac Systems, an empty folder (named *Empty Folder*) was always included on a startup disk. To make a new folder, you'd duplicate the empty folder and rename it.

Empty Folder

°°✥ **Folders can hold** almost anything—applications, documents, and other folders. What *can't* you store in a folder? A disk icon or the Trash.

You can put folders within folders within folders as much as you want—a veritable Russian nesting doll setup; putting folders within folders is, in fact, called "nesting."

One of the disadvantages of deeply nested folders in earlier systems was that you'd have to open several layers to get at what you wanted—say, open the Applications folder, then the Graphics folder, then the SuperPaint folder to open SuperPaint. But with System 7's aliases and the Apple menu for opening things, this isn't a problem anymore.

**THE WAY WE WERE ...**

Folders used to be just figments of the Finder's imagination. In the original Macs, you'd see folders in the Finder, but when you used an Open or Save box, everything was listed alphabetically, regardless of where you thought the items were stored—there were no folders except at the desktop. This wasn't much of a problem—the only disks available were 400K floppies, so there weren't that many files that could be stored on a single disk anyway.

But in 1986, HFS—the Hierarchical Filing System—was introduced with System 5.3/Finder 3.2. The hierarchy you created on your desktop with folders was reflected in Open and Save dialog boxes. Even more importantly, you could store more than 90–150 files on a disk, which was the previous limit (the actual number depended on your folder structure). The original setup was retroactively named MFS—Macintosh Filing System.

∞❧ **To put something in a folder,** just drag it into the folder's icon or into the folder's window. When a folder is opened, you can still drag something into its grayed, "open" icon.

∞❧ **Folders are an organizational tool**; there's no "best" way to use them, since everyone works differently and organizes things differently. But here are some guidelines anyway:

- Keep an application and its support files (like dictionaries) in the same folder.
- Keep applications together in an Applications folder. I have two application folders—one for the applications I use all the time, and another for ones I use less often. I happen to keep them on two different drives, too, but you can put *Applications2* inside *Applications*, or put them both into an outer folder. Variations on this theme include applications divided into folders by categories, like *Words* and *Graphics*.
- Put utilities together in a folder—either a subfolder of Applications or by itself. On my desk machine, my utilities folder is on the same level as the Application folder, but on my PowerBook, where I have fewer applications and utilities, it's a subfolder inside the Application folder.
- Keep related documents for a project in the same folder. This works a lot better than making separate folders for word processing documents, spreadsheet documents, and so on, which is what a lot of new users tend to do.
- Create a desk accessory folder for desk accessories you don't use a lot (like the Alarm Clock) instead of leaving them all loose in the Apple Menu Items folder. (More about this in Chapter 6.)

∞❧ **It's hard to figure how much** is in a folder. If you're using a list view, you can turn on the *Calculate folder sizes* option in the Views menu so you can see how much a folder holds—but even then you don't know how many items it contains—just their total size. On the other hand, if you open a folder window, the header tells you how many items are in the folder—but not how much room they take up on the disk.

*✳ Well, those were the stats when I first wrote this. Two months later, during the editing process, the numbers are: 35 items and 25,627K.*

Take my System Folder (please!). In a list view, I see that it totals an embarrassing 18,962K today; when I open it, I'm told there are 22 items in it, as you can see in the picture on the next page.*

But wait—you can leave the calculated sizes on for a list view and use the *Show disk info in header* option so you can get the size and item count at the same time. Right? Wrong. The item count in the window's header, as shown in the second picture here, counts everything in the window whether or not it's in the folder you're looking at; and it only counts the folder items it can "see"—the ones that are expanded.

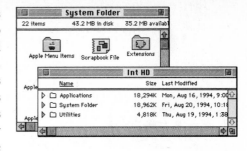

You can Get Info on a folder to get both the size and the item count for it. But guess what? It won't be the same item count as you see in the window. The last picture here shows that the Info window reports 600 items in the System Folder.

The difference isn't slight: 22 items versus 600 items! That's because in the folder's window, what you see is what you count—the file and folder icons that are showing. In the Info window, you get a count of *everything* in the folder, including what's inside any nested folders.

**POP QUIZ**                                    **[20 POINTS!]**

Tech editor Joe Holmes points out that the Finder is apparently influenced by quantum physics, since you can see either how many files are in a folder, or how much space they take up, but not both at the same time.

Now, just what does that have to do with quantum physics? What's the name of the principle that it's analogous to?

⌐•➤ **There's no limit** to the number of items you can put in a folder—or at least the limit is so high that we don't have to worry about it. But there are good reasons to keep the number of items in a folder down to a reasonable size. First, a folder with hundreds of items in it takes longer to open, while the Finder sifts through it and figures out how to display the icons, names, and so on. It also takes longer to sort. And, finally, the Open dialog does have a limit to the number of items it can include in a list. (Again, the limit's high enough that it's not a concern—unless you're producing a CD-ROM disk and expect all its contents to be displayed even if they're "unfolderized.")

•••➤ **You can create a folder on the desktop** although at first that doesn't seem possible, since a new folder is always created in the active window. Just make sure all the windows are inactive. You don't have to close them—just activate the desktop by pressing

Command-Shift-Up or by clicking on an icon that's already out "loose" on the desktop. Then, using the New Folder command creates a new folder right on the desktop.

Any folder created on the desktop belongs to the startup disk, even if another volume is selected on the desktop when you choose the New Folder command.

## USE FOLDERS TO ORGANIZE YOUR DOCUMENTS

•••❯ **There's more than one folder icon** that the system uses, although if you're a one-man, one-Mac setup (sexist, but alliterative) you won't see them. If you're on a network, the icon itself gives information about the folder's accessibility. So, a simple black slash at the top of the folder's tab means the folder is being shared under File Sharing; a slash and network connection beneath the folder means it's shared on an AppleShare network, and the addition of faces means it's shared for a group. If you're on a network and see a belted folder, that means it's locked and you can't open it; if it has a little arrow on top of it, you still can't open it, but you can put things into it.

*Chapter 5 discusses "The Folder from Hell"— one that refuses to be erased.*

•••❯ **Folders in System 7** on color or grayscale machines should be shaded in gray (as shown at left in the picture). If you have simple white folders with black outlines (as at right) although your screen is set for color or gray, it may be because a *minimal* system was installed on your hard drive and it's missing the color "resource" information for folders. You should install a full system for your specific Mac, as described in Chapter 23.

## Disk Icons

∞•❯ **When a disk icon appears on the desktop,** it's *mounted.* Hard drives, hard drive partitions, floppies, CD-ROMs, shared items on a network—all are *volumes* that can be mounted on the desktop, and each type has its own icon. For the most part, I use the word "disk" in this section to refer to any volume on your desktop.

Floppy    Hard Drive

Shared    CD ROM

The window that opens when you double-click on a disk is called the *disk window,* the *main window,* or the *root level* of the disk.

➔ **To eject a floppy,** or other "removable media," like a CD-ROM disk:

- Select the icon and use the Put Away command in the File menu. You'll see the icon's outline move to the Trash before it disappears from the desktop.
- Drag the icon to the Trash. I've always enjoyed making new users cringe when I do this to one of their disks. (Other than that, I'm a pretty nice person.) This procedure doesn't erase anything from the disk, although you might think of it as erasing the disk from the Finder's memory.

*Chapter 17 discusses how to get a disk out of a drive when it wants to stay in.*

➔ **You can't "put away" a disk** that's holding a file that's in use. When you try, you get this dialog:

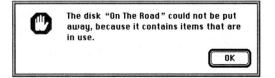

When you're working on a document that's stored on a floppy, it's pretty obvious it's in use; but sometimes it's a small utility, or a font or sound file, that may be open and in use from a floppy.

Then again, "in use" can sometimes be a pretty ephemeral concept. For instance, sometimes you can save a document to the floppy, close the document, go back to the desktop, and try to put away the disk—but you can't until you actually quit the application that created the document. An opened folder isn't considered "in use" by the finder. But if you open a *suitcase,* that's a different story—open a font suitcase, for instance, that's on a floppy disk, and even though you're not using the font, it's considered in use and you won't be able to put away the disk.

*This section covers disk icons; there's lots more information about disks in Chapters 17 & 18.*

But the clue here is in the phrase "put away": You *can* temporarily remove a disk from the drive and leave its icon on the desktop even when a file is in use. (More about this later.)

➔ **Copy an entire floppy disk** onto another disk by dragging one icon on top of the other. You don't need two floppy drives to do this. You can insert the first floppy, press Command-Shift-1 to eject it, then insert the other one; you'll wind up with both floppy disk icons on the desktop.

Make sure you're dragging the right icon for the copy—you'll get a dialog that confirms the procedure.

This confirmation dialog can be a little confusing, what with those empty parentheses after the second disk name. But that's just because the parenthetical phrase refers to the drive that's holding the disk, and the second disk isn't in any drive.

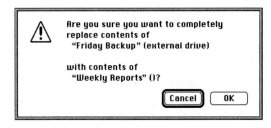

Be prepared for some disk swapping as you're prompted to insert one disk or the other during the copy process.

⟶ **Copy a floppy disk onto a hard disk** just by dragging the floppy icon onto the hard disk icon. A new folder will be created, with the name of the floppy, and all the floppy's contents will be copied into the folder.*

> *Doesn't that make sense—dragging a floppy to a hard drive and having its contents put into a folder? In early Mac systems, copying a floppy to a hard drive replaced the contents of the hard drive with the contents of the floppy. Honest!

⟶ **A floppy-to-floppy copy** with one disk drive is easier if you use the hard drive as an interim stop. Copy the floppy to the hard drive, eject it, insert the second floppy, and copy the information back from the hard drive. Even though there are two copy procedures with this method, it beats swapping those floppies—and it's often faster, anyway.

⟶ **A disk's Info window** provides some interesting information.

- *Size* gives a different report for what's on the disk compared to the report in the disk window. The report (like the one in a folder's Info window) includes all items, not just the ones on the main level.

- *Created* is not the date that the disk rolled off the assembly line at the factory, but the date that it was formatted.

- *Where*, for a hard drive, shows the name of the drive itself (where else could it be?). Then, if the disk driver software that lets your Mac and the disk talk to each other is anything other than Apple's driver, you'll see the driver identified; in this picture, the driver software is Drive7. Then, a sometimes-vital piece of information: the SCSI ID number of the drive. I'll save SCSI details for Chapter 18, but in the meantime if anyone tells you that you need a special utility to check SCSI ID numbers, you can show off. For a floppy disk, the "where" is which floppy drive it's in—internal or external, for instance.

⟶ **You can paste special icons** onto individual floppy disks (that's in the next section—*Editing Icons*) but SpeedyFinder7 includes an option for *all* floppies to appear with special 3D icons that match System 7's overall look. As a bonus, each disk is marked as double or high density, and if it's locked, there's a belt around it. [SpeedyFinder 7, shareware, Victor Tan]

⟶ **The best way to erase a floppy disk** is to select it and choose Erase Disk from the Special menu. Simply dragging all of a disk's files to the Trash is faster, but it leaves invisible files, leaves the information on the disk in a format that's recoverable with the right software tools (good for a rescue, but bad for security), and doesn't check the integrity of the disk media.

⟶ **The hard drive icon** on your desktop can have any of many looks. The thing that determines the icon's appearance (before you alter it by editing its icon) is the *driver* *software* that's installed when the disk is formatted, or later, if you update it. (That's all covered in Chapter 18.) Here's how some of the hard drives on my desktop look—only the one in the upper left is the standard Apple hard drive icon.

Int HD

PD Stuff

Ext 230  Ext 105

## Ghost Icons

∞◆ To temporarily eject a floppy disk, you can:

- Select the disk icon and choose Eject from the Special menu.
- Press Command-Shift-1 for the internal floppy drive; use Command-Shift-2 to eject a disk from an external floppy drive; Command-Shift-0 (that's zero, not the letter O) works for a second internal drive.*

✱You don't find too many Mac models with two internal floppy drives any more; most systems don't even have a place to attach an external floppy drive. For the earliest Macs, there was only a single floppy and not even an external floppy available. But for years a two-floppy configuration was enough to do some real work, keeping the system _and_ application on one floppy (imagine that!) and your documents on another.

With either of these procedures, the disk is ejected, but its icon remains on the desktop—that's why I referred to this as "temporarily" ejecting a disk.

∞◆ **The icon that stays** on the desktop when a disk is ejected is only a shadow of its former self, both in its closed and opened forms. I call this type of icon a "ghost." This picture shows closed disk icons on top, open ones on the bottom; the ones on the right are ghosts.

On The Road   On The Road

On The Road   On The Road

If the disk icon is selected, there's no visible difference between a standard icon and its ghost. In that case, you can get visual feedback from the contents of the disk window, which has ghost icons in it if the disk's been ejected. This picture shows an open, selected disk icon—you can't tell if it's a ghost or not. But if its window looks like the one at the left, it is a ghost; if its window is like the one on the right, it's not.

The ghost keeps the Finder aware of the disk and its contents. If you insert the disk again, the Finder doesn't have to read the disk's directory, build its windows, and so on—saving a lot of time. It can take 10–20 seconds for the Finder to read an inserted floppy; when you re-insert it, though, the Finder is instantly aware of its contents.

But you pay for the convenience of keeping the Finder aware of the disk. For one thing, every mounted volume takes another piece of the Finder's memory. For another, you'll occasionally be prompted to insert the disk if the Finder thinks it needs something from it; the prompts show up with annoying frequency when you're working in some applications and want to open or save something.

**WHERE GHOST ICONS COME FROM**

•••➤ **The Eject button** in Open and Save dialogs ejects the disk that's showing in the dialog, but it leaves the ghost icon on the desktop. (You probably won't notice this if you can't see your desktop when you're in an application, where you use the Open and Save dialogs.)

•••➤ **Get rid of a ghost disk** by dragging it to the Trash or by selecting it and using the Put Away command.

•••➤ **Some ghosts won't go away**—you drag the icon to the Trash, but it bounces right back up to where it was on the desktop. The Mac isn't letting you get rid of it because a file on it is still in use, by the System, or by an application—you'll get the same dialog you see when you try to put away a "real" disk with a file that's in use.

•••➤ **To get rid of the dialog** that asks you to re-insert a disk—when you don't want to insert the disk, that is—use Command-period. Sometimes you have to press it more than once to get the idea across. The dialog may not go away immediately, or it may reappear only a few seconds later. For instance, when I forced the dialog to appear so I could take its picture, I double-clicked on a ghost icon and got the standard dialog:

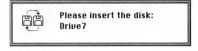

I pressed Command-period, and got this dialog:

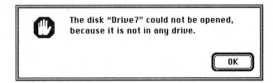

I clicked OK, and got the first dialog again; I pressed Command-period again, and the second dialog showed up again. Then the Finder finally gave up and let me get back to work.

⇢ **To avoid the Insert dialog,** lock the floppy disk before you insert it the first time—assuming, of course, that you're only going to be reading from it and don't need to save anything onto it. The Finder usually asks for the disk because it wants to update its (the disk's) desktop file, but it won't try to do that for a locked disk.

## ⇒⊩ EDITING ICONS ⊩⇐

### Basics

⇢ **You can customize desktop icons** in System 7. Most application icons and their documents describe pretty well what they are. But folders just beg to be altered.* Here's how BMUG's CD-ROM of public domain programs looks when you open it. Aren't these icons much more effective than plain ol' folders?

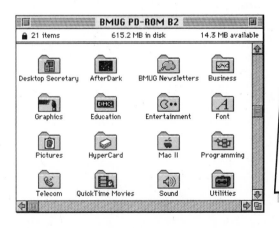

*Okay, I admit it: I haven't prettied up any of my folders. The only ones I've ever done are the ones for this book and other books that I've written. I can't seem to find the time. But then, I don't diddle with desktop patterns, or sounds, or any of the "environmental" things on the Mac. I just set them and get on with it. But most people I know prefer to pay more attention to their computing atmosphere.

Oh—and BMUG is the Berkeley Mac Users Group, whose name I drop several times throughout this book.

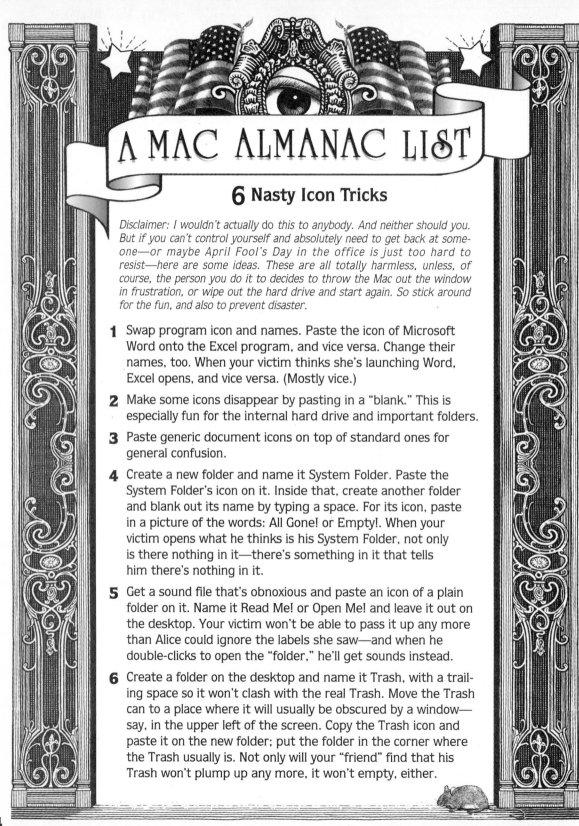

# A MAC ALMANAC LIST

## 6 Nasty Icon Tricks

*Disclaimer: I wouldn't actually do this to anybody. And neither should you. But if you can't control yourself and absolutely need to get back at some-one—or maybe April Fool's Day in the office is just too hard to resist—here are some ideas. These are all totally harmless, unless, of course, the person you do it to decides to throw the Mac out the window in frustration, or wipe out the hard drive and start again. So stick around for the fun, and also to prevent disaster.*

**1** Swap program icon and names. Paste the icon of Microsoft Word onto the Excel program, and vice versa. Change their names, too. When your victim thinks she's launching Word, Excel opens, and vice versa. (Mostly vice.)

**2** Make some icons disappear by pasting in a "blank." This is especially fun for the internal hard drive and important folders.

**3** Paste generic document icons on top of standard ones for general confusion.

**4** Create a new folder and name it System Folder. Paste the System Folder's icon on it. Inside that, create another folder and blank out its name by typing a space. For its icon, paste in a picture of the words: All Gone! or Empty!. When your victim opens what he thinks is his System Folder, not only is there nothing in it—there's something in it that tells him there's nothing in it.

**5** Get a sound file that's obnoxious and paste an icon of a plain folder on it. Name it Read Me! or Open Me! and leave it out on the desktop. Your victim won't be able to pass it up any more than Alice could ignore the labels she saw—and when he double-clicks to open the "folder," he'll get sounds instead.

**6** Create a folder on the desktop and name it Trash, with a trailing space so it won't clash with the real Trash. Move the Trash can to a place where it will usually be obscured by a window— say, in the upper left of the screen. Copy the Trash icon and paste it on the new folder; put the folder in the corner where the Trash usually is. Not only will your "friend" find that his Trash won't plump up any more, it won't empty, either.

➔ **To edit an icon**, select it and choose Get Info from the File menu. In the Info window, click on the icon so that a frame appears. Once the icon's framed, you can paste something over it. Or, you can copy it to the Clipboard, paste it into a paint program, alter it, and then paste the altered icon back in the Info window. The change to the icon itself appears immediately—you don't even have to close the Info window.

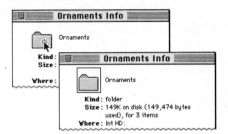

Selecting an icon for editing.

➔ **A locked file** can't have its icon changed.

➔ **If an icon's color on the desktop doesn't match** its color in its Info window, that means you've applied an extra layer of color to the desktop icon with the Label menu.

➔ **Some icons are locked** and can't be edited. This is *not* the same as a *file's* being locked and protected from all changes; it's just the icon itself that can't be changed. Most system file icons are locked, like the special folders inside the System Folder. And, unfortunately, the Trash icon is also locked from changes.

If an icon is locked, you can still select it in the Info window—in case you want to copy it—but you can't paste anything over it. The only way you'll know *that* is by trying to paste and failing. If you're pressing Command-V, you won't know what's going on—or *not* going on, to be more precise. But if you open the Edit menu, you'll see that the Paste command is dimmed.

➔ **When you want an icon to revert** to its original form, select it in its Info window and choose Cut or Clear from the Edit menu, or press the Delete key. The original version of the icon is always lurking behind the edited one.

➔ **If you paste in a picture** that's smaller than the normal 32x32-pixel icon, it will appear centered in the icon's rectangle. If you paste in one that's too big, it will be shrunk to fit.

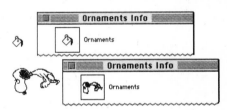

➔ **It's really hard to paste in a new disk or folder icon** correctly. The new icon is centered in the icon's area, so you wind up with a disk or icon floating too far above its name, like the altered icon in this picture.

When you're working in the paint program where you're editing the icon, you have to use a selection rectangle to select the white space around the icon (instead of a lasso that selects only the icon). But if you grab too much white space, the selection will be squeezed down to fit in the icon area, distorting the size and shape of the folder. Here's what to do: draw a square that's 34 pixels on each side—that makes the interior 32-pixels square. Keep the folder at the very bottom of the square. Remember that the frame around the icon in the Info window includes white space all the way around the icon to make it easy to see—so just because a folder floats a few pixels above the bottom of that frame, that doesn't mean you should keep it that way in your editing box. When you're finished editing the folder, select everything just inside the box, including the white area but excluding the frame itself (a magnified view sure helps), and copy that to the Clipboard for pasting back into the Info window.

The same technique works, of course, for any picture you're trying to size and position correctly for a new icon.

## Beyond Basics

➠ **Light colors disappear when** you paste in a new icon unless they're surrounded by a darker color. This is especially obvious when you're working in black and white, when it's easy to think of any white portion of your icon as being "solid" and therefore white when it goes back onto the desktop. In fact, the only parts of the icon that stay white—or, in colored versions, that remain visible—are the parts that are fully enclosed.

➠ **Another problem with black-and-white** icon editing is what happens when the icon is selected. Since the black-and-white parts of the icon simply switch, you get some strange looking figures. When an icon is designed as a *resource* (covered in Chapter 21) instead of being simply pasted in, there's a *mask* that defines how the icon should look when it's selected. The picture here shows a black-and-white panda icon, and how it looks when it's selected. The center icon is one that was pasted in; the one at the right was defined as a resource.

➠ **If you edit the icon of a shared volume** on a network, anyone who signs on afterwards will see the new icon—even though you may not see the altered icon on the file server.

➠ **The Mac doesn't have much of a problem** with storing a special icon for most files— it's just another item of information to be stored with the file. But disks and folders aren't files—and they don't consist of information the same way a file does. The Finder gets around the problem by creating an invisible file to store the icon. It stores this file inside the folder you've altered; for a disk, it stores the invisible file on the root level. You can see the file—cleverly named *Icon*—if you have a utility that lets you manipulate invisible files. Oddly enough, even if you return an icon to its original state by cutting or clearing the custom icon, the invisible icon files hangs around forevermore.

➠ **One of the most interesting dialogs** in the Mac lexicon is this one:

You get this cryptic message if you try to edit the icon of a folder or disk when it has been edited before and then had its

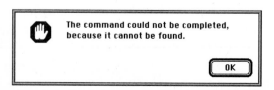

invisible file erased. (That's your punishment for messing around with invisible files that were made invisible in the first place so you wouldn't mess around with them.)

But, if you've erased the invisible file, that means you have a utility, like DiskTools, that lets you access invisible files. So, all you have to do is copy the invisible Icon file from some other folder and put it into the problem folder or onto the root level of the disk. Then you can go ahead and edit the icon as usual.

## Iconizing

••➤ *Iconizing* **is the process** of altering your desktop icons so you can get the most from them. The most what? The most information, the most fun, the most interesting looking desktop, the most time-wasting activity known to humankind … take your pick. And you can do it manually or use an iconizer—a program that lets you manipulate how your icons look. (Right, I made up both those terms. But they're handy.)

••➤ **Altering folders** is the most obvious, and the most useful, application of icon-editing, since it's a great way to see, at a glance, what's inside. (I refer you back to the picture at the beginning of this section that showed the folders on BMUG's shareware disk.) But you don't have to have a specific picture for a folder; you can change some of your folder icons to different styles of folders to prevent the tedium of those straight-manila icons.

••◇ **For instant folder gratification** without having to draw a thing, use Folder Icon Maker, Iconder, or I Like Icons. With Folder Icon Maker, for instance, all you have to do is drag a standard icon onto it and it creates a folder with the dragged icon miniaturized on it. Sorta cute when you have your Word folder stamped with the Word icon, and so on. [Folder Icon Maker, shareware, Gregory M. Robbins; Iconder, shareware, Stepan Riha, Steve Snyder; I Like Icons, Baseline]

Microsoft Word    Suitcase™

QuickTime    A. File Exchange

••➤ **Changing disk icons** is an easy way to tell at a glance which is which, whether you have several hard drives chained to your system, or you pop floppies in and out a lot.

••◇ **Make your document icons display** their contents with Thumbnail, which takes any graphics document and miniaturizes it for the desktop icon. Your icons could look like the ones here. [Thumbnail, free from ZMac, Robert S. Mah]

Babycarriage    Violin    Potogold    More Macs    Heart1

usflag    Moose    Angel    newton.gif    Black Bear

∞⟩ **Don't use a full-color paint program** to edit your icons—it's a waste of time (it takes relatively long to open) and memory (why give up a meg or more of space to edit a teensy weensy icon?). Besides, maybe you don't *have* a full-color paint program!

Icon Editor (shown in the picture), Icon 7, I Like Icons, and IconBOSS all provide full-color icon-editing capabilities with a range of drawing tools. You'll find an icon editor much easier to use than a paint program; aside from the time and space considerations—and cost! And an icon editor keeps your icons just the right size. You won't have to worry about copying the right-size square to the Clipboard to avoid distortion in the final product. [Icon Editor, Xtras for System 7, book/disk, Aker, Addison-Wesley; Icon 7, Inline Design/Microseeds; I Like Icons, Baseline; IconBOSS, shareware, Scott A. Johnson]

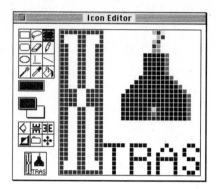

∞⟩ **Animate your icons** with I Like Icons—the all-purpose iconizer that slices, dices, chops and ... whoops, I got carried away there. I Like Icons, as I mentioned in some of the last few entries, lets you edit icons individually and automate the process of putting miniature icons on folders; it also makes icons based on a document's contents, like Thumbnail, but it works only with PICT-type graphics documents. What's special about it is that it can turn an icon into a mini-movie. It *looks* like a regular icon, but when you click on it, you get an animated sequence—complete with sound, if that's the way you want it. The program title seems a little wimpy until you see the packaging and realize it's a pun—you even get a pseudo-presidential campaign button in the box. [I Like Icons, Baseline]

A series of icons for a mini-movie in I Like Icons.

See Chapter 21 for information about customizing icons in the ResEdit program.

⊷ **Make icons invisible** by pasting in a white or light-colored block. What you're left with is simply the name of the icon. Why would you want to do this? It's the only way to get a list of file names out loose on the desktop, since there's no list view option except for inside windows. (More about this in the next chapter.)

Computer: A
high-speed idiot.

# CHAPTER 5
# STILL THE DESKTOP

In this chapter, you'll discover:

•••❱ More uses for aliases than you'll know what to do with.

•••❱ How the Trash is so tricky when it comes to locked files.

•••❱ What Help Balloons have in common with the Parthenon.

•••❱ The second reference in this book to the Beatles.

•••❱ Which Mac dialog says: "Oops!"

•••❱ How to find things with the Find command. And without it.

THE MOST FAMOUS
PERSON QUOTED IN
THIS CHAPTER

**O**scar the Grouch

–Includes–

147 Entries

9 Quotes

1 Terrific Table

2 Mac Almanac
Lists

*page 195*

## ❖❙ THE TRASH ❙❖

### The Empty Trash Command

∘∘❱ **When you drag something into the Trash,** the icon fattens to show there's something inside. The Trash doesn't empty itself when you shut down the computer or launch an application, as it did in previous systems. Trashed items stay in the Trash, and on the disk, until you use the Special menu's Empty Trash command.* Fortunately, although the Trash can bulges, it never overflows.

*✱Don't you think we're all old enough now to have a Delete command that would let us erase a selected icon without having to drag it to the Great Trash Can in the Corner?*

**MAC TRIVIA**

The Trash can didn't always bulge when you put something in it. That little nicety was added in 1987 with System 5.4 and Finder 4.0.

∘∘❱ **The Trash can is communal** property, much like the desktop. The files in it might belong to any mounted volume, and you can't erase, say, just the ones from the internal drive while leaving items from the external drive.

∘∘❱ **The warning dialog** (*Are you sure you want to permanently remove these items?*) that appears when you use the Empty Trash command is controlled by the setting in the Trash's Get Info window. With the *Warn before emptying* checkbox checked, you'll get the dialog every time you use the Empty Trash command. If it's unchecked, you bypass the warning dialog.

The setting in the Info window controls the warning dialog.

∘∘❱ **Check the warning setting** without opening the Trash's Get Info window. Since a menu command that opens a dialog box has an ellipsis (the three dots, like this ...) after it, just check the Empty Trash command in the Special menu. If there's an ellipsis after it, the warning is on; if there's no ellipsis, the warning's off.

In fact, if the warning's on and you hold down the Option key to temporarily turn it off, the ellipsis disappears from the command. The reverse isn't true, though—if the warning's off, holding down Option doesn't add the ellipsis to the command.

••➤ **You can temporarily reverse** the *Warn before emptying* setting by holding the Option key when you open the Special menu. So, if the warning is set to come on, it won't show up; if it's set not to come on, you'll get it. Of course, if you can remember to hold the Option key to get a temporary warning, you can certainly remember to check what's in the Trash—you're paying attention to what you're doing. The temporary reversal of the Get Info setting is really meant to temporarily bypass the warning, not to call it up.

••➤ **You can't trash a file that's in use.** You can put it in the Trash, but you can't erase it. A file is in use if it's open in some application. A folder is considered in use if contains a locked file. It's also often considered in use if—get this!—it's holding a document that you've used in the current work session and its application is still open! That is, you can close a document and then trash it with no problems even while its parent application is still open, but if you close the document and drag its *folder* to the Trash while the parent application is still open, you might not be able to erase the file. If you run into this problem, either take the document out of the folder, or quit the application.

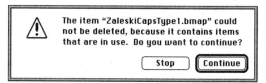

••➤ **Leave the Trash warning on** when you're cleaning up your hard drive because you're running out of space. It's really satisfying to see a report that you're going to free up 13.8 megs of disk space!

••➤ **Files aren't really erased** when you use the Empty Trash command. (Isn't that a shocker?) Instead, a trashed file's name is removed from the disk directory that the Mac uses to find things, and the areas of the disk that it was stored on are flagged as reusable. Until the actual information is overwritten by new information when you save a document or copy a file from another disk, it's still sitting there—even though you can't see it and the Mac doesn't know about it.

This fact of computing life is important to know for two reasons. First, it means that you can, with the right utility, recover a file you trashed by mistake and really really *really* need to get back. Second, it means that anyone else can, with the right utility, get at sensitive information you *thought* was safely erased from your disk.

## The Trash Can

••➤ **Take something out of the Trash** by opening the Trash icon (double-clicking on it's the easiest way) and dragging the icon out. Or, let the Mac do the work: open the Trash window, select the item you want to rescue, and choose Put Away from the File menu. The item zips back to where it was before you trashed it, no matter how many layers of folders it has to travel through.

••➤ **You can put two files** with the same name in the Trash at the same time. So, you can trash the *3rd Quarter Report* from your internal hard drive and your backup at the same

time. Of course, those two files still have different path names, since they're identified by their drive of origin. But, in fact, if you trash a file from a drive, then rename a file on that drive to match the one in the Trash, and then drag *that* one into the Trash, you won't get a *Do you want to replace … ?*
dialog. Instead, the Finder discreetly changes the name of the file that's already in the Trash, appending a *copy 2* to its name. If, for some reason, the name of the file can't be changed, you'll get this dialog:

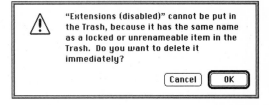

> ⚠ "Extensions (disabled)" cannot be put in the Trash, because it has the same name as a locked or unrenameable item in the Trash. Do you want to delete it immediately?
>
> [ Cancel ]  [ **OK** ]

•••➤ **The Trash can in System 7** must be heavier than the ones in previous systems, because it stays put. If you move it to a new position on the screen, it's still there when you restart, just as you'd expect. But before System 7, a restart always put the Trash icon back in the lower-right corner.

OSCAR THE GROUCH  I love trash!

•••➤ **The Trash shows in Open and Save** dialogs, but it's always dimmed, so you can't open it or get at anything inside it. Even Trash aliases show up in the list. I guess they were trying to be thorough, but it seems pretty useless.

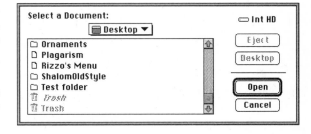

Select a Document:                    ▭ Int HD
            [ 🖥 Desktop ▼ ]
  📁 Ornaments                          [ Eject ]
  📄 Plagarism                         [ Desktop ]
  📄 Rizzo's Menu
  📁 ShalomOldStyle                    [ **Open** ]
  📄 Test folder                       [ Cancel ]
  🗑 *Trash*
  🗑 Trash

•••➤ **The Trash can serves as an eject** mechanism for floppy disks and other removable volumes, like CD-ROM disks and removable hard disk cartridges—just drag their icons into the Trash. You can also drag a network shared volume into the Trash to disconnect yourself from the network.

Many people have complained, and reasonably so, about this procedure over the years because it's so counter-intuitive. After all, the files you drag to the Trash are erased—shouldn't dragging a disk there erase it? Well, I remember when that feature was introduced (you couldn't always eject a disk that way) and we all loved the shortcut. And if Apple changes that now, a lot of us will be annoyed.

•••➤ **The Trash can in System 7** is basically a glorified folder. In fact, you can see the Trash folder—that's even it's name—under certain circumstances. If you boot up your system with a System 6 floppy, you'll see a folder named Trash on the root level of the drive with the waiting-to-be-trashed items in it. Or, if you're on a network and look at another Mac's drive, you'll see the folder sitting there on the root level. Some hierarchical

See Chapter 21 for more information about the Trash on networks.

Apple menu utilities (they're covered in Chapter 6) show the Trash folder as a sub-menu if you list the drive itself in the Apple menu.

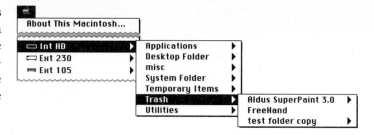

•••➤ **Sometimes there's a discrepancy** between the number of files the Trash's Info window reports as being in the Trash and the number of files you *know* are in there because you looked inside the folder that you dragged to the Trash.

The problem is invisible files that are inside folders. Occasionally an application will create an invisible file and forget to erase it, but the usual culprit is a folder's custom icon. When you paste an icon on a folder, the information for the picture is actually stored *inside* the folder, in an invisible file. You can't see it, but the Mac knows it's there and counts it as one of the files that's in the trash. What's that you say? That's a plain folder in the Trash? Well, if a folder *ever* had a custom icon, the invisible file stays inside even after you've erased the icon from the folder!

•••➤ **A Rescued Items folder** sometimes shows up in the Trash. The files in the folder are the temporary files an application makes while you're working; if the Mac crashes, it dumps the files into the Trash can.✱ Sometimes (never often enough) the information in the files is the stuff you didn't have a chance to save before the crash. You can't open a document that's in the Trash, so you have to drag the Rescued Items folder out of the Trash and, if you're lucky, you can open them in the parent application.

## Locked Files

°••➤ **There's no warning when** you drag a locked item to the trash, as there was in previous systems. In fact, the old trick of holding Option while you drag a locked item into the Trash to automatically unlock it doesn't work anymore either, although there is a related trick. (Read on.)

°••➤ **The way the Trash handles locked items** depends, oddly enough, on what else is in the Trash. If there's a mixture of locked and unlocked items in the Trash when you empty it, you'll get a dialog that tells you so, and asks if you want the unlocked items deleted. The locked items stay sitting in the Trash, and at first, it seems the only way to trash them is to open each locked file's Get Info window and unlock it. (This is definitely a teaser. Keep reading.)

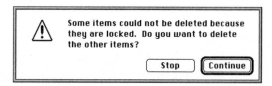

If *all* the items in the Trash are locked (or if there's a single locked item), you get a different dialog:

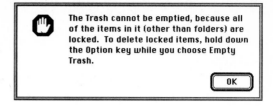

The Trash cannot be emptied, because all of the items in it (other than folders) are locked. To delete locked items, hold down the Option key while you choose Empty Trash.

OK

Aha! There's an important clue in that dialog that they didn't bother to put in the first dialog—you don't have to unlock the items in the Trash individually, because holding the Option key lets you erase them. I should be embarrassed to admit that I used System 7 for more than a year before I knew this; each time I got the first dialog, I opened the Trash, unlocked the items manually (well, not exactly manually, since I created a macro for it), and then emptied the Trash.

See Chapter 21 for information about macros.

••➔ **The Option key** both reverses the Trash warning and lets you erase locked files. Not a well-thought-out arrangement! What starts out as some basic idiot-proofing turns into a confusing setup. Here are the four possible scenarios for when all the files in the Trash are locked:

- *Warning on; Empty Trash command.* No problem: You get the *Hold down the Option key* dialog, as you'd expect.
- *Warning on; Option with Empty Trash.* The locked files get erased with no dialog. Not such a big deal—you probably held the Option key down specifically to turn the warning off anyway. And if you're bypassing the dialog on purpose, it's safe to assume you want that trash emptied, locked files or not.
- *Warning off; Empty Trash command.* You get the Hold down the Option key dialog. Perfect.
- *Warning off; Option with Empty Trash.* All the files are erased with no further ado. See the problem? The warning's off, so you hold Option to get the warning. But, not only is the warning skipped despite the Option key being down, even the locked files get erased without your having a second chance! Aha! Another idiot-proofed interface feature foiled.

**ADRIAN COBLENTZ**
(NJMUG's resident shrink)

It doesn't take a genius to get past idiot-proofing.

## More Trash

••➔ **The Trash window** shows less information in its header than most desktop windows, but it does tell you how many items are in it. It doesn't show how much is in the Trash (in K or megs), or how much room there's left on the disk, either. Like other desktop windows, it counts a folder as an item, but doesn't count the items inside the folder.

The Trash's Info window, on the other hand, gives a better count of what's in the Trash, even to the point of saying how many folders and how many files there are, along with the total size.

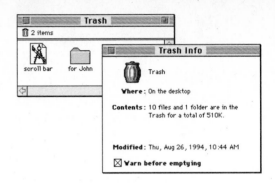

The Trash's Info window gives more information than its desktop window.

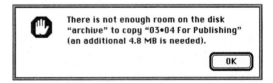

••▶ **When you drag items from a floppy** to the Trash and then eject the disk, it looks as though the items were erased from the disk because they disappear from the Trash—the Trash icon even slims down if the floppy's files were the only ones in there. This is particularly misleading for experienced Mac users because in previous systems, ejecting a floppy *did* erase the files you had dragged from it to the Trash. But the items are still on the floppy, in an invisible folder (cleverly named *Trash folder*).

In the generally balanced yin and yang of the Mac, when you insert a floppy with trashed, but not erased, files on it, they go back into the Trash can.

••▶ **If you want to erase some files from a floppy** to make room for new files you're copying to it, you can skip the Empty Trash command. First, drag the old files to the trash, then drag the new files to the floppy. You'll get this dialog:

Just hit Return and the Trash will be emptied (everything gets emptied, not just the stuff from the floppy disk in question). Now, isn't that easier than choosing the Empty Trash command before you drag the files to the floppy? It probably saves maybe about five seconds.

••▶ **When the Mac doesn't offer** to empty the Trash for you when you're dragging things to a floppy even though some of the floppy's items are in the Trash, that means there wouldn't be enough room on the disk even if the trashed files were erased. You get the same dialog that appears anytime there's not enough room on a disk:

••▶ **Erasing files is a background** operation. This means that while the dialog on the screen is counting down the 1,347 files you're erasing from your hard drive, you don't have to watch the progress report. You can go ahead and work in an opened application.

•••► **"Folder from Hell"** is the affectionate name given to a folder that refuses to be erased from the disk. You put it in the Trash, use the Empty Trash command, and you get a report that the Trash can't be emptied because the folder is locked or in use—but you know that it isn't.

There's a simple method for getting rid of this folder that works sometimes: with the Hell folder out on the desktop, create another folder with exactly the same name some-place else. Drag the newly created folder onto the desktop. You'll be asked if you want to replace the existing one; click OK. Now trash the new folder.

But the Folder from Hell syndrome is sometimes indicative of some serious problems with the disk directory—damage that can spread. Eventually, other folders won't be able to be erased; some will even refuse to open. If your disk directory is badly damaged, the Mac won't be able to find *any* of your files! Run Disk First Aid, the program that comes with your system disks. (If your computer came without system disks, get a set!) If running Disk First Aid doesn't solve the problem, try a heavy-duty disk utility like MacTools or Norton's Disk Doctor. If all else fails, plan to reformat your hard drive.

Disk First Aid, disk utilities and reformatting are covered in Chapter 18.

•••► **When you can't empty the Trash** because you keep getting a dialog telling you that the files (the ones in the Trash) can't be found, or that they don't exist, you definitely have directory damage. With luck, a disk utility will fix it up. Without luck, you'll have to reformat your hard drive to clean things up.

•••► **If you drag something into** the Trash and you get the dialog shown here, you might first wonder just which "it" can't be found—the item you dragged into the Trash (HyperCard, in this example) or the Trash.

Of course, either one of them being on the missing list is rather odd, since you have them both right under your mouse cursor when it happens. Sometimes this dialog seems to be triggered when you drag something to the Trash and there's

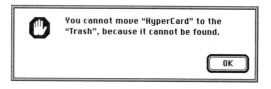

already a file there with the same name. Renaming either one of the files solves the problem. (Note this isn't the same as the last problem I described where the Trash won't erase something because "it can't be found"; this, less serious, problem occurs when you drag something into the Trash, not when you empty it.)

## Trash Tricks

∞► **You can rename the Trash icon.** (Why would you want to? Because it's there? To alle-viate the boredom, the utter sameness, of your day-to-day existence?) Although after nearly a decade of seeing *Trash* in the bottom corner of my screen, *Wastebasket* just doesn't seem right somehow.

∞► **Do you hate to throw anything away** because you know that as soon as you do, you're going to need it again? Let things sit around in the Trash can for a week or more before actually emptying it. Make it a Friday afternoon tradition. You can sort the items in the Trash window by date, drag the not-so-old ones temporarily onto the desktop or into a folder made especially for this purpose, and then use the Empty Trash command on the remaining items.

Or, create a "waiting for the trash" folder. Keep it sorted by date, and drag the oldest items to the Trash when a suitable time has elapsed. If you keep lots of files in the folder, you can even use the Find command, limiting the search to inside the folder, to select all the files older than a certain date; you can then drag the selected group to the Trash.

If you make a special folder to hold files before they go to the Trash, edit its icon to represent its purpose. A wastebasket, maybe. Or, just another Trash icon. You can move the real Trash to someplace less accessible (the upper-left corner of the screen, for instance, which is usually covered by some window or another) and put the pseudo-Trash folder in its place. You can even name it *Trash* if you include a leading or trailing space to differentiate it from the real thing.

•▸ **If the Trash is too small a target** for you, use the Trash window instead of the Trash can. Open the window and drag it as far to the right, or as far to the bottom of the screen, as possible, so only its edge is showing. You can make the window the length or width of the screen, or just a couple of inches tall or wide, as shown in the picture. Then, to drag things into the Trash, you just drag them off to the edge of the screen.

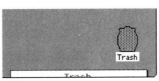

•▸ **Make an Eject icon** if you don't like dragging your disks to the Trash. First make an alias of the Trash, and name it *Eject*. Draw a picture in a paint program or icon editor that looks like the slot you put floppies in; paste the picture into the Eject icon's Info window. Put the icon next to or above the trash, or, even better, in a spot near the top of the desktop, where floppy disk icons appear. And there you have it: your very own disk-eject slot. Just drag the disk's icon into it to eject it from the drive. (This picture shows two Eject icons; one has a gray frame around its perimeter so the white area around it is preserved as a "solid" part of the icon so there's a larger target when you're dragging a disk to it.)

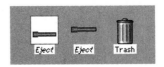

**P**utting aliases in the Trash, and making aliases *of* the Trash, are covered in the next section.

•▸ **You can't paste in a new Trash icon** because you can't edit the Trash. You can, however, edit any Trash aliases you make. For some reason, toilet variations are popular as icon replacements. A flushing toilet sound attached to the emptying of the trash was one of the first non-beep sounds I ever heard on an early Mac.

## Trash Utilities

∞➤ **The Trash can is a simple concept.** Too simple—because there are scads of utilities that enhance it. Or maybe not simple enough—after all, you do have to empty the trash. Maybe such a neat computer ought to take out the trash by itself.

∞➤ **Trash Chute** returns the Trash functionality from previous systems—it empties the Trash automatically when you shut down. (Well, it actually works at startup, but that amounts to the same thing from your point of view.) It also serves as an instant trash— drag an item into its icon, and it's erased without your using the Empty Trash command. [freeware, Melissa Rogers]

∞➤ **Xtras for System 7** is a bookware package that includes four Trash enhancers. [book/disk, Aker, Addison-Wesley]

- EmptyTrash empties the Trash can when you start up your computer. (This basically provides the same automatic emptying that previous systems had built in, where the Trash was emptied on shutdown.)

- Incinerate instantly erases files that you drag into it; you don't have to use the Empty Trash command.

- Shred•It overwrites any file that you erase with it so that the file's unrecoverable by any utility.

- Compost erases anything that's been in the trash too long—you define what "too long" is, in hours, days, weeks, and so on.

∞➤ **TrashPicker** lets you skip the Empty Trash command—just drag something into the Trash can while you hold the Option key, and the item is instantly erased. Or you can use its various settings to make it even more automatic (and let you work with only one hand): have it empty the Trash when the item you've dragged is from a floppy, or if it's an application, or an empty folder—or even at certain times of the day, or at startup or shutdown. [shareware, Bill Johnson & Ron Duritsch]

∞➤ **The best Trash tweaker** is Guaranteed Undelete, which comes with TrashMaster. You can set "filters" for your Trash can, defining what should be done with the different things that wind up in the Trash. This dialog, for instance, shows that the Trash is set to empty automatically once a day, except for large files which get erased immediately, and files trashed from floppies, which get erased when you eject the disk.

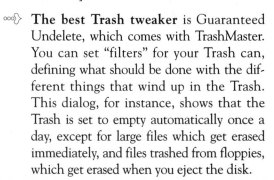

**GUARANTEED
UNDELETE**

The TrashMaster end of things also gives you a hierarchical Trash menu that lets you deal with items in the Trash can based on which disk they belong to, as well as an Incinerator function that overwrites files on the disk so they can't be recovered.

The Guaranteed Undelete part of the package ... well, I'm going to give that a separate entry because it deals with a very important issue. [Guaranteed Undelete, Utilitron]

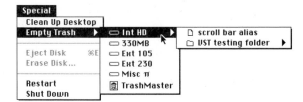

**Emptying the Trash doesn't mean** that the files are gone forever—unless you've used a utility that overwrites old files for security purposes. Since the normal "erasing" of files merely removes their names from the disk directory, the information is still on the disk—all you need is a utility that knows how to find it. Major disk utilities like MacTools and Norton Utilities for the Mac all include unerase options, but Complete Undelete makes unerasing its life work.

When you use an undelete utility, you get a list of what you've erased lately. Sometimes the list indicates whether the item is completely recoverable, or if parts of it—or all of it—have been overwritten by other information, and what the chances of successful recovery are. Complete Undelete simply changes the name of the Empty Trash command to *Recover Trash* when you hold down the Command key, and then lists all the deleted files that are still in its log. [MacTools, Central Point Software; Norton Utilities, Symantec; Guaranteed Undelete, Utilitron.]

THE MAC ALMANAC

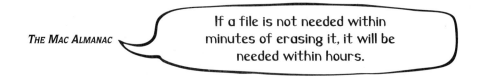

If a file is not needed within minutes of erasing it, it will be needed within hours.

## ➤ ALIASES ✦

### Alias Basics

**An alias is not a copy of a file.** It's more like a copy of the file's *icon*. The alias serves as a "pointer" to the original file. If you try to open an alias by using an Open command or double-clicking on it, it's the original item that opens. You can make an alias of anything: a file, a folder, a disk, the Trash, a control panel, an application ... anything.

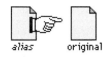

alias        original

Why use an alias?* Because, seemingly, it lets you keep an item in more than one place at a time: in an Application folder and in the Apple Menu Items folder; in the System Folder and on the desktop; in a Utility folder and in a Telecommunications folder. An alias is small—about half a K—so you won't waste space storing multiple copies of the same application. Just as importantly, you won't have to worry about having several versions of the same document on your disk and wonder which one is the most current.

*I added an external drive to my kids' Mac when the internal one overflowed (games take lots of room). My eleven-year old said he knew the internal was full, but couldn't he put just a picture of each game on the internal drive so he could get to it without opening the second drive's icon.

Now, if a kid intuits the need for something like an alias, it must be a <u>really</u> intuitive feature! (On second thought—if a kid can figure it out, what took Apple so long?)

∞➤ **To make an alias,** select an icon and choose Make Alias from the File menu. The alias has the same name as the original file, with *alias* tacked on to it. Aliases' names are always in italics, so they're easy to spot. This visual differentiation is really important for when you're trashing things or copying them to other disks. The alias inherits the original's icon—even if it's a custom one—and its label, if it has one.

FreeHand          FreeHand alias

The amount of room a file takes on a disk actually depends on the size of the disk! See Chapter 17.

∞➤ **The only thing you can do to an original** through its alias is open it. If you erase an alias, or copy it to another disk, it's the alias that's erased or copied, not the original. If you paste in a custom icon for an alias, or apply a label to it, the original is unaffected.

∞➤ **You can rename an alias** without affecting its tie to the original file. So, if you alias an application so that the alias can go into the Apple Menu Items folder, your Apple Menu doesn't have to have a list of names like *Microsoft Word Alias* and *Aldus PageMaker Alias*; it can be just *Microsoft Word* and *Aldus PageMaker*; or, even more simply, just *Word* and *PageMaker*.

The only time an alias can't have the same name as the original item is if it's in the same location as the original. (Of course, you wouldn't want it there, since that obviates the need for an alias; but when you first create the alias, it appears in the same place.)

∞➤ **The best time to rename an alias** is as soon as you create it, because its name is selected when it first appears—you can just go ahead and type. But if all you want to do is remove the *alias* suffix from the name, you don't have to retype the whole name. Double-click on the word *alias* to select it alone and erase it with the Delete key. Or, to work completely from the keyboard, hit the Right Arrow key to move to the end of the selected name, then hold down the Delete key to backspace over the word *alias*. In either case, leaving the space before *alias* as the last character in the alias's name differentiates it from the original so they can both exist in the same window until you move the alias where you want it.

⤳ **You can rename the original file** or move it to another location on the disk, and its alias will still find it. In fact, you can rename or move either the original or the alias, and they'll always find each other. (Isn't that romantic?) The only thing that breaks the connection between an original and its alias is if you erase one or the other from the disk. The magic of this alias link is due to the fact that every icon created on your disk—whether it's an application that you installed, a folder you created, or something you duplicated—has its own unique ID number. An alias doesn't track down the original by means of its name or location; it simply looks for the icon with the correct ID number.

Since moving and copying a file are so much alike—you move something to another folder, but when you "move" it to another disk, you're actually copying it—it's easy to get things confused here. For instance: You have a file, and you make an alias of it. Then you move the file to another disk, and erase the original because you have an exact duplicate on the other disk. The alias stops working, because it was hooked to the original file and doesn't know or care about the copy.

⤳ **You can alias more than one item** at a time: select as many icons as you want and choose the Make Alias command.

⤳ **You can find the original of an alias** by using the Get Info command on the alias and clicking the Find Original button in the window. This selects the original icon on the desktop, passing through as many folders as necessary to display it.

If you don't want to actually do anything with the item, and only want to know where the item is, you probably won't have to use the button: The path name to the original, identifying the disk that it's on and all the folders that it's in, is listed right in the Info window, under (well, next to) the label *Original*.

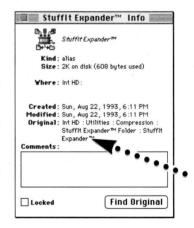

But if you've moved the original item since the last time you used the alias, the path name will still show the old location. When you use the alias, or the Find Original button in the Info window, the path name is updated to the original item's current location.

⤳ **Aliases and custom icons** have a somewhat fickle relationship, but three basic rules remain constant:

- If the original item has a custom icon, the alias inherits it.
- If you change the original's custom icon, the alias's icon won't change until you open the alias, at which point it's updated to match the original. *Unless* the alias is a program that you drag and drop something onto—the icon won't be updated as the result of a drag and drop operation.
- If you give the alias a custom icon, it won't update itself to match the original.

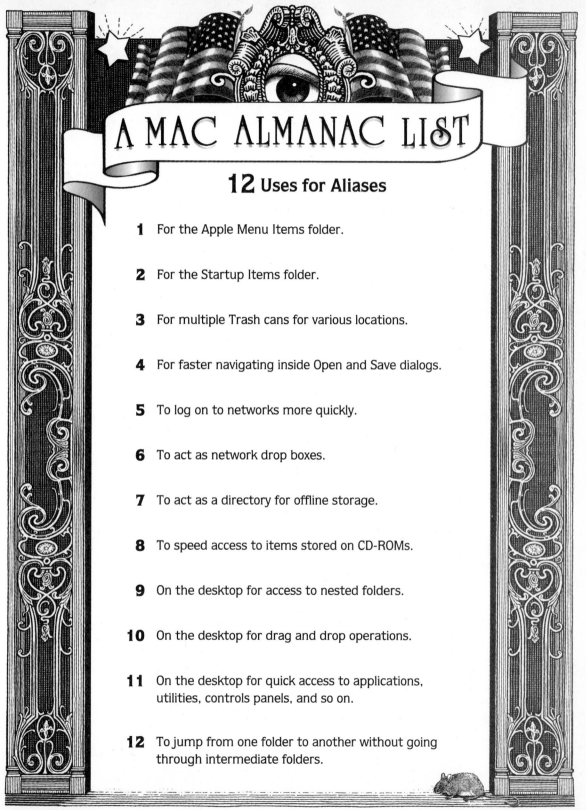

# A MAC ALMANAC LIST

## 12 Uses for Aliases

**1** For the Apple Menu Items folder.

**2** For the Startup Items folder.

**3** For multiple Trash cans for various locations.

**4** For faster navigating inside Open and Save dialogs.

**5** To log on to networks more quickly.

**6** To act as network drop boxes.

**7** To act as a directory for offline storage.

**8** To speed access to items stored on CD-ROMs.

**9** On the desktop for access to nested folders.

**10** On the desktop for drag and drop operations.

**11** On the desktop for quick access to applications, utilities, controls panels, and so on.

**12** To jump from one folder to another without going through intermediate folders.

◦•◗ **When an alias can't find its original,** it tells you so, in no uncertain terms:

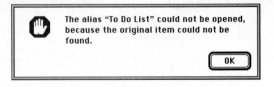

You may see this dialog when you try to open an alias, or when you use the Find Original button in the Info window. This will always happen if you delete the original item. But the Finder occasionally gets confused, and aliases sometimes lose their links to their originals, so don't panic when you see this. Use the Finder's Find command to search for the original.

•••◗ **An alias of an alias** seems to point to the original item: If you double-click on the second-generation alias, the original item opens. But things are not always what they seem. What's really happening is that the second alias thinks it's opening the first; but when the first one is "opened," it merely forces the original one to open.

Does this make any difference? It sure does—if you delete the first alias, the second one no longer opens the original because it can't route the Open command through the first alias.

For multiple aliases, make the first alias and then use the Duplicate command in the File menu. A *duplicate* of an alias, unlike an *alias* of an alias, retains its connection to the original file even when the "intermediary" alias is erased. You can also use the option-drag technique to make an exact copy of the original alias. Or just make all the aliases directly from the original item.

•••◗ **Erasing a file doesn't erase** any of its aliases, so you can wind up with aliases that don't point to anything anymore. To gather them up, use the Finder's Find command:

1. Use the More Choices button to get to the Full Find dialog.
2. Set the search for *Kind contains alias*.
3. Uncheck (if necessary) *All at once*.
4. Click *Find*.

Each alias on the drive will be selected in turn. You can check each one, bypassing it or dragging it to the Trash if you know you've trashed the original. Use Command-G to find the next alias each time. If you don't know whether you've trashed the original, use Get Info on the alias and try the Find Original button.

I know, I know—you were expecting something much more automated, but that's about the extent of the built-in capabilities for finding alias orphans. It's better than nothing—but nowhere near as good as using a utility to do it automatically.

•••◗ **Rebuilding the desktop** (covered in detail in the last section of this chapter) can solve some alias problems and cause others. If you find that many of your aliases seem to forget where their originals are, even though they (the originals) are readily available, rebuilding your desktop may help solve that problem. On the other hand, if you use aliases out on your desktop for drag-and-drop access to programs and utilities, you may find that after rebuilding the desktop, the alias won't highlight when you drag something onto it. This problem is more likely to crop up when you have multiple volumes mounted during the rebuild.

The only real solution is to recreate the aliases you need, unless you have a utility that lets you reconnect an alias to its original.

••} **An alias will open the wrong file** under one very specific circumstance: Replace the original file with one of the same name by dragging the replacement into the folder where the original was and clicking OK when you get the *Do you want to replace ...* dialog. From then on, the alias opens the replacement.

## Folders & Disks

oo•} **When you alias a folder,** its contents are not aliased—only the folder itself is. A folder alias is glued shut permanently; when you try to open a folder alias, it's the original folder that opens, not the alias. You'll even see that the folder's window zooms open from wherever the real folder is, not from the spot you double-clicked the alias.

In fact, a folder alias in a list view doesn't even have an arrow that lets you expand it. You have to double-click on the alias to open the original folder to see what's inside.

oo•} **When you put something into a folder alias,** the item moves directly into the original folder. The alias is somewhat like a chute (or, for physicists and Star Trek fans, a *wormhole*) that leads to the original.

oo•} **Aliasing folders means you can** keep the folder wherever it logically belongs, no matter how deeply nested, and yet make it easily accessible by keeping the alias on the desktop, in the Apple menu, or somewhere else closer to the surface.

An alias of the System Folder out on the desktop is especially convenient: Anytime you want to install a new font, extension, or control panel, all you have to do is drag it into the System Folder alias and it gets routed to the correct spot.

oo•} **If you move back and forth between** two specific folders frequently, keeping an alias of each one in the other saves time. I find that I often go from the Control Panels folder to the Extensions folder, or vice versa. With an alias of one in the other, I don't have to go back up to the System Folder to move from one to the other.

oo•} **Alias your hard drive** icon if you have a large monitor, or two monitors. Then you can double-click on it without traveling so far.

oo•} **An alias can point to an item** that's not on your drive at all. If you try to open an alias and it knows the original is on a disk that's not available, it will ask you to insert the disk, as this dialog shows.

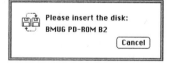

But you have to be careful if you set up aliases for items that are stored offline. You can't start with files on your hard drive, alias them, move the originals to a floppy, delete the originals from the hard drive, and expect the aliases to find the files that went to the floppy. (Well, you can *expect* it, but ... ) Because, of course, what's on the floppy are *copies* of the original files; the aliases point to the *real* originals, which you've erased.

For offline* storage, you have to make the alias *on the disk where the originals will be stored.* Then you drag the aliases back to the hard disk. You can delete the aliases from the floppy; the ones on the hard drive are exact duplicates and don't need the "first generation" aliases to find the files.

•••➤ **You can't create aliases on a locked** volume, like a CD-ROM disk or a networked volume where you don't have "write" privileges—or even a locked floppy. But you can create aliases *for* any item on the locked volume. Simply select the items you want to alias and choose the Make Alias command as usual. You'll get a dialog that asks if it's okay to put the aliases on your desktop—the desktop of your startup drive.

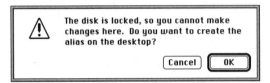

The disk is locked, so you cannot make changes here. Do you want to create the alias on the desktop?

Cancel     OK

•••➤ **You can't lock a folder but** you can lock its alias. Why would you want to? When it's locked, you can double-click anywhere on it to open it—including its name, which might otherwise be selected for editing. This makes for a bigger target when you're working on the desktop.

•••➤ **Create offline aliases quickly** even for a floppy by locking it before you make aliases for its contents. Then, instead of having to drag the floppy's aliases to the hard drive and delete the originals from the floppy, the aliases will be created directly on the desktop.

•••➤ **Alias offline files** so that when you double-click on them, you'll be prompted to insert the disk that holds the original item. This works particularly well for items that you need occasionally that would clutter up your hard drive if you left them there all the time—clip art or fonts, for instance.

To make offline aliases:

1. Store the original items on a floppy disk (or other removable media) if they're not already there.
2. Eject the floppy, lock it, and reinsert it.
3. Make aliases of the floppy's icons. Because it's locked, they'll appear on your desktop.
4. Drag the aliases to wherever you want them stored on your hard drive.

When you double-click on one of aliases, you'll be prompted to insert the disk that holds the original. (It would *behoove* you, as my high school principal Sister Theophane would say, to write the name of the disk on the disk label!)

•••➤ **Use aliases to speed up CD** retrieval. CD-ROM drives are inherently slow, at least when compared to hard drives. Rather than go through a series of nested folders on the CD to find the item you want when it takes *sooo* long for each folder to open and its contents be displayed, keep aliases of the items you'll need the most on your hard drive. Double-clicking on the alias will open the real file from the CD without your having to wade through the folders there.

## Aliases & the Trash

∞➤ **When you put an alias in the Trash** and erase it, the original isn't erased from the disk. But there are several Trash enhancement utilities that don't make this distinction, and trashing an alias might erase the original, so make sure you know just how your trash utilities handle aliases.

∞➤ **A Trash alias doesn't plump** up when you put something in it—because you never really put anything in it. A Trash alias, like a folder alias, is just a behind-the-scenes shortcut to the real thing.

∞➤ **Make aliases of the Trash can** and leave them around on the screen to make it easier and faster to drag things to the Trash—you won't have to always drag things down to the lower-right corner of the desktop. The multiple Trash can approach is especially convenient on a large screen or a multiple-monitor setup, but even on a standard or small screen it's a great idea to leave a Trash alias in the upper right, next to the disk icon. That way, when you want to drag a floppy disk icon into the Trash to eject it, the Trash icon is right there.

If you don't want the Trash aliases to be named *Trash alias, Trash alias 2,* and so on, rename the aliases using spaces so they all *look* like they're named simply *Trash.* For instance, the first alias can be named *Trash* with a trailing space; the next can use a leading space; the next can have a space both before and after the word. If you get tired of using spaces and need more aliases (I use five on my two monitors), you can always use a name like *Trash Can.*

## USING MULTIPLE TRASH CANS

∞➤ **You can put a Trash alias inside a window.** So, for instance, if you keep a Trash alias inside a folder of daily memos, it's easy to trash outdated ones when the window is open—you don't have to keep the desktop Trash can visible.

···➤ If you use a hierarchical Apple menu utility, put an alias of the Trash can in the Apple Menu Items folder. When you want to double check what's in the Trash before you empty it, it's easier to pop out a submenu and look at the list than to open the Trash

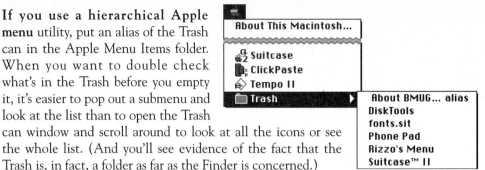

can window and scroll around to look at all the icons or see the whole list. (And you'll see evidence of the fact that the Trash is, in fact, a folder as far as the Finder is concerned.)

## More on Using Aliases

···➤ **Make desktop aliases** for any application or utility that you use with the drag-and-drop method. The instant gratification you get from many drag-and-drop setups fades when you have to open a window or two to access the program. (See Chapter 19 for drag-and-drop details.) I keep aliases of File Buddy (for getting more info than Get Info does on files), IntoApple (for creating and routing aliases), Incinerator (for instant erasing), and StuffIt Expander (for expanding compressed files) out on the desktop because those are items I use often—but I want the real items in their own subfolders inside my Utilities folder.

···➤ **Aliases in the Apple menu** aren't in italic, although they were in beta releases of System 7. This makes sense because you really don't need to know if you're selecting an alias or the real thing—all you're doing is opening it.

···➤ **An alias of the Control Panels folder** is automatically included in your Apple menu when you install your system. If you want a control panel, you open the folder from the menu and then double-click on the control panel you need.

If there are some control panels you use often—Monitors, for instance, if you flip between color and black and white, or maybe the Views control panel—it's easier to have them listed individually in the Apple menu so that a single selection opens the control panel itself instead of just opening the folder where it's stored.

To get at any control panel more easily, select its icon (the quick way to get that is to select the Control Panels folder from the Apple menu) and make an alias of it. Put the alias into the Apple Menu Items folder or leave it out on the desktop—or make two aliases and put one in each place.

···➤ **Make application aliases** so you can open the applications easily. The time is long past that you can just leave an application out on the desktop so you can double-click it and get started without digging through folders. Most applications now need to be in a folder that also holds all their support files. But with an alias, you can put an application in more than one place at a time. There are three popular places for application aliases: in the Apple Menu Items folder, in the Startup Items folder, and out on the desktop.

••➤ **Alias all your applications** for the Apple menu in a few easy steps:

1. Make an alias of the Apple Menu Items folder and put it out loose on the desktop, right above the Trash icon, for easy access. (You'll see why later.)

2. If all or most of your applications are in their own folders but inside another, general "Applications" folder, open that folder so the search can be done just through that folder.

3. Use the Finder's Find command in its full mode—use the More Choices button, if necessary, to open up the dialog.

4. Set the choices to *kind contains application*.

5. Set the search area to the correct drive if you have more than one. If you want to look through one folder and its subfolders, and you opened the folder before you used the Find command, that folder will be listed as one of the Search area choices, so select it from the popup menu.

6. Check the *all at once* box.

7. Click *Find*.

> The Find command is covered in detail later in this chapter.

If the search was wide-ranging—the whole drive, for instance—it's likely that it will come up with small utilities that you don't want included in this procedure. This next series of steps weeds out the little ones from the selection; if your search was done in a narrow area (say, an Application folder), you can probably skip these three steps:

1. *With the applications still selected,* open the Find dialog (Command-F) and set the search for *size is greater than 200K*.

2. Here's the important step in this one: Set the search to *the selected items* in the popup menu. This keeps the selection limited to within the already selected items, which makes the final selection applications that are over 200K in size.

3. Click *Find*.

Now, with all your applications selected, choose Make Alias from the File menu. All the selected applications are aliased; the originals are deselected and all the aliases are now selected. Grab any one of them with the mouse to drag all the selected items, and move them into the Apple Menu Items folder alias on the desktop. (And that's why the alias was there—otherwise, at this point, you'd have to open the System Folder to access the Apple Menu Items folder, deselecting all the selected files in the process.)

You can improve upon the end result of this process if you're using a hierarchical Apple menu utility (discussed in Chapter 6): Put all the aliases into a folder named *Applications* and drag that into the Apple Menu Items folder.

••➤ **Using aliases in Open and Save** dialogs is exceptionally handy—but seldom done. Even users who set up their desktop and Apple menu to make the most of aliases seldom think to create aliases specifically for navigating through Open and Save dialogs. Aliases are easy to pick out in the dialogs—their names are in italics. Here are some examples of how to make the most of aliases in these dialogs:

• Put a project folder alias inside an application's folder. When you launch a word processor, for instance, the first time you use the Open or Save As command, the dialog box defaults to the folder where the word processor is stored. If there are one or more specific folders you're most likely to want to move to, put an alias of it (or them) in the folder with the application. For instance, when I start my work session with Word and choose the Open command, I see the dialog shown here. Opening the Almanac alias (note the italics to indicate it's an alias), it's the real folder that opens. (Okay, that's not exactly what I do, since Word lets me put documents in its Work menu and I can open my chapters directly, but if I didn't have a word processor that let me do that, I'd do this.)

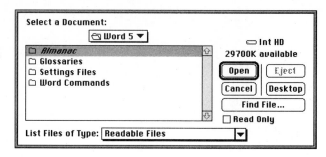

- Put a document alias in an application folder and use it to open a document that you work on often. (Maybe you start your day with a To Do list that you keep in your word processor.)

There's lots of information about Open and Save in Chapter 19.

- Create a Go To folder and leave it on either the desktop or the root level of your drive. Name it *Go To* (or something similar), but make sure you put a space as the first character in its name so it always percolates to the top of a list. Then, inside the Go To folder, put aliases of folders that you use a lot—your basic projects, maybe even the System Folder. Then, no matter what application you're working in and no matter where the Open/Save dialog puts you, it's simple to get where you want to go: Type Command-D to get to the desktop, type a space to move to the Go To folder, hit Return to open it, type a letter that will select the folder you want, and hit Return once more to move to the folder. The list in the Open/Save dialog would look something like the picture here. I find this setup incredibly convenient because no matter what I'm doing, the places I need to be most often are readily accessible.

**•➤ The best alias trick** in the Open/Save dialog is one that lets you move to another location instead of opening something. Of course, if you open a folder alias, you're moved to another location—that folder. But if you "open" a document with the Option key, you won't open the document—you'll be moved to the folder that it's in.

See Chapter 21 for ideas about using aliases on networks.

Say, for instance, you have an alias of your To Do document showing in the list. You don't want the To Do document opened, but you do want to get at another document that you know is in the same folder as the To Do original. Just use the Option key to jump to the alias's folder: Select the alias and press Option-Return, or hold Option while you click the Open button—or, more simply, press Option and double-click on the alias's name in the list.

**•➤ To alias compressed offline** files, you might find it makes more sense to alias the separate files before you compress them into a single package—that way, you can click on an alias called *telegraph* and be directed to a disk that holds a combined archive named *Communications*.

If the files are small, you can simply alias them on the floppy drive before you compress them so that the aliases will point to the disk. But if the files are large, you won't be able to put them on the floppy because they won't fit until they're compressed. In that case, cheat: Create empty folders on the floppy disk named for the items inside the compressed package. Alias the folders, copy them to the hard drive, and then delete the empty folders from the floppy. When you double-click on the folder alias, it will prompt you to insert the disk that holds the original file, even though that file doesn't exist separately anymore.

•••➤ **One of the Mac's more amusing dialogs** occasionally shows up when you try to open an original file that somehow thinks it's an alias—it even has the telltale italicized name.

The main reason for this problem is (warning: technobabble ahead) that the Finder sets a single bit of the information in a file as a flag to say that it's an alias. Older systems used the same bit for a locked file scheme; or, sometimes a file has an erroneous piece of data in that bit. In any case, the Finder at first thinks the icon's an alias—it might even give it an italicized name—but when you try to open the icon, it recognizes its mistake.

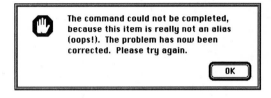

The command could not be completed, because this item is really not an alias (oops!). The problem has now been corrected. Please try again.

OK

∞⟩ **The alias feature** may be the single most versatile interface enhancement in System 7. Why shouldn't it, in turn, be enhanced? As usual, there are utilities that can do what the Mac can't.

- Alias Assassin finds all the alias "orphans" on your drive and lets you delete them—or reconnect them to their originals. [Free from ZMac, Bill Monk]
- Alias something directly into the Apple menu with IntoApple, which uses a drag-and-drop interface to let you quickly make an alias and put it into the Apple Menu Items folder. It automatically strips the *alias* suffix, but you can name the alias anything you want and direct it to somewhere besides the Apple Menu Items folder, too. Alias This also uses drag and drop so you can make an alias and put it in the Apple menu in one step. [Xtras for System 7 book/disk, Aker, Addison-Wesley; Alias This, freeware, Bruce Obervg and Gordon Sheridan]
- Change the italic style of aliases' names with any of several utilities. Some let you choose any style at all for the names, while others provide limited options, such as either italic or bold. The System 7 Pack includes a utility to redefine the suffix for an alias from *alias* to something of your own choosing. [AliasStylist, free from ZMac, Bill Monk; Alias Styler, freeware, Peter Kaplan; System 7 Pack, shareware, Adam Stein]
- TrashAlias takes care of a nagging problem. When you trash an item, any aliases you made of it still hang around. This utility erases all aliases associated with a file or folder that you trash. [shareware, Maurice Volaski]

Alias Assassin   Alias Styler   TrashAlias   Alias Stylist   IntoApple   AliasThis

**BY THE WAY ...**

*BiCapitalization*, or *InterCaps*, is putting uppercase letters in the middle of words. It probably started out way back when certain Neanderthalian computer systems couldn't handle spaces inside a file name, so if you wanted to use two words in a name, you'd cap the beginning of the second word, like this: MyFile. Most programming languages work that way, too.

It's not too awkward when the intercaps are used to denote the compound words, as in WriteNow and SuperPaint. Let's face it, it wouldn't be so difficult to read standard English if the habit crept in: DoorKnob, WindowFrame, FryingPan. But when the caps aren't limited to the first letter of the phrase and first letters of the embedded words—like NeXT, PBTools, QuarkXPress, ThinPacK, TidBITS—it gEts a liTTle riDicuLOUS—and difficult to type.

## ⤐ BALLOON HELP ⟵

## Balloon Basics

∞• **The Help menu** is at the right end of the menu bar—it's the one that has an icon of a question mark inside a cartoon speech balloon. The Help menu consists of only three commands. Well, three commands at a time, anyway—there are four different commands because one toggles between Show Balloons and Hide Balloons.

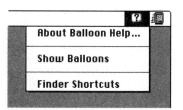

- About Balloon Help contains a simple explanation of balloon help.
- Show Balloons turns on the Balloon Help function. When Balloon Help is on, the command changes to Hide Balloons.
- Finder Shortcuts is the last command in the menu when you're on the desktop, but it changes according to the application you're in—sometimes it's a Shortcuts command, sometimes a Help command. In applications that don't support Balloon Help, there's no third item in the menu at all.

∞• **When Balloon Help is on,** balloons pop up on the screen when you're pointing to something. You *don't* have to press the mouse button to get the balloons. Point to almost anything on the desktop and you'll get a description of what it is, and sometimes even what it does.

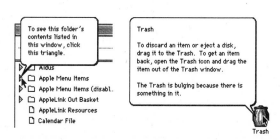

Even just pointing to various parts of a window gets you information:

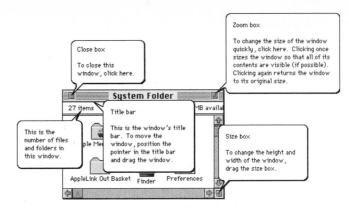

Chapter 21 shows how to connect the Help key on an extended keyboard to the Show Balloons command using a macro.

How much information you get from an item depends on how much information is available for it. Special system folders, for instance, have balloons that are different from the ones for generic folders.

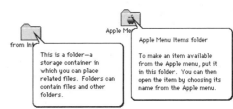

HELP BALLOON PROTOTYPE

THE BEATLES — Help, I need somebody. Help!

THE FIFTH DIMENSION — Would you like to ride on my beautiful balloon?

At my age, I don't remember what I had for breakfast. At the current rate of decay, I will need balloon help to tie my shoelaces.

BOB SEAVER
MAUG SYSOP

•❥ **Balloon Help is a system-wide feature**—the menu's always available—but the information for the balloons comes from individual applications. If you're in an application that doesn't support Balloon Help, you won't get anything except a few generic balloons supplied by the system, like "This is a title bar" and "This is an inactive window."

I have to admit that I looked askance at this feature at first. But I find that any time I put in a new or updated program, I turn to balloon help to identify unfamiliar icons or buttons—and I'm highly annoyed when there isn't any balloon information available in the program.

•❥ **You can continue working** while Balloon Help is on, although you won't want to because it's very annoying to have balloons continually popping out of your cursor as you move around on the screen. But it's important to know you can do this, because then you realize that you can open a menu and drag down to a command to find out what it does—even if it's dimmed.

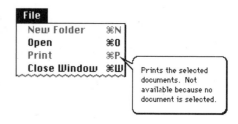

•••••••••••••••••••••••••••••••••••••••••••••••••

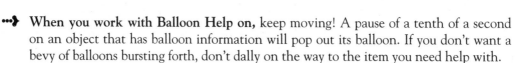

## BY THE WAY ...

The proportions of a Help balloon are beautiful—ask any architect, artist, or even mathematician of the last few thousand years. The relationship between the horizontal and vertical sides of the balloon's rounded rectangle shape can be mathematically described as the ratio 1:1.1618

This ratio is so pleasing that it has a name: the "golden rectangle." It's the basis for the proportions of the Parthenon. Béla Bartók divided his music into parts based on this ratio. Kepler thought it was described by the motions of the planets. Draw a spiral with nested golden rectangles as a guide and you get the curves of a Nautilus shell.

•❥ **When you work with Balloon Help on,** keep moving! A pause of a tenth of a second on an object that has balloon information will pop out its balloon. If you don't want a bevy of balloons bursting forth, don't dally on the way to the item you need help with.

•❥ **If your balloons aren't showing** up on the desktop, the Finder Help extension is probably missing from the Extensions folder. Use the Find command to see if it's someplace else on your drive. If not, look through your system disks for it. You don't have to do a re-install—just find the Finder Help file on the disks, drag it into your Extensions folder, and restart the Mac.

Finder Help

Chapter 18 talks about system disks.

∞﴾ **If your Help needs help,** here are some utilities you can get:

- Helium lets you turn Help balloons and on off as you need them, by pressing a few keys on the keyboard. That means you can point to something you want help on, press the keys, see the balloon, and when you release the keys, the balloon goes away—very convenient. It lets you print Help balloons, too. [shareware, Robert Mathews]
- Inflater changes the size of the type in Help balloons. [freeware, Peter Kaplan]
- SpeedyFinder7 removes the Balloon Help menu from the menu bar completely, which can be convenient if your menu bar is crowded. [shareware, Victor Tan]
- ClickChange, as well as some of the other interface-tweakers described in Chapter 2, changes the Balloon Help icon to any icon you want—and animates it when Help is on. I particularly like the heart that beats when Help is active. [Dubl-Click]

# ↭ THE FIND COMMAND ↫

## The Short Dialog

∞﴿ **The Finder lives up to its name** in System 7, with a real, honest-to-goodness Find command in the File menu.

There are two versions of the Find dialog. The short one searches by name only and shows one match at a time; the full one lets you define more specific criteria for the search, and can show you a whole list of matches. You toggle between the two dialogs with the More Choices and Fewer Choices buttons in the Find dialog.

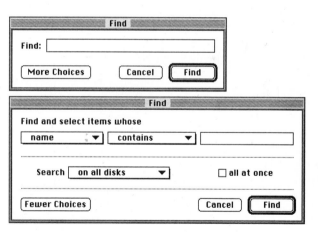

∞﴿ **The short dialog** for the Find command uses these criteria for matching a file's name to the text you type in the box:

- *Partial name:* It finds any file whose name includes the text you typed, whether that text is at the start, end, or somewhere in the middle of the file's name.
- *Case:* The search is "case insensitive"—there's no difference between capitals and lowercase letters.
- *Search area:* The Mac looks through everything it can find—all mounted volumes and inserted disks, and shared items on a network.

∘∘⟩ **When you click the Find button,** the dialog disappears while the Mac looks through all the mounted disks to find something that matches. When it finds a match, it opens the folder that contains the match, and selects the matching file for you.

∘∘⟩ **The Find Again command** is useful in two situations. If the Mac hasn't found what you're looking for on the first item it selects, you can use the Find Again command (Command-G) to look for the next one. The first match will be put away neatly—its window closes—and the next one will be found and displayed.

The other time to use the Find Again Command is after you've done something with the first item that was found and you then want the next matching item. Find Again works even if you've gone off to another application and then come back to the desktop. As long as you don't shut down, Find Again always uses the last thing you typed into the Find box.

∘∘⟩ **If the Mac can't find** what you're looking for, you'll get a dialog telling you so. But if you're using the Find Again command and there are no more matches, you'll simply get a beep indicating there are no more to be found. Ignore the beep and try Find Again again, and the basic Find dialog opens for you.

∘∘⟩ **Take advantage of the partial-name** searching capability to avoid the problem of misspelling the name you're looking for, or to compensate for misspellings or alternative names on the files themselves.

If you're looking for items that you've compressed for archiving (and you use special names for archival files), using *archiv* as the search name will find items with variations like *archive, archived,* and *archival.*

But, make sure that the partial name has enough letters in it to make it reasonably unique. Using *arch,* for instance, would select items with names like *March Memos, archetype,* and *Star Search.*

∘∘⟩ **The Find dialog forgets** what you were looking for when you shut down the computer. When you start up again, the dialog's blank.

∘∘⟩ **The Find function doesn't look inside files,** just inside disks and folders. So it won't find a sound file that you've put inside the System file, or a font that's in a suitcase (unless the suitcase has the same name as the font), or words inside documents.

∘∘⟩ **Skip looking through the rest** of an open window by closing it before using the Find Again command. The Mac displays one item at a time in a window, so normally you'd see the first one selected, then the next, and so on, before moving on to the next window. But if you close the window before using the Find Again command, the rest of that window is skipped. (And save another split second by pressing Command-W,G: that is, hold down the Command key and press W, then, with the Command key still down, press G. You don't need two separate presses of the Command key for the Close and Find Again keyboard commands.)

## The Full Dialog

∞→ **The full Find dialog** lets you search for files based on attributes other than their names. You can, for instance, search for files of a specific kind or size, or those with certain labels or creation dates. You also get to say *where* the search should be done, and whether you want to be shown one match at a time or all the matches at once.

∞→ **You still have choices to make** after deciding how you're going to look for a file (by its name, size, and so on.) You get to be more specific—whether, for instance, you're looking for a file created before, after, or on the date you specify. You enter all these criteria through a combination of choosing from popup menus, typing, and using arrow controls to change dates. Here's what it looks like when you're choosing how to match something to a file's name:

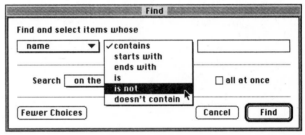

**BY THE WAY ...**

How many angels can dance on the head of a pin? I don't know, but there are some "how many's" we *are* able to answer. For instance, you can have:

| | |
|---:|---|
| **32** | disks or volumes mounted on the desktop |
| **53** | items in the Apple menu |
| **64** | folders nested inside each other |
| **256** | different colors in an icon at one time |
| **346** | files open at once on the Mac |
| **32,000** | items listed in a hierarchical view of a folder |
| **32,767** | resources (fonts, sounds, keyboard layouts) in the System file |
| **65,536** | files on a disk |

••▶ **Here's a chart of the combinations of search criteria** you can use in the full Find dialog. To easily make sense of the possible choices, read across the columns using the first column title as part of the sentence, and choosing any item, or each item in turn, from columns that contain multiple selections. For instance, the first sentence would be: "Search for a file whose name contains [text]." The next one would be "Search for a file whose name starts with [text]." The items in brackets, like [this], are items you type in yourself. Everything else is available as a menu choice in the dialog.

### Search Criteria in the Full Find Dialog

| Search for a file whose... | Choices | Match |
| --- | --- | --- |
| name | contains<br>starts with<br>ends with<br>is<br>is not<br>doesn't contain | [text] |
| size | is less than<br>is greater than | [number] |
| kind | contains<br>doesn't contain | alias<br>application<br>document<br>folder<br>stationery<br>[other] |
| label | is<br>is not | None<br>(label list) |
| date created | is<br>is before<br>is after<br>is not | [month/date/yr] |
| date modified | is<br>is before<br>is after<br>is not | [month/date/yr] |
| version | is<br>is before<br>is after<br>is not | [text] |
| comments | contain<br>do not contain | [text] |
| lock | is | locked<br>unlocked |

••▶ **Most of the items you can choose** from the first popup menu have their own little quirks. Here's a quick list of the things you should know:

- *Name:* As with the short Find dialog, it makes no difference whether you use capitals or lowercase letters.
- *Size:* The size is measured in K, and you can use only whole numbers.

- *Kind:* There are five menu choices, but you can type in something else entirely, like *suitcase* or *Word document.* (Look at a window's list view, in the Kind column, to get some ideas about how files are identified.) The choices for Kind searches are *contains* and *doesn't contain,* so a search for the kind *document* will find plain document types as well as anything with Kind identifications like *Word document* or *Excel document.* In fact, if you type *ord,* it will still find *Word document*—as well as several things you never meant to find.

- *Label:* The popup menu reflects the current contents of the Label menu.

- *Date:* The default is the current date. You can't type in the date, which is really annoying—you have to use the little arrows to increase or decrease the number. Click on the number (month, day, or year) that you want to change and then use the stupid little arrows. But the numbers for the month and day do at least cycle around from highest back to lowest again, so if the month is at 12 for December you can go "up" to 1 for January instead of clicking eleven times to get back down to it.

- *Version:* The Mac recognizes both standard decimal numbers and the double decimals often used for software versions. So, you can search for versions prior to 3.02 or 3.0.2. Remember, if you search according to version number, the Mac isn't looking at the *name* of the file, so a folder or file named *Word 3.01* won't be found using this criterion. The version number that appears in a file's Get Info window is the one that the Find command looks at.

  Unfortunately, manufacturers don't follow many conventions when it comes to version numbering, and it makes the version search pretty useless. One problem is there are often letters or whole words embedded in the version "number"—one of the files on my drive has the so-called number *Aldus PageMaker 4.2 ©1991 Aldus Corporation,* for instance. The Finder considers any alphabetic character higher than a number, so, if you do a search for versions greater than 5.0, you'll get every file whose version has a name in it, like *AppleTalk 3.0.* If a standard called for the number first, like *3.0 AppleTalk,* things would be easier. But, as tech editor Joe Holmes pointed out when he described the problem to me, if things were easier, this book would be half its size.

- *Comments:* In spite of the fact that there's room to display only about 20 characters in the text box for the Comments you're looking for, you can keep typing—you can search for up to 31 characters. Although when you sort by comments, it's the beginning of the comments that counts, a Find procedure looks through the entire contents field.

➔ **The Search popup menu** lets you narrow or broaden the scope of the search. The Mac can look at everything available, as it does when you use the short version of the Find dialog, or it can look at specific disks, in the active window, or through selected folders or files. The popup menu, in fact, is divided into three sections. At the top, there's the *on all disks* choice; in the middle section, you get a list of all the mounted volumes; at the bottom you see the name of the active Finder window (if there is one) and an option, *the selected items,* if anything's selected in the Finder. If there's no active Finder window, the menu lists *on the desktop* as a choice.

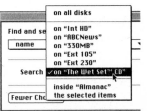

⤜➤ **See your matches one by one** or all at once by using the *all at once* button. If you leave the button unchecked, the Finder displays the matches one at a time, opening and closing windows as necessary. With *all at once* checked, the Finder opens the main search window (the disk window, or a folder window, depending on what you've specified as the search area) and uses a list view expanded as far as necessary so all the matches can be selected and displayed at the same time.

You'll get two progress reports during the searching process: one with a gauge somewhat like a spinning barber pole lying on its side while the Mac searches for matches, and another with the standard "thermometer" gauge while the window's being expanded and the proper items selected.

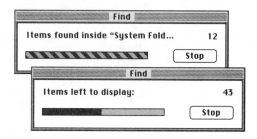

### MAC TRIVIA

The beta versions of System 7 didn't use the "barber pole" effect when a search was in progress. Instead, it used a spinning yin/yang symbol to show something was going on. While that worked for the search process, it didn't give enough feedback during the *Items left to display* process—there was no indication of how far along in the process you were, as there is with the "thermometer" gauge. Once they decided on the thermometer, though, I guess they needed something that matched it—hence the barber pole.

Tech editor Joe Holmes suggests that the yin/yang symbol was actually a cross-section view of a tube, and that, seen from the side, it's the barber pole. I think I'm working him too hard.

⤜➤ **When multiple items are selected** as a result of an all-at-once search, you're not limited to just *looking* at them. If you were searching for a particular file, fine—you can scan the selected items to find the one you want. But remember that you can do an all-at-once search specifically to act upon multiple files at once: you can alias them (the originals get deselected and the aliases are selected instead), move them to another folder, label them, duplicate them (leaving only the duplicates selected), and even open all of them at the same time—memory permitting—by double-clicking on any one of them.

⤜➤ **There are no keyboard shortcuts** in the Find dialog other than Return or Enter for the default button and Command-period or Esc for the Cancel button.

⤜➤ **Searching by name is the fastest** way to find something because the Finder keeps track of all its files' names in a special way. As a quick, though admittedly nonscientific, check, I searched through 185 megabytes of information—over 5,600 files on a CD-ROM—for the first file type of *suitcase* it could find; it took 9 seconds. Searching for that same file by name took 4 seconds. Searching for a nonexistent kind of file (an alias) took 7 seconds; searching for a nonexistent name took 4.

•⇥ **It was easy to hit a limit,** in early versions of System 7, on how many files could be displayed in a window when *all at once* was checked. But somewhere along the line—perhaps in System 7.0.1, or in a tune-up, that memory problem must have been addressed—because I just did a giant all-at-once search so I could take a picture of the dialog that would pop up, but there was no problem displaying the 4,500 files found on the CD-ROM that matched the search criteria.

•⇥ **When you switch back to the short** Find dialog after using the full version, all the criteria you entered are forgotten. If you go back to the full dialog, you'll find that everything is reset to the defaults: all drives, one at a time, and "name contains." If you were doing a name search, however, the name is carried back to the short Find dialog.

•⇥ **When matches are found on different volumes,** or in a window and on the desktop, the Mac has a problem—it can't display all the matches in the same window. Desktop items, of course, just aren't in windows, and neither are the folders that are out loose on the desktop. And files on different disks can't be shown in the same window, either. When you run into this problem, you'll get a dialog like this:

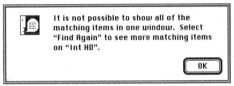

It is not possible to show all of the matching items in one window. Select "Find Again" to see more matching items on "Int HD".

OK

•⇥ **The *all at once* option** leaves a disk window opened with lots of expanded folders. Instead of collapsing them individually or in groups, use these keyboard commands to close up everything: Command-A, Command-Option-Left. The first selects everything, and the second collapses all the folders.

If you normally keep your main window in icon view, you can just switch back to the icon view without collapsing the outline. When you switch to a list view again, you'll get only the first level of folders showing.

•⇥ **You can't default to the full Find** dialog at startup. Even if you were using the full dialog when you shut down, it reverts to the short version when you start up the Mac. But the full Find dialog, once you use it, does stay around every time you use the Find command until you shut down or use the Fewer Choices button to return to the short dialog.

•⇥ **Semantics count for a search.** Select a mounted volume, and the Search popup menu says *on* "HD 80". But if the disk's window is active, it will be listed in the third section of the Search menu as *inside HD 80*. What's the difference between searching *on* a hard drive and *inside* its window? Searching *on* it includes any items that belong to the drive but are out on the desktop.

•⇥ **One-at-a-time searches are neater** than all-at-once searches. When you look at your matches one at a time, a single window opens to display the match, and it closes as soon as you use the Find Again command to look for the next match. So, unless you need multiple files selected at the end of a search for some sweeping action (like aliasing all of them), leave the *all at once* option off.

••◆ When you use the **Selected Items** choice as the search area in the Find dialog, the Mac looks *at* the selected items, but not *in* them. So, if the selected items include five files and two folders, the search is done by looking at those seven items, while the contents of the folders are ignored. To search inside a specific folder, you have to open it so it's the active window on the desktop—then it's listed in the popup Search menu.

## Using Find

••◆ **Find that file you created yesterday** even when you forgot where you put it, and exactly what you named it. Use the full Find dialog to search for files created on yesterday's date until you get the one you're looking for. (But first, look inside the folder of the application you used to create the document. That's where the Save dialog usually defaults to, and lots of documents wind up in application folders as a result.)

••◇ **The search procedure looks *at* files,** not in them. There are other utilities—GOfer, for instance—that look inside files for occurrences of specific text "strings," but you can't do it with the Finder. Some applications, like Word, also include this kind of capability—I can, for instance, have it look through all the chapters I've written so far to find where I used the phrase *hierarchical Apple menu.* [GOfer, Microlytics (also included with PrairieSoft's DiskTop); Word, Microsoft]

••◆ **Using Find is a quick way** of getting to something even if you know exactly where it is—it's often faster than clicking your way through several folder levels. It's a lot neater, too, because only the innermost folder will be opened to display the found item.

••◆ **Plan ahead** for searches you might want to do, and use the Label option, or Get Info comments, to identify certain desktop icons. You might want to be able to gather up all the items related to a specific project; maybe you need to keep track of where you downloaded certain files from; perhaps you need to differentiate between working files and online backups of those files.

••◆ **A disk housekeeping staple** used to be checking that there's no more than one System Folder on your hard drive; this doesn't happen much anymore since System Folders are too big to fit on a floppy and can't be copied over accidentally. But multiple copies of TeachText are still endemic; they won't hurt anything, but they are a waste of space, so you might as well scour the drive for that, too.

••◆ **Make manual backups** of important files on a daily or weekly basis by using the Find command. For a daily backup, do a search by modified date using the default options of *is* and the current date. For a weekly search, use *is after* and put in a date a week before the current date. Back up the found files by dragging them onto floppy disks. You might want to set the search area to a specific area of the disk.

••◆ **Do a search by date** when your hard drive is getting crowded and you need to get rid of the older files on the disk.

••◆ **Find the picture you need** by preparing your clip art files with comments in their Info boxes that use keywords to describe the picture—words like *Holiday, Halloween, black* *cat, witch, fence, scary, night* or whatever else describes the picture. Then you can search by comment to find all the pictures that have black cats, or some other connection to Halloween.

••➤ **A search is based on one criterion at a time**, even in the full Find dialog. So you can't, for instance, find all your Excel files created prior to a certain date, or all your applications that are over 500K in size. At least, you can't do it in one step—but you can do it in two. Here's how to do what's known as an AND search:

1. Do an *all at once* search based on one criterion—all your Excel files, for instance.
2. Without deselecting the items found in the search, use the Find command again, putting in the second criterion—files created before last month.
3. Keep *all at once* checked on.
4. Choose *the selected items* from the Search menu.

Since only the already-selected files will be checked, the matches you wind up with will meet both criteria.

Use the narrower criterion for the first search—for instance, you might have 200 Excel files, but only 30 files created since last week. Looking for the 30 dated files first and then searching within them for the Excel files takes less time than doing it the other way around. You'll also wind up with fewer expanded folders in your window if you do the narrow search first.

••➤ **Use an AND search to find** files created between two dates. If you want the files created between May 23 and June 20, first do an *all at once* search for files created *after* May 23. Then, with all those still selected, do another *all at once* search for files created *before* June 20. You'll wind up with all the files created between those two dates. (Not including either of the dates, by the way—the commands are *after* and *before*, so they won't include the dates you type in.)

••➤ **There's no easy way to do an OR search**—one that finds files that meet either of two or more criteria. (Finding files that meet multiple criteria, as described in the last entry, is known as an AND search.) For instance: If your hard drive is getting crowded, you might want to look through all the old files on it to see what you don't need anymore, and at all the files that are very large, to see what you might be able to live without. You don't need files that are both old and large—old files of any size, and large files from any date, are candidates for being cleared off the drive.

To set up an OR search, first make a new folder and put it out on the Desktop—call it anything you like, but *matches* will do. Do an *all at once* search for files that match the first criteria. While they're still selected, choose Make Alias from the File menu. Every selected file will be aliased, and all the aliases will be selected (the originals will be deselected when the aliases are made.) Drag the aliases into the Matches folder.

Do a search for the next criteria, alias the matched files, and drag them into the Matches folder. If you get a dialog that says *Replace some files with the same name?*, you can click Yes—it just means that some files on the disk met both criteria.

Now you have a folder that contains a list of the files that are either old, or large, or both, and you can decide which ones you want to erase or archive. To access the original for each alias, use the Find Original button in its Get Info window.

**You're not stuck with** the relatively weak Find capability of the Finder. There's always a utility that enhances or replaces a Mac system function, and the Find command is no exception.

- DiskTools is a utility that provides Find functions light-years ahead of the Finder. You can string the search criteria together with *and, or,* or *not*—for documents larger than 400K not created by PageMaker, for instance, or documents containing the word *chapter* modified after a certain date.

  DiskTools provides a list of the matches and displays their path names if you want to see where they are. You can mark any or all of the matches for manipulation—moving, copying, aliasing, and so on. There's more about DiskTools' other functions later in this chapter. [MacPak, Fifth Generation Systems]

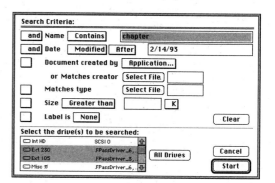

- DiskTop also has a wide array of Find options absent from the Finder. The fact that you can use multiple criteria in a single search (the name includes *memos* and the type is *folder)* makes things a lot easier than doing a double search on the desktop. [PrairieSoft]

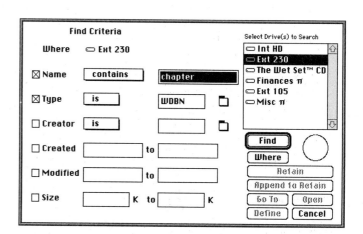

- FindPro (the one I have is FindPro III, but its version number changes at least annually) is a small application that mimics the Finder's Find command, so it will look very familiar to you. But—and this is a big "but"—you can specify multiple criteria for a search. So, you can look for applications over 500K in size, or Word documents less than a week old, or FileMaker documents that are locked and haven't been modified in

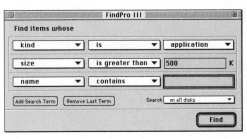

the last six weeks. There are also search criteria that the Finder doesn't provide, like creator and file type (they're covered in Chapter 21), whether an item has a customized icon, and even if a folder is empty. You can string together up to 13 criteria—the dialog box just grows along with your demands.

**FINDPRO**

But Find Pro's better-than-the-Finder functions don't stop there. What's great is what happens when it finds things. First it makes a list of the matches. If you click on an item in the list, it shows you the path to the item. You can select one

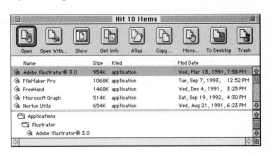

or more items in the list and tell Find Pro to do something with them—open, erase, alias, copy ... just look at this window with all the buttons for the various functions. [Free from ZMac, Bill Monk]

> If the Mac doesn't do it, a utility does. And if the Mac does it, a utility probably does it one better.

*THE MAC ALMANAC*

## ❧ BACK TO THE DESKTOP ❧

### Organizing the Desktop

•••➤ **Keep a "free space" report** for your hard drive hanging around in the corner of your screen. Create a folder on the desktop named *Free*, make it as small as possible, set it to icon view and drag it way down to the lower-left corner until it's nearly off the screen. All you'll be able to see is the name of the window and the amount of disk space left.

•••➤ **Small icons take less room** than standard icons for items out on the desktop. But as soon as you put something on the desktop, it turns into a standard icon. So, cheat: Edit the icon so that it's a miniature instead of full size. It won't look exactly like a small icon view in a window because small icon views have the icon in front of the name; whittling the icon down to size by editing it leaves the icon on top of the name. But it still takes up less room than standard icons.

The easiest way to get the small icon to paste in is to put the item in a window and set it for Small Icon view; then grab a picture of it with a screen-shot utility (described in Chapter 8) and paste that picture into the icon's Info window. You'll have to grab enough of the white area around the icon so it doesn't get distorted when you paste it into the Info window. (That's all covered in Chapter 4.)

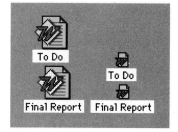

> How about a farm metaphor? The crops would replace the file folders. A goat would replace the garbage can. Here's where the mouse would have new meaning.

JOHN C. DVORAK
*MacUser*, DECEMBER 1988

•••➤ **Keep a list of items** on your desktop. That's right, a list—just names, no icons. Just paste a "blank" icon in through the Get Info window (that's back in the Chapter 4) and the icon disappears. Line up the icon names and access the files by double-clicking on the names in the absence of icons. Make a combined list of application and utility aliases, and documents that you use on a regular basis. Lock the aliases through their Get Info windows so you can be sure that a double-click will open them and not select the name for editing. If you want to get fancy, you can create folders with blank icons and name them with dots or dashes and use them as dividers for the list, as shown in this picture.

Even when a folder is boiled down to only its name, you can still drag something into it—just drag the item into the folder's name and it goes right into the folder.

**••▶ Make a launching pad** for applications. Use the Find command to find all your applications and make aliases of them; put the aliases in a special folder. Open the folder and set it to small icon view. With the icons arranged in a single vertical column, move the window way off to the right—off the edge of the screen except for the extreme left of the window. (You might want to add a leading space to the name of each icon so the letters don't butt up against the icons.) You wind up with a list of application icons peeking out from the window along the edge of the screen, where you can double-click any one that you want to launch, or drag and drop a file. You might not recognize all the icons shown in the picture here, but when you do it with your own applications, they're easier to recognize.

**POP QUIZ**                               **[3 POINTS PER "HIT"]**

Just what are the ten applications whose small icons are showing in the illustration for the "launch pad" tip?

**••▶ The Go To folder** described earlier in this chapter, under *Using Aliases*, is a good thing to keep out on the desktop. Although I previously described its use as a handy way to navigate in Open and Save dialogs, it's also useful on the desktop. With a Go To folder that contains aliases of all the folders you go to most often—whether it's the System Folder, one of its subfolders, or project folders whose originals are nested three or four levels deep—it's always easy to get right to the folder you want. You can keep it closed or set it up as a launch pad as previously described.

**••▶ Desktop access to** folders, applications and documents, and even desk accessories and control panels that you use often can really speed up your work. But there's only so much room on your desktop. My own setup is pretty generous—a 14-inch color monitor *and* a 21-inch grayscale monitor. That's a lot of room for leaving things hanging out on the surface. Here are some ideas for what you might want to leave out on your desktop, depending on the way you work. Don't forget that you don't have to leave the *real* thing out on the desktop: Use aliases. If the desktop is crowded and you want to make the most of it, try using small icons, lists of icon names, or the launch pad folder described earlier this section.

- A *project folder* that you open every day—or several times a day.
- *The System Folder* so you can easily install fonts, control panels, and extensions by just dragging them in without having to open the drive's main window.
- *The Apple Menu Items folder* so you can drag things into (and out of) your Apple menu with no fuss. You can put the alias up in the left corner of the screen directly beneath the Apple in the menu bar if your desktop windows don't always cover that spot.
- *Drag-and-drop utilities* for various handy operations. The ones I keep out are: IntoApple (for aliasing and putting things directly into the Apple Menu Items folder); Padlock (for locking and unlocking items); File Buddy (for super Get Info stuff); Incinerate (for instant erasing of files); and, StuffIt Expander (for expanding compressed files). A word processor like Microsoft Word is handy to have out, too, because it can open so many different types of files. Maybe a disk utility like Norton's Utilities so you can just drag the icon of a disk onto it to have the disk checked … well, maybe you just need a larger screen to take the fullest advantage of this approach.
- *Trash aliases* so you don't have to drag things too far to get rid of them.

••⤳ **Start with a clean desktop.** Hold down the Option key when you start the Mac and all the desktop's windows will be closed automatically.

## Rebuilding the Desktop

••⤳ **There's an invisible file** on every disk—the Desktop file—which the Finder uses to keep track of things. In System 7, there are actually two invisible files on any disk larger than 2MB (so, for now, that's everything but floppies). The two files are named *Desktop DB* and *Desktop DF*. Together, they keep track of where things are on the disk, where all the applications are, what icons look like, and the comments you put in a file's Get Info box. The phrase "the desktop file" is a little outdated because of System 7's two-file approach, but it's still used generally to refer to both invisible desktop files.

The desktop file—especially one on a hard disk—has new data written to it almost constantly. Any time you create a document, or move an item from one folder to another, or install a new application, the desktop file records the changes. As a result, the file is susceptible to both mild and severe corruption over a period of time.

Just in case you're wondering: The DF stands for Desktop Files. The DB stands for Desktop BNDL. BNDL is the code for *bundle*; the *bundle bit* keeps track of how a document icon looks based on its creating application. Do you realize what this means? The invisible files *Desktop DF* and *Desktop DB* are actually named *Desktop Desktop Files* and *Desktop Desktop BNDL!*

••⤳ **Reconstructing the Desktop file** is referred to as rebuilding the *desktop*, not rebuilding the desktop *file*, so if someone mentions "rebuilding the desktop," don't think that it's a procedure different from the one we're discussing here.

•••➤ **To rebuild the Desktop** on a hard drive, hold down the Command and Option keys when you start up. For a floppy, hold down the keys as you insert the disk. In either case, you'll get a dialog asking if you want to rebuild the desktop and a reminder that you'll lose your Get Info comments.

•••➤ **Rebuild the desktop for a hard drive** every month or so as a preventive measure. Also rebuild it right away if:

- Icons lose their looks and turn into generic icons, even though their parent applications are still around.
- Documents have the wrong icon—with all your MacWrite files looking like MacPaint documents, for instance.
- Double-clicking on a document gets a dialog that says *The document can't be opened because the application can't be found* when you know darn well that the application is on the drive.
- Desktop windows seem to take longer to open than they used to even if they have no more icons in them than usual.
- The desktop takes longer to appear on your screen on startup than it used to.

A monthly rebuild also purges the desktop file of unused icons, but that procedure is more important for a floppy disk. Read on!

•••➤ **Rebuild the desktop for a floppy** when you want to squeeze every K of space out of it. Because a floppy doesn't get quite as much intensive use as a hard disk, you won't run into desktop file-related problems too often. But the room that the desktop file takes up is more noticeable on a floppy. When you see that a floppy has no files on it but still has, say, 15K in it, the usual reason is the desktop file. (I checked four floppies at random, and their desktop files were 7, 15, 27, and 82K; the last one is probably pretty unusual.) The reason the file is so big is because you've had various files on that disk, probably with several different icons. Even though the files are gone, the icon information is still stored in the desktop file. Rebuilding the desktop purges the file of all the unnecessary icons. A floppy disk, in the normal course of events, has only about 1K used for the desktop file. So, if you want to get back 10 to 15K, or more, on your floppies, rebuild their desktops occasionally.

Even if you don't watch for the disappearance of space on a floppy, you may notice when its icon takes a long time to appear on the desktop after you insert it; that's usually a symptom of a bloated desktop file, and it's time for a rebuild.

•••➤ **Comments in Info windows** are lost when you rebuild the desktop. There are utilities, like CommentKeeper, that grab all the comments before the desktop is rebuilt and then write them back to the new desktop file, but most people deal with this problem by not using Comments at all. [shareware, Maurice Volaski]

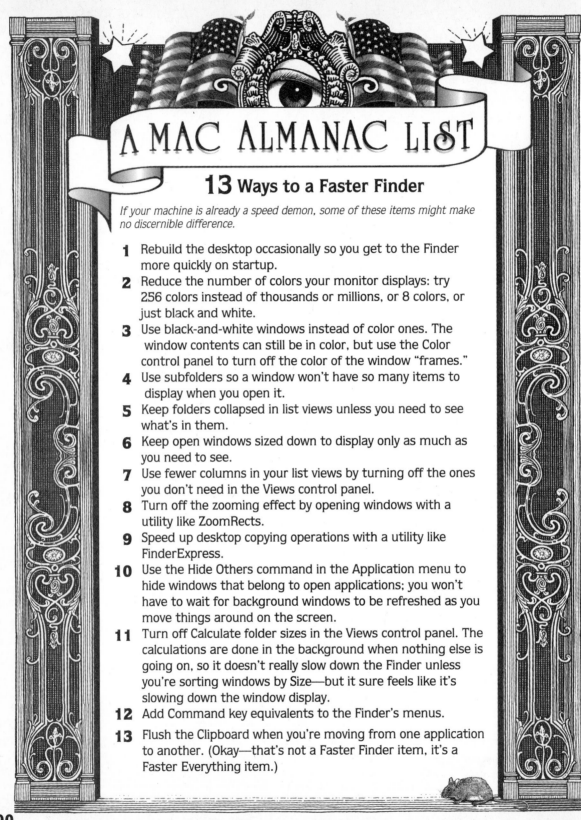

# A MAC ALMANAC LIST

## 13 Ways to a Faster Finder

*If your machine is already a speed demon, some of these items might make no discernible difference.*

1. Rebuild the desktop occasionally so you get to the Finder more quickly on startup.

2. Reduce the number of colors your monitor displays: try 256 colors instead of thousands or millions, or 8 colors, or just black and white.

3. Use black-and-white windows instead of color ones. The window contents can still be in color, but use the Color control panel to turn off the color of the window "frames."

4. Use subfolders so a window won't have so many items to display when you open it.

5. Keep folders collapsed in list views unless you need to see what's in them.

6. Keep open windows sized down to display only as much as you need to see.

7. Use fewer columns in your list views by turning off the ones you don't need in the Views control panel.

8. Turn off the zooming effect by opening windows with a utility like ZoomRects.

9. Speed up desktop copying operations with a utility like FinderExpress.

10. Use the Hide Others command in the Application menu to hide windows that belong to open applications; you won't have to wait for background windows to be refreshed as you move things around on the screen.

11. Turn off Calculate folder sizes in the Views control panel. The calculations are done in the background when nothing else is going on, so it doesn't really slow down the Finder unless you're sorting windows by Size—but it sure feels like it's slowing down the window display.

12. Add Command key equivalents to the Finder's menus.

13. Flush the Clipboard when you're moving from one application to another. (Okay—that's not a Faster Finder item, it's a Faster Everything item.)

••◆ **If there's more than one hard drive** on your system, you can pick and choose which desktop files you want to rebuild. Hold down Command and Option when you start up. You'll get the *Do you want to rebuild...* dialog for each drive in turn as it's ready to mount. It's not necessary to hold down the Command and Option keys throughout the first rebuild process just so you can catch subsequent drives as they're mounted. As long as you start with the keys down and get the first rebuild dialog, the Mac just stays in a rebuilding mood as each drive is mounted. You'll get a dialog for each drive in turn, whether you OK or Cancel any of the rebuilds.

••◆ **Don't rebuild the desktop on a running system** by using Command-Option-Escape to "quit the Finder," even though that was recommended early on in System 7's life. This emergency escape route (discussed in Chapter 24) might leave the computer's memory in a less-than-stable state; the procedure itself might even freeze up the system so you can't do anything. Since this "shortcut" necessitates quitting all your applications anyway, just go ahead and use the Restart command; it won't take that much longer to do it the right way.

••◆ **You can't rebuild a floppy's** desktop if there are no files on the disk. If you delete everything from the disk and then notice there's still 20K missing, you'd probably eject the disk and reinsert it to rebuild the desktop. But you'll find, despite the *Do you want to rebuild...* dialog, that nothing happens—there's still 20K missing. There's no indication that the desktop isn't being rebuilt, so you'd never know about it (that's what I'm here for). If you don't want to reinitialize the disk, you'll have to drag a single file over to it (or, better yet, leave a single file on it when you start erasing its contents), then eject and reinsert it to rebuild the desktop. *Then* you erase that single file. Unless, of course, you wanted the file on it after all.

••◆ **If a disk is used under System 6** and then used on a System 7 setup, there's no problem if it's only a floppy. Floppies, being under 2 megs in capacity, get a single Desktop file that both systems use without a second thought. But if you're using a larger disk on both systems—whether you're switching hard drive startups or using high-capacity removable media—System 6 still uses the single Desktop file while System 7 needs the double-file approach. As a result, under System 7 you'll get a dialog that says *Updating disk for new system software* when you try to mount the disk. The Mac is building the desktop files and creating invisible folders for the desktop itself and the Trash.

## Miscellaneous

∞◆ **Add more keyboard equivalents** to your Finder menus. SpeedyFinder7 makes some basic additions: Command-M for Make Alias, Command-U for Clean Up, Command-T for Empty Trash, and Command-R for Restart. The System 7 Pack lets you assign any Command key to any command, although it's limited to using the Command key alone and not, for instance, in a Command-Shift or Command-Option combination. [SpeedyFinder7, shareware, Victor Tan; System 7 Pack, shareware, Adam Stein]

For really keyboard-izing your Finder menus, you should use a macro utility, as described in Chapter 21.

∞•❥ **The Finder Shortcuts command** in the Balloon Help menu opens a window with five screens of information on navigating around the desktop. Here's one:

| Finder Shortcuts | | |
|---|---|---|
| Selecting icons | To select an icon by name | Begin typing the name |
| | To select the next icon alphabetically | Tab |
| | To select the previous icon alphabetically | Shift-Tab |
| | To select an icon to the left or right (in icon views only) | Left Arrow or Right Arrow |
| | To select an icon above or below (in any view) | Up Arrow or Down Arrow |
| | To select more than one icon | Shift + click the icons, or drag to enclose them |
| | To make the desktop active | ⌘–Shift–Up Arrow |
| 2 of 5 | | Previous   Next |

•••❥ **Several Finder procedures are background** operations: You can get them started and then go off and work in some application while the Finder goes on with its job. Of course, in each case, the operation would have to be long enough that you don't want to sit there and look at the screen—and emptying the Trash of a few files, or searching through a relatively small disk, or copying even a dozen little files hardly gives you enough time to go anywhere else and get anything done. In addition, when the Finder is working in the background, the Mac's attention is split between it and whatever you're doing. You'll find a significant slowdown until the background operation is over—your mouse moves erratically instead of smoothly, windows scroll slowly, even typing is slowed down. In all, it's not usually worth letting operations go on in the background. But the Finder's background operations include:

- Copying files from one disk to another
- Duplicating files on the same disk
- Emptying the Trash
- Find operations

•••❥ **The Finder Prefs file** in the Preferences folder keeps track of the settings you make in the Views control panel for things like the font you want used on the desktop and what's in the Label menu. If you find that the Finder doesn't remember some of the choices you've made in the Views control panel when you restart the computer, get rid of the Finder Prefs file and restart again. Everything will go back to default settings, but from then on your settings should "stick."

•••❥ **When there are lots of windows open** on the desktop, the Finder may tell you that it can't complete an operation because of all the open windows. Simply close a few and try again.

•••❥ **The Finder uses memory** from the portion that's allocated to the System as a whole. In earlier systems, the Finder was a separate application that got its own memory segment, like any other application. System 7's Finder is somewhat like a creature that's in between evolutionary steps—not entirely a separate application (although it's a separate file in your System Folder) and not yet absorbed by the System file itself.

Since the System grabs memory for itself as needed, the Finder should never (theoretically) run out of memory. And, in fact, the System 7.0.1 release vastly improved memory management and you'll seldom get out-of-memory messages on the desktop. But if you do, there's a way to force a larger memory allocation for the Finder: Start up your Mac with a System 6 floppy. Open the System Folder of your hard drive and find the Finder file inside the System Folder. Get Info on it, and increase the memory partition by 100K. Restart under System 7 and everything should be fine. If not, try another 50–100K until you find a satisfactory working space.

## JOE HOLMES' NEARLY USELESS TIPS

All this time you thought there was nothing you could do while waiting through a lengthy desktop rebuild. Here at Mac Almanac Research Labs we tirelessly labor day in and day out to debunk such myths. Take a close look at the dialog box that shows the rebuilding progress. It's a non-modal box. Apple designed the non-modal box to allow you to switch to another task without dismissing the box. So, theoretically, you should be able to switch to something more interesting than the sand-in-the-hourglass creep of the progress bar, right?

There is one serious obstacle to doing any useful work while the desktop is rebuilt: The rebuilding occurs before the Finder has launched. This means that, not only can you not launch applications, but nothing appears under the Apple menu except About This Macintosh. You can select About This Macintosh, but its window won't even appear until the rebuild is finished. If you're lucky enough to be rebuilding a disk other than your startup disk, you'll find the Apple menu is functional—at least to the extent that you can select items. But nothing will happen until the rebuild is finished, at which time everything you selected will launch. If you have a hierarchical Apple menu utility, you can select a control panel, and its window will open. If you try to click on anything in that window, however, you'll get only a beep.

So what *can* you do? You can turn Balloon Help on. Then, while the desktop is rebuilding, a help balloon can inform you, among other things, that you're pointing to the title bar in the desktop rebuild progress window.

And here you thought you couldn't accomplish anything useful during a desktop rebuild.

—*Joe Holmes*

⚫➤ **There have been many Finder replacements** over the years, but none ever really caught on. Apparently, despite the Finder's quirks and whatever it may be missing, it's still the best available way to handle things.

But that doesn't mean it's best for all the people all the time. You do have some choices.

- At Ease is Apple's "easy" interface. (Gee, they told us for years that the desktop was the easy interface.) At Ease comes with Performa system software and is also available as a separate product in both the basic form and a 2.0 version that's designed for network use; it was also included with some Mac models, and with some System 7 upgrade kits. At Ease shows a screen-size folder with large "buttons" that are application or document icons; you open an item by clicking on it. A single click does the trick—research indicated that a single click is easier than a double-click for beginners. (Hey, I just report the news.) You can easily move between At Ease and the desktop if the desktop hasn't been password-protected, an option that At Ease provides. It's good for beginners and great for young kids. I discuss it further in Chapters 19.

- Launching applications and documents is a Finder capability that's also offered by many different utilities; they're covered in Chapter 19.

- DiskTools has been one of my favorite utilities since it came out years and years ago. So long ago, in fact, that not only was there no System 7 on the horizon, there wasn't even a MultiFinder that let you get back to the desktop while an application was running. If you wanted to do any desktop copying, deleting, or so on, you had to quit the application that you were in. Utilities like DiskTools arrived as desk accessories that you could open on top of the current application and use to manipulate desktop files at a distance.

  DiskTools is still terrifically useful even if it is easy to get to your desktop now. It offers most desktop functions—getting info, copying, erasing, aliasing, even launching applications and documents—but you won't have to dig through folders to find them; you can work in DiskTools' list instead. It also offers things the desktop doesn't, like a Move function that copies a file to a new location and erases it from the old location in one fell swoop. And, by marking items and defining them as a set, you can view and manipulate any group of items together in a list even if they don't exist in the same folder. Although DiskTools offers a fancy Find function (which I described earlier), you don't have to use it to find and/or mark files, since you can just browse through DiskTools' list of what's on your desktop. In addition to all this, it provides "power tools" like seeing invisible files (you can see the two invisible Desktop files listed in its window in the picture) and manipulation file and creator types (more about that in Chapter 21). [MacPak, Fifth Generation Systems]

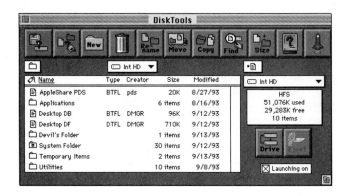

- DiskTop has enjoyed a loyal following for many years, too, and the advent of MultiFinder and then System 7 didn't kill it anymore than they killed DiskTools. In fact, the utilities are very much matched in their capabilities, although DiskTop begs for an update: it works under System 7, but is still in a pre-System 7 desk accessory suitcase. [PrairieSoft]

## THE WAY WE WERE

Before there was MultiFinder, there was MiniFinder. Actually, before there was MiniFinder, there was a MiniFinder.

The Open and Save dialogs were for a while referred to as MiniFinders, since they let you see what was on the desktop while you were still in an application. But somewhere around 1986, Apple came out with *the* MiniFinder, which let you open documents and applications without returning to the desktop. Why? A minor consideration was that the MiniFinder could, in a pinch, replace the Finder altogether; on a floppy-based system with an ever-growing System file, saving a few K helped. But the main reason for the MiniFinder was the original HD 20. As a non-SCSI device, it was as slow as (fill in your favorite trite expression here). To save the time-consuming return to the desktop when you quit one program so you could launch another, the MiniFinder filled the screen and let you double-click on one of the application or document icons you had installed in it. It saved a lot of time, although it wasn't much help when you wanted to copy or delete files.

Here's what it looked like—although I used current icons for the picture instead of the ones in use at the time.

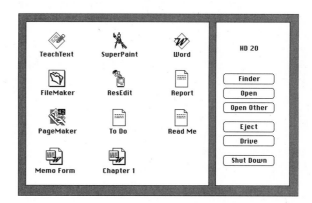

## ➤❙ SYSTEM 7.5 STUFF ❙◀

## Aliases

∘•➤ **There's a keyboard equivalent for** the Make Alias command in System 7.5's Finder; logically enough, it's Command-M. The only thing I can't figure out is why it wasn't in previous versions of System 7, since it certainly doesn't conflict with any existing desktop keyboard command.

∘•➤ **If you put a Trash alias in the Apple Menu Items folder,** System 7.5's hierarchical Apple menu displays the Trash icon in the menu. Most hierarchical Apple menu utilities reveal that the Trash is actually a folder when you alias it for the menu, since the icon is a folder icon.

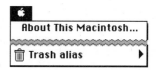

## The Apple Guide System

∞►  **Beyond Balloon Help**—that's the Apple Guide help system introduced with System 7.5. You can get help that's both *interactive* and *context-sensitive*, two buzzwords that earn their keep in this system. Turn on the help system by selecting Macintosh Guide from the Help menu. (Henceforth to be known as the Help menu, not the Balloon Help menu.)

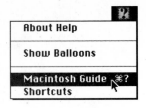

The window that opens gives you three ways to get help: Topics, Index, and Look For. Each approach provides the same information—it's just a matter of how you get there.

The basic Guide window gives you three ways to retrieve information.

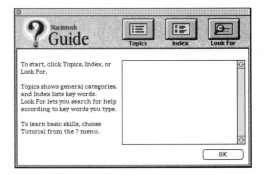

∞►  **To work with the Topics guide,** click the Topics button at the top of the window. Then click on a topic in the left panel and choose a subtopic from the right panel. For help, click OK—or just double-click on the subtopic in the first place.

Using the Topics button.

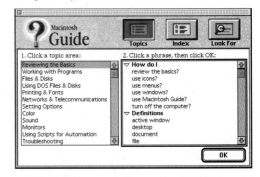

∞►  **To use the Index guide,** click on the Index button. This gives you an extensive alphabetical list of topics in the left panel. You can navigate the list in several ways:

Using the Index button.

- Scroll through the list until you find the topic you want.
- Click on a letter at the top of the panel to jump to that alphabetical portion of the list. Or, drag the pointer frame along the alphabet to the letter you want.

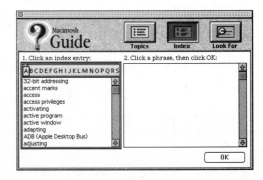

- Type the name of the item you're looking for. Use only as many letters as you need to uniquely identify it (*ic* will do for *icons*, for instance).

Once you find the topic and subtopic you want, click the OK button.

∞•➤ **The Look For button** lets you type in a word or phrase related to the question at hand; click the Search button to get the list of topics and subtopics in the panel.

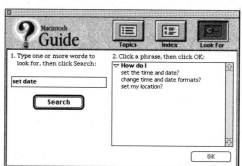

Using the Look For button.

∞•➤ **You can collapse any subtopic** in the right panel by clicking on its arrow; it's the same as working with hierarchical lists in Finder windows.

∞•➤ **The Guide window is standard throughout** this new help system. No matter how you look up your topic, you get to the same window. And when other applications learn how to hook into it, you'll be able to get help for more than just system software; in the meantime, it's pretty neat just in the Finder. The Guide window, and all the windows in the help system, are floating windows that stay on top of the current application, whether that's the Finder or something else. This picture shows what you see when you ask about using windows.

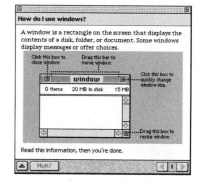

- The paging arrows in the lower-right corner are dimmed because this topic consists of a single page of information. For multiple-page topics, you use the arrows to move from one page to another.
- The up arrow in the lower-left corner of the window is used to move back to the main Guide window to select another topic.
- The Huh? button gives definitions of words and pictures displayed in the window, and sometimes covers related questions or information.
- The Zoom box in the upper-right corner shrinks the window to just its title bar, the topic question, and the strip of buttons along the bottom.

∞•➤ **When you need more help than just a window of information,** you'll get it. Apple Guide is designed to take you step-by-step through many procedures. It can show you one step at a time, or keep up with you if you know how to do some of the middle steps. For instance, if you ask to be shown how to set the time and date, you'll be told to use the Date & Time control panel. If you don't know where it is, you'll be told to open the Apple menu and choose Control Panels—and the Control Panels folder is underlined in the menu to catch your eye. If you've already opened the folder, but you're not sure what to do next, the instructions jump to that step.

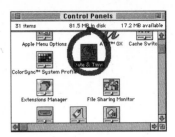

A red circle draws your attention to the item at hand.

But the best thing of all about the Guide (one might say it's *cool*, if one hadn't promised oneself to never, never use that overused word anywhere in this book) is how it guides you to things on the screen: It draws a red circle around the area in question. It doesn't just slap a circle up there—it *draws* it, from the top, around counterclockwise. You can't miss it. Really! This picture shows the Date & Time control panel highlighted for your attention.

## Find File

∞➔ **The Find command has been completely revamped.** In fact, it's not just a command: It's an application named Find File, and you'll find it listed in your Apple menu because it's stored in your Apple Menu Items folder. This means you can use it any time, no matter what application you're in; you don't have to move to the Finder first. But if you're in the Finder, using the Find command in the File menu, or pressing Command-F, also opens Find File.

The Find window is much more attractive in System 7.5, as you can see from the picture here. It might look familiar if you read the section earlier in this chapter that covers Find utilities, since it looks so much like FindPro; in fact, it pretty much *is* FindPro, since it's by the same author, Bill Monk.

∞➔ **Find File has more features** and works differently from the old Find command; it even looks for different categories of items, as you'll notice as soon as you pop up the first menu, shown here.

∞➔ **Basic search criteria rules** are the same as with the old Find command; that is, uppercase and lowercase letters are treated as identical characters. But Find File does have some new features for search criteria:

- For a *version* search, the choices are limited to *is* and *is not*. The old Find command included *is before* and *is after* as criteria, but they didn't do much good; version numbers are seldom actually numbers—they usually include letters, too.

- There's a new *folder attribute* criterion so you can look for folders that are or aren't empty, shared, or mounted.
- The *file type* and *creator* criteria could be really useful, if the Mac gave you some way of determining which applications use which creator codes and file types. There's some information about both in Chapter 21, but it's a little ridiculous to have a search tool that you can't make complete use of without *another* utility that lets you look at creator and file types!

This chart rounds up the search criteria available in Find File. As with the one earlier in this chapter, you can read across the columns to make sentences, like: *Search for a file whose size is less than....* Bracketed items in the Match column are things that you type into the Find File window. The bold items in this chart are the ones unique to Find File, not available in systems earlier than System 7.5; the crossed-out items are the ones dropped since System 7.1.

| Search for a file whose... | Choices | Match |
|---|---|---|
| name | contains<br>starts with<br>ends with<br>is<br>is not<br>doesn't contain | [text] |
| size | is less than<br>is greater than | [number] |
| kind | contains<br>doesn't contain | alias<br>application<br>document<br>folder<br>stationery<br>[other] |
| label | is<br>is not | None<br>(label list) |
| date created | is<br>is before<br>is after<br>is not | [month/date/yr] |
| date modified | is<br>is before<br>is after<br>is not | [month/date/yr] |
| version | is<br>~~is before~~<br>~~is after~~<br>is not | [text] |
| ~~comments~~ | ~~contain~~<br>~~do not contain~~ | ~~[text]~~ |
| lock | is | locked<br>unlocked |
| **folder attribute** | **is**<br>**is not** | **locked**<br>**shared**<br>**mounted** |
| **file type** | **is**<br>**is not** | **[text]** |
| **creator** | **is**<br>**is not** | **[text]** |

•➤ **Enter multiple criteria for a search** by clicking the More Choices button and selecting what you need from the menus. You can, for instance, look for all the PageMaker docu-

ments you created in the last week that are larger than 850K. The type of search you're doing with Find File is known as an AND search: It finds files that meet *all* the criteria you enter. The dialog pictured here shows how you'd search for Word documents larger than 600K with the word *chapter* in their title.

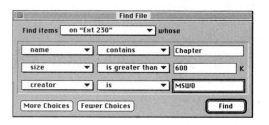

•➤ **When Find File finds the items** that match the search criteria, it opens the Results window. The upper part of the window lists all the "hits"; the picture here shows the result of a search for applications larger than 850K. The lower part of the window shows the path to the selected item.

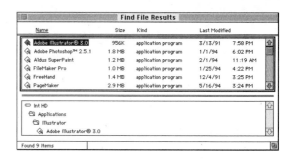

•➤ **The size box works in only one direction;** you can change the window's height, but not its width. You can easily change the relative height of the two lists in the window by dragging the double bar between them up or down. When the mouse cursor is over the bar, it changes into the Grabber (hand) cursor; when you press the mouse button, the hand closes around the bar to grab it!

•➤ **Organize the list of found items** by using the View menu, or by clicking on the column name in the window—the same way you sort things in Finder windows.

•➤ **Select items in either list with the Up and Down** arrows. The arrows affect the active list—the one with the dark frame around it. Use Tab to alternately activate the top and bottom list.

•➤ **Once you've selected an item** in the "hit list," you have several choices, although they're not apparent when you're looking at the window. But take a look at File menu. There are five commands that apply to a selected item: Open Item, Open Enclosing Folder (that opens the folder that the item's in), Print Item, Get Info, and Sharing. All but the last have keyboard equivalents.

This is very convenient—initiating an action (like opening or printing) on an item without having to actually go to its folder. But what about all those other things you might want to do with the items you've found? Gather them into a single folder. Erase them. Make copies to another volume. Make aliases. And so on. I guess I'll stick with Baseline's DiskTools (described earlier in this chapter), which gives me more options for dealing with found items.

| File | |
|---|---|
| Find... | ⌘F |
| Close Window | ⌘W |
| More Choices | ⌘M |
| Fewer Choices | ⌘R |
| Open Item | ⌘O |
| Open Enclosing Folder | ⌘E |
| Print Item | ⌘P |
| Get Info | ⌘I |
| Sharing... | |
| Quit | ⌘Q |

••➤ **Select multiple items in the list** by shift-clicking; select them all with the Select All command in the Edit menu. This is, in fact, the only command in the Edit menu you can use; the others remain dimmed.

| Edit | |
|---|---|
| Undo | ⌘Z |
| Cut | ⌘X |
| Copy | ⌘C |
| Paste | ⌘V |
| Clear | |
| Select All | ⌘A |

••➤ **You can "click" the More Choices and** Fewer Choices buttons by using Command-M and Command-R.

••➤ **Open any item in either list** by double-clicking on it. (Or by selecting it and then choosing Open Item from the File menu.) Since you can open anything in the lower list, that means you can get at any of the enclosing folders for an item in the upper list.

## Sticky Memos

∞➤ **Sticky memos are the electronic equivalent** of Post-It notes. I'm not sure if this is a great little feature or an annoyance—only time will tell. The picture here shows how you can tag an icon on the desktop with a little note; you could also leave a note on the desktop for the next person who uses the Mac. But it's easy for the screen to become cluttered in no time.

∞➤ **Sticky Memos is an application,** and the notes are its windows. So, for the notes to show, the application has to be the active one. When you open or move to Sticky Notes, all the notes you had open the last time appear on the screen again, wherever you positioned them last time; they float on top of whatever's on the screen.

That's the only way the notes exist: as open windows floating around on top of everything else. You don't close and open memos; if you try to close a memo, you're asked if you want to save the contents as a text file, but you can't reopen it as a note. You can use the Import Text command, but that's a lot of trouble for a little message.

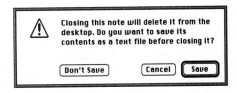

∞✦ **A sticky memo has basic window controls:** a title bar, close box, and zoom box. But the controls look different because the window behaves differently—and because the windows are so tiny that standard controls would overwhelm them. So, the size "box" is a little corner piece that you drag to resize the note, and there are no scroll bars.

∞✦ **The zoom box toggles** the note between two sizes, but you can set a preference (through the Preferences command in the Edit menu) that one of the sizes be just the title bar. Of course, there's nothing *in* the title bar—until you zoom the note down. The first line of the note appears in the bar that's left. (You can resize the bar to show more of the note if you want.)

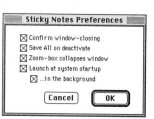

∞✦ **Set the default so that new memos start out** as closed title bars. When you type, the window opens a little at a time to accommodate the typing, and you'll wind up with a perfectly sized memo—no empty space at the bottom, and as little of the screen taken up as necessary.

∞✦ **Use the Page Up and Page Down** keys to scroll the text in a memo.

•••✦ **Option-clicking in the zoom box** sizes a memo just large enough to display its contents. When you press the Option key, you'll see the zoom box change to clue you in that something special will happen if you click in it.

•••✦ **Sticky Memos' menus are** pretty straight forward, with a few exceptions noted here:

- The Import Text and Export Text commands probably won't be utilized much; it should be quicker to retype, or copy and paste, a few sentences instead of importing and exporting them.

- The Use As Default sets the text and color—and even the position—of the currently active note as the default for all new notes.

- The Preferences command opens the window shown here, where you can set your program preferences.

- The Text Style command lets you choose a font, size, and style for the text in the active note. All the styles are applied globally to the note—you can't select a word or phrase and apply a style to it.

- The Note Info command opens the simple dialog shown here.

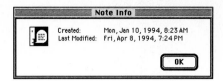

A roundup of Sticky Memos' menus.

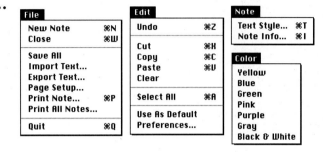

••➤ **A note sticks to a *spot* on the screen,** not to whatever's on the screen. So, you can't stick a note to something in a window and expect the note to stay with it if you move the window, or alter the window contents.

## Also ...

∞➤ **The Finder Shortcuts** command in the Help menu opens a shortcuts collection that's very different from the one in earlier versions of System 7. It's not half as cute as the old one, and it doesn't pack as much information into a window, either. Not surprisingly, it's modeled after the Guide system. The pictures here show the main screen and one of the information screens.

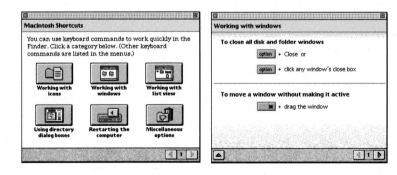

⇥·✳·I⇤

# More System Features

# CHAPTER 6
# THE
# SYSTEM FOLDER

> Computers can figure
> out all kinds of problems,
> except the things in the world
> that just don't add up.
>
> JAMES MAGARY

The pearls of wisdom in this chapter include:

**·►** Just how smart the System Folder is.

**·►** What all those pretty little folders in the System Folder are for.

**·►** Where and who the Blue Meanies are.

**·►** How to alter the contents of your System file.

**·►** Getting your Apple menu organized.

**·►** Why startup items don't go into the Startup·Items folder.

THE MOST NOSTALGIC
THING IN THIS CHAPTER

*The 200K System Folder.*

**About This Macintosh...**

- Calculator
- Chooser
- Note Pad
- Scrapbook
- Apple Menu Items
- Applications
- Control Panels
- DeskAccessories
- FileMaker Pro
- Projects
- System Folder
- Word

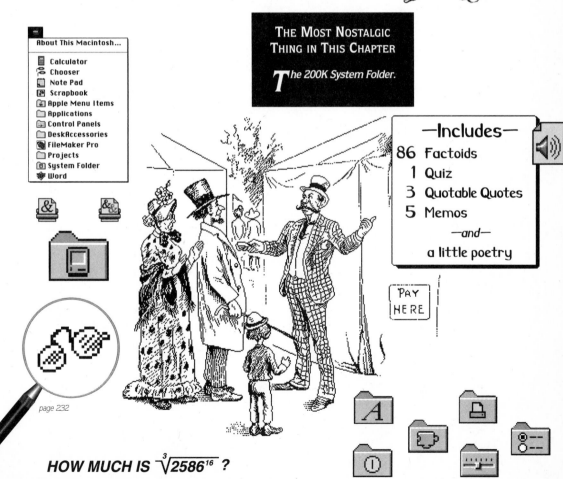

—Includes—

86 Factoids
1 Quiz
3 Quotable Quotes
5 Memos
—and—
a little poetry

PAY
HERE

*page 232*

**HOW MUCH IS** $\sqrt[3]{2586^{16}}$ **?**

## ⚓ FOLDER & SUBFOLDERS ⚓

### The Folder

∞⚓ **The System Folder** has a special icon on it so it's easy to pick out in a crowd—at least until you start editing folder icons. The icon on the System 7 System Folder is slightly different from the one used for System 6.

∞⚓ **Not everything in your System Folder** is neatly organized into special subfolders. You'll find loose files in the main level of the System Folder:

- The System and Finder files, the all-important components of your system software, are in the System Folder.
- The Clipboard icon comes and goes, depending on the state of the Clipboard.
- Desk accessory files like the ones for the Scrapbook and Note Pad, are also loose in the System Folder. Most have easily identifiable icons, but some (not the ones from Apple, of course) have generic icons.
- Enablers. If your Mac needs an Enabler for its system software (see Chapter 23), it will be in the main level of the System Folder.
- Preference files really belong in the Preferences folder, of course, but some programs don't follow the rules. Sometimes that's because the program was written before the advent of System 7 and its subfolders and, even though the program works under System 7, it doesn't know the details. Then again, some programs are just sloppy and leave their files up on the main level of the System Folder.
- Temporary files that applications create and use for their own purposes are erased when you quit the application. But if you look in the System Folder while the application is running, you may see a temporary file or two. Or, if a program crashes, its temporary files will be left behind.

This picture shows the loose files in my System Folder; the ones in the top row are all standard Mac items; the rest are from various applications.

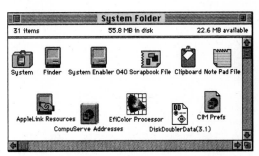

∞⚓ **The System Folder is smart.** When you drag certain items into it, they're routed to the correct subfolder. This won't happen behind your back, though: you'll get a dialog asking you if it's okay to put the item into, say, the Extensions folder.

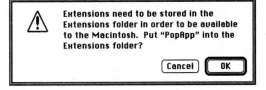

If you click the Cancel button, the item stays where it is—it won't go into the main level of the System Folder. This can be really annoying when you *want* the item in the main level of the System Folder—you'd think the dialog would let you prevent the item from going into the subfolder and still allow it to go into the main folder; instead the move is canceled altogether. If you want an item that's normally routed to a subfolder to stay on the main level of the System Folder, you have to drag it into the opened System Folder window.

The System Folder routes items like this:

- In System 7.1, screen fonts and printer fonts go into the Fonts folder. In System 7.0, screen fonts are routed to the System *file* and printer fonts to the Extensions folder.
- Extensions go to the Extensions folder.
- Control panels go to the Control panel.
- Desk accessories go to the Apple Menu Items folder.

⊶❥ **The System Folder is smart only** if you keep it closed. If you drag something into the System Folder's window, the item just stays in the main level of the folder even if it belongs in one of the special subfolders.

⊶❥ **The System Folder identifies** special files by their file types, as listed in the Kind column in Finder windows. A file that's a *system extension* or a *chooser extension*, for instance, is routed to the Extensions folder. A file that's of the type *desk accessory* is routed to the Apple Menu Items folder. But items like preference files are simply documents, and not special file types, so they won't be routed to the Preferences folder. And the various files you might want listed in your Apple menu can't be routed to the Apple Menu Items folder because the Mac can't read your mind. Yet.

⊶❥ **To take advantage of the System Folder's smarts,** leave an alias of the System Folder out on the desktop. Otherwise, every time you want to drag something into it, you'll still have to open the disk window and scroll around until you can see the System Folder icon.

⊶❥ **You can drag more than one item** at a time into the closed System Folder. The first dialog will be rather vaguely worded if you're dragging a mixture of different things into the folder, but when the procedure is finished, you'll get a full report on how many things went where.

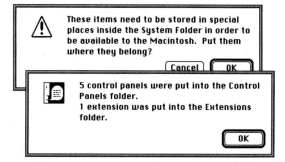

⚠ These items need to be stored in special places inside the System Folder in order to be available to the Macintosh. Put them where they belong?

Cancel    OK

5 control panels were put into the Control Panels folder.
1 extension was put into the Extensions folder.

OK

⊶❥ **If you drag a folder into the System Folder,** the Mac checks its contents. If there are System Folder or subfolder items in it (extensions, fonts, and so on), they'll be routed to the correct locations—and the folder dissolves away into nothingness.

•••❯ **It doesn't matter what you name your System Folder.** Any folder that holds the System and Finder files gets stamped with the special icon, and the Mac can work with it. If you remove either one of these special files from the folder, it loses its icon. In fact, this folder is so special (what with part of the Mac's operating system stored in it) that in programmer's parlance along Apple's guidelines, it's called the "blessed" folder.

Chapter 23 covers "System/system," "System Folder," "System file," and "operating system."

## WHAT DRIVING TO THE STORE WOULD BE LIKE IF COMPUTER OPERATING SYSTEMS RAN YOUR CAR*

**MS-DOS**: You get in the car and try to remember where you put your keys.

**Macintosh System 7**: You get in the car to go to the store, and the car drives you to church.

**Windows**: You get in the car and drive to the store very slowly, because attached to the back of the car is a freight train.

**Windows NT**: You get in the car and write a letter that says, "go to the store." Then you get out of the car and mail the letter to your dashboard.

**UNIX**: You get in the car and type GREP STORE. After reaching speeds of 200 miles per hour en route, you arrive at the barber shop.

*I think you can enjoy these jokes even if you don't know all the operating systems in question. I know I do, and I don't. (If you know what I mean.)

**Taligent/Pink**: You walk to the store with Ricardo Montalban, who tells you how wonderful it will be when he can fly you to the store in his Lear jet.

**OS/2:** After fueling up with 6000 gallons of gas, you get in the car and drive to the store with a motorcycle escort and a marching band in procession. Halfway there, the car blows up, killing everybody in town.

**S/36 SSP** (mainframe): You get in the car and drive to the store. Halfway there you run out of gas. While walking the rest of the way, you are run over by kids on mopeds.

**OS/400**: An attendant locks you into the car and then drives you to the store, where you get to watch everybody else buy filet mignons.

*—found circulating on the Internet*

•••❯ **Multiple System Folders on a hard drive** used to be a real problem. You still shouldn't have more than one System Folder on a single drive—you can get a lot of unexplained crashes that way. I say it "used to be" a problem because when the System Folder was small enough to fit on a floppy, along with an application (!), people tended to just copy over the entire floppy disk to the hard drive to "install" the software. As a result, there would be System Folders scattered all over the drive, buried inside application folders. Now that a System Folder barely fits on a floppy, even all by itself, it's unlikely you'll drag one over by accident.* The

*What this means is that Montclair State University's Bob Stephens will forever remain the all-time world record holder for accidental multiple System Folders, with a total of 19 on his hard drive at one time.

only software that even comes with a System Folder on its floppies is emergency disk recovery tools—which needs the system on the floppy because you use it when you can't get at the system on your hard drive.

•••▶ **If you don't know where something belongs,** drag it to the closed System Folder and see if the folder knows. Some extensions don't have the special puzzle-piece icon; not all control panels have the slider control incorporated into their icons. I remember what a pleasant surprise I had when I first installed System 7: I was dragging a bunch of printer fonts into the System Folder, since that's where they were stored in System 6, and I got the dialog that told me they belonged in the Extensions folder.

•••▶ **Clean up your System Folder.** Not with the Clean Up command—that would merely line up the icons neatly. Clean it *out*! If you're working with a small hard drive, dumping extraneous items is important, but even with a large hard drive you might prefer a lean, mean system. (Personally, I go for the bloated System Folder and buy bigger hard drives when needed.) Get rid of things you don't need. For instance:

Chapters 10 and 11 cover fonts.

- *Fonts.* If you really need to make room on your drive, trimming back on some fonts can help—unless, of course, you need that kind of variety in your printing. System-installed fonts (in the System file for 7.0, in the Fonts folder for 7.1) total around 1200K, and it's easy to cut that back by more than half. If you want the very basics in fonts, keep Geneva and New York (for easiest on-screen reading), Times and Helvetica (for PostScript printing) and Monaco (for programs that use a monofont). If you have a PostScript printer, you can dump all the TrueType fonts and keep only the screen versions in one or two sizes.

- *Printer drivers.* If you installed your system software and included the "all printers" options, you'll have many more printer drivers than you need, because you set up your Mac to work with every possible printer. If your Mac came with system software installed, it has too many printer drivers in the System Folder. Look in the Extensions folder and dump all the printer drivers except the one (or two) that you use. With printer drivers ranging in size from 70–400K, keeping a half-dozen around you don't need can eat up disk space.

  It's easy to find printer drivers: Their type is *Chooser extension* and their icons are little printers. You'll have only Apple drivers in your Extensions folder, but other printer manufacturers make drivers, too. Here's what some of the drivers look like:

LaserWriter

LaserWriter 8.0

StyleWriter

GCC Printing Extension

KodakDiconix 180si

DeskJet Portable

GCCWriteMove

Canon BJ-10ex

- *File sharing items.* If you're a single-Mac setup, you don't need the three file-sharing extensions (File Sharing Extension, Network Extension, AppleShare) or the three file-sharing control panels (File Sharing Monitor, Users & Groups, Sharing Setup). Together, they total about 350K.

- *Control panels.* If your system software was installed for "all Macs" instead of your specific model (see Chapter 8), there will be several control panels that you won't need. Brightness, for instance, is only for some Macs, like the Classic, that provide software-controlled screen brightness instead of a dial on the monitor. Caps Lock is only for PowerBooks. You may never need the Map, or Easy Access.

- *Miscellaneous system files.* DAL, which comes with 7.0 but not 7.1, is for accessing data on mainframes. You don't need it. Do you need Finder Help after you've looked at it a few times? (It provides extra Help balloon information on the desktop.) If you never do background printing, you don't need PrintMonitor.

- *Application subfolders.* Many applications create their own folders inside the System Folder. There might be extraneous files within these folders you don't need. Many programs, for instance, use *filters* or *translators* to help them convert a document created in another program. You probably don't need all the filters that the application comes with, so look through the folder and trash the ones you don't need. (They're easy to identify: they're named after the "foreign" program, so the Claris folder, for instance, might hold a file named *WordPerfect*.)

- *Mystery files.* Be careful here. Just because you don't know what something is, that doesn't mean you don't need it. Lots of applications install items in subfolders—especially the Extensions folder—without telling you. If you have some mystery files in your System Folder or its subfolders, try looking at their Get Info windows. If there's no identification in there, just drag them into a temporary folder or leave them out on the desktop for a week or two. If everything's still okay, you can trash the file—*after* copying it to a floppy disk to save just in case you find out that you need it after all.

**ADRIAN MELLO**
*MACWORLD, APRIL 1985*
*(When there were no hard*
*drives and a floppy held 400K.)*

A fully loaded System Folder can easily weigh in at 200K, which doesn't leave much room for application programs and documents on disk.

## The Subfolders

∞⤳ **The System Folder has special subfolders** in it to take care of the files that accumulate there. Prior to System 7, System Folder clutter was a big problem. Inits, control panel devices, printer fonts, preferences files—everything was just thrown into the System Folder, which could easily wind up holding a hundred or more items. It takes a long time to open such a stuffed folder, and even longer to track down any problem file that might be lurking there.

Like the System Folder itself, the special subfolders also have their own icons. The standard subfolders are: Apple Menu Items, Control Panels, Fonts (in System 7.1.),

There's also a Shut Down folder in System 7.5. See the end of this chapter.

Extensions, Preferences, and Startup Items. If you use background printing, you'll occasionally see a PrintMonitor folder, too.

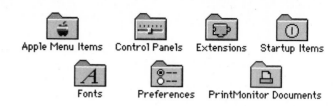

| Apple Menu Items | Control Panels | Extensions | Startup Items |

Fonts      Preferences      PrintMonitor Documents

⇝ **The icons on the special subfolders** appear and disappear almost magically. For the icon to be there, the folder must have the precisely correct name and be inside the System Folder. If you rename one of these special folders, the icon goes away. If you drag one of these folders out of the System Folder, its icon disappears; when you put it back, the icon reappears.

If you have nothing else to do, you can open your System Folder in an icon view and drag the System file or the Finder icon in and out of it. When either of these files is out of the window, the folder doesn't "count" as the System Folder anymore and the icons on the subfolders disappear, only to reappear again when you put the file back in.

⇝ **Some subfolders don't belong to the system,** but instead are used by applications or utilities. These subfolders contain information that the program needs to work, and often they're shared by more than one application from the same manufacturer. This is a great approach: a Microsoft folder, for instance, can contain files used by both Word and Excel, or a Claris folder can hold dictionaries common to ClarisWorks and MacWrite.

Usually these folders *must* be in the System Folder in order to work, although sometimes they can be stored elsewhere. They don't usually have icons of their own, but you can edit them so that they do. None of the 11 non-system subfolders in my System Folder has a special icon.

⇝ **New subfolders are created** on startup if any are missing from your System Folder.

⇝ **Don't restart** just to get new subfolders. If you happen to trash any of your special folders, just create a new, empty folder inside the System Folder and give it the right name. It gets stamped with the correct icon immediately. (Replacing the trashed contents will take a little more effort!)

⇝ **A "disabled" subfolder,** with a name like *Extensions (disabled)* or *Control Panels (disabled)*, inside your System Folder means you're using some sort of "manager" utility for your extensions to turn them on and off. There's more about this in Chapter 8.

## BY THE WAY ...

ENIAC is the computer equivalent of anthropology's Missing Link. It's the bridge between the mechanical calculators of its day and the modern computers that followed it. Here are some interesting facts about it:

- ENIAC stands for Electronic Numerator, Integrator, Analyzer, and Computer.

- ENIAC was 8 feet high and 80 feet long. It weighed in at 30 tons and used about 18,000 vacuum tubes and 70,000 resistors.

- ENIAC was originally part of the war effort, meant to calculate trajectory tables for missiles. Its design and construction were completed in November of 1945, three months after the war ended. Its destructive birthright was still accomplished however: Its first calculation was one that tested the feasibility of a hydrogen bomb design. (A month of calculations uncovered several significant flaws in the mathematical model of the H-bomb.)

- ENIAC went from a classified Army project known as Project PX to a recruitment inducement in three short years. By 1946, Army ads started with this headline:

$$\textit{HOW MUCH IS } \sqrt[3]{2586^{16}} \textit{ ?}$$

It went on to rave about ENIAC's capabilities: "... addition, subtraction, multiplication, division, square root, cube root, any root ... solved by an incredibly complex system ... The ENIAC is symbolic of many amazing Army devices with a brilliant future for you!"

- ENIAC was programmed by flipping its thousands of little toggle switches* into the right positions (off or on) and plugging and unplugging hundreds of cables.

> *One of ENIAC's input panels is on display in the Smithsonian. The front is covered with glass to protect it from fingers just itching to flip a switch. But I can tell you from personal experience that you can easily reach around and flip one of the switches on the rear of the panel.

## ⊁ THE SYSTEM FILE ⊁

## The System File

∞⟡ **The System file** that's in the System Folder works along with information stored in the Mac's ROM to provide an *operating system* for the Mac. (All the programs and support files that Apple provides to run the Mac come under the umbrella term *system software*.)

In System 7, the System file underwent both cosmetic and, you might say, philosophical changes. Its icon used to be a little Macintosh, and you couldn't open it to see what was inside; when you wanted to add or remove something, you needed a special utility, like Font/DA Mover. Now the System file has a suitcase icon and it's easy to open so you can change some of its basic contents.

**The Finder file** is the System file's partner; it provides your desktop and most of the operations you do there. The Finder file used to be much more independent—a separate application to which you could even allocate specific amounts of memory. It's unlikely the Finder file will survive as an independent file by the time we see another major system revision.

See Chapter 5 for details about the Finder file.

**The System file holds** more than meets the eye. I have no idea how anyone might run across this by accident (but then, I've often wondered how a coffee percolator could be accidentally discovered, too) since it involves a series of steps it would never occur to you to do. Try this: duplicate the System file. Use a good word processor that lets you open all sorts of files, and open the duplicate. It's amazing what's in there. But I'll save you the trouble and show you a picture of what will show up—bet you can figure out which one's from System 7.0 and which is from System 7.1.

There's more about ROM and system software in Chapters 13 and 23.

**POP QUIZ** [3 POINTS]

What groovy, gear animated movie introduced the Blue Meanies?

**The System file is a suitcase.** Not only because that's what its icon looks like, but because it's that specific file *type*. If you set the Fonts folder window to a list view, you'll see the System file's kind is identified as *suitcase*.

A suitcase is not the same as a folder, though there are many similarities: you double-click on it to open it and you can drag things in and out. An open suitcase window doesn't look much different from an open folder window, but you do get one visual cue: there's a little suitcase at the left of the window's header.

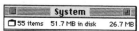

A suitcase differs from a folder both in what it can hold and how things are moved in and out of it. A suitcase can hold only certain types of items: The System file suitcase holds special resources, and font suitcases hold fonts. You can't put a folder, or another suitcase, inside a suitcase.

From your point of view, putting something into a suitcase or taking it out is the same as working with a folder—you drag the item in or out. But what's happening behind the scenes is considerably different. When you "move" something from one folder to another, the file itself hasn't moved on the disk. You've moved the icon from one spot to another, and that's what's been recorded on the disk—the file itself hasn't moved or changed. Moving things in and out of a suitcase, on the other hand, takes more time because the information is actually being added to or removed from the suitcase file itself, which means the information is being read from one spot on the disk and written to another spot. The information goes from being a separate file on the disk to being part of a larger file (or vice versa). It's like the difference between having two separate word processor documents in a folder or opening one, copying its contents into the other, and then getting rid of the original file.

**•••➤ The size of your System file** is *absolutely not* the same as the memory the System takes. The size of the file itself, available through Get Info or in any list view, indicates how much space it takes on the disk. A pretty bare System file—not much in the way of added sound resources—hovers around 1000K in System 7.1. For System 7.0, a small System file includes basic fonts and is around 1800K. In either case, the memory used by your system, as reported in About This Macintosh in the Apple menu, can be anywhere from around 1200K to 4000K. (This non-relation between a file's disk size and the memory it takes is also true for applications.) There's lots more about system memory usage in Chapter 9.

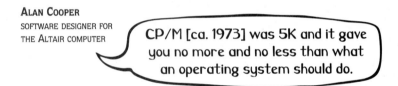

ALAN COOPER
SOFTWARE DESIGNER FOR
THE ALTAIR COMPUTER

CP/M [ca. 1973] was 5K and it gave you no more and no less than what an operating system should do.

## System Resources

**∞➤ The System file contains** not only operating system information, but also *resources* that any application can access and use, such as icons, dialog boxes, and sounds.

You can't get at the operating system instructions. You can't easily get at *all* the different resources in the System file, either, unless you use a program like ResEdit. But there are four types of resources that are easy to manipulate:

- *Sounds.* These include the basic system "beep" sounds and any others you want to add. (They're detailed in Chapter 2.)
- *Fonts.* In System 7.0, fonts are in the System file; in System 7.1, however, they're stored separately in the Fonts folder.
- *Keyboard layouts.* These layouts show up in the Keyboard control panel; they're discussed in Chapters 1, 8, 20, and 21.
- *Language scripts.* Don't worry about these—they're reserved for non-Roman-alphabet languages like Japanese and Hebrew, and they're not even included with your system. But I mention them here because this book aims to be painfully complete.

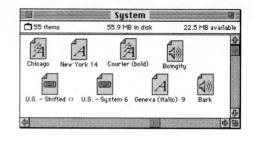

Basically, if you can see the resource when you double-click on the System file to open its window, then it's a resource that you can add or remove. Here's a picture of a System 7.0 System file, which includes fonts.

❧ **To add a resource** to the System file, you can drag it into the opened System file window, into the System file icon, or even into the closed System Folder. If you drag it to the closed folder, you'll get a confirming dialog before the resource is added.

❧ **To remove a resource** from the System file, double-click on the System file icon to open it, and drag out the resource you want to remove.

❧ **When you move a resource** into or out of the System file, the difference between the suitcase approach and folders becomes apparent. As mentioned earlier, the resource file information is actually erased from one place and written back to the disk someplace else. So, you'll get a series of dialogs that you never see when you're moving things from one folder to another.

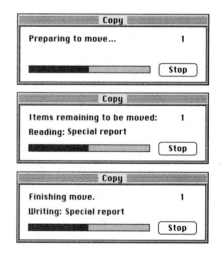

Note that the dialogs don't say that the Mac is *copying* something from one place to another; they say that something is being *moved*. Unlike a copy operation that puts a copy in a new location and leaves the original, a *move* makes the copy and then erases the original.

❧ **You can't add or remove** resources from the System file if any applications are running.

❧ **You can't rename** system resources while they're inside the System file, except for sounds.

❧ **Font files** in the System 7.0 System file can be of two different types. Standard screen fonts have a single letter A on them, while TrueType fonts have three As of different sizes. (This description also holds true for the font files in System 7.1's Fonts folder, but we're discussing the System file here.)

❧ **If you drag a suitcase** of fonts into the System file under System 7.0, the suitcase just sort of dissolves, and its contents are added to the System file. If you try the same thing under 7.1, you'll just get a dialog telling you that fonts belong in the Fonts folder.

## ◦H THE APPLE MENU ITEMS FOLDER H◦

### In General

◦◦→ **To list something in the Apple menu,** put it into the Apple Menu Items folder. A standard system installation starts with desk accessories and the Control Panels folder in the menu, but you can add anything you want. Items are listed alphabetically in the Apple menu, accompanied by their small icons.

You don't have to restart the Mac when you change the contents of the Apple Menu Items folder; changes appear instantly.

**About This Macintosh...**
- Alarm Clock
- Calculator
- Chooser
- Control Panels
- Key Caps
- Note Pad
- Puzzle
- Scrapbook

◦◦→ **Selecting an item from the Apple menu opens it,** so you have immediate access to desk accessories, control panels, applications, and even documents.

◦◦→ **The only "original" items you should put** in the Apple Menu Items folder are desk accessories, and any folders you create to divide the items in the menu. Everything else you want listed should be aliases of the originals: Leave control panels, applications, and documents all in their own folders.

### CHOOSING FROM THE APPLE MENU

◦◦→ **Aliases are listed in the Apple menu** in regular type, not in the italics used on the desktop and in Open and Save dialogs.

◦◦→ **You can put an entire folder** (or its alias) into the Apple Menu Items folder. In fact, an alias of the Control Panels folder is placed inside the Apple Menu Items folder when you install your system. When you select a folder from the Apple menu, you're switched to the desktop (if you're in an application) and the folder's window opens.

⚬••❯ **If you have a busy Apple Menu Items folder**—you change the contents quite often—leave an alias of it out on the desktop for easy access. Put an alias of it into itself (doesn't that sound weird?). Then you can select it from the Apple menu to open it.

⚬••❯ **The longer your Apple menu,** the longer it takes to open, since all those miniature icons have to be drawn. It can also take a long time to scroll through a few dozen items, so keep only the items you use the most frequently listed in the Apple menu.

⚬••❯ **There's a limit** to the number of items you can put in the Apple menu: 52. You can keep dragging things into the Apple Menu Items folder, but they won't show up in the menu—you'll get the first 52 alphabetical items listed. Oddly enough, though, "real" items take precedence: If you exceed the limit, aliases (no matter how they're named) drop out of the menu first.

## Organizing the Menu

⚬••❯ **You can set up either instant or secondary access** to the things you need by putting single items or folders into the menu. The way your menu is set up by the system, for instance, you have instant access to all your desk accessories because they're listed in the menu. You have secondary access to control panels, though, because you must select the folder in the menu and then you have to double-click on one of the control panels inside the window that opens.

⚬••❯ **Put some of your desk accessories** into a folder inside the Apple Menu Items folder. Leave the ones you use the most on the main level of the folder (maybe the Calculator, Note Pad, and Scrapbook) and put the others into the folder so they don't clutter the Apple menu. Put a special icon on the folder while you're at it.

⚬••❯ **Create aliases for the applications** you use the most and put them in the Apple Menu Items folder. Create an Applications folder for the menu, too, and put aliases of all your other applications in it. This gives you instant access to your main applications, and makes all the others easy to get at.

⚬••❯ **Put folder aliases in the Apple menu** for the folders you open a lot: the System Folder, for instance, or a Projects folder—maybe even the Apple Menu Items folder!

⚬••❯ **Rearrange the Apple menu** by renaming the items in the Apple Menu Items folder. Everything's listed alphabetically in the menu, so you can force things to the top or bottom of the menu the same way you can do it for desktop windows and the Open and Save dialogs, as discussed in Chapter 4. Group things by using leader characters that keep them together in the list.

An Apple menu created according to the suggestions so far, for instance, could look like the one at the left in the picture—a strictly alphabetical listing—or the one at the right, where things are grouped. The desk accessories, because their names are preceded by spaces, jump to the top of the menu; next comes applications (and the Applications folder), with a degree mark (Option-Shift-8) in front of them; miscellaneous folders are grouped with a bullet (Option-8); and the Projects folder is forced to the bottom with an Option-hyphen character.

**Organize the windows** of the folders you list in your Apple menu so that you can easily select items when the window opens. A quick way to open, say, the Control Panels folder, doesn't mean much if you then have to scroll around the window to find the control panel you want.

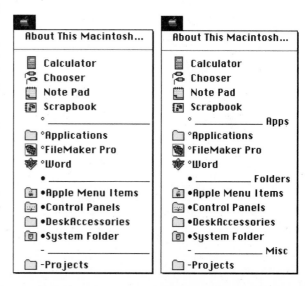

How to organize each folder depends on how you work. You might, for instance, simply set the folder to display things by name and make the window long and skinny so you can see the list of names but not be bothered by the rest of the information. You might try a small icon view with everything lined up along the left edge of the window, with the window, once again, long and skinny to display only the information you need. Or, if you prefer standard icon views, arrange the icons and size the window to display the items you're most likely to want; then, you'll only have to scroll occasionally for the less-used items.

**Put dividers in your Apple menu** by creating folders inside the Apple Menu Items folder and naming them with rows of dots, dashes, or underline characters. Get rid of the miniature folder icon that would otherwise be in the Apple menu by pasting a "blank" icon over the folder icon in its Info window. (That's in Chapter 4.)

Since these folder "names" will be sorted alphabetically, you have to start them with a leader character that will keep them in the correct spot. If you've already grouped your Apple menu items by using leader characters, this works perfectly. But you have to put a space after the leader character and before the "dividing line" name so that it stays at the top of the group. If you want all the divider lines to be the same length, copy the "name"—less the leader character—from one folder and paste it into the others. The picture here shows basic divider lines, and lines that incorporate the name of the group into the divider.

···❯ **You can select divider folders** by mistake as you're sliding down through the Apple menu. Genuine dividers in other menus can't be selected (and won't even highlight as you pass over them), but you can waste your time while a mistakenly selected empty folder opens on the desktop. To avoid this, first decide whether you generally mean to open the item above the divider or below it when you slip up. Then, make an alias of that item to replace the divider folder—give it the divider's "name" and a blank icon. The next time you select the divider by mistake, you'll still get the item you really wanted.

### WHAT'S IN A NAME?

Just because Apple became a company run by "suits" doesn't mean that the employees have lost their senses of humor, or whimsy. Programmers in particular are given to serious pun attacks (it must be all the Twinkies and Jolt cola). As a result, the CD disks that go out to Apple developers on a regular basis have some peculiar names. Many are named after current (at the time) movies; some after the classics, or TV shows. Here are some from the last few years—see if you can identify the original titles.

| | |
|---|---|
| The Postman Always Clicks Twice | The Byte Stuff |
| The Hound of Bitmapsville | The Silence of the ROMs |
| Gorillas in the Disc | Disky Business |
| Hex, Drives, and Videotape | Lord of the Files |
| Butch ASCII II and the Runtime Code | Code Warrior |
| Night of the Living Disc | Hack to Future |
| Desperately Seeking 7 | A ROM With a View |
| Other People's Memory | A Disc Called Wanda |
| Phil and Dave's Excellent CD | Northern Hexposure |
| On a Clear Day You Can CD Forever | ROM in Holiday |
| 2000 Leagues Under the CD | The Hexorcist |
| The Winter of Our Disc Content | New Hack City |

···❯ **Close the folder window** that you've opened from the Apple menu by option-double-clicking on the item you want to open—a desk accessory, for instance. As the item opens, the window closes.

···❯ **The Chicago font has some special characters** buried in it that you might want to use as leader characters (Chicago is the font used in menus). There's a solid apple as the Option-Shift-K character, for instance, which looks pretty neat in front of desk accessories. But there's also a hollow apple (maybe for folders) and a solid diamond (for applications?) that you might want to use—except that the Finder doesn't let you type them, since they're accessed by using the Control key (Control-P and Control-S, respectively). But all you have to do is use the Key Caps desk accessory, type the character there, copy it, and then paste it into the name of the icon in the Apple Menu Items folder. The sorting order of these special characters is: hollow apple, diamond, solid apple.

| | |
|---|---|
| ⚘ | **Control-P** |
| ◆ | **Control-S** |
| ⌘ | **Control-T or** |
| | **Option-Shift-K** |

There's also a check-mark and the command key symbol buried in the Chicago font. See Chapter 11.

System 7.5 includes a hierarchical Apple menu. See the end of this chapter.

## Hierarchical Apple Menus

∞❥ **You need a hierarchical Apple menu.** Trust me. It's the single most useful item you can add to your system to make things easier, faster, and more convenient. Hierarchical Apple menu utilities are available both as shareware and as reasonably priced (if not downright cheap) commercial products, so there's no excuse not to go out and get one.

In a hierarchical Apple menu, everything inside a folder is listed in a submenu; the things inside nested folders are subsubmenus, and so on. The Mac's system software allows up to five levels of subfolders (that's down to a subsubsubsubfolder), so all the utilities provide at least that level of access.

Not only do the utilities let you see what's inside folders, but most also let you reorganize the contents of the menus by name, size, kind, or in a custom order; add dividers in the main or submenus; and even let you change the font or size of the things listed in the menus. Some even provide the ability to open more than one item at a time—a whole subfolder of items, for instance.

∞❧ **You can get your hierarchical Apple menu** utility plain or fancy; the commercial ones are inexpensive, and some are really cheap.

- Now Menus gives you a hierarchical Apple menu, and more. You can pop up your Apple menu anywhere on the screen, for instance, and you get a "Recent" folder that keeps track of every file you've used recently so you can get back to work on it without rooting around on the desktop. [Now Utilities, Now Software]

- HAM stands for Hierarchical Apple Menu, a straightforward utility that provides a Recent folder and also offers "hamlets," groups of items for multiple-launching capability. [Microseeds]

- The Big Apple provides hierarchical structure and a choice of fonts and sizes for the submenus. [Xtras for System 7 book/disk, Aker, Addison-Wesley]

- MenuChoice allows for only limited reordering of the Apple menu (you can group folders at the top or bottom of the menu) and no sorting for submenus, but it does provide an unlimited number of submenus, where most other utilities are limited to five. It has a "recent" feature and lets you create a "Desktop" menu that lists items on the desktop. [Shareware, Kerry Clendinning]

∞❥ **Group. Most, first.** Those are the two rules for organizing your hierarchical Apple menu and its submenus. Group things together, and put the things you use most first in the list. Grouping lets you go right to a section without actually reading the items' names. Since hierarchical Apple menu utilities include custom organizing and divider lines, you won't have to resort to tricks like fake folders and renaming items to get things into groups. And, by keeping the most-used items at the top of a menu or submenu, it takes less time to get to it.

The top of my Apple menu looks like the picture here. The first item is the About command that belongs to the current application—I can't do anything about that, though I sure wish I could zap it down to the bottom, since I use it so seldom. The first group I have is simply the Applications and Utilities folders. Many of the utilities are also applications, of course, but I use my own personal sense of which is which when I divide them here. My next group is the folders for the kind of work I do most often. The folders come and go, depending on my current jobs, but there's always one (and sometimes two) for a book, there's one for *MacUser* magazine, and right now there's one for ABCNews. (Well, not *now* as you're reading this, but *now* as I write this. *Now* is in the eye of the beholder.) The next group is the desk accessories I use most often. That's just the top half of my Apple menu—I have a 21-inch screen, so I can see a lot in a menu without even scrolling it. But these are the items I access most often.

○○◆ **Make a Desk Accessory** folder inside the Apple Menu Items folder to hold the desk accessories you don't use very often. (I recommended that in the last section, too—but now, with a hierarchical Apple menu, you can select the secondary desk accessories from the menu instead of just opening the folder.) Leave the ones you use the most in the main level of the Apple Menu Items folder so that they're listed right in the Apple menu.

This was such an obvious move in the early days of System 7 that a book I worked on a year later blithely referred to the Desk Accessory folder as one of the subfolders in the System Folder—and not one of a half-dozen editors and tech readers caught the error.

○•◆ **The Control Panels folder** alias that the system puts in the Apple menu for you isn't the most efficient way to access control panels, especially when you start adding to your control panel collection. The alias will give you a submenu of *all* the control panels you have in the folder, and that can be a long list. I have control panels that I set once and ignore for the rest of their lifetimes; I have others that I access reasonably often, and some I use all the time. But I don't want to have to group and reorganize the 35 or so (!) items in my Control Panels submenu to keep things where I need them the most.

When it comes to desk accessories, you can leave some of them up at the top level of the Apple menu, put others in a folder, and even put others in a subfolder (for a subsubmenu). But you can't do the same thing with control panels because so many of them must be in the Control Panels folder in order to work. So, here's how to handle the problem:

1. Make a "fake" Control Panels folder for your Apple menu. Move the alias that's in the Apple Menu Items folder out to the desktop temporarily. Create a new folder in the Apple Menu Items folder, name it *Control Panels*, and edit its icon by copying the icon from the real Control Panels folder (or from the alias that's out on the desktop).

2. Put the Control Panels folder alias inside this new folder. (I renamed the alias *All Control Panels*.)

3. Open the *real* Control Panels folder and make aliases of the control panels you use most often. Put them in the "fake" control panels folder that's in your Apple Menu Items folder.

4. Group and arrange the contents of the "fake" folder so that the things you use most often are at the top of the submenu. List the loose control panel aliases first, then the real folder so you can get at all the others.

Here's what the control panel section of my hierarchical Apple menu looks like. The Control Panels folder listed in the Apple menu is the

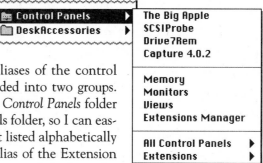

fake one. In the submenu, there are aliases of the control panels that I open the most often, divided into two groups. At the bottom of the submenu is an *All Control Panels* folder that's the alias for the real Control Panels folder, so I can easily get to any control panel—they're just listed alphabetically in the next submenu. (I also have an alias of the Extension folder in here in case I want to take a quick look at the extensions I have running.)

⊶ **Special control panels can be grouped** someplace other than in the Control Panels folder—the real one or the fake one. I keep aliases of network-related control panels in the section of my Apple menu that deals with my tiny office network.

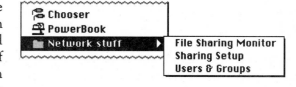

⊶ **Put an application folder** in your Apple menu. But if you use an Application folder on the main level of your drive, don't

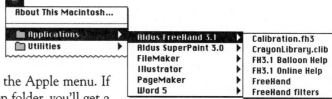

put it or even its alias into the Apple menu. If you use the real Application folder, you'll get a submenu that lists the folders for each of your applications, then a submenu that lists all the items in an application's folder. Sometimes it's not easy to pick out the actual application from its list of support files and folders—and you have to travel through an extra layer of submenus just to find the application's name.

Instead, create a new Applications folder for your Apple Menu Items folder. Alias your applications and put the aliases inside this Applications folder. Then you can just select the application you want from the submenu without going through any more folders, or browsing through a list of files. You can also get a list of applications in the submenu no matter where they actually "live"—even if they're on different drives.

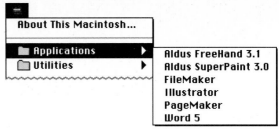

I keep my Applications folder arranged so that the items I use the most are on the main level, and others are in folders to keep the main submenu from becoming too crowded. There's a folder of telecommunication pro-

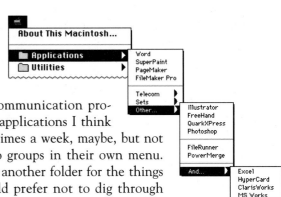

grams, for instance, and a folder of applications I think of as secondary—I use them a few times a week, maybe, but not every day; they're divided into two groups in their own menu. Inside that secondary folder, there's another folder for the things I don't use all that often but would prefer not to dig through folders to find.

••⋗ **Put your hard disk** in your Apple menu by making an alias of it for the Apple Menu Items folder. This provides five-levels-deep access to the contents of your hard drive. Want to get to yesterday's memo? Point to the name of the hard drive in the menu and follow the folder path down to the menu. I keep aliases of three hard drives, two partitions, and my PowerBook (a veritable embarrassment of riches) in my Apple menu.

••⋗ **Put an alias of the Trash** in your Apple menu. Then, if a window is blocking the Trash icon on the desktop, you can simply select the Trash from the Apple menu and the Trash window will open—you don't have to move the other windows around so you can double-click on

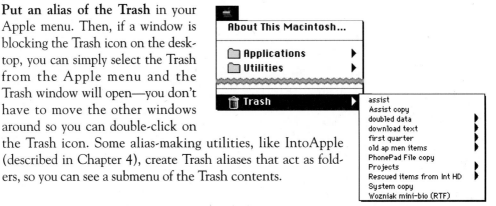

the Trash icon. Some alias-making utilities, like IntoApple (described in Chapter 4), create Trash aliases that act as folders, so you can see a submenu of the Trash contents.

••⋗ **If you put an Apple Menu Items folder** alias in the Apple menu, as suggested earlier so you can access it easily, you get a very strange effect once it's in a hierarchical Apple menu: Opening the Apple Menu Items folder's submenu shows a list identical to the Apple menu itself. The Apple Menu Items folder listed in *that* gives you another Apple menu, ad infinitum.

## MAC DOGGEREL

I've come to hate this darned machine.
I wish that I could sell it.
It never does just what I want,
But only what I tell it.

*—anon.*

•••➤ **If your hierarchical Apple menu** utility lets you launch more than one item at a time, set up subfolders with items that you use together. This might be a group of documents that belong to the same or different applications, or even a group of applications. I

keep a folder of "sets" in my application submenu so I can launch groups of applications at the same time, depending on the project I'm working on. Inside the Sets folder are folders named for combinations of applications; inside those folders are aliases of the applications themselves. By selecting the folder from the submenu with the Option key held down (the actual multiple-open technique varies from one utility to another), I can launch more than one application at a time.

•••➤ **If you use an alias of a file server** to log onto a network (that's covered in Chapter 21), putting it in the Apple menu makes it even easier to log on: You select the file server you want from the Apple menu and you're immediately presented with the log-on dialog asking for your password. I keep an alias of my PowerBook on my desktop system's Apple menu; I use it to make the connection between the two machines; then, when the PowerBook is mounted, the same item becomes a hierarchical menu that provides access to five levels of folders on the PowerBook's drive.

## ⊰ MORE SUBFOLDERS ⊱

## The Startup Items Folder

∞➤ **Any item in the Startup Items folder** opens whenever you start up your Mac. But don't put any "real" items in the Startup Items folder: It's a pretty awkward place to store applications or documents. Instead, put aliases in the folder.

∞➤ **Basic candidates** for the Startup Items folder include:

- *Applications* that you use all the time, every day, or at least at the start of every day. I keep an alias of Word in my Startup Items folder.

- *Desk accessories* that you use all the time. Maybe you like the Alarm Clock ticking away at the edge of the screen. Maybe you leave out the Note Pad (or a Note Pad-like accessory) to jot down notes all day. Maybe you have a big screen and like the Calculator hanging around all the time.

- *Any document* that you use constantly or first thing—a To Do list, say, that you check every morning. Or a special template that will both launch the application you want and give you a blank but formatted form to work in. I keep a SuperPaint document that's set to use a grayscale palette instead of a color one in my Startup Items folder so I can work on the illustrations for this book without having to open a new document and setting it to grayscale.

∘•◆ **The icon on the Startup Items folder** represents the power switch first used on the back of the early modular Macs—a round button with a vertical slash in it. (Bet you've been wondering about that!)

### BY THE WAY ...

Speaking of power switches ... the original Macs had rocker switches on their backs to turn them on and off. Why is this worth mentioning?

Well, the documentation that came with the very first Mac showed a studious young man concentrating on his Mac screen. Unless he was into Zen, though, he couldn't have been concentrating too hard on what must have been a blank screen. Only the back of the Mac showed in the photo—but the rocker switch is very obviously in the *off* position. (At least it's obvious to those of us who for years reached around to the back of the Mac to switch it on and off!)

∘•◆ **You can put a folder in the Startup Items folder** so it will be opened as soon as you start up—the folder's window will open on the desktop wherever you left it last. Why bother? Well, for instance, you could have a folder that contains aliases of the five applications you use the most. Then, depending on what exactly you're working on that day, you can select two or three of them and launch them all at the same time.

∘•◆ **Get a special startup sound** by putting a sound file in the Startup Items folder. Because "opening" a sound plays it, the sound will be played every time you start your machine. You can put more than one sound in. You can rename the sounds so that they play in a specific order, since they'll play alphabetically.

There are several different sound file formats that might be on your Mac, since different programs produce different files; the only one that will be played as a startup sound, though, is a Mac system sound file—the ones stored in your System file. These files have the speaker icon on them.

**···▶ Items in the Startup Items folder** are launched alphabetically in groups. Within each group, original items are opened before aliases. Here's the opening order of the types of items you're most likely to keep in your Startup Items folder:

1. applications
2. application aliases
3. documents
4. document aliases
5. desk accessories
6. desk accessory aliases
7. sounds
8. sound aliases
9. folders
10. folder aliases

Since the order in which you launch applications can have an effect on how memory is used, you might want to keep this ordering in mind. Generally (the specifics are in Chapter 9), you want to launch the application you'll be using most of the day first so that there aren't any unused blocks of memory later as you quit some programs and launch others. To force the launching order you want, keep track of how an application is being launched—from an original or from an alias, or from a document original or alias. You can rename any of the items in the Startup Items folder to change the launch order within groups.

**···▶ If you see this dialog on startup,** it means you've put an extension into the Startup Items folder by mistake. Just follow the instructions in the dialog!

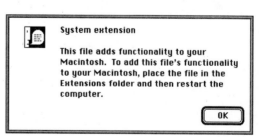

Lots of extensions seem to wind up in the Startup Items folder. Why? Because prior to System 7, extensions were called *startup documents* and lots of them are labeled as such if you check their *kind* in a list view window or Get Info. The Mac won't automatically put a file of this type in the Startup Items folder if you drag it to the closed System Folder, but *you* might put it there!

**···▶ There's an important difference between** init programs that run automatically on startup (they go into the Extensions and Control Panels folders) and the applications and documents that you want opened at startup which go into the Startup Items folder.

There's lots more about inits, extensions, and control panels in Chapter 8.

There's some confusion here because both things happen automatically at startup—and also because init programs used to be called *startup documents*.

Anyway, things in the Startup Items folder are *opened* at startup. What "open" means depends on the item: An application launches, a folder opens its window, a sound plays. Some items in the Extensions and Control Panels folder *load* at startup—that is, they're loaded into memory so they can lurk around in the background until you need them.

···➤ **Force the Mac to return to the desktop** after opening all the items in the Startup Items folder by including a desktop item in the folder. Alias any folder, or the hard drive itself, and put it in the Startup Items folder. There's also a public domain utility, FinderToFront, that brings the desk-top forward after getting everything else started. [freeware, Michael Pierce]

FinderToFront

···➤ **If you turn off Extensions** by holding the Shift key down at startup, nothing in the Startup Items folder will launch, either.

···➤ **You can prevent the startup items** from starting up when you still want your extensions to load by holding down the Shift key at *just* the right time during the startup process. If you press it too soon, you'll prevent extensions from loading; too late, and the startup items go their merry way. Press the Shift key after all the extensions have loaded—not after they've *started* loading, but after they've *finished*. (Some extensions turn themselves off if the Shift key is down when they're supposed to load.) After the last extension icon appears at the bottom of the screen, all the extension icons go away and you see the desktop pattern. There's a slight pause, and then the menu bar is drawn; another slight pause and the desktop icons appear. At this point, the startup items are ready to go. So, press the Shift key anytime while the menu bar or desktop are being drawn, and hold it down until the desktop and its icons are completely displayed on the screen.

···➤ **If a program begins to launch** because you didn't press Shift soon enough, or because you want the first few things in the Startup Items folder to launch but not *this* particular program, press Command-period *right away*. The program will quit before it has even finished launching, if you catch it soon enough. But this can be tricky, because if you launch multiple programs, you'll see that each one starts up briefly—its name flashes in the menu bar—and then the Mac goes on to the next one. Then it goes back to the first one and finishes launching it, creating the menu bar and opening windows.

···➤ **A startup screen** isn't a startup item—it doesn't go in the Startup Items folder, it goes in the System Folder. Ditto for a startup movie. (Startup screens and movies are covered in Chapter 1.)

## The Preferences Folder

∞➤ **The Preferences folder holds** special files that applications and utilities use to keep track of things like how you've configured their menu commands or the defaults in their dialog boxes. These files are generally referred to as "prefs" or "settings" files; the actual name of the file might include *preferences*, *prefs*, *settings*, *defaults*, or none of the above. (I was considerably surprised when I checked my Preferences folder while writing this and found no fewer than 49 items in it!)

➤ **The Preferences folder icon** is two radio buttons—indicating your choices that are stored in the prefs files.

➤ **Some utilities and desk accessories** keep more than just preference files in the Preferences folder. Sometimes an entire data file is stored in the Preferences folder, either "loose" or inside another folder that the utility creates specifically for that purpose. One of my favorite desk accessories—MacPak's PhonePad—keeps its data in the Preferences folder. I prefer this (get it?) to the way the Note Pad and Scrapbook keep their files out in the main level of the System Folder.

• • • • • • • • • • • • • • • • • • • • • • • • • • • • • • • • • • • • • • • • •

## MAC PEOPLE:          STEVE WOZNIAK

Steve grew up obsessed with technology. In high school, he designed computers in the margins of his notebooks while other kids were doodling. After school, he'd spend his time sneaking into local time-sharing computers.

Wozniak's forte was ingenious, highly efficient design—in digital circuits and in computer programs. If the book said you could perform a function with six chips, Steve would figure out a way to do it with three.* Better still, he would come up with a tricky software routine that did the same function without any extra chips at all.

After dropping out of college,** "Woz" got a job at Hewlett-Packard designing calculator circuitry. For a while he was content—but when the first microprocessor chips came out in the early seventies, he was seized by a passion to build his own personal computer. His typically clever single-board design, the Apple, made such a hit at the Homebrew Computer Club that his friend Steve Jobs talked Woz into forming a company to sell the computers. Wozniak was 22.

Actually, Woz wasn't particularly interested in business; in fact, he gave away schematics for the Apple and published chunks of its code in *Dr. Dobb's Journal*. But Jobs, a tireless promoter, put the company into high gear. Soon sleek Apple II computers were rolling off the production line—the first really successful "appliance" computer.

> *Most Macintoshes have an IWM chip. That stands for Integrated Woz Machine!
>
> **Woz later went back to college. By then, he had to duck his famous name and signed up at Stanford under the name Rocky Raccoon.

Apple grew and prospered, and Woz with it; but his next major project, the Apple ///, was a disaster. Plagued by design problems, poor quality control and inept marketing, the Apple /// hurt the company so badly that IBM's newly introduced PC was able to steal away the business market that Apple had dominated.

With Apple floundering, in came a new, expert manager: John Sculley from Pepsico. But things took an unexpected turn when Sculley, in a virtual coup d'état, assumed control and eased the two Steves out the door of their own company.

Woz, by then a fairly rich man, sponsored a couple of rock concerts, did a little tinkering (he invented the universal remote control) and settled into a comfortable semi-retirement in an elaborate underground house. When last heard from, he was living in a gadgeteer's paradise, surrounded by video games and the world's largest collection of laserdisc movies.

*—Andy Baird*

➤ **An application that doesn't know how to behave** under System 7 might leave its prefs file up in the main level of the System Folder instead of tucked away in Preferences where it belongs. (An application may *work* under System 7 without *behaving*. Miss Manners would grok the difference if, indeed, Miss Manners might be said to grok.)

⋯➤ **When an application or utility** seems to forget its default settings or otherwise starts acting strangely without actually crashing, sometimes trashing its prefs file will calm things down. Most applications will just create a new prefs file when you launch them and they can't find the old one.

## Other Subfolders

⋯➤ **The Extensions folder** holds *extensions*, programs, and files that add special features and capabilities to the Mac's operating system—hence the puzzle-piece icon. There are so many different extensions available, and things you ought to know about them, that they're covered separately in Chapter 8.

⋯➤ **The Control Panels folder** holds control panels—utilities that let you configure certain system settings, like the desktop pattern, the Label menu, the look of Desktop windows, how the mouse and keyboard work, and even what sound the Mac uses as an alert warning.

Some control panels are used so often (or should be) that your system comes with an alias of the Control Panels folder in the Apple Menu Items folder. Control panels are covered in Chapter 8.

The icon on the control panel folder is a slider control—something you use to adjust things like the volume in the Sound control panel.

⋯➤ **If you use the PrintMonitor** for background printing, it creates its own PrintMonitor Documents folder to hold its files. (The PrintMonitor is covered in Chapter 12.)

⋯➤ **The Fonts folder** showed up in System 7.1; it holds screen and printer fonts. In System 7.0, fonts go into the Extensions folder.

## ⌘ SYSTEM 7.5 STUFF ⌘

## Subfolders

⋯➤ **There's a new subfolder in the System Folder:** the Shutdown items folder. It's discussed at the end of Chapter 1.

⋯➤ **The two special subfolders** in the Apple Menu Items folder—Recent Applications and Recent Documents—are used by the Apple Menu Options control panel, which we'll get to in a minute. Sometimes there's a third folder, too: Recent Servers.

Recent Documents       Recent Servers
        Recent Applications

## The Hierarchical Apple Menu

∞⬦ **There's a built-in hierarchical Apple menu** in System 7.5. (Hallelujah!) The Apple Menu Options control panel gives you control over the few options there are: whether it's on or off, and how many items will be stored in the "Recent" folders for documents, applications, and servers.

∞⬦ **Using the On or Off button** in the Apple Menu Options control panel has an immediate effect on the Apple menu—you don't have to restart the Mac. You don't even have to close the control panel. But I can't, for the life of me, figure out why you'd want to turn off the hierarchical menus.

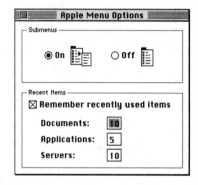

∞⬦ **The "Recent" submenus** list items you've used recently so you can reopen them without digging through folders to get to them. The picture here shows what a Recent Applications submenu looks like. If you don't want the Recent folders included in your Apple menu, uncheck the *Remember recently used items* button in the control panel.

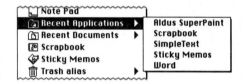

What's actually stored in the Recent folder (for Documents, Applications, and Servers) is an alias of any item you've used recently.

∞⬦ **Items in the Apple menu and its submenus are** listed alphabetically. To re-order them, use the various tricks described earlier in this chapter in the Apple Menu section.

∞⟨⟩ **Don't throw away your hierarchical Apple menu utility** if you used one for a system previous to System 7.5. And if you don't have one, consider getting one anyway. The built-in hierarchical Apple menu is better than none at all, but it's missing most of the features that make the utilities so handy—like dividers, definable fonts and sizes for the submenus, and the ability to list items in other than alphabetical order.

# CHAPTER 7
# DESK
# ACCESSORIES

The real problem is not whether machines think, but whether men do.

B.F. SKINNER

Some reasons why an entire chapter is devoted to desk accessories:

••▶ Desk accessories are not little applications, no matter what you've heard!

••▶ A Scrapbook page sometimes displays this notice: "This item has no text, picture, or sound."

••▶ There are ways to cheat with that stupid little Puzzle.

••▶ You can automatically dissolve the "suitcases" that old desk accessories are stored in.

••▶ Some space is devoted to explaining how the upgrade path from an original Mac to a Mac Plus cost $7600.

••▶ There are terrific replacements for the Calculator, the Scrapbook, the Note Pad, and even Key Caps.

••▶ There are quotes from Ben Jonson (b. 1572), the Grateful Dead, Chicago (or is it Blood, Sweat and Tears?), and Casey Stengel.

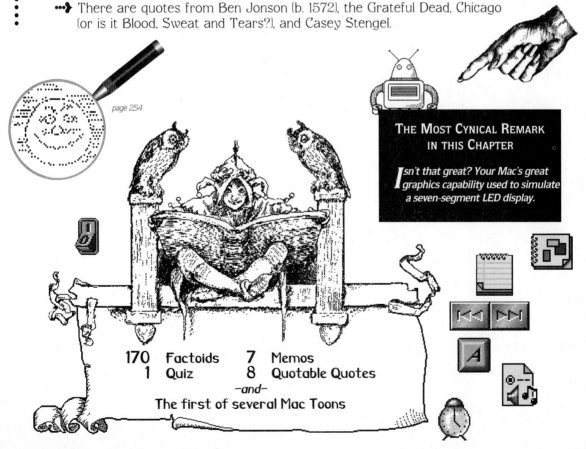

page 254

THE MOST CYNICAL REMARK IN THIS CHAPTER

*Isn't that great? Your Mac's great graphics capability used to simulate a seven-segment LED display.*

170 Factoids    7 Memos
  1 Quiz         8 Quotable Quotes
        *–and–*
The first of several Mac Toons

246

## ✦ IN GENERAL ✦

## Basics

∘•✦ **Desk accessories used to be** small programs inside the System file that were available only through the Apple menu. Now desk accessories can be larger, they exist separately from the System file, and you can open them directly as well as through the Apple menu.

Since the dawn of time, Apple has included seven basic DAs with its system software: Alarm Clock, Calculator, Chooser, Key Caps, Note Pad, Puzzle, and Scrapbook. The Chooser is the only one that's a necessity for most setups—and it's also the one that has changed the most. Most of the others have changed only slightly, and only recently. The only items added to the lineup in all these years are the Battery desk accessory for PowerBooks and CD Remote for systems with CD-ROM drives.

System 7.5 added the Shut Down DA. See the end of this chapter.

Key Caps   Scrapbook   Note Pad   Chooser

Alarm Clock   Puzzle   Calculator

CD Remote   Battery

∘•✦ **Desk accessories are listed in the Apple menu,** but that's only because a system installation automatically places them inside the Apple Menu Items folder. A desk accessory can be stored anywhere and it will still work.

∘•✦ **"DA" is the familiar,** almost *affectionate*, term for desk accessory. I'm tempted to point out that that's pronounced as two separate letters, but I don't suppose anyone would seriously contemplate saying "daah" or "duh." You might consider saying "day," but that would sound so much like "D-A" that you'd get away with it, anyway.

**About This Macintosh...**

🕭 Alarm Clock
🖩 Calculator
📷 CD Remote
🖆 Chooser
🅰 Key Caps
🗒 Note Pad
🎛 Puzzle
📇 Scrapbook

CLINT EASTWOOD
*(NOT!)*

Go ahead, make my DA.

∘•✦ **Some desk accessories are self-contained,** some use a single special document to store information, and some let you open and save documents the same way an application does.

The Calculator, for instance, is self-contained: It doesn't use any documents at all. The Scrapbook and Note Pad, on the other hand, each use a special document that has to be named in a particular way and stored in a specific place. From your point of view, though, it seems that the Scrapbook and Note Pad are self-contained because you never use an Open or Save command—the information is just there when you open the DA, and it stays there when you put it away.

Scrapbook   Scrapbook File

None of Apple's desk accessories uses regular Open and Save commands to handle different documents, but many desk accessories available from other sources work that way.

Note Pad   Note Pad File

⊶➤ **A desk accessory is not an application.** Hmm ... you've probably read, or been told, that under System 7, DAs are just little applications and that's why they're not in the System file any more, and that's why you can just double-click on them to open them. Not true! (The part about double-clicking is true; the statement that they're "just" applications isn't.)

It may seem hard to define a desk accessory now, since DAs have expanded in size and functionality, and anything can be accessed from the Apple menu. But System 7 actually provides a fairly strict definition: a file whose *kind* is Desk Accessory.

There are several results of this file definition, some behind the scenes, and some up front and visible. If you've included *Kind* as one of the items in the Finder's Label menu, there are some obvious results on the desktop:

- DAs are labeled as such in desktop list-view windows.
- When you sort by kind, DAs are grouped together.
- In the Find dialog, Desk Accessory is available as a criterion for a search.

Behind the scene, genuine desk accessories—as opposed to, say, a Scrapbook substitute that's actually an application—are also handled differently when it comes to memory usage (details to come!).

⊷➤ **The niftiest result of the special file type** for desk accessories is that you can drag a DA into a closed System Folder and you'll be asked if you want it placed in the Apple Menu Items folder. As with all the System Folder's "routing" dialogs, if you click Cancel, the DA stays where it is—it doesn't go into the System Folder itself.

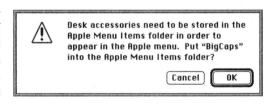

Desk accessories need to be stored in the Apple Menu Items folder in order to appear in the Apple menu. Put "BigCaps" into the Apple Menu Items folder?

[ Cancel ]   [ OK ]

⊷➤ **Organize desk accessories in your Apple menu** using the tips and techniques described in the last chapter. Here's a summary:

- Change the order of desk accessories in the Apple menu by renaming them.
- Group desk accessories by naming them with a special leader character.
- Put the least-used DAs in a folder for secondary access from the Apple menu. Leave the ones you use the most listed in the Apple menu itself.

- Arrange the window that holds your secondary DAs so they're all easy to get at.
- Use a hierarchical Apple menu utility so you can easily access the "secondary" DAs.

## THE WAY WE WERE ...

Desk accessories were a uniquely Macintosh feature when they were introduced with the Mac back in 1984. No other personal computer offered anything remotely like it. They were specifically made so that you could do something, like a calculation, without quitting your current application—the Mac could run only one application at a time back then. Desk accessories were necessarily small—they were limited to 32K in disk size (no problem for the 8K Calculator) and were installed directly into the System file.

In the very beginning, you had no choice about which DAs appeared in your Apple menu: If they were in the System file, they were in the Apple menu. And there was no way a "normal" user could get them in or out of the System file. Programmer Don Brown wrote a shareware utility called DAM—Desk Accessory Mover—that let us move those DAs in and out of the System file. (He later went on to write classics like DiskTop and QuicKeys, and found CE Software—not necessarily in that order.) Apple's great at copying good ideas (just look at its interface) and soon incorporated the Font/DA Mover into its system software.

At that point, users started making multiple startup disks (the system ran off a floppy disk in those days) so they could have different combinations of fonts and/or DAs depending on what project was at hand. After all, with both a System Folder and an application on the same floppy (imagine that!), it paid to get rid of fonts and DAs you didn't need so you'd have more room for documents. (Imagine *that*—we're talking about a single, 400K floppy disk!) Then we ran into the problem that altering the Scrapbook on one disk didn't affect the Scrapbooks on the other startup disks, something that really confused new users. ("*I know I pasted it in there yesterday!*")

As if that weren't enough of a concern, if you wanted to "waste" the disk space and install some of the nifty DAs available from third parties, the system limited you to only 15 of them in the Apple menu at a time. That seemed a low limit when using DAs was the only way to get pseudo-multitasking capability, since the Mac could run only one application at a time. There were some tricks to up the limit from within Font/DA Mover (and I vaguely remember some Font/DA Mover+ version that gave you a few extra "slots"), and a utility called DA Installer showed up that let you put 36 DAs in the menu at a time. But the entirely different approach of running a DA right from its suitcase instead of installing it in the System file first showed up in a utility called Other, by programming wiz Lofty Becker. Finally, Steve Brecher's Suitcase utility showed up—and it's still around, even for System 7 users, because of the way it handles fonts—which are, once again, stored in suitcases.

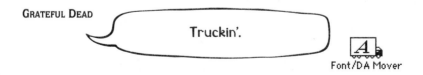

GRATEFUL DEAD
Truckin'.

Font/DA Mover

## Opening and Closing DAs

∞⟩ **Open a desk accessory** by selecting it from the Apple menu or by double-clicking on its icon.

∞⟩ **Make an alias of a desk accessory** and leave it "loose" on the desktop. That way, you can, for instance, keep the Calculator in the Apple menu but still be able to double-click on its icon if you're working on the desktop.

∞⟩ **If a desk accessory has a document file,** you *might* be able to open the DA by double-clicking on the document. This really varies from one DA to another. Apple's Scrapbook and Note Pad DAs can be opened this way as long as the DAs are in the Apple Menu Items folder and the files themselves are named correctly and are in the System Folder.* Few third-party DAs have this launching-from-a-document capability, but you can try.

> *Apple made a concerted effort to clean up the mess in the System Folder by providing official subfolders. So, why did they put desk accessories in the Apple Menu Items folder yet leave their files "loose" in the System Folder?

∞⟩ **The Application menu lists** open desk accessories, as it does for applications (although control panels don't get listed there). So if you open the Calculator and leave it hanging around on the screen, you can activate it by clicking on it if you can see it, choosing it again from the Apple menu, or selecting it from the Application menu if your mouse happens to be in that corner of the screen.

∞⟩ **You can "open" a DA that's already open.** That is, you can select a DA from the Apple menu even though it's already open (and, presumably, obscured by other windows on your screen or you wouldn't be looking for it in the Apple menu). Selecting an open DA merely activates it, bringing it to the top of the pile of windows on the screen. You won't get any weird happenings like a second version of the same DA opening up.

∞⟩ **Every DA has at least two menus:** File and Edit. Sometimes the File menu has only Close and Quit commands. The Edit menu contains at least the Undo, Cut, Copy, and Paste commands, although they're not always available. (Some programmers will follow Apple's guidelines to the letter—giving DAs these two menus with their basic commands—without following the *spirit* of the guidelines by providing the basic functionality of all those commands.)

∞⟩ **Look for a special menu!** Lots of DAs have a menu in addition to File and Edit. Does this seem obvious to you? I know someone who was annoyed for more than a year because Key Caps showed only the Chicago font—she never noticed the menu that would have let her change the font. (She'd probably be embarrassed if I mention her name. Hi, Carol!) Key Caps is the only one of Apple's desk accessories that has a menu—and it simply lists available fonts—but many third-party DAs have their own menus just chock full of commands. Most DA menus are named simply for the DA itself.

Key Caps has its own menu.

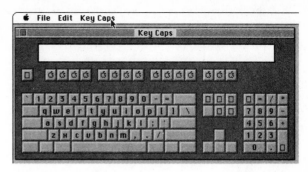

•••▶ **A desk accessory that's a single window** (like any of Apple's DAs) is closed when you click in its close box, but there are other ways to close DAs, too.

- Use the Quit command in the File menu, or Command-Q.
- Use the Close command, or Command-W, if the DA has no document windows.
- Try Command-period for single-window DAs.
- The Escape key* closes many third-party DAs, but doesn't work on Apple's collection.

*Tech editor Joe Holmes points out that, in Brooklyn, this key is known as the Excape key.

•••▶ **Desk accessories that can handle more than one document** (especially those that handle more than one at a time) usually stay open even after all their windows are closed. You may *think* you've closed the DA, because you'll see the desktop, or an application's window on the screen, but the DA itself is still active. This can be confusing, because your tendency is to click in an available window, which activates that application, and you'll forget that there's a DA open somewhere out there.

For these kinds of DAs, you *have* to use the File menu's Quit command or its equivalent; the Close command just won't work.

•••▶ **If you're launching a DA by double-clicking** on it and want the window that it's in to close, hold down the Option key while you double-click on the icon.

## Memory

•••▶ **A desk accessory gets 20K of memory** to itself when you open it, no matter how large or small it is. This picture shows the About This Macintosh dialog when four DAs are open. (And two applications—the one I'm writing in and the one I'm using to do these pictures.)

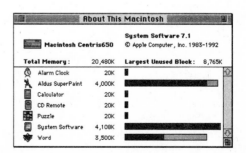

⋯**⟩ When a DA needs more than 20K** of memory, it grabs it from the system's allocation; the system, in turn, grabs some of the free memory that's still available in order to accommodate the DA's demand. These pictures, from the About This Macintosh window, show what happens behind the scenes. With two applications running, the system is using 3912K. When the Calculator is open, the system allocation has jumped to 3980K. When CD Remote—which does a lot more than the Calculator—is open, the system has grabbed 4133K.

| Aldus SuperPaint | 4,000K |
| System Software | 3,921K |
| Word | 3,500K |

| Aldus SuperPaint | 4,000K |
| Calculator | 20K |
| System Software | 3,980K |
| Word | 3,500K |

| Aldus SuperPaint | 4,000K |
| CD Remote | 20K |
| System Software | 4,133K |
| Word | 3,500K |

### THE WAY WE WERE ...

In the early days of DAs, whatever application was running (even if it was the Finder) "hosted" a DA, sharing memory with it. This was pretty transparent, since only one application ran at a time and used all the memory available. It became obvious, though, when Andy Hertzfeld's Switcher program let the Mac run more than one application—an open DA "lived" in whatever application you opened it in.

In later (much later) systems, under MultiFinder, desk accessories shared a common chunk of memory and lived in a common layer on your screen: Click on or open one DA, and all of the other opened ones would come forward, too. A little program in the System Folder called DA Handler took care of this—but it also slowed things down because the Handler had to launch first every time you opened a DA.

⋯**⟩ Opening lots of DAs at once can lead to memory fragmentation,** which means that although you may have plenty of free memory, it's in unusable small chunks. Here's an example of what might happen. Start with a 5-meg setup where the system software takes 1820K, leaving 3300K to work with: You open a word processor that takes 1300K of memory. Then you open three desk accessories, which use 20K each. Next, you launch a check-writing program that takes a slim 850K of memory. You're left with 1090K of memory, as shown here:

| Application | Allocation | Amount remaining |
|---|---|---|
| System | 1820K | 3300K |
| Word Processor | 1300K | 2000K |
| Calculator | 20K | 1980K |
| Scrapbook | 20K | 1960K |
| Note Pad | 20K | 1940K |
| CheckWriter | 850K | 1090K |

Next, you have a program that needs 1110K of memory. You figure that you can quit out of two of the DAs and, at 20K each, free up 40K of memory, giving you 1130K. But that won't work. The largest *block* of memory you have left is still 1090K; you have an extra block of 40K free, too, but the two blocks aren't connected. Programs can run only in *contiguous* memory—a complete chunk, not bits and pieces added together.

If, on the other hand, you had closed the DAs before launching the check-writing program, you would have had 1150K available, and the memory would be used more efficiently.

Now, with all that said ... if you find yourself continually *that* tight for memory, you should add more memory to your machine.

Chapter 9 covers memory allocations and fragmentation.

••➤ **A 20K slot left by a closed DA** is very efficiently used by the next DA that you open, so it's not totally unusable memory—it's just severely restricted as to what you can use it for.

## Old Desk Accessories

••➤ **Prior to System 7,** desk accessories that weren't in the System file itself were stored in files with suitcase icons. A desk accessory suitcase could hold a single desk accessory, or many. (The Font/DA Mover utility created the suitcases and manipulated their contents.)

But System 7 uses stand-alone DAs, out of their suitcases. If you have a suitcase file with one or more desk accessories inside, it's simple to take them out: Under System 7, double-click on the suitcase icon, and a window opens displaying its contents. Just drag the desk accessory icon(s) out of the window. (This window is a little different from a standard folder window—you'll notice a suitcase icon in the upper-left corner.) Once the desk accessory file is extracted from the suitcase file, you can put it in the Apple Menu Items folder.

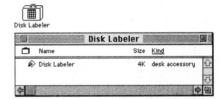

An old DA suitcase and its window.

Or let the Mac do the work: Drag the suitcase icon into the closed System Folder and you'll be asked if you want the DA put in the Apple Menu Items folder. Click OK, and the DA is automatically extracted from its suitcase.

••➤ **Make sure you duplicate a suitcase file** before extracting the desk accessory for System 7. Once a desk accessory is converted from its old form by being taken out of its suitcase file, you won't be able to convert it back to a form usable by System 6.

••➤ **An older DA won't necessarily work** under System 7 just because you successfully removed it from its suitcase file. You'll still have to test it under your new system.

Editing icons is covered in Chapter 4.

••➤ **Desk accessories "left over" from System 6** have generic icons. (The generic DA icon is a variation of the generic application icon: the hand that's writing on the diamond shape is a left hand instead of a right hand.) Take advantage of the fact that System 7 lets you edit desktop icons, and change the icon to something appropriate for the desk accessory.

➼ **Some old desk accessories that crash under System 7** (after behaving perfectly well in previous systems) will work under System 7 if they remain in their suitcase files. You can use a utility like Suitcase or Master Juggler to access the "suitcased" desk accessory. I used two of my favorite old DAs under System 7 with this trick for almost two years before I got around to updating them. (And, in fact, if I hadn't needed to check the newest versions so I could review them for this book, I'd probably still be using the old ones.)

A desk accessory that's opened by Suitcase or Master Juggler is listed in the Apple menu just as if it were in the Apple Menu Items folder, but you'll be stuck with a generic application icon for it.

### THE COSTLY UPGRADE PATH

By mid-1976, Mac hardware seemed to be growing by leaps and bounds. The Mac Plus with its mind-boggling full meg of memory was released; it included brand-new, larger ROMs and a floppy drive that handled 800K disks—twice the capacity of previous Mac floppies. And, miracle of miracles, there was finally a hard drive available: the Apple HD 20. The computer, hard drive, and the new improved ImageWriter II printer cost about $4700.

You think that was bad? Pity the poor pioneers who bought the original Mac and ImageWriter for a bundled price of $3000. They (oh, all right, *we*) grabbed the external floppy drive at $500 and thought it was a bargain, considering it doubled our disk capacity. (From a single 400K floppy to two 400K floppies at a time!) Then what? Ah, the memory upgrade. Finally! $1000 for less than a meg of memory. A hard drive! Damn the floppies, full speed ahead: $1500 for a vast 20 megs of storage—on a *slooow* non-SCSI serial device. But it didn't stop there— you could turn your ordinary Mac into a Mac Plus. All you needed was: new ROMs and internal disk drive ($300); a new logic board ($600); and the new keyboard ($130— about $45 per cursor key). But you couldn't stop there. No upgrade path for the printer, so just plunge in and buy the new ImageWriter II for $600. And the new adapter cable for it—a mere $30. Forget the external 800K drive ($500); use the old 400K external— 400Ks will always be around. Total for a one-megabyte Mac Plus, a 20-meg hard drive, and a dot-matrix printer? $7600.*

*The value of a Mac Plus at the end of 1993 was about $250. The original ImageWriter? Another $100. The original 20-meg hard drive would be thrown in the package for free.

ANON.

You can always tell the pioneers. They're the ones with arrows in their backs.

## ◄ THE SCRAPBOOK ►

### Scrapbook Basics

◦•➤ **The Scrapbook stores text, graphics,** and even sounds on an unlimited number of pages. You can use it to store text, graphics, and even QuickTime movies that you use repeatedly, or that you just don't want to transfer immediately through the Clipboard.

◦•➤ **When you open the Scrapbook it displays** the page you were looking at the last time you used it. You turn the pages by using the scroll bar and arrows at the bottom of the window. The numbers in the lower left show the current page and the total number of pages.

◦•➤ **When you paste something into the Scrapbook,** a new page is created to hold it, but the pages go in backwards. I mean, if you had a real Scrapbook, wouldn't you add things to the *back?* The Scrapbook creates a page on top of the currently displayed page, so if page 1 is showing, a new page 1 is created. If you want to add a page someplace else, move to a different part of the Scrapbook before you paste. But that still won't let you paste in the last page, because you can only paste on top of an existing page.

> A memento affixed to a scrapbook page is immutable. How much better to simply affix in memory that which may wax and wane as necessary in size, in importance, in truth.

ANNE BODNOY
1852

◦•➤ **To cut or copy something from the Scrapbook,** just turn to that page and choose Cut or Copy from the Edit menu—you don't have to select anything first. (It has always struck me as strange that Apple's own utilities defy interface conventions like this.)

◦•➤ **The Clear command** removes a page from the Scrapbook without putting it on the Clipboard.

**⋯➤ Some Scrapbook items can't be seen.** The solution for sounds is to display the sound icon, but sometimes you'll paste something in that can't be graphically represented—a QuicKeys macro, for instance. In that case, you'll see the somewhat Zen-like notice shown here.

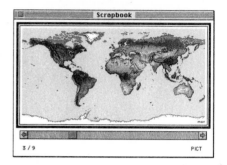

> This item has no text, picture, or sound.

**⋯➤ The color map that's in the Scrapbook** is made to be pasted into the Map control panel. (More about this in the next chapter.)

**∞⧸ The Scrapbook is undoubtedly the most useful** of Apple's DAs—not counting the Chooser, which is a necessity. (That's why it gets its own section in this chapter, while all the other DAs are lumped together in the next section.) But there's plenty of room for improvement. Just the addition of page titles and multiple Scrapbook files would increase its functionality. And a resizable window. And a shrink-to-fit option for large graphics. And the display of formatted text. And the ability to select only a portion of the page to copy …

- Now Scrapbook includes all the Scrapbook features I can think of—and several that I wouldn't have thought of. You can title the pages and add notes; you can view pages in miniature, then select one and either shrink it to fit the window or enlarge the window. It handles multiple files and even stores QuickTime movies. There's a Find function, a printing option, and import and export features. The pictures here show two views of the Now Scrapbook—the miniature page view, and a resized window with a full graphic showing. [Now Utilities, Now Software]

Different views of the Now Scrapbook.

- Publishist is the basic Apple Scrapbook plus: titled pages, a Find function, selection and the ability to open different files. It gets its name from the fact that it can publish any of its pages so you can subscribe to them from any application that supports Publish and Subscribe. [Xtras for System 7, book/disk, Aker, Addison-Wesley]

⊶⟩ **My absolutely most favorite Scrapbook replacement** isn't even a desk accessory, it's an extension—with a little DA component that lets you set a few parameters.

ClickPaste stores any kind of information—picture, text, movies, database text or form information, HyperCard buttons along with their scripts, PageMaker components, and so on—as a separate file in any subfolder in its main folder. To "paste" something into this collection, you copy it to the Clipboard and then pop up the ClickPaste menu anywhere on the screen with a click of the mouse and whatever key combination you've defined. (I use Option-Shift-Control, which are the three corner keys on my keyboard.) Use the Save Clipboard command to store the information wherever you want. When you want the information back, pop up the menu, slide down the list of folders, select something from a subfolder and presto! It's automatically copied from the stored file and

pasted directly into your current document; you don't even use the Copy or Paste command. You can even have a balloon pop out of any listed item to show you a miniature of the item before you select. It's incredibly convenient and on my can't-live-without-it list. [Mainstay]

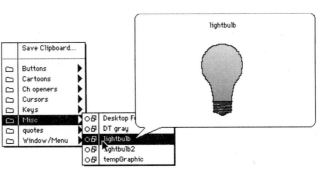

> Chapter 19 covers the Mac's Publish and Subscribe features.
>
> **CLICKPASTE**

## The Scrapbook File

⊶ **It's hard to remember that the Scrapbook and its contents** are two distinct files. The Scrapbook is a desk accessory. Its contents are in a document named *Scrapbook File* that's in the System Folder. Every time you open the Scrapbook, it finds the Scrapbook File and opens it, and any changes you make are saved to the file automatically when you close the Scrapbook.

Scrapbook  Scrapbook File

⊶ **If there's no Scrapbook File** in your System Folder, opening the Scrapbook creates a new file. You'll see a page that has the notice "Empty Scrapbook," a direct enough statement, with none of the whimsical charm of the original Scrapbook's approach to the situation.

⊶ **Double-clicking on the Scrapbook File icon** opens the Scrapbook, but *only* if the file is in the System Folder, where it belongs.

⊶ **Although the Scrapbook opens only one file,** you can have multiple Scrapbook files if you want. The procedure is a real pain, but it works. Keeping in mind that the Scrapbook opens the file with the right name in the right place, "all" you have to do is

> The end of this chapter describes the updated Scrapbook that comes with System 7.5

either shuffle Scrapbook files in and out of the System Folder or keep renaming files inside the System Folder so the Scrapbook DA opens the file you want.

Moving the files in and out of the System Folder is really time-consuming. You'd start by moving the original file out of the System Folder and opening the Scrapbook; that creates a new Scrapbook file. When you want to swap files, first you close the Scrapbook. But you can't just put the original file back in the System Folder, because it would copy over the new one you just created (and, presumably, entered information into). Dragging the new file out first into the same spot you put the old file would copy over the *old* file. So, you need a safe place to put one of the files while you're dragging the other into position. (And if you make more than two Scrapbook files, you can play even more elaborate games of Three-File Monte.) The alternative to shuffling the files around is keeping them in the System Folder, constantly renaming them so that only the one you want to access is named Scrapbook File.

So, if someone gives you a Scrapbook file of nifty pictures, you can open it without replacing your own Scrapbook file. To merge Scrapbook files, or add one of your friend's pictures to your collection, you have to continually rename the files, opening one, copying a picture, closing the Scrapbook, renaming the files, opening the other, pasting it in ... you get the picture.*

✳Don't you hate it when someone points out a pun? So, I won't.

**⟶ In the bottom right of the Scrapbook** you'll see some cryptic "words" that identify the type of information stored on the page. These are the *file types* that I refer to occasionally throughout this book and cover in detail in Chapter 21. The basic types you'll see reported in the Scrapbook are *PICT*, for images, *TEXT* for plain text, *styl* for formatted text, *snd* for sounds, and *moov* for QuickTime movies. Another format you'll see quite often is *RTF*, the *Rich Text Format* that's used by Microsoft for formatted text.

But the Scrapbook can store and will report on an almost bewildering array of file types—and a single item can have several "definitions." For instance, this picture shows what looks like a mere folder icon—but it's actually something that's been copied from the ResEdit program and it's more than just a picture of an icon. It's a real icon "resource" with information about its color, black and white, and small versions all stored together. You can paste it back into a ResEdit file and get all that information; or, you can copy it and then paste it into any program that accepts graphics and get just the picture of the icon. (Also involved here are the capabilities and limitations of the Clipboard itself in transferring information—which are covered in Chapter 2.)

Because the Scrapbook, like the Clipboard, can store information that's specific to an application, you'll often see a code for a program listed along with the main file type of the page. So, for instance, *PGMK, PICT* is a graphic element from Pagemaker, while *FMKR, TEXT* is text from FileMaker.

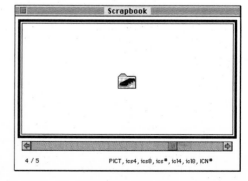

## THE WAY WE WERE ...

The original Macs, when faced with an empty Scrapbook, provided a much more whimsical notice than the current "Empty Scrapbook" statement: It used to say "This Space for Rent."

The pictures, too, have changed over time. If you know what I mean when I mention the Robot and the Fish, you've been around a long time, too.

I wanted to include the Robot and the Fish here for posterity, and was very surprised when I looked through a CD of old systems—starting with versions .1 and .3, as a matter of fact—and didn't find either picture. But I dug up the first Mac book I ever wrote and sure enough, there they were. Hmm. After much puzzlement, I realized that the book, written about MacWrite and MacPaint on a 128K Mac with a single 400K drive, included pictures from the Scrapbook that was on the MacWrite/MacPaint disk. Yep, a 400K disk contained a System Folder, MacWrite, and MacPaint! So, I called my friend Andy Baird, author of *The Macintosh Dictionary*, and sure enough, he still had his original MacWrite/MacPaint disk, so here are the famous early pictures.

The Scrapbook has evolved slightly to keep up with the Mac's capabilities, being able to store color pictures and sounds. The pictures, too have evolved slightly. Here, for instance, are the original Party picture and the one that comes with the current Scrapbook; the newer one, although shown in gray here, is basically a pink hat with multicolor confetti.

But here's a picture that really shows how the Mac has advanced in its graphics capabilities. I searched BMUG's PD-ROM for a picture of the original robot, and this is what I found. I wish you could see it in color.

**⊶ If you have trouble renaming** the Scrapbook File, that's probably because the Scrapbook itself is open. The file's not usually locked—but you can check with Get Info. Finally, if nothing seems to work for renaming the file, use the Duplicate command to make a copy, rename the copy, and trash the original.

⋯➤ **The Scrapbook File's file type changed** in System 7, as did its icon. The file's icon used to be a miniature Mac, as were all the system files in the System Folder. (The icon of the Scrapbook itself wasn't an issue—the DA lived inside the System file, so you never saw it.)

But the icon change is merely cosmetic. The file type and creator code changes go a little deeper. (Creator and file types are covered in Chapter 21.) As a result of the change, sometimes you can't open an old Scrapbook file with the new Scrapbook. The old creator and file types are MACS and ZSYS; the new Scrapbook file has *scbk* as both its creator and file type. Changing the creator and file type of an old Scrapbook file with a file utility like DiskTools usually lets the System 7 Scrapbook open the file.

## Text & Graphics

∞➤ **Text that's pasted into the Scrapbook** shows up in 12-point Geneva no matter how it was formatted when you copied it. But even though you can't see the formats, most of them are stored in the Scrapbook. When you copy the page and paste it back into the same application it came from, you'll get all your formatting back. If you paste it someplace other than its point of origin, you *might* get the formatting—it depends on whether or not the receiving application understands those formats.

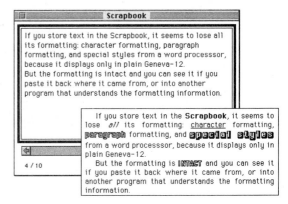

∞➤ **Bit-mapped and object-oriented images** in the Scrapbook are both identified as PICT images. The Scrapbook can store color and grayscale PICT images as well as black and white ones.

⋯➤ **The Scrapbook page can't be resized**, but you can paste a large picture into it. The whole image is stored even though only part of it is displayed. You'll get the whole picture back if you cut or copy the page and paste the image someplace.

⋯➤ **If you want to see the whole picture** that's on a Scrapbook page without having to paste it into a graphics program, copy it

The entire image is stored in the Scrapbook even when only part of it is displayed.

See Chapter 20 for more about bit-mapped and object graphics.

from the Scrapbook and then use the Show Clipboard command in the Finder's Edit menu. You can open the Clipboard window to the full size of the screen, if necessary, to see a large picture.

QuickTime is covered in Chapter 21.

••➤ **When you paste a QuickTime movie** into the Scrapbook, a single frame is displayed on the page. If you're using a special version of the Scrapbook (the one that came with the QuickTime Starter Kit), you'll even get the playback controls on the page with the movie, as shown at the right in this picture. But the standard Scrapbook stores the entire QuickTime movie even though it displays only the single frame.

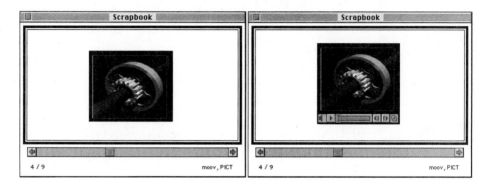

## Sound

∘••➤ **A page with a sound on it** gets a Play Sound button—which is a good thing, since that's the only way you'll be able to tell which sound is which. They all *look* alike, because each is simply a sound icon in the center of the page. (You'll see the same icon if you use a Show Clipboard command after you've cut or copied a sound from somewhere.)

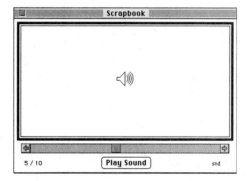

∘••➤ **How do you paste a sound** into the Scrapbook? Easy. Copy a sound to the Clipboard, then use the Paste command in the Scrapbook. Yeah, but where do you copy a sound *from?* That's a different story. Some programs handle sounds the same way they handle text or graphic objects, so you'll be able to select a sound and copy it to the Clipboard.

••➤ **Sounds get in and out of the Scrapbook** by copying and pasting. They get in and out of the system by their icons being dragged in and out of the System file. So, there doesn't seem to be any way to move sounds between the Scrapbook and System. Well, there isn't any *obvious* way, but that's what I'm here for—to find and share the subtleties of this machine.

You can use the Sound control panel to act as a transfer medium between the Scrapbook and the System file. With a sound on the Clipboard (from the Scrapbook), open the Sound control panel, and choose Paste. The pasted sound is added to the list of the system sounds.

To move a sound from the System file to the Scrapbook, you reverse the process: copy it from the list in the Sound control panel, and paste it into the Scrapbook.

**There's lots more about handling sounds in Chapter 2.**

➻ **You can turn a Scrapbook sound into** a stand-alone file by pasting it into the Sound control panel and then dragging it out of the System file.

## ⊁ FOR AUDIO CDS ⊁

### Playing CDs

➻ **If your Mac has a built-in CD-ROM drive,** it can play audio CDs—that's regular CDs, the kind you put in your stereo, not CD-ROMs, the kind made for computers. Although the later Macs have a surprising level of fidelity for playing CDs and other audios, it's certainly not as good as the CD player you probably already have for background music if you work at home or in a small office—unless, of course, you've beefed up your Mac system with special speakers. (But even the internal speaker is surprisingly good.)

Apple's first attempt at giving you control over audio CDs through the Mac gave us the CD Remote desk accessory; the second effort resulted in an application, AppleCD Audio Player. (I'm going to use the phrase CD controller as a generic reference to either of these items.)

➻ **You'll find your CD controller in the Apple menu,** whether it's CD Remote or AppleCD Audio Player—even though one's a DA and one's an application. During the system installation, each is placed in the Apple Menu Items folder on your drive.

CD Remote

AppleCD Audio Player

If neither controller is in your Apple menu, or anywhere on your hard drive (use the Finder's Find command to do a search), reinstall the CD software from the system CD (if your Mac came with one) or from a CD Setup disk (if that's what you have).

➻ **The CD controller can be kept anywhere** on your drive; it doesn't have to stay in the Apple Menu Items folder. You can even keep it in the Apple menu and also put an alias of it in any convenient spot.

➻ **Playing a CD in the background** isn't like performing a background task. The Mac manages background tasks, like copying files or downloading information from a remote source, by splitting its attention between whatever you're doing and what's going on in the background. As a result, overall operations slow down noticeably. But playing CD audio is not a background task: It's an independent operation that doesn't take up memory or time from your processor.

⋅⋅➤ **If you insert a data CD-ROM disc\*** in the drive when CD Remote is open, you'll get a subtle little notice over the time readout that there's no audio on the disc. In AppleCD Audio Player, the standard Audio CD popup menu is replaced by the title *Data CD*.

*\*"Disc" with a C is a compact disc. With a K, it's a floppy disk or hard drive. Picky, picky, picky.*

⋅⋅➤ **A data CD-ROM for the computer** might also have some audio tracks on it. But all the tracks—those with music and those with computer information—look alike. So if some tracks play and some don't, it's probably because there's no sound on some tracks.

⋅⋅➤ **When you insert an audio CD-ROM** in your Mac, you'll see an icon for each of the tracks on the CD. The CD itself is named based on how many CD's you've inserted since you turned on your Mac. You can't alter anything on the CD, but you can Get Info on any of the icons—and you'll get the playing time for the track.

A track icon's Info window shows its playing time.

An audio CD's window on the desktop.

The Apple documentation specifically states that you can't double-click on one of these track icons to play the music. Although that seems to hold true for most Mac models, I can double-click a track icon and get it to play on my Centris 650. (Which gives me the opportunity to use a quote from the eminently quotable Casey Stengel.)

CASEY STENGEL

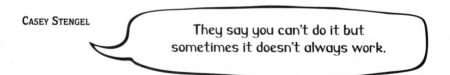

They say you can't do it but sometimes it doesn't always work.

⋅⋅➤ **You can record sound from a CD** directly into the Sound control panel, much the same way you use the microphone to record a sound. So, you can take any ten-second snippet of music and make it one of your system sounds: Just use the Sound control panel's Record button while the CD is playing. For Macs with built-in CD-ROM players, the sound is recorded directly—you don't have to use the microphone. In fact, using the microphone interferes with the direct recording.

But I did find a major glitch in this procedure with the CD Remote DA: If you record while you're using the Repeat button that lets you loop through a segment of music (the AB button), the sound resource that goes into the System file is reported in its Get Info window as being, oh, around 320 *megs!* I even had some files that said they were 570 megs and even over 4,000 megs! That's on a 230-meg hard disk, by the way, and inside a System file that reported its size as under a meg. I repeated this procedure on several different machines and the glitch showed up consistently. The really interesting part is that you can't get this resource out of your System file. Remember, when you drag something out of the System file, it's not *moved*, it's *copied*. Try dragging the weird file out of the System file into the Trash and you get a dialog telling you there's not enough room on the disk to copy the file. (Well, there's not enough room on the disk for the file to even exist in the first place, but that doesn't seem to bother it!) The trick here is to duplicate another sound resource and drag it out of the System file; rename it to match the weird sound, and then drag it back into the System file. You'll be asked if you want to replace the existing file; click OK (since there's no button that says *You bet I do!*) and the problem file is wiped out.

Using the Sound control panel is covered in Chapters 2 and 8.

Anyway, once the sound is in the System file, you can use it as a system beep. Or drag it out of the System file and put it in the Startup Items folder for a special startup sound.

••▶ **If an audio CD won't play** but you know your hardware is capable of it, you might be missing some of the extensions you need to work with CD Remote or AppleCD Audio Player. Reinstall your CD software from the CD Setup disk or from the system CD. You'll get a group of extensions in your Extensions folder: Audio CD Access, CD Remote Init, ISO 9600 Access, High Sierra File Access, and Foreign File Access.

••▶ **If an audio CD isn't playing on an** AV **Mac,** check the settings in the Sound control panel: Make sure the the built-in speaker is selected as the audio source.

••▶ **Installing AppleCD Audio Player** on your Mac with its Installer program erases CD Remote from your drive.

## Basic Functions

∞▶ **CD Remote has both a small and full version,** as shown here; you click in the zoom box to toggle between them. This DA's design was obviously influenced by the still-current style of black for high-tech stereo equipment. (Remember when brushed silver was the rage?) Anyway, except for this first picture, I'm going to use the magic of computer image editing to make it easier to see what's going on, by reversing the white-on-black approach.

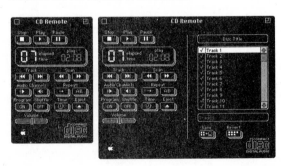

The small and full versions of CD Remote.

∞✦ **AppleCD Audio Player has both a small and a full version,** too. You toggle between them by clicking in the little arrow that's just beneath the Normal button. Once you're in the full version, you can use the scrollbar to go through the list of tracks, or you can use the size box to make the window larger so you can see all the tracks at once.

Esthetically speaking, the AppleCD Audio Player is way ahead of CD Remote, as you can see by these pictures—even if the basic playing buttons aren't labeled.

• • • • • • • • • • • • • • • • • • • • • • • • • • • • • • • • • • • • • • • • • • • • •
The small and full versions of AppleCD Audio Player (left), and the full version expanded for the entire track list (right).

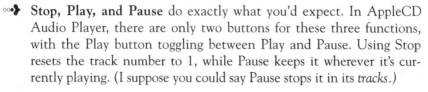

∞✦ **To start playing a CD** in your Mac, insert the CD, open the controller, and click the Play button. Or you can open the controller first and then insert the disc—the order doesn't matter, although it can take up to ten seconds or more for the controller to acknowledge the presence of an inserted disc. But whenever there's a CD in the drive, the controller will sense it—you don't have to "open" the CD, either on the desktop or from within the controller, to get it to play. You'll see the track number of the item that's playing and the elapsed play time displayed, just as you would on a digital readout on your stereo.*

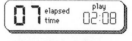

*Isn't that great? Your Mac's great graphics capability used to simulate a seven-segment LED display!

You don't have to keep the controller out while the music's playing—you can put it away until you need its controls.

∞✦ **Stop, Play, and Pause** do exactly what you'd expect. In AppleCD Audio Player, there are only two buttons for these three functions, with the Play button toggling between Play and Pause. Using Stop resets the track number to 1, while Pause keeps it wherever it's currently playing. (I suppose you could say Pause stops it in its *tracks*.)

∞✦ **The Track buttons** move you to the previous or next track.

•••➤ **Jump to a specific track** on the CD by using the Track menu in the AppleCD Audio Player. The popup menu is directly above the main play buttons, where it says *Audio CD*. When you're using a CD that you've identified before, the CD's title is displayed there, and the tracks are named by song titles instead of numbers.

•••➤ **The Scan buttons** let you fast forward (or backward) a track— and you can hear the track while it's moving. Keep the button pressed down for as long as you want to scan; when you release it, the scanning stops.

•••➤ **The Repeat button** controls whether the CD stops playing at the end of the last track or loops back to the beginning. (If you're playing a customized program, the Repeat button loops back to the beginning of the program.) Clicking on the button toggles you between the straight and the looped play, and the button icon changes to show you the current mode.

•••➤ **CD Remote's AB button** is a special repeat button that lets you "grab" part of the CD and repeat it—you can make it sound like a broken record if you want. First, you click the AB button: it turns into an A button and waits to mark the beginning of the segment you want repeated. Click the A button to mark the beginning of the passage you want repeated; the button turns into a B. Click the B button to mark the end of the passage. Then you have a button that shows A and B with a cycle symbol between them; as long as this button's showing, the segment is continually repeated. Click this special button to turn the repeat off and go back to the original AB button.

No matter how many times I do this, it just doesn't feel right. I want to click the first button to mark the start of the segment; and, when I see the A-cycle-B button, I want to click it to turn the repeat *on*, not *off*.

## Other Short-Version Functions

•••➤ **Adjust the volume of the CD** by using the slider control. This adjustment is independent of the setting in the Sound control panel. (Doesn't the CD Remote control look positively clunky next to the one from the AppleCD Audio Player?)

## AD HOC #1 AND #2

If there were awards for terrible grammar and spelling in computer ads, here are two that would be vying for first place:

A 1988 ad in the back of *MacUser*, even allowing for what was supposed to be partly a takeoff on the syntax of the HyperTalk programming language, surely couldn't have garnered too many clients for the promotional company that placed the ad. Here it is, with spacing and punctuation (or lack thereof) exactly as printed:

> Before you think of selling, linking up, or licensing away, any
> of your valuable stackware creations
> Aim, your stacks at our card. You'll find us, in the "Business
> Opportunities" stack, this folder.

Then there's the one that was doubly ridiculous because it was in the back pages of *MacWeek* magazine and the advertiser was *MacUser* magazine. They were looking for—oh, never mind what they were looking for; a single phrase from the ad is enough for the laugh:

> ... on the McIntosh ...

∞▸ **The Eject button**—well, you can guess what that's for. But remember you can also eject the CD the same way you eject any other disk: Drag it to the Trash, or use the Put Away command at the desktop. You don't have to turn off the music before you eject the disc.

∞▸ **The controller plays selections in one of three modes:** Normal, Shuffle, or Program.

- The Normal mode plays the CD tracks from first through last.
- The Shuffle mode plays the tracks in random order. Each time you click the Shuffle button, the order is randomized again.
- The Program mode plays the tracks in the order that you specify.

CD Remote provides only two buttons for the three functions because turning the Program button to Off automatically invokes the Normal mode; the Shuffle button also toggles between On and Off.

The AppleCD Audio Player provides one button for each mode; "LCD lights" over the buttons indicate which one is active.

∞▸ **Both controllers can tell you the elapsed time** and the time remaining on the current track; the AppleCD Audio Player can also report the elapsed time and time remaining for the entire disc. In CD Remote, click on the Time button to toggle between elapsed time and time remaining. In the AppleCD Audio Player, click on the little clock in the track and time readout area. You'll get a menu that lets you choose from among the four time reports.

•••➔ **Control the left and right audio channels** with the Audio Channels buttons in CD Remote or with menu commands in the AppleCD Audio Player.

In CD Remote, click on a button to turn a channel off; click it again to turn it on. The buttons reflect the current state of the channel—the icons show speakers with or without sound coming out of them. You can't turn both channels off—if one is off and you click to turn the other one off, the first comes back on.

In the AppleCD Audio Player, use the commands in the Sound submenu to control which channel is playing.

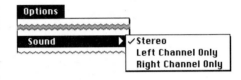

There's a difference between *audio channels* and *speakers*—at least when you're dealing with a single-speaker system like the Mac's built-in speaker. You can still turn either audio channel off even though you have a single speaker—the channel is really the music coming from the disc, not the music going to a speaker.

## CD Remote

∞➔ **In CD Remote's full version,** a panel opens to the right of the main controls. There's a list of numbered tracks in the panel, an area for the CD's title, and Save and Revert icons. If there are more than 11 tracks, there's a scroll bar in the list.

∞➔ **Play a specific track** by double-clicking on its name in the list. (If you double-click on the checkmark in front of the name, you'll merely check and uncheck it; you have to double-click on the name to jump to that track.)

∞➔ **Identify the CD** by putting its name (its real name or anything you want, like *My Favorite CD)* in the area above the track list. Name the tracks on the CD by selecting each one in turn and editing it in the area beneath the list.

The right panel of CD Remote, before and after entering the CD information.

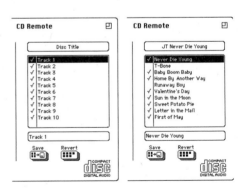

You can move from the CD name to the track name by pressing the Tab key. In black and white, it's easy to see that one or the other field is selected; in grayscale or color, though, it's almost impossible to see that the letters are selected—the inside of the name areas remains black and the letters turn gray instead of white.

Naming tracks one after the other can be done quickly: once you select and rename one, the Return key both enters the name in the list and selects the name beneath it so you can name that one—you don't have to work with the mouse.

When you reinsert an identified CD at another time, CD Remote displays its name and play list.

∘•❥ **Selecting an item in the list** with a single click (when you're going to change its name, for instance) doesn't make it play.

∘•❥ **Create your own play list** that includes only the tracks you want to hear, in the order you want to hear them:

- Click on the checkmark in front of a track title (not on the track title itself) to alternately check and uncheck the item; checked tracks are included in the play list.
- Change the play order of the tracks by holding down the Command key and dragging a track (either by its title or checkmark) into its new position.

∘•❥ **No matter where you drag a track** in the list, it retains its original track number; when it's playing, the track number is displayed. This picture shows what happens when you double-click on the third item in the play list: It's selected as a result of the clicking, and it's playing—but the indicator at the left reports that track 8 is playing because that's the song's actual track number.

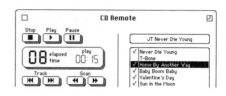

∘•❥ **Save the play list** if you're going to close CD Remote. Click the Save button or just close CD Remote (with the Close box, or with the Close or Quit command) and then click the OK button in the dialog that appears asking if you want to save the play list. Use the Revert button if you've edited the play list but you want to change it back to the last program that you saved.

∘•❥ **To use the play list,** click the Program button to ON. You can click the Program button back to OFF to play all the tracks, in order, without affecting the play list. You can even turn the program on and off with CD Remote in its smaller version—you don't have to display the play list.

•••❥ **Nothing is saved to the CD itself.** The play list information is stored in a file named *CD Remote Programs* in your Preferences folder inside the System Folder. CD Remote does read some specific information from an audio CD to be able to identify it the next time it's inserted, but nothing can be written to the CD.

•••❥ **Click on the Compact Disc** logo at the bottom of CD Remote to see who wrote the DA.

## The AppleCD Audio Player

∘∘❥ **In the AppleCD Audio Player full version,** the panel beneath the main controls lists the tracks and their running times. If the window isn't opened all the way, there's a scroll bar for scrolling through the track list.

∞→ **Play a specific track** by double-clicking on the track number in front of the track's title. (If you double-click on the title itself, you'll just select a word in the title for editing.)

∞→ **Identify the CD** by typing its name (its real name or one that you like better—you could, for instance, give a better title to the Beatles' White Album). Identify each of the tracks, too, by typing their names in the appropriate spots. You can use Tab or Return to move from the CD title to the first track, and from one track to the next; use Shift-Tab or Shift-Return to move up in the list. When you reinsert an identified CD at another time, its name and play list will be displayed.

The play list before and after identifying the tracks.

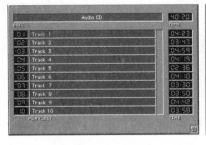

∞→ **Selecting an item in the list** with a single click (when you're going to change its name, for instance) doesn't make it play.

∞→ **Create your own play list** that includes only the tracks you want to hear, in the order you want to hear them:

Dragging an item from the track list to the play list.

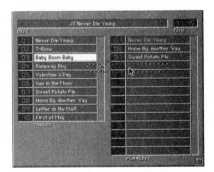

- Click the Program button. The bottom panel changes to show two lists: one for the way the CD is set up, and one for your own play list.
- To put something in the play list, just drag it from the list on the left and let it go anywhere within the left column; a copy of that title will go into the first available slot.
- Change a track's position in the play list by dragging it up or down into a new position; the other items in the list automatically move to accommodate the change.

The play list is automatically saved; you don't have to do anything. The next time the disc is inserted, AppleCD Audio Player displays the correct information.

∞→ **The commands in the Edit menu** apply only to the disc and track titles. You can cut, copy, paste, and select text; the commands won't do anything with the music on the CD.

→ **If the total time of a play list** is more than 99 minutes and 59 seconds, the time is reported as 99.99 in the display because that's the highest number AppleCD Audio Player is capable of displaying in those charming little LED-style digits.

⋯▶ **Nothing is saved to the CD itself.** The information in the play list is stored in a file named *AppleCD Audio Player Prefs* in the Preferences folder inside the System Folder. The application reads some information from the CD the next time it's inserted and matches it with information stored in the prefs file in order to identify the CD.

⋯▶ **If you have more than one CD-ROM drive** attached to your Mac, use the Startup CD Drive command to indicate which one the AppleCD Audio Player should be reading; drives are listed in a submenu according to SCSI ID number.

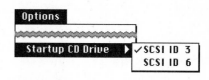

⋯▶ **Customize the AppleCD Audio Player** by using the Window Color and Indicator Color commands in its options menu.

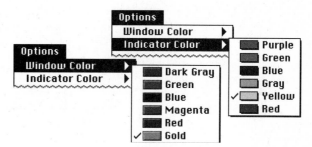

⋯▶ **The Open command** in the File menu only lets you open a track from an inserted CD. It's a convoluted way of selecting a specific track (since it's so much easier to do it from the Player's window); the command has nothing to do with opening a play list.

⋯▶ **There are keyboard shortcuts for** many of the AppleCD Audio Player controls:

- Click the Play/Pause button with the spacebar or the Enter key.
- Click the Stop button by pressing the Delete or Clear key.
- Change the volume with the Up and Down arrow keys.
- Move from one track to the next or previous one with the Left and Right arrows.
- Eject the disc with Command-E.

## ⊶ THE OTHER DESK ACCESSORIES ⊷

### Alarm Clock

∞▶ **Toggle the Alarm Clock** between the "time bar" and the full version by clicking on the handle in the right corner. (You don't have to drag the handle into position, the way I tried to every time I used it way back in 1984.)

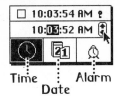

Time  Date  Alarm

You can also set the time and date from the General Controls control panel. See Chapter 8.

∘•➤ **Set the time or date** of the Mac's internal clock by clicking on the appropriate icon at the bottom of the full window and editing the numbers. The changes take effect as soon as you click on another icon at the bottom or when you put the Alarm Clock away.

∘•➤ **To set the alarm,** open the Alarm Clock to the full version and click on the alarm clock icon in the bottom-right corner. Click on the numbers in the central editing area and use the little arrows to change them; the arrows also change the AM to PM (and back) if you click on the letters first. Then—and this is the important part—click on the switch at the left of the numbers. The alarm is activated when the switch is in the *up* position. You'll know it's on because the alarm clock icon changes to show a ringing alarm.

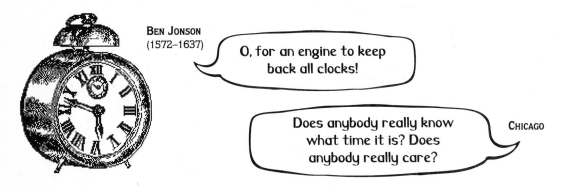

BEN JONSON (1572–1637)

O, for an engine to keep back all clocks!

Does anybody really know what time it is? Does anybody really care?

CHICAGO

∘•➤ **When the Alarm Clock "rings,"** you'll hear a beep and the Apple menu's icon will flash alternately with an Alarm Clock icon. The flashing continues, and is guaranteed to drive you nuts, until you turn off the alarm. (At least they finally made the menu flash with the alarm icon. The little apple used to just blink on and off, giving no clue as to why. Thousands of users were stymied by this flashing but finally learned to live with it, assuming it was a normal, if inexplicable, Mac function.)

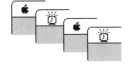

The alarm rings whether or not the Alarm Clock is open, so you don't have to leave the DA hanging around on the screen. To turn off the alarm, all you have to do is open the Alarm Clock—or, if you left it open, just click on it to activate it. You don't have to flip down the little handle that you used to set the alarm; just taking out the desk accessory stops the blinking in the menu bar. But that does leave the alarm still set to go off the same time the next day.

**If the computer is off** when the alarm time comes and goes, the alarm still "rings." Sort of. (It's a little like a tree falling in the forest when there's no one around.) You'll find the Alarm Clock icon flashing in the Apple menu when you start up the computer.

**Set the time, date, or alarm by typing.** You have to select the icon at the bottom of the window by clicking on it, but you can use the keyboard from then on. Hit Tab to select the first group of numbers and to move between them; Shift-Tab moves you backwards. The Right and Left arrow keys also move you from one block to another, while the Up and Down keys change the numbers (although typing the numbers is easier). Typing an A or P works for setting AM and PM—you don't have to type the M.

**You can leave the Alarm Clock out** on your screen, strategically positioned so it's easy to see while you're working in other windows. You'll always have a readout of the current time because the Alarm Clock is updated even when it's not the active window.

**If you want the Alarm Clock out all the time**, put it, or its alias, into the Startup Items folder in the System Folder. It will open automatically every time you start the computer, and go to the same spot that you left it in the last time you used it.

**You can copy the time and date** from the Alarm Clock: just use the Copy command while the Alarm Clock is active—you don't have to select anything first. You'll get something like this when you paste into an application: *6:20:10 AM 11/28/94.*

**To keep track of the time**, you don't need the Alarm Clock hanging around on the screen. There are many replacements available—and they're all improvements (although they're not all desk accessories).

- Wee Clock, for instance, is an application that puts a tiny time bar in the upper-right corner of your screen. You can choose to have the seconds displayed or not, and include the date or not. [freeware]

System 7.5 includes a menu bar clock. See Chapter 2.

- I'd say that SuperClock is ubiquitous, but that sounds like an insult. It's been around a long time and is a perfect little control panel. It puts the time right in the menu bar. You can choose the font and size, whether or not seconds are displayed, and lots more. (I'll just put a picture of one of its dialog boxes here so you can get the idea.) It lets you set alarms similar to the Alarm Clock, but can also chime on the hour for you. [freeware, Steve Christensen]

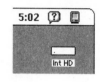

- General utility packages often include a menu bar clock. ClickChange provides all sorts of interface alterations and includes a menu bar clock that offers a wide variety of options. [Dubl-Click]

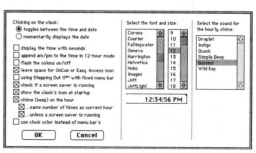

- What good is a clock you can't see? Invisible Clock states the time out loud at any interval you set. [freeware, Chris Holmes]*

- There are dozens of clock replacements available in public domain software, though not all of them ring alarms. You want digital? Analog? Roman numerals? How about Big Ben, or Albert Einstein to remind you of the relativeness of it all?

There's a little of everything out there. For instance—the Backwards Clock. It does exactly what it sounds like. (You can find real-world equivalents, by the way, in the same catalogs that offer signs for your backyard pool that say: *Our ool. Notice there's no P in it. Keep it that way.*) Burbank shows four clocks and time zones at a time, with nighttime clocks dimmed (of course); it includes an alarm and hourly chimes. Alarmist is a small, simple analog clock with a choice of a dozen faces (four of them are shown here); you can set up to 15 alarms with accompanying messages. [Backwards Clock, freeware, Kevin A. Beers; Burbank, freeware, Kelly Burgess; Alarmist, shareware, Jon Gary]

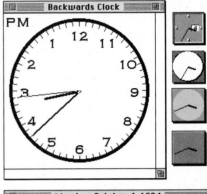

Monday, October 4, 1994

Burbank   Placid Lake   New York   Paris

## POP QUIZ                                    [5 POINTS]

The Burbank clock DA was inspired by a famous TV show—note that the time on the Burbank clock is out of sync with the others. So, what was the TV show? (Sock it to me.)

∞⧉ **To make sure you're setting the correct time,** try AutoClock. It sets your Mac's internal clock to the right time according to the atomic clock that even governments around the world agree is right. You need a modem, because running this little utility makes it call a special number that feeds it the information.

∞⧉ **For real reminders** about meetings, lunch dates, and quitting time, forget the Alarm Clock's little beep. Instead, get a calendar/appointment utility.

- Alarming Events rings an alarm when a scheduled event is due—although you could also use it schedule any alarming event you have coming up. Of course, it actually does more than ring an alarm—it pops up a dialog box for you, too, if that's what you prefer. [PrairieSoft]

- Now Up-To-Date is a full-blown calendar and appointment utility. Once you have your information entered, you can have the Mac remind you—with a dialog box that pops up on the screen—that your meeting is in 15 minutes, or you have one day left to prepare that report. And, because you're not always with your Mac, Alarming Events lets you print your calendar and appointments, too. [Now Software]

- IN Control is a "To-Do List Manager"—a combination To-Do/Calendar utility that's a really terrific piece of design and programming. It's basically a database. No, it's basically an outliner. Well, it's an outliner that uses columns—and any item with a date on it is automatically entered into an appointment calendar. You can sort and reorganize, prioritize, and, my favorite—check things off. (It's so much more satisfying when you have a list of checked boxes showing how much you've accomplished instead of *erasing* what you've done.) [Attain Corporation]

◦◦◊ **For dates instead of times**—when you don't need an alarm ringing, but you still want to keep track of your schedule, or just want to know what day the Fourth of July falls on—there are plenty of calendars out there.

- MacPak's Calendar is simple and straightforward; I've used it in its various incarnations on the Mac for almost as long as I can remember. It simply shows a month at a time with a notes area for each day; any day with a checkmark has notes attached to it. It's easy to move around in, has a Find function, and you can print from it. [MacPak, Fifth Generation Systems]

- For a little humor injected in your day, try the Gary Larson or Cathy cartoon-a-day approach—their calendars even include some animation. These are both terrific; I've had a picture of Gary Larson's "Boneless Chicken Farm" hanging around (on a wall) for years; Cathy's "The Worst of Both Worlds" (a working woman with a pile of laundry on one side and a pile of memos on the other) also adorned my office wall for a very long time. Having them on the computer is pretty neat. Here's a shot of the year-at-a-glance calendar; as you can see by the icons along the bottom of the calendar, you can view your schedule by the day, week, month, or year. [Amaze Computer Calendar, Delrina]

• When it comes to keeping track of even the simplest appointments or schedule, the Calendar from Seventh Heaven package isn't much help—but it has better-looking pictures in it than most wall calendars, so if all you need to know is what dates fall on what days, it might work for you. [Logical Solutions]

## Battery

∞ **The Battery DA is for PowerBooks.** It displays a gauge that purports to show the charge state of your battery and, in its full version, provides a Sleep button. (That odd little icon in the Sleep button is the late, unlamented Macintosh Portable.) You toggle between the short and full versions by clicking on the little handle in its right corner—it's just like the one in the Alarm Clock.

The short and full versions of the battery DA.

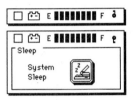

There's more about the Battery DA in Chapter 22.

∞ **The gauge bars change** from black to white as the battery loses its power. But the bars don't stand for any particular unit of time (like 15 minutes per bar), and they don't turn white in a steady manner. And, in fact, when they're all black, that doesn't necessarily mean that the battery's fully charged either.

∞ **A lightning bolt in the battery icon** in the Battery DA window usually means that the PowerBook is plugged in.

∞ **Put the PowerBook to sleep** by clicking in the Sleep button in the full version of the DA or by option-clicking on the little battery icon in the short version.

## Calculator

∞ **Click on the Calculator's keys** to enter numbers. The asterisk (*) is for multiplication and the slash (/) for division. The C is the Clear key, and it enters a zero into the number readout.

∞ **You can type numbers** into the Calculator using the numbers at the top of your keyboard or the ones on the numeric keypad. Both the equals sign on the keyboard and Enter key are the same as the Calculator's equals key.

∞ **To copy an answer from the Calculator,** just choose the Copy command from the Edit menu. You don't have to (in fact, you *can't*) select the numbers first.

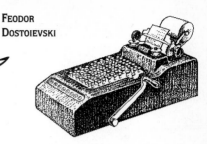

I admit that twice two makes four is an excellent thing, but if we are to give everything its due, twice two makes five is sometimes a very charming thing too.

FEODOR DOSTOIEVSKI

•••▸ **You can paste a number**, or even a problem (like 1024*9/.5) into the Calculator. Copy the numbers to the Clipboard from whatever application you're working in, open the Calculator, and choose Paste from the Edit menu. You'll see the numbers flashing on the Calculator as the keys are "pressed" and the answer appears in the readout.

If you try to paste in any special functions or operations that the Calculator can't handle, they'll just be ignored. Parentheses are ignored, too, so something like *3\*(10+2)* comes out as 32, not 36, since the operations are performed strictly left to right.

•••▸ **For any calculation involving more** than two or three short numbers, first type the calculation someplace and then paste it into the Calculator. This accomplishes two purposes: you can double-check the list of numbers you've entered if the answer seems off to you, and you can avoid having to retype the calculation from the beginning if you make a mistake during the number entry. If you don't have any text-processing program open, you can use the Note Pad to store the calculation.

•••▸ **The Calculator has two special spots** in its lower left and right corners that you can use to drag the Calculator around. There's one pixel in each bottom corner, right along the curve of the Calculator's edge, that are "draggable," although they're so hard to catch, you should stick to the title bar.

•∞◊▸ **There are several calculator DAs** out there in the public domain, as freeware or shareware. Here are some examples:

• **Calc+** has some unique properties—and a few problems. On the plus side (Calc+, *plus side*, get it?), it zooms down into an icon-sized tile you can leave hanging around on your screen; it turns into a graphics calculator, instantly converting inches to centimeters to picas to ciceros (that's another one of those things that if you don't know what it is, you don't need it!); you can slide the "paper tape" back and forth to see what you've done; and, it has printing functions. The main "minus" to the accessory is that you can't click on keys for the numbers—you have to type them in. And, some keyboard keys don't work as expected: when you type the equals key, for instance, it enters a percentage symbol. Minor complaints are the lack of a scroll bar for the paper tape area (you use the keyboard's arrow keys or drag the printout area with the mouse cursor) and the fact that the DA is, well … let's just say it's not esthetically pleasing. See what I mean? [Abbott Systems]

- **One of my favorite utility packages,** MacPak, includes two calculators which I don't need, but you might: Sci Calc and RPN. If you don't know what a scientific calculator is for, and you don't know or care what Reverse Polish Notation means (it *does* sound like an ethnic joke, doesn't it?), you don't need them any more than I do! [Fifth Generation Systems]

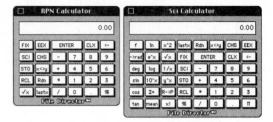

- **If you can't find just the calculator you need,** make one! The Calculator Construction Set is a terrific build-it-yourself utility. You create a window, drag keys around, decide on options like a paper-tape readout, and voilà—the calculator of your dreams! In fact, you can create calculators you never even dreamt of, since the "kit" includes functions for dates and times. The Construction Set creates stand-alone calculator DAs that you can use or freely give away for others to use. Some of the calculators that come as samples with the construction set are shown here. (The Good Time Charlie calculator has a read-out of different time zones!) [Dubl-Click]

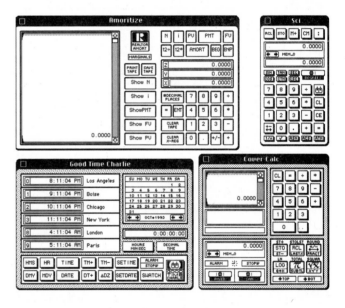

## Chooser

∞⊁ **The Chooser's basic purpose** in life is to let you choose your Mac's connections and how it interacts with its peripherals: printers, file servers, and fax modems. More than anything else, it's used for printer control—not only to choose a printer (if you have more than one) but also to turn "background printing" on and off (if your printer's capable of it).

∞⊁ **To choose something** in the Chooser, you click on an icon in the left panel and then choose from among the options in the right panel.

If you click on the LaserWriter icon, for example, you'll see a list of LaserWriters available on your network. For most people, that means one LaserWriter is listed, and automatically selected, as shown at the top of the picture here. If you're using an ImageWriter or StyleWriter, you click on its icon and get a choice of output ports in the right panel, as shown in the center of the picture. If you click on the AppleShare icon, you can choose from a list of file servers or shared volumes—the bottom of the picture here shows a simple network that lets a desk machine talk to a connected PowerBook.

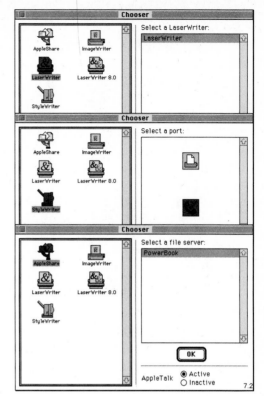

There's more about the Chooser and networks in Chapter 21.

∞•➤ **The Chooser is missing an OK button.** Just select your options and they'll be instantly activated, whether you leave the window open or close it. This seems to go against the standard interface, doesn't it? Doesn't it *feel* like you should have an OK button there?

But you don't have to reach for the mouse: Command-Q or Command-W closes the Chooser.

The Chooser also controls background printing. See Chapter 12.

∞•➤ **The icons that appear in the Chooser** are the ones you have in your Extensions folder inside the System Folder. Don't expect the LaserWriter icon to show up in Chooser just because you have a printer attached to your computer—you need the LaserWriter extension, or *printer driver*, in your Extensions folder, too.*

✳Don't you think there ought to be a Chooser folder inside the System Folder instead of mixing these things in with the extensions?

•••➤ **A LaserWriter won't show up in the Chooser's list** unless it's warmed up in addition to being turned on. If you open the Chooser before the printer's ready, wait a minute until the printer revs up, and its name will appear in the list.

•••➤ **The AppleTalk buttons** in the Chooser let you turn AppleTalk (Apple's networking protocol) on and off. Many networks need AppleTalk on—and sometimes a single LaserWriter connected to your computer is a network. (Check the manual that came with your printer to see if you need AppleTalk on.)

•••➤ **There's no User Name** entered in the Chooser now, as there was under System 6. Instead, you enter the *Owner Name* in the Sharing Setup Control panel. Chapter 21 covers this in more detail.

•••➤ **You can select Chooser items from the keyboard.** Use the Tab key to alternately activate each panel—the one with the extra frame around it is the active one. Then, select something in the panel by typing enough of its name for it to be identified, or use the arrow keys to select the "next" item. This picture shows what happens when I connect all the computers in the house into a network. I can press the letter A to select the AppleShare icon on the left, then press Tab to activate the list at right. Then I can press a single key to select the item in the list that I want to connect to.

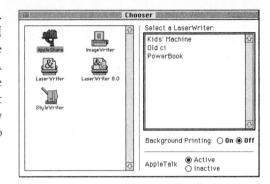

![ ]

## BY THE WAY ...

*Having a desk accessory immediately available sure is convenient. But even simply choosing it from the Apple menu sometimes seems a waste of precious time, what with reaching for the mouse when my fingers are on the keyboard. So I use a macro that calls up the DAs I use the most at the press of a key. This somewhat jaded view of "convenience" got me to thinking ...*

The first home computer, the Altair, came without many things, one of them being a keyboard. (Also among the missing: a monitor, and any storage device.) To enter information, you had to flip switches to send a stream of binary numbers into the processor. But it wasn't just data you had to enter this way—there were no programs around, either. So, if you wanted to, say, add 2+12, you couldn't just enter 10 for the two and 1100 for the twelve, even if you knew those were the binary equivalents. First, you'd have to enter the program that would know what to do with those numbers.

Imagine having to enter the equivalent of the Calculator DA into a computer. The Calculator is a compact little program, under 7K in all—about 7,000 bytes, which adds up to 56,000 bits of information. Since each flip of a switch entered one bit of information, that's how many times you'd have to flip switches; at one second per flip, it would take you nearly 16 hours of flipping before you could enter the two numbers you wanted to add.

By the same calculations, Microsoft Word 5.0's complete setup with all its support files would take around 45 million flips, or about a year and a half of constant effort—with no naps or coffee breaks.

And neither of these extrapolations takes into account the fact that both programs use information in the Mac's operating system—both the System Folder and the ROM—in order to work. Add another year or so for flipping *those* switches!

•••▶ **The newest LaserWriter driver** as of this writing is version 8.0 (well, actually, its descendant, 8.1.2), despite the fact it's for System 7. It changes the look of the Chooser a little bit, since it provides an extra button for printer setup. There's more about this in Chapter 12.

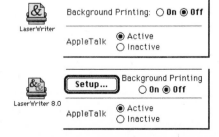

## Key Caps

⊶➤ **Key Caps lets you see** what characters are generated by different key combinations in any font. Select a font from the Key Caps menu to display it in the DA's keyboard. Pressing the Shift or Option key (or both) on the keyboard shows the characters you'll get if you type with those modifier keys held down. It's great for finding where those handy symbols like ¢, ™, and © are stored. The picture here shows how Key Caps look for the Chicago font with no modifier keys down, then with Shift, Option, and both Shift and Option pressed.

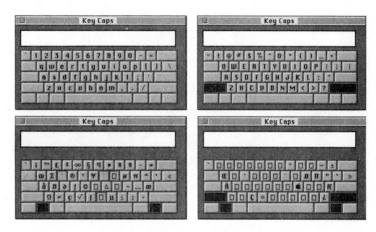

You can put characters into the Key Caps display area either by typing from the keyboard or by clicking on the Key Caps keys. But to press the Shift or Option key, you have to use the keyboard—then you can either type or click the character that goes with the modifier key.

⊶➤ **Use the Key Caps menu** to select the font you want to see in Key Caps. All the fonts that appear in your Font menus will appear in the Key Caps menu. (This wasn't always the case. The original Key Caps had no menu and displayed only the Chicago font. The menu was added in 1986, with the release of the Mac Plus.)

> **Key Caps**
> ✓Chicago
> Courier
> Geneva
> Helvetica
> Monaco
> New York
> Palatino
> Symbol
> Times
> Zapf Dingbats

⊶➤ **A rectangle in a Key Caps key** means there's no character for that key in the font you've chosen—at least not in the 12-point version that Key Caps uses for its display. (In the Key Caps picture, you can see a few where the Option key is pressed and lots where Shift-Option is pressed.) Some fonts have a character for every key combination, while others don't have much beyond the standard upper and lowercase letters.

⊶➤ **Key Caps doesn't remember** what you typed in it the last time you used it, even if you haven't shut off the computer since the previous use—unlike the Calculator, which stores the last number it displayed during a work session. Every time you take out Key Caps, its display area is blank.

•◦➔ **There's not much reason to paste into Key Caps,** but you can. The text appears in the display area—or at least as much of the text as can show on the one line.

•◦➔ **You can copy text from** the Key Caps window, and there's even a good reason to: once you've found, say, just the right Zapf Dingbats character, you may want to copy it so you can paste it into a document instead of trying to remember its key position so you can type it into the document.

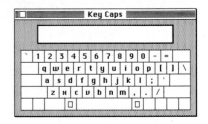

To copy something from Key Caps, first drag across the characters to select them. (This is in contrast to the Calculator where displayed numbers don't have to be selected in order to be copied.)

•◦➔ **Key Caps is smart.** It knows which keyboard you're using and matches its screen display to your actual keyboard. I've been faking the Key Caps pictures so far—it really comes up on my system showing all the function keys, the numeric keypad, and the keys in between, like the picture here.

If I take Key Caps out on my PowerBook, it looks like the smaller picture here (and it's in black and white), since that's the keyboard on my system.

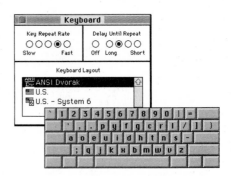

•◦➔ **Key Caps is keyed** (so to speak) to the keyboard resource you've selected in the Keyboard control panel. If you've installed any special keyboard resources and choose them in the control panel, the altered layout will show in Key Caps. With a Dvorak keyboard chosen, for instance, the new letter arrangements are displayed.

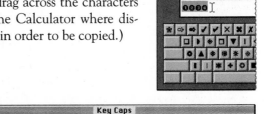

There's more about the Keyboard control panel in Chapter 8; the Dvorak layout is covered in Chapter 20.

•◦➔ **You can't print from Key Caps,** but that's just as well. Why would you want a printout of a keyboard with a gray background that makes letters, especially ones less bold than

Chicago, so hard to read? Instead, use a word processor to type each character, matching its position in the document to its position on the keyboard. Make one pass each for the plain, shifted, option, and shift-option characters; format it for the font(s) you want and print that out.

MAC TOON

HACKER™          by Vadun

Well, what new goodies did we get for Xmas ??? ☐ lots ☐ some ☐ none

Here's a new programming disk from Uncle Al ... a graphics disk from Mom ... and a hockey puck from Dad!!!

Whirrrrrrr Click

???

A hockey puck???

Well, you did tell him you wanted a hard disk!

—from the BMUG PD-ROM

···▶ **Key Caps works in the background.** If you size a document window so you can still see the Key Caps window, you'll see each letter you type highlighted on the Key Caps keyboard even while you're typing in the document window. So what? So if you're occasionally working with a symbol or picture font throughout your document, and you don't know where the characters that you need are, you can set Key Caps to that font and work in your document. Then, when you need a special character, you can glance at the Key Caps window to see where it is. If you hold the Shift key, the Key Caps display shows the shifted characters; pressing Option shows the option characters. In fact, the series of keystrokes you need for the special accented characters will be displayed in Key Caps even as you type in your document.

Keeping Key Caps open, though, can slow down your Mac, since it splits its attention between your current application and Key Caps, running back to Key Caps for a split second every time you press a key on the keyboard.

···▶ **You can see the special accented characters** in a font with a series of keystrokes in Key Caps. First, press the Option key. You'll see five keys—the first one in the first row, three in the second row, and one in the bottom row—framed in a dotted border instead of with the shades that make the keys look three-dimensional. These are the keys you use to put accents over letters. They're sometimes referred to as the *dead keys*: If you type them, nothing happens until you type another key—at which point you get an accented character. But certain accents can go only over certain letters, and that's where Key Caps can help. Press the Option key and click in any one of the framed keys. The Key Caps display changes to show what letters can be typed next with that accent mark—they're framed in black.

The pictures here show, at the top, what the Key Caps keyboard looks like when you press the Option key. The middle picture shows how it looks after you've pressed the grave accent in the upper left of the keyboard and then released the Option key. The bottom picture shows the display after holding Option and clicking the N key in the bottom row.

For more about accented characters, see Chapter 20.

•••▶ **Don't forget that the Control key** produces some characters in a few fonts (notably Chicago) and you can use Key Caps to check where they are. Not only can you find these characters in Key Caps, but Key Caps is often the only way you can use them. Some word processors let you type a character with the Control key, but few other programs allow it—even the Finder won't let you. If you want a special character in one of those programs, you can type it in Key Caps and then copy it and paste it into your program. The paste will be done in the application's current font, not in the font you're using in Key Caps, so you'll have to select the pasted character and change its font.

ASCII codes are covered in Chapter 20.

∞⟩ **Big Caps** is included with all of Dubl-Click Software's font packages, and it's a terrific replacement for Key Caps. The Big Caps window is resizeable, and you can change not only the font on its display, but also the font size (that alone is reason enough to switch). Big Caps also lets you access characters by their ASCII codes.

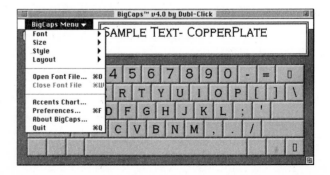

**⊶➤ If a key on your keyboard breaks**, or if the entire keyboard breaks down, you can use Key Caps to laboriously type in what you need—as long as you need only lowercase letters. Open Key Caps, click out the text you need, copy it, and then paste it where it's needed.

You wouldn't want to type an essay this way, but it works in a pinch. In fact, in the time between sending this chapter off to my tech editor and the time it came back, my PowerBook keyboard lost a few of its keys—*H* and *I* among them. (Not "lost" as in fell off—there was a problem on the motherboard that kept the keys from registering.) I had to use this copy-from-Key Caps procedure (which until then was strictly theoretical) to name a few backup files before I sent the PowerBook off for repair.

**⊶◊➤ PopChar** is a Key Caps substitute. (And it's *char* as in the first syllable of *character*, not *char* as in *chart*, as one person in my user group insists on pronouncing it despite many gentle, polite hints from the rest of us.) It's a control panel that puts a little symbol up in the menu bar that you can press to get a popup chart of the font you're currently using. All you do is drag to the character you want and let go, and it gets typed into your document. There's also a way to type more than one character at a time before the window closes, if that's what you need.

I haven't found PopChar to be the most stable of software under many different conditions, but lots of people I know swear by it. I'm just glad that Word, the program I use for my writing, provides a Symbol window that displays all the characters of a font any time I need them typed in. [freeware, Günther Blaschek]

Word's Symbol window.

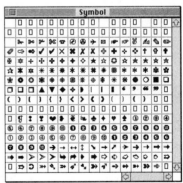

PopChar's window.

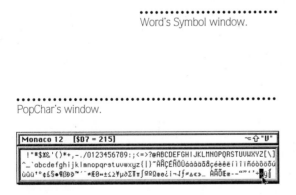

## Note Pad

**⊶➤ The Note Pad provides eight pages** for you to enter miscellaneous notes. There's not a lot of room on each page, and there's no way to change the size or style of the text, but, hey, it's free.

**⊶➤ Basic text editing techniques work** in the Note Pad, so you can double-click to select a word, drag to select text, and use arrow keys to move the insertion point around.

There's a new Note Pad in System 7.5. See the end of this chapter.

∘•➤ **Turn to the next Note Pad page** by clicking in the upturned corner of the current page. Click in the exposed corner of the next page to flip back to the previous page. (That doesn't make much sense logically, but once you do it a few times it comes naturally.) The Note Pad pages cycle around, so you can turn from page 8 back to page 1 or, if you're moving backwards, you can go from page 1 to page 8.

```
┌─────────────────────────────────┐
│ ▦        Note Pad             ▦ │
├─────────────────────────────────┤
│ You have eight pages to type on │
│ in the Note Pad.                │
│                                 │
│                                 │
│                                 │
│                                 │
│                                 │
│ ◣                          1    │
└─────────────────────────────────┘
```

∘•➤ **The Note Pad information is stored** in a file cleverly named *Note Pad File* in your System Folder. You never have to open the file or save information into it; that's all done automatically. If there's no Note Pad File available when you open the Note Pad desk accessory, a new one is created.

∘•➤ **Double-clicking on the Note Pad file** opens the Note Pad—but only if the file is in the System Folder and the Note Pad DA is in the Apple Menu Items folder.

∘•➤ **Cut, Copy, and Paste** work within the Note Pad (so you can move information from one page to another) and also between the Note Pad and any application you're using.

This ability actually gives a *raison d'être* to the Note Pad. (I want to pause here to point out that I paused here to use Key Caps to find where that circumflex accent was for the *e* in *être*.) You can keep a few names and addresses in the Note Pad and copy and paste them into letters if you use only a few, but use them often. Or maybe put *your* name and address in if your typing's so abysmal that it takes less time to open the Note Pad, copy the info, and paste it in as a return address in your document.

### ANOTHER JOE HOLMES NEARLY USEFUL TIP

The Note Pad is far too limited to be very useful for anything but the occasional phone number. It won't even accept a short paragraph. The commercial and shareware alternatives are nifty, but I can't keep up with the latest versions; I sometimes find they conflict or crash, and some cost actual money! Instead, I use genuine Apple-brand software as a replacement.

First, get rid of the original Note Pad from your Apple Menu Items folder (but save the Note Pad File, found in the System Folder, if you've got notes you want to keep). Then open up the TeachText utility and create a blank document. Title it *Note Pad*, and drag it to your Apple Menu Items folder. Now whenever you launch Note Pad from the Apple Menu, you'll actually be launching TeachText. Disadvantages? It takes more memory to run and you have to remember to save your work. Advantages? It holds 32K of text, you can copy pictures in and out using the Clipboard, and it will print.

Now here's the really tweaky part: copy the icon of the original Note Pad (in its Get Info window) and paste it in as the icon for your new Note Pad document. Now your Note Pad has the true Note Pad icon—an icon that will even appear in the Apple Menu!

Of course some people simply put TeachText into the Apple Menu and avoid the Note Pad altogether. But where's the sport in that?

*—Joe Holmes*

⊶➤ **If you want to print from the Note Pad,** you're out of luck—there's no Print command. You'll have to copy its contents into an application and print from there.

⊶➤ **If you need more than one Note Pad file** because eight pages isn't enough, there *is* a workaround: move the original file outside the System Folder and open the Note Pad to create a new file. Then, rename the files or shuffle them in and out of the System Folder so that the one you want to use is in the right place with the right name and will be opened. (A more complete description is in the Scrapbook section earlier in this chapter—the Scrapbook handles its file the same way the Note Pad does.)

Now, if you really need more than eight pages, and you have a job that pays you more than, say, $2 an hour, you'll save money buying a Note Pad replacement if you figure in how much time you'd waste futzing around with extra files.

⊶➤ **To consolidate the information** on the Note Pad pages, or to otherwise manipulate or store it, you can open the Note Pad File in any word or text processor that allows you to open "foreign" file formats—you'll get one document with all eight pages of information in it.

⊶➤ **My favorite Note Pad replacement** is the Phone Pad. It has 1000 (!) scrollable pages that use a 9-point font that lets you squeeze in a lot of information. It has a Find function so you can search for the text you've entered (it's the most convenient free-form database around—I use it constantly during the day to look up phone numbers, take notes during phone conversations, and so on.) In addition to the Find function, it even lets you

**MACPACK**

set up an index of names or keywords so a double-click can turn you to a specific page. If you've got your hardware hooked up correctly, it even dials the phone. You can change the font and size of the text, and re-size the pages. You can export the information so a word processor can read it; you can also print directly from the Phone Pad. It gets the Mac Almanac Blue Ribbon Award for Excellence—the only one awarded to a *segment* of a package instead of the whole package. (It's my book; I can do what I want!)

MockWrite is a venerable DA that provides a tiny word processor. You can have multiple documents, import text from another file, use a Find function, and print directly from it. It's been around seemingly forever (as has its author, Don Brown) and now that it has moved from its home with CE Software to a company started by old CE hands, it may get an update. It's still in old DA form, but it works under System 7 even in its current incarnation. (Please note that its name was a play on the only existing Mac word processor, MacWrite.) [Phone Pad, MacPak, Fifth Generation Systems; MockWrite, MockPackage, PrairieSoft]

## Puzzle

The Puzzle is a Jigsaw Puzzle in System 7.5. See the end of this chapter.

∞✦ **It's hard to find someone who's not familiar with** the plastic version of the Puzzle DA. To play it on the Mac, click on the tile you want to slide into the empty spot. You can shift two or three tiles at a time if the one you click on is separated from the empty space by one or two tiles, all in a horizontal line. Shuffle the tiles around the right way, and you solve the puzzle. You'll be rewarded by a rather bored voice saying "Ta-da." To start again (if you must) close the Puzzle and reopen. Each time you open the Puzzle, it's scrambled in a different order.

Clicking on a tile to move it (top); moving two tiles at a time (bottom).

⊶✦ **The Puzzle comes with two sets of tiles.** Use the Clear command in the Edit menu to toggle between them. Notice that the tiles around the edge of the Apple puzzle have a light border at the outside; that helps when you're trying to figure out which piece goes where while it's scrambled. If you actually solve these puzzles, the lines disappear from the Apple logo puzzle, and the blank space in the number puzzle gets a little apple printed in it.

⊶✦ **If you use the Copy command on a scrambled picture** and then paste it into a document, you'll see the unscrambled version of the picture, without the "tile lines." (You thought maybe I had time to *solve* the puzzles when I needed pictures for this book? Nope. I started with a shot of the Puzzle and its scrambled picture, then pasted the unscrambled picture on top and drew the lines in so it looked like puzzle tiles again.)

⊶✦ **You can paste any image into the Puzzle.** The picture is automatically scrambled into pieces when you paste it in. If it's too big, it will be scaled to fit.

⊶✦ **Using the Clear command on your own picture** erases it from the Puzzle; afterward, Clear once again toggles between the two standard Puzzles.

⊶✦ **Make an impossible puzzle** for someone you don't love. Start by copying the standard number puzzle and pasting it into a graphics program. If you're working in an object-oriented program, it's especially easy because each tile comes in as a separate object. In any case, create a puzzle picture in which the numbers are in a random order, and paste *that* into the Puzzle DA on someone's machine.

# -+| SYSTEM 7.5 STUFF |+-

## The Shut Down Desk Accessory

°°•❯ **The Shut Down desk accessory** is a tiny little thing that does the same thing as the Shut Down command in the Special menu. You don't get to open the Shut Down desk accessory and do anything with it; if you "open" it by double-clicking on it or selecting it from the Apple menu, the Mac starts its shutdown procedures, asking if you want your work saved, and so on. (This is pretty lame—you think you're opening a new desk accessory and you wind up shutting down the computer!)

The only reason it exists is because, as a desk accessory listed in the Apple menu, you can choose the Shut Down command no matter where you are—you don't have to go to the desktop first.

°°•❯ **The Shut Down DA's** name begins with a bullet (•) so that it sinks to the bottom of the alphabetical listing in the Apple menu. You can rename it if you want to.

• Shut Down

## Note Pad

°°•❯ **The Note Pad has finally been polished up** a little. You'll notice right away that there's a three-dimensional look to the corner where you flip the page, making it a little easier to figure out where you should click to move forward or backwards a page. (And you'll hear a little *swish* when you flip a page.) Other Note Pad improvements are:

- Resizable pages
- Scrollable text area on each page
- Definable font and size
- A Find function

°°•❯ **To change the font or size** of the text in the Note Pad, use the Preferences command in the Edit menu. You'll get a simple dialog where you can set the font and size, which will affect the entire Note Pad, not just a page or a selection.

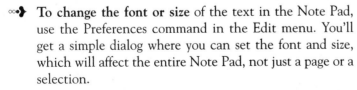

°°•❯ **The Find command** in the Edit menu lets you search through the Note Pad for specific text. You can choose to search a single page or the entire Note Pad by using the buttons in the dialog—the "notes" referred to in the dialog are pages.

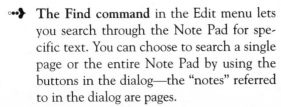

•••➤ **You can't go from the last page to the first** anymore: You have to flip back through all the pages to get to page 1. And there's only 6 pages now, instead of 8. (But who cares? They're so much bigger!)

## Jigsaw Puzzle

∘∘➤ **The Jigsaw Puzzle is** the logical successor to the Puzzle desk accessory. It starts with a simple picture of the alphabet (in fact, it's too simple, and unattractive—I hope it's only the picture they used for the beta copy of System 7.5 that I'm working with) but you can add your own picture.

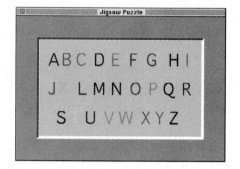

∘∘➤ **To break up the picture** into puzzle pieces, use the Start New Puzzle command in the Options menu. You'll get a choice of small, medium, or large pieces, and a chance to turn the sound effects on or off.

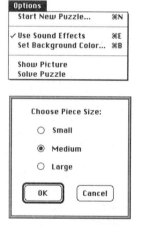

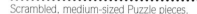
Scrambled, medium-sized Puzzle pieces.

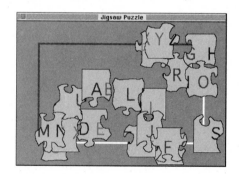

•••➤ **Paste your own picture** into the Jigsaw Puzzle by using the Edit menu's Paste command. The picture on the next pages shows what the Scrapbook's map picture looks like, broken into small pieces.

∘∘➤ **There are two ways to cheat**—oh, okay, "get help"—in the Jigsaw Puzzle. The Show Picture command in the Options menu opens a window with the Puzzle's picture in it; it's a floating window, so you can leave it on the screen for reference. And if you use the Solve Puzzle command, you have to watch one piece at a time being fitted into place.

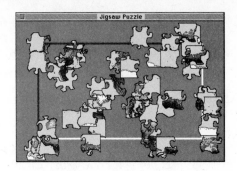

· · · · · · · · · · · · · · · · · · · · ·
The scrambled map.

●••▶ **You can "stick" pieces together** even if they're not in place in the puzzle. If you match two or more pieces correctly, they'll stay together and you can move them around as a single piece.

●••▶ **Maybe there's no Jigsaw Puzzle DA** in System 7.5. Apple's been known to promise features, and/or include them in beta versions of system software, only to pull them at the last minute. Here's what the Jigsaw Puzzle's About box says, in case you have to track it down as commercial software.

## Scrapbook

∞•▶ **The Scrapbook has undergone some long-needed changes** for System 7.5. Its window is finally resizable and it displays information about the item on each page. Now, if only they'd let us name the pages. And use a Go To command to get from one page to another. Or a Find command for a page's name. Or keywords. Or …

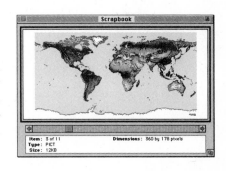

∞•▶ **The information given for a page** depends on what's on the page. You'll always get the type of the item—PICT, snd (sound), and so on—and the size of the item on the disk (as if it were a discrete disk file). But additional information depends on the item. In the last picture, for instance, you can see that the dimensions of the stored image are given as 360x178 pixels. For a sound, shown here, the duration of the sound is displayed.

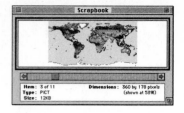

••▸ **When you shrink the Scrapbook window,** the image in it shrinks, too. The amount of "shrinkage" is noted in the window. When you make the Scrapbook larger than the picture, the picture stays at its full size and gets lots of white space surrounding it.

••▸ **The zoom box** in the Scrapbook window is very clever. (Well, not the box itself, of course, but you know what I mean.) It toggles the window between whatever size you set and the size that displays the image on the page at full size.

# CHAPTER 8
# EXTENSIONS & CONTROL PANELS

Technological progress is like an ax in the hands of a pathological criminal.

ALBERT EINSTEIN

In this chapter, you'll find out:

- ∞▸ When an extension isn't an extension. And when a control panel is.
- ∞▸ What an init conflict is, and how to deal with it.
- ∞▸ Where the Easter Eggs are hidden.
- ∞▸ Which two Apple extensions nobody needs.
- ∞▸ How to move the mouse cursor by typing.
- ∞▸ More about the Map control panel than any human needs to know.
- ∞▸ What the heck FKEYs are—and what they're not.
- ∞▸ That the original Control Panel was a desk accessory.

Slow    Fast

Black & White
4
16
256
Thousands

## THE LEAST IMPORTANT ITEM IN THIS CHAPTER

*T*he original release of the PowerBook's Caps Lock extension had a mistake in its Help balloon—but it was an interesting mistake.

Time

6:17:37 PM

Includes
159 Factoids
3 Quizzes
12 Quotes
—and—
1 Mac Almanac List

page 297

# EXTENSIONS

# THE EXTENSIONS FOLDER

# CONTROL PANELS

# FKEYS

# SYSTEM 7.5 STUFF

## ·H EXTENSIONS H·

## About Extensions

∞•❥ **An *extension* is** a small program that extends the capability of the Mac's operating system; it loads into memory at startup along with parts of the system itself. Extensions are like little pieces of the System file that exist separately so you can add or delete them according to your needs. Extensions let you, in effect, build your own Mac operating system.

Apple provides a certain number (growing all the time) of extensions that tweak problems in the System file, provide communication with peripherals, and give older Macs some of the capabilities of the newer ones. But there are hundreds of large and small third-party extensions out there that let you add functions to your Mac that Apple never even considered. An extension might be as simple as one that puts a clock in your menu bar. It can be more involved, like a spelling checker that watches as you type and lets you know when you've misspelled something. Or, it can be as complex as a macro utility that lets you automate many of your Mac operations

∞•❥ **The key difference between an extension** and an application or utility is that the extension is available on a system-wide basis. It's always there, ready and waiting, no matter what program you're in—you don't have to run it as you would a utility. So, a spelling checker that comes with your word processor works in that word processor. One that comes as a stand-alone utility has to be launched like any other program. But one that comes as a system extension works anywhere you care to use it.

Some extensions, such as ones that provide special capabilities in the Finder, aren't system-*wide* because their operations aren't necessary anywhere else. But they're still system-*level* functions, acting as built-in operations rather than as stand-alone utilities.

∞•❥ **An extension isn't always an extension.** That is, what we've defined as an extension isn't always labeled *extension* in a list view, and it doesn't necessarily belong in the Extensions folder.

It usually comes as a surprise to the uninitiated, but many control panels are actually extensions—they're extensions with a front end (the control panel) through which you can set your preferences. Just to confuse things, not all the items in the Extensions folder fit this definition of *extension*, either, because they don't all load into memory at startup.

The important thing to remember is that the word *extension* is more often than not generally used to refer to items loaded into memory at startup. This includes many of the items in the Extensions folder, but not all of them; it includes many items in the Control Panels folder, but certainly not all of them; it even includes some items that are loose in the System Folder. So when someone talks about turning off all your extensions, or about an extensions conflict, she's not referring to just the Extensions folder items.

**POP QUIZ** [10 POINTS]

There's an incredibly clever and subtle pun in the paragraph on the previous page that starts "It usually comes as a surprise ...". Old Mac hands should be able to pick it out.

•••➤ **An *init*** (the term comes from the word *initialize* and is pronounced *ih-NIT*) is a little program or utility that loads into memory at startup. Doesn't that sound familiar? That's how we defined *extension*. Most of the items in your Extensions folder are inits. Some of the items in your Control Panels folder are inits. The words *init* and *extension* are often used interchangeably.

The term *init* seemed destined for oblivion when System 7 was introduced, since what we used to call *inits* are now mostly extensions. If anyone uses the term *init*, you'll know they mean *extension*—in the general sense, not in the it's-in-the-Extensions-folder sense.

•••➤ **System extensions use memory.** The only way an extension can be ready and waiting no matter where you're working is by residing in memory. So the more extensions you have, the more memory is used up. Extensions that provide complex capabilities (like macro utilities) take up more memory than small ones.

The memory used by extensions is lumped together with the System memory in the About This Macintosh window. When I start my Mac with extensions off, the system takes 1176K of memory. With my extensions running, the system takes (are you ready?) 3462K!

System memory without and with lots of extensions running.

| | | |
|---|---|---|
| 🖳 System Software | 1,176K | ▬▬▬▫ |
| 🖳 System Software | 3,462K | ▬▬▬▬▬ |

Some extensions use only a little bit of memory when they load at startup and need more when they're being used; they "borrow" more from the System's memory allocation as needed, and the System grabs more free memory whenever it's necessary.

•••➤ **Extensions don't go in the Startup Items folder.** There's a big difference between extensions that *load* at startup and items that *open* at startup because you've placed them in the Startup Items folder. System extensions run and load themselves into memory in a very background kind of way. Documents and applications you put in the Startup Items folder open at startup so you can get to work.

···**➤** **If you have old inits from System 6,** they may still work under System 7. Use the Get Info command or look at the init in a list view and check its type. If the init's type is *cdev* (control panel device), try it in the Control Panels folder. If the type is *rdev* (Chooser device), put it in the Extensions folder. If the type is *startup document,* put it in the Extensions folder—not the Startup Items folder.

If the old init doesn't work at all, or it crashes, try it loose in the System Folder.

### Mac Wonk

Want to impress your friends with your vastly superior programmer-like knowledge of all things Macintosh? Just use the right words.

- Don't say *extension*. Say *init*.
- Don't say *control panel*. Say *cdev*. (But make sure you say it right: *SEE-devv*.)
- Don't say *Open dialog*. Say *GetFile dialog*.
- Don't say *Save dialog*. Say *SetFile dialog*.
- Optional: Refer to Open and Save dialogs in general as *SF dialogs*, for *standard file*. Or, even better, say *Set File* for the Save dialog and *Get File* for the open dialog.

## Using Extensions

∞•**➤** **Extensions belong** in one of three folders on your drive: the Extensions folder, the Control Panels folder, or the System Folder. How do you know which is the proper folder? First of all, 99 percent of the extensions will go in either the Extensions folder or the Control Panels folder, so you can forget about the System Folder as a candidate unless there are special circumstances (for older inits, or for special ones that absolutely have to load last into memory).

To choose between the other two folders, you can use any of a variety of methods to see where the item belongs:

- Check the icon. If it's a puzzle piece, it goes in the Extensions folder. If it has a slider control, it goes in the Control Panels folder.
- Use Get Info on the item. If its Kind is *control panel* or *system extension,* you'll know which folder to use.
- Double-click on the item. If it opens into a control panel interface with things for you to set, it goes in the Control Panels folder; if it belongs in the Extensions folder, you'll get a dialog saying it's a system extension.
- Point to the icon with Help balloons enabled and see how it's identified.
- Do what so few can bring themselves to do: Read the documentation that came with the utility!
- Easiest of all: Drag the item into the closed System Folder and let the Mac route it to the correct place.

∞→ **Regardless of where an extension** "belongs," it will in all likelihood still load if it's in any of the three folders that can hold extensions. So, a control panel in the Extensions folder loads; a puzzle-piece extension in the System Folder loads.

∞→ **You have to restart your Mac** after you install a new extension. Since it's loaded into memory at startup, you can't use an extension that wasn't *there* at startup!

Sometimes you have to restart the Mac after you've changed a setting in a control panel for the change to take effect. Changes made in the Memory control panel, for instance, require a restart before they work. Control panels that require a restart for changes almost always tell you so somewhere in a window.

∞→ **The icon parade at bottom of the screen** during the startup process shows the extensions being loaded into memory. Usually these are simply the same icons you see in the desktop window, but some are cute little animations which achieve their effect by simply cycling through two or more icons. Don't take this "init march" as a hard-and-fast guide to what's being loaded, though: many control panel extensions offer the option of turning off the icon display at startup, and some extensions load invisibly, never giving you the option of seeing a startup icon.

There's a sample icon parade at the bottom of this page and the following ones.

∞⟩ **When you have so many inits** that the icon parade is longer than the width of your screen, you don't have to worry—they'll just start a second row. This is automatic with System 7, although you used to need an extra init utility to get the icons to wrap.

∞→ **To prevent an extension** from loading at startup, move it out of its folder. Remember that moving an item out of the Extensions or Control Panels folder just one level—into the System Folder—won't keep it from loading.

Sometimes a control panel provides an "off" setting that lets you keep it from loading at the next startup without having to move it out of the folder. Some provide definable key combinations which, when pressed during the startup sequence, keep an individual extension from loading.

∞→ **An X through a startup icon** means it's been turned off temporarily. This usually happens only with control panels, there's no way to turn off a system extension in the Extensions folder.

A temporary turnoff isn't the same as dragging the control panel out of the Control Panels folder so it won't load. A temporary turn-off leaves the init in the folder so you can open it and turn it back on again. Sometimes turning it on means you can use it right away—the appropriate information was loaded into memory even though the control panel isn't "on" and ready for use; sometimes you have to restart the computer so the init portion of the control panel can be loaded.

init march init march init march init march init march init march init march init march init march init march init march init march init march init march init m

If you didn't explicitly turn off an init but there's an X through its startup icon, it might be because:

- It's a sample utility that has reached its expiration date and turned itself off.
- You may have pressed some key or combination of keys that turns off that specific extension at startup.
- The init uses some support file that's missing or damaged.

➡ **To prevent all extensions** from loading at startup, hold the Shift key down when you turn on the Mac. Keep the key down until you see the Welcome dialog, with its *Extensions off* subtitle.

➡ **Turning off all extensions** by holding the Shift key down at startup also prevents anything in the Startup Items folder from launching.

➡ **You can't always get rid of an init** simply by throwing it away and emptying the Trash. Since it's loaded into memory at startup, sometimes you can't erase it any more than you could get rid of an application that's running or a document that's open; you just get a dialog telling you that the Trash can't be emptied because the file's in use.

Erasing an init from your drive can be a three-step process. First, you have to drag it to the Trash; then you have to restart the Mac so the init is no longer "busy"; finally, you can empty the Trash.

Some inits that are loaded *entirely* into memory can be erased from the drive because they're not really open at all—a complete copy was placed into memory and the disk file isn't used.

➡ **Extensions load into memory alphabetically**, but in three distinct groups. The items in the Extensions folder load first. Then come the init portions of the control panels in the Control Panels folder. Finally, extensions that are loose in the System Folder load.

Since some inits fight over places in memory, and some won't work unless they're loaded first, and some insist on being last, where they're stored and what they're named become very important issues.

If you get an init that has a special lead character in front of its name, that's probably because it has to load first or last in a group, so don't rename it just for the heck of it, and follow the manufacturer's instructions when it comes to where the item belongs. Here are two perfect examples—two of the most popular and useful utilities around. Extensions Manager (which I describe later) has to load *before* everything else because it controls which other inits load into memory when you start up. So, its name includes a leading space and it goes in the Extensions folder to ensure that it loads first. ATM (Adobe Type Manager, covered in Chapter 10) has a squiggly tilde in front of its name (~ATM) and it goes in the System Folder so that it's loaded last.

⸳⸱➤ **Always turn off all your extensions** before using any software installer—whether it's the Apple system software Installer, or one that installs other applications.

What happens if you don't? Sometimes nothing happens. Sometimes bad things happen, like an application that won't work, or system software that keeps crashing. I received a call for help from someone who couldn't get his newly installed PowerPoint presentation program to run—it crashed every time it was launched. It was the newest version, his system software was up-to-date, his hardware was fine, and there weren't any problems with any other software. I suspected an extension conflict, so I asked him to start up with the Shift key down. When he saw the Welcome dialog with the *Extensions off* notice, he said, "Oh, *that's* what they meant in the installation instructions." Right. He hadn't turned them off when he installed the software. A re-install, the right way, solved the problem.

## Init Conflicts

⸳⸱➤ An *init conflict,* or *extension conflict,* is just what it sounds like: An init that conflicts with the system, an application, or another init. How do you know there's a conflict? Well, symptoms can vary from the obvious to the subtle, and from mild to disastrous. For instance:

- The extension or control panel doesn't work.
- Some other extension or control panel doesn't work any more, after having behaved prior to the new installation.
- The system behaves erratically. This includes anything from letters not being typed correctly to the mouse cursor looking funny or jumping around on the screen.
- The Mac crashes or hangs at startup, when you launch applications, or any old time it feels like it.

This is the cloud that goes with the silver lining of a system expandable through extensions. If these capabilities were built into the System file, they'd work together harmoniously. But with system functions added piecemeal, there's often discord.

Extension incompatibility isn't always immediately apparent, nor is it always easily identified. If your system crashes or freezes at irregular intervals for no apparent reason, suspect an extension conflict as the cause.

⸳⸱➤ **Tracking down an extension conflict starts** with turning off *all* your extensions (holding down Shift at startup) and seeing if your system behaves. If everything works when there are no inits, you can be sure that one or more inits are the cause of the problem.

**REALLY INSIDE MAC:
INIT CONFLICTS**

◦•➤ **When you suspect an extension conflict,** the most likely culprit is the most recent addition to your system. Take out the new kid on the block and see if your system works without it. (Remember: simply taking the init out of its folder isn't good enough—you have to restart the Mac to get the init out of memory.)

◦•➤ **If the Mac crashes during the icon parade** at startup, you can easily narrow down the probable culprit to one of two. Watch the icons and see which is the last to show up on the screen before the crash. The culprit is either the last one displayed or the one that was trying to load immediately after it. To check which one was going to come up next, restart (with Shift down to turn off all extensions and avoid the conflict on startup) and find the item that showed up last on the screen. Look for the file that comes after it alphabetically in the same folder, or what comes first alphabetically in the next folder.

**CLAUDE RAINS**
IN *CASABLANCA*

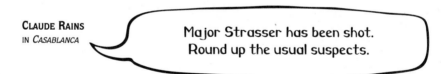

Major Strasser has been shot.
Round up the usual suspects.

◦•➤ **When the newest extension isn't** your problem, it's time for some real grunt work. You could take out all your extensions and add them back one at a time, restarting the Mac on every addition, until you find the one that's the problem. But a faster way is a method referred to as a *binary search*.

Create a folder to temporarily store the inits as you shuffle them around. Take out half your inits, putting them in the temporary folder, and restart. (I usually leave all my Apple system software inits in, plus a few other of my basics.) If everything's fine, put back half of the ones you removed and start again. Still fine? Put half the remaining ones

*march init march init march init march init march init march init march init march init march init march init march init march init march init march init march init march init march init march*

in. And so on, until your problem crops up; you'll know which subgroup the suspect belongs to, because it has to be in the most recently added group of extensions. Take out all the "good" extensions that behaved so far, and work with only the suspect group.

Once you have a small group of suspects (well, okay, it could be a big group of suspects, if the problem cropped up on the first round of the test), remove half of the suspect group and restart. If the problem persists, it's in the remaining half, so split it in half again. If the problem goes away, it's in the half you moved out. Move groups in and out—they'll be progressively smaller—until you've found the problem file.

(Ahh, if only I'd had this procedure as an example for my mother when my first son started eating real food. She said he should get only one new food a week, to make it easy to identify the culprit in case of allergic reaction. I said I could give him any number of new foods at one time and if there were a problem, I'd cut out half of them and see if the reaction stayed or went away. But Nick was born a few years before the Mac, so this example didn't spring to mind. Not that she would have approved anyway!)

✏➤ **When you think you've narrowed down** the problem to a single extension, make sure it's that extension alone and not how it's interacting with other extensions. Start up your system with nothing *but* the new extension in it, and work for a while to see if anything untoward happens. If you still have the problem, you have the criminal.

But it's entirely possible that the one extension that causes a problem when you add it to all the others—seemingly the straw that breaks the camel's back—will work fine when it's alone. In that case, you can be sure that the problem is not the extension itself, but in how it reacts with some other init in your system.

Figuring out which other init is the partner in crime means doing a binary search again, but always leaving the known "bad" extension running until you can figure out which other one it clashes with.

✏➤ **When you've identified a single** problem extension, what should you do with it? Well, sometimes there's no solution other than to get rid of it, but that's only the last resort. First, try these:

- Make sure that it's the most recent version. Check with the manufacturer, or, if the extension is shareware, check with your source for such software. If it's not System 7 compatible, there's nothing you can do. But many extensions, especially shareware ones, are updated at frequent intervals.
- If the extension causes a problem only when you're running a specific application, make sure that program is up-to-date.
- Change the name of the extension to force it to load first, or last, in your list of extensions. Move it to another folder if necessary, switching it from the Control Panels folder to the Extensions folder, for instance.

init march init march init march init march init march init march init march init march init march init march init march init march init march init march init march init march init march init march init march init march init t

- Make sure that your system software is up-to-date. You don't have to change from System 7.0 to System 7.1, but you do have to check if there are any recent updates or "tune-ups" to the system you're using to take care of any bugs.

**Make life easier** for yourself and use an extensions manager, a control panel that lets you easily turn inits (extensions, control panels, and even things in the Startup Items folder) on and off without doing any manual shuffling from one folder to another. Most extension managers create secondary folders called something like *Extensions (disabled)*, *Control Panels (disabled)*, and so on, putting the inits you want turned off into the disabled folders so they won't be loaded at startup. All you have to do is select or unselect the items in a list. You can even make "sets" so certain extensions always (or never) load together.

The aptly, if unimaginatively, named Extensions Manager is a solid utility with a price you can't beat—it's free. Startup Manager is one of the commercial extension manager utilities. Conflict Catcher and INIT Picker 3 have the added attraction of being able to help you through the dreaded binary search procedure in case of an init clash. [Extensions Manager, freeware, Ricardo Batista; Conflict Catcher, Casady & Greene; Startup Manager—Now Utilities, Now Software; INIT Picker 3, Inline Design]

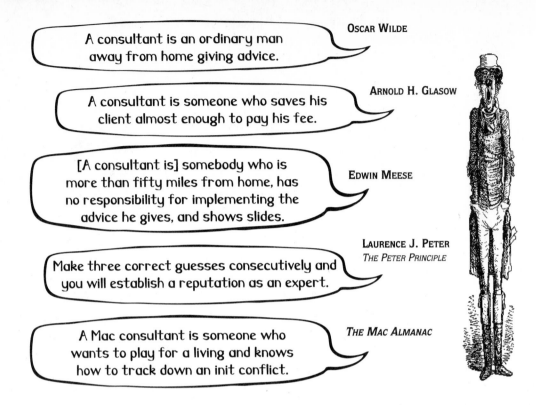

OSCAR WILDE

A consultant is an ordinary man away from home giving advice.

ARNOLD H. GLASOW

A consultant is someone who saves his client almost enough to pay his fee.

EDWIN MEESE

[A consultant is] somebody who is more than fifty miles from home, has no responsibility for implementing the advice he gives, and shows slides.

LAURENCE J. PETER
*THE PETER PRINCIPLE*

Make three correct guesses consecutively and you will establish a reputation as an expert.

*THE MAC ALMANAC*

A Mac consultant is someone who wants to play for a living and knows how to track down an init conflict.

## ⊱ THE EXTENSIONS FOLDER ⊰

### The Folder

∞➤ **The Extensions folder** is home to a wide variety of items, both from Apple and from third-party vendors. But two types of items make up the majority of the population: the puzzle-piece icons of *system* extensions (most of which are the kind of extensions that we've discussed so far in this chapter—the ones that load into memory at startup) and *Chooser* extensions.

∞➤ **A Chooser extension** is a file that lets your Mac communicate with another device— like a printer or fax modem—or connect to networks. These items deserve the name *extension* even if they don't load into memory at startup because they certainly extend the system's capability. Where would you be if your Mac couldn't talk to your printer? But how would you like a System file that's, say, 50 percent larger just so it could talk to *any* printer you're likely to use?

And, in case you didn't make the connection yet: Chooser extensions show up in the Chooser desk accessory so you can select the one you want to use. When you click on a Chooser extension, whatever's needed in memory is loaded at that point.

∞•❯ **You'll never want to sort** the Extensions folder by Kind since all the items in it are of the same type. *NOT!*

There are, in fact, an uncomfortable number of extension subspecies beyond system extensions and Chooser extensions. Even Apple provides items for the Extensions folder that aren't typed as extensions; look at your Extensions folder with the Kind listed, and you'll see items identified as *communications tool, application,* and even the all-purpose *file.* Since Apple seemingly declined to set an example for Extensions folder file types, third-party products can hardly be blamed for being less than proper about it. One of the files in my Extensions folder is *Disk Doubler Help*—and its file type is *document!* But they're all routed to the Extensions folder if you drag them to the closed System Folder.

A wide variety of file types is routed to the Extensions folder.

| Name | Size | Kind |
|------|------|------|
| Apple CD-ROM | 28K | system extension |
| Apple Modem Tool | 88K | communications tool |
| Apple Photo Access | 188K | system extension |
| AppleShare | 76K | Chooser extension |
| Finder Help | 36K | file |
| Foreign File Access | 36K | system extension |
| Hardware System Update | 8K | system extension |
| PrintMonitor | 64K | application program |

∞•❯ **The icon for a system extension** is a puzzle piece, indicating that it's part of the overall makeup of your operating system. The choice is amusingly ironic, as anyone who's dealt with extension incompatibilities will agree: Extensions are certainly a puzzle—and sometimes the pieces just don't fit together.

Most of Apple's extensions stick to the puzzle-piece theme, but third-party extensions generally have their own distinctive icons. Chooser extensions have icons that illustrate the device they help control—you'll see pictures of printers, for instance, for printer drivers.

∞•❯ **A printer font** might be considered a system extension—and in System 7.0, they are officially extensions, living in the Extensions folder. System 7.1 cleaned up both the Extensions folder and the concept by putting fonts in their own Fonts folder.

••❯ **If your printer fonts are loose** in your Extensions folder because you're not using System 7.1, use a utility like Suitcase II that lets the Mac access downloadable fonts from other folders. Keeping the printer fonts inside a folder in the Extensions folder is much more manageable than leaving them scattered in the Extensions folder with the other extensions.

Chapter 11 discusses fonts and the Suitcase utility.

## Apple's Extensions

∞⟍ **The Chooser extensions** included with your system software are the items that you see in the Chooser desk accessory—printer drivers and the AppleShare icon for networks. Just which printer drivers are in your Extensions folder—and whether or not the AppleShare icon is there—depends on how your system software was installed. If you installed a system that included the *Software for all printers* choice, you might have

a dozen printer drivers. If you didn't include any networking software during the installation, you won't see the AppleShare icon. (Wouldn't you think there'd be a separate Chooser folder, considering the potential clutter?)

∞⟍ **Apple's system extensions** can be loosely divided into three groups:

- *General extensions.* These can include the QuickTime extension so you can play QuickTime movies, and any system updaters that are released to tweak your system—sometimes to fix basic bugs in the System file, or to make an existing system version work with a new Mac model. A perfect example of a tweaker is the Basic Color Monitor extension, which takes care of a display problem when the Apple's Basic Color monitor is used with a Centris or certain Quadra models.

*QuickTime is covered in Chapter 21.*

- *Network extensions.* For simple Apple networks and basic file sharing, there are three extensions; for EtherTalk networks (if you have one of those, you either know all about them or you have a network manager who does!), there are two more. Whether or not these extensions are in your Extensions folder depends on what was selected during your system installation. (It's easy to think of file-sharing as built-in, since it works pretty invisibly once it's installed—so invisibly, in fact, that its icon doesn't show up during the startup init march.)

*Networks are covered in Chapter 21.*

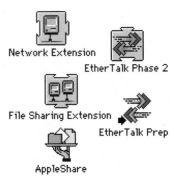

- *CD-ROM extensions.* Apple provides no fewer than seven items for complete CD control! Three of them have to do with accessing computer files on the CD, since a CD's file storage system is so different from the one used on hard drives. There's one each for accessing music and photos stored on CDs. And there's one

*init march init march init march init march init march init march init march init march init march init march init march init march init march init march init march init m*

**306** **CHAPTER 8** ⊬

that works in conjunction with the CD Remote desk accessory. These items are automatically included in your Extensions folder if you've installed basic system software for a Mac with a built-in CD-ROM drive. You'll also find them in your folder if you've used the *System software for all Macintoshes* install option with installation disks that were manufactured after the CD controllers became available.

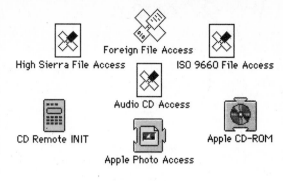

High Sierra File Access
Foreign File Access
ISO 9660 File Access
Audio CD Access
CD Remote INIT
Apple Photo Access
Apple CD-ROM

- **Communications tool is** another file type that goes in the Extensions folder. These files are used for various communications protocols for modems. The ones from Apple have a puzzle-piece icon that's a different style from the one used for system extensions.

- **The PrintMonitor** is an application—sort of. It's identified as an application when you look at it by Kind, and it certainly doesn't have a puzzle-piece icon. But when you drag it into the closed System Folder, it's routed right to the Extensions folder, where it needs to be to if you want it to work. (Chapter 12 covers the PrintMonitor in detail.)

- **Finder Help,** which provides special Balloon help on the desktop, is an odd hybrid. Sure, it has a puzzle-piece icon, but its Kind is *file*. Yet it gets routed to the Extensions folder when dragged to the closed System Folder. Go figure.

- **The Caps Lock** extension is for PowerBooks. It puts a little symbol up in the menu bar when the Caps Lock key is "locked"—because the Caps Lock key doesn't physically lock down on the PowerBooks.

### WHOOPS!

The Caps Lock extension released with System 7.0 for the early PowerBooks was never updated internally for the machines once they got past the code name stage. Balloon Help identified *TIM* and *Derringer* as the machines that Caps Lock worked on. They cleaned it up in System 7.1, though!

···❯ **The extensions nobody needs:** A/ROSE and DAL. A/ROSE is *Apple Real-time Operating System.* You need it only if you have an EtherTalk or TokenTalk network card installed in your Mac. DAL (for Database Access Language) was included with System 7.0 and dumped from System 7.1 (although made available separately, for a price); it's needed only for special access to data on a mainframe computer.

> Mainframe: A large, expensive peripheral for desktop computers.
>
> —ANON.

## ⊬ CONTROL PANELS ⊬·

### About Control Panels

∞❯ **A control panel is** something that lets you check and adjust system settings like how fast you have to click the mouse for it to be a double-click instead of two single clicks, or what the background of your desktop looks like, or how a certain extension will behave.

Control panels are placed inside the Control Panels folder in the System Folder when you install your system software. An alias of the Control Panels folder is put into the Apple Menu Items folder so it will be listed in your Apple menu.

∞❯ **Which control panels you have** depends on your hardware and on the version of system software you've installed. The Brightness control panel, for instance, is installed only on systems like the Classic that don't let you control screen brightness manually; the Cache Switch is only for Macs with '040 processors. There are a few control panels strictly for PowerBooks. The General Controls panel, on the other hand, comes in two versions: one for standard Mac systems, and one for the "P systems" for the Performas. Apple's basic control panels are:

- Apple CD Speed Switch
- AutoRemounter
- Brightness
- Cache Switch
- CloseView
- Color
- Date & Time
- Easy Access
- File Sharing Monitor
- General Controls
- Keyboard
- Labels

- Launcher
- Map
- Memory
- Monitors
- Mouse
- Number
- Sharing Setup
- Sound
- Startup Disk
- Users & Groups
- Views

## THE WAY WE WERE ...

The Mac system used to have only one control panel. Yep. Right up through System 6. Only one control panel. But it was Control Panel (capitalized). And it was a desk accessory.

When you opened *the* Control Panel, you saw a scrolling list of icons at the left that were *control panel devices*. (Items that are now independent control panels.) At the right, you got the controls for the selected control panel device. All in a neat little package. With the General device selected, as shown here, you'd get all the things that are now in General Controls, as well as elements of the Memory and Sound control panels.

But even this modular control panel wasn't always on the Mac. It showed up in mid-1987, in System 4.0/Finder 5.4—a full three years into the Mac's life.

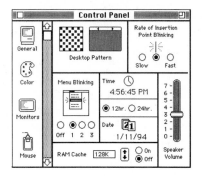

**Open a control panel** by double-clicking on its icon. If it's listed in the Apple menu, or one of its submenus (assuming you're using a hierarchical Apple menu utility), just select it from there. Most control panels have icons that incorporate a slider bar control into the design.

To close a control panel, you click in its close box. Unlike a desk accessory, which has a File menu with Close and Quit commands, control panels have no menus.

**When you change control panel settings,** sometimes the changes are immediate (like changing the desktop pattern), but sometimes you have to restart your Mac before they take effect (like the memory settings). You'll find that most control panels politely inform you when they can't make immediate changes.

**Since there's an alias of the Control Panels folder in the Apple menu,** it's easy to open the folder. But that means it's still a two-step process to open a control panel: Open the folder, then double-click on the icon. If there are certain control panels you use often, make aliases of them and put them "loose" in the Apple Menu Items folder so they'll be listed in the Apple menu. Then all you have to do is select the control panel from the menu to open it.

**Option double-click on** a control panel icon to open it and close the Control Panels folder window at the same time.

**Control panels don't have to be** in the Control Panels folder in order to work correctly. Control panels that load into memory at startup have to be either in the Control Panels folder, the Extensions folder, or the System Folder. But control panels like the Map will work no matter where they're stored.

Unless you're running into some conflicts as discussed in the last section, though, there's no reason to keep control panels anywhere but in the Control Panels folder. And, in fact, it's the best place for them because they're so readily available from there.

●●**➤** **A control panel is a Finder window.** Huh? Really, it is. Open a control panel directly from the Apple menu and you'll see you're returned to the desktop before it opens—it's not like opening a desk accessory, which opens right on top of whatever else is already running. All the Finder menus are active, too—control panels don't have their own menus. If you click an opened control panel to move to it from an application, you'll see you move back to the desktop; and if you move to the Finder from anyplace else, an opened control panel becomes the active window again if that's the way you left it.

●●**➤** **You don't always need a control panel** once you've set its parameters. You can set your mouse speeds, keyboard repeats, and color depth, and then get rid of the Mouse, General Controls, and Monitors control panels, for instance. The settings are stored in a special part of the Mac's memory—the PRAM—that doesn't forget things when the computer's turned off. This holds true for most of Apple's control panels, but many others need to be in the Control Panels folder in order to load at startup. In fact, as a general rule, keep in mind that the larger the control panel is, the more likely it is that you need it around at startup.

PRAM is covered in Chapter 9.

●●**➤** **It's hard to see the difference** between a control panel and a desk accessory when you're using it. The Map, for instance, certainly "feels" like a desk accessory. The easy way to tell if something is really a control panel is to check its "kind" as reported in its Get Info window or in a desktop window list. A control panel's Kind is listed as—you guessed it—*control panel*. Beyond that, however, there are several significant differences in the way the Mac treats control panels and desk accessories:

- An opened desk accessory is listed in the Applications menu; a control panel is not.

- When a desk accessory is active, there's a File and an Edit menu in the menu bar, as well as (sometimes) a menu that belongs to the DA. Control panels don't have any menus; the Finder menus are available whenever a control panel is open.

- A control panel is either loaded into memory at startup or when you open it (or both), but in either case it uses the same portion of memory as does the System. A desk accessory gets a 20K memory partition to itself when you open it, and borrows more from the system allocation when necessary.

- A desk accessory, even if it comprises only one window, is one of the many "layers" of application windows on your screen. A control panel lives in the desktop's layer and is treated like a Finder window.

●●**➤** **An option-click in a control panel's** close box closes *all* open control panels—as well as all open desktop windows. It works the other way, too: an option-click to close all Finder windows also closes any opened control panel. (Another result of a control panel being treated like a Finder window.)

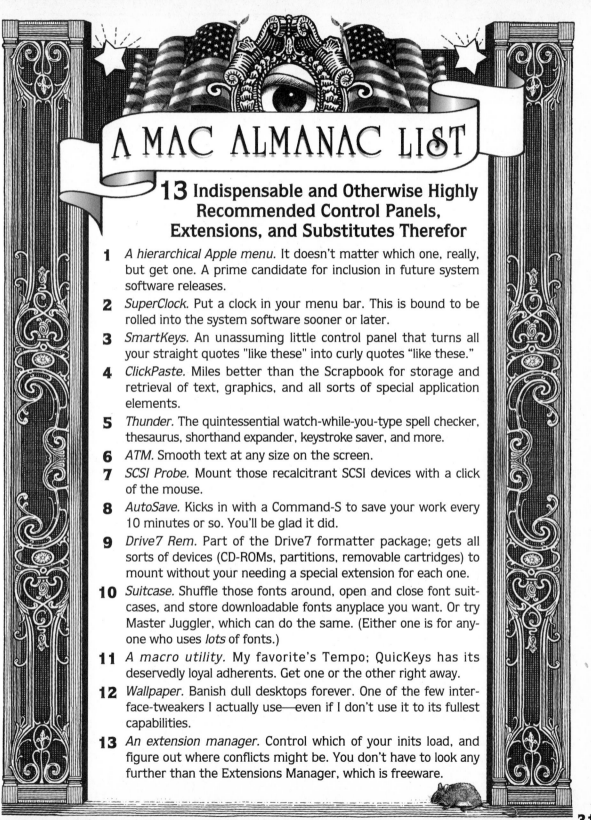

# A MAC ALMANAC LIST

## 13 Indispensable and Otherwise Highly Recommended Control Panels, Extensions, and Substitutes Therefor

1   *A hierarchical Apple menu.* It doesn't matter which one, really, but get one. A prime candidate for inclusion in future system software releases.

2   *SuperClock.* Put a clock in your menu bar. This is bound to be rolled into the system software sooner or later.

3   *SmartKeys.* An unassuming little control panel that turns all your straight quotes "like these" into curly quotes "like these."

4   *ClickPaste.* Miles better than the Scrapbook for storage and retrieval of text, graphics, and all sorts of special application elements.

5   *Thunder.* The quintessential watch-while-you-type spell checker, thesaurus, shorthand expander, keystroke saver, and more.

6   *ATM.* Smooth text at any size on the screen.

7   *SCSI Probe.* Mount those recalcitrant SCSI devices with a click of the mouse.

8   *AutoSave.* Kicks in with a Command-S to save your work every 10 minutes or so. You'll be glad it did.

9   *Drive7 Rem.* Part of the Drive7 formatter package; gets all sorts of devices (CD-ROMs, partitions, removable cartridges) to mount without your needing a special extension for each one.

10  *Suitcase.* Shuffle those fonts around, open and close font suitcases, and store downloadable fonts anyplace you want. Or try Master Juggler, which can do the same. (Either one is for anyone who uses *lots* of fonts.)

11  *A macro utility.* My favorite's Tempo; QuicKeys has its deservedly loyal adherents. Get one or the other right away.

12  *Wallpaper.* Banish dull desktops forever. One of the few interface-tweakers I actually use—even if I don't use it to its fullest capabilities.

13  *An extension manager.* Control which of your inits load, and figure out where conflicts might be. You don't have to look any further than the Extensions Manager, which is freeware.

## AppleCD Speed Switch

∞⦁➤ **The AppleCD Speed Switch** control panel is very simple: choose Standard or Faster speed for the data transfer between the CD-ROM drive and your computer. The warning in the window about some applications not working correctly is pretty succinct. But I haven't found any problems yet, and neither has anyone else I know. But if you have trouble running something from an older CD-ROM, try the Standard Speed button.

## Brightness

∞⦁➤ **The Brightness control panel** is for Mac models that don't have brightness control dials on their monitors, like the old Portable and the Classic. You just drag the bar on the brightness control to the left or right.

∞⦁➤ **Adjust the brightness level** in the control panel by typing a number from 1 (for the dimmest) to 9 instead of dragging the bar on the brightness control.

## Cache Switch

The cache that's in the Memory control panel is covered in Chapter 9.

∞⦁➤ **The Cache Switch** is strictly for Macs with '040 processors—Quadra and Centris models. Click the Faster button to use the full speed of your machine; use the More Compatible button if you're having trouble running older software on your newer Mac. (That is, in fact, the reason for the Cache Switch—when the Quadras first came out, software that didn't strictly adhere to Apple's programming guidelines often had trouble working at all.)

A cache is a temporary storage place in memory for something's that's normally on a disk; retrieving it from memory is a lot faster than getting it from the disk. Running with the Cache Switch off can cut your speed demon to half its normal pace, so don't do it unless you have to.

∞⦁➤ **There are two caches** that the Cache Switch controls. Did you notice that the buttons are subtitled *Caches enabled* and *Caches disabled?* There are separate caches for instructions and for data, but they're turned on and off together.

∞⦁➤ **You usually have to restart** for the changes you make to the cache switch to take effect. But if you option-click on the Faster or More Compatible button, the change takes effect immediately.

∞⦁➤ **To see who wrote** the Cache Switch, option-click on the version number in the corner of the control panel's window. Then, for a strange piece of non-information, point to the version number with Balloon Help activated.

## CloseView

∞❥ **CloseView was designed for** the visually impaired, but anyone can use it to magnify what's on the Mac's screen—it lets you do precision work in programs that don't provide magnification. It's not automatically installed in your system, but you'll find it on your system disks.

∞❥ **To work with CloseView,** you have to go through several steps:

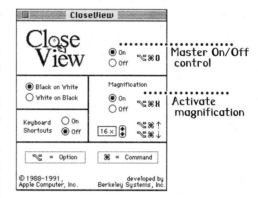

Master On/Off control

Activate magnification

1. Turn on the "master control"—click the On button at the top of the window.

2. Restart the Mac if CloseView wasn't in the Control Panels folder when you started the Mac.

3. Activate the magnification feature through the control panel, or with a keyboard command if you've set CloseView to use the keyboard shortcuts.

∞❥ **When CloseView's magnification is turned on,** a large black frame surrounds the mouse cursor. The size of the frame depends on what magnification level you've chosen in the CloseView control panel, because it's showing what will be enlarged if you activate the magnification. In this picture, the frame is around the arrow cursor on the desktop, and the magnification level is set for twice the normal size.

........................
When CloseView's magnification is turned on, a thick frame surrounds the cursor.

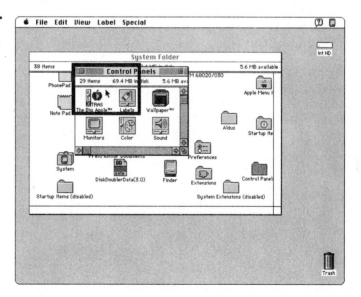

## EASTER EGGS

Lots of Mac programs have little hidden surprises in them. I don't mean hidden *features*, like a keyboard combination for a menu command that isn't listed in the menu, I mean *surprises*, like a keyboard combination that turns your screen upside down or something. These little hidden surprises are known as *Easter eggs*, in honor of the hunt for them.

To find an Easter egg, you pretty much have to Command-Option-double-click on everything in sight—sometimes several times in a row, with or without the Shift key, and maybe only on the third Tuesday of a month without an R. You get the idea.

Control panels are notorious for Easter eggs, where they are usually a way of burying the programmers' names in their creations. (Not for them the late-night but obvious Michelangelean chiseling of a name into a sculpture.) Here's a quick roundup of the ones mentioned in this chapter:

- Cache Switch: Option-click on the version number.
- Cache Switch: Point to the version number with Balloon Help on.
- Color: Click on the text sample: once for one programmer's name and a second time for the second programmer.
- Labels: Delete all the label names and then look at the Label menu.
- Map: Use the Find button for a place called "mid."
- Map: Click on the version number to see the programmer's name.
- Map: Scroll around to find the programmers' initials incorporated into the map picture.
- Memory: Turn on virtual memory and hold down Option while popping up the menu.
- Monitors: Press on the version number.
- Monitors: Press Option while pressing on the version number.
- Monitors: Press and release the Option key more than 12 times while pressing the version number.

∞❥ **Set the magnification level by** clicking in the arrows in the control panel—you can use anywhere from 2 to 16 times the normal size of the screen. If you've turned on the Keyboard Shortcuts, you can increase and decrease the magnification level by pressing Command-Option-Up and Command-Option-Down.

Here's what a standard, 2x and 4x magnification of part of a desktop window looks like with CloseView on:

○•◆ **If you want to use the keyboard commands** to turn CloseView on and off and to control the magnification, don't forget to enable the keyboard shortcuts by turning them on in the control panel.

○•◆ **CloseView provides a white-on-black** screen option that reverses the Mac's general black-on-white, or ink-on-paper approach. On a color screen, colors are inverted from the normal arrangement—with the inversion being an unexpected, somewhat psychedelic exchange of shades that I can't do justice in a picture here. (There's a reason for the options being labeled in terms of black and white rather than "invert": inverting color doesn't ease anybody's eyes!)

## Color

○•◆ **The Color control panel** lets you control two color factors on your screen: the color that highlights selected text, and the color of your window frames. To change either setting, choose the color you want from the popup menus in the window. If you choose the Other command from the Highlight popup, the Color Picker window opens so you can create a custom color.

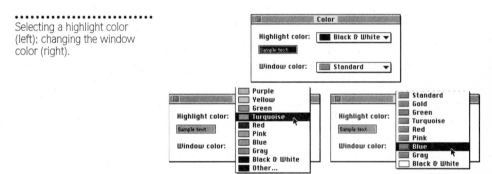

Selecting a highlight color (left); changing the window color (right).

Assigning highlight and window colors is covered in Chapter 2.

○•◆ **The Color Picker** lets you create and choose custom colors for your highlight color. The sample square in the Color Picker window shows the current color on the bottom and the new color on the top.

Colors on your monitor can be defined by an *RGB* value (how much red, green, and blue the color contains) or by a combination of *hue* (what you think of as the color—red or blue or green), the *saturation* (with a deep hue at one end of that scale, and the pastel version at the other), and *brightness* (how much light the color gives off—or how much black has been added to it). You can use the Hue, Saturation, and Brightness settings or the Red, Green, and Blue settings in the dialog to identify the new color: Either type in the new values, or use the arrows to change the numbers in each text box.

Of course, it's much easier to create a color by playing with the colors than by using numbers. There's a little marker that shows the current color on the color wheel. Click or drag anyplace in the wheel to pick a new color. Then use the scroll bar to change the brightness value. The numbers change as you interactively change the color.

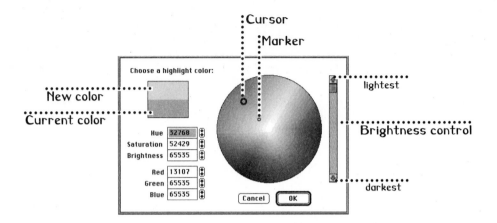

There's a new Color Picker in System 7.5. See the end of this chapter.

•→ **The more colors** your monitor is set to display, the smoother the gradations in the color wheel appear. These wheels, for instance, are from four different settings. Clockwise from the upper left, they show settings of 16, 256, Thousands, and Millions of colors.

•→ **Changing the window color** in the Color control panel affects only the window frame, not the window contents.

•→ **Use black and white windows** on a color system for some extra speed if you need it. This won't affect the color contents of windows, but will speed things like opening and closing windows, scrolling, and even some of the overall screen redrawing, especially on the desktop.

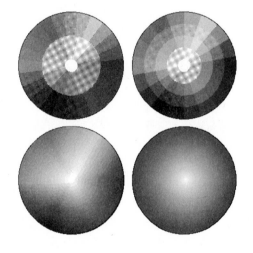

•→ **Selected text is inverted** to white only on a monitor set to black and white. If you use a dark color as the highlight on a color or grayscale monitor, the text won't invert, but disappears under the "highlight."

••→ **Your monitor must be able to display** at least 16 levels of gray or color for the color windows to be available.

••→ **The edit box** with the phrase *sample text* in it isn't editable—it's there just so you can see the effect of the color you've chosen. But if you click in it, you'll see the name of one of the programmers; click again and you'll see the name of the other programmer.

## Date & Time

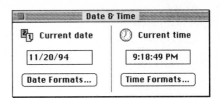

∞◆ **The Date & Time control panel** comes with System 7.1. You use it to define the way times and dates appear on the Mac. Any desk accessory, control panel, utility, or application that looks to the system to get the time or date without providing its own formatting will display the format you specify in the Date & Time control panel.

∞◆ **The Date Formats button** opens this dialog, where you can select or create date formats.

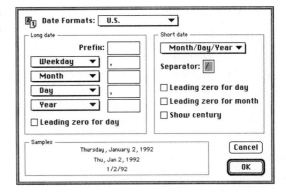

∞◆ **The Time Formats button** opens this dialog, where you can choose between a 12- and 24-hour clock, and how time readouts are formatted.

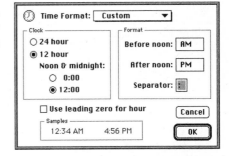

∞◆ **You can adjust the time or date** through the control panel by clicking in the text box for the date or time and then typing the new numbers or using the little arrows to adjust the numbers up or down.

🕐 **Current time**

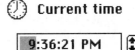

### POP QUIZ                    [3 POINTS]

Name three control panels and/or desk accessories in the Apple system software that let you adjust the time and date for the Mac's internal clock. (No points at all unless you can name all three.)

## Easy Access

∞♦ **The Easy Access control panel** was designed to help physically impaired persons bypass the mouse and also be able to type multiple-key keystrokes more easily with its three features: Mouse Keys, Slow Keys, and Sticky Keys.

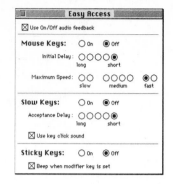

∞♦ **Mouse Keys** lets you use the numeric keypad for controlling the mouse cursor and clicking the mouse button. Turn it on and off through the control panel by clicking the buttons, or from the keyboard by pressing Command-Shift-Option-Clear.

The keys surrounding the 5 key move the cursor in any of eight directions. The 5 key itself acts as a mouse button for clicks and double-clicks. The zero key locks down the mouse button so you can use menus and drag things; the decimal point key unlocks it.

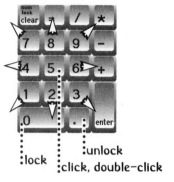

Keypad controls for the mouse cursor.

Pressing one of the controlling keys moves the mouse cursor one pixel on the screen. If you hold the key down, the cursor keeps moving in that direction. The *Initial Delay* setting in the Easy Access window defines how long it takes for that initial key press to be interpreted as a key being held down. The *Maximum Speed* setting sets the speed limit for the cursor once it gets going.

∞♦ **Slow Keys** adds a delay to each key press so an accidental press won't register. Turn it on and off with the buttons in the control panel. If you hold the Return key down for about 10 seconds (when you're someplace that the Return key doesn't *do* anything, like on the desktop with nothing selected), Slow Keys is supposed to be activated. But I've not found that method to be too reliable. Use the *Acceptance Delay* buttons to set how long a key should be down before it registers.

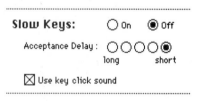

When Slow Keys is on, keys don't repeat no matter how long you hold them down. The "key click" sound that you can turn on or off with the checkbox in the control panel is a blip sound that sounds a lot like the one used in the early video game Pong.

∞♦ **Sticky Keys keeps a modifier key**—Command, Control, Shift, or Option—"stuck" down while you type another letter. So you can type a combination like Command-Q or Command-Option-S by pressing those keys in sequence instead of all at the same time. Turn Sticky Keys on and off with the buttons in the control panel or by pressing the Shift key five times in succession. You'll see a little bracket icon in the extreme upper-right corner of the screen when Sticky Keys is activated.

Pressing a modifier key while Sticky Keys is on "sets" the key so that the Mac thinks it's still down when you press the next key. So, Shift followed by the P key types a capital P; Command followed by the Q key issues the Quit command. When a modifier is set, the bracket icon in the menu bar has an arrow in it. A modifier is "unset" only when you type an alphanumeric character. So, if you press Command and then Option, both are set for the next key.

While "setting" a key keeps it down for only one more key press, "locking" it keeps it down for as many subsequent key presses as you want. You can make text both bold and italic, for instance, by locking the Command key down and then pressing B, then I. The menu bar icon changes to a filled bracket with an arrow when a modifier is locked.

To unlock a modifier, press it twice in a row again. (If you want to "unset" a modifier without using it, you have to press it a total of three times—once to set it, once to lock it, and once more to cancel it.)

The bracket icon that shows Sticky Keys is activated (top); a modifier is set (middle); a modifier is locked (bottom).

The icon in the menu bar indicates only that there's something set or locked; there's no indication as to which modifier, or how many modifiers, are actually in use. But you can get audio feedback as modifiers are set, locked, and canceled by checking the *Beep when modifier key is set* checkbox.

⤳ **The audio feedback setting** at the top of the control panel applies to each of the three features in Easy Access. With the feedback checkbox checked, you'll get a whistling sound whenever you turn any feature on or off—an especially appreciated touch when you're using keyboard commands instead of the buttons in the control panel. The sound is a little whistle—pitched upward when a feature is turned on, and downward when it's turned off. And if you don't *know* that, and you don't realize that Easy Access is in your system, and you happen to, say, press the Shift key five times, you'll be very puzzled as to why your Mac's whistling. I know I was!

⤳ **There are two extra keyboard** commands for turning off Sticky Keys: press any two modifier keys at the same time, or use Command-period.

⤳ **Do a shift-click equivalent** with Easy Access by locking the Shift key down with Sticky Keys and then manipulating the cursor and clicking the mouse button using Mouse Keys.

⤳ **Use Mouse Keys in graphics programs** that don't provide a "nudge" function to move a selection one pixel at a time. It often takes less time to activate and use Mouse Keys even for a single nudge than to repeatedly reposition a graphic, missing the exact placement you want.

## File Sharing

∞⁍ **File sharing on the Mac** involves three control panels—and three extensions and a Finder command. This unnecessarily complicated setup is covered in Chapter 21.

The three control panels, Sharing Setup, Users & Groups, and the File Sharing Monitor, will be in your Control Panels folder if basic file sharing software was installed during your system installation.

## General Controls

∞⁍ **The General Controls control panel** holds four items that, though important, just weren't big enough to deserve their own control panels: the desktop pattern, the insertion point blink, the menu blink, and time and date settings.

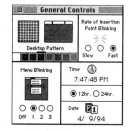

The standard General Controls control panel.

System 7.5 has a new General Controls control panel. See the end of the chapter.

∞⁍ **The Desktop pattern** in the standard General Controls control panel limits you to patterns of 8x8 pixels and eight different colors at a time. Using the control panel to set the desktop pattern is covered in Chapter 3, where there's also information about more interesting ways to color and design your desktop.

System 7.5 has a Desktop Patterns control panel. See chapter 2.

The General Controls control panel that comes with Performa systems provides eight pre-designed desktop patterns that you can choose through a popup menu.

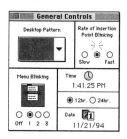

The Performa system's General Controls.

∞⁍ **The blink rate** for the insertion point (that blinking vertical line in text that shows you where you're typing) is demonstrated right in the control panel; you have three speeds to choose from. The quickest setting is a little too frenetic for me; it makes me feel like the Mac is impatient and demanding that I stop thinking and just type, type, type. The slowest setting, on the other hand, sometimes fails to catch my eye and I can lose where I am when I'm editing a document. I'm all for middle of the road in this instance.

∞⁍ **The menu blink** can be set to 1, 2, or 3 blinks, or turned off completely. What the heck is a menu blink? When you choose something from a menu, it's inverted while the mouse is pointing to it. When you let go of the mouse button, the black bar that's highlighting the choice blinks before the menu goes away. It's a subtle piece of feedback, but try turning it off and see how strange it is when there's no feedback at all!

∞⇥ **The Mac keeps track of the time and date** even when it's off or unplugged because it has an internal battery that supplies enough power to a special part of memory that stays alive and remembers a few things—like the time and date—even during shutdown. But you do have to tell it the information to start with.

- Set the time by clicking on the hour, minute, second, or AM/PM information and use the little arrows to change the numbers or type them in—you only have to type A or P for the AM/PM.

- Choose between a 12-hour clock (3:40:33 PM) or a 24-hour clock (15:40:33) by clicking one of the radio buttons.

- Change the date by clicking on the month, day, or year, and typing the new numbers or using the arrows to adjust them.

Once you click on the first set of numbers, you can tab from one number to the next instead of clicking on them.

∞⇥ **Changes made in General Controls** take effect immediately except for time and date, which take effect when you're finished editing them. "Finished" means you've moved on to something else in the control panel or left the control panel entirely, with or without closing the control panel as you leave.

∞⇥ **Clicking on the clock or calendar** after editing the time or date in the control panel deselects the time or date. You don't have to do this to set either piece of information, since doing something else in the control panel or leaving the control panel sets the information anyway. But you can!

∞⇥ **Time stands still when** you're editing it in the General Controls control panel. You'll see the seconds stop ticking by while you're editing; they'll resume when you're finished, without jumping forward to make up for the editing time itself.

∞⇥ **The 12-hour and 24-hour clock** settings are reflected in the Alarm Clock desk accessory. Some applications look to the system clock for information, so you may find it affects other programs, too.

∞⇥ **The time and date settings** in the General Controls control panel interact not only with the Alarm Clock but also with the Date & Time control panel that comes with System 7.1. So, if you've set your dates to be in a European format, or changed the hour/date/second separator to a hyphen, you'll see those format settings in the General Controls control panel.

## Keyboard

∞⇥ **The Keyboard control panel** lets you set the repeat rate and delay time for key presses, and choose a keyboard layout to work with.

∞⦁ **Adjust the repeat rate** by clicking in one of the five buttons. This is one of the differences between using a typewriter and typing on the Mac—hold down a key and the character is typed repeatedly.* The slowest setting is so slow it seems more like an *off* button; with the fastest setting, characters are typed onto the screen almost more quickly than you can control. It's great if you have to type a series of underline characters to draw a horizontal line. Most people don't need

*Okay, it's also one of the differences between manual and electric typewriters. But I went from a manual typewriter to a computer.

to type repeated characters very often, but do hold the Delete key down to erase a few characters or words in a row. So a good rule of thumb is to set the repeat rate to whatever's comfortable as a delete speed.

∞⦁ **The *Delay until repeat* setting** defines the time between the first character's being typed and when the repeat kicks in. Note this is *not* the same as the *Slow Keys* setting in Easy Access, which defines the length of time a key has to be down before the letter appears. Use the Off button to cancel the repeat capability completely.

⦁⦁⦁ **The keyboard layouts** listed in the bottom of the Keyboard control panel are the ones available in your system. In System 7.0, you'll see a single layout: *U.S.* In System 7.1, you'll see two: *U.S.* and *U.S.- System 6*. (There were slight changes in keyboard layouts from System 6 to System 7—that's covered in Chapter 20.) To use a specific layout, you select it in the list.

∞⦁ **Keyboard layouts are *resources,*** just like sounds. To install a keyboard layout (they have little keyboard icons on them), just drag it into the System file's window, the System file icon, or the closed System Folder. To remove the layout, open the System file and drag the keyboard layout out. As with other resources, you'll get a *Copy* dialog when you add or remove a keyboard to the System file.

## PRESS RELEASE?

*From Apple Computer, Inc:* Effective immediately, we are unbundling the "Return" key from Apple keyboards. This allows us to lower the price of our keyboards by $.01. Users wishing to buy a Return key will be able to do so through their local dealership. The kits will cost $99.95, with installation. "We think this will enable more users to get Return keys," says Apple chairman Sculley. "Also, we want the money."

—from the Internet,
in reaction to Apple's MacTCP pricing policy

Using keyboard layouts is covered in Chapter 1; altering them in ResEdit is in Chapter 21.

∞⦁ **A choice of keyboard layouts** is a necessity for bilingual typists, but why would you want more than one layout if you're typing in only one language? Well, don't you get tired of trying to type things like *New York, N.Y.,* or *U.S.* and having them turn out as *New York, N>Y>,* and *U>S>* because it's so hard to unshift for the period when you're typing capital letters? With a modified keyboard layout, the Mac interprets the Shift-period and the Shift-comma as period and comma instead of the greater than and less than signs. Or if you want to switch from the standard QWERTY layout to the Dvorak keyboard, all you have to do is change layouts through the control panel. PowerBook users will appreciate a layout that puts a numeric keyboard cluster in the center of the standard keyboard layout. You'll find alternate keyboard layouts online and through user groups.

## Labels

∞➜ **The Labels control panel** controls the contents of the desktop's Label menu. On a color system, you also use the control panel to change the label colors. To change a label, simply type in the new name in the control panel. The changes appear immediately in the Label menu

The Label menu reflects the entries in the Labels control panel.

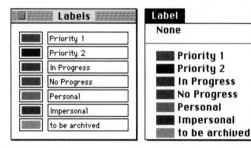

See Chapter 4 for details about labeling icons.

.∞➜ **To change a label color,** double-click on the color "swatch" in the control panel and then use the Color Picker (described earlier in this chapter) to alter the color.

••➜ **If you've altered the names and colors** in the Label menu and want to return them to the original values without reinstalling your system, the names are: Essential, Hot, In Progress, Cool, Personal, Project 1, and Project 2. The colors? Type these values into the fields in the Color Picker window:

### Default Label Menu Labels

| Label | Color | Red | Green | Blue |
|-------|-------|-----|-------|------|
| *Essential* | Orange | 65535 | 25738 | 652 |
| *Hot* | Red | 56683 | 2242 | 1698 |
| *In Progress* | Pink | 62167 | 2134 | 34028 |
| *Cool* | Light Blue | 577 | 43860 | 60159 |
| *Personal* | Dark Blue | 1 | 4 | 54272 |
| *Project 1* | Green | 0 | 25775 | 4528 |
| *Project 2* | Brown | 22016 | 11421 | 1316 |

••▶ **Programmers' names are** hidden in strange ways. Delete all seven labels in the Labels control panel so that they're blank, then take a look at the Label menu at the desktop.

## Launcher

∘∘▶ **The Launcher control panel** is a special feature of Performa system software. It provides a desktop window of "launch" icons so you don't have to dig through layers of folders to find your application and document icons. To open the window, double-click on the Launcher control panel or choose it from the Apple menu if it's listed there.

The launcher is part of standard Mac systems starting with System 7.5.

The Launcher window.

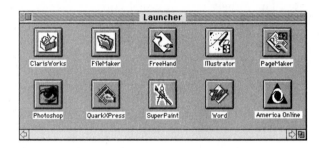

∘∘▶ **It takes only a single click** to launch something from the Launcher window, because the icons are buttons, not standard desktop icons. (I'm sure thousands of research hours went into discovering that a single click was easier for beginners than a double-click.)

∘∘▶ **To get an icon into the window,** put an alias of the item into the Launcher Items folder that's in the System Folder. You could put the original item in instead of the alias, but I can't thing of a single circumstance when doing it that way would be more convenient than the other way around.

To remove an icon from the Launcher window, take the alias out of the Launcher Items folder.

••▶ **You can put documents** in the Launcher window, but that clutters up the window very quickly. Stick with application icons for launching, with the possible exception of an oft-used document like a To Do list.

••▶ **The contents of the Launcher window** are updated automatically when you alter the contents of its folder. It might take anywhere from a few seconds to almost a full minute for the update, but it does happen.

## Map

∘∘▶ **The Map control panel** doesn't deserve to be a control panel—it ought to be a desk accessory. That issue aside, it's probably the least useful of any of the Apple control panels, though it sure can do a lot of little things. (Things that you don't need.)

You can check the latitude and longitude, and time zone, of any city that's in the map. You can also check the distance and time difference between a selected city and the "base" city. The problem is, there aren't all that many cities already on the map—you have to add the ones you want included.

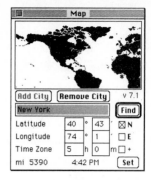

°°● **The blinking dots on the map** are cities. Click on one, or drag around until you touch one, and you'll get the information about that city. Once you touch a city, though, you have to release the mouse button and press down again before you can get the latitude and longitude to change while you're dragging.

The blinking mark that's a star of sorts is the currently selected city. The one that's sort of a Maltese cross is the "base" city from which distances and time differences are measured.

**ANNE BODNOY**
1852

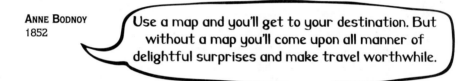

Use a map and you'll get to your destination. But without a map you'll come upon all manner of delightful surprises and make travel worthwhile.

°°● **Scroll the map** by dragging the mouse cursor against any of its edges. Or simply place the mouse on or right inside the border and press the mouse button to scroll without dragging—the "hot" area is only a pixel wide, so you have to be *right* next to the border. You can even scroll the map diagonally by pressing just inside any corner of its frame. And there's variable-speed scrolling, too: Start by dragging inside the map, and drag to outside its border. The further you move away from the border, the faster it scrolls.

°°● **Find a city** on the map by typing its name and clicking the Find button or pressing Return. You don't have to type capitals, and you have to type only enough of the city's name to uniquely identify it. Typing *new*, for instance, will get you to New Delhi, but typing *new y* gets you to New York. If the city you're looking for isn't on the map, the Mac beeps.

°°● **The checkboxes** at the right side of the control panel window help define the latitude and longitude, and time difference. If the N is checked, the measurement is North latitude; unchecked, the measurement is South. If the E is checked, the measurement is East longitude; unchecked, it's West. If the Plus (+) is checked, the time difference noted is that many hours later than the base city; if it's unchecked, the time is earlier than the base city.

⊠ N
☐ E
☐ +

**⟶** **Cycle through units of measure**—miles, kilometers, and degrees, by clicking on the measurement in the lower-left corner of the window.

**⟶** **Add a city** to the map by scrolling to the correct location (an amazing knowledge of geography, or an atlas, is helpful), clicking on the right spot, typing the city's name and clicking the Add City button. It's important to click the right spot because the latitude and longitude displayed for that spot are the ones that will be used for that city from then on.

**⟶** **To set the base city,** find it on the map (or, more likely, add it to the map) and, while it's selected, click the Set button.

**⟶** **Find the time difference** between the selected city and the base city by clicking on the *Time Zone* title. The title changes to *Time Differ* and the information readout changes from a time zone number (in relation to Greenwich Mean Time) to the time difference between the selected and base cities.

**⟶** **Option-click the Find button** or press Option-Return to jump to the next city in the alphabetical list of cities on the map.

**⟶** **The Scrapbook contains a color map** for use with the Map control panel. Just copy it from the Scrapbook and, with the control panel open, choose Paste. This is what the color map looks like—if you could see the whole thing at once. (Well, except that it's in *color*, and this book isn't!)

**⟶** **If you want to return to the black-and-white** map after pasting in the color one, too bad. In a slip of the interface conventions, pasting something into the Map control panel totally replaces the resource that's preserved internally as the map picture, and you can't undo the procedure. Nor can you copy out the existing map. But hey, why would you want to go back to the black-and-white one anyway? (You can always get the original from your system disks.)

**⟶** **Zoom in on the map** by holding Shift down when you open the Map control panel. Zoom in even further by holding Option down when you open it. You want closer? Hold down both Shift *and* Option while you open the Map.

Unfortunately, zooming in only magnifies the existing picture in the control panel; it doesn't provide any more detail. But it's much easier to work in a magnified view when you're adding cities to the map.

It's easy enough to hold either or both keys if you're selecting the Map from the Apple menu, or from one of its submenus if you're using a hierarchical Apple menu utility. If your Apple menu utility reacts to one of the keys by "forgetting" its submenus, no problem: find the Map in the submenu and just before you release the mouse button for the Map selection, *that's* when to press the modifier keys.

At the desktop, it's easy to Option-double-click on the Map icon for the magnified view. But using Shift or Shift-Option is a problem because the Shift key adds or deletes a clicked item from a selection—you'll wind up alternately selecting and deselecting the icon. The trick is to press Shift or Shift-Option immediately after you double-click the icon (you have to be *very* fast).

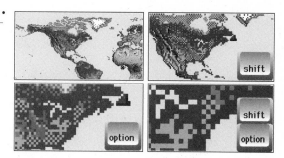

The standard Map and its magnified views of the New York area.

••◆ **You can paste any picture** into the Map and label its parts. (Although, if you have time for this, it would be better spent on any of dozens of more worthwhile hobbies.) You can also, if you want, copy the basic black-and-white map out of the Map control panel to paste somewhere else.

••◆ **If you want to know just where** the "middle of nowhere" is, type *mid* as the city and click the Find button.

••◆ **The Map's programmer hid** his name in two places. Click or press on the version number in the window, and you'll see his name where the city's name appears. And if you scroll around the world, you'll eventually find his initials embedded in the map. At least, I assume they're his initials, since the first and last ones match his name as it appears in the city field. On the other hand, there's a different set of initials stamped on the color version of the map, so maybe they're the artist's initials.

••◆ **Reset the base city** if you're traveling with a PowerBook; the time on your clock is automatically adjusted to the proper time zone without your having to use the Alarm Clock or General Controls panel.

## Memory

∘∘◆ **The Memory control panel** has up to four sections in it, depending on the capabilities of your Mac. You use it to control the disk cache, virtual memory, 32-bit addressing, and a RAM disk.

- *The disk cache* is a portion of memory used to hold information that's frequently accessed and would otherwise be retrieved, much more slowly, from a disk. The disk cache is available on all Macs.
- *Virtual memory* lets you use a segment of your hard drive as if it were RAM.
- *32-bit addressing* is needed to let Macs address more than 8 megs of memory.
- *A RAM disk* sets aside part of memory to be treated as a disk.

Chapter 9 deals with all these memory features in detail.

The Memory control panel changes to match your Mac's capabilities.

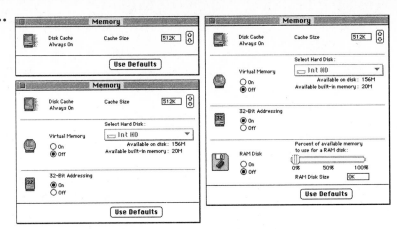

•••➤ **Any changes you make** in the Memory control panel won't take effect until you restart the computer.

•••➤ **For a strange cast of characters,** click the On button for virtual memory to activate the popup menu. Then, hold Option while you open the menu. Voilà!

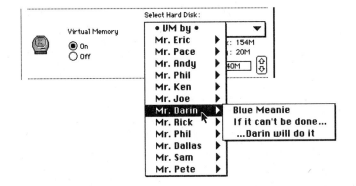

## POP QUIZ                                    [25 POINTS!]

In the cast of characters in the Memory control panel, Mr. Sam's submenu asks *Yngwie Who?* So, who *is* Yngwie? (Actually, if you get this one, I'd like to offer you a free dinner. But how could I be sure you didn't look it up in the back of the book first?)

## Monitors

•••➤ **The Monitors control panel** lets you set the number of colors or grays your monitor displays. (This is also known as the *color depth*.) If you're working on a multiple-monitor system, you can use the control panel to define the relative positions of the monitors and control which one is used as the main monitor.

∘∘✦ **To set the number of colors** to be displayed, click the Grays or Colors button, and then click on the choices in the list. Your choices, of course, are limited by the capabilities of your hardware. You can't get *more* colors out of a setup that allows 256 colors, or get any color at all out of a grayscale system. But you might occasionally want to display less than what your monitor's capable of in order to speed up the display itself.

Why does 8-bit color mean 256 colors? See Chapter 15.

The color bar at the bottom of the control panel shows the range of colors or grays available based on your choice in the list. This picture shows how the bar looks for four different grayscale choices.

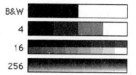

••✦ **The Options button** opens a small dialog with information about the video card that the monitor is connected to. Here, for instance, are the two dialogs I get for the two monitors connected to my screen.

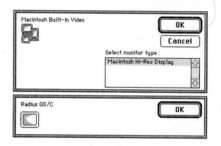

••✦ **There are Option options**—hold the Option key down while you click the Option button. You'll get a slightly larger dialog with a few options about the *Special Gamma*, depending on the hardware you're using. This dialog shows the Option options for the Mac's color display. With the Special Gamma button checked, a list of choices may appear (again, depending on your hardware). Stick with the Mac Standard Gamma, which is a slightly brighter overall picture than the Uncorrected Gamma choice. You may see other choices, such as *Page White*, which affects the white areas of the display rather than the mid-range of colors that the other choices correct.*

＊My real recomenda-tion here is to leave well enough alone. Unless you're having trouble with your monitor display, don't bother with the Options options.

For some monitors, there will be a list under *Select monitor type*. If your monitor can work in more than one mode—say 256 colors on a full screen or thousands of colors on a slightly smaller screen—the modes will be listed here so you can choose the one you want.

**⸭** **When you add a second monitor,** it won't be "acknowledged" until you open the Monitors control panel. That is, you can get everything hooked up and turned on, but you won't see anything on the new monitor, and you can't move the mouse cursor over to it, until you've opened the Monitors control panel.

**⸭** **For a multiple-monitor setup,** the Monitors control panel provides extra functions. When you open the control panel you'll see icons for both monitors, each with a number in it.

The Monitors control panel has been enchanced for System 7.5. See the end of this chapter.

- When you work with two (or more) monitors, you can slide the mouse cursor right from one monitor to the other, as if they were one screen. But for this to work correctly, you have to set the Monitors control panel to show the relative positions of the real monitors. Just drag the monitor icons around in the control panel until they're in the correct positions.

- To use any of the standard options (like setting the color depth), first click on the monitor you want and then choose the options. The selected monitor has its number highlighted and has a dark frame around it. (This picture shows a 13" color monitor and a 21" grayscale monitor, with the smaller monitor currently selected.)

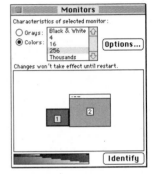

- To set the *main monitor*—the one that will have the menu bar on it—drag the miniature menu bar from one monitor to the other.

- To set the *startup monitor*—the one that gets the Welcome to Macintosh dialog—press the Option key until you see the miniature Happy Mac. Drag the Happy Mac to the screen you want as the startup. The startup monitor is also the one that's supposed to have the icons marching along the bottom of the screen at startup, but I find that my small color screen, which I have set as the startup, gets the Welcome dialog, but the icons still march on the larger, grayscale screen, which is set as the main monitor.

Move the Happy Mac icon to the startup monitor.

- When you click the Identify button, numbers flash on each screen so you can see which icon corresponds to which monitor.

While color-depth changes take effect immediately, changes to monitor positions or resetting the startup monitor need a restart to take effect.

**⸭** **If you set the smaller monitor** of a two-monitor setup as the default (the one with the menu bar) some applications get slightly confused and won't let you open a document window any larger than the small monitor—even if the window is on the bigger monitor.

**⸭** **If there are two monitor icons** in the Monitors control panel, you can move the selected one by using the Up or Down arrow keys. But this doesn't always just alter the relative positions of the monitors, as dragging the icon does. On some setups (mine, for instance—a color Apple and a large grayscale Radius), nudging the icon with the arrow results in the contents of the screen being shifted at the next startup with, for instance, the Trash can partially or entirely off the bottom of the screen. (If it happens to you, the fix is to open the control panel again, nudge the icon in the opposite direction, and restart.)

Tips for using large monitors and multiple monitor setups are in Chapter 15.

**••➤ Click on the version number** in the control panel to see a list of its programmers. Just for fun, see what happens when you repeatedly press and release the Option key while the list is showing—the little face will keep sticking out its tongue.

As if that weren't enough: Keep pressing and releasing that Option key. At the twelfth press, the famous Blue Meanies make an appearance, and something starts happening to the names. Try it and see.

**°°◌› Changing the color depth** on a monitor is simple enough—you don't have to restart the Mac for the changes to take effect. But if it's something you do relatively often during the course of your work session—say you keep your word processor in black and white for some extra speed, but want the graphics program you're running concurrently to be in 256 shades of gray—taking out the Monitors control panel repeatedly, or leaving it hanging around, gets annoying.

There are utilities that let you change the color depth more quickly, and even let you specify a color change as you switch from one application to another. Color Coordinator is one of them: it's a control panel that looks much like the Monitors control panel, but lets you set color depth for applications on an individual basis. It also provides a popup dialog to switch colors any time you want to do something other than your pre-programmed depths.

Working on a multiple-monitor setup, where one is a very large 21-inch screen, I find this automatic switching of color depths and its resultant flash-and-redraw of the screens too disconcerting. On the other hand, taking out the Monitors control panel to reset either the color or grayscale monitor is a pain, too. Instead, I use a macro to change either screen as necessary. The macro takes out the control panel, so it's not as fast as something like Color Coordinator, but it's not lack of speed I find annoying—it's having to do the changes manually. But I use Tempo for macros which, for all its power, is missing some things that QuicKeys can do—like automatically change color depth *without* opening the control panel. [Color Coordinator—Conflict Catcher, Casady & Greene]

## Mouse

∞•➤ **The Mouse control panel** lets you set the tracking speed (the relationship between how far you move the mouse on your desk and how far its cursor moves on the screen) and the double-click speed for the mouse. Just click the buttons for your choices—the specifics of both adjustments are covered in Chapter 1.

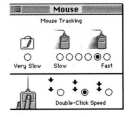

∞•➤ **The double-click speed setting** for the mouse also controls the "edit delay" for desktop icons—how long it takes for the editing rectangle to appear after you click on an icon's name.

**NAT AKER**
at age 5, when confronted with an IBM-PC.

> This is a stupid computer.
> It doesn't even have a mouse.

∞•⟩ **Speed up that mouse** beyond what the mouse control panel allows by using Mouse2, a control panel that lets you double the speed setting of the Mouse control panel. It's great for big screens. [shareware, Ryoji Watanabe ]

## Numbers

∞•➤ **The Numbers control panel** was introduced with System 7.1. You use it to specify your preferences for how numbers are formatted by the system. It's set to the U.S. as a default, which gives you a comma as the thousands separator, a period for the decimal, and a dollar sign in front of currency numbers.

The separator choice affects how numbers are reported in Finder windows, so if you use an apostrophe, you'll be told a file is 1'459K. Any application that looks to the operating system for number and currency formatting will be affected by the changes made in the Numbers control panel.

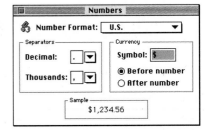

## PowerBook Control Panels

∞► **The Portable control panel,** left over from the Mac Portable, was still used for the first generation of PowerBooks under System 7. It was replaced by the PowerBook control panel in System 7.1. Either one sets the interval for drive and system sleep to conserve battery power.

### OLD CONTROL PANELS NEVER DIE ...

Macs evolve inside and out, but some control panel icons are stuck in the past.

The Portable control panel first showed up on—what else?—the Mac Portable. But it was also used for the first generation of PowerBooks. But take a look at the icon—it's a Portable, not a PowerBook.

The design of the mouse has changed during the Mac's life, with three significantly different major models. But the Mouse control panel's icon still has the unmistakable lines of the original mouse.

*Further details on using these control panels are in Chapter 22.*

∞► **The PowerBook Display** control panel controls the dimming interval for the screen (again, to save battery power) and how the PowerBook screen should act in relation to an external monitor.

∞► **AutoRemounter** is for PowerBooks attached to a desk Mac or other network—it automatically re-establishes the network connection when the PowerBook comes out of sleep.

## Sound

∞► **The Sound control panel** changes slightly depending on your hardware capabilities. And it changes a *lot* depending on the system software you're using.

The hardware-dependent features are the ones relating to the input and output of sound. On Macs with built-in sound recording capability, for instance, there's an extra section for recording.

Using the Sound control panel is covered in Chapter 2. Here's a quick roundup of facts and details:

*There's lots more information about using sounds and the Sound control panel in Chapter 2. System updates are discussed in Chapter 23.*

- Adjust the volume with the slider control. If you set the volume to zero, your menu bar blinks when the Mac would otherwise beep.
- Select the system beep from the Alert Sound list.
- The sounds listed in the control panel are the ones in your System file.
- You can use the Cut and Copy commands on any sound in the list.
- You can paste a sound into the list once it's on the Clipboard.
- To rename a sound, cut it out of the list and paste it back in; you'll get to rename it when you paste it.

○○•❯ **The standard Sound control panel** in System 7 and in the initial release of System 7.1 has all its controls in a single panel. The later Sound control panel has as many as four different panels for various functions. The later panel was introduced with one of System 7.1's hardware system updates.

The standard control panel.

The later control panel.

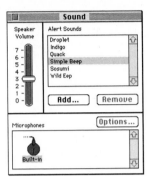
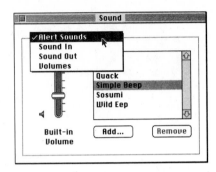

## Startup Disk

○○•❯ **Use the Startup Disk** control panel to specify which disk you want used as the startup for your system—assuming you have more than one attached and each has a System Folder on it. The Mac looks all over the place for a System Folder when it starts up, but it looks in a very specific order. To supersede that order, you can select the startup disk you want in the control panel.

There's more about the startup order and other startup concerns in Chapters 1 and 18.

•••❯ **Although you can select a disk partition** in the Startup Disk control panel—each partition appears as a separate disk—the Mac doesn't differentiate between partitions for startup, since they all have the same SCSI ID number. It scans the partitions in alphabetical order and uses the first one it finds with a System Folder on it.

•••❯ **A Mac Plus can't** use the Startup Disk control panel. The startup information is stored in PRAM, and the Mac Plus PRAM wasn't designed to retain that information.

## Views

○○•❯ **The Views control panel** lets you change the look of desktop windows. It's covered extensively in Chapter 3; here's a roundup of the things you can do with it:

- Choose a font and size for icon names.
- Select a straight or staggered grid for icon arrangements in windows.

- Keep icons snapped to the grid or not when you move them.
- Reverse the snap-to-grid setting by holding down the Command key when you drag an icon to a new spot.
- Control the list of items in the View label, and the columns that appear in list-view windows, with the "Show" checkboxes.
- Have folder sizes calculated and listed in list-view windows.
- Add a header to list-view windows that shows the amount of space used and remaining on the disk.

➡ **The popup menu for font size** in the control panel lists seven sizes from 9 to 24 points, but you can type in any point size from 6 to 36.

➡ **If your Mac seems to forget** the settings in the Views control panel, it's likely that the Finder Preferences file in the Preferences folder is corrupted (that's where your choices are stored). Trash the Finder Preferences file and restart; a new file will be created.

# ⊁ FKEYs ⊁

## Basics

➡ **Before there were extensions,** there were FKEYs. What were/are FKEYs? Little utilities that loaded into memory whose functions were available at the press of a key combination. Sound familiar? Yes, they were the precursors to extensions. But the big difference is that FKEYs were, and still are, installed into the System file itself rather than left loose in another folder. You can think of an FKEY (if you think about one at all) as an extension installed into the System file.

➡ **FKEYs are invoked** by pressing Command-Shift and a number, so there's only 10 slots available for FKEYs—zero through nine—and Apple reserved six of them right off the bat. When programmers started writing FKEYs, it was difficult to avoid clashes for key assignments.

But once the Mac's system software became extendable—and that was way before System 7, since control panels and inits have been around for years—FKEYs pretty much fell by the wayside.*

*As well they should! Why muck around in the System file when you can just drop a utility into a folder and remove it if it's giving you problems or needs to be updated?

➡ **An FKEY is not a function key.** A function key is one of those keys (labeled F1, F2, and so on) along the top of an extended keyboard. But the similarity in names isn't really coincidental. FKEYs, after all, provided specific functions at the press of a key—and since the Mac's keyboard didn't have any function keys until years after its original introduction, no confusion was anticipated.

○•➔ **The FKEYs** incorporated into the Mac system software are:

Command-Shift-1 ...... Ejects disk from first internal floppy drive
Command-Shift-2 ...... Ejects disk from second internal or from external floppy drive
Command-Shift-3 ...... Takes a snapshot of the screen and puts it on the disk.
Command-Shift-0 ...... Ejects disk from second internal or from external floppy drive

Wait a minute! Didn't I say that Apple reserved six FKEY slots? Yes, there used to be two more; one printed the screen directly to the ImageWriter printer, and the other printed the current window, but neither of these is available anymore.

Resedit is covered in Chapter 21.

••➔ **Of the four FKEYs** still in use, only one—the screen shot on Command-Shift-3—is actually an FKEY resource that you can see in the System file with a program like ResEdit.

## The Screen Shot FKEY

○•➔ **Take a picture of your screen** by pressing Command-Shift-3. You'll hear a camera click, and get a *screen shot*, or *screen dump*: a picture of the screen in a PICT-format file. It's named *Picture 1*, and if you take subsequent pictures, they're named *Picture 2*, *Picture 3*, and so on. The files are stored on the main level of the startup drive.

You can't invoke an FKEY while the mouse button is down, so you won't be able to take a picture of an opened menu.

Graphics formats are covered in Chapter 20.

••➔ **You can view the picture** in TeachText, or almost any Mac graphics program, since it's in the common PICT format.

### THE WAY WE WERE ...

The screen dump FKEY has been in the Mac's system since the very beginning, but its capabilities have evolved. First of all, it used to be a silent operation—sort of: there was no click of the camera in the early days, but there was the whir of the floppy drive spinning up so the picture could be stored on the system disk. The format of the screen picture was MacPaint, since that was the only graphics program around. And, of course, it was a strictly black and white world back then.

There was a limit of ten screens; the first was named Screen 0, the next Screen 1, and so on, through Screen 9.* The naming limit wasn't much of a problem, though, because what with a System Folder and even an application on the internal floppy, that didn't leave much room for more than a few snapshots. (Picture that!) When the first hard drives came out, though, tips abounded for surpassing the ten-picture limit; the main approach was to simply rename the existing pictures or move them into a folder to get them out of the way so you could start again.

✳I always thought it was stupid that the friendliest computer around sometimes insisted on counting like a computer, starting at zero instead of one.

••◄ **Taking a screen shot of** a large color monitor can take some time—up to a full minute—and during that time the mouse cursor won't move and you'll probably think you've crashed. Just be patient.

••◄ **With a multiple monitor setup,** the screen shot spans both monitors. (And takes a *long* time to process.)

∞◊ **There are many substitutes** for the built-in screen shot function, which has two inherent problems: You can't snap the picture while the menu is down, and you get a disk file that has the entire screen captured. Third-party utilities get around both those problems, and add other options as well, like keeping the picture on the Clipboard so you can paste it someplace immediately.

Capture is the aptly named utility that I used for all the screen captures in this book. Press whatever key you've assigned to activate it (I use F13 because it's labeled, right on some keyboard models, *print screen*) and you get a crosshairs cursor; drag across a section of the screen and it's copied to the Clipboard, the Scrapbook, or a disk file whose type you can specify. You can include the mouse cursor or not, force the screen capture to black and white on a color system, and say where you want a disk file to be saved—and you can name the files as you save them. [Mainstay]

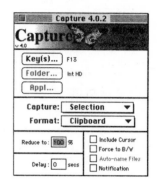

## ◄ SYSTEM 7.5 STUFF ►

### Control Panel Roundup

∞◄ **There are new control panels** in System 7.5, and a few changes to the old ones. Some of the additions to the Control Panels folder are: Apple Menu Options, ATM GX, Desktop Patterns, Macintosh Easy Open Setup, PC Exchange, Launcher, and WindowShade.

In addition to the new control panels, the General Controls control panel has undergone major modifications, the Monitors control panel has some new tricks up its sleeve, and there's an addition to the Date & Time control panel. The Color Picker, accessed through the Color control panel, has also been revised.

∞◄ **The Apple Menu Options** control panel controls the hierarchical Apple menu; it's described in Chapter 7.

∞◄ **ATM GX. Finally!** Built-in ATM (Adobe Type Manager), which was promised so many times—first for System 7.0, then System 7.1. The GX suffix differentiates it from Adobe's own product (although the functions are the same) and ties it in to the system software, what with QuickDraw GX technology. It's discussed in Chapter 10.

∞➤ **Desktop Patterns is a spin-off** from the old General Controls control panel, and is discussed in Chapter 3. But here are two shortcuts you'll find in it:

- Use the Left or Right arrow keys to flip through the patterns instead of clicking on the left and right arrow buttons.
- Double-click in the displayed pattern to put it on the desktop, instead of using the Set Desktop Pattern button.

∞➤ **The Launcher control panel** was always part of the Performa system software, so it's described earlier in this chapter. But with the advent of System 7.5, it's part of standard Mac systems.

∞➤ **Macintosh Easy Open Setup** lets you specify in what application "unattached" documents should open; it's described in Chapter 19.

Wouldn't you think they'd come up with a better name? First of all, almost all control panels provide setup options, and none of them has the trailer "Setup"—Mouse Setup, Keyboard Setup, Date & Time Setup …? Even worse, everyone's going to confuse this with Easy Access and At Ease.

∞➤ **PC Exchange lets you** open PC-generated files in Mac programs by double-clicking on them; you set up the "links" by showing which three-letter suffix PC file belongs with which Mac program. It starts with .TXT documents mapped to SimpleText, but you'll probably want to re-map them to your word processor. (PC Exchange, as an application, has been an overlooked part of system software for quite a while.)

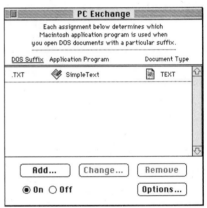

∞➤ **The nifty WindowShade control panel** lets you collapse windows down to their title bars; it's described at the end of Chapter 2.

To find out who programmed WindowShade, Command-Option-double-click on the mouse button in the window.

∞➤ **The Date & Time control panel now includes** a setting for the Menubar Clock, discussed at the end of Chapter 2.

∞➤ **The Monitors control panel** now does on-the-fly alterations: You don't have to restart the Mac to see a change to, say, which of two monitors has the menu bar. You can use the radio buttons at the bottom of its window to leave the changes until you restart or make them happen as soon as you close the control panel's window.

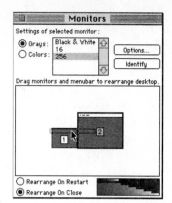

Changing which monitor has the menu bar like this doesn't require a restart to take effect.

**⠤⠴** **The new Color Picker**—the dialog you get when you're defining a new color because you've chosen *Other* from the Color control panel—is much more intuitive than the one we've been working with for so long. The most important change is that there are two separate dialogs, one for each approach to defining colors on the Mac. You click on an icon in the left panel of the dialog to choose which approach you want to work with.

Apple HSL stands for Hue, Saturation, and Light—the three values you worked with in the old Color Picker. The hue is the basic color, the saturation is how bright it is, and the lightness is how much black is added to mix. Apple RGB stands for Red, Green, and Blue, and it lets you define a color based on how much of each of these basic colors is in the mix.

Using Tab cycles you around the text fields in the right panel of the dialog, then selects the left panel and each of its icons in turn; more tabbing puts you back in the right panel again and selects each text field in turn. The "active" panel has a thick frame around it.

The RGB option, with the left panel active.

The HSL option, with the right panel active.

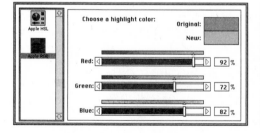

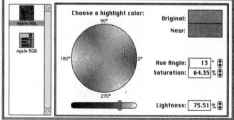

## General Controls

**∞⠴** **The General Controls control panel** has been completely reworked, with the desktop pattern section banished to its own separate control panel and a few items added. In fact, the only remnants of the old control panel are the Insertion Point and Menu Blinking rates.

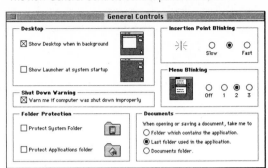

The new General Controls control panel window.

∘∘➔ **The Shut Down Warning**, if checked, displays a dialog on startup letting you know that the computer was shut down improperly. Not a big help—but you can use it as a reminder to look in the Trash for any files rescued at crash time.

The Shut Down Warning and dialog are covered in Chapter 1.

∘∘➔ **When you check *Show Desktop when in background*,** you'll be able to see desktop windows and icons even when you're in another application—as long as the desktop items aren't covered by the current application's windows. When you uncheck the option, you won't see the Finder's windows or icons in the background.

The difference between this option and the Hide command in the Application menu is that, first of all, although the Hide command will make the Finder's windows disappear, its icons remain visible. More importantly, when the desktop isn't set to show in the background, the desktop pattern that still serves as a background behind your application's windows isn't really the desktop—if you click on it, you don't get switched to the Finder.

Checking and unchecking this option changes the picture in the dialog box, just in case the name of the button doesn't do it for you.

∘∘➔ **The *Show Launcher at system startup*** button is a handier way of controlling the Launcher control panel than having to put its alias in the Startup Items folder (and taking it out again, as necessary). As with the Show Desktop option, the icon changes when you check and uncheck this button.

∘∘➔ **The Open and Save dialogs have always** defaulted to the folder that contains the application you're working in. The Documents setting in the General Controls control panel can change all that with a click of a radio button.

Clicking in the *Documents folder* button creates a Documents folder on the desktop so you can dump all your documents into it.

∘∘➔ **Protect your System Folder** from inadvertent changes by checking the button in the Folder Protection section of the control panel. With the System Folder protected, you can put things into it, but nothing can be removed until you uncheck the button. This low-level protection scheme is specifically for families with kids, or Macs exposed to other curious but not knowledgeable users.

You can put the same level of protection on your Applications folder. *What* Applications folder, you ask? The one that's created and placed on the main level of the drive when you check the *Protect Applications folder* button!

## The Control Strip

∞•▶ **The Control Strip is for PowerBooks.** It's a strip of, well, *controls* that sits at the bottom left of your screen. The one here shows seven icons, although there are eight basic ones—this one doesn't include the one for "video mirroring," since it's running on a Power-Book without a video out port.

The Control Strip combines the functions of the Battery DA and the PowerBook control panel in this series of icons with popup menus. It's included in System 7.5 for all PowerBooks, but was also included in the System 7.1 software for models in the 500 series and the 280 and 280c.

∞•▶ **The Control Strip is controlled by** the Control Strip control panel. (I've probably just broken some law about using the same word, or its variants, four times in one short sentence.) This control panel is about as simple as they come, as you can see by the picture here. You might expect that opening the control panel puts the Strip on the screen, but what you actually get is this window, which lets you open the Strip. To remove the Strip, you have to open the control panel again and click the Hide Button. (Isn't that stupid? Why not just open the Strip when the control panel is selected, and close it from a close box?)

∞•▶ **The Control Strip is modular,** and its modules are in a folder in the System Folder that's named, reasonably enough, Control Strip Items.

To add or remove an item from your Control Strip, move its module in or out of the folder and restart the computer.

*Chapter 22 has more information about Control Strip modules.*

∞•▶ **To change the size of the Control Strip,** use the tab at its right end. Clicking on the tab, or on what looks like a close box at the left edge, collapses the Strip down to nothing but the tab itself; click on the tab again, and the Strip opens up to whatever size you were using before you collapsed it.

Dragging the tab to the left or right makes the strip smaller or larger, although you can't make it any larger than a size that accommodates all the installed modules. If you make the strip smaller so that you can't see all the icons, use the arrows at the left and right ends to scroll through them.

⌒⬧ **Each item in the Control Strip has** a popup menu, as indicated by the little black arrow inside the icon. In some cases, it's pretty silly; the Sleep Now command, for instance, might as well be a button icon, since there's only one menu choice when you press the icon.

Be that as it may, these pictures show the menus you get for each icon. Note that there are two versions of the Battery Level icon, one of which displays the battery charge level right in the Strip. (If you're using a 500-series PowerBook with two batteries, there will be two gauges.)

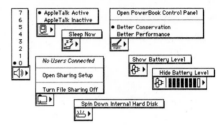

⌒⬧ **You can move the Control Strip,** although it's not immediately apparent. Hold down the Option key and drag the tab at the end of the strip. You'll find that the left end of the strip seems glued to the left edge of the screen, but it slides up and down very easily.

To switch the Control Strip to the other side of the screen, just option-drag on the tab, toward the other side. The Control Strip flips over and sticks to the right edge of the screen, with the tab facing left.

⌒⬧ **Change the order of the icons in the Strip** by option-dragging an icon to its new spot.

## Some New Extensions

⌒⬧ **The Apple Guide help system accounts for** most of the new items in the Extensions folder. There are no fewer than four files for the help system, although only one is actually an extension. (Apple Guide is covered in detail in Chapter 5.)

⌒⬧ **The GX printing technology,** covered in Chapter 12, means there are more printer drivers in the Extensions folder. Their icons are a combination of the standard printer icons and the standard extension puzzle-piece icon.

⌒⬧ **The nifty "clippings" capability** that comes in System 7.5 (it's covered in Chapter 19) is provided by the Clipping Extension extension. (My interactive spell checker just blipped at me because I typed a word twice in succession—but I had to; for some reason, this extension has Extension in its name.) In case you're wondering about the icon —it's a miniature Scrapbook page.

# CHAPTER 9
# USING
# MEMORY

> Everyone complains of his memory, and no one complains of his judgment.
>
> LA ROCHEFOUCAULD

Here are some of the things you might want to look through this chapter for:

- ➠ What RAM is and why it's volatile. (And what volatile is, in this case.)
- ➠ When an out of memory message doesn't meant that you're out of memory.
- ➠ Details about virtual memory, and its conceptual opposite, the RAM disk.
- ➠ What the heck "32-bit addressing" means.
- ➠ How to best divvy up the memory your Mac has when the System and your applications are all clamoring for more.
- ➠ Why January 1, 1904 is a significant date.
- ➠ What PRAM is. And how to zap it.
- ➠ Lewis Carroll, Everett Dirksen, Louisa May Alcott, Bob Hope, Ridley Scott, the Raiders and the Redskins, Ronald Reagan!

— Includes —
105 Entries
9 Quotes
1 Quiz
5 Memos
1 Mac Almanac List
—and—
a bit of poetry

**WHAT MAKES THIS CHAPTER UNIQUE**

*The elephants.*

page 354

NO PARKING BEYOND THIS POINT

# MEMORY IN THE MAC

# BASIC ALLOCATIONS

# MORE ON MEMORY

# SYSTEM 7.5 STUFF

## ⊣ MEMORY IN THE MAC ⊢

### RAM Basics

∞•➤ **RAM is *random access memory*.** When someone refers to the computer's memory, it's RAM that they're talking about. It's called "random access" because the computer can access the information that's stored there in any order, jumping to any spot to grab what it needs. It's also sometimes referred to (almost archaically) as *read-write memory* because you can both get information from it and put information into it.

∞•➤ **RAM is *volatile*.** That sounds as if it might blow up if the computer gets too warm, but all it means is that any information in RAM disappears when you turn off the computer, or when anything else interrupts the power to the computer.*

> *Maybe ephemeral would be a better word than volatile.

On the electronic level, RAM is hundreds, thousands, or even hundreds of thousands, of tiny electronic switches in on or off positions that represent the zeros and ones of the computer's binary language. But the switches on a RAM chip need a constant electric current to stay set, so even a temporary power glitch can wipe out the contents of RAM. That's why it's so important to save your work at frequent intervals: You never know when you might be zapped.

**LEWIS CARROLL**
**(1832–1898)**

> ... the King went on, " I shall never, never forget!" "You will, though," the Queen said, "if you don't make a memorandum of it."

∞•➤ **Memory is generally measured** in K and megs, the larger units of binary measuring (covered in detail in Chapter 1). Although we always talk about megs of memory (at least since the Mac started coming with at least a meg of memory as standard), memory is reported in K in the About This Macintosh dialog. With 1024K to a meg, here's a sample of how megs and K measure up:

| | | | |
|---|---|---|---|
| 1024K | .....................1 meg | 8192K | ................8 megs |
| 2048K | .....................2 megs | 10,240K | ..................10 megs |
| 4096K | .....................4 megs | 16,384K | ................16 megs |
| 5120K | .....................5 megs | 20,480K | ................20 megs |

••➤ **Disk space is not RAM,** although many beginners have trouble differentiating the two—maybe because they're measured the same way (in Ks and megs) and in both cases you have to worry about running out of room. Or maybe because there's some archetypal memory trace about disks being referred to as *slow memory* back in the early days. There's some logic behind this: You store computer information on disks, and retrieve it from them—hundreds of times more slowly than you can access RAM. But I *never* refer to disks as memory, and neither should you. Don't perpetuate the confusion.

In any case, be sure you understand the difference between RAM and disk space, so you'll know the difference between the two alerts shown here; few people misunderstand the one that says *the disk is full*, but many mistakenly interpret the *not enough memory* warning as being out of disk space, too.

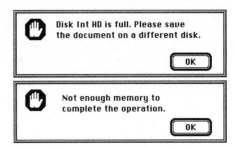

ROM, RAM chips and SIMMs, and installing memory in your Mac are covered in Chapter 13.

•••❯ **ROM is often** spoken of in the same breath as RAM, at least when you're comparing the specs of two different computers. ROM is *read-only memory*, permanent information in the Mac that it can access but can't change.

•••❯ **Video RAM** is another specialized use of RAM, but it's usually separate from the main RAM in your machine; Chapter 15 discusses video RAM.

## Memory in the Mac

For System 7.5, you need even more memory. Check the end of this chapter.

∘∘❯ **Officially, you need 2 megs** of memory to run System 7. And 2 megs is fine—if the system is all you're running.

You really need 4 megs of memory to get any work done. Luckily, we're far past the days that memory cost $400 a meg; 1-meg SIMMs run about $40 now. (In the really old days, RAM cost way more than $400 a meg, but that was when a computer could work with memory in amounts like 2K, 16K, and 64K.)

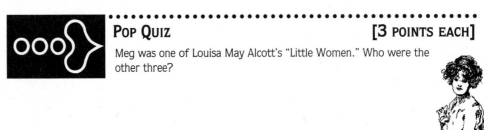

**POP QUIZ**  [3 POINTS EACH]

Meg was one of Louisa May Alcott's "Little Women." Who were the other three?

∘∘❯ **To see how much memory you have** (well, not *you*, but your computer—you can assume your memory is diminishing with age), use the About This Macintosh command in the Finder's Apple menu. The figure next to *Total Memory* is the amount of RAM in your Mac. (Remember, we talk about RAM in megs, so if your About dialog reports 4096K, you've got 4 megs of RAM.) The dialog also shows how the rest of RAM is being used by any applications that are running.

The dialog here shows the memory report for my Mac, which I upped to 20 megs during the course of this project.

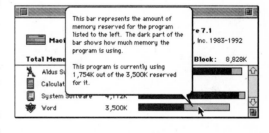

○•⤳ **The overall length of a bar** in the About This Macintosh dialog represents the total memory allocation for an application, but the black area shows the amount currently being used.

What's the difference? Each application needs a certain amount of memory for its own "code" (programming instructions) to work in, but it also needs room for part or all of the document you're working on; it even needs room reserved for other documents that you might open. If you have the application running, but no documents open, there will still be plenty of room showing in the memory bar. The bigger your document gets, or the more documents you have open in an application, the more black there is in the bar.

○•⤳ **To see how many K the black part of the bar** represents, turn on Balloon help and point to the bar.

○•⤳ **The *Largest Unused Block* report** in the About dialog won't always be the total amount of memory less the numbers reported as used by various applications. That's because the *largest unused block* is just that—the largest *contiguous* piece of memory that's available. The total of unused memory might be a little more—or a *lot* more—than that block, depending on how you've been working, since you can leave separate, unusable blocks of memory in your wake.

•••⤳ **Macs have inherent memory limitations,** some of which can be worked around, and some that can't. Sometimes it's as simple as the fact that there's just no place to plug in more memory. For instance, a Centris with 8 slots for memory modules might actually be able to use 136 megs of RAM, but with 8 slots and the largest modules available being, say, 16 megs, you can install only 128 megs.

More important, though, are the Mac's internal limitations for handling information and accessing memory; no matter what you do, it can't use anything beyond its internal limits. The Mac Plus and the SE—the oldest Mac models that can run System 7—are limited to 4 megs of memory; the early PowerBooks are limited to 8MB; the Classic II and LC max out at 10MB; other Macs go as high as 256MB.

Mac models' memory limitations are covered in Chapter 13.

**•••➤** **Sometimes things just don't add up** on the Mac (as in life). If you look at your About This Macintosh dialog when there are no programs running and the largest unused block reported is several hundred K smaller than the amount of total memory, it might be because your Mac model reserves some RAM to manage its internal video card; the IIci and IIsi both do this.

**DAVID BUNNEL**
MACWORLD, JULY 1985

> Wouldn't it be great if the Mac had 4 megabytes of RAM? Going from 512K to 4 megabytes on a Macintosh would be like trading in a Volkswagen for a Ferrari.

**MACWORLD**
FEBRUARY 1986

> More memory is on many a Mac owner's wish list. When you use Excel a sizable portion of the Mac's 512K of RAM is taken up by the program.

**DOUG CLAPP**
MACUSER, FEBRUARY 1986

> One of my nerdy friends has a megabyte of linear RAM in his Macintosh. What's he do with it? He installs six applications in Switcher. What's he doing with the applications? Not much ... Everybody needs a hobby.

**MACWORLD**
APRIL 1986

> A megabyte of memory provides a flexible environment to tailor to your own work habits and style.

**MICHAEL D. WESLEY**
MACUSER, APRIL 1987

> And it's possible to build the [Mac II's] RAM up 2 gigabytes by filling the slots with RAM cards. Those numbers are so staggering that they made me break out laughing when I first read the specs. What could anyone possibly do with 2 gigabytes of RAM?

## Memory Shortages

∞•➤ **When you get an Out of Memory dialog,** don't assume you have to add memory to your computer. You might just need to reorganize the memory you're using. For instance:

- You may have run out of memory within an application's allocation (its working space) but by increasing the allocation, you get more working room.
- An application can refuse to launch because there's not a large enough space left in RAM, but by reorganizing the other applications you're using, you can make a space that's large enough.

When you become familiar with how the RAM in your Mac is divvied up for various tasks, you'll be able to tell if you *really* need more memory or if you need to be more efficient with the memory you have.

•••➤ **Warning signs for low memory** situations aren't always as obvious as a dialog telling you so. Here are some other general symptoms that mean you're working in a tight memory situation:

- Applications quit unexpectedly.
- The Finder says to close some windows.
- You can't save a document.
- Documents print slowly.
- Documents won't print at all.
- The Mac is scaling fonts even though you have TrueType installed.

∞•⟩ **Add memory without adding memory.** (Don't you love it when I say stuff like that?) RAMDoubler is an amazing utility that pretty much tricks your Mac into thinking it has more RAM than it really does. The behind-the-scenes wizardry includes a little bit of disk use (like virtual memory, discussed later in this section), and a little bit of compression technique, and some juggling around of what memory is allocated to—but isn't currently being used by—other running applications. However they perform the magic, it's great. I'm generally wary of such miraculous tricks, since they work on such deep levels that they can royally mess up your system when you're not looking, but this product is solid so far. [Connectix]

•••➤ **Tune up your system if** you're running System 7.0.1. With the tuneup, memory is handled in a much better fashion and you'll get fewer out of memory messages.

•••➤ **QuickTime versions** earlier than 1.5 often hold on to extra memory even when you're not using a program that needs the QuickTime extension. Use version 1.6 or later.

•••➤ **For the IIci and IIsi,** you can free up a few hundred K of memory by running the monitor in black and white instead of color. Because of the way these two models handle their video, they have to devote over 300K of RAM to the display when there's a 14-inch monitor running in color. If it's running in black and white, only about 40K is used.

•••➤ **You'll get a false** *Not enough memory to complete this operation* report sometimes when you're dealing with a corrupted resource—a font, sound, or keyboard layout. Trying to drag a damaged file in or out of the System file, System Folder, or Fonts folder often results in a dialog that says there's not enough memory to copy the file somewhere else—even if you have 20 megs of free memory.

## 32-bit Addressing

∞⤙ **Most Macs are prepared to use 8 megs of memory.** Go beyond that, and you have some problems—the Mac can't keep track of all those little bits of memory without a little extra help. That help comes in the form of something called *32-bit addressing*, a setting in the Memory control panel. With 32-bit addressing on, the Mac can "see" beyond 8 megs of memory.

Turn on 32-bit addressing in the Memory control panel.

```
          32-Bit Addressing
  [32]    ● On
          ○ Off
```

∞⤙ **32-bit addressing is available** in System 7, and its heirs, but not in its predecessors.

### SHAVE AND A HAIRCUT*

There are times when the Mac feels more like a computer than a friendly little appliance. And 32-bit memory addressing is one of those times. But the actual background behind the concept is relatively simple.

Everything that's stored in the Mac's memory is stored in a specific place, at something called an address. Every address is identified with a number, just like a street number on a house. With 8 megs of memory, there are already millions of addresses, but the highest one is numbered 111111111111111111111111 in the Mac's binary numbering scheme. That's the highest number you can write in binary using 24 digits, which is the way the Mac was designed to refer to memory locations. It's a 24-bit number, or 24-bit addressing.

Like the phone company adding area codes or the post office going to Zip+4, the Mac needs an additional group of numbers to get past that 8-meg wall. So it now uses an additional byte of information (8 bits) to refer to memory locations. 8 bits on top of the 24 bits already used is—you guessed it—32-bit memory addressing. With a number that large, the Mac can keep track of 4,096 megs of memory—more than any current Mac can physically accommodate.

∞•⤙ **Some applications are *32-bit clean*;** others are 32-bit dirty, meaning they don't work with 32-bit addressing turned on. Older applications that didn't take into account for the possibility of using memory addresses beyond the 8-meg mark also didn't take into account the possibility they might freeze or crash when you try to run them with 32-bit addressing on. There's no easy way to tell if an application is clean or dirty; but if it runs without 32-bit addressing on and crashes when it's off, that's pretty much an indictment.

Keep in mind that extensions and control panels can be 32-bit dirty, too!

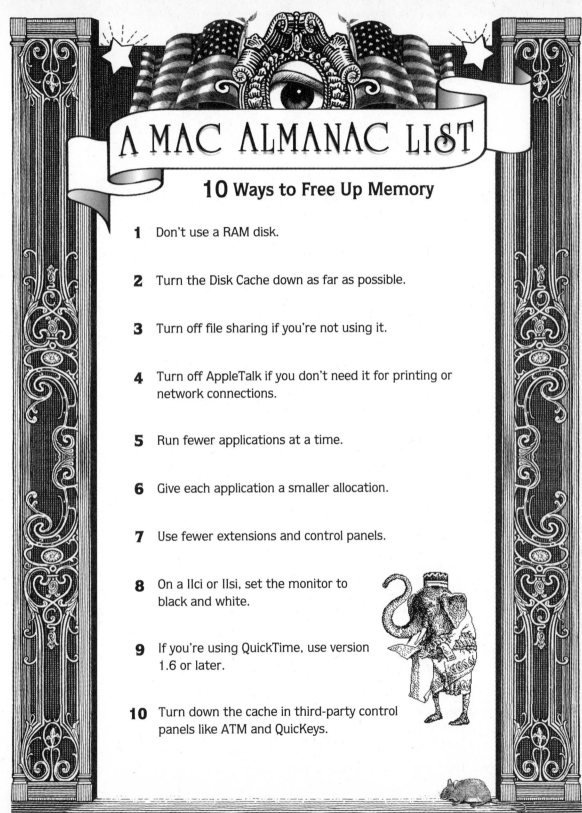

# A MAC ALMANAC LIST

## 10 Ways to Free Up Memory

**1** Don't use a RAM disk.

**2** Turn the Disk Cache down as far as possible.

**3** Turn off file sharing if you're not using it.

**4** Turn off AppleTalk if you don't need it for printing or network connections.

**5** Run fewer applications at a time.

**6** Give each application a smaller allocation.

**7** Use fewer extensions and control panels.

**8** On a IIci or IIsi, set the monitor to black and white.

**9** If you're using QuickTime, use version 1.6 or later.

**10** Turn down the cache in third-party control panels like ATM and QuicKeys.

**•→ Not all Macs can use 32-bit addressing.** Yep. Some *Macs* are dirty. More specifically, they're referred to as having *dirty ROMs* because they can't see beyond 8 megs of physical memory. All Macs before the IIci—including the Mac II, IIx, IIcx, and SE/30—have dirty ROMs.

But that doesn't mean you can't ever go beyond 8 megs of memory on one of these machines. There's always (well, almost always) a workaround.

The first fix offered was from Connectix: An extension called Mode32 that let the older Macs break the barrier. Apparently in response to disgruntled "dirty Mac" users, Apple bought Mode32 from Connectix and provided it free to Mac owners. Then, a year or two later, it came up with a replacement: an enabler called, reasonably enough, the 32-Bit Enabler. It was also provided free to the needy, although it had some of its own compatibility problems.

So, if your Mac has dirty ROMs and you want to get at more than 8 megs of memory, you need one or the other of these solutions. Mode32 is quite stable, and available through user groups and online services, but is no longer supported by anyone; if you have a problem, you're on your own. In addition, Mode32 isn't compatible with virtual memory, and won't run at all under System 7.1. The 32-Bit Enabler isn't quite as reliable, but it runs with virtual memory and under System 7.1; and, at least you'll have someone to complain to if there are problems.

### Mac Doggerel

There was a young lady named Gertie
Who had purchased a Mac SE 30
She expected to stuff it
With RAM but she muffed it ...
She forgot that the ROMs were all dirty.

—*Bob Seaver*

**•→ Constant crashing with *bus errors* reported** in a dialog when 32-bit addressing is on usually means that your hard drive driver needs to be updated. Your *what?* This is covered in more detail in Chapter 18, but briefly: There's a piece of software on your hard drive that lets it communicate with your Mac. It's called the *driver*, and it has to be updated when you move from System 6 to System 7. Luckily, it's a cinch to do, and the software for doing it comes with your Mac.

**•→ With virtual memory, your Mac can address** 14 megs of memory without 32-bit addressing, but 14 megs is the limit of combined RAM and virtual memory. (More about this in the Virtual Memory section later in this chapter.)

**•→ Some Mac models have permanent** 32-bit addressing—it's always on. The AV models and the Power Macs, for instance, are always in 32-bit addressing mode.

# ⊱ BASIC ALLOCATIONS ⊱

## System Memory

∞⫽ **The memory assigned to the system** varies according to how the system is set up and what machine you're running it on. A minimum system setup under System 7.0 starts at around 1600K, but an average one is more likely to be around 2500K. (I just checked mine: it's 3206K; my PowerBook, which I also just checked, is 2074K; on the kids' machine, it's 4324K—they have a *lot* of junk in there!)  ⬜ System Software  3,206K  ████████████████

∞⫽ **The system's memory allocation is *dynamic*:** it grows or shrinks as necessary. The amount of memory assigned to the system—especially the part known as the *system heap*—used to be a concern for people who used a lot of inits. But with System 7's dynamic memory allocation, you don't have to worry about manually adjusting the size of the system heap anymore. You also don't have to worry about how much free space is left showing in the System bar in the About This Macintosh dialog.

∞⫽ **The more you do, the more memory** the system uses. Look at these two pictures of the About This Macintosh box; one is how it looks before any applications are launched, the other is after two applications and a desk accessory are opened. That's the *only* thing that was done—the programs were opened; I didn't even do any work in them! Yet the system allocation jumped 221K.

The system's memory use grows in response to just opening applications.

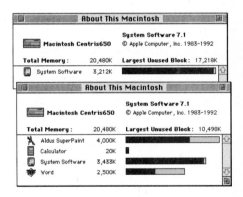

∞⫽ **The system's memory allocation grows** as necessary when you work, but occasionally forgets to shrink back down. Sometimes this is because an application misbehaves and doesn't release back the memory it may have borrowed from the system; sometimes its just a quirk of System 7's. This was a major problem in the early releases of System 7—there were times when I'd start out with as little as 1700K allocated to the system and after several hours of work, opening and quitting applications, it had grown to about 3000K. But neither System 7.0.1 with its tune-up nor System 7.1 are quite as prone to this "memory creep" effect.

If you're suffering from memory creep, first make sure you're running at least System 7.0.1 tuned-up; moving up to System 7.1 helps, too. Other than that, the only way you can get the system's allocation block back down is to restart the Mac.

⌘▶ **Major portions of the System file** are held in RAM, but that's not the only thing that's in the system memory allocation. It includes many different things, which is why it's large to start with and gets larger as you add things to your system.

> ✳The Finder gets nearly 500K of memory. That's about four times the total memory of the original Mac!

- The Finder used to get a separate allocation of memory and in previous systems had its own bar in the About This Macintosh dialog. Now the Finder's portion of memory is rolled into the system allocation.✳
- Inits—the parts of extensions and control panels that are loaded into memory at startup—are part of the system allocation.
- If you use a RAM disk, the amount you set aside for the disk is added to the system's allocation.
- The Disk Cache is lumped in with the system allocation.
- Desk accessories get their own 20K allocations of memory, but many need more than that—and the extra comes out of the system's allocation.

⌘▶ **Inits are the biggest memory eaters.** My system is around 3200K at startup, but with all extensions off, it starts out at 1256K.

You don't need to be using a lot of inits for the memory total to get out of hand; a few major extensions and control panels can add up to major amounts in no time. (Even the little ones nibble away at RAM, though.) Here's what some popular, basic system extensions use:

| | |
|---|---|
| Hierarchical Apple menu | 43K |
| Macro editor | 125–200K |
| FileSharing | 300K |
| AppleTalk | 400K |
| Interactive spell checker | 220K |
| ATM | 256K–1200K |

SENATOR EVERETT DIRKSEN

> A million here, a million there. Pretty soon it adds up to real money.

⌘▶ **An extremely large allocation** for the system—on the order of 5 or 10 megs or more—is usually due to one of two factors:

- You have more than 8 megs of memory in your Mac but you didn't turn on 32-bit addressing in the Memory control panel. As a result, all memory beyond 8 megs is dumped into the system allocation.

- You're using a RAM disk and the amount of RAM allocated to the disk is being reported in the system allocation.

Freeze? See Chapter 23.

➡ **Leave the system some room to grow.** Don't allocate every last K to applications. Always leave a few hundred K—say, 400—free for the system to expand; otherwise, you'll find your Mac freezes and crashes frequently.

➡ **The Finder's memory partition** isn't adjustable—at least, not directly, as it was in previous systems. The Finder is an application with its own memory partition—but the memory it uses is just rolled into the System allocation in the About This Macintosh dialog.

It's doubtful you'll need more Finder memory than what the system provides by default—about 475K. But there are ways to up the memory allocation, which I'll describe only briefly, since it's unlikely you'll be needing to do it anyway:

- Start up your Mac with a System 6 disk and Get Info on the Finder that's on your hard drive. You'll see a box in which you can type a higher-than-standard number for the memory allocation; try an extra 100K.
- If your Mac model is one that won't start up under System 6 (none of the late-model ones can), copy your Finder icon to a disk and insert it in someone else's Mac—someone who's running System 6. Alter the memory allocation there.
- Use ResEdit to find the SIZE resource on a *copy* of your Finder file, and up the allocation by a 100K or so.

If you can use the first method, all you have to do is restart the Mac as usual and you'll be using the new Finder. But if you use either of the other two methods, you'll have to replace the current Finder in two steps, since you can't replace an active Finder. Drag the Finder out of the System Folder and put it into the Trash; drag the altered Finder into the System Folder. Restart the Mac so the altered Finder is the one being used, and then empty the Trash of the old Finder.

Once again, however, I recommend that you update your system—7.0 to tuned-up 7.0.1, or either to 7.1—if you're running out of memory during desktop operations.

## For Applications

➡ **Every application needs its own *memory partition,*** the chunk of memory where it lives when it's running. This memory allocation has to be large enough to hold both the application and any documents you open in it.

Some applications load completely into memory and hold all their open documents in memory, too. Most applications load only a core part of themselves into memory and then load and purge other portions in and out of memory as necessary while you work. Documents are also often held only partly in memory, with other parts read in from the disk as necessary.

➡ **The size of an application's partition** depends on what's set in its Info window. The Info window changed slightly from System 7.0 to System 7.1. Under System 7.0, you'll see two items listed under Memory Requirements: *Suggested size* and *Current size*. The later system keeps the *Suggested size* item, but has two adjustable items: *Minimum size* and *Preferred size*.

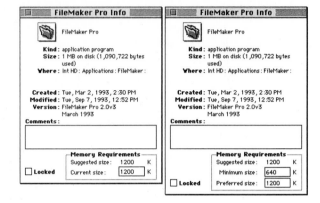

An application's Info window in System 7.0 (left) and in System 7.1 (right).

- The *Suggested size* is the RAM allocation recommended by the manufacturer for either minimum or optimum performance, depending on what he's is trying to prove. (*Hey! We can run in less than a meg of memory!* or *Wait till you see how fast this runs even in just the standard memory allocation!*)
- When you run an application in System 7.0, it uses the allocation listed in *Current size*, regardless of the manufacturer's suggested size.
- Under System 7.1, the amount listed in *Preferred size* is used as the application's allocation, again regardless of the manufacturer's recommendation. But it will automatically run in a partition smaller than that if necessary, as long as it's at least as big as the amount listed in *Minimum size*.

∞•❥ **Adjust an application's memory partition** in its Get Info window. In any allocation change, start with the Suggested Size as a guide. Temper the recommended amount with how you work: do you need more speed, or doesn't that matter? Are you annoyed by how often the application has to go to get information from the disk? Do you always work with multiple documents, or with very large documents? Do you need to run multiple applications at one time?

You can specify a number far larger than the manufacturer recommends; in many cases, you can also use a partition that's quite a bit smaller than the recommended dosage.

∞•❥ **It's first come, first served for memory** allocations. If you want several programs open at the same time and you're not sure if they'll all fit, launch the ones you need the most first.

∞•❥ **When there's not enough memory left** for an application to launch, you'll get a dialog telling you so. (Of course you will! This is a Mac.) But what the dialog says depends on what system version you're running; the Mac gets a little more intelligent with each revision.

System 7.0 will tell you there's not enough memory; it merely suggests you quit another program to make room. A tuned-up System 7.0.1 reports on how much memory is left and asks if you'd like to open the application in that smaller partition.

System 7.1 takes the best approach. First of all, since it already knows what the minimum partition size for an application is, it doesn't bother asking you if it should launch in less than the full partition—it just does it. If there's not enough room to launch in even a minimum partition, it looks around to see if one of the currently running applications has no open documents, and asks if you want to quit out of it to make room. If you choose to quit the program, the other application that you're trying to open will then launch automatically. This saves you several steps over the System 7.0 approach.

The dialog you get when there's not enough room to launch an application depends on which version of the system software you're running.

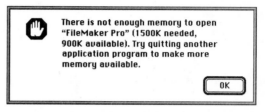

There is not enough memory to open "FileMaker Pro" (1500K needed, 900K available). Try quitting another application program to make more memory available.

OK

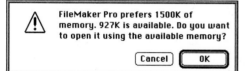

FileMaker Pro prefers 1500K of memory. 927K is available. Do you want to open it using the available memory?

Cancel   OK

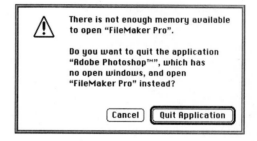

There is not enough memory available to open "FileMaker Pro".

Do you want to quit the application "Adobe Photoshop™", which has no open windows, and open "FileMaker Pro" instead?

Cancel   Quit Application

## BIGGER AND BETTER

It used to be a point of pride for programmers to write programs that worked in very little memory. Of course, it was a necessity, too, since memory was so expensive and there was very little in the average personal computer.

But times change. And, boy, so do memory requirements! Take a look at this brief chart of recommended memory allocations for four programs that have grown over the years:

|  | 1986 | 1991 | 1994 |
|---|---|---|---|
| Finder | 106K | 190K | 476K |
| Excel | 304K | 900K | 2048K |
| Word | 160K | 512K | 1024K |
| PageMaker | 256K | 1500K | 1500K |

•••❥ **An application uses more memory as you work,** so most start out by using only about half of the allocation you assigned. The rest is used both for temporary "code segments" that the application loads into memory when needed, and for documents.

The picture here shows how the "in use" part of the allocation—the dark area—grows as you do things in an application. The first bar shows the initial status; all I did was launch Word. The second bar shows how more memory is used when I opened a document. Then I invoked the spelling checker function, and the third bar shows how the memory use crept up in response, since the spelling checker isn't a function that's initially loaded.

This is why an application can run out of memory even if it launches without a problem. When you see a dialog box like the one here, or one that says anything about a memory shortage (*Not enough memory to complete the operation; Running low on memory—save your documents and quit the program; Low memory—close other documents*), sometimes you can get around it by closing other open documents in the application. Other times, you'll just have to quit the program, up its memory allocation, and launch it again.

> ✋ **Not enough memory to open the document.**
>
> [ OK ]

•••❥ **To make an application work faster,** give it a larger memory allocation. With a larger allocation, more of the application can be loaded into RAM, avoiding the delays caused by accessing the parts of the program still on the disk. The larger allocation also lets more of the document stay in memory, making operations like scrolling and editing much faster.

For an application that already loads entirely into memory, or keeps the entire document in RAM, a larger allocation won't change the speed at which you can work—but it will let you use larger documents and have more open at a time.

•••❥ **When the *Application unexpectedly quit* dialog** shows up right after your application disappears from the screen, it's often a memory problem. Sometimes this happens as soon as you launch a program; sometimes it happens unexpectedly while you're working, in which case it takes your document—probably unsaved—with it. Upping the application's memory partition often takes care of this problem.

*MACWORLD*
APRIL 1986

> Primarily due to the bulkiness of a System file containing several fonts and desk accessories, hardly enough room remains in 512K for more than one program and an open document.

⋯⋗ **When you get an Out of Memory** message while you're working in an application, regardless of the warning's specific wording, your first step should always be to save your work. Working in really tight memory situations often leads to freezes and crashes, and you'll lose any unsaved work you've done.

⋯⋗ **In a memory emergency**—you're in an application and it won't even let you save a document, or type another word in—try flushing the Clipboard. Sometimes a large item on the Clipboard eats away at the application's memory partition just enough to keep it from being able to function. To flush the Clipboard of its contents, copy something small, like a single word, to it *twice*—the original item is kept around the first time in case you choose the Undo command. If the memory shortage keeps you from even using the Copy command (and it happens!), switch to the desktop, and copy something there—the name of a file, for instance. Do it twice. Then switch back to the application and try saving the document.

⋯⋗ **Disk space and RAM allocation** are two different things for an application. For one thing, most applications don't load completely into memory; for another, they need room in memory to do calculations and other processing, and to hold document information. Generally, however, the larger a program is on the disk, the more memory it needs to run properly because larger programs do more complex operations. Here's a short list of the disk size and recommended memory requirements of some popular programs:

| Application | Disk Space | RAM |
|-------------|-----------|------|
| TeachText | 36K | 192K |
| Word | 884K | 1024K |
| FileMaker | 1072K | 1200K |
| SuperPaint | 1028K | 2500K |
| PhotoShop | 1872K | 5120K |
| QuarkXpress | 2612K | 3000K |

## Memory Fragmentation

∞⋗ **Applications need *contiguous* RAM**—memory that's in one large chunk instead of in little pieces.

Think of the memory in your computer as one long curb where several cars are going to park. The first, a stretch limo, slides into place at the beginning of the block. Next comes a Volkswagen Beetle, which pulls in right behind the stretch. Then comes, say, a Camry, which parks right behind the Bug; a Jeep parks right behind it. Then an Infiniti shows up—but there's no room left. The Bug and the Jeep both pull out, but even though the *total* empty space at the curb is sufficient, you still can't park the Infiniti because the available space is split into two sections, separated by the Camry. There's still room for another Bug and a Jeep, or even two Bugs, since one can fit into the Jeep's space, but you can't park the Infiniti.

The new car can't park even though the total curb space is sufficient.

Launching programs on the Mac is like parking cars on the curb. (Stay with me here.) Say the first thing you open is a big word processor, and then you launch a calendar utility. The word processor takes the first chunk of memory, and the calendar takes the next piece; it's like the limo in the first spot at the curb with the Volkswagen behind it. You open a small database next, and then a spreadsheet. These each take their own chunks of memory, in order, like the Jeep and the Camry parking in line behind the other two cars. You quit the calendar program and the database, and try to launch a graphics program. (Right, that's the Infiniti.) But you can't. When you closed the two other programs, they left unused chunks of memory, but the graphics program needs memory that's in a single chunk; it can't run in the discontiguous pieces of memory any more than a full-size sedan can park in two small open spaces when there's a car in the intervening space.

But, just as you can park a small car in an existing space, a program that fits into any existing chunk of memory can still be launched—even if, like a Bug going into the vacated limo's space, the parking job leaves yet another small and perhaps unusable chunk of memory (or is it curb?) available.

∞•❯ **Memory fragmentation** is what happens when you repeatedly launch and quit programs leaving unusable chunks of memory around instead of one free block of memory that could be put to better use.

∞•❯ **Avoid memory fragmentation** by paying attention to the order in which you launch and quit programs. The program you use the most should be opened first because it's less likely that you'll quit out of it, leaving a "hole" and fragmenting memory. Launch the second-most-used application next, and so on.

∞•❯ **To defragment memory,** quit the applications that are running and then re-launch them. If you know what order they were launched in, quit them in reverse order until you're down to the first one.

Applications are listed alphabetically in the About This Macintosh dialog and in the Application menu, not in the order in which they were opened and assigned RAM partitions, so there's not much help there. Keep an eye on the *Largest Unused Block* report in the About dialog to see when you have enough room to launch the application you want to work with.

## ◂╂ MORE ON MEMORY ╂▸

## PRAM

∞▸ **PRAM** (*PEA-ram*, not *pramm*) stands for parameter RAM. It's a small chunk of memory reserved for storing some basic, important information—certain *parameters* that your Mac uses. How small is small? In this case, it's 256 bytes (that's *bytes*, not K).

The information stored in PRAM includes:

- time and date settings
- the desktop pattern
- insertion point and menu blink rates
- keyboard repeat rate
- mouse tracking and double-click speed
- volume setting
- modem and printer port settings
- startup disk setting

∞▸ **PRAM is special** not because of its size or what it holds, but because it "lives" even while the Mac is turned off. It's like regular RAM in that it needs constant electrical refreshing to hold its memory, but it gets that electricity from the Mac's battery. (Did you ever wonder how the Mac remembers what time it is even though you shut it off, and even unplug it?)

∞▸ *Zapping the PRAM is* a uniquely Macintosh activity. Sometimes the information stored in PRAM gets corrupted, or confused, so you have to clear it and reset the parameters; the procedure is known as *zapping*. How does it get corrupted? Something to do with absolute power, maybe? No, generally it's from a misbehaving program that has the nerve to write to the wrong section of memory—the PRAM.

To zap PRAM, restart the computer and hold down Command-Option-P-R while it's starting up. (It's a great finger-stretching exercise.) You'll hear your usual startup tone, the screen will flash, and the system will restart all over again with the startup sound. Make sure you let go of the keys on the second startup sound, or you'll just zap and restart again.

This procedure resets all the options in PRAM to their defaults, except for the time and date, which remain set.

∞▸ **Zap the PRAM when** odd things start happening on your computer, like:

- The time or date don't remain set or consistent.
- Basic control panel settings aren't remembered between shutdowns.
- The Mac seems to forget what printer you selected in the Chooser and you have to select it again to get anything to print.
- Your communications software can't find your modem even though it's plugged into the modem port.

- When you run into those special situations that we experts sometimes refer to as "random weirdness": Minor things are going wrong and you can't put your finger on why. Zapping PRAM is in the list of basic troubleshooting techniques you should keep in your arsenal and use at the first sign of trouble.

### MAC TRIVIA

Zapping the PRAM used to reset the time and date as well as other settings. The date defaulted to January 1, 1904.

What's so special about that date? A reference to H.G. Wells' Time Machine? Nope, that was 1900. It's special because it makes the date calculation easier from the Mac's point of view. The year 1900 was not a leap year, despite the fact it's divisible by 4. By not starting at 1900, but four years later (in the leap year), the Mac and its programmers don't have to worry about convoluted calculations to figure out how many days in a given month or on what day of the week a certain date falls. It's the earliest date in this century that could be used without running into a mathematical problem.

The divisible-by-4 but not-a-leap-year coincidence doesn't occur again until the year 2400. But the Mac tells time by counting seconds—the seconds since 1904 started. With its 32-bit capability for storing numbers, the Mac can count up to 4,294,967,296. That's a lot of seconds, but they'll run out sometime in 2040—well before the next non-leap year problem rolls around.

···❯ **Since zapping the PRAM resets most control panel settings** to their defaults, you'll find that after a zap you have to set all your preferences again. You may find your mouse moving very slowly, if you normally use a faster-than-standard speed; your desktop pattern reverts to plain old gray; 32-bit addressing is turned off (except on late-model Macs that have permanent 32-bit addressing), so you can't use more than 8 megs of memory. And so on.

···❯ **A RAM disk is wiped out** by a PRAM zap. Absolutely wiped out—its contents and its very existence, although it's normally recreated at startup and even its contents live through normal restarts.

···❯ **On a Mac Plus, zap the PRAM** by taking out the battery for about 10 minutes.

## The Memory Control Panel

See Chapter 8 for some more information about the Memory control panel.

···❯ **The Memory control panel** lets you control the four main memory features of the Mac: the Disk Cache, Virtual Memory, 32-Bit Addressing, and the RAM disk. The appearance of the Memory control panel depends on your Mac model; if your Mac can't use one or more of these memory features, it won't be in the control panel at all. The picture here shows what a full control panel looks like, and how it looks on a Mac with fewer features.

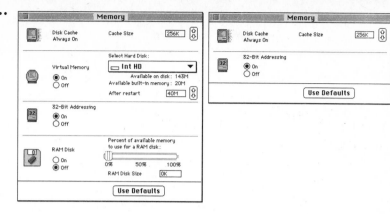

The Memory control panel changes depending on the capabilities of your Mac.

## The Cache

∘•❯ **The *Disk Cache* setting** in the Memory control panel used to be called the *RAM cache* (that's why I called this section simply "The Cache"). This cache—pronounced *cash*, not *catch*—acts as a temporary storage space for information that's frequently accessed; in fact, the word is French for *hide*.

Few applications load completely into memory; the core of the program is there for speedy operation, but other parts stay on the disk until you need them. The operating system works the same way. Since it takes longer to get information from the disk than from memory, getting disk information slows down your work. With the cache storing pieces of information in RAM that would otherwise be on the disk, things speed up. (That's why the cache is sometimes called the *disk* cache and sometimes called the *RAM* cache. It depends on how you look at it: It's storing disk information, but the information is being stored in RAM. If you cached supplies for your trek across the frozen tundra, you might refer to it as the *food cache*, for its contents, or as the *cave cache* for its location.)

The increased performance you get from a cache depends on the speed of your Mac and the speed of its hard drive.

∘•❯ **The memory allotted to the cache** is part of the overall allocation to the system memory. So as you increase the cache size, you'll see more memory used by the system, as reported in the About This Macintosh dialog.

∘•❯ **You don't choose the information** that goes into the cache—the Mac takes care of all that. It watches what you do and stores oft-repeated operations in the cache. When things get too crowded, some of the old information is purged—whatever information was least recently used is dumped.

∘•❯ **You can change the size of the cache** but you can't turn it off. (Before System 7, you could turn it off entirely.) You adjust the size of the cache in the Memory control panel, where you use the little arrows to

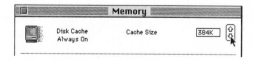

change the size of the cache. The change doesn't take effect until you restart the computer, even though (in a minor interface transgression) there's no note in the control panel that tells you so.

⊸❥ **How much of a cache you should set** is a hard call. It seems a logical assumption that the larger the cache, the better. Logical, maybe—but wrong. Increasing the cache beyond a certain point doesn't get you any increase in performance. Using a gigantic cache can be slower than using a more moderately sized one, since the Mac has to look through more stored items in the larger cache. The cache's efficiency is also affected by whether or not you're using virtual memory, the size of your hard drive, and even how you work.

As a general rule of thumb, use 32K of cache for each megabyte of memory in your Mac. That means:

| Memory | Cache |
|--------|-------|
| 2MB | 64K |
| 4MB | 128K |
| 8MB | 256K |
| 10MB | 320K |
| 12MB | 384K |
| 16MB | 512K |

Some experts question whether any cache over 256K is efficient; most seem to agree that more than 512K isn't going to get you any performance increase except under very special circumstances. In any case, if you want to try a gigantic disk cache, limit it to a quarter of your total RAM—that's 1 meg (1024K) on a 4-meg machine.

⊸❥ **Using the cache is efficient when** you're dealing with data that doesn't change a lot, or at all. If you're working mostly in one program, its instructions that aren't already in RAM can be stored in the cache, significantly increasing its speed. On the other hand, if you switch around among several running programs, you're not going to see much of a benefit since by the time you need something stored in the cache from one program, it may have already been replaced by code from another program. (On the other other hand, the switching process itself is speeded up with the cache on, so the benefit, or lack thereof, depends on how you're using the programs that you're switching around in.)

Along the same lines, a large cache can help when you're retrieving data from a CD-ROM, since its contents are static. But if you're working with a database, changing its records as you go along, your work might be even slower with a cache than without it because each time you change something on the disk, corresponding information in the cache has to be purged.

⊸❥ **The default size for the cache** is set to 32K per meg of RAM in your machine; if you have 20 megs or more of RAM, you'll find that the default falls short of 32K per meg, since it's unlikely you'll benefit from a larger and larger cache as your physical memory increases. You get this default when you click the Use Defaults button in the Memory control panel.

••➔ **If you zap the PRAM,** the disk cache is reset to its minimum of 32K. (*Not* the default of 32K per meg of RAM, but 32K.)

> Cache as cache can.
>
> ANON.

••➔ **On a Mac IIci or IIsi,** upping the cache can really boost performance because of the way these two models use regular RAM to help the video display. On a IIsi with color or gray set to four levels (in the Monitor control panel) or higher, set the cache to 768K. This way the RAM needed for the video and the cache are placed in the main memory chips (on the motherboard) and everything else uses the SIMMs that are installed, resulting in much faster performance.

To get the same benefits for the IIci, there are several conditions:

- The monitor should be set to four or more grays or colors.
- There should be 5, 9, or 11 megs of RAM installed.
- The four 256K SIMMs that help make up the total of RAM have to be in Bank A, the one closest to the disk drive.

••➔ **Macs with 68040 processors** have built-in caches you can turn on and off with the Cache Switch control panel. These caches act totally independently of the disk cache.

••➔ **The Mac IIci has a cache card** that boosts its performance, but it's separate from the cache you can set in the Memory control panel. The very earliest IIci's came without this card but there's a space for it inside the computer.

••➔ **Some programs are incompatible** with the disk cache. Actually, PhotoShop is the only one I know of that specifically wants you to keep the cache to its minimum size, but some other high-end programs may want the same thing. It doesn't hurt to check your manuals. You don't have to read the whole thing—just check the index under *memory* or *cache*.

Cache card? See Chapter 13.

••➔ **Sometimes a humongous disk cache** works to your benefit. Both Rich Wolfson and Joe Holmes, tech reader and tech editor for this book, use large disk caches to "trap" an entire online session in the Navigator program so the hard drives in their PowerBooks won't spin up unnecessarily.

## AD HOC #2

... why 1984 won't be like 1984.

That's the tag line of the infamous one-time-only SuperBowl commercial for the Mac, just weeks before its official introduction.

If you've never seen it, picture this: Rows of zombie-like shaven-headed downtrodden citizens funneled into a dim auditorium to watch Big Brother lecture on a large screen. A woman with a sledgehammer jogs down the center aisle. She halts in front of the screen, then twirls in place building up momentum, releasing the sledgehammer right into the screen. And then the scrolling text: *On January 24th, Apple Computer will introduce Macintosh. And you'll see why 1984 won't be like "1984".*

Here are some key moments in the commercial. Enjoy the following trivia about it.

- About 43 million people saw it.

- Ridley Scott directed it. He had already done Blade Runner, and was to go on to do the Alien films.

- It was filmed in England, and used real skinheads as the craven crowd.

- The actual hammer throw was done by an Olympic athlete.

- The blue haze overlying the commercial wasn't supposed to refer to IBM, known disaffectionately as Big Blue. Scott decided the blue filter set the right mood.

- What Big Brother was really saying:

  *Each of you is a single cell in the great body of the State. And today, that great body has purged itself of parasites. We have triumphed over the unprincipled dissemination of facts. The thugs and wreckers have been cast out. Let each and every cell rejoice! For today we celebrate the first glorious anniversary of the Information Purification Directive. We have created, for the first time in all history, a garden of pure ideology where each worker may bloom secure from the pests purveying contradictory and confusing truths. Our unification of thought is more powerful a weapon than any fleet or army on earth. We are one people. With one will. One resolve. One cause. Our enemies shall talk themselves to death, and we will bury them with their own confusion. We shall prevail!*

- It was never run again after the SuperBowl game. Except for a few dozen times on newscasts, which, in commenting on its innovative approach, replayed it in its entirety.

- It played once in December of 1983 (at 1:00 in the morning) in an inconspicuous northwestern television market (Twin Falls, Idaho) so it would be eligible for the Clio advertising awards for that year.

- Apple's Board of Directors tried to kill the spot. It ran only because the advertising agency couldn't resell the air time.

- The Raiders and the Redskins played that day: Raiders 38, Redskins 9.

## RAM Disks

◦◦➤ **A RAM disk is** a somewhat imaginary disk. Although you'll see it on your desktop and can treat it like any other disk, it exists only in the Mac's memory, in its RAM—hence the name.

Aha! You're thinking (if you've been paying attention) that it doesn't make much sense to use RAM as a disk, since it disappears when you turn off the computer. Well, you're partly right—it *does* disappear when you turn off the computer, but that doesn't mean it doesn't make sense to use it.

Remember that RAM is a lot faster than a real disk; that is, you can access information in RAM a hundred times faster than you can access it from a disk. Now what do you think? Right, speed is a good reason to use a RAM disk.

◦◦➤ **Create a RAM disk** with the Memory control panel: click the On button, then use the slider control to set the RAM disk size, or type in the number directly. The slider control is easier to use

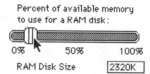

in that it represents all the currently free memory in your Mac and you can easily set it to use, say, 25 percent of your memory for the disk.

You have to restart the Mac for the RAM disk to appear. When it does, you'll see a floppy-disk shaped icon on your desktop. (That centipede-like creature on the icon is actually a RAM chip.)

◦◦➤ **Treat a RAM disk** like any other disk: change its name; double-click to open it; drag things onto it; drag things off it. You can save things to it, too, from within an application, but that's not recommended. About the only thing you can't do to a RAM disk that you can do to a regular disk is lock it—but you can lock the RAM disk's *contents*.

◦◦➤ **The RAM you assign to the RAM disk** becomes part of the System RAM allocation, so you'll see that allocation jump when you're using the RAM disk.

◦◦➤ **To get rid of a RAM disk,** you can't just drag it to the Trash or use the Erase Disk command.* You have to first get rid of anything that's on the RAM disk—the Erase Disk command is handy for that and works in a fraction of a second, although you could use the two-step process of dragging the contents to the Trash and emptying it. Then open the Memory control panel and click the Off button. The RAM disk disappears from the desktop.

> *That would give a deeper meaning to the Erase Disk command, wouldn't it, since it wouldn't just erase the disk contents but actually obliterate the disk!

◦◦➤ **Even when a RAM disk disappears** from the desktop, it's not really gone. Or you might say that it's gone but not forgotten. The memory it used is still tied up, part of the System memory allocation. It isn't freed up until you restart the Mac.

◦◦➤ **The contents of a RAM disk survive a restart**. If you want to restart your Mac (with the Special menu's Restart command) because, for instance, you just changed a control panel setting or added a new extension, you don't have to worry about losing the items on the RAM disk.

RAM disks on PowerBooks are power-savers. See Chapter 22.

- **RAM disk contents don't survive a shutdown,** or restart that's caused by a power interruption. Whatever was there is lost forever. In the case of using the Shut Down command, you'll get a dialog warning you about the RAM disk so you can copy whatever you might need to a real disk. Power interruptions, of course, don't provide any dialogs before they zap you.

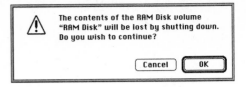

The contents of the RAM Disk volume "RAM Disk" will be lost by shutting down. Do you wish to continue?

Cancel    OK

- **Put an application on a RAM disk** when you want the application to run quickly and not bog down every time you use a feature that's not normally instantly available. With the application on the RAM disk, even when the application goes back "to the disk" for some of its information, you won't notice the delay. Of course, with applications getting bigger and bigger, you need a sizeable RAM disk to hold the application and its support files, like dictionaries or glossaries.

- **Don't store documents on a RAM disk.** RAM contents disappear if you crash and it's not worth the risk for the little extra speed you might gain—documents are pretty much held in RAM anyway when you're working on them. (RAM disks on PowerBooks are not as dangerous, though, since battery power keeps them going.)

*Think about that: An invisible file on a nonexistent disk!*

- **If the Off button is dimmed** in the Memory control panel when you go to turn off the RAM disk, that's because there's something on the disk so you're not allowed to turn it off. If you could *swear* there's nothing on the disk, maybe you dragged things to the Trash but didn't empty it. Or maybe there's an invisible file on the disk that was placed there by some program you were using.* In either case, the Erase Disk command will surely wipe out the disk contents so you can turn the RAM disk off.

- **Put your System Folder on a RAM disk** if the disk is large enough and the folder's small enough. Nothing soups up a system like running it from a RAM disk. (And on a PowerBook, it saves a lot of battery power.) The trick, of course, is to make sure you're running from the RAM disk and not your hard disk: use the Startup Disk control panel to select the RAM disk as the startup, and then use the Restart command in the Special menu so "control" passes to the system on the RAM disk.

**MACWORLD** APRIL 1986

If you want to see a speed demon in action, load a 512K RAM disk with the System, the Switcher, and ... [spreadsheet] MultiPlan and [communications program] MacTerminal.

- **An application on a RAM disk still needs** its RAM allocation to live in when it's launched. Remember that what you're doing by putting the application on a RAM disk is just storing it on a different disk—albeit an extremely fast one. It *still* needs RAM to live in once it's launched no matter what disk it's stored on. You can, however, assign it a smaller RAM allocation than usual because when it goes back to the disk to get pieces of itself while you're working, it's retrieving things from a RAM disk and you won't even notice the delay.

But consider this: Say you normally run an application in a 2000K partition to get good performance but would like to crank it up a bit. So you create a RAM disk that's 1500K to store the application and its support files. Since it's on the RAM disk, it doesn't need as large a partition as it used to; say you reset the partition to 1500K. You're using a total of 3000K for the program—1500K each for the RAM disk and the memory alloca-tion. You might find that simply upping the allocation to 3000K while running the application from the hard drive gets you the speed increase you want while saving over-all memory and avoiding the extra steps of creating the RAM disk. And working in a larger partition instead of from the RAM disk means that if you're short of memory for another application, you only have to quit the first application to free up space. To free up the RAM disk space, you have to erase all its contents, turn it off in the Memory control panel, and restart the Mac.

••▶ **The PowerBook 100 retains** all RAM disk information even when you shut it down. (But *not* if you turn the storage switch to Off, disconnecting the battery.)

∞◦⧽ **Only later model Macs** (from around late 1992 on) come with the RAM disk option in their control panels. If you can't update your system software to provide this option on your Mac, there are several utility programs that offer the capability.

- AppDisk is a little different from other RAM disk utilities, since it runs as an application whose memory allocation serves as the RAM disk; as a result, it frees up the memory it was using as soon as you quit it—you don't have to restart. [shareware, Mark Adams]
- Maxima provides a standard RAM disk approach, much like Apple's. But it can save its contents to a hard disk when you shut down, then recreate the RAM disk and restore its contents on startup. [Connectix]
- RamDisk+ is a control panel that provides a RAM disk capability on any Mac. [shareware, Roger Bates]

••▶ **Zapping the PRAM wipes** out a RAM disk—it even turns off the RAM disk setting in the Memory control panel. Make sure you don't have anything important stored on a RAM disk if you're doing a restart in order to zap the PRAM.

## Virtual Memory

∞◦▶ **Virtual memory is** a sort of pseudo-RAM; it's a way of using part of your hard drive as RAM. (Conceptually, it's pretty much the opposite of a RAM disk, which lets you use part of RAM as a disk.)

∞◦▶ **Virtual memory is slow.** Since accessing real RAM is so much faster than getting something from a disk, at first glance it doesn't make much sense to use the disk as additional RAM. But there are two good reasons. Physical RAM costs about $40 a meg;

a meg of hard drive space is about $3. Then there's the issue of the RAM barrier: Macs are limited to using (or *addressing*) specific amounts of *physical* memory, but most can address additional virtual memory.

**Not all Mac models can use virtual memory**. A 68030-based machine can use virtual memory because it includes a special chip called the *PMMU (paged memory management unit)*. 68000-based Macs like the Plus, Classic and LC don't have this capability. The Mac II, a 68020 machine, can't use virtual memory unless it's had a PMMU upgrade. And if you use a 68030 accelerator on one of the slower models, that still won't solve the problem, since there's information in the Mac's ROM that's needed for virtual memory and the accelerator doesn't usually provide it.

If you're not sure what processor your computer uses, how can you tell if you can use virtual memory? Easy: Check the Memory control panel. If your machine can't use virtual memory, there won't be any virtual memory section in it.

**Macs that normally can't use virtual memory** can use it if you use a program called Virtual, which provides the capability to virtual memory-impaired Macs. [Connectix]

**Activate virtual memory** through the Memory control panel:

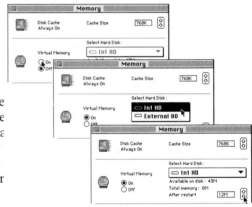

1. Click the On button to activate the popup menu.
2. Select the drive you want to use for virtual memory storage from the popup menu.
3. Set the total amount of memory you want to use by clicking in the arrows. The number represents the of actual standard RAM in your ma plus the amount of virtual memory going to use. So 8 megs of regular more of virtual memory means you r as the number in this dialog.
4. Restart the Mac to activate virtual memory.

**The disk space put aside** for virtual memory isn't the amount of virtual memory: it's the *total* amount of memory, virtual and physical.

If you don't have enough room on your hard drive for the amount of virtual memory you want to set up, you'll find that the control panel won't let you set that amount. In fact, if there's not a minimum amount of room on the hard drive, you'll find that the disk name is dimmed in the popup menu so you can't even select it.

What's really happening when you use virtual memory is that the Mac uses a complicated process of swapping information between what's in physical RAM and what's on the disk; it's faster when the entire contents of memory—RAM and virtual together—are mapped onto the disk.

Just where is all this information? You'll see the amount of free space on your disk drop precipitously, but you won't see the virtual memory information anywhere. It goes into an invisible folder named VM Storage.

◦•➤ **How much virtual memory** you set up depends not only on available disk space but also on how much real RAM you have. The more virtual memory you use in relationship to physical RAM, the slower things get. Using the same amount of virtual memory as real RAM works all right, but don't go beyond twice your RAM size for virtual memory if you don't want things to bog down. That means you should, on an 8-meg system, restrain yourself to 16 megs of virtual memory, for a total of 24 megs of working memory.

◦•➤ **The About This Macintosh dialog** changes when virtual memory is being used, with two additional items being reported. Since the normal *Total Memory* report now includes the virtual memory, there's a separate report for *Built-in Memory*. And there's an entry that notes how much of the hard drive (and which hard drive) is being used for virtual memory.

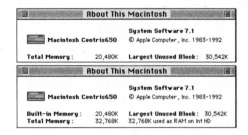

◦•➤ **The best use of virtual memory** is where you need to run lots of little programs and move back and forth among them. You won't derive much benefit from virtual memory when you need a very large portion of it to handle a complex document in a single application. It might let you open that document when you would otherwise be unable to open it at all, but the system will be so sluggish you'll want to run out and buy more RAM chips right away.

••➤ **The virtual memory allocation is limited** not only by available disk space, but also by the amount of RAM your Mac model is able to address.

Most later-model Macs (starting with the IIci) can address more than a gigabyte—over a thousand *megs*—of virtual memory. But models earlier than the IIci that can handle virtual memory because they have a 68030 chip have a special limitation: they can use a maximum of 14 megs of *total* memory, *minus* 1 meg for each NuBus slot in use. So, say you have a IIcx with 8 megs of RAM and one slot being used for a special video display card. You'll be able to use a maximum of 13 megs of memory, 5 of which will be virtual memory.

Memory limits for different Mac models are discussed in Chapter 13.

You don't really have to worry too much about what your Mac's virtual memory limitation is—you won't be able to set more than the maximum in the Memory control panel.

••➤ **A hard drive used under System 6** needs its driver software updated if you want to use it for virtual memory storage. You should be updating a disk's driver if you're running System 7 from it, but a System 6-formatted external disk normally presents no problem to a System 7 setup. So remember: If you're using an external disk drive for virtual memory storage, its driver needs to be updated. Actually, you don't have to remember—you'll be reminded when you try to turn on virtual memory and the Mac checks the disk you're trying to use. It will even remind you to use HD SC Setup to do it—that's covered in Chapter 18.

••➤ **Don't use virtual memory on a PowerBook** unless it's absolutely necessary, because virtual memory means disk access and disk access means draining the battery. Virtual memory is such a power-eater that you get a special warning when you go to use it on a PowerBook.

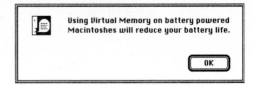

Using Virtual Memory on battery powered Macintoshes will reduce your battery life.

OK

••➔ **You need 32-bit addressing turned on** in the Memory control panel to go beyond 8 megs of physical RAM, but you also need it on to go past 14 megs of combined physical and virtual memory.

••➔ **Some programs aren't compatible** with virtual memory. PhotoShop, for instance, uses its own virtual memory scheme; combine that with a virtual memory setup on the system level, and you've got so much disk access that the program slows down to a crawl. And, if you're already on a system that pretty much crawls with a program like PhotoShop anyway, you might as well give up and work with Crayolas rather than slow it down any further.

••➔ **Don't mix QuickTime and virtual memory.** QuickTime movies need a lot of speed to play without being choppy; some of that speed comes from the computer's processor, and some comes from the fact that lots of the QuickTime movie goes into RAM. Using virtual memory instead of the real thing slows down the movie, since the disk is accessed so often.

## ✠ SYSTEM 7.5 STUFF ✠

### Memory Requirements

••➔ **System 7.5's memory requirements are** pretty heavy: 4 megs of memory at the very least, assuming you don't want to use the PowerTalk or QuickDraw GX features. Add those in, and you need a minimum of 8 megs of RAM.

But if you're using a Power Mac, you need even more: 8 megs without PowerTalk or QuickDraw GX; with those features, the minimum requirements jump to 16 megs!

••➔ **The About This Macintosh** dialog has a nice, full-color (which, of course, you can't see here!) icon in it under System 7.5.

Thanks for the memory.

Uh. I don't recall.

# Fonts & Printing

# CHAPTER 10

# FONT TECHNOLOGIES & TYPE

> I am the voice of today, the herald of tomorrow ... I am the leaden army that conquers the world. I am TYPE.

FREDERIC GOUDY

Whatever could you learn from a chapter with the dry title "Font Technology and Type"? Well, how about:

•••❯ What WYSIWYG stands for.
•••❯ Whether to use PostScript or TrueType fonts—and how to use both.
•••❯ Why PostScript fonts have such strange names.
•••❯ How to mix all the Mac font technologies harmoniously.
•••❯ How to count fonts. (There's more than one way.)
•••❯ What "leading" is and how to pronounce it.
•••❯ How to build a font library.

Serif

A B C
A B C
ABC

*page 398*

### THE MOST AMUSING INFORMATION IN THIS CHAPTER

*How a shipping clerk forced a big manufacturer to spend millions of dollars tracking him down.*

~ATM™

JOHANNES GUTENBERG

-Includes-
112 Factoids
4 Quotable Quotes
7 Memos
—and—
The Font Family Vacation!

Sans. Serif

FLEXIBLE
PARALLEL
SQUARED
RECTANGULAR

# ➤ FONT TECHNOLOGIES ➤

## Overview

∞✦ **WYSIWYG** (*wizzy-wig*) is a term that was launched into general usage by the Mac. Text on the Mac's screen was represented by dots, or *pixels*, and printed with dots on its only printer—the ImageWriter I (although it didn't have a numeral at the time). By no mere coincidence, the size of the dots on the screen and those on the printer matched, at a measurement of 72 dots per inch (dpi). This perfect screen-to-printer translation was christened *What You See Is What You Get*. (Of course, other printers used dots, too, but other screens didn't—they used a character-based system that put letters up in little blocks on the screen and represented boldface, for instance, by little symbols before and after the bold characters.)*

> *I remember how hard it was to talk to PC people in the beginning, because they kept asking how wide the Mac screen was: 70 characters? 80 characters? The answer "It depends on the size of the character" just didn't make any sense to them.

∞✦ **As printer technology advanced** and became more affordable, the 72-dpi Mac screen (basically still the same as the original, even though screens are larger and in color) fell way behind the 300 and even 600 dpi resolution of printers. And so the problems started. Why have one of those printers if the printouts can't look as good as possible? But if you get the perfect fonts for the printer, they can look miserable on the screen. And the information the Mac needs for screen fonts isn't the same information a LaserWriter needs for its high-resolution printing.

So, there are several screen and printer font technologies in the Mac world. Two of them (bitmapped and TrueType) come with your Mac system; a third (PostScript) may be built into your printer; another (ATM) is available as a commercial product at such bargain rates that it's a standard on most Macs. But don't despair: The different systems are easy to understand; you don't need them all; and, if you have them all, they can coexist peacefully.

∞✦ **A bitmapped font** is designed and displayed as a series of dots. It's also sometimes referred to as a *fixed-size* font. In the Mac's case, the dots are square, since the Mac's screen pixels are square. (*Dots* and *pixels* are interchangeable words in this case.) The Mac knows how to interpret the information in a bitmapped font to display it on the screen. A bitmapped font can also be used for printing, but provides good output in only limited situations.

Bitmapped font characters are made up of square dots.

∞✦ **An *outline* font** is designed as a set of instructions instead of a series of dots. The instructions describe how lines and curves should be drawn from one set of coordinates to another to form the letter. Once the outline is drawn, it's filled in to make the letter.

An outline character is filled with black.

•→ **A PostScript font** is an outline font that's described in Adobe Inc.'s PostScript language. (PostScript is actually a "page description" language, so it can describe more than just fonts—it can be used to do all sorts of graphics tricks. But more about that in other chapters.) Since PostScript fonts were built into the first LaserWriter, and PostScript fonts are the most-used printer fonts in the Mac world, lots of Mac people use the phrases *PostScript font* and *outline font* interchangeably, but that's not strictly correct. PostScript fonts are outline fonts but not all outline fonts are PostScript fonts.

A PostScript font is designed for the printer—for PostScript printers, in fact. The Mac doesn't know how to display PostScript information on its screen, so a coordinating bitmapped font is used for the screen when you're using PostScript fonts.

A$_{TM GX is}$
included
with System 7.5.

•→ **ATM** (Adobe Type Manager) was the best thing that happened to Mac fonts since square pixels. ATM is an extension that lets the Mac take the information in the PostScript printer file and use it to display smooth characters on the screen in any size, not just the ones for which bitmapped versions were available. It makes any non-installed size better looking, but its effect is particularly noticeable on large-size text, as you can see in this picture.

Large text on screen without ATM (left) and with it (right).

✽Okay, he meant "letter" as in "missive," not alphabetic character, but it's a nifty quote. And it's from the man who had a computer programming language named after him.

I have made this letter longer than usual only because I have not had the time to make it shorter.*

**BLAISE PASCAL**
(1623–1715)

•→ **Apple's TrueType technology** was designed to deal with the screen-versus-printer problem. TrueType is an outline font—its characters are mathematically described—but the Mac can interpret the information both for the screen and for high-resolution printers, overcoming the PostScript font problem of needing two versions of every font. So, you get smooth text at any size for the screen *and* for the printer, all wrapped up in a single font file.

•→ **A *printer* font is** an outline font. It's the file that describes a font in a way that only the printer understands. The Mac doesn't know how to take those same directions and display the font on the screen. A printer font is also called a *downloadable* font because it's downloaded from the Mac to the printer when it's time to print. So that means there are four different terms you'll see for this kind of font:

printer = downloadable = PostScript = outline

··→ **Screen font is** another term for *bitmapped font*. But it's sometimes used in the stricter sense of a bitmapped font that acts as a companion to a printer font so the Mac has something to display on the screen. So, you'll see three different terms for this kind of font:

bitmapped = fixed size = screen

··→ **A bitmapped font is always used** on the screen, no matter what technology you're using—because *everything* on the screen is bitmapped, using the pixels on the monitor as dots that are on or off. A TrueType font is an outline font, but the information in the font is used to create a bitmap of the correct size for the screen. But when we refer to a bitmapped font, we mean one that was designed as a bitmap.

··→ **The word *outline*** is used in three ways in relation to fonts. There's the outline font that I've been describing here—the one that's formed from mathematical descriptions. Then there's the outline style that looks like this. Finally, there are *font outlines*, or *character outlines*, that come with some outline fonts. These are individual files of editable characters that you can alter if you have the right graphics program.

## Bitmapped Fonts

∞→ **The number of dots available** for a bitmapped character's design is limited by the point size of the font. (A point is actually a very specific measurement, but for the most part in this chapter we can assume that *dot=pixel=point*.) A standard 12-point font is 12 dots high. But that height has to include both the tallest letters in the font—the capitals—and the "tails" on some of the lowercase letters, like *g* and *y*. At smaller and smaller point sizes, it gets harder and harder to design readable fonts since there are fewer dots to work with.

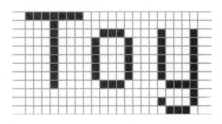

Letters in a 12-point font are designed on a grid 12 squares high.

∞→ **Enlarging a bitmapped font** creates distortions. If you display a 24-point font that's derived from a 12-point design, every dot in the original design becomes four dots on the screen. (Doubling the size makes one dot into four dots because the size is doubled in both the horizontal and vertical directions.) Creating a 48-point display from a 12-point design means every dot in the original becomes 16 dots. This enlargement doesn't matter much when you're working with horizontal and vertical lines, but angled lines and curves become a series of stairsteps known as *jaggies*.

The distortion is even worse when you try to display a font that's not a multiple of the original size. If you want a 30-point font from a 12-point design, every original dot needs to be turned into

The jaggies show up in the 24- and 48-point fonts derived from the 12-point design at the top.

two and a half dots vertically and horizontally. There's no such thing as a half-dot on the screen, though, so sometimes a full dot is used and sometimes a dot just drops out. As a result, you get variations in line thickness and blobs around curves.

A derived font size that's not a multiple of the original design is very uneven.

**30 points**
12 points

∞➡ **Shrinking a bitmapped font** isn't any cleaner than enlarging it. Even cutting a 24-point design in half doesn't get you a good 12-point solution. Dots drop out (or stay) at unpredictable spots and you get odd line widths and blobs. This picture shows a 24-point font; to the right is the "real" 12-point font (top) and the one the Mac would come up with in the absence of a 12-point design (bottom).

A B C   A B C
           A B C

> The big print giveth and
> the fine print taketh away.

**ARCHBISHOP FULTON J. SHEEN**
*(Referring to a television appearance contract)*

∞➡ **All large fonts aren't jagged** because some are specifically designed to be a large size, where there are plenty of dots available to make a smooth line instead of a jagged one. Compare the 24- and 48-point designs

A B C   A B C
ABC ABC

here: The ones on the left are the designs derived from the 12-point version of the font, while the ones on the right were hand-tooled for the larger point sizes.

The large-designed fonts are good-looking because everything that would be a stairstep is smoothed out during the design. This magnified view of the 24-point letters shows the differences. At the top is the derived font; at the bottom is the hand-tooled one.

Notice that designing a font at a specific size isn't just a matter of smoothing out the jaggies, though. Letters at different sizes sometimes need different proportions entirely. The large A, for instance, doesn't have as much of a point at its top as the small A did. And, while the small B was divided exactly in half for its curves, the large B is has a larger bottom curve to keep it from looking top-heavy.

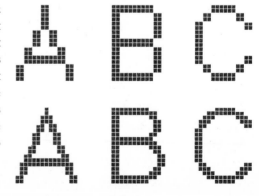

•••❥ **A true-size bitmapped font is always best** for the screen. It's better than something that's derived from a bitmap of another size, a TrueType font, or a PostScript font. But it's not feasible to keep a bitmapped font in every size you're likely to use, since that would take too much room on the disk. Bitmapped fonts are designed in only a handful of sizes, anyway, usually ranging from 9 to 24 points.

## Printer & PostScript Fonts

∞•❥ **Characters in an outline font** are still represented by dots both on the screen and on printers because screens and printers work with dots. Once an outline is drawn, it's not filled with black the way you might pour something into a frame. Instead, the outline is placed on a grid of dots and the dots that fall inside the outline are used for the letter-form; this process is called *rasterization*. That, of course, leaves the letter a little raggedy around curves, but the dots used on a printer are so small that you don't see the rough edges.

The outline laid on a grid (left) and the pixels that finally get included in the letter (right).

**"Hinting" is the method behind the magic** of PostScript fonts. Here's the problem: Trying to fill in a character outline—especially a small one—leads to problems when the outline doesn't fit on a grid of dots too well. The lowercase *f* outline shown here is fitted to a grid in different positions with differing results. In each sample, any dot partially within the outline was turned on. The third sample is undoubtedly the best, but still won't print as well as the separate figure shown, which none of the grid characters generated. But hinting instructions in a printer font file take care of such problems and make sure that letters are always formed and printed the best way possible for the output device's resolution.

Hinting is needed for small type on low-resolution printers—but in this case, your 300-dpi LaserWriter is considered low resolution, since it's being compared to devices in the printing industry that output at 1200, 2500, and even higher dpi resolutions.

The results of fitting an outline to a grid in different ways.

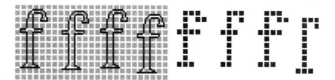

None of the grid figures came up with this, the best bitmap for printing.

## WHEREFORE ART THOU ADOBE, ALDUS?

In a world of high-tech names which, if they don't bring to mind at least some kind of machinery, they recall something from Star Trek or the Star Wars trilogy, where did the premier names in desktop publishing—Aldus and Adobe—come from?

Aldus Manutius was a fifteenth-century printer and font designer who created one of the first italic font faces. He printed the first small, almost pocket-sized, books, cheaply enough so that more people could afford to buy them. When he died, he was buried surrounded by books.

And Adobe? It's the name of a creek that runs behind the Northern California home of the company's founder. (If a dry creek can be said to run.)

**Type 1. Type 3. Type A.** One's a personality type that's heading for ulcers or a heart attack. The other two are types of PostScript fonts (Type 2 never made it off the drawing board and into use).

Type 1 fonts are encrypted to hide their design details and hinting from prying eyes and copycats. Type 3 fonts aren't encrypted or hinted and were, until relatively recently, the only type of PostScript font someone besides Adobe could create. But now the cat's out of the bag—or, speaking more formally, Adobe decided to open up its architecture and share the Type 1 approach. (This was hardly altruistic. There was a distinct possibility that Apple's TrueType, with Microsoft behind it on the PC front, would outpace the use of PostScript fonts in the computer world.)

Type 1 fonts are generally better looking than Type 3 fonts, and are the only ones that ATM can use to render type on the screen. But if you're printing at resolutions greater than 300 dpi, or not using text smaller than, say 10 points, a Type 3 font still looks good.

➤ **You don't need a decoder ring** to figure out the name of an outline font, although sometimes it might help. There's actually a very strict naming convention for printer fonts. The first five letters name the font family (unless the font name is less than five letters, like *Jott*). Any other words in the font's name are then given three letters each. So, Tekton Oblique becomes TektoObl. This gives rise to some strange combinations.* Here are some that are lurking around on my drive:

> *I did this late at night. So when I looked through the folder and saw Franklin Gothic Demi and then Frutiger Bold, all I could think of was "FrankGotDem" and then he put them in the "FrutiBol." And then I ran across TradeGotBol and TradeGotBolTwo. If you don't think that's funny, try reading it at around 2:00 a.m. after a very long day.

| | |
|---|---|
| CheltUltIta | Cheltenham Ultra Italic |
| CoppeThiThrBC | Copperplate 33BC |
| QuoruBoo | Quorum Book |
| FolioBol | Folio Bold |
| FrizQuaBol | Friz Quadrata Bold |
| GaramThrBolItaOsF | Garamond Three Bold Italic Old Style Figures |
| GillSanUltBolCon | Gill Sans Ultra Bold Condensed |
| SnellRouScr | Snell Roundhand Script |
| TiffaHeaIta | Tiffany Heavy Italic |
| UniveConLigObl | Univers Condensed Light Oblique |
| UtopiExpSemIta | Utopia Expert Semibold Italic |

➤ **Some printer font names** are impossible to translate if you don't know the name of the screen font, because the three-letter abbreviations shorten multiname fonts to nonsense. UtilCitLas, for instance, is Utility City Laser. But the majority of three-letter abbreviations in printer font names refer to weights or styles and conform to certain standards. Here's a list of the common ones.

| | | | |
|---|---|---|---|
| Bol | bold | Kur | kursive |
| Boo | book | Lig | light |
| Bla | black | Med | medium |
| Con | condensed | Obl | oblique |
| Com | compressed | Reg | regular |
| Dem | demi, demibold | Rom | Roman |
| Ext | extra, extended | Sem | semi |
| Hea | heavy | Thi | thin |
| Ita | italic | Ult | ultra |

•◆ **PostScript fonts are** *downloaded* to the LaserWriter at print time if they're not built into the printer. The application you're printing from takes care of the downloading. When the document is all printed, the font information is flushed from the LaserWriter's memory.

> ✳Information and files are <u>downloaded</u> and <u>uploaded</u> from one place to another.

You can manually download* fonts to the LaserWriter independently of a document's application, so they stay there instead of having to be downloaded over and over. That's covered in Chapter 16.

•◆ **PostScript fonts can be stored** in many different places and the Mac can still find them when it's time to send them to the printer. The Mac looks in these places, in this order:

- In the LaserWriter's ROMs.
- In the LaserWriter's memory.
- On a hard drive attached to the LaserWriter.
- In the Fonts folder (System 7.1) or Extensions folder (System 7.0) on the system disk.
- In any other folder specified by a font utility like Suitcase.

> FOND, and other font resources, are covered in Chapter 11.

•◆ **NEVER rename a PostScript** font or the Mac won't be able to find it when it comes time to download it to the printer. The name of the correct printer font is actually stored in the FOND resource of the bitmapped font, so renaming the bitmapped font to match a renamed PostScript font won't work. (On the other hand, it means you can rename a bitmapped font without affecting the link to its printer font.)

•◆ **The main problem with PostScript** fonts is that they're designed for *PostScript devices*—devices that include a PostScript interpreter to turn the font file information into characters. And guess what? The Mac is not a PostScript device, so it can't use PostScript information to put letters on the screen. When you're using PostScript printer fonts, you still need something for the screen, so you need a bitmapped font in at least one size for the screen display—*and* to get the font listed in your Font menus, since the Mac ignores printer fonts when it's building menus.

•◆ *Multiple masters* is probably the future of computer font design; its beginnings are already here. It's from Adobe, the PostScript people, and it's sort of a Super Hints for fonts. A standard font is defined with certain characteristics in common for all of its characters: the thickness of its lines (standard, semibold, bold, extra bold), style (serif or sans, italic, oblique or roman), and width (standard, condensed, expanded). A multiple master font contains several definitions, or *master designs*, each of which defines an extreme in a category such as weight or oblique angle. With the right utility (or, eventually, with an application that knows how to interpret multiple masters), you can create a font that uses any of the characteristics anywhere between the extremes. Imagine the Style menu choices: *Extra thick bold, Pretty bold but not too much, Only a slight lean, Just short of toppling over angle, …*

•◆ **AFM files** come with many Adobe PostScript fonts. These files (Adobe Font Metrics) contain special information that describes the dimensions of the font for applications that need the information provided that way. (I know only of two applications that use

AFMs—FrameMaker and InterLeaf. Bet you never even heard of InterLeaf. Bet most of you never heard of FrameMaker, either.)

So, you can get rid of any AFM files you have hanging around. (They're text files, by the way, so you can read through them with a word processor if you don't have a life.)

## TrueType

∞➤ **Apple's TrueType technology** solves several font problems, the most obvious being the distorted characters you wind up with when you use a bitmapped font at an odd size. This picture, for instance, shows samples of a bitmapped and a TrueType font in corresponding sizes; the bitmapped version on top was installed in only one size, the smallest one in the sample. This smooth-at-any-size approach is echoed in the printing process, too, on any printer.

Before TrueType (top) and after (bottom).

Type  Type  Type **Type**

Type  Type  Type Type

➤ **The TrueType and bitmapped** version of the same font can look quite different.

Here, for instance, are some magnified samples of two versions of the same font. The top one is the hand-tooled bitmapped version; the bottom is TrueType. The 9-point TrueType looks larger than the bitmapped version because its lowercase letters are

designed to be a little taller; the characters have lost almost all their serifs (the bars at the end of the long lines in characters, like at the bottom of the *p*). The 14-point TrueType *o*, *i*, and *1* are clunky compared to the bitmapped version, the *n* has a small piece missing, and the *i* and the *n* are touching.

Magnified bitmapped font (top) and TrueType (bottom).

9 point  14 point

9 point  14 point

➤ **Some TrueType fonts come in "families"** of plain, italic, bold, and bold italic, just like PostScript fonts. Some come in smaller families—you'll find both a Courier and a Courier (bold) TrueType font in your Courier suitcase. Times, workhorse that it is, has all four family members in TrueType inside your Times suitcase.

Times   Times (italic)   Times (bold)   Times (bold, italic)

*F*ont families are covered in detail a little later in this chapter.

➤ **You can't turn off TrueType.** It's built into the Mac's system, right there in the System file where you can't get at it. But you *can* remove the TrueType file for any font if you want to "turn off" a specific font. Why would you want to? Sometimes you'll have both a TrueType and a PostScript version of the same font, and using ATM to display the PostScript version gives you a more accurate screen representation.

••◗ **You don't need the TrueType init,** an extension you might have around, or might have seen, running under System 6.0.7. The only way you could use TrueType technology before System 7 was with 6.0.7 and the init; but the information in the init is rolled into System 7's System file.

### HMM ...

Ever wonder why Apple bothered inventing a font technology when PostScript was working so well for printing and ATM let the PostScript fonts be displayed on the screen?

Wounded pride? Or because they paid more than $700 per LaserWriter as a licensing fee to Adobe for the fonts included with the printer? Hmm ... Adobe fonts are still bundled with the LaserWriters, but the prices have really dropped. Maybe it's just that manufacturing costs dropped.

••◗ **Printing TrueType to an old LaserWriter** is sometimes hard or impossible because of memory constraints. TrueType won't even print on the original LaserWriter; you'll have serious problems on a LaserWriter Plus with less than two megs of RAM. Here's the problem: The Mac has to send both the *font scaler* to interpret the TrueType font, and the font itself. There's just not enough room in memory for both. When the Mac realizes this, it generates a PostScript version of the TrueType font which has no hints at all to hone problem characters, and sends that version to the printer. The result? A bad-looking printout that's slow to come out.

You don't get this problem on lesser printers with no memory at all, like the ImageWriter—because the Mac doesn't even try to send the scaler and the outline font information. It just sends the same bitmap that it used to display the font on the screen.

## ATM

∞◗ **ATM** was the first solution to the jaggies on the Mac screen. It took the information in a PostScript printer font file and interpreted it to be displayed on the screen. For the first time, Mac users could have smooth text at any size without a bitmapped version of the font installed to provide it.

Text without ATM.
Text with ATM.

At one point, rumor had it that Apple planned to roll ATM right into System 7; when that didn't happen, it was assumed that System 7.1 would have ATM with it. But it hardly matters that it's not actually system software since you can, at this writing, get it for $7.50. Anyway, ATM is so endemic in the Mac community, I'm giving it its own little section here as if it came with the Mac. And who knows—it may be rolled into the next round of system software.

°•◆ **ATM is a two-piece utility**, a control panel and a *driver*, both of which work only from the System Folder because they have to load last or near-to-last in order to work. Their names begin with the tilde (~) character to keep them loading last.

~ATM™      ~ATM 680x0

Chapter 8 discusses the loading order for control panels and extensions.

°•◆ **Although the name of ATM's control panel** has steadfastly been ~ATM all along, the driver portion has been renamed several times as it's updated for new Macs. The driver uses the Mac's processor chip as the identifier, although there's been a lot of condensing of the name along the way. So, it's gone from ~ATM 68020/68030 to ~ATM 68020/030/040 to ~ATM 680x0.

°•◆ **You need a bitmapped version** of a PostScript font even if you're using ATM because otherwise the font won't appear in the menu, and you won't be able to select it. The bitmapped font also contains the information that tells the Mac which printer font to send to the printer.

There's more about font families and applying styles in the next chapter.

But you can get away with using a single bitmapped font for a whole family of printer fonts. You select the plain version from the menu and apply bold from a Style menu; the bold printer font is the one that's sent to the printer. This isn't always the best solution, since the derived bold on the screen may have significant spacing differences from the one in the printout, but you should know it's an alternative to filling your System file or Fonts folder with four bitmapped fonts for every basic font family.

°•◆ **Even if a PostScript font is** built into your printer, you still need the printer file on your Mac if you want ATM to render it for the screen.

°•◆ **ATM gives you a choice between** having the individual letters on your screen formed to match how they'll look on the printout ("preserve character shapes") or formed and spaced to match the *spacing* you'll get on the printout ("preserve line spacing"), which is a little different. The picture here shows Times in four varieties; the top sample of each pair preserves the character shape, while the bottom preserves the line spacing. You can see that the italic spacing is actually narrower than can be displayed when all the characters are kept as perfect as possible, while the other three examples take up more room on the line when the spacing is matched to what will happen on the printout.

Preserving character shape or line spacing changes the length of a line of type. The bottom sample of each pair preserves the line spacing.

The Times font in plain.
The Times font in plain.
*The Times font in italic.*
*The Times font in italic.*
**The Times font in bold.**
**The Times font in bold.**
***The Times font in bold italic.***
***The Times font in bold italic.***

Stick with the spacing option, even though it doesn't look as good on the screen. It shows for sure where the lines will break in a paragraph of text, and that's much more important than getting the individual letters represented more perfectly.

•••❯ **ATM uses only Type 1** PostScript fonts. This isn't too much of an issue any more, since there are very few Type 3 PostScript fonts around.

•••❯ **ATM lets you print** PostScript fonts on non-PostScript printers. It renders the type for the printer the same way it renders it for the Mac screen, so you can take advantage of some of the zillion PostScript fonts out there no matter what printer you have. But since PostScript fonts were designed for high-resolution output, you won't be happy with ATM-produced text unless it's quite large (as for a headline) or you're using a high-resolution (300-dpi or better) printer that doesn't have PostScript already built in.

•••❯ **ATM doesn't always run the screen** display. If there's a bitmapped font of the correct size, that's used instead of the ATM version. (This is the same setup that TrueType uses—it bows to the superior-for-screen-display bitmap of the right size.)

•••❯ **ATM "breaks" under new system software** more than just about anything else I've ever used on the Mac since the Mac began. That is, if you update your system software to a new version, or for a different machine, your current version of ATM is unlikely to work. Luckily, Adobe updates ATM constantly. Here are a few guidelines about different versions:

- For any version, make sure if you've changed your hardware to a new Mac with a different processor that you have the correct extension—one that includes your new machine. The ~68020/68030 that worked fine on your IIci won't work on your new Quadra.
- Versions earlier than 2.0 won't run under System 7.
- Version 2.0 works with System 7.0 but looks only in the System Folder for the printer font file. It doesn't work with System 7.1.
- Version 2.0.2 works with System 7 and looks in both the Extensions folder and the System Folder for printer fonts. It doesn't work with System 7.1.
- Versions earlier than 3.0 are not "32-bit clean," so they won't work on machines using 32-bit addressing.
- Versions 3.0 and higher look in the Fonts folder and work with System 7.1.

Clean?
Dirty?
32-bit
addressing?
See Chapter 9.

•••❯ **Later versions of ATM are** significantly faster than the earlier ones. So even if everything's working all right and you're not upgrading your hardware or your system software, you should still upgrade to the most recent ATM version available.

•••❯ **ATM clashes with MenuFonts,** one of my other favorite font utilities. But it's simply a classic case of which extension's loading when. By renaming MenuFonts to ~MenuFonts and leaving it in the System Folder, it loads after ATM and they're both happy.

∘∘◊❯ **Look, up on the screen!** It's a B! It's an N! It's *SuperATM!* SuperATM is *not* the latest version of ATM, although it's easy to think so, considering the name. SuperATM is a different product that happens to incorporate ATM as part of it. SuperATM's function is to create "fake" fonts for documents on systems that don't have the fonts that were originally used in the document's creation. The fake imitates the original's general look, but more importantly, preserves its weight and the line breaks it causes in the document so someone can view it even if he doesn't have the original font in his system.

So, don't think you're missing the latest ATM just because you don't have SuperATM; it's a different product entirely.

## TrueType vs. PostScript

➔ **TrueType is self-contained**. You need only one font file (stored in the System file in System 7.0, in the Fonts folder in System 7.1) for any size display on the screen and for use with any printer. For the same results with a PostScript font, you need the PostScript printer font, at least one screen font, and ATM to display the font at every size on the screen and to print to a non-PostScript printer.

➔ **A TrueType font file** takes more room on the disk than a PostScript font file. The TrueType Times, for instance, is 67K, while the PostScript version is 36K; even adding the 7K for a Times bitmap to the PostScript file size (since you need it for the Font menu), the PostScript setup takes less room.

But, realistically, the TrueType is going to take less room overall. For one thing, you'll generally have four PostScript files for a font (the plain, italic, bold, and bold italic versions) and of course you need ATM for the screen rendering.

➔ **TrueType works for any printer** because it's the Mac that does the work. It can send the right information to any printer. PostScript fonts work only for PostScript printers unless you also use ATM.

➔ **TrueType uses more printer memory** in most LaserWriters. First of all, the TrueType font files are bigger than the corresponding PostScript font files not only in disk space, but in the memory needed to hold them in the printer. But the font information has to be interpreted for printing, and while most LaserWriters have the PostScript interpreter built in, they need the TrueType *scaler* downloaded to memory. (The download itself is invisible; the Mac takes care of it for you.)

➔ **TrueType is slower** than PostScript on PostScript printers. Many LaserWriters have PostScript fonts built in, so the Mac doesn't have to download the font information for a print job. But even when the font information is downloaded, the interpreter is already in the printer. Not so for TrueType, which needs both the font information and the interpreter sent to the printer for the print job.

➔ **TrueType fonts are resources** stored in the System file (System 7.0) or the Fonts folder (System 7.1). PostScript fonts are data files that exist independently and whose information is downloaded to the printer as necessary.

➔ **Choosing between TrueType and PostScript** isn't all that difficult. If you're pretty much a self-contained operation, using a non-PostScript printer, TrueType is the way to go. If you have a PostScript LaserWriter, you can use the PostScript fonts that come with it and the TrueType fonts that you have for variety beyond the built-ins.

If you're doing very high-resolution printing with something like a Linotype at a print service bureau, stick with PostScript fonts.

••◆ **PostScript won't be going away.** Even with TrueType technology growing in speed and in variety, and crossing platforms with Microsoft using it in Windows, it can't replace PostScript. TrueType is strictly a font technology. PostScript is a complete page description language and encompasses more than fonts: it includes graphics, and, by extension, complete laid-out pages.

••◆ **If a font is jagged** on the screen even though the TrueType version is installed, you may be running low on memory.

## Mixing Technologies

∞◆ **To use a font,** it has to be in a Font menu. To get it into a Font menu, you need at least one bitmapped version (in any size) or a TrueType version installed in your system. This means that if you're using PostScript fonts for the printer and ATM for the screen display, you still need a bitmapped version of the font just so it will be in the font menu.

### CLEANLINESS IS NEXT TO ...

A clean, dust-free environment is a necessity for manufacturing computer chips. The clean-room environment in the industry is beyond that needed in a surgical operating room.

At one point (the actual point is obscured by the mists of time—call it a couple of decades ago), the Intel company blamed its poor production yields of computer chips on Monsanto, the company providing silicon wafers used to make the chips. Monsanto already had a spic and span facility, but it spent several millions of dollars in research and revamping. To no avail: Intel's yields were still very low, despite Intel's also-immaculate environment.

Monsanto got tired of being unfairly blamed for the contaminants. Someone at the company had a brainstorm: if neither company was at fault, why not check what was happening to the wafers during shipment? Ah ha! A clerk at Intel, upon receiving each shipment of wafers, opened the boxes and counted the wafers by (presumably dirty) hand to make sure they were all there.

∞◆ **You can mix technologies** without worrying too much. In each instance, for each font and size, the Mac will choose what's best for the screen and then what's best for the printer based on what's available. In fact, it's difficult *not* to work with mixed technologies, since the Mac comes with both bitmapped and TrueType fonts and most LaserWriters come with PostScript fonts.

But mixing technologies gets a blessing based on an assumption: that you're mixing bitmaps and TrueType for some fonts, and bitmaps and PostScript for other fonts, but not TrueType and PostScript versions of the same font. Mixing PostScript and TrueType won't blow anything up—I kept several duplicates around during the course of writing these chapters—but it's considered very poor form. And your printout won't match your screen display if you're printing PostScript fonts but TrueType is taking care of the screen.

⋙ **A font displayed on the screen** can come from one of four places. It can come from a bitmapped font of the size that's being displayed; it can be derived from a bitmapped font of different size; it can be a TrueType font; or, it can be a PostScript printer font that's displayed with the ATM extension.

But the Mac knows best, and it looks in a specific order for screen font information. If it can't find the best thing, it looks for the next best thing. (Don't we all?!) The Mac first looks for a bitmapped font in the correct size. If it can't find that, it looks for the TrueType version. If there's no TrueType for the font, the Mac checks if ATM is running and uses the PostScript file to create the screen font. If none of those strategies is successful, it falls back on using a bitmapped version of the font to create the size you need.

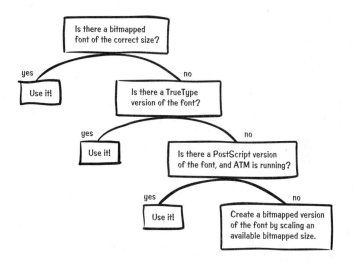

⋙ **For printing,** the Mac once again looks for the best possible way to create text. "Best" in this case, though, differs according to the printer that's available—whether it's PostScript capable or not.

The hierarchy of choices for printouts is pretty much the opposite of that for screen display. PostScript fonts take priority if they're available: if they're built into the printer, that's all well and good, but if they're not, they get downloaded to the PostScript printer. In fact, if you're running ATM and using a non-PostScript printer, the PostScript font still gets priority. If there's no way to do a PostScript font, the Mac will settle for sending a TrueType font to the printer. Finally, with no PostScript or TrueType font around, the printer is stuck with the bitmapped font or its derivative for different size.

So, the priority is:

1. PostScript font, with ATM if necessary
2. TrueType font
3. Bitmapped font

P*ostScript fonts can be stored in many different places and still be available to the printer. See Chapter 12.*

❖ **If you forget to install** a printer font in your Extensions folder or Fonts folder, but you've installed the screen version for the Font menu, the screen font will be used as a bitmap for the printer. (Assuming the font isn't built into the printer.)

If you do the reverse—install a printer font but forget to install the screen font—you won't be able to access the font because it's the screen font installation that puts the font's name into the menu.

❖ **Your PostScript printer might print a TrueType font** despite a PostScript version of the font's being built in if you turn Font Substitution off in your printing options. And if you're using the right—or wrong, in this case—combination of printer and driver. (And if it's a waxing half-moon on a winter Tuesday.)

F*onts and printing are covered further in Chapters 11 and 12.*

❖ **The problem with mixing technologies** is that you get one thing on the screen and another in the printout. So what, if you're looking at the best for each situation? Well, they don't always match. And the problem with *that* is that three lines of text on the screen may turn into four lines, or two, on the paper.

If you start running into these kinds of problems, try trimming down the variety of fonts available to your Mac. Don't use both TrueType and PostScript versions of the same font, since TrueType will win on the screen and PostScript in the printout. If you're printing PostScript, use ATM for the screen display; totally remove the TrueType versions of the font.

Sometimes the bitmapped font that looks so great on the screen has very different line spacing from the TrueType or PostScript version that's going to be printed. So, despite that terrific on-screen look, you might have to remove the bitmapped version of a font in all but a single size.

## Font Editing

FONTOGRAPHER

❖ **Fontographer is for font artists.** Or font artist wannabes. Use it to design your own PostScript or TrueType fonts from scratch. Or alter an existing font to suit your purposes by adding characters or by making an entire font lighter or heavier. We used Fontographer to create a special font for this book—one that includes the curly arrows used for each entry, the ornaments in the headings, and the special characters for the Shift, Option, and Command keys that I use in tables and charts.

The most recent version of Fontographer includes a tool palette that rivals that of PostScript drawing programs, so there's not much you can't do with it. Assuming, of course, you have the talent! [Altsys]

**TypeStyler** doesn't create fonts, as does Fontographer, but lets you create graphics with type. You can twist or distort any text to fit into any shape and/or apply special effects to the type. You can use the supplied "envelopes" for the basic shape or create your own. The altered type can be exported as a graphic to be used in other programs. The one dialog shown here, out of dozens available, gives you some idea of the kind of control you have over the type. As you can see, even within the basic roller coaster shape chosen, you get four different ways to squeeze the letters in. [Broderbund]

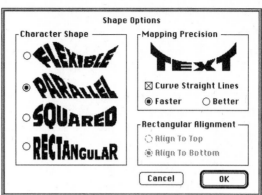

**TYPESTYLER**

**You can do font manipulation** without a font-specific utility, since most graphics programs let you handle text. Of course, you won't be creating a font, but you'll be creating a graphic from text. You can also manipulate text right in some word processors. In Microsoft Word, for instance, you can turn any text selection into a graphic. Then you can resize the graphic, perhaps widening it to create an eye-catching headline like this:

# LOOK AT THIS

**You can change fonts from one type** to another—TrueType to PostScript, Type 3 to Type 1, PostScript to TrueType—with any of several utilities, like FontMonger, Metamorphosis Professional, and ParaFont. Most utilities also let you alter the fonts somewhat, and combine characters from different fonts into a single font, or use a graphic as a font character. [FontMonger, Ares Software; ParaFont, Design Sciences; Metamorphosis Professional; Altsys]

# ➤ FONTS & FACES ◄

## Of Fonts & Families

**A** *font* **is,** in the world of computer technology, a certain typeface no matter what its size or style. You can use Times at 12 points, or at 18 points, or with bold or italic styles applied, but it's all still the Times font.

In traditional typography, each size and style of a typeface design is considered a separate font. So, 12-point Helvetica is a different font from 14-point Helvetica, or even 12-point italic Helvetica. This made perfect sense when the cast letters for each "font" had to be physically separated for easy handling and quick access, but that's not the case anymore.

Trying to define point sizes as different fonts in this age of computer-scalable fonts is a lost cause, especially because there are programs that can print fonts at fractional point sizes, say 10.5 or 8.25 points. So despite the tradition of a few hundred years, we use *font* to describe all the versions of a related font and then refer to its various *styles*.

∞❥ A *font family* is the traditional term for a group of related font designs that share the same basic name—like Times, Times Italic, Times Bold, and Times Bold Italic. It's what we call a font in the Mac world.

But you'll see a reversion to the more traditional terminology for *font* and *font family* when someone is trying to impress you, the presumably impressionable consumer, with the vast number of fonts built into a printer or included in a font package. All of a sudden, Helvetica, Helvetica Bold, Helvetica Italic, and Helvetica Bold Italic are four different fonts.

∞❥ Most font families consist of a basic gang of four: the basic font, a bold version, an italic version, and a bold italic version. You'll find plenty of variations, and family groups larger and smaller than four, but those are the four standards.

You don't have to worry much about this when you're using the Mac; if you select text that's in a certain font and apply bold, the Mac will substitute the bold member of the family for you if it's available—you don't have to choose a separate font.

••❥ Many basic families keep the plain/italic/bold/bold italic relationship among their four members, but those aren't actually the true weights and styles in the family. A LaserWriter, for instance, has Avant Garde and Bookman built in, but these are the actual fonts:

| | |
|---|---|
| Avant Garde Book | Bookman Light |
| Avant Garde Book Oblique | Bookman Light Italic |
| Avant Garde Demi | Bookman Demi |
| Avant Garde Demi Oblique | Bookman Demi Italic |

For Avant Garde, Book is the normal weight, but Demi (for demibold) is the bold version, while Oblique is the italic version. For Bookman, Light is what's being used as the normal weight with Demi as the bold, while there's a true italic style for each of those weights.

••❥ Why do you need a family of fonts when the Mac can change the basic font by applying a style to it? Because although the Mac can take a font and make it bold or italic, it does it in a rough—one might say *sloppy*—fashion. You want italic? The Mac takes the basic font and slants its letters by shifting the pixels at the top of the characters to the right and the bottom ones to the left. You want bold? The Mac adds an extra pixel along the vertical edges of letters so that they're thicker. But these *derived* fonts are nowhere near as good as a *designed* font. (Designed variations of a basic font are called "cuttings" in traditional typography.)

••❥ A designed italic font is very different from the computer-generated one. A derived italic is merely slanted; the designed one is, well, sort of *curled*. You can see the differences in the picture here, which shows how the fonts look on the screen.

In the designed italic, the letters are more rounded, and the serifs—the little straight lines at the ends of the long lines in a character—are curled instead of flat as in the derived font in the middle of the picture. The lowercase *a* is entirely different from the ones in both the plain and slanted versions, and the lowercase *f* extends below the base line of the text in the designed font. All together, the designed font is much more attractive than the derived font, and it's much more readable when printed out.

The basic font (top), a derived italic (middle), and a designed italic (bottom).

A sample of the Times font.
*A sample of the Times font in italic.*
*A sample of the Times font in italic.*

**A designed bold font** is also quite different from the derived version, as you can see here. The derived bold font merely thickens every vertical line. The designed bold doesn't thicken every line, but the ones that are thickened are much wider. The serifs are generally straight, as in the base font, but some—like the one in the lowercase *f*— end in knobs; the dot for the i and the period are much larger and rounder. Altogether, the much heavier-looking designed bold takes less room on the line because its letters stay closer together.

The basic font (top), a derived bold (middle), and a designed bold (bottom).

A sample of the Times font.
**A sample of the Times font in bold.**
**A sample of the Times font in bold.**

When you combine bold and italic and let the Mac derive the font from the standard one, you get just what you'd expect—slanted, thickened letters. A font designed for bold and italic, however, is much more attractive—and, once again, takes less room on the line.

The derived font (top) and the designed font (bottom).

***A sample of Times in bold italic.***
***A sample of Times in bold italic.***

**The other styles** that you're used to on the Mac—underline, outline, shadow—aren't designed fonts, but computer enhancements to the basic designed fonts. They're always derived fonts.

**An *expert set*** or *expert collection* is like an extended family—it's a font in a myriad of versions, including different weights, small caps, and fractions (which are pretty much in short supply in any font). There aren't that many expert collections around, and they're expensive, but if you're an expert, you probably need a few.

Styles that you apply to fonts are covered in the next chapter.

### THE FONT
### FAMILY VACATION

## Basic Typography Terms

∞•❯ **Fonts are measured in *points*.** A point is about 1/72 of an inch—approximately the size of a single dot on a standard Mac screen (not exactly a coincidental occurrence). If you want to be very specific, a point is .0138 of an inch.

∞•❯ **The six basic terms that describe** character design are: *baseline, cap height, x-height, ascender, descender,* and *counter*. This is one of those times when a picture is worth about a hundred words, so you can check the picture for the definitions of these terms.

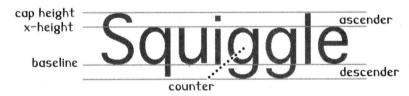

There are, of course, many more terms in typography and type design, and many more details. Like, for instance, the cap height isn't always the same as the ascender height—sometimes it's shorter; and there are words like *arm* for the short diagonal or horizontal projections in letters like y and k. But the basic terms here are enough as points of reference when you're talking or reading about fonts.

••❯ **A *monofont*,** or *monospaced* font gives equal horizontal space to every letter no matter how wide the letter is. Most fonts are *proportional*, giving less space to skinny letters than they do to wide letters. Logical enough, right? After all, an *m* needs more space than an *i*. But that's not the way it always is. Monospaced fonts make your printouts look typewritten, or computer-generated. (Well, non-Mac-computer-generated.)

Monospaced (top) and proportional (bottom) fonts.

| m m m m<br>i i i i | This is a monospaced font. |
|---|---|
| m m m m<br>i i i i | This is a proportional font. |

➤ **Characters in a *serif* font have** some sort of cap at the end of the lines that make up the letters. A *sans serif* font doesn't have these end strokes. (*Serif* rhymes with *sheriff*, not Omar *Sharif*. *Sans*, like *sands* without the *d*, is French for "without.")

Sans.
Serif
Serif

### KEEPING THINGS IN PROPORTION

Proportional spacing for type seems so much more "advanced" than monospacing that one is tempted to assume that we started out monospaced and evolved to proportional spacing, but that's not the case. (And the first automobiles didn't have manual transmissions, either.) Early printing—*really* early, like Gutenberg—was all proportional, since the letters used in printing presses were handmade and cast in "slugs" of the appropriate width. But our immediate printing predecessor is the typewriter, which gave the same amount of line space to each character.

➤ ***Leading* is** the space between lines; it's pronounced *ledding*, not *leeding*, because it comes from the lead strips printers used to space lines of lead type. Leading is measured in points, usually from the baseline of the text in one line to the baseline of the text in the next line.

leading { Leading is measured from one baseline to the next.

Except for page layout programs, most Mac applications refer to *line spacing* rather than leading. Most programs provide *auto leading* or *auto spacing* that adjusts the line spacing to accommodate the largest character in the line, even (or especially) if you insert a larger character, say 24-point, in the midst of 12-point text.

This book is using a 10.5-point font for the main body text, with a leading of 12.5 points. That's referred to in writing as 10.5/12.5, and in speaking as "ten and a half on twelve and a half." You might find it interesting to take a look at some of the bulleted lists throughout the book. The text is in the same point size, but with a tighter leading—it's 10.5/11.5—the text has an overall darker look. That, along with the nested margins for bulleted text, makes it easy to see where lists start and end as you read along—you get subtle visual clues as to where the lists begin and end.

➤ **A point isn't the only unit** of measure in typography. A *pica* is a useful unit because it's larger—it's 12 points. (It's easier to talk about a 1.5-pica margin than an 18-point one.)

The other two measurements you might run across in your Mac usage are *em* and *en*, units without absolute sizes—they depend on the font you're using. An em is as wide as the widest letter in the typeface—usually the letter M. An en is half the typeface's point size, about half of an em. So, you may see references to an em dash or an en dash, or an em space, all of which are slightly different from regular dashes or spaces.

## More Font Facts

∞❯ **Fonts can be described** in general terms beyond the common dividing lines of serif and sans serif. There are four basic categories:

- A text font is, of course, for text—the kind you read in paragraphs and paragraphs of fact or fiction.
- A display font is designed to look good at large (more than 14 points or so) sizes, for headlines.
- A decorative font is pretty fancy and meant to catch your eye and convey a certain feeling or, shall we say, *attitude*.
- A specialty font is one that's, well, special. It might be filled with foreign-language characters, or pictures.

Fonts can also be described according to the way they're designed. Fonts that imitate handwriting, for instance, are *cursive* or *script*, while fancy, ornate letters are *blackletter* or *Old English*.

∞❯ **A *roman* font** is what we call "plain": It's not bold, and it's not italic.* Roman fonts are also sometimes referred to as the *book* version of the font.

∞❯ **Italic isn't always italic.** Sometimes it's oblique.

> *A Gothic font, by the way, is actually a pretty plain font, despite the word's connotation of "fancy."

An oblique font is one that's slanted; an italic is a much more flowing, curly design. Generally speaking, *oblique* and *italic* are interchangeable terms when it comes to Mac fonts. But you should be aware of the shade of difference, since sometimes the on-screen font will be oblique and the printout a true italic. But some fonts are truly oblique—designed that way on purpose— instead of italic.

*This is oblique*
*This is italic*

∞❯ **It was easier when plain and bold** were the only *weights* available for a font. Easier, but not so interesting.

A font's weight is basically the thickness of the lines that make up its letters. You can be bolder than bold, or less bold but not quite plain. Or you can be lighter than plain. There are many words used to describe various weights. In order, they are:

ultra light
thin/extra light
light
roman/book/regular/plain
medium
demi bold
bold
black/heavy/extra bold
ultra bold

There is, of course, a lot of leeway here. One font's bold may in fact be heavier than another's black version. Most heavy fonts include the weight right in their names, like Helvetica Black. Here's a sample of five weights of one of the fonts used in this book:

Quorum Light
Quorum Book
Quorum Medium

**Quorum Heavy**
**Quorum Black**

➤ **A font's point size** is not always apparent. If you want a 4-foot picket fence or a 4-foot chain-link fence, they're both going to look the same height despite their styles, but not so for fonts. A font height is measured from its highest ascender to its lowest descender, but your eye registers the x-height as the "size." There can be a vast difference between the 12-point version of one font and the 12-point version of another. These are both 12 points, for instance:

# Bookman          *Garton*

➤ *Kerning* **is changing the space** between letters. A letter normally lives in its own little box. Even in proportional fonts, where a box's width varies with the size of the character itself, the letters never go past the box's boundaries, and the boxes never overlap. But there are lots of times when the box approach really makes the type look bad. Sometimes you want a lowercase letter to nestle beneath a capital T's overhang; sometimes letters like W, A, and V just beg to be a little closer together. The pictures here show the difference between unkerned letters (at the top) and kerned letters in two sample words.

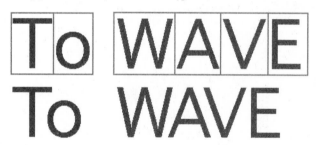

➤ **Some fonts have** *kerned pairs,* and some fonts claim more pairs than others as a sales point, as if the more there are, the better. They are. So what's a kerned pair? It's a pair of letters, like *To, Te, Wa,* or *We* that are automatically kerned to nudge the second one closer to the first than the standard spacing allows. If a font has a *To* kerned pair, for instance, you just type *T* and *o*, but at printing time the letters come out closer together so they look better—*if* the program you're using supports the use of kerned pairs. Most page layout programs support kerned pairs, but few other programs do.

➤ *Ligatures,* or *ligated* characters, are not the same as kerned pairs. Ligated letters actually touch each other. The Times font, for instance, has the ligated pairs *fi* and *fl* as Shift-Option characters; the true letters are shown at the top here, while the ligatures are at the bottom. Another difference is that, for kerned pairs, you type normally and the kerned pairs are substituted; for ligated pairs, you have to type the key combination that produces them in order to get them.

fi  fl
fi  fl

••✦ If you see the phrase *old style* used to describe the numbers in a font, it means many of the numbers drop below the baseline of the font.

## Design Guidelines

∞✦ **Faced with a menu full of font** choices, most beginning Mac users succumb to the temptation of using as many as possible in a document, showing off just how much their Macs can do. No doubt they've been subliminally influenced by one of the original Mac fonts, San Francisco, a font made up of different fonts, so to speak. This has come to be known as the ransom note style.

Anyway, the suggestions in this section are guidelines, not rules, since a good designer can break any, or possibly every, rule and still have a great-looking document.

Less is more.

LUDWIG MIES VAN DER ROHE
1886-1969

∞✦ **Use a serif font** for body text; serif fonts are generally easier to read within a large block of type.

∞✦ **Use a sans serif font** for large-type headlines; serifs in large print are very distracting.

∞✦ **Mixing a serif font** for body text with a sans serif for headlines is fine; mixing different fonts in the body text, or as headline fonts, is something best left to professionals.

••✦ **The size of the font** for a body of text should be keyed to the width of the column; the narrower the column, the smaller the font. The rule of thumb is that a column should hold an alphabet and a half (A through Z plus A through M, typed as a single word) of the font.

∞✦ **Use a single style option** for emphasis: **bold** or *italic*, for example, but ***not both***. Leave ugly <u>underlining</u> to typewriters,* and avoid using ALL CAPITAL LETTERS for emphasis within text.

> *Unless, of course, if you're imitating handwriting, which gets <u>underlined</u>, not italicized!

∞✦ **Use fonts from the same family** where you can to achieve an overall unity in your document. Since families come with a lot of members, in a wide range of weights and styles, you can still get a lot of variety in your document for its different elements yet be sure that everything works well together.

••✦ **For fax documents,** be careful about which fonts you choose, whether you're faxing directly from your computer's modem or if you're printing out for a standard fax. Use a reasonably large size; 14 points is good, but some 12-point fonts work well. Use a simple font; sans serif is more likely to come out clear at the other end. The font should have large counters (the round areas inside a lowercase g, for instance) so they won't bleed closed at the other end of the fax transmission.

# Printing Samples

∘∘➤ **It helps to have printed samples** of your fonts, even if you don't have an extensive collection. Why?

- To familiarize yourself with the look of the basic font.
- So you can see what the variations on the basic font (bold, italic, small, large) look like.
- To check the "character set" for each font, since fonts vary greatly in how many characters are included.

∘∘➤ **Make a template** in any word processor. Type an upper- and lowercase alphabet, numbers, and punctuation. Type Option and Shift-Option characters. Copy and paste several copies of this, formatting each block for different sizes and styles. Add a paragraph of narrow-margined text in a 10- or 12-point size.

For each font you have, format the entire document for that font, type its name at the top, and print it out.

∘∘➤ **The LaserWriter Font Utility** included with your system software can print out samples of any font built into the LaserWriter or downloaded to it. And since the utility also downloads fonts to the LaserWriter, it's one-stop shopping.

The samples are skimpy—just your basic *The quick brown fox jumps over the lazy dog* sentence, but it gets printed in plain, italic, bold, and bold italic for any font that has those variations available.

> The Laser-Writer Font Utility is covered in Chapter 11.

∘∘⟩ **If the LaserWriter utility isn't** enough, and making your own template is too much trouble, there are several commercial and shareware products that can help catalog your fonts.

- AboutFace is not only cleverly named, it's terrifically implemented. You can choose any of six styles of sample pages (one is shown at right), including one that shows which characters are mapped to which keys, for any font. [Big Rock Software]

- FontCharter is from one of my favorite software companies. It's not available as a separate utility, but comes with Dubl-Click's fonts and their MenuFonts utility, too. You can print samples of keyboard arrangements or a chart with a sample alphabet in any size; the chart includes the ASCII code for each character. [Dubl-Click]

- The TypeBook (or, to stick with its author's naming convention, *theTypeBook*) is a full-featured font sampler that prints your fonts in all sorts of sizes, identifies characters' keyboard positions, and shows the complete character set for a font. [shareware, Jim Lewis]

**ABOUTFACE**

# ❖ YOUR FONT COLLECTION ❖

## Choosing & Collecting Fonts

**If the fonts that came with your Mac** just aren't enough for you, there are tens of thousands of fonts out there to choose from. You can buy PostScript or TrueType fonts; you can get *free* fonts, for that matter. Although we all succumb to font mania eventually, if you're on a budget, you'll have to build your font library slowly.

Try to keep your collection balanced. Since the Mac provides a decent variety of text fonts, especially if you've purchased a later-model LaserWriter with its bundled Apple Font Library, you should start by adding some decorative fonts, then some display (headline) fonts. After that, you can add to the text font collection.

**Fonts with the same name aren't** necessarily the same font. Font designs aren't copyrightable, so you'll often find fonts from different companies that have the same name and the same overall look. But they're seldom identical, so be careful. Either one may suit your purposes just fine, but if you use, say, ImageClub's University Roman on your computer and bring the document to a service bureau for printing, they'll probably be using Adobe's University Roman. Without any judgment about which one may be *better*, you have to be aware that they may be *different*, affecting not only the look of certain letters, but possibly the overall look of the document and where its line breaks occur.

The Apple Font Library is covered in the next chapter.

**Fonts with different names** are sometimes the same font, more or less. I've always liked Dubl-Click's version of the classic Adobe font Hobo—which Dubl-Click cleverly calls Hoboken. On the other hand, the same design from Casady & Green is called Harlequin. I've seen the aforementioned University Roman also under the names University and Universal Roman. The point is, if you're looking for a certain "feel" with a font, look at font samples, not font names.

**Count fonts.** Or count font families. But know what you're counting. Don't buy a package touting 60 fonts and be surprised if it's only a dozen fonts, each with several variations, like bold and italic and bold italic. And when someone says you can buy a font for only $10, check what's meant—you may have to purchase each of the basic family members separately, which means you'll be paying $40 for what you really think of as a single font.

**When it's PostScript, does it have to be Adobe?** Yes and no. While using an Adobe font pretty much guarantees top-quality output, other vendors make excellent PostScript fonts, too, even the ones that already exist in the Adobe library. But what I ran into over and over in my research, and in talking to graphic designers is the practical consideration that if you're taking your work to a service bureau for printing, you should stick to Adobe because that's what they'll be using.

**Unless you need a specific font** for a specific job, your best approach for growing a font collection is a *bundle*—a package of a dozen or two unrelated fonts. In the last year, I've seen dozens of packages for under $100. Under $70, for that matter. I've even seen them for $35. As a matter of fact, there were so many inexpensive but *nice* collections, that I couldn't round them up here without turning this font chapter into a font book. (It turned into two chapters anyway!) Of course, you can also get packages of *related* fonts—ones that work well together, for instance, or ones that all fall into the same category, like display fonts. Casady & Greene and Dubl-Click are two companies that offer low-priced bundles, but there are dozens of others.

**Need a *large* collection** because you're a designer—or a font freak? You can take the opposite approach from the little bundle: get a CD with an entire font library on it. Adobe offers its collection on CD: so does ImageClub, and Monotype. In each case, you don't have to buy the entire library outright, although if you have $10,000–$20,000 to spend, you could. Otherwise buy the CD, get to see and use all the screen fonts, and then when you need a specific font, you call the company and get a code that "unlocks" that font from the CD—and you get charged for the font at that point.

**There's an incredible number** and variety of free and shareware fonts out there. And just because they're free (or almost) doesn't mean they're not as good as commercial fonts.

In my travels through the font world of the Mac, I've found that public domain and shareware fonts are likely to have fewer characters than commercial fonts—there won't be any Option or Shift-Option characters, for instance. But many free fonts are also missing characters you really need from the main keyboard sets, like quotes, apostrophes, and even parentheses. Many of the screen fonts are not especially well-designed even when the printer font is.

But there are so many to choose from that are both well-designed and complete that you should avail yourself of them at any opportunity. After all, even the shareware ones let you try before you buy! I'm closing out this chapter with just a small sample from the BMUG PD-ROM, which includes lots and lots and lots of PostScript and TrueType fonts. These fonts are also available through regular shareware channels.

ANN STONE

**Bell Bottom**

Black Chancery

ERASER DUST

FLINTSTONE

Handwrite Inkblot

JoePerry

LOGGER

MardiGras

PigNose*

POSTCRYPT*

Ransom Note

SillyconValley*

STARS & STRIPES

Sumdumgoi*

TRIBECA

*Don't you just love those names? PigNose is a takeoff on (from??) Peignot. The second from the last one, in case you can't read it, is Sumdumgoi. Hey, wait ... you don't think that's really a homonym for Some Dumb... nah!

## ❧ SYSTEM 7.5 STUFF ❧

### Yet Another Font Technology

➤ **The QuickDraw GX technology** that's incorporated into System 7.5 encompasses both graphics and text. For text, GX will allow greater control over font-manipulation, with easy-to-do fractions, simple kerning, automatic ligatures, and almost anything else a programmer chooses to add to a program. But the trick is this: you'll need "GX-savvy" applications—programs that take advantage of QuickDraw GX's power. So, you'll be missing many of the promised features until programs are rewritten and you upgrade to the new versions.

And, of course, Apple's pushing a new font type—GX fonts. GX supports both standard Type 1 and TrueType fonts, but Apple's pushing the new standard. TrueType didn't make any inroads with professional users, though, who are completely wedded to PostScript, and it's unlikely that GX fonts will, either.

➤ **A special version of ATM** is included with System 7.5: ATM GX. (What else?) It works the same as the current Adobe Type Manager, discussed earlier in this chapter, and handles both TrueType and Type 1 PostScript fonts.

# CHAPTER 11
# USING FONTS

> Any sufficiently advanced technology is indistinguishable from magic.
>
> — ARTHUR C. CLARKE

Some of the incredibly interesting details covered in this chapter:

- ⟶ Get a sample of any font, right on your desktop.
- ⟶ There's more to a font than the letters on the keyboard.
- ⟶ The differences between handling fonts under System 7.0 and System 7.1.
- ⟶ Font menus can be cleaned up so that "family members" are in submenus.
- ⟶ Italic is not always italic.
- ⟶ Why sometimes when you choose one font another gets printed.
- ⟶ Font ID conflicts, the result of poor planning on Apple's part, are not yet a thing of the past.
- ⟶ There are two versions of the Chicago font in your Mac— and one has more characters than the other.

**THE STUPID INTERFACE DETAIL EXPOSED IN THIS CHAPTER**

*There's no easy way to create a new, empty font suitcase.*

100 Entries
5 Quotes
3 Memos
3 Quizzes

—and—
1 Mac Almanac Chart

page 416

405

# FONTS ON THE MAC

# CONFLICTS AND CORRUPTION

# APPLE FONTS

# SYSTEM 7.5 STUFF

# ➤ FONTS ON THE MAC ◆

## Basics

∞➤ **Both bitmapped and TrueType** fonts come with your system. They have similar but distinctly different icons: bitmapped fonts have a single A on the icon, while TrueType fonts, advertising their resizability, have multiple As in different sizes on the icon.

New York 9   New York

Names for bitmapped and TrueType fonts are also easily distinguishable. Bitmapped fonts have a size incorporated into the name: *Geneva 9, New York 12,* and so on. A TrueType font has a name with no size: *Geneva, New York.* Some TrueType fonts include a style in the name, like *Times (bold).*

∞➤ **The icon for a printer font** varies with the manufacturer or designer. A standard Adobe PostScript font has a striped icon with a large letter A on it—it's in the upper left in the samples here. Many downloadables show something being loaded into a LaserWriter; some have very inventive icons that have something to do with the font itself.

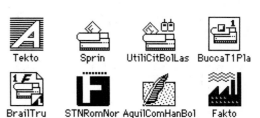

Tekto   Sprin   UtiliCitBolLas   BuccaT1Pla

BrailTru   STNRomNor   AquilComHanBol   Fakto

∞➤ **For a sample of a bitmapped or TrueType** font, double-click on its icon. Bitmapped fonts display a single sample in the appropriate size; TrueType fonts display three different sized samples.

Double-clicking a printer font doesn't give you a sample of the font; since it's basically an extension, you get a helpful little dialog about the file.

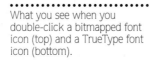

What you see when you double-click a bitmapped font icon (top) and a TrueType font icon (bottom).

What you get when you double-click on a printer font icon.

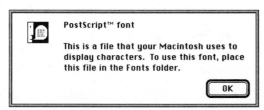

> **Mac fonts can provide up to four keyboards** of characters for each font: the unshifted and shifted groups (usually lowercase and capitals), one accessed with the Option key, and another with Shift-Option. There's some standardization of these characters, but the specifics can vary from one font to another. Bitmapped fonts especially are lacking in many of the Option and Shift-Option characters. (It's a great way to utilize the Key Caps desk accessory—see what's where on the keyboard for a specific font when you're pressing any of the modifier keys.) Here's the basic standard set of characters for a font that uses all four groups:

The placement of some keyboard characters changed from System 6 to System 7. That's covered in Chapter 20.

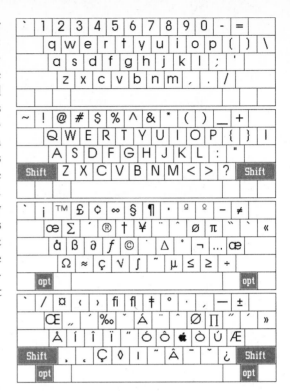

> **There are some repeated characters** on the Option and Shift-Option keyboards; they're marked in this picture. What's the difference between them? If you type them with Shift-Option, you'll see the character, as you'd expect. But when you type them with only the Option key, nothing appears on the screen unless you type a space. That's because those Option characters are accents meant to be used with other characters. (We'll get back to this in a minute.)

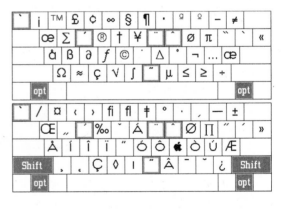

> **Some bitmapped fonts have different** sets of characters in their different sizes—a few option characters in New York-12, say, might be different from the ones available in New York-20. To add to the mild confusion, the TrueType version of a font often has a different character or two (or more) from its bitmapped version. So, you can't be sure as you switch from one size to another, or even from the screen to the printout, that you'll always get the same special characters.

**There's a whole 'nother set** of characters in most fonts accessible through a two-step key sequence. The characters are set up so you can type accent marks on top of letters (as I mentioned in passing when describing the Option/Shift-Option duplicates).

To get an accented character, you type Option and a key (at the same time, as usual), but nothing appears on the screen.* Then you release those keys and type a letter, with or without Shift down. So, when you type Option-E, nothing happens, but when you follow it by Shift-A, you get Á.

> *That's why certain combinations are referred to as "dead keys"—nothing happens when you type them.

These keyboard sequences don't always produce an accented character, especially when you're working with a picture font. Sometimes it produces nothing at all, depending on the font. Here's a chart of which Option sequences *can* produce characters, and which ones they produce in a standard, full font. To utilize the chart, you'd type the Option combination in the first column, followed by a letter in the top row; a capital letter in the top row means you need to use the Shift key with the letter. (And that first Option character is the tilde (~) key in the upper left of the keyboard.)

Accented characters are covered in more detail in Chapter 20. Using Key Caps to find the accents is covered in Chapter 7.

The standard accent characters.

|         | a | A | e | E | i | I | o | O | u | U | n | N |
|---------|---|---|---|---|---|---|---|---|---|---|---|---|
| OPT `   | à | À | è | È | ì | Ì | ò | Ò | ù | Ù |   |   |
| OPT e   | á | Á | é | É | í | Í | ó | Ó | ú | Ú |   |   |
| OPT i   | â | Â | ê | Ê | î | Î | ô | Ô | û | Û |   |   |
| OPT u   | ä | Ä | ë | Ë | ï | Ï | ö | Ö | ü | Ü |   |   |
| OPT n   | ã | Ã |   |   |   |   | õ | Õ |   |   | ñ | Ñ |

## THE WAY WE WERE ...

It's hard (or perhaps almost embarrassing) to describe the thrill of discovery in early Mac days when you'd be playing around on the keyboard and all of a sudden you'd type a rabbit, or a robot, instead of a letter. The early fonts each had a small picture on the Shift-Option-tilde key. In fact, some of the fonts had a different picture in each font size. But from the user's point of view— who knew from bitmapped fonts and character sets at different sizes?—if you changed the size of the picture character, the picture changed.

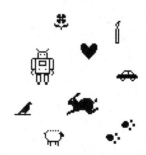

Geneva had a sheep, a rabbit, and a bird. New York alternated between a heart and a robot at each size. Monaco had a candle, Athens bear paw prints, San Francisco a car, and London a flower. The figures are recorded here for posterity.

*Hey, do you think that's why they call it _hard_ copy?

•→ **Key Caps can't print,** so it's difficult to get a printout* of what's on which key for a font. There are keyboard charts in Chapter 20 and at the back of the book, but they show only one font. If you want to do printouts for other fonts, you can create one in any word processor.

Just type the keys on the keyboard in order, starting with the top row, leaving a space between each one. When you're finished, type them again with the Shift key down; do it again with the Option key, and then the Shift-Option key. Type the name of the font at the top of the page, format it for that font, and you have your keyboard printout.

Or you can create a keyboard chart in table form, the way you'll see charts later in this book. Make a column for each of the "keyboards"—plain, Shift, Option, and Shift-Option—and type a row for each key, something like this:

| Key | (plain) | Shift | Option | Shift-Option |
|-----|---------|-------|--------|--------------|
| A | a | A | å | Å |
| B | b | B | ∫ | ı |
| C | c | C | ç | Ç |
| D | d | D | ∂ | Î |

Some of the utilities I mentioned in the last chapter for printing font samples, like AboutFace and FontCharter, also print keyboard charts. [AboutFace, Big Rock Software; FontCharter, Dubl-Click]

•→ **If the sample in a font's Info window has bars** in place of letters, like the one shown here, that's because it's a caps-only font. Since most of the sample consists of lowercase letters, there's nothing to show in those spots.

## Suitcases

∞→ **A suitcase is** a special way of storing fonts in System 7.1. Interestingly enough, suitcases were used before System 7, too (for both fonts and desk accessories); so, in fact, it's only System 7.0 that _doesn't_ use suitcases for fonts!

But even if you're using System 7.0 (or System 7.0.1, to be exact), you should still know about suitcases, since it's likely you'll run into them—what with all the font suitcases around—and because your system can still use the fonts once they're extracted from their suitcase files.

∞→ **A suitcase file** can hold any mix of bitmapped and TrueType fonts. Suitcases are special types of files, since they hold _system resources_. Moving things in or out of a suitcase isn't like dragging something in and out of a folder; you get a Copy dialog on the screen during the operation, the same way you do when you're moving a sound resource in or out of the System file.

➤ **Open a suitcase** the way you open almost everything on the Mac: double-click on it. You'll see icons of bitmapped and TrueType fonts inside. You can tell when a window is for a suitcase instead of for a folder, because a suitcase window has a suitcase icon in its header.

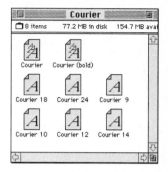

An opened suitcase file with the suitcase icon in its header.

➤ **Change a suitcase's contents** by opening it and dragging out the font(s) you want to remove. To put a font into a suitcase, drag it into the opened suitcase window or the closed suitcase icon.

➤ **The phrase "an installed font"** is left over from earlier versions of the Mac operating system, when the only place a font could be stored was inside the System file itself. But it's a useful phrase—sometimes replaced by the more awkward and slightly wimpy *available to your system*—to mean any font that's, well, available to your system for use. Depending on whether you're using System 7.0 or System 7.1, and whether you're using a utility like Suitcase or Juggler, the font itself could be in the System file, the Extensions folder, the Fonts folder, or any folder that's been included in the "search path" by a font utility.

➤ **Create a new, empty suitcase by** (get this!):

1. Selecting an existing suitcase.
2. Duplicating it with the Duplicate command in the File menu.
3. Renaming the duplicate.
4. Selecting all the fonts in the suitcase and dragging them to the Trash.

Sad, but true. Don't you think a New Suitcase command is called for?*

➤ **Keep an empty suitcase around** so you don't have to duplicate and empty an existing one every time you want a new one. Name it *Empty Suitcase* and leave it someplace convenient; duplicate it whenever you need a new suitcase.

> *The early Macs had no New Folder command, and we had to continually duplicate the Empty Folder folder on the desktop to create new folders. Wouldn't you think the programmers would have learned from past mistakes?

➤ **The Simsonite utility** (there's a joke in there about either luggage or a dysfunctional cartoon family) creates an empty suitcase for you. All you do is leave it in your Apple Menu Items folder; when you want an empty suitcase, you select it, and the empty suitcase appears on the desktop.

The Apple Menu Items folder location is recommended by Simsonite's author, but you might consider leaving it in your Fonts folder or even out on the desktop for double-clicking. Or, if you leave it in your Apple menu, you can rename it *Empty Suitcase* so it "feels" more like choosing a command from the menu. [freeware, Elsewhere Corporation, Don Munsil]

∞⟩ **If someone says "Suitcase"** with a capital S, he or she is referring to the utility Suitcase II, which has been around a very long time. (Isn't it too bad we can't *hear* capitals?)

Suitcase, and a rival utility called Juggler, both handle suitcase files more conveniently than the Mac system does. (And they did it *before* the Mac system could, too!) In fact, they also handle sounds, desk accessories, and FKEYs, all system resources that used to be stored exclusively inside the System file.

Using either Suitcase or Juggler adds a layer of convenience to your system if you use a lot of different fonts at different times—say, for different projects. It's much easier to manipulate the fonts using these utilities. You can, for instance, open a font suitcase no matter where it is on your disk; and, once a suitcase is open, any printer fonts in the folder where the suitcase is located are included in the Mac's search for printer fonts at printing time.

My personal favorite is Suitcase, but either one is highly recommended for the fontmaniacs among you. [Suitcase II, Fifth Generation Systems; Master Font Juggler, ALSoft]

••➤ **There are several ways to install fonts** and/or suitcases in your system, and they're covered in the next two sections—one for System 7.0, one for System 7.1. But dragging a font icon or a suitcase into the closed System Folder is the only way you can get the Mac to check the font/suitcase for file corruption and font ID conflicts.

## In System 7.0

∞➤ **In System 7.0,** bitmapped and TrueType fonts go into the System file; printer fonts belong in the Extensions folder.

To install a font into the System file, you can drag it into:

- the opened System file window
- the closed System file icon
- the closed System Folder

The printer font can be dragged directly into the Extensions folder or into the closed System Folder.

When you drag any font into the closed System Folder, you'll be politely asked if you'd like it routed to where it belongs (the System file or the Extensions folder).

∞➤ **To remove a font** from the System file, double-click on the System file icon to open it and drag out the font icon.

Removing a font from the System file.

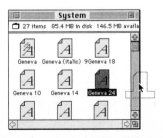

## CLEAN AND REVERENT? THRIFTY?

Take a company started in a garage by two kids and turn it into a multimillion dollar corporation, and there are bound to be growing pains. In the early years of the Mac, Apple's corporate structure was ... well, unstructured. And this was one of the jokes going around:

**Q.** What's the difference between Apple and the Boy Scouts?

**A.** The Boy Scouts have adult supervision.

•••➤ **Installing and removing fonts** isn't exactly like putting something into and taking it out of a folder. The System file is actually a kind of suitcase file, so you'll see the little suitcase icon in its window's header, and you'll get a *Copy* dialog as the font information is written into or erased from the System file itself.

•••➤ **You can't install or remove** fonts while any applications or desk accessories are open. If you try to, you'll get a dialog telling you to quit all applications before trying again. There's some logic to this limitation: An application builds its Font menu when you first launch it; adding or removing fonts after an application is launched means it won't know what fonts are *really* there and its menu won't match reality.

•••➤ **If you have a font suitcase**, you can install its contents into the System file very easily. If you want to use only a few of the fonts in the suitcase, open it by double-clicking and drag the font files from the suitcase window into the System file or the closed System Folder. If you want to use all the fonts in the suitcase, just drag the suitcase itself into the System file or closed System Folder: The suitcase "dissolves" and the fonts are installed.

## In System 7.1

•••➤ **In System 7.1,** all types of fonts—bitmapped, TrueType, and printer—go into the Fonts folder. Bitmapped and TrueType fonts are usually stored in suitcase files first. You can put any font or suitcase directly into the folder, or drag them into the closed System Folder for automatic routing.

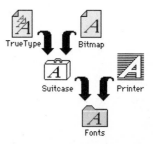

⋯➤ **You can install a font** into the Fonts folder while applications are running, but you'll get a dialog telling you that applications that are already running won't be aware of its existence. You can't remove fonts from the Fonts folder while applications are open— even if they're the ones you just dragged in and the open applications don't know about them.

Printer fonts can be dragged in and out with impunity—it's the bitmapped and TrueType fonts that get listed in Font menus which have this restriction.

⋯➤ **Combine suitcases** by dragging one icon onto the other one. The first suitcase dissolves and all its contents are transferred to the other.

### THE WAY WE WERE ...

Adding fonts to the Font menu in the early days—the days of the original and the 512K Mac—posed several problems to the pioneers.

First, of course, there were few fonts around. Second, there was no easy way to get the fonts in or out of the System file where they lived—even the venerable Font/DA Mover wasn't around the first year. If you had a utility that let you add fonts, and you managed to get a collection of bitmapped fonts, you ran into the problem of having non-scrolling, 20-item limit Font menus. And, finally, there was this endearing little feature: Fonts appeared in the menu not alphabetically, but in reverse order of their installation!

⋯➤ **You can store single-font files** in the Fonts folder. That is, your fonts don't have to be in suitcases, but can be "loose" files the way they were in System 7.0. But this doesn't make much sense unless you're temporarily testing a font and plan to either get rid of it or incorporate it into an existing suitcase.

⋯➤ **There's a limit of 128 font suitcases** for the Fonts folder. But since each suitcase can hold so many different fonts, there's no serious limitation on the number of fonts you can actually use.

⋯➤ **If you have a lot of fonts,** it's much easier if you do some suitcase combining. You can start with the ones that come with your Mac, putting them all into one suitcase. I keep them in three suitcases, actually: Mac Fonts holds things like Geneva, New York, and even Cairo; LW Fonts holds the bitmaps for the fonts built into my LaserWriter, like Times and Avant Garde; LWTT Fonts holds the TrueType fonts that came on disk along with my LaserWriter—fonts like Nadianne and Zeal. Besides the Mac's fonts, I have a suitcase of PostScript fonts that I like and use a lot. Those are my permanent suitcases; others come and go according to the projects I'm doing. So, for instance, one of the other suitcases I'm using right now holds all the fonts for this Almanac; another contains the ones I used for the book *The PowerBook Companion*; another has fonts for a project I did for ABCNews Interactive.

Installing and reinstalling systems is covered in Chapter 23.

⋯➤ **If you install System 7.1** "over" System 7.0—that is, if you install it without removing your 7.0 System file from the System Folder—you'll find that your new System file contains the same fonts the old one did, even though they're repeated in the Fonts folder under System 7.1. You should open the System file and remove the duplicated fonts.

••◆ **Font aliases don't work.** That is, you can't put an alias of a suitcase in the Fonts folder and get it to point to the real thing on another drive. Too bad—that would be a neat way to save space on your main drive if things were getting crowded.

## Font Menus

∞◆ **The Size menu** in an application (sometimes it's a submenu) lets you know which screen sizes are available for the current font by outlining those sizes in the menu. If only a few sizes are available, you can be sure that bitmapped fonts of those sizes are installed in your system. If all the sizes are outlined, you can be 99.9 percent sure that you have a TrueType font available, since it's unlikely that you'd have more than a half-dozen sizes at most available for any font.

A size that's not outlined isn't entirely unavailable to you—you can still choose it. But the screen representation will be distorted since that specific size isn't installed in your system or available from TrueType. (If it's available through ATM, it won't be outlined in the menu, since ATM doesn't interact with the Mac on that level.)

The outlined numbers are the sizes available for the chosen font.

| Size | Size |
|------|------|
| 9 point | 9 point |
| 10 | 10 |
| ✓12 | ✓12 |
| 14 | 14 |
| 18 | 18 |
| 24 | 24 |
| 36 | 36 |
| 48 | 48 |

∞◆ **The Font menu in some applications,** like FileMaker Pro, displays the actual fonts instead of listing their names in the Chicago font. Of course, that can make it difficult when you have picture and symbol fonts installed. The sample menu here is culled from my current Font menu—I took out all the readable ones and this is what's left.

••◆ **What are those stupid font names** in your Font menu? Names like *B Muscovite Bold* and *I Muscovite Italic* when all you did (you thought) was add the Muscovite font to your collection of fonts?

Since many printer fonts come as a family of fonts, including bold, italic, and bold italic (and other) versions, there can be many different screen fonts to go with them—you may not have noticed if you didn't look inside the screen fonts' suitcase. So, each screen font gets listed in the menu. But why aren't they simply Muscovite Bold, Muscovite Bold Italic, and Muscovite Italic, all grouped together in simple alphabetical order? Because some programs don't display font names only in Font menus, but also in scrolling lists in dialog boxes—lists that are of limited widths and display only a certain portion of the font names. So, you'd see *Muscovit* listed four times without being able to tell which was which. The identifying letters that differentiate the fonts need to be at the beginning of their names.

This picture shows the listings for the various forms of the Univers font I have in my menu. Most of them are clumped under C (since they're condensed versions), which isn't much help when I'm already sliding down U for Univers. And in my real menu, the Chicago and Cheltenham fonts are interspersed in the Univers list. One of the Univers fonts is under L, and there's one under (gasp!) U.

```
C Univers 57 Condensed
CB Univers 67 CondensedBold
CBO Univers 67 CondBoldObl
CL Univers 47 CondensedLight
CLO Univers 47 CondLightObl
CO Univers 57 CondOblique
L Univers 45 Light
Univers 55
```

•••••••••••••••••••••••••••••••••••••••••••••••

## POP QUIZ                                [4 POINTS EACH]

*You don't need a classical education to be able to read Greek. I mean, come on, can't you see that Συμβολ in the menu means Symbol? Then you probably can also translate these common sayings and proverbs into English, too. (Hint: It's the lowercase pi that stands for P; the uppercase pi is an apostrophe.)*

Τηε εαρλψ βιρδ χατχηεσ τηε ωορμ.

Α στιτχη ιν τιμε σαϖεσ νινε.

Α βιρδ ιν τηε ηανδ ισ ωορτη τωο ιν τηε βυση.

Βεττερ σαφε τηαν σορρψ.

Α πεννψ σαϖεδ ισ α πεννψ εαρνεδ.

Λοοκ βεφορε ψου λεαπ.

Φοολσ ρυση ιν ωηερε ανγελσ φεαρ το τρεαδ.

ΔονΠτ λοοκ α γιφτ ηορσε ιν τηε μουτη.

**For a true-font Font menu,** you don't have to wait for your applications to provide them. There are several utilities that can do the same for you.

But why would you want to? Well, compare these two menus, for instance (another sample right from my Font menu). It's hard enough to distinguish among the true fonts; it's

| Font |
|------|
| Copperplate29ab |
| Copperplate29bc |
| Copperplate30ab |
| Copperplate30bc |
| Copperplate31ab |
| Copperplate31bc |
| Copperplate32ab |
| Copperplate32bc |
| Copperplate33bc |

| Font |
|------|
| COPPERPLATE29AB |
| COPPERPLATE29BC |
| COPPERPLATE30AB |
| COPPERPLATE30BC |
| COPPERPLATE31AB |
| COPPERPLATE31BC |
| COPPERPLATE32AB |
| COPPERPLATE32BC |
| COPPERPLATE33BC |

impossible when they're all in Chicago. Displaying the true fonts sometimes takes longer, depending on the utility you use—you press on the Font menu and a few seconds (or more) go by while it slowly appears on your screen, but it can be worth the wait. Some of the utilities that provide true font menus are:

- MenuFonts [Dubl-Click]
- Suitcase II [Fifth Generation Systems]
- WYSIWYG Menus [Now Utilities, Now Software]

➤ **What do all those leading letters** in font names *mean*? (Now that you know why they're there.) Here's a list of the common ones:

| | | | |
|---|---|---|---|
| B | Bold | K | Kursiv |
| Bk | Book | L | Light |
| Blk | Black | N | Narrow |
| C | Condensed | O | Oblique |
| D | Demi | P | Poster |
| E | Extended | S | Semi |
| H | Heavy | U | Ultra |
| I | Italic | X | Extra |

The letters are often combined, like XB for Extra Bold and CL for Condensed Light.

➤ **A grayed font name** in a Font menu usually means the document was created using that font but the font isn't available in the system you're using now. This only works in clever programs that keep track of fonts by name, like PageMaker; other programs blithely substitute some other stupid font for the missing one, and the substitution sticks even when the font is available later.

(Do I sound bitter? Look at this and the previous chapter. See how many fonts are included. I was working away from home and copied this file to someone else's computer to work on it, in Microsoft Word. All the fonts went away, changed to Geneva. I had to reapply *all* the fonts all over again when I got home.)

➤ **You can fix messy Font menus** with a utility that clumps together related fonts under a single name, with the different versions appearing in a submenu. This picture shows part of my Font menu before and after using one of these utilities. At the left is the original menu; at the right is the condensed menu that has all the fonts grouped into families. Beneath the condensed menu are a few samples of its submenus. As you can see, even the submenus don't use the names with the extra letters in front of them.

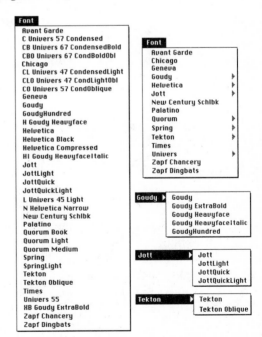

Utilities that can create this kind of Font menu include:

- MenuFonts [Dubl-Click]
- Type Reunion [Adobe]
- WYSIWYG Menus [Now Utilities, Now Software]

**MENUFONTS**

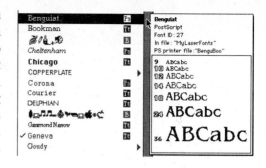

ᵒᵒᐛ **MenuFonts is my favorite** Font menu utility, so it gets a separate entry with a little more information about it. The two main things it does for you are true-font menus and family grouping. But you can turn several options on and off, including one that labels each font in the menu as bitmapped, TrueType, or PostScript, and a bar along one edge that lets you access samples and information about the font.

## From the Style Menu

ᵒᵒᐛ **Applying bold or italic** to selected text ain't what it used to be. If you're using strictly bitmapped fonts for both the screen and printing, you don't have to worry. But if your printer uses separate printer fonts, you may find that applying italic or bold styling actually means the Mac is going to print using a different printer font from the same family. What you have to keep in mind is that the screen version of the bold font that the Mac creates for you may be slightly or significantly different from the printer version in line spacing, as you can see here (the bottom sample is the printer font).

A sample of the Times font in bold.<br>A sample of the Times font in bold.

ᵒᵒᐛ *Italic* and *Oblique* are two different design styles, but not only do *people* use the word pretty interchangeably, the Mac also doesn't care much about the difference. If you apply Italic to selected text and what's really available in your system or for your printer is the oblique version, the Mac uses the oblique version. The Helvetica fonts built into a LaserWriter, for instance, include Helvetica Oblique, not Italic. But all you do is select the Italic style from a menu and you get the oblique version.

ᵒᵒᐛ **When you use the Bold style,** the Mac substitutes a true bold font when possible. The really interesting substitutions, though, come when you're working with more than just two weights of a font.

I noticed, for instance, that although I have five weights of the Quorum font in PostScript font files, the suitcase of its bitmapped fonts held only three: Quorum Light, Quorum Book, and Quorum Medium. (The PostScript fonts included Quorum Bold and Quorum Black.) At first I thought I was missing two of the bitmaps, but a little experimentation showed that applying the bold style to Book printed the Bold font, while applying bold to the Medium font printed the Black font. This can get confusing, because although it's easy to see the weight difference on the screen—that the bolded Book, for instance, is definitely heavier than the Medium, and that bolded Medium is the heaviest of all—the fonts aren't substituted in the document: select the bolded

Book version, and you'll see your Font menu reports Quorum Book being used, with the Bold style.

What can be more confusing than anything else is a situation that crops up with this Quorum set of weights: bold the Light font and *nothing* happens! Here's what's going on for the screen and in the printout for this font:

| This font... | PLUS BOLD | Prints this font... |
|---|---|---|
| Quorum Light | | Quorum Light |
| Quorum Book | | **Quorum Bold** |
| Quorum Medium | | **Quorum Black** |

You'll have to experiment with your fonts to find out for sure when substitutions will be made and when they won't. Not that it occurs randomly—the substitution information is built into the screen version of the font, but you can't get at that information. The clue that should set you to experimenting is if your screen fonts don't exactly match the printer fonts, in name or number, as was the case with my Quorum fonts.

GEORGE JACQUES DANTON
1792

Boldness, and again boldness, and always boldness!

➤ **The Underline style** looks considerably different on the screen and in a printout that uses printer fonts. On the screen, the underline is broken for the descenders in lowercase letters (and any fancy swashes on uppercase letters that extend below the baseline). It can even, as in one of the examples here, cleverly show up in the middle of a round descender.

But the printout is a different story. First, the underline is a solid line. Second, it's not always the same thickness as shown on the screen, nor is it always the same distance from the baseline of the characters as expected. Both the thickness of the underline and its position depend on the individual font.

Underlines on the screen (left) and in printout (right).

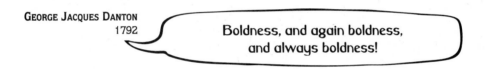

•••❯ **The Small Caps style** that some applications let you apply to text is actually another instance of a derived font—the Mac works with what's there and comes up with something else. In this case, what it works with is two different sizes of the same font: it takes the capital letters of the current font size for any shifted letter you type, and it grabs the capital letters from a smaller font size for any unshifted letter. The result is that you're typing all capital letters, in two different sizes, with the shifted letters bigger than the unshifted ones.

But there are two problems with this approach. First, the shifted, larger, letters are noticeably thicker than the smaller letters. It's unlikely that's the look you're going for when you want to use small caps:

## A SAMPLE OF SMALL CAPS IN TIMES

There's also the problem of the difference in size between the shifted and unshifted letters, which varies according to the size you're using. In the samples here, 48-points looks fine because the 36-point font is used for the smaller letters. But the 50, 55, and 60-point versions all use the 48-point font for the smaller letter. The difference is barely discernible at 50 points, and it isn't much better at 55 points; it's not until 60 points that the difference becomes obvious.

TIMES (48)  TIMES (55)
TIMES (50) TIMES (60)

Fonts *designed* as Small Caps don't suffer from distortions, as you can see in this sample.

| 12 | THE DERIVED FONT | THE DESIGNED FONT |
|----|------------------|-------------------|
| 18 | THE DERIVED FONT | THE DESIGNED FONT |
| 24 | DERIVED FONT | DESIGNED FONT |
| 36 | DERIVED | DESIGNED |

•••❯ **The Condensed style** you find in Style menus isn't the same as a font designed as condensed or *compressed*. The picture here shows, on the top line, a basic font. The second line is how the Condensed style is applied by the Mac; most programs allow you to specify the amount, in hundredths of a point, up to about 2 points. This sample in the second line is condensed by 1.7 points. As you can see, all that's happened is that the letters are closer together. The sample on the bottom line, though, is a font that's designed as a condensed version of the basic font. It's not just the line spacing that's changed, it's the design of the letters themselves. They're still obviously the same font, but everything's narrower—you can see that the O's are no longer round, for instance.

An open mind—or a hole in the head?

An open mind—or a hole in the head?

An open mind—or a hole in the head?

If you condense a font with the Condensed style, there won't be any font substitution at print time, as there is for bold or italic/oblique fonts. A condensed font is an entirely different font family, usually with its own members, like HelveticaCondensed, HelveticaCondensedItalic, HelveticaCondensedBold, and so on.

•••➤ **The Expanded style** in a Style menu isn't the same as a font that's designed as expanded, or *extended*. As with the Condensed style, Expanded simply adjusts the spacing of the letters along the line; a designed expanded font changes the letters, making them wider without changing their weight. In the examples here, the top is plain, the middle is an applied Expanded style, and the bottom is a designed expanded font.

STEPPING STONE, OR STUMBLING BLOCK?

STEPPING STONE, OR STUMBLING BLOCK?

STEPPING STONE, OR STUMBLING BLOCK?

Once again, as with the condensed fonts, applying an Expanded style won't get the Mac to substitute the condensed font design.

•••➤ **For an exercise in futility,** try taking each of your PostScript fonts and print a four-line sample: plain, italic, bold, and bold italic. Then print them out and see which ones actually print in all four styles.

Conventional wisdom says that unless you have a printer font for a particular style, it won't print that style at all. Lots of times that's borne out. Using Hobo, for instance, here's what I get on the screen (left) and from the printer (right) for each of the four styles:

Hobo plain     Hobo plain
Hobo italic     Hobo italic
Hobo bold     Hobo bold
Hobo bold italic  Hobo bold italic

Right, no styles because the plain Hobo printer font is all I have available. (The printer doesn't care that the Mac is adjusting things on the screen.)

But then I pick another font that has only a single printer font, and here's what I get on both the screen and the printout:

Black Chancery     Black Chancery italic

Black Chancery bold     Black Chancery bold italic

Leave aside the issue of why you wouldn't want to bold or italicize this lovely font; the point is, you *can*, despite there being no styled printer fonts around.

There's information in each font that tells the printer whether it's allowed to alter the basic printer font to get the styles you've chosen. So, for instance, it can forbid the obliquing of a font when you use the Italic style; it can allow a bold derivative through smearing the existing font a little or by using a slightly larger font size than is called for; it can specify an Outline style to be white against a black shadow, or to be an outline of the font character shape. The only way you'll know whether your font will print with the style you see on your screen is by printing out a sample.

# ❖ CONFLICTS & CORRUPTION ❖

## Resources & ID Numbers

⚬•❥ **Fonts are a** *resource*—a word I've been throwing around mildly on and off since the beginning of the book. (Resources being a special kind of information available to the system and shared by any running application that wants it—sounds are resources, too.) Every resource has a *type*, a special four-letter identification. Fonts and font technologies have evolved over the Mac's life, so there are now four different font-related resources used by the Mac: FONT, FOND, NFNT, and SFNT.

You normally don't have to worry about, or even know about, resource-level goings on in your Mac. But in the case of fonts it's helpful because if you use a lot of different fonts, you may run into problems, and understanding a little about the underlying causes can help you solve them.

⚬•❥ **The FONT resource** was the original, logically named resource for fonts. A FONT resource stores all the information about the font—how the letters looked, how they were spaced, and so on. Each installed bitmapped font—that is, every size of a font— had its own FONT ID.

Pretty straightforward and simple. But too much so. Apple, in one of its greatest Mac miscalculations, allowed for 256 different font ID numbers (every resource has an ID number), and reserved the first 128 for its own use. It never occurred to anyone that a computer user would ever even need that many different fonts, never mind more than that!

⚬•❥ **The FOND resource** was added to the Mac universe when PostScript was released. It helped the Mac keep track of the relationship between the various components of a font—the screen font and the printer font, all the different sizes of the bitmapped version, and the separate styles (regular, bold, and italic, for instance) for a single font. This is the resource that keeps track of what can be substituted when you bold or italicize a font, or what happens (if anything) when you apply a style to a font and there's no printer font in that style. The FOND approach relieved some menu clutter problems (the italic and bold versions showing up as separate items), but it didn't alleviate the shortage of ID numbers.

⚬•❥ **The NFNT resource** replaced the original FONT resource approach and provided 16,000 different ID numbers for fonts by cooperating with a corresponding FOND resource. (It actually provides numbers as high as 32,767; but almost half of the numbers are reserved by Apple.) This is the first unpronounceable font resource; if you have to say it, say: *en-font*.

⚬•❥ **The SFNT resource** is the newest of the font resources; it stands for "scalable font" and is especially for TrueType fonts. (Say *ESS-font*.)

> When Apple introduced the LaserWriter, Mac users looked forward to a profusion of high quality typefaces. Now, almost a year later, all that is available are the original four ... Why haven't any new fonts appeared?

MACUSER
DECEMBER 1985

••➤ **You can find out a font's ID** number without doing any hardcore programming or using a font utility. The MenuFonts utility from Dubl-Click, for instance—which I raved about earlier in this chapter—incidentally identifies the ID number for each of the fonts in its menu if you want to access it.

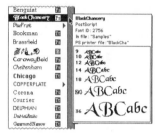

Microsoft Word also has a way of identifying font numbers for you. In Word 5, here's what you do:

1. Create a new document.
2. Use the Preferences command to set your preferences for the Open/Save options so that *Always interpret RTF is unchecked.*
3. Save the document in RTF format: Use the Save command, and select *Interchange Format (RTF)* from the Save File as Type popup menu at the bottom of the dialog.
4. Close the document.
5. Open the document. You'll be presented with a dialog that asks if you want the RTF text interpreted; click No.

The document that opens lists a lot of cryptic commands, but you'll see all the fonts installed in your system listed in the beginning of the document. Each font name is preceded by a backslash, the letter *f*, a number, another backslash, and a word which we're going to completely ignore. It's the number that counts—that's the font ID number between the backslashes. So you can see that Chicago's ID is 0; New York's is 2; Geneva's is 3, and so on. (It's no coincidence that the Apple fonts have the first group of numbers!)

```
{\rtf1\mac\deff2 {\fonttbl{\f0\fswiss Chicago;}{\f2\froman New
York;}{\f3\fswiss Geneva;}{\f4\fmodern Monaco;}{\f5\fscript
Venice;}{\f6\fdecor London;}{\f7\fdecor Athens;}{\f8\fdecor San
Francisco;}{\f11\fnil Cairo;}{\f12\fnil Los Angeles;}}
```

## Font Conflicts

∞➤ **Having around 16,000 possible** font ID numbers doesn't solve a central font problem—conflicting IDs. Why? Because there was no central registry arrangement set up.

So font creators assigned their own numbers, and, sometimes, they happened to assign the same ones to different fonts.

When you use two different fonts with the same ID numbers, you can run into the nether world of *ID* or *font conflicts*.

◦•▶ **A font conflict problem** can rear its ugly little head in several different ways. For instance:

- A document created on one computer is opened on another and different fonts show up in the document.
- You open an old document on your computer—one that was created before you added some new fonts—and the fonts you originally used in the document have been replaced by other fonts.
- You choose a font from a menu but a different font is applied to the selected text—even though the font you selected is the one checked in the menu.
- When you make a style change, like adding bold or italic, the font itself changes. Changing the style back restores the original font.

◦•▶ **Applications that use font names** instead of font IDs (as Apple has been recommending for years in its programming guidelines) are less likely to have font conflict problems in their documents whether the documents stay on one system or are passed from one to another.

◦•▶ **You can avoid font conflicts by** sticking to fonts from one vendor, if possible.

◦•▶ **The Mac cures many potential conflicts** by renumbering a font when you add it to your system if a font with the same ID is already installed. But the only time it checks an incoming font is if you drag it into the closed System Folder—*not* if you drag it into the System file icon (in System 7.0) or into the Fonts folder (System 7.1).

> What businessman knows about point sizes on typefaces or the value of variable point sizes? Who out there in the general marketplace even knows what a "font" is?

**JOHN DVORAK**
(predicting the Mac's failure)
*SAN FRANCISCO EXAMINER*,
FEBRUARY 1984

◦•▶ **Renumbering conflicting IDs** avoids font problems on your own system, but it doesn't do anything for material that's being moved from one system to another. In fact, it can *cause* problems when you start moving material around because your renumbered font might exist with its original ID on that other system and/or the new number might conflict with another font on that system.

•••▶ **Using a font utility like** Suitcase or Juggler means you can open font suitcases and use fonts that haven't been vetted by the Mac's system to check for ID conflicts. Both utilities come with their own way of identifying and handling font conflicts, and renumbering offending fonts. This, for instance, is the dialog that shows up courtesy of Suitcase when you open a conflicting font:

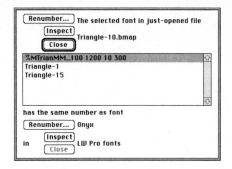

➤ **Once you have a font conflict,** tracking down the culprit is somewhat like tracking down an extension conflict as described in Chapter 8. The newest font is most likely the problem, but it's difficult to find which other font it's conflicting with. If you run into font ID problems, strip your system down to only the necessary fonts—and reinstall those fonts from their original sources so that you're working with the original ID numbers.

## Corrupted Fonts

➤ **A corrupted font file or suitcase** can cause all sorts of weird problems. Suitcases in particular are prone to corruption if you keep altering their contents or keep them open on the desktop while the system is using their contents. Replace corrupted fonts by trashing the ones on your hard drive and replacing them with fresh copies.

➤ **A corrupted bitmapped font** may cause system crashes when:

- You select the font from a Font menu
- You try to open the suitcase the font is stored in
- You open a document that uses the corrupted font

➤ **A corrupted printer font** may cause a system crash when you try to print a document that uses the font; it also might just keep the document from printing at all—you may or may not get a PostScript error report.

➤ **A jagged font on the screen while ATM's** running can mean the printer font is corrupted. (Or else it means you don't have the correct printer font around!)

➤ **A corrupted font in the System file** in System 7.0 means you'll probably have to reinstall your system because sometimes it's difficult or even impossible to remove a corrupted resource from the System file.

➤ **Worst case scenario** for a corrupted font suitcase (and it happened to me while I was writing this chapter): Every time I selected a certain font from my Font menu, in any application, the Mac crashed. Assuming it was a corrupted bitmapped font, I opened the suitcase where it was stored and tried to drag the font out. The Mac refused to let me do that, citing a shortage of memory every time—*There's not enough memory to complete that operation*—despite the 20 megs of memory on the machine. Sometimes it just froze up without the report, or right after the dialog appeared on the screen. Sometimes I couldn't open the suitcase at all. I had the same problems if I tried to drag the damaged suitcase file out of the Fonts folder.

Quite a dilemma: I couldn't use the font, and I couldn't throw it away, either! On the assumption that the Mac was having a *really* hard time working with this damaged resource that was in use by the system (since it was in a font suitcase in the Fonts folder), I dragged the entire Fonts folder out of the System Folder and onto the desktop. I created a new Fonts folder in the System Folder and moved my basic suitcases from the old Fonts folder into the new one. Then I restarted the Mac. I still couldn't open the damaged suitcase, but since it was no longer being used by the system, I was able to drag it out of the old Fonts folder and throw it away.

## ≫ APPLE FONTS ≪

### System & Bundled Fonts

∞▸ **There are four "system" fonts** that the Mac uses on the desktop, in menus, and in dialog boxes: Chicago-12, Geneva-9, Geneva-12, and Monaco-9.

The Chicago font, the one used in menus, is so crucial to the look and feel of the Mac that it was finally built right into the ROMs so it would always be available. The two Geneva sizes and Monaco are inside the System file, but they're invisible—you won't see them even if you open the System file. This is, of course, to keep you from accidentally (or mischievously) deleting them. You can remove all the Geneva and Monaco fonts you see, but the system can still get the sizes it needs.

Geneva Italic-9 really deserves status as a system font—it's what's used as the default for alias names. But it's not invisible, so you can remove it from the System file (in System 7.0) or from the Geneva suitcase (in System 7.1). If you remove it, your alias labels will be a little harder to read, since the Mac will invent a slanted font to replace the italic one.

∞▸ **The fonts that come** with the Mac operating system are shown in the table on the next page. What's that? You've heard San Francisco *used to be* supplied with the Mac but it's not in your Font menu? And Athens, and London? Apple's "classic" fonts that come in bitmapped versions only (and limited sizes at that) are on your system disks—they're just not automatically installed on your hard drive. Check the Fonts disk of your system disk set for a folder called *Classic Fonts*.

∞▸ **Courier and Monaco are** the Mac's monospaced fonts, and, ugly as they are, they have their purposes. Monaco's handy on the desktop in its 9-point size to keep list views looking neat and easy to read. And both are handy when you're looking at documents generated on lesser computers that use repeated spaces to define columns in a table—using a monofont slaps everything back into line immediately.

## The Original Mac Fonts

| Font | Bitmapped versions | TrueType versions |
|---|---|---|
| **Athens** | 18 | - |
| 🍇✒🖌🏺 (Cairo) | 18 | - |
| **Chicago** | [12] | Chicago |
| Courier | 9, 10, 12, 14, 18, 24 | Courier<br>Courier (bold) |
| Geneva | [9], 10, [12], 14, 18, 24;<br>Geneva (italic) 9 | Geneva |
| Helvetica | 9, 10, 12, 14, 18, 24 | Helvetica<br>Helvetica (bold) |
| London | 18 | - |
| Los Angeles | 12, 24 | - |
| ➡🖫🎙🎵❖ (Mobile) | 18 | - |
| Monaco | [9], 12 | Monaco |
| New York | 9, 10, 12, 14, 18, 24 | New York |
| Palatino | 10, 12, 14, 18, 24 | - |
| San Francisco | 18 | - |
| Σψμβολ (Symbol) | 9, 10, 12, 14, 18, 24 | Symbol |
| Times | 9, 10, 12, 14, 18, 24 | Times<br>Times (bold)<br>Times (italic)<br>Times (bold italic) |
| Venice | 14 | |

*[Bracketed] numbers are fonts that are built into the ROM.*

➤ **The fonts built into the LaserWriters** have changed over the years, with more being added in newer models of LaserWriters. The original LaserWriters had four fonts:

| | |
|---|---|
| Courier | Helvetica |
| Times | Σψμβολ (Symbol) |

By the time the LaserWriter NTX came out, the list had expanded to include:

| | |
|---|---|
| Palatino | Bookman |
| Avant Garde | *New Century Schoolbook* |
| Helvetica Narrow | ✳●□❖ (Zapf Dingbats) |
| Zapf Chancery | |

And those are the fonts that are still built into even the newest LaserWriters.

→ **LaserWriters have 35 built-in fonts.** What? Didn't I just list what's built in, and wasn't it a short list?

Well, the difference between "font" as it's used in the Mac world and in typography was discussed in the last chapter. And here's where the traditional definition of font holds—every style of the font is counted as a different font. So, in fact, there are four Courier fonts (Courier, Courier Oblique, Courier Bold, and Courier Bold Oblique), four Times fonts, and so on. Here's the list, according to family:

- Courier: plain, Oblique, Bold, Bold Oblique
- Helvetica: plain, Oblique, Bold, Bold Oblique
- Helvetica Narrow: plain, Oblique, Bold, Bold Oblique
- Times: Roman, Italic, Bold, Bold Italic
- Symbol
- Palatino: Roman, Italic, Bold, Bold Italic
- Bookman: Light, Light Italic, Demibold, Demibold Italic
- Avant Garde: Book, Book Oblique, Demibold, Demi Oblique
- New Century Schoolbook: Roman, Italic, Bold, Bold Italic
- Zapf Chancery: Medium Italic
- Zapf Dingbats: plain

See? 35 fonts!

→ **The Apple Font Library** of TrueType fonts comes bundled with most of Apple's printers. The selection of TrueType fonts keeps growing—especially the ones from Apple—and the collection even includes TrueType versions of fonts that were previously offered only in one or two bitmapped sizes as screen fonts to match built-in LaserWriter fonts. Here's what's included in the Library:

| | |
|---|---|
| Avant Garde | *Nadianne* |
| Bookman | ***New Century Schoolbook*** |
| DELPHIAN | Old English Text |
| Garamond Narrow | **Onyx** |
| **Helvetica Black** | *Oxford* |
| **Helvetica Compressed** | Palatino |
| Helvetica Narrow | *Swing* |
| Lubalin Graph | *Zapf Chancery* |
| Lucida Bright | ✷✾❒❄ (Zapf Dingbats) |
| **MACHINE** | Z̄ ⇩ ⇧ ➘ (Zeal) |

→ **By the usual fancy font count,** the Apple Font library—whose fonts I just listed, and, boy, it sure *looked* like 20 fonts—has 60 fonts. There are four variations for ten of the fonts, three of the fonts have two variations each, and 14 fonts come as single styles.

# Chicago

∞➤ **The Chicago font** that's used for menus and dialog boxes comes in two flavors: bitmapped and TrueType. Any time you use the 12-point version, you're looking at the bitmapped font; at any other size, you're looking at the TrueType font. So? So they have different character sets, and you may be in for a surprise as you change type sizes on the screen, or when your printout doesn't match your screen display. Remember, a bitmap is used for the screen whenever possible, but the TrueType version takes over for printing; so, your 12-point display on the screen won't match any other size *or* a printout.

The standard and shifted keys are the same in both fonts, but the Option and Shift-Option sets are significantly different, with the TrueType version having many more characters available. (You won't be able to see the TrueType font set in Key Caps, which displays only at 12 points. But if you could, this is what it would look like!)

The bitmapped Chicago font (left) and the TrueType version (right).

As you might guess, the accented characters available in the TrueType version also outnumber those in the bitmapped font. The items in the chart highlighted in gray are characters that are also available from the Option or Shift-Option keyboards.

Accents in bitmapped Chicago.

|        | a | A | e | E | i | I | o | O | u | U | n | N |
|--------|---|---|---|---|---|---|---|---|---|---|---|---|
| OPT `  | à | À | è |   | ì |   | ò |   | ù |   |   |   |
| OPT e  | á |   | é | É | í |   | ó |   | ú |   |   |   |
| OPT i  | â |   | ê |   | î |   | ô |   | û |   |   |   |
| OPT u  | ä | Ä | ë |   | ï |   | ö | ö | ü | Ü |   |   |
| OPT n  | ã | Ã |   |   |   |   | õ | Õ |   |   | ñ | Ñ |

Accents in TrueType Chicago.

|        | a | A | e | E | i | I | o | O | u | U | n | N |
|--------|---|---|---|---|---|---|---|---|---|---|---|---|
| OPT `  | à | À | è | È | ì | Ì | ò | Ò | ù | Ù |   |   |
| OPT e  | á | Á | é | É | í | Í | ó | Ó | ú | Ú |   |   |
| OPT i  | â | Â | ê | Ê | î | Î | ô | Ô | û | Û |   |   |
| OPT u  | ä | Ä | ë | Ë | ï | Ï | ö | Ö | ü | Ü |   |   |
| OPT n  | ã | Ã |   |   |   |   | õ | Õ |   |   | ñ | Ñ |

∞➤ **The standard alphanumeric sets** for bitmapped Chicago and TrueType Chicago are identical with one exception: the zero is slashed in the TrueType version, like this: **0**.

### WHAT'S IN A NAME?

The original Mac fonts were copies of existing fonts in the printing industry—licensing the real ones would have cost money! At the beginning, all bitmapped fonts were named after cities. (Which knocked out the original name for the San Francisco font: Ransom.) Some were almost named Rosemont, Merion, and Ardmore after train stops in designer Susan Kare's home town, but Steve Jobs, who was running the show, wanted more *important* cities to be commemorated in the Font menu.

The original Mac fonts had some gentle puns built into their final names. For instance:

| | |
|---|---|
| (Cairo) | What else would you call a picture font—unless after some other Egyptian city that calls to mind the hieroglyphs used by the ancients? |
| Geneva | The Swiss name for Switzerland is Confoederatio Helvetica. Geneva is the Mac version of the classic Helvetica font, which was designed in Switzerland. Need I say more? |
| London | A classic Old English style font. (Recently replaced by the TrueType Old English Text font.) |
| Monaco | Simple—it's a monofont. What else could you call it? |
| New York | This is actually a pun gone awry because someone was laboring under a misunderstanding early on. New York is the Mac version of the staid, traditional Times font used in the newspaper of the same name. But it was the London Times, not the New York Times, that used it. |
| San Francisco | I don't have anything to prove my theory about this name, but just look at the font, and think about the sixties. You know what I mean? Groovy! |
| Venice | Ah, a really subtle one here. Venice is an italic font. Italic. Italy. Think about it. |

∘•◆ **Did you notice the special character** on Shift-Option-K in both the bitmapped and TrueType Chicago? It's the Apple logo that's at the top of the Apple menu:  .

∘•◆ **Both Chicago fonts have three** special characters that appear in menus: the command symbol, the checkmark, and the diamond. But they're almost inaccessible, since you need the Control key to type them, and not too many applications pass Control characters through so you can type with them. Here's where the symbols are (including the Apple symbol, which, although it's a Control key character, is more easily accessed through Shift-Option-K):

[CTRL] **Q** = ⌘          [CTRL] **R** = ✓

[CTRL] **S** = ◆          [CTRL] **T** = 

If you want to use these symbols but can't type them in your application, you can open Key Caps, press the Control key, click the key with the symbol you want, and then copy the symbol out of the edit area in Key Caps and paste it into your text.

••◆ **TrueType Chicago** has a full set of symbols in its Control character set, as you can see in this picture. It's the only font I know of that actually has a set of characters stored this way.

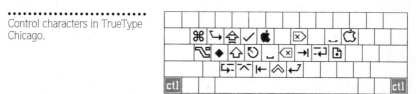

Control characters in TrueType Chicago.

Many of these characters are practically impossible to type, even in an application that lets you type with Control characters. There are some keyboard codes, for instance, that mean "delete"—and boy, do they mean delete: Type the sequence and it's the same as hitting the delete key—so you erase a character instead of typing it. (Try typing Control-H, where, fittingly enough, the Delete symbol is stored in Chicago TrueType. But try typing it in any font!)

Except for those extra-difficult key sequences, you can get these special characters out of Key Caps even though you can't *see* them in Key Caps! Press the Control key and you'll see the four symbols in the bitmapped version of Chicago, as well as a lot of "blanks"—squares that stand for no characters. Click on the square that's on the key for the symbol you want (the Shift symbol, for instance, is on the A key). A box is typed into the edit area of Key Caps, but have faith. Copy the box and paste it into your document; format the box for Chicago in a size other than 12, and you'll see the symbol.

Alternatively, if you have a utility or program that lets you specify the ASCII number of a character, you can use the symbol's ASCII number. This chart rounds up the symbols in TrueType Chicago, and describes what they stand for and how to access them from the keyboard, whether you're using the Control characters to type, clicking in Key Caps, or using the ASCII number to get at them.

## Control Characters in TrueType Chicago

| Name | Symbol | Type | ASCII |
|---|---|---|---|
| Option | ⌥ | CTRL A | 1 |
| Control | ⌃ | CTRL B | 2 |
| Enter | ⌤ | CTRL C | 3 |
| Shift | ⇧ | CTRL D | 4 |
| Caps Lock | ⇪ | CTRL E | 5 |
| Rotate | ↻ | CTRL F | 6 |
| Delete | ⌫ | CTRL H | 8 |
| Space | ␣ | CTRL G | 7 |
| Left tab | →| | CTRL J | 10 |
| Switch right | ⇲ | CTRL K | 11 |
| Page down | 🗎 | CTRL L | 12 |
| Return right | ↪ | CTRL N | 23 |
| Fixed space | ⎵ | CTRL O | 15 |
| Apple key | ⌘ | CTRL P | 16 |
| Command key | ⌘ | CTRL Q | 17 |
| Check | ✓ | CTRL R | 18 |
| Diamond | ◆ | CTRL S | 19 |
| Apple | 🍎 | CTRL T | 20 |
| Forward delete | ⌦ | CTRL U | 21 |
| Right tab | |← | CTRL U | 22 |
| Return left | ↵ | CTRL W | 14 |
| Switch left | ⇱ | CTRL X | 24 |

## Cairo

∞❥ **Cairo** was among the original Mac fonts, and you'll still find it on your system disks, although it's not automatically installed in your system. In comes as a bitmapped font in an 18-point size and its characters are of limited usefulness (though enduring charm).

Almost all of Cairo's characters are on the plain and shifted keys. There's only one additional character you can get at with Shift-Option. There is one more character in Cairo, hidden away in the double-keystroke accent list: a baseball is on Option-U, Shift-A.

The pictures and charts on the next page round up the Cairo character set.

Cairo has a full set of unshifted and shifted characters, but no Option characters and only a single additional character on the Shift-Option keyboard.

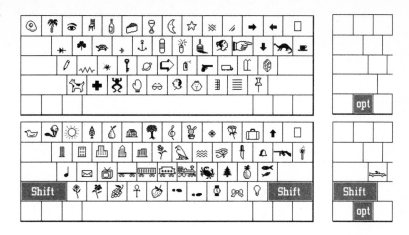

Cairo has a single accented character.

| | a | Å | e | E | i | I | o | O | u | U | n | N |
|---|---|---|---|---|---|---|---|---|---|---|---|---|
| OPT ` | | | | | | | | | | | | |
| OPT e | | | | | | | | | | | | |
| OPT i | | | | | | | | | | | | |
| OPT u | 🜨 | | | | | | | | | | | |
| OPT n | | | | | | | | | | | | |

## POP QUIZ  [2 POINTS]

What's wrong with the die that's in the Cairo font on the apostrophe key?

---

**Many of Cairo's characters** are designed to go with each other. You can make a skyline (here threatened by a Jurassic Park escapee), a train, or a picket fence, for instance:

You can type a couple having a dialog, or being interrupted by a baby.

Then there's the clef, staff lines, and the double bar for the staff end that all coordinate. Unfortunately, typing in a note interrupts the staff.

**The famous Dogcow** is part of the Cairo font. You'll find more about the Dogcow in the next chapter.

## Mobile

∞❥ **The Mobile font** wasn't one of the original fonts, but was added to the list early on. (I have a version of it under the name Fallingwater, as a matter of fact, which must have been a prerelease version.)

Anyway, it's a picture font that's heavy on trees, and pretty much slanted toward people and furniture, too. It comes in an 18-point bitmapped font only, and doesn't even have any Option or Shift-Option characters. Here are the two keyboard sets, the sum and total of the Mobile font:

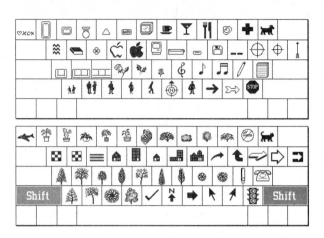

## Symbol

∞❥ **The Symbol font** is filled with characters needed for mathematical operations, even if at first glance it seems to be just a Greek alphabet.

In the font charts here, you'll notice that there are four characters on the Option keyboard framed in gray; they match the four characters in the same position on the Shift-Option keyboard.

Symbol has quite a few characters on its accent chart. (All those straight lines are actually slightly different; read the next few entries to find out about them.) The items in the accent chart on the next page that are available as Option or Shift-Option characters are highlighted with gray.

The repeating characters on the Shift and Shift-Option keyboards are explained earlier in this chapter.

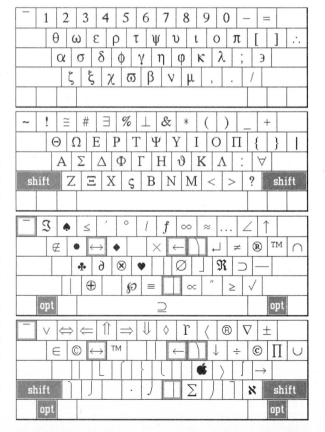

Accents in Symbol.

| | | a | A | e | E | i | I | o | O | u | U | n | N |
|---|---|---|---|---|---|---|---|---|---|---|---|---|---|
| OPT | ` | ⊄ | | | ⌈ | | { | | ⟩ | | \| | | |
| OPT | e | \| | | | | | \| | | ⌊ | | ∫ | | |
| OPT | i | Σ | | | ( | | ⌊ | | \| | | ⌠ | | |
| OPT | u | | | | \ | | ⌊ | | | | | | |
| OPT | n | ⊂ | | | | | | | ⊆ | | | | |

•➤ **Many of Symbol's symbols are pieces** for larger symbols, meant to be typed on top of each other in subsequent rows of text to make tall brackets and braces for mathematical formulas. So, you can type a small right bracket with the bracket (]) key; you can type a medium size one by typing Shift-Option-period, moving down to the next line, and typing Option-K. The tops and bottoms of the characters meet to form solid lines. For a larger bracket, type the top part with Shift-Option-period, move down a line, add an extension by typing Option-H, and move down again to type the bottom piece with Option-K. For even larger brackets, type additional extensions in the center:

*Small bracket* ........ Bracket key          ]          *Large bracket*... Shift-Option-period  ⌉
*Medium bracket* .... Shift-Option-period  ⌉               ... Option-H               |
          ..... Option-K          ⌋               ... Option-K               ⌋

### Brackets and Braces in Symbol

| Figure | Section | | Type: |
|---|---|---|---|
| left bracket | top | ⌈ | OPT ~, SHIFT **E** |
| | extension | \| | SHIFT OPT **S** |
| | bottom | ⌊ | SHIFT OPT **D** |
| right bracket | top | ⌉ | SHIFT OPT period |
| | extension | \| | OPT **H** |
| | bottom | ⌋ | OPT **K** |
| left brace | top | ⌠ | SHIFT OPT **F** |
| | middle | { | OPT `, SHIFT **I** |
| | extension | \| | SHIFT OPT **J** |
| | bottom | ⌡ | SHIFT OPT **H** |
| right brace | top | ⌉ | SHIFT OPT **Z** |
| | middle | } | SHIFT OPT **G** |
| | extension | \| | SHIFT OPT **J** |
| | bottom | ⌡ | SHIFT OPT **Ж** |
| left parenthesis | top | ( | OPT **I**, SHIFT **E** |
| | extension | \| | SHIFT OPT **Y** |
| | bottom | ( | OPT **U**, SHIFT **E** |
| right parenthesis | top | ) | SHIFT OPT **I** |
| | extension | \| | SHIFT OPT **N** |
| comma | bottom | ) | SHIFT OPT |
| integral | top | ⌠ | OPT **I**, SHIFT **U** |
| | extension | \| | OPT `, SHIFT **U** |
| | bottom | ⌡ | SHIFT OPT **B** |

☜ **Symbol contains an entire Greek** alphabet, both upper- and lowercase. Here's where you'll find all the characters:

### The Greek Alphabet in Symbol

| Letter | Uppercase | Type: | Lowercase | Type: |
|--------|-----------|-------|-----------|-------|
| alpha | A | [SHIFT] A | α | A |
| beta | B | [SHIFT] B | β | B |
| gamma | Γ | [SHIFT] G | γ | G |
| delta | Δ | [SHIFT] D | δ | D |
| epsilon | E | [SHIFT] E | ε | E |
| zeta | Z | [SHIFT] Z | ζ | Z |
| eta | H | [SHIFT] H | η | H |
| theta | Θ | [SHIFT] Q | θ | Q |
| iota | I | [SHIFT] I | ι | I |
| kappa | K | [SHIFT] K | κ | K |
| lambda | Λ | [SHIFT] L | λ | L |
| mu | M | [SHIFT] M | μ | M |
| nu | N | [SHIFT] N | ν | N |
| xi | Ξ | [SHIFT] X | ξ | X |
| omicron | O | [SHIFT] O | o | O |
| pi | Π | [SHIFT] P | π | P |
| rho | P | [SHIFT] R | ρ | R |
| sigma | Σ | [SHIFT] S | σ | S |
| tau | T | [SHIFT] T | τ | T |
| upsilon | Y | [SHIFT] U | υ | U |
| phi | Φ | [SHIFT] F | φ | F |
| chi | X | [SHIFT] C | χ | C |
| psi | Ψ | [SHIFT] Y | ψ | Y |
| omega | Ω | [SHIFT] W | ω | W |

☜ **At first glance, the sigma** character in Symbol seems to be repeated: on Shift-S and Option-I, Shift-A. But the latter one is actually the mathematical character for summation. Of course, the character is still the sigma, but it's bigger, even at the same point size, and its bottom drops below the baseline for the rest of the font. Here they are, both at 12 points:

sigma    Σ          summation    Σ

For mine own part, it was Greek to me.

SHAKESPEARE
*JULIUS CAESAR*
ACT I, SCENE II

•••✦ **There are card suit symbols** in two of the fonts that Apple provides. This could come in handy if you write a Bridge column, because you can describe hands like this, where you can talk about going for a small slam in Hearts if your partner bids Diamonds:

♣ 8          ♥ 4, 6, 7, 10, J, K, A

♦ 2, J, K       ♠ K, A

Does anybody write Poker columns? Anyway, here's the two fonts that provide card symbols, and where they are. I think the similarity in keyboard combinations was done to purposely confuse us and force us to use Key Caps.

### The Card Suits

| | | Symbol | Zapf Dingbats |
|---|---|---|---|
| ♣ | | OPT S | OPT R |
| ♦ | | OPT R | OPT G |
| ♠ | | OPT G | OPT 2 |
| ♠ | | OPT 2 | OPT E, space |

## Zapf Dingbats

∞•✦ **Zapf Dingbats is** such a handy little font. Need a bullet that's larger than the one on Option-8 in your text font? Zapf Dingbats has it. How about circled numbers? There are four sets. Arrows? Checkmarks? The ubiquitous pointing hand? They're all there. Here are four keyboards that show you what's available in Zapf Dingbats. The items in the chart that are on both the Option and the Shift-Option keyboards are framed in gray.

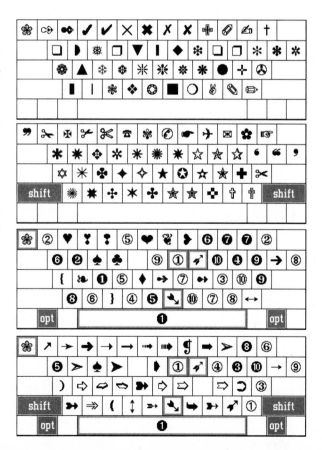

Zapf Dingbats has lots of characters in its accents chart. Some of them, though—the ones in the table shaded in gray—are also on, and more easily accessed from, the Shift-Option keyboard.

Accents in Zapf Dingbats.

| | | a | A | e | E | i | I | o | O | u | U | n | N |
|---|---|---|---|---|---|---|---|---|---|---|---|---|---|
| OPT ` | | ( | ❷ | | ⇨ | | ◇ | | ⇨ | | ↘ | | |
| OPT e | | ⟩ | ➤ | | ) | | ⇨ | | ◇ | | ⊃ | | |
| OPT i | | ⟩ | ➡ | | ➡ | | ⇦ | | ⇨ | | ≫⊸ | | |
| OPT u | | ( | ( | | ➡ | | ⇦ | | ) | | ⟨ | | |
| OPT n | | ) | ❸ | | | | | | ❹ | | | | ( |

**POP QUIZ**                    **[2 POINTS EACH]**

Who called his wife by the questionably affectionate term Dingbat? And what unquestionably unaffectionate term did he use for his son-in-law?

**There doesn't seem to be rhyme** nor reason to the arrangement of Zapf Dingbat characters on the keyboard. The sets of circled numbers are scattered all over, and some are well-hidden; and few of the related characters (there are, for instance, four pairs of scissors) are bunched together.

Would you believe that it's not the Zapf Dingbats arrangement that's out of order, but the keyboard? Every character in a font has a code number; when you arrange the Dingbats in order according to their ASCII code numbers, this is the arrangement you get. It does make sense, doesn't it? And this chart is a handy way to see the groups of characters that are available: four scissors, four hands, three pencils, two checks, four Xs, and so on.

More about ASCII codes in Chapter 20.

•••➤ **There's no plain checkbox** in Zapf Dingbats, although there are four drop-shadowed boxes. But there's a plain black box on the N key (unshifted). Format it as Outline, and you'll get a plain checkbox.

•••➤ **Aren't four sets of circled numbers** overkill? Not really—there's two sets each of serif (fancy) and sans serif (plain) numbers, one set black-on-white and one set reversed. The real killer is remembering where they are—and finding the three hidden ones that don't appear in Key Caps. Here's a chart to make your life easier:

### Circled Numbers in Zapf Dingbats

| | | | | | | | |
|---|---|---|---|---|---|---|---|
| ① | OPT SHIFT ? | ❶ | OPT [space] | ① | OPT U,[space] | ❶ | OPT D |
| ② | OPT 1 | ❷ | OPT ~, SHIFT A | ② | OPT = | ❷ | OPT W |
| ③ | OPT L | ❸ | OPT N, SHIFT A | ③ | OPT SHIFT " | ❸ | OPT SHIFT P |
| ④ | OPT U | ❹ | OPT N, SHIFT O | ④ | OPT SHIFT O | ❹ | OPT P |
| ⑤ | OPT F | ❺ | OPT SHIFT Q | ⑤ | OPT 5 | ❺ | OPT B |
| ⑥ | OPT X | ❻ | OPT Q | ⑥ | OPT SHIFT + | ❻ | OPT 9 |
| ⑦ | OPT J | ❼ | OPT - | ⑦ | OPT , | ❼ | OPT zero |
| ⑧ | OPT \ | ❽ | OPT SHIFT - | ⑧ | OPT . | ❽ | OPT Z |
| ⑨ | OPT SHIFT \ | ❾ | OPT [ | ⑨ | OPT Y | ❾ | OPT " |
| ⑩ | OPT ; | ❿ | OPT SHIFT [ | ⑩ | OPT M | ❿ | OPT O |

•••➤ **"Derived" is pretty much a dirty word** when it comes to fonts, as you may have noticed, because it usually refers to a jaggedy size derived from an existing bitmapped font. But Dubl-Click's UtilityCity is a font derived from other fonts: it takes pieces of Helvetica, Times, Symbol and Zapf Dingbats and puts them together to make very necessary little characters. (Note: you have to have those fonts in your printer, or downloaded to it, for this font to work.)

When you type plain and shifted numeric keys, you get sans serif numerators and denominators 1 through 0; the Option and Shift-Option numbers give you serif numerators and denominators. And the numbers are kerned very close to the slash character, so you get fractions that look like this:

$$\frac{1}{12} \qquad \frac{34}{43} \qquad \frac{3}{4} \qquad \frac{56}{786}$$

UtilityCity also provides a complete five-size set of boxes, shadow boxes, and circles in both plain and marked versions; here are some samples:

□ □ □ □ □     ○ ○ ○ ○ ○     ⊠ ⊠ ⊠ ⊠ ⊠     ◉ ◉ ◉ ◉ ◉

Finally, you get some of your favorite Zapf Dingbats in a variety of orientations:

UtilityCity comes with two other symbol fonts, SymbolsGalore and MathWhiz, as well as Dubl-Click's terrific utilities BigCaps and FontCharter.

# A MAC ALMANAC CHART

## Zapf Dingbats Character Set

| Key | SHIFT | OPT | SHIFT OPT | Key | SHIFT | OPT | SHIFT OPT |
|-----|-------|-----|-----------|-----|-------|-----|-----------|
| A | | | | Y | | | |
| B | | | | Z | | | |
| C | | | | 1 | | | |
| D | | | | 2 | | | |
| E | | | | 3 | | | |
| F | | | | 4 | | | |
| G | | | | 5 | | | |
| H | | | | 6 | | | |
| I | | | | 7 | | | |
| J | | | | 8 | | | |
| K | | | | 9 | | | |
| L | | | | 0 | | | |
| M | | | | ` | | | |
| N | | | | - | | | |
| O | | | | = | | | |
| P | | | | [ | | | |
| Q | | | | ] | | | |
| R | | | | \ | | | |
| S | | | | ; | | | |
| T | | | | ' | | | |
| U | | | | , | | | |
| V | | | | . | | | |
| W | | | | / | | | |
| X | | | | [spc] | | | |

| | a | A | e | E | i | I | o | O | u | U | n | N |
|------|---|---|---|---|---|---|---|---|---|---|---|---|
| OPT ` | | | | | | | | | | | | |
| OPT e | | | | | | | | | | | | |
| OPT i | | | | | | | | | | | | |
| OPT u | | | | | | | | | | | | |
| OPT n | | | | | | | | | | | | |

# Zeal

∞➤ **Zeal is** Apple's third pictorial font, and its most recent. It's a TrueType font that comes bundled with most of Apple's printers and is included in the Apple Font Library.

Zeal has a lot of arrows, clocks, zodiac, and miscellaneous symbols from a recycle symbol to a skull and crossbones, but its main design is an all-capitals font that has bars above and below the letters.

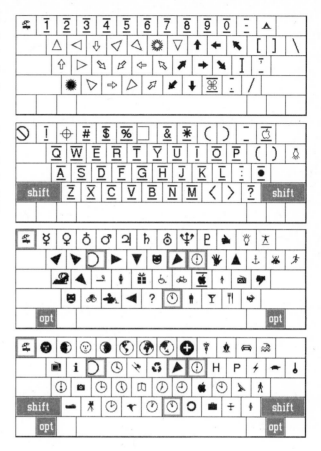

Zeal has plenty of characters in its accent chart, although many of them are repeats of items on the Shift-Option keyboard (they're the ones highlighted in gray frames in this chart).

Accents in Zeal.

**◦•▸ The alphabet in Zeal** is an all-caps alphabet with bars above and below the characters; the bars extend beyond the letters so that when you type, there's a solid bar above and below the words.

THE BARS IN ZEAL LOOK LIKE THIS

**◦•▸ If you don't want breaks between words** in a Zeal banner, use Shift-hyphen instead of typing a space.

THE BARS IN ZEAL LOOK LIKE THIS

**◦•▸ There's a complete set of clocks**—one for each hour—in Zeal, scattered all over the place. Unlike the astrology symbols, which are at least in order if you view the font characters according to their ASCII codes (as mentioned in the section on Zapf Dingbats), the clocks have no order whatsoever. Here's a chart for your convenience:

## Clocks in Zeal

| Clock | Type: | Clock | Type: |
|-------|-------|-------|-------|
| ① | [SHIFT] [OPT] I | ⑧ | [SHIFT] [OPT] H |
| ② | [SHIFT] [OPT] B | ⑨ | [OPT] ` , [SHIFT] E |
| ③ | [SHIFT] [OPT] C | ⑩ | [SHIFT] [OPT] J |
| ④ | [SHIFT] [OPT] D | ⑪ | [SHIFT] [OPT] L |
| ⑤ | [SHIFT] [OPT] R | ⑫ | [SHIFT] [OPT] N |
| ⑥ | [OPT] F | ⑬ | [SHIFT] [OPT] A |
| ⑦ | [OPT] ` , [SHIFT] I | | |

**◦•▸ There are three very special** characters in Zeal; each prints right over whatever character precedes it. Why in the world would you want that? Because the characters are circle, a square, and the slashed circle that's used to indicate "forbidden."

The circle is on Option-E; the square is Shift-6; the slashed circle is Shift-~. If you look at the keyboard chart, or in Key Caps, you'll see that each of these characters is printed slightly off the key, to the left, to indicate how the character will be printed.

Use the circle and square characters to make circled numbers or letters by combining them with the numbers and letters from another font. Type the number or letter in the font you want, then choose Zeal from the Font menu, then type the circle or square character. It takes some experimentation to find which sizes will work together.

You can combine the slashed circle with pictures from Zeal or from other fonts to indicate forbidden activities. (The last one is "no bright ideas")

**◦•▸ Zeal has a double set of zodiac** symbols in it—the astrological symbols as well as more common icons (like the Crab for Cancer). The chart on the next page shows what they are, and where you'll find them.

## Zodiac Symbols in Zeal

| Sign | Icon | Type: | Symbol | Type: |
|------|------|-------|--------|-------|
| Capricorn (goat) | | OPT A | ♑ | OPT `, O |
| Aquarius (water carrier) | | OPT C | ♒ | OPT I, O |
| Pisces (fish) | | OPT E, E | ♓ | OPT U, O |
| Aries (ram) | | OPT A | ♈ | OPT `, E |
| Taurus (bull) | | OPT N, SHIFT N | ♉ | OPT I, E |
| Gemini (twins) | | OPT U, SHIFT O | ♊ | OPT U, E |
| Cancer (crab) | | OPT U, SHIFT U | ♋ | OPT E, I |
| Leo (lion) | | OPT E, A | ♌ | OPT `, I |
| Virgo (virgin) | | OPT `, A | ♍ | OPT I, I |
| Libra (scales) | | OPT I, A | ♎ | OPT U, I |
| Scorpio (scorpion) | | OPT U, A | ♏ | OPT N, N |
| Sagittarius (archer) | | OPT N, A | ♐ | OPT E, O |
| Mercury | | | ☿ | OPT 1 |
| Venus | | | ♀ | OPT 2 |
| Earth | | | ♂ | OPT 3 |
| Mars | | | ♂ | OPT 4 |
| Jupiter | | | ♃ | OPT 5 |
| Saturn | | | ♄ | OPT 6 |
| Uranus | | | ♅ | OPT 7 |
| Neptune | | | ♆ | OPT 8 |
| Pluto | | | ♇ | OPT 9 |

# ➤ SYSTEM 7.5 STUFF ➤

## New Apple Fonts

∞➤ **It's always fun to peruse new system disks for fonts.** Fortunately, a few new ones have shown up in System 7.5; unfortunately, I'm using a beta version of System 7.5 for this, and I can't be sure that what I have is what you'll have! But look on the bright side— maybe you'll have even more than I'm listing here!

The table on the next page rounds up what you'll (probably) get with the new system.

## New Mac System Fonts

| Font | Bitmapped versions | TrueType versions |
|---|---|---|
| *Apple Chancery* | - | Apple Chancery |
| Hoefler Text | - | Hoefler Text |
| | | Hoefler Text (bold) |
| | | Hoefler Text (italic) |
| | | Hoefler Text (bold italic) |
| (Hoefler Text Ornaments) | - | Hoefler Text Ornaments |
| Skia | - | Skia |
| Tekton Plus Regular | 10,12 | Tekton Plus Regular |

∞❥ **All but one of the new fonts** are text fonts. Here's what they look like:

- *Apple Chancery is certainly a derivative of Zapf Chancery. The big difference between them is just that: BIG! Apple Chancery's high x-height makes it look much larger, at the same font size, than Zapf Chancery.*
- Hoefler Text is a nice, clean text font.
- Skia is a nifty little font that keeps its easy-to-read quality even at small sizes, even in bold. There's no doubt in my mind that it was designed for use in dialogs (specifically, inside Help systems).
- Tekton Plus Regular is a TrueType variation of the terrific (if lately over-used) Tekton font.

∞❥ **You'll see the Hoefler Text Ornaments font** in your Font menu, but not in your Fonts folder, because it's in the same suitcase as Hoefler Text. This isn't unreasonable; what's unreasonable is the oxymoronic name Hoefler Text Ornament!

•••❥ **Hoefler Text Ornament** has a relatively small character set; there are blanks even on the unshifted and shifted keys. The majority of the characters are swirly little ornaments on the unshifted keys, with outlined or black-and-white versions of the same character on the shifted keys, like this:

There are also a few whimsical characters in the font, including hands (both right- and left-pointing) whose jester-style cuffs are a relieve from the hackneyed standard dingbat approach of white cuff and black sleeve edge:

The Hoefler Text Ornaments character set.

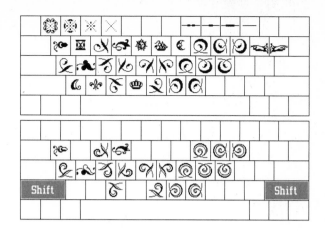

➤ **Some of the ornaments in Hoefler** (I think we can proceed on a first-name basis now) are made for each other—literally. Here, for instance, are five pairs of characters that combine to make larger ornaments. In fact, the last two pairs consist of the same characters, with their positions reversed.

And, some of the characters are made to join in a long line, like this:

# CHAPTER 12
# PRINTING

Where a calculator on the ENIAC is equipped with 18,000 vacuum tubes and weighs 30 tons, computers of the future may have only 1,000 vacuum tubes and perhaps weigh 1.5 tons.

POPULAR
MECHANICS
1949

There's more to printing than using the Print command and clicking the Print button—that's why this is one of the longest chapters in the book. Here's a small sampling of what you'll learn:

•••} What a printer driver is. And, even better (or worse) what a PPD is.

•••} What to do with the Chooser Setup button.

•••} How to print in miniature, upside down, or sideways. Or all three at once.

•••} The special concerns for printing bitmapped graphics on different types of printers.

•••} How to set up background printing. And when not to.

•••} How to use the LaserWriter utility program.

•••} What the dogcow is. Where it comes from. And what it says.

•••} How to set up a document's pages for printing what will become a folded booklet..

## WHAT'S NOT IN THIS CHAPTER

*L*ots of information about printing with QuickDraw GX—because its release was so delayed.

Printer has no paper tray

-Includes-

160 Factoids
  7 Quotes
  9 Memos
  2 Quizzes
    -and-
  1 Mac Almanac List

page 470

## ❧ PRINTER DRIVERS ❧

### The Chooser & Drivers

∞❥ **The Chooser desk accessory** is your main access to your printer. With it, you can specify the printer you're using if you have more than one available, and turn background printing on and off for printers with that capability. Chapter 7 covers using the Chooser DA.

∞❥ **The printer icons in the Chooser** are the *printer drivers* stored in your Extensions folder. A printer driver translates printing information from an application into instructions that the printer can understand. With this type of system-level printer control, an application doesn't have to contain instructions for every type of printer that might possibly be connected to your Mac. Instead, it sends out sort of generic instructions which the printer driver translates for a specific printer. Which drivers are in your Extensions folder depends on how your system was installed.

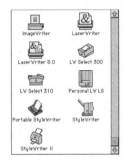

The Chooser has some new functions in System 7.5. See the end of this chapter.

∞❥ **You don't need the Chooser every time** you print something. The Mac remembers your printer setup, so you have to open Chooser only if you're changing printers or turning background printing on and off.

∞❥ **If you get a new printer** for your Mac setup, you might be missing the correct printer driver in your Extensions folder—it depends on how your system was installed, and how new the printer model is (compared to how old your system disks are). But the disks that come with your printer will have the correct printer driver, as well as an updated Chooser if necessary.

The printing process is covered in this chapter, but printers themselves are covered in Chapter 16.

∞❥ **Keep your printer driver updated.** Sometimes an updated driver has only cosmetic changes, but often an update fixes a bug in an older version or improves general performance.

Updated printer drivers are generally released with system "tuners" or "hardware updates." You can also often get them through online sources or user groups.

∞❥ **When you switch printers** in Chooser and close it, you get a dialog telling you to choose Page Setup in any open applications. This is one of those mysterious little messages that the Macintosh provides, which most people either follow without knowing why it needs to be done or completely ignore.

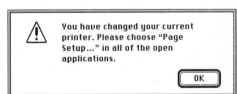

System tuners and updates are in Chapter 23. Online services and user groups are in Chapter 21.

Since different printers have different capabilities, especially when it comes to output resolution for text, a document printed on one printer can look significantly different when printed on another: With higher resolution, more characters can fit on a line, changing line breaks and, eventually, page breaks. By invoking the Page Setup command while a document is open, you force the document to reformat with the currently chosen printer in mind.

••▶ **The Laser Prep file** that worked in tandem with the LaserWriter driver under System 6 is no longer needed under System 7.

••▶ **The System 6 and System 7 LaserWriter drivers** differ in how they prepare the LaserWriter to receive information. If you switch from one to the other, the printer has to be reset to erase what's in its memory and have the new information downloaded to it. You don't have to actually turn it off and back on again—the Mac takes care of resetting the LaserWriter when you switch drivers. But when you're sharing a LaserWriter on a network and the Macs attached to it are using different versions of system software, this continual resetting eats up a lot of time. You can alleviate the reset problem by putting new drivers on the System 6 Macs. System 7 system disks include a special version of the System 6 LaserWriter Prep file that's compatible with the System 7 driver; use it and the System 7 driver on the System 6 Macs.

∞⧘ **Try the BetterWriter driver** for your ImageWriter if you want it to print faster and with more options—like scaling anywhere from 10 to 400 percent instead of just normal or 50 percent. It also lets you flip the page vertically or horizontally, or invert the image to white on black. (Although printing mostly black will kill your ribbon pretty quickly.) [GDT Softworks]

••▶ **Use the StyleWriter II driver** for your StyleWriter I. It prints faster, and with better grays. Just skip the *Clean ink cartridge* option that you'll find in the Print dialog's Option dialog. (You know ... you click the Options button in the Print dialog.) There's some evidence that the mechanics of cleaning the printhead on a StyleWriter II can ruin the printhead on the original StyleWriter.

••▶ **You don't just choose a printer in the Chooser.** You choose a printer *driver*. Then you choose a printer, but that second step's not necessary. This means you can work with a driver for a printer that's not attached to your Mac. This is handy when a document you create will be printed from another system, on a different type of printer. Since changing printers can also change the way a document looks, you can check your document formatting even without having the right printer.

••▶ **You need AppleTalk turned on** in the Chooser if you're using an AppleTalk connection for your printer. All LaserWriters and StyleWriters are AppleTalk printers. The AppleTalk On and Off buttons are in the Chooser.

••▶ **You need AppleTalk *installed*** if you want to turn it on! AppleTalk is installed automatically if you use the Easy Install option for your system installation. But if you use the Customize option, you have to specifically select AppleTalk as one of the options you want installed.

∞⧘ **Skip the Chooser for switching printers** by using the Choosy function in QuickKeys. You can select a printer with a single keystroke, which is a blessing if you switch printers often. [CE Software]

## The 8.0 Driver & PPDs

∞➤ **The LaserWriter 8.0 driver**, despite its number, is for System 7 setups. It offers speedier performance and advanced features for many printers. It takes advantage of the PostScript "Level 2" language built into the latest LaserWriters, but it also improves performance of older models. (It's sometimes referred to as the Level 2 driver.)

LaserWriter   LaserWriter 8.0

∞➤ **The Page Setup dialog** with the 8.0 driver has a few things shuffled around; actually, it's a much more logical organization of commands and options divided between the main dialog and the Options dialog.

- All the Paper options are in a popup menu.
- The Printer Effects checkboxes have been moved into the Options dialog, under Visual Effects.
- The *Faster Bitmap Printing* option has been dropped.
- A Layout option—printing multiple, miniature document pages on a single page of paper—has been added to the main dialog.

The LaserWriter 7.0 Page Setup dialogs.

```
LaserWriter Page Setup                              [ OK ]
Paper: ● US Letter  ○ A4 Letter                     [ Cancel ]
       ○ US Legal   ○ B5 Letter  ○ [ Tabloid    ▼]  [ Options ]
Reduce or [100]%   Printer Effects:
Enlarge:           ☒ Font Substitution?
Orientation        ☒ Text Smoothing?
                   ☒ Graphics Smoothing?
                   ☒ Faster Bitmap Printing?
```

```
LaserWriter Options                                 [ OK ]
  ☐ Flip Horizontal                                 [ Cancel ]
  ☐ Flip Vertical
  ☐ Invert Image
  ☐ Precision Bitmap Alignment (4% reduction)
  ☐ Larger Print Area (Fewer Downloadable Fonts)
  ☐ Unlimited Downloadable Fonts in a Document
```

The LaserWriter 8.0 Page Setup dialogs.

```
LaserWriter 8.0 Page Setup                          [ OK ]
              Paper: [ US Letter ▼]                  [ Cancel ]
              Layout: [ 1 Up ▼]                      [ Options ]
              Reduce or [100] %                      [ Help ]
              Enlarge:
              Orientation:
```

```
LaserWriter 8.0 Options                             [ OK ]
              Visual Effects:                        [ Cancel ]
              ☐ Flip Horizontal
              ☐ Flip Vertical                        [ Help ]
              ☐ Invert Image
              Printer Options:
              ☒ Substitute Fonts
              ☒ Smooth Text
              ☒ Smooth Graphics
              ☐ Precision Bitmap Alignment (4% reduction)
              ☐ Larger Print Area (Fewer Downloadable Fonts)
              ☐ Unlimited Downloadable Fonts in a Document
```

∞➤ **The Print dialog** under LaserWriter 8.0 has undergone a major overhaul. There's so much new stuff that there's an Options button in the main dialog to get to the rest of the choices. The options that are available depend on your specific printer's capabilities.

The LaserWriter 7.0 Print dialog.

```
LaserWriter                                              [ Print ]
Copies: [1]      Pages: ● All  ○ From: [    ] To: [   ]  [ Cancel ]
Cover Page:  ● No ○ First Page ○ Last Page
Paper Source: ● Paper Cassette  ○ Manual Feed
Print:        ● Black & White   ○ Color/Grayscale
Destination:  ● Printer         ○ PostScript® File
```

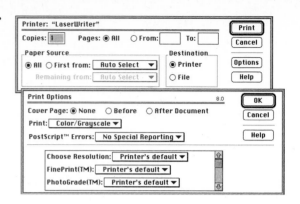

The LaserWriter 8.0 Print dialog and its Options dialog.

**⫸ PPD? Printer description files?!** What kind of computer is this, anyway? Once I started using the 8.0 driver, I felt as if I'd left the easy days of Mac printing behind. That's because, to some extent, I did. Not only are there so many choices in the Print dialog that it needs a secondary dialog, but there are these things called *PostScript printer descriptions*, or *PPDs*, that you have to keep in your Extensions folder, inside a folder predictably named Printer Descriptions. (Sometimes PPD is translated as *Printer Page Description*. They're also called *printer description files*, or *PDFs*.)

Since there are so many LaserWriter models around with so many different capabilities, a single LaserWriter driver can't take care of all of them. All the driver itself can do is let you get at the common capabilities, like font substitution and print size scaling—all those options that have always been in the Page Setup and Print dialogs. But in order for you to get at the unique capabilities of your LaserWriter—600 dpi printing, say, or multiple paper trays—the driver needs a list of the capabilities of your particular printer. That's what the PPD is—a list of your printer's specifications. With these specifications at hand, the Mac knows which options to put in the Print dialogs.

※Look at those icon names. I find it hard to believe that the LaserWriter Pro PPD has gone through more than 2000 versions, don't you? Maybe it's a stardate: Captain's log: Stardate 2010.130

The contents of the Printer Descriptions folder.*

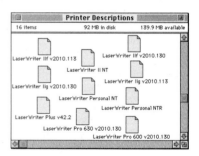

**⫸ PPD files are installed automatically** when you run the Installer program that's on the disks that come with your printer; the Installer creates a folder inside the Extensions folder and puts all the printer files in it. You'll find, however, that it installs the PPDs for all LaserWriters. You don't have to keep them all in the Printer Descriptions folder, though, small as they are (about 15K each); trash whichever ones you don't need. Or use the Customize button in the Installer dialog and select only the PPDs that you need.

## IT COULD BE WORSE ...

Although I shudder at the thought of thinking about drivers, dealing with PPDs, and an Option button in the Print dialog, I have to admit we still have it better than the users of those *other* computers. Here's something that made the rounds of electronic bulletin boards some time ago. It was gleefully posted by someone who works at a "mixed shop"—a place that uses both Macs and PCs. A new printer was added to the network, and the users needed instructions for accessing it. Apocryphal? Maybe. But here's the note:

The Phaser II PX is now online and accessible from both the Mac and the PC. The drivers are in Y:\ALDUS\DRIVER\PHASER. To use the printer, do the following.

For Mac System 7.0:

    1. Select the printer in the Chooser and print.

For Windows:

1. Replace the Capture command for LPT3 in your startnet.bat file with the following: *Capture1=3 q=PHASER_II s=VCSLIB a nob NT.*
2. Reboot your computer.
3. Run startnet.
4. Start windows.
5. Double-click on the Control Panel dialog box.
6. Double-click on the Printers icon in the Control Panel dialog box.
7. Click on the Add Printers button.
8. Select the Apple LaserWriter II NT/NTX PostScript printer.
9. Double-click Install.
10. When the Use Current of New Driver prompts comes up, click on Current.
11. Click the Configure button.
12. Select : for the printer port.
13. Click on the Setup button.
14. Click on the Add Printers button.
15. Type in the path Y:\ALDUS\DRIVERS\PHASER\WINDOWS in the path prompt.
16. Select Tektronix Phaser II PX printer.
17. Click on the Add button to add the printer.
18. Click the Done button.
19. Click OK in the Add Printers dialog box.
20. Click OK in the Configure dialog box.
21. Click Active in the Printers dialog box.
22. Click OK in the Printers dialog box.

••▶ **The LaserWriter Prefs file** for the 8.0 driver seems particularly prone to corruption, although all new system software goes through a breaking-in period.* If you run into strange printing problems—your settings are forgotten, a print job stops halfway through, or constant paper jams that don't seem mechanical in nature— trash the LaserWriter 8.0 Prefs file that's in your Preferences folder.

*That's the period of time in which the original keeps breaking and during which they write the update to fix the problem.

## The Chooser Setup Button

∞→ **There's a Setup button in the Chooser when** you're using the 8.0 driver. Clicking it opens a setup dialog that you can view in one of two ways—short or full—by clicking the More Choices or Fewer choices button in each dialog.

Use the Chooser's Setup button the first time you set up your system with your printer so you can select the proper PPD for your printer. You don't need to use it again unless you want to change some of the settings for your printer, or if you switch to a different LaserWriter model for a print job.

The Setup dialog offers a confusing array of buttons. At least, it's pretty confusing when for years you've just chosen a Print command and clicked the Print button. But even the full dialog, which has eight buttons, has only four you have to learn about—after all, you already know about the More Choices/Fewer Choices button, and you can figure out Help, Cancel, and OK.

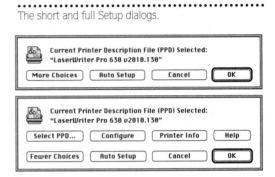

The short and full Setup dialogs.

∞→ **The Select PPD button** lets you do just that. The first time you get your printer set up, there's no PPD selected at all; if you change printers, the wrong PPD is selected. In either case, you use this button to open a dialog that presents a scrolling list of PPDs available in the PPD folder.

∞→ **The Configure button** opens a dialog that lets you specify which options you've installed in your printer. Note that this refers to the "add-on," hardware type of option like extra paper trays, not the built-in options that you can turn on and off, like FinePrint or 600 dpi resolution. For most printers, there *aren't* any options available, but the picture here shows how the dialog looks for the LaserWriter Pro 630.

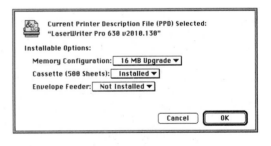

∞→ **The Auto Setup button** makes everything easy. It tells the Mac to look at the printer you've selected in the Chooser and figure out which model it is; then it selects the correct PPD for you. A cinch! Use it when you're not sure which PPD you need, or which printer model you've hooked up to. (Okay, you'll *usually* know what model printer you're connected to, but you might be hooking up to someone else's temporarily, or you may be on a network and the LaserWriter's in the next room.) But if you know what printer you have, it's faster to set it up by using the Select button and selecting the right PPD because you won't have to wait for the Mac to figure out which one it is.

➤ **The Printer Info button** lets you check on the printer you're using. If you don't know which model you're connected to, or how its default options are set, click this button. The Mac checks out the printer and provides a report like this:

Here's the complete report provided in the scrolling area of the Printer Info dialog for my LaserWriter:

> Printer Name: LaserWriter
> Zone: *
> Product Name: LaserWriter Pro 630
> PostScript Level: 2
> PostScript Version: 2010.130
> Resolution: 300 dpi
> Fax Support: No
> Total Memory Installed: 8 MB
> Total Memory Available: 2.3 MB
> Binary Communications Supported: Yes
> Color Supported: No
> PPD File: LaserWriter Pro 630 v2010.130

One of the reasons this information is so handy is that some of these options are originally set through the LaserWriter Utility and if you occasionally switch between, say, 300 and 600 dpi resolution, you may forget what the current setting is. You can get that information here instead of running the utility.

➤ **So what's in a PPD file,** exactly? Lots of boring stuff, except for one line. You can open a PPD file in any word processor, or even in TeachText, since they're only text files. Here's a sample for the curious (remember what happened to the cat!). It's only the first of many pages in the file for the LaserWriter Pro 630.

The line that's not boring? The last line in the first section. What kind of nickname is that? Aren't nicknames supposed to be shorter than the real name, and kinda cute?

> *PPD-Adobe: "4.0"
> *FormatVersion: "4.0"
> *FileVersion: "1.6"
> *LanguageVersion: English
> *PCFileName: "APTOLD81.PPD"
> *Product: "(LaserWriter Pro 600)"
> *PSVersion: "(2010.130) 1"
> *ModelName: "Apple LaserWriter Pro 600 with 8MB"
> *NickName: "Apple LaserWriter Pro 600 with 8MB v2010.130"
>
> *% === Options and Constraints =========
> *OpenGroup: InstallableOptions/Options Installed
> *OpenUI *Option1/Memory Configuration: PickOne

```
*DefaultOption1: None
*Option1 None/Standard 8 MB RAM: ""
*Option1 16Meg/16 MB Upgrade: ""
*Option1 32Meg/32 MB Upgrade: ""
*CloseUI: *Option1

*OpenUI *Option2/Cassette (500 Sheets): Boolean
*DefaultOption2: False
*Option2 True/Installed: ""
*Option2 False/Not Installed: ""
*CloseUI: *Option2

*OpenUI *Option3/Envelope Feeder: Boolean
*DefaultOption3: False
*Option3 True/Installed: ""
*Option3 False/Not Installed: ""
*CloseUI: *Option3
```

••◗ **For a non-Apple laser printer** that doesn't have a PPD of its own, click the Use Generic button when you're in the dialog that lets you choose PPDs. There's no generic PPD in the Printer Descriptions folder; clicking the button makes the Page Setup and Print dialogs default to their general, common options.

## ⟿ PRINTING COMMANDS & OPTIONS ⟵

## The Commands

∞◗ **There are two basic printing commands**, available in almost every application's File menu: Page Setup and Print. The options available in the dialogs that appear when you use either of these commands depend on which printer you're using.

More specifically, the options depend on which printer driver you've selected in the Chooser, but the assumption is that you've chosen the icon that matches your printer.

| File | |
|---|---|
| New... | ⌘N |
| Open... | ⌘O |
| Close | |
| Save | ⌘S |
| Save As... | |
| **Page Setup...** | |
| **Print...** | **⌘P** |
| Quit | ⌘Q |

∞◗ **The Page Setup command** lets you set overall parameters for printing a document: the paper size, orientation, printout size, and "special effects."

The specific choices available depend on the printer you're using—and the version of the driver you're using, too. Here, for instance, are the Page Setup dialogs for some of Apple's many different printers.

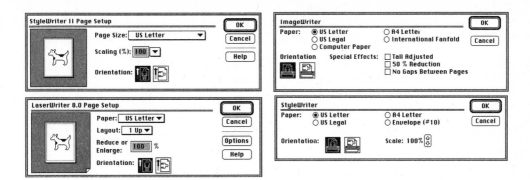

PostScript printers have so many capabilities that you'll find an Options button in the Page Setup dialog when you're using a PostScript printer. It opens a dialog something like the one shown here, with even more options in it.

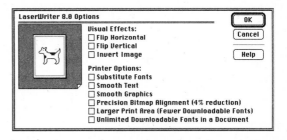

∞❯ **Some printing options** are available for all printers, others only for specific printers. But they can be broken down into three groups based on what they affect: the overall page, text, or graphics. Here's a roundup of the options you'll find in the various Page Setup dialog boxes (and their Options dialogs):

For the page:
- Paper/Page Size
- Scaling/Size/Reduction
- Orientation
- Special Effects/ Visual Effects
- Layout
- Larger Print Area
- No Gaps Between Pages
- Flipping Vertical, Horizontal
- Invert Image

For text:
- Text Smoothing
- Font Substitution
- Fewer Downloadable Fonts
- Unlimited Downloadable Fonts

For graphics:
- Graphics Smoothing
- Faster Bitmap Printing
- Precision Bitmapped Alignment
- Tall Adjusted

You'll find more information about each of these options later in this chapter.

∘◦➤ **The Print command** opens a dialog box that, like the Page Setup dialog, changes according to the printer you're using. Some options, like how many copies you want printed, are always available; others depend on the printer you're using. Here are four sample Print dialogs:

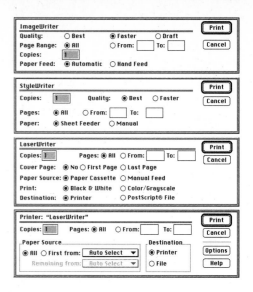

With the LaserWriter 8.0 driver, there are so many options that there's a separate Print Options dialog, accessible through an Options button in the main Print dialog.

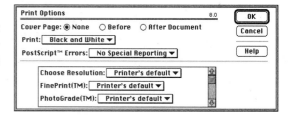

The options in the Print dialog (and its Options dialog) can include:

- Number of copies
- Page Range
- Print Quality
- Paper Source
- Destination
- Cover Page
- Black & White or Color/Grayscale output
- PostScript Error reports
- Overrides for default settings on later LaserWriter models

You'll find more information about each of these options later in this chapter.

∘◦➤ **To cancel a print job** after you've clicked the Print button, press Command-period. Almost every application reminds you of this, keeping a Cancel box on the screen while the printing's in process.

> Printing in progress.
>
> Press Command-. (period) to cancel.

It's not likely that the printing will stop immediately, since the Mac may be talking to the printer at the moment you press the keys, and it can be several seconds—even 15 or 20 seconds—until it checks in with the keyboard. The Command-period you use, though, is stored in the keyboard buffer until the Mac is ready to attend to it, so you don't have to repeatedly press the keys.

Even if the Cancel dialog goes away, the printer may still be churning out another page, or even several more, since information goes to the printer in large chunks. What you've done is cancel the Mac's involvement in the printing process so it won't send any *more* information to the printer; but you can't send a message to the printer saying *Hey. Stop that. Right this minute! I mean it. Now!* like some ineffectual parent dealing with a wayward child.

**⌁➤ You can turn off a printer in the middle** of a print job without causing any harm. The worst that can happen is that you'll have to pop the top of a LaserWriter to pull out a paper that's gotten only halfway through its trip through the rollers.

Why might you turn off a printer while it's working? Well, you can't cancel some print jobs. For example: Tell the LaserWriter to print 45 copies of something (which I did by mistake, instead of telling it to print pages 4 to 5) and unless you cancel the job immediately—before the information goes to the LaserWriter—you can't cancel it at all. The LaserWriter ignores instructions from the Mac while it's doing multiple copies of a page. You'll have to actually turn the LaserWriter off to stop it.

**⋯➤ Page Setup options are document-specific**. If you have more than one document open and use the Page Setup command, it applies only to the active document. If you save the document after using the Page Setup command, the settings are saved with it and used when you open the document again.

**⋯➤ There's two-way communication between** the Mac and your printer. A printer like the LaserWriter can send messages to the Mac, so you'll get notices on the screen like the one shown here.

> Printer has no paper tray

**⋯➤ The LaserWriter is** such an involved piece of machinery—it's actually a computer all by itself—that you'll get dialogs on the screen during the printing process letting you know what's going on. Here's what you'll see:

- *Looking for LaserWriter*. The Mac is looking for a specific LaserWriter—the one you selected in Chooser.
- *Initializing printer:* The Mac sends some initial information to the printer to get it ready for printing. You see this only the first time you print after turning on the LaserWriter, or if you're sharing the LaserWriter with someone who's using a different driver that's initializing the LaserWriter differently.
- *Starting job*: Finally, the document is being sent to the printer for processing. (Each document you print is considered a "job.")
- *Processing job:* The printer is interpreting the PostScript information being sent to it and is preparing a page for printing.

**⋯➤ Many applications have customized** Print and Page Setup dialogs with extra options at the bottom. These are some of the more common additions:

- *Fractional Character Widths:* This little-understood option is something that deals with the screen/printer dichotomy. No matter how your screen text is displayed, it's limited to its 72-dpi display and letters have to be placed along a line in $1/72$ of an inch increments. The printer, despite its ability to place letters at, say, $1/300$

of an inch intervals, will try and match the spacing as shown on the screen so all your line breaks will match—even if that occasionally leads to awkward spacing on a line. Turn on this option to let the printer do its thing and, consequently, to make your screen display look a little squished since letters in your document will try to match their ultimate spacing in the printout.

- *Print Odd/Even Pages:* When you want to print both sides of the paper, you need page 2 on the back of page 1, page 4 on the back of page 3, and so on. An option that prints only odd or only even pages makes this a lot easier.
- *Print Selection Only:* You'll find this in some word processors and many spreadsheets; it prints only the selected portion of the document.
- *Print Back to Front:* Some LaserWriter models—mostly the early ones—had the printed paper come out face up into the paper bin; with the first page on the bottom of the pile and all the pages face up, you had a document whose pages were backwards so you had to shuffle them back into order. This option prints the document starting with the last page so everything's in order when you're finished.

••❥ **Help is only a button click away** in most Print dialogs.* Here's what you see when you click the Help button in the LaserWriter's Page Setup dialog:

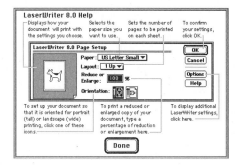

✳Guess you don't need to read this chapter, huh?

OLIVER HARDY TO STAN LAUREL
*DRIVER'S LICENSE* SKETCH, 1947

Why don't you do something to *help* me?

∘∘❥ **Forget all the Page Setup and Printout options** for setting up special print jobs. DynoPage is a control panel that lets you easily arrange things like: special page sizes for personal organizers and appointment books; printing booklets; and printing both sides of the paper. [Portfolio Systems]

## Copies & Page Ranges

∘∘❥ **Specifying the number of copies** for a printed document is the most straightforward item in the Print dialog (with the possible exception of the Print button itself).

But when you print multiple copies of multi-page documents, keep in mind that what you'll get is, say, five copies of page 1, then five copies of page 2, and so on, which you'll have to collate by hand. Printing multiple copies this way is faster than issuing the Print command five times, though, because there's something called *imaging time* that has to be considered—it takes time for the Mac to send information to the printer and for the printer to figure out how the page should look before it actually gets printed. With multiple copies specified, you don't repeat the download or the imaging time; repeated printings mean the process starts all over again.

∞⧽ **You can limit the number of copies** anyone can print on a LaserWriter by using the LaserOneCopy driver, a totally unofficial but solid tweak of the basic Apple driver. Here's what happened, many years ago: Montclair State University in New Jersey set up an open-access Mac lab for its students and faculty. This was in the early days—it was filled with Mac Pluses and two LaserWriters. Students would come in and want to print 20 copies of their resume; even if everything was fine, that tied up the printer unfairly for the other users. But more often than not, they'd find a mistake on the page and then print *another* 20 pages. So we tweaked the LaserWriter driver so there would be no Copies option in the Print dialog, limiting every printout to a single copy. The driver's available free to anyone who wants it; each time a new driver comes out, we tweak that one, too. If you have access to the Internet, you'll find it posted in standard Mac archive sites. If not, contact Rich Wolfson at one of these e-mail addresses: CIS 72467,617; AOL WolfsonR; Internet Wolfson@Apollo.Montclair.edu.

∞⧽ **Press Tab to cycle** through the boxes in the Print dialog—from Copies to From to To, and around to Copies again. Use Shift-Tab to move in reverse.

**Copies:** ⟦1⟧    **Pages:** ⦿ **All**   ○ **From:** ⟦  ⟧   **To:** ⟦  ⟧

∞⧽ **You don't have to click the From button.** If you type in a range of pages, the From button is automatically selected.

∞⧽ **When you want a single page** printed, type the same page number in the From and To boxes.

⦿ **From:** ⟦4⟧   **To:** ⟦4⟧

∞⧽ **To print from a specific page** to the end of the document, whatever that page number might be, put the beginning page number in the From box and leave the To box blank.

⦿ **From:** ⟦5⟧   **To:** ⟦  ⟧

•⧽ **The Print dialog deals with *physical* pages,** not numbered pages. You might have a word processor document, for instance, that has a title page with no page number on it, and a second page that starts with the number 1. If you use the Print command to print pages 1 and 2 you'll get the unnumbered title page and the page numbered 1—the first two physical pages of the document, not the pages numbered 1 and 2.

The same principle applies when you're printing a document that has sections with separate page numbering. If your document has a five-page first section and a ten-page second section, and you specify pages 3 through 7 in the Print dialog, you'll get the last three pages of the first section and the first two of the second section.

## MAC TOON

—*from the BMUG PD-ROM*

**⋯❯ You don't have to wait for the Print dialog** to appear on the screen. If you know the default settings (1 copy, all pages) are fine, just hit Command-P for Print, followed by Return. The Return counts as clicking the Print button in the dialog even though the dialog's not on the screen yet.

If you want a specific number of pages, or a page range, you still don't have to wait for the Print dialog. Say you want a copy of page 4. You type:

Command-P, Tab, 4, Tab, 4, Return

This gives the Print command, tabs past the Copies box (even though you can't see it), types a 4 in the From and To boxes, and clicks the Print button.

**⋯❯ Many applications offer their own** options for printing multiple copies and page ranges—especially word processors and page layout programs. A word processor that divides its document into sections, for instance, with page numbering restarting at 1 for each section, might let you specify which pages from which sections you want printed by typing something like S2P2 and S2P4 in the standard From and To boxes in the Print dialog for pages 2 through 4 of the second section of the document. Or you may find that you can have the document printed already collated—that is, you just say you want five copies and the Mac prints five copies in a row, start to finish, instead of five copies of each page at a time.

## Paper & Image Size

∞◆ The *paper size* option is provided in all Page Setup dialogs either through radio buttons, a popup menu, or a combination of those controls. The available sizes depend on the printer you're using—some have no special envelope feed, for instance, while others can't handle legal-size paper.

Here's a list of the standard sizes (since a button labeled B5 isn't very helpful).

| Description | Size (inches) |
|---|---|
| Computer Paper | 8.5 x 11 |
| International Fanfold | 8.3 x 11.7 |
| US Letter | 8.5 x 11 |
| US Legal | 8.5 x 14 |
| A4 Letter | 8.3 x 11.7 |
| B5 | 7.2 x 10.1 |
| B4 | 10.1 x 14.3 |
| 10 envelope | 9.5 x 4.125 |
| Tabloid | 11 x 14 |
| A3 Tabloid | 11.75 x 16.5 |

∞◆ The *printout size*, or *image size*, is not the same as the paper size. Regardless of the size paper you're using, you can still control the size of the image on the page to some extent—sometimes to a *great* extent. Use the Scaling option, which goes by various names in different dialogs.

- With an ImageWriter, you can choose a 50% reduction.

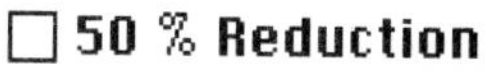

  ☐ **50 % Reduction**

- Early StyleWriters were limited to reductions of 80, 60, 40, and 20%, the sizes that look best based on how the StyleWriter works; you chose the size by clicking on arrows that paged through the available sizes.

  **Scale: 100%** ⬍

- Later StyleWriter drivers and the Color Printer driver have a popup menu that lists those recommended sizes, but you can also type in any size you want—from 5% to 999%!

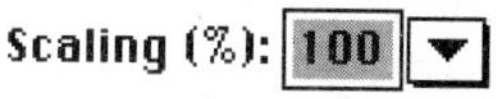

  **Scaling (%):** **100** ▼

- Non-PostScript LaserWriter printers provide 75% and 50% reduction.

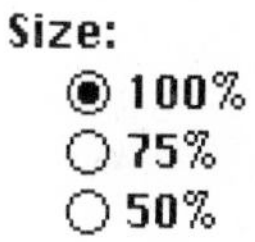

  **Size:**
  ⦿ **100%**
  ○ **75%**
  ○ **50%**

- PostScript printers let you type in a reduction or enlargement factor anywhere from 25% to 400%.

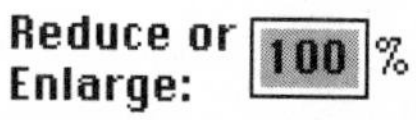

  **Reduce or Enlarge:** **100** %

•❥ **The reduction percentage used** in these dialogs is a *reduced to* percentage, not a *reduced by* number. The difference? A picture reduced *to* 75 percent is three-quarters of its original size. A picture reduced *by* 75 percent is only a quarter of its original size.

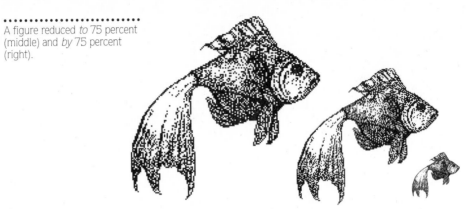

A figure reduced *to* 75 percent (middle) and *by* 75 percent (right).

•❥ **Changing the image size** doesn't put multiple miniature pages on a sheet of paper. It simply shrinks the image of the entire page and prints it on the paper starting in the upper-left corner.

•❥ **The *Page Layout* option** in the LaserWriter 8.0 driver *does* put multiple miniature pages on a single page—two of them at a time, or four. All you have to do is choose 1 Up, 2 Up, or 4 Up in the popup menu.*

When you print multiple pages, you get very neat miniatures that include frames around them to delineate the page. And you should note that printing two pages to a page (so to speak) actually gives you a sideways, or landscape, printout, as the pictures in the Page Setup dialog indicate.

*The "Up" is terminology from label layouts, where you can choose things like 3 up for 3 columns of labels. Don't you wish there were a choice 7 Up?

Use the 2 Up and 4 Up options to print miniature pages (also called "thumbnails") for proofing a layout, or for printing samples of a graphics collection.

1 Up ▼    2 Up ▼    4 Up ▼

•❥ **Specifying pages with a Layout option** refers to the document's pages, not the papers coming out of the printer. So, if you say you want pages 1 through 4 printed 4 Up, you get a single sheet of paper with the four pages printed on it.

•❥ **Reducing or enlarging your printout** may have surprising results. Reducing the page size by 50 percent doesn't give you something that covers half a page—it covers a *quarter* of the page, because both the horizontal and the vertical dimensions have been cut in half. By the same token, doubling the size of a full page document gives you *four* pages of printout, because both dimensions have been doubled.

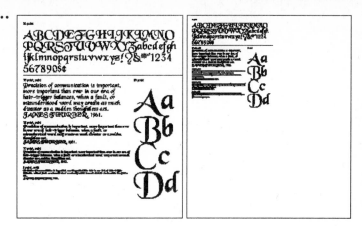

A 50 percent reduction takes up a quarter of the page.

➤ **Using 2 Up layout doesn't shrink** the document to half its size, though that seems like a reasonable assumption. The page image is shrunk to fit on half the page, which means it's about 65 percent of its original size. So a 12-point font in the document prints, not at 6 points, but to a very readable 8-point (or thereabouts) font.

➤ **To find out the page size and margins** for the paper size you've selected in the LaserWriter 8.0 driver's Print dialog, just click on the sample page, and you'll get all the information you need. (The margins are the area that the LaserWriter can't print to, not any page margins you might have set for paragraphs in your document.)

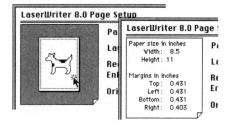

➤ Use the **2 Up layout to make a booklet**—the kind where you fold the paper over in half to make a little book. All you have to do is make sure the pages print where you need them to. This means that after your document is finished, you have to rearrange its pages by cutting and pasting. To make a four-page booklet out of a single piece of paper, you need pages 1 and 4 printed on one side of the paper (with page 4 on the left of the printout) and pages 2 and 3 printed on the other side of the paper (with page 2 on the left). That means you need to reorganize the document so the pages are in this order: 4, 2, 3, 1. Of course, most word processors won't let you actually shuffle pages around as such: you have to paste your page 4 material at the beginning of the document, and the page 1 material at the end, and you won't be able to use any automatic page numbering because the numbers would be in their standard order no matter where you put what material.

Once you have your pages reorganized—and manually numbered if you want page numbers—you print the first two pages using the 2 Up option. Then you put the same paper through the printer again and print the next two pages. The front and back of your paper have pages printed like this when you're finished (with page 2 printed at the back of page 1, and 3 on the back of page 4). All you have to do is fold the paper in half to make the booklet.

For a four-page booklet, a single piece of paper needs pages 1 and 4 on one side and pages 2 and 3 on the other, printed so that page 2 is on the back of page 1, and page 3 is on the back of page 4.

An eight-page, two-paper booklet is a little more complicated, but follows the same general procedure. Reorganize your document so the page material is in this order: 8, 1, 4, 5, 6, 3, 2, 7. Print the first four pages of the document—which will put four pages on two sheets of paper. Put the papers back in the printer and print the next four pages. What you'll wind up with is one sheet of paper with pages 1, 2, 7, and 8 on it, and the other paper with pages 4, 5, 6, and 3 on it. Fold both papers together to get your booklet.

For an eight-page booklet, one paper has pages 8, 1, 2, and 7 printed on it; the second paper needs pages 4, 5, 6, and 3 on it.

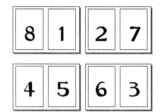

## MAC PEOPLE                                       SUSAN KARE

Susan Kare may be the best-known unknown artist in the world. Every day, tens of millions of computer users look at her work without realizing it. Kare, you see, is responsible for much of the graphical look of the Mac, Windows 3, and NextStep; every time you drag something to the Trash Can, you're looking at a Susan Kare original.

Her doctorate in art history might not seem like the best preparation for a computer interface designer. But when high-school classmate Andy Hertzfeld recruited Kare to be the original Mac team's Resident Artist, she looked at pixel-by-pixel icon editing and saw a modern cousin of the ancient arts of mosaic tile and needlepoint. Carefully placing each screen dot for best overall clarity in the tiny icons, buttons, and low-resolution typefaces, she gave the Mac its distinctively refined look.

When her old boss, Steve Jobs, left Apple and formed NeXT, Kare followed him. She used the four levels of gray in the NeXT display to create a subtle but effective three-dimensional look. Later, working as a freelance interface designer, Kare went on to do the same job for Microsoft, overhauling the terminally ugly Windows 2 operating system to produce the attractive, clean looking Windows 3. (Too bad it doesn't work as well as it looks!)

The importance of Susan Kare's work is demonstrated by the fact that every graphical operating system in the past ten years—and every program written for those systems—has been heavily influenced by her clean, instantly understandable graphic designs. More than any other single individual, she has defined the look of the computers we all use.

*—Andy Baird*

••◆ **A screen inch isn't always a real inch.** That nifty ruler along the top of your screen in your word processor might show your text as 6 inches wide, and it will print at 6 inches wide, but if you measure it while it's on the screen, you won't necessarily get 6 inches.

The resolution of the Mac screen started out at 72 dots per inch, and it's generally referred to as 72 dpi. But Mac screen resolution actually varies from 70 dpi on the 12-inch black-and-white monitor to 90 dpi and higher on some PowerBook screens and monitors from other manufacturers.* Your ruler is based on the fact that an inch should be 72 dots—so that's how it works: Every 72 dots on the screen, no matter their actual size, make up an inch.

> *I know, I know. All along, I've been referring to the 72-dpi Mac screen. I lied. But it was for your own good.

This actually makes a lot of practical sense. Create a document on a 90-dpi PowerBook and then open it on a 72-dpi desk Mac, and what happens? Nothing much—because of the 72 dots-to-the-inch approach. The text, picture, whatever, takes more room on the screen—its lines and dots are thicker—but it still measures 6 inches on the ruler.

## Orientation

∞➤ **The *orientation*** choice is simple: regular or sideways. The official names are *portrait* and *landscape*. Just click on the icon that shows the orientation you want.

∞➤ **If printing 2 Up layouts** gives you sideways printing, what happens if you *choose* sideways (landscape) printing and then use 2 Up layout? You get miniature pages printed sideways on the paper—which are right side up when you hold the paper vertically.

2 Up pages with normal orientation are printed sideways (left); 2 Up pages with landscape orientation are printed vertically (right).

∞➤ **Sideways printing for spreadsheets** is great, since so often you have more columns than rows that you want to print. In fact, sideways printing coupled with a reduction in size squeezes a lot onto a paper but keeps it very readable.

Printing a spreadsheet in portrait orientation (top): printing the same one in landscape mode (bottom).

## Other Basic Options

∞➤ ***Print Quality*** **is an issue** only for ImageWriters and StyleWriters.

For an ImageWriter:

- *Draft* is a low-quality but speedy printout. The ImageWriter ignores fonts and graphics from the Mac and prints only text in its own built-in font. A draft printout is oddly spaced because despite the use of a simple font, the text is still printed with line breaks preserved—that is, each word prints on a line starting at the same spot it would if the printer were using the proportional font and styling

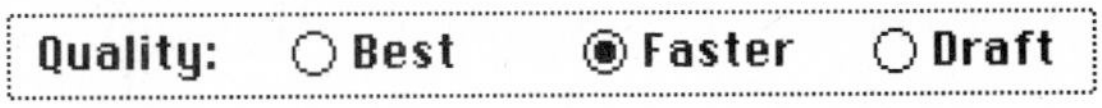

**Quality:** ○ Best ● Faster ○ Draft

that you used in the document. This is obviously only for proofreading text, since formatting isn't even preserved in draft mode printing.

- *Faster* prints everything as it as it exists on the screen, at 72-dpi resolution. What it's faster than is the Best mode, not the Draft mode!

- *Best* is best because then the ImageWriter uses its 144-dpi resolution. But it's slower than Faster mode because to get the 144 dpi, the printhead makes two passes for every line, offsetting the second line slightly from the first to minimize any jagged lines. The ImageWriter driver takes the 72-dpi information from the document (since that's the resolution of the screen fonts and graphics) and creates a bitmapped image of the page that's twice the size of the original; then, it shrinks it by 50% to get it to the 144-dpi resolution of the printer's Best mode.

For a StyleWriter:

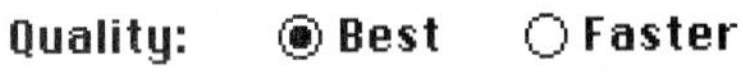

- *Faster* prints in the StyleWriter's lesser-quality mode of 180 dots per inch.

**Quality:** ● Best ○ Faster

- *Best* mode gives a 360-dpi printout—a resolution greater than the basic LaserWriter resolution of 300 dpi. But it can take up to a full two minutes for even an uncomplicated page to be printed in this mode.

∞❥ **The *Paper Source*** (or *Paper Feed*) option used to be very simple: The paper was fed to the printer automatically or manually. The automatic feed might have been tractor-feed paper or a sheet feeder, but it was still automatic and controlled by the printer. Clicking the Manual Feed button would make the printer print a single page at a time and display a dialog with a Continue Printing button that you'd click when you had the next sheet of paper ready to go.

But as sophisticated printers become more affordable, you see more options in the Print dialog. For my LaserWriter Pro, for instance, I have an option of printing the first page from one tray and the rest from another. This is great if I want to print the first page on some special letterhead paper and the rest of the document on plain paper. (I never do, but the option would be a great convenience if I did.) Or if I want to set up the printout so that first an envelope is printed and then the five-page letter that's going in it. (I don't do that either, but I like to know that I *can!*) Anyway, I normally leave the dialog set so that all the pages come from the same source, the main cassette tray. But if I want to print the first page differently, I would click the *First from* button that activates the menus for both the first and remaining pages. All I'd have to do is select the paper source from each menu.

• • • • • • • • • • • • • • • •
When the *First from* button is clicked, both popup menus are activated. The menu, shown at right, is identical for both.

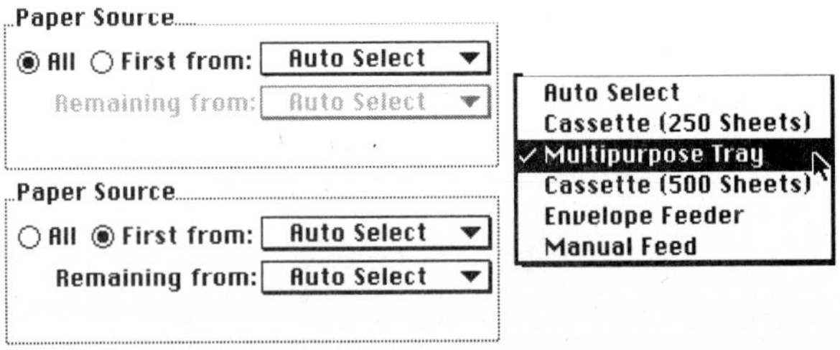

Paper Source
● All ○ First from: [ Auto Select ▼ ]
　Remaining from: [ Auto Select ▼ ]

Paper Source
○ All ● First from: [ Auto Select ▼ ]
　Remaining from: [ Auto Select ▼ ]

Auto Select
Cassette (250 Sheets)
✓ Multipurpose Tray
Cassette (500 Sheets)
Envelope Feeder
Manual Feed

∘•❥ **The overall page appearance** is affected by four Page Setup options, most of which are pretty self-explanatory; all are accompanied by visual aids that demonstrate their effects.

- Flip Horizontal
- Flip Vertical
- Invert Image
- Larger Print Area
  (Fewer Downloadable Fonts)

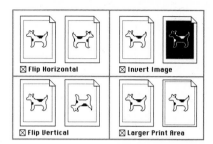

∘•❥ **The *Larger Print Area* option** has a subtitle because it triggers a trade-off: You can have lots of downloadable fonts in a document, or you can have a larger print area, but you can't have both, because they both eat up the LaserWriter's memory.

How much larger is the larger print area? It varies from one printer to the next and according to the options you've already set for the printer (if it has options like 300- vs. 600-dpi printing), since the printout area is dependent upon available memory. You can look for a difference of a quarter-inch to more than a half-inch in the margin width. These are the differences with my LaserWriter for letter- and legal-size pages:

|        |                     | Top  | Left | Bottom | Right |
|--------|---------------------|------|------|--------|-------|
| Letter | Standard print area | .431 | .431 | .431   | .403  |
|        | Larger print area   | .111 | .139 | .208   | .153  |
| Legal  | Standard print area | .75  | .889 | .75    | .889  |
|        | Larger print area   | .111 | .139 | .208   | .153  |

## POP QUIZ                                                    [5 POINTS]

That little animal in the Page Setup and print dialogs is a dog ... isn't it? Not really. Look at the shape of its muzzle, cover the tail for a minute—it's more like a cow, especially with those markings.

Actually, this strange little creature is the famous dogcow who first made an appearance in technical note 31 of the Macintosh Technical Notes HyperCard Stack v3.1. Although all dogcows look the same, this is probably the very one that appeared in that stack, in which case his name is Clarus. And what sound does a dogcow make? Moof!

Now, on to the quiz: What is this thing pictured here? It's remotely related to the subject at hand.

∘•❥ ***Unlimited downloadable fonts*** is a LaserWriter option that lets you use more fonts in a document than you might normally be able to. The LaserWriter retains downloaded font information during the course of printing a document in case you want to use the font again; the font isn't flushed from memory until the entire document has been printed. But memory can fill up quickly, especially on older LaserWriters, and you may find the Courier font being substituted when there just isn't any more room for another font to be downloaded.

Keeping this option checked lets the LaserWriter flush a font from memory when it's time to download another one for the same document. Of course, that means it needs to download the first one again if it's used again in the document, and that slows down the overall printing process. But that brings to mind the adage: *A slow print is better than a Courier print.*

••➤ **No Gaps Between Pages** is an ImageWriter-only option, since that's the only printer that can use tractor-feed paper. Tractor-feed paper, being one very long sheet of paper, has a perforated area that shouldn't be printed across. The ImageWriter normally advances the paper a little bit before it prints a page in order to avoid printing on the perforation. But when you're using single sheets of paper, or special tractor-fed items like envelopes or labels, check this button to avoid the extra paper advance.

••➤ **You can override a LaserWriter's default settings** when you're using the LaserWriter 8.0 driver, through the Print dialog's Option dialog. There's a scrolling list of popup menus (an odd hybrid of interface elements) that refer to each of the defaults you set for your printer through the LaserWriter Utility. Only certain LaserWriters have these capabilities built in, so don't be surprised if there's nothing like this showing in your Options dialog!

FinePrint? PhotoGrade? They're covered in Chapter 16.

••➤ **PostScript printers offer grayscale** printing that's unavailable in other printers. Of course, the printer is still printing black dots, but by varying their size and placement, the printer simulates a gray tone.

Depending on the printer and driver you're using, the Black & White versus Color/Grayscale choice might be right up in the Print dialog or in an Options dialog you reach through the Print dialog. (Unless you're working with a color printer, color items in your document will print as grayscale when the Color/Grayscale option is on.)

If you print a color or grayscale image in a document with Black & White selected, all the colors or grays lighter than a certain shade are printed as white while all the ones darker than a certain shade print as black. But black-and-white printing goes much

A grayscale and a black-and-white print of a color image.

faster, so when you're proofing the text of a document and don't need to check the graphics, it makes sense to keep the black-and-white setting for printouts.

## Printing from the Desktop

∞➤ **To print a document from the Desktop,** select its icon and then choose Print from the File menu. Both the document and its application open. Then the application's Print dialog appears so you can select options—so make sure you're paying attention, not just issuing a Print command from the Finder and then walking away.

Whatever Page Setup options you used the last time you printed the document are used for this printing; you don't get a chance to choose the Page Setup command. When the print job is finished, the application automatically quits.

∞➤ **You can print multiple documents** from the desktop. Just select all the ones you want to print and choose the Print command. This is a great option, since so few applications let you print more than one document at a time.

∞➤ **There's a single Print dialog** used by the application when you're printing multiple documents from the desktop. The options you choose in the dialog box—the number of copies, for instance—apply to all the documents that are going to be printed.

∞➤ **You can print documents from different applications** from the desktop. This wasn't always the case: multiple-document printing used to work only for documents from the same application.

When you select documents from different applications and use the Print command, each application opens, prints its documents, and quits in turn. You'll have to attend to a Print dialog for each application as it opens.

•➤ **Clicking the Cancel button** in a Print dialog that's there because you chose Print from the desktop not only cancels the printing, it quits the application, too, just as it would if the print job were done. If you've selected multiple documents to be printed, too bad: Everything's canceled.

•➤ **Using Command-period** to cancel a print job that's in progress—one that started from the desktop, that is—cancels the printing of the current document as well as any others that were included in the selection. It quits the application, too.

•➤ **If an application's already open** when you use the Finder's Print command on one of its documents, the document is opened, printed, and closed, but the application doesn't quit.

# ✦ PRINTING TEXT ✦

## Fonts & Printer Resolution

∞✦ **The quality of your text printout** depends on both the kind of printer you're using and the kind of fonts you've chosen. The higher your printer's resolution, the better your text will look because a high-resolution printer can print very tiny dots very close together and therefore make both very thin lines and very smooth curves. The correct choice of fonts can improve the look of text on lower-resolution printers.

A brief reminder of the information covered in the last two chapters:

- Bitmapped fonts, no matter what their size, are designed at 72 dots per inch (dpi). Letting the Mac create a font in the size you need from an existing size introduces distortions.
- PostScript fonts are outline fonts, designed as mathematical descriptions so their resolution can match that of the printer and they can be resized with no distortions. But the printer has to be a PostScript printer in order to interpret the font information correctly. Or you need ATM to interpret the PostScript information to make a bitmapped font for a non-PostScript printer.
- PostScript fonts can't be displayed on the screen unless you use ATM, which takes the printer font information and interprets it for the Mac's screen. You don't need ATM: You can use a bitmapped version of the font for the screen and the PostScript font for the printer.
- TrueType fonts from Apple are outline fonts so they can be resized without distortion and they can take advantage of the printer's resolution. And they work for both the screen and the printer.

∞✦ **An ImageWriter prints at 144 dpi** in its best mode. TrueType fonts, or PostScript fonts with ATM to handle the interpretation for the printer, take advantage of this resolution which, although relatively low, is still twice that of the standard Mac screen.

The resolution is also twice that of a standard bitmapped font. So if you're using a bitmapped font, you should have in your system a font that's twice the size of what you want printed. If you print 12-point Balloon, for instance, you should have the 24-point Balloon version available. The Mac uses the more detailed information from the 24-point map, shrinking it 50 percent to get it to the size you want, and you wind up with a better printout. The problem, of course, is that your document might include headings at, say, 14 and 18 points, and footnotes at 10 points. That means you'd also need a 28, 36, and 20-point version of Balloon for the best printout (while keeping the original sizes for the best screen display).

You can, of course, print documents without the right bitmapped size available—the text just won't look as good. (In fact, it might look *terrible*.)

∞✦ **A StyleWriter prints at 360 dpi** in its Best mode. Once again, TrueType fonts or PostScript fonts with ATM will take advantage of the printer's resolution.

But you've got a real problem with plain bitmapped fonts: the StyleWriter's resolution is five times that of the font. This means that for the best printout, you'd need a bitmapped version in a size five times the one you want. For a 12-point version, you'd need a 60-point design to take advantage of the printer's capabilities—if you could find a font that comes with a version that big!

As with the ImageWriter, though, you don't *need* a font in the larger size in order to get a printout—you just need it to get the best-looking printout possible.

∘∘⟩ **A LaserWriter prints at 300 dpi;** later models have a 600-dpi option. Forget bitmapped fonts entirely. Because 300 isn't a multiple of 72, you'd need a font that's *twenty-five* times the size of the printout to really take advantage of the 300-dpi resolution without introducing any distortions. For non-PostScript LaserWriters, use TrueType fonts, or PostScript fonts with ATM; for PostScript LaserWriters, use TrueType or PostScript fonts.

### POP QUIZ                                    [10 POINTS]

This is really more of a riddle than a quiz, but still:

There were at least two computers in the Garden of Eden. Eve used an Apple. What did Adam use?

## Other Concerns

∘∘⟩ **Strictly WYSIWYG** (What You See Is What You Get) printouts pretty much went out the window once we got beyond the combination of Mac, bitmapped fonts, and the ImageWriter. With printers that have different resolutions from the screen, and different fonts for the screen and for the printer, what you see on the screen is sometimes nowhere near what you get on the printer. (Many times it's very close, though!)

Generally speaking, though, the printout of a text document will always look better than it did on the screen, so don't despair when your screen letters look jagged or crookedly formed.

∘∘⟩ **Text on LaserWriters can be affected** by two Page Setup options.

  • *Text Smoothing.* This affects only fonts created from a bitmapped font file, not TrueType or PostScript fonts. It smoothes out characters a little bit by adding extra dots along the 90° and 45° lines in the character. (Since printers use smaller dots, and therefore have a higher dots-per-inch rating, it's easy for them to print dots that are too small to be displayed on the screen.)

- *Font Substitution.* This option replaces certain bitmapped fonts in your document with fonts that are built into the printer. Geneva is replaced by Helvetica; New York is replaced by Times; and Monaco is replaced by Courier. (Of course, Monaco and Courier don't look at all alike, but they're both monofonts.)

Both these options are pretty much relics of the early days and should be left off. You should be using either PostScript or TrueType fonts for printing, so Text Smoothing should never come into play. And font substitution is pretty ridiculous, since if you swap fonts at print time, your line breaks and page breaks change. This was a crutch Apple offered in the early days of LaserWriter printing because everybody was used to using Geneva and New York on the screen and continued to do so even after trading in their ImageWriters for LaserWriters—and those fonts printed out very poorly on LaserWriters. (They print out much nicer now, since Geneva and New York are both TrueType fonts and not mere bitmaps anymore.)

✦ **Styled text on the screen** won't always print out as styled if the printer is using an outline font. Sometimes the differences between the screen version and the printer version are minor; sometimes they're major. The last two chapters dealt with the whys and hows of bold and italic styling because they're often part of a font family and you need a separate printer font for each of those. But take a look at what can happen to the other styles, the ones the Mac or the printer creates for you when you choose Underline, Outline, or Shadow from a Style menu.

In these samples of Zapf Chancery, the screen version of the underlined style has nice-looking breaks for the letters with descenders; the printed version has a straight line that plows through the descenders. The Outline style looks much cleaner on the printout than on the screen, which is no great surprise. But on screen, the Shadow style simply has dark lines around the edges of its letters, while the printed version really looks like there's a shadow cast by the letters that are in the foreground. On screen, you can create an Outline Shadow version that looks different from both the Outline and the Shadow styles. But the printout of Outline Shadow is identical to the Shadow style—because, if you notice, the plain Shadow style already includes the outline version of the font.

| Style | Screen | Printout |
|---|---|---|
| Underline | *Zapf Chancery* | *Zapf Chancery* |
| Outline | *Zapf Chancery* | *Zapf Chancery* |
| Shadow | *Zapf Chancery* | *Zapf Chancery* |
| Outline & Shadow | *Zapf Chancery* | *Zapf Chancery* |

The results of using Underline, Outline, and Shadow individually or in combination vary from one font to another, so plan to do test printouts if you find yourself using these styles for special effects.

•••➤ **The empty boxes that** show up when you type some Option or Shift-Option characters won't print as boxes. The boxes indicate that there's no character in the font for that key. So that's what prints—no character!

There is an exception to this: When there's no character in the bitmapped font that's being used for the screen display, but the key combination does produce a character in the TrueType or PostScript font that's going to be used for printing, you'll get a box on the screen and a character in the printout.

•••➤ **When a different font is printed** than the one that's displayed on your screen, it might be because:

- You have *Font Substitution* checked in the Page Setup options. This substitutes Times for New York, Helvetica for Geneva, and Courier for Monaco.
- Your LaserWriter ran out of memory during the page imaging and substituted Courier for whatever font it couldn't manage.
- It's actually the same font. The screen representation just doesn't match the printed version too well. Sometimes that's because the screen will be using the bitmapped font, or a scaled TrueType font, but the printer's using the PostScript version. And sometimes it's because all the designer's efforts went into the design of the PostScript font and he or she didn't spend much time on the screen font.
- The text is embedded in a graphic inside the document and wasn't downloaded at all. If this happens, download the embedded font manually so that it's there waiting, or format a blank line or space in the regular text as that font so it gets downloaded normally.

Printing trouble-shooting is covered in Chapter 24.

## ➤ PRINTING GRAPHICS ◄

### Printing Bitmapped Graphics

∘∘➤ **Standard bitmapped graphics** have a resolution of 72 dots per inch (dpi)—perfect for the Mac's screen. But only the ImageWriter in its Faster printing mode matches that resolution. The ImageWriter's Best mode is 144 dpi; the StyleWriter can do 180 dpi and 360 dpi; LaserWriters print at 300 or 600 dpi. A 72-dpi graphic can't always take advantage of a printer's higher resolution, and sometimes (more often than not) it's slightly distorted when printed unless you pay some special attention to it.

∘∘➤ **The *Graphics Smoothing* option** in some Page Setup dialogs does just what it says: it smoothes the edges of bitmapped images by adding a few extra dots where otherwise there would be a small jagged edge. If you're using bitmapped images for their textured "feel," you don't want to turn on the smoothing option, because the texture changes. A picture that's mainly a line drawing may benefit from smoothing; one that has a textural pattern shouldn't be smoothed.

∘∘➤ **The *Precision Bitmap Alignment* option,** also called *Exact Bit Images* in some Page Setup dialogs, is available for printers that print at 300 and 600 dpi. It shrinks bitmapped images by 4 percent so that their resolution matches the printer's capabilities.

A basic LaserWriter printout, for instance, is 300 dpi, while the bitmapped image is 72 dpi. If you send a 72-dpi image to the printer, every dot that's in the image has to be represented by about 4.17 dots in the printout. But there's no such thing as a fraction of a dot, so most dots in the image are replaced by 4 dots, but every sixth dot or so is represented by 5 dots in the printout. The result? A distorted image or pattern in the printout.

By reducing the image 4 percent, the computer sends a 75-dpi image to the printer. (Squeezing down the picture a little gets that many more dots per inch.) That number can easily be quadrupled to the printer's 300-dpi capability for a perfect printout.

A standard bitmapped image printed on a LaserWriter (left); the image printed with the Precision Bitmap Alignment option (right).

••➤ **You can increase the resolution of a graphic** by resizing it before you print it. But how, and how much, you shrink it makes a big difference.

First, consider that if you take a 72-dpi image and shrink it 50 percent, you then have a smaller image that has 144 dots squeezed in per inch. The smaller image has a higher resolution. But if you do this in a program that works with bitmapped images strictly on a dot-by-dot basis (like MacPaint or the paint layer in SuperPaint), the Mac shrinks the picture by throwing out every other dot, so what you really have is a smaller, muddy picture that's still 72 dpi. You haven't changed its resolution, you've just ruined it.

Shrinking the image in any program that treats it as a *bitmapped object*, though, means you have indeed increased the resolution because the Mac keeps track of where every single dot is—it doesn't throw any away to achieve the smaller size. You won't be able to see this increased resolution on your screen, since the screen is still a 72-dpi (or thereabouts) display. In fact, a bitmapped image scaled down the right way (as an object) and one scaled the wrong way (as a bitmap) look exactly the same on the screen. But the important difference will show up on your printout.

Top: The screen image (left) and the printout (right) of a bitmapped image reduced incorrectly. Bottom: The screen image (left) and the printout (right) of a bitmapped image reduced correctly.

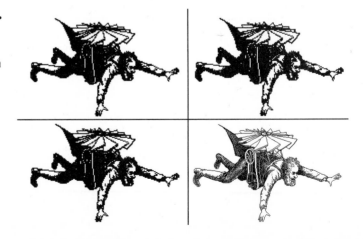

The more you shrink the image, the more you increase the resolution. These pictures show part of a full-size bitmapped picture and the complete picture that's been reduced by about 50 percent. You can see that the smaller picture has much finer, and smoother-looking lines in it.

Bitmapped and object-oriented graphics are covered in Chapter 20.

**NORMA DESMOND***
SUNSET BOULEVARD (1950)

> I am big. It's the pictures that got small.

*Am I the only one who can visualize only Carol Burnett's takeoff on Norma Desmond instead of the original?

➤ **Bigger is never better** when it comes to bitmapped graphics. No matter what the percentage of enlargement, no matter which printer, no matter *anything*, an enlarged bitmap gets distorted and jagged

The bigger it gets, the worse it gets!

when you print it—it's no better on the printer than on the screen. That's because if you start with a picture that's 72 dpi and enlarge it, it's enlarged based on the bitmap as it already exists—it's like enlarging a bitmapped font, where every existing dot becomes multiple dots in the enlargement, creating a very chunky look.

➤ **Your printer's resolution determines** the best reduction size for your pictures. You need to reduce the image so that its new increased resolution will match the printer's, or be a factor (mathematically speaking) of the printer's resolution. For instance:

- The ImageWriter has a resolution of 144 dpi in Best mode. So scaling a 72-dpi graphic 50% is perfect, because it increases the resolution to 144 dpi.
- The StyleWriter prints at 360 dpi in its Best mode. That means you have to reduce a bitmapped image to 20% of its original size to get the full benefit of the printer's resolution. But you can increase the image's resolution without introducing any distortions by shrinking it to 80%, 60%, or 40% of the original size.
- For a LaserWriter printout at 300 dpi, you have to shrink a bitmapped image to 24% of its original size to get the best possible printout. But a reduction of 96%,

72%, 48%, or 24% keeps the picture's resolution in the right ratio to the printer's and prevents any distortion of the image. If you're working with a 600-dpi LaserWriter, the same proportions apply, but using a 72-dpi image at 12% of its original size takes complete advantage of that resolution.

It's no coincidence that the ImageWriter's Page Setup allows for a 50 percent reduction and the StyleWriter's Page Setup provides choices of 20 percent, 40 percent, 60 percent, and 80 percent. But remember, using the page reduction size in the dialog shrinks the entire page, not just the picture.

••➤ **Instead of using the Precision Bitmap Alignment** option to adjust the look of bitmapped graphics on a LaserWriter printout, you can specify that the entire document be reduced in size. Use a 96 percent reduction to get the same effect.

••➤ **Altering the size of a graphic** through a Page Setup or Print dialog option doesn't work if you've already resized the graphic in the document you're printing. If I put a bitmapped graphic in a Word document, for instance, and shrink it to 96 percent, I don't have to make any adjustments in the print dialogs—and if I do, they'll mess up the sizing I already did in the document!

••➤ **The *Faster Bitmap Printing*** option available in some LaserWriter Page Setup dialogs, like Text Smoothing and Font Substitution, is just left over from the early days. It originally forced the Mac to "preprocess" bitmapped images before sending them to the printer because the Mac could do the figuring so much faster than the printer could. But today's LaserWriters are so fast that using this setting *slows down* the printing process! As a matter of fact, you won't even find the option in the newest LaserWriter drivers. In the meantime, keep it turned off—sometimes it even keeps documents from printing at all.

••➤ **The *Tall Adjusted* option is** unique to ImageWriters because ImageWriters have a unique printing problem. In Faster mode, the ImageWriter prints at 72 dots horizontally and 80 dots vertically; in Best mode, it prints at 144 by 160 dpi. But the Mac screen (and its bitmapped images) has an equal number of dots horizontally and vertically. So no matter how you print things out, there's going to be some distortion in the translation from screen to printer—

Standard printout (left) and with Tall Adjusted (right).

circles, for instance, are printed as ovals that are about 11 percent taller than they are wide. The Tall Adjusted option prevents the vertical distortion by making everything slightly wider. But that means that text is wider, too—a 6-inch wide paragraph will cover more than 6.5 inches.

••➤ **Dithered patterns in small pictures** are a big problem on high-resolution printouts. A dithered pattern is one that uses alternating dots of black and white to simulate gray—or alternating dots of any color to simulate another color.

The proof of this widespread problem is in almost every book about the Mac under System 7. Take a look at the pictures in one of those books—the pictures of the System Folder and its subfolders. You'll see plaids and checkerboard patterns in the folders where you see gray or light blue on your own Mac. Why? Take a look at the magnified view of the folder here. It's not a solid gray or light blue—it's a dithered pattern.

The pattern is an 8 by 8-pixel repeating one. That just doesn't translate mathematically for the resolution of a 300 or 600 dpi LaserWriter, or a 1200 or 2400 Linotronic output, even without shrinking the picture. And you can't shrink it much because it's so small to begin with. Besides, there's the problem of these folders just being part of a larger picture (a screen shot of an open desktop window, say) that has to be reduced by a certain percentage to fit the layout of the book—and that's rarely going to be the percentage needed to keep the distortion pattern from the folder. So, you'll see a lot of plaids and checkerboards. But why won't you see them in this book (except where they snuck by me)? Because I re-drew the folders in every picture so that they're a solid color instead of a dithered pattern. (What I don't do for you!) Here are the two folders—the genuine one and the edited one; it's easy to figure out which is which.

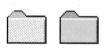

QuickDraw's in Chapter 13. Object-oriented (and other) graphics are in Chapter 20.

**•••➤** **Printing *object* or *vector* graphics** doesn't pose problems the way printing bitmaps does. Object-oriented graphics pretty much carry their definitions with them (*I'm a rounded rectangle with a 2-pixel border and a striped pattern fill*) in any program, and the Mac's inner QuickDraw routines take care of rendering the picture correctly at any size you choose to print them.

## PostScript Graphics & Files

**∞➤** **A PostScript graphic is** an image that contains a description of itself in the PostScript language that a PostScript *device* (most LaserWriters are PostScript devices) can understand. A PostScript device interprets the description and prints the graphic so that it uses the highest capability of the printer, whether that's 300 or 600 dpi on a LaserWriter or 2400 dpi or more on high-end printers.

But the Mac can't interpret the PostScript description for its screen display. (If you've already read through the font chapters, this problem should sound familiar, since the Mac can't display PostScript fonts, either.) But the solution for PostScript graphics is nothing like the solution for screen display of PostScript fonts, which is to use a special utility to translate the font information for the screen. Instead, a PostScript graphic for the Mac contains two descriptions: one for the printer, and one for the screen. This is called *encapsulated PostScript*, or *EPS*. (Or sometimes, EPSF, for *encapsulated PostScript file*, which leads to the redundant phrase *EPSF file*.)

Graphics file formats are covered in Chapter 20.

**∞➤** **Printing an EPS graphic** on a PostScript LaserWriter is a breeze. (Okay, sometimes it's a very gentle breeze, since complicated graphics print slowly on older LaserWriters.) You can resize it smaller or larger without introducing any distortions.

CINDERELLA
at her old LaserWriter

Someday, my prints will come.

⟶ **A PostScript file** is an entire document—text, graphics, or both, along with other document information like margin sizes and the page layout—that's been translated into the PostScript language. Unlike an encapsulated PostScript file that includes a special representation for the screen, a PostScript file is simply a series of commands for the printer. Since PostScript is a

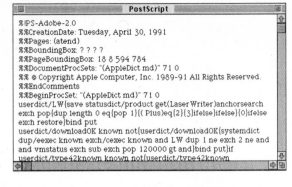

"high-level" programming language, its commands are reasonably English-like—at least when compared to "low-level" languages. Anyway, you can actually open a PostScript file and read the commands (for all the good it will do you). The picture here shows what a simple PostScript file looks like. The document that was PostScripted (isn't that a handy word?) was from a graphics program, and it was simply a single page with a single box drawn on it.

⟶ **Create a PostScript file** by using the Destination option in the Print dialog—it will be there if you're using a printer with PostScript capabilities. Instead of printing to the printer, the document can be saved in PostScript definitions to the disk. Here's how:

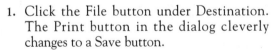

The Save dialog for a PostScript file.

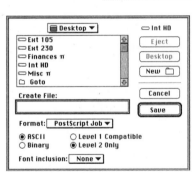

1. Click the File button under Destination. The Print button in the dialog cleverly changes to a Save button.

2. Click the Save button. You'll get a Save dialog with several options along the bottom.

3. Choose a format from the popup menu. A standard PostScript file is plain text, so you can leave the menu at PostScript Job. But if you know what you're doing and want to create a PostScript file that's going to be placed within another document instead of downloaded to the printer, use one of the three EPS choices; two of them will create a screen image for the document separate from that of the printer information.

4. Click the ASCII or Binary button. For a downloadable PostScript file, you'll want the ASCII format. In fact, for most purposes you'll want ASCII (text) format. A binary file will print faster, but will print only on printers like the LaserWriter Pro 630, which understand the binary format.

5. Choose between the Level 1 and Level 2 buttons based on the capabilities of the PostScript printer you'll be printing to; all PostScript printers can handle Level 1, so if you're in doubt about the final destination printer, click that button.

6. Use the Font Inclusion popup menu to exclude or include fonts in the file. If you include fonts, the file will be much bigger but will be able to print from any Mac system, even if the document's fonts aren't there. The All But Standard 13 choice will include fonts in the file except for the 13 that are built into most LaserWriters.

| None |
|---|
| All |
| All But Standard 13 |

7. Give your file a name and click the Save button.

•••➤ **To print a PostScript file,** you can't just open the document and print it: you'll get a printout of text commands. Instead, you have to *download* it to a PostScript printer, which will interpret the commands and print the original document. Use the LaserWriter Font Utility, or its update, the LaserWriter Utility, to download the file to the printer. All you have to do is use the Download PostScript File command and select the file in the Open dialog.

### THE WAY WE WERE ...

Things on the Mac are getting more complicated, but they're also getting easier. Consider, for instance, how you had to make PostScript files from an application that didn't provide the capability (and most didn't):

First, you'd prepare the document as usual and use the Print command. You'd even click the Print button. Then, quick as a wink (approximately), you'd have to press Command-F. Or Command-K. One key combination included the fonts and the Laser Prep information in the file and one didn't. Really intuitive, right?

# ⇒ THE PRINTMONITOR ⇐

## Printing in the Background

•••➤ *Background Printing* **buttons** appear in the Chooser desk accessory when you're using a printer (a LaserWriter or StyleWriter) that's capable of background printing. What *is* background printing? Well, usually when you print something you see a dialog on the screen that tells you printing is in progress; the Mac is totally tied up with the printing process. What's happening is that the information from the document is being translated by the printer driver into a file that the printer understands; then, the information is fed to the printer. But the information is processed and sent in relatively small amounts since the printer prints so much more slowly than the Mac processes. The Mac waits, twiddling its thumbs, until the printer signals that it's ready for the next batch (which might be as little as a single page, or as much as a dozen pages of text).

Background Printing
◉ On ○ Off

When background printing is enabled, instead of the printer driver interpreting the document's information and sending it to the printer, it stores the interpretation in a disk file. This information is fed to the printer in whatever size chunks it can handle. But between feedings, the Mac is yours to use.

Well, it's *mostly* yours. During background printing, the Mac splits its attention between the printer and what you're doing. Even when it's not downloading a new chunk of information to the printer, it has to keep checking with the printer to see if it's ready for more or if a problem has cropped up (like running out of paper). So you'll notice a slow-down on your Mac. The mouse cursor sort of jerks around on the screen instead of describing a smooth path; or there might be a delay between the time you press on a menu name and when the menu opens.

∞•❯ **The PrintMonitor** is the application that controls background printing. Although it's an application, it's installed in your Extensions folder when you set up your system. You can open it directly by double-clicking, but you never have to: it's launched automatically when needed. (See that hand on the icon? It's the traditional application icon approach.) Just click on the icon of your printer in the Chooser DA and then click the On or Off background printing button.

∞•❯ **AppleTalk has to be turned on** for background printing to work. This is not usually an issue, since it also has to be on to print at all to a LaserWriter or StyleWriter—the only Apple printers that can do background printing. And once it's on (in the Chooser DA), there's no reason to turn it off unless you're using a PowerBook and are trying to conserve battery power.

AppleTalk   ● Active
          ○ Inactive

∞•❯ **A special folder is created** in the System Folder to hold the files that PrintMonitor is sending to the printer. It's cleverly named *PrintMonitor Documents*. Once it's created (automatically, by PrintMonitor), it hangs around even if it's empty.

> ✳The word spool is sometimes defined as having come from the phrase simultaneous peripheral operation off line, but many old hands claim that's a contrived back-formation. Whatever the origin, it's a handy word.

Sending files someplace temporarily until they're processed or sent someplace else is called *spooling*,* so the print files are spooled to the PrintMonitor folder, and the PrintMonitor itself is a *print spooler*.

•••❯ **You use the standard Print command** for background printing; there's nothing in the Print dialog that indicates anything different's about to happen. In fact, you even get the standard printing dialog on the screen as if the document were going to the printer instead of the disk. But you'll probably notice how quickly the dialog goes away, compared to when a document goes to the printer.

•••❯ **Pressing Command-period** while the Print dialog is still open stops the spooling process and erases the file that was being saved. If you press Command-period towards the end of the process, you may think the dialog went away because you canceled it but it might have disappeared because the disk file was completed—and in a few minutes or less, your printer's going to start printing the document you thought you had canceled. You have to cancel a spooled document through the PrintMonitor window.

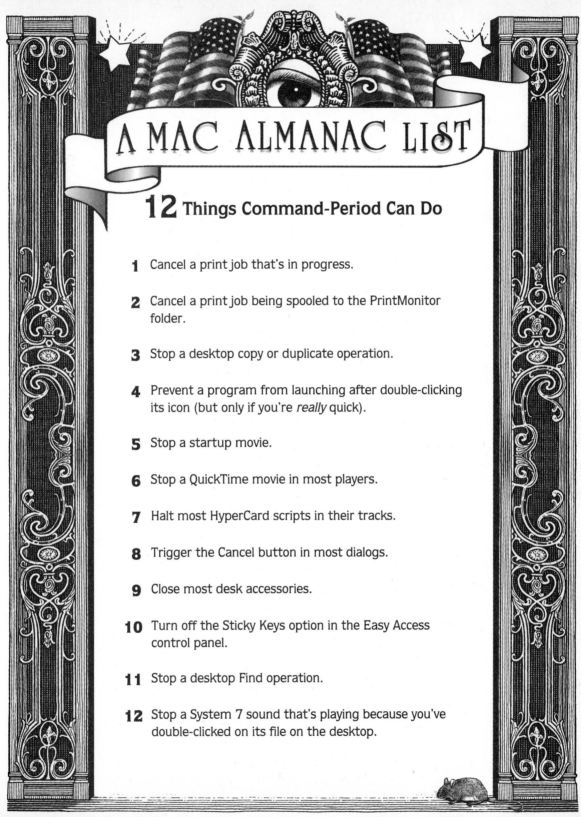

# A MAC ALMANAC LIST

## 12 Things Command-Period Can Do

**1** Cancel a print job that's in progress.

**2** Cancel a print job being spooled to the PrintMonitor folder.

**3** Stop a desktop copy or duplicate operation.

**4** Prevent a program from launching after double-clicking its icon (but only if you're *really* quick).

**5** Stop a startup movie.

**6** Stop a QuickTime movie in most players.

**7** Halt most HyperCard scripts in their tracks.

**8** Trigger the Cancel button in most dialogs.

**9** Close most desk accessories.

**10** Turn off the Sticky Keys option in the Easy Access control panel.

**11** Stop a desktop Find operation.

**12** Stop a System 7 sound that's playing because you've double-clicked on its file on the desktop.

•••❥ **A document doesn't have to stay open** once it's been spooled to the PrintMonitor folder, or—in another handy piece of jargon—after it's been printed to the disk. In fact, the application that created the document doesn't even have to stay open. As long as you keep the Mac on so PrintMonitor can handle the print job, you can work on something else.

## Using the PrintMonitor

∘∘❥ **When the PrintMonitor is active,** it's listed in the Application menu with the other applications. Selecting it from the menu opens its window, shown here.

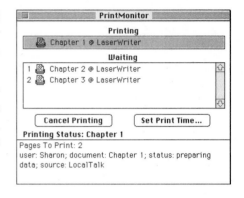

You don't need to open the PrintMonitor window for basic printing, since it works invisibly in the background once you turn on background printing in the Chooser. But the window does provide:

- A status report on the current print job
- A list of waiting documents
- A way to cancel a print job
- A way to delay printing
- A way to change the order of the documents waiting to be printed

∘∘❥ **The PrintMonitor has a Preferences command** but a lot of people don't realize it. Why? Because it's there in a File menu that nobody ever notices, either. But you can use the Preferences command to determine what happens to the PrintMonitor window during a print job, how it should report problems, and how it should handle manual-feed print jobs.

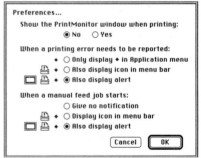

PrintMonitor's Preferences dialog, which so few people ever see.

To get at the File menu, you'll have to double-click PrintMonitor and run it like a regular application; otherwise, the only time it's available is when the print job has already started.

∘∘❥ **The Open and Close commands** in the PrintMonitor's File menu have nothing to do with the documents waiting to be printed; they Open and Close the PrintMonitor window.

∘∘❥ **To cancel a print job** after it's been spooled to the disk, open the PrintMonitor window and click the Cancel Printing button or press Command-period.

➤ **Set the PrintMonitor window to stay open** during a print job. That way, you can get a constant report on how many pages are left to print for the current document. You can position the window so just the line with the page countdown is visible at the bottom of your screen, just peeking out from beneath whatever document you're working on in another application. (I'm spoiled—I can leave the PrintMonitor window open on my second screen.)

➤ **Use any Print or Page Setup options** you want for a print job going to the PrintMonitor, just as if you were printing the document normally.

➤ **When the PrintMonitor needs your attention,** it can discreetly blink its icon in the Application menu, or put up a dialog on the screen to really get your attention. The third option is for its title to be marked with a diamond in the Application menu, but this is so subtle as to be useless. I find that the in-your-face dialog is the best choice in the Preferences dialog.

The PrintMonitor can warn you of printing problems in subtle or obvious ways.

There is a printing problem. Please choose PrintMonitor from the Application menu or click the PrintMonitor window.

OK

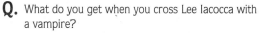

### GET THIS ...

Well, maybe you won't get this, since it's based on at least a surface knowledge of that other operating system.

**Q.** What do you get when you cross Lee Iacocca with a vampire?

**A.** Auto.exec.bat

➤ **When a print job chokes before it's finished** for some reason—maybe the printer was turned off by mistake, or there was a paper jam—you'll see this dialog. If more than just a few pages of the document have already printed, don't use the Try Again button—the entire document is printed again, from

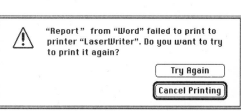

"Report" from "Word" failed to print to printer "LaserWriter". Do you want to try to print it again?

Try Again

Cancel Printing

the first page, no matter where the problem cropped up. Instead, use the Cancel Printing button and start a new print job, specifying a starting page later in the document. UNLESS you don't have the original document available—in which case, let

PrintMonitor start it all over again; if you cancel the printing, the spooled document is erased from the PrintMonitor folder and you won't be able to print it at all.

···❥ **The PrintMonitor needs memory** to do its work. It comes set to about a 115K partition. If it needs more for the current job, a dialog pops up asking if it can allot itself more memory. If you agree, the partition is automatically reset to a higher amount. You can avoid the dialog by upping the PrintMonitor's partition in its Get Info window. Or, if circumstances are more dire, you may see this dialog, which lets you either delay printing or let the Mac give it its full attention.

M<sup>emory</sup>
alloca-
tions are
covered in
Chapter 9.

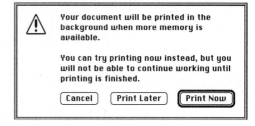

···❥ To **delay a printing job** until a more convenient, time:

1. Turn on background printing through the Chooser.
2. With the document open, use the application's Print command.
3. Choose PrintMonitor from the Application menu. It might take up to half a minute to appear there, but if you wait too long, the print job will start!
4. If the document you just "printed" is the current print job, its name will be selected in the top box. If it's one in a list of waiting documents, select its name in the list.
5. Click the Set Print Time button.
6. In the dialog that opens, set a specific print time (you can type the numbers after you select them, or use the little arrows to change them), or click the Postpone Indefinitely button.

If you have a print job waiting, the document will be listed in the Waiting list, with a clock icon and date if you've set a time, or with a postponed notice if that's the option you chose.

The Set Print Time dialog and how waiting documents are noted in the PrintMonitor window.

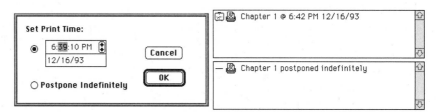

There are good reasons to delay a print job. I just can't think of any. But if I say there aren't any good reasons, somebody will write or call with perfectly valid situations where a delay makes sense and I'll feel very stupid. If you're on a network with high-volume printing during office hours, you could set a print job to start after you've left, I suppose—but then you wouldn't see any reports of problems, and there's no reason you can't just send the print job and let it wait in the queue of waiting documents anyway.

PowerBook users may have more valid reasons—get a document finished, spool it to the PrintMonitor with an indefinite hold order, and print the work when you get back to your printer.

◆ **Another way to delay a printout job** is to open PrintMonitor by double-clicking on its icon (in the Extensions folder) and selecting Stop Printing from its File menu. Any printing you do from then on—with background printing, that is—will be queued in the Waiting list. Nothing will be printed until you use PrintMonitor's Resume Printing command, also in the File menu.

◆ **Beginners and PrintMonitor just don't mix.** Ask any Mac troubleshooter.

The real problem is that most beginners don't even know about PrintMonitor. And here's what happens: Background printing is on. Why? Who knows. The user clicked the button in Chooser, not really knowing what it was. Or figured out what it meant without knowing the details. Or someone else clicked the button. In any case, it's on. But the LaserWriter is off. So the user issues a Print command, clicks the Print button, and sees the usual printing progress reports on the screen—but nothing's coming out of the printer. The document's being sent as a print file to the PrintMonitor folder, where it can't be fed to the printer because the printer's off.

In the meantime, the PrintMonitor preferences are set to discreetly mark the PrintMonitor name in the Application menu if there's a problem—so the user never sees a dialog or a blinking icon to signify a problem. So what happens next? He uses the Print command again. And again. And maybe again.

Eventually—maybe the next day—the LaserWriter gets turned on. And the PrintMonitor jumps into action, sending all those stored print files to the printer. From the user's point of view, the Mac's haunted—the file that refused to print is spewing out of the printer five times the following day, with no print command used at all.*

*Yes, this is an actual case study. The names were omitted to protect the embarrassed.

◆ **Using the LaserWriter 8.0** driver with PrintMonitor has one subtle but, to some people, important difference: with the new driver, the name of the document you're printing isn't broadcast all over the network on everyone else's screens while they're waiting for the printer to be free.

◆ **Your mileage may vary.** Background printing isn't the miracle it sounds like. Since the Mac has to handle both the print job and whatever you're doing, what you're doing slows it down. On older and slower Macs, background printing is nearly useless. On the newer and faster Macs, it can be a boon when the document is short and/or uncomplicated and what you're doing isn't so fancy, either. But try working in something like a graphics program when the Mac isn't always responding immediately and you're courting disaster. You'll click and drag to draw something, and nothing happens, so you do it again. All of a sudden the Mac catches up with you and gives you two objects on the screen when you only wanted one—and your picture is ruined. I never used background printing until I graduated to a speedy '040 machine, and even now I use it only when my "foreground" task is writing that has a lot of thinking behind it—not writing that's hammering out a lot of formatted text.

## Multiple Documents

∞❥ **You can send another document to be printed** even before the first is finished; in fact, the PrintMonitor can keep a whole list of documents in its print queue. If you open PrintMonitor after sending several documents, you'll see the list in the "Waiting" area.

| Waiting | |
|---|---|
| 1 🖳 Chapter 2 @ LaserWriter | |
| 2 🖳 Chapter 3 @ LaserWriter | |
| 3 🖳 Chapter 4 @ LaserWriter | |
| 4 🖳 Chapter 5 @ LaserWriter | |

∞❥ **To get information about a waiting document,** select it in the Waiting list. You'll see how many pages it is, what application created it, and when it was sent to the PrintMonitor.

∞❥ **Remove an item** from the list by selecting it and clicking the Remove button.

•••❥ **Reorganize items in the list** by dragging them up or down; you have to grab an item by its little printer icon (ouch!). If items have a delayed printing set, you won't be able to move them, but all the others can be dragged.

## ❧ THE LASERWRITER UTILITY ❧

## Basics

∞❥ **The LaserWriter Font Utility** program that comes with System 7 has already been superseded by the LaserWriter Utility that comes with the LaserWriter 8.0 driver. Notice the subtle name change? There are also some changes in capabilities, but the basic *raison d'être* for both utilities is the same: you can interact with your LaserWriter in ways that no other part of the Mac's system software makes possible. You can use it for things like checking what fonts are installed in the printer, which are in the printer's memory, what fonts are on the disk attached to the printer (if there is one), download fonts to the printer or its hard drive, set the defaults for the printer … you get the idea.

The LaserWriter Utility (in either incarnation) isn't automatically installed on your hard drive during a system installation, but you'll find it on your system installation disks—probably on a disk named Printing Tools, although system disk names and organization are subject to fluctuation.

∞❥ **Run the LaserWriter Font Utility** or the LaserWriter Utility by double-clicking on it. The earlier version starts out with a brief explanatory dialog; when you click OK, it goes away and you have nothing on the screen that belongs to the program, which can be disconcerting. Run the later version and you'll see a dialog that tells you it's checking the characteristics of your printer; it goes away in a minute or so and there you are facing a blank screen. (Or, more confusingly, a screen that shows only windows that belong to another open application.) Despite the lack of any window, though, the Utility's running, as you can tell from the menu bar. (From here on in, "Utility," with the capital, refers to either version of this program.)

Both versions of the utility
have the same File menu.
The Utilities menu for the
LaserWriter Font Utility (top) is
much smaller than the one in
the newer LaserWriter Utility
(bottom).

**File**
Download Fonts...                ⌘D
Display Available Fonts...       ⌘L
Initialize Printer's Disk...

Page Setup...
Print Font Catalog...            ⌘P
Print Font Samples...

Quit                             ⌘Q

**Utilities**
Download PostScript File...
Start Page Options...
Remove TrueType™...
Restart Printer...

**Utilities**
Name Printer...
Set Startup Page...
Get Page Count...
Imaging Options...
Calibrate Printer...
Configure Communication...
Print Configuration Page...
Download PostScript File...
Remove TrueType™...
Restart Printer...
Change Zone...
Print Density...
Paper Handling...
Power Saving...

The File menus in the two utilities are identical, but the
Utilities menu has been greatly expanded in the later version, as you can see in this picture.

**Utilities**
Name Printer...
Set Startup Page...
Get Page Count...
Imaging Options...
Calibrate Printer...
Configure Communication...
Print Configuration Page...
Download PostScript File...
Remove TrueType™...
Restart Printer...
Change Zone...
Print Density...
Paper Handling...
Power Saving...

∘•➔ **The commands that are actually available** in the
LaserWriter Utility's menus—that is, the ones that aren't
dimmed—depend on the printer you're using.

Remember that flash of a dialog that said *Getting printer
characteristics* when you started the program? Well, that
means the program knows which printer you have and what
it can do. If your printer can't handle multiple printer trays,
the Paper Handling command is dimmed; if there's no hard
disk attached to the printer, the Initialize Printer's Disk
command is dimmed, and so on. The picture here shows
how the Utilities menu looks for my LaserWriter Pro 630.

∘•➔ **If the Utilities menu** is dimmed when you run the Utility, that means your LaserWriter
isn't turned on.

∘•➔ **Keep the Utility listed in the Apple menu** if you find you use it a lot for downloading
fonts, resetting the LaserWriter, or changing its defaults. It's especially handy as a listing
in a submenu if you're using a hierarchical Apple menu utility.

## The File Menu

∘•➔ **A LaserWriter can access fonts from** three places:

- Its ROMs. These are the built-in fonts, also called the *resident* fonts.
- Its memory. These are also referred to as *downloaded* fonts. A printer font is sent
  to the LaserWriter memory from your Fonts folder or Extensions folder at printing
  time. Fonts can also be *manually downloaded* ahead of time by a separate utility.
- A hard drive that's connected to the printer, internally or externally.

Of course, the printer fonts you have on your Mac's hard drive can be sent to the
LaserWriter, but the Mac's in charge of that—the LaserWriter doesn't do the accessing
until after they've been sent to the printer by the Mac.

The commands in the Utility's File menu—with the exception of Page Setup and Quit—let you send fonts to the printer's memory or its hard drive, and check what's already there.

∞❥ **The Display Available Fonts command** lets you see what fonts are built into the LaserWriter or are being held in its memory, and which ones are stored on its hard drive (if it has one).

To see what's on the disk, you click the Printer Disk(s) button. (Bet you could figure that out without me.) But when you click the Printer button, you see a combined list of resident and downloaded fonts, and there's no indication which is which. This picture shows the BluePrint font in the middle of the list of built-in fonts—you can see that you can't tell from how it's listed that it's not one of the built-in ones.

∞❥ **The Print Font Catalog command** prints a list of all the fonts currently available to the LaserWriter: resident, downloaded, and the ones on any attached hard drive.

✳Ever wonder what's so special about that sentence? It has every letter of the alphabet in it.

∞❥ **You can print samples** of all the fonts available to the LaserWriter (resident, in memory, and on its hard drive) with the Print Font Samples command. The samples are a simple *The quick brown fox jumps over the lazy dog\** line for each font available.

••❥ *Manually downloading* **a font** means to send it to the LaserWriter, where it's stored in memory for when it's needed. The advantage to this procedure is that you don't have to wait for the font to be downloaded to the LaserWriter each time you print a document that uses that font. Normally, a font is downloaded by an application and then flushed from the LaserWriter's memory right after the print job, so it has to be downloaded again the next time you print the document. A manually downloaded font remains in the LaserWriter's memory until you turn off the printer. Other fonts may be automatically downloaded and flushed from the memory that remains, but the manually downloaded ones stay there.

To download fonts:

1. Choose Download Fonts from the File menu.
2. Click the Add button in the dialog that opens.
3. In the next dialog, find and select the font you want to add to the download list. Click the Add button. (Or just double-click on the font in the list and skip the button click.)
4. Use the Add button for any other fonts you want downloaded at the same time. Use the Done button when you're finished selecting fonts.

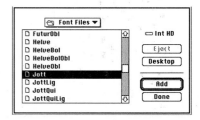

5. The next dialog lets you review the list of fonts to be downloaded. If everything's okay, click the Download button. Make sure, if you have a hard drive attached to the printer but you want to download the files to the printer's memory, that you have the Printer button, not the Printer's Disk button, selected at the top of the dialog.

You'll get a progress report during the download process, and a confirmation dialog when it's finished.

• • • • • • • • • • • • • • • • • • • • • • • • • •
The series of dialog box you'll see while setting up a font download.

• • • • • • • • • • • • • • • • • • • • • • • • • •
The download progress and confirmation reports.

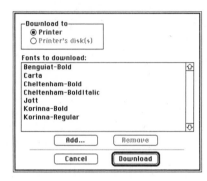

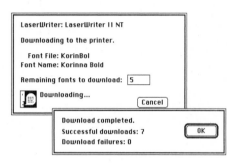

Working with a LaserWriter's hard drive is covered in Chapter 16.

••➤ **Remove downloaded fonts** from the printer's memory by selecting the Download Fonts command, but then use the Remove button after selecting a font in the list. You'll have to do this if the LaserWriter is running out of memory because you're using so many fonts or printing complicated graphics. Resetting the LaserWriter (by turning it off and then on again, or by using the Reset command in the Utilities menu) removes *all* the downloaded fonts from its memory, but the Remove button lets you remove just a select few.

∞➢ **LaserStatus** is a nifty font-downloading utility that's much more convenient to use than the Apple utilities. It lets you create and use "sets" of fonts to download all at once, so if you're working on a project that requires certain fonts, you don't have to pick them one by one from a list every time you want them sent to the LaserWriter. [CE Software]

•••➤ **You can't download TrueType fonts** to the LaserWriter's memory, but you *can* download them to a LaserWriter's hard drive, where they'll be accessed faster than if you leave them on the Mac's drive.

## The Utilities Menu

∞➤ **The Utilities menu** changes according to which version of the Utility you're using, and which printer you're working with, as I mentioned before. But I mention it again in relation to this sad fact: The days when I used to be able to round up every detail of every printer in a short book chapter are gone. So I'm wimping out and covering only the most common and most useful of the commands here. For the rest, you'll have to (*gulp!*) see your printer manual!

◦◦◗ **Each time you start the LaserWriter,** it prints a test sheet that identifies the characteristics of the printer and how many pages it has printed so far in its lifetime. Pretty much a waste of paper—though it kept us tipsters in business with clever ways to avoid that printout (like pulling out the paper tray a little bit when you start the printer). But both versions of the

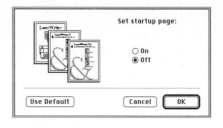

LaserWriter Utility provide a simple command to suppress the *start page,* or *startup page,* as it's called. In the older Utility, use the Start Page Options command; the newer one has a Set Startup Page command. In either case, you get a dialog something like the one shown here.

◦◦◗ **When the startup page** doesn't print, you don't get constant reports of how many pages your printer has churned out. So, to satisfy your curiosity (or that of the person who's buying your used printer), use the Get Page Count command and you'll see a dialog like the ones here. (Oh, okay—it's only the middle one you'll see. I got carried away doing the illustration.)

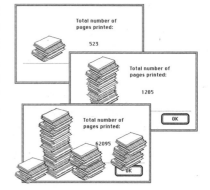

◦◦◗ **Restarting the printer** erases what's in its memory—downloaded fonts and certain initialization information. Sometimes you need the fonts cleared because you need the memory to print a complicated graphic. Or, sometimes the printer has been initialized (started up) with a driver that's incompatible with the

one you're using. Turning the printer off and on again clears its memory. But if the printer isn't easily available physically (as when you're on a network) or if, as in my case, the on/off switch isn't easily reached, you can use the Restart Printer command instead.

◦◦◗ **Give your LaserWriter a name.** You think it likes being identified by its generic model name, like tens of thousands of other printers with no personality?

Actually, naming a LaserWriter is only necessary if you're on a network where you have to be able to tell the difference between printers so you don't mistakenly print to a different office or building. But you can name your printer just to personalize your system if you want. Use the Name Printer command in the LaserWriter Utility.

The LaserWriter Font Utility doesn't have a Name Printer command, but it comes with a little application called Namer that you use to name the printer.

## A ROSE BY ANY OTHER NAME ...

There must be a lot of clever LaserWriter names out there, don't you think? At Montclair State University in New Jersey there are several Mac labs with named printers. The lab that's in the same building as the traditional printing equipment has printers named A.B. Dick and Davidson. But the inspired names are in the lab in Chapin Hall: They're named Harry and Tom. I asked online for comments on interesting LaserWriter names. Here are some of the notes I received back:

- One of my favorites was at a bank in NYC: Gzunda, because the printer goes under the desk.—*Wiggo*

- The nicest I've seen is Aethelred. If you're an English history buff, no doubt you remember Aethelred the Unready. Need I explain?—*Lofty Becker*

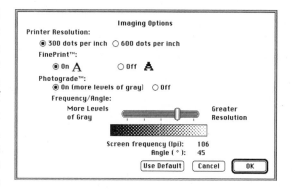

- Our original LaserWriter II NTX is named "Lasey Boy" (Lasey from Laser), and our new IIg is named "gThePrinter," which is a MacApp joke. In our contest to name the IIg, other suggestions were "Linkletter," and "Chia Print" (late night TV references). "Thighmaster" could also be considered because it's a kind of "toner."—*Stoney Ballard*

- One of our original LaserWriters (not even a LaserWriter Plus) is named "Decrepit Paper Creaser," because that's what it does if you print too many pages at one time. I also heard of a guy who had a printer that he didn't want people on the network to use because he kept it loaded with special paper, so he called it "Broken."—*Phil Reed*

- The best name I've seen is "Godot." Of course, it's only effective if you don't use background printing.—*Manuel Veloso*

SHAKESPEARE
*ROMEO AND JULIET*, II:2

What's in a name?

**The Imaging Options command** lets you set defaults for your LaserWriter if it has options like 300 vs. 600 dpi resolution, or FinePrint or PhotoGrade that can be turned on and off. This is one of those items I'm leaving to your LaserWriter manual to detail; but, since I mentioned earlier in this chapter how to override these options through the Print dialog's Option dialog, I did want to mention them in passing here.

# ❧ SPECIAL PRINTING CONSIDERATIONS ❧

## Paper & Special Stock

○○◗ **For an ImageWriter,** the quality of the paper is not as much of an issue as for other printers; a lot more depends on the ink ribbon. What you really want to watch for on ImageWriter paper is how cleanly the edges tear off when you're using tractor-feed paper.

○○◗ **For a StyleWriter,** clay-coated paper made especially for inkjet printers works the best. Because the ink is sprayed onto the paper by the StyleWriter, the tiny blobs spread on porous paper, making the printout less sharp than it should be. Clay-coated paper—if you're willing to pay the extra money for it—keeps the spread from spreading.

○○◗ **"Laser paper" isn't just a marketing ploy.** Special papers really do work better with LaserWriters than standard typing paper. But that doesn't mean that the laser paper is expensive—because it's the same type of paper that photocopiers use. Both LaserWriters and photocopiers use an electrical charge to put flakes of toner onto the paper in the right spots, then fuse the toner to the paper with heat. So, you need paper that reacts well to both an electrical charge and heat.

> The American wasps form very fine paper ... they seem to teach us that paper can be made from the fibers of plants without the use of rags and linen ....

RENÉ-ANTOINE FERCHAULT DE RÉAMUR
1719, when paper was still being made from cloth

○○◗ **Extra-smooth paper** isn't good for LaserWriter printing, since the toner won't stick. On the other hand, toner flakes off paper that's too textured. (The last time I was rounding up this type of information was when I was working on the 3rd Edition of the Macintosh Bible. My friend Carol showed me some paper that didn't work well with LaserWriters; the paper was of a textured type referred to in the business as *laid*. I was going to write it up under the heading *Don't get laid*, but I thought better of it.)

○•◗ **Paper should be stored** in its wrapping even, or especially, after opening a package to use some of it. Paper that's exposed to air absorbs moisture, and moist paper—even though it feels dry to the touch—tends to curl as it goes through the printing process.

○•◗ **Sometimes cheaper is better.** Expensive paper is "dusted" to keep the pages from sticking together in high humidity. But on a LaserWriter, the powder used for the dusting sometimes gets fused right onto the paper along with the toner, resulting in a slightly bumpy surface.

○•◗ **Printing on thick stock**—special papers or envelopes—takes a little extra attention.

Most LaserWriters let you open a secondary output door to let thick stock come through without having to be bent around a second set of rollers to come out normally. Check your LaserWriter manual for your specific model instructions.

On StyleWriters, there are two manual adjustments you should make. The first is easy to remember—it's the lever on the feeder tray, which has to be in the "envelope" position, by the envelope icon. The second adjustment is on the ink cartridge itself: open the front panel of the StyleWriter to get at it, and flip the little blue lever pointing to the envelope icon.

➤ **Printing envelopes** can really be a chore. There's the mechanical problem of getting them through the printer, and the formatting problem of getting everything to print correctly. Here are some pointers:

- For an ImageWriter, tractor-feed (perforated) envelopes probably feed through the best—but they're the least convenient if you're only printing a few envelopes—and then you have to tear them apart, too.
- For a LaserWriter, make sure you get envelopes whose glue can make it through the heat of printing without sealing themselves closed.
- You can get envelopes attached to full-size sheets of paper that are made for using with computer printers that don't like handling something the size of an envelope by itself.
- Test your output on plain paper first to see if things are landing where you expect them to. Then test a single envelope, not an entire print job. You'll find you'll have a lot of tweaking to do to get the return address and the main address in the right spots. (You might not even get them on the right *side* of the envelope the first time.) Use the Page Setup options to arrange sideways printing; that usually works better than the normal vertical orientation (which is the *short* dimension of the envelope, top to bottom).
- Feed an envelope through the LaserWriter longways so it won't drop out between the sets of rollers that bring it into the LaserWriter and the ones that feed it back out.

➤ **Don't print transparencies** on a LaserWriter unless the film is made to take the heat of a LaserWriter. Standard transparency film can melt inside the LaserWriter, where the temperature can reach 400° to melt the toner. Imaging Products provides a wide range of laser printer products, including five different colors of transparencies.

➤ **Printing labels** has always been more difficult than it should be. On the ImageWriter, you had the problem of labels peeling off when the ImageWriter rolled the platen backwards at the beginning of a page. (Or when *you* rolled it backwards while getting it aligned.) On a LaserWriter, programs always allowed for the fact that LaserWriters can't print to the edge of a page—but the sheet of labels didn't, with the labels evenly distributed across the length and breadth of the sheet.

Here are some things to keep in mind when you're printing labels, whether you're working in a program that specifically makes labels, or from a word processor document that you've set up:

- Never roll a sheet of labels backwards in an ImageWriter.
- On a LaserWriter, use labels specifically made for laser printing. The heat in the LaserWriter can melt the glue on the back of standard label sheets, even those labeled "for computers"—because the assumption is that they're being printed on

a dot-matrix printer like the ImageWriter. Avery and 3M both make a wide variety of LaserWriter labels.

- Do a test print on regular paper. Sacrifice a sheet of labels for a template by peeling off the labels, leaving only the surrounding gridwork still stuck on the sheet. Put the sheet over the test printout and hold them up to the light. Does everything line up? Fine, print the labels. If not, go back and tweak the document. This low-tech approach is the only one guaranteed to work.

❖ **Print in color** without a color printer. When you need color to make an impact, there are several ways you can go about it:

- Use colored paper. You can buy laser paper in pastel or neon shades. My kids use the neon shades when they're printing up party invitations or school report covers. I use bright colors for special lists, like project due dates, that I stick up on my bulletin board. I sometimes use pastel shades to color-code things for special projects. You might want to perk up a newsletter with a nice colored stock.

- Use colored toner for a LaserWriter. You can get toner cartridges in blue and brown, and sometimes in other colors. Brown print on cream paper is classy; so is dark blue ink on light blue or gray paper.

- Use color ribbons in an ImageWriter. Ribbons come in the one-color variety as well as a multi-colored style with four bands of color: black, yellow, red, and blue. A multi-color ribbon doesn't last long, though, because to get any colors besides the ones on the ribbon, multiple passes are used, ruining one band or another pretty quickly. (What happens, for instance, with printing green is that a pass is made using the blue band of the ribbon, and then a pass with the yellow band. As the pins from the printhead hit the yellow part of the ribbon against the area of the paper that's already been printed in blue, some of the blue ink gets smeared onto the yellow, ruining that part of the ribbon for any further yellow printing.)

- Use printed paper. PaperDirect is one of the companies that provides pre-printed papers for LaserWriters in many styles, ranging from marbleized patterns to fancy borders. They even have paper that's pre-printed so you can make a trifold brochure out of it.

- Apply spot color after the fact. You print your document as usual, then stick a small piece of special colored film over the areas you want colored. You run it through the LaserWriter again by printing a blank page from your word processor; the heat from the LaserWriter melts the film only onto the areas that already had toner applied from the first printing. When the paper comes out, you peel away the extra, leaving colored highlights where you need them. You can get the special film from companies like PaperDirect and through mail-order catalogs that offer computer printing supplies.

attributed to
HENRY FORD

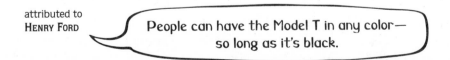
People can have the Model T in any color—
so long as it's black.

➤ **Print on a T-shirt.** Well, not directly—but you can print with special ink in the LaserWriter to make an iron-on transfer that you can put onto the T-Shirt. Easy Transfer Cartridges—that's the name of both the company and the cartridges—are filled with special color ink that dries on good paper to make an iron-on transfer. (Don't forget to choose the Flip Horizontal option in Page Setup first so that by the time you iron the image onto the fabric, it prints the right way instead of as a mirror image.)

## Service Bureaus & Printers

➤ A *service bureau* is a place you take your files to be processed and printed at a higher resolution than you can do on your printer. It might offer laser printing, if that's what you're looking for, but most service bureaus offer *imagesetting* on a device that offers resolution way higher than your LaserWriter. Most use Linotronic imagesetters.

Whether you're taking your files to a service bureau for a hundred copies of a collated newsletter, or a thousand business cards, or a single high-resolution or color print, you have to keep in mind that your file's going to be printed from a different Mac than you used, and on a different printer than you used for your proofs.

Some service bureaus offer only the imaging end of things, giving you a single film or printout that you would then take to a traditional printer for a copy or copies to be made. But these days, a service bureau and printer are usually the same shop, so I'll be using the terms interchangeably.

➤ **Make sure the printer has the right fonts.** (I'm referring to the printer *person* here, not the printer *machine*, but I guess you can read that either way.) If the Mac at the service bureau doesn't have the font you used, bring it with you so it can be installed for your print job.

Most font vendors realize that this kind of font use is necessary and have no objections. The implicit understanding is that when the print job is over, you or the printer will remove the font from the shop's Mac so no one else will use it.

➤ **See if the printer has the application** you used to create your document. If he has Quark Xpress and PageMaker available and yours is a LetsDoLayout document, he's not going to be able to open and print it. You can either bring your application (although the printer's not going to like having to do a temporary install job just to print your document), or create a PostScript file of your document that the printer can download directly to his machine.

➤ **Prepare your document with the right driver.** If you use an ImageWriter and want a final LaserWriter printout, you're going to have a problem: a LaserWriter puts a lot more on a page because it can put a little more on each line of text. You'll find your line breaks, and then your page breaks, will change going from one printer to another. To proof your document for a printer you don't have, all you need is the printer driver. Select the printer driver in Chooser (it doesn't care that the actual printer is nowhere to be found) and then open your document. Choose the Page Setup command, then cancel the dialog. The document will reformat itself as it will be printed on the remote printer, and you can check where your line breaks and page breaks are.

Ask your service bureau what driver you should use to format your document.

···❯ **Get all your support files together.** Some applications, like QuarkXpress don't store all the document elements in the document itself. You may think you've imported a graphic to an Xpress document, but the real thing is still a separate file on the disk. Try printing the document without the original file, and you'll get a blank spot in the document or an ugly print of the screen representation of the image.

### THE MAC MAN

I had the pleasure of hearing Andy Hertzfeld, Mac programmer extraordinaire, speak at Princeton, ages ago when his Switcher utility was the way you ran more than one program at a time on the Mac. He described one of Steve Jobs' unimplemented Mac ideas: the Mac Man.

Jobs, whose moods apparently fluctuated between rage and euphoric enthusiasm during the course of the Mac project, came into the programmer's den all excited one day, with a great idea: How about if, at random intervals—say every thousandth or so menu pull-down—a little Mac man appeared on the screen waving at you. Wouldn't that be *great?*

And the marketing people fussed about the frivolity of the Puzzle desk accessory!

···❯ **Theoretically, you can proof on a LaserWriter** and do a final print to an imagesetter like a Linotronic, because they're both PostScript devices and should handle the page the same way. But that's theory. In practice, there are differences between the LaserWriter and an imagesetter that can affect the final output:

- There's no font substitution available on imagesetters. Don't count on the LaserWriter's automatic font substitution (Times for New York, Helvetica for Geneva, Courier for Monaco); make sure your document is formatted with the fonts you want printed.
- Most LaserWriters have Helvetica Narrow built in. Imagesetters don't. You'll need the right printer file if you're using Helvetica Narrow in your document.
- LaserWriters can't print to the edge of the page. Imagesetters can.
- Imagesetters don't offer any bitmap smoothing for graphics the way LaserWriters do.
- The shades of gray available from a LaserWriter pale in comparison (literally) to the ones available from an imagesetter. Or is it the other way around? If your graphics include grays, even if it's just gray boxes behind print for shaded areas of text, plan a test print to see what shade of gray you're really going to get.
- Imagesetters don't always handle PICT format images too well. Save them as TIFFs or EPS documents, where you can, for more foolproof printing.

···❯ *Going to Lino* is a phrase that means you're getting a high-resolution imagesetter printout. It comes from the name of the machine, a Linotronic—the first imagesetter to offer an easy hookup for a Mac. But the service bureau may well be using a different brand imagesetter, like VariTyper. It surely upsets the Linotronic company to have its name used generically, since that's how companies lose trademarks. But wouldn't you think that the other companies that make imagesetters get even *more* upset?

## → SYSTEM 7.5 STUFF ←

### Desktop Printing

∞→ **The GX technology in System 7.5** promises better fonts and graphics printing—but you need the cooperation of the application you're using to fulfill that promise. Until applications are re-written to use GX capabilities, we'll have to make do with what we already have—except for *desktop printing*, which is a provided in System 7.5 with a new Chooser and GX printer drivers.

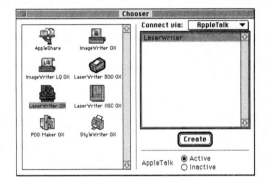

The new Chooser has two new items in it which are immediately obvious: a Connect popup menu and a Create button. (You'll also see some new printer drivers displayed in the left panel.)

∞→ **Use the Connect menu** to specify the type of connection you're using for printing.

∞→ **Use the Create button** to create a "desktop printer" from the printer you've selected in the Chooser's list. What's a desktop printer? Well, first it's an icon that looks like the one here—the dark outline around it means that it's currently the default printer.

How do I know this is a desktop printer? Its Info window tells me so, as you can see here.

Okay, but what can you *do* with it? Well, if you drag a document icon into this icon, it will print to that printer. Pretty neat, but not revolutionary—there have been utilities around that do the same thing, and besides, who wants to go from an application to the desktop, dig through folders, find a document and then drag it onto this icon?

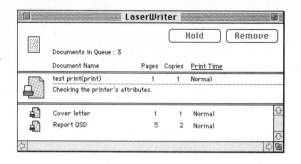

•••❯ Double-clicking on the desktop **printer** icon opens a window that gives information similar to the PrintMonitor: you'll see a list of print jobs, and the status of each. You can remove an item from the list with the Remove button, or set it to print at another time by using the Hold button.

PART FOUR

# Hardware

# CHAPTER 13
# HARDWARE BASICS

I can design computers. I know I can.

STEVE WOZNIAK
designer of Apple computers

The fascinating tidbits you'll find in this chapter include:

- The difference between RAM and ROM.
- How the size of the Mac's ROMs has increased from 64K to 4096K over the years.
- How the Mac's clock rate compares to your heartbeat.
- What a "zero footprint" is.
- What a SIMM is, and what kind your Mac needs.
- Just how short a picosecond is.
- Why a 20-meg Mac could be worth $768,000.
- The first two light bulb jokes.

## WHY THIS CHAPTER IS SPECIAL

*I*t has more acronyms than any other chapter. For instance: SIMM, PMMU, ROM, RAM, FPU, DSP, SCSI, PDS, ADB.

page 520

—Includes—

100 Factoids
3 Memos
7 Quotable Quotes
*and* 12 tables!

## → COMPONENTS ←

## The ROMs

∘∘•⟩ **This entire section** is written apologetically. I'm really sorry you have to know about all these terms and technical issues; it doesn't feel much like a Mac anymore when we lapse into real computerese, talking about *chips* and *clock speeds* and *data paths*.

But when you're making decisions about buying or upgrading equipment, or even about which kind of software to use, you really do have to know about these things. How else can you figure out what you want and need, and what's compatible with what?

Chapter 23 discusses the software end of the operating system.

∘∘•⟩ **ROM stands for** *read-only memory*. It's read-only because you can use the information that's in it, but you can't change it or add to it. The information in the Mac's ROMs works along with that in the System Folder to act as the Mac's *operating system*.

∘∘•⟩ **There are lots of programs stored** in the Mac's ROMs. QuickDraw, a set of routines that controls how lines, shapes, and colors are displayed on the screen, is there, as are all sorts of "managers," like the Menu Manager and the Window Manager. Having all these routines stored in ROM makes the Mac a Mac, and makes it consistent. A programmer doesn't have to write a routine to create a window or make it scroll, or to make a menu. The programmer has only to specify certain parameters (like the size of the window, or the commands in the menu) and then use the routines already built into the Mac.

∘∘•⟩ **The ROMs in the original Macs** were 64K. The Mac Plus ROMs were 128K, while the Mac II debuted with hefty 256K ROMs. By the time Macs started using 68030 chips, beginning with the SE/30, they needed 512K ROMs. It didn't stop there: The Quadras' ROMs are a full megabyte—1024K of permanent instructions. The AV's doubled that. And the Power Macs doubled *that*, so they have an incredible 4 megs of ROM.

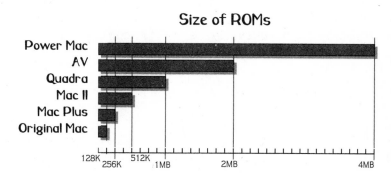

Size of ROMs

∘∘•⟩ **The phrase** *color ROM* has nothing to do with the color of the ROM chips themselves. It has to do with what's *in* the ROMs: the ability to "think" in color, creating color images on a color-capable screen. A Mac with color ROMs can produce color even if, like the SE/30, it has only a black-and-white monitor. What's the use? If you connect a color monitor to the system, you can get color output.

## The Processor

∞♦ **The Mac's brain is its CPU,** or *central processing unit*. It's also referred to as the *processor*, *processor chip*, or just *chip* (although there are plenty of other chips in there).

Processor chips are usually referred to by the numbers the manufacturer uses to identify them. The Mac's CPUs are Motorola chips; early Macs used the 68000 chip, but other models have used the 68020, 68030, or 68040 chip. (Power Macs use an entirely different processor chip—more about that later.)

∞♦ **The higher a chip's number,** the more advanced it is; this results in a faster, more powerful computer. There are also some things that you just can't do without a more advanced chip. System 7's virtual memory feature can't be used, for instance, without a 68030 chip or its equivalent.

**SQUEEZE PLAY**

Ever wonder why the number 68000 was used to identify the chip that was used in the original Mac? No, you probably didn't. But you're about to find out why anyway.

The chip is so named because it has 68,000 transistors inscribed on it. Really! This is, of course, even more impressive than the current record for inscribing the most characters on a grain of rice (1,749).

So, does the '040 chip have 40 more transistors? No, it's more like 40 times as many: 1.2 *million* transistors are etched into that little baby!

Now, how many angels, do you suppose, can dance on the head of a pixel?

∞♦ **Chips have nicknames,** more or less. There's no affectionate little appellation for the 68000, but a 68030 is referred to as an "oh-thirty" for its trailing numbers, which are the important ones; the written abbreviation is *'030*. It's handy to have these brief names because it makes it easy to refer to a whole class of Macs—the '040s, for instance. Here's a quick chart of chip names:

| Chip | Pronounced... | Short name | Pronounced... |
|------|---------------|------------|---------------|
| 68000 | sixty-eight thousand | - | - |
| 68020 | sixty-eight oh-twenty | 020 | oh-twenty |
| 68030 | sixty-eight oh-thirty | 030 | oh-thirty |
| 68040 | sixty-eight oh-forty | 040 | oh-forty |

When you're referring to any of the chips in the 68000 line, without wanting to specify only one of them, you use the number 680x0. (I suppose you could *say* "oh-ex-oh," but I've never heard anyone do that.)

•••♦ **The phrase CPU** (well, it's not really a *phrase*, exactly) also refers the boxy component of a modular Mac's setup—the part that contains the real CPU as well as the internal hard drive. So, you can say, "Connect the monitor to the CPU," and you're talking about the box, not the processor chip.

···❯ **The differences from one processor** to the next are sometimes subtle and sometimes major. If you're just dying to know a little more about the technical end, here it is:

- The 68020 was an improvement over the 68000 by, first and foremost, being a true 32-bit processor. The 68000 chip handles information 32 bits at a time internally, but talks to the rest of the computer in 16-bit chunks. The 68020 handles 32-bit bundles all the time. It also contains a 256-byte instruction cache to hold recently (and frequently) used information for faster reference; the cache can increase some areas of performance by 40 percent. Finally, the '020 can work at faster clock rates—up to 33 MHz, as opposed to the 68000's 16 MHz limit.

- The 68030 chip has several improvements over the '020. First, it has a built-in PMMU, the *paged memory management unit* that lets the Mac use System 7's virtual memory feature. It has a 256-byte data cache in addition to the instruction cache, and it has two "data paths" (buses), that each handle 32 bits at a time—giving it the power to process two things at the same time.

- The 68040 chip includes most of the functions of an FPU (math coprocessor). Like the '030, it has two caches, one each for data and instructions; but, at 4K, the caches are *sixteen* times the size of the '030's.

- The 68LC040 is a special version of the 68040 that doesn't include the math coprocessor functions.

- The 68HC000 is a special low-power version of the 68000 chip, used only in the PowerBook 100.

## THE MAC'S ORIGINAL PROCESSOR

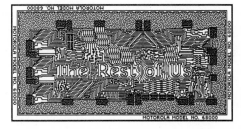

*—from BMUG PD-ROM*

···❯ **The Power Macs** use a processor that's also from Motorola, but it's not in the 68000 family. It's an entirely new chip, one that uses RISC (reduced instruction set computing) technology that is not only inherently faster, it also can run at clock speeds of 60, 80, and 100 MHz! (It's not often that you get to use exclamation points in a computer book.)

Power Macs have their own section later in this chapter.

## Coprocessors

···❯ A *coprocessor* is pretty much what it sounds like—another processing chip. Although the *co* prefix makes it sound like an equal partner, the common coprocessors used in the Mac are pretty much subordinate to the main processor.

∘•➔ **The *FPU* is the most common** coprocessor in the Mac world. In fact, it's so common that when Mac people use the phrase *the coprocessor*, they mean the FPU.

FPU stands for *floating point unit*. That may sound like an anti-gravity component or some transcendental meditative assistant, but a *floating point* is just a kind of number. The FPU is a *math coprocessor*. It handles complicated calculations more quickly than the main processor can. The main processor hands off difficult math problems to the coprocessor chip, and everything works much more quickly. One of the reasons it works faster is that it has certain values—numbers like 0, 1, and even pi (more or less)—and some basic mathematical functions built in. This saves a lot of basic calculating time.

The Mac's math coprocessor, like its main chip, is from Motorola. The Mac II had the 68881 coprocessor; since then, the faster 68882 has been used instead.

∘•➔ **Speed isn't the only benefit** derived from an FPU; accuracy is another. With the coprocessor, the Mac is mathematically accurate to 18 places after the decimal point; without the coprocessor, accuracy drops to 14 places.

∘•➔ **You don't need an FPU. Maybe.** It depends on what you're doing with your Mac. Word processing, doing even reasonably complicated spreadsheets, working with a database, using page layout programs, or playing QuickTime movies—none of these is speeded up by a math coprocessor.

A math coprocessor crunches the numbers in an extremely complicated spreadsheet more quickly than the main processor can, but it's not just number-crunching programs that the FPU speeds up. *Everything* in the Mac is numbers—even if *you're* working with pictures. So, high-end graphics programs like CAD (computer-aided-design) and 3-D modeling programs both need a math coprocessor, too, because of the vast number of calculations needed to keep track of complicated images.

∘•➔ **A PMMU is another coprocessor** commonly used in the Mac. PMMU stands for *paged memory management unit*; this processor is necessary for virtual memory.

Since the PMMU is built into the 68030 (and later) processors, you don't hear much about it anymore. But it wasn't built into the 68000 or 68020 chip, so sometimes you'll see a phrase like: *an '030 machine or a Mac II with a PMMU*.

••➔ **The '040 Macs** (see, I told you the name comes in handy to refer to a class of Macs) don't need separate math coprocessors. Most of the FPU's functions are built into the '040 chip.

••➔ **There are several other** coprocessors built into later-model Macs. The AV's, for instance, have special coprocessors (called DSPs—*digital signal processors*) that help speed up data transfers, especially when you're working with sound. But the FPU and the PMMU are the coprocessors you should know by name and function.

## Speed

∞→ **A computer's *clock rate*,** or *clock speed*, governs how fast it can do its processing, which, in turn, controls things like how often the picture on the screen is redrawn and when the CPU checks the mouse or keyboard for input.

A computer's clock is a quartz crystal that beats millions of time each second in response to an electric current. *Hertz* is a measurement of cycles (or beats) per second; *megahertz*—abbreviated *MHz*—is a million cycles per second. The earliest Macs ticked away at a mere 8 million cycles per second, or 8 MHz. Today's models using the same 680x0 chip family run at 16, 25, 33, or even 40 MHz. (Power Macs whiz by at 60 and 80 MHz with a different processor chip.)

### PALPITATIONS

The quartz crystal that keeps ticking inside your Mac beats more often in two minutes than your heart will in your entire lifetime.

∞→ **The *data path*, or *bus*,** is what information travels on inside the Mac's circuits. The wider the path, the faster the machine works because more information can be moved at one time, without the data moving any quicker. The path is measured according to how much information can be moved in one chunk: a 16-bit or a 32-bit path.

Macs based on the 68000 chip move 16 bits at a time on the bus; the data buses in most other Macs are usually twice as wide, handling 32 bits at a time.

A narrow data path can cripple the speed of a computer. The LC uses an '020 processor; the LC II an '030. They both run at 16 MHz, but the LC II should be faster because the '030 chip is inherently faster. But they both perform at just about the same overall speed because despite the faster processor in one, they both use a 16-bit data path.

•••→ **There are many factors that affect the speed** of your Mac—it's not just a matter of the clock rate and data path. There are so many different components, and there's a wide range of speed capabilities for each. Unless all the components are matched in speed, there'll be a bottleneck someplace. Here are some of the things that affect the overall speed of your system:

- The processor is the crux of the matter. Each advancement in chip design increases the Mac's speed because there are more instructions and routines built in, which means there's less to be figured out on the fly. In fact, the speed improvement with each chip advancement is enough to outweigh a faster clock rate: An '040 chip at 25 MHz will outperform an '030 chip running at 33 MHz.

- The presence of various coprocessors speeds up the Mac's operations in many ways. An FPU, for instance, take a lot of the processing burden off the main processor for complicated calculations; a PMMU helps manage memory details.

- The clock speed paces the computer's processor, telling it when to move on to the next item in its series of instructions. You can't just put a super-fast clock in your Mac to increase its speed, because each processor has an upper limit at how fast it can work; but an '030 chip running at 25 MHz will give you a faster computer than an '030 running at 16 MHz.

- The size of the data path (the bus width) affects how quickly information can move from one place to another inside the computer. You might have a speedy processor with a fast clock rate which sometimes twiddles its thumbs, because the information coming into or leaving it isn't moving fast enough.

- The speed of the Mac's hard drive(s) is something most people forget to take into account; there's a considerable difference from one drive to another both in *access time* (how long it takes to find something) and *data transfer rate* (reading or writing the information).

- The SCSI transfer rate is another bottleneck for the Mac. You can move information through a SCSI connection only at a certain speed, and no faster, no matter how much work your Mac has done internally. SCSI transfer rates vary in different Mac models.

- The monitor is often the slowest component of a Mac system. The monitor itself is not usually the problem (although monitors vary in their "refresh rates," as discussed in Chapter 15); the real bottleneck is getting the screen information, which is in QuickDraw format, through the video card to the monitor. Some video cards include acceleration for this part of the Mac's performance.

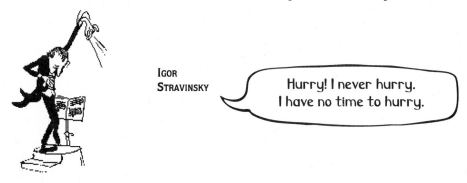

IGOR
STRAVINSKY

Hurry! I never hurry.
I have no time to hurry.

## Slots

°°•➤ **A *slot* is** an internal connector in the computer that accepts *cards* or *boards*—additional computing power that you can just snap in. A *video board*, for instance, contains all the circuitry you'd need to run an extra-large video monitor. One edge of the card slides into the slot inside the computer case, and one edge, with its connector for the video cable, pokes through an opening in the CPU case.

SIMMs? More about them a little later in this chapter.

°•➤ **There's a PDS slot** in some Mac models. This *processor direct slot* is special in that any board in the slot is connected directly to the main logic board and becomes a working part of the main processor.

°•➤ **A SIMM slot** is a slot that holds a SIMM—a small board that contains extra memory for your Mac. Most Macs have SIMM slots, although their size and number vary from one model to another.

•→ **Most modular Macs have NuBus slots** for expansion purposes. You slide the card—which can range from 4 to 14 inches in length—into the slot and off you go. Okay, maybe you'll need a new control panel or extension to control the settings for the new card or whatever's attached to it, but the installation is still a breeze due to the NuBus architecture, which is *self-arbitrating*. Huh? On a PC, when you install a new board, you have to fiddle with tiny switches and jumpers so the computer knows the card is there. Even worse, when you have more than one card, you have to set them up correctly so the computer will know which one has priority. The NuBus architecture takes care of all of that for you: The Mac knows what cards are installed and they all work together harmoniously without your having to do anything.

•→ **The most popular NuBus card** is a video card for a monitor hookup. But there are many other types of cards that go into NuBus slots. A NuBus card can basically have a whole computer in its circuitry, so there's a wide range of cards that can go in the slots. For instance:

- An accelerator card boosts your Mac's speed either by helping with the processing or by taking over from a slower built-in processor.
- A network card can provide Ethernet capability to the Macs that don't come with it.
- A frame-grabber board lets you capture video images from an attached video setup so you can manipulate them on the Mac.
- Houdini. Who? DOS emulation for the Mac: Plug in this whimsically named card and your Mac pretends to be an IBM-PC clone. (This was a long-awaited capability quickly eclipsed by the Power Mac approach of being able to run either (or both) operating systems.)

•→ **The AV Macs have a special type of NuBus** slot that uses a standard known as *NuBus-90*, which provides faster data transfer than the standard NuBus.

## Ports

•→ **A *port* is an external connector** on your computer that's used for plugging in peripheral hardware. *Port* is the general term out there in computerdom, but you may find that the more generic term *connector* is often used in Mac discussions.

You won't have much trouble connecting peripheral devices to your Mac. With few exceptions, the ports are different shapes so you won't be able to plug cable A into port B. The only shapes that are interchangeable are the sound input and output ports, and the printer and modem ports. But each is clearly labeled—and nothing terrible will happen if you switch the printer to the modem port or vice versa.

•→ ***Serial* and *parallel*** are the two main types of ports. The words describe how information travels across the cables and through the connectors. A serial port handles a stream of data one bit at a time; your Mac, which is dealing with 16- and 32-bit chunks of data, has to break up the chunks and make the bits walk single file through a serial port. A parallel port handles at least 8 bits at a time, the way a multi-lane highway lets cars travel in parallel instead of in a single line. Obviously, parallel ports keep data moving faster than do serial ports.

ANON.

Any port in a storm.

∘∘◗ **The ADB port** on your Mac is the one you use for your keyboard and mouse. ADB stands for Apple Desktop Bus (remember, a *bus* is what information travels on); as you might suspect, it's a Mac-specific connection you don't find elsewhere in the computing world.

Most Macs have a single ADB port; some have two. Since you can chain ADB devices—you plug your mouse into the keyboard, for example, and the keyboard into the ADB port on the computer—one ADB port is enough for several devices.

ADB issues are covered in Chapter 14.

∘∘◗ **Macs have internal speakers**—that's how you can hear the various warning beeps and startup chimes that they make. But they also have a sound output port so you can hook up external speakers or (for kids playing invading alien games) earphones.

Later Mac models have sound input capabilities, too. In some cases, the microphone is built-in, but in others there's a sound input port (marked with an icon of an old-fashioned microphone).

∘∘◗ **The floppy drive port,** available on fewer and fewer Mac models, is for connecting an external floppy drive. Oddly enough, its icon is the practically ancient 5.25-inch floppy disk that was never used on any Mac.

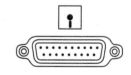

∘∘◗ **The video port**—on Macs with built-in video support for an external monitor—is marked with what's supposed to be a monitor icon. If you're using a separate video card, its connector will protrude through an opening in the case, but there won't be any icon identifying it.

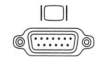

∘∘◗ **There's a SCSI port** on every Mac model since the Plus. SCSI (pronounced *scuzzy*) stands for *small computer serial interface.* SCSI devices that connected to this port or chained through other SCSI devices include storage devices like hard drives and CD-ROM drives; there are even a few SCSI printers and monitors available. The SCSI port on PowerBooks is smaller than the ones on the back of desktop Macs and needs a special cable.

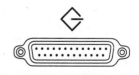

SCSI is an industry standard, but Apple implements it in a non-standard way, so you need Mac-specific SCSI devices for your computer.

### THE WAY WE WERE ...

The SCSI standard was around in the computer industry before the Mac used it. And it was pronounced with a vowel sound between the C and the S: *scuzzy*.

Mac people don't mind being different. In fact, we enjoy it. In fact, we practically insist on it. So, when the Mac Plus debuted with a SCSI port, there was a movement afoot to pronounce it with the vowel sound between the S and C: *sexy*. The movement didn't last. (Which is just as well.)

**The printer port** is used for most printers, although there are a few SCSI-connection printers around. This port is also used as the connection for an AppleTalk network.

The printer and modem ports are identical, so you can use the modem port for a separate printer if the printer port is being used for a network connection. (The printer and modem ports are the Mac's serial ports.)

**The modem port** is, of course, for connecting a modem to your computer. The modem is what translates the numeric information of a computer into a signal that can be sent over telephone lines. If you look closely at the icon, you'll see that's a string of ones and zeros next to the telephone handset.

Modems are covered in Chapter 14.

**The Reset and Interrupt buttons** aren't ports, but this seems a good place to mention them, at least in passing. Most Mac models have these buttons someplace on the case; in the earliest Macs, you had to install the little plastic piece with the "buttons" yourself; it was known generically as the *programmer's switch*. Some Macs don't have the buttons at all, but provide special keyboard combinations instead to act as the buttons. There's more about these buttons in Chapter 24.

**The GeoPort** is pretty much the port of the future; so far, it's on only the AV models and the Power Macs. It's a special version of the modem and printer serial connections; it's so fast that it can be used for multiple purposes—send a fax over a phone line, feed a document to the printer, and maintain a network connection—all at the same time.

## Odds & Ends

*Hardware* is the physical computer itself: its electronic and mechanical components and casings. *Software* is what makes the hardware do something—the *programs* that you run. Software is stored on disks and is loaded into memory as necessary. There's another word you may run into occasionally: *firmware*. That's something that is somewhere in-between hardware and software—like the ROMs in the machine, which are physical items that have permanent, unchangeable programs stored on them.

∞•❯ The term *microcomputer* comes not from your desktop computer's size in relation to its big mainframe cousins, but from the fact that its CPU is a single component, or *microprocessor*. (A CPU in a large computer consists of many components.) But it's a logical assumption that *microcomputer* refers to the overall size because the term *minicomputer* was used to describe the machines that were smaller than the original mainframes.

∞•❯ The computer's *footprint* is the area it occupies on your desk. At about one foot square, the original Mac had an incredibly small footprint for a computer—even a desktop one. A *zero footprint* peripheral—as many external hard drives for compact Macs are advertised—is one that sits under the Mac so it doesn't take up any additional room. (Although the *zero footprint* phrase as an absolute value rather than a relative one has always had pretty fascinating implications.)

∞•❯ A *chip* is a little silicon wafer with thousands, or even millions, of circuits etched into it. Its more formal name is *integrated circuit,* or *IC chip.* You don't usually see or handle the actual chips; they're encased in little plastic or ceramic blocks with protruding metal connectors—the overall effect is somewhat like a centipede.

✳Why, do you suppose, that in such a male-dominated industry, these components are gender-typed as female? Maybe for the same reason a ship is a she. (Not that I know what that reason is, either—"it" pretty much does it for me when it comes to boats and computers both.)

∞•❯ A *board* is, well, a *board*, with circuits etched, or printed in metal, on it. In fact, it's called a *circuit board.* When it's the main board in the computer, the one with the ROM chips on it, it's called the *logic board.* The main board is also called the *motherboard;* boards that connect to the motherboard are called *daughterboards.*✳

### CRYSTAL BALL GAZING

Editorials in computer magazines talk about the future as much as they talk about the present. Back in June of 1988, the Mac SE was the basic Mac, the Mac II was the high-end machine, and Steve Bobker was ... well, his title was Chief Scientist at MacUser magazine.

Steve, who I'm pleased to count among my friends, wrote a column about the future *appliance Mac.* The concept was vintage Steve Jobs: the Mac would be an appliance, easy to use, not a complicated computer. Bobker editorialized that the appliance Mac had never really happened, and listed some of the things such a machine would need. How well did he do? You be the judge. I took his comments and compared them against three of the current low-end Macs (there were so many to choose from!).

| What Steve said: | Some of today's appliance-like machines: | | |
|---|---|---|---|
| **Based on what currently exists, here's what I think the appliance Macintosh will be like:** | Color Classic | Quadra 605 | LC520 |
| The highest possible list price figure is $995 (with keyboard and monitor). | $900 | $900 | $900 |
| Will probably have 2.5 megabytes of RAM unless the differential cost of providing 4 megabytes is only $25 or so. I don't see that happening for at least a few years. | 4 MB | 4 MB | 4 MB |
| | Prices dropped radically in the next few years, and the latest machines often come with 8 megs of memory. | | |
| The central processing unit will be the 68030 running somewhere between 16 and 25 MHz. | 6830 25 MHz | 68LC040 25 MHz | 68C040 25 MHz |
| | Pretty close to the mark on this one! | | |
| It will have a built-in hard disk ... 20 megabytes will be more than ample for the situations where [this] Mac will be used and the rumored new, very small 10-megabyte drive will also be adequate. | 40-160MB | 80-160MB | 80-160MB |
| | Hey, when you're working with 400K disks, 60K System Folders, and 200K applications, 10 megs really did seem adequate! | | |
| One external floppy drive capable of reading any format (800K, SuperDrive, and MS-DOS). | Internal, but capable of reading any format. | | |
| Don't expect to see anything too radical in storage such as CD-ROM ... | No CD-ROM storage built in models, but the external one is popular | | Built-in CD-ROM drive |
| There will be an expansion port or two. These will not be card slots, however, but cartridge openings accessible without opening the case. | Right about the expansion slots, but wrong about the approach: Macs never used the cartridge approach. Each of these models provides 1 PDS slot. | | |
| The monitor will be a separate unit allowing a choice for those affluent enough to take advantage of it. The basic monitor will be a black and white, portrait-format, page-size box. | Built-in, but standard format, and in color. | Separate monitor, but standard format and color are still the most popular. | |
| The keyboard will probably remain an ADB unit. | And so it has. | | |
| Radically new system software ... nearly totally self-contained in a greatly expanded ROM, will rely heavily on artificial intelligence to learn its users' ways and wishes. | The ROMs are certainly greatly expanded, but the system software is neither self-contained there nor radically new—nor reliant upon artificial intelligence. But it's still a good idea! | | |

•→ **Numbers in a computer's name**—besides the model number, like LC III or Centris 650—usually refer to the amount of RAM and the size of the hard drive in it. So, a 4/80 PowerBook 170 has 4 megs of RAM and an 80 MB hard drive. These numbers are seldom in a computer's "official" name, but are often listed when you're comparing models: a Quadra 900 4/120 versus a Quadra 900 8/160, for instance.

It used to be pretty clear that the slash between two numbers referred to the RAM/drive configuration. There was also that little glitch in the SE/30's name, though, where the number referred to the 68030 processor, to differentiate it from the SE with the 68000 processor. Now, the newest wrinkle is the slashed numbers in the Power Macs' official model names: 6100/60, 7100/66, and 8100/80. For these models, the first number is the model number, and the second is the clock speed of the processor.

•→ *Multi-tasking* is a computer doing more than one thing at a time. Because a computer works so quickly, lots of times you may think you're multi-tasking, but what's really happening is that the computer is splitting its attention between operations, a few milliseconds here, a few milliseconds there. For true multi-tasking, the computer has to be actually processing more than one thing at a time; no Mac can do that yet.

For years, my stock answer to the question "But can you multi-task on your Mac?" has been: "Of course I multi-task. I'm a working mother."

**THE MULTI-TASKING COMPUTER**

### → MEMORY ←

## SIMMs

•→ **A computer's RAM** is easy to think of as a vast empty space that gets filled up by data as you work—a somewhat nebulous electronic cavern. If you know a little bit (no pun intended) about how information is stored in memory, you might visualize RAM as a series of cubbyholes waiting for items to be sorted into them.

But RAM is actually a series of tiny electronic switches that keep track of information by being in either On or Off positions. A *memory chip* for a computer is a collection of these little switches that are set in their positions by instructions from the computer, and held there by a constant flow of electricity. Turn off the electric power, and the switch positions are forgotten. That's why information you've stored in RAM disappears when you turn off the computer or restart it.

⚬•→ **A SIMM** is a small board (about the size of a stick of chewing gum) with memory chips on it. The chips themselves are somewhat insectoid in form: dark bodies with lots of little "legs" that serve as connectors to the board. *SIMM* (pronounced as a single word) stands for *single inline memory module*—the memory chips are in a single line on the board.

You add memory to your computer by snapping SIMMs into the slots inside the CPU.

A chip (left) and a SIMM (right).

⚬•→ **The size of a SIMM** is its memory capacity, not its physical dimensions; memory capacity is also sometimes referred to as the *density*. SIMMs range in size from 256K to 16 megs and more. So, by using four 256K SIMMs, you get 1 meg of memory; four 16-meg SIMMs give you 64 megs of memory.

⚬•→ **A SIMM is rated by the speed** with which its memory can be accessed. The speed is measured in *nanoseconds*—billionths of a second; the abbreviation is simply *ns*.

The speed rating of a SIMM is expressed according to how long it takes to do something (rather than how many things can be done in a set period of time). So, a lower rating means a faster SIMM: A 100ns SIMM is faster than a 120ns SIMM.

### TIME IS RELATIVE

A second is a very long time in the world of computers. Even a millisecond (a thousandth of a second) is a long time; after all, in a millisecond, electricity can travel the length of Manhattan—and then some.

But a nanosecond—a billionth of a second—is a unit of time that computers are comfortable with. In a nanosecond, electricity travels about 10.6 inches.

And what about the next unit: a picosecond, which is a trillionth of a second? Well, take that 10.6-inch wire whose length is traversed by electricity in a nanosecond. Pulverize it. In a picosecond, electricity has a chance to travel about the length of one of those powdery flakes.

⚬•→ **You can tell the speed of a SIMM** by looking for a number printed somewhere on the board. Of course, it would be much too easy if the actual speed rating were printed on the board. Instead, there are only two digits that stand for the speed. In the case of 60ns and 80ns chips, that's not a problem, but other speeds are also marked with only two digits. The first two digits? No. The last two? Nope, still too easy. They're identified like this:

$$10 = 100ns$$
$$20 = 120ns$$
$$15 = 150ns$$

••→ **A SIMM has either 30 or 72 *pins*,** the connectors along its bottom edge. The 72-pin design is relatively new to the Mac and is used in only the later models.

••→ **Most SIMMs have eight** chips on them; some have only two, and some 16. Sometimes a SIMM is referred to as a *one-by-eight*, or *one-by-two*, and so on, referring to the number of rows of chips, and the number of chips in each row.

••→ **A *low-profile* SIMM** will fit in any Mac that uses SIMMs for memory expansion. Low profile refers to how the chips sit on the board. Some Macs have their SIMM slots very close together and have trouble accommodating anything except low-profile SIMMs. Stick with the low-profile ones even if your Mac can handle the bulkier SIMMs, since you never know when you might want to sell the SIMMs and replace them with higher-capacity ones; the low-profile models are much more marketable.

••→ **A composite SIMM** is one that has double the usual number of chips on it. Some current 16-meg SIMMs, for instance, use 16 chips (eight on each side of the board) instead of only eight chips total. Composite boards have some timing problems in some Macs, especially the AVs, so it's best to avoid them completely.

••→ **You can use a faster SIMM** than your Mac needs, but it won't speed up your Mac; the extra speed capability is wasted. But using a slower SIMM than your Mac can handle *does* slow down the computer, so do your best to get the correct chips.

••→ *Dynamic* **RAM** is used in most Macs; it needs constant electrical refreshing to keep its electronic switches in place. It's sometimes called DRAM (*DEE-ram*), but since it's the most common type of RAM chip used, it's usually the one we mean when we say RAM. *Static RAM* chips don't need a constant electrical flow to keep their switches in place; the switches stay set until you change them. Static RAM is significantly more expensive that dynamic RAM; it was used in the much-maligned (and rightly so!) Mac Portable. Then there's the *pseudo-static RAM* used in PowerBooks. It needs electric power to keep the switches set, but it takes very little power to do so; it's a lot less expensive than true static RAM.

••→ **PowerBooks don't use SIMMs** because of their cramped innards. The memory boards used in PowerBooks are called just that—*memory boards*, or *memory modules*. The arrangement of memory chips on the boards is different from the in-line design of a SIMM.

## Adding Memory

••→ **Additional memory for your computer** is the easiest, most cost-effective upgrade you can make. With more memory, you can run more programs at one time, and each program can run faster inside a larger memory partition. You can beef up your system with more inits, too, when you have memory to spare.

∘∘→ **Some Macs have *soldered* memory:** RAM chips permanently attached to the main logic board. (That's why it's also referred to as *on-board* memory.) On-board memory is a relatively recent development in the Mac world. Low-end systems generally have 1 meg of soldered memory; others might have 4 or 8 megs. The amount of on-board memory counts towards the maximum that your computer can have installed.

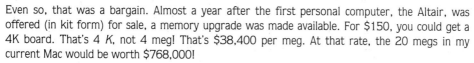

## THANKS FOR THE MEMORY

The cost of memory chips has gone up and down over the years; luckily, it has mostly gone down. When the PowerBooks were introduced, for instance, a 6-meg upgrade cost around $800. Ten months later, I bought a 6-meg board for $219. And even that's a little expensive compared to the kind of memory used in desk Macs, which has hovered around $30 a meg for years. Just think: the original Mac came with 128K. The cost to upgrade to the Fat Mac, with its 512K memory, was $1000: That's a little over $2600 a *meg*, since all you got was an extra 128K.

Even so, that was a bargain. Almost a year after the first personal computer, the Altair, was offered (in kit form) for sale, a memory upgrade was made available. For $150, you could get a 4K board. That's 4 *K*, not 4 meg! That's $38,400 per meg. At that rate, the 20 megs in my current Mac would be worth $768,000!

∘∘→ **Add memory to your Mac by installing SIMMs.** In all but the older compact Macs, this is pretty much a cinch because the SIMMs snap into small slots made expressly for that purpose. (Older compact Macs have SIMM slots, too, but it's hard to get at them because it's difficult to open the case.) Different Mac models have different numbers of slots, anywhere from a single slot to as many as 16.

∘∘→ **The number of SIMM slots** in your Mac isn't a serious limitation on the amount of memory you can use, since SIMMs come as small as 256K (a quarter of a meg) and as large as 32MB. The sizes in between, of course, follow the binary numbering units that you're used to seeing for memory amounts: 512K and 1, 2, 4, 8, and 16 megs. As you might expect, the larger sizes cost more; the largest at this point (16 and 32MB) are more expensive per meg than the smaller ones because of the cost of technology— squeezing more and more memory into the same size package.

∘∘→ **You have to add 30-pin SIMMs in groups** because of the way a Mac moves data around internally. A standard SIMM sends or receives data 8 bits at a time. A Mac model like the LC uses a 16-bit data path, and so needs information in 16-bit chunks. You have to install SIMMs in pairs in an LC because that way there are 16 bits of information moving in and out of the SIMMs at a time. Other Macs move data in 32-bit chunks. To get a piece of information that size in and out of memory, you need the SIMMs in groups of four, since each handles 8 bits at a time.

●•◗ A *bank* is a grouping of 30-pin SIMM slots, although the physical arrangement isn't always clear; four slots may be a single bank, or two banks of two slots each.

A bank of slots has to be treated as a group: the bank has to be entirely empty or entirely filled, and each slot has to be filled with the same size SIMM as the other slots in the bank. So, in a Mac that has two banks of four slots each, you could put 1-meg SIMMs in one bank and 4-meg SIMMs in the other for a total of 20 megs of memory. But you can't fill one bank with 1-meg SIMMs and the other with two 1-meg and two 4-meg SIMMs, or with a single 8-meg SIMM.

Some Macs have a few other quirks, like a particular bank is the one that has to be filled first if only one is being used, or hold the lower-density SIMMs if the banks are getting different SIMMs. Here's the general rule: Use Bank A first, and use it for the lower-density group of SIMMs. The banks are usually identified (in very tiny print) right on the logic board where they're positioned.

> To cope with the fact that many new programs have outgrown [512K of memory in] the Macintosh, some Mac owners are installing memory upgrade boards [that] can boost the amount of RAM to as much as 2 megabytes. Many of the upgrades void the Apple warranty, however.

*MACWORLD*
FEBRUARY 1986

●•◗ 72-pin slots aren't arranged in banks; a 72-pin slot is, for all intents and purposes, a bank in and of itself in most Macs (all but the Power Macs) because 72-pin SIMMs send and receive information in 32-bit chunks. So, you can add 72-pin SIMMs one at a time; you can put a SIMM in any available slot; and, you can put any size SIMM in any slot in any order.

●•◗ **Don't worry about which SIMMs** you need or how many can fit into your Mac. If you're calling to order SIMMs from any mail-order place, or going to a dealer, all you have to do is tell them which Mac model you have and they'll know what you need.

There are two situations where you should know specifically what type of SIMMs your Mac needs:

- If you're buying SIMMs from another Mac owner because she's upgrading to even larger ones. If it's the same model of Mac, there's no problem (unless she's been using the wrong ones—like maybe the wrong speed). If it's a different model, you'll have to double check that they'll work in yours.
- If you expect to upgrade your Mac to a faster model that might need faster SIMMs.

An anticipated upgrade isn't far-fetched at all, as I know from experience. I had a 20-meg IIci and decided to get a Centris 650 for the extra speed; it came with 8 megs. The ci had four 1MB SIMMs and four 4MB SIMMs in it. Since it was going to the kids (while their LC II was sold), it didn't need that much memory. I took out the 4-meg SIMMs and replaced them with the four 1-meg SIMMs that I saved when I had upgraded from 8 megs to 20. That left the kids with an 8-meg machine (plenty) and me with an 8-meg machine and four 4-meg SIMMs that didn't fit in the Centris because it takes the 72-pin style. So, I sold the 4-meg SIMMs and had to buy more memory for the Centris. But, finally, the real problem: Should I get the 80ns chips that the Centris needs, or pay extra for 60ns chips that I figured I'd need in a year or so if I boosted the Centris's clock speed to 33MHz to turn it into a Quadra 800? I settled for the 80ns chips only because a colleague who had just purchased an 800 had bought the wrong SIMMs—he needed 60ns but had the 80ns minimum that I needed. So, I bought his.*

> *And now I'll just skip to a Power Mac as my next machine and the 80ns chips will be fine.

**••→ Buy your SIMMs through mail order.** It's absolutely the best way. You can install them yourself or find someone who knows how to do it in a local user group. Unless you have a compact Mac whose case is difficult to open, it's the only way to go.

What kind of mail order? Directly from a chip specialist is the cheapest way to go: say about $35 per meg and overnight shipping. You get great service, guarantees, and the SIMMs—but nothing else (like instructions). For a little more money, say $45 per meg, you can get them through a general Mac mail-order concern and get instructions, too. But there's not much instruction needed, so you can save $40 on 4 megs by getting them from the specialist.

There are many mail-order services around, but I can personally recommend The Chip Merchant and TechWorks because I've been using them for years; I've also seen them replace bad chips on the few occasions customers received them. On the general mail-order side, I've used both MacConnection and MacWarehouse for many things over the years.

**••→ SIMMs are easy to install,** but you do have to be careful. The first precaution is protecting against static—that little spark that discharges from your fingertip after you shuffle across a carpet on a cold day is deadly to computer circuitry. Basic static precautions: touch something else to discharge the static from your body before you touch anything on the inside of the Mac.

The second precaution: the little plastic clips that hold the SIMMs in place are easy to break, and expensive to replace—and a SIMM that's not firmly in place won't work. So handle everything gently.

Most SIMM slots need the board to be inserted at a slight angle, then straightened, at which point the plastic tabs lock the SIMM into place. To remove existing SIMMs, you can gently push the top edge of the board so the SIMM is at an angle; this usually releases the clips. Sometimes you have to use a fingernail or a small screwdriver or other implement to release the board from the clips.

••◆ **Turn on 32-bit addressing** (in the Memory control panel) if you install more than 8 megs of memory in your Mac. Otherwise, any amount over 8 megs gets dumped into the system allocation and is unavailable for applications.

••◆ **A Sad Mac on startup** can be from a bad SIMM. It can also be from many other things. But if you get the black screen with the Sad Mac and hear a single note that's different from the usual startup sound, or a two-note sequence, it's likely a SIMM problem. A Sad Mac with a four-note sequence is not a SIMM problem.

## Special Considerations

∞◆ **The amount of memory your Mac can use** is affected by a number of factors:

- How much memory a specific model can *address*, or use, when it's looking for RAM. This maximum amount is a solid wall that you can't get around.
- The amount of soldered RAM.
- The number of SIMM slots inside.
- How (and if) the slots are arranged in banks.
- The size SIMM that the model can use.

Say a Mac has 2 megs of on-board memory and a single bank of two SIMM slots that can handle 1-meg or 4-meg SIMMs. Keeping in mind the rules about filling banks (all slots in a bank must be filled if any are filled, and they must have the same size SIMMs in each bank), this fictitious model could have 2, 4, or 10 megs of memory because:

| On-board | + | Bank A | + | Bank B | = | Total |
|----------|---|--------|---|--------|---|-------|
| 2 | + | 0 | + | 0 | = | 2 |
| 2 | + | 1 | + | 1 | = | 3 |
| 2 | + | 4 | + | 4 | = | 10 |

A table showing Mac memory configurations is on the next page.

∞◆ **Macs with dirty ROMs** can't use more than 8 megs of memory unless you use the Mode32 extension or Apple's 32-Bit Enabler, both described in Chapter 9. The dirty Macs are: the Mac II, IIx, IIcx, and the SE/30.

∞◆ **To upgrade a Classic,** you have to buy a special expansion kit. There's a meg of soldered memory in the Classic, and the expansion attachment gives you another soldered meg as well as two empty SIMM slots for additional memory. The two slots are a single bank, so you have to treat them equally when it comes to SIMM installation.

••◆ **The Mac II has several special needs** when it comes to memory upgrades:

- It can't see more than 8 megs of memory unless it has a PMMU installed.
- If you're using anything larger than 1-meg SIMMs, they have to be PAL SIMMs. A PAL (*programmable logic array*) SIMM has eight standard memory chips and a ninth PAL chip on it.
- If you fill both banks with SIMMs, Bank A (closest to the edge of the case) has to be filled before Bank B. The Bank A SIMMs can't be larger than the Bank B

SIMMs or the memory won't be recognized. And, Bank A can't use larger than 1MB SIMMs.

If the Mac II was upgraded with the SuperDrive Upgrade Kit, many of these limitations don't apply, because the upgrade includes new ROM chips that fix several problems in the original ROMs. If you have the SuperDrive Upgrade Kit in a Mac II:

- It can use standard SIMMs instead of the PALs
- You can use 4-meg SIMMs in Bank A
- You can use 4-meg or 16-meg SIMMs in Bank B

## Memory Configurations

| Model | Max. | On-board | Slots | Banks | Type | SIMM sizes (MB) | Speed (ns) |
|---|---|---|---|---|---|---|---|
| Plus, SE | 4 | 0 | 4 | 2 | 30-pin | 256K, 1 | 150 |
| SE/30 | 128 | 0 | 8 | 2 | 30-pin | 256K, 1, 4 | 120 |
| Classic | 4 | 1 | 2 | 1 | 30-pin | 256K, 1 | 120 |
| Classic II | 10 | 2 | 2 | 1 | 30-pin | 1, 2, 4 | 100 |
| Color Classic | 10 | 4 | 2 | 1 | 30-pin | 1, 2, 4 | 100 |
| LC | 10 | 2 | 2 | 1 | 30-pin | 1, 2, 4 | 100 |
| LC II | 10 | 2 or 4 | 2 | 1 | 30-pin | 1, 2, 4 | 100 |
| LC III, 520 | 36 | 4 | 1 | - | 72-pin | 1, 2, 4, 8, 16, 32 | 80 |
| LC 475 | 36 | 4 | 1 | - | 72-pin | 4, 8, 16, 32 | 80 |
| II | 20 | 0 | 8 | 2 | 30-pin | 256K, 1, 4 | 120 |
| IIx | 32 | 0 | 8 | 2 | 30-pin | 256K, 1, 4 | 120 |
| IIcx | 32 | 0 | 8 | 2 | 30-pin | 256K, 1, 4 | 120 |
| IIci | 32 | 0 | 8 | 2 | 30-pin | 256K, 512K, 1, 2, 4 | 80 |
| IIsi | 17 | 1 | 4 | 1 | 30-pin | 256K, 512K, 1, 2, 4 | 100 |
| IIvi, IIvx | 68 | 4 | 4 | 1 | 30-pin | 256K, 1, 2, 4 | 80 |
| IIfx | 128 | 0 | 8 | 2 | 64-pin | 1, 4 | 80 |
| C 610 | 136 | 4 | 2 | - | 72-pin | 4, 8, 16, 32 | 80 |
| C 650 | 136 | 4 or 8 | 4 | - | 72-pin | 4, 8, 16, 32 | 80 |
| C, Q 660av | | 4 | 2 | - | 72-pin | 4, 8, 16, 32 | 70 |
| Q 605 | 20 | 4 | 1 | - | 72-pin | 4, 8, 16 | 80 |
| Q 610 | 68 | 4 | 2 | - | 72-pin | 4, 8, 16, 32 | 80 |
| Q 650 | 132 | 4 or 8 | 4 | - | 72-pin | 4, 8, 16, 32 | 80 |
| Q 700 | 64 | 4 | 4 | 1 | 30-pin | 1, 16 | 80 |
| Q 800 | 136 | 8 | 4 | - | 72-pin | 4, 8, 16, 32 | 60 |
| Q 840av | | 0 | 4 | - | 72-pin | 4, 8, 16, 32 | 60 |
| Q 900, 950 | 256 | 0 | 16 | 4 | 30-pin | 1, 16 | 80 |
| Performa 200 | 10 | 2 | 2 | 1 | 30-pin | 1, 2, 4 | 100 |
| Performa 400, 405, 410, 430 | 10 | 4 | 2 | - | 30-pin | 1, 2, 4 | 100 |
| Performa 450 | 36 | 4 | 1 | - | 72-pin | 1, 2, 4, 8, 16, 32 | 80 |
| Performa 460, 466, 467 | 36 | 4 | 1 | - | 72-pin | 1, 2, 4, 8, 16, 32 | 80 |
| Performa 475, 476, 550 | 36 | 4 | 1 | - | 72-pin | 1, 2, 4, 8, 16, 32 | 80 |
| Performa 600, 600CD | 68 | 4 | 4 | 1 | 30-pin | 256K, 1, 2, 4 | 80 |
| Quadra 660av | 68 | 4 | 2 | - | 72-pin | 4, 8, 16, 32 | 70 |
| Quadra 840av | 128 | 0 | 4 | - | 72-pin | 4, 8, 16, 32 | 60 |
| Power Mac 6100 | 72 | 8 | - | - | 72-pin | - | 80 |
| Power Mac 7100 | 136 | 8 | - | - | 72-pin | - | 80 |
| Power Mac 8100 | 264 | 8 | - | - | 72-pin | - | 80 |

••➔ **The Mac IIx needs special SIMMs.** Like the Mac II, it needs PAL SIMMs with the ninth chip on the board for anything larger than 1-meg SIMMs.

••➔ **On a IIci using the internal video card,** keep Bank A (the one closer to the drive) filled with the smaller SIMMs if you're using different densities in the two banks. The ci's built-in video steals RAM from the first bank; with the arrangement recommended here, you can keep things from slowing down any more than necessary.

••➔ **The LC II can address** only 10 megs of memory, despite the fact that there's 4MB of soldered memory and two SIMM slots. There's a real catch here (sort of a "Catch LC II"): You have to use both slots, since they make up a bank. Putting 2-meg SIMMs in each gives you a total of 8 megs of memory, counting the on-board memory; that means you're not using as much memory as you can. But putting 4-meg SIMMs in each slot means there's a total of 12 megs installed—and two megs will be wasted because the LC II can't see anything beyond 10.

••➔ **The Quadra 700 has the same problem** as the LC, but bigger: you waste memory if you fill all its slots with large SIMMs, but if you don't, you won't get as much memory as you can. The 700 has 4 megs of memory on board and four slots. The four slots are a single bank, so you have to use them all. Put 16-meg SIMMs in them and you get 68MB of total memory—but the machine can use only 64!

••➔ **The Power Macs have two SIMM-related** features worth noting:

- Although they use the 72-pin SIMMs, which other Macs use singly, the Power Macs use them in pairs. The Power Mac transfers information internally in 64-bit chunks, so it has to work with two 72-pin SIMMs at a time, since each provides 32-bits of information.
- The Power Mac uses slower SIMMs (80ns) than some Quadras and AVs (which use 60 and 70ns). Since the Power Mac can move information in 64-bit chunks, addressing two SIMMs at a time, it's still a lot faster with 80ns SIMMs than the other machines are with the faster chips that use 32 bits at a time. (The Power Mac's addressing scheme with the 80ns SIMM would be the equivalent of another Mac working with 40ns chips.)

••➔ **The Mac IIfx uses different SIMMs** from any other Mac: It needs special 64-pin SIMMs.

••➔ **For the Centris 650 and Quadra 800,** keep adjacent slots filled with SIMMs of the same size so the computer can use its special memory interleaving technique to access the two SIMMs as a single large area of RAM. This can increase the operating speed of the computer by as much as 10 percent.

••➔ **The Mac Plus and SE** have four SIMM slots that are paired in two banks. These models can't address any more than 4 megs of memory, so you'll want to put a 1-meg SIMM in every slot; you don't have to worry about the banks at all.

But you do have to worry about the special attention these two machines need if you're adding memory. Not only are they difficult to open, they also have special jumpers or resistors on their motherboards that must be adjusted if you want to install their 4-meg maximum memory. This is not a do-it-yourself job unless you really know what you're doing yourself, so it's best to let an experienced person handle the job. That doesn't necessarily mean an Apple technician—it's likely that someone in your local Mac user group has done this before.

User group? See Chapter 21.

···→ **The Mac Portable needs a special** memory card for memory expansion. The card can contain either 3 or 4 megs of RAM; together with the 1 meg on the logic board, that gives the Portable 4 megs of memory (in the standard model) or 5 megs (in the backlit model).

## → MEET THE MACINTOSHES ←

## Compact Macs

∞→ **The three earliest Macs,** prior to the Mac Plus, are, sadly, totally out of the running as viable systems—unless you can be satisfied with ancient system software and applications. Neither System 7 nor any program released in the last few years can run on one of the early machines. Want a quick trip down memory lane? Here we go:

- The original Mac had 128K of memory. That's about it. For $2500 you got a machine with a single internal floppy drive—for floppies that held 400K of information. No hard drive, no expansion capabilities, not even an external floppy drive was available at first. But it was bundled with MacWrite and MacPaint, and it was a miracle.

- The Fat Mac, introduced only nine months after the original, had 512K of memory. That was simply its popular name—the official name was the Macintosh 512K. But it was fat because it quadrupled the amount of memory previously available.

- The 512Ke came out about a year and a half after the Fat Mac. The *e* was for *enhanced*; the enhancement was an 800K drive. This model is "prior" to the Mac Plus only in abilities, since it was actually introduced after the Plus, and the 800K drive was for compatibility with that drive in the Plus.

∞→ **The second group of compact Macs,** starting with the Mac Plus, are still usable systems today, although their capabilities are somewhat limited, especially if you want to run System 7 on them.

- The Mac Plus had a lot of pluses when it was introduced: a full megabyte of memory (eight times the amount of the first Mac); a floppy drive that handled 800K floppies (twice the capacity of the previous disk standard); a SCSI port for an external hard drive; and, the ability to address 4MB of RAM—although few users thought at the time they'd ever need more than the 1 meg that came with it. The Plus's minuses as a working system today are its limited ability to work with System 7: it's much too slow, and with an upper limit of 4 megs of memory, the memory-hungry system doesn't leave much working room for applications. It's also slow at running newer applications, even if you can get them to work under System 6.0.7.

- The Mac SE introduced Mac users to several new features, including a choice between an internal hard drive or two internal floppy drives and, in a major philosophical change, an internal fan. Another philosophical change of cosmic proportions was the inclusion of an expansion slot inside—but this hardly counts, since you couldn't get at it. The SE's produced at the end of the model's lifetime included the new FDHD floppy drive. Although it's about 20 percent faster than the Plus, the SE is no more usable with System 7: it's still too slow, and has the 4-meg memory limit.

- The SE/30 was a giant step forward in many ways. First and foremost, it used the 68030 processor (hence the name); it included an FPU; it had the FDHD drive that read 1.4-meg floppies; it could use up to 128 megs of memory (although there were no SIMMS large enough, at the time, to provide that configuration). And—its most subtle improvement—it had ROMs that could drive a color display. Of course, it still had the standard 9-inch black-and-white screen, but it was theoretically possible to attach a color monitor to its internal PDS slot.

### Old Compact Mac Specs

|          | CPU   | Speed  | FPU | Max. RAM | Slots |
|----------|-------|--------|-----|----------|-------|
| Mac Plus | 68000 | 8 MHz  | no  | 4MB      | none  |
| Mac SE   | 68000 | 8 MHz  | no  | 4MB      | none  |
| Mac SE/30| 68030 | 16 MHz | yes | 128MB    | 1 PDS |

••▶ **The Mac Classic line** is in many ways a return to the Mac's roots.

- The Mac Classic is a real throwback. After years of powerful processors and larger, color screens, the Classic showed up with a black-and-white 9-inch screen and the old 68000 processor. It had no FPU and a RAM limit of 4 megs. Apple was trying to provide a low-cost, entry-level system to users who didn't need the speed and power of the larger systems. It only lasted a year though, since even budget-minded buyers couldn't see buying a machine barely better than the Mac Plus so many years after that model had been laid to rest.

- The Classic II addressed the problems of the first Classic model: it uses a better processor at a faster speed (the 68030 at 16 MHz instead of a 68000 at 8 MHz); has sound input; and can address up to 10 MB of memory.

- The Color Classic took a good idea and added color—the first time a color screen had been built into a compact Mac model. It was also the first desktop model with a built-in microphone.

### Classic Specs

|              | CPU   | Speed  | FPU  | Max. RAM | Slots |
|--------------|-------|--------|------|----------|-------|
| Classic      | 68000 | 8 MHz  | no   | 4MB      | none  |
| Classic II   | 68030 | 16 MHz | no   | 10MB     | none  |
| Color Classic| 68030 | 16 MHz | opt. | 10MB     | none  |

## T-Shirt Sighting

This was a favorite in the early days, especially at the Mac Expo trade shows. In large letters on the front: IBM. In smaller print, following the letters:

**I**

**B**ought

**M**acintosh

## Modular Macs

∞→ **The Mac II line started** with—what else?—the Mac II, which introduced a number of important innovations: more advanced processors, modular design, expansion slots, and, the most obvious and longed-for improvement, color.

- The Mac II is one of the very few Macs that uses the 68020 processor. (It was advanced at the time, but was immediately superseded by the even better 68030.) It was the first Mac with slots—six of them, in fact, a number that only the IIx and some of the Quadras match. And, as the first modular Mac, it was the first one that needed a video card installed in order to run a monitor.

- The Mac IIx was the first Mac to use the 68030 processor chip and include an FPU as standard. It was also the first model to offer the FDHD Super Drive as standard.

- The Mac IIcx is a compact version of the IIx, with three slots instead of six. The only other difference between them is that the cx was designed with money-saving manufacturing in mind: Most of its components snap together rather than being screwed in.

- The Mac IIci looks just like a IIcx, but it's a speed demon in comparison: Its processor runs at 25MHz rather than at the cx's 16 MHz. It was the first modular Mac to have a built-in video card and provide the option of a cache card for even speedier processing. (More than a year after the ci's introduction, Apple started including the cache card as standard.)

- The Mac IIsi introduced a few new ideas: a very low-profile CPU case (sometimes referred to as the *pizza box*), a sound input port and microphone, and a meg of RAM on the main logic board. At 20 MHz instead of 25, it's a little slower than the ci, but it wasn't meant as a replacement—it was a lower-cost alternative. In fact, it was one of a group of low-cost alternatives at the time, the others being the Classic and the LC.

- The Mac IIvx replaced the IIci. It has a slightly faster clock speed, and an internal video card that doesn't pay any penalty in system speed because, unlike the ci, it has separate VRAM (video memory) for the monitor. It was the first Mac to include a CD-ROM drive. It also had the shortest shelf life of any Mac model, having been discontinued in its first year of life. VRAM? See Chapter 15.

- The Mac IIfx was the first model to run at a zippy 40 MHz. It uses the original Mac II case, and so has room to offer six slots. A 32K built-in RAM cache for oft-repeated instructions adds to this speed demon's capabilities.

## Original Modular Macs Specs

|          | CPU   | Speed  | FPU  | Max RAM | Slots           |
|----------|-------|--------|------|---------|-----------------|
| Mac II   | 68020 | 16 MHz | opt. | 20MB    | 6 NuBus         |
| Mac IIx  | 68020 | 16 MHz | yes  | 32MB    | 6 NuBus         |
| Mac IIci | 68030 | 25 MHz | yes  | 32MB    | 3 NuBus         |
| Mac IIcx | 68030 | 16 MHz | yes  | 32MB    | 3 NuBus         |
| Mac IIsi | 68030 | 20 MHz | yes  | 17MB    | 1 PDS or NuBus  |
| Mac IIvx | 68030 | 32 MHz | yes  | 68MB    | 2 NuBus         |
| Mac IIfx | 68030 | 40 MHz | yes  | 32MB    | 1 PDS, 6 NuBus  |

**⊶➤ The LC line** started in late 1990 with the Macintosh LC, which was meant to offer a low-cost color alternative to the Macs in the II line.

- The original LC was a slight step backwards when it came to its processing power. It's the only Mac besides the long-gone Mac II to use the 68020 chip. One reason it was so inexpensive (besides the cheaper chip) was that it offered a single expansion slot, the less-popular PDS instead of a NuBus slot; the FPU was optional. With its relatively slow speed and 10MB memory limit, it's not an optimal system to run System 7.

- The LC II was a short-lived improvement on the LC, quickly squeezed out of the lineup by the LC III. The LC II improved upon the LC by using the '030 processor, which not only improved performance but also provided virtual memory capability. But it still has a 10MB memory limit without virtual memory, and needs an upgrade to an LC III to make it a truly viable machine for System 7.

- The LC III betters the LC II by running at 25MHz instead of 16 MHz and by being able to address up to 36MB of RAM. Its built-in VRAM is larger, too, so it can display more colors on the standard 14-inch monitor.

- The LC 520 is a very strange machine—not in or of itself, but in the way it's marketed and how it fits into the Apple lineup. Come to think of it, it's intrinsically a little strange, too, being an odd hybrid of an LC II and a Color Classic: a one-piece unit with a built-in 14-inch monitor. In addition, it has a built-in CD-ROM drive and microphone, as well as special stereo speakers unavailable on any other Mac. It's only available through educational channels, though, so unless Apple changes its marketing mind, you won't ever see one in a store—except under the name Performa 520.

- The LC 475 is a slight improvement on the 520. It's faster, since it uses an '040 chip—but it uses a special version, the 68LC040, which doesn't include the functions of an FPU as does the standard '040 chip.

## Specs: Mac LC's

|        | CPU     | Speed  | FPU  | Max. RAM | Slots  |
|--------|---------|--------|------|----------|--------|
| LC     | 68020   | 16 MHz | no   | 10MB     | 1 PDS  |
| LC II  | 68030   | 16 MHz | yes  | 10MB     | 1 PDS  |
| LC III | 68030   | 25 MHz | opt. | 36MB     | 1 PDS  |
| LC 520 | 68030   | 25 MHz | opt. | 36MB     | 1 PDS  |
| LC 475 | 68LC040 | 25 MHz | no   | 36MB     | 1 PDS  |
| LC 550 | 68030   | 33 MHz | opt. | 36MB     | 1 PDS  |
| LC 575 | 68LC040 | 33 MHz | no   | 36MB     | 1 PDS  |

## The '040 Modulars

••◆ **The Quadra line** is built around the 68040 processor, a better and faster chip than the ones used in previous Macs. The Quadras were also the first Macs to include built-in Ethernet networking capability. Quadras are designed differently from other Macs when it comes to the case, too: They're designed as vertical towers that stand next to a desk rather than on it.*

> *So much for desktop computing!

- The Quadra 700 was the first of the line and beats the former speed champ (the IIfx) by about 20 percent. It's the only Quadra that can be used as either a tower or horizontally as a desktop unit.
- The Quadra 900, introduced at the same time as the 700, offers the ability to address more memory and hold more internal add-ons: up to four hard drives, for instance. It also has more NuBus slots—five instead of two.
- The Quadra 950 is a faster 900: It runs at 33 MHz instead of 25 MHz and has a faster data transfer rate for its hard drive.
- The Quadra 800 is faster than the 900, despite the same processor and clock rate, because it uses faster memory chips. It addresses less total memory, but its 136MB limit will probably keep most people quite happy.

The Quadra line keeps growing, although when the Power Mac line is robust enough to satisfy users who need high-end speedy equipment, many models will drop out of the lineup. It's hard to make sense of the model numbers, since the originals were the 700, 900, and 950, but later, better ones were 800. (And then there are the AV models, but that's in a different section.) Anyway, the Specs chart here includes the models already described separately as well as some of their cousins.

### Quadra Specs

|     | CPU | Speed | FPU | Max. RAM | Slots |
|-----|---------|--------|------|----------|------------------|
| 700 | 68040 | 25 MHz | opt. | 64MB | 1 PDS, 2 NuBus |
| 900 | 68040 | 25 MHz | yes | 256MB | 1 PDS, 5 NuBus |
| 950 | 68040 | 33 MHz | yes | 256MB | 1 PDS, 5 NuBus |
| 800 | 68040 | 33 MHz | yes | 136MB | 1 PDS, 3 NuBus |
| 605 | 68LC040 | 25 MHz | none | 20MB | 1 PDS |
| 610 | 68040 | 25 MHz | opt. | 68MB | 1 PDS or 1 NuBus |
| 650 | 68040 | 33 MHz | yes | 132MB | 1 PDS, 3 NuBus |

••◆ **The Centris line** was short-lived under that name. The Centris models were released in early 1993 in the midst of a model blitz: Every week, it seemed, Apple was announcing a new computer. When they tried to straighten up their act and tighten up the line, the Centris was combined with, or rechristened, Quadra. (Except for the Centris 660AV, which is exactly the same as the Quadra 660AV, except for its name.)

- The Centris 610 is a strange, slightly crippled model. It uses a relatively slow 20 MHz '040 chip—but a special version of the chip that lacks the built-in FPU functions. It has a limit of 68MB of RAM—high enough for most users, but low compared to the other Centris and Quadra models. It lacks a ready-to-go expansion slot: you need a $100 adapter to make the slot usable as either NuBus or PDS.

- The Centris 650 is a beautiful machine, but I'm not that objective because I'm working on one right now. It was the model that convinced me to give my IIci to the kids and get a new, faster machine. Its '040 processor runs at 25 MHz—that's almost the only difference between it and the Quadra 800. In fact, the week I bought my Centris—only a few months after its introduction—a 33 MHz model called the Quadra 650 replaced it when Apple rolled the Centrises into the Quadra line.

### Centris Specs

| | CPU | Speed | FPU | Max. RAM | Slots |
|---|---|---|---|---|---|
| 610 | 68040 | 20 MHz | yes | 136MB | 1 PDS or NuBus |
| 650 | 68040 | 25 MHz | opt. | 136MB | 1 PDS, 3 NuBus |

••→ **There's really no Quadra/Centris** model, or Centris/Quadra. But you'll see the compound name quite often because the Centrises were renamed as Quadras. *But*—they were slightly upgraded when they were renamed, with the Centris 610's 20 MHz clocking changed to 25 MHz and the Centris 650 changed from 25 MHz to 33. When you see the slashed name, it's merely referring to either of the machines, with the clock rate a moot point for the issue at hand. The Quadra 660AV and the Centris 660AV, however, are identical.

## WHAT'S IN A NAME?

There used to be some logic behind the Mac naming conventions. Not a lot, but some.

The second and third Mac models were named simply 512 and 512e (although the popular name was Fat Mac). The Mac Plus had a lot of pluses; the Mac SE was so named apparently for *system expansion* because it had an expansion slot; the SE/30 was an SE with an '030 processor.

In the meantime, there was the Mac II line which started with, of course, the Mac II and then the Mac IIx, whose capabilities *extended* beyond those of the II. (It could have been called the Mac II/30 to echo the name change from the SE to the SE/30, but II/30 would be too much like the two numbers used to indicate memory and hard drive size. And they couldn't use the x suffix for the SE because … well, you figure it out.)

The *c* suffix is for *compact*; *i* is for *integrated* video; *s* is for *slim*. So, the cx is *compact extended*; the ci is *compact integrated*; the si is *slim integrated*.

LC is probably for *low cost*, or *low-cost color*. The Quadras were named for the *4* in the '040 chip. The AV's are *audio-visual*, the multimedia machines. Centris was named to suggest the middle of the Mac line.

And the rest? Sorry, I'm tired of trying to make sense of these things. It's possible they have no meaning at all.

**SHAKESPEARE**
*ROMEO AND JULIET*, II:2

What's in a name? That which we call a rose
By any other name would smell as sweet.

## Special Macs

∞→ **The Performa line was designed** for the mass market retailers like Sears, office-supply stores, and, one supposes, KMart. Apple couldn't sell *Macintoshes* through these outlets because of promises to its dealers; but there's a sizeable entry-level market out there whose shoppers don't go into computer stores. So, Apple repackaged the basic Mac, added a few extra interface options to make the Mac even easier for a novice, installed some basic software on the hard drive, and *voilá!* A Performa.

- The Performa 200 is simply a repackaged Mac Classic II.
- The Performa 400 line consists of repackaged LC II's. All but the 400 model itself include a built-in modem. The other things that differentiate the 400's from each other are things like the size of the internal hard drive (that's the only difference between the 405 and 430, for instance), the clock speed, whether an FPU is out of the question or at least an option, and the amount and kind of memory they can use.
- The Performa 520 and 550 are repackaged LC 520's. (Aha! A pattern is emerging!) That's the strange, one-piece design with a 14-inch built-in monitor.
- The Performa 600 is similar to the IIvx, except that it's lacking an FPU (math coprocessor) and the vx's high-speed memory cache; the 600CD model has a built-in CD-ROM player.

### Performa Specs

| | CPU | Speed | FPU | Max. RAM | Slots |
|---|---|---|---|---|---|
| 200 | 68000 | 16 MHz | no | 10MB | none |
| 400, 405, 410, 430 | 68030 | 16 MHz | no | 10MB | 1 PDS |
| 450 | 68030 | 25 MHz | opt. | 36MB | 1 PDS |
| 460, 466, 467 | 68030 | 33 MHz | opt. | 36MB | 1 PDS |
| 475, 476 | 68030 | 25 MHz | no | 36MB | 1 PDS |
| 520 | 68030 | 25 MHz | opt. | 36MB | 1 PDS |
| 550 | 68030 | 33 MHz | opt. | 36MB | 1 PDS |
| 600 | 68030 | 32 MHz | opt. | 68MB | 2 NuBus |

∞→ **Performas are equivalent,** for the most part, to standard Mac models; they're just sold in different types of stores. For instance:

Performa 200 = Classic II

Performa 400 = LC II

Performa 600 = Mac IIvx (without a cache card and FPU)

Performa 405 = LC II (plus a built-in modem and larger internal hard drive)

Performa 430 = LC II (plus a built-in modem and even larger internal hard drive)

Performa 450 = LC III

∞→ **The AV line** started with two machines, one a Centris and one a Quadra. Why, then, do I refer to an AV line instead of to models in the Centris and Quadra lines? Because the AV's are unique, with capabilities that set them apart from other Macs. The 660AV and the 840AV are specially enhanced to work as multimedia machines. Through a combination of redesigned circuitry and an additional processor (AT&T's DSP chip, a *digital signal processor*), the AV's do special work at especially fast speeds. Some of their features include:

- Permanent 32-bit addressing, with all internal components having direct access to memory.
- Built-in output capability for TV in NTSC, PAL, and S-video signals.
- Voice recognition for a limited number of commands and with the additional purchase of a special microphone.
- Speech. That's right, speech. Choose man, woman, or child (and set other parameters for the voice) from the control panel and have the Mac speak selected portions of text.
- High-fidelity sound recording right to your disk. (As high as that used on audio CDs.)
- Video digitizing, with the camera as a separate purchase.
- The new GeoPort connector for high-speed serial communication.

## AV Specs

|  | CPU | Speed | FPU | Max. RAM | Slots |
|---|---|---|---|---|---|
| Centris/Quadra 660AV | 68040 | 25 MHz | yes | 68MB | 1 NuBus or 1 PDS |
| Quadra 840AV | 68040 | 40 MHz | yes | 128MB | 3 NuBus |

The AV capabilities will last, but the AV's won't. They seemed to be a stopgap measure for people who needed more power in specialized areas than even a Quadra could provide. The introduction of the Power Mac and its optional AV card pretty much spelled out the end of the separate AV line.

### BRIGHT IDEAS #1 & #2

**Q.** How many software engineers does it take to change a light bulb?

**A.** "It's a hardware problem."

**Q.** How many hardware engineers does it take to change a light bulb?

**A.** "Tell software it has to code around it."

••▶ **The TV Mac** is one that few people ever heard of—it sounds like a joke. But the Macintosh TV, as it's properly called, is a 32 MHz 68030 machine with a built-in CD-ROM and a 10-meg RAM limit. It comes with a 14-inch cable-ready color TV monitor and a remote control for the TV and the CD drive. This "special edition" model may still be available—who knows? It's not like Apple is actually trying to sell it.

••▶ **PowerBooks.** The portable Macs. (And, oh, yes—their ancestor, the Mac Portable.) The PowerBooks are standard Macs in so many ways, and yet have many special abilities and concerns, especially the LCD display, battery handling, and power usage.

There's so much that's special about PowerBooks that I could write a separate book about them. Wait! I already did that, with co-author Rich Wolfson. I'll limit myself to a separate chapter about PowerBooks in this book.

## Power Macs

∞◆ **PowerPC. Power Mac:** one of the worst-kept secrets in the computer industry. The fruit of a surprising marriage between Apple and IBM, a PowerPC is a speed demon that's a totally different animal from either a Mac or an IBM-style PC. These computers, based on the *PowerPC 601* processing chip, can work like a Mac or like a DOS/Windows-based machine.

*PowerPC* is not only the name of the chip, but also the generic reference to these machines, which are manufactured by several different companies. The Apple-brand PowerPC is named the Power Mac.

∞◆ **The Power Mac is a screaming fast machine** because it uses RISC technology. RISC stands for *reduced instruction set computing*; it's a way to get more speed out of a processor chip.

In addition to the inherent speed in the PowerPC 601 processing chip, the Power Macs run at speeds of 60 to 80 MHz, well beyond the speeds of previous Macs. (The 100 MHz model was announced, but not released, as this book was finished.) To top it all off, the Power Macs have several internal features that speed operations even more, like a 256K cache and the ability to move data in 64-bit chunks instead of the standard 32-bit size.

∞◆ **A Power Mac is still a Mac.** What makes the Mac a Mac (I know I've said this before) is its interface, and the Power Mac runs System 7, so it works like a Mac. (The Power Mac version is System 7.1.2.)

∞◆ **A Power Mac works in two modes:** *native* and *emulation*. Native mode uses the Power Mac's processor chip (the PowerPC) and can take advantage of all its power and speed. But programs written for standard Macs don't know how to talk to a PowerPC chip. So, the Power Mac also runs in an emulation mode, where it pretends to be a 680x0 machine that can run all the current Mac software. Emulation mode gives you a slower environment than native mode, but still works at about the speed of a Centris or Quadra, which aren't exactly snails—except in comparison to the Power Mac's native mode, which is around five times faster.

∞◆ **The three initial models** of the PowerPC have the worst names yet of any Macs:

- The Power Mac 6100/60 is the low-end model, with a 60 MHz processor; it's packaged in a Quadra 610 case. It provides a single NuBus slot, but only if you buy a special $99 adapter.
- The Power Mac 7100/66, packed in a Quadra 650 body, has a 66 MHz processor.
- The Power Mac 8100/80 looks like a Quadra 800; if you're observant, you will have guessed that it runs at 80 MHz.

There are a lot of other special things about these machines. For instance: each supports not one, but *two* monitors with built-in video capabilities; the optional internal CD-ROM drive has a new mechanism that doesn't require using the caddy we've been stuck with for CDs on other Macs; you can buy it bundled with SoftWindows, a Windows emulator; and, the serial ports for modem and printer are high-speed GeoPorts.

The most unusual option for a Power Mac, though, may be the AV card; it's certainly the option that tolls the death knell for the AV machines. Buy a Power Mac with an AV card in it (it's not available as a separate purchase), and you get all the special video capabilities of an AV model, but in a faster machine. There's no DSP chip on the AV card, since the PowerPC RISC chip can handle all its functions at speeds rivaling that dedicated chip.

Upgrades from standard Macs to Power Macs are covered in the next chapter.

## Power Mac Specs

| | CPU | Speed | FPU | Max. RAM | Slots |
|---|---|---|---|---|---|
| 6100/60 | PPC601 | 60 MHz | - | 72MB | 1 NuBus |
| 7100/66 | PPC601 | 66 MHz | - | 136MB | 3 NuBus |
| 8100/80 | PPC601 | 80 MHz | - | 234MB | 3 NuBus |

**••▶ The Power Mac will get faster** over the first few months or even the first year of its life. There's no black magic at work here, and the hardware will still be the same. But you'll be able to work faster as the months go by for two reasons: more and more applications will become available in native mode, and a greater portion of the system software will be translated into native code as the months go by. With the initial Power Mac release, its version 7.1.2 of System 7 was only about 10 percent native code—but the most commonly used portions of the system were the ones that were converted first.

GEORGE LUCAS
(His most frequent direction
to the actors in Star Wars)

Faster, faster!

# CHAPTER 14
# MORE ON HARDWARE

> What we did was follow our own instincts and construct a computer that was what we wanted.
>
> STEVE JOBS

Some of the information you'll find in this chapter:

- ••◆ What an ADB device is, and how many you can attach to your Mac.
- ••◆ The evolution of the mouse.
- ••◆ A mouse pad is not a cool rodent's apartment.
- ••◆ How to make your Mac louder or silence it completely.
- ••◆ How to turn one Mac into another one.
- ••◆ What differentiates the Performas from other Macs. (And what doesn't.)
- ••◆ Where the hidden pictures are buried inside certain Mac models.

THE LAST PERSON YOU'D EXPECT TO FIND QUOTED IN A COMPUTER BOOK WHO IS ACTUALLY QUOTED IN THIS CHAPTER

*Henry Kissinger*

*page 537*

—Includes—

| | |
|---|---|
| 129 | Factoids |
| 10 | Quotes |
| 6 | Memos |
| 1 | Quiz |

# MOUSE & KEYBOARD

# OTHER INS & OUTS

# BASIC UPGRADES

# MAC BY MAC: QUIRKS & COMMENTS

## → MOUSE & KEYBOARD ←

### ADB Chains

∞→ **The keyboard and the mouse are ADB devices**—they use the Apple Desktop Bus to communicate with the Mac. There, wasn't that a helpful definition? Remember (from Chapter 13), a *bus* is a path for data to travel on, so ADB is simply a special kind of communication setup for certain Mac peripherals: the mouse and keyboard, numeric keypads, some scanners, trackballs, and so on.

### THE APPLE DESKTOP BUS (*NOT*)

The Journey is the Reward

SLIGHTLY MODIFIED THUNDERSCAN BY B. MAPLE

—from the BMUG PD-ROM

∞→ **ADB devices can be *chained***—linked to one another in a line. That's what you do, in fact, when you plug the keyboard into the computer and then plug the mouse into the keyboard—you've created a chain of two devices.

∞→ **There are several ways to plug in** an extra ADB device:

- If your Mac has a second ADB port (in the back with all the other ports), use that one.
- Use the pass-through ADB port on the extra device if it supplies one. Many trackballs, for instance, hook up to the keyboard's ADB port (where you normally plug in the mouse) but also provide a port that the mouse can then be connected to.
- Get a Y- or a T- connector that plugs into an existing ADB port and provides two ADB connections.

∞→ **Don't connect or disconnect ADB devices** on older Macs unless the computer is turned off—you can blow the ADB driver circuit on the motherboard if you're plugging in at exactly the wrong moment. (If you've been doing this with no problems so far, you're pushing your luck.)

Starting with the IIci, this is no longer a concern because the later-model Macs have a self-resetting fuse to take care of any problems on an ADB plug-in.

••→ **Don't chain too many ADB devices** to the Mac. The theoretical limit on an ADB chain is 16 devices, since there are 16 different "addresses" that the Mac can assign to ADB devices to keep track of them. But the practical limit is three, or maybe four at the most; beyond that, the signal from the last device(s) is usually too weak to make it to the computer. If you have more than one ADB port on the Mac itself (not an extra one because you used something like a Y-connector), they're separate chains when it comes to the signal being passed through, but the Mac still has the 16-device limit for both chains together.

••→ **There's a limit to the length** of an ADB chain independent of the number of devices; the limit is always given as five meters, which—for those of you who can't think in metric—is about 16 feet. That's not much, really: I have a six-foot cord to the keyboard, the keyboard is nearly two-feet long, the mouse wire is more than two-feet long—that's about 11 feet just for the two main devices. No wonder you can't get beyond three or four devices in the chain: The overall length limitation kicks in first!

••→ **You don't need a specialized ADB cable** for your ADB connections. The cable known as Super VHS has the same connectors and internal wiring; you can get it at any electronics store.

••→ **The Mac Plus** keyboard and mouse are not ADB devices; they have an entirely different setup, one that matches that used on the earliest Macs.

## The Mouse

∞→ **There have been three distinct mouse designs** used for Mac mice, but the second design actually had three different versions. The various models are easily differentiated, since the three main designs are completely different, and the variations of the second design have different color track balls and styles of retainer rings. And most of the mice are marked with their place of manufacture. (When was the last time you read the bottom of your mouse?)

• The original mouse used on all the Macs through the Mac Plus is, in retrospect, fairly clunky in design. It plugs into a special mouse port at the back of the Mac; unlike later mice, it's not an ADB device. It's forever enshrined as the icon for the Mouse control panel.

*✻I think we can assume the complaints were about the weight, not the color of the trackball.*

• The first ADB mouse introduced the lower, sleeker design that was used for the next several revisions of the mouse. It has a heavy gray ball and a retainer ring that slides forward to release; it was made in the USA. The second version has a lighter (in weight) black ball held in with a rotating retainer ring; it was made in Taiwan. The third version of the ADB mouse was made in Malaysia; in response to the complaints of users of the first and second versions, it used a heavier, gray, trackball.*

- The latest mouse design is a total departure from both the original and the previous one: It's very rounded and the trackball is forward, nearer to the fingertips than in the earlier mice. It's made in—wait, let me turn mine over and see—well, this one's from Malaysia, too.

## THE EVOLUTION OF THE MOUSE

The Macintosh mouse has gone through three major designs, changing shape and losing weight each time.

When Apple engineers were designing a mouse—originally for the Lisa (the Mac's predecessor)—they went through over 150 test models, many of which included more than one button. In fact, the action of double-clicking on the Mac to make something happen is a direct result of the decision to go with a single button on the mouse instead of multiple buttons to provide different functions.

∞•> **The Mouse control panel** lets you set the tracking speed and the double-click interval for your mouse. The details are few, but they're in Chapter 8.

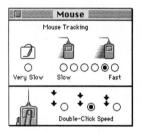

∞◦> **Speed up that mouse** beyond what the mouse control panel allows by using Mouse2, a control panel that lets you double the speed setting of the Mouse control panel. It's great for big screens. [shareware, Ryoji Watanabe]

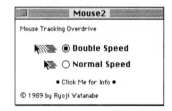

∞•> **Use a mouse pad.** Go ahead—splurge a few bucks on an actual mouse pad to keep under the mouse. Don't worry about clever substitutes like spiral notebook covers or a little cutting board covered in art paper—you'll be spending just as much money, for something less efficient. A mouse pad stakes out an area of your desk that's specifically for the mouse, provides an excellent rolling surface (just the right amount of traction), and keeps dust and dirt in the rolling area to a minimum.

There's an astounding variety of mouse pads available, from designs that advertise companies and products to artistic ones that you might be tempted to frame and hang on a wall on a day when you've totally lost sight of reality. You can get a mouse pad that has a clear cover under which you can place a calendar, a list of shortcuts for your favorite programs—or one of the Mac Almanac Charts from the back of this book. There are even mouse pads that offer extra wrist support for those of us being crippled by overuse of our computers.

**SAKI**
*THE SQUARE EGG,* 1924

... always leave room for the mouse.

•••▶ **You can wax** your mustache, your legs, your surfboard, or your car (although probably not both your mustache and your legs, if you catch my drift), but don't wax the surface beneath your mouse. With nothing between a waxed desktop and a mouse ball, the wax gets transferred to the ball and then to the rollers inside the mouse—and you'll have a useless mouse in a very short time. Cleaning wax off the ball and the interior rollers is more difficult than removing dirt and lint.

∞◊ **Replace a worn out ADB mouse** with another Apple mouse, a third-party mouse, or a trackball. Logitech makes two replacement mice. One's called the MouseMan, and it has three buttons whose functions you can define. Their Kidz Mouse is for little kids: It's shaped like a real mouse, but it's small, for young hands—and the two flat ears are the buttons.

∞◊ **The Mac Plus mouse** is really aging by now. Although later mice have Teflon areas that slide around on your desk surface, the Mac Plus mouse had four little nubby feet made of the same plastic material as the casing itself. If you've been using the mouse since the Plus was introduced in 1986, it has put on many miles—and those feet are somewhat worn down. But you don't need a whole new mouse, or even foot transplants. Try any of these:

- Add small stick-on felt pads over what's left of the feet.
- Use the rounded ("eye") half of Velcro stick-on pads on the feet. These glide nicely over a hard surface and work well as long as you don't mind a slight scritchy sound as you move the mouse around.
- Try Mouse-Ease, Teflon stick-on nubs for the bottom of your worn-out mouse. [Taclind]

•••▶ **Unplugging and reattaching the mouse** while the computer's on—for models where this isn't a danger (ci's and later)—can have one of several consequences. You may find that the mouse cursor is moving more quickly or more slowly than before, and resetting the tracking speed in the Mouse control panel fixes the problem. Or, you may find the cursor speed has changed but you can't reset it—only a restart of the Mac fixes the problem. Or you may find no problem at all.

Which of these three scenarios is yours depends on which Mac and which mouse you're using, but you can count on its being consistent.

## The Keyboard

**Keyboards have evolved** along with the Macs. The clunky arrow-less keyboard of the original begat the Mac Plus keyboard—still clunky, but with cursor keys and a numeric keypad. The Mac Plus keyboard miraculously begat a line of ADB keyboards:

- The Apple Keyboard is pretty much an ADB version of the Mac Plus keyboard. It's sleek and the keys are clicky instead of spongy, but the keyboard layout is pretty much the same, with the arrow keys all in a row at the bottom right of the alphanumeric keys. There is the addition, however, of the Power On key for Macs that can be started from the keyboard.

- The Apple Keyboard II, also referred to as the "extended keyboard," offers more keys than the standard keyboard: important modifier keys like Command and Option appear twice; there's a cluster of keys that let you jump around in documents, access online help, and use a forward delete function; and, there's a row of 15 function keys that provide shortcuts in many programs. The layout of the keyboard differs from the standard one, with the Esc key placed at the top of the keyboard, and a few other minor keys (like the backslash) moved around.

- The Apple Extended Keyboard II is the same as the first version except that it has feet at the back to hold it at a tilted angle that's more comfortable for typing.

- The Apple Adjustable Keyboard is an odd-looking piece of work; its main keyboard is split and the two pieces rotated slightly away from each other to provide a more comfortable position for your hands and wrists.

Chapter 3 discusses the functions of all the special, non-typewriter, keys on the keyboard.

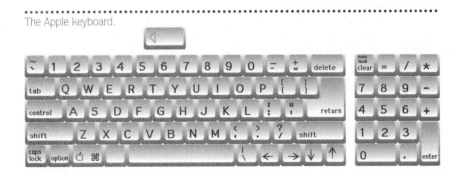

The Apple keyboard.

The Apple Extended keyboard.

◦•→ **The "feel" of a keyboard** is very important, but there's not much you can do ahead of time—you won't find any "try before you buy" deals anywhere. You can console yourself with the idea that, for the most part, you get used to a keyboard's touch—and its key arrangement—after using it for a while.

If you hate your keyboard, though, you don't have to stick with it. You don't even have to stick to Apple's keyboard lineup, since other manufacturers make ADB keyboards for the Mac. You might consider ordering a keyboard from a mail-order catalog that offers your money back if you don't like the product. Try the keyboard for a week (taking *very* good care of it) and if it just doesn't please you, then send it back.

◦•→ **The Keyboard control panel** lets you set the key repeat rate, the delay until the repeat, and the keyboard layout if you have more than one. The details are covered in Chapters 1 and 8.

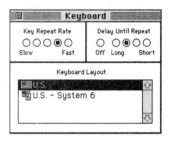

### STROKE, STROKE!

A single keystroke contact lasts about 500 microseconds and uses about 4 ten-millionths of a watt-hour. You could type nearly 200,000 standard double-spaced pages and your keyboard uses only as much electricity as a 100-watt bulb does in an hour.

> ✳That's an aircraft
> carrier you can land
> a plane on ... get it?

◦•→ **Get the extended keyboard** if you have a choice. (Some Macs come bundled with the standard keyboard, but for most models you buy the keyboard separately.) This keyboard, because of its size, is often disparagingly referred to by its original code-name *USS Saratoga*,✳ but I love it. The function keys across the top are being used for shortcuts by more and more programs; and they give me quick access to lots of features that I've programmed in as macros. The Page Up/Down, Home, and End keys are terrific, as is the Forward Delete key (once you start using it in word processing, you'll wonder how you lived without it). What's a few more square inches of desk space compared to all that convenience?

> Macros are
> covered
> in Chapter 21.

I love my PowerBook, but I miss that big keyboard when I'm away from my desk machine. I've set up macro substitutes for the function keys and Forward Delete, but it's just not the same. I'll just have to get a newer PowerBook, one with function keys on it.

◦•→ **There are two extended keyboards:** The Apple Keyboard II and the Apple Extended Keyboard II. What's the difference? About $80. What do you get for that $80? Not much. Same number of keys. Same layout. A slightly different feel on the keys—no better or worse, just different. Feet at the back to raise it to an angle you like for typing. That's about it.

**The adjustable keyboard** is a nifty idea, but it just doesn't go far enough. I know: as I type this, I'm wearing wrist braces because I type so much that I have tendinitis and have to keep my wrists in a certain alignment in order to keep it from flaring up. The adjustable keyboard is certainly an improvement over the standard one, because you don't have to bring your arms in front of you (angled in from your shoulders), and then rotate your hands outward at the wrist to line them up on the keys. But Apple's Adjustable Keyboard keeps the numeric keypad, cursor keys, and function keys on a separate unit. The function keys are ugly little rubbery ovals, and the page control keys are rubbery little circles. Both are awkward to get to, and hard to press. You can't just quickly jab at them the way you can standard keys—you have to aim more precisely, and then *press*, to get the keys to register. And take it from me: If you have long fingernails, the buttons are almost impossible to press since you can't use your nail or the tip of your finger—you have to approach them sort of sideways with your finger.*

> *For those of you without manicures, who might be wondering: Regular keyboard keys can be pressed easily with either the fingernail itself, or with the fingertip while the nail sort of slides in the crack above the key you're pressing. Isn't it amazing what you can learn from this book?

Did you ever wonder why you don't hear much about this keyboard? I don't think it's because it wasn't the perfect answer to an endemic problem. I think Apple has a real problem pushing this new ergonomic keyboard in a litigious society. How long do you think it would take someone to say: "Well, if you know this is a better keyboard, then you must have known that the other keyboards you're selling are ruining my wrists, so..." The adjustable keyboard costs about $220.

**Does your keyboard have feet** that you don't know about? Let me tell you a story. About my sister-in-law. (Wait, that's my *ex*-sister-in-law. My new sister-in-law shouldn't get blamed for this.) When she was first married, she and her husband bought a coffee table for their apartment—a modernistic wood-and-glass design that they both loved. But she was disappointed that the model they had looked at in the showroom glided easily on hidden casters, while hers simply rested on its wood-frame bottom and had to be lifted to be moved—and that glass was heavy! Years later they moved from the apartment to their first house and, of course, the coffee table went with them. But, as it was lifted into the moving van, they caught their first glimpse of the bottom of the table: And there in the hollow formed by the wooden base, were the wheels, in factory-fresh condition, still sealed in plastic bags taped to the bottom of the table.

Are you looking underneath your keyboard now? Is there a thin strip the length of the keyboard, along the edge that's underneath the function keys? Aha! You've found your hidden feet! Many users never realize that the latest extended keyboard—The Apple Extended Keyboard II—is adjustable. There's a slider control at the back edge of the keyboard (the part that faces the computer). It's ridiculously hard to move, but when you do move it, the keyboard support moves up and down out at the back of the keyboard.

**Give your wrists a rest.** When I first got my PowerBook, I couldn't figure out why typing on its even-more-cramped-than-usual keyboard was so comfortable. Then I realized that the heels of my hands were resting on its built-in wrist rest while my fingers did their walking.

✳No doubt, there'll be
a product named Wrist
Wrest before long.

Adding a wrist rest to your desktop keyboard is a simple and inexpensive way to make keyboarding less stressful. (It's really the heels of your hands that rest on the support, but *wrist rest* ✳ is so much more alliterative than *heel rest*.)

∞﴾ **You can get a separate numeric keypad** if your keyboard doesn't have one. A keyboard as a stand-alone unit was popular after the Mac Plus came out, but the demand faded away after all the Mac keyboards started coming out with integrated keypads. You'd be hard-pressed to find a keypad for the Mac Plus these days, because there's so little demand. However, the advent of the keypadless PowerBook created a demand for an ADB keypad, so you'll find several models available. If you bought a small keyboard several years ago, when Apple was marketing one that was used on both Macs and the Apple IIGS, this is a great way to add a keypad.

There's not much that sets most of the keypads apart from one another; you get pretty much the same capability from most. You can get good units from Sophisticated Circuits and from Kensington. But the MacAbacus from Key Tronic is really special: it's a calculator—LCD display and everything—that can paste the results of its calculations directly into the document at the touch of the Send button. In its keypad mode, it offers the numeric keypad; in function key mode, it offers the standard 15 function keys. In any mode, it provides four arrow keys in a convenient inverted-T formation.

∞﴾ **If you work in a dirty environment** and want to keep your keyboard clean and clear, especially from particulates that can sift down between the keys, or if you're just an Oscar Madison type who needs to protect the keyboard from spilled coffee or soda, get a keyboard cover for about $20. This clear plastic film fits snugly over the keyboard; it's strong, but so thin that it doesn't interfere with the feel of the keys. Honest, it doesn't— I've tried them!

∞﴾ **Get an extra-long keyboard wire** if the standard one is too short. My CPU is to my left, on a raised part of the desk, with external hard drives stacked on top of it, rather than in front of me under the monitor, as in most setups. As a result, the keyboard wire just doesn't reach comfortably. I have a 6-foot coiled keyboard wire that reaches, with room to spare—one of the best $15 that I ever spent on computer equipment. You can get this kind of wire from several sources; mine is from Kensington.

∞﴾ **Where can you buy all the odds and ends** I mention in this chapter: extra-long cables, ADB Y-adapters, trackballs, mouse pads, wrist rests? Do it by my favorite method: catalogs. A good catalog is a great shopping experience—you'll find things you didn't know existed, and didn't know that you needed. For instance, I just gathered up several catalogs so I could write this entry and thumbed through the APS catalog. In amongst their cable collection was an item I hadn't noticed before: a switch cable. It's a perfect solution for a common problem: one serial port free on your computer and two devices you need to attach; you don't need to use both at the same time, but it's a pain to swap the cables at the back of the computer. If you attach both devices to this switch, all you have to do is flip the switch to let one or the other use the serial port. Now, I don't need this handy little critter—but you might. On a different page, I see another product I was unaware of—a mouse ball replacement. Anyway, the point is that catalog browsing is a great way to see what's out there.

There are some very reliable Mac mail-order catalogs around. The service is fast—overnight, if you need it—and, for the most part, the personnel are knowledgeable. Look through a recent issue of *MacUser* or *Macworld* magazine—almost every Mac owner gets one or both of them. You'll find inserts from the catalog companies, and once you order, you'll get the full catalog directly (for the rest of your natural life and perhaps beyond).

I use APS for PowerBook stuff, hard drives, and odds and ends like cables. I've used MacConnection and MacWarehouse for years for software (okay, what little I have to actually buy since I'm constantly getting review copies) and for smaller odds and ends like floppy disks and labels. You can even buy memory through these catalogs (instead of through a memory-only mail-order place). I've never had a problem getting stuff in a rush, or returning it for whatever legitimate reason may have cropped up. In addition to these three places, which I can personally recommend very highly, The MacZone is another mail-order place with a good reputation.*

*Apple had a catalog for a while. The most interesting thing about it was that you could, for a mere $2000, order a year's worth of technical support from an Apple engineer!

Here are their numbers:

| | |
|---|---|
| APS | 800-926-0390 |
| MacConnection | 800-800-2222 |
| MacWarehouse | 800-255-6227 |
| The MacZone | 800-436-8000 |

## → OTHER INS & OUTS ←

### Trackballs

∞→ **A trackball is essentially an upside-down mouse.** Some people swear by them; others swear *at* them. I've never found a trackball comfortable to use at my desk machine, yet on my PowerBook, I don't have a problem. I think the difference is the placement: On a PowerBook, the trackball is right there beneath the spacebar, right where your thumbs are hovering anyway.

∞→ **Trackballs have more than one button.** That's because it's easy to keep the mouse button down while you're moving the mouse, but it's difficult to roll a trackball while holding down one of its buttons. The usual approach is that one button is used for clicking, while the other one is for dragging—when you press it, the button stays locked down in position until you press it again.

PowerBook trackballs are covered in Chapter 18.

Some trackballs provide more than two buttons, or special functions, when you press both buttons at the same time. The functions are usually user-configurable, so you can use them as a Paste command, or as Save or Undo, for instance.

∞→ **If you're getting a trackball,** find the right balance (for you) between size and weight. A heavier trackball usually provides smoother operation, but smaller trackballs provide finer control. Most trackballs are in the $100 range.

The Turbo Mouse from Kensington has a nice, heavy ball with smooth action and includes software that lets you jump the cursor to predefined spots on the screen. (And you can get custom-color trackballs for it!) CoStar's Stingray has a beautiful, sleek design, with the sides—which are the buttons—sloping away from the trackball in the center, and comes in platinum or black; its shape certainly resembles the marine animal for which it's named. LogiTech's TrackMan is an odd-looking item, a flat rectangular body with the ball off to one side for your thumb to manipulate while your fingers can fiddle with the three programmable buttons.

∞➢ **Get a keyboard with a built-in trackball** for your desk machine. Key Tronic's TrakPro combines the arrow keys with the Page Up/Page Down and other cursor control keys so there's room for a small trackball right on the keyboard, where the arrow keys are usually placed. If you use the arrow keys and the page control keys a lot, this setup isn't for you, since one set of keys has to toggle between two modes; but if you don't use the page control keys often and don't have room for a mouse or a separate trackball, this is a compact approach. It costs about $230, what you'd wind up paying for a good keyboard and separate trackball.

PETER MACWILLIAMS
THE WORD PROCESSING
BOOK, 1983

The Lisa [the Mac's immediate predecessor] uses a device known as a mouse to move a pointer around the screen. A mouse is a sort of executive joystick. If you want to file something, you move the pointer to a picture of a little folder and push a button. Business, then, becomes a computer game.

Man's fear of ideas is probably the greatest dike holding back human knowledge and happiness.

MORRIS LEOPOLD ERNST

## Tablets & Scanners

∞➤ **A *graphics tablet* provides** a flat area that you draw on with a special pen; the motions of the pen are considered mouse motions, so what you draw on the tablet appears on the screen. The way you actually press the "mouse button" on the pen varies from one model to another.

Graphics tablets are great for artists who just can't do what they need to with a mouse, which, after all, is somewhat like drawing with a bar of soap. They range in size (the tablets, that is, not the artists) from about 7-inches square to the more standard 12x18 inches to an incredible drafting-table size of 35x45 inches.

⤙ **Graphics tablets use *absolute positioning*** instead of *relative positioning*. A mouse uses relative positioning: You can put it down anywhere on your desk and when you move it, the cursor on the screen just moves relative to the starting position of the mouse. On a graphics tablet, if you touch the pen to the center of the tablet, the cursor jumps to the middle of the screen; touch it to the lower-left corner of the tablet, and the cursor moves to the lower-left corner of the screen. It's really a great feature, and it's a shame there's no special mouse pad that would provide that option for mouse positioning.

⤙ **Some tablets are *pressure sensitive*** so that the harder you press the pen, the darker or wider the line on the screen becomes. This is analogous to pressing harder with a paint-brush to use the thicker gathering of bristles instead of its tapered point. (Of course, the software you're using has to know how to interpret that kind of information coming in from the tablet.)

⤙ **Once you decide you need a tablet,** and about what size it should be, how do you pick a brand? Two manufacturers that get consistently high ratings from reviewers and other hard-to-please users are CalComp and Wacom. CalComp's DrawingBoard II has both a pen and a "puck" for input, and both come in cordless versions. Wacom's SD420E (don't you think they could have worked on that name a little bit?) also has both a pen and a puck with cordless versions.

I checked with two artistic friends—Carol's a graphic designer who designed this book, and Andy did many of the drawings for the book—and they both use Wacom tablets; I suppose that's a substantial endorsement.

⤙ **A scanner is** a miraculous device that puts what you have on paper onto your computer screen. They come in black-and-white and in color models. (I'm referring, of course, to the type of materials they can scan, not to the color of their cases.)

Most scanners are *flatbed* models, which means you can simply lay the paper flat inside (as in a copy machine) and it's scanned by a mechanism that moves beneath it. Other scanners roll the paper through, past a stationary scanning mechanism; still others, *hand scanners*, let you roll a small hand-held unit over the paper.

Flatbed scanners, as you might have guessed, are both the most sophisticated and the most expensive for desktop systems—but for the most part, they're worth every extra cent because you don't have to worry about getting the paper in perfectly evenly, or piecing together multiple passes of a hand-scanned document.

If you want to scan in transparencies-slides, you need a scanner with higher capabilities and should expect to spend more money. Scanners start at around $600 and can cost many thousands of dollars at the top end. Companies whose scanners have generally received good reviews from the Macintosh community include: Abaton, Agfa, Barneyscan, Hewlett-Packard, Leaf Systems, Microtech, and Thunderware.

⤙ **Scanners can also scan text.** Then, a special program called OCR (*optical character recognition*) software converts the picture the scanner takes into true, editable text. When you see good software working, it is an amazing procedure. If you think about it, it's hard to differentiate an *m* from *ni*, and so on. Good software can recognize different font types and even handle multiple-column scans; combined with a good spelling checker, you can easily get 98-percent accuracy on a single pass.

## Sound

☞ **Every Mac has an internal speaker** that's perfect for system sounds like beeps and chirps, and is sufficient for any other kind of sound that might accompany a special program, like a game. But there's also a sound output port for when you need better-fidelity sound. The Mac produces sounds of a much better quality than you're able to hear through its speaker.

☞ **Make your Mac speak up** with external speakers. You don't have to be playing beautiful music on your Mac to want better sound output. My kids love turning on their speakers for playing certain games.

The speakers don't have to be fancy; you don't even need two of them. The first time I hooked up any speaker at all to my Mac (it was a Plus), I used a speaker from a kid's stereo set; I wired a miniplug to the end of the speaker wire so I could plug it in to the sound port. It was great.

But if you want external speakers, you may as well take a more formal route:

- You can plug into your stereo set if you want to use its speakers. Get a cable from an electronics or stereo store that has the miniplug at one end (for the Mac's sound port) and two RCA plugs on the other. Use the line inputs on your stereo's receiver (they're marked *aux* on mine).
- Buy speakers made for your computer. They should be *powered* so they don't have to be plugged into an amplifier—they can be plugged directly into an outlet. And they should be *shielded* because the electromagnets used in speakers can interfere with your monitor, if they're allowed to leak their signals unimpeded.

☞ **Try earphones with the Mac.** Or, more to the point, leave them there for the kids to use when they're playing games that you don't want to hear.

The little earphones that come with personal players like Walkmans have plugs that are the correct size for the Mac's sound port; the earphones are compact, too, so you can hang them on the side of the Mac with a little Velcro strip. If you want to use standard stereo earphones, you'll need an adapter because the larger plug won't fit into the Mac. Stereo and electronic stores carry these $1/8$-inch-to-$1/4$-inch adapters.

☞ **The Mac is very loud.** If you've hooked up earphones to the sound jack, make sure the volume is way down to 1 or 2 in the Sound control panel before you put the earphones on. You can then try the 3- or even the 4-level volume, but you'll probably find it uncomfortable.

☞ **Silence your Mac completely** by putting a plug in it. You can get a single plug that doesn't even have a wire on it at any electronics store. Or you can snip one off an old broken pair of earphones. Or plug the earphones in but don't put them on. When anything's plugged into the sound out port, the internal speaker isn't used.

## Modems

∞→ **A *modem* is a device that** lets your computer communicate over phone lines. It takes the *digital* signals that the computer uses (strings of ones and zeros) and changes them into *analog* signals (sound, in this case) that can be

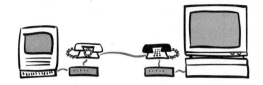

transmitted on phone lines. At the other end of the connection, another modem takes that analog signal and converts it to digital form again for the computer at that end. The signal is being *modulated* and *demodulated*, which is where the word *modem* comes from.*

> *I expect that origin to become shrouded in mystery sometime in the next few decades, as modems become standard equipment.

A digital signal from the computer is converted to an analog signal for the phone by the modem; at the other end of the connection, the analog signal is changed back to digital for the other computer by another modem.

∞→ **The speed at which a modem sends** and receives information is known as its *baud rate*. Early modems worked at 300 and 1200 baud; 2400-baud modems are now considered slow. Now, 9600-baud is almost considered the slow standard, with 14,400 baud being the preferred rate.

We're in the midst of a jargon evolution when it comes to speed, and more and more often you'll see speed measured in *bps*, or *bits per second* instead of in baud.

∞→ **A modem can work at a slower rate** than its maximum. And many times it has to: If you're communicating with another computer whose modem can't match your modem's top speed, the faster modem can notch down to talk at the slower speed.

∞→ **What difference does the baud rate make?** Just before I replaced my older modem on my desk setup, I was preparing to send a file to someone and noticed that the transmission time, as reported by the software ahead of time, would be about half an hour at 2400 baud. Having better things to do with that half-hour, I transferred the file across my tiny network to my PowerBook, which is equipped with a 14,400-baud modem. The file was transmitted at 9600 (the capacity of the receiving modem) in less than three minutes. I ordered a faster modem for my desk machine the next day.

∞→ **An older 2400-baud modem** is sufficient for some people. If, for instance, your modeming is going to be basically reading through bulletin board notices and transmitting short text files, 2400-baud won't seem all that slow. But it's getting harder to acknowledge the usefulness of a 2400-baud modem when the 14,400 versions are well under $200.

∞→ ***Hayes compatible* is** a label you'll probably see on about 99 percent of modems. Hayes Microcomputer developed a set of commands for its modems way back when, and they're an industry standard now. If the modem is Hayes compatible, it can send and respond to the basic modem commands. I don't think I've ever run across a modem that wasn't 100-percent Hayes compatible—except for some of the ones from Apple!

Using your modem for telecommunications is covered in Chapter 21.

••◗ **MNP? v.32bis? What?** When you're shopping for modems, you'll see all sorts of specs—few of which you'll be able to translate. Most refer to the special protocols used by the modem when transmitting data, all meant to speed up the transmission. Some are compression schemes which squeeze the data into smaller chunks before sending them, with the understanding that they'll be expanded back to their original sizes at the other end. Some are error-checking schemes that make sure the transmission is correct—that what shows up at the other end is the same thing as you sent. There are only two things you need to keep in mind: As the numbers get higher (MNP5, MNP10; v.32bis, v.42bis), performance gets better; and, advanced capabilities in the modem on your end can't be used if the one on the other end can't do the same tricks. Luckily, all that is automatic—*you* don't have to figure out what the other modem can do. Oh— and you say *v.32bis* as *vee-dot-thirty-two-biss*.

••◗ **Almost every modem is a fax modem** these days. I know; I tried to buy one that *wasn't* a fax modem and couldn't find one. I already had a fax modem in my PowerBook, and a standard fax machine, too, and didn't need any more faxing capability.

Using a fax modem and faxing software (bundled with the modem), you can send a document from your computer to someone's fax machine. This beats printing the document and then faxing it on a standard machine because the image the fax modem sends is much cleaner (and because you may not *have* a fax machine!). You can also receive faxes from a standard fax machine directly into your computer—but keep in mind that you'll get an *image* of a document, not editable text on your screen from a fax. (Some fax software offers the capability of translating the images into true text, but the accuracy is far from acceptable at this point.)

I did see one item advertised as a fax modem that was actually a standard fax machine with a modem built into it. If you see a fax modem advertised for around $800 instead of, say, $300, you're probably looking at that fax/modem hybrid rather than a modem that knows how to send and receive faxes.

> Just the fax, ma'am, just the fax.    DRAGNET

## → BASIC UPGRADES ←

### Apple Upgrades

∞◗ **Apple's not known for upgradeable** equipment—ask any Mac owner who's been stuck in an evolutionary dead end. (I mean, whose *computer* is an evolutionary dead end. Although there *are* some people I've met that … never mind.) But some Macs are upgradeable in minor and in major ways with Apple-supplied parts. You'll probably have to go through an authorized dealer or technician for these upgrades, but I've included the Apple part numbers where possible.

∘•▶ **Beef up an older Mac model** with one of the little things it might be missing, like a coprocessor or the 1.4MB SuperDrive floppy drive. The upgrades from Apple are:

| For this model... | Get a... | Part # |
|---|---|---|
| Mac LC III; Color Classic; Performa 450, 460, 466, 467 | math coprocessor | M6775LL/A |
| Mac IIsi | math coprocessor (included on PDS adapter) | M0480LL/A |
| Mac IIci | cache card | M0326LL/B |
| SE | SuperDrive upgrade | M6052/B |
| Mac II | SuperDrive upgrade | M6051/C |
| Mac II | PMMU | M0221 |

∘•▶ **Some Macs can be changed into other models** by an Apple upgrade: You swap the logic board of your computer for that of another model. These are the upgrades that Apple can provide:

| Turn this... | Into a... | Part # |
|---|---|---|
| Mac Classic | Mac Classic II | M1545LL/A |
| Mac LC or LC II | Mac LC III | M1386LL/A |
| Performa 400, 405, 410, 430 | Performa 450 | M0375LL/A |
| Mac II or IIx | Mac IIfx | M1330LL/A |
| Mac IIvx, Performa 600, 600CD | Quadra 650 | M1421LL/A |
| Quadra 900 | Quadra 950 | M6940ZA |

Interestingly enough, the upgrade to the Performa 450 is by means of the LC II logic board upgrade—further proof of the "equivalencies" mentioned in the last chapter. (Not that you doubted me, of course.) Many late-model Macs can be upgraded into Power Macs—that's covered in the next section.

•••▶ **Don't upgrade an LC** to an LC II. It costs about $700. You get an '030 chip instead of the LC's original '020, but you won't see much of a speed increase. Instead, upgrade it to an LC III—for over a hundred dollars less! You'll practically double the power of the LC when you transform it into an LC III—the best upgrade deal Apple ever offered.

There is a certain relief in change, even though it be from bad to worse; as I have found in traveling in a stage-coach, that it is often a comfort to shift one's position and be bruised in a new place.

WASHINGTON IRVING

···◆ **Before upgrading to a new logic board,** think twice. Or three times. Some upgrades make a lot of sense: the LC or LC II to an LC III; the Classic to a Classic II. But in many cases, if you need an upgrade because your needs are outstripping the computer's capabilities, it makes more sense to sell your current machine to someone who needs that level of computing power and buy a new machine. In fact, the difference between what you get for your old system and what you pay for the new one might be not too much more than the cost of an upgrade.

Personally, I use the trickle-down method most of the time: I get a new system, the current one goes to the kids, and the kids' setup gets sold. Not that the kids need the level of computing power that they have now (a IIci with 8 megs of memory, 160 megs of disk space and a CD-ROM player), but it serves as a second work station for me when I need it.

···◆ **Can you PowerPC it?** Can you change your computer into a Power Mac, or add a card that has the PowerPC chip and increase your Mac's capabilities? Before upgrading any mid-range or high-end Mac to something a step or two beyond its original capabilities, look into the possibility of leapfrogging beyond the incremental upgrade and getting PowerPC power.

Turning a Quadra 900 into a 950, for instance, was never a bargain at about $1900, since all you really got was a faster machine—something you could achieve with a third-party accelerator for a lot less money. But now it makes no sense at all, because you can add a PowerPC card for the extra speed, for less money.

···◆ **Donate your old system** to a charitable organization. Some really old systems are impossible to sell, especially since the cost of new systems keeps dropping. Help someone out and get a tax break at the same time. Lots of organizations can use a Mac Plus or SE for basic word processing and record keeping.

## Upgrading to a PowerPC

···◆ **Upgrading to a Power Mac** is easy for many users. Knowing that sales of late-model pre-PowerMac machines would drop precipitously in anticipation of the PowerMac's release, Apple made sure that upgrades from a standard Mac to a PowerPC would be possible. You can replace the logic board of your computer with a Power Mac logic board and, to all intents and purposes, you'll have a Power Mac. Which Power Mac you can upgrade to depends on which Mac model you started with. Here are the possibilities:

| Upgrade to a... | From a... |
|---|---|
| Power Mac 6100/60 | Quadra/Centris 610, 660AV |
| Power Mac 7100/66 | Mac IIvi, IIvx |
| | Performa 600 |
| | Quadra/Centris 650 |
| Power Mac 8100/80 | Quadra 800, 840AV |

At the time the Power Macs were released, these three upgrades cost $1000, $1500, and $2000. I'd expect those prices to remain stable for nearly a year before the price comes down. Power Mac AV upgrade cards are also available for each of these models.

HENRY KISSINGER

Power is the ultimate aphrodisiac.

•→ **A semi-upgrade to a Power Mac** is available for many Quadra, Centris, and Performa models. This upgrade isn't a logic-board exchange, but a PDS card that adds the PowerPC 601 chip to your computer; this doubles the clock speed of your computer and gives it the capability of using applications written in PowerPC native code. You don't get all the features of a Power Mac this way, but it is a way of increasing the power of your existing machine. The models that can use this $700 upgrade are:

- Centris/Quadra 610, 650
- Quadra 700, 800, 900, 950

To differentiate between the logic board upgrade and this one, this is referred to as the *PowerPC Upgrade Card*—the "card" part that gives it away.

∘∘⟩ **Apple isn't the only one with PowerPC upgrade** cards. DayStar's PowerPro 601 upgrades offer even better performance than Apple's cards (for, of course, a little more money). The PowerPro upgrades are 66- and 80-MHz cards that get the upgraded Mac to run at those speeds. The Apple upgrades, on the other hand, double the existing speed of the Mac model you're upgrading. So, a 25-MHz Quadra 700 runs at 50 MHz with the Apple upgrade but at 80 MHz with the better of the two PowerPro upgrades.

In addition, the DayStar upgrade cards include SIMM slots right on the card. The PowerPC chip on the card can access this memory more quickly than the one on Apple's card can access the memory in the standard SIMM slots in your Mac. [DayStar]

•→ **Upgrading a Centris 610** with a PowerPC Upgrade Card is a bad idea. You need a PDS adapter to be able to use the upgrade card, raising the total cost of the upgrade to $800. For that, you get the ability to run PowerPC native applications and a doubled clock speed—40 MHz, not that much at all. For $1000, you can get the logic board upgrade, which gives you the native mode capability, the new GeoPorts, and the 60MHz processor—a much better deal.

•→ **Upgrade your hard drive driver** if you upgrade your Mac to a Power Mac. Your what? This is discussed in Chapter 18, but, briefly: the hard drive driver is the software that lets the Mac talk to the hard drive. The ROMs in the Power Mac and PowerPC upgrade cards can work up to 25 percent faster on SCSI transfers when the driver is updated.

## Other Upgrades

∞✦ **The easiest and most** cost-effective upgrade for you computer is additional RAM. Chapter 13 covers this in detail.

### A DIFFERENT TYPE OF **RAM** UPGRADE

Back in 1985, a "fat" Mac meant 512K of RAM, and SIMMs were as yet unheard of in the Mac community.

But if the 512K machine just didn't provide enough RAM for everything you wanted to do, there was an alternative: the Dasch (Disk Acceleration/Storage Control Hardware). Since the Mac itself wasn't upgradeable, a Dasch provided *external* RAM; the unit connected to the printer or modem port and multiple units could be chained together to provide 16 megs of RAM (!).

The cost? Let me quote from the October, 1985 issue of *MacUser*:

> ... And the price is pretty reasonable. DASCH comes in three versions. The 500K version lists for $495, the 1 MB version is $975, and the 2MB monster is $1785.

Pretty reasonable at the time, I suppose. There's no such thing as a "2MB monster" anymore: 2MB is positively wimpy these days. And it costs about $70.

∞✦ **An accelerator board** replaces your Mac's processor with a faster one: a 68030 instead of a 68000, or an '040 instead of the '030. Although a logic board replacement from Apple that turns your Mac into a completely different model certainly accelerates your system, there are also separate accelerator boards from other companies that get installed in a NuBus or PDS slot instead of replacing the logic board itself.

∞✦ **You can add an FPU** to several of the Mac models that come without them. The models that can be upgraded this way are: the LC III, Color Classic, Performa 450, 460, 466, and 467.

∞✦ **A QuickDraw accelerator** is a different kind of accelerator; instead of making the processor work faster, it makes your screen work faster. Many times the bottleneck of a Mac system is not a slow processor, but the time it takes to draw the processed information on the screen. This is especially obvious when you're using a double-page display in grayscale or color. QuickDraw is the set of routines in the Mac's ROMs that draws things on the screen, so accelerating this process speeds up the screen display.

Many specialized video cards that enable you to connect a monitor to your Mac include QuickDraw acceleration.

∞✦ **A cache card** provides special storage (in high-speed memory chips) for data and instructions that have been used recently and are likely to be needed again. The IIci has a special slot for a cache card; the earliest models came with an empty slot; later, the cache card was included as standard.

The '040 Macs include cache memory; some Quadras, though, have a slot for an additional cache card.

••→ **You can upgrade the video capabilities** of many Mac models by increasing the amount of *video RAM* in the machine. With an upgrade, a Mac that previously could display only 256 colors would be able to display thousands; one that displayed thousands originally could display millions. That's all covered in the next chapter.

## Installing Cards

∞→ **When you are buying any type of board** to upgrade your computer, make sure it's the right kind, made for your specific Mac model. The "right" kind is not just a PDS versus a NuBus card, because NuBus slots come in several varieties. Some Macs have short slots that are only 7 inches long; most accommodate cards that are 12 inches long.

THE MAC ALMANAC

> If it ain't broke, you can still upgrade it.

∞→ **Watch out for static when** you're installing a card—even when you're just handling one. Cards come in anti-static bags for a reason! The little spark of static that might jump from your finger to the board can fry its circuits; if your Mac is open, a static spark can fry *its* components!

The most basic static precaution is to discharge any static buildup by touching a ground before you touch the card or any computer component. If your Mac is open, you can touch the metal covering of the power supply inside the case to discharge the static from your body before you touch anything else. Many cards come with an anti-static wrist strap: if you have one, wear it. Work in a low-static environment—in an uncarpeted area, for instance. Rubber-soled shoes aren't going to do you any good; contrary to anything you may have heard, they can make matters worse. In fact, bare feet are best.

Do I follow all this advice? Only when I've opened the PowerBook, whose miniaturized circuits are especially prone to static damage. For my main machine, I don't worry about moving it someplace or wearing a wrist strap. I work on it where it lives (on an area to the left of my desk) because I don't have a carpet in the office. I *do* always discharge the static from my body before touching anything inside the case.

∞→ **Opening an older compact Mac is a project** unto itself. They weren't meant to be opened by the user, so there's no convenient way to do it. You need two special tools: a long-shafted #10 Torx screwdriver and a "case cracker." Here's what you do:

1. Lay the Mac screen-side down on a safe surface.
2. Loosen all the screws that hold the case together. There are two hidden deep inside the well that forms the carrying handle—that's why you need the long

screwdriver. On a Plus, there's one screw hidden beneath the battery cover. It's easiest to leave the screws right in position even after they're completely loose.

3. "Crack" the case—separate the front part that frames the screen and floppy drive opening from the main body of the case. This is the tricky part; Apple technicians actually have a special case-cracking tool. But it's possible to separate the two parts of the casing by inserting a wide putty knife in the crack where the two parts join (it's about an inch behind the front face of the computer, and runs entirely around the top, sides, and bottom of the computer) and carefully prying the sections apart.

4. Lift the back part of the case completely off the computer, without tipping it even after it's free of the computer's innards—don't forget, those loose screws are still in the casing's holes.

•••> **Opening a new compact is easy:** A tray at the bottom of the unit slides out from the back after you take out the retaining screw with a #10 Torx driver.

•••> **Opening a modular Mac** is the easiest of all. There's usually a single screw someplace at the back that must be removed first; how the case opens after that depends on the model. On the older models, the "lid" just lifts right off the top of the CPU case. (Opening an old Mac II case is a scary proposition because it makes a terrible cracking, snapping sound as the top comes off.) Newer models like Centrises and even the Quadra "towers" have the back of the case attached to the base of the unit where all the innards are attached; to pull the case apart, you slide the rest of the case away from the back/bottom unit—although "slide" may be too gentle a word to describe the firm pulling you might have to do. In any case (no pun intended) the modulars were made to be taken apart, so it's all relatively easy.

•••> **Before you insert a card,** check to see if it's one that has a connector at one side that will serve as a port for something to plug into. If it is, you have to poke out the little cover at the back of the Mac's case so the connector will be accessible. Then push the card gently but firmly into the slot; sometimes you have to push one end in a little bit, then the other, then back to the first end so the card goes in a little at a time with the rocking motion.

•••> **If you move "old" cards to your new Mac,** don't assume they'll work—or that they'll work efficiently. Video cards that work in one Mac model may fit in another, and may even work (that is, you'll see stuff on the monitor), but you may need the card itself upgraded for the best performance.

When I went from a IIci to a Centris, for instance, the video card for my 21-inch Radius screen didn't work at all. I had to get the card upgraded (a simple matter of changing a ROM chip on the card) in order to work with the new system.

Another example: the Radius PrecisionColor Pro24X, an accelerated video card, works in both a Quadra 840AV and in a Power Mac 8100/80. But it works seven times *faster* in the Quadra than in the Power Mac unless it's upgraded to work with the newer model.

So, when you switch Macs, always check with the manufacturer of any devices you're using, to see if you need any upgrades for optimum performance.

# → MAC BY MAC: QUIRKS & COMMENTS ←

## General

∞→ **Every Mac has a battery.** Or two. That's how it can keep track of the date and time when it's shut off and even unplugged. The battery keeps PRAM powered, too, so your control panel settings are remembered between settings. But batteries run out—and the way you can tell is that your time and date are reset to January 1, 1904 after each shut-down, and control panel settings are forgotten, too.

The Mac Plus has a simple battery compartment at the back of its case. The Mac II and IIx have special lithium batteries soldered onto the motherboard, so you'll have to get a dealer or authorized technician to replace them for you. Other modular Macs use snap-in lithium batteries you can replace yourself, every five to seven years, as needed.

∞→ **The On/Off button on some modular CPUs** can remain locked in the On position so that the computer immediately comes back on if power returns after an interruption. This is very useful for machines being used as file servers, where the box itself is usually hard to get at.

Quirks regarding memory and SIMMs for each model are in Chapter 13.

∞→ **Increase the number of colors displayed** on your monitor by increasing the amount of VRAM (video RAM) in your computer. Not all models can handle a VRAM upgrade, and those that do have different maximums, but you should know that you're not stuck with, say, the 256 colors that come as standard on the Color Classic screen—you can increase that to 32,768 colors. Monitors and VRAM are covered in the next chapter.

## Mac Plus

∞→ **Let the Plus breathe.** It was the last Mac designed without an internal fan for cooling, and, in most cases, that's not a problem. But leave room at the side and top of the computer where the vents are, so nothing impedes the natural flow of air.

∞→ **To zap the PRAM** on a Plus, shut it off and take out its battery for about 10 minutes, then put it back in.

∞→ **Replace the battery.** It lasts for only two years. Since the Mac Pluses in use at this point are anywhere from six to eight years old, they've all had their batteries replaced several times by now. Probably. The battery compartment at the back of the case is easy to open. Replace the battery with the same 4.5-volt type (it's *not* your basic AA battery, even though it's the same size).

Since the battery keeps the internal clock going when you shut down, you'll have to reset it when you start up again. In fact, the battery keeps PRAM alive during shut-down, so you'll have to reset all your control panel options, too, because they're stored in PRAM.

∞→ **The Mac power supply** was infamous for its poor performance; when it died, it took the screen with it. A power supply replacement runs about $200. But when your screen dies—sometimes a little at a time, shrinking in from the edges—it might not be the power supply itself that's the problem. Many Pluses have a bad solder connection on the power supply and *that's* the problem. How can you, a mere mortal, tell the difference without even opening the case? Thump the Plus's case in the middle of its left side: a good thump, now, don't be shy. If the screen comes back up, it's the solder connection, not the power supply. Ask a technician or a knowledgeable friend to resolder the connection.

• • • • • • • • • • • • • • • • • • • • • • • • • • • • • • • • • • • • • •

### MULTIPLE CHOICE

A Macintosh enthusiast's reaction to the breakdown of a Mac Plus after only one week of use would most likely be:

a) "You have to expect a few 'Bad Apples'... ha ha ha!"

b) "Apple's expert technical support dudes will be certain to correct the problem in a meticulous, efficient, and courteous manner!"

c) "Think about how much more quickly and easily the Mac did it, compared to the IBM PC!"

*—Andy Ihnatko, The Macintosh Summertime Funtime Quiz,*
*The Active Window newsletter, February 1989*

••▶ **Just for fun:** Press the interrupt switch at the left side of the computer—assuming it was installed. (See Chapter 24 for more about that.) Type: G 40E118. Make sure you type the space, and a zero—not the letter O—after the 4. Then press Return. You should get a secret message on the screen. (Well, it's secret until it shows up on the screen.) To get things back to normal, press the reset switch to restart the machine.

## SE & SE/30

••▶ **The SE has the same secret message** hidden inside as the Mac Plus. To see it, press the interrupt switch and type: G 40E118, then press Return. To restart normally, just press the reset switch.

••▶ **There's also a slide show built into** the SE. Press the interrupt switch at the back of the case and type: G 41D89A, then press return. Enjoy. To get things back to normal, press the reset switch to restart the machine.

••▶ **A different secret message** is buried in the SE/30. Press the interrupt switch and type: DM 4082E853 20. Type the spaces, and use zeros, not O's, and then press Return. After you read the message, restart normally by pressing the programmer's switch.

••▶ **Screens on older compact Macs tend to shrink** with age. (Well, not the *screen*, exactly, but the *display area*.) This applies to the SE, SE/30, and the Plus. Just another one of those things where art imitates life, I suppose. But you can adjust the screen controls easily if you know how to open a compact's case (which is described earlier in this chapter).

Once the case is open, you'll see two screws on a side panel; they may or may not be labeled as monitor adjustment controls. The one at the upper left controls the width; at the lower right is the height control. You should use a TV alignment tool to make the adjustment—it's a very inexpensive plastic screwdriver-like tool. Turn the screws a very little bit at a time to get the image back up to its normal size.

This is an instance where you'll have to have the computer plugged in and turned on while you make the adjustment (after you open the case), so you can see how the screen changes. Make sure that the aspect ratio of the screen is correct after the adjustment—that is, that you've changed the vertical and horizontal size in tandem. Run a graphics program and draw a perfect circle. Make sure it's still a circle, not an oval, after your adjustments.

**POP QUIZ**            **[5 POINTS]**

Name the '60s TV show that began with an announcement along these lines:

*Do not attempt to adjust your television. There is nothing wrong with the picture. We control the horizontal. We control the vertical.*

## The Classics

∘∘▶ **The Classic II is actually slower** than the SE/30 that it replaced. Why, when they both have '030 processors running at 16MHz? Because the Classic II has a 16-bit data path, only half the size of the SE/30's 32-bit data path, slowing down the internal transfer of information between the processor and RAM.

∘∘▶ **The Color Classic is a little slower** than the Classic II, despite the fact that they have the same processors running at the same speed, because processing color takes a little longer.

∘∘▶ **The Classic II can't read old 400K disks.** (It can't read *new* 400K disks, come to think of it!) 400K disks are read by varying the speed of the spinning disk because of the way information is stored on them. But the Classic II preempts the variable speed signal for its screen brightness control.

∘∘▶ **Shut down the Color Classic** with the Power On key on the keyboard. That makes more sense if we just call the key the Power key, since it's acting as an On/Off switch for the Color Classic. You'll get the usual shutdown dialogs prompting you to save your work.

•••▶ **Start up the Classic without a startup disk:** Hold down Command-Option-X-O. The Classic's the only model with a *ROM disk* inside: a ROM chip whose contents appear as a disk on the desktop when you start up this special way. The disk has a system on it—System 6.0.3—so it acts as a startup.

## Mac II

∘∘▶ **To make the Mac II a viable system** today, you definitely need some upgrades. Although you can turn it into a IIfx with a major upgrade, the minimum you need to do is upgrade the floppy drive(s) to FDHD drives instead of the 800K models it came with. You say you can live with just 800K capability? Sure, you probably can for a while longer. But the FDHD upgrade includes a new ROM chip; without the upgrade, you won't be able to use more than 8 megs of memory, or use virtual memory at all.

••◆ **Early Mac II's have some NuBus problems.** (Not surprising, I suppose, when you consider that it was the first model to have NuBus at all.) The problem seems to be limited to NuBus cards with more than 1 meg of memory on them. For a while, Apple was providing a free upgrade to solve the problem, and you may still be able to avail yourself of that offer.

## Mac IIci

∞◆ **If you're using the internal video card** for any monitor setting other than black and white, you can speed the ci's overall performance by setting the Disk Cache in the memory control panel to 768K. This works only if there are four 256K SIMMs in Bank A and the total memory is 5, 9, or 11 megs.

∞◆ **Using a separate video card** instead of the built-in one increases the ci's speed by a considerable amount. I had two monitors on my ci: the standard Apple color monitor, using the internal video card, and a Radius two-page display using its own card. When I switched the color monitor to its own video card, the change in speed on the Radius display was incredible: I was finally able to keep it in grayscale instead of black and white and not twiddle my thumbs while the screen was being redrawn.

∞◆ **Speed up the ci** by turning on 32-bit addressing in the Memory control panel even if you're not using more than 8 megs of memory. (It's a minor increase of, say, about 2 percent—but every little bit counts.)

32-Bit Addressing
◉ On
○ Off

∞◆ **If yours is an early production** model ci, it may not have the cache card installed. Using a cache card significantly increases the overall speed of the ci, so it's worth the $75 or so for the upgrade. How do you know if you're missing the cache card? Open the ci's case and look at the motherboard (you can't miss it, honest!). There's a slot for the cache card right in the center.

••◆ **Access the hidden picture** of the ci's design team by setting the Mac's clock to 9/20/89, the monitor to 256 colors, and then restart holding down Command-Option-C-I. (That's the letter I, not the number 1.)

## Mac IIsi

∞◆ **Running the monitor** in black and white can almost double the si's overall speed when you're using the internal video connection for the monitor.

∞**→** **If you're using the built-in video** connection for any monitor setting other than black and white, you can speed the si's overall performance by setting the Disk Cache in the Memory control panel to 768K.

 Disk Cache   Cache Size   768K
Always On

∞**→** **Using a separate video card** instead of the built-in one increases the si's speed by a considerable amount.

∞**→** **The si's sound output** is notoriously quirky; sometimes it just stops working completely. The problem is a finicky connection between the motherboard and the speaker. Here are three different ways to deal with it:

- Set the volume to maximum in the Sound control panel and then reset it to the volume you want.
- Attach an external speaker to the sound port. Since the main problem is the connection for the internal speaker, this bypasses the problem completely.
- Open the si case, unplug the speaker cable, clean the contacts, and plug the cable back in.

**→** **The Power key** serves a special function on the si. The si lacks a reset/interrupt switch, but pressing Command-Control-Power is the same as pressing a reset switch.

**→** **The PDS slot** in the si isn't really a PDS slot. At least, it's not a *standard* PDS slot. You can plug in a PDS card with no problem, but you can also use it as a NuBus slot if you get the correct adapter from Apple (for about $200.) The si is the only Mac with this semi-dual-purpose slot.

## Mac IIfx

∞**→** **When it comes to termination** (which is covered in detail in Chapter 18), the IIfx is special: it needs a special terminator known as the "black terminator."

**→** **Access the hidden picture** of the fx's design team by setting the Mac's clock to 3/19/89, the monitor to 256 colors, and then restart holding down Command-Option-F-X.

## The LC's

∞**→** **The Power key** on the LC's keyboard doesn't turn it on or off; you have to turn it on at the back of the unit and turn it off with that same switch after you've used the Shut Down command. But the Power key does serve a special function: Pressing Command-Control-Power is the same as pressing a reset switch.

## Centris & Quadra

⚬•**➤** **Centris and Quadra are** often the same thing. Take the 660AV, for instance: The Centris 660AV is the same machine as the Quadra 660AV—it just depends when it was "born." There are slight differences between the Centris 610 and the Quadra 610, and between the Centris 650 and the Quadra 650; in each case, the Quadra version has the faster clock speed, but that's the only difference. So, you'll often see references like this: Centris/Quadra 610. Or just: 610. That just means that whichever model you have, the advice applies.

⚬•**➤** **Use the Basic Color Monitor extension** for a Centris or Quadra running the Apple Basic Color Monitor to clear up greenish or washed-out blue display problems.

⚬•**➤** **The number of PDS and NuBus** slots in Centrises and Quadras varies with the specific model, but they're among the few Macs that provide both kinds of slots. But the tricky part is that sometimes you have to choose *either* the PDS or the NuBus slot: installing a PDS card blocks the NuBus slot. In models with three NuBus slots to begin with, losing one isn't so bad; but in models that offer only a single NuBus slot to begin with, you have to choose which slot is more important.

⚬•**➤** **The 610 uses special NuBus cards**—they can be only 7 inches long instead of the standard 12 inches.

Termination and other SCSI matters are covered in Chapter 18.

•••**➤** **The Quadra 900 has a special rule for** internally mounted SCSI devices. Normally, any internal SCSI device needs its own internal termination. But the 900's SCSI bus is terminated on both the motherboard and the cable, so internal SCSI devices need to be unterminated on this model.

MacUser
June 1988

The Mac, some Mac, any Mac that's any good will be cloned.

John Ruskin
(1819–1900)

There is hardly anything in the world that some man cannot make a little worse and a little cheaper.

•••**➤** **The Quadra 950 needs a special extension** if you're using the built-in video card and setting the monitor to millions of colors. The 950 Color Addition extension takes care of a little bug that sometimes prevented color graphics from displaying images properly. The extension is available from Apple dealers, user groups, and online services.

⚬•**➤** **The Quadra 700 has a unique hardware feature:** a key. The key sets the 700 to *On*, where everything works as usual; *Off*, where you can't turn it on; or *Secure*, where the mouse, keyboard, and floppy drive are disabled—a great setup if you're using it as a file server on a network.

•••→ **The 660AV** needs a special 7-inch NuBus card instead of the standard 12-inch one, so if you're upgrading to the AV, you won't be able to just take your NuBus cards with you.

System software is covered in Chapter 23.

•••→ **A Quadra 950** filled to its maximum with RAM—256MB—can't use a RAM disk. Believe it or not!

## Performas

•••→ **The Performas are standard Macs.** The things that differentiate them from "real" Macs are:

- They're sold in different *types* of stores, like Sears, instead of in computer stores.
- All Performas are bundled with keyboards; for most Mac models, you purchase the keyboard separately.
- Some Performas include an internal modem; no regular Mac has this option.
- Most Performas come with applications already installed on their hard drives.
- The system software installed on Performas is slightly different than the standard Mac system software, providing a few features that make using the Performa extremely simple for beginners.
- Performas come without a set of system disks.

•••→ **Software included; instructions not.** I was floored when I took a look at a Performa, saw that it had ClarisWorks installed on it, and found out the only documentation for the program was the "Getting Started" quick reference that usually comes with ClarisWorks, but not the standard full reference manual that also comes with it. So, for whatever program is installed on your Performa, plan a trip to the bookstore to buy a book about it. (Luckily, there's a wide selection of books on every popular Mac program.)

At Ease and Launcher are in Chapter 19.

•••→ **The desktop alternative** that the Performa provides is a full-screen folder, or series of folders, with large icons that need to be clicked to launch a program or document. But this isn't built-in to the Performa; nor is it an integral part of the Performa system software. It's a utility called At Ease that's running the show—a utility that Apple sells separately, as a matter of fact, for any Mac.

•••→ **The special Launcher window** on the Performa's desktop isn't hard-wired into the Performa or its system software any more than At Ease is. The Launcher, which gives you special launching icons in a separate window (so you don't have to dig through folders to find the applications or documents you want to open) is a control panel that comes with the Performa system software.

The Launcher window.

→ **You can tell if a machine is running Performa system software** by checking the About This Macintosh window from the Finder's Apple menu. If there's a P after the version number, the Mac is running the Performa software.

→ **There's a special General Controls** control panel on the Performa that provides desktop background patterns based on larger "tiles" than the 8-by-8 pixel blocks used by the standard General Controls control panel. But either control panel—standard or Performa—works on any kind of Mac. In fact, you can have both of them on your machine at the same time, although there's no reason to. (I happen to have them both going right now because I was comparing them.)

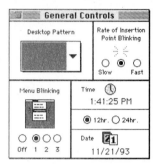

The Performa system's General Controls control panel.

→ **The Documents folder** on the Performa desktop—where *all* your documents go when you save them, unless you specify otherwise—is actually a feature of the Launcher control panel. Turn the control panel off, or even simply rename the folder, and your Save dialogs will open to the most recently used folder, as they do on standard Mac systems.

→ **The self-hiding Finder** *is* a special feature of the Performa system software, unlike At Ease and the Launcher, which are separate, removable utilities. When you launch any application on a Performa, the Finder disappears and can be accessed only through the Applications menu at the far right of the menu bar. This feature prevents beginners from accidentally clicking on the desktop background and being switched to the desktop when they didn't mean to be there.

→ **Buy system disks.** Performas don't come with system disks that you can use to reinstall a system when you're having problems. Instead, it comes with a special backup utility that puts a copy of your system onto floppy disks so you can replace a misbehaving hard disk system with the version you saved on the floppies. But this isn't a great approach: You either replace your configured and tweaked system with a plain one from the floppies, or you back up the tweaked one and hope that there are no incipient problems backed up with it.

→ **Install standard system software** on a Performa if you want to; the Performa really is a standard Mac inside. If you like the special things that the Performa software provides, like At Ease and the Launcher, and maybe even the General Controls control panel, you can add them to the standard system after it's installed. You'll find that it's much easier to get help and hints from others (at a user group, for instance) if you're using the standard system software that the vast majority of users have.

## Power Macs

∞❱ **You need special versions of your applications** if you want to be able to take advantage of a Power Mac's speed and power. Applications written for other Macs will run in the Power Mac's emulation mode; but an application written specifically for the Power Mac—written in *native code*—will be able to run a lot faster. When you run a standard Mac application in emulation mode, you'll find it runs a little more slowly than it would on the fastest standard Macs—Centrises and Quadras. So, if you move up to a Power Mac from a Centris or Quadra without getting new software (assuming a native-code version is available), you may find that you're actually slowing down a little.

### FARGO NORTH, DECODER

As with most products that take research and development, Macs live under code names until their real names are figured out or ready to be released. Here's what some of them look like:

| | |
|---|---|
| Mac Plus | Mr. T |
| Mac SE | Aladdin, Chablis |
| Mac 30 | Green Jade |
| Mac Classic | XO |
| Mac IIx | Spock |
| Mac IIcx | Aurora |
| Mac IIci | Aurora II; Pacific |
| Mac IIsi | Ericson, Raffica |
| Mac LC | Elsie |
| Mac LC II | Foster Farms |
| Quadra 700 | Shadow |
| Quadra 900 | Darwin |
| Mac II | Jonathan, Milwaukee, ParisMac |
| Portable | Esprit, Laguna, Malibu |
| PowerBook 100 | Derringer, Rosebud |
| Duos | BOB (Best of Both Worlds) |
| PowerMac 7100-66 | BHA |
| PowerMac 8100-80 | Cold Fusion |
| PowerBook 500's | Blackbird |

Are you wondering about that BHA code name for one of the PowerMacs? Is it an additive you'll find listed on cereal boxes? No, it stands for *Butt Head Astronomer*, after the astronomer in question found out that the original code name was his name and objected to the use of his name on a product, even one under development, without his permission or endorsement. I won't use his name, but Apple's probably hoping to sell *billions and billions* of the machine.

# CHAPTER 15
# MONITORS

> And thus the native hue of resolution is sicklied o'er with the pale cast of thought.

SHAKESPEARE
HAMLET, III:1

The valuable information presented in this chapter includes:

••▸ Why smaller pixels on a screen mean higher resolution.
••▸ Why diagonal monitor measurements mean nothing.
••▸ What the difference is between dots per inch and dot pitch.
••▸ Why, when it comes to pixels, square is beautiful.
••▸ How to test your monitor flicker with Wintergreen Life Savers.
••▸ What VRAM is, and why it's so important.
••▸ Why 8-bit color means you have 256 different colors.

## THE ODDEST ITEM IN THIS CHAPTER WHEN TAKEN OUT OF CONTEXT

*N*o matter how many dots-per-inch your monitor uses, 72 dots always equal an inch.

—Includes—
75 Factoids
11 Quotable Quotes
5 Memos
and
a computer on drugs

| Black & White |
| --- |
| 16 |
| 256 |
| Thousands |
| Millions |

*page 580*

# MONITOR BASICS

# YOU & YOUR MONITOR(S)

# → MONITOR BASICS ←

## Size & Resolution

∞→ **A monitor's *resolution*** is not the same as its *size*. Resolution, measured in *dots per inch*, depends on the size of the dots, or *pixels* on the screen. The smaller the dots, the higher the resolution. A 78-dpi monitor has higher resolution (and smaller dots) than a 70-dpi monitor. The two squares here are the same size, but the one on the right has smaller dots, so there are more dots per inch in it—its resolution is higher.

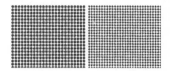

If these blocks were screens, the one on the right would have a higher resolution.

∞→ **What's the *display area* of a screen?** Now, there's a question to keep in mind when you're looking at monitors that are close to each other in size. There's always a black, unused border around the perimeter of the screen which cuts down the size of the screen image. Apple has manufactured two 12-inch screens; the display area on the color monitor is about a quarter inch larger in each direction than that of the monochrome monitor, for a total difference of more than 3.5 square inches.

∞→ **Increase the display area** of a 13-inch monitor by using that black border. The MaxAppleZoom utility works only for an Apple 13-inch monitor being used with the Apple Mac II High-Resolution 4- or 8-bit video card. But with that setup, it gives you a 704x513-pixel display instead of the default 640x480 measurement. [freeware, Naoti Horii]

∞→ **A larger monitor doesn't always show more.** It might simply show the same amount of information, but bigger—the way a large-screen TV gives you a bigger picture, not additional parts of the picture around the edges. A monitor with a low-resolution might show only as much, or possibly even less, than a smaller monitor with a high resolution. Since the images on the screen are made of dots, it's the number of dots per inch that regulates how much of an image can be displayed on the screen.

So, the 9-inch screen on an old compact Mac or the Classic seems to be much smaller than Apple's 12-inch black-and-white monitor. But the 9-inch screen has a resolution of 72 dpi and the 12-inch screen is 64 dpi, so they show the same amount of information— 512 pixels—across their widths. The 12-inch monitor is a little taller, by an extra 40 pixels along the bottom, but how much does that count? It gets you only two extra lines of text in a word processor document, for instance.

Just keep in mind that a physically larger screen doesn't necessarily mean you're going to see any more information.

The screen on the left is a lower resolution than the one on the right, although they're both the same size.

•••⟩ **The Mac's beautifully clear, readable screen** is due to not only its resolution, but the fact that it uses *square* pixels, while most other computers produce round pixels inside a square grid. What difference does that make? When you're drawing things with round shapes in a square grid, the only time one pixel touches another is when the line is verti-

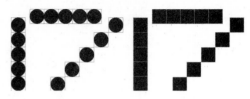
Vertical, horizontal, and diagonal lines with round and square pixels.

cal or horizontal—and even then, the dots barely kiss each other in the line; in a diagonal line, the pixels don't touch at all. With square pixels, though, horizontal and vertical lines are solid because the sides of the pixels meet; in diagonal lines, their corners meet to give a continuous line. You can see the difference in the magnified examples here; you can imagine the effect each approach has on how things look on the screen.

## SPEAK TO ME ONLY ... #1

There's a humorous look at various operating systems ("If Operating a Computer Were Like Driving a Car") back in Chapter 3. I said there that you didn't have to really know the operating systems to enjoy the jokes. Here's a similar approach to programming languages. This little farce was found floating around on the Internet, so its author is unknown—most likely, there are several authors. The list was so long I broke it into three parts. It starts with the following introduction:

*The proliferation of modern programming languages which seem to have stolen countless features from each other sometimes makes it difficult to remember which languages you're using. This guide is offered as a public service to help programmers in such dilemmas.*

**C:** You shoot yourself in the foot.

**C++:** You accidentally create a dozen instances of yourself and shoot them all in the foot. Providing emergency medical care is impossible since you can't tell which are bitwise copies and which are just pointing at others and saying, "that's me, over there."

**Fortran:** You shoot yourself in each toe, iteratively, until you run out of toes, then you read in the next foot and repeat. If you run out of bullets, you continue anyway because you have no exception-processing ability.

**FORTH:** Foot in yourself shoot.

**SNOBOL:** If you succeed, shoot yourself in the left foot. If you fail, shoot yourself in the left foot.

**APL:** You shoot yourself in the foot, and then spend all day figuring out how to do it in fewer characters.

**HyperTalk:** Put the first bullet of the gun into foot left of leg of you. Answer the result.

**Picospan**. You can't shoot yourself in the foot, because you're not a host.

**Paradox:** Not only can you shoot yourself in the foot, your users can too.

•••◆ **72 dots always equal an inch** no matter what the resolution of your monitor. That is, every 72 dots on the screen equals an inch in a printout, and if you're using a program with a ruler in it, the ruler's inch marks will be at every 72 dots, no matter what the true on-screen measurement is. As odd as it might sound, this quirky rule of measurement ensures that as you move from Mac to Mac, or change monitors on your own system, what you intended to design in your document stays the same. It also means that the higher your monitor's resolution, the smaller the 72-dot inch measurement. On an 86-dpi screen, for instance, a ruler inch actually measures about .84 inches; on a 65-dpi screen, a ruler inch's actual measurement is about 1.11 inches.

∞◊ **Work on a "virtual screen"** that's larger than your monitor's screen with Stepping Out. Once you define the size of the window you want to work on, Stepping Out takes over and your monitor acts as a window onto the larger picture.

Stepping Out II lets you work on a *smaller* screen than your display, too. This is handy if you work on a large monitor but you're designing a database or HyperCard stack that will run on a smaller monitor. [Berkeley Systems]

## How a Monitor Works

∞◆ **Computer monitors using glowing phosphors** to display images. On a black-and-white monitor, the back of the screen is coated with white phosphors. An electron gun inside the monitor shoots a stream of electrons at the screen; the phosphors glow briefly wherever the electrons hit. The combination of glowing phosphor dots and the ones that haven't been activated gives you the black-and-white dots—*pixels*—on your screen.

In a grayscale monitor, the electron gun shoots at varying intensities to provide shades of gray. A color monitor's screen is coated with colored phosphors so that each pixel is made up of a red, a green, and a blue dot. The electron gun (or, in many monitors, one of three electron guns) fires at one or more of the dots, whose combined colors appear as a single colored pixel on the screen.

∞◆ **A monitor's *scan rate* determines** whether or not the screen image flickers. The electron gun that's shooting at the back of the screen starts by aiming at the upper-left corner and moves in a horizontal line; when it reaches the right edge, it goes back to the left and shoots another stream of electrons in a line slightly lower than the previous one.

Since the phosphor glow fades quickly, the gun zigzags its way down the screen and quickly moves back to the top of the screen to refresh the phosphor with another dose of electrons to keep it glowing in the right spots. If it doesn't do this quickly enough, the image flickers. (Much like the juggler on the Ed Sullivan show trying to keep a dozen plates spinning on sticks—he'd get them all twirling but by the time the last one got going, he'd have to rush back to the first one which by then had started to wobble.)

How quickly a monitor does this (refresh the phosphor, not spin the plates) is called the *scan rate* or the *refresh rate*. Scan rates are measured in *hertz* (cycles per second). The Apple 16-inch Color Display, for instance, has a scan rate of 75 Hz, which means the entire screen is being redrawn 75 times a second.

## TWO, TWO, TWO TESTS IN ONE

Here's a little trick that's on a par with noticing how spinning wagon wheels seem to roll backwards on film: you can make yourself see your screen flicker no matter how stable it seems to you under normal conditions.

Nope, you don't need a strobe light. Just get a piece of hard candy and start crunching while looking at your monitor out of the corner of your eye. A good enough crunch and you can even look at it straight on. The sharp but tiny jarring of your jaw gets your vision out of sync with the monitor's scanning, and you'll see a definite screen flicker.

Any hard candy will do, but Wintergreen Life Savers are highly recommended. That way, you can perform a second experiment at the same time—do it in a darkened room and see if they really emit sparks when crushed!

**Apple's monitors vary** in size, resolution, and scan rates. Although I've referred to the Mac screen as 72 dpi throughout this book, the truth is that the resolution varies from 70 to 80 dpi, depending on the monitor. Monitors from other manufacturers sometimes offer even higher resolutions, of up to 85 dpi.

Here's a quick chart of some of Apple's current (and recently past) monitors, so you can see how they vary. I've stuck with Apple's terminology for the monitor names (sometimes *Color*, sometimes *RGB*; sometimes *monitor*, sometimes *display*; sometimes diagonal measurement, sometimes orientation description, sometimes no measurement at all), so don't blame me for the inconsistencies here! I've also included the specs on the compacts' built-in black-and-white screen for comparison.

| Monitor | Color | Diagonal size (inches) | DPI | Pixels | Display area (inches) | Scan rate (Hz) |
|---|---|---|---|---|---|---|
| Compact | b&w | 9 | 74 | 512 x 342 | 7 x 4.75 | 60.15 |
| Macintosh 12" Monochrome Display | gray | 12 | 76 | 640 x 480 | 8.35 x 6.26 | 66.7 |
| Macintosh 12" RGB | color | 12 | 64 | 512 x 384 | 8.08 x 6.02 | 60.15 |
| AppleColor Hi Res RGB Display | color | 13 | 80 | 640 x 480 | 9.3 x 6.9 | 66.7 |
| Macintosh Color | color | 14 | 70 | 640 x 480 | 9.3 x 6.9 | 66.7 |
| Apple Macintosh Portrait | gray | 15 | 80 | 640 x 870 | 8 x 10.87 | 75 |
| Apple 2-Page Monochrome Monitor | gray | 21 | 77 | 1152 x 870 | 15 x 11.3 | 75 |
| Macintosh 16" Color Display | color | 16 | 70 | 832 x 624 | 11.8 x 8.9 | 75 |
| Macintosh 21" Color Display | color | 21 | 79 | 1152 x 870 | 14.6 x 11 | 75 |
| AudioVision 14" display | color | 14 | 70 | 640 x 480 | 9.3 x 6.9 | 66.7 |
| Multiple Scan 20" | color | 20 | 79 | 1280 x 1024 | 14.2 x 10.6 | 29 to 82 |

···→ **The picture tubes used in Apple's displays** vary from one model to another. For instance:

| | |
|---|---|
| 12-inch monochrome | ........ Clinton |
| 15-inch portrait | ................. Toshiba |
| 13-, 14-, 16-inch color | ........ Trinitron |
| 21-inch color | ..................... Phillips |

···→ **Monitors emit ELF magnetic fields**: that stands for *extremely low frequency,* and there's some controversy about what kind of health hazard ELFs might pose to the computer user. There are radiation screens that can be added to your screen—but there's also lots of controversy about their effectiveness (or lack thereof). It's generally agreed that sitting 30 inches away from a 19-inch monitor decreases your exposure dramatically. (Also note that the ELF emissions at the back of a monitor are stronger than those coming from the front. If you want to sit behind your monitor, stay about 45 inches away.)

···→ **Macs and TVs just don't mix.** The signal generated by the Mac for its screen is nothing like the signal a television set uses; TVs use an *NTSC* signal (*National Television Standards Committee*). There are video boards that can turn your Mac output into an NTSC signal so you can create a videotape to be played on a television. But *don't* bother trying to hook your Mac up to a television as a monitor: even if you find a card that lets you do it (and I do know of one, which I refuse to recommend), you'll never be satisfied with the quality of the screen—even if your standards are not the highest.

PowerBook screens use LCD technology. They're covered in Chapter 22.

···→ **Terminology? You want terminology?** Have we got terminology for you! Here's a quick roundup of some of the terms I haven't defined elsewhere:

- *Pixel:* Of course, we've defined this several times throughout the book as one of the dots on your screen. But this chapter's a good place to point out that the word itself comes from the words *picture element.*

- *RGB:* All this time, you thought the primary colors were red, yellow, and blue, right? Well, that holds true for Play Doh and finger paints—which is why you learned that in kindergarten—but when it comes to mixing *light* instead of pigments, the three primaries are red, green, and blue. RGB is just another word for "color," as in *RGB monitor.*

- *CRT:* This is practically archaic terminology, even if the technology hasn't really changed much. The initials stand for *cathode ray tube,* because the electron gun at the back of early monitors (and TVs, for that matter) were cathodes. Sometimes you'll see the phrase by itself, or as *CRT screen* to refer to a monitor. (If you do see or hear it, though, you can be sure the writer or speaker is an old-timer.)

- *Hi-Res:* This is simply shorthand for *high resolution.*

- *VGA:* In the PC world, CGA stands for *color graphics adapter,* but VGA apparently stands for *video graphics array.* In any case, a VGA monitor is one made for the "other" computers, but many later model Macs can use one as long as you have the right cable.

- *Multisync:* Most monitors are built to handle a certain type of signal—a certain number of pixels in a certain pattern and a specific refresh rate, for instance. A multisync monitor can work in a number of different modes, with different refresh rates and resolutions.

- *Dot pitch:* On color screens, each pixel is made of a red, a green, and a blue dot. The dot pitch is the distance from one red dot to the next red dot, or one green dot to the next green one, or one blue dot to the next. A smaller dot pitch means a higher-resolution screen; most of Apple's monitors have a .26 millimeter dot pitch.

- *Interlace:* Mac monitors draw their images one line at a time, from top to bottom. Television screens, and some monitors for other computer systems, draw alternate lines on the screen: On one pass, the odd-numbered lines are drawn, while the even-numbered lines are drawn on the next pass. Drawing alternate lines is called *interlacing*, and it reduces flicker on systems that aren't as fast as the Mac's *non-interlaced* setup.

- *Degaussing.* Does your monitor have automatic or manual degaussing, and what the heck is it? If you move your display and put it down a little roughly, or bump into it, you may find that the colors change because the jarring might shift the magnetic field. Degaussing corrects the colors by resetting the field.

## Color ROMs & Video Cards

∞► **There are three basic varieties** of monitors, despite the wide choice of sizes and shapes:

- A black-and-white monitor can produce only a black-and-white display, no matter what you do.
- A grayscale monitor can produce shades of gray on the screen.
- A color monitor displays any of the colors that the Mac can produce.

∞► **What can be displayed on the Mac's screen** depends on four interdependent factors:

- The capability of the specific Mac model.
- The capability of the specific monitor.
- The *video card* used to run the monitor, or the internal video circuitry for Macs with built-in video.
- The amount of memory available for the video display.

∞► **A Mac has to be able to "think" in color** in order to produce a color display. Its ROMs have to be able to produce color images or you won't be able to see color on the screen, no matter what you do.

Of the older compact Macs, only the SE/30 has color ROMs; of the new compact Macs, only the Classic *doesn't* have color ROMs. Yep, that means that, despite the built-in black-and-white screens on the SE/30 and Classic II, these models actually can provide color output. On the other hand, the Mac Portable and the PowerBook 100 are missing color ROMs.

∞► **There's color, and then there's color.** The SE does indeed have color ROMs; so does the Classic. But these 68000-based machines produce only eight colors: black, white, red, green, blue, cyan, magenta, and yellow. This limited capability was put in to satisfy those who needed color output for charts and graphs on a plotter or printer; no one expected the Mac to actually *display* colors.

> ... someday a Mac or the equivalent of a Mac with color would be wonderful.

**BILL GATES**
INTERVIEWED IN *MACWORLD*, 1985

> My own conclusion is that color, while it's a definite enhancement, is not really all that crucial to a PC.

**DAVID BUNNELL**
*MACWORLD*, JANUARY 1986

> I don't think that Apple is going to come out with a Macintosh that features absolute built-in color. It will always be an option.

**NEIL SHAPIRO**
*MACUSER*, APRIL 1987

**MAC**azine
SEPTEMBER 1988

> Sources claim the next-decade [the '90s] agenda includes plans to ... unveil a color SE.

•••➤ **A non-68000 Mac with color ROMs** can produce about 16.7 million colors. This is enough for true photographic realism on the screen, since your eyes can't discern that many different colors. But just because the Mac can produce that many colors, that doesn't mean the screen can display them: Remember the other factors—the monitor itself, the video card or internal video circuitry, and the video memory.

•••➤ **A *video card* provides** the connection between the innards of a modular Mac and its monitor. The card contains the video circuitry that drives the monitor, and also often includes extra RAM that's dedicated to the screen display. The kind of circuitry and the amount of memory on the card determine what type of monitor it can control.

•••➤ **A *monochrome* monitor** is *not* a black-and-white monitor. *Monochrome* refers to a single color, but includes many shades. A black-and-white TV, for instance, or a black-and-white photograph actually include many shades of gray. And a *monochrome monitor* is another phrase for *grayscale monitor*. But so many people confuse monochrome with black and white (and that includes people at monitor companies and advertising agencies) that you should double-check, or triple-check, any monitor labeled monochrome to be sure whether it's grayscale or just black and white.

## Video RAM & Color Depth

•••➤ **RAM that's dedicated to the screen display** is called, predictably enough, *video RAM*, or *VRAM (VEE-ram)*. The amount of VRAM controls how many colors or grays can be displayed on various-size screens. So, even with a Mac that can produce color, and a monitor that can display color, VRAM can be a limiting factor for your screen display.

There are three different approaches to VRAM in various Macs:

- Part of the standard system RAM can be used for the video display.
- Special dedicated RAM chips can be built into the Mac for use as video RAM.
- Video RAM can be included on the video card you're using for an external monitor.

**On a black-and-white system,** each pixel on the screen corresponds to one bit in the computer's memory. Because a bit can represent one of two things (that's back in Chapter 1), there's a perfect correspondence between a single bit in memory and a single dot on the screen that can be either on or off. That's where the phrase *bit-mapped* comes from: Every dot on the screen is *mapped* to a bit in memory.

On the 9-inch black-and-white screen used on compact Macs, there are 175,104 pixels. That many *bits* of memory are needed to map the screen; that's 21,888 bytes, or about 21K of video RAM.

**On a grayscale or color screen,** you need more than one bit of memory to keep track of each pixel on the screen. If there were two bits of memory per pixel, the computer could keep track of four possible shades for that pixel, since there are four possible combinations of two bits of information. (A reminder from Chapter 1: Two bits gives four combinations because both bits can be on, both can be off, the first can be on and the second off, or the first can be off and the second on.) So, with two bits of information per pixel, you can have four (that's $2^2$) different colors.

**T-SHIRT SIGHTING**

Front (picture of a Mac): This is your computer.

Back (picture of IBM-PC): This is your computer on drugs.

*Color depth* **refers** to how many different colors can be displayed on the screen at one time. You can speak in terms of either the total number of colors available—256, for example—or how much VRAM is allotted to each pixel—8-bit, for instance. Aha! The mystery is solved! *That's* why 8-bit color is actually 256 colors!

Here's a quick color depth table (note that 2 colors means black and white):

| | | |
|---|---|---|
| 1-bit | = | 2 colors |
| 2-bit | = | 4 colors |
| 4-bit | = | 16 colors |
| 8-bit | = | 256 colors |
| 16-bit | = | 65,536 colors |
| 24-bit | = | 16.7 million colors |

**There's no such thing as 32-bit color,** really. Even though the Mac is a 32-bit machine, the last 8 bits beyond the 24 that give you 16.7 million colors are reserved for other information that's not yet standardized; it's often used as a "masking channel" for on-screen animations.

∘∘◊〉 **Change color depth as you move** from one application to another with Color Coordinator. When you want to work in black and white in your word processor but switch to color for the charts in your spreadsheet, you don't have to take out the Monitors control panel every time. Color Coordinator lets you specify color depths on an application-by-application basis so the switch occurs automatically. [Color Coordinator-Conflict Catcher, Casady & Greene]

••◊ **Larger screens need more video RAM** because every pixel on the screen needs a certain amount of memory. So, a Mac and a video card that can give you millions of colors when you connect a 14-inch screen might provide only 256 colors on a larger screen, and might not be able to drive a very large screen at all. This sample chart shows various combinations of a Mac IIci with five of Apple's monitors and three different Apple video cards: the one that's built into the IIci, the 4•8 card, and the 8•24 card; the difference between the cards is the amount of VRAM. (Note that the Portrait and 2-Page monitors are monochrome, so they produce only grays, not color.)

### Video Capabilities for a Mac IIci

| Card | Monochrome Monitors | | | Color Monitors | |
|---|---|---|---|---|---|
| | 12-inch | Portrait | 2-Page | 12-inch | 13-inch |
| Built-in | 256 grays | 16 grays | - | 256 colors | 256 colors |
| 4•8 | 256 grays | 16 grays | 16 grays | 256 colors | 256 colors |
| 8•24 | 256 grays | 256 grays | 256 grays | 16.7 million colors | 16.7 million colors |

••◊ **The VRAM in some Mac models** is upgradable; by adding more video RAM, you can get more colors on your screen or run a bigger screen when you're using the Mac's internal video capabilities. VRAM upgrades are easy to obtain and easy to do; any place that sells regular RAM SIMMs (see Chapter 9) also sells VRAM SIMMs. Most Macs use 256K VRAM SIMMs, although 512K SIMMs are also available for VRAM.*

*Aren't all those necessarily CAPITALIZED words a pain to READ?

There's a quick chart on the next page of some the Mac models that offer VRAM expansion capabilities, and the difference the expanded memory can make when it comes to running certain monitors.

### VRAM and Video Output for Apple Monitors

| Model | VRAM | Portrait (grays) | 13-, 14-inch (colors) | 16-inch (colors) | 21-inch (colors) |
|---|---|---|---|---|---|
| LC, LC II, | on-board | - | 16 | - | - |
| Performa 400 | 1 256K | - | 256 | - | - |
| IIvx, IIvi, | on-board | - | 256 | - | - |
| Performa 600 | 2 256K | - | 32,768 | - | - |
| Centris/Quadra | on-board | 16 | 256 | 256 | 16 |
| 610, 650 | 1 512K | 256 | 16.7 million | 32,768 | 256 |
| Quadra 700 | on-board | 16 | 256 | 256 | 16 |
|  | 2 256K | 256 | 16.7 million | 256 | 256 |
|  | 6 256K | 256 | 16.7 million | 16.7 million | 256 |
| Quadra 900, 950 | on-board | 256 | 32,768 | 32,768 | 256 |
|  | 4 256K | 256 | 16.7 million | 16.7 million | 32,768 |
| PowerBook Duo Dock | on-board | 16 | 256 | 256 | - |
|  | 1 512K | 256 | 32,768 | 32,768 | - |

•••➤ **Grayscale monitors are limited to** 256 shades of gray at the most because of the way the shades are produced, with the electron gun at the back of the screen shooting at various intensities to produce the different shades. So, limited VRAM can keep you to *fewer* shades of gray, but extra VRAM won't get you past 256 shades.

### MULTIPLE CHOICE

"Obviously, color images should be our ultimate goal" was one of Steve Jobs' earliest quotes concerning:

a) The video screen of the Macintosh

b) The printing mechanism of the ImageWriter

c) The first Macintosh T-Shirts

—Andy Ihnatko, *The Macintosh Summertime Funtime Quiz,*
*The Active Window newsletter, February 1989*

•••➤ **A color Mac can always produce 16.7 million colors.** The color depth of a monitor refers to how many different colors from that 16.7 million-color palette can be displayed *at one time*. If you're running your monitor in 256 colors, there's a standard "palette" of colors that's used for the desktop, in icons, and so on. But many graphics programs let you change the palette while you're working in a specific document so, for instance, you can work with 256 different pastel shades, or 256 brilliant colors, and so on. The same holds true for working in thousands of colors on the screen: the Mac has a basic "system palette" that it uses, but an application can alter that.

A well-behaved application always returns you to the system palette when you quit the program. Not all programs are well-behaved, though, so sometimes you'll find your desktop icons in different colors, or even in black and white, after moving to the desktop from, say, Photoshop or SuperPaint.

## Choosing a Monitor

°°→ **70 dots per inch might sound small** (after all, that means each dot is only 1/70th of an inch), but it's actually a little rough: even 72 dpi can seem pretty chunky if you're used to 76 dpi or higher. If you're shopping for a monitor and you have a choice, look for a resolution of 76–82 dots per inch. (On the other hand, some people with minor vision problems may prefer the relative chunkiness off a 70- or 72-dpi display because of the slightly larger text.)

°°→ *Orientation* **may be the most important factor** in deciding on a monitor. The orientation can be the standard horizontal (*landscape*), or it might be vertical (*portrait*). Orientation and size are also described with the terms *full-page display* or *two-page display*.

If you do page layout, a full-page display is a must, so that you can see an entire page at one time without scrolling around. Heavy-duty layout work really calls for a double-page display so you can see facing pages next to each other on the screen. A two-page display generally measures 19 inches diagonally; a 21-inch display—I have one and I *adore* it—gives you two full pages and an extra inch or so along the right edge so you can still see the disks and the Trash on the desktop.

°°→ **Diagonal measurements mean nothing,** unless you're talking about televisions—and even that standard may be falling by the wayside as "letterbox" screens become affordable.

But a diagonal measurement for a Mac monitor is practically useless information. Wouldn't you think that Apple's 14-inch monitor is bigger than the 13-inch monitor, and the 16-inch larger than the 15-inch portrait? In fact, the 13-inch and 14-inch monitors display exactly the same amount of information (640 pixels across and 480 pixels down); the 15-inch monitor, because of its vertical orientation, can show you a full page of text, while the 16-inch monitor chops off the bottom of a page. (Not to mention the fact that a diagonal measurement usually includes the entire screen area, the outside edge of which isn't normally used for the screen image. Wait—didn't I say I wouldn't mention that?)

Diagonal measurements aren't much help since they don't define the screen orientation at all.

°°→ **Pixel count doesn't count much, either.** An overall pixel count is how many pixels are on the screen. But that doesn't tell you how many there are per inch (the resolution) or how they're arranged (the screen's orientation). Apple's 15-inch monitor has a pixel count of 556,800; the 16-inch monitor's pixel count is lower, at 519,168. There's a clue in there, since the larger screen has the lower count: it probably has a lower resolution. (And, it does, at 70 dpi to the other's 80 dpi.) But neither the count nor the presumed resolution makes any difference if what you need is a full-page display for page layout work.

What are you going to do, anyway? Figure out the price per pixel and buy the best bargain? Forget the pixel count and look at the pixel *measurement:* how many pixels across and down the monitor displays. The 15-inch monitor with the 556,800 pixel count is 640x870; the 16-inch, 519,168-pixel monitor's measurement is 832x624. Now, *those* are helpful measurements, since they define the orientation of the screen.

MAC TOON

I asked for more PIXELS, not PIXIES!!

•••▶ **A SCSI-based monitor** is one that hooks up through your computer's SCSI port. The signal going through this port is nowhere near the speed of the one using the normal route through the video circuitry, but it's sometimes the only solution—to add a large or color monitor to a Classic II, for instance, or to one of the first-generation PowerBooks. A SCSI monitor, even with built-in acceleration, is too slow for heavy-duty graphics work; in fact, quirks such as the inability to display certain images from major graphics programs like FreeHand keep a SCSI monitor from being a solution even more than its lack of speed does.

There are also SCSI adapters that let you hook a standard monitor to the SCSI port of your Mac. But be very careful before going the SCSI route: make sure that you see the monitor in use—using the applications that you need to run, connected to the Mac model that you use—before purchasing one.

Oh, and one more thing: Using a SCSI monitor invites other problems that are intrinsic to SCSI devices attached to your Mac—chaining and termination considerations if you're also using an external hard drive or CD-ROM drive. (More about this in Chapter 18.)

•••▶ **You don't need an Apple monitor** for your Mac. Other companies make monitors for Macs, too. My personal favorite has always been Radius: great technology, terrific technical support, upgradable video cards, and good prices. RasterOps and NEC are the two other manufacturers that immediately come to mind as having great products for the Mac; and, of course, there's Sony, who makes the innards of many of Apple's monitors.

**A *non-Mac* monitor** is not the same as a *non-Apple* monitor for the Mac. A monitor made for the Mac by any company is a cinch to use and hookup; that's a non-Apple, but still Mac, monitor. A non-Mac monitor manufactured for IBM and its compatibles can cause some problems.

First and foremost, there's the cabling problem. The Mac's video port is not a standard one in the industry, so you'll need a special cable to attach a non-Mac monitor. More importantly, non-Mac monitors don't necessarily accept the output from the Mac and turn it into a screen image, since the Mac uses "synchronization signals" that are different from other computers. Later Mac models provide a signal that a standard VGA monitor needs, but you still need the correct cable.

## SPEAK TO ME ONLY ... #2

Part two of a continuing series! A tongue-in-cheek multi-lingual* exposé of programming languages. I'm repeating the first example, in the C language, which in this instance is identical to English, so you can see how the other languages handle the same procedure.

*I guess that would make it *tongues* in cheek!

**C:** You shoot yourself in the foot.

**Pascal:** The compiler won't let you shoot yourself in the foot.

**Lisp:** You shoot yourself in the appendage which holds the gun with which you shoot yourself in the appendage which holds the gun with which you shoot yourself in the appendage which holds the gun with which you shoot yourself in the appendage which holds ...

**COBOL:** USEing a COLT45 HANDGUN, AIM gun at LEG.FOOT, THEN place ARM.HAND.FINGER on HANDGUN.TRIGGER, and SQUEEZE. THEN return HANDGUN to HOLSTER. CHECK whether shoelace needs to be retied.

**Modula/2:** After realizing that you can't actually accomplish anything in the language, you shoot yourself in the head.

**Ada:** If you are dumb enough to actually use this language, the United States Department of Defense [which developed the language] will kidnap you, stand you up in front of a firing squad, and tell the soldiers, "Shoot at his feet."

**Concurrent Euclid:** You shoot yourself in somebody else's foot.

**BCPL:** You shoot yourself somewhere in the leg—you can't get any finer resolution than that.

**APL, version 2:** @#&^$%&%^ foot

**VMS:** %SYS-F-FTSHT, foot shot (fifty lines of traceback omitted)

**Unix:** % ls foot.cfoot.hfoot.otoe.ctoe.o % rm * .o rm: .o: No such file or directory % ls %

**Some monitors offer multiple resolutions** because they can sense and interpret different synchronization signals coming from the computer. This multisync capability (from *multiple synchronization*) has been around in the PC world for a long time, but is relatively new to Macs.

In addition, some newer Macs can send different types of signals, actually working in different resolutions. The way you match the Mac signal to the monitor's capability varies.

- For a standard Mac connected to a non-Apple multisync monitor, the signal is strictly controlled by the cable itself—a special one that allows only the one correct signal to be transmitted.
- Sometimes the choice of signals (and, therefore, resolutions) is wider, and you make the choice through the Options button in the Monitors control panel; this requires a restart to switch to the new screen resolution.
- Some utilities offer on-the-fly resolution switching that doesn't require a restart to take effect.

···❯ **If you have a multisync monitor but no cable** because the manufacturer doesn't support the Mac (and you know that the monitor can use the signals that the Mac produces), you can use Nanao USA's VGA-to-Mac cable. [Cadlax Micro Distribution]

···❯ **The wrong signal can damage a monitor.** If your monitor software utility provides a way to switch resolutions by selecting a frequency, make sure you check the Mac's output against the monitor's capability. If you choose an incompatible signal, at best you'll get gibberish on the screen; at worst, you'll damage the monitor. If you get gibberish, you can clear it up by shutting down, disconnecting the video cable, resetting the resolution, reconnecting the cable, and starting up again. If you damage your monitor … well, don't blame me!

This isn't an issue for newer Mac monitors that are controlled through the Monitors control panel; it's the "foreign" hardware you have to be careful with.

···❯ **Apple's bottom-of-the-line color displays** are the Apple ColorPlus Display, the Performa Display, and the Performa Plus Display. They're not terrible, and, in fact, are perfectly serviceable for a kid's setup or for a home computer that gets relatively light use. But their quality isn't anywhere near that of Apple's other displays.

Each of these monitors has a 640x480-pixel display at 68 dots per inch; they all have the same scan rate, too. But the dot pitch—the distance between the red, green, and blue dots that make a single colored pixel on the screen—varies from one to the next, and makes a great difference in the crispness of the display. So, the Performa Display's .39mm pitch makes it the worst of the bunch; the Performa Plus has an improved .29mm dot pitch; the ColorPlus Display uses a .28mm dot pitch.

···❯ **Apple makes two 14-inch color** monitors. Don't confuse them, because one is definitely better than the other. The standard 14-inch color monitor is called the Macintosh Color Display; with its .26mm dot pitch, it's the better of the two. Its Apple part number is M1198LL/B. The other 14-inch display is the ColorPlus, or Basic Color Display, described in the previous entry; its Apple part number is M2346LL/A.

···❯ **The AudioVision display** is an awkward-looking beast that was designed for the AV systems. The screen is fine: a 70-dpi 14-inch color display with a Sony Trinitron tube. What makes it look odd is the built-in microphone and stereo speakers in the cabinet that's beneath the screen.

# → YOU & YOUR MONITOR(S) ←

## Tidbits

∞● **Monitors for modular Macs have their own On/Off** switches, but with most Mac models, the monitor is automatically turned on and off along with the computer as long as you leave the monitor's switch in the On position. It's very easy to leave a monitor on by mistake when you're working with a model that doesn't provide this convenience. When my kids had an LC II, I was constantly nagging them about turning the monitor off; finally, I plugged the external hard drive and the monitor into a separate power switch so they could turn both off at the end of a computer session.

∞● **Any monitor can work in a "lesser" mode:** a grayscale monitor will work in black and white, and a color monitor can display grayscale or black and white. A monitor can display fewer colors or grays than its maximum, too. All these things are adjustable within the Monitors control panel.

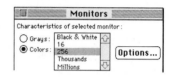

But why would you want to work at less than the maximum? Because the monitor works faster in black and white than in gray, in gray than in color, and in fewer grays or colors than maximum. If you're working on a page layout where you don't have to see the colors of the objects, switching to grayscale or black and white can speed the screen redrawing considerably.

∞● **Running your monitor in black and white** makes it faster—it takes much less time to calculate and manipulate a single bit of memory for every dot on the screen than to work with eight bits for every pixel. If you're simply word processing or working with a spreadsheet, you may want to set your color monitor to black and white; you'll be amazed how that can speed up basics like window scrolling on a slower machine. Keep the color mode for artwork and games.

∞● **Clean your screen only with** a non-abrasive cleaner; most monitors have special glare-reducing coatings that can be damaged by abrasive cleaners. You can get special computer-screen cleaners at most computer stores.

Don't spray anything directly on the screen—it can drip down inside the monitor casing at the bottom edge of the screen. Always spray the cleaner onto the cloth.

∞● **There's only a slight chance** that leaving the computer on indefinitely might damage the monitor. The image on a screen is kept there by a bombardment of electrons that "excite" particles on the phosphor coating on the inside of the screen. If the particles stay excited for too long, they might never calm down, and you wind up with a "burned-in" image that won't go away. The chance of this happening is extremely slight—you'd have to leave your Mac on and unused for weeks—but it has been used as the excuse to start an amusing sub-industry of "screen-savers," programs that use the Mac's screen when you're not. These programs ensure that you won't think the computer's off (as you might assume if you merely turned down the screen brightness or shut off just the monitor) and at the same time make sure that the screen image isn't static. Screen savers can be set to kick in after a definable amount of idle time, or when you click in a certain spot on the screen.

I have to admit I just can't understand the incredible growth of this market, and the direction of that growth. Some of the screen images are incredibly fascinating; some of the modules are actually games. I thought that they were for when you're away from your computer—so why do you need a wide variety of fascinating images, or a game to play, if you're not even there? Oh well, I never saw a single episode of Dallas, either, or any of the Rocky movies; I'm just out of sync with the general population in some areas of interest.

There's a wealth of screen savers available for the Mac. The first one, Pyro, was by Steve Brecher (who also wrote Suitcase) and Bill Steinberg, one of my favorite programmers. (I'm not just saying that because we had dinner together in Chinatown and in Soho during the course of my writing this book; he didn't pick up the check. Okay, okay—neither did I.) Pyro displayed some nifty little fireworks (pyrotechnics, get it?) on the screen during idle time.

- Pyro's still around, and it does a lot more than just fireworks. It works, as most screensavers now do, with a variety of modules whose parameters you can set; you can choose the module you like best, or let them come up randomly. [Fifth Generation Systems]

- After Dark is the most popular of the screen savers. It made Flying Toasters and the Lawn Mower Man famous. There's an intimidating number of modules available, and more, seemingly every day. Its MultiModule option lets you combine elements from different modules to make new screens. [Berkeley Systems]

- Star Trek: The Screen Saver is a special After Dark package with images from—you guessed it. We're talking the original cast here—Kirk, Spock, McCoy, Scotty—not Picard and his crew. My kids are nuts about this one. You can set the parameters for each module—I'm sick of hearing "Scotty, get us out of here," but I particularly like the one where amoeba-like organisms splay on your screen—from the inside, so you see their undersides, like snails on the side of the aquarium. Tribbles are also included! [Berkeley Systems]

- Wallpaper is basically a desktop background utility, but its related Wallpaper/Light & Dark program takes the backgrounds and makes them foregrounds as screensavers in many interesting approaches. I especially like the patchwork quilt option that slaps varying sized rectangles of different background patterns onto the screen. [Thought I Could]

MR. SPOCK?

Live long and phosphor.

"Grays" on a black-and-white screen are actually *dithered* patterns of black-and-white dots that look pretty gray. The original Mac's desktop always looked pretty gray, but it was a dotted pattern of alternating black-and-white dots.

Dithering is also used to create colors or shades that wouldn't normally be displayed on the screen. If you're using 8-bit color, for instance, a program can dither some of those 256 colors to represent the truer color that would be available on a 24-bit screen. This approach is very effective: did you ever notice, for instance, that the light blue of a standard desktop folder is actually a dithered pattern of not-so-light blue and white?

Magnified view of the desktop "gray" pattern.

●➤ **The brightness of a screen fades** over time. It's so gradual that you probably won't even notice. But after two years of constant use, my old monitor paled in comparison (as it were) to the one that came with my new computer.

●➤ **Trade off screen size for more colors** on your monitors. Some models—the LC III and a Duo 270c, for instance, let you sacrifice a little screen size to get more colors displayed in the display area that's left.

The LC III's default VRAM, for instance, can display 8-bit color on the standard 14-inch monitor; that's enough to give you 256 colors on the screen at once in the monitor's 640 by 480 display area.

You can get 16-bit color, though, if you give up the bottom 80-pixel strip. Open the Monitors control panel and click the Options button. You'll see two choices listed: the default *Macintosh Hi-Res Display* and *640 by 400 Hi-Res*. Select the second option, and your monitor displays thousands of colors on the slightly abbreviated screen.

The Monitors control panel is covered in Chapter 8.

It's not often that you'll want to give up an inch of the screen for extra colors, but if you're looking at QuickTime movies or photographs, the extra colors provide the photographic realism that's missing in the 256-color world.

●➤ **There are two ways to speed up your display:** with a video accelerator or with a CPU accelerator. (Assuming, of course, that either is available for your particular monitor and Mac.)

Which method to use depends on what's slowing you down. If you're using a program that creates complex graphics, the Mac sometimes takes quite a while to figure out how the picture should look—and it can't put the picture on the screen until it has finished thinking. If this thinking time is slowing things down, a CPU accelerator will help considerably.

If your display takes a long time to scroll large windows, move graphics objects around, or generally refresh the picture from top to bottom after even a minor change, a video accelerator (also called a graphics accelerator) is what you need.

●➤ **The Mac's graphics are unique in computerdom** not because of any particular monitor, but because of the Mac itself.* The Mac generates graphics from routines built into its ROM; the routines are called *QuickDraw* and they're responsible for the consistency of Mac graphics

*Sort of the opposite to the saying "The music's not in the piano." The graphics are—at least to some extent—in the Mac.

from one program to another. With the routines in ROM, each program doesn't have to draw its own graphics; it can grab the necessary information from the Mac itself.

*Color QuickDraw* first came out as an extension for color monitors, but now it's built into the ROM of every non-68000 Macintosh. As you might guess, this controls how color is handled on the Mac.

## Add-Ons

∞◊ **Screenies are the most amusing peripheral** to come along in quite a while; they're cardboard frames for your monitor that Velcro on to surround the screen. The amusing part is what's on the Screenie; you can, for instance, make the monitor look like a TV set, or an Etch-a-Sketch. [Screenies]

∞◊ **Most monitors have anti-glare** coatings that help in standard office lighting situations. But don't count on the built-in protection if there's a sunny window behind you. Several manufacturers make anti-glare covers in various sizes for different monitors; I use one from Kensington on the smaller of my two monitors. You can expect to pay from $50 to $170, depending on the size of your screen.

∞◊ **Get a monitor stand.** Many large monitors come with built-in tilt-and-swivel stands, but you can buy separate ones for other monitors, and you should. Even if you think you've got the perfect setup, sometimes you'll find that the lighting in the room calls for a slightly different angle, or you may change the height of your chair and need a different tilt to the screen. Or somebody joins you at the computer and can't quite see the screen. And, of course, *any* tilt is difficult and dangerous without a stand that holds the monitor securely, even though the height is relatively easy to adjust by putting something underneath the monitor.

Or consider a monitor swivel arm, which dangles the monitor from a wall or ceiling, making it easily adjustable to any height or angle, and leaves you more desktop space for other things.

## Large Screens & Multiple Monitors

∞➔ **Who would use a multiple-monitor setup?** Well, I do, for one. My Mac came with a color monitor, and I do need one for testing certain features and using certain software. But when I got to the point that I needed a double-page display for layout work, I couldn't see spending that much money for a double-page *color* monitor. A grayscale monitor filled the bill nicely for layout work, but I still need color for some things; so, I have both monitors attached to my Mac. I do the bulk of my work on the big screen, and the small screen serves as a day-to-day luxury for leaving calendars, note pads, and control panels hanging around within easy reach; on a part-time basis it earns its keep as the working screen for certain applications.

I suppose that one of these days I'll graduate to a big-screen color monitor (tell *all* your friends to buy this book), but then I'll really miss the little sidekick. These days the most likely user of a multiple-monitor setup is probably a PowerBook user who hooks into a larger screen for desk work.

∞•▶ **Multiple monitors are treated as one** giant monitor by the Mac. So, you can slide your mouse cursor directly from one monitor to the other (right through the intervening space), and drag windows and other objects back and forth.*

> *Tech editor Joe Holmes points out that this can really impress DOS and Windows users, who think the coolest thing in the world is that a press of a keyboard key can switch them from one monitor to another.

∞•▶ **If you want two monitors, you need** two video ports. On Macs with internal video support, that usually means you're running one monitor from that internal video circuitry, and the second from a video card installed in one of the Mac's slots. For Macs without internal video that have multiple slots, you can use two video cards. The Power Macs have built-in video support for two monitors.

And, yes, you can have more than two monitors if special circumstances require it.

∞•▶ **The Monitors control panel** provides control over a multiple-monitor setup so you can define such things as where the monitors are in relation to each other (so that the mouse cursor can just glide from one to the other at the appropriate spot) and which serves as the main monitor. These details are covered in Chapter 8.

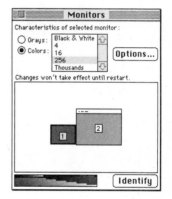

∞•▶ **Use the Mouse control panel** to increase the mouse's tracking speed so you can get the cursor across a big screen without the mouse falling off the edge of the desk.

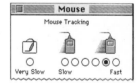

The Mouse control panel is covered in Chapter 8.

∞•◇ **Speed up the mouse** for a big screen even beyond the highest tracking speed in the Mouse control panel with Mouse2. [shareware, Ryoji Watanabe]

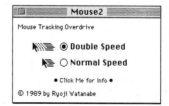

## SPEAK TO ME ONLY ... #3

The third and final installment of this series starts, once again, with a repeat of the example of how the procedure works in the C programming language so you can compare the other alleged approaches.

**C:** You shoot yourself in the foot.

**APT:** You cut a perfect bullethole in your foot, and shoot through it. [Note to the uninitiated: APT is the oldest computer language currently in use—Automatic Programming of Tools.]

**Assembly:** You crash the OS and overwrite the root disk. The system administrator arrives and shoots you in the foot. After a moment of contemplation, the administrator shoots himself in the foot and then hops around the room rapidly shooting at everyone in sight.

**SmallTalk:** You spend so much time playing with the graphics and windowing system that your boss shoots you in the foot, takes away your workstation, and makes you develop in COBOL on a character terminal.

**BASIC:** Shoot self in foot with water pistol. On big systems, continue until entire lower body is waterlogged.

**Motif**: You spend days writing a UIL description of your foot, the trajectory, the bullet, and the intricate scrollwork on the ivory handles of the gun. When you finally get around to pulling the trigger, the gun jams.

**JCL:** You shoot yourself in the head just thinking about it.

**MSDOS**: You shoot yourself in the foot, but can unshoot yourself with add-on software.

**Revelation**: You'll be able to shoot yourself in the foot just as soon as you figure out what all these bullets are for.

**Oracle:** The menus for coding foot_shooting have not been implemented yet, and you can't do foot shooting in SQL.

*—from the Internet*

**TI Calculator:** Enter 10045, turn calculator upside down, drop on foot.

*—Joe Holmes*

•••➤ **Two monitors provide a lot of real estate,** and lots of miles for the mouse to travel. Save some of that travel time by using aliases liberally: Sprinkle Trash aliases around both screens, and keep aliases of your internal drive and any other drives on both screens.

•••➤ **If you don't want your mouse cursor to slip** over to the second screen accidentally, redefine the relationship between your two monitors in the Monitors control panel. The definition doesn't have to match reality. (In fact, if you're jealous of a friend who has a two-monitor setup and want to cause him some grief, switch the monitor positions in the control panel.) Back to the main point: if you set the control panel monitor icons as shown here, the only time you can get the cursor from one screen to another is if you go through the bottom corner of one and the top corner of the other.

I don't care for this setup myself, since I like to slide back and forth between the screens in a way that more closely resembles the actual physical setup.

A possible arrangement of monitors in the Monitors control panel.

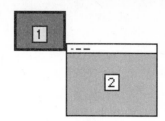

•→ **Don't forget CloseView,** the control panel that enlarges the contents of your screen and lets you switch from black-on-white to white-on-black screens. It's discussed in detail in Chapter 8.

A desktop window (left) and two magnifications from CloseView.

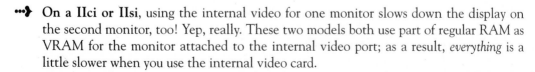

•→ **On a IIci or IIsi,** using the internal video for one monitor slows down the display on the second monitor, too! Yep, really. These two models both use part of regular RAM as VRAM for the monitor attached to the internal video port; as a result, *everything* is a little slower when you use the internal video card.

When I was using a ci's internal video for a color monitor while I ran the second, large monitor from its own card, I generally kept the big monitor in black and white because things scrolled so slowly in the word processor. When I added a separate video card for the color monitor, the speed increase on the big monitor increased dramatically: Even when using 256 grays, it was faster than it had been in black and white under the previous setup.

**⋯▶ One or both displays might jiggle** or be a little wavy on a multiple-monitor setup because they're being affected by the electromagnetic waves that the other monitor is outputting. Separating the monitors by a few inches should solve the problem.

**⋯▶ When you add a second monitor**, it won't be "acknowledged" until you open the Monitors control panel. That is, you can get everything hooked up and turned on, but you won't see anything on the new monitor, and you can't move the mouse cursor over to it, until you've opened the Monitors control panel.

## Monitor Problems

**⋯▶ If your monitor stares at you blankly** when you start up your system, don't panic. Check the easy things first : Is it plugged in? Is it turned on? Are the brightness and contrast controls at settings that let you see something? Most monitors don't die without being sick first—or at least without smelling pretty bad in their death throes. For a monitor with no symptoms other than a blank screen, the easy things are the most likely problem.

**⋯▶ There are many lines in your monitor**, but only one that you can see. The Apple 13- and 14-inch monitors are Sony Trinitrons inside, one of the best technologies available. But the construction is such that there's a thin gray line stretched across the screen about an inch and a half from the bottom. If you haven't noticed it, *don't* go looking for it—once you find it, you'll keep seeing it! The line is actually a shadow of a stabilizer wire inside and you can't do anything about it. Except maybe get a bigger monitor, which might give you *two* shadow lines!

**⋯▶ If a 13-inch monitor occasionally** goes blank and then finally stays dark, it's most likely a problem with the high voltage transformer inside—a component that caused problems in many of these color monitors. A replacement will cost about $125.

... we've had a very in-depth involvement. Whenever you get involved with prototype machines that early on, you are essentially part of the engineering team ... Microsoft has been an extension of the internal Mac software team for the last few years.

BILL GATES
1984

BRUCE HORN
(Finder programmer),
1984

I've noticed that Microsoft's taken a lot more credit than they deserve.

•••▶ **Apple's 8•24GC card,** its first and last accelerated video card, turned out to be incompatible with … System 7! There's no fix for this, and, in fact, the card was discontinued.

Well, there's no fix, but there is a stupid workaround. Remove the card's software from the Extensions folder. This runs it in unaccelerated mode—or, you might say it *walks* it, since you're losing the acceleration for which you paid extra.

•••▶ **When the Mac Plus screen** starts shrinking, flickering, or occasionally going black (or all three), that's symptomatic of a bad power supply, a problem that was endemic in the Pluses. The power supply inside the Mac needs to be repaired or replaced.

•••▶ **A blank screen on a Centris or Quadra** that *isn't* an Apple monitor may be caused by Apple's Basic Color Monitor extension, an extension that corrects some slight color problems between the Quadra/Centris and Apple's basic color monitor.

Restart (right, you can't see the screen to get to the Restart command, so reset the machine with the programmer's switch or by turning it off and on again), holding Command-Option-P-R down to zap the PRAM, since the extension stores some information there. As soon as you hear the Mac restart after the zap, hold the Shift key down to finish the startup without any extensions loading. Get rid of the Basic Color monitor extension and restart again.

Zapping PRAM is covered in Chapters 9 and 24.

# CHAPTER 16
# PRINTERS

> The printing press is either the greatest blessing or the greatest curse of modern times, one sometimes forgets which.

**J. M. BARRIE**
1896

Here are just a few of the things you'll learn from this chapter:

→ There was never an ImageWriter I printer.

→ The Portable StyleWriter is portable, but it's not really a StyleWriter.

→ Which LaserWriters speak PostScript and which don't.

→ Re-inking ribbons is a messy business.

→ How to print a test sheet for any Apple printer.

→ ImageWriters sometimes revert to a primitive form of communications known as "hex-dumping."

→ Why you might want to attach a hard drive to a LaserWriter.

→ There's no such thing as a QuickDraw printer.

→ What PhotoGrade and FinePrint are.

THE SENTENCE IN THIS CHAPTER THAT MOST NEEDS TO BE KEPT IN CONTEXT

A *LaserWriter isn't a printer.*

page 612

-Includes-

109 Factoids

2 Quotable Quotes

1 Quiz

1 Mac Almanac List

—and—

Another light bulb joke!

*at absolutely
no extra cost

# Printer Technologies

# ImageWriters & StyleWriters

# LaserWriters

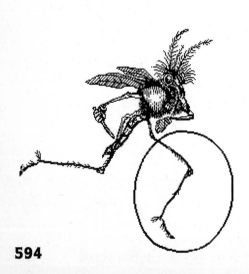

# → PRINTER TECHNOLOGIES ←

## Types of Printers

∞•➤ A *dot-matrix printer* puts an image on paper by using a moving *printhead* whose "pins" fire against an inked ribbon to form dotted patterns of letters or other figures. Because these printers work by pressing the ribbon against the paper to transfer the ink, they're also referred to as *impact* printers. The phrase *dot matrix* comes from the fact that the pins on the printhead form a matrix of dots. The ImageWriters are Apple's line of dot-matrix printers.

∞•➤ An *inkjet printer* sprays ink from the printhead's cartridge onto the paper in a dotted pattern to create letters and shapes. The dots from the spray are much smaller than the ones that come from a firing pin pressing against a ribbon, so inkjets usually have much better resolution than do dot-matrix printers. The inkjet printout is also better because each dot is made of a little splotch of ink that spreads slightly on the paper, so it comes in contact with the ones next to it and creates continuous, smooth lines even around curves. Apple's StyleWriters are inkjet printers.

∞•➤ A *laser printer* uses the same technology as a copy machine. It uses a laser to etch an image onto a drum; the etched areas attract particles of toner (powdered ink), which are then melted onto the paper in the right spots. Apple's laser printers are myriad: All the LaserWriters, no matter what else their capabilities, are laser printers.

∞•➤ **All three printing technologies work with dots.** The computer (or the LaserWriter, which has its own brain) figures out which dots go where on the paper and then prints them according to the capability of the printer. Even the LaserWriters use dots to draw letters—their terrific resolution comes from using very tiny dots. But the phrase *dot matrix* is reserved specifically for printers that use a firing-pin printhead against a ribbon.

All the printers use dots to create images, but smaller dots mean clearer images, as you can see here: As the dots get smaller, the closer the character comes to the original letterform.

∞•➤ **A quick comparison of printer technologies** shows the pros and cons of each in relation to the other:

- A dot-matrix printer is cheap (although not much cheaper than inkjets these days). It's slow, noisy, and has low-resolution output. It's the only one you can use if you have to print on multiple-layered pre-printed forms.
- An inkjet printer offers high resolution at low prices, but Apple's inkjet printers are very slow.
- A laser printer offers quiet operation and clean, high-resolution printouts. They're considerably more expensive than other types of printers, but the price of some models is well within the modest budget of a home or small office.

•••→ **Dot-matrix printers have a bad reputation** because early ones used a very small matrix of pins to define a letter. With such a limited number of dots to print out a letter, the letterforms were crude and had obvious gaps between the dots. There are many people who still insist that a dot-matrix printout is entirely unsuitable for even casual business use, but that's because they've never taken the time to inspect a printout done in the last ten years or so.

## PostScript & Non-PostScript

•••→ **A PostScript printer** is a printer that knows how to interpret PostScript commands.

PostScript is often thought of as merely a way to get terrific type in all sorts of fonts and sizes. But PostScript is actually a programming language—a "page description" language. It can describe in great detail how a page should look, including fonts and graphics—so, we have not only PostScript fonts, but PostScript graphics, too. Another special thing about PostScript is that it isn't *device dependent* (or, that it is *device independent*.) This means that the same information can go to any PostScript printer and come out at that printer's highest resolution.

Not all LaserWriters, or all laser printers, are PostScript printers.

### AD HOC # 4

Two of the cleverest ads, in terms of word play, that I've ever seen for Mac products are these:

For Timbuktu, a program that lets you see and control a remote Mac (on a network, or even over a phone line) from your Mac:

*The next best thing to being there.*

For Retrospect, a backup program, touting the necessity of keeping backups so you can keep going if you lose the originals:

*To go forward, you must back up.*

•••→ **There's no such thing as a QuickDraw printer.** Wait! I have right here in front of me a chart from Apple that lists its current printers and their features. Reading across the "Languages & features" row, there it is: QuickDraw. Looks like the suits in marketing out-voted the techies on that one.

There really isn't any such thing as a QuickDraw printer. QuickDraw is not a capability of the printer. It's what the Mac uses to create images—letters and pictures—on the screen. That image is easily sent to the printer, but that doesn't mean the printer has any inherent QuickDraw capability. *QuickDraw printer* is just a phrase used to describe a printer that can't interpret PostScript—it's just so much more positive than saying *non-PostScript* printer.

⋯➔ An *imagesetter* is a very high-resolution device that works with images set onto film. They're in a class separate from computer printers not only because of their high-resolution output (and because you can't afford one for your desktop system), but because they don't have to work with dots. With the other printer technologies covered here, even a straight line is drawn by using a series of dots; on an imagesetter, which works with film, a line is actually a line. These are the devices used to create pages for most magazines and books (including this one).

## ➔ IMAGEWRITERS & STYLEWRITERS ⟵

## Models

⋯➔ **There was no ImageWriter I.** There was an *Imagewriter*, though—no numerical suffix or capital W; both were added only after the ImageWriter II came out, in what might be referred to by semanticists as a product name back-formation.

In any case, the ImageWriter I, which is what we'll call it for clarity, was something of a minor miracle when it came out with the first Mac. You saw something on the screen, and it printed to the paper exactly the same way. The WYSIWYG (*what you see is what you get*) miracle of the Mac wasn't due solely to its on-screen magic—the printer that could echo that magic with a matching printout completed the output revolution.

For almost two years the Image Writer I was the only printer that worked with a Mac, and there are many still in service.

⋯➔ **Did you ever hear of the wide-carriage ImageWriter?** Probably not. But there was such an item available, not too long after the original ImageWriter was released. Except for its wide orientation, it was the same as the ImageWriter. I guess market research showed that people were complaining that they couldn't use the then-standard wide computer paper (you know, that green-and-white striped stuff) in an ImageWriter, so Apple released this short-lived model that nobody really wanted, anyway.

⋯➔ **The ImageWriter II** is still in the product line—probably the longest-lasting item in Apple's long list of products. The ImageWriter II, introduced in 1986, had several important improvements over the ImageWriter I:

- Faster printing.
- Smaller pins in the printhead for higher-resolution printing with the same number of pins.
- An add-on cut-sheet feeder to handle multiple pages of standard paper.
- An add-on (the *ImageWriter II/LQ LocalTalk Option*) that provides a slot for a networking card so the printer can be shared by more than one Mac.

It also came in a new color—platinum—instead of the original's beige. But it wasn't any less noisy than its predecessor.

✳The Feldsteins—Joel and Susan, Glenn and Carin—were the most recent users of this particular marvel of technology.

ImageWriters are real workhorses. I replaced my I with a II in 1986 and used it for several years. Since then, it's been on loan to various people as they bought their Macs and weren't sure of what printer they wanted.✳ So, it has had eight years of heavy-duty use by a half-dozen people, most of them novices, many of them with kids, and it's still going strong.

•••➤ **The ImageWriter LQ** was a doomed machine from the moment of its release, when reports of problems started pouring in. LQ stood for *letter-quality*—there were more pins on the LQ's printhead than on the other ImageWriters, for a better output. No one I know bought an LQ. Except my sister. (Against my advice. Why should she listen to me? What do I know? After all, she's the *older* one!) She didn't like it much, but it's long gone and replaced by a LaserWriter. (One of mine, coincidentally enough!)

•••➤ **The StyleWriter I** (which, of course, didn't have the I in its name at the time) was Apple's first effort at an inexpensive, high-resolution printer. The only way to combine those two qualities is with inkjet technology, so the StyleWriter I was also Apple's first inkjet printer.

The StyleWriter offers 360-dpi printing (that's higher than a basic LaserWriter) at a painfully slow one page per minute; its draft mode gets you a page in half that time, but with a lower-resolution trade-off. The operation is silent—you can't hear the cartridge squirting away—and the quality is excellent. The life expectancy of an ink cartridge is 500 pages; at Apple's suggestion that this printer is for those who print "as many as 20 pages a day," the cartridge should last for five weeks of weekday use.

•••➤ **The StyleWriter II** has several improvements over its immediate predecessor. It has the same slow, silent, 360-dpi printing, but it's in a redesigned case that's both smaller and lighter than the original. The StyleWriter II can handle 100 sheets in its paper tray instead of only 50, can automatically feed up to 15 envelopes, and can use Apple's GrayShare software that both lets you share the printer with another Mac and provides grayscale printing.

•••➤ **The Portable StyleWriter** isn't a StyleWriter at all, but Apple's too embarrassed to advertise the fact that it's selling someone else's printer, so it had to change the name. It's actually a repackaged Canon BJ-10ex and is aimed at PowerBook users who need a lightweight traveling printer. Because it's an inkjet, they slapped the StyleWriter name on it.

## Using an ImageWriter

More details on print qualities in Chapter 12.

•••➤ **There are three printing modes** for an ImageWriter, which you can select from in the Print dialog: Draft is low quality, but speedy at two (ugly) pages per minute; Faster is faster than Draft and prints one dot on the paper for every dot on the screen, at 72 dots per inch; Best is best quality—144 dpi—but slowest, at about a half-page per minute.

> Quality:   ○ Best      ⦿ Faster    ○ Draft

•••••••••••••••••••••••••••••••••••••••••••••••••••
## USING AN IMAGEWRITER (AND CHECKING IT TWICE)

∞•❯ **For round circles,** you have to keep the *Tall Adjusted* option ☐ **Tall Adjusted**
checked in the ImageWriter's Page Setup dialog. In Faster mode,
the 72-dpi printout is actually 72 dots horizontally but 80 dots vertically; Best mode
prints 144 dots horizontally and 160 dots vertically. This causes circles to print as ovals
unless you keep the adjustment checked.

∞•❯ **Print in color** by changing ribbons. ImageWriter ribbons come in various single colors,
as well as in a multi-color ribbon that's made of bands of black, yellow, red, and blue; by
overprinting two colors, you get a third. You need software that prints in color in order
to make use of the color ribbons.

∞•❯ **You can print a test sheet** from the ImageWriter II without using the Mac at all. (It's
called a self-test, since the printer can do it all by itself.) In fact, you can print tests for
each print-quality mode.

  • For a Draft-mode test sheet, shut off the printer and then turn it back on while
    holding down the Form Feed button.
  • For a Faster-quality test, start with the Draft-mode page. While that's printing,
    press the Line Feed button, then the Print Quality button, and then the Line
    Feed button again. The Faster-quality print sample starts with the next line that's
    printed.
  • For a Best-quality test (I bet you could figure this one out by now without me),
    start the Draft printout, switch to the Faster printout, and then press the Line
    Feed button, the Print Quality button, and the Line Feed button again.

∞•❯ **New ribbons don't always give the best printout.** I always found a little smearing—
resulting in slightly thicker letters—with the extra ink in brand-new ribbons. Use
brand-new ribbons for printing drafts, and slightly used ribbons for final printouts.

∞•❯ **Don't stockpile ribbons** no matter how great a bargain you run across: Ribbons dry up in
storage, and you may find that they're useless by the time you get to them. If you're storing ribbons for more than a few weeks, seal them in a plastic bag to keep the ink moist.

∞•❯ **It's normal for the printer to start and stop** several times while printing a page. The
ImageWriter is so small-brained that it can't keep an entire page in memory at once.

So, it prints one "band" and then waits for the next chunk of information to come from the Mac. There are more pauses in higher-quality printouts than in lower-quality ones because more information is needed to print the high-quality page.

•→ **For the fastest Draft mode** printing on an ImageWriter, you not only have to choose it in the Print dialog, you also have to set it on the print quality switches on the ImageWriter itself.

•→ **You don't need ImageWriter ribbons** for the ImageWriter. If you're ordering mail order, or shopping in a business-stationery store, ribbons made for the C. Itoh 8510, NEC 8023, and DEC LA50 printers are all the same.

•→ **You can re-ink ImageWriter ribbons** instead of always buying new ones. Re-inkers are clever little machines that wind the ribbon around felt-covered posts. The posts are hollow and filled with ink, which flows through little holes in the posts into the felt, and from there to the ribbon.

In all the years that I used ImageWriters (and there were many), I was never completely happy with the re-inked ribbons, since they tended to smear the output and, in all, I felt they were not worth the trouble. (And this was during some very tightly budgeted years.) If you do want to re-ink ribbons, keep these guidelines in mind:

- Don't be too generous with the ink. If there's too much applied to the ribbon, the type will always smear.
- Use an ink specifically designed for dot-matrix printers, since it contains a lubricant that's necessary for the pins in the printhead.
- Don't re-ink a ribbon more than three or four times. The ribbon eventually wears out, but before you notice the wear and tear, tiny shreds of ribbon can get caught on the firing pins and ruin the printer's printhead.
- Use rubber gloves! The procedure gets messy, and the ink is hard to get off your hands.

•→ **Do you ever get rows and columns of numbers** printed out—when you're *not* working with a spreadsheet? If your ImageWriter starts spewing forth gibberish, you'll be just tickled to know that what it's doing is a *hex dump*—dumping information to the printer in its hexadecimal form rather than translated into English (or other human language). To stop it, just turn the printer off and on again. To prevent it, make sure you turn the printer on after you turn on the Mac, and restart the printer each time you restart the Mac.

You can, by the way, *hear* when this is happening, because the very regular pattern of pin-firing used to print the groups of hexadecimal numbers is significantly different from the irregular striking needed to print text and graphics.

•→ **LQ's have problems on networks**—sometimes or most of the time, depending on which disgruntled owner you talk to. They just stop or reset at unpredictable intervals (the printers, not the disgruntled owners). The models manufactured from February to April of 1989 (serial numbers lower than 183181813) are particularly prone to this problem. The only fix seems to be a new logic board—available only from Apple, of course.

••→ **The LQ's printhead often sticks.** What you need to fix it is something called the *Home Position Switch Kit* from Apple.

## Using a StyleWriter

∞→ **There are two printing modes** for a StyleWriter; you can choose between them in the Print dialog. *Faster* prints at 180 dots per inch; *Best* prints at 360 dpi, at a speed of about one page per minute.

Quality:   ⦿ **Best**   ◯ **Faster**

∞→ **For the best-looking text,** use TrueType fonts, PostScript fonts with ATM as the "interpreter," or, if you're using plain bitmapped fonts, install one that's five times the size of the final output. Yep, that's a 60-point bitmapped font for 12-point print.

Chapter 12 deals with font types and print resolutions in more detail.

••→ **Use high-quality paper for better-quality printouts.** Low-quality paper lets the ink spread before it dries and gives blurry letters. (We're not talking terribly blurry here—the letters don't turn into blobs. But there's a definite sharpness to the printing on the higher-quality paper.)

∞→ **StyleWriter ink smears** if you touch it before it dries. Although it dries quickly, this is an issue when the paper is first coming out of the printer.

••→ **Don't let a StyleWriter printout get wet.** No matter how long the ink's been dry, moisture will make it smear.

••→ **Print a test page** by keeping the On button pressed down when you turn on the printer.

••→ **For thick paper stock** and envelopes, there are two adjustments you have to make. One lever is on the paper tray; move it so that it points to the envelope icon. Then comes the tricky part: Open the front panel and move the lever on the ink cartridge to the envelope icon. Both levers need to be flipped back when you switch to printing on regular paper again.

••→ **A StyleWriter II can be shared** among several Macs. Of course, it has to be connected to the main Mac's *modem* port, since the printer port will be used for the network connection.

To activate printer sharing, you open the Chooser, select the StyleWriter II driver, and click the Setup button. You'll get a dialog like the one shown here, where you can name the printer, give it a password, and turn sharing on and off.

••→ **If you can't share your StyleWriter II**—the Name and Password labels in the Sharing dialog stay dimmed—you're missing the Printer Share extension that you need. It's on the StyleWriter's Install disks, though, so just run the Installer again.

••◆ **Sharing a StyleWriter means sharing your Mac.** The StyleWriter doesn't have much of a brain: It needs a computer to figure out what the page looks like. And guess what? The Mac it's connected to does the figuring, no matter which Mac sent the print job. And that makes the main Mac *slooow!*

••◆ **The holes in the ink cartridge** can clog if you haven't used the StyleWriter II in a while—which, of course, means that it can't print. But if you click the Options button in

> **StyleWriter II Print Options**    [ OK ]
> ☐ Clean ink cartridge before printing    [ Cancel ]

the Print dialog, you'll get another dialog, with a single option: a *Clean ink cartridge before printing* checkbox. Click it, start your printing, and the StyleWriter will try to blow through the crud on the cartridge before it starts printing.

You don't have to worry about turning off this option; it's turned off automatically after one use.

••◆ **Speed up a StyleWriter I with the StyleWriter II driver.** But rumor has it that the *Clean ink cartridge before printing* option in the StyleWriter II's Print dialog's option dialog can ruin the StyleWriter I's cartridge. So, use the driver but don't use that option.

StyleWriter

StyleWriter II

## → LASERWRITERS ←

## Features

∞◆ **A LaserWriter isn't a printer.** It's a computer. Okay, it's a computer whose sole purpose in life is to print. But because it's a computer, you have some of the same components, with the basically the same functions, as a computer: a processor with a certain clock speed, for instance, and memory. There are many LaserWriter models out there. Some are differentiated from their brethren by only minor details; some models, or model lines, incorporate major feature changes.

DAVID RAMSEY
*MACWEEK* COLUMNIST

> Many Mac users have yet to come to grips with the fact that their PostScript printers, far from being simple output devices, are separate computers of labyrinthine complexity, and that the printer's internal page description language is understood completely by only three people, all of whom work at Adobe Systems, Inc.

∞◆ **A LaserWriter's resolution is** at least 300 dpi. Later models can switch between 300 and 600-dpi modes. The LaserWriter Pro 810 was the first to offer even more choices and higher resolution, with 300-, 400-, 600-, and 800-dpi options.

It's hard to see the difference between 300- and 600-dpi text printouts coming from the same printer, except with the smallest and finest of fonts. But the difference in basic graphics at those two resolutions is obvious—not a jaggy to be seen on curves or angled lines when they're printed at 600 dpi, while you can still see them at 300 dpi.

∞◆ **PostScript capability** is the largest dividing line between LaserWriters and Apple's other printers. But even some LaserWriters don't have built-in PostScript capability. If the LaserWriter can't do PostScript, you can't print PostScript fonts or graphics without some special utility to do the interpretation—which slows things down and often gives you output of a lesser quality. PostScript Level 2 capability is even more advanced and is in later-model LaserWriters.

∞◆ **The processor in most LaserWriters** is the same as the one in most Macs: a Motorola 68000 series chip—a 68000, 68020, or 68030. The clock speeds on the processors range from 5.5 MHz to 25 MHz.

Some LaserWriters use a RISC (*reduced instruction set computing*) processor instead, for extra speed. The models in the Select and Personal lines that incorporate RISC technology use AMD RISC chips with a clock speed of 16 MHz. The LaserWriter 810 uses a Weitek RISC chip, which is so much more advanced that even at its 7.5-MHz speed it outpaces every other LaserWriter.

∞◆ **Some LaserWriters have no processors.** These are the ones that don't do PostScript, either, since the processor is there to interpret the PostScript commands. These are generally referred to, inaccurately, as QuickDraw printers. (The one exception to this is the Personal LaserWriter SC, which has a processor, but doesn't have PostScript capabilities.)

∞◆ **The number of PostScript fonts built into** the LaserWriters has increased over time, from 13 in the first LaserWriter to a standard 35 now. But you have to be careful how you count the fonts—there are 35 individual fonts, sure, but that's when you count Times, Times Bold, Times Italic, and Times Bold Italic as four separate fonts instead of as one "family."

The first LaserWriter had four font families (13 fonts) built-in:

| | |
|---|---|
| Courier | Helvetica |
| Times | Σψμβολ (Symbol) |

All other models include the first four families as well as:

| | |
|---|---|
| Palatino | Bookman |
| Avant Garde | *New Century Schoolbook* |
| Helvetica Narrow | ✳❂◻✿ (Zapf Dingbats) |
| *Zapf Chancery* | |

Wait! Did I say *all* later models? All but one, actually: the LaserWriter IIg, for some reason, didn't include Zapf Dingbats. (But see the upgrade section later in this chapter for more about that.)

Lots more about fonts and families in Chapter 11.

•••➤ **The more memory a LaserWriter has,** the more complicated the documents it can print. With more memory, it can print a page of intricate graphics and multiple fonts without "choking"—either taking just short of forever to print, or failing to print at all. Some LaserWriters are limited to the amount of memory that's initially built in; others can be upgraded with additional memory.

There's a whole section on LaserWriters and hard drives later in this chapter.

•••➤ **You can connect a hard disk** to some LaserWriter models to hold downloadable fonts. Some models offer a SCSI port for an external hard drive, some can accommodate an internal hard drive, and some offer both options.

•••➤ **A LaserWriter's "interface" is** the way it connects to the computer; in this case, the word is used in its older, more traditional sense instead of in its current popular usage that refers to how you interact with the computer.

You might be tempted to simply use the word *port* for the LaserWriter's connector, but then run into a problem: one port—the standard printer port—might be used for a regular serial connection, a high-speed serial connection, or an AppleTalk network connection. So, I'll stick to referring to the *interfaces* available for different LaserWriter models.

There are several different interfaces on various LaserWriter models; some models offer more than one option. The various interfaces are:

- *Serial.* This is the standard printer port and it lets you connect the printer directly to the computer. It's sometimes referred to as the *RS-232* serial port.
- *High-speed serial.* This interface is just what it sounds like; it's sometimes referred to as *RS-422.*
- *Parallel.* This connection gets information to the printer more quickly than a serial interface, because the data travels along sets of parallel wires instead of being funneled through a single skinny one. But it's not an option you can use with your Mac setup: it's made for connecting LaserWriters to Windows machines—that is, IBM PC-compatibles running Windows software.
- *LocalTalk.* This is the standard network connection between the Mac and the LaserWriter, even if you're not on a network; LocalTalk is the "protocol" used for the exchange of information between the computer and the printer. It's a serial connection, using the standard printer port.
- *Ethernet.* This is a connection for high-speed Ethernet networks; its data transfer rate is about ten times that of LocalTalk.
- *SCSI.* A very few LaserWriter models actually connect through the SCSI port of the Mac. But don't confuse this with a LaserWriter's having a SCSI port for attaching a hard drive—that's a different matter altogether.

•••➤ **Multiple paper trays are** a convenience you shouldn't discount too quickly: with one to feed in letterheads and the other to hold standard paper, or one for paper and one for envelopes, the later LaserWriters that offer this capability are a boon to many businesspeople.

•••**➤** **The speed of a LaserWriter** is usually given in *ppm—pages per minute*. But you shouldn't count on the rating, except as a general rule for comparing one model to another. Just don't expect to get that many pages printed out each minute, because it's always fewer unless you're printing straight text in a built-in font, or multiple copies of the same page.

The pages per minute rating refers to how quickly the "engine" of the LaserWriter can print a page; it's pretty much the speed of the *mechanical* end of things. But remember that a LaserWriter has to process information before it can print it, so several other factors come into play for the true ppm rating: the amount of information on a page, and its complexity; the type of processor the LaserWriter has; and, the clock speed of the processor.

As a general rule, if your pages are complicated, you want a fast processor—and that's not reflected in the ppm rating. If you do multiple copies of the pages you print, a higher ppm rating is better because the LaserWriter can churn out the multiple copies very quickly—the image of the page has to be processed only once.

•••**➤** *FinePrint* **is** the name of the technology built into the latest round of LaserWriters. It smoothes lines in text and graphics by printing dots of different sizes when necessary to round out a curve. How much difference does it really make? I printed out some samples from my LaserWriter Pro 630 and not one of a dozen people could see a difference between the FinePrint and the non-FinePrint. (But everyone could see the difference between my LaserWriter printout and the ones they got from their older LaserWriter models; the newer models use finer toner particles and so can produce finer lines.)

•••**➤** *PhotoGrade* **is** a later-model technology that prints better grayscale graphics, whether computer artwork or scanned photos. It enables LaserWriters to print using 91 levels of gray instead of the previous limitation of 33. The PhotoGrade difference (unlike the FinePrint one) is breathtaking, and not just if you're doing photographic printing. If, for instance, you're using a gray screen behind text, even the best of the LaserWriters without PhotoGrade prints dots that make any normal-sized text difficult (or impossible) to read. With PhotoGrade, a LaserWriter prints what looks like a true gray screen—you can't see the dots without *really* squinting.

•••**➤** **FinePrint and PhotoGrade** are built into certain LaserWriters by means of an *ASIC*— an *application-specific integrated circuit*. (Just thought you'd like another piece of jargon.)

•••**➤** **TrueType is built into** a very few LaserWriter models. That is, the TrueType *scaler*, or *rasterizer*—the part that figures out how to translate the TrueType font information into actual letters—is built-in. Normally, the Mac sends the scaler information to the printer, and then sends the font. Having built-in TrueType scaling doesn't save any time, though: The scaling information is still downloaded to the printer, which then discards it as extraneous information. I suppose that leaves the only advantage to having TrueType built in is that you save a little memory; no wonder built-in scaling didn't become a standard.

## Models

⚬•➤ **LaserWriter models can be grouped** loosely by their model names. You'd think that the names would indicate their capabilities, and that models in each group would sport certain features in common, but you'd be wrong. There's quite a bit of overlap from one group to another, and there's sometimes a wide range of abilities within a group. But the handy classifications are:

- LaserWriter I
- LaserWriter II
- Personal LaserWriter
- LaserWriter Select
- LaserWriter Pro

⚬•➤ **The first two LaserWriters** were named LaserWriter and LaserWriter Plus. (They're generically referred to as LaserWriter I's, even though the number was never used in their names.) The original LaserWriter had 4 font families (counted as 13 fonts); the Plus had the full complement of 35 that's still used in Apple LaserWriters. There are still plenty of these early models around, which is testimony to their ruggedness. The only problem with them is their relatively slow speed and limited memory compared to the latest models. If your needs are relatively simple (no intense graphics or fancy font mixtures), however, these older models are still perfectly serviceable.

There were actually two LaserWriter Plus models: The later one had an upgraded ROM that used version 47 of PostScript, but it (the LaserWriter model) was never given a separate name or number.

⚬•➤ **The LaserWriter II line** was introduced in 1988 with three models, and expanded with two more models in 1991. The II line was marked by better, faster printing: the Canon engine that's inside a LaserWriter II prints faster and with darker, more solid blacks. Some of these models are still in production, and most (if not all) are certainly still in use. The difference from one model to another is simply the card that controls what's going on inside; from the outside, they all look the same.

The II line consists of:

- *LaserWriter II SC.* The SC stands for SCSI, because this printer hooks up through the Mac's SCSI port. It doesn't support PostScript (which also means it has no built-in fonts) and can't be shared among multiple Macs because of the SCSI connection.

- *LaserWriter II NT.* The NT is for *new technology*—the new Canon engine that's also in the other II models. It sports full PostScript capability and built-in fonts, a faster clock speed, and twice as much memory as the SC, and it's networkable.

- *LaserWriter II NTX.* The X is for *expandable*, because its 2-meg memory is expandable to 12 megs. It also has a 68020 processor running at 16 MHz, so it's much faster than the NT's 12-MHz 68000.

- *LaserWriter IIf.* This and the IIg are the first printers to use PhotoGrade, FinePrint, and PostScript Level 2. The IIf runs at 20 MHz and comes with 4 megs of memory that can be expanded to 32 megs.

- *LaserWriter IIg.* This model comes with 8 megs of memory and runs at 25 MHz, so it outperforms the IIf. The only other difference between the two models is that the IIg has built-in Ethernet support.

### MAC TRIVIA

The LaserWriter II's (the SC, NT, and NTX) have an ADB port. Why? So you can hook up your keyboard and type directly to the printer?

In fact, the port's totally useless. It was meant for expansion capabilities later in the development of the II line—for multiple cut-sheet feeders, for instance. But few add-on devices were developed, and the II's ROM was never even upgraded so that it could fully recognize the port!

So what does ADB stand for? *A Dubious Blunder?*

**The Personal LaserWriter** line consists of a variety of low-cost alternatives. Although the capabilities of the models vary considerably, they're generally slower and have less memory than the models in the II line. They use a different Canon engine than the II's do, which accounts for the slower printing. Since they're made for *personal* printing, there are cutbacks in other areas, too, like a paper tray that holds fewer pages.

- *Personal LaserWriter SC:* Once again, the SC stands for SCSI because that's how it connects to the Mac. It uses a 68000 processor running at a sluggish 8 MHz, but it doesn't do PostScript.

- *Personal LaserWriter LS.* This replaced the SC in the lineup within a few months of the SC's introduction. It doesn't do PostScript, and, although it connects through the printer port rather than the SCSI port, it's not networkable. It has only 512K of memory, but uses a special compression scheme so it can sometimes perform as if it had as much as 2.5 megs.

- *Personal LaserWriter NT.* Not to be confused with the II NT, this NT in the Personal line uses a 68000 processor running at 12 MHz. It comes with 3 megs of memory, upgradable to 4. It's a PostScript printer that's networkable, and it lasted a year in the model line before being replaced by the Personal NTR.

- *Personal LaserWriter NTR.* This NTR (once again, not to be confused with the II NTR) uses a RISC chip instead of one in the 68000 series and works more than twice as fast as the Personal NT that it replaced. But wait! When you look at a chart (there's one coming up soon), you'll see that both models—in fact, all the models in the Personal line—are rated at 4 pages per minute. How can one be faster than another? Remember, the popup menu rating is for the mechanical churning out of pages; the NTR *processes* the image for the page faster than the NT does. So if you're printing simple text, you probably won't see a speed difference; fancy text (multiple fonts) or complex graphics will definitely show a speed difference. The NTR is also the first LaserWriter to offer a parallel port for use with PC-compatibles.

- *Personal LaserWriter 300.* I have no idea where this number came from, although I suspect it's a nefarious scheme to confuse us, since 300s are used mainly in the Select line of LaserWriters. In any case, this 300 seems to be a replacement for the Personal LS, since most of the features are the same but the 300 is a smaller, lighter machine with better grayscale printing and a larger paper tray.

••➤ **The LaserWriter Select line** so far consists of three models.

- *Select 300.* This non-PostScript printer is rated at 5 pages per minute. It uses the same compression scheme as the Personal LS to make its 512K of memory work more like 2.5 megs, but it is expandable to a true 4.5 megs. It has FinePrint built in, and you can add a PhotoGrade upgrade.

- *Select 310.* This is a PostScript printer with a RISC processor, rated at 5 pages per minute. It comes with 1.5 megs of RAM that can be upgraded to 5.5. It has both a high-speed printer port and a parallel port for PC-compatibility. Oddly enough, it has only 13 PostScript fonts built in, as did the very first LaserWriter. And it supports neither FinePrint nor PhotoGrade—not even as options.

- *Select 360.* This one's a step ahead of the other Select LaserWriters in several ways. The three most obvious are: it prints at 10 pages per minute; it can be upgraded to 16 megs of memory; and, it prints at a beautiful 600 dpi. In addition, you can add a PostScript fax card to enable it to send, receive, and print plain-paper faxes.

••➤ **The LaserWriter Pro series** has three models at this point: the 610, the 630, and the 810. (There's no rhyme or reason to these numbers; in my more paranoid moments, I think they were invented so I could confuse my Centris 650 with my LaserWriter Pro 630. Or is that the Centris 630 and the Pro 650? Or is it a Quadra 650 now anyway? See what I mean?)

The LaserWriter Pros were the first Apple LaserWriters to break the 300-dpi barrier, with 600-dpi options on all of them, and up to 800 dpi on the 810. In addition, the 600's run the 68030 processor at a zippy 25 MHz and include some specialized chips to speed things up even further. Multiple paper trays in these models mean you can feed in two different types of paper (letterhead and plain paper, or envelope and paper) automatically.

- *Pro 600 and 630.* There are only a few differences between these printers: the 630 has SCSI ports for both internal and external hard drives while the 600 has none, and the 630 has built-in Ethernet capability. Oh—and the price, of course!

- *Pro 810.* This is a monster of a machine that churns out 20 pages per minute. As you should know by now, that number describes strictly the mechanical end of things. But the 810 also has a special RISC processor; it's so much more advanced than the chip used in the other RISC-technology LaserWriters that it outstrips them even running at a seemingly slow-sounding 7.5 MHz. It can print at 300, 400, 600, and even 800 dpi—the highest resolution of any Apple LaserWriter. Its multiple paper trays hold a whopping 750 pages at a time—obviously a printer made for an office network. It takes an optional PostScript fax card so it can send, receive, and print plain-paper faxes. Oh, and as if all that weren't enough, it's also the only Apple printer that lets you print on tabloid (11x17-inch) paper.

## LaserWriter Model Specs

| Model | PostScript | Processor | Speed (MHz) | Built-in Fonts | Pages per Minute | Dots Per Inch | Interface | Max. RAM (MB) | Hard Drive | PhotoGrade | FinePrint |
|---|---|---|---|---|---|---|---|---|---|---|---|
| LaserWriter | 1 | 68000 | - | 13 | 4 | 300 | serial | 1.5 | - | - | - |
| LaserWriter Plus | 1 | 68000 | - | 13 | 4 | 300 | serial | 1.5 | - | - | - |
| II SC | - | 68000 | 7.5 | | 8 | 300 | SCSI | 1 | - | - | - |
| II NT | 1 | 68000 | 12 | 35 | 8 | 300 | serial | 2 | - | - | - |
| II NTX | 1 | 68020 | 16 | 35 | 8 | 300 | serial | 12 | √ | - | √ |
| IIf | 2 | 68030 | 20 | 35 | 8 | 300 | serial | 32 | √ | √ | √ |
| IIg | 2 | 68030 | 25 | 35 | 8 | 300 | serial EtherTalk | 32 | √ | √ | √ |
| Personal SC | - | 68000 | 8 | 35 | 4 | 300 | SCSI | 1 | - | - | - |
| Personal LS | - | - | - | - | 4 | 300 | high-speed serial | .5 | - | - | - |
| Personal NT | 1 | 68000 | 12 | 35 | 4 | 300 | serial | 4 | - | - | - |
| Personal NTR | 2 | AMD RISC | 16 | 35 | 4 | 300 | serial, parallel | 4 | - | - | - |
| Personal 300 | - | - | - | - | 4 | 300 | high-speed serial | - | - | - | - |
| Select 300 | - | - | - | - | 5 | 300 | high-speed serial | 4.5 | - | - | √ |
| Select 310 | 1 | AMD RISC | 16 | 13 | 5 | 300 | high-speed serial, parallel | 5.5 | - | - | - |
| Select 360 | 1 | AMD RISC | 16 | 35 | 10 | 600 | high-speed serial, parallel | 16 | - | - | - |
| Pro 600 | 2 | 68030 | 25 | 35 | 8 | 300, 600 | serial, parallel | 32 | - | √ | √ |
| Pro 630 | 2 | 68030 | 25 | 35 | 8 | 300, 600 | serial, parallel, EtherTalk | 32 | √ | √ | √ |
| Pro 810 | 2 | Weitek RISC | 7.25 | 35 | 20 | 300, 400, 600, 800 | serial, parallel, EtherTalk | 32 | √ | √ | √ |

···❯ **LaserWriter is an Apple trademark;** *laser printer* is generic, and there are other laser printers out there besides Apple's. Testing and reporting on various brands is not only beyond the scope of this book, it's outside the realm of possibility considering the author's budget and time constraints. But ... I sure have seen and heard a lot over the years when it comes to printers and Macs. And three brands of non-Apple printers consistently get high marks for compatibility, dependability, and output quality: QMS, Hewlett-Packard, and NEC.

## Options & Upgrades

∞•❯ **LaserWriters are the most upgradable** of Apple's products (with the exception, perhaps, of late-model Macs designed to be upgradable to Power Macs). Most models beyond the II NT accommodate additional memory, and some have minor upgrades available—for PhotoGrade capability, for instance. Many models can be turned into entirely different machines by a logic board change. Then there are the *options*, as opposed to upgrades: things like larger, or extra, paper trays.

∞•❯ **You're not always stuck with the paper tray** your LaserWriter came with. The way you get additional paper capacity for automatic feed-in depends on which LaserWriter you own, although every model within a line of LaserWriters usually has the same options because their "bodies" are the same. Some LaserWriters are designed to let you swap the standard paper cassette for one that holds legal-size papers, or envelopes. Some models have bins you can add to the bottom of the printer to hold hundreds more pages for printing. Others accommodate multi-purpose trays that hold letter-size papers or envelopes. Here's a quick chart of what comes as standard with late-model LaserWriter models and what's available as accessories:

| Model | Standard | Options |
|---|---|---|
| IIf, IIg | 200-letter | letter cassette<br>legal cassette |
| Personal LS, NTR | 70-letter/15-envelope | 250-letter<br>letter cassette<br>legal cassette |
| Select 300, 310 | 250-letter/15 envelopes | 250-sheet letter<br>500-sheet letter<br>250-sheet legal<br>30-envelope<br>50-letter/5-envelope |
| Select 360 | 50-letter/5-envelope<br>250-sheet letter | 250-letter<br>500-sheet letter<br>250-sheet legal<br>30-envelope |
| Pro 600, 630 | 100-letter/15-envelope<br>250-letter | 500-letter<br>75-envelope |
| Pro 810 | (3) 250-sheet universal size<br>(letter, legal, tabloid) | 250-sheet universal<br>250-sheet folio<br>100-sheet/15-envelope |

∞•❯ **Upgrade a LaserWriter's memory** to improve its performance. More memory means you can:

- Process more complicated graphics.
- Use more fonts on a page.
- Download more fonts for faster operation.
- Generally print faster.

∞➤ **Adding memory is easy:** you just get SIMMs and snap them in, the same way you put memory in a modular Mac. Get the SIMMs from the same place you'd get memory for your computer (some suggested resources are listed in Chapter 14).

•➤ **Not all LaserWriters** can accommodate more memory. Here's a quick list of how much memory different models come with, and how far they can be upgraded:

| Model | Standard (MB) | Maximum (MB) |
|---|---|---|
| LaserWriter | 1.5 | - |
| LW Plus | 1.5 | - |
| II SC | 1 | - |
| II NT | 2 | - |
| II NTX | 2 | 12 |
| IIf | 4 | 32 |
| IIg | 8 | 32 |
| Personal SC | 1 | - |
| Personal LS | .5 | - |
| Personal NT | 2 | 4 |
| Personal NTR | 3 | 4 |
| Select 300 | .5 | 4.5 |
| Select 310 | 1.5 | 5.5 |
| Select 360 | 7 | 16 |
| Pro 600 | 4 | 32 |
| Pro 630 | 8 | 32 |
| Pro 810 | 8 | 32 |

•➤ **Change one LaserWriter model into another** by changing its *logic board* (also referred to as the *controller card*). You won't be able to turn a Personal LaserWriter into a LaserWriter Pro, but many of the low-end models in a line can be upgraded to the higher-end models within the same line by the simple swapping of a logic board. (It's so simple you can do it yourself.)

Here's another chart, showing which models can be upgraded to what.

| Model | Upgrade to... |
|---|---|
| II SC, II NT | NTX, IIf, IIg |
| II NTX | IIf, IIg |
| IIf | IIg |
| Personal SC, NT | Personal NTR |
| Select 300 | Select 310 |
| Pro 600 | Pro 630 |

•➤ **If you upgrade, go all the way.** Just because you can upgrade a II SC to an NTX, and an NTX is so much better than the SC, that doesn't mean it's the best thing to do. Go for the highest upgrade you can get: a II SC, for instance, can be turned into a IIf or IIg. The only reason there's an NTX upgrade for it is that the NTX came out before the IIf and IIg, and was, for a while, the only upgrade for the II SC.

•➤ **Most upgradable LaserWriters use standard SIMMs**—the same 32-pin SIMMs that most Macs use. So, if you upgrade your computer's memory with larger SIMMs, and you have, say, 1-meg SIMMs left over, you can use them in any LaserWriter except the NTX.

**··►** **The II NTX uses special SIMMs** that are more expensive than standard SIMMs. So be careful if you're changing printers—you can't always take your memory with you.

**··►** **The Select 300 has a PhotoGrade upgrade** option; without the upgrade, it's the only LaserWriter that has FinePrint without having PhotoGrade.

**··►** **A Select 300 to 310** upgrade gets you PostScript capabilities, a selection of built-in fonts, the capacity for more memory, and overall faster operation. But you'll lose the FinePrint and PhotoGrade capability of the 300. (Wouldn't you think they'd set it up so that you could have it all?)

### THE WAY WE WERE ...

It's hard to believe that the program Just Text actually received favorable reviews when it was released at the end of 1986. (To get yourself oriented in time: The LaserWriter had just been introduced, and the Mac Plus with its 1 meg of memory and 800K disks was the cutting edge of Macintosh technology.)

At its introduction, and for at least a year afterward, the PostScript capabilities of the LaserWriter were unused except for printing one of its four built-in fonts. No graphics. No other fonts. Not even any typographic control over the fonts—there was no such thing as non-standard or fractional font sizes, no kerning of letters—there was no program that took advantage of the LaserWriter's PostScript capabilities.

The Just Text program gave a great deal of control over the size and exact placement of text, and even graphics, in a document. But it did it all in a window that showed only 9-point Geneva, and could hold only 32K of information. And it did it with commands like this:

- For an em dash (a long hyphen), you'd type {md}.
- For italics, you typed {f6} at the beginning and {f4} at the end of the italicized word or phrase.
- To begin a new paragraph, you typed {ql} (for *quad left)* at the end of the previous paragraph. For a little extra spacing, you'd use something like {ql}{a6}.

So, to get a line of text like this:

> You *like* this—this *program*?

You would type it like this (including some initial commands for where the text begins on the page, and the font and size):

> {il9}{ir9}{p12}{l213}You {f6}like {f4}{md}this {f6}program{f4}?

And that's not all. Once you finished typing the gibberish, you couldn't just print it. Oh, no. First it had to be compiled, which is the process of taking "raw" code that humans use and turning it into a language that the computer understands. In this case, the computer was the LaserWriter and the language was PostScript. If the compiler program found any errors (and you can imagine how easy it was to make a few mistakes), it told you where they were. Or it just crashed. Once you managed to get the compiled PostScript code, which was a text file, it had to be downloaded to the printer with yet another utility, since downloading a file isn't the same as simply printing it. And if you were very, very lucky, the page that came out was what you meant to print.

···➔ **You can get a free ROM upgrade** for the IIf or IIg if you're having certain problems with it, for instance:

- The printer status light flashes to indicate the printer's busy, even when it's not doing anything.
- The LaserWriter Utility can't see a hard drive attached to the printer.
- Printing errors and incomplete print jobs using print spoolers.
- Certain font manipulation programs can't get the font information they need from the LaserWriter.
- You can't rename the IIg on an Ethertalk network.
- You can't place the IIg in different zones on an Ethertalk network.

Now, here's the interesting thing: The 2.0 ROM upgrade includes Zapf Dingbats, which the IIg is missing in its 1.0 ROM. But if you just want the upgrade for the Dingbats, that's not a free fix; you only get the free upgrade if your LaserWriter is having problems. Let me say that again: the upgrade is free only when you complain about the LaserWriter's exhibiting some of the problems that crop up with the 1.0 ROMs. Get it?

This 2.0 ROM, by the way, is strictly a fix for reported problems; it was never incorporated into the IIf or IIg later in their production runs.

···➔ **Add a PostScript fax card** to a Select 360 or a Pro 810 to turn it into a plain-paper fax machine—albeit an *expensive* fax machine, but then plain-paper faxes are expensive anyway, and we can assume you'll be using the LaserWriter as a printer as well.

The fax card lets you receive standard faxes that get printed out beautifully on regular paper instead of that waxy, flimsy fax stuff. You can send standard faxes, too, as long as you're sending computer files as the fax document; you can't run a printed page through the LaserWriter and have it sent as a fax.

···➔ **Are upgrades worth the money?** Well, say you're a graphic designer who's printing test sheets of complicated graphics, and your printer spends about 45 minutes processing the page. What's it worth to you to get that page in 10 minutes instead? Or what if you use a lot of fonts (tastefully, we'd like to think) on a page and they all come out printed as Courier because there's not enough memory in the LaserWriter to handle more than three fonts? What's that worth to you?

As with all upgrade or new purchase decisions, "worth" is in the productivity level of the user.

## Using a Hard Drive

···➔ **Attach a hard drive to your LaserWriter** to store font files for speeding up the overall printing process. Not all LaserWriter models offer this capability—but if you see a SCSI port on your LaserWriter, you can plug in an external hard drive.

What normally happens when you use a font that's not built into the LaserWriter is that the Mac has to send the font information to the printer; the font files in your

Extensions folder (System 7.0) or Fonts folder (System 7.1) are downloaded to the printer. This, of course, ties up your Mac longer for a print job when it's downloading a font than when the font's already in the LaserWriter. You can send fonts to the LaserWriter's memory and store them there, but that's a limited storage situation, and they disappear when the LaserWriter is turned off.

By storing font information on a hard drive attached to the LaserWriter, the font information is transferred from the hard drive to the LaserWriter when needed. Although this isn't as fast as dealing with a font that's already *in* the LaserWriter's memory, that memory is limited; and the speed of the SCSI transfer from the LaserWriter's hard drive is much faster than the rate data can move across the AppleTalk connection between the Mac and the printer. In addition, your Mac finishes the print job faster than if it were sending the fonts.

∞♪ **You can't use a Mac-formatted hard drive** on a LaserWriter. The LaserWriter needs an entirely different setup of information storage, so you can't set up the hard drive while it's attached to the Mac and then connect it to the LaserWriter. Instead, you connect the hard drive to the LaserWriter, and then use the LaserWriter Utility to initialize the printer: Just choose the Initialize Printer's Disk command, and the Mac takes it from there.

∞♪ **To store fonts on the printer's drive,** use the Download Fonts command in the LaserWriter Utility. Make sure that the *Printer's disk* button is selected in the dialog. After that, it's the same as downloading a font to the printer's memory, as detailed in Chapter 12. (Don't forget: you're downloading the *printer* fonts, not the screen fonts. I don't know why the bitmap fonts even show up in the list when you click the Add button!)

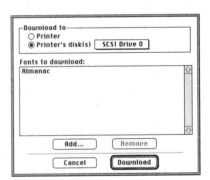

∞♪ **TrueType fonts can be downloaded** to a printer's disk the same way that PostScript fonts can.

∞♪ **The entire hard drive is not used** for font storage. Only a portion of it is actually used for storing font files. The exact proportion? That seems to be a closely guarded secret, but estimates range as low as only 20 percent of the drive.

The rest of the drive is used as a *font cache.* If the LaserWriter has a font downloaded to it from the Mac, it processes the information and creates a bitmapped font of the right size to use for the printing. Normally, that font information gets bumped from the LaserWriter's memory when more recent information is downloaded to it. But when there's a hard drive available, the information is stored on the hard drive instead, and it is retrieved if it's needed again.

Font files, however, are very small. With only a 40-meg drive attached to the printer, 20 percent of its storage space can store around 230 font files.

°•➤ **The LaserWriters that can use hard drives** can't always use each others' hard drives. Well … they can use the drive itself, but not the way it was set up for the other model. So, if you used a hard drive with your II NTX and then upgraded to a IIf, IIg, or a Pro, you'd have to reinitialize the hard drive and download the fonts all over again.

°•➤ **There's no way to see what's really on** the printer's hard drive. You can get a list of the fonts you've downloaded, through the LaserWriter Utility's *List Available Fonts* command, but that won't tell you how much room is left on the drive, or how much of the drive is used for the font cache, or what's in the font cache. Isn't that ridiculous? Maybe it will be in the next version of the LaserWriter Utility. But for now, you just keep downloading fonts until you get a *disk full* message. In the meantime, you have no idea how much of the drive is used up, or what's stored in the font cache portion of the drive. (They probably don't want us to see how little of the drive is actually used for font storage!)

°•➤ **Some printer hard drives** can be read by the Mac. If you detach a drive from a LaserWriter IIf, IIg, or Pro 630, and attach it to the Mac, you can see what's on the disk. Isn't that an easy way to check its contents?!

°•➤ **If you're using Adobe Type Manager,** it won't "see" the printer files on the printer's hard drive. So you'll still need to keep a copy of the printer font on your Mac's hard drive for good-looking screen text even if it's on the printer's hard drive for speed.

➤ **A hard drive used with a IIf or IIg** needs the special black terminator that the Mac IIfx uses.

Termination for hard drives is covered in Chapter 18.

➤ **There's one way to get a minimal report** about the printer's drive and how much room is used and how much is still free, although there's no differentiation between the font storage portion of the drive and the font cache partition. Here's the multi-step process, which has you writing a PostScript program (remember, it's a programming language) and sending it to the printer.

    1. Type this program *exactly* as it's printed here, in a word processor or TeachText:

```
/Helvetica findfont 14 scalefont setfont
statusdict begin
30 100 moveto
(*A page is 1024 bytes — a K. ) show
30 115 moveto
(Total number of pages: ) show
diskstatus
10 string cvs show
30 130 moveto
(Number of pages free: ) show
10 string cvs show
showpage
```

2. Save the file as a text file—most word processors offer that as an option.

3. Launch the LaserWriter Utility.

4. Use the Download PostScript file command and send the text file to the printer.

5. You'll be asked where you want to save the PostScript Log for the download. Put it anywhere—it won't even be saved if everything goes well; it's only for error reports.

That's it. If you typed everything in correctly, you'll get a printout that looks something like this:

Number of pages free: 34235
Total number of pages: 39991
*A page is 1024 bytes — a K.

This report is for a 40-meg drive attached to the LaserWriter. With 34,235 pages free, and a page equaling 1024 bytes (a single K), the total free space is still over 33 megs.

**••◆ Multiple hard drives on a II NTX** are treated as a single giant drive, so you can't make sense of anything if you try to hook up one of them directly to the Mac. Nor can you detach one of them and expect the remaining one to work—you'll have to reinitialize the drive and download the fonts all over again.

**••◆ "Left over" hard drives from PowerBooks** are a popular choice for installing in LaserWriters that take internal hard drives. The early PowerBooks came with 20- and 40-meg drives, and thousands of users upgraded to larger drives when they became available. With the right brackets, you can use these drives inside a LaserWriter. (The brackets are available from a terrific mail-order company that specializes in Mac peripheral hardware, APS.) But the Conner brand 20- and 40-meg drives, for some unknown reason, just don't seem to be able to make the transition. The Quantum and IBM* brands work fine.

> ✳Yes, IBM. That IBM. Their internal hard drives are used in many PowerBooks.

## Toner Cartridges

**∞◆ Adjust the density of the toner** your LaserWriter's using to make the cartridge last longer.

The LaserWriter I and II models have density control dials; on the earliest models, it's on the outside, while for the II line, it's inside, just under the lid. The settings on the dial are 1 to 9, with 9 being the lightest. (Hey, I didn't design it, I'm just reporting the facts.) When the toner cartridge is new, set the dial to 9; when the printouts seem a little light, turn the dial down.

Other LaserWriters have software-controlled density settings. You use the Print Density command in the LaserWriter Utility to access a little slider control to set the density. (I have to admit that I've yet to see any difference from one extreme setting to the other with my LaserWriter Pro 630.)

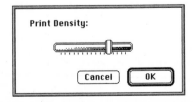

○○○⟩ **Print draft copies** in a perfectly readable gray instead of black, and cut your toner usage in half. Toner Tuner is a utility that cuts back the toner density more than a density dial or a LaserWriter Utility adjustment can. [Working Software]

•••⟩ **Pay no attention to that blinking yellow** light on the LaserWriter that says you're out of toner. If your printouts look right, you're not that much out of toner! In fact, you'll notice that when the toner gets low, it's almost always just the center of the page that stops printing (or starts printing in light gray, or in mottled black and white). You can get more toner from the cartridge, though: Take the cartridge out and rock it from side to side to redistribute the toner inside. You'll be amazed at how many pages you'll still be able to print. I did this recently (I'm printing *lots* of pages as I work on this book) and, after having a completely white streak down the center three inches of the page, a little rocking gave me about 400 more pages before the toner was really gone.

•••⟩ **Toner cartridges can be *recharged***—reconditioned and filled with new toner. I can't recommend any particular company for this—it's almost always a small local business that offers this service. Ask around at a User Group to make a connection in your area, or check the back pages of your favorite Mac magazine.

A properly refilled cartridge is just as good as a new one. Cartridges can be refilled, on the average, about three times with good results. After that, the drum inside has to be recoated—at which point it's good for three or four fills again.

A caveat: Make sure that you get a totally reconditioned cartridge, not one that's been through a "drill and fill" procedure. A good refill includes not only new toner, but a thorough check on all components and replacement parts when necessary.

 **POP QUIZ**          **[10 POINTS EACH]**

Here's a double quiz, based on the last two entries. Clues: Both answers are both books and movies! In fact, the two movies vied for Oscars in the very same year.

*Have some madiera, my dear*

1. One entry started with the phrase *Pay no attention to the blinking yellow light.* That's a twist on the phrase *Pay no attention to the man behind the curtain,* an oft-repeated utterance from a classic movie.

2. The last entry ended with a caveat; that word's from the phrase *caveat emptor,* which means *let the buyer beware.* Now, what very, very famous work of fiction had the suave, mustached, big-eared hero convince the tough but charming heroine to name her new shop the *Caveat Emporium*—which she did, unwittingly, to his great amusement?

•••⟩ **Toner cartridges are very warm**—one might even say *hot*—when they're in use. And that means they're still hot immediately after being used. So if you're reaching in to remove a cartridge for a little rocking or a replacement, give it a cool-down period.

••→ **You don't need cartridges made specifically for LaserWriters.** If you're shopping and you can't find anything except cartridges labeled for Hewlett-Packard laser printers, here's an equivalency list:

> HP II, II D, III, III D .......... LaserWriter II series
> HP Laser Jet 4-L, 4-ML ...... Personal LaserWriter 300
> HP Laser Jet 4 .................... LaserWriter Pro 600 models

••→ **Recycle empty LaserWriter cartridges.** Don't just throw them out; they're non-biodegradable, to say the least—and just picture the amount of landfill used cartridges can create. Even if you don't want to use a refilled, tuned-up cartridge, others will. And when a cartridge has gone through its maximum number of refills, its case can be melted down and the material used again.

Apple makes it exceptionally easy to recycle cartridges—they come in boxes that you can ship them in, and there's even a prepaid label to the recycling center. Other cartridge manufacturers also have recycling programs. For more information, call:

> Apple: 800-776-2333
> Xerox: 800-822-2200
> Canon: 800-962-2708
> Qume: 800-421-4326
> International Cartridge Recycling Association: 202-857-1154.

## Odds & Ends

∘∘→ **Telling LaserWriters apart** within a model line can't be done from just the outside—mine, for instance, simply says LaserWriter Pro on it, and there's nothing to show whether it's a 600 or a 630. All the II's look alike, too, and most of the Selects are identical to each other.

But there are three easy ways to check what's really inside (when, for instance, you're purchasing a used LaserWriter):

- Check the odometer. Print a startup page, which identifies the printer and also tells you how many pages it has printed in its lifetime.
- Use the LaserWriter Utility to print a Configuration Page. This not only identifies the model, it tells you how much memory's installed, too.
- Look at the logic board inside. The name of the model is printed on it. On the earliest LaserWriters, you'll find the name on a plate near the printer's cables.

*✳The way I have my equipment set up, I can't see any of the lights. Oh well, I'm moving as soon as this book is finished— maybe my new office will work a little better.*

∘∘→ **There are four lights and symbols** on a LaserWriter for various status reports.* The colors of the lights have changed from one model to another, with various combinations of red, yellow, and green being used, so I'll refer to them by number, from left to right. The icons by the lights, shown in the picture on the next page, have remained standard.

- When the first light is on continuously, the printer is ready and waiting for work. When it's flashing, the printer is "thinking"—processing the image for a page.
- When the second light is on continuously, the paper tray is either empty or not in the machine. When it's flashing, the printer's waiting to be fed a piece of paper—you've selected the manual feed option in the Print dialog.
- When the third light is on, the toner in the cartridge is low.
- When the last light is on continuously, there's a paper jam.

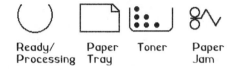

Ready/    Paper   Toner   Paper
Processing  Tray            Jam

∘∘• **The LaserWriter IIf and IIg** have a TrueType scaler built in. As I mentioned before, this doesn't save any time, since the scaling information is still downloaded to the printer, then discarded as unnecessary.

∘∘• **Turn FinePrint and PhotoGrade defaults on or off** and choose the printing resolution you want with the Imaging Options command in the LaserWriter Utility. (Only for those Laser-Writers, of course, that have those options at all.) The dialog shown here lets you choose your default settings. You'll find that if you choose 600 dpi as the resolution, FinePrint is no longer available as an option—you won't need it if you're printing at that resolution.

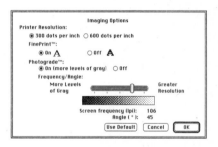

∘∘• **Bypass the imaging defaults** through the Print dialog's Options dialog: Choose Print and then click the Options button. The dialog has a scrolling list of printer options (the one you can't see in the first picture here is for paper trays) that let you leave things at the printer's default or at an override setting.

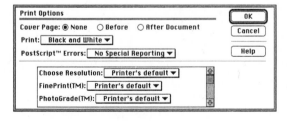

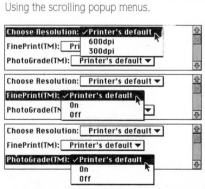

Using the scrolling popup menus.

⊶❥ **To clear a paper jam,** lift the lid of the printer and pull gently on the page that's stuck. If you pull too quickly, you may find *half* a paper in your hand and the other half with no exposed edge to grab. (Reminds me of the old joke—what's worse than finding a worm in an apple?)

You don't have to turn off the printer—and, in fact, you shouldn't, because it will merrily complete the print job once the paper path is clear. All you'll have to do is reprint the page that was caught in the mechanism.

⊶❥ **Paper jams are caused** by any of several factors. The paper may be too thick to feed through the rollers. The paper may be too thin to make its way through. A folded or wrinkled edge may catch on the way in or out. Sometimes a page that's been printed with no problem the first time might not make it through a second time for printing on both sides—the heat from the first printing curled the paper just enough that the edge won't feed through cleanly.

But the oddest reason for a paper jam is one that took us (me and my trusty sidekick Rich Wolfson) nearly two weeks to figure out. I kept getting paper jams at unpredictable intervals. The whole thing started immediately after the installation of an internal drive in the LaserWriter, so that was the immediate suspect, though neither of us could figure out what that could possibly have to do with paper jams. There were two additional clues in the situation. The paper jammed at different spots—sometimes it was just barely feeding in, sometimes it was part way through the cycle, sometimes it was all but in the printed pile and the last inch would get stuck; we were suspecting a problem ROM in the LaserWriter at that point. And, what struck me as very odd for what was apparently a hardware problem, the print job wouldn't continue after the paper path was cleared. It wasn't exactly canceled, either—it just sort of disappeared, with the Mac behaving as if the entire print job had been completed.

The culprit turned out to be a corrupted LaserWriter 8 Prefs file, a troublesome little item discussed in Chapter 12.

⊶❥ **The IIf can print legal-size pages only if** it has been upgraded from its standard 4 megs of memory to 5 megs, since it needs that extra meg to image the larger page size.

⊶❥ **You know your LaserWriter needs more memory** when you constantly get *Can't print—not enough memory* dialogs. But there's a more subtle clue, too: If any of the fonts in your document get converted to Courier (the one that looks like a typewriter typed it), you probably don't have enough memory in your LaserWriter to handle the jobs you're printing.

*Probably?* Can't I be more definite? Sure. Even if you have plenty of memory, Courier gets substituted for Monaco if you have Font Substitution checked in your Page Setup dialog options. It also sometimes substitutes for a font that's missing from your system. Occasionally, a font is embedded in a graphic (not a bitmapped graphic, but an object graphic that stores fonts as fonts instead of as dots), and the application you're using doesn't "see" it in order to download it for printing. If none of these is the reason you're getting a Courier printout, then you definitely have a low-memory problem in your LaserWriter.

And remember: Even if your LaserWriter doesn't *need* more memory, that doesn't mean it can't *benefit* from additional memory—if you often use fonts that aren't built-in, more memory to store downloaded ones can speed the printing process.

Chapter 20 covers bitmapped and object graphics.

⌐•❯ **A LaserWriter is attached** to the Mac by means of a LocalTalk cable—Apple's network wiring. That is, that's how it's attached if you follow the recommended procedure. But you're talking about a $50 cable and connector that you probably don't need. If you're just attaching one Mac and one LaserWriter, use a plain ImageWriter cable (an 8-pin serial cable); It works fine, and costs less than $20.

And if you need a network connection—for two Macs and a printer, say—use Farallon's PhoneNet connectors, which are just as good as LocalTalk connectors, but less expensive. [Farallon]

∘∘❧ **Print PostScript without PostScript** if you really have to with Freedom of Press. That is, if your printer doesn't have PostScript built in but you have to print PostScript graphics, there's a software utility that processes the PostScript information and turns it into page images before it goes to the printer. But because Freedom of Press is not an Adobe product (they own and license PostScript) and doesn't use a true PostScript interpreter, it's very expensive ($500) and *very* slow (an hour for a not very complicated graphic). In fact, at that price, and with the price of PostScript LaserWriters dropping every few months, you're much better off buying a new printer. [Custom Applications, Inc.]

⌐•❯ **Where are your fonts coming from?** There are three main places a PostScript font can be stored: in the ROM of the LaserWriter, on a hard disk attached to the LaserWriter, and on your Mac's hard disk. In addition, it might be residing temporarily in the LaserWriter's memory. Come to think of it, the font might also be in the font cache portion of the printer's hard drive.

In some cases, the printer file might be stored in more than one place—a font that's in the ROM or on the printer's hard disk might also still be on the Mac's hard drive because you need it for ATM's screen display; a font residing in either the LaserWriter's memory or the disk's font cache is certain to be stored somewhere else, more permanently, as well.

ATM is covered in Chapters 10 and 11.

When the LaserWriter needs a font, it looks to the fastest storage place first (that is, the place where it's fastest to retrieve the font information from), then the next fastest, and so on. It looks in this order:

1. In memory
2. In font cache of attached hard drive
3. In ROM
4. On attached hard drive
5. On Mac's hard drive

⌐•❯ **You can't use the Level 2** PostScript capabilities of your printer unless you update the printer driver to the LaserWriter 8 driver. There's more about printer drivers in Chapter 12.

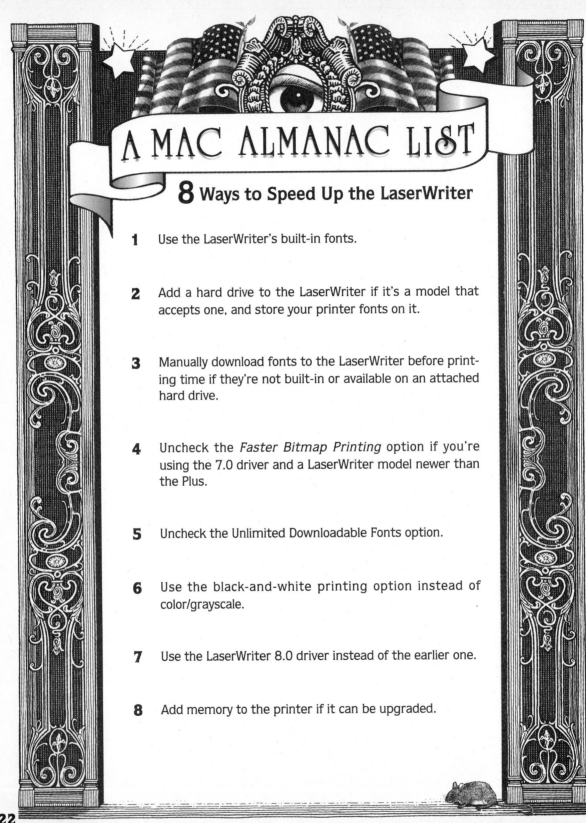

# A MAC ALMANAC LIST

## 8 Ways to Speed Up the LaserWriter

**1** Use the LaserWriter's built-in fonts.

**2** Add a hard drive to the LaserWriter if it's a model that accepts one, and store your printer fonts on it.

**3** Manually download fonts to the LaserWriter before printing time if they're not built-in or available on an attached hard drive.

**4** Uncheck the *Faster Bitmap Printing* option if you're using the 7.0 driver and a LaserWriter model newer than the Plus.

**5** Uncheck the Unlimited Downloadable Fonts option.

**6** Use the black-and-white printing option instead of color/grayscale.

**7** Use the LaserWriter 8.0 driver instead of the earlier one.

**8** Add memory to the printer if it can be upgraded.

# CHAPTER 17

# STORAGE BASICS & FLOPPY DISKS

**GANTZ & ROCHESTER**
THE NAKED COMPUTER

> People who build computers worry about things such as whether dots of magnetism are standing up or lying down.

Here are some things you absolutely have to know, and some that you don't. But they're all covered in this chapter.

- ••▶ Disk space is not memory.
- ••▶ Formatting and initializing are interchangeable terms in the Mac world.
- ••▶ Every disk has one or more invisible files on it.
- ••▶ Floppy disks are not delicate creatures.
- ••▶ The Mac has used three different floppy disk formats and four different floppy drive models so far in its life.
- ••▶ Emptying the Trash doesn't erase files from the disk.
- ••▶ There are many things you can do to rescue an unreadable floppy. On the other hand, sometimes you can't do anything to rescue one.

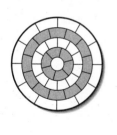

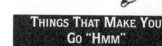

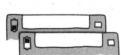

**THINGS THAT MAKE YOU GO "HMM"**

*The size of a file depends on the size of the disk it's stored on.*

*page 629*

**—Includes—**

| | |
|---|---|
| 71 | Factoids |
| 2 | Quotable Quotes |
| 2 | Memos |
| 1 | Mac Almanac List |

# DISK BASICS

# FLOPPY DISKS & DRIVES

# USING FLOPPIES

## → DISK BASICS ←

### In General

°°→ *Disk storage* **and** *memory* are two entirely different things, although beginners often confuse the two. *Memory* stores information temporarily with little electronic switches. A *disk* stores things on a long-term basis, in a magnetic format. An *out of memory* message refers to RAM; a *disk full* message refers to the disk.

Unfortunately, the vocabulary waters are muddied by the fact that, strictly speaking, disk storage is a kind of memory, since it stores information; and, in fact, it used to be (in its infancy) referred to as *slow memory*. But forget I even brought this up.

°°→ *Volume* **is a handy,** and necessary, term that refers to disks and things that are treated like disks on your desktop. A volume is represented by an icon that you can open to see its contents. So, a volume can be:

- a floppy disk
- a hard drive
- a hard drive partition
- a removable hard drive cartridge
- a magneto-optical disk
- a CD-ROM disc
- any disk or folder that's shared across a network

Floppy

Hard Drive

Optical

Shared

CD ROM

SyQuest

°°→ **A volume is** *mounted* if its icon is showing on your desktop. When you get rid of the icon (by ejecting a disk or signing off from a network, for instance), the volume is *unmounted*, not *dismounted*.

°°→ **Two volumes can have the same name** on your desktop without the Mac's getting confused because volumes are also assigned numbers when they appear on the desktop. You don't ever see these numbers—and they're *not* the same as SCSI ID numbers—because the Mac just uses them internally.

••→ **Every disk has an invisible** *desktop file* on it that stores information about where things are on the disk, where the applications are, how your windows are arranged, the Get Info comments you typed, and what the icons are supposed to look like. The *Rebuilding the Desktop* section of Chapter 5 covers this in detail, but here's a quick roundup:

- There's a single file called *Desktop* on System 6 disks and on floppies.
- There are two files on System 7 hard drives: *Desktop DF* and *Desktop DB*. They're still referred to collectively as "the desktop file" for convenience.
- The desktop file gets bloated keeping track of icons you might not need any longer; sometimes the information in it gets corrupted. *Rebuilding the desktop* means making the Mac clean up the file.
- You rebuild the desktop by holding Command and Option down at startup (for a hard drive) or when you insert a floppy disk.

- Rebuilding the desktop erases all the comments in Get Info windows.
- Rebuilding the desktop should be a monthly maintenance procedure on a busy hard drive.

••► **When the computer puts information on a disk,** it's *writing* to the disk; when it's getting information from the disk, it's *reading* from it.

*Reading* and *writing* are technically accurate and are reasonably friendly expressions for terms that have been around in computerdom for a long time. They're even used in the Finder when you're copying from one disk to another—you'll see a dialog that gives a continuous progress report, like: *Reading Int HD: MyFile* and then *Writing BackupDisk: MyFile*. But when you're in an application, the correct terminology is *opening* and *saving*. I've seen programs—SuperPaint, for instance—that, despite their Open and Save commands in the File menu, have progress dialogs that use the phrases *Reading from disk* and *Writing to disk*. This is a symptom of programmers with the bends—they can't quite make it all the way to the surface where we users live.

## How Disks Work

∘∘► **Information is stored magnetically** on disks. The bi-polarity of magnetic material is a perfect match for the binary language of computers. So, the ones and zeros that the computer understands are stored as north or south magnetized particles on a disk's magnetic coating.

### HOW SMALL IS IT?

Just how big are those magnetic particles that store information on a disk? Their size varies with the density of the disk.

But take, as an example, a high-density Mac floppy that stores 1.4 megs of information. That's 11,744,051 *bits* of data, so that's the minimum number of particles on both sides of the disk. (There's actually more, because that's just the capacity for *your* data; there's also formatting information and invisible files for the Mac.) Working with a round 12 million, then, that's still 6 million bits per side. With the surface area of a 3.5-inch disk being about 8.5 square inches (after subtracting the center hub), that's about 706,000 bits of information, or magnetic particles, per square inch. And floppies are not nearly the densest storage media available for the Mac!

∘∘► **The physical size of a disk** isn't half as important as how the information is packed onto it. The first 3.5-inch floppy disk the Mac used stored 400K of information; later came 800K capacity; now, the standard is 1.4 megs—all on the same size disk. Apple's first Mac hard drive was about a foot square and 3 inches high, and stored 20 megs of information; a PowerBook's hard drive is about the size of a deck of cards and can store over 500 megs of information.

A PowerBook internal drive and a deck of cards.

•••→ **Information is stored in *tracks* and *sectors*** on a disk. Tracks are concentric rings; sectors, also sometimes called *blocks*, are sections of the ring. The actual number of tracks and sectors varies from one type of disk to another. A 1.4 meg floppy, for instance, has 80 tracks with 18 sectors on each track; an 800K disk has 80 tracks, too, but the number of sectors ranges from 9 to 12, depending on which track you're looking at. Initializing a disk creates these tracks and sectors by building the magnetic fences that define them.

A disk is divided into concentric tracks made up of sectors.

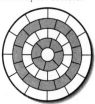

•••→ **A new disk has to be *initialized*** so the Mac can use it. A disk isn't inherently a Mac disk or not (the *This is not a Macintosh disk* dialog notwithstanding). A computer recognizes a disk by the way the information is organized on it. Initializing a disk organizes it into divisions that the computer understands, laying down the magnetic dividers for tracks and sectors.

•••→ ***Initializing. Formatting.*** Is there a difference? Yes and no. Strictly speaking, *initializing* means just erasing the disk directory—the invisible file that acts like a table of contents for the computer, to tell it where everything is stored. *Formatting* means erasing the entire disk and redrawing all those magnetic lines for tracks and sectors.

But on the Mac, the terms are interchangeable. Even Apple's HD SC Setup utility has an Initialize button that is actually for formatting the disk.

•••→ **Parts of the disk are reserved for the Mac**, which stores information in invisible files. You can't see these files on the desktop, although many utilities let you see them in their Open dialogs. That's one reason why you'll see a floppy with no icons in its window, with the header reporting zero items, and yet there's still a certain number of K missing. The same thing happens with hard drives, although you're less likely to notice the missing space since there's still so much left.

166K is used on this disk even though there are no files on it.

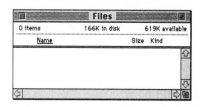

•••→ **Your files aren't where you think they are** on your disk. You think they're in your folders, don't you? Well, folders are to some extent a figment of the Finder's imagination, because a file can actually be anywhere on the disk and, in fact, is often stored piecemeal across several different areas of the disk. Folders are a graphical metaphor.

The next chapter describes the "file directory" and other invisible files on the disk.

## File Size & Disk Size

∞→ **The size of a file changes depending** on the size of the disk it's stored on. Go ahead, read that sentence again; no one ever really believes it the first time they hear it.

Here's what happens: When a disk is formatted, it's divided into tracks and sectors. But there's another division, too, referred to as the *allocation block*. This isn't a physical division like tracks and sectors are. An allocation block is a "logical" division—a way the Mac can treat a sector or a group of sectors as a single unit even though they're separate.

An allocation block is the smallest unit the Mac works with when storing a file. The block can never hold parts of two different files; if it isn't completely filled by a single file (or a portion of a single file that's overflowed from its other storage blocks), the remainder stays empty. So, if you put a very small file into a very large block, you wind up with room left over—unusable room, unless you edit the file so that it's bigger and fills the block when you save the edited version. (At which point it probably spills into the *next* block, taking only a tiny bit of it and wasting the rest.)

⟶ **A file's true size, and the room it takes** up on the disk, is easy to check with the Get Info command. Here, for instance, is a very small file—an alias. The Size report shows how much room it takes on the disk (4K) and how much of that space is actually used (787 bytes). 787K is only about three-quarters of a K; that means that more than 3K is being wasted for every alias that's on this drive.

⟶ **The bigger the drive, the more room a file** takes up. I put copies of an alias (remember, that's 787 bytes) on the various hard drives and partitions attached to my system. Here's the amount of room they actually occupied:

| Disk Size | File Size |
|---|---|
| 800K | 1K |
| 1.4MB | 1K |
| 20MB | 1K |
| 80MB | 2K |
| 105MB | 2K |
| 120MB | 2K |
| 170MB | 3K |
| 182MB | 3K |
| 230MB | 4K |

The pattern isn't easily discernible, but there is one. A sector is 512 bytes, half of a K. On volumes up to 32 megabytes, an allocation block is the same as a sector; so, anything less than 512 bytes still takes up 512 bytes on the disk, while a file that's 787 bytes, like the alias shown above, takes a full K because it overflows into a second allocation block.

Every time the size of a volume increases by 32 megabytes, the allocation block increases by another 512 bytes. So, this is the pattern:

| Disk Size | Allocation Block Size |
|-----------|----------------------|
| 32MB | .5K |
| 64MB | 1K |
| 96MB | 1.5K |
| 128MB | 2K |
| 160MB | 2.5K |
| 192MB | 3K |
| 224MB | 3.5K |
| 256MB | 4K |
| 288MB | 4.5K |
| 320MB | 5K |
| 352MB | 5.5K |
| 384MB | 6K |

## PRE-MAC PUNCH-IN

# → FLOPPY DISKS & DRIVES ←

## Floppy Basics

∞•▸ **A floppy disk doesn't seem floppy** because it's encased in a plastic shell. But the actual disk is very floppy—it's similar to the material used in audio and video tapes. The thin plastic material is coated with iron oxide particles (yep, rust!) that respond to the magnets in the drive's read/write heads.

∞**➤** **The metal shutter on a floppy case** opens automatically when you insert it into the drive. Early 3.5 disks on some other computers didn't do that: you had to manually slide the shutter over to an open position, where it would stay until you squeezed it to snap it shut again.

There's a reason for the shutter: It's there because of you, not because of the Mac. Information on 3.5-inch disks is squeezed in so tight that dust and dirt—including fingerprints—can interfere with the Mac's reading the information on the disk.

### AD HOC #5

Companies that specialize in computer products may be on the cutting edge of technology, but their marketing departments often lag behind.

Maxell's full page ad that ran in Mac magazines in the first year or two of the Mac's existence is a case in point. Maxell was one of the few manufacturers of the relatively new 3.5-inch disks that the Mac used. The text of the ad read: Maxell. Floppy Disks. The Gold Standard. The picture was of a classy dining room in a turn-of-the-century men's club. The figures at the table in the foreground, and the waiter, were golden robots, apparently cousins to C3PO, the prissy language droid in Star Wars. The waiter is lifting the cover from a silver platter which is holding … a 5.25-inch, paper-sleeved disk for PCs.

∞**➤** **Floppies are not delicate** little creatures, although you should treat them with a modicum of respect. When I started with the Mac, I had an infant and a toddler; there was no such thing as a hard drive, so I had lots of floppies around. They (the floppies) survived inquisitive little hands and even a little chewing; they served as thin blocks for building tower stacks and as indoor frisbees. Now the boys are 12 and 14, with their own Mac, and they treat their hardware a little better.

∞**➤** **Floppies are not overly sensitive** to magnets, despite all the warnings you've read. I've even written some of them—better to be safe than sorry, especially if you're talking to beginners! One of the standard warnings is to keep them away from ringing telephones. I've had a disk sit *under* a telephone for … well, I don't know how long, since I didn't put it there on purpose. But it certainly didn't suffer (except perhaps from claustrophobia, poor thing). Even real, genuine, actual magnets haven't hurt my disks. What kind of magnets came in contact with my disks? That old standby, the refrigerator magnet. That silly desk ornament, the paper clip dispenser. A kid's toy (the wand from Wooly Willy). An executive's toy—a steel marble stacker.

These were all accidental incidents. The one experiment I did set up was ruined by an overly helpful accomplice. I was having an MRI done—magnetic resonance imaging, a procedure that, basically, magnetizes your body so its hydrogen molecules line up temporarily so that their subsequent falling out of ranks can be recorded and produce terrific pictures of your innards. I wondered how far out of the machine the magnetic field traveled, so I brought a floppy into the room with me, meaning to leave it somewhere

around the outer perimeter. (Right, that was me, shuffling along the hall in a hospital gown and robe, in paper booties, with the floppy disk in my hand.) When I started to explain to the technicians just why I had a computer disk with me, one of them took it from me, held it in the MRI tube for a few seconds, then told me to do the same. It was difficult to hold on to—it waved back and forth in my hand! The magnetic field in the tube pushed against the metal parts of the disk (the shutter and the hub), much as if I were holding it under water in a strong current. Needless to say, the information on it was wiped out.

••◆ **A floppy drive has a pair of *read-write heads*** that check and change the magnetic particles on the surface of the disk. When you insert a disk into a drive, it's sandwiched between the heads, which move in and out. Since the disk spins around and the heads move in and out, every spot on the disk can be accessed. (The earliest Mac drives had a single read-write head, since only one side of the floppy was used.)

## Three Disks & Drives

∞◆ **Three different types of floppy disks** have been used with the Mac during its decade of existence. The evolution of the floppy started with the 400K single-sided model, which is referred to by either one of those descriptions—400K or single-sided. The next disk was the 800K double-sided disk; once again, it's called by either of those descriptions, or sometimes referred to as *double-density*. The evolution seems to have peaked, for now, with the double-sided, high-density 1.4-megabyte version; they're referred to as either high-density, 1.4-meg, or, very commonly, as *superfloppies*.

∞◆ **Telling the difference between floppies** is a simple matter of sticking them in the computer and checking the reported capacity.

Oh—you mean you want to know the size of the disk *before* you insert it? Okay. Identifying a high-density floppy is easy. It has an extra square hole in its case, across from the locking tab. When 800K disks first came into use, they were marked somewhere on the case as *800K*, or *double-sided*, or *double-density*, but they've been standard for so long that most have no identifying marks. Unless you've had a Mac for ages—since before the Mac Plus—or you're exchanging disks with an old-timer, all your disks without the extra hole will be 800K versions; you can't even buy 400K disks anymore.

••◆ **Three different floppy disk drives** have been used with Macs over the years, to accommodate the changes in the floppy disks themselves. Disk drives are usually described by the capacity of the disks they can handle, so we've had the 400K drive, and then the 800K drive. When the current drive was developed, Apple named it the FDHD drive—for *floppy drive high density*—but no one ever calls it that, since it's difficult to pronounce (*fudhud?*). It's called the *SuperDrive*.

◦•◗ **There's actually a fourth floppy drive** model, but to all intents and purposes it's the same as the SuperDrive. The only difference is that it doesn't automatically suck in the disk when you've inserted it most of the way; you actually have to push the disk in completely. This new design costs less to manufacture.

(Before these drives were released, rumor had it that the new design would do away with the auto-eject mechanism that we've always enjoyed with the Mac. Thankfully, that wasn't the case. But the redesign—and the reconsideration of the auto-eject mechanism, if the rumor had any basis in fact—was certainly in response to the complaints of how expensive Mac floppy drives are compared to those for other computers—three to four times as much!)

◦•◗ **Each floppy drive can read** its own disk format and earlier ones. So, an 800K drive can read 400K and 800K disks; a SuperDrive can read all three types of floppies. A SuperDrive spins superfloppies at a constant speed, but switches to variable-speed disk spinning when it's dealing with lower-density disks, which have differing numbers of sectors on different tracks.

### SUPER WOZ

The first floppy drives for the Mac had the unusual feature of variable speed spinning. You could hear the speed change because the normal humming sound the drive made changed pitch when the speed changed. This "tune" was sometimes referred to as MacDirge.

There was a very special reason for the variable speed. When a disk is divided into the concentric circles of tracks and their sector slices, there are fewer sectors on the inner circles than on the outer ones. If a disk is spinning at a steady rate, there are more sectors passing under the read/write head in a given time period when it's positioned at the outer tracks than when it's at the inner tracks. Since the computer can digest information coming from a disk only at a constant rate, the usual solution was to leave blank sectors on the outer tracks so there wouldn't be any more information there than on the inner tracks.

The Mac needed a lot of information squeezed onto a disk—a System Folder, an application, and a few documents; this was not a system that could afford to waste disk space. So, one of Apple's most famous resident geniuses, Steve Wozniak, designed a floppy drive controller that let the disk slow down or speed up depending where the read/write head was; this meant that data was streaming in at a constant rate, no matter where the head was positioned, and the entire surface of the disk could be packed with information.

•••◗ **You don't need disks made *only* for the Mac**; the 3.5-inch floppies are the same for any computer. Just check whether they're high-density or not; high-density formats to 1.4 megs on the Mac and 1.44 megs on a PC, while the lower density (usually just labeled "double-sided," with no mention of density) formats to 800K on the Mac and 720K on a PC.

## Initializing Floppies

◦◦◗ **When you insert a new, blank disk** into the Mac, you're asked if you want to initialize it, but the dialog that you see depends on both the disk and the drive that you're using.

○•→ **A SuperDrive can format any kind of disk.** Inserting a high-density disk into a SuperDrive is the most common scenario, and it's a no-brainer: You can choose to initialize the disk, or cancel the operation and eject the disk.

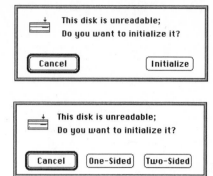

When you put an 800K disk into a SuperDrive, the initialization dialog lets you choose between one-sided (400K) and two-sided (800K) formatting.

As a matter of fact, if you put a 400K disk in a SuperDrive, you get the same dialog as when you insert an 800K disk. But you shouldn't format 400K disks to 800K, for reasons we'll get into soon. But the assumption here (by both me and the Mac) is that you're using 800K disks that you may want to format as 400K for someone with an antique Mac.

○•→ **An 800K drive can format only** for 800K or 400K disks. You get the same dialog as you get with the SuperDrive—with Cancel, One-Sided, and Two-Sided buttons—but you get it no matter what kind of disk you put it: a superfloppy, an 800K, or a 400K.*

> *I don't suppose the 400K formatting option is going to be around much longer. I know I'm getting tired of it!

○•→ **A disk isn't stuck with its original formatting** forever; as long as you don't mind erasing its contents, a disk usually can be reformatted to a greater or lesser capacity, depending on your needs.

○•→ **With two kinds of drives** and two kinds of disks (ignoring both 400K disks and drives as rare these days), here's a summary of your formatting options:

| Disk | 800K Drive | | SuperDrive | |
|------|------------|--------------|------------|--------------|
| | Single-sided | Double-sided | Single-sided | Double-sided |
| 800K | 400K | 800K | 400K | 800K |
| 1.4MB | 400K | 800K | automatic to 1.4MB | |

○•→ **The wording in the Initialize dialog** varies depending on the system version you're using. It may start with any of these three statements: *This is not a Macintosh disk; This disk is unreadable; This disk is unreadable by this Macintosh.*

But all the dialogs have the same question: *Do you want to initialize it?*

○•→ **You don't have to return to the desktop** to initialize a new disk. Just pop the disk in no matter where you're working. The Initialize dialog will show up on the screen, and you'll be able to name the disk, without leaving your application.

•••▶ **There are three dialogs that offer an Initialize** button. One is the basic initialize dialog that appears when you insert a blank disk. If a disk is damaged (that is, the information on it is damaged, as opposed to physical damage to the disk itself), the Mac offers to re-initialize it for you. And, finally, if you use the Erase command from the Finder's special menu, the confirming dialog offers to initialize the disk, not simply to erase it.

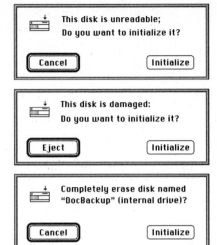

Dialogs for: a blank disk (top); a damaged disk (middle); the Erase command (bottom).

•••▶ **Don't format a lower-capacity disk** to a higher one. That is, don't try making 400K disks 800K, or 800K disks superfloppies. As each new disk format became available, the new disks were much more expensive than the older ones, and cost-cutting tricks abounded—or ran amuck.

There was a lot of controversy about the reliability of 400K disks formatted as 800K. Physically, they were the same disks; it's just that the manufacturer never tested the quality of the second side, since it wouldn't be used. So, it seemed safe to assume that if the Mac could initialize and verify both sides, everything would be fine. This is no longer an issue for new disks, since you'd be hard pressed to find any single-sided disks for sale, and, if you did, the price difference between them and the double-sided ones would be negligible. Reformatting old, used, 400K disks as 800K is an even shakier proposition. The 400K drives used mechanical pressure on one side of the disk to keep the other side close to the read/write head, making the likelihood of damage to the "pressed" side very high.

As for formatting 800K disks as 1.4 meg disks—well, at first it doesn't even seem possible, does it, since the superfloppies need the little holes in them? Some fearless souls actually drilled the holes into the case; a few enterprising individuals even made and sold special disk-hole punchers. But, aside from the fact that physically altering the disk case usually lets particles of plastic (and who knows what else) slip into the case to later wreck the medium, forcing the high-density formatting is still a bad idea. That's because high-density formatting is for disks that have high-density material on them—finer magnetic particles that can pack more information per square centimeter. You might be able to initialize the disk, and you might even be able to use it for a while, but you'll never have a disk you can rely on.

**•→ If the initialization fails,** you'll know it because you'll get a dialog that tells you so. A disk can fail for several reasons, but don't despair: Eject the disk, re-insert it, and try again. If it fails a second time, get rid of it; unreliable disks aren't worth the dollar it costs to replace them.

## JOE HOLMES' INCREDIBLE FLOPPY-FORMATTING TIP

This is one of the neatest, most useless tips I've ever discovered. If you have two floppy disks to format, you can save, maybe, a *quarter second* of your valuable time by this simple method of telling the Finder to format both floppies in a row.

If you have two floppy drives, insert both floppies and select their icons on the desktop. Choose Erase Disk from the Special menu, and you'll get a dialog asking if you want to erase one of the disks. Click on the appropriate button *and then click on that same spot again.* That second click will wait in the keyboard buffer while the first floppy is formatting. As soon as the progress box for the first disk disappears, the Finder displays a dialog asking whether you want to erase the second disk; at that point, the second mouse click you pressed registers, and the second disk gets formatted. *Even if you're out walking the dog!*

Incredibly, this trick works even with only one floppy drive. Mount one disk and then eject it with Command-E. Now insert the second disk, select both icons, and follow the steps outlined above. You'll have to insert the ejected disk when prompted, so you can't take the dog for a walk, but the second mouse click will still be in the buffer and will click the button to format the second disk once it's been inserted. Two in a row!! This trick works even with mixed low- and high-density disks, since the buttons line up in the different dialog boxes.

Even more amazingly, you can theoretically format an infinite number of disks in a row (given infinite time and RAM and some minor fiddling with the keyboard buffer). For four disks and two floppy drives, for example:

Put a floppy into each drive, select both disk icons, and then eject them by hitting Command-E. (If the Finder asks for them back again, obey and eject with Command-E a second time.) Insert the third and fourth floppies and select all four icons (two of which are grayed because the disks were ejected) and choose Erase Disk. Click on the Two-Sided button in the dialog box that appears, and then click the exact same spot *three* more times. As each disk finishes, the Finder will eject it and ask for another one. Obey. The three mouse clicks are kept in the keyboard buffer and are accepted one at a time as each floppy is finished and the next begins. All you have to do is swap disks. A lot. In fact, the more disks you ask the Finder to juggle, the more often you have to swap them in and out. But you'll have to choose the Erase Disk command only once!

*—Joe Holmes*

**•→ Frequent failures in floppy disk initialization** may be due to a bad lot of disks—but it might also be due to a faulty drive. If two or three out of ten new disks are bad, don't jump to the wrong conclusion: Try formatting them on someone else's Mac. If there's no trouble formatting them elsewhere, it's probably your drive, even if you're not having any trouble reading pre-formatted disks. (This is the voice of experience speaking.)

••◆ **A disk formatted for one computer system** can't be read by another—usually. The Apple File Exchange utility that comes with your system software lets the Mac read an IBM-formatted disk. (But it doesn't do anything to let the Mac read the *files* on that disk, which is an entirely different matter!)

••◆ **If the Mac spits out a floppy** without even *trying* to read it, you can try this old trick: Insert any disk, and choose the Erase Disk command from the Special menu. While the Initialize dialog is on the screen, use a paper clip to manually eject the disk that's in the drive. (More about the paper clip trick later.) Insert the rejected disk—in effect, you're doing it while the Mac's back is returned. Then click the Initialize button.

## Mixing Disks & Drives

•••◆ **Put a formatted superfloppy into an 800K drive** and you get a dialog that says *This disk is unreadable; do you want to initialize it?* Don't panic. And don't click Initialize, which erases all the information on it. Click the Cancel button and the disk will be ejected, with its information still intact—presumably to be read by the proper drive.

•••◆ **A SuperDrive can't read** a superfloppy that's been formatted to 800K in an 800K drive. As soon as the SuperDrive sees the extra hole in the high-density disk, it looks for high-density formatting. When it doesn't find it, it doesn't look for any second-choice 800K formatting; it just tells you that the disk is unreadable.

If you need to read an 800K-formatted superfloppy in a SuperDrive, cover the telltale hole with a piece of tape. But don't consider this a long-term solution: The piece of tape is bound to come off sooner or later—and it's likely to come off while the disk is in the drive, causing all sorts of problems

•••◆ **You can force a 1.4MB disk to be formatted as 800K** in a superfloppy drive if, for instance, you have to give a file to someone who has only an 800K drive.

When you insert a high-density disk and the SuperDrive sees the extra hole, it automatically formats it to its greatest capacity. But you can circumvent this automation by taping over the hole so the Mac thinks it's dealing with an 800K disk. (The tape doesn't have to stay on for later use in the 800K drive, since that drive doesn't know anything about high-density disks.)

•••◆ **A superfloppy formatted as 800K** in an 800K drive often can't be reformatted to its 1.4-meg capacity. The magnets used in an 800K drive are brutes compared to the ones in a SuperDrive. The magnetic particles on a high-density disk are finer, ready to respond to the more delicate magnets in the SuperDrive. Once the disk is divided into tracks and sectors by an 800K drive, it's possible that the SuperDrive won't be able to budge those magnetic fences.

It's no wonder Mac users looked for ways to "cheat" with floppies, trying to format them to ever-higher capacities: Floppy disks were an expensive necessity in the early days.

I remember very clearly the original prices for floppy disks: $35 for a box of ten. Ten 400K floppies! Prices varied depending on the brand, but even the cheapest were well over $2 throughout the first year of the Mac's life. Things got better every year, though. Here are some sample prices, *per disk*, culled from old issues of Mac magazines. The parenthetical numbers are the approximate cost-per-meg of storage space.

|  | *400K Disks* | *800K Disks* | *1.4MB Disks* |
|---|---|---|---|
| Jan. 84 | $3.50 ($10.50) | | |
| Nov. 85 | $1.99 ($5.97) | | |
| May 88 | $1.09 ($3.27) | $1.39 ($2.85) | |
| Apr. 92 | | $ .90 ($1.22) | $1.50 ($1.29) |
| June 94 | | $ .80 ($1.20) | $1.20 ($1.02) |

## → USING FLOPPIES ←

## Using Floppies

∘•❥ **Floppy disks like temperate climes,** as do most of us. If your disks are exposed to extreme heat or cold, let them return to room temperature before you use them. If you bring a sealed box of disks in from the cold, leave the box alone until it reaches room temperature to avoid condensation problems on individual disks.

∘•❥ **Lock a disk** by sliding the plastic tab in its corner. It's an intuitively backward setup, though: When the hole is *uncovered*; it's locked. So, an open hole means a locked disk, while a closed one means the disk is unlocked.

∘•❥ **You can't change anything** on a locked disk. You can copy files from it, but not to it. You can open a file that's on a locked disk, but you won't be able to save the changes back to the same disk. You can open disk and folder windows, change their views, and even move icons around, but the changes are made only in the Finder's memory; they won't be there the next time you insert the disk.

∘•❥ **The windows of a locked disk** display a little lock icon in their headers.

∘•❥ **Trashing files from floppies** is covered in Chapter 5, but here's a reminder of the main points:

• Files dragged to the Trash are not automatically erased from the floppy when you eject, although this is the way it worked prior to System 7.

- If you try to copy files to a floppy that has trashed (but not yet erased) files, you'll get a dialog asking if you want the trash emptied. But you'll only get the dialog if erasing the trashed files will make enough room on the disk for the files you're trying to copy.

And here's something that wasn't in Chapter 5, because I didn't know about it when I wrote that chapter. (Which, in the peculiarly charming way of publishing a computer book, is already set in cement and has no room for changes.) If you drag files from a 400K disk to the Trash and try to eject the disk, you'll get the dialog shown here.*

*How was I supposed to know this would happen? Who uses 400K disks with System 7?

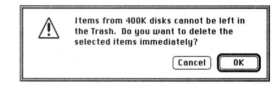

⚠ Items from 400K disks cannot be left in the Trash. Do you want to delete the selected items immediately?

[Cancel] [ OK ]

## FREE FLOPPIES

Are you always short of floppy disks? No matter how many you buy—and no matter how often you think that you don't need floppies, since you use a hard drive—there never seems to be one around when you need it.

Here's the cure for your floppy shortage woes. Type the following letter into your Mac, putting your name and address in the last spot. Through the miracle of word processing and the Print dialog, make six copies of it and send it to six superstitious friends. In six weeks, if no one breaks the chain, you'll receive 46,656 disks in the mail.

Dear Fellow Disk User:

This chain was started in the hopes of keeping everyone supplied with a sufficient number of floppy disks at a reasonable cost. Within a week, send a floppy disk to the person at the top of the letter. Make six copies of this letter, leaving off the top name and inserting yours at the bottom.

When your name reaches the top, you'll be the grateful recipient of over 45,000 floppy disks from other participants.

If you should be so careless as to break the chain, you can expect untold disk problems that no amount of desktop rebuilding will cure.

| | |
|---|---|
| Sharon Aker | Andy Baird |
| 9 Winding Way | S-2 Avon Drive |
| North Caldwell, NJ 07006 | Hightstown, NJ 08520 |
| | |
| Craig Chananie | Rich Wolfson |
| 42 Francisco Drive | 9 Winding Way |
| Little Falls, NJ 07424 | North Caldwell, NJ 07006 |
| | |
| Joe Holmes | *(Your name here)* |
| 410 Ninth Street | |
| Brooklyn, NY 11215 | |

°•**→** **If the Trash plumps up when you insert** a floppy, that means there were items that you dragged from the disk to the Trash the last time you used the disk, but you didn't empty the Trash.

°•**→** **Removing a disk label** is usually more difficult than you expect. Even when the paper part of the label comes off without too much fuss, there's often adhesive left on the disk case that will keep the next label from adhering smoothly and securely.

There are three different fluids you can use, on a clean cloth, to rub off the adhesive residue: rubber cement thinner, WD-40 lubricant, or lighter fluid.

°•**→** **You don't have to remove disk labels.** There's plenty of room for three or four labels on top of one another on the disk—the layers won't interfere with the drive mechanism. Just make sure that each new label is sticking securely to the one beneath it—the little edge that wraps around the top of the disk is a problem sometimes.

After the fourth label or so, you might want to start peeling some of the labels off; you may find that one label comes off another more easily than it would come off the plastic of the disk case.

°•**→** **Where are all those missing K?** You put in a floppy, there are no files on it, but there are hundreds of K still reported as being used. Here's where they might be, and what to do to recover them:

- There are files dragged to the Trash, but not yet erased. Use the Empty Trash command.
- The desktop file is bloated with old icons that have been used for files on this disk. Re-insert the disk while holding down Command and Option to rebuild the desktop file.
- There are invisible files on the disk (besides the desktop file) that were put there by some utility or program. You can delete invisible files with the correct utility, but it's easier to just reformat the disk.
- There are some bad sectors on the disk that were set aside as unusable when the disk was formatted. There's nothing you can do about this.

You don't have to guess at which of these is the problem; using the Erase disk command will erase trashed files and invisible ones, rebuild the desktop file, and check for any bad sectors.

Rebuilding the Desktop file is covered in Chapters 5 and 24.

## Erasing Files & Disks

°•**→** **Information isn't actually erased from a disk** when you drag a file to the Trash and then empty it. Instead, the file's name is erased from the disk directory, and the sectors it was stored in are marked as free so they can be re-used.

Since files aren't immediately erased from a disk, that means they can be retrieved with the right tools. Some utility programs keep track of where "deleted" files were stored so you can get them back; even if some of the original sectors have been overwritten with new files, sometimes parts of the original file can be recovered.

∘•**➤** **Erase a disk** by selecting it on the desktop and choosing Erase Disk from the Special menu. Erasing a disk re-initializes it; you'll get basically the same dialog as when you insert a blank disk.

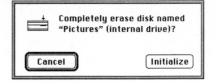

## MAC TRIVIA

The icon that appears in any dialog referring to a floppy disk changes based on where the floppy drive "lives"—what computer it's in. The two pictures here show how the internal hard drive is referred to in a IIci (the top picture) and a Centris 650 (the bottom picture).

I remember the momentary panic I felt when I first saw this dialog, telling me a disk was unreadable. With the picture of my Mac's CPU right there in the dialog, I though at first it was referring to the internal hard drive!

∘•**➤** **Since erased files aren't really erased,** this poses a security problem when you *think* you've erased confidential information from a disk but it's really still there for some spy with the right software tools and secret access to your disk. But, the world can stay safe because there are utilities that *really* erase a file, by writing over the file with random information.

Re-initializing a disk really erases all the information in it: it doesn't just change or wipe out the directory. That's fine for a floppy, but you won't want to reinitialize a hard drive just to completely erase a few files.

∘•**➤** **Erasing a disk takes longer than** just dragging its contents to the Trash, but there are several advantages to using the Erase command:

- Everything on the disk is erased, including invisible files that may be taking up needed space.
- The Desktop file is re-created from scratch, with old icons purged from it, freeing up more room on the disk.
- The initialization process checks the entire disk for any flaws, so you can be more certain of the disk's reliability.

## Ejecting Floppies

∘•**➤** **There are many ways to eject a disk.** Some of them leave the disk's icon (a "ghost") on the desktop, and in the Finder's memory, while some eject the disk and make the Finder forget all about it.

To eject the disk temporarily, letting its icon remain on the desktop:

- Select the disk's icon on the desktop and choose Eject from the Special menu.
- Press Command-Shift-1 to eject the disk in an internal floppy drive. Command-Shift-2 works for an external drive, and Command-Shift-0 (zero) works for a second internal drive. You can use these FKEY commands whether you're on the desktop or working in an application.
- Use the Eject button in an Open or Save dialog when the disk is selected in the dialog's list.

To eject the disk and make its icon disappear from the desktop:

- Select the icon and choose Put Away from the File menu.
- Drag the icon to the Trash.

Floppies are also automatically ejected on shut down and at a restart.

→ **You can't eject a disk** (except temporarily, leaving its ghost on the desktop) if one of its files is in use. You just get the dialog shown here. An opened document is obviously in use, but sometimes a small utility, a font, or a sound may be the opened file that's preventing the disk from being "released."

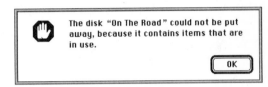

The disk "On The Road" could not be put away, because it contains items that are in use.

OK

Ghost icons, and other disk-on-the-desktop information, is covered in Chapter 4.

→ **When a disk won't eject,** use the emergency eject mechanism: Straighten a paper clip and push it, gently but firmly, into the little hole near the floppy drive opening. The thicker, heavy-duty paper clips are the best. This almost always gets the disk out. DON'T, under any circumstances, forcefully pull a disk out (don't reach for the needle-nose pliers, for instance) if this emergency eject doesn't work, or you might damage the drive.

If you're sure it's not your drive at fault, get rid of any disk that has been stuck in the drive—you don't want that kind of trouble. You can be relatively sure it's not your drive if it happens only with specific disks, few and far between.

And if you're disk is *really* stuck and just won't come out, plan a trip to a computer store with a technician who can take apart the machine and get the disk out without ruining the drive mechanism.

→ **To eject a disk at startup,** hold down the mouse button when you turn on the Mac. This isn't normally an issue, since disks are automatically ejected at shutdown and on restarts. But a disk may have been inserted before you started up the Mac, or the computer may have been shut down improperly (like someone's pulling the plug, or a power outage). It's *still* not an issue unless the disk is a startup disk—regular disks are automatically ejected at startup if they happen to be in the drive. But *if* there's a disk in the drive and *if* it's a startup disk and *if* you don't want to start up with it, hold down the mouse button during startup and the disk will be ejected.

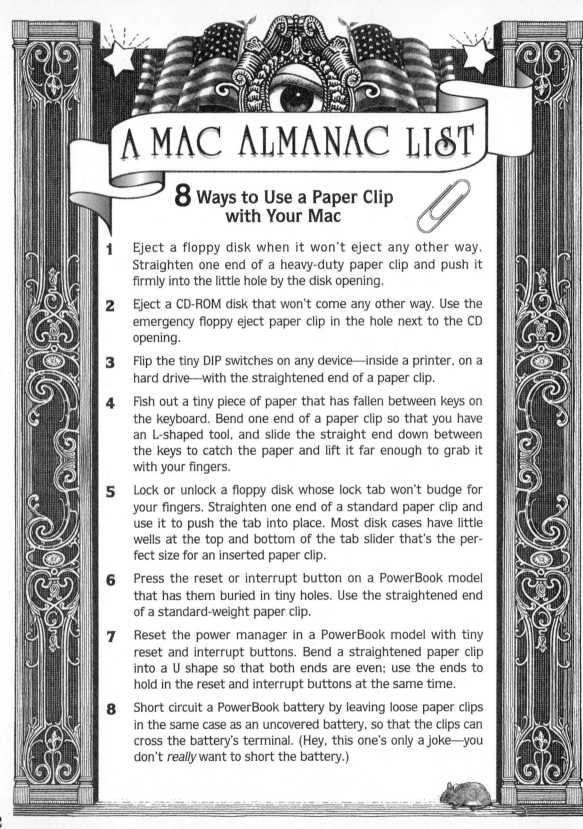

# A MAC ALMANAC LIST

## 8 Ways to Use a Paper Clip with Your Mac

**1** Eject a floppy disk when it won't eject any other way. Straighten one end of a heavy-duty paper clip and push it firmly into the little hole by the disk opening.

**2** Eject a CD-ROM disk that won't come any other way. Use the emergency floppy eject paper clip in the hole next to the CD opening.

**3** Flip the tiny DIP switches on any device—inside a printer, on a hard drive—with the straightened end of a paper clip.

**4** Fish out a tiny piece of paper that has fallen between keys on the keyboard. Bend one end of a paper clip so that you have an L-shaped tool, and slide the straight end down between the keys to catch the paper and lift it far enough to grab it with your fingers.

**5** Lock or unlock a floppy disk whose lock tab won't budge for your fingers. Straighten one end of a standard paper clip and use it to push the tab into place. Most disk cases have little wells at the top and bottom of the tab slider that's the perfect size for an inserted paper clip.

**6** Press the reset or interrupt button on a PowerBook model that has them buried in tiny holes. Use the straightened end of a standard-weight paper clip.

**7** Reset the power manager in a PowerBook model with tiny reset and interrupt buttons. Bend a straightened paper clip into a U shape so that both ends are even; use the ends to hold in the reset and interrupt buttons at the same time.

**8** Short circuit a PowerBook battery by leaving loose paper clips in the same case as an uncovered battery, so that the clips can cross the battery's terminal. (Hey, this one's only a joke—you don't *really* want to short the battery.)

## Also...

→ **One of the Mac's most annoying dialogs** is the one that says *Please insert the disk MyFiles* (or whatever the disk name is). Dealing with the dialog on an occasional basis when you're working on the desktop and copying things to or between floppies isn't so bad. But when you leave a disk icon on the desktop after the disk's been ejected, this dialog can pop up at unpredictable and inopportune moments. And if, heaven forbid, you don't have the disk at hand, you're stuck with an insistent Mac.

Pressing Command-period usually make's the dialog go away. Sometimes you have to type it several times before the Mac is willing to accept the fact that you really mean it.

→ **If you alter the contents of a disk while** its ghost is still on the desktop (of course, you'd need a second Mac to do that, but the scenario's not farfetched in an office situation where a disk may be used to make a quick transfer of a small file), the Mac won't recognize the disk as the same when you put it back in. That means that when you get the *Please insert* dialog, you won't be able to satisfy it, because that disk doesn't exist anymore. If the Command-period cancellation just won't work, you may have to restart the computer the hard way—shutting it off with a switch rather than with the Restart or Shut Down commands. Luckily, you save your work at such frequent intervals that this won't bother you a bit, right?

→ **You can use or ignore the plastic sleeve** that many floppies come in. The little baggies are just meant as extra protection from dust and dirt by the shutter. They don't afford static protection; nor do they build up static that might adversely affect the disk.

→ **Macs used to come with a yellow "disk"** inserted in the floppy drive; it was just a piece of plastic, not really a disk. It was, in fact, an unnecessary piece of plastic, since the drive's heads need no protection even when you're shipping the computer.

→ **Know what kind of disk is in your drive** at a glance by using SpeedyFinder7. One of its options gives disks nice 3-D shading; as a bonus, each is marked as single-sided, double-sided (also sometimes referred to as *double-density*, hence the DD label on the icon), or high-density. And, as if that weren't enough, there's a special icon for locked disks, and one for a disk that has some sectors "roped off" by the Mac as unusable. The icons are here; I'll bet you can figure out which are which. [SpeedyFinder7, Victor Tan]

→ **When you drag a file to a floppy,** the Mac copies it over and then double-checks that the new copy matches the original, in a process called *verification*. If a file can't be verified, you'll get a dialog telling you so and offering to continue copying whatever other files you copied over to the disk. Don't continue! If a file can't be verified because of a disk error, don't use the disk! Reinitializing the disk usually takes care of things, since it can rope off any problem sectors from being used.

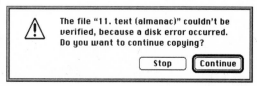

The file "11. text (almanac)" couldn't be verified, because a disk error occurred. Do you want to continue copying?

Stop    Continue

••▸ **When the Mac sees a problem on a floppy** that it can do something about, you'll get a dialog that says *This disk needs minor repairs. Do you want me to repair it?* or something along those lines. Go ahead and click Yes. First of all, it won't be able to read the disk unless it's repaired; secondly, it won't erase the disk or any of the files on it.

••▸ **Don't panic when you can't read a floppy,** even though *This is not a Macintosh disk* is a dire message when the floppy has something important on it. Other problem alerts, like the one shown here, are just as heart-stopping.

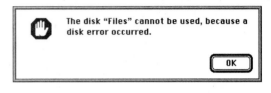

Here are some things you can try when the Mac can't read a floppy:

- First, make sure you have the right disk in the right drive. Is it a 1.4-meg disk in an 800K drive? Is it a 1.4-meg disk that was formatted as 800K in an 800K drive but is now in a SuperDrive? In either case, take the disk back to wherever it came from and read it from that machine.
- Try re-inserting the disk while holding down Command and Option to rebuild its desktop.
- Eject the disk. Snap the shutter open and closed a few times to make sure it's working. Turn the disk inside the case by rotating it with the metal hub while holding the case. Slap it flat against a table top. Re-insert the disk and see if it's readable.
- If the disk has recently been exposed to extreme temperatures (outside in a car, or pocket, when it's really hot or really cold), let it reach room temperature before trying again.
- Try the disk in another drive, or on another computer.
- Run Disk First Aid (it's on your system disks, or on your hard drive already, since it's part of the Mac's system software) and see if it can repair or read the disk.
- Use a heavier-duty disk utility like MacTools or Norton's to try and recover the information from the disk.

If the Mac ejects the disk every time you insert it, without even the courtesy of a dialog, try running MacTools or Norton's, and then inserting the disk. Sometimes they can read it when the Finder can't.

D isk utility programs are covered in the next chapter.

••▸ **On a Mac with two internal floppy drives** (a convenience that's not been built-in since the SE/30 and Mac IIfx), the one at the right or on the bottom is the first drive, while the one at the left or on the top is the second drive. This is useful if you want to know which one is checked first for a startup disk, or which keyboard eject combination (Command-Shift-1, Command-Shift-0) works on which drive.

••▸ **Disk drives get pretty dirty,** as do the read/write heads inside. There are cleaning kits that provide a felt circle inside a disk case; you put cleaning fluid on the felt, put the disk in the drive, and let it wipe down the heads. This is a pretty clever approach, but many experts point out that you may wind up scratching the read/write heads as a result; other experts swear by regular cleaning.

The other type of cleaning is a quick vacuuming right at the drive opening to suck out the dust that's been accumulating. (If you ever open your Mac case—to put in memory chips, for example—you'll be amazed at how dirty things get in there!)

In ten years of Mac use, I've had one floppy drive problem, which had nothing to do with accumulated gunk. I've never used cleaning solutions; I've occasionally vacuumed things out—on the order of once a year or so, when I have to open the Mac to swap cards or SIMMs or something along those lines.

# CHAPTER 18
# MASS STORAGE & SCSI STUFF

Computer:
One who computes.

WEBSTER'S
COLLEGIATE
DICTIONARY
1929

The mysteries explained, and otherwise unraveled, in this chapter include:

- ••➤ Why your hard drive needs a driver.
- ••➤ How you can unerase erased files.
- ••➤ Why daisy chaining is no longer a pastoral pastime.
- ••➤ What's even worse than black arts.
- ••➤ Formatting, defragmentation, interleaving and partitioning.
- ••➤ Why you should never go forward without backing up.

## FROM THE "WE HOPE THERE'S NO DEEPER MEANING TO THIS" DEPARTMENT

*In the battle of acronym pronunciation, "sexy" lost out to "scuzzy."*

page 664

### —Includes—

| | |
|---|---|
| 148 | Factoids |
| 10 | Quotable Quotes |
| 2 | Mac Almanac Lists |
| 1 | Mac Almanac Chart |

*—and—*

another light bulb joke

## HARD DRIVE BASICS

## WORKING WITH HARD DRIVES

## SCSI DEVICES

## CD-ROM (& OTHER) DRIVES

## BACKING UP

# → HARD DRIVE BASICS ←

## About Hard Disks

∘∘❥ **The difference between a *disk* and a *drive*** is easy to see when you're using floppy disks: The disk is that square plastic thing and the drive is the mechanism that you put it into. Or, more formally, the disk is the *storage medium* and the drive manipulates the disk so you can put information on it and retrieve the data when you need it.

A hard disk, however, combines the storage medium and the mechanism into one unit, which is why the phrases *hard drive* and *hard disk* are used interchangeably.

*See Chapter 23 for info about minimal systems.*

∘∘❥ **You need a hard drive.** That's all there is to it. Although they've always been highly recommended for Mac systems, they became a necessity with the advent of System 7, which can't fit on or run from a floppy (except in a minimal configuration for emergencies).

*MACWORLD, JULY 1985*

> The whole notion of computing takes a quantum leap when you discover that information can be stored in one place rather than scattered over hundreds of little disks.

∘∘❥ **A hard drive uses basically the same mechanism** as a floppy drive, but usually consists of a series of stacked metal or glass platters, with a set of read-write heads for each platter.

∘∘❥ **Hard drives are not only bigger, they're faster** than floppies. And they're faster for several reasons:

- Information is packed more tightly on the platters of a hard drive than on a floppy disk, so it takes less time for the read/write heads to get to the information.
- The hard drive platters spin much faster than a floppy—ten times faster for even the slowest hard drive.
- A floppy disk sits still until you need something from it; then it starts spinning, but it takes a few seconds for it to get up to speed. A hard disk is always spinning, so you don't have to wait through a spinup every time you want to access it.

∘∘❥ **Hard drives are sealed shut** because even a small speck of dust could spell disaster. Unlike a floppy's read/write head, which touches the floppy disk media, a hard drive's read/write head floats just microns above the platter surface, and even tiny particles can cause problems. I mean, *really* tiny, like a speck of dust, a smoke particle (not an ash, but *smoke!*), or even the oils left behind in a fingerprint.

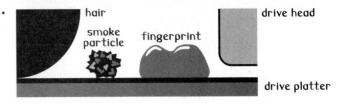

A hard drive is sealed shut to keep it clean.

hair

smoke particle

fingerprint

drive head

drive platter

••→ **All hard drives die eventually.** There's a nifty little misleading acronym that manufacturers use: MTBF. That stands for *mean time between failures* and it's meant to be a guideline as to how long the drive will last. But it's misleading for several reasons. It's not really the time *between* failures. It's the time *until* a failure. And the failure isn't just a little glitch—it's a major failure, a death with little possibility of resurrection. Finally, keep in mind the phrase *mean time*. That's not a life span prediction for the hard drive; that's the *average* life for a model. This means that some will die later; *yours* may die quite a bit sooner. In all, MTBF really means *probable life span*.

Always remember that a hard drive is one of the few computer components that has mechanical parts. The parts have high speeds and small tolerances, and are in constant use. When you think about it, it's a miracle they last as long as they do.

All that said, it's a relief to know that no MTBF rating is less than several years, and some are a decade or more. Only one of my drives has ever really, totally, died in all the years and dozens of drives that I've used. And I have no doubt that it was a manufacturing flaw anyway, since it died at a young age and was from what turned out to be quite a disreputable company—which is no longer in existence.

••→ **There are some terms and issues** that mere mortals shouldn't have to deal with, but if you have a hard drive, there are a few advanced items you ought to have at least a passing acquaintance with—if for no other reason than you might have to deal with *boot blocks* or *extents tree* when you have a hard disk problem.

Here, then, is a brief description of some of the terms I wish we could avoid. Most of these terms have to do with invisible files and roped-off sectors of the disk that the Mac uses to keep things going.

- The *boot blocks* are the first two sectors on a hard drive (which, in the charming counting habits of a computer, are numbered 0 and 1). They contain the information that the Mac needs to start up, or *boot*. This information includes the name of the System file, the name of the startup screen file, and how many files can be opened simultaneously.
- The *master directory block* keeps track of which file system is being used (HFS, in most cases), and how many files and folders the disk contains.
- The *directory* is a file that keeps track of where every file is on the disk; since files can be split into pieces, the directory also keeps track of the order the pieces were stored in. (*Let's see … the first piece is in 12:1, then comes 17:4 through 17:9, and the last piece is in 42:7 through 42:12.*) On the Mac, the directory is actually made up of two different files: the *Extents B-Tree* file and the *Catalog B-Tree* file.

- The *volume bit map* has one bit reserved for, or *mapped to*, each sector on the disk. When the bit is on, it means the sector is in use; when it's off, or zero, it means the sector is available.
- The *volume information block* stores information about the disk itself: when it was initialized; when it was last modified; how often it's been written to; and, the sizes of the other reserved areas of the disk.

You can easily imagine how damage to any one of these sectors, or the information stored in them, can keep a disk from mounting, or cause you to lose files—even though the files themselves may be sitting there on the disk where they were stored originally.

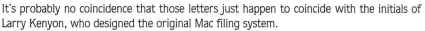

 **MAC TRIVIA**

The first two sectors of a disk are known as the *boot blocks* because they store information that lets the Mac start up, or *boot*. When you format a Mac disk, there's special information written to the first two bytes of the boot blocks: the letters LK.

It's probably no coincidence that those letters just happen to coincide with the initials of Larry Kenyon, who designed the original Mac filing system.

## Buying a Hard Drive

∞→ **You need a hard drive that's at least** twice as big as you think you need. With the size of the System Folder for System 7 (especially one you've beefed up with a few special extensions) and the size of some applications (with their supporting files), 20 megs of hard drive space is needed just for the system and a few applications. If your work is mainly word processing and using a spreadsheet, you can get away with an additional 10 megs for documents, so a 40-meg hard drive would last you for a long time. But it's unlikely you'll be able to *find* a 40-meg drive these days unless you buy a used one. It's even hard to find 80-meg drives these days!

But do you want a few terrific games? Add another 20 megs. Do you work with page lay-out, complicated graphics, color graphics, sound, or QuickTime movies? 200 megs will be used up in no time, what with the size of the programs for those activities, and the large documents they create.

The picture here shows the window that holds only some of the applications on one of my drives—the folders add up to well over 40 megs, and there's at least that much for other applications—and my System Folder is weighing in at 30 megs right now with all the fonts I'm using for this book and the extensions that I'm testing.

| Applications | | |
|---|---|---|
| 9 items | 141.2 MB in disk | 90.7 MB available |
| **Name** | Size | Kind |
| ▷ ☐ FreeHand | 2,280K | folder |
| ▷ ☐ Aldus SuperPaint | 4,432K | folder |
| ▷ ☐ FileMaker | 3,816K | folder |
| ▷ ☐ Illustrator | 960K | folder |
| ▷ ☐ PageMaker 4 | 2,584K | folder |
| ▷ ☐ PageMaker 5 | 4,828K | folder |
| ▷ ☐ PhotoShop | 13,736K | folder |
| ▷ ☐ QuarkXpress | 5,900K | folder |
| ▷ ☐ Word 5 | 5,620K | folder |

> Average users can store all their programs as well as a year's worth of files on a 10-megabyte hard disk—and theoretically never have to look at a floppy again.

DAVID BUNNEL
*MACWORLD, JULY 1985*

•••➤ **The *drive mechanism* refers** to the guts of your hard drive. You can pick up a catalog and find dozens of drive brands but, in fact, there are only a few companies that actually make the drive mechanism. Other companies buy the internal stuff, package it (usually providing the power supply and case), and sell it to you. Quantum, Conner, and IBM probably make 95 percent of the drives you'll see available for the Mac; Seagate manufactured many of the internal drives for Macs when they first started sporting this feature. (This is a good place to mention another acronym you'll see around: *OEM*. That's for *Original Equipment Manufacturer*, which is what Quantum, et al., are when it comes to drives.)

Here's a snapshot of the items on my SCSI chain, courtesy of the SCSIProbe control panel described in detail later in the chapter; I'm using it here because it lists the brand of the internal mechanism for each device, not the vendor's name. At ID 0, there's the Mac's internal hard drive—a Quantum mechanism that Apple puts in many of its computers. At ID 1 is a SyQuest drive from APS; ID 2, another Quantum mechanism, is an external drive

| ID | Type | Vendor | Product | Version |
|----|------|--------|---------|---------|
| 0 | DISK | QUANTUM | LP240S GM240S0... | 6.3 |
| 1 | DISK | SyQuest | SQ5110C | D7F |
| 2 | DISK | QUANTUM | LP240S GM240S0... | 6.4 |
| 3 | ROM | SONY | CD-ROM CDU-800... | 1.9a |
| 4 | | | | |
| 5 | OPTIC | EPSON | OMD-5010 | 3.09 |
| 6 | DISK | QUANTUM | LP105S 9101094... | 2.8 |
| 7 | CPU | APPLE | Sharon's 650 | 7.1 |

from APS; at ID 3 is Apple's internal CD-ROM, manufactured by Sony (Sony makes Apple's floppy drives, too); ID 5 is a magneto-optical drive from APS, manufactured by Epson; ID 6 is yet another Quantum mechanism, this time a LaCie drive; finally, there's the Mac itself at ID 7.

•••➤ **A fast hard drive** is always good, but there are many ways to measure a drive's speed:

- Platters spin at a minimum of 3600 rpm, but some models whirl them around even faster.
- *Access time* is the time it takes the read/write head to get to a specific spot on the disk. Access times are measured in milliseconds, so the lower the number, the better for you.
- *Latency* is the time it takes for a specific spot on the disk to pass beneath the positioned read/write head.
- The *data transfer rate* is probably the most important measure of speed, since it's the rate at which information can be transferred from the disk to the Mac.

Interleaving and fragmenting are both covered later in this chapter.

In addition to these built-in speed factors, the way the hard drive is set up also affects its speed. The wrong *interleave factor*, for instance, can slow down performance, as can fragmented files.

•••➤ **If the drive is faster than the Mac**—that is, if its data transfer rate is more than the Mac can handle, the drive's extra speed is wasted. Anything less than an '030 Mac can't handle the faster transfer rates that new drives can deliver.

•••♪ **How big can you get?** The Mac's original filing system (MFS, Macintosh filing system) choked on as few as 400 files. Then HFS (Hierarchical Filing System) came along, and upped that limit considerably, but we're not past it yet. With HFS, the Mac uses a 32-bit number to keep track of each byte of information on a volume. That's 2,147,483,648 bytes—two gigabytes. The Mac can't handle a single volume larger than that.

> ✳System 7.5 upped the ante on file storage to four gigs.

∞◊〉 **There are many reliable hard drive manufacturers** around, and the cost of large hard drives has done nothing but drop over the years. And, as I mentioned before, the innards of hard drives are actually manufactured by only a few companies.

APS Technologies currently gets an A+ in my book. (Hey, *this* is my book, isn't it?) While not always the lowest in price, they're one of the lowest, and they don't skimp on the important things. Instead of offering you just 20 megs of public domain software on a drive, they supply you with heavy-duty SCSI cables and a reliable terminator. And their tech support is absolutely outstanding—even if you have a general question rather than an actual problem. Microtech is another company that gets good marks for price, product, and support.

APS
TECHNOLOGIES

LaCie is also a highly rated drive company, and I have several of their units around, all of which have seen heavy use and been perfectly reliable; in fact, the company is owned by hard-drive manufacturer Quantum. They also are one of the lowest-priced brands around. I have to admit, though, that I stopped ordering from them when I found that a drive I had bought from them, which was supposed to be internally terminated (and which I used, as a sole external drive, with no problems) acted up when I had a longer chain of SCSI devices attached. Deciding I would take the termination out of the drive and put it in the middle of the chain instead of at the end, I opened the case to find it wasn't terminated at all. I can forgive things like this—but the failure of their tech support people to get back to me when I called about the issue ... well, that makes it hard to recommend the company even when I know that their hardware is excellent.

•••♪ **The important things to consider when buying** a hard drive are:

- *The price.* A high price doesn't guarantee high quality, and a low price doesn't guarantee a bargain. But lets face it, all things being more or less equal, you'll want the lower-priced unit. Keep in mind that the price-per-meg of storage goes down as the capacity of the drive goes up, since there's a certain cost for the case, power supply, and cables for each unit.

- *Speed.* Is it fast enough for your Mac? Most drives are faster than the older Macs, and fast enough for the newer ones, but you might want to get more specific if you have a Quadra or Power Mac.

- *The case.* Do you want a "zero footprint" drive that sits under a compact Mac? Do you need something smaller for transportability? Do you want one that stands on end to take less room on your desktop next to the CPU?

- *The SCSI connector.* Life is easier if you stick to units that use the standard 50-pin SCSI port, since the standard cabling assumes that's what's on an external device. Some drives, however, have 25-pin SCSI connections.

- *Cables.* Does a cable come with the unit? (It should.) Which cable? Cables are discussed in the SCSI section later in this chapter, but take a look at your setup and make sure that the cable you're getting with the drive is one that lets you hook it up to your Mac or to your other peripherals, if you have them.

- *Termination.* Avoid internally terminated units, but try to get a drive that comes with an external terminator so you don't have to buy one separately.
- *SCSI ID setting.* Get a drive that has an easy way to set its SCSI ID number: an easily accessible wheel or buttons with numbers at the back of the case is best. DIP switches are a pain to use, and *internal* setting of ID numbers is ridiculous.
- *Bonus software.* Not the public domain stuff—by the time you get the drive, it's probably outdated anyway. But many drives come bundled with terrific disk utilities, either for formatting or for taking care of disk problems.

> The number and size of files expand to fill all available disk space in a time span that's inversely proportional to the cost of the hard drive.

*THE MAC ALMANAC*

••▶ **You can buy a new internal hard drive;** you don't have to increase your overall storage capacity by buying external units. Of course, that leaves you with an extra internal hard drive mechanism and no place to put it. You could always sell it to someone who has an even smaller hard drive, and let them handle the leftover problem.

This trickle-down is endemic in PowerBook circles. My PowerBook's hard drive used to belong to Vernon Huang, who I "met" online and, much later, in person. My old PowerBook drive is in Andy Baird's PowerBook (he did many of the illustrations, and the "Mac People" entries for this book). Rich Wolfson, the tech reader for this book, has Steve Bobker's (MacUser's former Editor-in-Chief) hard drive in his PowerBook. And Joe Holmes, my terrific tech editor, has *another* of Bobker's hand-me-down drives in *his* PowerBook.

An alternative is to keep the hard drive yourself, and turn it into an external unit by getting a case and a power supply from a company like APS Technologies.

## Formatting Hard Drives

*✴Remember, initializing and formatting are the same thing when it comes to Mac disks.*

∞▶ **You don't usually have to initialize** a hard drive, since most come ready to go. An internal drive that comes in a Mac is set up at the factory and even has a System Folder on it already. Many external hard drives come from manufacturers with systems on them, or at least formatted* and with various utilities and other programs on them.

But if you have a truly blank hard drive, or you want to wipe out the contents of your current hard drive and start again, it's easy. If the drive is not the startup drive, simply select its icon on the desktop and choose Erase Disk from the Special menu. If the disk is the startup drive, you have to start your system with a different volume: either another hard drive, a CD-ROM, or a floppy, if you have one with a minimal system on it. Once again, just use the Erase Disk command on the hard drive's icon.

∞§ **The HD SC Setup utility** comes with your system software, and it can be used to format or reformat an Apple drive. Many hard drive manufacturers provide their own formatting utilities—or one from a software company—along with the hard drive itself. There are also utilities that provide formatting and other capabilities, like partitioning and SCSI mounting. SilverLining has long enjoyed a good reputation among Mac experts, as has Drive7, the one I swear by, and FWB's HD ToolKit. There's some evidence that these third-party utilities actually get your drive to work a little faster with their drivers than with the Apple driver.

DRIVE7

HD SC Setup works only on Apple drives, but you can reformat an Apple drive with any other commercial drive utility. [SilverLining, LaCie; Drive7, Casa Blanca Works; HD Toolkit FWB]

∞♦ **To reformat your internal drive,** you have to start up your Mac with the Disk Tools floppy disk or an external hard drive that has a system on it. This is, of course, *after* you've backed up everything you want to save.

Run HD SC Setup from the floppy or from the other hard drive, click the Drive button until you see the drive you want to format, and then click the Initialize button.

•••♦ **Reformat your hard drive annually.** Why? Especially when it's such a pain to back up and restore the data? Because the reformatting process checks the disk for any bad spots and if there are any, they're excluded from the overall map of available space on the hard drive; this way, the Mac won't try to store information there—and later lose it. Occasional reformatting is great preventive medicine.

•••♦ **Hard drives aren't always formatted to their full** capacity. Until the advent of the HD SC Setup version 7.3.1 that came with a system update in the spring of 1994, Apple's drives were always formatted with a partition that was less than their full capacity. What? Your drive isn't partitioned? Oh, yes it is! Every Mac drive that comes from Apple is partitioned—but it's one giant partition, so you think you're using the whole drive. But you may not be. Many drives are formatted to nice round-sounding numbers like 40, 80, 120, and 230 megs, even though their actual capacities might be 41.5, 83, 128, and 243 megs. Wouldn't you like to get at that extra space (an extra meg and a half per each 40 megs on the drive)? You can, even with the older version HD SC Setup program that's on your system disks.

First, check if your drive is formatted to its fullest:

1. Run HD SC Setup and click the Partition button in the main dialog.
2. Click the Custom button in the next dialog, ignoring all the suggested partitioning schemes in the list.

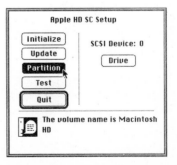

3. The next dialog shows the *partition map*. Don't touch the 16K partition at the top, since it's reserved for the disk driver. The white area, with your drive's name in it, is the main partition that's already in use. At the bottom is a gray area that represents the unused portion of your drive. If there's no gray area, the disk is already formatted to its maximum capacity.

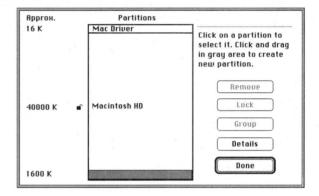

The partition map.

4. Click the Done button and get out of there! If you continue, you'll erase everything on your hard drive.

If there was a gray area at the bottom of the partition map representing unused space on the disk, you'll want to repartition your drive. The repartitioning procedure will erase everything on your hard drive. Let me say that again: *This procedure will erase everything on your hard drive*. Got that? Good. Back up everything on the hard drive and tell yourself this is a great opportunity to defragment the whole thing anyway.

Run HD SC Setup (from a floppy, since you're erasing the hard drive), and follow steps 1 through 3 above; continue with these steps (you're looking at the partition map at the end of step 3):

4. Before you can make the new, larger partition, you have to remove the current one. Click in the middle of the white area, and then click the Remove button. You'll get a dialog that warns you that you're about to erase the hard drive. If you've backed everything up, go ahead and click OK.

5. The partition map is now totally gray beneath the driver partition. Drag the mouse from a point near the top of the gray area to the bottom. The gray block won't change as you're dragging, but you'll see a line and brackets on the side as you move the mouse. Let go of the mouse button when you reach the bottom.

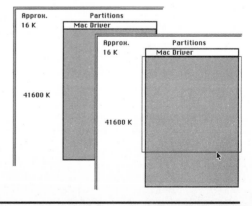

Dragging the new partition.

6. The dialog that pops up as soon as you let go of the mouse lists possible partition types for the area that you just dragged through. Click on *Macintosh Volume*.

7. Click OK.

Click on *Macintosh Volume* and leave the maximum number suggested.

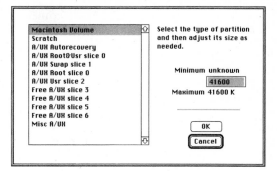

That's it. The Mac will churn away for awhile, reformatting your drive, and then you'll have to copy back all your software to it.

## Interleaving

⊶❯ The *interleave factor* (doesn't that sound like a good science fiction title?) of a drive is how its sectors are numbered for reference in data retrieval. You have to know about this only if you're using a Classic, an SE (not the SE/30), or a Plus, since all other Macs use a standard 1:1 ratio. Huh?

It's simple, really. As a hard disk spins around, the Mac is reading the information flying by; it reads what's in one sector, transfers it to memory, and then goes back to read the next sector. A fast Mac (68020 or better) can read the data, transfer it, and be ready to read again in time to catch the next sector whizzing by. So, the sectors are numbered in order around the track because when the Mac is finished with sector 1, it wants sector 2, then sector 3, and so on.

Numbering sectors in order gives a 1:1 interleave.

But now consider a slower Mac, and what happens when it tries to read information from the disk. It reads sector 1, transfers it to memory, and returns for sector 2—only to find that sector 2 has already passed by and sector 3 is the one it's looking at. It has to wait for the disk platter to spin all the way around again, past all the sectors, through number 1 again, before it can see sector 2. And when it returns for the sector 3 information, it has to wait for a full spin once again. And so on.

The best setup for the sector numbering on a hard drive used by a slower Mac is one that matches its "reading" speed. Since the SE and the Classic can grab only every other sector, the sectors should be numbered differently to accommodate those Macs. The first physical sector is still 1, but it's the third sector that's numbered 2, and the fifth one is 3. This way, when the Mac looks back at the disk, the sector that's numerically after the one

An interleave of 2:1 numbers alternate sectors on the disk.

it just read is the one that's in position under the read/write head. The intervening sectors aren't left blank: alternate sectors are numbered all the way around the track, then the numbering continues in the sectors left blank on the first round. This is an interleave factor, or ratio, of 2:1; sometimes it's simply referred to as an interleave value of 2.

The Mac Plus is the slowest of the Macs (we're discounting its predecessors entirely, since they can't run System 7), and needs an interleave of 3:1 for optimum performance.

⚬•➤ **A hard drive's interleave ratio** is automatically set to match the computer you're using when you format the drive with HD SC Setup.

⚬•➤ **If your hard drive comes from another Mac,** and that other Mac was an older, slower model, reinitialize the hard drive from your system to make sure the drive's interleave factor is right for your Mac.

••➤ **Force a specific interleave ratio** for a hard drive when you're formatting it with HD SC Setup by pressing Command-I (that's I, for Interleave) after you launch the utility. You'll get the dialog shown here. Other formatting utilities usually provide a way to specify the ratio, too.

••➤ **An older Mac with an accelerator needs** a different interleave factor for its drive. An SE that has an '030 accelerator behaves like an SE/30 and needs a 1:1 interleave ratio for best results instead of the 1:2 interleave that the SE should have.

So, if you have an accelerated system, reinitialize the drive and force the format to the proper interleave; the formatting utility will recognize only the basic model you're using, and won't be aware of any accelerators.

••➤ **A hard drive with built-in *data caching*** lets you use a 1:1 interleave ratio with even the older Macs, with no performance penalty. With data caching, an entire track is read at once and stored in memory that's installed in the hard drive unit; when the Mac needs another sector from that same track, it's retrieved from memory instead of from the disk.

> Given Apple's history ... the hard disk is nice, but the price is phenomenal! It's realistic, reasonable, responsible, affordable, and most of all, totally uncharacteristic.

**MacUser**
January 1986
(in regard to Apple's
first hard drive for the Mac—
20 megs for $1500)

## Hard Drive Drivers

⚬•➤ **A *driver*** is a piece of software that regulates how the Mac interacts with a peripheral device. The icons in your Extensions folder for various printers are printer drivers, for instance.

A hard drive needs a driver, too, but you won't find it in your Extensions folder. Hard drive drivers are stored on the hard drive itself, tucked in some inconspicuous spot—so inconspicuous, in fact, that it's invisible: It's in an invisible partition. Driver software is automatically installed when you initialize the hard drive with HD SC Setup or some other hard drive utility.

••▶ **Update the hard drive driver** if your hard drive was used with System 6 and now you're using System 7. This is essential for any drive that is a startup disk; it's also highly recommended for any other hard drive that's being used with System 7. Without the update on a system disk, you may get frequent system crashes, and you won't be able to use System 7's virtual memory.

••▶ **Updating a driver doesn't disturb the data** on the drive. It's not like erasing or initializing the drive. An update merely replaces the driver software on the drive. But you should always have current backups available before you do anything to your drive, so don't skip it for this operation, just because it's not *supposed* to touch the rest of the drive.

••▶ **To install a new driver with HD SC Setup,** first make sure you have the latest version of the utility. It comes with your system disks, but if your system disks aren't any newer than your Mac's hard drive, you won't be updating anything. The assumption here is that you've updated your system, so your system disks are newer than your hard drive driver.

Launch HD SC Setup and use the Drive button, if necessary, to display the name of the "target" in the dialog. Then click the Update button. That's all there is to it. And it takes all of about five seconds.

••▶ **The driver doesn't take much room** on the disk. This is part of one of the pictures used earlier to show how you can repartition a drive; notice that the top part is partitioned off for the driver—and it's only 16K.

| Approx. | Partitions |
|---------|------------|
| 16 K | Mac Driver |

## Disk Utilities

°°▶ **Disks are often described as electronic filing cabinets,** and with good reason. But they're much more complex, more than just magnetic repositories for your applications and documents. There's lots going on behind the scenes—and lots that can go wrong.

No computer user should be without several good disk utilities to take care of problems that can crop up. In fact, no Mac user is without at least two disk utilities: HD SC Setup and Disk First Aid come with the Mac system. But you probably need more than just these two basics if your Mac sees a lot of use.

∞•→ **The HD SC Setup program** that comes with your system disks is a basic formatting utility that many Mac owners never touch, since their internal drives come pre-formatted. But this bare-bones program (it doesn't even have any menus) can perform four functions, each at the click of a button:

> ```
> Apple HD SC Setup   v7.2
>
> [ Initialize ]      SCSI Device: 0
> [  Update    ]      [   Drive   ]
> [ Partition  ]
> [   Test     ]
> [   Quit     ]
>
>        The volume name is Int HD
> ```

- Initialize, or reinitialize, a hard drive. Reinitializing the drive erases everything on it.
- Update the hard drive driver. Updating the driver doesn't affect the data on the drive.
- Partition the hard drive for use with the Mac or for sharing between a Mac and a PC. Partitioning, or repartitioning a drive, erases everything on it.
- Test the hard drive for basic hardware problems. This is strictly a diagnostic test; it's only looking for hardware problems, and can't fix anything it finds wrong. Running this test doesn't affect any data on the drive.

∞•→ **HD SC Setup works only with** Apple's hard drives. You can use other formatting, partitioning, and testing utilities on Apple's drives, but you *must* use a third-party utility on a non-Apple drive. In fact, if you've formatted an Apple drive with something other than HD SC Setup, you won't be able to use HD SC Setup for anything on that drive except reformatting it: you can't update the driver, partition it, or test it.

∞•→ **Disk First Aid** is an often-overlooked tool when Mac users run into disk problems; maybe, because it's free (it comes with your system disks), people assume it's not very good. Although it doesn't have the power or

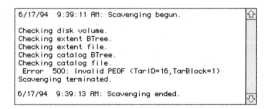

Disk First Aid

scope of larger, commercial utilities, it does a good job of repairing minor disk problems—even before you know they're there. And each version of Disk First Aid that's released with system updates is a little more sophisticated than the last.

Disk First Aid is easy to use. Launch it, select your hard drive in the main dialog box, and choose the Automatic Repair command from the Options menu. (It's the only command, other than Erase, that the program offers.) If it encounters any problems in the disk's data structures, it repairs them.

∞•→ **Run Disk First Aid every month** or two for your hard drive as simple preventive maintenance. You can often catch, and fix, a disk problem before it affects your drive.

∞•→ **If you want to watch what Disk First Aid is doing**, press Command-S after clicking the Start button for the Automatic Repair. You'll get a window like the one shown here (for all the good it'll do you).

> ```
> 6/17/94  9:39:11 AM: Scavenging begun.
>
> Checking disk volume.
> Checking extent BTree.
> Checking extent file.
> Checking catalog BTree.
> Checking catalog file.
>  Error  500: Invalid PEOF (TarID=16,TarBlock=1)
> Scavenging terminated.
>
> 6/17/94  9:39:13 AM: Scavenging ended.
> ```

∞••} **A SCSI utility** is a program that lets you check the ID numbers of the SCSI devices in your chain and mount volumes that, for one reason or another, didn't mount automatically. The freeware SCSIProbe control panel is the best-known of these in the Mac community. (The one pictured here has the SyQuest logo on it—and the *sq* in its window title—because it's a special version that comes with SyQuest drives.) SCSI Identifier is another, similar utility. Most formatting programs include mounting utilities; Drive 7, for instance, includes the awkwardly named but very handy Drive7rem control panel.

Some SCSI utilities, like SCSI Evaluator, test and report on the SCSI chain and the devices on it. [SCSIProbe, freeware, Robert Polic; SCSI Identifier, freeware, Laurie Gill; Drive 7, Casa Blanca Works; SCSI Evaluator, shareware, William A. Long]

**SCSIPROBE**

∞§ **A heavy-duty, full-fledged disk diagnostic and repair** utility is a must for all but the most casual Mac user. What can such a disk utility do? Well, things like:

- Defragment the files on the disk.
- Scan the disk and recreate a file directory if the main one's been damaged. Without a file directory, you can't find your files. Some utilities work behind the scenes while you're working and create a second invisible file directory that can be used if the Mac's file directory fails.
- Recover "erased" files. When you empty the Trash, the file itself isn't erased: the directory entry for that file is erased. A disk utility can keep track of erased files for you and often recover them if you've changed your mind.
- Access any part of the disk without going through the Finder. The Finder can only find and manipulate information if everything is in order and where it belongs. A disk utility can recover a file that may be missing its middle or end section, or its directory entry.
- Repair the boot blocks of the disk if they're damaged. Corrupted boot blocks mean your hard drive won't mount—and on the system disk, that means the Mac can't start up.
- Repair the file information blocks—the extents tree or the volume bit map, for instance.
- Check for and eradicate viruses on the disk.

**MACTOOLS & NORTON UTILITIES**

Norton Utilities for the Mac has enjoyed a deservedly great reputation for a long time; some of its fame initially spilled over from the PC world, but its success on the Mac is due to its excellence. MacTools is an excellent utility, in its third version as I write this, and is my utility of choice. But the truth is that heavy-duty users and consultants usually

Viruses are covered in Chapter 24.

**SAFE & SOUND**

[Blue Ribbon Award — THE MAC ALMANAC BLUE RIBBON AWARD FOR EXCELLENCE]

keep both of these programs in their arsenals, since problems missed by one are generally picked up by the other. Safe & Sound is a subset of MacTools, aimed at the beginning or casual user, and it's simply terrific—it's all most people need in the way of preventive medicine and diagnostic/repair power, and the price is fantastic. [Norton Utilities, Symantec; MacTools and Safe & Sound, Central Point Software]

••→ **Two kinds of utilities can increase the storage capacity** of your drive. One kind is a file compressor, a utility that squeezes down files so they occupy less room. They've long been popular in telecommunications, because smaller files take less time to transfer (and therefore cost less to transfer, too). These utilities are covered in Chapter 21.

The second type of utility is one that works its magic at a much lower level, replacing the disk's driver software and fooling the Mac as to how items are stored on the disk; this can double the capacity of a drive. In fact, these utilities are sometimes referred to as disk doublers, which can cause some confusion because there's a program called Disk Doubler that uses file compression to get more storage space on a drive. In any case, the driver-replacement method is one that I'm very uncomfortable with; utilities that work on such low levels (that means way down in the guts of things) often cause many unexpected problems. And, indeed, early users of these utilities ran into many problems, not the least of which was the fact that replacing the drivers often interfered with disk recovery utilities. I'm not a technological Luddite by any means, but this is an approach that I avoid, and recommend that you do, too. Save your money and buy a larger hard drive if you really need the space. Or take the middle road and use a utility like Disk Doubler that compresses and decompresses files in the background as you save and open them.

> If I doubled the size of my hard drive, it would be about 2 feet by 18 inches by 8 inches.

LOUISE KOHL,
former executive editor,
*MacUser*

## → WORKING WITH HARD DRIVES ←

### In General

∞→ **The icon used for a hard drive** on the desktop depends on the driver software that's installed when you format the disk or that's later updated. Here are a few samples—the one in the upper left is Apple's basic hard drive icon; the others are some of the ones provided by other formatting software. (And, of course, you can always just edit the icon yourself, as described in Chapter 4.)

Int HD

PD Stuff

Ext 230    Ext 105

∞→ **Hard drives aren't delicate,** no matter what their manufacturers' warnings. Most of the drives I know (and use) have been backpacked through airports and transported in car trunks over bumpy roads with no damage. But let's be reasonable here—I wouldn't *throw* the drive into the trunk, or drop it from my shoulder to the floor.

◦•▶ **The internal hard drive is the *startup disk* in** most Mac systems. That means it's the one with the System Folder on it that the Mac uses to run its operating system, and its icon appears in the upper-right corner of the desktop.

The startup drive is always on top.

Startup disk issues are covered in Chapter 1, but here's a roundup of the main points:

- Any attached disk can serve as the startup disk; specify the one you want through the Startup Disk control panel.
- Bypass the internal hard drive as the startup by holding down Command-Option-Shift-Delete at startup; the startup will pass to the next system disk that the Mac finds. (Sometimes you have to try this three or four times before it "catches.") The internal hard drive won't mount at all when you bypass it as the startup.
- A floppy can be a startup disk if you install a minimal system on it.
- External hard drives need time to warm up before the Mac starts. If the external startup disk isn't ready when you turn on the Mac, you'll get the blinking question mark on the screen; just start the Mac all over again.
- The Mac scans all attached devices for a System Folder and starts up with the first one it finds. The scan order is: floppy drives, device specified in the Startup Disk control panel; internal hard drive; external SCSI devices starting with the highest SCSI ID number.

◦•▶ **To force the Mac to use the internal hard drive as the startup**, zap the PRAM, holding down Command-Option-P-R at startup. A setting in PRAM keeps track of the startup device you've chosen, and zapping it returns it to its default of the internal drive.

Why would you need to do this instead of using the Startup Disk control panel? Well, you could do something mildly stupid like I did. I wanted to compare a specific point of System 7.0.1 with System 7.1, so I installed 7.0.1 on one of my external drives and set it as the startup. Well, I had recently changed from a IIci to a Centris—which doesn't work under anything less than System 7.1 with the correct enabler. So, it wouldn't start up at all—I just got a dialog that told me I needed a different version of the system software to run this Macintosh. Restarting didn't help, since it kept looking for a good system on the device I had chosen. Could I find a startup floppy anywhere? No. But zapping the PRAM returned things to normal.

Enabler? See Chapter 23.

◦•▶ **When a hard drive is in use**, treat it nicely. Don't jar it, or you could ruin parts of the platters that are whizzing around so close to the read/write heads. You can move a spinning hard drive—a little bit, slowly and gently—if you have to, but not if it's in the process of actually reading or writing data. PowerBook drives are, of necessity, very hardy creatures even when in use.

•• ► **If you can't rename your hard drive**—you just can't select the name, no matter what you do—there's one of three factors at work:

- You've run into an early System 7 bug that you can get rid of by installing System 7.0.1 and its updater.
- The disk icon is locked. Get Info on it, and unlock it.
- The disk is being shared (or thinks it's being shared) on a network. Turn off file sharing by selecting the icon, choosing the Sharing command from the File menu, and unchecking the *Share this item and its contents* button.

### PRICING STRICTURES

Prices of almost everything always creep up. Except the price of technology, which constantly creeps down. Take early hard drives for the Mac, for instance: Everyone was relieved when Apple announced its $1500 price tag for a 20-meg hard drive because that was far less than the non-Apple alternative at the time.

Here, culled from old issues of Mac magazines, are some dates and drive prices (all neatly and approximately rounded).

| Date | Size (MB) | Price | Price per MB |
|------|-----------|-------|--------------|
| Feb 85 | 5.5MB | $1800 | $325.00 |
| Jan 86 | 10 | $1000 | $100.00 |
| | 20 | $1500 | $75.00 |
| Jun 86 | 74 | $7000 | $94.50 |
| Jul 89 | 20 | $550 | $27.50 |
| | 40 | $700 | $17.50 |
| | 80 | $1000 | $12.50 |
| | 140 | $1500 | $10.75 |
| Mar 94 | 170 | $300 | $1.75 |
| | 340 | $525 | $1.55 |

•• ► **You can turn off a hard drive** and turn it back on again and your Mac might not know the difference. I know, I've done it several times over the years. Years ago, I had a hard drive that sat beneath a Mac Plus; its on/off switch was in the front, low on the case and easy to push. If I slid the keyboard too far under the Plus's front overhang, it would hit the drive's switch. As long as the Mac wasn't reading or writing anything at the time, it just sat there as if nothing had happened. I could turn the drive back on and get back to work.

This has happened more recently, too, to one or more of the devices in my chain of peripheral storage devices. Some are plugged into a separate power strip, and it was flipped of by mistake. The Mac sat patiently and went back to work when I turned everything back on. Nothing was lost or corrupted.

So if this happens to you, turn the hard drive back on right away; don't do any work—not even a Save for the current document as a precaution, even if the document is stored on a different device that's still turned on. You don't want to do *anything* while one or more items is turned off in a SCSI chain.

···→ **Don't wait for disaster to strike.** Keep your hard drive in good shape by running a disk diagnostic utility at frequent intervals; a good utility can catch problems before they cause any grief at all. Although an extensive disk check can take upwards of an hour for a large hard drive, you don't have to do much; it's as easy as selecting a disk icon and clicking the Check button in this window from Central Point Software's Safe & Sound.

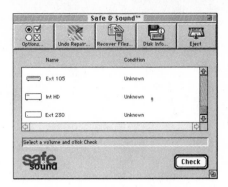

## Fragmentation

∞→ *Fragmentation* **slows down a disk's performance.** Although fragmentation occurs on both floppies and hard drives, it's an issue for only hard drives because you change the contents of the hard drive—copying files to it, deleting files from it, editing the files on it—so often.

Files are often stored piece-meal in several sectors across the disk.

Most files are stored in more than one sector on a disk. When the disk is relatively empty, it's easy to store the pieces of a file in contiguous sectors. But if you edit a file so that it's larger than it was originally, the sectors next to its current storage spots might not be available. Parts of the edited file wind up being stored in spots on the disk that are nowhere near each other.

When you erase a file, you free up the sectors it was stored in. But it's unlikely that a new file will fit in the same number of sectors, so it might fill them all and then have its other pieces elsewhere on the disk.

Although it's actually the files that are fragmented across the disk, this mess is referred to as *disk fragmentation*. And now, back to the first sentence of this entry: fragmentation slows down a disk's performance. After all, it takes time to run around and collect a file from various spots on a disk.

∞→ **You can defragment a hard drive** by backing up its contents, erasing the drive (with the Finder's Erase command, or with HD SC Setup), and putting the contents back. If that seems a little drastic to you, you're right—it is drastic. But reformatting a hard drive completely also gets rid of any problems waiting to happen, like corrupted directory entries.

∞→ **Defragment a drive without erasing it** by using defragmenting software. Most high-end disk utilities include defragmenting options—sophisticated ones that can check just how fragmented your disk is in terms of both how many files are chopped up, and how many pieces they're chopped up into. MacTools (my personal favorite) and Norton Utilities are the disk utilities of choice in the Macintosh community, and both provide defragmentation options. DiskExpress II specializes in defragmenting drives. [MacTools, Central Point Software; Norton Utilities, Symantec; DiskExpress, AlSoft]

••➔ **Cut down on file fragmentation** by starting out right. When you're starting with a fresh hard drive, first copy the System Folder to it, and your extra system utilities—fonts, extensions, and control panels. Then copy the applications you use the most.

The logic behind putting these things on your hard drive first is two-fold. First, since they don't change too much, you won't have anything fragmented on this part of your drive. A fragmented system file or application will slow you down more than a fragmented document.

I can't find any expert confirmation to this, but many people recommend that you plan ahead and create room for your system to grow. So, you should put your System Folder on the hard drive, and then copy something else to the hard drive that will serve as "place holders": extra copies of your fonts, for instance. Then copy the applications. When you want to add new extensions or control panels to your system (or new fonts, for that matter), you delete some of the placeholders and then copy the new stuff onto the drive; on the assumption that the new stuff gets copied into the recently vacated sectors, you'll still have all your system files in contiguous sectors on the drive.

••➔ **Do some mini-defragmenting** of a few important files so that they'll be stored in contiguous sectors. Use the Duplicate command on the desktop, and then get rid of the original file. The duplication is likely to be written to contiguous sectors if your hard drive isn't too full. This is a good approach for database files, which are particularly prone to fragmenting because they're changed so often, and they suffer the most from fragmented slowdown because the application hits the disk so often for the database information.

••➔ **Defragmenting isn't of vital importance.** For many people, doing it once a year or every two years is plenty; for some *never* doing it is fine, since it will take more time to defragment than you'd save with an unfragmented setup. If your drive gets a lot of use, with files being added, edited, and erased to the tune of a dozen or so a day, and every last ounce of speed is vital to you, you might consider defragmenting twice a year.

## Partitioning

••➔ *Partitioning* **a drive is** just what it sounds like: dividing it into smaller pieces. When you split up the room on a hard drive like this, each partition appears as a drive icon on your desktop.

One disk divided into three partitions looks like three drives on the desktop.

I have one of my large drives divided into one large and two relatively small partitions; the smaller ones are "Finances" (checkbooks and taxes) and that old standby "Miscellaneous." They look like this when they're on the desktop: the π in their titles stands for (at least in my method) *partition*.

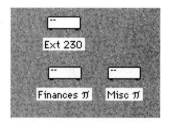

∞➔ **Why partition?** Because partitions don't have to be mounted at all unless you need the information on them, you can save time (the Finder doesn't have to scan the contents of the partitions at startup), Finder memory, and desktop space by ignoring the partitions until you need them.

In addition, partitions provide a measure of security because everything's not right there on your desktop for everyone passing by to see. In fact, there's no way to tell that there's a hidden partition somewhere on your drive just by looking at the desktop, and partitions can be password-protected.

**MAC TOON**

I teach UNIX.

Really? What do you teach them?

∞➔ **Don't partition for speed.** Theoretically, working with smaller volumes speeds things up because the desktop file with the disk directory for each volume is smaller, meaning the Mac can figure out where something is. But if you keep your system and related files on one partition, and your applications on another, and the documents on a third, the read/write heads are going to be jumping around a lot more. The only sure speed increase that comes with partitioning occurs if you don't automatically mount each partition at startup, but only when you need it.

∞➔ **Partitioning a small drive** doesn't make much practical sense, unless you want to set aside a small amount to "hide" some material from prying or idly curious eyes. But there's an extra benefit to partitioning a very large drive. If you recall from earlier in this chapter (you did read it, didn't you, and you were paying attention?), files take more room on larger drives because each "block" is bigger. So, a 1K file might take as much as 10K of space on a large drive. While that doesn't mean that a 100K file will take 1000K, since we're not talking about a factor of 10, but a unit of 10, that still means that you could be wasting an average of, say, 5K on each file. I have nearly 2000 items on my 140-meg partition. That means you could have maybe 7500 items on a 500-meg drive. At a 5K-per-file wastage, that's 36 megs of wasted space! Dividing the giant drive into smaller partitions means you're wasting less space because you're dealing with smaller blocks.

∞➔ **You can't repartition a disk without erasing it.** Since changing the size of a partition counts as repartitioning, that means the partition sizes are set in stone unless you want to erase all your files and reformat the disk. There are, however, some formatting utilities that let you plan ahead for increasing the size of a partition and will allow some minor repartitioning without erasing data.

•••► **HD SC Setup doesn't provide partitioning** the way I'm referring to it here. The only partitioning HD SC Setup does is setting a single giant partition for the Mac, or dividing the available space between a Mac and a non-Mac computer.

•••► **You can't set a partition as a startup.** You'll see each partition of a hard drive in the Startup Disk control panel, but the only thing the Mac keeps track of is the SCSI ID number of the device you select. Since all the partitions have the same device number, there's no way to differentiate among them, and the Mac looks only at the partition that comes first alphabetically at startup.

•••► **Avoid** *software partitioning.* Standard partitioning divides the drive magnetically, in much the same way that tracks and sectors are created. Software partitioning is a "fake" partitioning scheme that tricks the Mac into thinking it's dealing with a volume filled with different files when in reality, there's a single file on the disk that contains all your other files. Think about the nightmare of having a problem with any part of that giant (20-50 meg) file and losing the entire thing!

## Mixing System 7 & System 6 Disks

°°►  **Disks are handled differently under System 6** and System 7. That is, the way their contents are tracked is different. System 6 used a single desktop file to keep track of things. System 7 uses a special desktop database file to keep track of disk contents for any volume that's over 2 megs—in effect, everything but floppies.

So, you can use floppies back and forth between the two different systems with no problems; but, there are some minor concerns about other volumes—hard drives or removable media—that go from one system setup to another. (I'm talking about "data" disks here—ones that store information but aren't *startup* disks.)

°°►  **When you mount a System 6 drive** on a System 7 setup, you get a dialog that says: *Updating disk for new system software.* What's happening is that the Mac is creating the desktop database file it needs to keep track of the disk's contents. It's not installing system software, it doesn't change any of the other information on the disk, and you can still use the disk again on a System 6 setup.

Updating disk for new system.

°°►  **A System 7 disk can be used** on a System 6 setup with no problems, and no dialogs when you try to mount it. But you will find two extra folders on the disk: the Desktop folder and the Trash folder. They'll contain anything that the disk displayed on the desktop under System 7, or was holding in the Trash waiting for emptying.

Desktop Folder

Trash

This applies to any large disk used with System 7, whether it was always a System 7 disk, or if it had been used with System 6 previously and then was temporarily switched to System 7.

**⋯➤** **If the disk is going to stay under System 7,** you can delete the invisible file named Desktop that System 6 used. It's still on your drive and can be taking up quite a lot of room, even after a desktop rebuild under System 7.

How do you find an invisible file? With the proper utility. ResEdit is the tool of choice for hacker wannabe's, but many DAs also let you see invisible files. My favorite is DiskTools, from Fifth Generation Systems' File Director package. Any utility that lets you see an invisible file also lets you erase it, so go ahead and delete that file. DON'T delete *Desktop DB* or *Desktop DF*, the invisible files that System 7 uses.

## Disk Problems & File Recovery

**∞➤** **When you run into a serious** hard disk problem—it won't mount at all, or you get a *This disk is unreadable* dialog—don't panic. The problem may be as simple as a loose cable connection. It might be a SCSI chain problem, or it might be that one of the important files on the drive—one that keeps track of the disk contents—is corrupted. Keep in mind that it's seldom actually the disk itself—the mechanical parts or the disk media—that's at fault. All your data is still on the drive and is often recoverable. But even when you can't recover the data, the drive is usually perfectly reusable after being reformatted.

Even when you get the *disk is damaged* dialog, the Mac is seldom referring to an actual hardware problem; that's the message it gives you when it can't read the information on the disk, and that's often because a directory file is garbled.

**∞➤** **If you erase a file by mistake**, it's not necessarily gone forever. Remember, the file itself isn't erased (unless you use a special utility that overwrites a file for security reasons); the directory entry for the file is what's deleted from the disk.

As soon as you realize you've mistakenly erased a file, DON'T DO ANY MORE WORK. If you save a document, or copy a file to the disk, it's possible that the new information will be stored right over parts of the old file, making it impossible to recover. Although many recovery utilities can piece together incomplete files, you want to stack the odds in your favor.

**∞➤** **Recover trashed files with** any of the major disk utilities—MacTools or Norton's—or with a Trash-specific utility like Guaranteed Undelete (which was awarded a Blue Ribbon for Excellence back in Chapter 5).

With Norton's, for instance, you start with the first dialog shown on the following page, and choose the Quick UnErase method. Then the program searches for recently erased files and sees if their pieces are still on the disk or have been written over. It reports on the chance you have—excellent, fair, or poor—of recovering each of the files in the list, as shown in the second picture.

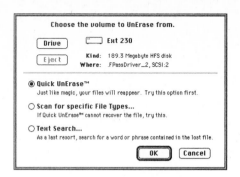

Norton's UnErase main dialog.

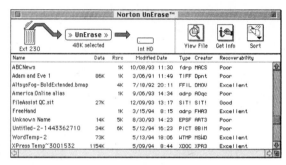

The results of a Quick UnErase

**When your hard drive won't mount,** it's not necessarily the end of the world. (Although sometimes it might as well be.) There are lots of things you can try before assuming you've got a *real* problem on your hands. But here's the main rule: *If you get the drive to mount, immediately back up any important files that are on it.* Don't tempt the SCSI gods and disk deities by shutting down the system, assuming that if you recovered it once, you can recover it again. You may never get it to mount again.

When the startup disk won't mount, you'll get the blinking question mark on startup. When it's an external drive that won't mount, everything else might be working perfectly but its disk just doesn't show up on the desktop. Or, a problem with an external drive could mess up the whole SCSI chain and not let anything else mount either—even the internal system disk.

**To mount a hard drive that won't mount** by itself, there are lots of cures to try. This list is pretty much in order of easiest to hardest, not in a "most likely to work" order:

- Shut everything off and restart. Sometimes an external hard drive doesn't mount because it wasn't ready when the Mac looked for it; turn externals on first, then the Mac.
- If it's a removable disk (CD, SyQuest, or magneto-optical), make sure you have the right extension in your Extensions folder for mounting the disk. If it is there, replace it with a fresh copy.
- Check that all cables are attached securely—while the Mac and its peripherals are turned *off*.
- Make sure there are no SCSI ID conflicts.
- Check for proper termination on the SCSI chain.

- Zap the PRAM (hold Command-Option-P-R at startup). Corrupted PRAM information sometimes keeps a hard drive from mounting.

- Rebuild the desktop at startup with Command-Option. This sometimes fixes things for a system that crashes every time it tries to mount the hard drive.

- Use a utility like SCSI Probe to mount an external drive that didn't mount at startup. If it's the internal that didn't mount, try starting with an external drive or a floppy disk and mount the internal with a SCSI utility.

- Reinstall the system software on the startup disk if that's the one that's the problem and you can see it when you start up with a different disk.

- Replace the hard drive's driver software if HD SC Setup, or the formatting utility you use, can "see" the drive.

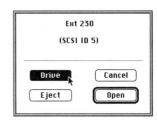

Selecting a drive in the Disk First Aid window.

$S$CSI chains and IDs are covered in the next section.

- Try Disk First Aid: click the Drive button until the problem disk is listed, click the Open button, and choose Repair Automatically from the Options menu.

- Bring out the heavy artillery: use the disk repair utility of your choice to try to get the disk mounted and repaired, or at least to recover as many files as possible from it.

Unfortunately, disk problems are frequent enough that I'm also making this list into a chart that you can tear out and stick on your wall someplace near the Mac.

•→ **When you've had major problems with a drive**, even if your disk utility has been able to repair damaged files, you should back everything up and reformat the entire drive at the earliest convenient time.

•→ **One of the scariest false alarms for a hard drive** occurs when you start up and get nothing but the question mark icon, despite the fact that the hard drive you're using (or trying to use) as the startup is spinning merrily along. This isn't always a false alarm, of course—you could have a severely damaged disk. But you might have fallen prey to an odd bug in the Mac's ROM that cropped up with the advent of System 7 and the widespread use of very large hard drives.

Here's the scenario: the Mac crashes, for one reason or another. At the next startup, the Mac checks for any hard drive damage. But to test the drive, the Mac uses a program that's in ROM—and there's a bug in the ROM. If you're using a large hard disk, and many of the files on it are fragmented, an invisible file called the *extents tree* gets very large, too, because its job is to keep track of where files—and their fragmented pieces— are stored. If the extents tree file is over 760K, and happens to be a multiple of 64, the ROM program thinks the disk is damaged. Since it can't start up from a damaged disk, it puts the blinking question mark on the screen.

But the disk isn't really damaged, and is easy to recover with the right software. Any good disk recovery program (MacTools, Norton's) will get it up and running again. In fact, the program will probably tell you that it didn't find any problem—but will go ahead and fix it anyway.

If you're wondering if your disk is susceptible to this bug, get yourself a copy of Disk Bug Checker, which Central Point Software made available free to every Mac user; you can get a copy from a user group or an online service. The program diagnoses your disk structure and lets you know if you're at risk.

To prevent the problem, if your disk is over 80MB, defragment it at reasonable intervals. Or, back it up and reformat it with the latest version of HD SC Setup (version 7.3.1 or later), which fixes the bug. Use the latest hardware system updates—versions 2.0 and later take care of the bug.

→ **When you can't revive your drive,** the data isn't necessarily lost. Some companies specialize in data recovery; it can be very expensive, but it might well be worth it. DriveSavers is one recovery company that comes highly recommended.

→ **Encrypting the data on a drive**, or using password protection for access can foil attempts to recover files when something goes wrong. If you use a security utility, make sure that it works with the disk utilities that you use.

→ **The 40- and 80-megabyte hard drives that** came in Mac II's, IIx's and SE's (Seagate mechanisms) were prone to a special problem called *stiction*—a nifty combination of stick and friction. (Well, the *word* is nifty, not the problem.) Insufficient lubricant in the spindle would keep the platters from spinning up after a shutdown. If you have one of these drives and all of a sudden it stops working, give the case a good thump with the side of your fist and try again. (And if at first you don't succeed, thump, thump again.) If you get the drive to spin up, back up all your data, because it's bound to fail again.

Apple had a free replacement policy for these drives, even if they were out of warranty, for a long time, but it's unlikely that's still going on. I guess it wouldn't hurt to ask. There was actually a formal recall on the 40-meg drives with serial numbers 335507 to 12500863.

### MAC DOGGEREL

Some drives have a dire affliction
Which is known by the epithet *stiction*.
But give them a whack,
A smack, or a thwack,
And the pounding wins over the friction.

# A MAC ALMANAC CHART

## How to Mount a Disk That Won't

•••➤  Shut down and restart.

•••➤  Make sure you have the correct extension for mounting removable media.

•••➤  Check cables and connections.

•••➤  Correct any SCSI ID conflicts.

•••➤  Check SCSI termination.

•••➤  Rebuild the desktop.

•••➤  Zap the PRAM.

•••➤  Use a mounting utility.

•••➤  Reinstall system software if it's the system disk.

•••➤  Replace the drive's driver software.

•••➤  Use Disk First Aid.

•••➤  Use a disk recovery utility.

# → SCSI DEVICES ←

## SCSI Basics

◦•→ **SCSI stands for** *small computer system interface*. It's pronounced *scuzzy*, which has an appropriately derogatory ring to it, considering the problems that sometimes plague SCSI setups.

At its heart, SCSI is simply a specific type of connection between certain computer devices. All internal hard drives and most external ones are SCSI devices. Most storage peripherals—CD-ROM drives, removable hard drives, magneto-optical drives—are also SCSI devices. There are even some printers and monitors that use SCSI connections.

> SCSI (pronounced "scuzzy" or, in the Mac community, "sexy")...

**MICHAEL D. WESLEY**
*MacUser, September 1986*

◦•→ **A SCSI connection is fast** because it's a *parallel* connection that lets more than one bit of information at a time be channeled from one place to another. Unlike the ADB *serial* bus that makes bits travel single file, a SCSI connection lets eight bits move together from one place to another.

◦•→ **SCSI speed varies from one Mac model** to another. A Classic's SCSI bus, for instance, can send 650K per second (you can think of that as 650,000 letters or characters), while a Quadra 900 speeds things along at 5MB (five million characters) per second.

◦•→ **For the fastest SCSI rates,** make sure your hardware's capabilities are matched. A fast hard drive won't do you much good on a Mac Classic; a slow hard drive will negate the Quadra's speed capability.

••→ **The SCSI-2 standard** is just starting to appear on Macs and in other computer systems. Based on how entrenched the current SCSI standard is, how many machines use it, and how long those machines last, it's going to be quite a while before it takes over. But since it offers faster transfer rates and better reliability, there's no doubt it will win in the end.

## Cables & Connectors

◦•→ **The Mac has a single SCSI port** for external connections, so if you have more than one SCSI device, you have to connect one to the other in a chain. SCSI chains cause more user grief than any other single Macintosh feature.

Since SCSI devices are connected in a single line rather than in any other formation (looped around, for instance, or in some sort of branching formation), the connection is called *daisy chaining*, after the pastoral pastime of braiding flowers together into a long rope—a connotation entirely too pleasant and benign to be intimately associated with SCSI operations.

∞♦ **The Mac can handle seven SCSI devices** in a chain, including the internal hard drive. Actually, there can be *eight* SCSI devices on a chain, but the Mac itself counts as one, so saying you can attach seven devices to it is a little clearer.

Do seven devices sound a little ridiculous? Who would ever need that many? Well, let's see what I've got here. (Okay, okay, maybe I'm not your normal user, but still ...) An internal hard drive. An internal CD-ROM drive. Two external hard drives (the 105-meg model pretty much filled up after a year or so, so I added a 230-meg model). A SyQuest (removable cartridge) drive. That's five right there. And I'd really like to add a scanner; and, every once in a while a friend comes by with an MO drive or another SyQuest when we're working on a project that needs large-file transfers. It adds up quickly!

∞♦ **The total length of a SCSI chain** should not exceed 20 feet. This actually includes the cabling *inside* the devices, so you have 6 to 12 inches per device in addition to the cables you can see. Keep the cabling as short as possible in any case: don't use a 3-foot cable when a 1-foot one can reach.

*THE MAC ALMANAC*

A SCSI chain is only as good as its weakest link.

∞♦ **There many different SCSI cables**, some of which are very common, and others for special situations.

SCSI connectors come in two different widths: 25 pins and 50 pins. The Mac has a 25-pin SCSI port, and most external devices have 50-pin SCSI ports; the ports on the Mac and on external devices are always female. So, it's left to the cable to provide male connectors in various combinations of 25- and 50-pin ends. A cable is often referred to simply by the size of the connectors on each end: a 25x50, a 50x50, and so on. A connector is often described by the number of pins it uses, with the prefix DB: DB-25, for instance.

The arsenal of SCSI cables includes:

- The *SCSI system cable* is the one that goes from the back of your Mac to the external device. It has a 25-pin male connector at one end, and a 50-pin male connector at the other. Because of the 25x50 arrangement, it can also be used to connect an external SCSI device with a 25-pin connector to another, standard 50-pin peripheral.
- The *peripheral interface cable* has 50-pin male connectors at both ends; it's made to connect one SCSI peripheral to another in a chain.

- A *cable extender* has a 50-pin male connector at one end and a 50-pin female connector at the other. If your SCSI peripheral isn't very close to your Mac, you can attach the SCSI system cable to the Mac, and then use the extender to connect the cable to the peripheral.
- A *25x25 cable* has two male 25-pin connectors. It's used for connecting the Mac to a 25-pin SCSI peripheral, or for attaching two 25-pin peripherals to each other.
- An *HDI-30 system cable* is for a PowerBook's special SCSI port; it has the standard 50-pin male connector on the other end.
- An *HDI-30 disk adapter cable* is for connecting a PowerBook to another Mac as an external drive.

Once you start hooking things together and you find you're somehow stuck with two male connectors, or a 25-pin male connector and a 50-pin female port, don't despair. There are all sorts of adapters that solve these problems. A *gender changer*, for instance, is a short adapter with either both ends male or both ends female; by attaching it to the end of one cable, you switch the gender of the connector. There are also adapters that change your 25-pin connector to 50 pins, or vice versa, without your having to use an entire cable to do it.

**PowerBooks and SCSI concerns are in Chapter 22.**

⊶❯ **Use good cables.** More than anything else—once you've followed the basic laws of cabling and termination—good, extra-heavy cables can ensure a trouble-free SCSI chain. You can usually tell a good cable from a cheap one at a glance: the good ones are thicker: they use heavier-gauge wires and thicker shielding wrapped around them. Good quality cables also have better grounding and better connections to the "hood" of the connector.

Mixing the cheap cables and the better ones in the same chain can result in some problems, too, so stick to one kind of cable. In fact, sticking to one brand is best, since cables that are constructed with different wire placements or impedances can affect the signal on the bus.

⊶❯ **Be nice to your cables.** Don't bend them any more than necessary. Don't shove the devices right next to the wall so that there's a 90-degree bend right after the connector; the wires inside the cable can break. And use the screw-in or snap-in fasteners that are on the connectors to assure a tight, firm connection.

•••❯ **One way to keep cables short** is to avoid using cables at all. If you're going to need a stack of external devices, both APS and LaCie make special connectors for stacking their drives that are more like clamps than cables, keeping the distance the SCSI signal travels to its barest minimum.

## ID Numbers

⊶❯ **Every SCSI device has an ID number,** from 0 through 7. (That's the way computers count—starting at 0, not 1.) The Mac itself is ID 7, and the internal hard drive is 0.

⊶❯ **Every device in a chain needs a unique ID** number. Most devices have little number wheels that you can adjust to set their ID numbers. Some less friendly models have little DIP switches that you have to set in various combinations to represent numbers. For instance: There are four switches and one up and three down means 1; the first and third ones up and the other two down means 3, and so on, in some ridiculous non-intuitive pattern. Some extremely unfriendly models have their SCSI numbers set internally; avoid these like the plague.

However you set the ID numbers on your SCSI peripherals, make sure they're set to be unique in the chain.

•••♦ **You can easily find out the SCSI ID number** for any hard drive: just use the Get Info command on its icon on the desktop. The Info window displays the ID number in the *Where* information.

•••♦ **When the Mac is scanning for external devices** at startup, it looks for and mounts them according to their SCSI IDs, not according to the order in which you've connected them to the Mac.

•••♦ **Set an external CD-ROM drive's ID** to 3. That's the number that internal CD-ROM drives are set to, and you're less likely to run into problems with swapping other components if there's some standard to follow. (Unless, of course, you're connecting an external CD-ROM drive to a system that already has an internal one—then, it should be anything but 3!)

•••♦ **Internal hard drives are set to ID 0.** This rarely presents a problem, since you have only one internal hard drive in a Mac. But if you take the internal hard drive out because it's being replaced with a larger one, you can put the old one in a case, add a power supply, and use it as a supplemental external hard drive. But if the ID number is hard-wired on the drive, you can't use a second ID 0 with another Mac.

Internal hard drives use jumpers on the circuit board to indicate the SCSI ID. There's a set of six pins (three pairs of two), usually at the edge of the board; no jumpers between them means the ID is 0. Adding a jumper between one or more pairs of pins changes the number. (Obviously, this is not a project for the faint-of-heart.)

•••♦ **The internal hard drive in a PowerBook** is, as usual, set to ID 0, but when it's used as an external SCSI device for a desk Mac (in SCSI disk mode), it defaults to an ID of 1. A factory-installed internal drive in a Duo Dock defaults to 1, too.

S CSI disk mode is covered in Chapter 22.

## Chains & Termination

°°•♦ **SCSI devices need *termination*** somewhere along the chain. (Even just your Mac and its internal drive constitute a chain, albeit a short one.) Termination keeps the signal on the SCSI chain from echoing back on the chain and disrupting the signal, which would interfere with the data being passed along.

∘•◗ **Termination is usually added by** means of a (guess what!) *terminator*, which looks somewhat like the connector on a SCSI cable, but without the cable attached. Some terminators are basically dead-ends: a 50-pin connector on one side and a "blank wall" on the other. Some are *pass-through* terminators that have 50-pin connectors on both sides so you can connect another cable if you have to. You can use a pass-through connector at the end of a chain the same way you would a dead-end one.

∘•◗ **A *self-terminating* device** has termination built into it. This was very popular, and pretty handy, when most Macs had, at the most, a single external device that had to be terminated. But a self-terminating device is a real pain when you have multiple SCSI devices, since it always has to be the last item in the chain.

If you're the intrepid type, you can open the case of a self-terminating device and remove the termination; usually it's three little resistor packs, and sometimes there's a separate cover in the case so you can get at them without having to open the whole case. Make sure you note exactly how they're connected, since they shouldn't be reinserted backwards.

••◗ **The basic rule of termination** is that the first and last devices in a chain need to be terminated, but none of the middle devices should have any termination at all. Since a Mac's internal hard drive is terminated, this means that all you have to worry about is slapping a terminator on the last device in a chain—whether that's the single external hard drive you're using, or the fourth item in a daisy chain.

••◗ **Extra termination is sometimes needed on a long** SCSI chain. The general recommendation is that if the chain is over 10 feet in length, you should add a terminator around the 10-foot mark; this is in addition to the termination at the beginning and the end of the chain. But if you have a long chain that's not giving you any problems—leave it alone!

### OOH, EEE, OOH AH AH ...

Working with SCSI chains—or getting them to work—is often referred to as a *black art*. *The New Hacker's Dictionary* (MIT Press) provides several other phrases along those lines, to describe procedures and issues that require varying degrees of arcane knowledge. In order of seriousity, we have:

- black art
- black magic
- deep magic
- heavy wizardry
- voodoo programming

•••◗ **Later-model Macs have *active termination*.** This is a very intelligent type of termination that provides the proper amount of termination for internal devices (the hard drive and CD-ROM drive, for instance) when there are no external SCSI devices, but turns itself off when it detects the presence of an external SCSI device that provides its own termination.

*Active termination* is also the phrase used to describe a terminator that also provides some diagnostic capabilities for problems in the SCSI chain.

•••◗ **For a Mac without an internal hard drive,** you need to terminate the external hard drive you're using. This is usually a simple matter of using one of the SCSI connectors on the hard drive to attach it to the Mac and the other for the terminator.

If you're connecting more than one device to a Mac without an internal hard drive, you should use one terminator *before* the first hard drive, and another at the end of the chain. This means you need a pass-through terminator that connects to the back of the drive and lets you hook up the cable from the Mac. A standard terminator on the last device takes care of the other end of the chain.

•••◗ **The Mac IIfx has special termination** requirements because it uses a slightly different SCSI chip. You need something known as the *black terminator* for items on an fx's SCSI chain.

•••◗ *Termination power* is different from termination; termination power—"term power" to the techies—helps send the signal along the bus, and is usually provided by the Mac itself, as well as by the external SCSI device.

The only time this becomes an issue is if you hook up a device with no termination power to a Mac that provides no termination power. Most devices provide power; some older hard drives don't. And all the Macs except the Mac Plus and the PowerBooks (and Mac Portable) provide termination power. Without termination power, the SCSI chain can't work, so hooking up a PowerBook as an external SCSI device to a Mac Plus turns into a problem.

## Also...

∞◗ **Keep every device in a chain turned on** when you're using your Mac. Just because you're not going to use, say, the scanner during a work session doesn't mean you can leave it off. A properly working SCSI chain can fast lose its manners if any one of the devices in the chain is off.

∞◗ **Don't turn on or connect** a SCSI device if your Mac is already up and running.

∞◗ **A SCSI chain problem** can make itself known in several ways. Here are the most common, listed in rough order of how likely they are to occur:

- The icon of a hard drive or other device doesn't show up on the desktop.
- The icon of one of the devices shows up intermittently on the desktop.

- The Mac refuses to start up at all, displaying either the Sad Mac on a dark screen, or not getting past the blinking question mark icon.
- The Mac crashes at startup, or soon thereafter, or unexpectedly during use, or especially when trying to access an external device.
- There are continual read-write errors with a SCSI device.
- You get a Sad Mac and the Chimes of Doom at startup.

Chimes of Doom?? See Chapter 24.

⦿→ **When you think you have a SCSI problem,** it takes a little detective work to narrow down the cause. If everything works until you add a new device to the chain, and then it stops working, you can be sure beyond a reasonable doubt that it's a SCSI problem. If you're not sure, remove all your SCSI devices and see if your Mac works (especially if you're getting a Sad Mac on startup). Here are some of the SCSI gymnastics you'll have to try when you run into a problem:

- Check the ID numbers on each device.
- Remove and reattach all the cables, in case one wasn't seated properly the first time. (Do this with all devices *off*.)
- If you have more than one device on the chain, test each device alone with the Mac to make sure they all work.
- Replace or swap cables to test that each cable you're using is working properly. Check that all the pins in the connectors are straight and clean. (Minor oxidation on connectors can be rubbed off with a pencil eraser.)
- Change the way cables go in and out of the devices: if the "in" cable is in the top port, put it in the bottom, and put the "out" cable or the terminator in the top port. (Strange, but it has made a difference for some people!)
- Try to shorten the overall length of the SCSI chain by using shorter cables from one device to another.
- Double-check the termination of each device—you may have something in the middle of the chain that's internally terminated.
- Add or remove terminators, even if you're already following the basic termination rule of one at the beginning and one at the end of the chain. Keep in mind that the terminator device itself might be defective.
- Swap the order of the devices in the chain. (Strange, but true: sometimes a different order works even with all the same devices, cables, and termination.)

SCSI SENTRY

⦿→ **SCSI Sentry** is a great little device that can analyze and straighten out SCSI and termination problems. It's not much bigger than a terminator, and has several lights on it that let you know what's going on in the SCSI chain—when information is being requested, and when it's being provided. Checking which lights are on or off can help determine what the SCSI problem is: a bad or loose cable, a problem in the Mac itself, a lack of power, an ID conflict. SCSI Sentry also provides termination and termination power if it's needed on the chain. [APS Technologies]

# A MAC ALMANAC LIST

## 7 Ways to Avoid SCSI Problems

**1**    Use good-quality cables.

**2**    Keep all cables the same quality—and the same brand.

**3**    Keep total cabling as short as possible.

**4**    Fasten all connectors securely.

**5**    Provide proper termination.

**6**    Keep all devices on the chain turned on.

**7**    Avoid ID conflicts.

# ☆ CD-ROM (& OTHER) DRIVES ☆

## Removable Media

•••❯ ***Removable media* refers to** high-capacity storage systems that let you change disks or cartridges. (Isn't that a clever definition? The "high-capacity" adjective rules out floppy disks.) Removable media combine the storage capacity of a hard drive with the convenience of a floppy drive.

The most popular types of removable media for the Mac are CD-ROM discs, SyQuest cartridges, and magneto-optical (MO) drives. I'll deal with each of them in more detail later.

•••❯ **Removable cartridges or disks** are used in SCSI devices, which presents a problem: When the Mac starts up, it checks the SCSI chain for devices that are present, and it doesn't check for them again. So, an empty CD-ROM drive has nothing to mount at startup, but when you insert a CD later, the Mac isn't looking there. The same holds true for SyQuest and MO drives. And if there's an inserted disk at startup, the Mac has no way of knowing when you eject the disk, because it doesn't expect SCSI devices to change after startup.

If you've already used CDs with your system, you're wondering what I'm talking about, since you know that if you insert a CD it appears on your desktop with no further ado, and you can eject it the same way you eject a floppy. But this works because you have the proper extension in your Extensions folder—one that watches for activity with the CD-ROM drive. And, in fact, SyQuest drives and MO drives also come with system extensions that let the Mac keep track of what you're doing with their disks. If you watch an empty CD-ROM drive while you're working, you'll notice its read/write light flashing every once in a while as the Mac checks whether it has anything in it.

•••❯ **If you use more than one removable disk system** at a time (right now, for instance, I have all three—a SyQuest, an MO, and a CD-ROM drive—attached to my Mac), you don't need an extension for each one. There are utilities that will take care of all of them. I use Drive7Rem, which comes with the Drive 7 formatting utility. It works in the background to mount and dismount any of the removable media, and I can also use the control panel to check all the SCSI devices in the chain and mount any of them on an individual basis if there's a problem. [Casa Blanca Works]

•••❯ **Removable cartridges don't have to mount automatically.** If you keep a SCSI device on your Mac but use it only occasionally, you might not want an extension that continually scans the SCSI chain for disk "events." You can use a utility like SCSI Probe to manually mount and dismount cartridges as you need them. There's also an FKEY, MountEm, that lets you mount volumes with a simple key combination. [Billy Steinberg]

•••❯ **Removable cartridges** (SyQuest or MO, since you can't write to CDs) are great for making backup or archival copies of your work. You don't have to tie up a regular hard drive with this relatively static information, and you don't have to juggle a hundred floppies to store a lot of information.

•◆ **You can't dismount a volume**—whether it's a floppy, a file server, or some removable media when one of its files is in use; you just get the dialog shown here.

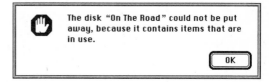

An open document is obviously in use, but sometimes a small utility, a font, or a sound may be the opened file that's preventing the dismount. Sometimes a CD disc that's set to be shared across a network won't dismount even though none of its files is actually in use.

When all else fails, and you just can't figure out what's preventing the disk from being freed up, you can always shut down and start again without that disk in the drive.

•◆ **Sometimes you can't dismount** a disk or cartridge because the Mac thinks it's being shared on a network, even when it's not, and even when you're not on a network. You'll get a dialog like the one shown here if you try to eject the disk.

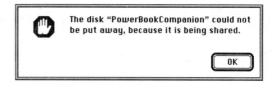

The problem stems from the fact that the disk was already in the drive when you started the Mac, and file sharing was turned on in the Sharing Setup control panel. Although you never explicitly shared the disk with the Finder's Sharing command, you have to turn off file sharing in the control panel in order to "release" the disk.

## Removables as Startups

•◆ **Removable disks can be used as startups**, which is particularly handy when there's system software on the removable disk that you want to install on your internal drive. In fact, Macs with built-in CD-ROM drives come with a CD system disk.

Use the Startup Disk control panel to choose the startup device. As long as any disk is inserted in the device, it appears in the control panel—it doesn't have to be a disk with a system on it. This picture shows six items in my control panel. Only one, the Int HD, is actually a system disk. The two other hard drives contain data; AlmanacBackup is a SyQuest data cartridge; Wet Set is a CD of clip art; PowerBKCompanion is an MO data disk.

When you select a disk in the Startup Disk control panel, you're actually selecting the *device*, not the particular disk inside it. So, as long as there's a system disk in it at the next startup, you can start from it.

∞❥ **If you haven't selected an external device** as the startup, but want the Mac to start up from there, hold down Command-Shift-Option-Delete to bypass the internal hard drive as the startup. The time you'll *really* need this trick is when there's something wrong with the hard drive that's keeping the Mac from starting up at all. But remember that the internal won't mount at all when you bypass it—you'll need a utility like SCSIProbe to get it on the desktop.

∞❥ **Reset the startup drive to the internal** hard drive when you're finished with the external disk as the system disk or installer so the Mac won't keep looking to that drive as the startup. You'll find that an empty removable drive still set as the startup makes the Mac cycle around the SCSI chain several times before it finally uses the internal hard drive.

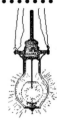

**BRIGHT IDEAS #4**

**Q.** How many Microsoft programmers does it take to change a light bulb?

**A.** None. Bill Gates will declare darkness a new world standard.

## CD-ROM Drives & Disks

∞❥ **CDs are one-way media:** you can read them, but you can't write to them. They're great for storing a ton of information (oh, okay—550 megs or so) that you want to retrieve but not change—like dictionaries, encyclopedias, font and graphic collections, and even large-scale games.

The CD-ROM drives built into the Mac can play regular audio CDs as well as retrieve information from those formatted for computer use. There are even disks that combine audio and computer information.

∞❥ **There are seven extensions** in Apple's system software for complete CD access: Foreign File Access, High Sierra File Access, ISO 9660 Access, Audio CD Access, Apple CD-ROM, Apple Photo Access, and CD Remote INIT.

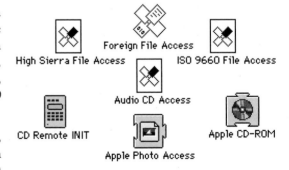

In addition, there's a control panel, AppleCD Speed Switch (covered in Chapter 8 and later in this chapter) and a desk accessory, CD Remote (covered in detail in Chapter 7).

∞❥ **CD-ROM drives are slow** compared to hard drives. This is obvious when you compare their specifications: Average access time on a hard drive is 10-30 milliseconds, while on a CD it's 300-650 milliseconds. (This is probably one of the few times in your life you'll consider 600 milliseconds *slow.*) But you don't need to look at the numbers to see the difference: when you're retrieving information from the CD, you'll notice right away.

If you're shopping for a CD-ROM drive, make sure it has an access time of no more than 300 ms, or it will drive you crazy; it won't be worth the money you save buying a slower drive.

→ **The AppleCD Speed Switch** control panel lets you choose between two speeds for the data transfer between the CD-ROM drive and the Mac. Leave it at the Faster speed unless you're having problems with a program that's retrieving data from the CD. (Some older programs don't know how to deal with the now-standard double speed operation of most CD-ROM drives.)

→ **You can set the CD-ROM drive to be the startup** if you want to temporarily run the Mac from a CD system disk. You'll want to do this only temporarily because CD retrieval is too slow to make it a viable system disk; but if you want to install new system software from a CD to the internal hard drive, it's the best way to do it. (Using removable disks as startups is covered a few pages back, under—you guessed it— *Removables as Startups.*)

→ **Some Macs can't use CDs as startups.** All the early compacts, the Plus, SE, SE/30, Mac Portable, Mac II, IIx, IIcx, and Classic share this flaw.

→ **The SCSI ID** of an internal CD-ROM drive is set to 3.

→ **PhotoCD is a technology from Kodak**, the picture people. It's a way of putting pictures onto a CD in a digital format that a computer can access. Kodak's PhotoCD players are made to hook up to television sets, but when you use a computer CD-ROM drive and let the computer access the pictures, you can play all sorts of electronic games with the images. Here are the things you need to know about PhotoCD:

- To access a PhotoCD disk on the Mac, you need the Apple Photo Access extension in the Extensions folder.
- About 100 color photos fit on a CD.
- Most Kodak film processing labs can put the photos from your negatives onto a CD.
- A lab that can process negatives to a CD can also process prints *from* your CD images.
- *Multi-session* is the technology that lets photos be put on a CD at different times instead of all at once. If your CD-ROM drive doesn't have multi-session capability (the Mac's built-in drive does), you won't be able to access any but the first group of images.

## SyQuest

∘∘➤ **SyQuest drives were the first** removable media available for the Mac. SyQuest drives use mechanisms built by—who else?—SyQuest, but the overall drive usually has another manufacturer's name on it. These drives use cartridges (SyQuest cartridges, of course) that hold 40-270 megabytes of information on them.

∘∘➤ **Time was, I wouldn't touch a SyQuest with** a ten-foot SCSI cable. On Mac systems, they seemed to cause nothing but trouble, and there was never a User Group meeting that didn't include questions asked and frustrations aired by SyQuest users.

Things have improved, to say the least. But I was burned by early experiences, and didn't want to invest in a SyQuest drive, even though I needed one for this book project. (Boy, those laid-out pages sure take a lot of room!) I mentioned this to the president of APS Technologies and asked him to reassure me as to the current state of SyQuest. His reply was the loan of a SyQuest drive. I had no cartridge problems, no SCSI problems, no problems of any kind, after months of heavy duty use. So, I bought it!

∘∘➤ **The standard cartridge size** for SyQuests was 44MB for a long time. 88MB cartridges became available after several years, but before they became a standard of any kind, 105-meg cartridges were introduced.

The trick here is that, much like the floppy drive evolution, new, higher-capacity cartridges require new drives. The most common technologies at this point are:

- 44 drives that format, read, and write 44MB cartridges.
- 88 drives that format, read, and write 88MB cartridges.
- 44/88 drives that read and write 44MB cartridges, and format, read, and write 88MB cartridges.

Note that the 44/88 drives can't format 44MB cartridges, although they can use them. This isn't a problem because you can buy pre-formatted disks, and you can always erase their entire contents when you want to.

In addition, there are SyQuest cartridges that hold 105 and 270 megs of data, and the drives that can handle those capacities.

## Other Drives

∘∘➤ **A magneto-optical drive,** commonly referred to as MO, is one that uses an entirely different technology to store vast amounts of information in a very small space. A 128MB disk is about 3.25 inches square—a little smaller than a floppy disk—and it's only about twice as thick. AND (that's a big "and," get it?) information on an MO disk will last for decades, unlike the relatively fragile magnetic media in other drives. An MO drive works a little more slowly than a SyQuest, but it's very likely going to take over as the removable media of choice.

••➤ **Bernoulli drives never caught on much** in the Mac world; I'm not sure they're still famous in the rest of the computer world, either.

The eighteenth-century physicist Daniel Bernoulli put forth the Bernoulli Theorem: air pressure, or fluid pressure, decreases when it's moving (relative to an object, which actually might be the moving part of the setup).* A Bernoulli drive uses this effect to keep a flexible disk inside a cartridge floating on a cushion of air, spinning very close (to within a few thousandths of an inch) to the read/write head. The air stream inside a Bernoulli drive also serves to puff away any particles of dust that might be on the disk; and, since the disk is so flexible, an errant particle caught between it and the read/write head won't cause any damage—the disk bends away from the head and you get a temporary read/write error on the Mac.

> *You trust this theorem every time you step onto an airplane.

I don't know why Bernoulli drives didn't make an impact in the Mac market. My guess is that their manufacturers ignored it for too long, and other storage media became standard.

···➤ **A RAID is an interesting** concept for hard drives (not to mention an interesting acronym). It stands for *redundant array of inexpensive disks*. Isn't that cute? It means you have a stack of hard drives attached to your Mac that are pretty much treated as a single unit. In one approach, the data going to and from the disks is split across the two disk to save time by having two read/write operations going at once. But if either drive fails mechanically, you lose all your data because everything exists split across the two drives. Other arrays work with more disks, and they mirror the disk operations so you're always making two copies at a time.

A RAID is very expensive, despite the I in its name; each disk might be inexpensive, but by the time you stack them up and get the right hardware and software to make use of them, they're very expensive, and unnecessary for most Mac users—even in business situations.

## → BACKING UP ←

## Backup Basics

∞➤ **The most important preventive medicine** in computing is easy, and it's also free—how can you *not* do it?* *Backing up* your work means making an extra copy of it so that if something happens to the original, you don't have to start all over again. You can start with the copy and update it to include whatever was added to the original since the copy was made.

> *Of course, wearing a seatbelt is easy and free and can prevent major disasters like disfigurement and death, but an awful lot of people don't do that, either.

Making backups is tedious and time-consuming, even if it's "only" from a 40- or 80-meg drive. Start with a 105- or 230-meg drive full of information, and you're talking *major* time invested every time you back up. That's probably why so many people avoid it. But, trust me, it's worth the time.

> There are only two kinds of computer users: those who have lost data, and those who are about to.
>
> — *THE MAC ALMANAC*

••→ **Sometimes a single file** gets corrupted and can't be opened, even though everything else on the drive is fine. In fact, losing a file to the occasional vagaries of electronic storage is more common than losing an entire hard disk. So, making two copies of a file on the same disk is an easy strategy to prevent some disasters.

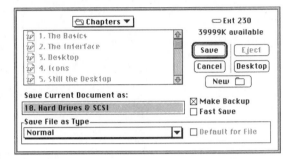

Word's Save dialog offers an automatic backup copy.

You won't want to bother with, say, a thank-you note that you type, but for a large file that you work on over the course of days or weeks, an extra copy right in the same folder as the original might come in handy some day. Some applications, like Microsoft Word, give you the option of saving two copies of the file automatically.

••→ **Backups can be full, partial, or incremental.** A full backup is pretty much a mirror image of your hard drive. A partial backup, which is plenty for most people, backs up only the data (documents) on the hard drive. An incremental backup is one that preserves the previous version of a changed document as well as making a copy of the new version.

••→ **The safest backup strategy** is to keep *three* copies of everything—the working copy on your hard drive, the main backup on another disk, and a third backup "offsite." This may seem like over-kill, but if your business depends on your records, and something disastrous happens to your office, destroying all its contents, both the working and the backup copies are going to be lost. For a home computer, an offsite backup might not be possible or necessary, but at least two copies of important items are still called for.

••→ **You don't have to back up everything.** You should reinstall your system and applications if your drive is ruined; you can do that from the master disks. So, it's your documents that you really need to back up.

Reinstalling a system is covered in Chapter 22.

It's also handy to back up the utilities that make your system special. Having your fonts, sounds, extensions, and control panels in one place to add to a freshly installed system instead of having to gather them up from their original sources again makes a system reinstall much less painful.

••→ *Archive* **generally refers to** a file that's no longer in use but is saved in case you ever need it again. Sometimes backup copies are called archives, and the word is also used to describe files that have been compressed, especially into a single file.

# A MAC ALMANAC LIST

## 6 Things You Forget to Back Up

**1** Desk accessory files (the Scrapbook, a Calendar DA, the Note Pad or its replacement)

**2** Preferences and Settings file for your applications and utilities

**3** Address books for email programs

**4** Dictionaries for applications and spelling checkers

**5** Glossaries for applications

**6** Macro files for macro utilities

## How & When

∞♦ **How often you should back up** depends on how much information and/or time you stand to lose. Do you want to re-create a day's work, a week's work, or a month's? You may not even want to re-create more than a couple of hours' work, but you will be forced to if your drive dies unexpectedly.

∞♦ **What backup media you use** depends on how much you have to back up, and what program you have to back it up on. Your choices range from floppies to external hard drives to removable hard drives to tape backup machines.

It's not impossible to back up to floppies. In fact, for many people, it's the perfect solution. Since you're only backing up your documents, and not your whole drive, floppies might work for you—if your documents are of reasonable size. If you do graphics or layout work, forget it. But simple word processor and spreadsheet documents easily fit onto floppies.

∞♦ **Don't scoff at paper backups.** They're not much good for complicated graphics, but for straightforward data—your checkbook, for instance—they're extra insurance if all your electronic copies dissolve in the great electronic ether.

> A good scare is worth more to a man than good advice.
>
> E.W. HOWE
> (1853-1937)

∞♦ **For manual backups,** use the Finder's Find command to help you find the files modified after a specific date, or created by a certain program.

∞♦ **Backup utilities take different approaches** to saving your work, and which one is best for you depends on how you work, what you have to back up, how often you do backups, what media you back up onto, and so on. Here are some of the things you should consider when looking for a backup utility:

- Can you back up onto the media of your choice? Will the utility back up onto floppies, another hard drive, removable disks, a tape back up?
- Can the utility run unattended so you won't have to spend hours watching the Mac do backups?
- Can you specify which files will be backed up, or are you forced to back up the whole drive each time? And can you specify *types* of files (all PageMaker files, for instance) instead of just naming the files you want backed up?
- Are the backups files that the Finder can read so you can copy them back easily, or are they in a special format that only the backup utility can handle? Although it's nice to have Finder-readable files, utilities that work in their own formats generally work much faster, and the backups take less room.
- Can the utility store large files on floppies, either by compressing them, splitting them across floppies, or a combination of the two methods?

∞◊ **There are many backup utilities** in the Mac market; Retrospect, DiskFit, Redux, and FastBack are all excellent programs, but Retrospect usually comes out ahead in roundup reviews of point-by-point feature and performance comparisons. In addition, many general disk utilities, like MacTools and Norton Utilities, include backup programs. [Retrospect and DiskFit, Dantz Development; Redux, Inline Design; FastBack, Fifth Generation]

∞◊ **"File-synching" programs made to keep PowerBook files** in "sync" with a desk Mac also double as backup utilities. In fact, that's all I use now as backup software. I waffle between PowerMerge and FileRunner; Inline Sync has also received many favorable reviews, but I think it needs an interface overhaul. [PowerMerge, Leader Technology; FileRunner MBS Technology; Inline Sync, Inline Design]

There's more about syncing utilities in Chapter 22.

••◊ **Turn up the disk cache in** the Memory control panel when you're using a backup utility; most backup programs work faster with a larger cache. Don't forget that you'll have to restart the Mac after you set the cache for it to take effect. You might also want to give the backup program a larger memory allocation when you're backing up a lot of files.

••◊ **If your backup utility insists on doing the entire drive,** get another utility. Well, okay, consider this alternative: partition your drive so that the backup software backs up only the items on a smaller partition instead of the whole drive. Of course, that means you'd still have to buy another utility—the partitioning software.

# Using the Mac

# CHAPTER 19
# APPLICATIONS & DOCUMENTS

In a few minutes a computer can make a mistake so great that it would take many men many months to equal it.

MERLE L. MEACHAM

The incredibly useful information in this chapter includes:

•••> 34—count 'em!—ways to launch an application.

•••> Just what all those decimal and double-decimal numbers mean in software version numbers.

•••> How to buy software. And how not to.

•••> The difference between commercial and freeware/shareware software.

•••> How to get the most out of your software.

•••> How to launch, run, and hide.

•••> Which Apple utility started out with the name Tiny Toons.

•••> Umpteen shortcuts in Open and Save dialogs.

•••> What "drag and drop" is in System 7. And what it becomes in System 7.5.

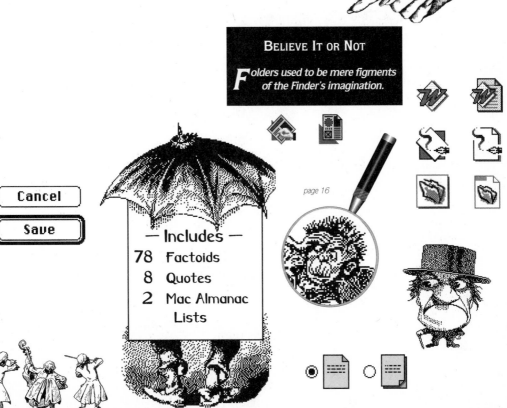

**BELIEVE IT OR NOT**

*F*olders used to be mere figments of the Finder's imagination.

page 16

Cancel

Save

— Includes —

78 Factoids

8 Quotes

2 Mac Almanac Lists

# ≕ SOFTWARE BASICS ≔

## In General

∞•❱ **Software is** the stuff that makes the Mac do things for you—or with you. The Mac without software would be pretty much like a stereo setup with no tapes or CDs—you have the machine, but there's no music to play on it.

∞•❱ **A software program is continually developed** into something slightly different and, usually, better. Sometimes the development is a result of operating system enhancements, sometimes it's a response to user feedback, and sometimes it's just trying to keep up with or beat the competition. Oh—and sometimes it's because the current version doesn't work right. Whatever the reason, the result of this continual development is that users need to keep updating their software to keep up with the latest versions.

A total reworking of a product usually results in its getting a new name: FileMaker, for instance, became FileMaker Plus, FileMaker II, and then FileMaker Pro. But you can tell the extent of an upgrade by its version number, too. A whole-number jump indicates as major an upgrade as a new name: Excel 1.0, Excel 2.0. A decimal number tacked onto a version number is more minor: HyperCard 2.1, or PageMaker 3.01. Whether the number is a tenth or a hundredth is usually indicative of how many changes were made, whether they were minor or major—and how much you'll pay for the upgrade. Some minor upgrades fix obscure (and sometimes not-so-obscure) bugs; some update the program so that it stays compatible with another upgraded program, or with new system software.

Roman numerals, by the way, aren't the same as version numbers. Roman numerals are part of the name; so, you can have FileMaker Pro II 2.0 and one number's the name, and the other is the version.

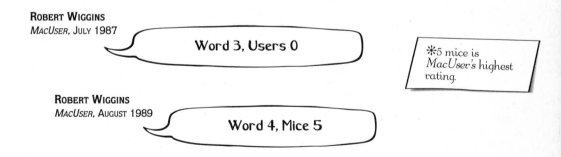

ROBERT WIGGINS
*MacUser*, JULY 1987

Word 3, Users 0

*❋5 mice is MacUser's highest rating.*

ROBERT WIGGINS
*MacUser*, AUGUST 1989

Word 4, Mice 5

•••❱ **You don't own the software you buy.** You purchase a *license to use the software*. And the licensing agreement—which you agree to just by opening the package (or so you're told by the manufacturer), usually allows you to run a single package on a single Mac. That sounds reasonable, but it's easy to start running into problems. What if you own a desk Mac and a PowerBook? Sometimes you need the software on one, sometimes on the other, and it's ridiculous to have to buy two copies of a $600 word processor just so you can keep typing no matter where you are.

But licensing agreements are becoming a little more reasonable. Some of them are *single-user* licenses instead of *single-machine* licenses, which lets you legally run the software on any machine you happen to be using. And some programs are *meant* to be run on more than one machine—a syncing program, for instance, that keeps your PowerBook and desk machine up-to-date with each other.

••**◗ Piracy hurts everyone.** Piracy is the unauthorized copying and distribution of software—cheating the publisher of its profits. In fact, piracy is so rampant that sometimes the publisher is cheated of its *costs*, never mind its profits. There are costs associated with the research and development of a product; without profits from one version, development on the next version suffers. Some experts estimate that for every legal copy of a popular piece of software sold, there are five illegal copies being used.

••**◗ *Copy protection* is** any scheme used by a software manufacturer to prevent piracy. Due to so many consumer complaints, restrictive copy protection schemes—like having to insert a master "key" disk every time you launch a program from a hard drive—are seldom used; unfortunately, that approach is still used on many games. Another approach that's popular for games is making you type in something from the documentation (" the third letter of the fourth word in the eighth line of page 28"). This sounds benign at first—until you've told the kids to put away that booklet for the zillionth time, or they've lost it. (And can't you just copy the documentation, anyway?)

Publishers have the right to protect their work, but often the protection interferes with your using the program. The most popular, and least intrusive approach for single-machine users, is that of serial numbers: Each copy of a program has an individual serial number. You have to type it in when you install the software on your hard drive. You need it if you call in for support. But if you're working on a network, the program won't run if another copy with the same serial number is running; while that seems fair enough, the fact that it continually checks the network for other copies of itself adds traffic to the network and can slow things down or cause other problems.

••**◗ You benefit from the leapfrog effect** in software design. What's that? Well, when BitDiddler comes out with ten nifty features, and then ByteDabbler comes out with fifteen, BitDiddler is rewritten to give you *twenty* features. As a result, users get to choose from programs that can do all sorts of things.

••**◗ You pay for *creeping featuritis*.** What's that? It's the leapfrog effect gone wild. As competing programs add features so they'll look good in a comparison chart, you can't find a simple program anymore. And you pay for features you can't use in many ways: money, learning time, disk space, speed, and memory when you run the program.

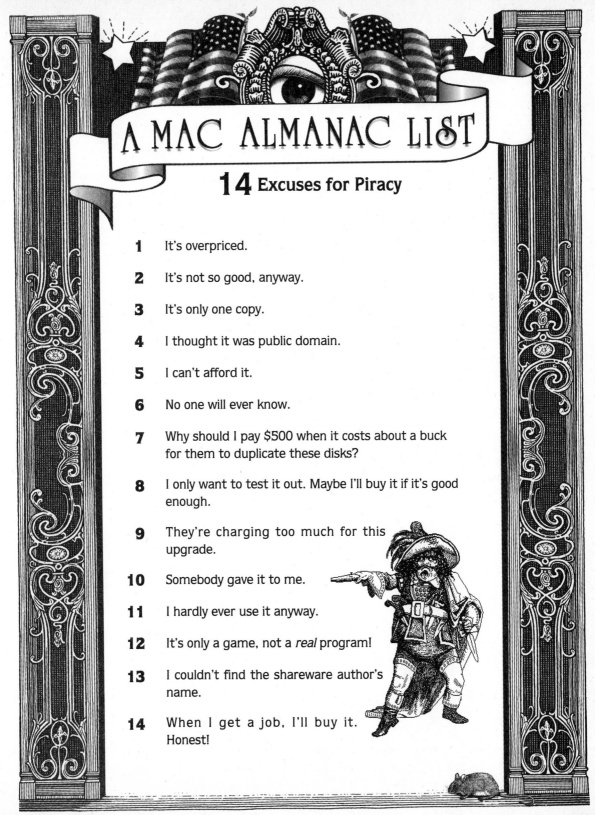

# A MAC ALMANAC LIST

## 14 Excuses for Piracy

1  It's overpriced.

2  It's not so good, anyway.

3  It's only one copy.

4  I thought it was public domain.

5  I can't afford it.

6  No one will ever know.

7  Why should I pay $500 when it costs about a buck for them to duplicate these disks?

8  I only want to test it out. Maybe I'll buy it if it's good enough.

9  They're charging too much for this upgrade.

10  Somebody gave it to me.

11  I hardly ever use it anyway.

12  It's only a game, not a *real* program!

13  I couldn't find the shareware author's name.

14  When I get a job, I'll buy it. Honest!

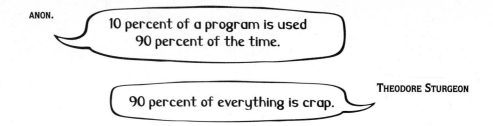

ANON.

> 10 percent of a program is used
> 90 percent of the time.

THEODORE STURGEON

> 90 percent of everything is crap.

⮞ **Don't use beta software.** When a program is in the very early stages of development, it's referred to as an *alpha* version, or *being in alpha*. The second stage, when the program looks like it's supposed to look and, theoretically, behaves the way it's supposed to, is called *beta*. But beta is strictly a testing stage, where the programmers work out all the bugs. Beta software can be pretty dangerous—you can wind up with corrupted files and disks if it's *really* buggy. Many beta versions of software keep a *b* or *ß* character in their version numbers.

**BRIGHT IDEAS #5**

**Q.** How many beta testers does it take to change a light bulb?

**A.** "We just find problems. We don't fix them.

⮞ **Compatibility with System 7** is less and less of an issue as time goes by. Most programs on the market today will run under System 7 even if they don't take advantage of all its features. But you do have to watch out for compatibility problems as minor updates to System 7 show up: there were problems for some programs from System 7.0 to System 7.1, and from System 7.1 to System 7.5. Some utilities, especially shareware programs, have problems when there's even a minor update to a current system.

Don't ever update your system unless you're absolutely, positively, without a doubt *sure* that the applications and utilities you need to use will work under the update.

## How to Buy (& Upgrade)

⮞ **Picking the right program** isn't as simple as it may seem at first: after all, you want an application that does what you need at a price that fits your budget. But in any major software category, you'll find several programs that meet your basic needs, and they'll probably be comparably priced. So, here's a list of questions you should ask about a program before buying it:

- Is it free from bugs that would keep it from running smoothly?
- Is it easy to learn? Does it have good, clear documentation?
- Is it easy to use? There's always a trade-off between ease-of-use and power, but

that's no reason for a powerful program to make things even more difficult by bad interface implementation and poor design decisions.

- Is it powerful enough? It should have all the features you need, and then some, so you'll have room to grow.
- Is it compatible with the other software you use?
- Is the manufacturer a reputable company that's been around for a while and gives every indication that it will be around in the future? (But don't ignore a new company if it has a terrific product.)
- Does the publisher provide support—free or inexpensive upgrades, a telephone help line—an 800-number support line?

**Most people find the answers** to the questions posed in the last entry *after* they buy the software. That's when they find out that the software doesn't work with their system or utilities, or that the company provides little or no technical support, and no free upgrades for buggy programs. So, how do you avoid buying a pig in a poke?

- Read product reviews in the major magazines (*MacWeek, MacUser, Macworld*). They're not always on the mark, but they're sure to provide helpful information and general advice.
- Talk to other people. Start at your Apple dealer or software store, but don't limit yourself to store personnel—strike up a conversation with other customers. Find a user's group and ask questions there. If you use an online service, ask there— you'll get more answers than you can deal with.
- Ask a dealer for a hands-on demonstration. (Okay, that's a long shot—but you can *try!*)
- Check with the manufacturer to see if there's a demo version of the program available. Some programs have demonstration versions that do everything but save or print a document.
- Find a book about the product at a computer or bookstore. A major program may have several how-to books written about it; you'll get much more information about the product's features than can be squeezed into a 2500-word magazine review. If you're considering the purchase of a $600 program, a book is a wise $20 investment.
- If you're in the vicinity of a Macintosh show—major ones are held in Boston and San Francisco every year, and hundreds of smaller and special-interest ones are held around the country—stop in and watch some demos and ask questions.

**Buy cheap. Buy mail order.** Unless you live in one of the few metropolitan areas that has a computer store that actually demonstrates the software it sells, with knowledgeable personnel, there's no reason to buy your software in a store. Reputable mail-order companies offer the best discounts around, and you can even have your software delivered overnight: *and* most offer money-back guarantees. I've dealt with both MacConnection and MacWarehouse, so I can recommend them personally.

**Sometimes bandwagon buying** can be very important. No, not buying a bandwagon (just what *is* that, anyway?), but jumping on the bandwagon and buying what everyone else is buying. Why? Because sometimes you need the advantages of being in a crowd. Say you run into a problem with LayoutKing, or just want to learn more about its fine points. Who you gonna call? It's not a big enough company to supply telephone techni-cal support except for one hour a week, on Fridays, 4:30–5:30 p.m. Pacific Standard Time. It's not a popular enough program to have its own newsletter, or hints and tips in Mac magazines. People in your user group use PageMaker and Quark Xpress for layout. Don't underestimate the advantage of these resources.

**⋯❯ When a major new version of a program** comes out, buy the old one right away! Because sometimes it works like this: WordMangler 1.0 sells for $80. The 2.0 version ships, and since it's a major upgrade, it's going for $190. But there's a special offer for current users of the 1.0 version, who can upgrade for only $50. So, you spend $80, regis-ter, and upgrade for $50, for a total of $130 instead of $190. Sometimes special offers are extended to people who bought the "old" version within weeks of the new version's announcement, so keep your receipt.

**⋯❯ Upgrading to a new version** of your favorite software isn't something to be done in haste. Granted, you may get a "limited time only" upgrade offer that lets you move up to the new version of DrabPaint for only 75¢ if you do it *right away, this week.* So, send your money and get the upgrade. But don't use it—or at least, don't replace the old ver-sion right away. Let the versions live side by side for a while until you're sure the new version works reliably, can read documents created in previous versions of the program, and so on.

RICHARD HOOKER
(1554–1600)

> Change is not made without inconvenience, even from worse to better.

**⋯❯ *Sidegrading* is** an interesting concept. That's when you upgrade from a program to a competitor's product. Sidegrades are sometimes offered by publishers for new or upgrad-ed programs—you send them the documentation or the master disk from the rival product PhoneMan, and they'll send you their new TalkTone software for half price. You can get some great deals this way.

## What's a ... ?

**⋯❯ A word processor is** an application that lets you, at the very least, enter, edit, and print text. At the other end of the extreme, a word processor lets you create graphics and play QuickTime movies within a document. In between the extremes, you get varying levels of capability, like spelling and grammar checkers, thesaurus functions, and page layout options.

The best thing that ever happened to word processors (other than computers, of course) was the concept of *style sheets.* In one fell swoop, you can apply a combination of para-graph and character styles to selected text. Many word processors also include basic page layout functions, allowing you to arrange text in multiple columns and around embedded graphics. I don't think there's any word processor that doesn't come with a spelling checker now, and many also offer grammar checkers and thesauruses. (Maybe that should be thesauri?)

The best-selling word processor for the Mac is Microsoft Word. Whether that's because it's the best, or it's been around so long, or because Microsoft is an incredible selling machine doesn't really matter. I know I can't live without it. But there are other word processor programs for the Mac that are excellent. Nisus is terrific and has its rabid fans; WriteNow is an elegant program that more than satisfies users with less than power-user needs. WordPerfect, the word processor of choice in the PC world, was long referred to as Word Imperfect in its Mac versions; but the 3.0 version finally got it right. MacWrite, despite the benefit of being published by Apple and Claris, and being bundled with the early Macs, never quite took over as the word processing standard.

> 85 percent of Microsoft Word's users swear by it. The other 15 percent swear *at* it.

THE MAC ALMANAC

∞•➔ **A spreadsheet is** an application that manipulates numbers in a fascinating variety of ways and at speeds to warm the cockles of an accountant's heart.* You can do anything from adding up simple rows and columns of numbers to financial and statistical analysis. Most spreadsheets also have charting capability, for when a picture is worth a thousand numbers.

*Just what <u>are</u> cockles, anyway?

In the Mac world, the word *spreadsheet* is synonymous with *Excel*, Microsoft's take-over-the-world spreadsheet program.

A typical spreadsheet window.

| | A | B | C | D | E | F | G | H | I |
|---|---|---|---|---|---|---|---|---|---|
| 1 | | Rent | Heat | Elec | Phone | Income1 | Income2 | | Total |
| 2 | Jan | 385.00 | 75.00 | 65.00 | 75.00 | 1500.00 | 2200.00 | | 3700.00 |
| 3 | Feb | 385.00 | 75.00 | 75.00 | 84.00 | 1500.00 | 2200.00 | | 3700.00 |
| 4 | Mar | 385.00 | 75.00 | 57.00 | 65.00 | 1500.00 | 2200.00 | | 3700.00 |
| 5 | Apr | 385.00 | 0.00 | 65.00 | 32.00 | 1500.00 | 2200.00 | | 3700.00 |
| 6 | May | 385.00 | 0.00 | 70.00 | 84.00 | 1500.00 | 2200.00 | | 3700.00 |
| 7 | Jun | 385.00 | 0.00 | 65.00 | 95.00 | 1500.00 | 2200.00 | | 3700.00 |
| 8 | Jul | 385.00 | 0.00 | 72.00 | 87.00 | 1500.00 | 2200.00 | | 3700.00 |
| 9 | Aug | 425.00 | 0.00 | 56.00 | 54.00 | 1500.00 | 2200.00 | | 3700.00 |
| 10 | Sept | 425.00 | 50.00 | 87.00 | 54.00 | 1500.00 | 2700.00 | | 4200.00 |
| 11 | Oct | 425.00 | 75.00 | 65.00 | 54.00 | 1500.00 | 2700.00 | | 4200.00 |
| 12 | Nov | 425.00 | 125.00 | 89.00 | 84.00 | 1500.00 | 2700.00 | | 4200.00 |
| 13 | Dec | 425.00 | 130.00 | 65.00 | 54.00 | 1500.00 | 2700.00 | | 4200.00 |
| 14 | | | | | | | | | |
| 15 | Total | 4820.00 | 605.00 | 831.00 | 822.00 | 18000.00 | 28400.00 | | 46400.00 |
| 16 | Avg | 771.25 | 94.58 | 133.08 | 130.75 | 2875.00 | 4550.00 | | 7425.00 |
| 17 | Max | 425.00 | 130.00 | 89.00 | 95.00 | 1500.00 | 2700.00 | | 4200.00 |
| 18 | | | | | | | | | |

➤ A *database* **program is** basically an electronic index card filing system. Each "index card" is a *record*; records hold information in *fields* like "name" and "phone number"; the "box" that holds the index cards is the database file.

The main advantage of an electronic filing system over its paper counterpart is the speed at which you can find and manipulate information. In a paper system for libraries, for instance, you need three cards for each book so that you can have one group sorted by author, one by book title, and one by topic. In an electronic system, one file serves all three purposes because it takes only seconds to change the sorting order. And if you want all the books by a specific author, or all the books on Renaissance gardening techniques, a subset of the file can be created instantly.

Most databases use *calculated fields* to perform mathematical operations based on the other fields in the record. Most can generate *reports* that consist of information garnered from all the records, or from a subset of records. A report function usually provides mathematical operations that can be used for calculations across a group of records.

A *relational database* links its various files so they can exchange information automatically in a variety of sophisticated ways. A database that doesn't have relational ability is a *flat file* database.

Mac databases offer many kinds of graphics capabilities, both for creating professional-looking forms and to make data entry and manipulation easier. In fact, many databases will even let you store graphics for later retrieval.

Claris' FileMaker is the best-selling Mac database; it's elegantly designed and full-featured. (Microsoft somehow lost its early lead with Microsoft File, which was for a while the *only* Mac database around.) On the relational end of things, you pretty much get to choose between 4D and FoxBase Pro, both of which work very well but are guaranteed to drive you nuts during the design stage.

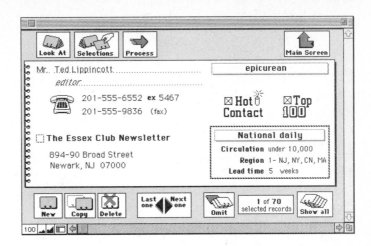

..............................
A Mac database screen.

**The Mac is a graphics-oriented machine,** so it's no surprise that there are many different kinds of graphics programs available. From kid's scribbling programs through artistic painting and drawing packages, to professional-level photo-retouching, it's all available for the Mac.

MacPaint came bundled with the Mac, but once it was unbundled, it lost its lead to SuperPaint. SuperPaint is still around, in ever-more-complex versions, and has been joined by Fractal Painter, Canvas, and PixelPaint as top-end painting programs. Freehand and Illustrator are high-end illustration programs; each has its proponents, but the truth is that graphic designers need both programs. PhotoShop just about owns its category of high-end graphics/retouching software (and deservedly so). [SuperPaint, Aldus; Fractal Painter, Fractal Design; PixelPaint, SuperPaint; Illustrator & PhotoShop, Adobe; Freehand, Aldus]

Types of graphics, and graphics programs, are covered in the next chapter.

**Page layout.** Arranging things on the page. How much could there be to a program that lets you do that? Lots. PageMaker was for a long time the premier layout program, but lately it's been playing catch-up to QuarkXpress.* Personally, I vastly prefer PageMaker's elegant interface; Quark is clunky in comparison, requiring several steps for many basic procedures that are done in a single step in PageMaker. But each program has its strengths and weaknesses, and a few things the other program doesn't provide.

\*Probably the only program known by its publisher's name, "Quark," instead of the program's name, "Xpress."

Low-end layout programs just don't seem to make it on the Mac, although several have tried. That's probably because word processors supply so much in the way of basic layout that people who buy layout software are the ones who need the high-end features. [PageMaker, Aldus; QuarkXpress, Quark]

**Communications, or telecom programs** (short for *telecommunication*) are programs that let computers talk to each other over phone lines. With a modem to connect the Mac to the phone and translate its signals from digital to analog—and another modem on the other end to do the reverse—your computer can talk to Macs, and other computers, all over the world—if you have the right software.

There's more about telecom and online services in Chapter 21.

There are general telecom programs that let you talk to any other similarly equipped computer, typing information back and forth or transferring files. There's also dedicated software used for specific online services like CompuServe and America Online.

While online services provide e-mail (electronic mail) functions, there are also programs specifically for e-mail within an office network, like QuickMail and Microsoft Mail—although they both also provide links to the greater world of telecommunications, too.

•••❯ **An *integrated program* is** one that combines different types of programs into one application. An integrated program usually offers a word processor, a spreadsheet, a database, and some sort of graphics capability; it might even include basic telecommunications. For a long time, Microsoft Works was the reigning integrated champion, and it deserved the title. But ClarisWorks is the one to have now; its level of integration, and overall power and elegance is a joy.

Some programs that advertise themselves as integrated are actually just *suites:* a collection of separate applications sold in one box. Sometimes the programs in the suite have special links between them for shared data, but they're seldom as smooth as a truly integrated program.

### BETTER LUCK NEXT TIME

Perhaps its copy-and-paste approach to exchanging information between programs influenced program designers, but whatever the reason, integrated programs became popular early in the Mac's existence. Some of the choices were:

- Jazz
- Ensemble
- Harmony
- Quartet
- Ragtime
- Executive Office

Does any one of these even ring a bell? (And why, do you suppose, were there so many musical names?) Or do you remember the page layout program to replace all others: Scoop?

•••❯ **An educational program** is something that parents can buy to make themselves feel better for having bought such an expensive toy for the kids.

There are some great programs out there that are truly educational, specifically targeting certain areas of knowledge or learning skills. But many are merely games in disguise—and poor games at that, unlikely to hold a kid's interest for long. Keep in mind that programs not meant for kids, nor meant as educational, can actually be quite educational. There's more about this in Chapter 21.

••➤ **A** *utility* is difficult to define. Generally, it's a small program that doesn't create any documents, but enhances your system or other applications in some way. It can be a tiny program that performs one little but important function (like letting you capture a picture of the screen), or it can be a major piece of software that diagnoses and fixes hard drive problems.

••➤ **The terms** *public domain* **and** *freeware* are often used interchangeably, but they're not the same thing. Public domain software is free; it's created by a programmer or an artist who wants to share something nifty with the Mac world and doesn't want to be paid for it. Strictly speaking, when something is put in the public domain, the author doesn't even own it anymore. So, most items put out for free by their authors are known as *freeware*—software that's free but the author retains rights to it.

*Shareware* is pretty much the same thing, but it's not free. You don't have to pay for it until *after* you get it, use it, and (presumably) like it. There's usually a notice within the program, or in a separate file, that tells you who the author is, how much the program costs, and where to mail the check.

Freeware and shareware software get distributed through the same channels—through online services and user groups—so it's no surprise that people confuse the two. But it's *really* important to support shareware authors, so they get enough money to pay for their time, and will continue improving the program or creating others. A big problem these days is buying a book with a disk in it, or with a whole CD full of shareware programs. You've paid for the book or CD, but you *haven't* paid the shareware authors; the book or CD is merely the distribution method for the software, but the money doesn't get to the programmer unless you send it separately.

## Making the Most of Your Software

∞➤ **Register your software** when you buy it. Registered users may get several "perks":

- Notice of upgrades, bug fixes, and so on.
- Special deals on upgrades, and/or other products from the company.
- Free telephone support—sometimes for a limited period of time.
- Free or trial subscriptions to a newsletter about the product.

∞➤ **Learn how to use your program** to its fullest extent. Here's the best way to go about learning it:

1. Use the tutorial provided in the manual, following it step-by-step on your computer.
2. Read the manual. Give it a full read-through right away even though many of the features or procedures may not be entirely clear to you until you've used them. Even if you don't remember how to do a specific procedure, you'll remember that it's possible.
3. Use the program. *Really* use it, for real projects.
4. Read magazine articles that describe how to use the program's more advanced

features, or subscribe to a newsletter devoted to it, or get together with other people who use the program. (Or all of the above.)

5. After you've used the program for two or three months, or even a few weeks of intensive work, go back and read the *entire* manual again. You'll understand all the references to the program's features, and you'll pick up all the little details this time around.

Dealing with technical support people is covered in Chapter 24.

> If you are sure you understand everything that is going on, you are hopelessly confused.
>
> WALTER MONDALE

### RTFM

Here's a great acronym which I'm not going to completely define, so as not to offend anyone. (It was totally edited out of one of my previous books, but I'm dealing with a more mature crowd—well, the ages haven't changed, but the attitudes have.)

Tech support people—both official ones and ones like me—are continually frustrated by people who call with questions that are clearly answered in a program's manual. The traditional answer, seldom voiced by those of us raised or paid to be polite and helpful to the questioner is: "RTFM!" That stands for "Read the manual!" Oops, I left a word out ....

## ⬱ APPLICATIONS ⬱

### Installing Applications

∘∘❥ An *application* is a program that lets you create or do things. Most applications create files called *documents*. A word processor is an application; the memo, or the Great American Novel, that you write with it is a document.

> ✳This is sound advice; I <u>know</u> it is. And I still don't do it—but that doesn't mean you should live dangerously!

∘∘❥ **When you buy software, don't copy it just to your hard drive.** Make another copy onto a floppy disk (or a *set* of disks). That way, if something happens to the copy on your hard drive *and* to your master disks, you'll have a backup available.* You might have a problem with your hard drive a year or more after installing the software and need to reinstall it from the masters—only to find that the master is unreadable.

It's not always possible to make backup copies of master disks, since some are designed *not* to be copied, but make your copies whenever you can.

◦◦► **An application is a single file on the disk,** but more and more applications come with support files like dictionaries, import filters, translators, and so on. Support files usually have to be in the same folder as the application, or in a subfolder—or sometimes in a special folder inside the System Folder. (Companies like Claris, Aldus, and Microsoft coordinate their products to share a single support folder, usually kept in the System Folder.)

◦◦► **If an application has an installer program,** use it! Large applications don't even fit on a single floppy disk, so the information is compressed on the floppy and the installer expands it back into a usable form on your hard drive (sort of like reconstituted orange juice). In many cases, an application is split across two or more disks, and the installer sews it back together. Installer programs also put an application's support files in all the correct places.

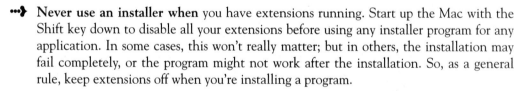

**BRIGHT IDEAS #6 AND #7**

**Q.** How many software developers does it take to change a light bulb?

**A.** "The light bulb works fine on the system in my office."

**Q.** How many product managers does it take to change a light bulb?

**A.** "Let's get marketing involved. I think we can sell this as a feature."

••► **Never use an installer when** you have extensions running. Start up the Mac with the Shift key down to disable all your extensions before using any installer program for any application. In some cases, this won't really matter; but in others, the installation may fail completely, or the program might not work after the installation. So, as a general rule, keep extensions off when you're installing a program.

••► **Some programs need to be *de-installed*** instead of just erased. If a program uses an installer, check whether it provides a de-install option, and use it if you're getting rid of the program. A de-installer will get rid of all the support files scattered around on the drive in addition to erasing the main file. More importantly, a de-installer will get rid of any items that were installed in your System file without your knowing it. (Yes, it happens!)

Many programs that use the Apple Installer (the one that installs your system software) provide a de-install option but forget to tell you about it. Go to the Customize installation screen, and hold down the Option key: The Install button changes to Remove.

## Launching Applications

◦◦► **When you open an application,** you're *launching* it, or *running* it. These terms apply only to applications—you open folders and disk icons, but you don't *launch* or *run* them. The fine difference seems to be that when you open a folder, it just sits there with its window open. When you open an application, it's off and running and it helps you *do* something.

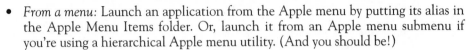

∞•⟩ **The basic ways to open an application** from the desktop have remained the same since the dawn of Macintosh: double-click on the application's icon, or select it and choose Open from the File menu. You can also select the icon and press Command-O or Command-Down. Or ... wait a minute, there are more ways to open an application than meet the eye, and you don't have to be on the desktop to do it. For instance:

- *From a menu:* Launch an application from the Apple menu by putting its alias in the Apple Menu Items folder. Or, launch it from an Apple menu submenu if you're using a hierarchical Apple menu utility. (And you should be!)
- *With an alias:* Use any of the methods for opening an application on its alias, and the application opens.
- *Through a document:* Open a document by any of the methods discussed later in this chapter, and the application that created it opens, too.
- *Automatically:* Put an application or its alias in the Startup Items folder so it opens automatically at startup.

•••⟩ **There are utilities that make launching** easier and even more convenient:

- The Launcher control panel in the Performa system creates a separate window of buttons for application and document launching.
- At Ease, also with the Performa system, but also available as a separate utility from Apple, replaces the Finder with a series of application and document buttons.

U sing the Launcher control panel is described in Chapter 8.

•••⟩ **There are several launching tricks** covered in other chapters. Here's a quick roundup:

- Make a "launch pad" on the desktop with a special window of mini icons. (Chapter 5)
- Keep a folder of application aliases in the Startup Items folder. The folder will open at startup, letting you pick the applications you want to run without looking for them on the drive. (Chapter 6)
- If you launch applications from the Apple menu, keep the applications together in the alphabetical listing by altering their names to keep them in a group. (Chapter 6)
- Use a hierarchical Apple menu utility that lets you launch more than one item at a time. (Chapter 6)
- Launch applications with keystrokes by using a macro utility. (Chapter 21)

•••⟩ **Hold down Option when you double-click** an icon to launch an application, and the window that the icon is in will close.

•••⟩ **To cancel a program launch,** (maybe you didn't *mean* to double-click that icon), press Command-period. But you have to be *really* quick!

•••⟩ **Every application needs enough memory** to work in. Applications and memory usage are covered in detail in Chapter 9, but here's a roundup of the most important points:

- Adjust an application's memory partition—both its preferred size, and the one it will settle for if there's not enough for the preferred size—in its Get Info window.
- Applications need more memory if you're going to be working on complex or multiple documents.

- Continual launching and quitting of programs during a work session fragments the Mac's memory. You may find that although you have enough total memory for an application, there's not enough in an uninterrupted chunk for it to run.

◆ **You can launch two or more applications at the same time** using any of several different techniques:

- Select their icons and then use the Open command from the File menu or from the keyboard. If the icons are in different folders, you can still select both applications as long as *those* folders are in the same folder: Use a hierarchical view and Shift-click to select the icons.
- When multiple icons are selected, double-clicking on any one of them opens all of them—as long as you have enough memory.
- Put their aliases in the Startup Items folder so that they're all launched automatically at startup.
- Opening multiple documents at the desktop opens the various programs that created them. Once again, that's assuming there's enough memory for all the programs.*

> *This deserves special mention because it wasn't possible before System 7. If you tried to open two documents created by two different applications, you'd get a dialog politely informing you that you had to open the documents from within the applications in question.

## At Ease

◆ **At Ease comes with** Performa system software, but it's also available as a separate utility from Apple; in fact, for a short time it was bundled with System 7.1 when that system was first released. (I think it was just to make people feel better that it was the first operating system that actually had to be *paid* for.)

At Ease* is a Finder alternative; when it's running, you don't have a desktop. You get a screen that looks like a manila folder (more or less) with icon buttons on it. The icons are for your applications and documents— they're stored on separate "pages" of the folder—and clicking an icon launches the item.

> *The original name— before it was ever released, that is—was Tiny Toons. Sounds like something Roger Rabbit would use!

Authorized persons—and that might exclude others in your office, or the kiddies at home—can get to the desktop if they know the password you've set up in the control panel.

◆ **At Ease is a control panel, but** you can't install it like every other control panel, by just dragging it into the Control Panels folder or System Folder. You have to use its installer program, then restart the Mac. Then you have to open the control panel, click the On button, and restart the Mac again to switch into At Ease instead of the Finder.

◆ **Set up the At Ease icons** using the Select Items and Set Up Documents buttons in the control panel. The dialog that opens lets you select programs and documents from your hard drive that will be placed in buttons on the At Ease screen.

◆ **There are features in At Ease that can drive you crazy** if you're anything but a rank beginner. In fact, even beginners might have some problems with the fact that you can't delete or rename icons, and you can't even organize them the way you want— they're always alphabetical.

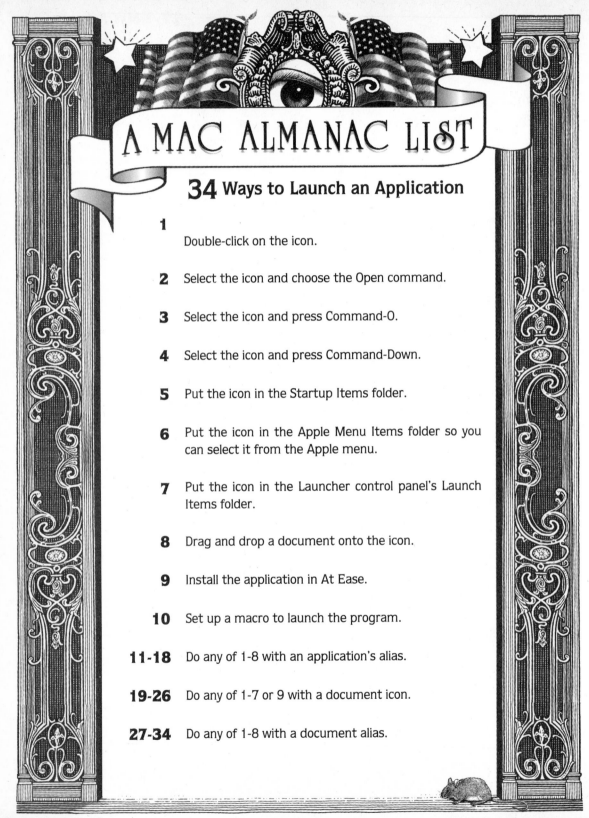

# A MAC ALMANAC LIST

## 34 Ways to Launch an Application

**1** Double-click on the icon.

**2** Select the icon and choose the Open command.

**3** Select the icon and press Command-O.

**4** Select the icon and press Command-Down.

**5** Put the icon in the Startup Items folder.

**6** Put the icon in the Apple Menu Items folder so you can select it from the Apple menu.

**7** Put the icon in the Launcher control panel's Launch Items folder.

**8** Drag and drop a document onto the icon.

**9** Install the application in At Ease.

**10** Set up a macro to launch the program.

**11-18** Do any of 1-8 with an application's alias.

**19-26** Do any of 1-7 or 9 with a document icon.

**27-34** Do any of 1-8 with a document alias.

**Don't remove At Ease from your hard drive** without turning it off first. And that means turning it off in the control panel, restarting the Mac with At Ease still in your Control Panels folder so the "off" setting registers, and *then* taking it out of your Control Panels folder.

But this still doesn't remove At Ease permanently. You have to use its Installer program to remove it, as described in the manual: click Customize, hold down Option, and click Remove. Why all these fancy steps? Because At Ease alters the *boot resource* in the System file; these are the first instructions the Mac follows when it's starting up. If it's still looking for At Ease, and At Ease has been removed from the drive, you'll crash every time you try to start up.

If you've already messed things up and you've looked up this entry hoping for a solution, there is one: re-install your system from system disks, and the problem is solved.

# ◄ USING MULTIPLE APPLICATIONS ►

## Handling Multiple Applications

**You don't have to do anything special** to run two or more applications on your Mac at the same time. Just launch them one at a time, or together, with any of the methods described above. There's no MultiFinder to set up the way there was in earlier systems.

Application memory is covered in Chapter 9.

**The number of programs** you can have going at the same time depends on how much memory your Mac has, since each application needs its own chunk of memory to live in.

**There's only one *active* application** when you're running multiple applications. It's easy to see which program is active: Its windows are on top of all the others. If all its document windows are closed, you should be able to recognize what application you're in by the menus on the menu bar. If *that* doesn't do it for you, check the mini icon in the right corner of the menu bar—it belongs to the current application. When all else fails and you forget where you are, click on that icon, because it opens the Application menu, where the current application is listed with a checkmark.

**⋯⋗** **A background application** like Print Monitor used to take over the Apple menu icon when it wanted attention. Now, a background application whining for attention flashes its icon alternately with the Application menu's icon.

## Moving Around & Hiding Windows

**⋯⋗** **The Application menu** at the far right of the menu bar (its "title" is a mini-icon of the active application) lists all open applications and desk accessories. The way an item is displayed in the menu tells you what state it's in:

- An application whose icon is normal has all its windows showing—they haven't been hidden to stay out of the way. Even if they're totally obscured by other windows, they're there and you'll see them if you move the windows that are in the way.
- An application with a dimmed icon is open, but its windows are currently hidden from view because one of the Application menu's hiding options was used.
- The active application is checked.
- An application marked with a diamond is running in the background and asking for attention.

| |
|---|
| Hide Word |
| Hide Others |
| Show All |
| A Aldus SuperPaint |
| ♦ 🖥 Finder |
| ✓ 🐾 Word |

**⋯⋗** **Switch to an open** application by:

- Choosing it from the Application menu.
- Clicking in any exposed part of one of its windows.
- Using any of the methods that would normally launch it, such as selecting it from the Apple menu or double-clicking one of its document icons. You can even double-click on the application's icon, which will be gray because it's already open.

**⋯⋗** **Use the Application menu to hide** and show windows for running applications:

- The Hide command hides all the windows belonging to the current application. The actual wording of the command changes to reflect the name of the current application—*Hide Word, Hide SuperPaint, Hide Finder,* and so on. Of course, if you hide the application's windows, you can't do any more work in it. So, choosing the Hide command also moves you to another application—the last one you were using before you moved to the current one.
- The Hide Others command hides everything *except* the current application. It doesn't provide a drop-cloth effect behind the current application, though, blocking out everything; although Finder windows are closed with the Hide Others command, you'll still see the desktop in the background, and any icons that are "loose" on the desktop.
- The Show All command displays all the windows for all running applications.

**⋯⋗** **The Hide command is dimmed** if all the other applications are already dimmed. That's because when you hide the current application, you move to the last application you worked in, but you can't move to it if you hid its windows, except by specifically selecting it from the Application menu.

➤ **You can choose a dimmed application** from the Application menu; the dimmed icon merely indicates that its windows are hidden. You're moved into the application when you choose it, and its windows re-appear.

➤ **Floating windows** like the tool palettes in SuperPaint and PageMaker disappear when you switch to another application even if you're not hiding windows as you leave.

### THE TWELVE BUGS OF CHRISTMAS

*Posted on various electronic bulletin boards by an anonymous source, this is the jolly song of a software support technician. You know the tune. (I left out the repeats.) Sing along ...*

For the twelfth bug of Christmas, my manager said to me:
Tell them it's a feature;
Say it's not supported;
Change the documentation;
Blame it on the hardware;
Find a way around it;
Say they need an upgrade;
Reinstall the software;
Ask for a dump!
Run with the debugger,
Try to reproduce it,
Ask them how they did it, and ...
See if they can do it again!

➤ **To hide the current program's windows** as you move to another application, hold the Option key while you select the destination program from the Application menu. Or, option-click in a window of the program you want to move to.

➤ **Clicking on the Application menu's icon** doesn't do anything but open the menu. What should it do? Before System 7, under MultiFinder, clicking in the icon in the upper-right corner of the menu bar switched you to one of the other programs running. Do you miss that click-and-switch function? JustClick is a utility that brings it back for you. [shareware, Louis A. Bardi]

➤ **If you're tired of manually hiding** application windows, try the HideAlways utility, which automatically hides the windows of the application as you leave it. [freeware from ZMac, Mike Throckmorton]

## Finder Considerations

➤ **If you hide the Finder,** only its windows are hidden—you'll still see the desktop in the background, disk and Trash icons, and any icons that are out on the desktop.

••❯ **To move to the desktop, you can click** not only on one of its windows, but also on any desktop icon or even on the desktop background itself.

••❯ **Option-clicking on an exposed part of the desktop** when you're in an application moves you to the Finder, hiding the windows of the application you're leaving.

••❯ **The Launcher control panel** that comes with Performa system software automatically hides the Finder whenever you're in an application.

# ⮌ CREATING & SAVING DOCUMENTS ⮌

## In General

••❯ **A document is not a part of the application that created it,** somehow stored within the application. That might seem obvious to you, but it's a common misperception among many beginners who don't spend much time on the desktop and never see a document as a file completely independent from its application.

••❯ **A document's icon is usually** related visually to the application that created it.

••❯ **When you open a document, the file on the disk** isn't affected—a *copy* of it is placed into memory and the original file isn't altered until you use the Save command to save the changes you make. If a program doesn't use a Save command (as in most databases), then the changes you make to the document on screen are made to the disk file automatically, at an interval that depends on the application you're using.

••❯ **It's hard to save "over" a document** accidentally—that is, to replace an existing document by mistake because you've given a new document the same name. You'll get a dialog like the one shown here. In fact, many applications have a second cautionary level built in: If you try

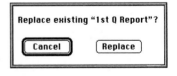

and save over another document, and the existing document is a different file type than the one you're saving, you may get another dialog double checking that you *really* want to do it. Some applications won't let you replace one document type with another at all.

••❯ **Although documents are generally stored in memory** until you save them to the disk, sometimes there's not enough memory available—especially for a large document. Many applications create temporary disk files while you're working to store the document information that doesn't fit in RAM. The original file, though, is not altered until you save it, and the temporary files are erased by the application when you quit. If you move to the desktop while the program's still running (or if the application or the Mac crashes before you quit the program), you might see icons in the application's folder or the System Folder labeled "temp" or something similar; don't throw them away as long as the application is still running.

## New Documents

∞•► **Most applications start with an empty window**—a blank document. (When you're in an application, *document* is just about synonymous with *window*. When you're on the desktop, *folder* is almost synonymous with window.) If there's no window to work in, or you've used the original one and want to start a new one, choose New from the application's File menu.

∞•► **Some applications won't give you a window** to work in, even in response to the New command, unless you name the file first; this happens in most databases. Other programs, notably graphics and page layout applications, ask for additional information before giving you a new window—like what size page you want, how many colors you're going to be working in, and so on.

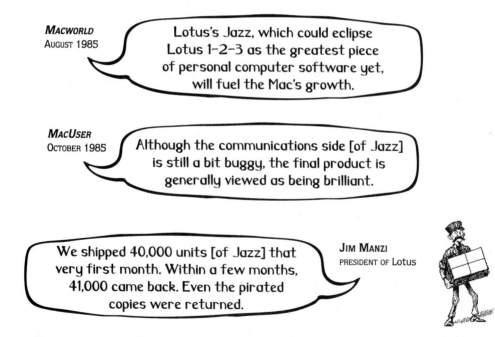

**MACWORLD**
AUGUST 1985

Lotus's Jazz, which could eclipse Lotus 1-2-3 as the greatest piece of personal computer software yet, will fuel the Mac's growth.

**MACUSER**
OCTOBER 1985

Although the communications side [of Jazz] is still a bit buggy, the final product is generally viewed as being brilliant.

We shipped 40,000 units [of Jazz] that very first month. Within a few months, 41,000 came back. Even the pirated copies were returned.

**JIM MANZI**
PRESIDENT OF Lotus

## Handling Multiple Documents

∞•► **When you have more than one document open in an application,** the basic window-handling rules apply: only one window can be active (it will have a striped title bar) and clicking in any window activates it and brings it to the top of the pile.

∞◆ **Some applications provide a Window menu** that lists all the opened documents; choosing one from the menu brings it to the top of the pile.

## Save & Save As

∞◆ **Everything you do while a document is open** is stored in RAM, which disappears when you turn off the computer. For a more permanent copy of the document, you use the Save command to put it on the disk.

∞◆ **There's no difference between the Save and Save As commands** if you've never saved the document before. Some very prissy programs will dim the Save command until you've used Save As the first time. This makes logical sense—after all, you have to name the new document, so you're saving it *as* something—but common usage lets us use Save even for a new document.

Using either Save or Save As as the initial command opens a dialog box—cleverly referred to as the Save dialog—that lets you name the document and specify the folder you want it saved in. The basic Save dialog is shown here, although it can really vary, depending on the program you're using.

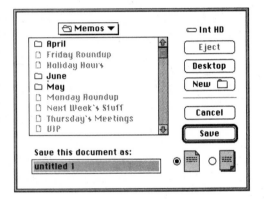

∞◆ **Once a document's been saved, the Save command** saves the changes you've made to the document. You won't see a dialog box; the last version of the document is replaced by the current version, under the same name and in the same place. Some applications display the progress of the save operation, which is great feedback when you're working with large documents. Others give no indication at all as to what's going on or when the save is completed—you have to keep an eye on the mouse cursor and see when it changes from a wristwatch back to the arrow.

∞◆ **The Save As command** lets you rename a document, or save it in a different folder, or on a different disk, or in a different format, leaving the original version of the document untouched. The Save As dialog is the same as the Save dialog, but the current name of the document is usually already entered, and selected, in the text box.

∞◆ **Using Save As** after you've opened a document and made a few changes to it *doesn't* save the changes in the original document. This is a handy approach when you want different versions of a document. But it can be a real problem if you open a document, edit it, and do a Save As to a separate disk to give to someone else, and assume that the changes have been recorded in the original file.

◌◦♦ **You can't forget to save a document** or the changes you made to it before you close it because the Mac reminds you. (You think that's not worthy of noting? Then you haven't worked on other computers, with poorly designed software. I have—but not since I got my first Mac.)

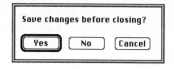

◌◦♦ **You don't have to worry about wiping out** an existing document if you inadvertently use the same name again. When you try to save a document into a folder that already contains a document with that name, you'll get an alert that looks something like this:

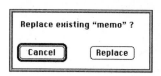

◌◦♦ **Some applications save information automatically** without your having to use a Save command. This is common for most database programs.

◌◦♦ **The Mac is generous when it comes to document names**—at least, more generous than most computer systems. But it does have certain rules and limitations; not at all coincidentally, they're the same limitations as those for naming icons on the desktop. All this is discussed in Chapter 4, but here's a quick roundup:

- The name can't be longer than 31 characters.
- You can't use a colon in a file name.
- Two files in the same folder can't have the same name.
- There's no difference between capitals and lowercase in file names, so *Memo*, *memo*, and *MEMO* are all considered the same and can't co-exist in the same folder.
- When you want documents to appear in a window or list in a certain order, keep in mind the Mac's alphabetization rules: numbers come before letters; numbers are sorted "alphabetically" (so 10 comes before 2); most punctuation characters come before letters or numbers; option characters get sorted before, between, and after letters.

◌◦♦ **Save your document early and often.** How soon, and how often, depends on how much work you want to do all over again if something happens before you save the document or the changes you've made to it.

- You should save the document before certain operations that traditionally trigger crashes on an unstable system, like printing or launching another application. But learn to let other things trigger the Command-S reaction, too: I save the document I'm working on every time the phone rings, for instance. There are days when it rings often enough to keep my work safe.
- Some programs have auto-save functions that will save your work at some definable interval, like every 10 or 15 minutes.
- Use a product like AutoSave, which can be set to save your work in certain applications at any interval from 1 to 99 minutes. [Magic Software, Inc]
- If you use Tempo or QuicKeys, you can make a macro that saves your work at intervals.

Macros are covered in Chapter 21.

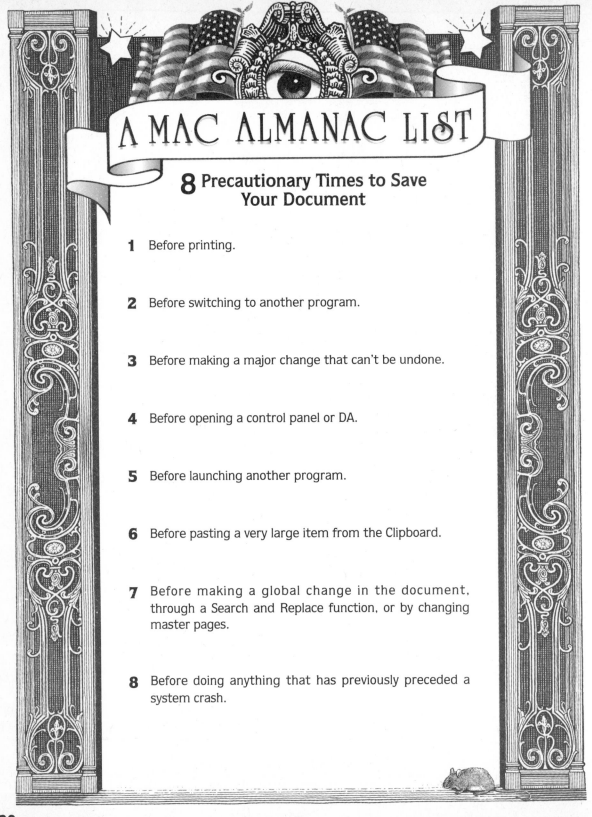

# A MAC ALMANAC LIST

## 8 Precautionary Times to Save Your Document

**1** Before printing.

**2** Before switching to another program.

**3** Before making a major change that can't be undone.

**4** Before opening a control panel or DA.

**5** Before launching another program.

**6** Before pasting a very large item from the Clipboard.

**7** Before making a global change in the document, through a Search and Replace function, or by changing master pages.

**8** Before doing anything that has previously preceded a system crash.

## Stationery

◦•➤ **The concept of** *stationery* comes from the real-world procedure of tearing a piece of paper from a pad of printed stationery: Each piece is blank except for pre-printed items like a letterhead or checklist or other fill-in-the-blank features.

Macintosh stationery is a document that you can use as a template for other documents. It may already have something in it, like a letterhead, or it may be a blank page that's formatted with the margins, and the text and paragraph styles you want to use.

◦•➤ **Stationery was around before System 7,** but now it's a system feature; this means that programmers can just hook into it without having to create the routines from scratch. This *should* mean that every application handles stationery the same way, but most applications have either stubbornly clung to their own methods—usually dealing with documents called *templates*—or ignored the stationery concept altogether, despite Apple's best intentions.

◦•➤ **Stationery buttons in a Save dialog** let you choose between saving your work as a standard document or as stationery. The icon that looks like a single page is for normal documents; the one that looks like a pad of paper—oh, okay, it looks like maybe two pages—is for stationery. You click the button you want before you save the document so that it's saved in the right format.

But you know what? You won't see many stationery buttons; not too many programs use them. But if you're just dying to see them in person, you can run the TeachText or SimpleText program that comes with your system software and look at them in the Save dialog.

◦•➤ **When you close a document that's been saved as stationery,** you may get the standard *Do you want to save changes before closing?* dialog because, as far as the application is concerned, you haven't really saved the *document* just because you made a stationery pad out of it.

◦•➤ **When you open a stationery document**, you don't really open the stationery document—you get an untitled document in the application with the same formats and information as were in the stationery document. You add the material that you want, then save the document as usual; because it started out as untitled you have to give it a new name—and the original stationery document remains unchanged.

◦•➤ **If you want to change the stationery document itself**, open it, make the changes, and then save it as stationery using the same name as before. You'll be asked if you want to replace the existing file, and you can click *Yes*.

◦•➤ **Stationery documents have their own special icons** in lists and on the desktop. A stationery icon usually looks like the application's standard icon with an extra page behind it. Here's what Microsoft Word's icons look like.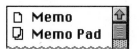

Memo   Memo Pad

••➔ **You can make stationery for an application that doesn't provide** the option. Create a document that you want to use as stationery, and save it in the normal fashion. Then, go to the desktop and find the document's icon; select it and choose the Get Info command. Click the *Stationery pad* checkbox at the bottom of the window.

Creating stationery from an Info window.

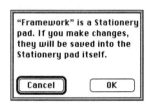

What happens when you open stationery that you've made this way depends on the application. Applications that aren't "aware" of the stationery concept just open the document as if it were nothing special. But the Mac may intervene briefly with the dialog shown here. Since the application doesn't know anything about stationery, though, once the document actually opens, it's just the original document and saving any changes will affect your "stationery." Or, the stationery document may just open as Untitled as if the program knew about stationery all along—it just didn't want to provide stationery buttons in its Save dialog.

••➔ **To prevent accidentally changing a document** that you've defined as stationery on the desktop when the application doesn't know anything about stationery, check the Locked button in the document's Get Info window.

## Publish and Subscribe

∞➔ **Publish and Subscribe** was a major new feature introduced with System 7. Was? Right, "was," because nobody really made much use of it. Without enough applications including the capabilities, users just don't get used to it and demand that it be included in other programs. There were just enough interface issues left open for Publish and Subscribe at the release of System 7 that programmers were wary of implementing it. In any case, as a system feature, it fizzled. But I'll cover some of the highlights in this section, just in case there's a resurgence soon.

You'll know if a program has Publish and Subscribe capabilities because it will have the appropriate commands in its Edit menu.

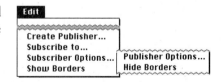

∞➔ **You can link parts of documents** with Publish and Subscribe. You select part of a document—or *all* of a document, and *publish* it. The material in the document that you're publishing is called, awkwardly, the *publisher*. (Neither the application nor the document is the publisher—the selected material is.)

Publishing part of a document creates a separate disk file, called an *edition*, that's linked to the original document.

When you are working inside another document, even one that was created in a different application, you can *subscribe* to the edition, and that material appears in your current document. The material in this document is called the *subscriber*. (Again, it's neither the application nor the document that's the subscriber; just the shared section.)

A publisher in one document (left, framed in gray) sends information to the edition file (center) which sends information to the subscriber in another document (right, framed in gray).

So far, it sounds pretty much like copying and pasting, with the added aggravation of a disk file as an intermediary. But the trick is that, when you change and save the material in the original document, it updates the edition, which, in turn, updates the second document.

•➤ **The Show Borders command** highlights any publishers or subscribers in a document by framing them in gray. Hide Borders, of course, turns off the frames.

•➤ **Edition file icons** usually look something like the document icon of the application that published them, but the standards call for the icon to be shorter than document icons and to incorporate the gray publisher/subscriber frame.

If you double-click on an edition icon on the desktop, you'll get a window that shows what's in the file, with an Open Publisher button so you can open the document the material's in.

Edition

•➤ **The Publisher Options and Subscriber Options** commands let you specify things like when the edition should be updated, and when the publisher should get the update from the edition. The Subscriber Options dialog looks like the one here. You can set the updates to be automatic or manual; if manual is set, there's a Get Edition Now button for that purpose. You can also cancel the link to the subscriber, leaving the material as-is in the current document, or open the document that contains the publisher.

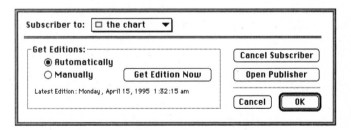

•➤ **A subscriber is a part of the document** where it resides, so you can give the file to someone else, without providing the edition file, and the material will be in the document.

## ⇥ OPENING DOCUMENTS ⇤

### From the Desktop

⊶➤ **To open a document from the desktop,** double-click on its icon, or select it and use the Open command from the File menu or from the keyboard. This opens the application that created the document, then opens the document.

⊶➤ **If the application is already open** when you try to open a document from the desktop, the Mac should switch you into the application and then open the document. Some applications don't seem to be able to deal with this situation, though, so you wind up with a polite dialog that suggests you open the document from within the application.

⊶➤ **Open multiple documents simultaneously** by selecting them on the desktop and using the Open command. Or, if you have several documents selected, double-clicking on one of them opens all of them. Before System 7, you couldn't open multiple documents from the desktop if they belonged to different applications, but now you can (as long as there's enough memory).

⊶➤ **When you try to open a document and its application can't be found,** you'll get a dialog telling you so—the first dialog shown here.

> 🛑 The document "Cubic World short" could not be opened, because the application program that created it could not be found.
>
> [ OK ]

If the document is in a format that TeachText or SimpleText can handle—and one of those programs is on your drive—you'll get the second dialog shown here.

> ⚠️ The document "Tennis" could not be opened, because the application program that created it could not be found. Do you want to open it using "SimpleText"?
>
> [ Cancel ]  [ OK ]

⊶➤ **"Rewire" the Finder for opening documents** whose applications can't be found, or to bypass TeachText or SimpleText as the application of choice for plain text and PICT files. Many utilities provide this function. Some utilities provide it as one of many functions; for other utilities, it's their sole purpose in life.

HandOff is one of the utilities whose main function is to let you rewire documents launched from the Finder. SpeedyFinder7, a nifty collection of tweaks to the Mac interface, includes document-linking options. [Handoff, Connectix; SpeedyFinder7, shareware, Victor Tan]

System 7.5's Easy Open control panel "rewires" double-click launching options. See the addendums at the end of this chapter and Chapter 8.

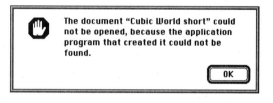

SpeedyFinder7's document-linking option dialog.

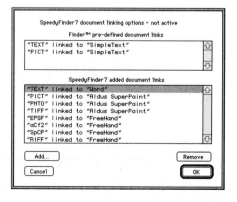

## Other Ways to Open Documents

∘•▸ **The Open command in an application's** File menu lets you open documents that the application created. Here's the basic Open dialog, though the specifics vary from one program to another. There are so many controls in this dialog, and tricks and shortcuts, that they're covered in a separate section later in this chapter.

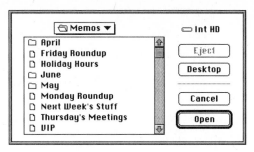

∘•▸ **Many applications provide special ways** to open documents so you don't have to wade through a series of folders in an Open dialog. Word, for instance, lets you add document names to a Work menu, and both Word and Excel keep the names of the last four files you used listed in the File menu for easy access.

∘•▸ **Make a document open automatically** when you start up the Mac by putting it or its alias in the Startup Items folder inside the System Folder. (Most people put only applications in the Startup Items folder, but the whole idea of using a Macintosh is not to be hidebound!)

∘•▸ **Keep a document in the Apple menu** if it's one that you use often. Put its alias in the Apple Menu Items folder so it will appear in the menu. Selecting a document from the menu is the same as opening it from the desktop: It opens both the document and the application that created it. If the application is already open, the document should open up inside it.

∘•▸ **Many applications let you open "foreign"** documents—compatible files created by other applications. This doesn't mean that the file will be totally compatible with the application, though. You may find lines and lines of "garbage characters"—boxes and squiggles and nonsense words—before the actual text of the document is displayed; and, in fact, you may not find any usable text at all simply because your word processor let you open the file.

## Drag and Drop

∘•▸ **Launch an application with the "drag and drop" method:** On the desktop, drag a document into an application's icon. Both the application and the document open.

Using drag and drop.

∘•▸ **The drag and drop advantage isn't immediately apparent,** since you can just as easily (and usually *more* easily) double-click the document icon to open both it and the application. But, here's the real trick: The document doesn't have to belong to the

application that you drag it onto. You're not going to be able to, say, open a PhotoShop picture inside Microsoft Word, but the trick works for compatible files. So, you can drag a text document created anywhere onto the Microsoft Word icon and it will open.

## WHAT A DRAG ...

The "drag and drop editing" that some programs (notably, Microsoft's Word and Excel, and Quark Xpress) offer is not the same as drag and drop document opening. Drag and drop editing is a terrific little feature with which you can simply drag selected text to a new spot in a document instead of cutting and pasting. Drag and drop document opening is a desktop procedure provided by the Mac system itself.

Other companies misuse the phrase, too. Connectix's CPU package for PowerBooks calls its file-syncing interface "drag and drop," but all you're doing is dragging a file from one place to another. The *drop* in drag and drop should refer to dropping an icon on top of another icon, not into another disk or window, or onto the desktop.

So, keep in mind that if a piece of software claims it has a drag and drop feature, it's *not* talking about the ability to open documents from the desktop. Thanks to Microsoft, especially, for introducing a terrific new concept and, at the same time, confusing Mac users everywhere.

System 7.5 gives a new definition for drag and drop editing, as described at the end of this chapter.

∘•➤ **The document icon stays** in its original location after a drag and drop operation. You can drag a document from its window to the application's window, or onto a desktop icon, without worrying about messing up whatever level of organization you've set up. The document icon itself never really moves at all—you're dragging only its outline into the application icon.

∘•➤ **You can drag an icon and drop it** into an application icon even if the application is open—in which case, the application icon is gray.

••➤ **If you can drag but can't drop**—the application doesn't highlight when you drag the document icon over it—then that application can't open that document format from the desktop. But when you can't open a document into an application by the drag and drop method, sometimes you can still open it from within that application because some programs offer "filters" that let you open "foreign" documents.

## ⊯ THE OPEN & SAVE DIALOG BOXES ⊫

### In General

∘•➤ **The dialog boxes that appear when you open or save** a document are officially dubbed *directory dialogs*—not one of Apple's better dubbings, especially since it smacks of PC-carryover. Programmer-types refer to them as the *GetFile* (for Open) and *SetFile* (for saving) dialogs. Old—and I mean *ancient*—Mac hands may even use the word *MiniFinder*, which was the dialog's nickname for a brief time (because it gave you some of the Finder's functionality from within an application). But that was before Apple actually created a program named MiniFinder that let you launch programs without wading through your desktop folders. And *that* fell by the wayside a long time ago, although the concept was resurrected for the At Ease software.

Most people (including *moi*) just call them the Open and Save dialogs.

∞► **The Open and Save dialogs in System 7 differ** quite a bit from their predecessors. The main change is that the desktop is a separate level in the hierarchy of folders and disks; it used to be combined with the main level of the hard drive. In addition, Save dialogs that follow the rules let you create a new folder from within the dialog. Dialogs that *really* follow Apple's guidelines, instead of reality, provide buttons for standard and stationery documents. The samples here show standard Open and Save dialogs. They have many features in common, but the Save dialog offers more options. And rightly so: When you're saving a document, you have to name it and indicate where it's going to be saved. The Open box only has to let you look around to find what's already there.

•••••••••••••••••••••••••••••••••••••••••••••••••••••••••••••••••••••••••••••••

A standard Open dialog (left) and a Save dialog (right).

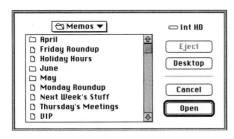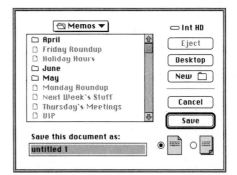

•••► **Minor changes to Open and Save dialogs** crop up at unexpected times—in the middle of this chapter, for instance! I installed the latest system hardware update, and found that the Open and Save dialogs all of a sudden displayed true mini icons in the list instead of generic ones. In addition, long titles no longer appeared condensed in the list—an innovation with System 7—but reverted to the earlier approach of dropping the last letters and replacing them with an ellipsis.

While the minor details of these dialogs may change from time to time, and you may find some differences between the pictures shown here and what you'll see on your Mac's screen, the main functions and shortcuts are standard.

•••► **The most important thing when** it comes to Open and Save dialogs is to get a feel for how the information you see in them relates to what's on your desktop. Here, for instance, is an Open dialog and the desktop window it refers to. This is the main disk window, so the disk's name—which is also the window's name on the desktop—is in the popup menu in the dialog. The list displays the contents of the window.

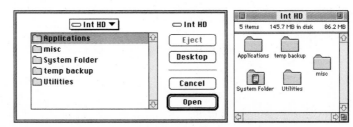

When you open one of the folders in the list, its name goes into the popup menu, and the list displays what's in *that* folder, as shown in this picture:

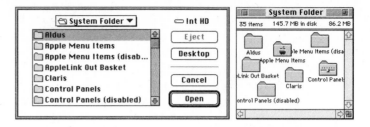

As you move down through folders in the dialog box, each folder is added to the popup menu so that the menu lists all the folders you've gone through. Using the menu is the same as using the popup menu that's built into desktop windows, except that the menu in the dialog includes a Desktop level that you don't need when you're actually on the desktop.

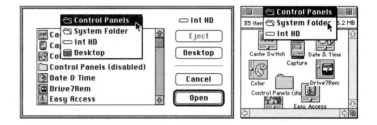

◦•◗ **The "location" showing in a dialog**—the folder and disk in its menu and list—is the last place you opened or saved something. When you first launch an application, that application is the last thing you opened, so when you save a new document, you're in that application's folder to start with.

Luckily, when you have several programs running, each application keeps track of where its Open and Save dialogs "are" so you can work in different locations with different applications. (This is a great relief to those of us who suffered through the quirks of earlier dialog design for multiple-program setups prior to System 7.)

◦◦◗ **Even something as basic as the Open/Save dialogs** begs for improvements over Apple's implementation. The main complaint has always been that it's just too hard to get from here to there—you have to go up a few levels, and down again along another path, to move from folder to folder. There have been several utilities over the years that offer better navigational options inside the dialogs, with SuperBoomerang the long-lived champion; it's included with Now Utilities. Norton Utilities has a hidden little gem included with it—Directory Assistance—that also enhances the dialogs. Both these utilities add a menu bar to the dialog box, giving you plenty of options for finding files and jumping to various folders that you use often. [Now Utilities, Now Software; Norton Utilities, Symantec]

···❱ **Dialogs differ from one application to the next** because high-end applications provide many options when it comes to opening and saving documents, dealing with many different formats. But the basic rules and functions remain the same—the changes are not really changes, they're additions. Here are four examples.

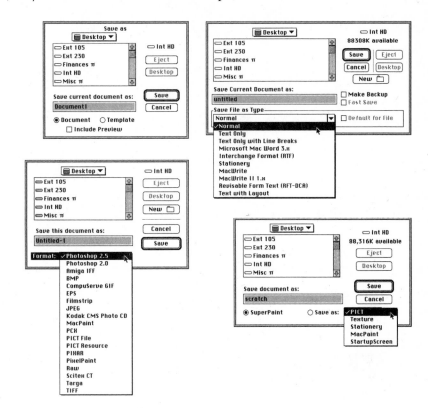

## The List

◦◦❱ **The list in an Open/Save dialog** is always alphabetical (except when it's displaying the desktop level, but let's ignore that for now). In the Save dialog, you'll see everything listed—folders and volumes, which you can open, are listed in normal text, and files (which, of course, you can't open when you're saving something) are listed in gray. In an Open box, the list includes volumes and folders, and any files that the application you're using can open. Here's how the list for the same folder looks in an Open and in a Save dialog.

An Open dialog list (left) and the same list in a Save dialog (right).

∞•❥ **Long file names are treated in a special way**, but which special way depends on exactly what System 7 version you're using. The first version of System 7 introduced condensed characters in dialog lists, which was great—even if it looked a little odd sometimes. In an update for System 7.1, the condensed characters disappeared and the approach reverted to using ellipsis for missing characters. I much prefer the condensed font to the ellipsis, but this isn't a user-configurable option. (Well, it will probably change again, anyway.)

Two ways of dealing with long names in lists.

| 🗀 a folder name | 🗀 a folder name |
| 🗀 a longer folder name | 🗀 a longer folder name |
| 🗀 a very much longer file name | 🗀 a very much longer folde... |

∞•❥ **A list displays icons** next to a item's name. Up until recently, the icons were generic icons for just a few categories of items, like volumes, folders, applications, documents, and desk accessories. An update to System 7.1 started a new approach: using true mini-icons, just like the ones on the desktop, in the list. Most of the pictures in this and later chapters in the book show the mini-icons. Earlier chapters sometimes show the generic icons because I updated my system half-way through the book!

∞•❥ **An alias appears in a dialog list** in italicized type, just the way it does on the desktop. If you open an alias, it's the original that actually opens—again, just like on the desktop.

Although opening an alias from the Open dialog opens the original file, you stay in the alias's folder. That is, the next time you use the Open or Save command, you'll still see the folder you were working in last time, not the folder that the opened file is from.

### THE WAY WE WERE ...

When you're in a Save dialog now, you can see what's already in a folder. All the files are listed in dimmed letters because you can't select them when you're saving something; but they're listed so you don't have to wonder what's already in the folder you're looking at.

It wasn't always like that. In days gone by, the only thing you could see in a Save dialog's list was any folders that were there, in case you wanted to Open them to save the current document inside. So, often you'd try to save your document under a name that was already used. Although a dialog showed up to tell you about the problem and ask if you really wanted to replace the document that was already there, it was frustrating.

And if you think *that's* bad ...

Prior to the HFS system, which debuted with the Mac Plus in 1986, there were no folders inside dialog boxes. No popup menu, no way to navigate through the contents of the disk. Navigation wasn't necessary—everything on a disk was listed in a single list, alphabetically. Oh, sure, there were folders on the desktop for organizing things, but they were strictly a figment of the Finder's imagination—a shared hallucination among Mac users—that were ignored by Save and Open dialogs.

∞•❥ **To open an item in the list**—whether it's a folder you want to look in, or a file that you're actually opening into the application—click on it to select it and then click the

Open button. If you're in a Save dialog, the Save button temporarily changes to an Open button when a disk or folder is selected in the list.

Of course, that's not the *only* way to open something in the list. First, you can select an active (not dimmed) item in many different ways:

- Click on it.
- Use the Up and Down arrows to move up and down in the list.
- Type the name of the item. You need only a few letters—just enough to differentiate it from another item with a similar name. If you type something that isn't in the list, the nearest alphabetic equivalent is selected.

Then, there's more than one way to open a selected item:

- Click the Open button.
- Press Return.
- Press Command-O.
- Press Command-Down.

Or, you can open an item in a single step: Double-click on it in the list.

All these opening options echo exactly what you can do on the desktop to select and open icons.

°•◆ **For keyboard commands to work in the Save** dialog's list, the list has to be the active box, because otherwise the keystrokes are sent to the text box where you name the file. When the list box is active, it has an extra black frame around it. When the text box is active, its contents are selected or it has the blinking text cursor in it.

To activate either the list box or the text box, click in it or use Tab to move from one to the other.

An active list box (left) and an active text box (right).

°•◆ **What's that Open button** doing in the Save dialog? When the item selected in the list is "openable"—a folder or a volume—the button says Open instead of Save.* When you want the Save button back because you've found the spot you want to save your document, any of these actions changes the Open button to a Save button:

- Click in the file name box to de-activate the list.
- Tab to the file name box to de-activate the list.
- Click on a dimmed item in the list to deselect whatever's selected.

*It was always a pet peeve of mine that this button used to say Save even when you were using it to open a folder. (If Apple keeps polishing its interface, I won't have a lot left to complain about.)

••➤ **Sometimes you'll see invisible files** in a list—that is, they're invisible if you're on the desktop, but they show up in a dialog's list. If I use Word's "All Files" option in its Open box and look at the main level of my hard drive, for instance, I see Desktop DB and Desktop DF listed—the two invisible files that make up the Mac's all-important desktop file.

••➤ **A strangely named folder** sometimes shows up on the main level of a drive in a list: *Move&Rename*, with a prefix of several boxes. It's actually an invisible folder that you can't see when you're on the desktop, and it comes and goes in response to the file sharing setup in the Sharing control panel; it keeps track of the changes that a "remote" user makes to the local disk.

## The Desktop Level

∞➤ **The desktop level in the Open/Save dialog** is new with System 7. Before that, items on the main level of the disk and those on the desktop appeared together in the same list. Now there's one list for a disk's main window, and the desktop level is separate. The desktop level list displays everything that's on the desktop—disks, loose files and folders, and even the Trash.

∞➤ **Having the Trash listed** at the desktop level is pretty useless: it's always dimmed so you can never open it. It's reasonable to be "forbidden" from working on trashed files—after all, you might retrieve one and alter it, use a quick Command-S save and save it right back into the Trash where, no doubt, it would be flushed into oblivion before you remembered to take it out. But why doesn't the Mac let you open the Trash to look inside, and if you open a document, immediately re-locate it to the desktop?

∞➤ **You can move to the desktop level** in the dialog box in any of four ways:

- Select *Desktop* from the popup menu over the list.
- Click the Desktop button.
- Press Command-D.
- Press Command-Shift-Up.

This last option is an interesting one: It's the same as the sequence that lets you activate the desktop itself when you're in the Finder. So, while the key combination makes no sense within the list of Open/Save dialog keyboard commands, it's perfectly logical in the overall Mac interface.

••➤ **The desktop you see in the list is shared** by all the disks you have attached or inserted in drives. So, if you have an internal and external hard drive, and an inserted floppy, what you see might belong to any of the three disks.

••➤ **How can you tell which disk** an item belongs to when it's in the desktop-level list? Select the item in the list, and the disk that "owns" it is identified with the icon that's over the buttons.

···▶ **The desktop-level list** uses two alphabetical groupings. First come all the volumes, and then the items that are out loose on the desktop. The picture here shows three volumes and then the files and a folder that are on the desktop. Finally, there's the dimmed Trash icon, always at the bottom of the list.

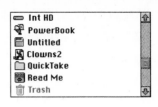

···▶ **Typing to select something in the desktop list** is a little awkward because of the two alphabetical groupings. You may be looking at a list of volumes (like the one shown here) and type a single letter, expecting to select one of them. But there might be a file lower down in the list that matches the typed letters more closely, and it will be selected instead. Typing an *I*, for instance, selects a file on my desktop named *Incineration* rather than the Int HD volume in the list.

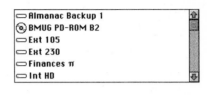

···▶ **To save a document onto the desktop,** where it will cry out for constant attention, you have to be at the desktop level. But which disk are you really saving something to if you save on the desktop level? The disk whose icon is showing in the dialog (over the buttons) is the one where the file gets saved.

If you want to save a document to the desktop of a specific disk, different from the one whose icon is in the dialog, first go to the desktop level, and then click on the name of the disk in the list.

···▶ **All of the standard options for jumping to the desktop level** in a dialog move you to the desktop of the system disk; that is, no matter which disk icon was showing in the dialog when you started, it's the system disk that's displayed by the time you jump to the desktop level.

There are two ways to get to the desktop of the current disk instead of the startup. You can click on the icon of the disk as many times as necessary to get to the desktop—each click moves you up through one folder level. Or, you can jump to the desktop level with any of the shortcuts I listed earlier, and then type the first letter or two of the disk's name so that it's selected.

···▶ **Mounted volumes on a network,** even a little one that's using file sharing between two Macs, don't share their desktops the way standard mounted disks do. Instead, each volume you access on the network has a Desktop Folder on its root level that holds all the items that are on that volume's desktop. In fact, there's a Trash folder, too, that holds the items trashed but not erased from the shared volume.

An Open/Save dialog list for a shared volume includes Desktop and Trash folders.

## Menus & Buttons

∞▸ **Create a new folder** with the New Folder button. You'll get a dialog asking you to name the new folder when you click the button. Before you click the button, though, make sure you're in the right spot: The new folder will be placed inside the folder that's currently displayed in the list box.

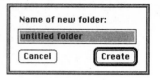

∞▸ **Move up to any folder** that's in the dialog's menu by selecting it from the menu. But if you want to move up just one level, there are two alternatives:

- Press Command-Up.
- Click on the disk icon that's above the buttons.

Even when you're moving up several disk levels, it's usually faster to use the keyboard option; pressing Command-Up, even three or four times, is faster than reaching for the mouse for a menu selection.

∞▸ **The Eject button** ejects a selected volume—if it's ejectable, that is. You'll find that the button is dimmed if you select a hard drive in the list. But select a floppy, or a CD, or even a removable SyQuest cartridge, and you can use the Eject button.

But: The ejection doesn't remove a disk's icon from the desktop. It leaves the "ghost" icon discussed in Chapter 4, and you'll be asked, sooner or later, to re-insert the disk unless you go back to the desktop and get rid of the ghost.

### NOT KASEY KASEM'S!

You can probably identify today's best-selling software without thinking too hard. Microsoft Word. Excel. Quark Xpress. And so on. But what about yesteryears? Try these on for size:

| | Dec. 85 | Apr. 86 | July. 86 | Sept. 88 | Nov. 88 |
|---|---|---|---|---|---|
| 1. | Jazz | Excel | Excel | MS Word | MS Word |
| 2. | MS Word | Jazz | MS Word | PageMaker | Excel |
| 3. | MS Multiplan | MS Word | MS File | Excel | TOPS |
| 4. | MS File | MS Multiplan | MacDraw | FullWrite | MS PowerPoint |
| 5. | MS Chart | MS File | MacProject | MacProject | MacDraw |
| 6. | Dollars & Sense | MacDraw | PageMaker | TOPS | Flight Trainer |
| 7. | MacDraw | Dollars & Sense | Jazz | MacDraw | SUM |
| 8. | MacProject | Helix | Omnis 3 | MS PowerPoint | PageMaker |
| 9. | Back to Basics | pfs:file | MS Multiplan | Cricket Presents | Quicken |
| 10. | pfs:file | MegaForm | MS Chart | 4th Dimension | FileMaker |

## Terrific Tricks

∞▸ **To select the first or last item in the list,** try using the space bar or the tilde key. These actions are only taking advantage of the alphabetization of the items in the list: the space bar, coming before A in the Mac's alphabet, selects the nearest alphabetic equivalent—

usually the first item in the list. The tilde key, unshifted, types an accent mark, which is alphabetically after Z, so it usually selects the last item. Of course, if you've used some clever naming conventions to circumvent the natural order of things, you might have a file or folder that comes before space or after the accent, but that's seldom the case.

But there is a key that *always* selects the last item in the list, no matter what its name: the Forward Delete key on the extended keyboard. (It doesn't make any sense to me, either, but, hey—it's there.)

**Use keyboard commands instead of clicking buttons** in the dialog:

| | |
|---|---|
| Open/Save | Return or Enter |
| Open | Command-O |
| Save | Command-S |
| Cancel | Command-period or Esc |
| New Folder | Command-N |
| Desktop | Command-D |

**Use keyboard editing techniques** for changing the name of a document when you do a Save As; you don't have to reach for the mouse when you want to alter the name that's in the text box.

Say you're saving a document named *Picture* as *Picture2*. When the Save As dialog opens, *Picture* is selected, and you could type *Picture2* to replace it, since selected text is replaced by new typing. Or, you can simply press the Right arrow key, which deselects the text and places the text cursor at the end of the text in the box, and just type a *2*. And if you wanted to rename it *2Picture*, you'd press the Left arrow before typing because deselects the text and puts the editing cursor at the beginning of the text.

Text editing techniques are covered in Chapter 20.

**When you move up a folder in the list** by using the popup menu in a Save dialog, the text box stays active and any selected text in it stays selected. But when you move up by using Command-Up, the list box is activated.

**There's no Drive button** in dialogs anymore, so at first it seems that the only way to look at a different disk is to move up to the desktop level and find the disk in the list. But there is a terrific keyboard shortcut to cycle around any and all mounted volumes: Command-Left moves you from one disk to the next, and Command-Right moves you in the opposite direction.

**If you're going to insert a disk** to save or open something, insert it *after* the dialog opens. Why? Because it will save you time.

If you insert a disk, then use the Open or Save command, you'll have to move to that disk, using several keystrokes or mouse moves to get there. But if you insert a disk after the dialog opens, the disk is automatically displayed in the dialog.

**The Home, End, Page Up, and Page Down keys** on the extended keyboard serve a special function inside an Open/Save dialog. Home and End display the top and bottom of the list. They don't select anything—it's just the equivalent of dragging the scroll box to the top or bottom of the scroll bar. Page Up and Page Down also scroll the list up and down without selecting anything; these keys are the equivalent of clicking in the scroll bar above or below the scroll box.

**•••▶** **This is my favorite hidden trick** in the Open/Save dialog. If you select an alias and add the Option key to whatever open routine you use—that is, hold Option and double-click on the alias, or hold Option while you click the Open button, or hold Option while you press Return to activate the Open button—the dialog list displays the *original* of the alias, jumping to whatever folder the alias is in. The original will be selected in the list, but won't be opened unless you click the Open button or press Return.

You can use this trick to both open the file and move to its folder. (I noted before that opening a file through its alias leaves you in the alias' folder.) It's a shame this procedure isn't echoed on the desktop—it would be nice to option-double-click on an icon and have its original found.

## ⇥ SYSTEM 7.5 STUFF ▷

## Launching

°°▶ **There are new ways to launch** both applications and documents in System 7.5:

- Use the Launcher Control panel. This used to be part of only the Performa system, but now it's part of mainstream Mac system software. Any items in the Launcher folder will show up in the desktop Launcher window.
- Select the document or application from the Recent folder in the Apple menu. If there are no Recent folders available, turn them on with the Apple Menu Options control panel.

```
┌─ Recent Items ─────────────────────┐
│ ⊠ Remember recently used items     │
│                                     │
│   Documents:        [20]            │
│   Applications:     [10]            │
│   Servers:          [2]             │
└─────────────────────────────────────┘
```

## Open & Save Dialogs

°°▶ **The list in Open and Save dialogs** defaults to showing the last place you worked from in the application. That means your first Open or Save during a work session always shows you the application's folder (although some applications are smart enough to default to a document's folder if you launched the application by double-clicking on the document).

But System 7.5 lets you define where the Open and Save dialogs default to: the folder which contains the application, the last folder used in the application, or the Documents folder. Use the buttons in the General Controls control panel to make your choice.

```
┌─ Documents ────────────────────────┐
│ When opening or saving a document, take me to │
│ ○ Folder which contains the application. │
│ ● Last folder used in the application. │
│ ○ Documents folder. │
└─────────────────────────────────────┘
```

What's that you say? Your application already puts you in the last folder you used? Well, now you'll get the last folder you used even if the last time you used it was last week—it's the first one you'll see when you launch the application again.

As for the Documents folder: If you choose it as the default, a Documents folder will be created on the desktop.

## The New Drag and Drop

∞▸ **Do you have the drag and drop concept** down flat now? You know it means that you can drag one icon onto another on the desktop and something happens, like a document opening into an application? Well, forget it. Apple has, without a backward glance, without apology, without a single thought for the confusion they might be sowing, introduced a new feature with System 7.5 that's named … *Drag and Drop!*

What is it? Actually, it's the only really exciting new feature as far as I'm concerned, because not only is it useful, but it's *new*, not just a previous feature being tweaked with minor improvements. Picture this: You have two applications open—a page layout program and a graphics program. You've laid out your document and left a space for the graphic. You move to the graphics program, draw the picture, select it … and *drag* it from its own window right into the window holding the layout document!

This feature is built-in to System 7.5, but you won't be able to use it until the applications you use are rewritten to take advantage of it. But System 7.5's Scrapbook and Note Pad can use the feature, so the pictures here illustrate dragging text from the Note Pad into the Scrapbook.

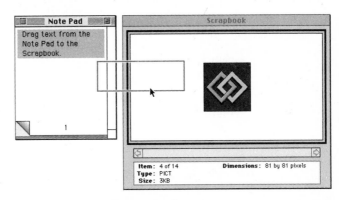

●●◗ **You can drag and drop a selection** from a document right onto the desktop, and later drag the item—called a *clipping*—into another document. This is what the clipping icons look like on the desktop.

text clipping

picture clipping

# CHAPTER 20

# TEXT & GRAPHICS

> But computers will never be perfected until they can compute how much more than the estimate the job will cost.

LAURENCE J. PETER

A representative, though incomplete, list of the kernels of knowledge in this chapter:

- ••◆ The Caps Lock key is not a Shift Lock key.
- ••◆ How to type in "shorthand."
- ••◆ TeachText and SimpleText aren't much on input, but they can open all sorts of basic files for you.
- ••◆ The Mac is not a typewriter.
- ••◆ The key combinations for typing certain special characters changed from System 6 to System 7.
- ••◆ You type invisible characters all the time.
- ••◆ You need an eraser to get rid of text in some graphics programs.

**THE SMALLEST ITEM IN THIS CHAPTER THAT YOU SHOULD KNOW BUT MAYBE YOU DIDN'T**

*You can drag backwards while selecting text.*

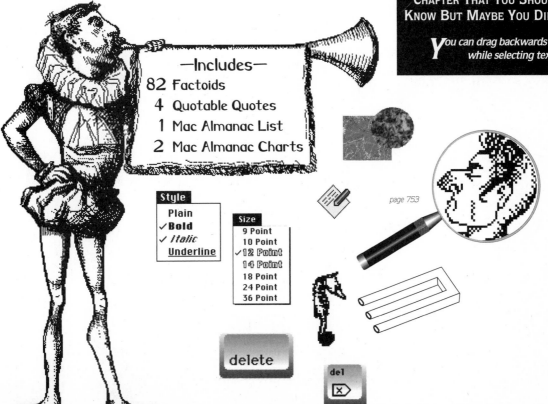

—Includes—

82 Factoids

4 Quotable Quotes

1 Mac Almanac List

2 Mac Almanac Charts

*page 753*

**Style**
Plain
✓**Bold**
✓ *Italic*
<u>Underline</u>

**Size**
9 Point
10 Point
✓ 12 Point
14 Point
18 Point
24 Point
36 Point

delete

del

## ≡ TEXT BASICS ≡

### The Insertion Point

∞➤ **When the mouse cursor is within a text area,** it changes to the *text*, or *I-beam*, cursor.

| The mouse cursor changes when it's in a text area. | I The mouse cursor changes when it's in a text area. |
|---|---|

∞➤ **The basic rule of Mac text handling is:** *everything happens at the insertion point.* The insertion point, often referred to as the *blinking cursor*, is a blinking vertical line. As you type, letters appear at the insertion point. If you use the Delete key, the insertion point moves backwards, erasing text as it goes. If you paste something into a text document, it's inserted at—you guessed it— the insertion point. The insertion point is *not* the same as the I-beam cursor. You have to click the I-beam to place the insertion point in text.

Typing, deleting, and pasting are all done at the insertion point.

| T| | Delete| | Paste|in |
|---|---|---|
| Ty| | Delet| | Paste this in |
| Typ| | Dele| | |
| Typi| | Del| | |
| Typin| | De| | |
| Typing| | D| | |

∞➤ **Since you can move the insertion point,** you can enter or edit text anyplace in your document. Small moves—one character left or right, or one line up or down—are easiest with the arrow keys on the keyboard. Moving farther than that is easiest by using the mouse: Just click where you want the insertion point to go.

| clicking in|text |
|---|
| clicking in|text I |

∞➤ **The Home, End, Page Up and Page Down keys** also control the position of the insertion point. Depending on the application you're in, Home and End may move you to the beginning and end of the document, or just to the top and bottom of the screen; Page Up and Page Down might move you a "windowful" at a time, or shift the cursor to the previous and next printed page. Many applications, especially word processors, have special key combinations that move the insertion point by handy increments like words, sentences, and paragraphs.

∞➤ **The insertion point can be placed** only within existing text. So, for instance, you can't click halfway down in the blank window of a new document to begin typing there. Instead, you have to "type" your way to that spot by pressing Return to move the insertion point there.

∞➤ **Basic text handling techniques** for moving the insertion point, and selecting and editing text, work almost everywhere, not just in word processors. You can use them in desk accessories like the Note Pad, on icon names on the desktop, and even in dialog boxes that have text boxes.

### Entering & Editing Text

∞➤ **Holding down a key** repeatedly types the character. There's a slight hesitation before the second letter appears on the screen—to give you a chance to get your finger off the key. But after that, the letters appear without any delay.

Set the delay rate with the Keyboard control panel. See Chapter 8.

•➤ **Entering text is straightforward** typing *except* that you don't press Return at the end of one line to move down to the next. The insertion point automatically moves down to the next line as you type. If you're in the middle of a word the entire word is shifted down to the next line. This is called *text wrap* or *word wrap*.

| |
|---|
| Keep typing as you rea| |
| Keep typing as you reach the end of a line| |

•➤ **To insert text,** put the insertion point in the right spot and type. (Early word processors on other computers had "insert" and "overtype" modes, but the Mac is always in insert mode.)

Simple editing

Simple|editing

Simple text|editing

•➤ **Delete text** with the Delete key, which moves the insertion point backwards, erasing letters as it goes. The Forward Delete key on an extended keyboard erases the letter in front of the insertion point. Holding down Forward Delete turns it into a vacuum cleaner that sucks up all the text in front of it. (Early keyboards had a Backspace key instead of Delete.)

| | |
|---|---|
| Deleting all\|the text | Deleting all\|the text |
| Deleting al\|the text | Deleting all\|he text |
| Deleting a\|the text | Deleting all\|e text |
| Deleting\| the text | Deleting all \|text |

> The biggest obstacle to professional writing is the necessity for changing a typewriter ribbon.

ROBERT BENCHLEY
1889-1945

•➤ **To start a new paragraph,** press the Return key. A new paragraph is really just starting a new line before you've typed all the way to the end of the current one. So, in a list of single short lines, each line is really a paragraph as far as any word processor is concerned.

•➤ **The Caps Lock key** is just that: *Caps* lock, not *Shift* lock. What's the difference? Well, using it gives you capital letters when you type an alphabetic key, but you don't get the shifted characters on other keys; so, you still get 5 when you type that key, not the % character, while Caps Lock is down. You also get all the unshifted punctuation marks instead of the shifted ones, so that when you're typing in all caps, you can still type a comma and period instead of < and >.

*Change the highlight color with the Color control panel, described in Chapter 8.*

## Selecting Text

•➤ **You select text to** format it, delete it, or replace it. Selected text is *highlighted:* inverted to white on black, or, on color and grayscale systems, marked with a color behind it.

•➤ **The basic way to select text** is to drag across it with the mouse. All the text from the beginning of the drag to the end gets selected.

| | |
|---|---|
| The\|easiest way to select small portions of text is by dragging the mouse across it. | The easiest way to ⌶ select small portions of text is by dragging the mouse across it. |

**Take drag shortcuts.** You don't have to drag to the end of one line and around to the beginning of the next: Just take the shortest path from the starting point to the end spot.

| The easiest way to select a small portion of text is by dragging the mouse across it. | The easiest way to select a small portion of text is by dragging the mouse across it. |
|---|---|

**You can drag backwards.** Okay, that may seem obvious to you, but a lot of people don't realize that dragging works both ways.

**Double-click on a word** to select it. In some programs, this selects only the word itself; in others, it conveniently selects the trailing space, too, so if you

Double-clicking selects a single word.
Double-clicking selects a single word.

hit the Delete key to delete the word, you're not left with two spaces between the words on either side. *Really* smart programs select the trailing space, but if you type to replace the word (instead of deleting it), the trailing space is left in after all, so you don't have to type it again.

**Shift-click to select** large areas of text: Put the insertion point at one end of the area you want to select, find the other end (even if you have to scroll the window to get there), and click again while you hold the Shift key. This selects everything from the first click, where the insertion point is, to the shift-click spot. The picture here illustrates a click before the word *shift*, which leaves the insertion point there, and a shift-click after the word *areas*.

| The shift-click method of selecting text is a quick way to select larger or irregular areas of text. | The shift-click method of selecting text is a quick way to select larger or irregular areas of text. | The shift-click method of selecting text is a quick way to select larger or irregular areas of text. |
|---|---|---|

**The Shift key extends** a selection even if you drag instead of click with the Shift key down.

**Shift-clicking changes the size** of a selection, making it larger or smaller. Just shift-click at the new end point for the selection. If you shift-click beyond the original selection, you get a bigger selection; if you shift-click within the selection, it gets smaller. (This is like shift-clicking on icons on the desktop, where you can add an icon to, or subtract it from, the selection, by shift-clicking on it.) The selection you're left with after the second shift-click depends on the original position of the text cursor. The top part of the picture here shows where the insertion point is to start with, and the original selection. The samples at the bottom show what happens if you shift-click beyond the original selection (left), within it (middle), or in front of the original cursor position (right).

| | |
|---|---|
| Everything depends\|on the initial position of the insertion point. | Everything depends on the initial position[of the insertion point. |

| | | |
|---|---|---|
| Everything depends on the initial position of the insertion]point. | Everything depends on the initial[position of the insertion point. | ]Everything depends on the initial position of the insertion point. |

☞ **There's no insertion point when text** is selected, so whatever would normally happen at the insertion point happens to the entire selection instead:

- Typing replaces the selection with whatever you're typing.
- Pasting replaces the selection with the current contents of the Clipboard.
- The Delete key erases the selected text.
- The Forward Delete key also erases the selection.

There are also several things you can do to selected text that don't apply to the insertion point:

- The Cut or Copy command puts the selection on the Clipboard.
- The Clear command (if there is one in the Edit menu) deletes the selection without putting it on the Clipboard.
- Character formats (fonts and styles, for instance) are applied to the selected text.

☞ **Deselect text** by:

- Clicking anywhere in the text of the document. This deselects the text and puts the insertion point at the clicked spot.
- Making another selection. This is handy to keep in mind—you don't have to, for instance, click someplace to deselect something and then make a new selection. Save yourself a step.
- Using an arrow key to deselect the text and move to the beginning or end of the selection. In my totally unscientific yet relatively broad-ranging experiments, all applications seem to support the left arrow key for this technique, leaving the insertion point blinking at the beginning of the selection (well, what *used* to be the selection—you know what I mean). *Most* applications also support the right arrow key for this, and *many* of them leave the insertion point at the end of the selection; unfortunately, some let you deselect text with the right arrow, but put the insertion point at the *beginning* of the selection, which is very disconcerting. (The Interface Police ought to go after them.) Some applications let you use the up and down arrow keys to deselect text, leaving the insertion point at the beginning or end of the selection; many programs inexcusably ignore those keys altogether while there's a selection on the screen.
- Using the Home, End, Page Up, and Page Down keys on the extended keyboard usually deselects text, too, and moves the cursor to the beginning or end of the page or document. This varies from one program to the next.

••♦ **Using Shift to change a text selection** extends (or shortens) a selection in the unit of the original selection. So, if you double-click to select a whole word and then click or drag with the Shift key down, the selection jumps forward word by word, not to the exact spot where your mouse cursor is. If you're in an application that lets you select sentences or paragraphs as a unit, shift-clicking or shift-dragging selects entire sentences or paragraphs afterwards.

••♦ **Watch out for off-screen selections.** If you make a selection and then scroll the window, the selection is off-screen—but it's still what will be affected by any editing action. You might hit delete and erase it, or you might start typing and replace it. Most applications will immediately display the area you're working in when you start typing, so the window should jump to that part of the text (the part you're changing by mistake). That's when you'll catch on to what's going on (at least, we can hope so!) and you can use the Undo command.

## TeachText

••♦ **TeachText is a simple** text utility that's been bundled with Mac system software for many years. It can't do much except create and open simple text files, and open simple graphics files. But since everybody has it, it serves as a common denominator for *Read Me* files—a document that accompanies many Mac products. Read Me's contain late-breaking information that didn't make it into the documentation. Sometimes a Read Me *is* the documentation, when it accompanies shareware.

TeachText is usually put onto your hard drive, in its main window, during a system install.

••♦ **You can't do much in a TeachText** document except type basic text. The two menus here are the sum total of the commands available—no fonts, sizes, or styles; we're talking *plain* here. In fact, it's so plain that you can't even open more than one document at a time. You can't paste a graphic in either, although TeachText can open a graphics file.

| File | | Edit | |
|---|---|---|---|
| New | ⌘N | Undo | ⌘Z |
| Open... | ⌘O | | |
| | | Cut | ⌘X |
| Close | ⌘W | Copy | ⌘C |
| Save | ⌘S | Paste | ⌘V |
| Save As... | | Clear | |
| | | | |
| Page Setup... | | Select All | ⌘A |
| Print... | ⌘P | | |
| | | Show Clipboard | |
| Quit | ⌘Q | | |

••♦ **Double-clicking on a text file** or a PICT-type graphics document when its parent application isn't around gets you the dialog box shown here. This polite offer and capability for opening basic text and graphics files is what makes TeachText so handy.

The document "PICTure" could not be opened, because the application program that created it could not be found. Do you want to open it using "TeachText"?

Cancel    OK

**G**raphics formats are covered later in this chapter.

••♦ **Change the width of a TeachText window,** and you change the margins of the texts in it; the text automatically rewraps to fill the width of the window.

•••➤ **You can select any part of a TeachText graphic** to copy it. This certainly isn't immediately apparent, because there's no selection tool available; most people settle for the Select All command in the Edit menu before copying a graphic.

But as soon as you put the mouse cursor anywhere in the window of a document that contains a graphic, the cursor changes to a crosshairs; you can select any rectangular portion you want before using the Copy command. (You can't use the Cut command because you can't alter a graphics file in TeachText.)

You can select a part of a graphic in the window; the selection tool appears automatically.

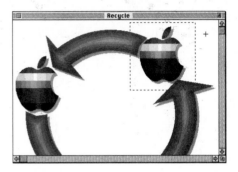

•••➤ **Check for extraneous copies of TeachText** on your hard drive; you need only one, and it's installed with system software. But TeachText comes with many commercial applications and shareware utilities, so it's easy to wind up with multiple copies on your drive. Use the Find command at the desktop to see how many you have, and get rid of the extras.

## SimpleText

∞•➤ **SimpleText, TeachText's replacement** somewhere around the third hardware update for System 7.1, isn't all that simple. That is, it's simple to use, but it can do more things than its predecessor. Just comparing its File and Edit menus with those of TeachText shows some basic differences.

| File | | Edit | |
|---|---|---|---|
| New | ⌘N | Undo | ⌘Z |
| Open... | ⌘O | | |
| | | Cut | ⌘H |
| Close | ⌘W | Copy | ⌘C |
| Save | ⌘S | Paste | ⌘U |
| Save As... | | Clear | |
| Page Setup... | | Select All | ⌘A |
| Print... | ⌘P | | |
| Print One Copy | | Next Page | ⌘= |
| | | Previous Page | ⌘- |
| Quit | ⌘Q | Go to Page... | ⌘G |
| | | Show Clipboard | |

∞•➤ **SimpleText offers true text formatting**, with Font, Size, and Style menus. Apply the formats as you type, or to selected text after you type.

| Size | Style | |
|---|---|---|
| 9 Point | Plain Text | ⌘T |
| 10 Point | ✓**Bold** | ⌘B |
| ✓12 Point | *Italic* | ⌘I |
| 14 Point | Underline | ⌘U |
| 18 Point | Outline | |
| 24 Point | Shadow | |
| 36 Point | Condensed | |
| | Extended | |

•••••••••••••••••••••••••••••••••••••••••••••••••••••

## MAC PEOPLE                                     JOHN SCULLEY

Prince of Pepsi turns computer visionary? Such is the story of John Sculley. Although in boyhood he dreamed of being an inventor, he ended up in architecture school. After a brief stint in advertising, he got into Pepsico, the world's second-largest soft drink company, by the time-honored method of marrying the chairman's daughter.

If mere nepotism had been at work, Sculley would have puttered along in safe mediocrity at Pepsico. But he made real contributions as he worked his way up the corporate ladder, promoting the highly successful Pepsi Generation and Pepsi Challenge ad campaigns and reorganizing the company's snack foods division. Still, he must have felt there was something missing, because when Steve Jobs invited him to join Apple's top management in 1985, Sculley didn't take long to make up his mind.

By the time Sculley came on board, Apple was a billion-dollar corporation, and the *ad hoc* management style of its two Founders (Jobs and Wozniak) was no longer workable. Steve Jobs knew Apple needed some real management expertise, and Sculley was brought in to supply it. What Jobs didn't know was that within a little over a year, he and co-founder Steve Wozniak would both be forced out of Apple by John Sculley, leaving Sculley in control.

Initially ridiculed by many as a "bean-counter" and computer illiterate, Sculley set Apple on a steady course toward increased Macintosh sales and more responsiveness to the customer. If the closed architecture and tiny black-and-white screen of the original Mac typified Steve Jobs' "I know what's best for you" philosophy, then the modular, expandable architecture of the Mac II was Sculley's response to customers' demands for expandability and speed—and color. Under Sculley's leadership, Apple enjoyed steadily increasing sales while introducing innovations such as HyperCard and the PowerBooks.

But even bean-counters can dream of greater things, and Sculley's famous "Knowledge Navigator" video (a simulation of possible future computer technology) showed his visions had become rather grandiose. Eventually Sculley himself was forced out of Apple, replaced in 1993 by the stolid, unimaginative Michael Spindler, a hard-driving executive from Apple Germany who bears the nickname "Diesel." After leaving Apple, Sculley moved to the chairmanship of a small telecommunications company—but left within a month in a series of ugly recriminations and lawsuits. Thereafter, John Sculley simply sank from sight. Prince of Pepsi turns computer visionary turns invisible, you might say.

**STEVE JOBS**
(to John Sculley, when wooing him away from Pepsico)

> Do you want to spend the rest of your life selling sugared water, or do you want a chance to change the world?

•••► **To change paragraph margins** in SimpleText, you change the width of the window. The text always goes from one edge of the window to the other, no matter how wide or narrow you make it. There aren't any other paragraph formatting options available.

•••► **SimpleText's Sound menu** is intriguing, but it's only a teaser if your Mac can't input sound and handle speech. The dialogs that appear in response to the basic commands look like their control panel counterparts.

# A MAC ALMANAC CHART

## Keyboard Guide for the Basic Character Set

| Key | | SHIFT | OPT | SHIFT OPT |
|---|---|---|---|---|
| A | a | A | å | Å |
| B | b | B | ∫ | ı |
| C | c | C | ç | Ç |
| D | d | D | ∂ | Î |
| E | e | E | | ´ |
| F | f | F | ƒ | Ï |
| G | g | G | © | ˝ |
| H | h | H | ˙ | Ó |
| I | i | I | | ˆ |
| J | j | J | ∆ | Ô |
| K | k | K | ˚ |  |
| L | l | L | ¬ | Ò |
| M | m | M | µ | Â |
| N | n | N | ˜ | ˜ |
| O | o | O | ø | Ø |
| P | p | P | π | ∏ |
| Q | q | Q | œ | Œ |
| R | r | R | ® | ‰ |
| S | s | S | ß | Í |
| T | t | T | | ˇ |
| U | u | U | | ¨ |
| V | v | V | √ | ◊ |
| W | w | W | ∑ | „ |
| X | x | X | ≈ | ˛ |

| Key | | SHIFT | OPT | SHIFT OPT |
|---|---|---|---|---|
| Y | y | Y | ¥ | Á |
| Z | z | Z | Ω | ¸ |
| 1 | 1 | ! | ¡ | ⁄ |
| 2 | 2 | @ | ™ | ¤ |
| 3 | 3 | # | £ | ‹ |
| 4 | 4 | $ | ¢ | › |
| 5 | 5 | 5 | ∞ | fi |
| 6 | 6 | ^ | § | fl |
| 7 | 7 | & | ¶ | ‡ |
| 8 | 8 | * | • | ° |
| 9 | 9 | ( | ª | · |
| 0 | 0 | ) | º | ‚ |
| ` | ` | ` | ~ | ` |
| - | - | _ | – | — |
| = | = | + | ≠ | ± |
| [ | [ | { | " | " |
| ] | ] | } | ' | ' |
| \ | \ | \| | « | » |
| ; | ; | : | … | Ú |
| ' | " | ' | æ | Æ |
| , | , | < | ≤ | ¯ |
| . | . | > | ≥ | ˘ |
| / | / | ? | ÷ | ¿ |
| [spc] | | | | |

| | a | A | e | E | i | I | o | O | u | U | n | N |
|---|---|---|---|---|---|---|---|---|---|---|---|---|
| OPT ` | à | À | è | È | ì | Ì | ò | Ò | ù | Ù | | |
| OPT e | á | Á | é | É | í | Í | ó | Ó | ú | Ú | | |
| OPT i | â | Â | ê | Ê | î | Î | ô | Ô | û | Û | | |
| OPT u | ä | Ä | ë | Ë | ï | Ï | ö | Ö | ü | Ü | | |
| OPT n | ã | Ã | | | | | õ | Õ | | | ñ | Ñ |

748

## ◄ SPECIAL TYPING CONSIDERATIONS ►

### Character Sets

∞► **The characters available from the keyboard** vary from one font to the next, but a font can have up to four sets of keyboard characters: unshifted, shifted, option, and option-shift. As described in Chapter 11, you can use Key Caps to view and find all these characters, but here's a picture of the four basic keyboard sets.

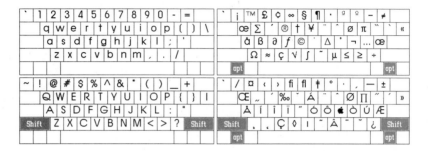

∞► **Some keyboard combinations changed** from System 6 to System 7 for certain characters. There's no effect on documents created in one system and opened in another—it's just the way you type them in that has changed. This is why there are two keyboard layouts in your System file, accessible from the Keyboard control panel: U.S. and U.S.-System 6. If you select U.S. (the default), you'll need the current key combinations to type the characters; if you select U.S.-System 6, you'll need the old ones.

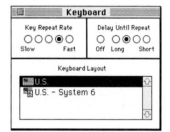

| Character | System 7 | System 6 |
|---|---|---|
| Â | Shift-Option-M<br>Option-I, Shift-A | Shift-Option-R |
| È | Option-`, Shift-E | Shift-Option-I |
| Ë | Option-U, Shift-E | Shift-Option-U |
| Ê | Option-I, Shift-E | Shift-Option-T |
| Ì | Option-`, Shift-I | Shift-Option-G |
| Ù | Option-`, Shift-U | Shift-Option-X |
| Û | Option-I, Shift-U | Shift-Option-Z |
| Ÿ | Option-U, Shift-Y | Shift-Option-` |
| ´ | Shift-Option-E<br>Option-`, space | Option-`, space |
| ^ | Shift-Option-I | Shift-Option-N |
| ~ | Shift-Option-N<br>Option-N, space | Shift-Option-M<br>Option-N, space |
| ¨ | Shift-Option-U<br>Option-U, space | Option-U, space |
| ‚ | Shift-Option-Z | [none] |
| „ | Shift-Option-G | [none] |
| ‰ | Shift-Option-R | Shift-Option-E |

‣ **It's not too difficult to remember where special** characters are because so many are placed on the keys or key combinations in some logical manner. And where there's no logic found—or intended, for that matter—you can usually make up some connection between what you see on the keyboard and what you type. For instance:

| Character | Type | Logic |
|---|---|---|
| • | Option-8 | Asterisk is on 8 key; it's pretty round, too. |
| ° | Shift-Option-8 | Similar in shape to bullet and asterisk on 8 key. |
| ō | Option-0 (zero) | Looks like underlined zero; or, since 0 is after 9 on the keyboard, it looks like a sideways 10. |
| ® | Option-R | The R key, of course. |
| ∞ | Option-5 | Percent sign also on 5 key; this looks a little like a squashed and flattened %. |
| … | Option-semicolon | There's a colon on this key, with two dots; this is three. |
| ¿ | Shift-Option-/ | Shift-/ is the question mark. |
| ¨ | Option-U | This is an umlaut character; that starts with U. |
| √ | Option-V | A basic V-shape. |
| ◊ | Shift-Option-V | Two V shapes together. |
| ¬ | Option-L | Looks like an L lying down (and flipped over). |
| – (n-dash) | Option-hyphen | A short hyphen. |
| — (m-dash) | Shift-Option-hyphen | A long hyphen. |
| ≠ | Option-equals | The *does not equal* sign. |
| ± | Shift-Option-equals | The Shift-equals key gives you the plus sign; this is "plus or minus." |
| ≤, ≥ | Option-comma, Option-period | These keys also have the < and > symbols on them. |
| ÷ | Option-/ | The slash is used for division on the keypad. |
| ¡ | Option-1 | Looks like upside-down exclamation point; exclamation point also on the 1 key. |
| ƒ | Option-F | Looks like a lowercase f. (Many people use this to stand for "folder," as in Games *ƒ*.) |
| ¢ | Option-4 | Dollar sign also on 4 key. |
| † | Option-T | It looks like a T, doesn't it? |
| ¥ | Option-Y | Looks like a Y. |
| fi | Shift-Option-5 | "Five" starts with the first two characters of this ligature. |
| å, Å | Option-A, Shift-Option-A | They're special A's. |
| ç, Ç | Option-C, Shift-Option-C | Just fancy lowercase and uppercase C's. |
| ø, Ø | Option-O, Option-Shift-O | They're just slashed O's. |
| π, ∏ | Option-P, Shift-Option-P | P for pi, lowercase and uppercase. |
| µ (mu) | Option-M | Mu starts with M. |

‣ **Every letter has a number** in the numeric world of computers. And, in order to make the exchange of information between computers easier, there's long been a standard code used to identify each character you type. The standard is *ASCII*—American Standard Code for Information Interchange; it's pronounced *ask-key*. (Oh, all right, it's pronounced *ASS-key* but that doesn't look very polite.) Codes 1 through 31 are reserved for nonprinting items like tabs, newlines, and returns; numbers 32 through 255 are shown in the chart on the following page. (And there's a tear-out version at the back of the book.)

Why 255? Because, along with the zero used for the first character, that makes 256, which, as you should know by now, is one of the more magical binary numbers.

## ASCII Code Chart

| | | | | | | | | | | | | | |
|---|---|---|---|---|---|---|---|---|---|---|---|---|---|
| 32 | spc | 64 | @ | 96 | ` | 128 | Ä | 160 | † | 192 | ¿ | 224 | ‡ |
| 33 | ! | 65 | A | 97 | a | 129 | Å | 161 | ° | 193 | ¡ | 225 | · |
| 34 | " | 66 | B | 98 | b | 130 | Ç | 162 | ¢ | 194 | ¬ | 226 | ‚ |
| 35 | # | 67 | C | 99 | c | 131 | É | 163 | £ | 195 | √ | 227 | „ |
| 36 | $ | 68 | D | 100 | d | 132 | Ñ | 164 | § | 196 | ƒ | 228 | ‰ |
| 37 | % | 69 | E | 101 | e | 133 | Ö | 165 | • | 197 | ≈ | 229 | Â |
| 38 | & | 70 | F | 102 | f | 134 | Ü | 166 | ¶ | 198 | ∆ | 230 | Ê |
| 39 | ' | 71 | G | 103 | g | 135 | á | 167 | ß | 199 | « | 231 | Á |
| 40 | ( | 72 | H | 104 | h | 136 | à | 168 | ® | 200 | » | 232 | Ë |
| 41 | ) | 73 | I | 105 | i | 137 | â | 169 | © | 201 | … | 233 | È |
| 42 | * | 74 | J | 106 | j | 138 | ä | 170 | ™ | 202 | | 234 | Í |
| 43 | + | 75 | K | 107 | k | 139 | ã | 171 | ´ | 203 | À | 235 | Î |
| 44 | , | 76 | L | 108 | l | 140 | å | 172 | ¨ | 204 | Ã | 236 | Ï |
| 45 | - | 77 | M | 109 | m | 141 | ç | 173 | ≠ | 205 | Õ | 237 | Ì |
| 46 | . | 78 | N | 110 | n | 142 | é | 174 | Æ | 206 | Œ | 238 | Ó |
| 47 | / | 79 | O | 111 | o | 143 | è | 175 | Ø | 207 | œ | 239 | Ô |
| 48 | 0 | 80 | P | 112 | p | 144 | ê | 176 | ∞ | 208 | – | 240 |  |
| 49 | 1 | 81 | Q | 113 | q | 145 | ë | 177 | ± | 209 | — | 241 | Ò |
| 50 | 2 | 82 | R | 114 | r | 146 | í | 178 | ≤ | 210 | " | 242 | Ò |
| 51 | 3 | 83 | S | 115 | s | 147 | ì | 179 | ≥ | 211 | " | 243 | Ú |
| 52 | 4 | 84 | T | 116 | t | 148 | î | 180 | ¥ | 212 | ' | 244 | Û |
| 53 | 5 | 85 | U | 117 | u | 149 | ï | 181 | µ | 213 | ' | 245 | ı |
| 54 | 6 | 86 | V | 118 | v | 150 | ñ | 182 | ∂ | 214 | ÷ | 246 | ^ |
| 55 | 7 | 87 | W | 119 | w | 151 | ó | 183 | Σ | 215 | ◊ | 247 | ~ |
| 56 | 8 | 88 | X | 120 | x | 152 | ò | 184 | Π | 216 | ÿ | 248 | ˘ |
| 57 | 9 | 89 | Y | 121 | y | 153 | ô | 185 | π | 217 | Ÿ | 249 | ˇ |
| 58 | : | 90 | Z | 122 | z | 154 | ö | 186 | ∫ | 218 | ⁄ | 250 | ˙ |
| 59 | ; | 91 | [ | 123 | { | 155 | õ | 187 | ª | 219 | ¤ | 251 | ˚ |
| 60 | < | 92 | \ | 124 | \| | 156 | ú | 188 | º | 220 | ‹ | 252 | ¸ |
| 61 | = | 93 | ] | 125 | } | 157 | ù | 189 | Ω | 221 | › | 253 | ˝ |
| 62 | > | 94 | ^ | 126 | ~ | 158 | û | 190 | æ | 222 | fl | 254 | ˛ |
| 63 | ? | 95 | _ | 127 | none | 159 | ü | 191 | ø | 223 | fi | 255 | ˇ |

## Accent Marks

∞▶ **Using accent marks** is easy, although the method is far from obvious. You type the key combination that provides the accent, but nothing appears on the screen. Then you type the letter to be accented and—*voilà!*—the letter and the accent appear together. So, for instance, I just typed *v,o,i,l,Option-`,a* to get that nicely accented *voilà*, although the Option-` combination didn't put anything on the screen.*

There are five basic accent marks included in most fonts:

| Name | Keys | Accent | Sample |
|---|---|---|---|
| Acute accent | Option-e | ´ | é |
| Grave accent | Option-` | ` | è |
| Circumflex | Option-i | ^ | ô |
| Umlaut | Option-u | ¨ | ü |
| Tilde | Option-n | ~ | ñ |

*To everyone in my friend Joanne Ferreri Coté-Bonanno's office in the Life Skills Center at Montclair State University: Type Option-e and then e for that accent!

Chapter 11 covers using accents, which ones are in which fonts, and using Key Caps to help find them, but here's a repeat of the standard accents chart from that chapter to show you where everything is in a font that provides a full set of accented characters. The chart shows how using Option plus a character (in the first column) and following it with an unshifted or shifted letter produces an accented character.

## Standard Accents Chart

| | | a | A | e | E | i | I | o | O | u | U | n | N |
|---|---|---|---|---|---|---|---|---|---|---|---|---|---|
| OPT | ` | à | À | è | È | ì | Ì | ò | Ò | ù | Ù | | |
| OPT | e | á | Á | é | É | í | Í | ó | Ó | ú | Ú | | |
| OPT | i | â | Â | ê | Ê | î | Î | ô | Ô | û | Û | | |
| OPT | u | ä | Ä | ë | Ë | ï | Ï | ö | ö | ü | Ü | | |
| OPT | n | ã | Ã | | | | | õ | Õ | | | ñ | Ñ |

••➤ **There are some accent combinations** that you can't type. The tilde, for instance, won't go over an *e*: You'll get just a box and then the *e*. (This is no great loss, since no language uses such an accented character.)

••➤ **Three of the basic accents** are available in the main character set of each font—they're printed right on the keyboard keys. The tilde (~) and the grave accent (`) are both on the key in the upper-left corner; the circumflex, or carat (^), is on the 6 key. You can't type the accents from these keys on top of other letters, but the arrangement makes it easy to type the accents by themselves if you need to.

••➤ **To type either of the two accents** that aren't on the keyboard—the umlaut and the acute accent—type the key combination for the accent (Option-u or Option-e), and then type a space.

*✳Did the bold phrase catch your eye? You shouldn't get stuck in a typewriter, either.*

## Type Right

∞➤ **Don't get stuck in a typewriter** mode.* Here's the difference between typing as if you were using a typewriter and as if you knew what you're doing on a Mac:

| Typewriter | Mac |
|---|---|
| Use <u>underline</u> for emphasis. | Use *italic* or **bold** for emphasis. |
| Use two spaces after the end of a sentence. | Use a single space after the end of sentence; proportional type provides the visual clues needed in a body of text. |
| Use two dashes--like this--for setting off text. | Use an em dash—like this—by typing Shift-Option-hyphen. |
| Use straight quotes "like this" and straight apostrophes ('). | Use curly quotes "like these" from Option-[ and Shift-Option-[. The curly apostrophe is on Shift-Option-]. |

### AD HOC #6

Outliners were a dandy invention—a whole new category of software introduced by a product named ThinkTank from David and Peter Winer's company Living VideoText. Outlining hardly exists as a separate category anymore, thanks (sort of) to the inclusion of outlining capabilities in most word processor programs. One of the most amusing Mac ads over the years was for the outliner Acta, which showed how Julius Caesar might have used it to organize his thoughts (not to mention Gaul):

Things to Do Today

> Come, see, conquer

> Make salad for toga party

> Something different ... romaine,
  garlic, eggs, anchovies and croutons?

> Send thank you to Cleo for pyramid tour

> RSVP to Senate for Ides of March event

> Invade Carthage

> Take chariot in for tune-up

> Remember to have wheel hubs greased

> Set date for next bocce game

> Series stands at 8-2 Brutus

### POP QUIZ                    [5 POINTS]

What's the clever little pun hidden in Caesar's outline?

••▶ **There are hyphens and there are hyphens.** The hyphen that's on the key next to the zero key is a true hyphen and should be used for hyphenation, as in Julien Bennett-Holmes. The Option-hyphen character, called an *en dash*, should be used for math: 5–2. The Shift-Option-hyphen character, called an *em dash*, is longer, and is used to set off text—like this. The characters get their names from the fact that they're supposed to be the same width as an *n* and an *m* in a given font.

••▶ **Typing fractions is always a problem** in almost any font. Just typing with the slash makes it look like this: 1/2. That's a good reminder that a fraction is, after all, a division problem, but it's easy to misread (*take one divided by two cups of water...*).

The first, partial, fix is to use the special *virgule* character that's on Shift-Option-1 in most fonts; it's a slash that's at a better angle for fractions: 1⁄2 instead of 1/2. How effective this is depends on what font you're using.

Next, assuming that you're using a word processor that lets you superscript characters, superscript the numerator and set it to about three-quarters of the point size you're using in the text—say, 8 points for 12-point text. Change the denominator's size to match—but *don't* subscript it. You get this: ½. If you're in a good program, one that lets you kern letters, you can push the characters closer together or further apart.

Many fonts include specially designed characters to be used as fractions. The Utility City font from DublClick that I describe in Chapter 11 as providing arrows and check-boxes also does little tricks with the Helvetica and Times fonts built into the LaserWriter to make real fractions; although you're limited to Helvetica and Times, no matter what font you're using for the body text, that at least gives you a choice between serif and sans serif type.

> ✳This led, in a roundabout way, to one hell of a problem in the production of this book. Details in Chapter 24.

•••❯ **The relative sizes of a hyphen,** an em dash, and an en dash change from font to font.* All fonts keep an en dash shorter than the em dash but just how long is long, and how short is short, varies, as you can see in the samples here.

| Font | hyphen | em | en |
|------|--------|----|----|
| Times | - | — | – |
| Helvetica | - | — | – |
| Avant Garde | - | — | – |
| *Zapf Chancery* | - | — | – |
| Courier | - | — | – |
| Palatino | - | — | – |
| New York | - | — | – |
| Geneva | - | — | – |
| **Chicago** | - | — | - |
| Bookman | - | — | – |

∘∘◇ **You don't have to remember where special characters are** when you use a program that takes what you actually type and changes it to what you *wanted* to type. Many word processors have built-in curly, or *smart*, quotes: You type a quote or apostrophe from the standard key, and the program substitutes the correct curly character for it. Most programs can figure out whether to use an open or close quote (or standard or reverse apostrophe, also called close and open single quote) based on the character you typed before it. So, if you type it [apostrophe] s, you'll get it's; but if you type it [space][apostrophe] s, you'll get it 's because the space indicates you're starting a quote, not contracting two words.

Even clever programs can get mixed up when you're editing. Say you finish a sentence, type a space, and then go back to change an *its* to an *it's* by inserting an apostrophe. All the program knows is that the last character you typed was a space, so it puts in a reverse apostrophe. But a *really* smart program, like Word, can look at what's around the insertion point before it inserts the apostrophe or quote, and can get it right every time.

If you're using a program that doesn't provide smart quotes, you can get a system-level utility that does. The aptly named *SmartQuotes* provides curly quotes and apostrophes, and can even turn a double hyphen into an em dash. It's just about perfect, doing only one small thing, but doing it extremely well.

The Thunder spelling checker is a full-fledged typing utility that I describe elsewhere in this chapter; it also provides smart quotes and the double-hyphen-into-em dash. [Thunder, Baseline Software; SmartQuotes, shareware, Philip Borenstein]

## Pop Quiz [5 points]

*Mad* magazine's optical illusion object was called The Mad Poiuyt. Where did they get that name? (And if you know the answer, you'll know why it's in this section of the book.)

## Odds & Ends

∞•➤ **There are invisible characters** in almost any text document. When you type a Tab, for instance, the insertion point moves over to a tab mark, but you don't actually *see* a tab; the same goes for a paragraph mark. But a computer needs a symbol for everything you type, so there's a character of one kind or another stored  every time you use an alphanumeric key. Most word processor and page layout programs let you turn invisible characters on and off for editing purposes, and that's very helpful when you have formatting problems that need attention—you'll be able to see, for instance, where multiple spaces were typed instead of a tab.

•➤ **Word processor programs often use special characters** that affect how words are treated when they're at the end of a line; page layout programs use them, too.

- A *newline* character (which is invisible) begins a new line without starting a new paragraph. If you have special formatting for the first line of a paragraph, like an indent, or the paragraph is formatted for an extra space before it, starting a new line instead of a new paragraph ignores the indent and the open spacing, but keeps the other characteristics of the paragraph, like its margins.

- A *hard space*, or *nonbreaking space*, keeps two words from being separated at the end of a line. You might, for instance, want to make sure that the phrase *Mac Plus* always stays together instead of being split, so you could type a hard space between the words.

- A *soft hyphen*, or *optional hyphen*, appears only when a word has to be split at the end of a line. You type the soft hyphen, but it's used only if the word falls at the end of the line and has to be hyphenated; otherwise, the hyphen isn't printed at all. (Sometimes the standard hyphen character is referred to as a *hard hyphen* when someone's trying to differentiate the two.)

The specific characters, and how you type them, depend on the application, but these are pretty much the standard ones:

Newline ...................... Shift-Return
Hard space .................. Option-spacebar
Soft hyphen ................ Option-hyphen

☞ **Avoid mistakenly typing the < and > characters** instead of the comma and period when you're using the Shift key to capitalize letters. (This isn't an issue if Caps Lock is down, since you get the standard characters on the lower part of the key for non-alphabetic keys.) There are two ways to solve the problem:

- The QuicKeys macro utility lets you re-assign keys, so you can simply re-assign the Shift-comma and Shift-period combinations to the comma and the period.
- Alter the keyboard layout, or get a copy of one that someone else altered, so that typing with the Shift key still gives you the period and comma. (This involves using the ResEdit program, as described in the next chapter.)

☞ **A *text file*, or *plain text file*, is** one that has no special formatting included for either characters or paragraphs. It includes paragraph breaks and tabs—in fact, it can include anything that's in the basic ASCII text code—but there's nothing fancy. Most programs can save their documents as a text file; most programs can open a text file. (Except, of course graphics programs; I'm referring to word processors, spreadsheet, and databases here.) So, a text file is easy to transfer between programs and even between computers, no matter what their operating systems.

Special character and paragraph formats can be embedded in a plain text file by using codes made up of standard, but seldom-used ASCII characters. This is sometimes, logically enough, referred to as *rich text format*, and it means you can transfer formatted text between programs that can't read each other's files but can interpret the rich text commands.

☞ **Change your QWERTY keyboard to** a Dvorak layout. QWERTY is the standard keyboard layout—its name comes from the first five letters in the top row. The Dvorak layout, shown here, puts the most frequently used letters in more easily typed spots. You don't have to change your physical keyboard—in fact, if you change *just* the keyboard, the Mac still thinks it's a standard one—but it helps to put stickers or something on the keys. But it's easy to change *layouts*: drag a keyboard layout into your System file (as described in Chapter 6), and select it in the Keyboard control panel. You can get Dvorak layouts from most user groups or online services.

The Dvorak keyboard.

**TAKE A LETTER ...**

Our current QWERTY keyboard layout has been standard since 1873. But there were many keyboard layouts experimented with at the dawn of typewriting, including a semi-circular arrangement of the keys that particularly lent itself to the two-fingered typing that was used so much.

The QWERTY layout is often described as one invented to slow down typists. Many of the early layouts resulted in a typist's jamming the mechanism when typing very fast. Our current layout solved that problem by putting common letter pairs on opposite sides of the then-current typing mechanism, so the type bars would be swinging in from opposite sides as much as possible, reducing the probability of crashing into each other on their way to or from the paper. So, the QWERTY layout actually speeded up the whole typing process by avoiding mechanical hangups.

With mechanical problems prevented by electronic keyboards, the layout can be redesigned to be efficient for today's typists, with the most-used letters near the strongest fingers, and so on. That's what the Dvorak layout is all about.

You may have noticed a few quotes by John C. Dvorak sprinkled throughout this book. They are almost all derogatory about the Mac and its interface; in fact, Dvorak is mainly known to Mac readers as the *MacUser* magazine's anti-editor! Back in March of 1989, a curious reader wrote in and asked if John was related to the Dvorak of the Dvorak keyboard, or, possibly, was *the* Dvorak—with the side comment: *It would be just like him to invent something that won't be universally acceptable till after he's dead.* This was John's reply in the Letters to the Editor section, where he answered in lieu of one of the editors:

> Cu C daew yd.f-e x. yflcbi nct. ydco!

○○◇ **Don't type if you don't have to:** Let the Mac do it for you by using an interactive spelling checker glossary expander. A *what?* I don't know what to call it, generically, but here's what it does: You get an interactive spell checker that watches you as you type, signaling you when there's a spelling error or typo, like *hte*. Instead of just telling you you're wrong, however, it checks its glossary of misspelled terms and finds that you really meant *the*. So, without stopping you from typing, it quickly erases the misspelled word and replaces it with the correct one. The real trick is that you can teach it that *wp* is a misspelling for *word processor*, and all you have to do is type two letters and let the Mac do the rest. If I want to type the phrase *hierarchical Apple menu utility*, or *in the Apple Menu Items folder inside the System Folder* (and you have a pretty good idea of how many times I had to do that recently), all I type is: *hier apm ut* or *in the amif inside the sf.**

> *It was extremely difficult to type those abbreviations, since every time I did, they were automatically expanded.

I use Thunder, which is an interactive spell checker with this glossary expansion feature; it can also check already-typed text and has several other nifty features, including a full-fledged thesaurus. It's one of the most elegantly designed utilities you'll ever see, all due, I'm certain, to the exquisite style and skills of its programmer, Evan Gross. (He also designed and programmed one of my other favorite utilities, DiskTools.) [Baseline]

**THUNDER**

## ⭐ CHARACTER & PARAGRAPH FORMATS ⭐

## Character Formats

∞⬦ **Character formatting** is the characteristics you assign to text: the font, size, and style of the letters. Some applications have menus for each of these options; many have one menu for fonts and another that combines sizes and styles. Apply character formatting to existing text by selecting the text and then choosing the font, size, or style from the appropriate menu.

∞⬦ **The fonts listed in your Font menu** are the ones available in your system—either in the System file or in the Fonts folder, or through a special utility, like Suitcase, that makes the contents of font suitcases available to the system. The details on fonts, font menus, and font sizes are in Chapter 11, but here are the other main points:

The outlined numbers are the sizes available for the chosen font; when all the choices are outlined (right), that usually means you're working with a TrueType font.

| Size |
| --- |
| 9 point |
| 10 |
| ✓12 |
| 14 |
| 18 |
| 24 |
| 36 |
| 48 |

| Size |
| --- |
| 9 point |
| 10 |
| ✓12 |
| 14 |
| 18 |
| 24 |
| 36 |
| 48 |

- An outlined size in a font menu means the font is available in that size; either the bitmapped version of that size is installed, or it's a TrueType font that works in every size.
- A font size is measured in *points*; a point is a 72nd of an inch.
- The sizes available in a Size menu vary with the application. Some give a limited list of font sizes, some have long lists, and some even have an *Other* command so you can specify a size that's not listed in the menu.

∞⬦ **You can combine character styles** so that your text can be, for instance, ***bold italic,*** *italic underline,* or a totally tasteless and almost unreadable combination like ***bold italic outline shadow.***

∞⬦ **The standard styles are** Bold, Italic, Underline, Outline, and Shadow. They're standard because those were the options in MacWrite and MacPaint Style menus when the Mac first came out. (The *real* standards are Bold and Italic, since that's what most fonts are designed for.) Whatever you consider the actual standards, there are lots more character formatting options available in most Mac programs. You'll find, for instance:

- *Strike Thru* ~~looks like this~~. It's handy to use for editing when you want to show what's being removed.
- *Small Caps* looks LIKE THIS. IT CONSISTS OF CAPITAL LETTERS IN TWO DIFFERENT SIZES—ONE FOR THE "UPPERCASE" LETTERS AND ONE FOR THE "LOWERCASE" ONES. IT'S GOOD FOR HEADLINES AND SUBHEADINGS IN DOCUMENTS.
- *All Caps* is sometimes provided as a style option so you don't have to use the Caps Lock key when you want LETTERS THAT LOOK LIKE THIS. The advantage to Caps as a style is that if you want to change a headline that you

typed in normally as capitals, you don't have to retype it—you just apply the All Caps style. And, of course, when you realize that all capitals make it look like you're YELLING, it's easy to remove the style without retyping.

Chapter 11 describes how to avoid the distortion that sometimes occurs with the All Caps style.

- *Initial Caps*, or *Title Case*, puts a capital letter at the beginning of each word. You Wouldn't Want To Use This In A Regular Sentence, But It's Handy For Headings And Subheadings, and for tyro novelists and screenwriters.

- *Sentence Case* puts a capital at the beginning of each sentence, just in case you don't. (I used it for both these sentences, but you can't tell.)

- *Uppercase* and *Lowercase*, or *Caps* and *Uncaps*, make sure you've got all capital, or all lowercase, letters.

- *Condensed* and *Expanded* text changes the space between letters so they're closer together—like this, for condensed text—or further apart—l i k e  t h i s ,  f o r  e x p a n d e d  t e x t .

- *Underline styles*: The normal underline <u>includes the spaces between words</u>; there's also <u>word</u> <u>underlining,</u> <u>like</u> <u>this</u>; <u>double underlining</u>; and even <u>dotted underlining</u>.

- *Colors*: This is, of course, of dubious value in general word processing and a world of black-and-white printouts, but it counts as a character format. And, on a color screen, it can actually serve as a good way to denote the importance of certain things while you're working, or to differentiate between original and edited text.

- *Superscript* and *subscript* raise and lower the letters in relation to the baseline of the text. A smart program will automatically make the superscripted or subscripted numbers smaller than the main font, so things look like this: $3^3$ or $H_2O$.

## Applying Formats

◦•➤ **Style commands in menus** are toggle commands: You choose one to turn it on, and choose it again to turn it off. The exception is the Plain style, which turns all the other styles off.

◦•➤ **Currently *active* styles**—the ones that are applied to the text that's selected, or the ones you'll get if you start typing at the current cursor position—are checked in the menu.

◦•➤ **Apply formats to text** by choosing from menus or using the appropriate keyboard commands.

Apply formats to existing text by selecting it and then using the format command. Or, you can apply formats before you type by using the formatting commands and then continuing your typing.

When there are keyboard commands for character formats, it's easier to type the style changes as you go along, especially when there's a change for only a word or phrase.

◦•➤ **When you have a text selection that includes a combination** of fonts, styles, or sizes, nothing will be checked in the menus as the current font, style, or size. But if you're working in an application that gives you a dialog box with checkboxes in it to represent styles, and the selection has more than one style, the checkboxes involved will be filled with gray. Clicking on a gray checkbox changes it from gray to checked to unchecked and to gray again; in this way you can apply the style to the entire selection, take it off from the entire selection, or return the selection to its mixed state. In the sample here, starting with the selection at the top left, both checkboxes are gray; altering them to on or off gives the results shown.

The original selection (top, left) and the results of cycling through some of the checkbox options.

## Paragraph Formats

∞▶ **You can apply paragraph formats** to any selected paragraph(s) in a document. Most word processors consider a paragraph selected if the insertion point is in the paragraph, or if any part of the paragraph is selected—you don't have to select the entire paragraph for it to be the one targeted for formatting.

∞▶ **Paragraph formatting** options vary from one program to another, but the basic ones are:

- *Margins.* The left and right paragraph margins set the outer limits for the left and right edges of the text on the page. The *first line indent* is a separate setting for the first line of a paragraph, which can be set to automatically indent so you don't have to press Tab at the beginning of each paragraph. Setting the first line indent out further than the left margin gives a *hanging indent,* or *outdent.*

- *Alignment,* or *justification,* is how the lines of a paragraph align with the left and right paragraph margins. Left alignment gives you an even left edge; because of the way this leaves the right edge, it's also referred to as *ragged right.* Right alignment is the opposite, of course. *Justified,* or *fully justified,* text keeps the text aligned on both left and right margins by spacing the words and letters on the line. Because the last line of a paragraph (or a single-line paragraph) isn't stretched out to the right edge in fully justified text, some word processors, and most page layout programs, supply a *forced* justification option that will force a single line to span the full width of a text margin. This is useful for headlines that have to fill a fixed width.

- *Line spacing* is the space between the lines in a paragraph. At the very least, a word processor will provide the single, space-and-a-half, and double-space options that are carryovers from typewriting. Page layout programs define line spacing in terms of *leading,* the space between the baselines of text.

- *Paragraph spacing,* available in most word processors, adds extra space before or after a paragraph; when it's added before the paragraph, it's referred to as *open spacing.* This isn't like pressing Return—you don't get any extra, blank lines that you can delete.

- *Tab stops* are the places the cursor moves to when you use the Tab key. Many programs provide several kinds of tabs.

**There are four different types of tabs** in most word processors: left, right, decimal, and centered. It's important to use the correct one for each situation. The standard left tab gives you left-aligned text in the tabbed column.

| 14.2 | 14.2 | 14.2 | 14.2 |
| 273.5 | 273.5 | 273.5 | 273.5 |
| 62.79 | 62.79 | 62.79 | 62.79 |
| 7.956 | 7.956 | 7.956 | 7.956 |

Right-aligned tabs are useful for items like page numbers that need to butt up against the right edge of the page. Don't use right-aligned tabs for numbers, although it's tempting, and, for some columns of numbers, it may work; use the decimal tab even if the numbers you're typing don't have decimals in the them. The center tab should be used only when a column of text has to be centered; for items that take up a full line, like titles, you should be using a center paragraph alignment, not a tab.

The picture here shows the results of using the four different tabs with a column of numbers; the gray line shows where the tab was actually set.

**Tabs can have "leaders" attached** to them to fill in the space from one item to the next in a line when you use a tab. You see dotted leader tabs in tables of contents all the time, between a chapter title and its page number. Some programs provide only dotted tabs; others let you choose the leader character that you want, so it can be dashes, or bullets, or anything you can type from the keyboard.

The leader tab matches the large size and bold formatting of the text (top); the leader tab selected (middle); the leader character in the tab formatted for plain text (bottom).

**Chapter 2** ............................... 54

**Chapter 2**................................. 54

**Chapter 2**.................................. 54

Sometimes you have to adjust the size or style of the leader character to get the effect you want. Since the tab is actually a character, you can select the area between the two typed items where the tab is (a tab is easy to see when it's filled with a repeating character) and change its format, making it bold, or plain, or larger or smaller.

**Style sheets are** the best thing since sliced bread. (At least, that's the phrase that jumps to mind; I'm sure there have been many better things since the invention of sliced bread that style sheets are as good as or better than.) Anyway, a style sheet feature lets you apply both character and paragraph formats in one fell swoop. You define a paragraph, for instance, as being 14-point bold Times, centered text with double-line spacing. Or 10-point Helvetica italic, single-line, fully justified, with a half-inch indent and four tabs at specific spots.

Not only is applying formats a breeze with styles (each definition is a *style*; the collection of style definitions for a document is a *style sheet*), reformatting is a cinch: Change the style definition, and everything in the document defined as that style changes to match the new definition. And with a style definition that's "based on" another one, changing one style definition also changes the related style.

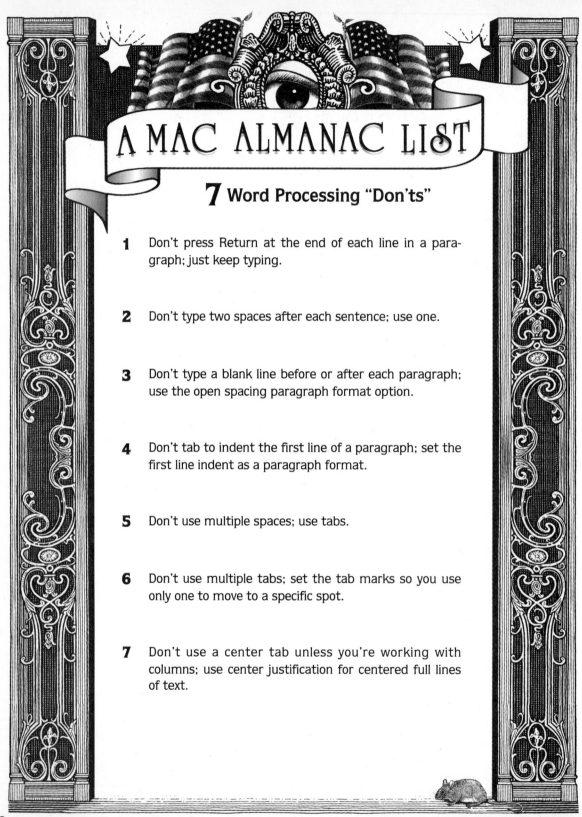

# A MAC ALMANAC LIST

## 7 Word Processing "Don'ts"

**1** Don't press Return at the end of each line in a paragraph; just keep typing.

**2** Don't type two spaces after each sentence; use one.

**3** Don't type a blank line before or after each paragraph; use the open spacing paragraph format option.

**4** Don't tab to indent the first line of a paragraph; set the first line indent as a paragraph format.

**5** Don't use multiple spaces; use tabs.

**6** Don't use multiple tabs; set the tab marks so you use only one to move to a specific spot.

**7** Don't use a center tab unless you're working with columns; use center justification for centered full lines of text.

## ◄ ABOUT GRAPHICS ►

### Bitmapped vs. Object-Oriented

∞◆ **The two basic types of graphics on the Mac** are *bitmapped* and *object-oriented* graphics.

∞◆ **Bitmapped graphics** are made from individual dots. Once you draw a square, for instance, the Mac doesn't know it's a square: it's just dots on the screen that have no special relationship to each other. If you make a circle that overlaps the square, that's just some more dots; the Mac doesn't see two distinct shapes. If you try to separate the images, you'll find that the "covered"

Bitmapped images don't exist as independent shapes.

part of the shape "in the back" doesn't exist. It's like sketching something on paper with a pencil and then cross-hatching another shape over it—the "shapes" are just bits of graphite on the paper, and you can't erase a top layer to get to the figure below.

∞◆ **In object-oriented graphics,** items are discrete objects. If you make a shape, or "object," the Mac recognizes it as a distinct object with certain characteristics. If you make a square, and then draw a circle over it, you can move the circle to see the square that's beneath it. You can even change the relative positioning of the objects, moving the one that's in front to the back. While bitmapped graphics are like pencil drawings on paper, object-oriented graphics are a little like playing with Colorforms shapes.

You can change certain *properties* of an object—its size and proportions, the thickness of its outline, or the color or pattern of its outline or its inside—very easily. But the basic definition of the object doesn't change: it's still a square, or an oval, or a rounded rectangle.

Object-oriented graphics exist as independent shapes.

∞◆ **Working with bitmapped graphics** is called *painting* because the original bitmapped graphics applications for the Mac was named MacPaint. Working with object-oriented graphics is called *drawing* because ... right, because the first object-oriented graphic program for the Mac was called MacDraw.

∞◆ **High-end illustration programs** generate PostScript output for the graphics you create on screen. While you're in the program, it's basically an object-oriented program. Its tools are more sophisticated than most drawing programs, but most of the basic working rules are the same: You create discrete objects that are easily altered individually without affecting anything else that's in the document. But instead of using the Mac's QuickDraw routines for rendering the final output, an illustration program turns your creation into a PostScript file that's sent to the printer (presumably a PostScript model). The advantage to these programs, beyond their sophisticated drawing tools, is that their output always takes advantage of the highest resolution of the output device.

## Working with Bitmapped Graphics

∞•➔ **You create bitmapped graphics** with a variety of tools. All you do is click on a tool and then use it to make a shape or an image.

Here's a tool palette from SuperPaint and one from PhotoShop. You'll notice a lot of basic tools in common, as well as a wide variety of specialized tools.

∞•➔ **The *selection rectangle*** is one of the basic tools for selecting bitmapped images on the screen. When you drag a rectangle around part of an image, everything inside it is selected, including any "empty" space that's around the image.

Dragging a selection rectangle.

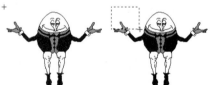

When you move the selection, or copy and then paste it someplace, the "empty" area is part of the image and covers whatever's behind it.

Moving a rectangle selection ruins part of the background image.

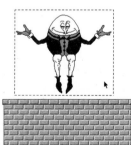
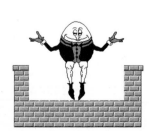

**➤ The *lasso*** is the second standard selection tool for bitmapped graphics. When you drag the lasso around an image and then let go of the mouse button, it tightens up around the colored parts of the image and excludes the empty space around it.

When you let go of the mouse button, the lasso line is drawn to the original spot (bottom, left) and then tightens up around the image.

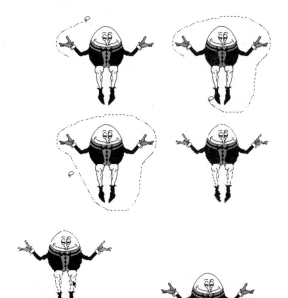

When you move or paste a lassoed selection against a background, there's no surrounding white space ruining the image.

## THE ANTS GO MARCHING ...

When there's a rectangle selection on the screen, the dashed lines that make up the rectangle move around the rectangle's edges much like the flashing lights along the edges of an old-fashioned movie marquee. This tool was, in the early days of looking for new terminology, often called the *selection marquee*, even though the tool itself certainly wasn't a marquee.

Most lassoed images just shimmer around their edges, but in some programs, the entire image shimmers as dark and light pixels keep reversing themselves—in an effect also known as *marching ants*.

**➤ When you change the size of a bitmapped selection,** it gets distorted. If you make it twice its original size, its "frame" and fill are also doubled in size. With some very limited shapes and patterns—something based on straight lines, say—this won't matter too much, as long as you change the length and width of the image proportionately. But if you make a disproportionate size change (making it just taller, or just wider), or use curved lines, or more intricate patterns, changing the size of a bitmapped image seriously distorts it.

Changing the size of a bit-mapped image distorts it.

°•➤ **Text in a paint program is** just part of the bitmap. Whether you type it in the program, or paste it in from somewhere else, it's not editable text—it's just a series of dots that are no longer really letters.

Erasing text in a paint program.

To li₂.    vour load,
whistle ʋ    ᵓ you work.
You may ₂ ☐.red.

## Working with Objects

°•➤ **You use tools to draw objects,** too, but the variety of tools is usually smaller than the one in bitmapped programs. However, they generally offer greater precision and control.

Draw objects are easier to edit, and they print out at better quality than bitmapped items. An object has a basic definition—"oval," for instance—but all its other properties can be easily redefined. So, you can start with a dark blue striped fill inside a small vertical oval with a thin black outline, and after a few clicks and drags, you'll have a light gray checkered large horizontal oval with a thick red outline.

°•➤ **Selecting an object in a draw program** is like selecting an icon on the desktop: You click on it. A selected object has "handles," little boxes on the corners of the rectangular area that surrounds the object. Dragging on a handle changes the size of the object.

Clicking on an object to select it.

°•➤ **When you change the size of an object,** its other definitions don't become distorted. The line thickness for the outline, and the fill pattern, don't get larger or smaller as the object itself grows or shrinks.

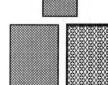
The same small square (top) enlarged as an object (left) and as a bitmapped item (right).

°•➤ **Select multiple objects** in a document the same way you select multiple icons on the desktop: Shift-click on the objects, or draw a rectangle around them to "catch" them all.

°•➤ **Drawing programs let you "group"** objects so they can be treated as one object. A grouped object gets one set of handles, and editing it changes all the objects in the group.

## BRIGHT IDEA #8

**Q.** How many graphic designers does it take to change a light bulb?

**A.** "Does it have to be light bulb?"

◦•▶ **Text in a draw program** is editable, and you can apply basic formats to it, too. Each block of text you create is a separate object which acts like a mini-word processor.

Text in a draw program is editable.

> To lighten your load, whistle while you work. You *may* get fired.

## Also...

◦•▶ **When you paste a graphic** that's on the Clipboard, what happens to it depends on both what it is, and where you're pasting it.

- A bitmapped selection pasted into a paint program is usually slapped right into the middle of the document, but it remains an active selection that you can move to the right spot before it becomes part of the document. If it was copied as a rectangular selection, it's pasted as one; if it was copied as a lassoed selection, that's how it's pasted.

- A bitmapped selection pasted into a draw program becomes a *bitmapped object*. A bitmapped object can be selected and moved the way a regular object can, but the only alteration you can make is changing its size, distorting it in the process. If you shrink it, however, the distortion will be only on the screen; the printout, depending on the printer, may be improved.

- Pasting an object into an draw program is the same as creating an object there—the result is a fully editable item.

- Pasting an object into a paint program turns it into a bitmapped item—forever: You can't select it and put it back into a drawing program, except as a bitmap object like any other bitmapped selection.

- Pasting an item from an illustration program into a paint or draw program creates a bitmap or an object, but one without the embedded PostScript definitions that it had in the originating program.

- Pasting an object or bitmap into a PostScript program isn't even usually possible, although some programs let you put the item in a separate layer to use as a template for tracing.

◦•▶ **You can paste a graphic into most text programs,** but how it's handled depends on the program. On the most basic level, the graphic is embedded into the text, appearing at the insertion point. It's treated as a single character within the text; as shown here, an embedded graphic usually throws off line spacing. More advanced word processors let you put text

> To lighten your load, whistle while you work. You may get fired.

> To lighten your load, whistle ♫ ♪♩ while you work. You may get fired.

and graphics at least side-by-side, with the graphic in its own "frame." Sophisticated word processors, and page layout programs, let you define how the text will wrap around the graphic.

◦•➤ **The quality of a printed graphic** depends on what kind of graphic it is, and what kind of printer you're using. Sometimes what you see on the screen isn't at all what you get in the printout. If there's a difference, however, the printout is usually better, because its resolution may be higher than that of the screen. And the Mac, though it can display the image at only 72 dpi, can store the information for a much higher-resolution printout. The *Printing Graphics* section of Chapter 12 covers all this in detail.

The printout (left) and the screen image (right).

••➤ **There are several standard graphics formats** that make it easy to transfer graphics from one program to another. The basic formats are:

- *Paint* (or *MacPaint* or *PNTG*) graphics are basic 72-dpi bitmap graphics that are on a standard 8.5x11 page and are strictly black and white. This is "left over" from the original Mac art program, MacPaint and, while the real standard for basic Mac Graphics is PICT, most programs can handle the Paint format. Most of the pictures that accompany the anecdotal material in this book are Paint images.

- *PICT* graphics are the most common graphics on the Mac; they contain QuickDraw instructions that the Mac can translate into an image. A PICT file can contain bitmapped or object-oriented graphics, or text—or a combination thereof. The PICT2 file format is an enhanced format that can store grayscale and color images.

- *EPS* stands for *encapsulated PostScript*. This file format encapsulates PostScript information for the printer and QuickDraw information for the Mac's screen.

- *TIFF* (*tagged image file format*) is a bitmapped graphics format, but it's way ahead of the standard Paint format. In can, for instance, be of any resolution (instead of the Paint's limitation of 72-dpi) and the document can be any size. The "tags" in the file format identify the document size, resolution, and whether it contains any grayscale or color resolution. The full-page graphics for the Almanac Lists and Charts in this book are TIFF images.

- *GIF* (*graphics interchange format*) is a file format developed by the CompuServe information service so its clients, who use all sorts of computers, would have a standard file format. (And it's pronounced *jiff*, although I always say "*Giff*, I mean *jiff*."

◦◦◌ **The *clip art* available for the Mac** is vast in scope. A whole book could be devoted to it. (Wait, one has! Maybe even more than one!) It would also be easy to devote a chapter to it, or at the very least, an entire section of a whole chapter. Instead, I'm limiting myself to this single entry. (You'll thank me in the end; it's for your own good.)

Electronic clip art is the same as its real-world counterpart in the graphics industry. It's instant art—you buy the pieces and incorporate them into your work. You can get clip art in each of the main graphics types—bitmap, TIFF, and EPS. There's clip art for almost any conceivable use; you can buy packages that cover specific topics—holidays, business, animals, children, religion—almost any category you can think of. I've narrowed down my clip art coverage to the best of the best—one package of bitmap art, and one of EPS graphics. Each is available as a CD-ROM collection, although separate, smaller, packages of the collections are available on disk from both publishers.

If you want a collection of bitmap art, get WetPaint from Dubl-Click. I've used its art throughout this book, on the chapter title pages and in the anecdotal material—all the old-fashioned-looking pictures are from WetPaint. It also includes other styles of art—there's a whole collection of people, for instance (the Font Family cartoon back in Chapter 10 was from that group), and one of animals (the sea horse I used a few pages ago). All the art is repeated several times on the CD—there's *lots* of room on those discs!—so you can get at the art in several different ways: as separate documents sorted alphabetically; as separate documents grouped according to their original disk releases; through a search-and-retrieve engine called Mariah, and so on.

If it's EPS clip art you want, you want Images with Impact! from 3G Graphics.* The CD gathers together all the art from their various disk packages, provides color versions of much of the previously released material, and includes the excellent manuals that came with the originals; you'll find great information and suggested uses for the clip art. There are a lot of

✳The three G's are from the owners' names: Gail and Glenn Giaimo.

accents and borders, in groups that can be used for matching announcements, stationery, brochures, and business cards. The business images are useful for newsletter production, and the people collection is terrific. One of the things that makes this work stand out is the attention to detail and consideration for the Mac artist using it. If, for instance, you work with a bowl of fruit, you'll find that un-grouping it gives you the bowl and the fruit pieces separately; most EPS images are not so lovingly crafted and don't bother with "hidden" parts of the picture. I've included a few samples of the art here and on the next page, because I can't resist it. In all, the company could change its name to "3 G's and a Q"—for quality.

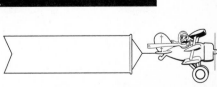

# CHAPTER 21
# HodgePodge

We don't know a millionth of one percent about anything.

THOMAS ALVA EDISON

The far-ranging information in this chapter includes:

> Some advice about mixing computers and little kids.
> What kind of computer printouts the IRS accepts.
> The silly acronyms that supposedly turned into Lisa, Mac, and PowerPC.
> How to "macromize" basic desktop functions.
> What the mysterious ResEdit program is.
> A list of "smilies" for telecommunications.

## No Kidding!

*In the early stages of this book, a developmental editor at the publisher's office reviewed the outline and complained that none of the items in this HodgePodge chapter were related to each other.*

—Includes—

94 Factoids
2 Quotes
3 Memos
1 Quiz

—and a lightbulb joke—

Find Original

KEY ASC

KCHR

AppleShare

*page 774*

# ◄ THE AT HOME MAC ►

## Kids

◦◦➤ **You're never too young for a Mac.** Well, almost never. My youngest was two and a half when I got my first Mac, and he and his brother (two years older) used it. There wasn't much software, of course, but there was MacPaint, and I wrote a few programs for them to play with. (Now they're 12 and 14—or 13 and 15, depending on when you read this book—and have their own setup.)

But don't buy a Mac for a little kid; buy it for yourself, or for the whole family—just remember that even the littlest ones can be easily taught to press a few keys and enjoy seeing something happen on the screen. Realistically, don't expect someone younger than three years or so to be able to do much, especially with the mouse, which takes more coordination than poking a few keys.

◦◦➤ **Protect your computer equipment** from accidents. Make it an absolute rule: No food or drinks around the computer—especially the keyboard—or wherever disks are stored. (This should be a rule for you, too!)

◦◦➤ **Protect your data from** accidental erasures or alterations. How you protect it depends on the age of the kids. The youngest ones will seldom be at the computer alone, so they may not be a problem. But pre-schoolers through pre-teens can wreak havoc on your neatly organized desktop, and it's easy—and *fun*—to drag things to the Trash and watch it plump! Here are some things you can do to protect the files on your drive:

- Use At Ease (described in Chapter 19) to keep everyone away from your desktop. You can set a password so that only you (or other authorized person) can get past the At Ease screen, which provides nice, big single-click icons for launching programs. Even the youngest Mac user can handle that.
- Try the Launcher control panel that comes with Performa system software 7.0 and 7.1, and with all Mac system software version 7.5 (and later, we presume). This won't protect your files, since the Launcher window is on the desktop, so it's for slightly older children, who still aren't old enough to go digging around looking for their games and other files.
- Lock all applications, and important files, so they can't be erased by mistake.
- Make sensitive files invisible on the desktop with a file utility like DiskTools. You'll still be able to see "invisible" folders and files in the open box of your applications, but no one will be able to drag them to the Trash accidentally, or even double-click on them to open them.

◦◦➤ **Don't stick to kids' programs for kids.** By the time they're 10 or 12, they can make use of many standard Mac programs. They don't have to use the fancy features in a word processor, but they can type in a school report. My boys liked experimenting with numbers in a spreadsheet; all they had to learn was how to refer to a block of cells, and then they could try all sorts of things on a list of numbers, like finding the sum, or the average, or the mean—and they could turn the numbers into charts, too. As for a

File utilities are covered later in this chapter.

database—it's a great way to keep track of a baseball card collection. And a basic paint program that you like is often simple enough for a child to master, too. (Don't let that make you feel bad!)

⌐→ **Get a typing program.** Even the ones aimed at adults have games built in for practice. There's nothing more frustrating than hunting and pecking out a school report. If your kid's hands are big enough to rest on the home keys, encourage him or her to really learn to type.

⌐→ **Get a CD-ROM drive** if your Mac doesn't have one built in. It's the single best addition you can make to your system if you have kids. With the amount of information that can be stored on a CD, it's the ideal medium for both reference materials (encyclopedias that include movies and sound, for instance) and graphically rich games.

 **MAC TOON**

—from the BMUG PD-ROM

⌐→ **A home computer needs a good home.** It needs a good *spot* in the home. If you store the computer in a corner and put it on the dining room table when you want to use it, it's not going to get much use. Give it a permanent spot someplace—even if the spot is a corner of the dining room. A corner of the family room works great.

⌐→ **Get earphones *and* speakers.** Earphones for when the kids are playing games that you don't want to hear. Speakers for when you don't mind hearing the nifty sound effects in SuperBonkerWomper, which is even more super when it's loud. (Hmm ... I just realized: When I make up a program name in a *serious* category, like WordMangler, you know it's not a real program, but just an example. Don't write to ask about SuperBonkerWomper. I made it up.)

## Educational

⌐→ **For a young child,** everything's educational. Trust me. I have a degree in psychology; I'm a mother; I've even taught nursery school (and college—and sometimes there wasn't much difference). You don't *need* educational programs for the kids. You don't have to avoid them, either, but there's nothing wrong with straight-out games. (Or do you always keep your television tuned to just PBS and National Geographic specials, too?)

••❯ **Some standard games are educational without** meaning to be. Consider a standard "text adventure": Aside from general reading skills, solving—or even just playing—a text adventure requires a lot of logical thinking, planning, and even map-making skills.

••❯ **One of the best educational items** around isn't a game or an educational program; it isn't even for kids. If your child's old enough to type a school report, use an interactive spell checker like Baseline's Thunder. Every time there's a misspelled word, you get *immediate* feedback—a signal that it's wrong, and the correct spelling if you want it (although you can backspace and try again before looking). What more can you ask for in a learning experience?

> *Okay, okay. It's not spell checker, it's spelling checker, but that leads us to the awkward action of spelling checking, so I'll stick with the common, low-brow phrase spell checker!*

Second to an interactive approach is the after-the-fact spell checking* that most word processors provide. Encourage your child to use it!

∞❩ **There's a ton of educational software out there.** And even if I list just the good 10 percent, that's a lot of pages. So, I'm picking only four programs to recommend, in various topics and for various age groups. You can't go wrong with any one of them—and it's unlikely you'll go wrong buying other programs from the companies that publish them.

**READER RABBIT & WHERE IN THE WORLD IS CARMEN SANDIEGO?**

- Reader Rabbit, for pre-schoolers and Kindergartners, is a terrific little program consisting of several reading-readiness games. As with the best of educational software, the kids won't even notice that it's educational. There's a Reader Rabbit II, too, for the 6-8 age group. [The Learning Company]
- Where In the World is Carmen Sandiego? One sentence can sum up the popularity of this game: it spawned a TV series on educational TV. It and its sequels, Where in Time, Where in the U.S, and Where in America's History, take kids through geography and history as they search for Carmen; the games come in both disk and CD versions, and research materials are included. [Broderbund]
- Fun geography (How's that for an oxymoron?) for the 10 through early teen age group: That's Swamp Gas Visits the United States of America and Swamp Gas Visits Europe—Swamp Gas being the name of an alien space craft. Find your geographical goal, and you're rewarded with an arcade game. [Inline Design]
- Learn to type with Mario, of Nintendo fame. All the basics on plenty of levels, with, of course, plenty of games along the way. [MacPlay]

## Entertainment

∞❯ **There's a wide range of games** available for the Mac, which is just proof of the insatiable human need for playtime. "Games" usually connotes some give and take with the material on the screen, whether it's an arcade-style shoot-'em-up or something a little more benign. But for the youngest Mac users, a "game" might also be a beautiful on-screen book with sound and animation included. That's why this section is titled *Entertainment.*

I'm not devoting lots of space to game reviews. We've spent a year collecting some of the best, and testing them with friends and family. This section describes the best of the best, a list that will serve to get you started on your game collection.

## PLAYTIME

In the Mac's early days, Steve Jobs, et al., were concerned that the Mac might not be taken seriously. It was, after all, just so damn *cute!* In striving to establish the Mac as a real computer and not a toy, Apple made it difficult for programmers to write games for the Mac; rumor had it that while developers of application software were wooed and treated with kid gloves in the early days, game developers were actually discouraged from getting their products out the door. Then, of course, there was a glaring lack on the hardware side: no port that could accommodate that hallowed instrument of game interaction, a joystick. (There was also the minor problem of strictly black-and-white graphics.)

Despite all this, the games showed up anyway. The best ones of the early crop didn't make you move the mouse like a joystick, or stick to just the keyboard, but made use of the mouse in a way that was, well, *mousier* than a joystick. One of the best was a program whose name unfortunately escapes my slowly decaying memory: It had a shower of knives and other objects (including, oddly enough, a shopping cart) raining down on the poor mouse you were trying to move around on the screen. I can still hear the *blip, blip, blip* of those falling objects. (And they say that hearing's the *first* thing to go!) Another early winner is more easily recalled: Airborne, from Silicon Beach Software, the company that later got serious and developed SuperPaint. Anyone who ever played it knew what the ominous silence at certain points meant: One of the *big* planes was about to swoop in, with its jets screaming. Programming wiz Eric Zocher managed to invent *RealSound* for Airborne, the first use, to my knowledge, of digitized sound on the Mac. (A system, the game, *and* the specially compressed sounds all fit on a floppy!)

☞ **The kids can play with programs that aren't games.** The Star Trek screen saver is a terrific example—setting various parameters and trying them out is an interesting activity. Utilities that let you create desktop patterns is another artistic activity for kids. My kids also like toying with ClickChange (described in Chapter 2), which lets them change the colors and designs of their menu bar and windows.

☞ **For the young crowd,** there are two CD series that are the epitome of children's software. Just Grandma and Me, recommended for ages 3 to 8, and Arthur's Teacher Trouble, for ages 6 to 10 are part of a "Living Books" series that are incredibly charming programs for young kids. The picture and text of the story appear on the screen; the text is spoken, and clicking on almost any item gives you some little animation and sound. These are so well done that my 12- and 14-year-old sons enjoyed going through them (one time, anyway) and even showed their friends, who pronounced both CD's "cool," the penultimate accolade (the ultimate being "awesome"). The other series for the young set is Putt Putt (Joins the Parade, Goes to the Moon). The child is presented with a goal (joining the parade) and some simple problems to solve (get the birds in the road out of your way by honking your horn). [Living Books, Broderbund; Putt Putt, Humongous Entertainment]

○○◇ **For the 8 to 12 age group** (what I refer to as middle-aged kids), you can't beat the Kid Pix paint program and its attendant packages like Kid Pix Companion. The painting tools have sound effects (like splashing paint from the paint bucket) and you can erase by dropping a bomb on your picture. For a change of pace, try Spelunx and the Caves of Mr. Seudo. It's sort of an adventure, sort of a mystery, sort of a wander around and discover things game that even young teens will enjoy. [both from Broderbund]

○○◇ **For teens to adults,** there's a wealth of entertainment in many different categories.

- Pinball games get better and better: try Amtex's Tristan, Bally's 8-Ball Deluxe (distributed by Amtex), or Starplay Productions' Crystal Caliburn.
- Play a board game on-screen: Virgin Designs' Monopoly is the traditional board game with sound effects (an auctioneer's voice when a property's being sold) and someone to do the math for you (those mortgage rates haven't changed much over the years); and, you can play against the computer when there's no one else around. [distributed by Inline Designs]
- Thinking can be fun, and some computer games prove it. Try Darwin's Dilemma, a strategy game where you move from screen to screen based on how you merge tiles that represent increasingly complex life forms. It doesn't sound like much, but it's intriguing. Ask Addy Giuliani or Lara Masker, my son's friends who didn't test all the games I wanted them to look at because they liked this one too much! SimCity and SimAnt are "simulation" games where you get to design a city or an ant colony, and see how it thrives or dies as a result of your design and decisions. And then there's chess—Chessmaster 2100 being one of the best. But one of the cleverest thinking games—which you can use for experimentation if you don't feel like thinking—is The Incredible Machine, and its sequel, Even More Incredible Machines. You construct Rube Goldberg-type devices out of a myriad of objects (matches, buckets, pulleys, ramps, bowling balls) and then set the whole thing in motion. [Darwin's Dilemma, Inline Design; SimCity and SimAnt, Maxis; Chessmaster, Software Toolworks; Incredible Machines, Dynamix]
- Myst and Seventh Guest are adventure games that are breathtaking in their graphics; Myst is mind-boggling in its puzzles; both come on CD's and will keep even the most expert gamer working for weeks to learn their intricacies. Prince of Persia is a game on disk, with amazingly fluid graphics; it, too, is an adventure game, but of the type where there's a lot of action that needs speed and coordination to get from one level to the next. [Myst and Prince of Persia, Broderbund; Seventh Guest; Virgin Interactive]

EVEN MORE
INCREDIBLE
MACHINES

## Finances

○○➤ **Early home computer marketeers** tried to come up with a definitive use for a computer in the home, and kept coming up with … *recipes!* Just think, with a few keystrokes, you can call up a recipe, let the computer calculate the measurements you need for the number of servings you want to make, and print it out. Wow.

As far as I'm concerned, the definitive use for a home computer is keeping track of family finances: checkbooks and taxes. While I was working on this very chapter, for instance, the bank through which we applied for a mortgage called: My credit check showed a late payment to Macy's in May of 1992—what was the reason? 1992? May? *Macy's?* Before he was off the phone, I had called up my combined 1992-1994 checkbook and found that the payment had indeed been made in March of 1992, and offered the bank a confirmation of that from the computer checking service that I use.

∞⟩ **You should have two home finance** applications: a checkbook program and an income tax program.

- The two premier checkbook programs are Quicken and CheckFree. CheckFree is the service that I use, and it's been a lifesaver because while I was working on this book, I didn't have time to pay bills—but they got paid because I have all of that set up ahead of time. But Quicken, which is much stronger in the bookkeeping area and also prints checks for you, has a CheckFree module available. It's an incredible convenience to just set up payments months in advance (how often does your rent or mortgage payment vary?) and have the checks sent out automatically; for "merchants" like banks where you have credit cards, the payments are transferred electronically from your bank account to theirs. You do the work on your computer, your computer calls their computer … and it's done. The cost isn't much more than the cost of writing real checks and mailing them; the convenience is incredible. [Quicken, Intuit; CheckFree, CheckFree Corp.]

- Unless you do the short form when it comes to income taxes, get a tax program; I've always used Macintax. It's great to type in a few numbers and let everything else be done for you—and even get reminders about which spaces you inadvertently left blank. The printouts from the program are perfectly acceptable to the IRS. (Whether or not your numbers are is another matter.) [ChipSoft]

If you have a spreadsheet program, or an integrated program with a spreadsheet module, you can easily set up a checkbook register. Unlike the checkbook programs mentioned above, it won't print any checks or make any electronic payments for you, but it does the balancing for you and it's great for looking up items, or sorting them into categories and subtotals at tax time—as long as you input the information as you go along.

## ⊨ MACROS ⊨

## In General

∞⟩ **A *macro* is a combination** of commands or steps that you can execute with a single keystroke. You use a macro utility to create and play back the macros. There are only two macro utilities in the Mac marketplace: Affinity's Tempo and CE's QuicKeys; each has its fans. I've used both extensively, but prefer Tempo for some of its more advanced features.

But I'm not doing a comparative review here. Most people don't need the more advanced features of either program, and people who do still use the basic "record" mode of the utility to create the majority of their macros anyway. Either utility will do all the macros I discuss in this section.

**It's easy to make a macro.** In effect, you say "watch me do this," then you do whatever it is you want repeated later. When you're done, you give the macro a descriptive name and a key combination that will replay it.

There are other nifty tricks you can do without needing any advanced, programming-like tricks that a macro utility might provide. It's simple to chain certain macros together into something more complicated, or to set one up to repeat a specific number of times.

**Macros can be "universal" or "local";** that is, a macro can work no matter what application you're in, or it can be specific to a single application. This makes it easy to re-use certain key combinations for program-specific operations; otherwise, you might run out of unique combinations long before you run out of ideas.

**AppleScript is not a built-in macro editor,** even if it is reasonably easy to use on its simplest level (and I'm not sure that it's reasonably easy to use even on that level). You can't just say "watch me do this, and do this again later" as you can with Tempo or QuicKeys. Besides the "scriptable" Finder comes only with System 7.5 (although I think it was also part of the special System 7 Pro software), and not all applications can interact with AppleScript. So, I still highly recommend that you get a third-party product to automate your computer.

## Desktop Macros

**The most obvious use for macros in the Finder** is to make keyboard equivalents for all those commands that are missing built-in equivalents. The hardest part is coming up with unique, but logical, key combinations for all the commands. So, I did the hard part for you; the table on the next page (because I couldn't fit it on this page) includes the commands already in the Finder and the ones that you can add (in italic). The commands in the View menu get Command-Shift combinations; all the others get Command plus a single key—*except* the potentially dangerous commands in the Special menu, which get Command-Shift-Option combinations to make you think twice before you use them, and to keep you from hitting the macro accidentally.

**Even if you don't assign a key** to every Finder command, the Make Alias command should get a Command-M because it's so convenient. (System 7.5 finally added the keyboard equivalent.)

| File | |
|---|---|
| New Folder | ⌘N |
| Open | ⌘O |
| Print | ⌘P |
| Close Window | ⌘W |
| Get Info | ⌘I |
| Sharing... | |
| Duplicate | ⌘D |
| Make Alias | |

## Keyboard Equivalents for Finder Commands

| File Menu | |
|---|---|
| New Folder | Command-N |
| Open | Command-O |
| Print | Command-P |
| Close Window | Command-W |
| Get Info | Command-I |
| Sharing | *Command-H* |
| Duplicate | Command-D |
| Make Alias | *Command-M* |
| Put Away | Command-Y |
| Find | Command-F |
| Find Again | Command-G |
| Page Setup | *Command-J* |
| Print Window | *Command-T* |

| Edit Menu | |
|---|---|
| Undo | Command-Z |
| Cut | Command-X |
| Copy | Command-C |
| Paste | Command-V |
| Clear | *Command-B* |
| Select All | Command-A |
| Show Clipboard | *Command-K* |

| View Menu | |
|---|---|
| Small Icon | *Command-Shift-S* |
| Icon | *Command-Shift-I* |
| Name | *Command-Shift-N* |
| Size | *Command-Shift-Z* |
| Kind | *Command-Shift-K* |
| Date | *Command-Shift-D* |
| Label | *Command-Shift-L* |
| Comments | *Command-Shift-C* |

| Label Menu | |
|---|---|
| None | *Command-0* |
| Labels/Colors | *Command-1 through 7* |

| Special Menu | |
|---|---|
| Clean Up | *Command-U* |
| Empty Trash | *Command-Shift-Option-T* |
| Eject Disk | Command-E |
| Erase Disk | *Command-Shift-Option-E* |
| Restart | *Command-Shift-Option-R* |
| Shut Down | *Command-Shift-Option-S* |
| Sleep (PowerBooks) | *Command-L* |

☞● **Make a better Alias command.** Instead of just making a keyboard equivalent for Make Alias (which you should do even if you don't make equivalents for the other commands) do something really useful: Record a macro that creates an alias and then gets rid of the annoying "alias" suffix.

Select an icon before recording and then record:

1. Choose Make Alias from the File menu.
2. Press the Right Arrow key once. When the alias is created, its name is automatically selected for editing; pressing Right Arrow moves the insertion point to the end of the file's name.
3. Press Delete 5 times. This erases the word "alias" from the file name.

That's all. By erasing the word *alias* but not the space preceding it, you keep the alias's name different from the original file name so they can co-exist in the same window (or on the desktop) until you move the alias to where you want it. I just use Command-M for this, since there's no reason to use the Make Alias command without removing the word *alias*; but if you want two different commands, Command-Option-M works fine.

☞● **Find an alias's original** item with a single keystroke. Don't start recording until after you've selected the alias icon. Record these two steps:

1. With the alias icon selected, press Command-I. This opens the Info window for the alias.

[ **Find Original** ]

2. Click the Find Original button.

## TAKE A LETTER, MARIA

The computer world practically resonates with acronyms; it's probably second only to the military in the use of letters to stand for complicated phrases. But sometimes the names come first, and then someone insists that it's an acronym, like:

*Lisa:* Locally Integrated Software Architecture

*Mac:* Mouse Activated Computer

*PowerPC:* Performance Optimization With Enhanced RISC

## POP QUIZ                                   [2 POINTS EACH]

Sometimes acronyms turn into real words—like *scuba* and *snafu.* Where did these two military acronyms come from?

•◗ **Lock and unlock icons** with a keystroke instead of reaching for the mouse. With the icon already selected:

1. Press Command-I to open the icon's Info window.
2. Click in the Locked checkbox.
3. Press Command-W to close the Info window.

Depending on which macro utility you're using and how fancy you want to get, you can make a single macro that toggles the checkbox on and off so you can use it to lock or unlock an icon. But I find it easier to use two macros so that I know for sure which state the icon will be in when I'm finished. I use Command-L for locking and Command-Shift-L for unlocking.

•◗ **Open the main window of your startup drive** by recording a double-click on the icon; you can assign it to Command-1. If you normally have two or three volumes displayed on your desktop, you can record double-clicks on them, using Command-2 and Command-3, and so on.

You can use this macro not only to open the main window, but also to move an already-open drive window to the top of other windows on the desktop.

•◗ **If you'd like to see *just* the root level** of *just* the startup drive, you can make a macro that clears the desktop of all the windows except that one. Record these steps:

1. Use Command-Option-W to close all the windows on the desktop.
2. Double-click on the icon of the startup drive.

This should work no matter where you start from, since if there are no windows open, Command-Option-W won't hurt anything, and the startup icon is always in the same spot no matter what its name. And, if the root level was already open, it will just close and then open again. If you've already recorded a macro that opens the root level of the drive, you can just include it as step 2 in this macro, or branch to that macro after the first step. And, you can make it a universal macro by starting it with a move to the Finder through the Application menu.

••⮞ **Select and eject a floppy disk** from the keyboard. Exactly what you record depends to some extent on how you keep your desktop arranged. Where does a floppy icon appear on your desktop? Immediately beneath the startup drive, or two or three spaces below that? Record:

1. A single click on the spot where the disk icon is.
2. Command-Y, or choose Put Away from the File menu.

## Universal Macros

••⮞ **A macro is a great way to turn on Balloon help** and turn it off again quickly, easily, and without the mouse when you just want to check a few things. Record selecting the Show Balloons command from the Help menu (which, of course, changes to Hide Balloons). I keep this macro on the Help key on the extended keyboard.*

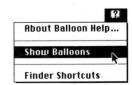

> ✳Doesn't that make sense? Why isn't it hard-wired in?

••⮞ **Click buttons with key presses.** I'm so used to working in Word, which lets you simply press a key to trigger a button click (like N for No, Y for Yes, and so on), that I get very annoyed when I'm in programs that don't provide the same convenience. I keep a set of universal macros for button presses, using the Control key as the modifier, so that Control-N clicks No, Control-Y clicks Yes, and Control-O clicks OK (for those dialogs where OK isn't the default and can't be triggered by pressing Return).

••⮞ **When you're ready to shut down,** you don't have to quit your programs and go to the Finder for its Shut Down command. Your macro can take you to the Finder and choose Shut Down. All you have to do is hang around in case the Mac asks you if you want to save documents in case you have any open ones.

> System 7.5 has a Shut Down command in the Apple menu. See Chapter 1.

Record this simple sequence, making sure you store it as a universal macro, and not one that's available only from a specific application:

1. Move to the Finder. How you move depends on your macro utility and the other macros you've created. You can select Finder from the Application menu, or invoke any "move to Finder" macro you've already made.
2. Choose Shut Down from the Special menu.

## Desk Accessories & Control Panels

••⮞ **Open any desk accessory or control panel** with a simple keystroke. I have the accessories I use the most "wired" into my numeric keypad; I use Control-Shift-Option (the three corner keys) and the numbers on the keypad to open the DAs that I need. I even have little labels right on the keys.

∞•▸ **Make a date stamp** macro using the information in the Alarm Clock. Click in the spot where you want the date pasted, and record these steps:

1. Choose the Alarm Clock from the Apple menu.
2. Choose Copy from the Edit menu.
3. Press Command-Q to close the Alarm Clock.
4. Press Command-V to paste the time and date in the document. You'll get both the time and the date, like this: 7:40:17 AM 7/25/94.
5. Press the combination you need in your word processor to move the insertion point five *words* to the left, to place it before the date. In Word, for instance, Command-4 (keypad) moves the cursor word by word to the left. The date consists of five "words" because each group of numbers, and each dividing slash, is considered a word. You can't simply use the left arrow key, because sometimes the month or day will consist of a single digit, and sometimes double digits.
6. Press the key combination you need to move *and select* six words to the left, to select the entire time; the *AM* or *PM* is a word, as is each set of digits for the time, and the colons between them. In Word, using Command-Shift-4 (keypad) selects words to the left of the insertion point.
7. Press Delete to erase the time.
8. Use the key combination you need to move five words to the right, to put the insertion point at the end of the date.

Does this sound like more trouble than glancing at a wall calendar and typing the date in? The macro plays it back in less than two seconds on my Mac.

∞•▸ **It's easy to store something in the Scrapbook.** First, make a selection in your document. Then record:

1. Use Command-C to copy the selection.
2. Choose the Scrapbook from the Apple menu.
3. Use Command-V to paste the item into the Scrapbook. (It automatically goes on the top page.)
4. Use Command-Q to close the Scrapbook. You'll be returned to the document where you started from.

Getting an item from the Scrapbook isn't quite as simple, since you need to flip through its pages to look for the text or picture that you want. So, you'll just have to open the Scrapbook with whatever key combination you assigned to it (if you gave it one) and find the picture you want. But you can automate the rest of the procedure:

1. Use Command-C to copy the Scrapbook page.
2. Use Command-Q to close the Scrapbook. Assuming you were working in a document before you opened the Scrapbook, that's where you'll be returned to.
3. Use Command-V to paste the Scrapbook page into your document.

∞•▸ **Add calculating capability to any application** by using a macro that whips out the Calculator to figure out whatever expression is selected in the text.

First, type the expression you want evaluated, using an asterisk for multiplication and a slash for division. (You can only add, subtract, multiply, and divide, since that's the extent of the Calculator's capabilities.) Next, select the expression so that it's highlighted. Then, record:

1. Use Command-C to copy the expression to the Clipboard.
2. Press Right Arrow to deselect the text.
3. Press the spacebar to move the insertion point over, ready for the answer to be pasted in.
4. Choose the Calculator from the Apple menu.
5. Use Command-V to paste the expression into the Calculator.
6. Use Command-C to copy the result from the Calculator.
7. Use Command-Q to close the Calculator. Your application's window will become active again, with the blinking text cursor in place.
8. Use Command-V to paste the Calculator's answer in the document.

If you want the pasted answer to replace the expression instead of being typed next to it, then skip steps 2 and 3; when the macro brings you back to the document and the expression is still selected, the pasted answer will replace the selected text.

⦿•➤ **If you're using a printer that supports background printing,** (like a LaserWriter) you can turn the background feature on and off with macros.

1. Open the Chooser.
2. Type L to select the LaserWriter driver in the left panel. With a LaserWriter selected, the Background Printing buttons appear. (If you're using something besides a LaserWriter, or a special driver with another name, type as many letters as you need to select the correct icon.)
3. Click the On or Off button, depending on which macro you're working on. (You need two different macros because they're radio buttons and not a single toggle.)
4. Use Command-Q to close the Chooser.
5. Click the OK button that shows up reminding you to choose Page Setup in all open applications because you've changed your printer. (You haven't really changed your printer, but the Chooser thinks you did because you chose it again.)

> ✳System 7.5 has a menu bar clock built in.

⦿•➤ **Check the time or date instantly** if you're using SuperClock (and you should be).* Just record a click on the time in the menu bar, which switches the readout to the date. Record two clicks on the date in the menu bar to get back to the time, because you have to cycle through SuperClock's stopwatch to get back to the time display. I use Control-Shift-Option (my combination for desk accessories and control panels) with D for the date, and T for the time.

## For Applications

⦿•➤ **My favorite way to launch** an application is with a macro from the keyboard. I don't assign anything to the first four function keys, since I use them for Undo, Cut, Copy, and Paste, but the next two groups of four keys have two and three programs assigned to each one of them. For the applications I use the most, all I have to do is press the key. Applications that I launch less frequently are assigned to a combination of Control and a function key; some others are on Control-Shift plus the function key.

The "launch keys" even work to move me from one program to another when more than one is open (which is all the time).

I have even been known to actually write directly on the keyboard (gasp!), above the function keys, so I don't have to remember which keys are for what. But that was before I got my Brother P-Touch labeling system, so now the keys are neatly labeled. (As are so many other things around the house—that commercial showing a new P-Touch owner labeling everything in sight, including his body, is not far from the mark.)

∞➤ **Applying multiple character styles** with a macro is really convenient. Do you need capital bold italic underline? (I didn't say this would be *tasteful*, I said it would be *convenient*.) Record a macro that selects each of those options from a menu or in a character format dialog. Then, when you select text and play the macro, all the character formats are applied in one fell swoop.

∞➤ **Add a forward delete** function to applications that don't support the forward delete key be recording a press of the right arrow followed by a press of the standard Delete key.

∞➤ **You can reverse two letters** with a single keystroke, so when you forget that it's *i before e except after c,* you can switch the letters to the way they're supposed to be. With the text cursor right after the second letter of the reversed pair:

1. Press Shift-Left to select the letter to the left of the text cursor.
2. Use Command-X to cut the selected letter.
3. Press the left arrow to move the blinking cursor in front of the first letter.
4. Use Command-V to paste down the letter you cut.
5. Press Right Arrow to move the text cursor back to its spot after the second letter of the pair—which is now in the right spot!

Now, at first glance, calling up this macro isn't much of an improvement over a manual fix, since it takes two key presses (Control-Left, say) instead of four: two deletes and retyping both letters. But I've found that I often repeat the same letter-reversal sequence because my fingers aren't cooperating with my brain. So, I'll type *recei*, see the mistake, backspace twice, and retype *ei*. So—two more deletes, two more typed letters. When I use the macro, I end up using two keystrokes instead of six or more.

•➤ **Sometimes you have a parenthetical passage** that you'd like to release from its parentheses; sometimes you'd like to put a word, phrase, sentence, or even paragraph into parentheses.

To add parentheses, select the words you want put inside the parentheses before you start recording. Then:

1. Use Command-X to cut the selected material.
2. Type the left parenthesis.

3. Use Command-V to paste the material back in.

4. Type the right parenthesis.

If you forget to select the text before you run this macro, you'll get two parentheses with nothing between them.

To remove parentheses, select the text within them—but not the parentheses themselves—and then:

1. Use Command-X to cut the selected material.

2. Press Delete to backspace over the left parenthesis.

3. Press Forward Delete to erase over the right parenthesis. (If you don't have a Forward Delete key on your keyboard, press Right Arrow followed by Delete.)

4. Use Command-V to paste the original material back in place.

## ⇛ TINY NETWORKS ▷

### Basic Setup

∞▸ **There are WANs** (Wide Area Networks) and LANs (Local Area Networks); there are also, in the Macintosh world, something you might call TANs: Tiny Area Networks, consisting of only two computers hooked to the same printer or to each other. Because Macs have built-in networking capabilities, it has always been easy to hook them up to each other; with the advent of System 7 and its personal file-sharing capabilities, it's a cinch to get them to talk to each other, too. This section is assuming that you're working with a TAN—a PowerBook and a desk machine, or two desk Macs—but the networking basics are much the same for a larger group of computers, too.

∞▸ **The Macs have to be physically connected** for the network to work. If they're both connected to a printer—usually a LaserWriter—then they're actually connected to each other already.

How do you hook two Macs to the same printer when each of the three devices has one connection port? Apple would have liked you to use its original LocalTalk connectors, but Farallon's PhoneNet connectors were smaller and less expensive—even Apple used them. Now you can buy LocalTalk RJ11 Connectors from Apple—they're actually PhoneNet connectors.

A connector—whether it's LocalTalk or PhoneNet—has a standard connector on one end for the printer port (of the Mac or of the printer) and two openings on the other end. The openings accommodate standard phone wire—the kind that goes from the phone to a wall jack. With a connector in each of the three devices, you can run a wire from each of the Macs to the printer, whose connector has two openings available. The "left over" openings get plugged with terminating resistors, which are included with the connectors.

Connecting two computers to a printer with AppleTalk or PhoneNet connectors.

∞♦ **You need file-sharing software installed** on the Macs for this networking to work. File sharing is a smooth process once it's going, but underneath it's a messy collection of extensions, control panels, and a Finder command. A factory-installed system, or one you did with the Installer's Easy Install option, includes everything you need. Check in the Chooser; if you see the AppleShare icon, file-sharing software is installed. If not, use the Installer for your system software. You don't have to re-install your entire system; use the Customize option and click on File Sharing in the list of software options to be installed.

Installing system software is covered in Chapter 23.

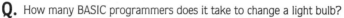

## BRIGHT IDEAS #10, 11 & 12

**Q.** How many Windows programmers does it take to change a light bulb?

**A.** 472. One to write WinGetLightBulbHandle, one to write WinQueryStatusLightBulb, one to write WinGetLightSwitch Handle, one to write ...

**Q.** How many BASIC programmers does it take to change a light bulb?

**A.** Five. Four never find their way back from GOSUB GetLadder.

**Q.** How many C++ programmers does it take to change a light bulb?

**A.** You are still thinking procedurally. A properly designed light bulb object would inherit a change method from a generic light bulb class, so all they'd have to do is send it a bulb change message.

∞♦ **The Sharing Setup control panel** is the crux of the file-sharing system. You use it to identify yourself, indicate a password, and give the Mac a name. The Mac name you enter here is the one that will show up in the other Mac's Chooser. For a tiny network, you can skip the password. Once the information is entered in the top part of the window, click the Start button. (And *never* use the Program Linking button. You don't want to share programs; they work so slowly across networks that it's not a convenience at all—it's a nefarious torture device.)

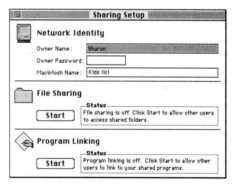

∞♦ **You still have to specifically share** material on your Mac's drive after enabling file sharing in the control panel. You can share an entire drive, or only specific folders; or, you can share one hard drive that's connected to the Mac, but not another. To share a drive, or any item on it, select the icon on the desktop and choose Sharing from the File menu.

The choices in the Sharing window are meant to define "privileges" for anyone accessing your drive on the network. For a tiny network—which assumes you've got nothing to hide because both machines are yours—just leave all the boxes checked.

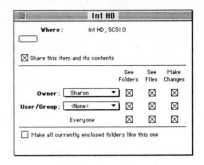

⬅❯ **Use the Chooser to access a shared** volume on your network. It's a quick four-step process:

1. Click on the AppleShare icon in the Chooser.

2. Click on the name of the other Mac, which is listed as a "file server" and click OK. (Or, as you might do just by habit, you can double-click on the name of the Mac.)

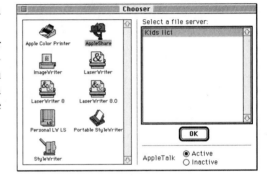

3. The window that opens lists the items on the other Mac that are set up to be shared; the picture here shows the internal hard drive on the "remote" Mac is a shared item. Select the item in the list that you want and click OK.

4. Finally, you get to the actual Connect dialog, where you type in your name and, if you used one, a password.

Like magic (or, "automagically," as they say in the programming biz), the drive shows up on the desktop as an AppleShare volume. The picture here shows how the internal hard drive of my kids' computer, which is as imaginatively named as mine is, looks on my desktop—it has the same name, but it has an AppleShare icon because it's a volume being shared across a network.

Another Mac's internal hard drive mounted as a shared volume on the desktop.

●●▶ **When your Mac is being shared,** its folder icons change to indicate they're available for anyone who logs on with the proper authority: there's a black line along the top edge of the folder's tab.

●●▶ **The Trash and Desktop folders** you see on a remote volume hold the items that are, on that disk, in the Trash and on the desktop. Interestingly enough, when you open the desktop folder, items are arranged in it exactly the way they appear on that volume's desktop.

●●▶ **Logging off a network**—breaking the software connection between your Mac and the mounted volume—is a simple matter of dragging the volume's icon to the Trash. (Selecting it and choosing Put Away works, too.)

●●▶ **There are two file-sharing control panels that you don't need** for a simple networks: Users & Groups and File Sharing Monitor. Users & Groups lets you identify the people (individuals and groups) who are allowed to access your shared Mac. The File Sharing Monitor, whose window is shown here, lets you check the activity on your shared Mac—and disconnect anyone you don't want connected!

Users & Groups

File Sharing Monitor

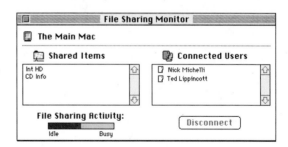

## Network Shortcuts

○●▶ **You can connect two computers without** any networking cables at all. A standard Mac-to-printer cable (also called an ImageWriter cable or, more formally, the Macintosh Peripheral 8) goes from the printer port on one computer to the printer port on the other; after that, you can use file sharing software as if they were both connected to a printer.

●●▶ **Use an alias for instant network sign-ons.** First, log onto a network volume the usual way: use the Chooser and its AppleShare icon, and the ensuing dialogs. When the shared volume is mounted on your desktop, make an alias of it.

Next time you want to log on to the volume, skip the Chooser. Double-click on the alias, and you'll jump right to the Connect dialog.

⮞ **Connect to a network volume through a menu** selection: Put an alias of the volume in the Apple Menu Items folder. Just select it from the Apple menu (or a submenu) and you get the Connect dialog.

⮞ **Make a "drop box" on your desktop that** sends items directly to a folder on another volume on the network. Sign on to the network and find the folder where you want to send the material. Make an alias of it, and copy that alias to your desktop. Dragging a file into the alias on your drive sends it to that folder on the networked volume.

⮞ **Using a macro to sign on** is the easiest way to establish a network connection (macros are covered earlier in this chapter). Make an alias of the network volume or folder, and record a macro that double-clicks the icon or opens it from the Apple menu, types in your name and password (if necessary) and clicks the OK button in the connect dialog.

⮞ **The steps involved in file sharing** are pretty Byzantine for a Mac operation, what with so many control panels and extensions, and the Sharing command in the Finder. Somebody tried to make it a little easier in one spot: If you choose the Sharing command but file sharing hasn't yet been enabled, you get the first dialog shown here; clicking OK opens the control panel for you.

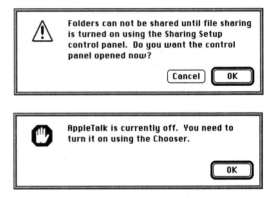

But make any other mistakes, and you're on your own. The second dialog here, for instance, shows up when you try to set up file sharing but AppleTalk hasn't been turned on. Does it offer to open the Chooser for you? Nope.

## ⮞ ADVANCED TOPICS ⮜

### ResEdit

⮞ **ResEdit is** Apple's infamous resource-editing program. (It's pronounced *REZZ-edit*.) Macintosh programs consist of two "forks": the data fork and the resource fork. The resource fork holds things that are pretty much reusable at different points in the program, like icons and dialog boxes. Dialog boxes, in fact, are made up of other resources: icons, "strings" (text), menus, and buttons. The data fork of the program contains the code that makes the program work. But in the code, there are instructions like: *Okay, when this happens, go get dialog #5, put strings #3 and #17 in it, along with icon #12, and put these buttons in there, with the first one highlighted as the default.*

Font files, sounds, menus—they're all resources, and ResEdit lets you get at them.

> Apple is considering voiding the warranty for consumers who use ResEdit. Some factions at Apple wants to forbid sales entirely to anyone who's even *heard* of ResEdit. "Ever heard of a program called ResEdit? You have? Sorry, we can't sell you a Macintosh. How about an Amiga?"

DOUG CLAPP
*MacUser*, 1986

∞♦ **Work on *copies* of files ONLY!!!** Especially when you're playing with the System file or Finder! You may unintentionally change a vital resource that might corrupt the entire file and make it unusable. The rest of this section is going to give you *brief* instructions on changing a variety of resources, so you get an idea of how simple it can be.

∞♦ **To use ResEdit,** launch it and use it to open the file you want to play with. You'll get a window that displays the types of resources in the file; the picture here shows some of the System file's resources.

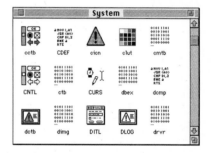

When you double-click on one of the resource icons, you get a list of the resources of that type that are in the file; the second picture here shows what you see if you double-click on the CURS (cursor) resource. (You don't recognize that circle cursor? It's used in the Color Picker.)

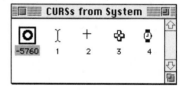

Next, you double-click on the specific resource that you want to edit. Here's what you see if you double-click on an icon resource; it's the window in which you do the actual editing.

ResEdit has no Save command. Instead, you'll get a dialog asking you if you want to save the changes you've made when you close the resource you've been editing.

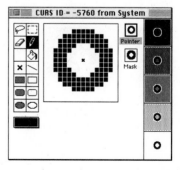

⚬•❯ **There are many different types of resources,** and new ones cropping up all the time. Here's a partial list of common ones. (Note that a resource name is *always* four letters; if you only see three, there's a space being used as the last character.)

| | | | |
|---|---|---|---|
| ALRT | Alert dialog | NFNT | Font family information |
| BNDL | Bundle—files and Finder icons | PAT | QuickDraw patterns |
| CNTL | Control template | PAT# | Pattern list |
| CODE | Programming code | PICT | PICT format graphic |
| DITL | Dialog item list—what's in a dialog | PREC | Print record |
| DLOG | Dialog box | STR | Dialog box string |
| DRVR | Desk accessory or driver | STR# | Dialog box string |
| FKEY | F KEYs | WDEF | Window definitions |
| FOND | Font family information | cicn | Color icon |
| FONT | Font information | clut | Color lookup table |
| FREF | File reference | crsr | Cursor color table |
| ICON# | Icon lists | scrn | Screen configuration |
| ICON | Icons | snd | Sound |
| MENU | Menu items | | |

•••❯ **Grab the "Ta-Da" sound** from the Puzzle and use it as a system sound. (If you've never heard the sound, that means that you've never actually solved the puzzle!)

snd

1. Open the Puzzle in ResEdit.
2. Double-click on the snd resource icon.
3. There's only one sound listed in the window that opens. Click on it to select it, and choose Copy from the Edit menu.
4. Open the Sound control panel (the regular way — not in ResEdit) and choose Paste. You'll be asked to name the sound when you paste it in.

That's it. No sense in opening the System file and adding a resource to it when you can just paste it in through the control panel. (You can also paste it into the Scrapbook if you want, and click the Play button to hear the sound.)

### HEY THERE, HI THERE, HO THERE ...

So many humorous little items are hidden from mortals' eyes. Here's another piece of programmer whimsy: the resource type for the mouse. Think about it.

mcky

•••❯ **Add Command key equivalents to Finder menus** by editing the Finder itself—working on a copy, of course. You might want to add Command-M for Make Alias, or Command-J for Page Setup, or other equivalents for items in the View menu. Open your Finder copy in ResEdit and:

fmnu

1. Find the fmnu resource icon and double-click on it.

2. In the window that opens, double-click on the line for ID 1252—that's the File menu.

3. The next window that opens has columns of numbers and letters in it. The far-right column has, mixed in with boxes and odd characters, the Finder menu commands. Find the command you want to add a command key to.

4. The command key equivalent is stored in the third character before the menu command. The commands without keyboard equivalents have four boxes before them.

Selecting the correct character for the Make Alias command.

| | | | | | |
|---|---|---|---|---|---|
| fmnu ID = 1252 from Finder | | | | | |
| 000070 | 6E66 | 6F00 | 7370 | 7276 | nfo□sprv |
| 000078 | 1002 | 0000 | 0853 | 6861 | □□□□□Sha |
| 000080 | 7269 | 6E67 | C900 | 7364 | ring...□sd |
| 000088 | 7570 | 1002 | 4400 | 0944 | up□□□□□□ |
| 000090 | 7570 | 6C69 | 6361 | 7465 | uplicate |
| 000098 | 7361 | 6C69 | 1002 | □□□□ | sali□□□□ |
| 0000A0 | 0A4D | 616B | 6520 | 416C | □Make F |
| 0000A8 | 6961 | 7300 | 7370 | 7574 | ias□sput |
| 0000B0 | 1002 | 5900 | 0850 | 7574 | □□Y□□Put |
| 0000B8 | 2041 | 7761 | 7900 | 7878 | Away□xx |
| 0000C0 | 7830 | 0000 | 0000 | 012D | x0□□□□- |
| 0000C8 | 6669 | 6E64 | 8110 | 4600 | find□□F□ |
| 0000D0 | 0546 | 696E | 64C9 | 6669 | □Find_fi |
| 0000D8 | 6E6E | 8100 | 4700 | 0A46 | nn□□G□□F |
| 0000E0 | 696E | 6420 | 4167 | 6169 | ind Agai |

5. Select the third box before the command you're working on, and type, in uppercase with the Shift key, the character you want to use for the keyboard equivalent. DON'T erase a box and then type; type over the selected box so you can be sure the character is going into the correct "slot."

6. Close the windows, saving the changes, and quit ResEdit.

You'll have to replace your current Finder with this altered one and restart to see your menu changes.

Here are the codes for the other Finder menus:

Edit = 1253
View = 1254
Special = 1255
Labels = 1256

••➤ **Edit a keyboard resource** to make the layout more convenient. Here's how you can keep from typing < and > when you're holding down Shift and really want just the period and comma. For this, you'll be working on the keyboard resources stored in the System file, so make a copy of the System file and open it in ResEdit.

1. Double-click on the KCHR resource. You'll see a list of the keyboard layouts in the system that matches the icons you'll see if you double-click on the System file in the Finder—except that you can see the standard U.S. keyboard, too, which isn't visible in the System file.

KCHR

2. Click on the U.S. keyboard and press Command-D to duplicate it; you'll get a second listing of the same name, with a new ID number.

| | KCHRs from System | | |
|---|---|---|---|
| ID | Size | Name | |
| 0 | 1422 | "U.S." | |
| 128 | 1422 | "U.S." | |
| 501 | 1422 | "ANSI Dvorak" | |
| 16383 | 1422 | "U.S. - System 6" | |

3. With the duplicate keyboard selected, press Command-I to get Info on the resource. In the Info window, change the name of the keyboard; the picture here shows it named *MyKeys*. Close the Info window.

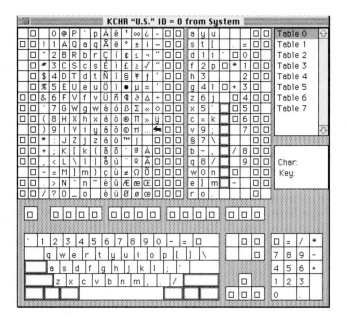

4. Double-click on the newly named resource in the KCHRs window; the window that opens looks something like the picture here. The only parts you'll be using are the large chart of characters in the upper left (the "array"), and the keyboard arrangement at the bottom.

5. Since we're going to put the comma and period on the shifted comma and period keys, the < and > symbols have to go someplace else; in addition, since the comma and period will be duplicated (for both the unshifted and shifted keys), something has to go! I suggest putting the < and > on the shifted bracket ([ ]) keys, and dropping the braces ({}) from the character set. So, move the < symbol onto the shifted [ key: Hold the Shift key so that the keyboard shows the shifted characters and drag the < symbol from the array (it's near the bottom of the fourth column) right onto the keyboard where the { is being displayed. Then drag the > symbol from the array to the shifted ] key.

6. Keeping the Shift key down to display the shifted character set, drag the comma from the array (near the bottom of the third column) onto the < key. Drag the period onto the > key.

7. Close all the windows; when you close the last one, you'll be asked if you want to save the changes you made. Click Yes, and quit.

8. At the desktop, open the System file duplicate you just worked on. You'll see the new keyboard layout inside it. Drag it out, and right into your working System file.

MyKeys

To use your new layout, open the Keyboard control panel and select it.

•••▶ **Make a keyboard layout menu** so you don't have to open the Keyboard control panel to switch layouts. You have to alter the System file itself, so make a copy of it and work on the copy:

1. Double-click on the *itlc* resource icon.

2. Double-click on the single line of information that's in the window that opens.

3. In the next window, look for the label *Always show* and its two radio buttons. The zero is selected; click in the one instead.

4. Close the windows, saving the changes when you're asked.

Move your current System file out of the System Folder and put this altered one in its place, and restart. You'll find a Keyboard menu in your menu bar, between the Help icon and the Application menu's icon. Select the keyboard you want to use from this menu any time you want to switch layouts.

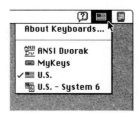

## File Types, Etc.

∞•▶ **A file utility lets you** see and manipulate files in ways you can't on the desktop or in other applications. You can even tweak the definitions of your files to change or fix some problem. You can, for instance, make a file invisible, or "un-invisible" it.

I use DiskTools, which, as described in Chapter 5, lets me find and manipulate files in more ways than the Finder lets me; it's a great utility even if you don't want to some of the more "power user" stuff. But since it lets you see invisible files and change file attributes (like invisibility, and file and creator codes), it's a handy tool for the tricks described in this section. The window here shows the main level of my startup drive; you can see the invisible desktop files listed—and you can see how much room they take on the disk!

DiskTools' listing of a startup drive—and its invisible files.

| Name | Type | Creator | Size | Modified |
|------|------|---------|------|----------|
| 🗀 Almanac backup | | | 1 items | 6/5/94 |
| 🗀 Applications | | | 9 items | 5/27/94 |
| 📄 Desktop DB | BTFL | DMGR | 160K | 6/17/94 |
| 📄 Desktop DF | DTFL | DMGR | 1,216K | 6/17/94 |
| 🗀 misc | | | 5 items | 10/2/93 |
| 📁 System Folder | | | 36 items | 6/15/94 |
| 🗀 Temporary Items | | | 1 items | 6/18/94 |
| 🗀 Utilities | | | 11 items | 12/5/93 |

(A not-so-brief aside: Why would you want to make a file invisible? Here's a situation that you probably won't run into: I was staying at a friend's house for the weekend, with my kids. I knew there were "adult" games on the computer—yes, I mean "adult." I also knew the kids would be up and at the computer in the morning before we were. So what was I supposed to do? Tell them, "Okay, boys, when you play on the computer tomorrow, here's the stuff you're not supposed to look at." Sure. I made the folder invisible, instead.)

⊷♦ **Every file has two four-letter codes** attached to it: a *creator code* and a *file type*. The creator code tells the Mac which application created the file—it's how the Finder knows which application to open when you double-click on a file. Creator codes are registered with Apple, so no two programs can have the same code. (An application's creator is itself.) The file type is, well, the type of file. Word, for instance, can create its own "native" files, text files, support files like Glossaries—they're all different file types with the same creator.

When you change a file type or creator code with a file utility, you can force items to open in applications that don't normally handle them.

⊷♦ **When you use an older drive,** one that was used under System 6, the Mac updates the desktop file so that System 7 can find things on the disk. But it doesn't erase the old desktop file. Use a file utility to erase it: it's named *desktop*. Don't erase *Desktop DB* or *Desktop DF*, because they're the System 7 desktop files.

⊷♦ **Every file has certain *descriptors*** that describe (of course) certain of the file's properties. Here are the common ones that you may see if you're using a file editing utility:

- *Protected*: The Finder can't duplicate the file or move it to the Trash.
- *Locked*: The Finder can't trash, rename, or replace the file.
- *Invisible*: You can't see the file on the desktop, though often you can still see it in Open dialogs.
- *Bundle*: The file contains resources like an icon list and version data that the Finder copies to its desktop file.
- *Busy*: The file is open.
- *Inited*: The file's icon has a specific location on the desktop.

⊷♦ **If you can't move or Trash a file,** you might be able to "cure" it with a file utility. If you get the message *Cannot be duplicated or moved*, you can be relatively sure that its *Protected* flag has been set. Use a file utility to turn the Protected attribute off, and you should be able to trash it afterwards. If not, it's time for MacTools or Norton Utilities.

## ⊰ LAST, BUT NOT LEAST ... ⊱

### Telecommunications

⊷♦ **No Mac is an island** if you have a phone line and a modem. You can call another similarly equipped Mac—or computer of any brand—to exchange information.

This information exchange can be generally divided into four types.

- It can be real-time typing with someone doing the same on the other end.
- You can leave messages in an open forum that everyone calling in to the same service can read and respond to, even if the message was directed to a specific individual's attention.
- You can send private messages to someone using the same service; this is called *electronic mail*, or *e-mail*.
- You can send or receive files—documents or applications—to and from other computers.

Basic modem information is in Chapter 14.

**You need a communications program** to let your Mac communicate with the rest of the online computer world. Many online services, and some bulletin boards, have proprietary software that you have to use in order to use their services. General telecommunications (*telecom,* for short) programs let you call other telecommunicating Macs directly, and also let you log in to some services that don't require specific software. There are many good general telecom programs in the Mac world: Software Ventures' MicroPhone, Hayes' SmartcomII, and FreeSoft's White Knight are among them.

**An *online service* is,** in general terms, a giant computer that all of our little computers can hook into. It's a place to get and exchange information both in open forums and through private e-mail, and even in live group conferences. To give you an idea of what's available, let me list a few things I've used my online services for lately:

- I send my monthly *MacUser* columns, and any other work I do for the magazine, across the country from here in New Jersey to there in California in only a minute.
- I've checked airline schedules and flight availability for various trips, late at night when my travel agent wasn't available.
- I downloaded the *exact* factory cost for the base model and all options for the car I wanted to buy. When I was dickering with the salesman and he exclaimed, as if I were crazy for offering the amount that I did: "Do you know what the markup is on these things?!" I looked him straight in the eye and replied, "Eighteen point two percent." It was great.
- Towards the end of this project, I was selling my house, buying another, and packing to move. Mortgage hunting? A cinch: We went online and downloaded the rates for 100 banks that gave mortgages in the area. We called the dozen best ones and within ten days applied for and received our mortgage at a rate that surprised all our friends and family.
- When my son couldn't find the information he needed on a specific, very esoteric topic (the actual topic escapes me at the moment) and the library was closed, we went online to an encyclopedia service and found what he needed.
- When I upgraded my computer equipment and had a few items "left over" in the move, I put a notice online and sold them that way; that's also how I've bought used equipment occasionally.
- My cousin moved across the country, and although I had his phone number, it was months before I needed his address. When I needed it he wasn't home; but I accessed an online database that is, in effect, a giant phone book for the whole country, and found his address in only a few minutes.

This is only a brief sampling of the kinds of things you can do online. You can meet people and make friends; some remain disembodied online typing, but are friends nonetheless, while others turn into real live relationships. (Ask former *MacUser* editor Steve Bobker, who met his wife online.)

∞⧉ **Subscription to an online service** is a great investment for a Mac owner, whether for business or pleasure. With the wealth of information, and the wide range of experts and other Mac users available at your fingertips, you can get an answer to almost any question you have—whether you're looking for Mac information or something in almost any other category. Costs for the services vary; most charge a flat monthly rate for a certain level of service, and more for "extras"; add in your phone bill, and you're looking at an expense of $30 to $60 a month.

**NAVIGATOR**

* CompuServe is probably the best known of the online services. Its full name is CompuServe Information Service, or CIS. (Pundits referred to it as CI$ for a long time, in honor of its hourly connect charges, which have since dropped considerably). You can access its services with a general communications software package or by using either of two terrific programs: CompuServe Information Manager (CIM) or CompuServe Navigator. CIM takes a Mac-like iconic approach to managing your telecom sessions; Navigator lets you set everything up ahead of time, runs the online session unattended, and lets you review everything later, reading and replying to your messages and marking areas of interest at your leisure. (The "Nav session" is a bone of contention in my house, where it is a significant addiction for my significant other; I, on the other hand, use it in perfect moderation.) [CIM and Navigator, CompuServe Information Services.]

  * MAUG is a special part of CompuServe: the *Micronetworked Apple User Group* that Neil Shapiro started for Apple II users. Neil migrated to Macintosh—in fact, he's the founding editor of *MacUser* magazine although he's no longer connected with it—and so did MAUG, which is made up of many different forums devoted to Mac use and Mac people. Post a question and get an answer in hours, or even minutes; MAUG is so highly trafficked, someone passing through is bound to have experienced whatever's bothering you!

✳Since the time this book first went to press, I've become a sysop in MAUG; as a MacUser writer, I hang out in ZiffNet, too. You can message me at 74774,27 in either place—in a public forum is better than private email, so anyone who wants to can chime in.

  * ZiffNet, or ZMAC, is a special service from Ziff-Davis Publishing; although it's a separate service, separately billed, you can access it through CIS. There are forums for each of Ziff's publications (*MacWeek* and *MacUser* for Mac people; *PCWeek* and *Computer Shopper* for others) where you can download articles ahead of time, look up a catalog of published reviews, drop letters to the editors, and hang out with experts and the rest of us. ZMAC commissions certain software utilities from programmers which it then posts online for its members; it's freeware that you can use and even give away to others, but the only online source is ZMAC. That's why, throughout this book, you'll find the phrase "free from ZMAC" as the description for a program described in the text. (The Find File utility included with System 7.5 was originally a ZMAC item.)

* America Online (AOL) is a very Mac-oriented service, and you can find your way through its various folders with little or no instruction or practice. Because it has less traffic than CompuServe, you might find that it takes longer to get replies to your Mac questions (a matter of days instead of hours) but that's not a concern for most people. I'm uncomfortable with the folder setup that most message areas in

AOL use; I much prefer the "thread" system that CompuServe uses to track the various replies and branches to an original comment by someone. But AOL's friendly approach is hard to beat.

- Prodigy is not. A prodigy, that is. The objections from Mac users in particular started right at the beginning, since the graphical interface was designed for "all" computers, and therefore doesn't follow the Mac interface at all. It also didn't work under MultiFinder, which was the pre-System 7 way to run multiple programs, and didn't even leave your Apple menu available to you. And then there are the constant advertisements displayed on the bottom part of your screen (Prodigy is a subsidiary of Sears and IBM). And *then* there was the problem of censorship in public messages, accusations of *private* e-mail being read and censored (anti-Prodigy remarks, in particular, were deleted), and an abrupt about face regarding the cost of e-mail after people signed up. In all, Prodigy wasn't a service that started out on the right foot. But it started with the right price, and that means a lot.

- eWorld is Apple's long-awaited online service that's based on AOL. I can't say much about it because it's still awaited as I write this; if it follows Apple's usual method of offering something that other people also offer, it will be well done but cost more.

- The Internet … ah, the Internet. It's hard to pick up even a noncomputer magazine and not run across a reference to it (this week's Time magazine, and this month's Smithsonian both mention it in passing). What is it? It's a giant monster of a communications network that ties the whole country together. The Internet wasn't planned; it just grew. It's doubtful that anyone anywhere really knows its full extent. Now, it also serves as the link between the major commercial networks: I can, for instance, send a message from my CompuServe account to someone's AOL account by sending it through the Internet. Here's an interesting address you can try if you have access to Internet services: president@whitehouse.gov

◆ A *bulletin board service,* or just *bulletin board* or BBS, is a mini-online service where you can post notes and get replies; most also offer a library of downloadable files and utilities, and some offer private e-mail between users.

The person running the BBS is the *sysop* (SISS-op), for *system operator.* Most BBSs are free, except for your phone bill; many are sponsored by user groups, or devoted to specific interests. Find one BBS and you'll find them all, more or less, because most keep a list of bulletin boards that you can download and then call. Here's one to get you started, the one my User Group, NJMUG sponsors: 908-388-1676. Tell sysop Mike Bielen I sent you.

◆ A *compression* utility makes a file smaller so it takes less room on the disk, and less time to transfer from one computer to another; the utility can also, of course, expand the file back to its original size so it can be used again normally. One of the most popular compression utilities on the Mac is StuffIt; it's so popular, in fact, that the phrase "stuffed file" has come to mean any compressed file, not just one compressed by StuffIt.

Some files compress more tightly than others: a straight text file might shrink down to only 35 percent of its original size, while a graphics file might not get down past 85 percent.

## IMHO, You Should LOL

Online messages often contain abbreviations; some are to save time typing, others are to express some emotion, since there's no tone of voice that goes along with a typed message. A line that might be taken as insult but is meant in jest might have, for instance, a <g> appended to it, to show the person who's "saying" it is grinning. Sometimes a "sound effect" is put in brackets or double colons; often it's when someone's signing off, like this: <poof> or ::poof::. An "action" that you're trying to "do" to the other person goes in brackets, too, like (hug).

But there are two major categories of abbreviations that are used very often and are unintelligible to the uninitiated. The first is using the initial letters of the words in a phrase. Here, for your edification, are the six most popular ones:

IMO ......................In my opinion

IMHO ....................In my humble opinion

BTW ......................By the Way

OTOH ....................On the Other Hand

LOL ......................Laughing Out Loud

ROTFLOL ...............Rolling On The Floor Laughing Out Loud

Tech editor Joe Holmes suggests we start using TNOWEMN for *the name of which escapes me now.*

The second set of conventions is usually referred to simply as "smilies," although I prefer the more technical term *emoticons.* They're sets of punctuation marks that, when looked at sideways, make faces. This, for instance, is your basic smiley face :) although it also sometimes comes with a nose, like this :-) or a different mouth, like this :->.

With only a few different symbols, many different faces or emotions can be expressed. For instance:

| | | | | |
|---|---|---|---|---|
| :>) | different nose | | :^ | different nose |
| :-( | frown | | :-< | frown |
| :-D | laughing | | :-* | kiss |
| ;-) | winking | | :-X | keeping mouth closed |
| :-P | sticking tongue out | | :-o | surprised |
| :-(O) | yelling | | ~ :-( | very angry (steaming) |
| 8-) | wearing glasses | | B-) | wearing sunglasses |
| O:-) | halo (innocent) | | ]:-) | devil (guilty, sneaky) |
| \:-) | wearing beret | | *=:-) | wearing chef's hat |
| o-) | cyclops | | ) | Cheshire cat |

•••➤ **When you see a file with a three-letter extension** on its name, like *file.sit,* or *file.sea,* that usually means the file is compressed. The *.sit* means it was compressed with StuffIt. The *.sea* means it's a *self-extracting archive:* You don't need a compression utility to expand it—just double-click on it and it expands itself.

○○◇ **Most compression utilities can expand** the files created by other utilities as well as create their own compressed files. There's always a trade-off between speed and size: if you want to compress a file quickly, it won't be quite as small as if you had let the utility take its time to do a better job. StuffIt Deluxe is a full-featured compression program; the shareware version, StuffIt Classic, offers all the basic features. There's also a freeware StuffIt Expander utility (its icon is in the margin here) which can expand compressed files from various programs, although it offers no compression capability. Compact Pro is a terrific shareware utility that compresses and expands files. [StuffIt, Aladdin Systems; Compact Pro, Bill Goodman]

## QuickTime

○○● **QuickTime is** Apple's movie-playing technology. It's also the name of the extension that helps the Mac play movies. If you have the extension (it comes with your system software), you still need a program that can play, or let you edit, QuickTime movies. If you have a QuickTime player or editor, you'll still need the extension for it to work.

QuickTime is usually thought of as synonymous with *movies*—I even defined it that way. But it's actually for *dynamic* information, as opposed to the *static* information in text documents and single-frame pictures. So, QuickTime encompasses sound; usually, the sound is part of a movie, but a QuickTime file can be only sound, too.

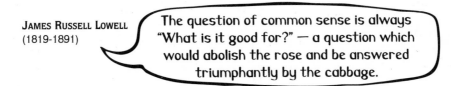

JAMES RUSSELL LOWELL (1819-1891)

The question of common sense is always "What is it good for?" — a question which would abolish the rose and be answered triumphantly by the cabbage.

○●● **You need a fast Mac to see a good movie.** The QuickTime technology is smart: If you're using a slow Mac, it doesn't show every frame of the movie. On an LC, for instance, it plays 8 frames a second; as you might guess, this makes for pretty choppy motion. On a Quadra, you get smooth motion at 30 frames per second. But on any Mac, the sound portion of a QuickTime clip stays intact and plays in full, even when the movie is skipping frames.

○●● **You need a small window and a big disk for a good movie.** The larger the movie, the more pixels are used on the screen—and that means more memory is needed to store the information, and more processing power for handling the information being displayed. In addition, bigger windows and longer movies mean more disk space storage.

○●● **You need 5 megs of memory** to run even a tiny QuickTime movie.

○●● **The *Standard Controller*** is a strip of controls at the bottom of a QuickTime display; programs that provide just the simplest of QuickTime operations (that is, playback but no editing) provide the standard controller.

- The sound icon in the left corner lets you click the sound on and off. If there are no "sound waves" coming out of the speaker icon, it's a QuickTime movie with no sound. If there are sound waves, you can press on the icon to get a slider volume control.

- The Play button lets you start the movie; when the movie's playing, the button is a double-bar Pause icon.

- The Slider beneath the picture shows you what part of the movie's playing by its position on the bar. You can drag it to any part of the bar and skip to that part of the movie.

- Clicking on the Step Backward or Step Forward buttons plays the movie frame by frame in either direction.

- The resize box changes the size of the window, as it does for any Mac window. But changing the size of a QuickTime window also changes the size—and therefore the resolution—of the image inside it.

**⋯➤ There are several tricks buried** in the Controller's controls, and there are keyboard alternatives for manipulating the playback. For the most part, they're standard no matter where you're playing a QuickTime movie.

- Turn the sound on and off by option-clicking on the sound icon.

- Use the Up and Down arrow keys to adjust the volume.

- Use the Right and Left arrow keys to play one frame at a time.

- Option-click on the Play button to see every frame of the movie. On a fast Mac, you're already seeing every frame, but on a slower one, you may be seeing only about a quarter of the total. Option-clicking the Play button displays every frame in sequence.

- Click directly in the QuickTime image itself to stop the movie; double-click on the picture to start it again.

- Press the spacebar or Return to alternately start and stop the movie.

- Click anywhere on the slider bar to move to that part of the movie—you don't have to drag the slider.

- Option-click on the Step Forward or Step Backward button to jump to the first or last frame of the movie.

- Control-click on either Step button to get an entirely different control, shown in the picture here. Drag the little slider to the left of the white 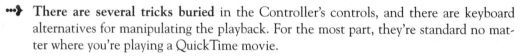 center or the bar to play the movie backwards; drag it to the right to play the movie forwards. The farther you get from the center, the faster the movie plays; the closer you are to the center, the slower it goes. (Normal speed for each direction is somewhere in the middle of the gray area to either side of the white center.)

## THE FOURTH DIMENSION?

The Macintosh has always been anthropomorphised. It has more than a brain, it has a soul; it has a personality; it even has a sense of humor. When it was first introduced, it wasn't *the* Mac, it was simply *Mac*, as if it were a person's name. Mac is a great computer. Buy Mac. Mac is the computer for the rest of us.

In the beginning, this was the corporate marketing approach. The word *the* crept in sometime after the machine's first birthday. But it doesn't matter, because the Mac is imbued with its heart, soul, and sense of humor by the very type of engineers who supplied the Help balloon for the QuickTime extension icon.

And if that weren't enough: The file type (a four-letter code that all files need) for a QuickTime movie is *mooV*. (The V is pronounced separately.)

Time n. A nonspatial continuum in which events occur in apparently irreversible succession from the past through the present to the future.

QuickTime™

**⋯➤ When a QuickTime movie is embedded** in another document—a word processor document, for instance— the controller bar detracts from its looks, but the absence of the controller makes it look like a regular picture. The solution is something called the *badge:* a little filmstrip icon in the lower-left corner. Click on the badge and it expands into a full controller bar.

**⋯➤ You don't have to buy an expensive program to play** QuickTime movies. Apple's QuickTime Starter kit is inexpensive; the Popcorn utility ("the perfect movie companion") from Aladdin Systems is freeware.

**⋯➤ The Scrapbook that comes with** Apple's QuickTime kit can play QuickTime movies.

**⋯➤ There's one way to play a QuickTime movie** with no extra "equipment" other than the movie and the QuickTime extension: name the clip Startup Movie and leave it loose in your System Folder. When you start your Mac, the movie plays.

## And ...

**⋯➤ A User Group.** It sounds like something to do with drugs. But the connotation isn't all that far off the mark: a user group is a self-help club where computer users meet to ask questions and exchange information. A meeting usually consists of a question-and-answer session and a demonstration of some new product. Many user groups sponsor SIGs—*special interest groups*—that meet at other times to address issues of interest to those who use specific programs or types of software. User groups are a great source for public domain software and a way to stay current on your system software and hardware updates, too; most sponsor a monthly newsletter, too.

Call 800-538-9696, extension 500, to find the user group nearest you.

In addition to local user groups, there are some that work nationally. The venerable Berkeley Mac User's Group—BMUG—offers membership benefits that are advantageous even if you can't go to meetings: their semi-annual "newsletter" is a book of several hundred pages, a collection of helpful articles on a wide range of topics: They offer an incredible collection of public domain fonts, graphics, and utilities on disk and CD; and, they have a bulletin board system with its own sign-on software.

**HyperCard.** You can't write a Mac book without reading about it, so this is the obligatory entry. The problem with HyperCard (besides the fact that its first four letters spell *hype*) is that Apple could never decide how to treat it. It was first bundled with the Macs. Then it was sold to—and by—Claris, while a limited version stayed bundled. Then it was sold only by Claris, with nothing at all bundled with the Macs. The current status seems to have settled on Claris's selling HyperCard, but anyone who creates "stacks" can license the HyperCard Player to give to users so they can play back the stacks if they don't have HyperCard itself.

HyperCard was supposed to be a programming tool for the rest of us, but those of us who needed it clamored for more power, and so it soon became too complicated for the rest—without offering some of the main benefits of a real programming language, primarily the ability to create stand-alone applications. But as a tool for information retrieval, the HyperCard approach of button-clicking and jumping around between "cards" is a smooth, convenient, intuitive one.

# CHAPTER 22
# POWERBOOKS

A few reasons why a whole chapter is devoted to PowerBooks:

- ••▶ Desk machines don't sleep.
- ••▶ You can't trust the Battery desk accessory.
- ••▶ HDI cables and connectors are unique to PowerBooks.
- ••▶ You can brighten up your PowerBook with a colorful trackball.
- ••▶ PowerBooks opened a can of worms labeled "file synching."
- ••▶ Some PowerBooks can be a computer, or just a hard drive.

THE ONE FACT IN THIS
CHAPTER THAT SOME PEOPLE
REFUSE TO BELIEVE

X-rays won't harm your PowerBook.

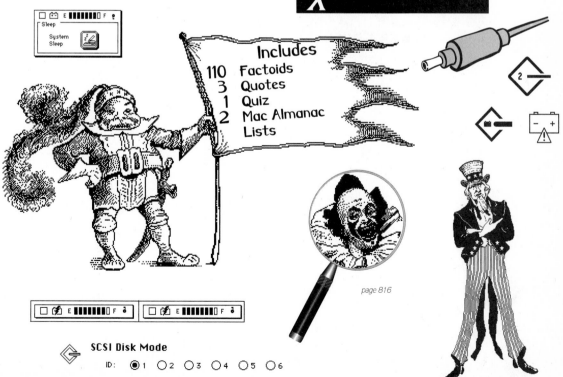

Includes

110 Factoids
3 Quotes
1 Quiz
2 Mac Almanac
Lists

page 816

SCSI Disk Mode
ID:  ●1  ○2  ○3  ○4  ○5  ○6

## ≈ MODELS & COMPONENTS ≈

### The PowerBook Roundup

∞➔ **The PowerBook 100**, although one of the original PowerBook models, has always been in a class by itself. It's the only one that:

- has a 68000 processor
- uses a lead-acid battery
- has no internal floppy drive*
- uses a 1-inch trackball
- doesn't recognize the difference between shutting down and sleeping

> ✳The only non-Duo, that is!

In addition, the 100 has features that weren't added to other PowerBooks until much later down the line, like the SCSI disk mode capability that lets you use the PowerBook as an external drive.

#### PowerBook 100 Specs

| Model | Screen | Colors | Battery | Chip | Speed | FPU | Max. RAM |
|-------|--------|--------|-----------|-------|-------|-----|----------|
| 100 | passive | b&w | lead-acid | 68000 | 16MHz | no | 8MB |

∞➔ **The original PowerBooks** (not including the 100) are differentiated chiefly by their screens and processor speeds. There are other, minor, differences, such as the size of the hard drive and the amount of on-board RAM, but it's easy to look at these PowerBooks as a group. They all use NiCad (nickel-cadmium) battery technology, but what they particularly have in common is the lack of a video out port for connecting to an external monitor.

- The PowerBook 140 was the original middle-of-the-road computer. If the 100 was a little too slow and you wanted the convenience of an internal floppy drive but the 170 was out of your price range, the 140 fit the bill perfectly.
- The 145 model quietly replaced the 140 not long after its introduction; the single difference was its clock speed.
- The 145B was the same as the 145, except that its insides had been redesigned to make manufacturing easier and cheaper.
- The 170 was the original top-of-the-line PowerBook. It stood out not only by virtue of its price, but because of its beautifully crisp, clear, active-matrix screen; it also included an FPU, absent from the other original PowerBooks.
- The 150 is included here with the original PowerBooks because, despite its being the newest of all the PowerBooks discussed in this chapter (in fact, it's not even released as I write this!), it was introduced to replace the 145B. At 5.5 pounds, it's lighter than the other originals, yet is more advanced in several ways, since it has the advantage of two additional years of technological development behind it. One of the reasons it's smaller, though, is because it has fewer ports: SCSI, one serial, and an optional internal modem port. It comes with a 120MB hard drive

Chapter 24 discusses cleaning a PowerBook's screen and trackball.

and can be expanded to 40 megs of RAM; its screen offers 4 levels of gray in the 640x480-pixel mode; and it retains RAM information in sleep for a short time even when the battery's removed—long enough for you to swap batteries.

### Original PowerBooks Specs

| Model | Screen | Colors | Battery | Chip | Speed | FPU | Max. RAM |
|-------|---------|---------|---------|--------|--------|-----|----------|
| 140 | passive | b&w | NiCad | 68030 | 16 MHz | no | 8MB |
| 145 | passive | b&w | NiCad | 68030 | 25 MHz | no | 8MB |
| 145B | passive | b&w | NiCad | 68030 | 25 MHz | no | 8MB |
| 170 | active | b&w | NiCad | 68030 | 25 MHz | yes | 8MB |
| 150 | passive | 4 grays | NiCad | 68030 | 33 MHz | no | 40MB |

⋯▸ **The second wave of PowerBooks** introduced two major items lacking in the first line-up: screens in grayscale and color, and video output ports. In addition, they offered the capability of greater memory expansion. Since they were introduced at about the same time as the PowerBook Duos, they were christened "all-in-ones," because you didn't need to dock them to another unit or attach peripheral items in order to access things like an FPU, a floppy drive, or standard I/O ports.

- The PowerBook 160 offers a passive-matrix screen, but in grayscale.
- The PowerBook 165 is a 160 with a 33MHz processor.
- The PowerBook 180's grayscale screen is active matrix.
- The PowerBook 165c was the first color PowerBook, but its passive-matrix screen offered somewhat washed-out color and most buyers sat back and waited a few months for the rumored active-matrix color machine.
- The PowerBook 180c offered a beautiful (if tiny) active-matrix color screen. It was also the first PowerBook display to use the standard 640x480-pixel proportion found on standard monitors.

### Second-Wave PowerBook Specs

| Model | Screen | Colors | Battery | Chip | Speed | FPU | Max. RAM |
|-------|---------|----------|---------|--------|--------|-----|----------|
| 160 | passive | 16 grays | NiCad | 68030 | 25 MHz | no | 14MB |
| 165 | passive | 16 grays | NiCad | 68030 | 33 MHz | no | 14MB |
| 165c | passive | 256 | NiCad | 68030 | 33 MHz | yes | 14MB |
| 180 | active | 16 grays | NiCad | 68030 | 33 MHz | yes | 14MB |
| 180c | active | 256 | NiCad | 68030 | 33 MHz | yes | 14MB |

⋯▸ **The PowerBook Duos** took a new approach to computing: Why carry the whole thing with you when you didn't *need* the whole thing with you all the time? Especially when leaving all that stuff at your desk meant you were also leaving a lot of *weight* at your desk? A Duo by itself is a portable computer, with a minimum of I/O ports. Slid into a Duo Dock, it serves as the CPU and hard drive of a larger system. The Dock provides a floppy drive, all the standard ports, extra video RAM to run a standard monitor, and even a place to plug in an FPU chip. The Duo Dock II includes an Ethernet connector and provides more video RAM. The Duos also introduced a new battery technology to PowerBook users, since they use nickel-metal-hydride (NiHy, or NiMHy) batteries.

- The Duo 210 and 230 were the original Duo offerings. Oddly enough, the only thing that differentiated them was their clock speeds. Neither has an FPU, which can be installed in the Duo Dock if you need the functionality.

- The second round of Duos offers active-matrix screens and 33 MHz speeds. The 250 has a 16-level grayscale screen; the 270c offers 256 colors in its 640x480 pixel mode or thousands of colors in the smaller 640x400 mode. The 270c was the first Duo to include an FPU and the capability of going to 32 megs of RAM.

- The 280 and 280c Duos are, in effect, '040 versions of the 250 and 270c. Although the clock rates of the 280's are the same as their predecessors', their more powerful processor chip makes them speed demons.

### PowerBook Duo Specs

| Model | Screen | Colors | Battery | Chip | Speed | FPU | Max. RAM |
|-------|--------|--------|---------|------|-------|-----|----------|
| 210 | passive | 16 grays | NiHy | 68030 | 25 MHz | (Dock) | 24 |
| 230 | passive | 16 grays | NiHy | 68030 | 33 MHz | (Dock) | 24 |
| 250 | active | 16 grays | NiHy | 68030 | 33 MHz | (Dock) | 24 |
| 270c | active | 256 or thousands | NiHy | 68030 | 33 MHz | yes | 32 |
| 280 | active | 16 grays | NiHy | 68LC040 | 33 MHz | no | 40 |
| 280c | active | 256 or thousands | NiHy | 68LC040 | 33 MHz | no | 40 |

••▶ **The '040 all-in-one PowerBooks** offer new designs both inside and out. Their processor chip, the 68LC040, is a special low-power version of the standard '040; it's missing the built-in FPU functions of the standard chip. The 520 and 520c run at 25 MHz, while the 540 and 540c run at 33 MHz; all are able to address up to 36 megs of RAM. Another feature that sets these PowerBooks apart from their predecessors is the fact that they run on *two* batteries, one of which can be replaced by a module that connects to the PDS slot hidden in the battery bay. With an adapter, the slot accepts PCMCIA cards—a new standard that squeezes even more information into even smaller areas. (A PCMCIA card can hold a few megs of memory, or even a modem.) Finally, there's the special *touchpad* that these computers have instead of a trackball. Oh, and one more thing—there's a row of tiny function keys* along the top of the keyboard, for those of us who can't function without them.

*✳Function keys, not FKEYs. But the occasional name confusion reminds me of a list I meant to include earlier in the book—about names for the Command key. So, I'll slap it in this chapter!*

It's important to note that the passive-matrix screen on the 520c uses a special *dual scan* technology that refreshes the screen more quickly and makes them much better than previous passive-matrix screens.

### 500-Series PowerBook Specs

| Model | Screen | Colors | Battery | Chip | Speed | FPU | Max. RAM |
|-------|--------|--------|---------|------|-------|-----|----------|
| 520 | passive | 16 grays | NiHy | 68LC040 | 25 MHz | no | 36 |
| 520c | passive | 256 or thousands | NiHy | 68LC040 | 25 MHz | no | 36 |
| 540 | active | 16 grays | NiHy | 68LC040 | 33 MHz | no | 36 |
| 540c | active | 256 or thousands | NiHy | 68LC040 | 25 MHz | no | 36 |

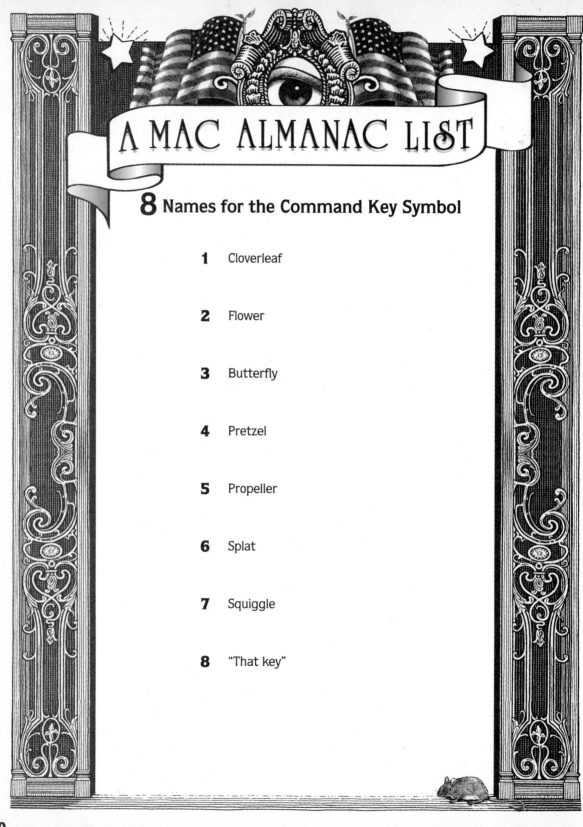

# A MAC ALMANAC LIST

## 8 Names for the Command Key Symbol

**1** Cloverleaf

**2** Flower

**3** Butterfly

**4** Pretzel

**5** Propeller

**6** Splat

**7** Squiggle

**8** "That key"

## Screens

∞► **Many PowerBooks have nonstandard screen proportions,** measuring 640x400 pixels instead of the usual 640x480 pixels. In many ways, this doesn't matter, and it's a small price to pay for portability. But you have to keep in mind that if you're preparing a presentation on the PowerBook that will be delivered from another Mac, or preparing it on a desk Mac to be displayed from a PowerBook, you're going to have a problem because of the 80 pixels missing in the PowerBook's screen height.

All models prior to the 180c have the shorter screen. Later models, although they offer a 640x480 screen, can work in either of two modes: On the full screen you get 256 colors, but if you switch into the smaller 640x400 mode, you can use thousands.

∞► **There are two types of PowerBook screens:** active and passive matrix. Active-matrix screens are a thing of beauty, with sharp, clear pictures. If you do a lot of word processing, or work for hours at a time with your PowerBook, the active-matrix screen is almost a must.

Passive-matrix screens are a little slow. You wind up "typing ahead," with letters appearing on the screen as if they're floating up toward the surface of the display; if you move the cursor too fast, it disappears. The original passive-matrix screens are completely viable as a work "surface," but not recommended if you need to work for hours at a time with them.

The passive-matrix screen introduced on the 520c uses a special scanning approach that improves its look considerably.

∞► **A black-and-white or grayscale PowerBook** still "thinks" in color, so you can use it to prepare and/or project full color presentations that will be funneled through a color display or projection unit or hook up the PowerBook to an external monitor and work in color.

••► **The early PowerBook models have no video out port** and can't be easily connected to an external monitor. There are several products that came to market in the first year of the PowerBook's introduction that let it hook up to a monitor. But I can't heartily recommend any of them, because I don't believe they'll be around to support the product much longer since all new PowerBook models have had video outs—there's just not enough of a marketplace out there to keep them in business.

If you need to hook up to an external monitor, don't buy a used PowerBook 100, 140, 145B, or 170. If you already have one of those models, consider selling it and buying a newer model with video out.

••► **Some active-matrix screens have flaws** called *voids* (where a pixel never turns on, staying white) and *stuck pixels* (where a pixel never turns off, staying black). There's an average of two voids per active-matrix screen.

Apple doesn't consider voids a serious defect unless there are more than five of them on the screen, or two within an inch of each other. Then it's serious enough to warrant a free replacement.

A single stuck pixel, however, is enough to get you a new screen because when a pixel is stuck on, it uses up battery power. You can inspect the screen by using the General Controls control panel to turn the desktop completely white and then completely black, moving the control panel's window and any desktop icons in each case so they're not concealing flaws.

•••▶ **PowerBook displays can't suffer from burn-in**, since that's strictly a problem with phosphor screens used in standard monitors. But they can suffer from a temporary shadowing problem if you leave the screens on too long—say, 24 hours—without changing the displays.

If you find your screen suffering from this problem because you left it on (and plugged in, obviously, or the battery would run down before the screen could have a problem), put it to sleep. The longer you left the screen on, the longer it has to sleep for the problem to go away, but overnight should do it.

## Memory

∞•▶ **PowerBooks don't use SIMMs** because of their cramped innards. The memory boards used in PowerBooks are called just that—*memory boards*, or *memory modules*. The arrangement of memory chips on the boards is different from the in-line design of a SIMM. Each new crop of PowerBooks has greater memory capacity than the last, as you can see in the PowerBook Memory Configurations chart.

### PowerBook Memory Configurations

| Model | On-board (MB) | Max. RAM (MB) | Speed (ns) |
|-------|---------------|---------------|------------|
| 100 | 2 | 8 | 100 |
| 140 | 2 | 8 | 100 |
| 145 | 2 | 8 | 100 |
| 145b | 4 | 8 | 100 |
| 160 | 4 | 14 | 85 |
| 165 | 4 | 14 | 85 |
| 165c | 4 | 14 | 85 |
| 170 | 2 | 8 | 100 |
| 150 | 4 | 40 | 85 |
| 180 | 4 | 14 | 85 |
| 180c | 4 | 14 | 85 |
| 520 | 4 | 36 | 70 |
| 520c | 4 | 36 | 70 |
| 540 | 4 | 36 | 70 |
| 540c | 4 | 36 | 70 |
| Duo 210 | 4 | 24 | 85 |
| Duo 230 | 4 | 24 | 85 |
| Duo 250 | 4 | 24 | 85 |
| Duo 270 | 4 | 32 | 85 |
| Duo 280 | 4 | 40 | 85 |
| Duo 280c | 4 | 40 | 85 |

## Cables & Connectors

⊶ **Don't use a Mac Portable power adapter** or the one from a StyleWriter to charge your PowerBook, even though the connectors are the same. The cords are *not* interchangeable, and you could damage the adapter, the PowerBook, or both.

⊶ **PowerBooks introduced a new connector** for SCSI cables, since the standard connector was way too big for the back of such a small machine. The HDI-30 SCSI connector (HDI stands for *high-density interface*) is a port that squeezes the 30-pin SCSI connection into a square configuration that, of course, requires a special cable (the HDI-30 SCSI System Cable) if you want to connect a SCSI device to the PowerBook. But, as tech editor Joe Holmes pointed out when he read this, there's no excuse for using the HDI-30 connector on the back of the Duo Dock, where there's plenty of room for a standard SCSI port.

There's also an HDI-20 connector on the PowerBook 100, and on the Duo's MiniDock and Floppy Disk Adapter, for connecting an external floppy drive.

⊶ **The HDI-30 SCSI Disk Adapter cable** is used for turning your PowerBook into an external hard drive for your desk machine (or for another PowerBook, come to think of it!); most PowerBooks are capable of this *SCSI disk mode*, which is covered later in more detail.

This cable is often confused with the HDI-30 system cable, which is used to attach SCSI devices to the PowerBook. Here's how to tell them apart:

| | System Cable | Adapter Cable |
|---|---|---|
| Use | attaching SCSI devices to the PowerBook | attaching the PowerBook as a SCSI device |
| Length | 18 inches | 10 inches |
| Color | light gray | dark gray |
| Pins | 29 | 30 |
| PowerBook connector | HDI-30 | HDI-30 |
| Second connector | 50-pin male | 50-pin female |

⊶ **SCSI Boy** is a small, very handy, 30-to-25-pin adapter for the PowerBook. It plugs into the HDI-30 port and gives you a standard 25-pin SCSI connection at the other end. It's easier, smaller, and cheaper than using Apple's HDI-30 system cable. The SCSI Doc provides the same hookup, with an extra feature: At the flip of a switch, it turns into an adapter for a SCSI-mode hookup. [APS Technologies]

**SCSI Boy & SCSI Doc**

⊶ **Many of the original PowerBook power adapters** had a defect that can damage the motherboard. If your adapter is model #5140 (check its label), you could have a major problem. Inspect the black ring at the tip of the plug that goes into the PowerBook; if the black part is chipped or cracked at all, get a replacement *immediately*.

## ⊰ TIDBITS ⊱

### General

∞•➤ **A slight clicking sound** from your PowerBook at odd intervals is nothing to worry about. Its sound circuit is shut down periodically to save battery power, and the click you hear is the circuit shutting off. Another "clicker" inside the PowerBook can be the hard drive; the IBM drive (yes, Virginia, there are many an IBM drive in PowerBooks) makes a clicking sound when the drive arm parks and unparks.

My PowerBook hard drive clicks, and I remember being concerned the first time I heard it. I had just upgraded to an 80MB hard drive from the 40MB model that came with the machine; the 80 was a used hard drive that I bought from someone online. That someone showed up on the front page of *MacWeek* not long afterward, with his new 165c, sitting in the cockpit of a plane—or was it a helicopter? Vernon Huang was a Navy flight surgeon at the time; now he's finished his hitch and is a medical software developer. And I'm happy to say that we generally meet in Boston and San Francisco during the Macworld Expos and do lunch or dinner and hang out. (Of course, I don't do that with *everyone* I buy something from online …)

∞•➤ **PowerBooks are easier to fix** than any other Mac because they're the easiest to ship off to a repair technician.

Apple's approach to computer repair changed when the PowerBooks were introduced—after all, when you're traveling with a portable computer, it's not likely you'll be able to reach your local Apple dealer when you run into a problem. Apple SOS is a great deal: you call 800-SOS-APPL and describe your problem, they send you a shipping carton, you ship the computer to them, they fix it and ship it back. Three days—five days, tops. It's great.

### MOMMY, WHERE DID I COME FROM?

Your PowerBook's serial number tells when and where it was created. The first two characters identify the place:

CK ..............Cork, Ireland

SS ................Sony in San Diego

SQ................Sony in Nagano, Japan

F1 ................Plant 1, Fremont, California

F2................Plant 2, Fremont, California

FM ..............consolidated facility in Fremont

FC................Fountain, Colorado

The next digit is for the year: 1 is 1991, 2 is 1992, and so on. The next two digits stand for the week of the year; 01 is the first week of January, 10 is around the second week of March, and so on.

The last set of numbers identifies your individual PowerBook.

∞◊ **My PowerBook isn't unrelieved granite gray.** When I open the case, I'm greeted by an orange trackball. It's the perfect touch—unless you'd prefer green, yellow, or hot pink. Or you can buy a four-pack of PowerBalls and change them weekly! [APS]

◦•▸ **Attaching an external SCSI device** to a PowerBook is relatively simple if you have an HDI-30 SCSI cable and the device you're connecting has the standard 50-pin SCSI connector.

As for termination requirements, the general guideline is the same as for a desk Mac: Terminate the last device in the chain. But Apple recommends that for PowerBooks you also add termination *before* the first device for "optimum performance." (That means that you can do without it unless you're having some SCSI problems.) A simple chain then consists of: the PowerBook, the HDI-30 SCSI system cable, a pass-through terminator, the external drive, and the drive's terminator.

If you're attaching a SCSI device to a Duo, you'll need the Duo Dock or the MiniDock to provide the connector—but you won't need the extra terminator, because there's termination in the Dock and in the MiniDock.

∞◊ **Connecting an all-in-one PowerBook** to a network—even if it's just your desk machine—can involve lots of cables. On my simple setup, for instance, the PowerBook needs three connections: the power adapter that I leave at my desk (I use a second one for travel); the phone line for the modem; and, the network connector for the desk machine and printer. Not only does it take time to connect and disconnect all these cables when I'm coming and going, there's considerable wear and tear on the connectors themselves because it's not likely that they're inserted and detached straight on, with no angled wobble or wiggle each time.

But the BookEndz unit solves the problem: It holds all the connecting wires, and the PowerBook just slides in and out of a little docking station. It's a great convenience. [Pilot Technology]

◦•▸ **Don't run on batteries when there's a monitor** connected to the PowerBook. The monitor has its own power supply, but the power to the video circuitry comes from the PowerBook, and the battery will drain quickly.

**POWERBALLS**

**BOOKENDZ**

## PowerBook 100

◦•▸ **The three backup batteries** in the PowerBook 100 are easy to replace: Just swing out the storage compartment at the back of the case, remove the old ones, and put the new ones in, making sure that the positive sides of the battery are facing up. These batteries aren't rechargeable, but they should last for years.

◦•▸ **Never let the main battery drain too far.** "Too far" doesn't mean the last low-battery warning before the computer shuts itself off. Draining it too much beyond that point, though, can ruin it. Remember that a battery is continually (though very slowly) drained just by being in the 100, so don't delay recharging. If you can't recharge it, remove it from the 100, or flip the storage switch to Off.

···➔ **If you use the 100 in SCSI disk mode**, there's no obvious way to turn off the PowerBook. The Shut Down command shuts down the desk Mac, but the 100's drive keeps spinning and it stays in disk mode. To turn it off, press the Reset and Interrupt buttons simultaneously.

### YET ANOTHER JOE HOLMES NEARLY USELESS TIP

(This one's really from my brother Chris.) Turn off or put your PowerBook 100 to sleep; turn off your desktop Mac. Use an ADB cable to connect the ADB ports of the PowerBook and the desk Mac. Start up the desktop Mac. Guess what you've got? A new keyboard and trackball for the desk machine. That's right: The PowerBook 100 keyboard and trackball will now operate your desktop Mac!

If the PowerBook is shut down, the little thing will act just as a keyboard and trackball attachment—a very expensive second-rate keyboard and third-rate trackball, that is.

But, if you've only put the PowerBook to sleep, the first key press wakes it. From then on, you'll be typing into both the PowerBook and the desk Mac every time you press a key on the PowerBook keyboard. Run a word processor on both machines, and you've got a hardware-based simultaneous-entry backup program that records all your text input.

Or, how about this: Place one hand on each keyboard, with the keyboards tilted at a comfortable angle toward each other, and you've got a homemade version of Apple's ergonomic split keyboard.

And here's one we haven't tried yet, because all our machines are out of warranty: What if the ADB hookup still works while you've docked the PowerBook in SCSI disk mode? It's a hard drive! A keyboard! A trackball! Three devices in one!

Boy, I'll bet Apple is really gonna regret dropping the PowerBook 100!

*—Joe (& Chris) Holmes*

···➔ **If the 100's battery won't charge** when it's in the PowerBook, but it takes a charge when it's in a recharger unit, there's almost certainly a problem with the solder connection between the adapter connector and the motherboard. This needs to be fixed by a dealer or Apple SOS—it's a $400 fix. But you can easily do it yourself if you're used to working inside a PowerBook and are handy with a soldering iron (the soldering pads are fairly large and easy to repair).

···➔ **If the 100 turns on only when it's plugged in** and not when it's on only the battery, check that the storage switch is in the On position; if you've shipped it off for repairs, you'll almost certainly get it back with the storage switch flipped to Off. If the storage switch isn't the problem, you may have a blown fuse, which is a $400 fix from Apple. (It's about $125 if you know any technicians who do component-level repairs. And it's about a buck if you do can do it yourself.)

···➔ **Improve the trackball performance** on the 100 with this simple adjustment:

1. Take out the trackball by removing the retaining ring around it and then taking out the ball.

2. Locate the shafts to the left and bottom of the trackball well; each has a blue roller on it.

3. Slide the blue roller on the left shaft down from its original position. Slide the blue roller on the bottom shaft further to the right.

4. Return the ball to the well and replace the retaining ring.

By moving the rollers this way, the ball comes in contact only with their edges and there's less movement of the rollers and the shafts while you're using the trackball; as a result, you get smoother trackball action.

⚫➤ **The 100 *meltdown* problem** was infamous not for the number of cases (only three reported out of 60,000 units sold), but for the fact that it resulted in Apple's only product recall. A protruding pin on one of the internal components apparently shorted out against the inside of the case, generating enough heat to melt through the bottom of the case. PowerBooks with serial numbers below SQ211xxx and SS216xxx are the only ones prone to this problem. The fix is easy, since the protrusion needs only to be clipped down to size. A "clipped" PowerBook gets a small sticker with an ® symbol near the serial number. (PowerBook 100's sent in for any type of repair are normally fixed for this, too.)

⚫➤ **The PowerBook 100 retains all RAM disk** information even when you shut it down. (But *not* if you turn the storage switch to Off, disconnecting the battery.)

⚫➤ **Change the 100's battery while it's sleeping** and everything will still be there when you wake it up.

## PowerBook 140/145/170

⚫➤ **A problem screen on a 140 or 145** might be due to a too-thin cable inside the PowerBook, an acknowledged problem on the early production models. If the display works correctly when you squeeze the right side of the frame around the screen, you've probably got the cable problem. The fix is a simple shim that's easy for a technician to install. And, in fact, it might be a fix that you can get for free even if the machine is beyond its one-year warranty date. Try calling Apple SOS and see what they have to say.

*See Chapter 24 for more about Apple SOS.*

PowerBooks with serial numbers later than CK121xxx or higher, or F2208 or higher, or any number beginning with FC, already have the shim installed.

⚫➤ **The floppy drives in the 140 and 170 models** had some significant problems in the early production models—the ones manufactured before April of 1992. They're very finicky when it comes to reading disks, and the *This is not a Macintosh disk* dialog is the frequent response to insertion of a perfectly good disk. The problem was apparently caused by inadequate shielding on the backlight converter, a problem attended to later in the production runs of both models—first with a shield, and later with a new, less sensitive, floppy drive. These models had shielding installed at the factory:

- 140s with serial numbers higher than F2150xxx
- 170s with serial numbers higher than CK205xxx

These models have the new (rev B) drive:

- 140s in any configuration other than 4/40 or 4/80 (4 megs of RAM and 40 MB or 80 MB hard drives)
- 140s in a 4/40 configuration and serial numbers starting with or higher than F2211xxx
- 140s in a 4/80 configuration and serial numbers starting with or higher than F2212xxx
- 170s with serial numbers starting with or higher than FC213xxx or CK213xxx

••➤ **Disk-reading problems on a 140 or 170** may be due to inadequate backlight shielding as described above, but you might be able to work around the problem until you get the PowerBook fixed. When you get a *This disk is unreadable* dialog, eject the disk, turn the backlight off, and re-insert the disk; this often makes the disk readable. If the problem disk is one that was mass-produced, try making a copy of it at a desk Mac; the PowerBook might be able to read the copy when it can't read the master.

## Duos

∞➤ **Early Duo 210 and 230 models** had some significant keyboard problems—keys that repeated and a spacebar that wouldn't work at all. These need total keyboard replacements. But if the Duo's been opened for memory or modem installation, the problem may be simply from a too-tight screw at the bottom of the case: Turn your Duo over and loosen the screw that's at the center of the case.

∞➤ **If you connect a monitor through the MiniDock,** make sure you keep the Duo plugged in. The monitor will have its own power supply, but the power to the Duo's video circuitry comes from the Duo—and the battery can't handle that kind of power draw for very long.

● ● ● ● ● ● ● ● ● ● ● ● ● ● ● ● ● ● ● ● ● ● ● ● ● ● ● ● ● ● ● ● ● ● ● ● ●

**POW! SHAZAM!**                                    **[3 AND 5 POINTS]**

For 3 points: Who are the Dynamic Duo—the Caped Crusader and the Boy Wonder? And for 5 points: What were their names back in real life—the millionaire and his ward?

∞➤ **Skip the Shut Down command** on your Dock system if you're going to eject the Duo anyway. Just press the Eject button; the system will still go through the standard shutdown procedures.

••➤ **You can lock an empty Dock.** You already know you can lock your Duo in the Dock, and you can think of several reasons why you might want to. But why lock an empty dock, preventing the insertion of Duo? Because if you have an internal drive mounted in an unlocked Dock, someone can come along, insert his Duo, and access the contents of your hard drive.

**•••➤ You can insert a sleeping Duo into the Duo Dock** but you can't use it that way—when you press the Power On key on the main keyboard, the Duo is ejected. But you might want to insert a sleeping Duo anyway—the Dock serves as a handy recharging station for the Duo's battery, and the Duo can charge in the Dock while it's asleep. Or, you might want your sleeping Duo to be locked safely in the Dock when you're not looking.

**•••➤ Set the Dock's internal drive** to be the startup disk by installing system software on it and using the Startup Disk control panel on the inserted Duo to specify the Dock's drive as the startup. But once you do that, the Duo will always give preference to an internal Dock drive as the startup—even if you insert it into someone else's dock! This amazing little twist is a result of the fact that the Startup Disk control panel stores the ID number of the desired startup drive in the Duo's PRAM; Dock drives are typically set to ID 1 no matter what Dock they're in.

**•••➤ You can't get FPU functions on the** 280 or 280c Duo models. The 68LC040 chip they use is missing the built-in FPU functions of the standard '040. But since the chip is an '040 (of sorts), software programs won't look beyond it to an FPU that's been installed in a Duo Dock. So, there's no way to get FPU functionality on these models!

## File Synching

**∞➤ *File synching* is a phrase ushered in** with the PowerBooks: How do you synchronize the files that you keep on both your PowerBook and on a desk machine?* You work at your desk, you put some files on the PowerBook when you're leaving on a trip, you put them back on the desk machine when you get home. It sounds simple—until you consider that the files on the desk machine might change while you're gone (because "home" might be an office with other people in it), or, worse, changes might be made to both files—the one at home base and the one on your PowerBook—while they're separated.

> *Since a Duo is your desk machine, synching's not an issue for Duo owners!*

But even if you know that both files (or folders) have been changed, what good does that do you? How can you tell the difference between an item that's been added on one machine and one that's been deleted from another—whether that item is a file in a folder, or a record in a database? You can't. Some file-synching utilities can—but they can't resolve the problem of updating information within a file, or combining the changes if both files were changed.

**∞➤ If you sync files manually,** you have to look at their modified dates to see which is the most recent version, and copy files back and forth accordingly—presumably across the network that's set up between your PowerBook and the desk machine. The modified date on a file serves as a time and date "stamp" for the file.

**∞❨ A synching program** is a great convenience for a PowerBook owner, since it takes care of checking the files on both the PowerBook and a desk machine and updates whatever's necessary—in either direction. A sync program even tells you if both versions of the file have been changed since the last synching operation, although it can't do much about reconciling them. Synching programs can also serve as backup programs for users who don't even own PowerBooks, since you can set the sync to go "one way," from your main drive to the backup disk.

**POWERMERGE**

My loyalties in this arena swerve between PowerMerge and File Runner. PowerMerge is very straightforward and simple to use, but still allows lots of variety in the setup (like "sync the contents of this folder to that one, but skip these particular files each time"). It's my current favorite, and I used it for backup operations during the course of this book project. File Runner is also very good, allowing you to do all sorts of "inclusions" and "exceptions" in a sync, and even provides file compression if you're using a floppy as the medium between two Macs that aren't connected. Inline's Sync! is a powerful program that lets you script sync scenarios, but its current insistence on reading the *entire* contents of *both* drives even when you want to sync only a folder or two, and the abysmally brief documentation for its scripting capability, keep me from recommending it. [PowerMerge, Leader Technology; File Runner, MBS Technologies]

### SAY WHAT?

A Newton isn't a micro-Mac, but it's hard not to think of it when discussing the miniaturized Macs that are PowerBooks. And, in fact, the Newton's mis-interpretation of its owner's handwriting is more amusing than running Lewis Carroll's Jabberwocky through a spell checker.

I asked my kids to come up with famous sayings from American history, and other patriotic phras-es, and I wrote them into a Newton that hadn't been "trained" to recognize my handwriting. Here are the results—see if you can figure out the originals.

- No key atlas without representation.
- Give me likely, or give me drink.
- 1 midnight that I have but one life to guy for my country.
- We the people if the united states in order to Burma mine perfect review...
- Forward and severe years ago, or factors brought faith lot this continent a new Watson knows a in liberty once dedicated to Are purposes Thatcher men all created equals.
- Ask nut what your country can door you, but rural give can do for your country.
- Oh say can you see legs the Donna early light. Oh the rounded we watched were so brilliantly straining.
- Girl mess America, bond that I love...
- Oh beautiful air Spokane skies, for Aruba circuits of grain...

⊶**◗** **The modified date showing in the Finder** isn't always the perfect guide for checking which version of a file or folder is the most recent. Here are some of the things you need to keep in mind for synching:

- Check that the time, as well as the date, is set correctly on both machines.
- If the PowerBook has been taken apart for a repair or upgrade, and the time and date weren't immediately reset, your most recent files may be dated 1904.

- If you travel to different time zones and reset your PowerBook's clock, the time/date stamp on your files won't reflect the right relationship to the ones on the home machine. Not only that, you'll get internal conflicts, like a saved *copy* of an edited file's being dated *before* the original. It's best not to change the time on the PowerBook if you don't absolutely need to.

- Some files (particularly databases) get a new date stamp if you simply open them to look up something. If you're going to use a file as "read only," lock it with Get Info at the desktop so the date stamp won't change.

- A folder's modified date changes when you save a new document into it. But if you alter an existing file in the folder, its date doesn't change. On the other hand, some applications create and then erase temporary files while you're working, which changes the modified date of the folder even though its contents haven't changed. In all, don't trust modified dates on folders: Always look at the files inside.

- If you save a new document into an open folder on the desktop, it shows up with the correct date stamp. But change an existing file, and its stamp isn't updated as long as the window is open. You can force the update by closing and reopening the window. So, if you habitually leave certain windows open on the desktop, close and reopen them before you sync any files in them.

⊶➧ **It's easy to forget about "background" files** when you're synching your PowerBook and desk machine. There are all sorts of peripheral files we use every day that we don't think about too often, since they're not actually documents that we create and save in the normal way. For instance:

- Custom dictionaries and glossaries for word processors, spell checkers, and thesauruses.

- Macros. Did you ever try to run a macro on one machine that only exists on the other? I do it quite often. Sometimes it's easier just to record a fresh one on whatever machine I'm on, but synching the macro file would take care of the problem.

- Desk accessory files. Whether it's Scrapbook pages or a rolodex-type accessory, desk accessory files contain information that needs to be updated. (Make sure you sync the desk accessory *files*, not the desk accessories themselves.)

- Telecom files. How many times have you saved someone's address during an online session and then tried to retrieve it to send her a note when you're on your other machine? Or saved an entire message or thread to review later, but it's on the other drive when you're ready to read?

## ◄ SPECIAL SYSTEM SOFTWARE ►

## The Portable Control Panel

⊶➧ **The Portable control panel** is left over from the old Mac Portable system software; it was included with the System 7.0.1 that shipped with the original PowerBooks but was later replaced by the PowerBook control panel. You'll be using the Portable control panel only if you have a 100, 140, 145, 145b, or 170, since all other models need System 7.1 at the least, which doesn't include this control panel. What's included in the Portable control panel depends on what machine you're using, and its hardware components.

The configuration of the Portable control panel depends on your PowerBook.

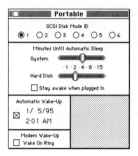

∞➜ **Set the sleep intervals for the system and the hard drive** by adjusting the slider controls. System sleep, of course, also puts the hard drive to sleep, but you can also separately stop the hard drive from spinning. (It's easier to use the word *spindown* when you're talking about the drive's sleep state.) When your PowerBook is idle for the number of minutes you've set in the control panel, it goes to sleep.

You'll find that you can't set the system sleep interval shorter than the drive sleep—move the system sleep control too far to the left and the drive sleep control moves with it. This, of course, makes perfect sense, since the drive isn't going to keep spinning when the system is sleeping.

∞➜ **Other options** in this control panel are:

- SCSI ID number selection (for the 100 only).
- Automatic wakeup (for the 100 only).
- Wake on ring for an incoming modem call, specifically for the internal or an external modem.
- Stay awake when plugged in setting.

All these options are also provided in the PowerBook control panel, so they're covered in that section.

••➜ **There's a hidden option in** the Portable control panel: Option-click where it says *Minutes Until Automatic Sleep* and you'll get a dialog about the PowerBook's special *rest* state (which is covered a little later, under *Power Concerns*).

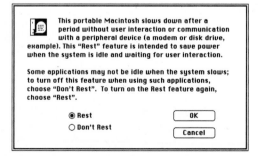

This portable Macintosh slows down after a period without user interaction or communication with a peripheral device (a modem or disk drive, example). This "Rest" feature is intended to save power when the system is idle and waiting for user interaction.

Some applications may not be idle when the system slows; to turn off this feature when using such applications, choose "Don't Rest". To turn on the Rest feature again, choose "Rest".

◉ Rest
○ Don't Rest

[ OK ]
[ Cancel ]

## The PowerBook Control Panel

∞◆ **The PowerBook control panel,** introduced with System 7.1, replaced the Portable control panel. It provides all the functionality of its ancestor in a neater package. Like the previous control panel, its actual appearance depends on which PowerBook it's running on.

The look of the control panel depends on which system it's on.

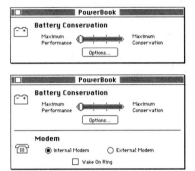

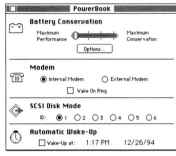

The next version of this control panel showed up with the 3.0 Hardware Update for System 7.1. Although the functions are basically the same, they're approached in an even easier way—with the Options right in the control panel instead of hidden or stored in a separate dialog. Clicking the Easy/Custom button changes the full control panel to a small one that displays only the Conservation/Performance slider bar. The picture here shows what the control panel looks like on a PowerBook 170. (Did you notice that the picture is black and white? That almost all the pictures are black and white in this chapter? That's because I have a black-and-white PowerBook!)

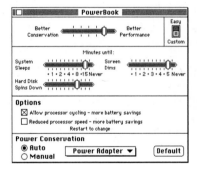

Hardware updates are covered in Chapter 23.

∞◆ **The Conservation/Performance settings** changed a little from one version of the control panel to the next. In the first version, you have the labels *Maximum Performance* and *Maximum Conservation*; in the second, they're *Better Conservation* and *Better Performance*. Each slider control pretty much defines the trade-off: more power means less battery time. In the original

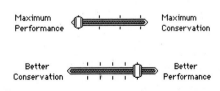

control panel, this setting combines the system and drive sleep settings of the old Portable control panel. In the new control panel, the slider control also includes screen dimming.

**ASK ANDY**

The PowerBook control panel doesn't display any specific times for drive or system sleep, but the slider control does mark a specific number of minutes for each.

My friend Andy Baird—who's done the Mac People bios and some of the artwork for this book—tested the parameters and altered his control panel accordingly. It looks like this:

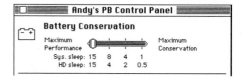

°•▶ **Select a SCSI ID number** for a PowerBook that can use SCSI disk mode by clicking in the numbered button. The default of 1 is usually fine, but it depends on the rest of the setup. This is discussed in more detail later in this chapter under Odds & Ends.

°•▶ **Some models can be awakened automatically** at a preset time by the setting in the control panel. This is handy if you set up an automatic telecommunications session so that the PowerBook wakes up and then the telecom program takes over, sending or receiving information when you're not even around—like in the middle of the night when you're sleeping but the telephone rates are really low.

°•▶ **A PowerBook modem can wake up for an incoming call** if you check the *Wake on Ring* setting in the control panel and specify the internal or external modem. This setting isn't available in the updated System 7.1 control panel, but the update does provide a separate control panel—PowerBook Setup—for these functions.

Since the SCSI Disk Mode and Automatic Wake Up settings were banished from the newest version of the PowerBook control panel, you'll find them in the new version of the PowerBook Setup control panel.

•••▶ **Leave the *Stay awake when plugged in* option checked**, since there's no reason to save battery power if you're plugged in.

➡ **You can make two different "sets" of** settings in the new PowerBook control panel, one to be used when you're on battery power, and one for when you're plugged in. The PowerBook will automatically switch to the settings you've defined when you attach the power cord or unplug it.

To define your sets, click the Auto button at the bottom of the window, and choose Power Adapter or Battery from the popup menu. Then set the controls in the window to whatever you want used in that situation. When you want to temporarily override your settings without redefining the set, click the Manual button and change the settings.*

> *This is one of Apple's lesser efforts in the interface department. Why isn't "manual" just one of the menu choices?

## The Battery DA

➡ **Toggle between the short and full** versions of the Battery DA by clicking on the little handle in its right corner. The bars in the gauge change from black to white as the battery loses its power.

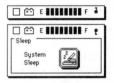

The short and full versions of the battery DA.

➡ **Don't count on the power level reported** in the Battery DA's gauge. It's only a very loose approximation, at best. And the bars in the gauge don't stand for any unit of time—10 minutes per bar, for instance. In fact, all the bars could be black and that wouldn't even necessarily mean that the battery is fully charged!

➡ **A lightning bolt through the battery icon** means your battery is being recharged. Usually. If you're using a Duo or a 500 series PowerBook, it really does mean the battery is charging. On other PowerBooks, however, the situation is trickier: The lightning bolt appears if the battery is low (below 80 percent charge) and the adapter is plugged in; it doesn't appear if the battery is more than 80 percent charged even if the adapter is plugged in.

But this assumes that not only is the adapter plugged into the PowerBook, it's also plugged into a powered outlet at the other end. This isn't always a safe assumption—the outlet might be switched off or otherwise have no power, or the plug may have pulled out of the wall and you don't realize it.

Unfortunately, the Battery DA doesn't seem to care much about whether the battery is actually being charged—it usually assumes that if the adapter is plugged into the back of the

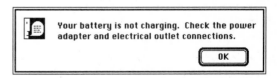

PowerBook, it's being charged. It's counting on a human to check the other end of the cord. (Oh, foolish machine!) If the battery is still over the 80 percent charge threshold, you still won't see any lightning bolt. When it drops below the 80 percent threshold, you get the lightning bolt again—even though there's no charging going on. This is particularly cruel, since you're being told the battery is charging when in fact it's slowly draining. It's not until the battery charge dips well below that 80 percent mark that the Battery DA smartens up and realizes what's going on, at which point you'll get the dialog shown here.

••➧ **Check whether the power adapter is actually** supplying power to the battery with this little test: Open the Battery DA so you can watch the gauge, unplug the cord from the back of

the PowerBook, and then reinsert it. The gauge will drop a few notches as soon as you re-insert the power cord. If there's power available, the gauge will go back up in about 15 seconds; if there's no power, the gauge will stay at the lower readout.

## Also ...

∞➧ **The PowerBook Display** control panel that came out with System 7.1 lets you automatically dim the screen brightness, much as you can control the sleep intervals for the drive and system. You can turn the dimming on or off, specify an

inactive interval of 1 to 5 minutes, and disable it when the PowerBook's plugged in. Since the backlighting is a major power-eater, it's important not to keep the screen lit when you're not actually using it.

••➧ **AutoRemounter** is another System 7.1 addition to the PowerBook collection of control panels. With it, you can have the PowerBook automatically reconnect itself to a network when it comes out of sleep, mounting the network volume(s) on its desktop. (Unfortunately, it can't do what I want—mount itself back on my desktop machine when it wakes up.)

The original version of AutoRemounter didn't work with the PowerBook 100, 140, 145, or 170 even if you installed System 7.1 on those models. A later version, that came with the 2.0 Hardware Update for System 7.1, works fine on these models.

There's more about the Control Strip in Chapter 8's System 7.5 section.

••➧ **The Control Strip is** a nifty piece of software, although it's hard to pinpoint as to what system software it comes with. Unlike most items that were included in System 7.5, it's not also included in the 3.0 Hardware Update to System 7.1. On the other hand, it was included with System 7.1 on machines sold in the latter part of 1994, in that period between the releases of the 3.0 Update and System 7.5.

The Control Strip is completely customizable with the functions of the Battery DA and all the PowerBook's control panels.

❖ **The Control Strip is modular,** so watch for plug-in modules for it. The whole concept is new as I write this, but there's already a terrific product that makes use of the Control Strip. PBTools, which I describe later in the chapter, has a single module that replaces Apple's modules with PBTools' more advanced ones. It also uses PBTools' more advanced concept of SmartClick—a click on some icons toggles a state (like AppleTalk on or off, or hard drive spinup or spindown)—instead of your needing to select from a menu.

The picture here (which is in color—well, grayscale by the time you see it—because PBTools' author, Bill Steinberg, provided it)  shows the PBTools module. The first two icons show the charge levels in the batteries (on a two-battery system); the icon changes when the PowerBook is being charged, and clicking on either one puts the PowerBook to sleep. The next two icons are for hard drive spindown and spinup, and AppleTalk on and off. The next icon shows the processor speed, or a dimmed Z when it's in the rest state. Next comes the modem status, with the icon dimming when the modem isn't drawing power. The last icon shows whether Ethertalk is on or off. Then there's the "time remaining" readout for Duos and 500 series PowerBooks, which know how to provide this information.

## ◄ POWER CONCERNS ►

### Power States

∞► **The PowerBook's sleep state** differentiates it from all other Macs and, since saving battery power is a primary concern for PowerBook users, sleep is an extremely important issue. When a PowerBook is sleeping, its drive isn't spinning, the screen is blank, and there's no power being supplied to the trackball, the modem, or the floppy drive. Other components, like the CPU and RAM, are in a special standby mode rather than being fully on and drawing power.

Putting your PowerBook to sleep when you're not using it—even for only a few minutes—is the best thing you can do to preserve battery power. There are many ways you can do this:

- Use the Sleep command in the Finder's Special menu.
- Use the Battery DA.
- Set the interval for automatic sleep in the PowerBook control panel (System 7.1) or the Portable control panel (System 7.0).
- For a Duo, close its case.
- Run the battery down so low that the PowerBook goes to sleep automatically because of the emergency low-power situation. (This is not the recommended solution!)

•••→ **Power cycling, or processor cycling,** is a power-saving technique that goes on in the background while you're working. If the CPU isn't being used, it goes into a *rest state*—which, as the name implies, is somewhere between awake and asleep. The PowerBook sort of catnaps, looking around every three seconds to see if there's anything that needs to be done. If not, it goes back to the rest state. (Three seconds doesn't seem like much to us, but for a processor doing 30 or 40 million operations every second, that's a significant coffee break.)

EVELYN WAUGH

One needs more rest if one doesn't sleep.
That's why I go to bed early.

•••→ **Prevent processor cycling** through a setting in the PowerBook control panel. In the original System 7.1 control panel, click the Options button in the main window, and use the buttons in the secondary dialog to enable or disable processor cycling. In the updated System 7.1 control panel, the buttons are on the main level of the dialog.

Don't turn off the cycling unless it's absolutely necessary, because it's a great battery saver. Some applications slow down when processor cycling is on, and it particularly affects many games—but then, if you're playing games while on battery power, I have no sympathy for you.

In System 7.0.1, the processor cycling control is hidden in the Portable control panel. Option-click on the *Minutes Until Automatic Sleep* title and you'll get a dialog that gives you Rest and Don't Rest buttons to click.

## Sleep

∞→ **Put the PowerBook to sleep with the Battery DA.** If the DA is open to its full version, click on the Sleep icon. In the short version of the DA, Option-click on the little battery icon.

∞→ **Wake up a PowerBook by** pressing any key (except Caps Lock). Pressing the Power On key also wakes up a sleeping PowerBook.

∞→ **If a PowerBook doesn't wake up when** you press a key, maybe it isn't sleeping—it might have been shut down. Use the Power On key instead.

Life is something to do when
you can't get to sleep.

FRAN LEIBOWITZ

•→ **Don't shut down the PowerBook.** Put it to sleep. There are very few occasions when you need to actually turn off the PowerBook at all. My poor PowerBook has probably been turned off not more than a dozen times in two years, and those times it was for repairs or upgrades. Basically, you need to turn off the PowerBook if:

- You're connecting it to another Mac in SCSI disk mode.
- You're connecting a SCSI device to the PowerBook.
- You're connecting an external floppy to the 100.
- You're connecting a monitor directly to an all-in-one PowerBook.
- You're inserting a Duo into the Duo Dock.
- You won't be using the PowerBook for more than a week or two.
- It's being opened for a repair or upgrade.

•→ **You get a network disconnect warning** before the PowerBook goes to sleep whether or not you're actually attached to a network—what counts is the AppleTalk setting in the Chooser. If AppleTalk's activated and you want to bypass this network

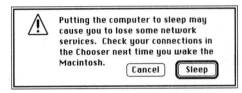

dialog, hold Shift while you "click" the PowerBook to sleep through the Battery DA: shift-click on the Sleep button or shift-option-click on the battery icon.

•→ **Many things cause insomnia** in a PowerBook. If your PowerBook isn't going to sleep when you expect it to, investigate these possibilities:

- When AppleTalk is On in the Chooser, the PowerBook won't go to sleep.
- Check the *Stay awake when plugged in* setting in the PowerBook control panel.
- Opened applications may be doing background processing that keep the PowerBook from going to sleep.
- Timed events in open applications or inits may be kicking in at short intervals, constantly resetting the "clock" that's keeping track of how long the computer's been idle.
- The PowerBook won't go to sleep when certain peripherals—some monitors and SCSI devices, for instance—are connected.

## Conserving Power

•→ **The CPU eats more power** than anything else on the PowerBook. That's sometimes a surprise, or even a difficult concept, since the CPU isn't something a computer user ever has to think about once the computer's purchased. But the CPU takes a lot of energy, and the faster it runs, the more power it uses. And there's the clue: On a PowerBook that can run at either of two speeds (that's every model except the 100 and the 140), setting the clock rate to the lower speed saves a lot of battery power.

To reset the clock speed, use the PowerBook control panel. Depending on what version you're using, you'll find the "Reduced processor speed" option in either the main level of the control panel or in its Options dialog. On a 170 that's running System 7.0.1, use the Battery DA to control the clock speed. You'll see On and Off buttons under the label *Power-Saver*. The On button means you've turned on the power-saver mode by reducing the clock speed.

Changing the clock speed through either method doesn't take effect until you restart the PowerBook.

∞➤ **Turn down the screen lighting.** The backlight uses more power than anything except the CPU. If you're working in a bright room, or near a lamp, you can even turn off the backlight completely—unless you're using a color active-matrix screen, which always needs some backlighting for good viewing. If there's not enough ambient light for you to see the screen, turn down the light as much as possible. And when you're not using the PowerBook for a few minutes, turn the light all the way down until you need it again.

∞➤ **Minimize use of the floppy drive.** Most people use it only for installing software, anyway, but if you also use it to back up the files you're working on (a good idea), do it when you're plugged in.

### TAKE CHARGE

A woman trudged through the airport terminal, lugging an oversized suitcase in each hand. Every few minutes she stopped, put the luggage down, and glanced at her wrist; occasionally she'd mutter something with her cuff close to her mouth. Then she'd pick up the luggage and continue towards the gate.

An airport official noticed her behavior and finally walked up to her. "Excuse me," he began, "But I wonder why you keep stopping like that. Can I help you?"

The woman pulled up her sleeve slightly and exposed, not a watch, but a wrist-sized, full-color, voice-activated Macintosh. The man immediately, but jokingly, offered to buy the computer right off her wrist. To his surprise, she jumped at the offer, and a bargain was struck. As the man strapped the Mac to his arm, the previous owner walked away with a spring in her step.

"Wait," he called. "You forgot your luggage!"

The woman turned around. "Luggage?" she asked, shaking her head. "That's not my luggage."

She grinned. "That's the batteries!"

◦•❯ **A spinning hard drive is a drain** on the battery. Unless there's information being written to or read from the disk, there's no reason for it to be spinning. Set the drive sleep to a short interval, or use a utility that lets you stop the drive from spinning whenever you want.

◦•❯ **Spinning up the hard drive from** its sleep state takes more power than does just keeping it spinning—about four times as much. So, if you figure that the spinup itself takes about 10 seconds, that's the same as 40 seconds of spinning. Keep this in mind when you're trying to find the correct balance between keeping the drive in sleep and how often you'll have to spin it up.

••❯ **Use a RAM disk** whenever possible to avoid using the hard drive. If you don't have at least 8 megs of memory, setting up a RAM disk will be nearly impossible—the RAM has to be divvied up among the disk itself, the operating system, and whatever application you're running. Even with a reduced System Folder (assuming you're putting the system on the RAM disk, too), there's just barely enough memory even with 8 megs, to make a really workable setup.

••❯ **Keep AppleTalk turned off.** When AppleTalk is turned on (the setting is in the Chooser), the CPU constantly checks for AppleTalk activity. This constant work keeps the PowerBook from slipping into its rest state and burns up more power. You need AppleTalk on only when you're connecting to some printers or network services, so it's unlikely you'll need it while running on battery power.

••❯ **Don't use virtual memory on a Power-Book** unless it's absolutely necessary because virtual memory means disk access and disk access means draining the battery. That doesn't mean you should *never* use virtual memory on a PowerBook. In fact, it

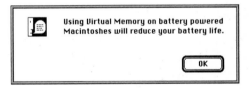

got me through a tough time. My PowerBook was still quite new and had only the 4 megs of RAM it came with; additional RAM was running $800, which just wasn't in the budget. But I was in bed after surgery and working on the PowerBook all day. Since the PowerBook was always plugged in, power wasn't an issue, but shortage of memory was; using virtual memory made the whole thing workable. (That and the fact that I actually called my main computer downstairs to retrieve files when necessary, on a phone line specially set up for that purpose! Ah, technology!)

Virtual memory is such a power-eater that you get a special warning when you turn it on.

••❯ **The contrast setting** for the screen—for models that have manual contrast control—has only a negligible effect of the power drain, so set it for the best-looking screen you can get and don't worry about it.

◦◦❯ **The best way to keep track of power use**—and minimize it—is to use a PowerBook utility that provides greater control over power-eating functions like the CPU speed, the backlight, the spinning drive, and the sleep interval. There are several packages available, but the two foremost are CPU (Connectix PowerBook Utilities) and PBTools

**PBTOOLS**

by Billy Steinberg (known to Mac people as the author of many public domain utilities and the screen saver Pyro!). Both provide functionality beyond that of the system's control panels and desk accessories; PBTools provides state-of-the-art battery management by tracking the charge and discharge cycles of your batteries.

And, as mentioned earlier in this chapter, PBTools 2.0 comes with a module for the Control Strip control panel.

I was at a PowerBook seminar at a Mac Expo not long after PBTools was released. The audience was polled as to which utility they used. About 85 percent said CPU (which got a year's jump on every other utility, it was released so soon after the PowerBooks), but the entire panel of experts used PBTools. [CPU, Connectix; PBTools, VST Systems]

## ☜ BATTERIES ☞

### In General

∞➤ **There are three basic battery technologies** used by PowerBooks:

- Lead-acid. This is the same type of battery that your car uses. It's used only in the PowerBook 100.
- NiCad, or nickel-cadmium batteries, are used in the all-in-one models.
- Nickel-metal-hydride (NiHy, or NiMHy) batteries are used in Duos.

∞➤ **You can charge a battery inside the PowerBook** or in a separate recharging unit; the time for recharging, and the net results, are the same. For most models, the power adapter that's used for the computer is the same one used for the recharger.

•••➤ **Power adapters have been improved** slowly and quietly for the all-in-one PowerBooks. Later ones, phased in with later-model PowerBooks, will recharge your battery faster than the older ones. Make sure you get the latest model if you're buying a second adapter, or a replacement.

Check model numbers and hold out for the 24-watt model. The first version (model #M5140) was 15 watts; the second version is 17 watts (model #M5651); the 24-watt version is model #M5652. (The 500-series PowerBooks use 40-watt adapters, with 20 watts going to each battery.)

•••➤ **Later-model batteries are better.** All NiCads for the all-in-one PowerBooks may look the same, but they differ significantly in how long they take to recharge and how long they'll last. And there are three types of NiHy batteries, too, with the later ones being more efficient than the earlier ones.

- The original, 2.3 amp-hour, NiCad is labeled 140/170, since it only needed to be differentiated from the battery used for the 100; its model number is actually 5417.
- The second-generation NiCad is 2.5 amp-hours, and its model number 5653.
- The third generation NiCad is 2.9 amp-hours and has the model number 5654.

••▸ **Those nice, neat battery packs** you use in your PowerBook are chock full of caustic and toxic materials. Just thought I'd mention that so you'd realize there are some basic precautions you should keep in mind:

- Try not to drop the battery—don't take it out and just toss it on a table. Don't puncture it or try to open the case.
- Occasionally inspect the battery for damage—a cracked case, a seam that's coming apart, or anything leaking from it. A lead-acid battery can leak sulfuric acid; a Duo battery might leak a little sodium hydroxide out onto your skin. Get rid of a damaged battery—and wash your hands after handling it. If any leakage comes in contact with your skin, rinse the area with water for five minutes.
- Don't let anything cross the terminals of the battery. The terminals are the little metal tabs along one edge of the case, and a large paper clip or a metal pen barrel could touch them both at the same time, shorting out the battery and heating the metal contact material to the point where it can be a fire hazard.
- Never incinerate a battery.

### NOT SO RICH, BUT FAMOUS

I was lucky enough to spend not one, but two weekends in the Bahamas last winter. I was unlucky enough to be working on this book, and couldn't really take the time off, so I brought my work with me, on my PowerBook.

You need a passport, of course, but I don't have one—I get around, but not much, and not too far. It's also permissible to show a birth certificate and a photo ID. On the first trip, they never asked for the photo ID; on the second trip, I neglected to bring it. They let me out of Newark Airport with just the birth certificate, but there I was in the Bahamas, with no photo ID—and they wouldn't let me in.

Then, it hit me! Right there in my PowerBook case was an issue of *MacUser* magazine. Right there in *MacUser* was my Mobile Mac column—with my picture on it. I took out the magazine, showed them the picture, pointed out how the middle name (Sharon *Zardetto* Aker) was the one on my birth certificate, and guess what? They laughed, but they let me in.

••▸ **Recycle a dead battery.** A really dead one, that is—one that can't be recharged anymore due to either damage or age. Those same toxic materials that keep you handling your battery with a modicum of respect warrants care in its disposal, too—so return it to your Apple dealer, or to Apple, when it's time to get rid of it. Most new batteries come in packaging designed for the old one to be packed up and shipped back to Apple for recycling.

**THINPACK**

••◊▸ **An external battery** is often the best way to power your PowerBook when you can't tether it to an outlet. Your best bet is the ThinPack, a three-quarter pound, half-inch thick external battery with a footprint slightly smaller than the PowerBook itself. It comes with PBTools, *the* best PowerBook utility, and will provide several hours of battery life for your PowerBook. [VST Systems]

## Recharging

∞**❯** **A rechargeable battery has a limited number of** *cycles*—the number of times it can be recharged. With most PowerBook batteries having a 500-cycle lifetime, they should last for about two years of normal, careful use.

∞**❯** **To make your battery last** through as many cycles as possible, follow these guidelines:

- Keep the battery in a cool, dry place when it's not inside the PowerBook.
- Charge a battery fully before storing it.
- If a battery is in storage, don't leave it there for more than three to four months without taking it out and recharging it,
- Don't leave a battery inside an unused PowerBook indefinitely; batteries drain even when the PowerBook's not in use. Don't ignore the lead-acid battery in the PowerBook 100 for more than two weeks. NiCad and NiHy batteries shouldn't be left in an unused PowerBook for more than a month without plugging the PowerBook in to recharge the battery (or inserting a Duo in its Dock).
- Don't let the 100's battery run down any further beyond the last low-battery system warning.
- Discharge NiCad batteries completely at regular intervals.
- Use only PowerBook-specific adapters and rechargers.

∞**❯** **Some batteries have charging** *modes*. Actually, its the charger that has the "modes"; the battery just goes along for the ride. Both the charger unit inside the PowerBook and the external charger for NiCads are "smart" and charge the battery faster or slower depending on how charged it is already. The batteries get charged to 80 percent capacity very quickly, in *fast charge* mode; they're charged more slowly the rest of the way in *trickle* mode. So, a PowerBook 100 battery can reach 80 percent charge in two hours but take another four hours to charge the rest of the way. This method strikes a nice balance between getting a good, usable charge as soon as possible and avoiding ruining a battery by overcharging it.

••**❯** **A charger can get stuck in trickle mode.** If you charge a NiCad or lead-acid battery long enough so that it's in trickle mode and then swap the battery with one that's more depleted, the charger won't know the difference and will stay in trickle-charge mode. It could take close to forever to completely charge a battery in trickle mode. If you swap batteries in the PowerBook or in a recharger, unplug the power cord momentarily and plug it back in again to reset it to fast mode for a low battery.

## ⇒ ODDS & ENDS ⊫

## SCSI Disk Mode

∞**❯** *SCSI disk mode* **lets you** attach your PowerBook to another computer and use the PowerBook as if it were an external hard drive. Of the original PowerBooks, only the 100 has this capability, so the 140, 145, 145b, and 170 can't be used this way. All other PowerBooks, and Duos with a MiniDock, can be used in SCSI disk mode

When a PowerBook is attached in SCSI disk mode, you can transfer information from it to another computer much faster than if they're just connected as a network.

∞► **The cables you need for SCSI disk mode** are an HDI-30 disk adapter cable *and* a standard SCSI system cable. This is the chain you create: The disk adapter cable goes into the PowerBook; its 50-pin female end attaches to the male end of a SCSI system cable, whose other, 25-pin male, end connects to the desk Mac. (Use an HDI-30 system cable if you're hooking up to another PowerBook.)

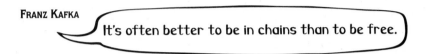

FRANZ KAFKA

It's often better to be in chains than to be free.

∞► **Check your SCSI ID numbers** when you're going to use the PowerBook in SCSI disk mode. Every device in a chain needs a unique ID number, and the PowerBook is set to a default SCSI ID of 1 for SCSI disk mode. A desk Mac is ID 7, and its internal drive is 0; an internal CD-ROM drive is 3. If you're simply connecting the PowerBook to your desk machine, there's no problem. But if you have other SCSI items already connected (another external drive, for instance), its number might clash with the one assigned to the PowerBook.

To change the PowerBook's SCSI ID number for SCSI mode, use the PowerBook control panel; click in the number you want to use as the ID. (Do this *before* you switch into SCSI disk mode, while the PowerBook is still running on its own normally!)

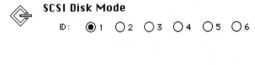

**SCSI Disk Mode**

ID: ◉1 ○2 ○3 ○4 ○5 ○6

∞► **Turn off *everything*** when you're getting SCSI disk mode set up. Turn off both the PowerBook and the desk machine, as well as anything attached to either one of them. Then hook up the cables, turn on the PowerBook, and then turn the desk Mac back on.

When you want to disconnect the PowerBook, turn off everything again. Use the Shut Down command for the desk Mac, turn it (and its peripherals) off, and turn off the PowerBook.

∞► **The PowerBook appears on the desktop** of the desk Mac as a standard hard drive when it's in SCSI disk mode. The PowerBook screen displays a SCSI disk mode icon moving across the lit screen when the PowerBook's acting as a hard drive. (You can't change the screen backlight level when in SCSI disk mode; it stays lit.) The number in the icon indicates the ID number for the PowerBook's drive.

···◆ **If the PowerBook is sleeping** instead of being shut off when you hook it up for SCSI disk mode, you'll get this dialog on its screen when you wake it up (or think you're turning it on). Follow the instructions, disconnecting the cable immediately. Then shut down, re-attach the cable, and start again.

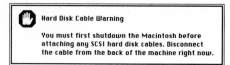

> ✋ **Hard Disk Cable Warning**
>
> You must first shutdown the Macintosh before attaching any SCSI hard disk cables. Disconnect the cable from the back of the machine right now.

···◆ **Don't use battery power for SCSI disk mode.** A spinning drive eats up a lot of power, and the drive keeps spinning if it's serving as an external drive; and, you can't turn off the screen backlight during SCSI disk mode. If you're running on battery power and the battery charge gets low, the SCSI mode icon on the PowerBook screen changes to a low-battery icon as a warning. Just which icon depends on your PowerBook model and what system you're running. If your PowerBook is forced to shut down because of a low battery, the only warning will show up on the PowerBook screen—you won't see anything on the desk machine's monitor. The desk machine will just give up and crash.

## Travel

···◆ **Travel with the PowerBook in sleep,** despite your manual's warning about shutting down the PowerBook when it's being transported. The basis for that warning is the off-chance—the *way* off-chance—that jostling the PowerBook around when it's slung from your shoulder or on the back seat of a car might jiggle a key *just* enough to register a key press—and wake up the PowerBook. Since it's in its case, you won't know it's awake, and the battery will be draining, unbeknownst to you.

First of all, the chances of this happening are so remote as to be laughable: More than a million PowerBooks out there for years now, and not a single such incident reported. Besides—your PowerBook is set to go back to sleep, isn't it?

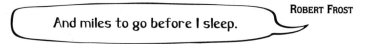

ROBERT FROST

And miles to go before I sleep.

···◆ **X rays absolutely, positively, definitely** can't hurt your PowerBook. Really. Honest. Send it through the X-ray security check at the airport without a second thought. Trust me!

I don't mean to sound as if I'm begging; I'm trying to be reassuring. Because despite the laws of physics, which guarantee that X rays won't harm anything in your PowerBook, many portable computer users still insist on being "safe" and not exposing their machines to X rays—just in case. These are probably the same people who still don't step on the cracks in sidewalks, just in case.

I'm going to borrow from another book here, The PowerBook Companion, which I wrote with Rich Wolfson. We X-rayed some PowerBooks (mine went first) while at my friend's office. My friend Steve Blazar happens to also be my orthopedic surgeon, and as long as they were X-raying my back … well, here are two of the pictures they took that day.

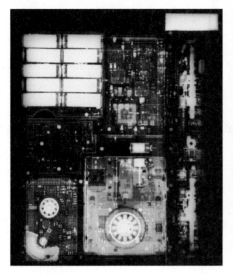
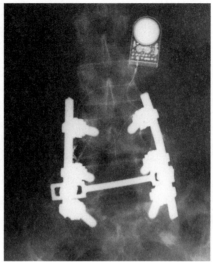

**POP QUIZ**                        **[20 POINTS]**

What type of astronomical object is surrounded by an accretion disk that gives off X rays? Clue: It's the only evidence we have of the existence of these objects. (Aren't you glad I didn't simply ask which comic book hero used X-ray vision?)

◦••➤ **Don't worry about the conveyer belt motor, either.** Conventional wisdom says that when you put the PowerBook through security X ray, you should place it as close to the mouth of the tunnel as possible, to avoid the magnetic field generated by the motors that run the conveyer belt (the motors being at the beginning of the conveyer belt). Forget it. Any magnetic field there is so weak it's not going to harm anything.

◦◦◦➤ **To print in a "hostile" environment**—that is, a non-Mac environment—when you're traveling, you need two things: the correct printer driver for the PC printer, and the correct cable. Actually, you need only one thing: PowerPrint, a package that contains a standard printing cable that you'll need to hook up to a non-Mac printer, and several drivers that work with over a thousand different PC printers. [GDT Softworks]

•••➤ **Few airlines object** to your using a PowerBook while in flight. Some scaremongers will tell you that electronic devices can foul up cockpit readings so your PowerBook (or GameBoy) can crash the plane. Few pilots voice any concerns, especially about in-flight use of electronic devices—it's the takeoffs and landings where instrumentation is

**POWERPRINT**

crucial. So, all airlines will ask you to stow the PowerBook during takeoff and landing—but all potential projectiles need to be stowed during those times anyway, so this shouldn't be a hardship or seen as a condemnation of the PowerBook.

All that said, the pilot is the final authority when you're flying; if you're asked to put away your computer at any time during the flight, be cooperative. (She can arrange for your arrest on landing if you aren't!)

••◗ **Pack emergency disks when you travel,** because if your PowerBook won't start up, or continually crashes, you're not going to get any work done. Emergency disks include: a full set of system disks in case you need to do a reinstall; an emergency startup/disk repair floppy with your disk utility of choice—MacTools or Norton Utilities; and, a minimal-system startup disk so that, failing everything else, you should be able to at least start up your PowerBook and retrieve whatever file you need.

And: Test that emergency disk *before* you need it! If you didn't put the right system on it, or you're missing an enabler, or there's any other glitch, you want to find out before it's too late.

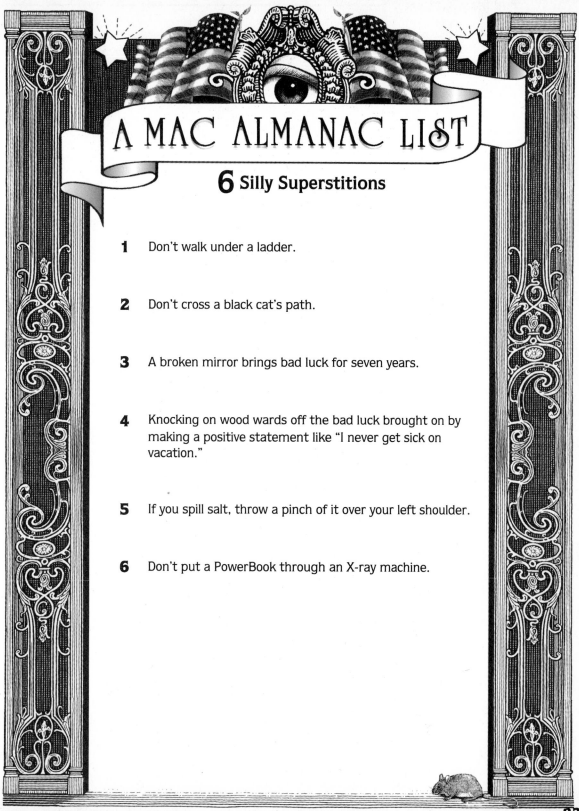

# A MAC ALMANAC LIST

## 6 Silly Superstitions

**1** Don't walk under a ladder.

**2** Don't cross a black cat's path.

**3** A broken mirror brings bad luck for seven years.

**4** Knocking on wood wards off the bad luck brought on by making a positive statement like "I never get sick on vacation."

**5** If you spill salt, throw a pinch of it over your left shoulder.

**6** Don't put a PowerBook through an X-ray machine.

# CHAPTER 23
# SYSTEM SOFTWARE

Learn how to operate a Macintosh computer.

H. JACKSON BROWN
*LIFE'S LITTLE INSTRUCTION BOOK*

Let's face it: System Software can be a pretty dull topic. But here are some of the things you'll find in this chapter:

***→ The demystification of system software version numbers. (As far as is possible.)

***→ The sad biography of Lisa.

***→ What Tune-Ups and System Updates are. And what a mess Enablers turned out to be.

***→ The author's favorite episode of Jeopardy.

***→ The difference between "all Macs" and "any Macs" installation.

***→ How to tweak your System Folder.

ANOTHER MYSTERY SOLVED

*Why Macintosh is misspelled.*

-Includes-
76 Factoids
3 Memos
2 Quotes
3 Mac Almanac Charts

page 859

Team

HERE, KITTY KITTY KITTY!!

Easy Install

**841**

## ◄ THE BASICS ►

## System Software

∞▶ **System software is the behind-the-scenes stuff** that runs your Mac. It gives you the desktop where you organize your files and disks, and it provides the standard interface components (like dialogs and menus) that you find in all Mac applications. System software also lets the Mac control hardware peripherals like hard drives and printers.

The System Folder, with its System file, Finder, control panels, and extensions holds the Mac's system software.

∞▶ **Other computers\* have *operating systems*,** but that term was, until rela-tively recently, foreign to Mac users. As the Mac strives for legitimacy in the business world (since *ascendancy* is an impossible dream), there's lots of cross-over jargon, so you may hear or see references to the Mac's operating system, or the *Mac OS*. (I mention this only in passing, because I'm trying to be thorough. I'm not *encouraging* the phrase Mac OS—which, by the way, is pronounced as separate letters, not *oss*.)

*\*We won't mention any names!*

If you see the term Mac OS instead of *system* or *Finder* or *desktop*, you can be pretty sure that you're reading something meant for non-Mac users who wouldn't recognize the term *Finder*, or something that was written by someone who's come over (but not all the way) from the "other side."

Since the Mac's operation is a combination of its system software and the information in its ROM, there's an argument to be made that OS is a handy term that includes both the hardware and software components of the Mac's internal workings. But I'll let oth-ers make that argument.

### LEGAL EAGLES #1

In early 1990, Xerox filed a suit against Apple claiming copyright infringe-ment because Apple derived the Lisa and Mac interface from programs developed at Xerox PARC (Palo Alto Research Center). The suit asked to have Xerox declared the sole owner of the graphical user interface that was first demonstrated on the Xerox Star—where Steve Jobs and his friends saw it and went away inspired for the Lisa system.

In response to the suit, an Apple spokesperson said that although they acknowledged Xerox's pioneering role, ideas can not be copyrighted.

In June of 1993, Apple lost its five-year copyright-infringement case against Microsoft and Hewlett-Packard for copying the Mac's graphical interface.

An Apple spokesperson declared: "We think it is important that innovative graphical computer works receive the protection to which they are entitled under the copyright law."

Yeah, right.

∞•❥ *System* **terminology:** The *System file* (the first word capitalized) is the very important file in the System Folder that looks like a suitcase. A *system file* (lowercase) is any file inside the System Folder—the Scrapbook file, for instance—or any of the files inside the System Folder's subfolders.

When the word *System* stands by itself, it still usually refers to the System file, as long as it's capitalized. But when it's lowercase, it can be referring to:

- The version of the system software you're using *(What system are you running?)* or your system software in general *(My system crashed)*.
- The environment you've created with specific fonts, sounds, and system extensions *(What's your system like?)*.
- Your hardware configuration—a Mac LC with a 40-meg internal drive and a LaserWriter SC printer, for example *(Which Mac system do you use?)*.

∞•❥ **The Mac needs a disk with a System Folder** on it in order to start up. The disk with the System Folder on it is called, reasonably, enough, the *startup disk*. These days, except in emergency situations, the startup disk is always a hard drive, because it's just too difficult to squeeze a workable System Folder onto a floppy. (Well, okay, you can squeeze an *emergency* system on a floppy—but I don't consider it a *workable* system— and you don't have to put the System and Finder inside a folder on the floppy …)

∞•❥ **An external drive used just for extra storage** doesn't need system software on it at all. System software's necessary only for the startup drive.

## System Versions

∞•❥ **System software versions** are identified by numbers. A major change is reflected in the main number—System 6 to System 7, for example. Although we usually just say "six" or "seven," the official name of an initial version of new software includes a decimal point and a zero: *System 7.0.*

The numbering for system software updates pretty much matches that for software applications, as explained in Chapter 19. Minor bug fixes or simple changes for matching new hardware releases get a second decimal point, like 7.0.1. Enhancements to the basic system version increases the first decimal number: 7.1, for instance.

LORD RANDOLPH CHURCHILL
(1849–1895)

> I could never make out what those damned dots meant.

∞•❥ **There are two ways to check** what version of the system you're running: Choose *About this Macintosh* from the Finder's Apple menu, or select the System file icon and use the Get Info command on it. Both dialogs identify the current system version number.

Checking the System version number.

◦•▶ **There are two special symbols** that might appear next to the system version number in the About This Macintosh dialog. A bullet ( • ) after the number means the system's been tuned up with a Tuner extension. A *P* after the number means you're using Performa software. (And if both symbols are there, you're using tuned-up Performa software.)

Tuners, or Tune-Ups, are covered later in this chapter.

◦•▶ **If you want to sound as if you know** what you're talking about, *never* say "zero"; say "oh." And don't mention the decimal point. So, it's "Seven-oh" and "Seven-oh-one" for 7.0 and 7.0.1. If you mention the decimal, you can sound *really* wonky if you say "dot" instead: "Seven dot oh dot one."

◦•▶ **When there's an *x* in a version number** (like 7.x) it's referring to seven-point-anything: 7.0, 7.0.1, 7.1. The x might be at the later decimal point, like this: 6.0.x, in which case … oh, come on, you can take it from there.

## MAC TRIVIA

You think you have it bad, trying to keep track of system version numbers with double decimal points? Pity the poor pioneers: Apple didn't start using system "sets" until something called "System Tools 5.0"—which consisted of a System file version 4.2 and a Finder version 6.0. (It seems they used a special formula to arrive at that number: $MOD(SystemVersion+ (FinderVersion/3))$

Here's the sad history of version number pairings of System and Finder files up to System 6:

| System number | System file | Finder |
|---|---|---|
| - | 1.0 | 1.1 |
| - | 2.0 | 2.0g |
| - | 2.0 | 4.1 |
| - | 3.0 | 5.1 |
| - | 3.1 | 5.2 |
| - | 3.2 | 5.3 |
| - | 3.3 | 5.4 |
| - | 4.0 | 5.4 |
| - | 4.1 | 5.5 |
| 5.0 | 4.2 | 6.0 |
| 5.1 | 4.3 | 6.0 |
| 6.0 | 6.0 | 6.1 |

•→ **Don't practice one-upmanship** with friends who have system version numbers higher than yours if the number is a second decimal place, like 7.0.1 versus 7.0.2. Apple tried to standardize version numbers so that a second decimal number indicated a change that's strictly an update for a new machine. So, running 7.0.1 on one machine would be the same as 7.0.2 on another. (It's bad enough that your friends will lord it over you that their hardware is newer and better; don't let the system version number bother you!) The big exception to this is 7.0 versus 7.0.1: You need 7.0.1 because 7.0 was so buggy.

•→ **Don't upgrade your system software as soon as** a new version is available. Wait a month or two (or three) and let thousands—*tens* of thousands—of other Mac users test it for you. If there are no major problems at that point (or there are problems that you can avoid, or that won't affect you), then go ahead and upgrade. If it's a minor upgrade that fixes some bugs, or provides an enhancement like faster printing, you might want to take a chance and upgrade sooner if the bug or the slow printing's been affecting you.

•→ **What system should you be using?** Unless you have an exceptional reason to stay with System 6, you should be using some version of System 7. If your machine can't run System 7 because it doesn't have enough memory, get more memory as soon as you can—it's relatively cheap, especially compared to your overall investment in hardware and software.

But which system you should run also depends on which Mac you have, because some older models don't support the newest software, and most later models can't run with earlier systems. There's a chart on the next page (because we couldn't fit it on this page) that shows which versions of System 6 and System 7 work on which machines. A bullet means the system works on that machine; a dash means it doesn't; an asterisk means that system works on the model but needs an enabler (enablers are covered a little later).

## System 7 Variations

•→ **System 7 is** a major step forward in Macintosh system software; not revolutionary, to be sure, but certainly an evolutionary leap beyond System 6. Some of the major changes from System 6 to 7 are:

- A new System Folder and a set of subfolders for it
- TrueType fonts
- Multiple programs running without a special application like MultiFinder
- Hierarchical window views in the Finder
- Aliases
- New, easier, ways to handle fonts and desk accessories
- Built-in Color QuickDraw
- File sharing for connected computers without a file server
- Balloon Help
- Virtual memory
- 32-bit memory addressing, breaking the 8-meg memory barrier
- Publish and Subscribe capabilities

## Which System to Use with Your Mac

| Model | 6.0.2 | 6.0.3 | 6.0.4 | 6.0.5 | 6.0.7 | 6.0.8 | 7.0 | 7.0.1 | 7.1 | 7.1.2 |
|---|---|---|---|---|---|---|---|---|---|---|
| Mac Plus | • | • | • | • | • | • | • | • | • | - |
| Mac SE | • | • | • | • | • | • | • | • | • | - |
| Mac SE/30 | • | • | • | • | • | • | • | • | • | - |
| Mac Classic | - | - | - | - | • | • | • | • | • | - |
| Mac Classic II | - | - | - | - | - | - | - | - | • | - |
| Mac Color Classic | - | - | - | - | - | - | - | - | • | - |
| Mac Portable | - | - | • | • | • | • | • | • | • | - |
| Mac II | • | • | • | • | • | • | • | • | • | - |
| Mac IIx | • | • | • | • | • | • | • | • | • | - |
| Mac IIcx | - | • | • | • | • | • | • | • | • | - |
| Mac IIci | - | - | • | • | • | • | • | • | • | - |
| Mac IIfx | - | - | - | • | • | • | • | • | • | - |
| Mac IIsi | - | - | - | - | • | • | • | • | • | - |
| Mac IIvi,IIvx | - | - | - | - | - | - | - | - | * | - |
| Mac LC | - | - | - | - | • | • | • | • | • | - |
| Mac LC II | - | - | - | - | - | • | • | • | • | - |
| Mac LC III | - | - | - | - | - | - | - | - | * | - |
| Mac LC 475 | - | - | - | - | - | - | - | - | * | - |
| Mac LC 520 | - | - | - | - | - | - | - | - | * | - |
| Centris 610 | - | - | - | - | - | - | - | - | * | * |
| Centris 650 | - | - | - | - | - | - | - | - | * | * |
| Centris 660AV | - | - | - | - | - | - | - | - | * | * |
| Quadra 605 | - | - | - | - | - | - | - | - | * | - |
| Quadra 610 | - | - | - | - | - | - | - | - | * | * |
| Quadra 650 | - | - | - | - | - | - | - | - | * | * |
| Quadra 660AV | - | - | - | - | - | - | - | - | * | * |
| Quadra 700 | - | - | - | - | - | - | - | • | • | * |
| Quadra 800 | - | - | - | - | - | - | - | - | * | * |
| Quadra 840AV | - | - | - | - | - | - | - | - | * | * |
| Quadra 900,950 | - | - | - | - | - | - | - | • | • | * |
| PowerBook 100 | - | - | - | - | - | - | - | • | • | - |
| PowerBook 140, 145,145B,170 | - | - | - | - | - | - | - | • | • | - |
| PowerBook 160,180 | - | - | - | - | - | - | - | - | * | - |
| PowerBook Duo 210,230,250,270c | - | - | - | - | - | - | - | - | * | - |
| PowerBook 165c,180c | - | - | - | - | - | - | - | - | * | - |

• system works on this model
- system doesn't work on this model
* system works on this model but needs an enabler

∞◗ **To run System 7, you need** a hard drive and 2 megs of RAM. There's no argument about the hard drive—after all, a basic System Folder takes more room than a floppy provides—but the RAM requirements are questionable. Apple's party line is that you need 2 megs to run System 7.0. They're right, if that's all you want to run; you'll get your desktop, and maybe you could run TeachText, but that's about it. If you want to do real work in a reasonably powerful program, you need 4 megs of memory. And 4 megs lets you run only one program, if it's a large one. So, 5 megs quickly becomes the minimum for running two programs at the same time under System 7.

⚫➤ **Don't use System 7.0.** At the very least, use System 7.0.1, since the original release of System 7 was so buggy. And use it with its Tune-Up—version 1.1.1 at the least, since the early Tune-Up versions were buggy, too. The worst of the 7.0 bugs was one that caused folders to just up and disappear—sometimes to never re-appear.

⚫➤ **System 7.1 is** basically a tweak of System 7. The major difference is that it provides a handy Fonts folder in the System Folder, instead of insisting that you put screen fonts into the System file and printer fonts into the Extensions folder. There are other, minor, differences, too—like a different approach to application memory allocation in the Get Info box, better memory management, and faster printing—but there's not much of a change, overall, from System 7.0.

System 7.1 has basically the same memory and disk space requirements as System 7.0.

⚫➤ **The main difference between 7.1 and *all*** earlier system versions is that it's the first one you have to *buy*. It comes free with your machine (depending on when you bought your Mac), but people who had System 6 or even System 7.0 Macs can't upgrade to it for free. This was a major departure from Apple's previous policy of providing free system software upgrades online and through user groups, but the screaming has died down and we're getting used to it now.

⚫➤ **The Performa system software** is basic Mac system software with a few additions and deletions. The main additions are the Launcher control panel (added to System 7.5 for regular systems) and the At Ease replacement for the Finder. The deletions are all sorts of separate system files that you just don't need for a Performa—in fact, you don't need them for most Mac models. There are minor differences, too, like a different General Controls control panel, but for the most part, Performa system software is still the Mac system software.

The really special thing about Performa system software is that you don't get system disks when you buy the machine. Everything's on the machine's hard disk, and you have to back it up onto floppies in case anything ever goes wrong and you want to replace the System Folder. (Shame on Apple: The set of customers presumed to be the least sophisticated in computer use gets no backup disks for their system software!)

If you have a Performa, keep in mind that you can install regular system software on it and you'll have a regular Mac: The hardware's the same. But whether you want the standard Mac system or the Performa version, get yourself a set of system disks immediately, if not sooner.

⚫➤ **System 7 Pro was**—oh, I suppose maybe it still *is*—a version of System 7.1 (7.1.1, actually) that included some of the things that had been promised for System 7.0 but didn't make it into system software until System 7.5; most people never heard of it. It was just an interim release to keep a small portion of Mac power users happy, since it includes the first released version of AppleScript, and a "scriptable" Finder.

● ● ● ● ● ● ● ● ● ● ● ● ● ● ● ● ● ● ● ● ● ● ● ● ● ● ● ● ● ● ● ● ● ● ● ● ● ● ● ● ● ● ● ● ●

## MAC PEOPLE                                                    LISA

Lisa, Mac's ill-starred aunt, was born in the Spring of 1983 and died less than two years later. Yet in her short lifetime she paved the way for the younger Mac's success, and her genes helped to determine his personality.

The offspring of Steve Jobs, Lisa was conceived during a visit to Xerox's famous Palo Alto Research Center, where Jobs first encountered the exotic beauty Alto. Early in her life, Lisa's godfather, Bill Atkinson, taught her to draw, and she developed a precocious skill with graphics of all kinds. Like her mother, Alto, Lisa grew up to be exotic and beautiful. Unfortunately, she was also high-strung and undependable. Her health was shaky at best: for example, her floppy drive, known as "Twiggy," had to be surgically replaced before she was a year old.

When Mac was born in the winter of 1984, Lisa had already acquired a most unfortunate reputation: slow and very pricey. At $12,000, she could hardly compete with the $2,500 Mac. Her agent recommended a name change—"let's show the public a new Lisa!" And so her name was legally changed to Mac XL.

Too late ... Mac had already won the hearts of the public, who cruelly joked that "XL" stood for "ex-Lisa." Brokenhearted, Lisa pined away, almost unnoticed. Her tragic death was unmourned even by her parents: Steve Jobs was too busy playing with his new favorite child, Mac, and Lisa's mother, Alto, had long since slipped into a coma from which she would never recover.

Unappreciated and unlamented, Lisa finally expired just short of her second birthday. But her heritage lives on in her cousin Mac and his descendents, reminding us of a valiant pioneer who was just a bit too far ahead of her time.

*—Andy Baird*

**••▶ System 7.5 is another big step** in system software development, though it's not, as seemingly indicated by its number, halfway to System 8—whatever and whenever that might be.

System 7.5 changes include:

- An enhanced Apple menu, with hierarchical capabilities and new subfolders.
- Built-in ATM (Adobe Type Manager) technology
- A hideable Finder
- A menu bar clock
- The Apple Guide interactive help system.
- New printing capabilities with QuickDraw GX.
- New and updated control panels and desk accessories.
- AppleScript and a scriptable Finder.
- The ability to drag selections from one document to another, even between applications.

**••▶ To run System 7.5, you need** lots more memory. Even Apple says you need 4 megs of RAM—which means, of course, you really need 8 to get anything done. But Apple's guidelines call for even more memory* depending on the Mac and System 7.5 features you're using:

> *If Apple says you need 16MB for a PowerMac with System 7.5 and QuickDraw GX, how much, do you suppose, do you really need?

for basic System 7.5 ........................................................4MB
for basic System 7.5 on Power Mac ............................8MB
System 7.5 with QuickDraw GX .................................8MB
System 7.5 with QuickDraw GX on Power Mac ..........16MB

••▶ **You need at least a 68020 Mac** to run System 7.5 with its QuickDraw GX features.

••▶ **How can you keep track of system software updates,** and where can you get them? The best way to find out what's going on is to join a user group; there's *always* someone there who knows the latest developments. There's also always someone online who knows what's going on, so if you belong to any of the online services, you can keep current. The Mac magazines aren't much help on this, since there's so much lag time—generally three months—between the time articles are written and the magazine hits the stands. (*MacWeek,* since it's a weekly newspaper, doesn't suffer from this lag time, but it's relatively expensive and not as widely read as the monthlies.) But if you're not in a user group or online, you can always call Apple, or Apple SOS, to find out what's the latest system version.

*Getting* the software is a different issue. System 7.0 (and its update, 7.0.1) was the last of the free system software packages. You can buy later system software from Apple, at large computer stores, and through mail order. The Hardware Updates are somewhat easier to get ahold of; since they're good only for someone who already has the basic system, they're generously distributed. Apple SOS currently sends out Hardware Update disks for about $10; sometimes the Updates are available online, or user groups get permission to distribute them.

## Enablers

∞▶ **An *enabler* is** a system file that enables the current system—whatever its version number—to work with different Mac models. Apple's switch to the enabler technology was to get rid of the constant second-decimal system updates. Prior to enablers, a new machine, because of minor differences in its circuitry, would need an updated version of the system—7.0.2 instead of 7.0.1, for instance. But with an enabler providing machine-specific information, a new Mac can use the already current system software.

••▶ **If you need an enabler, you *really* need** an enabler. A Mac that uses an enabler absolutely can't start up without one in the System Folder. It's easier to list the models that *don't* need enablers:

| | | | | | | |
|---|---|---|---|---|---|---|
| Plus | Classic | LC | Mac II | Mac IIsi | PB 100 | Quadra 700 |
| SE | Classic II | LC II | Mac IIx | Mac IIci | PB 140 | Quadra 900 |
| SE/30 | | | Mac IIcx | Mac IIfx | PB 145 | Quadra 950 |
| | | | | | PB 170 | |

••▶ **The enabler setup is a mismanaged nightmare** thus far. The enablers have terrific names like System Enabler 040 and System Enabler 088, with no indication of which machines they're for. You can't make a minimal-system emergency startup floppy that can be used on different Mac models, because you can't fit more than one or two enablers on the disk. And the enablers themselves are occasionally updated to iron out problems or otherwise improve them, so you have items like System Enabler 131 version 1.0.3. And then you have to deal with things like System Enabler 111 and System Enabler 121 being replaced with System Enabler 131. It's all just so *intuitive!*

There is at least some hope, since some recent updates include enablers that are good for a whole model line and they even come with names, like *PowerBook Duo Enabler*.

···➤ **Which Macs use which enablers?** Good question! Here's a handy-dandy chart listing Mac models, their enablers, and the enablers' version numbers. The version numbers are, of course, subject to change, since they might be updated after this book is printed. But at least you can be sure that you need *at least* this version number to be current.*

> *Come to think of it, the enabler numbers may be changed eventually, too. Oh well, this is the best I can do for you.

| Model | Enabler | Version |
|---|---|---|
| Centris 610 | System Enabler 040 | 1.1 |
| Centris 650 | System Enabler 040 | 1.1 |
| Centris 660AV | System Enabler 088 | 1.2 |
| Color Classic | System Enabler 401 | 1.0.5 |
| IIvi | System Enabler 001 | 1.0.1 |
| IIvx | System Enabler 001 | 1.0.1 |
| LC III | System Enabler 003 | 1.1 |
| LC 475 | System Enabler 065 | 1.2 |
| LC 520 | System Enabler 403 | 1.0.2 |
| LC 550 | System Enabler 403 | 1.0.2 |
| LC 575 | System Enabler 065 | 1.2 |
| PowerBook 160 | System Enabler 131 | 1.0.3 |
| PowerBook 165c | System Enabler 131 | 1.0.3 |
| PowerBook 180 | System Enabler 131 | 1.0.3 |
| PowerBook 180c | System Enabler 131 | 1.0.3 |
| PowerBook 520 | PowerBook 500 Series Enabler | 1.0.2 |
| PowerBook 520c | PowerBook 500 Series Enabler | 1.0.2 |
| PowerBook 540 | PowerBook 500 Series Enabler | 1.0.2 |
| PowerBook 540c | PowerBook 500 Series Enabler | 1.0.2 |
| PowerBook Duo 210 | PowerBook Duo Enabler | 2.0 |
| PowerBook Duo 230 | PowerBook Duo Enabler | 2.0 |
| PowerBook Duo 250 | PowerBook Duo Enabler | 2.0 |
| PowerBook Duo 270c | PowerBook Duo Enabler | 2.0 |
| PowerBook Duo 280 | PowerBook Duo Enabler | 2.0 |
| PowerBook Duo 280c | PowerBook Duo Enabler | 2.0 |
| Quadra 605 | System Enabler 065 | 1.2 |
| Quadra 610 | System Enabler 040 | 1.1 |
| Quadra 650 | System Enabler 040 | 1.1 |
| Quadra 660AV | System Enabler 088 | 1.2 |
| Quadra 800 | System Enabler 040 | 1.1 |
| Quadra 840AV | System Enabler 088 | 1.2 |
| Macintosh TV | System Enabler 404 | 1.0 |
| Power Mac 6100 | PowerPC Enabler | 1.0.2 |
| Power Mac 7100 | PowerPC Enabler | 1.0.2 |
| Power Mac 8100 | PowerPC Enabler | 1.0.2 |
| PowerPC Upgrade Card | PowerPC Upgrade Card Enabler | 1.0.1 |

···➤ **Enablers are installed** during a system installation as long as you start with the *Install Me First* disk and use the Installer on it. Don't lose that disk! And make a copy of it so if the disk is damaged, you'll still have the enabler you need.

## Tune-Ups & System Updates

∞▶ **Apple's Tune-Up approach to interim system upgrades** was short-lived. The Tune-Up approach was supposed to save worry about decimals in system numbers—which ones were for bug fixes and minor enhancements, and which were releases for new hardware. The Tune-Up was strictly for fixes and enhancements.

When the initial release of 7.0 turned out to have some problems, Apple released Tune-Up 1.0. It also, coincidentally, released System 7.0.1 at the same time, for some new machines; 7.0.1 had the 1.0 Tune-Up fixes incorporated into it. So, what happened? Users moved to 7.0.1 whether they needed it or not, then needlessly tuned up *that* system release (although it later had a necessary Tune-Up of its own). Then, of course, there were revisions to the Tune-Ups. Oh well, so much for a simpler approach.

Using the Tune-Up is simple, though: You simply run the Installer on the Tune-Up disk, and it replaces the files on your hard drive that need to be tuned or changed, and adds a Tune-Up extension to your System Folder.

System 7.0x is the only one that gets a Tune-Up. Later systems use a different method for bug fixes. If you're using System 7.0, you should be using, at the very least, System 7.0.1 with the 1.1.1 Tune-Up, which has been proven dependably stable.

∞▶ **The Hardware System Update** approach in System 7.1 replaced 7.0's Tune-Up approach; its title quickly transmuted to simply *System Update* since the "Hardware" in the original name was so misleading.

A System Update is a combination of bug fixes and minor system enhancements, like new printer drivers. System 7.1's first System Update was 1.0, but 2.0 and 3.0 soon followed. System Update 3.0 included several items that turned out to be part of System 7.5. (Some people felt that it was generous of Apple to give out pieces of the new system software; personally , I think they wanted us to beta test those new components.)

A System Update is easy to use: It comes with the basic Apple Installer, and all you do is double-click on it to have it install the new and improved files in your System Folder. You'll get updated drivers and things like that, as well as a System Update extension whose icon is a just too-cute-for-words little Mac with a screwdriver.

### MAC TRIVIA

Did you ever notice that *Macintosh* is misspelled? Or do you just misspell kinds of apples now because you're so used to your computer's name? In the early days at Apple, code names were given to projects in one of two categories: female names and apples. So, there were Annie and Sara, as well as the well-known Lisa. And there were Pippin and Golden Delicious, as well as … McIntosh?

Jef Raskin originated the Macintosh project and named it after his favorite type of apple. And mispelled it. I mean *misspelled* it.

## ◄ SYSTEM INSTALLATION ►

## System Disks

⚬•➤ **You need a set of _system disks,_** or _install disks,_ to put system software on a hard drive. Even if your drive had a system installed on it when you bought it, you'll eventually need to reinstall or upgrade the system software. A set of installation disks is an absolute necessity.

System disks come with your Mac, unless you bought a Performa. (And, I believe, one of the PowerBooks—the 145B—was unaccompanied by system disks.) If your Mac comes with a built-in CD-ROM drive, you won't get a set of floppy system disks, but you will get a system _disc_—a CD with system software on it.

Systems prior to 7.1 are available free or for a nominal fee from users groups and Apple dealers, although they're also available for purchase if you want to get the documentation with them. You have to pay for disks for System 7.1 and later versions, though, and user groups are no longer allowed to distribute the system software

⚬•➤ **System software comes on superfloppies**: 1.4-meg disks. If your hardware can't handle these high-density disks, you can call Apple and ask for the 800K-disk set.

⚬•➤ **If your Mac has a built-in CD-ROM,** you have a CD of system software—it's named InstallMeFirst; the picture here shows the main window of the CD.

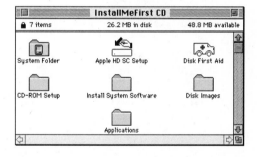

The Install System Software folder contains the Installer and all the files needed to install system software on your Mac. You can start up the Mac from the CD, and install the system on any attached hard drive.

••➤ **The Disk Images folder on the startup CD** contains special files called (what else?) _disk images_. With them, you can make a complete set of floppy system installation disks. Use the DiskCopy utility in the CD's Applications folder to create the disks.

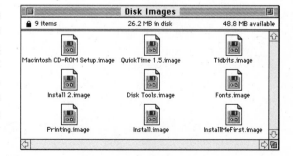

## System Installation

∘∘➤ **You can install, reinstall, or update** the system software on your hard drive.

- *Install* the system software if your hard drive has no System Folder on it. Without a System Folder, the hard drive can't act as the *startup disk* for your computer. When you buy a Mac with a hard drive, the system software is already installed, but sometimes you'll buy an empty drive, or erase one and have to start from scratch.

- *Reinstall* the system software when things aren't working right. On a reinstallation, you're replacing the existing system software with a fresh copy of the same system version.

- *Update* the system software when you want to use a higher version number.

∘∘➤ **Never run the Installer while any inits** (extensions or control panels) are running. Start up the Mac with the Shift key down to disable all inits before doing any system installation. You shouldn't have any applications running, either, but the Installer will check that and offer to quit them for you.

∘∘➤ **There are several files on the installation disks** that the Installer might not put on your hard drive. I say "might not" because Apple continually improves and changes the Installer and how it handles system files.

Here are the files that, historically speaking, haven't made it to the hard drive during system installs. Pop in each of the system install disks and look around for interesting stuff! You can just drag most of it right from the floppy to your hard drive.

| Files | on | for... |
|---|---|---|
| Apple File Exchange | Install 2 | ... transferring files from an IBM-compatible disk to the Mac. |
| Fonts | Fonts | ... fun in formatting—not all the fonts are automatically installed in your system. |
| Disk First Aid | Disk Tools | ... checking and making minor repairs to disks. |
| LaserWriter Font Utility | Tidbits | ... downloading fonts and other PostScript files to a printer. |

∘∘➤ **Different Mac models need different system software,** even when the System version number is identical. The Mac has grown more sophisticated over the years, with more information built into its ROMs. The System files for earlier machines include the information—called "patches"—that's built into later machines; this way, the older machines can behave the same as their more sophisticated descendants. Programmers don't have to worry about which machine their software might be running on, because all the Macs will act the same and have the same system information on hand.

And it's not just the System file that's different from one machine to the next. There are "support files" that might be needed on one machine and not another. For instance, while every Mac needs a Mouse control panel, a black-and-white Mac doesn't need the Color control panel.

When you use the Installer to install a system for a specific Mac model, you get the right System file for the machine. What's the difference between this and the enabler approach? Basically, the altered System file takes care of machines born before the system software you're installing; enablers take care of machines born *after* the system software you're using!

## The Installer

∞•➤ **Use Apple's Installer program** whether you're doing a new installation, a reinstall, or an update. Don't just drag the System Folder files from the installation disks to the hard drive and expect things to work correctly. The Installer makes sure that you're installing the correct system for your specific machine. It's a cinch to use: Double-click on the Installer icon and follow the prompts on screen.

The Installer's main dialog.

∞•➤ **Updating or reinstalling** system software with the Installer preserves the items you've already added to your system, like special fonts or sounds.

∞•➤ **Don't copy the Installer to your hard drive** and try to run it from there. I'll give you two good reasons (neither of which will be "because I said so," no matter how tempted I am in several places not to explain myself, an attitude that comes along automatically with motherhood). First, the Installer needs to grab information from the System Folder that's on the floppy disk it came on. Second, the Installer can't alter a System file that's active—the one on your hard drive is active if it's the startup drive for your computer. (And third, because I said so!)

•••➤ **Although you shouldn't drag the System or Finder files** from the Installation disks to your startup disk, other system files don't have to be "officially" installed. If you get a new printer, or eventually need networking software, you can just drag the correct extensions from the installation disks to your drive.

•••➤ **There's a hidden trick in the Installer.** When you're looking at the main, Easy Install, screen, hold down the Command and Option keys. The Help button changes to an About button, and clicking on it gives you a More About button. Here's one of the credits you'll see.

Quality

The best testing ever! Guaranteed by:

Rob "lunatic" Moore
and thousands of wily Beta testers.

[ More About ]

## HOBBIES FOR $100, ART ... I MEAN, ALEX!

I'm not rich, but I've reached the epitome of fame, indirectly. To misquote Weird Al, I've won at Jeopardy.

The picture here shows what the TV screen looked like on the night of September 7, 1993. The category: non-fiction. The answer: as shown on the screen. The correct question, as posed by a teacher from Austin, Texas: *What is operating a computer?*

What does this have to do with me? That's *my* book up there (the Macintosh one, not the DOS one!), right on TV, on the Jeopardy screen. It's better than being a contestant!

> **NON-FICTION**
>
> To become literate in this field, try "The Macintosh Companion" or "DOS for Dummies"

Now, did I see this brief flash of fame? Nope. But one of the editors of the book, Elizabeth Rogalin, just *happened* to be dressing for dinner in her hotel room in Boston and had the TV on in the background. She called me the next day, but I didn't believe her—well, not at first, anyway.

Then, the big problem: I had to see this for myself. How in the world do you get a tape of last night's Jeopardy? Well, lucky for me it's broadcast on the ABC network in my area. Lucky for me I've written documentation for ABCNews InterActive over the years. Lucky for me that Lew Strauss knows how to get favors from the entertainment division even though he's in news. So, I have a 30-second tape of that show: the opening theme, the contestant introduction, and then a cut right to my answer and question.

(I was going to grab a frame from the tape, convert it to a TIFF image, and print it here. But it's sort of a dull picture—in fact, it looks exactly like the facsimile here.)

⬤⬤➧ **There's lots of disk-swapping during system installation**, especially if you're installing from 800K disks. And it's not just because there are so many floppies involved: You may find that the main Installer disk is asked for several times during the installation.

You can avoid the extra disk swapping by allocating more memory to the Installer program itself. Unlock the first disk from the installation set and insert it; open the disk icon if necessary, and select the Installer icon. Choose Get Info from the File menu and change the number in the Application Memory Size box (System 7.0) or the Preferred Size box (System 7.1 and later) to about 1200. The next time you use the Installer, you'll probably have to insert each disk from the set only once.

⬤⬤➧ **Use the Installer to remove items** that it installed by making a Remove button magically appear! Use the Customize option, then hold down the Option key while the Custom dialog is open. The Install button in the dialog changes to Remove, and clicking it removes any of the software that's selected in the list. It's an easy way to remove, say, file-sharing software without having to figure out just which extensions and control panels have to be dragged to the Trash.

Using the Option key changes the Install button to a Remove button.

> Click the items you want to select;
> Shift-click to select multiple items.
>
> System Software for any Macintosh
> Software for all Apple printers
>
> **File Sharing Software**
>
> [ Remove ]

## Easy Install

◦•▸ **The Easy Install option** in the Installer installs the System Folder files specific to the Mac model you're using, basic network and file-sharing software, and updates any existing printer software on your drive.

Use the Easy Install option if you're installing the system on an internal hard drive *and* the drive already has printer software on it for the printer you'll be using. (If you've been using your setup with a printer and you're not changing printers, then the printer software is already on the drive.)

Since the Easy Install option installs a system that works only for the Mac that you're using and you won't be using the internal hard drive to run another machine, this hardware-specific easy installation is all that most people need. (This is perfectly good advice— installing hardware-specific system software on an internal drive. Perfectly good. Unless you do what I did: I sold my IIcx when I got a IIci, but I swapped

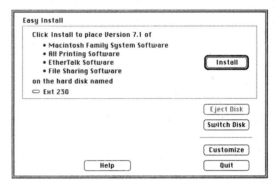

the internal hard drives so I wouldn't have to copy everything over to the new machine. So I wound up with an internal drive in the ci that would start up only a cx!!)

◦•▸ **Easy Install updates *existing* printing software.** Say you've been using an ImageWriter and you've treated yourself to a StyleWriter or LaserWriter along with your system software upgrade. You run the Installer, using the Easy Install option, hook up your printer … and find that you can't access the printer because its icon doesn't show up in the Chooser. That's because you had only the ImageWriter driver for the Chooser in your previous system, and the Installer updated only that existing printing software.

If you're changing or adding printers while you're upgrading your system software, you can opt for the Customize install option, or use the Easy Install option and then just drag the proper printer icons from the installation disks to your hard drive.

## Customized Installation

◦•▸ **You can customize your System installation** in three areas: basic system software, printing software, and networking software.

Use the Customize option if you're installing the system on an external hard drive that will be used as a startup for a Mac model other than the one you're using for the installation—or if the drive will act as the startup for more than one Mac model (both your home and office computer, for instance).

Although you can specify an external hard drive with the Easy Install option, the Installer still assumes you want a system for the Mac you're using. Using the Customize option lets you specify which model Mac will be using the hard drive.

∞•→ **There are four options for basic system software.** The first, at the top of the scrolling list in the Installer dialog, is for *any* Mac model. The next is later in the scrolling list (after printers and networking): software for *specific* Mac models. The difference is that the software for *any* Mac model will run *every* Macintosh. The software for a specific Mac model will run only that model. Finally, at the very end of the scrolling list, you have an option for a *minimal* system for any Mac or for a specific Mac.

Here's when to use each of these choices:

| Option | Use it for ... |
| --- | --- |
| System software for any Mac | An external hard drive that might be moved from one Mac to another as the startup disk. |
| System software for a specific Mac | An internal hard drive, or an external hard drive that's going to be used as a startup for only one machine. |
| Minimal system software for any Mac | Never. Use minimal software for a specific Mac model. |
| Minimal system software for a specific Mac | A floppy disk for an emergency startup disk. |

∞•→ **If space is not an issue on your external hard drive,** use the "for any Macintosh" option—you never know when you're going to travel with the hard drive and hook up to another Mac but will still need *your* fonts and system utilities.

∞•→ **Customize your printer software** by selecting your printer from the list. Or, install all the printer software by selecting *Software for all Apple Printers* at the top of the list, even though you're customizing the rest of the system software.

Some printer software options displayed in the list.

∞•→ **You probably don't need all the network software** the Installer can provide. The network section of the list displays three choices: File Sharing Software, EtherTalk, and TokenTalk. If you're not on an EtherTalk or TokenTalk network (if you are, you'll know it—and you'll probably have a network administrator taking care of things, too), skip them. But do choose File Sharing Software even if you're not on any network. If you want to hook up someone else's Mac and send files back and forth, you'll need that software on your drive.

Choosing just the file sharing software from the network options.

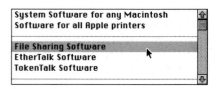

••➤ **If you're installing a system** on a hard drive that will be used as the startup for two different systems, and only two (say, for your office and home), you can Shift-click on the two different sets of system software in the Installer's Customize list instead of installing the software for any Mac. You can save quite a bit of room on your hard drive this way.

Selecting two systems.

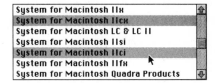

## LEGAL EAGLES #2

*Item*: When the New York Mac Users' Group tried to register its newsletter's name—*the Mac Street Journal*—as a trademark, it was sued by both Apple Computer and McDonald's. (The Wall Street Journal either didn't know or didn't care.)

*Item*: Infocom published a terrific series of text adventure games, including the popular Zork series. It also published a newsletter for enthusiasts which was originally named the New Zork Times. Guess who threatened to sue?

*Item*: Back in 1988, *MacUser* magazine used the phrase *The Big Picture* as a headline for information about a large-screen display. That caused a ruckus, because E-Machines registered that phrase as a trademark for its big screens. *MacUser's* comment:

"We recommend you take an x-acto knife, remove the offending page from the magazine, shred it, and hoover up the pieces. Then reward yourself with a coke and a twinkie from the frigidaire. (You might want to xerox this page for future reference.)"

And I'm sure the editors wiped the tears from their cheeks with a kleenex.

*Two more items:* Berkeley Systems sued the publishers of copycat screen saver Bill and Opus, and won. Then Jefferson Starship (nee Airplane) sued Berkeley Systems for stealing the *original* flying toasters from *30 Seconds Over Winterland*. Case pending as of this writing.

••➤ **Create a startup floppy by using** the minimal system option in the Custom section of the Installer. A minimal system consists of a System and Finder and not much else—no extensions, control panels, or desk accessories, although you'll see the subfolders in the System Folder. And you get only a single font: 9-point Geneva.

A startup floppy is for emergencies only; not only is the system minimal on a floppy, it runs *very* slowly from a floppy. In an emergency, when your Mac won't boot from the hard drive because its system is somehow corrupted, you can start it up with a floppy system disk to take a look—and rescue the files you need.

A partial list of the minimal system installations available.

Min System for any Macintosh
Min System for Macintosh Portable
Min System for Macintosh PowerBook 100
Min System for Macintosh PowerBook 140/145
Min System for Macintosh PowerBook 170
Min System for Macintosh Plus
Min System for Macintosh SE

•••➤ **An external drive with model-specific system software** on it can still be used with another model—it just can't be used as a startup disk. Say, for instance, you have a friend with a Mac Performa which is running from an internal hard drive. You run your LC II from an external hard drive that has system software specifically for the LC II. You're a wiz at Excel, and your friend wants to learn it. She doesn't always have to come to your place: You can take your hard drive and hook it up to her Performa and run your copy of Excel. Her hard drive is running the Performa, but your hard drive is accessed as an extra storage device.

## Reinstalling a System

•••➤ **If you're reinstalling your System** because you've had a series of unexplained crashes and think some of the system files have been corrupted, you should first erase the old system files. Otherwise, the Installer will simply check files like the printer drivers, see that they're the right versions (without knowing or caring if anything's wrong with them) and not change them at all. System files that tend to get corrupted are the System file itself, the Finder, enablers, and printer drivers.

Of course, you can't just erase the System file or the Finder, since they'll be in use when your system's running. So, move the System file out of the System Folder, and rename the folder something like *old system*. Run the Installer, and you'll get a brand new System Folder created on the disk; you can drag special programs from the old folder to the new one to get your old system setup back.

## Tweaking the System Setup

•••➤ **Trim down your System Folder** by getting rid of the files you don't need—there's always extra, especially if you've done an install For Any Macintosh or an Easy Install.

Start with the Extensions folder, and get rid of some or all of these:

- *Printer drivers:* You only need the one for your printer. Each driver is named for the printer it controls (ImageWriter, Personal LaserWriter, etc.).
- *DAL:* This isn't even included with 7.1 or later systems, but it's in 7.0 and 7.0.x. It's used for accessing remote databases on a network; trust me, you don't need it.
- *Finder Help:* This contains the five screens you see when you choose Finder Shortcuts from the Balloon Help menu. So read them, then get rid of them.

Consider taking these out of the Control Panels folder:

- *Easy Access:* This lets you control the mouse cursor from the keyboard, and do multiple-key combinations with one hand. It's meant for people who don't have the physical ability to control the mouse or handle the keyboard to its fullest extent.
- *Color:* Depending on which installation option you used, this might not have been installed in the folder of a black-and-white machine, but if it was, and your Mac is black and white, you don't need it.

- *Monitors:* You don't need this if you have a black-and-white machine with only a single monitor.

In the Apple Menu Items folder, check each of the desk accessories. If you're replacing any of them with something better from a third party, you can get rid of them.

••➔ **You can get rid of fonts** you don't want or need. A newly installed system includes over a megabyte of fonts.

In System 7, double-click on the System file to see the font files inside. In 7.1 and later, open the Fonts folder. The suitcase icons hold groups of fonts; you can get rid of an entire suitcase, or double-click on it to see the fonts inside and get rid of only some of them.

*Font handling is in Chapter 11.*

••➔ **If you delete files from the System Folder** and realize later that you need them, you don't have to use the Installer to put them back on your startup disk. Just drag them from one of the installation disks to the System Folder on your hard drive.

**MAC TOON**

## Two Systems on Two Drives

∞➔ **Sometimes you need two systems** around for a while. You may need (okay, maybe you just *want*) the capability of a new system right away, or have an application that works only with that system; in the meantime, some of your applications might work only under the older system.

The only safe way to keep two systems around is to use two hard drives, putting one system on each. Use the Startup Disk control panel to indicate which drive you want used as the startup at any given time.

⚫➤ **Bypass the internal hard drive as the startup** by holding down Command-Option-Shift-Delete when you start the Mac. Release the keys as soon as you see the flashing question mark icon during the startup procedure. This forces the Mac to ignore the internal hard drive during the startup scan, so it starts up with the external hard drive instead. (This is in case you forgot to specify the external drive with the Startup Disk control panel.) Of course, then you can't see the internal drive at all, so you'll have to mount it with a utility like SCSI Probe.

⚫➤ **Pretend you have two hard drives** by partitioning one hard drive into separate volumes, and put a system on each one. A drive partition is treated as a totally separate volume, so you won't have any system clashes. You do have a problem with setting the startup, though: You'll see both partitions in the Startup Disk control panel, but choosing either one does nothing but set the drive itself in general as the startup device because what's stored is the drive's SCSI ID number, not the partition's name. But if you rename the partitions so that the one you want as the startup is alphabetically earlier than the other partition, it will be the startup. Rename the partitions each time you want to change startups.

There's more about partitioning in Chapter 18.

# ⬅ FROM SYSTEM 6 TO SYSTEM 7 ⬅

## Upgrading from System 6 to 7

○○➤ **If you're upgrading to System 7 from 6.x,** we can assume that your hard drive is already pretty much filled with applications and documents. Make sure you back up everything before you start the installation. Let me say that again: *make sure you back up everything before you start the installation.*

> And now for something completely different.

MONTY PYTHON'S FLYING CIRCUS

Fragmentation is covered in Chapter 18.

○○➤ **You don't have to reformat your hard drive** before installing System 7. (Although if you can take the time to do so, you'll find you've optimized your disk speed as a side benefit of the defragmentation that occurs.)

○○➤ **System 7 needs hard drive drivers** that are different from the ones System 6 used. You need to update the driver on the disk, unless you're reformatting the drive with a utility that installs the updated driver during the formatting.

Huh? A hard drive driver? "Driver" in this case doesn't stem from the "drive" in hard drive; instead, it's used in the same sense that "printer driver" is used. A driver is a small program that helps control a piece of hardware and how the computer talks to it. Even experienced Mac users seldom realized there were disk drivers because they didn't have to pay attention to them before System 7 showed up. You can update the driver on an Apple drive with the HD SC Setup utility that comes with the system software, as explained in Chapter 18. For other drives—or even for Apple drives—you can use a third-party product like Drive7, which is also discussed in Chapter 18.

◄ **You lose all your Get Info comments** when you upgrade to System 7 because the first thing that happens when you restart after the installation is rebuilding of the desktop— and the comments are stored in the desktop file that's erased.

◄ **The best way to move from System 6 to System 7** is to take the time and opportunity to optimize your hard drive set up, erasing everything on it and starting fresh. Here are the steps you should follow:

1. Back up everything.
2. Reformat the hard drive. Use the HD SC Setup utility that comes with the System 7 disk for an Apple drive. For a non-Apple drive, use a formatter like Drive7.
3. Install the new system.
4. Tweak the System Folder, deleting items you don't need and adding extensions and utilities you can't live without.
5. Copy back the applications and documents that were on the drive before you reformatted it.

If you want to do a less than optimal, but perfectly workable installation, do these steps:

1. Install the new system.
2. Update the hard drive drivers.

◄ **The invisible Desktop file that System 6 uses** to keep track of what's where on the disk isn't needed by System 7, but it's still there on your hard drive when you move from System 6 to System 7.

Since the Desktop file is no longer necessary, you can delete it and reclaim some disk space.

How do you find an invisible file? With the proper utility. ResEdit is the tool of choice for hacker wannabe's, but many DAs also let you see invisible files. My favorite is DiskTools, from Fifth Generation Systems' MacPack. Any utility that lets you see an invisible file also lets you erase it, so go ahead and delete that file. (If you're reformatting the hard drive as part of upgrading to System 7, you don't have to erase any old files—the whole drive will be erased anyway.)

The Desktop file is discussed in Chapter 5.

## System 6 Fonts & Desk Accessories

∘•◆ **System 7's basic fonts are TrueType** versions of the bitmapped ones used in previous systems. When you upgrade from System 6 to 7, the Installer replaces what fonts it can with the TrueType versions. So, for instance, the bitmapped Monaco and Geneva used in System 6 get replaced with their TrueType incarnations.

Special bitmapped fonts that you put in your old system will be carried forward to your System 7 System file or Fonts folder if there's no TrueType equivalent.

∘•◆ **System 6 stored desk accessories** in the System file. When you upgrade to System 7, the Installer removes the old Apple DAs from the System file and puts the new System 7 versions in the Apple Menu Items folder. Non-Apple DAs are removed from the System file and placed as individual desk accessories in the Apple Menu Items folder. (Of course, just because they're in the Apple Menu Items folder doesn't mean they'll work under System 7. You'll have to try each one and see if it's compatible with your new system; if they don't work, contact the manufacturer to see if there's an update.)

*More about old and new desk accessories in Chapter 7.*

## ⇐ SYSTEM 7.5 STUFF ☞

### The New Installer

∘•◆ **There's a new, friendlier, Installer** with System 7.5 (finally, after all these years). It's not only better in that you can more easily pick and choose from among the various installation options, and select specifics in categories (like control panels), but it's prettier, too, as you can see here.

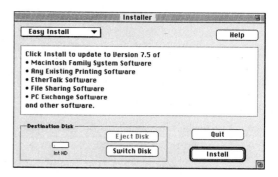

∘•◆ **The popup menu** in the corner lets you choose between the Easy and Custom installation procedures, *and* provides a Remove option—it's about time that was up on the surface instead of a hidden little trick!

∘•◆ **The list in the Custom Install dialog is hierarchical.** You can click the checkbox on the main level, or click the arrow in front of it to see what's listed beneath it. In the picture on the next page, the figure on the top shows the main level of the list. The middle figure shows the System Software item expanded. You can choose a specific system to install, or leave the main level checked for an "Any Macintosh" installation.

The figure at the bottom shows two other items—Compatibility Software and Multimedia Software—expanded.

∞**➤** **The little i icon in the list** is an information button. Click in it and you get an information window like the one shown here.

# CHAPTER 24

# PROBLEMS & PREVENTIONS

A chapter about nothing but problems can get really depressing. That's why there are solutions and preventions in here, too. Like:

➻ The care and feeding of your hardware components.
➻ What to do (and not do) during thunderstorms.
➻ What the heck a programmer's switch is.
➻ How to keep your computer free from viruses.
➻ Where to go for help.
➻ How to diagnose a problem.

THE PERSONAGE LEAST EXPECTED
TO POP UP IN A COMPUTER BOOK
WHO'S ACTUALLY IN THIS CHAPTER

***N**oah*

Includes

85 Factoids
9 Quotes
1 Memo
1 Quiz
2 Mac Almanac
    Charts

—*and*—

the final 2 light
bulb jokes

Force "Word" to quit?
Unsaved changes will be lost.

( Force Quit ) ( Cancel )

*page 878*

FileMaker Pro prefers 1500K of memory. 927K is available. Do you want to open it using the available memory?

( Cancel ) ( OK )

## ⇥ PREVENTIVE MAINTENANCE ⇤

### Care & Feeding

∘•➤ **The best way to handle a problem** is to prevent it altogether. General system maintenance—both hardware and software—can prevent many problems.

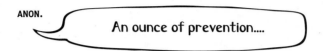

ANON.

An ounce of prevention....

∘•➤ **Clean the keyboard** with a soft cloth moistened with a mild cleaning solution. Don't let any liquid drip into the keyboard itself. Use a can of
compressed air to spray between the keys and clear out any dust or dirt particles. The APS Technologies Catalog carries a nifty product called
KeyKleen,* a box of premoistened swabs for cleaning the keys—the flat
swabs reach between the keys easily.

> *Nifty product,
> stupid name. The
> population in general
> already has a severe
> problem with spelling.

∘•➤ **Wiping a screen can make it dirtier.** If you wipe it with, say, a dry tissue, you'll build up
a static charge which will actually attract more dust. Use a special anti-static cleaner,
and *never* spray the cleaner directly on the screen—it could drip down into the monitor
case at the bottom of the screen. Spray the cleaner on a soft, lint-free cloth and then
wipe the screen. Make sure you don't use an abrasive cleaner, since it can ruin the anti-
glare coating that's on most displays.

Klear Screen and Klear Kloth are products obviously from the same company that
makes KeyKleen; if you can get past the name, the products are just what you need.
There's also a terrific, super-fine, multi-thousand-per-inch threadcount cloth called
Luminex that is wonderful for cleaning screens (and other glass surfaces—it's made for
eyeglasses). You can find it at opticians, and it's also been sighted in Sporty stores and
catalogs (800-543-8633), where it's known as simply "lens cleaning cloth."

∘•➤ **Keep the mouse as clean as possible** by using a mouse pad that defines a reasonably
clean rolling area. An extremely dirty surface will keep the mouse from rolling smoothly, and you'll probably notice that. But dust and paper particles count as "dirt" and will
wind up *inside* the mouse because they're picked up by the ball on the underside of the
mouse and delivered to the rollbars (and beyond) inside. Using a mouse pad is the best
approach. (Right, there's a MouseKleen Kit, too, but I cringe to mention the name. At
least they spelled *Kit* correctly.)

∘•➤ **Clean the inside of a mouse or trackball** at regular intervals; how often depends on
how clean its environment is. A mouse rolls around and collects lint and dirt. A trackball (on a PowerBook, or one that you use with your desk machine) doesn't collect
desktop dust, but it's more exposed to airborne particles, and the natural oils (not to

mention Dorito grease) on your fingers gunks up the ball's rollers pretty quickly. Whether you're cleaning a mouse or a trackball, the steps are basically the same:

1. Remove the retaining ring. (Most need a counterclockwise twist to unlock.)
2. Take out the ball.
3. Blow out the dust inside the assembly with a can of compressed air. (Not the *whole* can, of course!)
4. Clean the rollers and support posts inside the assembly. A gentle scraping with a blunt instrument—a toothpick or a fingernail works well—is sometimes enough to get the accumulated dirt off. Don't use a hard or sharp object that could score the rollers. If they don't come clean with a *gentle* scrape, use a cleaning solvent on the grime. Sometimes you'll need to loosen the gunk with a cotton or foam swab dipped in isopropyl alcohol or tape head cleaner. When fibers wrap themselves around the rollers they're hard to scrape out, but tweezers easily pull out the mess.
5. Wipe the ball itself with the dampened cloth.
6. Return the ball to the well and replace the retaining ring.

> If I'd known I was gonna live this long, I'd have taken better care of myself.

EUBIE BLAKE
(1883–1983)

## General Precautions

☞ **Don't move a hard drive** while it's turned on. The real danger is moving the drive while the disk is being accessed by the read/write heads, but consider a turned-on drive an unmovable object. (And don't forget that also applies to the Mac itself, if you have an internal drive.)

The smaller, lighter, drives inside PowerBooks withstand jarring without much effect even when they're spinning. as befits a *mobile* computer.

☞ **Don't block** any cooling vents on any of your computer equipment. Leave several inches of air space free along any vented side, back, or top for air currents.

☞ **Electrical storms** are hazardous to your computer's health. Don't just turn the computer off: Unplug it. Don't count on a surge protector to save you from a lightning strike. Unplug a modem not only from the power supply, but also from the telephone line. (The following quote is paraphrased from the original—I didn't save the *MacWeek* column in which it appeared a long time ago, but the thought stayed with me!)

> The only thing you can put between your computer and a power outlet to guarantee safety is about two feet of air.

DAVID RAMSEY

∞✦ **Don't shut off the computer** without using the Shut Down command in the Special menu. (Or, in System 7.5, the Shut Down DA listed in the Apple menu.) When you shut off without shutting down, you run the risk of losing information in unsaved documents as well as whatever else is in RAM and not yet written to the disk. You might also corrupt some system files that will then prevent the Mac from starting up again, and you'll have re-install the system.

∞✦ **Don't connect or disconnect any equipment** while the computer is on. Well, hardly any. Attaching or removing a cable from the printer or modem port won't do anything but interrupt a data transmission. But connecting things like hard drives or other SCSI devices while the Mac's on can damage your equipment (and not just the equipment you're plugging *in*, but the stuff you're plugging *into*—your Mac). On older Macs (pre-IIci), connecting an ADB device while the computer's on risks damage to the components.

∞✦ **Don't vacuum the inside** of a modular Mac or a compact Mac, if you should open it for any reason. The static charge that can build up during vacuuming (especially with a Dustbuster-type handheld vacuum, or any plastic-nozzled vacuum) can zap the circuit boards inside. If you don't want to invest in a special no-static vacuum made for computers, use compressed air to blow the dust out of the components.

## Software

∞✦ **Keep your system software** up-to-date. Don't jump on the update bandwagon—let everyone else test a new release. But if the new release fixes some bugs in the current release, and the bugs have been bugging you, upgrade as soon as possible..

∞✦ **Keep your applications in step** with your system software. Major upgrades to your system software might make some of your applications work a little strangely, or not at all. Keep track of the current version of any application you're using. You may be waiting breathlessly for the next major upgrade with umpteen new features, but minor upgrades that fix lurking bugs are more important to your workaday operations. User groups and online services are good places to keep abreast of recent updates.

## Hard Drives

∞✦ **If you take care of only one of your computer components,** make it the hard drive—that's where all your important, and perhaps irreplaceable, information is stored.

∞✦ **The particulars of disk care are covered** in Chapter 18, but here's table of what you should do, and when—and why. (There's also a Mac Almanac Chart of disk-care steps in this chapter—you can tear out the copy in the back of the book and stick it on your wall someplace in full view so you won't forget to do what it tells you.)

## Disk Maintenance

| | How | Why | When |
|---|---|---|---|
| MAKE BACKUPS | Manually or with disk backup software like Retrospect or DiskFit. | Because you'll be very sorry if you don't. | Depending on your work schedule and how important the files are. Once a day for some things; less than once a week is asking for trouble. |
| | *Comment:* It's not necessary to back up your system or applications, since they can be reinstalled. Backing up documents is what's important. Remember to back up desk accessory files, too, if you have lots of names and addresses in a Rolodex-type DA. Consider backing up "background" files like personal dictionaries, glossaries, and preferences files. | | |
| REBUILD THE DESKTOP | Hold down the Command and Option keys right after extensions load; for floppy, hold down Command and Option as you insert disk. | To avoid Disk is damaged and Disk needs minor repairs dialogs; speeds up the appearance of a disk on the desktop, and recovers disk space wasted on outdated icons stored in desktop file. | For a hard drive, once a month, or whenever documents seem to lose their links to the applications that created them. For a floppy, whenever it seems to take a long time to appear on the desktop after you insert it, or when you notice a large discrepancy between the size of the files on the disk and the header report of how much of the disk is used. |
| | *Comment:* Rebuilding the desktop erases all Get Info comments. | | |
| RUN VIRUS CHECKER | Follow program's instructions. | To detect and remove viruses. | Once a week as a general rule, but it depends on your "level of exposure." Always check bulletin board downloads, other public domain software/disks. |
| | *Comment:* Some virus checkers run as inits, automatically scanning any inserted floppy. Most are good only as long as you keep them current, since they scan for "known" viruses. | | |
| RUN DISK FIRST AID | This program is on your system disks: just double-click to launch it, and use the Repair Automatically option. | To nip problems in the bud. | Once a month unless disk problems ("repairs" dialog or problems recognizing a disk) call for it sooner. |
| | *Comment:* Not the best or most sophisticated disk utility, but it's free and takes care of basic problems. | | |
| RUN DISK DIAGNOSTICS | Follow program's directions; consider MacTools or Norton Utilities. | To nip problems in the bud. | Once a month. |
| | *Comment:* Disk diagnostic utilities go far beyond Disk First Aid and can find and fix problems before they even affect your work. They also usually include disaster relief like file recovery tools, virus checkers, and a disk optimizer for defragmenting files. | | |

continued...

## Disk Maintenance (continued)

|  | How | Why | When |
|---|---|---|---|
| DEFRAGMENT DRIVE | Use a disk utility like MacTools, Norton's, or Disk Express. | When files are fragmented on a disk, it slows down overall disk performance. | Three–six months, or even annually, depending on how you use your Mac. |
| | *Comment:* Always make sure your files are backed up before you defragment. | | |

## Be Prepared

◦◦➤ **Save early and often.** If your system crashes or the power goes out, you'll lose whatever's in the computer's memory—and most documents are held in memory. If you haven't saved the document on the disk, or the changes you've made to a document during a work session, all that work will be lost.

If the applications you use have auto-save functions that either save automatically or prompt you to save at intervals, use it!

◦◦➤ **Backup. Backup. Backup.** If your hardware breaks down, it can be fixed or replaced. If you lose your files, you have to re-create them—if you can.

HOWARD RUFF

It wasn't raining when Noah built the ark.

◦◦➤ **Tool kit. Arsenal.** Whatever you want to call it, you need certain things on hand to deal with minor and major disasters, and general disk maintenance. Some of the tools are free—they come with your system software. Others are commercial items that you should buy, but it will be money well spent. Make sure you have all of these around *before* there's any problem:

- A *startup floppy*. Make a startup floppy by installing a minimal system for your computer on a floppy disk. If the Mac won't start up because of a problem with the internal hard drive, a floppy can get you going so you can see the hard drive and perhaps rescue the files you need, or even get at the problem on the hard drive.
- *Disk First Aid*. This comes with your system software. Keep a copy on your hard drive so you can run it for any other volume you have connected to your Mac, and for floppy disks. Also keep it on a startup floppy for when your hard drive won't start the Mac. If you have a set of system disks, the Disk Tools disk is a startup floppy with Disk First Aid on it. If you have a CD with system software, use it to make a Disk Tools disk.

- *Virus Detector.* Whether it's a commercial package, part of a general disk utility package, or a stand-alone freeware or shareware item, get one.
- *Disk Diagnostic Utility.* Get MacTools or Norton Utilities. Or both. (Or get Safe & Sound, a subset of MacTools.) All three packages provide disk diagnostics and fixes. The two larger packages also include virus checkers, defragmenters, and several other useful items.
- *Defragmenter.* If you need to defragment, you can use the tools in your general disk diagnostic software rather than buy a separate piece of software.

∞◊ **Get insurance.** You can get a policy that covers anything that might happen to your hardware, and even the software that you own. (Although earthquake damage is often excluded—sorry, California.) At less than $100 per $5000 worth of equipment, you can be covered for almost everything, including data recovery or re-entry, and the rental of equipment until yours is fixed or permanently replaced. There are two companies I can recommend highly because of friends' experiences: Data Security Insurance (800-822-0901) and Safeware (800-800-1492).

# ☜ CRASH! REBOOT! ☞

## About this Bomb ...

∞➤ A *crash,* or *bomb,* is the general term for when the system software misbehaves itself to the extent that it stops working. You'll usually get a dialog with the non-apologetic message *A system error has occurred.* The dialog also has a Restart button, which rarely works. Often there's an icon of a bomb with a burning fuse (a little piece of misplaced humor considering the grief that crashing causes). Sometimes there's an error ID number, which does you no good at all because they're meant for programmers, and even the error definitions make no sense to the rest of us. Your only choice is to restart your computer—and, as I mentioned, the Restart button seldom works, so you'll have to use the reset switch.

∞➤ A *freeze* or *hang* is a type of crash, one where your computer just stops what it's doing and refuses to even let the mouse cursor move around on the screen—never mind display a dialog telling you that you've crashed. Once again, you have no choice but to reset the computer.

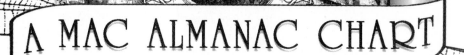

## Hard Drive Setup & Maintenance

**Setup:**

•••❯ Update the driver software to the most current available.

•••❯ Format the drive to is fullest capacity.

**Daily:**

•••❯ Backup important files.

**Weekly:**

•••❯ Backup important files if you don't do it daily.

•••❯ Scan for viruses. (Daily or monthly for high- or low-use systems.)

**Monthly:**

•••❯ Rebuild the desktop.

•••❯ Run Disk First Aid.

•••❯ Run MacTools, Norton Utilities, or other disk diagnostic utility.

**Semi-Annually:**

•••❯ Defragment hard drive. (Or only annually, depending on level of use.)

● ● ● ● ● ● ● ● ● ● ● ● ● ● ● ● ● ● ● ● ● ● ● ● ● ● ● ● ● ● ● ● ● ● ● ● ● ● ● ● ● ● ●

### POP QUIZ                              [5 POINTS]

What's the name of the company where Wiley Coyote buys his explosives in his never-ending quest to catch that Road Runner?

⬧ **When something's wrong in the initial stages** of the startup procedure, while the Mac is going through its internal hardware check, you get a black screen, an icon known as the Sad Mac, and a disconcerting series of notes known as the *Chimes of Doom*—an arpeggio that strikes terror into the heart of Mac owners everywhere. But sometimes the Sad Mac isn't as disastrous as you might assume; there are more details later in this chapter.

⬧ **An error ID number isn't very helpful** to "the rest of us," but if you continually crash, make a note of any error ID that's displayed. It can be useful information to whatever technician you wind up going to for help, whether it's for a software or a hardware fix. I'm not going to make a chart of the esoteric bomb ID explanations; if you're a glutton for punishment, you can try the freeware desk accessories System Errors Table by Bill Steinberg, or Easy Errors by Dave Rubinic.

## The Programmer's Switch

⬧ **The *reset* and *interrupt* buttons** are pretty much the Mac's panic buttons. They're located at the front or side of most desk Macs, and at the back of most PowerBook models—and some Macs, like the LC, don't have them at all.

If you have reset and interrupt buttons, they'll have cryptic little marks on them so you can tell which is which: The reset button is marked with a triangle (or arrow, depending on how you interpret these things), and the interrupt button has a circle on it.

Sometimes the phrase *programmer's switch* is used to refer to the interrupt button, which is, indeed, needed and used by programmers. Sometimes, though, it refers to both switches together; this is left over from the early days when the switches were on a separate, little piece of plastic that you had install on a compact Mac yourself—the plastic piece itself was called the programmer's switch.

⬧ **The reset button** resets everything in the computer's memory; it's like turning the computer off and then on again, but doesn't place quite as much electrical stress on some of the components.

⬧ **The interrupt button** puts the Mac into a special mode that programmers use to test what's going on in the guts of the machine. If you press it, you'll get a blank dialog with an arrow prompt (>) waiting for you to type something. (Well, not *you*, but someone who knows what to do next.)

⬧ **If your Mac has no reset or interrupt** buttons, use the Power On key in combination with other keys as a substitute. Command-Control-Power is the same as pressing the reset switch. On most models, Command-Shift-Power is the same as using the interrupt button.

●●●●●●●●●●●●●●●●●●●●●●●●●●●●●●●●●●●●●●●●●●●●●●

## AMAZING GRACE

Here's the story about how the word "bug" came to mean a glitch in a computer program: Sometime in the forties, Grace Hopper, the developer of the COBOL language, pulled a moth out of a malfunctioning Harvard Mark II computer, and from then on, "bug" was used to describe anything that kept a program from running correctly.

That's the *story*. But it's not accurate. First of all, Admiral Hopper wasn't there; she just liked to tell the story of the incident. Yes, it was an actual incident; the insect in question was indeed pulled out of the computer's relays. But the record of the occasion, a log entry dated September 9, 1945, said: *"Relay #70 Panel F (moth) in relay. First actual case of bug being found."* From the wording, it's obvious that the term itself was already in use. The logbook, with the unfortunate moth taped onto that page, was on display for years at the Naval Surface Warfare Center.

And when Grace Hopper retired, she gave a speech in which she used one of my all-time favorite quotes: "It's easier to get forgiveness than permission."

••◆ **There's a big difference between the reset button** and the Special menu's Restart command. Using the Restart command is basically the same as using Shut Down: The Mac has a chance to do its disk housekeeping before RAM is cleared. The reset switch—and any Restart button that's in a system error dialog—immediately clears RAM without saving anything to the disk.

## ◄ OTHER THINGS TO KNOW ►

## Viruses

∞◆ **A *virus* is a computer program** designed by (at best) a careless or (at worst) a pathological mind. A virus hides itself somewhere on your drive, usually inside other programs, and reproduces itself, spreading from file to file and disk to disk.

A virus can be benign, designed to put a message on your screen on a certain date, or it may be purposely destructive, erasing disk files or slowing down network operations. But even benign viruses can unwittingly ruin your files, or at the least, interrupt your work.

∞◆ **You catch a virus** by using an infected file. Exchanging disks with other users and downloading files from a communications network are the main ways your computer exposes itself to viral programs. All online services do their best to post only "healthy" files, but some problems can slip past even the most vigilant sysops.

∞◆ **It's hard to tell when you have a virus.** Your computer isn't going to cough, sneeze, and complain of stomach pains. But viruses can cause all sorts of symptoms, ranging from unexplained system crashes to disappearing or corrupted files, and almost anything in between.

## CHECKING FOR VIRUSES

∞▶ **Run a virus-checker** at regular intervals. If you use a lot of floppies that have been in other machines, if you're on a network, or if you do a lot of telecommunicating, check for viruses at least once a week. If your machine is more isolated, once every month or two is often enough. I've had one virus in 10 years of Mac use, and it was picked up in a college computer lab where I connected my hard drive to one of its Macs. And that was the only virus ever on the campus in all the years they've been using Macs. So, keep things in perspective: Viruses are not all that endemic in the Mac world.

∞▶ **An anti-virus program** works in one (or more) of several ways. Some programs read through a disk, checking for either known viruses or suspiciously-altered files, or both. Some programs can scan a disk and also remove any virus that's found. Sometimes an anti-virus program will check every disk you insert in a floppy drive, or ask you each time you insert a disk if you want it scanned.

But because a virus-checker looks for specific viruses, it's good only for viruses that have been identified before you get the checker program. Virus-checkers have to be updated at regular, and frequent, intervals in order to keep you protected.

**DISINFECTANT**

∞▷ **Virus-checking utilities** come with disk maintenance programs like MacTools and Norton Utilities, but the best solo virus program is Disinfectant. Not only is it good, it's free, with immediate updates anytime a new virus rears its ugly little head . What more could you ask for? [freeware, John Norstad, distributed by Northwestern University]

## PAX VOBISCUM

The first virus on the Mac was known as the Peace virus because that's the message it displayed on the Mac screen when the internal clock hit the date March 2, 1988—the first birthday of the Mac II. This sounds benign, of course, but that's not the point. First of all, you never know when even a well-tested program is going to mess up your system; who knows what an untested program will do—especially one that can only survive by burrowing deep inside some other program or system file. Secondly, you have a right to control the contents of your computer system.

Since people who create and knowingly spread viruses are sometimes in it for the "fame," I'm not going to mention the name of the perpetrator here. But some of his statements in an interview with Neil Shapiro in *MacUser* magazine are ironically interesting. When Neil pointed out that even if his virus was benign, maybe others would adapt it into something more harmful, Neil was told that his fear was a "cultural problem" because "here in Canada, we don't have nuclear weapons. We are not allowed to own guns. Not like in the United States, where people are nasty." And, a little later in the conversation, he (not Neil!) said: "Perhaps because I am a Canadian, I don't do nasty things."
Right.

•••▶ **When a computer "expert" says you have a virus,** don't believe him or her unless the virus is specifically identified in the diagnosis (and, presumably, eradicated). Claiming a virus infection is always a good out when someone can't figure out what's wrong.

## Getting Help

∞▶ **The first place to turn to for help** is the manual. Look it up! Whatever your problem is, there's a chance it's covered in the documentation. Look through related materials, too: manual addendums, Read Me documents, and any online help the program provides. Sometimes what you think is a bug may be simply (but annoyingly) a non-intuitive way of doing something, or a feature that you thought was in the program but actually isn't. (And, of course, sometimes it's a bug.)

Please refer to the RTFM information in Chapter 19!

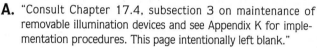

**BRIGHT IDEAS #13**

**Q.** How many manual writers does it take to change a light bulb?

**A.** "Consult Chapter 17.4, subsection 3 on maintenance of removable illumination devices and see Appendix K for implementation procedures. This page intentionally left blank."

•••▶ **If you're an online junkie**—or even a judicious user of your online service—you'll probably find lots of people who use the same program you're having trouble with. In fact, you'll find whole sections devoted to certain popular programs and utilities. It's likely you'll find a solution for your problem, in the form of either an updated program or an explanation of what's causing it, or a workaround. If nothing else, you'll find company in your misery.

•••▶ **If you're in a User Group,** describe the problem there and see if anyone else has run into the same problems and can provide some helpful advice.

•••▶ **Call the manufacturer.** Most manufacturers provide telephone technical support for their products, although the degree of expertise and helpfulness certainly varies from one company to the next—and some of the large companies charge for phone support. But when and if you call, be ready with a list of information so the tech support person can better understand what the problem might be. You should know:

- The program's serial number, if there is one. Some companies provide support only to users who have purchased a legitimate copy of the program. Check the About box, the master disk, and the packaging for a serial number.

- What version of the program you're using. It's usually available in the About dialog from the Apple menu, or in the application icon's Get Info window. (Check for the decimal numbers: PerfectProgram 2.1 may have a different set of problems than PerfectProgram 2.0.)

- What version of the system software you're using. Again, decimals are important; there might be differences between the program's behavior under System

7.0.1 and 7.1. Also know what, if any, tune-ups or updates you've made to the system software.

- What extensions you have in your system, especially the non-Apple ones. You should be able to tell the tech support person if there are specific inits the program seems to be clashing with, because you will have already done some troubleshooting of your own.

- The specifics of the problem. "It keeps crashing" or "I can't print this document" aren't very descriptive or helpful. But "The program crashes every time I have a lot of material on the Clipboard and then try to create a new document" or "I can't print this document, but all the other documents I created can be printed with no problems, and the only difference seems to be the extra fonts" can help the technician pinpoint the problem more easily.

### BRIGHT IDEAS #14

**Q.** How many technical support people does it take to change a light bulb?

**A.** "We have an exact copy of the light bulb here and it seems to be working fine. Can you tell me what kind of system you have? Okay. Just exactly how dark is it? Okay. There could be four or five things involved. Have you tried the light switch?"

•••➤ **Send out an SOS.** That is, call Apple SOS. More specifically, call 1-800-SOS-APPL for problems with your Macintosh hardware or Apple software—especially if the hardware is still under warranty.

## ⊰ TROUBLESHOOTING ⊱

## Diagnosing the Problem

•••➤ **What's new in your system?** That's the first thing to ask yourself when you run into a problem. Or, rephrased: "What changes did I recently make to my system?" If you just added a new extension, or changed printer drivers, or updated other system software, the new item is likely to be the culprit.

•••➤ **Try to isolate the problem.** Consider all the components of the operation, and change one at a time to see if you can find the root of the problem. For instance: A document won't print. Well, is it the document? The application? The printer? The printer driver? A background printing problem? How about memory? Maybe the connection between the printer and the computer? Or a general system software problem that's affecting printing? It gets daunting when you consider all the things that might be causing a single problem.

But it's relatively easy to narrow down the problem to just a few possibilities. If a document isn't printing, can you print other documents from the same application? If not, can you print from other applications? Or, if other documents print from the first application, can you print different parts of the problem document separately? You might find that the problem is a specific font, or a single graphic on a complex page.

SCANDAL OF FATHER BROWN
*POINT OF A PIN* (1935)

> **It isn't that they can't see the solution.
> It's that they can't see the problem.**

**See if the problem is reproducible** more or less on demand. That is, see if you can figure out the specific circumstances under which the problem occurs—especially if it's a system crash. For instance, is it when you try to paste something into a document, and there's something really big on the Clipboard every time? Or you brought information in on the Clipboard from another application that's running? Figuring out the specifics that lead to the problem often point to the cause, and, therefore, a solution—or at least a workaround.

For instance: Even before I finished writing this book we were laying out the earlier chapters. Although I didn't have time for most of the layout myself, I did prepare each QuarkXpress file, importing the original Word document, checking the style sheets, and so on. Quark often crashed soon after the import, as soon as I tried a cut or copy operation. But it didn't *always* crash, and it didn't seem to depend on the size of the chapter I had just imported. Then I realized: After I imported the Word file, the first thing I would do is cut some of the beginning material (the chapter title and contents) from the main text to put it into a separate box on the first page. If I did the cut or copy *before* I saved the document (after the import), Quark would quit on me. But if I imported the file, saved the document, and *then* cut or copied the initial material, everything was fine. Aha! Obviously poor memory management on Quark's part—it choked after a big import followed by my trying to put something on the Clipboard. But once the document was saved to the disk, Quark wasn't holding quite so much in memory, and could handle the next operation. Could I fix the bug? No—even allotting more memory to Quark didn't take care of it. But I could make sure I saved the document as soon as I imported the file, and avoid the problem.

### THE THREE L'S

To troubleshoot Mac problems, you need to *learn* all you can and use *logic* for deducing causes. But some problems are so unexpectedly ridiculous, only *luck* gets you through. Take the production of this book (please!).

Despite the fact we're in the electronic age, at one point this manuscript was actually processed on paper, as it went through the copy-edit process. The copy editor suggests changes and I agree or argue; this is all marked on a printout. When the changes are finalized, they go to the word processing people, who work on the electronic files I provide. (I guess they don't want me slipping a new word in here and there.) In this case, though, I got the files back to do the layout, and that's when the fun began.

I imported the edited Word file into QuarkXpress (which I call QuirkXpress for reasons too numerous to mention here). Before the text appeared in the document, I got a dialog box telling me that font 14760 was unavailable. 14760? I just okayed my way out of the dialog and poured the text, which imported with no regard to the styles that had been painstakingly designed and applied during the writing process just so the layout would be a smooth process. Instead, fonts, sizes, and styles changed in the middle of sentences whenever they felt like it, and sometimes changed back pages later (and sometimes not). It happened to every file, no matter what I did. I tried re-applying, re-naming and re-defining styles on the Word end, and again on the Quark end. No effect. But that missing font dialog kept showing up on the import. Wait a minute! How about importing the file that I sent to the word processing people? Yep, it came in with everything intact. Obviously, something was happening on their end, but what? It may have been their fault, but it was certainly my problem. Faced with the task of manually reformatting 1000 pages of text, or re-inputting editorial changes, I kept experimenting.

Back to the "missing font" clue. Which was font 14760? I looked through my fonts—no such ID. Wait, this is impossible! Word is unkind to fonts that don't exist in the system it's running on—it replaces any missing font with an existing one, and even when you open the document back on the original system, the substituted font remains. So how could a font introduced in the Ziff offices still affect a file that I'd run through Word on my machine afterward? I saved the word processed file in Word's special RTF format that defines all the components of the document, and took a look at it; the fonts in the document and in my system were listed by ID number at the top, but there was no 14760. Hmm .... On a hunch, I searched the document for any mention of font 14760. Yep, there it was—each time there was an em dash in the document, it was preceded by the code for switching to font 14760. I called CharleyΔ Cowens, the production manager and told him it may sound crazy, but files were being corrupted on their end by something to do with em dashes. What did he think? He thought he finally found a good reason to make them stop a process that seemed silly but, till now, harmless. It seems that no matter what typeface a ZD Press book uses, it uses an extra-long em dash from a special Times font. Every time there was an em dash in one of my files, the word processing people pasted over it with an em dash from the special font.

So, I did a global search and replace for all the em dashes in the files, and everything imported correctly after that. There's still no explanation for why Word left the nonexistent font marker in place, and I lost two days of work tracking down the problem, but, gee ... it makes for an interesting example of bug hunting.

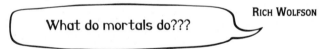

What do mortals do???

RICH WOLFSON

## General-Purpose Fixes

∞•➔ **No matter what the problem seems to be,** there are several all-purpose fixes that you should always try, pretty much in this order:

- Start up without extensions and see if the problem persists.
- Rebuild the desktop: Hold down Command and Option when you start up.
- Zap the PRAM: Hold Command-Option-P-R at startup.
- Check for viruses.
- Reinstall the system.
- Run Disk First Aid.

- Run disk diagnostic software.
- Backup the drive and reformat it.

These procedures are so often the cure for general problems that I've also put them in an Almanac Chart for you to tear out.

•◆ **Is it plugged in?** That's the old TV-repairman joke, but it applies to all your hardware. Of course, it's probably plugged in, but what about all the cable connections—are any of them loose? And are the cables themselves in good condition? Check that the pins on all connectors are in good shape, too.

## ◄ **PROBLEM AREAS** ►

### Startup Problems

•◆ **Problems at startup can be hardware- or software-based** and they can be minor or truly disastrous. But based on when exactly during the startup the problem occurs—and what exactly is occurring—you can narrow down the scope and usually solve the problem.

•◆ **If the question mark icon stays on the screen,** the Mac can't find a startup drive.

- If the startup is an external drive maybe it wasn't spinning up to speed when the Mac "looked at" it during the startup sequence. Leave the drive on and restart the Mac.
- For an external startup, make sure all the cables are connected and that it's plugged in to its own power source.
- If the startup is your internal drive, just restart the Mac and see if it starts up the second time. If not, get it going with a floppy startup and see if your hard drive icon appears. If you can see the hard drive when you start up with a floppy, there's something wrong with the system software on the hard drive; reinstall it. If you can't start it with a floppy, try a disk repair utility.

•◆ **If you crash or freeze when the init march** starts on the screen, it's almost certainly an init conflict causing the problem. See Chapter 8 for details on how to track down and handle init conflicts.

•◆ **If an external drive doesn't mount** at startup—its icon doesn't show up on the desktop—it might be that:

- The drive wasn't up and running when the Mac looked for it. Leave the drive spinning and restart the Mac.
- There's something wrong with the SCSI connection or chain.
- The drive's driver is corrupted. Re-install the driver, as described in Chapter 18.

> The computer is down.
> I hope it's something serious.

STANTON DELAPLANE

# A MAC ALMANAC CHART

## Trouble-Shooting Procedures

**For general system problems:**

- ⇢ Start up without extensions and see if the problem persists.

- ⇢ Rebuild the desktop: Hold down Command and Option when you start up.

- ⇢ Zap the PRAM: Hold Command-Option-P-R at startup.

- ⇢ Check for viruses.

- ⇢ Reinstall the system.

- ⇢ Run Disk First Aid.

- ⇢ Run disk diagnostic software.

- ⇢ Back up the drive and reformat it.

**For general application problems:**

- ⇢ Allocate more memory to the application.

- ⇢ Trash the application's Prefs or Settings file.

◦•▶ **If the desktop takes a long time to show up** after all the inits have loaded, it's probably time to rebuild the desktop file.

◦•▶ **If there's a longer-than-usual delay before the Welcome dialog** shows up after you start the Mac, it may be because you've recently upped the memory. The Mac checks all its memory as part of the startup procedure, and there's a noticeable difference between the time it takes to check 4 or 8 megs of memory and 20 megs. You may also notice that it takes longer to start up after a system crash—that's normal, and you won't get the delay again after a clean shutdown.

◦•▶ **If you see this dialog at startup** right after the desktop appears, it means you have an extension in your Startup Items folder. Anything in the Startup Items folder opens as soon as the Mac is up and running, but you can't really open an extension. If you double-click on an extension icon to open it, this is the dialog you get—and leaving it in the Startup Items folder is just like double-clicking on it.

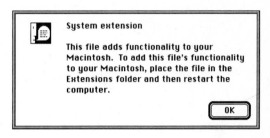

•••▶ **When the Happy Mac icon blinks,** or shows up and then the screen reverts to the question mark icon, it's usually indicative of a problem with system software. Start up with your system disks and reinstall the system.

•••▶ **If you get a Sad Mac on startup**—on a black screen and accompanied by the Chimes of Doom—it can indicate one of many problems.

- Try starting up with a floppy disk. If you can start the Mac that way, then the Sad Mac indicates a problem with the system files on the hard drive; reinstall the system software.
- If you installed SIMM chips recently, they're probably not firmly seated. Re-seat them and try again. Even if you haven't put them in recently, check them out. In fact, *take* them out, and see if the Mac starts up without the extra memory chips.
- For a PowerBook whose case has been opened recently, check that both the memory modules and the daughterboard are firmly seated.

•••▶ **The code numbers under the Sad Mac**, starting with the SE, indicate what's wrong. Here's a brief list of what the codes refer to. (The numbers are the last four digits in the first row under the icon):

| | |
|---|---|
| 0001 ......ROM chip | 0008 .......ADB problem |
| 0002 ......SIMMS in bank B | 000A ....NuBus slots |
| 0003 ......bank B SIMM slots | 000B .......SCSI chip |
| 0004 ......SIMMs in bank A | 000C......floppy drive |
| 0006 ......ADB port | 000D......printer or modem port |

**⋯➤ A corrupted disk driver** can cause a Sad Mac at startup, but there's no easy way to fix it because the driver will cause the crash even if you try to start up with a floppy. But there are two things you can try. First, hold Command-Shift-Option-Delete on startup (with the Disk Tools startup floppy in) to try and bypass the internal drive completely. If it works, install a new driver.

Disk drivers are covered in Chapter 18.

If bypassing the internal drive doesn't work, here's a really hard-core fix: If you know how to disconnect the internal drive, disconnect it and try starting up with the Disk Tools floppy; if the Mac starts, you'll know for sure it's the driver causing the problem. Once the Mac is up and running on the floppy, you can reconnect the hard drive and reinstall the driver.

## General System Crashes

**⋯➤ A general system crash is** one that gives you a *Sorry, a system error has occurred* dialog box, or one that just freezes up the computer so you can't do anything at all. Sometimes the crash is totally unrelated to what you're doing at the time, and happens inconsistently but frequently. Sometimes it's a little more predictable, happening only within certain applications or during particular operations.

**⋯➤ Extensions can cause system crashes,** so restart without extensions and see if the crashes continue. If they stop, you'll have to go through the init-conflict procedures described in Chapter 8.

**⋯➤ Try curing the problem with** one or all of the cure-alls: rebuild the desktop, zap the PRAM, run Disk First Aid, reinstall the system software.

**⋯➤ Use the emergency escape route:** press Command-Option-Esc when the computer isn't responding to anything else. You'll get a dialog asking if you really want to force the current application to quit (the current application might be the Finder), with buttons letting you force the quit or cancel; the dialog notes that all unsaved changes will be lost.

Since you won't have a chance to save your work, this emergency escape doesn't seem to make much sense—until you realize that, if it works, it will have gotten you out of the application that froze or crashed

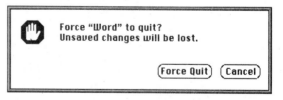

and let you get to any *other* running applications that might have unsaved work. If the emergency escape works, save all your work anywhere you can and then restart the computer right away.

**⋯➤ When you can't restart the computer** after a crash or freeze because it's not responding to the mouse or keyboard, use the reset button. You'll lose everything in memory, but you'll get your computer back.

**System 7 introduced a new error dialog:** your system cra<sup>,</sup>
*f-line instruction*. In early versions of System 7, this cro<sub>f</sub>
referred to as the *f-word* dialog. It still pops up occasior
can do about it. You can try the emergency escape r<sup>,</sup>
reset the computer to get going. If you see this dialo<sup>,</sup>
sure your system software is up-to-date, and reinsta<sup>,</sup>

## Mouse & Monitor

**If the mouse cursor is moving erratically,** or not moving at all,

- The mouse (or trackball) needs a cleaning.
- There's some background processing going on—printing ι
  PrintMonitor, or file copying.
- The ADB cable isn't in firmly, or the cable or connector needs replacing.

**When the mouse moves too slowly** or too quickly, adjust the tracking speed with the Mouse control panel. If the adjustment makes no difference, you may need to simply restart the computer—sometimes disconnecting and reconnecting an ADB cable while the Mac is running slows down the mouse and makes it immune to its control panel settings.

**If the mouse cursor freezes** on the screen:

- See if the ADB cable connector came loose, and reconnect it.
- See if the keyboard still works. If it doesn't, check the keyboard's cable. If the keyboard works but the mouse doesn't, save as much of your work as you can before you're forced to reset the computer. If you have a macro utility like QuicKeys, a Shut Down macro that uses the command in the Special menu can be a lifesaver.
- Restart the computer with the reset switch.
- Shut down the computer, disconnect and reconnect the mouse, then restart.

If the cursor is frozen on startup—usually in the upper-left corner of the screen, near the Apple menu, try restarting. If it's still stuck, try restarting again, zapping the PRAM this time around.

But before you try any of these fixes—did you just try a screen dump with Command-Shift-3 or some utility that you have? The cursor won't move until the screen dump is completely finished and stored on the disk; with a large screen set to many colors, this can take up to a full minute.

**The most common monitor problems** are discussed in Chapter 15. Here's a roundup:

- A blank monitor may be unplugged or turned off (even though the computer's actually on), or the brightness and contrast settings may be set to extremes.
- The Trinitron monitors have a perfectly normal thin gray horizontal line about two-thirds of the way down the screen.

Intermittent blackouts followed by a permanently blank screen may mean you need the high voltage transformer replaced.

A flickering, shrinking screen on a Plus or SE means the power supply needs repair or replacement.

- Apple's 8•24GC video card is incompatible with System 7.
- A blank screen on a Centris or Quadra using a non-Apple monitor may be due to the Basic Color Monitor extension; get rid of it (the extension, not the monitor!).

## Applications

⚬•➤ **If there's not enough memory to launch** an application, you'll get a dialog telling you so, although the exact wording of the dialog, and your options, vary a bit from System 7.0.1 to System 7.1 and later. You may have to quit other running applications, or defragment the available memory, in order to make room for the application you want to launch.

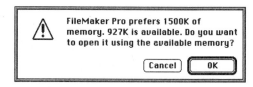

⚬•➤ **When a program unexpectedly quits,** you usually get a dialog telling you so, but sometimes the program, and any of its opened windows, simply disappear from the screen. It's very disconcerting, since (although you don't realize it) you're very used to seeing windows close by zooming down into nothingness.

Memory allocations are covered in Chapter 19.

A program's quitting unexpectedly is more often than not due to a memory problem—that is, a lack of memory. Try allocating more memory to it in its Get Info box on the desktop.

The application WordPlay has unexpectedly quit.

(many software developers)

It's not a bug, it's a feature!

⚬•➤ **Try allocating more memory to a program** whenever you have any kind of problem with it; this probably cures at least half of all application problems.

⚬•➤ **My favorite all-purpose application-fixer** (besides allocating more memory) is getting rid of the application's prefs or settings file. Often—especially often with Microsoft Word—it's the settings file that's corrupted and causing all the weirdness in the application itself. I've seen this cure quits, crashes, printing problems, on-screen text and formatting problems … it might even cure warts. Recreating Prefs files can be a pain, so keep a copy of a clean, uncorrupted one around in case you need to replace the working copy.

○•◗ **Crashes, freezes, and unexpected quits** might also be due to the application's conflicting with an extension. Try running with extensions turned off and see if the problem goes away.

○•◗ **Sometimes a utility stops working after** you've reinstalled the system to cure some other problem. Quite a few utilities work by altering the System file; some even alter the Finder file. Installing a clean system means you've lost the special resources the utility installed in one of the system files. Even though everything looks fine on the surface because you can still see the extension, or the control panel, or whatever it is you use to control the utility's functions, it's lost its underpinnings. Try reinstalling any utility that suddenly stops working.

••◗ **The application or its supporting files** may have been corrupted by a system crash, so reinstalling the application can often cure its general woes.

## Documents

○○◗ **When an application can't be found**—that is, you double-click on a document and get a dialog that says *An application can't be found for this document*, you can:

- Find the application and install it on your hard drive.
- Try to open the document in another application, one that accepts the general file format of the document.
- Drag the document onto an application icon to force it to open there if it can.

You can also use a utility like HandOff or SpeedyFinder7 that lets you "rewire" specific types of documents to open in the applications that you have instead of "giving up" when they can't find the application that created them. [HandOff, Connectix; SpeedyFinder7, shareware, Victor Tan]

The Easy Open control panel in System 7.5 takes care of the "orphan" document problem. See Chapter 19.

○•◗ **When a document won't open** with a double-click (all you get is a dialog that says it's damaged) try opening it from within the application that created it. If you manage to open it, do a Save As right away and trash the original.

○•◗ **Copy a damaged document** that won't open into an application by using the Finder's Duplicate command, and see if you can open the duplicate.

## Printing

○○◗ **The Chooser desk accessory** may present you with any of three basic problems:

- If the icon for your printer is not in the left panel, the printer driver is not in the Extensions folder. Reinstall it with the Installer program.
- If you select a LaserWriter icon and the LaserWriter's name doesn't show up in the right panel, the LaserWriter isn't turned on. Or, if it's on, it hasn't warmed up yet. (Or, it's the old standby—a cable is loose.)
- If you select the LaserWriter's name in the list and the Background Printing buttons don't appear or remain dimmed, the PrintMonitor program is not in the Extensions folder.

⚬•➤ **Blank pages coming out of a LaserWriter** might be due to:

- *Really* bad formatting. For instance: You formatted everything for hidden text (which shows on the screen) but used a default setting of No Hidden Text for printing.
- Blank pages. You may have multiple blank pages in the document because you entered several page breaks in a row. Or, you have only one blank page—but you asked for 10 copies of it instead of a printout of pages 1 through 10.
- Grayscale graphics. The lighter values in grayscale graphics print as white if you've checked the black-and-white printing option. If the entire page is relatively light-shaded, nothing at all will print.
- You're printing color-separated pages and one of the pages is a color you don't have in the document.
- The cartridge is really, truly, completely out of toner.
- You forgot to remove the protective plastic strip from a new toner cartridge.

⚬•➤ **When pages don't come out at all**, but from the Mac end of things everything seems to be fine (you don't get any dialogs indicating a printing problem), it might be that:

- The document is too complicated for the printer's memory. The things that take up memory are complicated graphics and lots of fonts on a single page. The problem may also be just that a complicated page is taking a long time to process, and waiting it out will solve the "problem"; see if the printer's light is blinking, indicating that it's still processing the page. (Complicated pages, especially printed with the color/grayscale option, can take 5 or 10 minutes to process, even on a reasonably fast printer model; *very* complicated graphics can even take an hour, especially on an older LaserWriter.)
- The Faster Bitmap Printing option in Page Setup is turned on—turn it off.
- Background printing is on, but PrintMonitor is set to print at a different time or date.
- Background printing is on, and PrintMonitor is waiting for you to check it—because it's trying to tell you that the paper tray isn't inserted all the way, or that it's out of paper.
- The printer you selected in Chooser the last time you used it is no longer attached to the Mac.
- The LaserWriter Prefs file (in the Preferences folder inside the System Folder) is corrupted; trash it and try again.
- You're on a network and your document is being printed on a different printer than the one you intended to print from.

⚬•➤ **The *Can't open printer* dialog** may show up after you've clicked the Print button. If it does, it might be because:

> Can't open printer.

- The printer isn't turned on.
- The printer isn't connected to the computer.
- A printer wasn't selected in Chooser.

THE WAY WE WERE ...

### MACS WHO?

MacsBug is a famous (within in a small circle) debugger for the Mac—a utility that helps track down what's going on when and where in another program. But the *Macs* in MacsBug doesn't stand for our beloved computer; it stands for *Motorola Advanced Computer Systems*.

•• **When fonts or graphics don't come out** the way you expect them to, there are many possible causes. Chapter 12 covers basic printing problems for fonts and graphics.

•• **General troubleshooting steps** for non-specific printing problems are:

- Check the printer cable.
- Restart the printer.
- Reselect the printer in Chooser.
- Trash the printer's Prefs file from the Preferences folder.
- Reinstall the printer driver (put a fresh copy of the driver in the Extensions folder).
- Restart the computer.
- Zap the PRAM.

## Also ...

•• **The most frequently asked memory-related question** is: *Why is all the memory I just added to my computer showing up in the system allocation, where I can't use it to run more applications?* The answer: Because you forgot to turn on 32-bit addressing in the memory control panel.

•• ***Out of memory* messages** don't necessarily mean there's not enough memory in your computer; you may have too little allocated to a specific program, it may be fragmented and therefore unusable, or your thousand inits may be eating it up. These, and other, memory issues are detailed in Chapter 9.

•• **Disk problems range from simple** to disastrous, whether it's a hard drive that won't mount, an unreadable floppy, or an important file that you've erased by mistake. These problems (and more) are covered in Chapters 17 and 18.

# Reference & Index

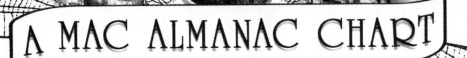

## Desktop Keyboard Shortcuts

### To close all desktop windows

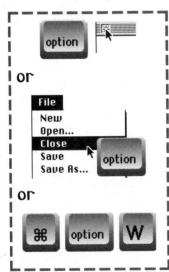

option

**or**

```
File
New
Open...
Close
Save
Save As...
```
option

**or**

⌘ option W

### To activate the desktop

⌘ shift ↑

### To open and close windows

Open selected folder — ⌘ ↓

Open selected folder and close its parent — ⌘ option ↓

Activate parent of current window — ⌘ ↑

Close current window and activate parent — ⌘ option ↑

### To expand and collapse folders

Expand selected folder — ⌘ →

Expand all levels of selected folder — ⌘ option →

Collapse selected folder — ⌘ ←

Collapse all levels of selected folder — ⌘ option ←

# A MAC ALMANAC CHART

## Zapf Dingbats Character Set

| Key | | SHIFT | OPT | SHIFT OPT | Key | | SHIFT | OPT | SHIFT OPT |
|---|---|---|---|---|---|---|---|---|---|
| A | ❀ | ✡ | ❴ | ❵ | Y | ❘ | ☀ | ⑨ | ▸ |
| B | ❁ | ✢ | ➎ | ➭ | Z | ❙ | ✴ | ⑧ | ➾ |
| C | ✻ | ✣ | ❲ | ❨ | 1 | ☞ | ✂ | ② | ➚ |
| D | ❂ | ✤ | ➊ | ☞ | 2 | ☛ | ✠ | ♥ | → |
| E | ❃ | ✥ | ♠ | 3 | ✓ | ✄ | ❣ | ➡ |
| F | ❄ | ✦ | ⑤ | ☜ | 4 | ✔ | ✄ | ❢ | → |
| G | ✽ | ✧ | ◆ | ➡ | 5 | ✕ | ✗ | ⑤ | ➞ |
| H | ✾ | ★ | ➜ | ⇨ | 6 | ✖ | ❉ | ♥ | ➠ |
| I | ❋ | ☆ | ↗ | 7 | ✗ | ❡ | ❧ | ➟ |
| J | ✺ | ✪ | ⑦ | ⇨ | 8 | ✘ | ☛ | ❦ | ❡ |
| K | ✼ | ✩ | ➤ | 9 | ✚ | ✈ | ⑥ | ➡ |
| L | ● | ✭ | ③ | ⇨ | 0 | ✎ | ✉ | ⑦ | ➢ |
| M | ○ | ✮ | ⑩ | ➡ | ` | ✽ | ❞ | | ✿ |
| N | ■ | ✯ | ➥ | - | ✍ | ✿ | ⑦ | ⑧ |
| O | ❑ | ✰ | ⑩ | ④ | = | † | ☞ | ② | ⑥ |
| P | ❒ | ✫ | ➍ | ➌ | [ | ✳ | ✻ | ❛ | ⑩ |
| Q | ❏ | ✱ | ➏ | ➎ | ] | ✳ | ❝ | ➜ | → |
| R | ❐ | ✲ | ♣ | ➤ | \ | ✳ | ❞ | ⑧ | ⑨ |
| S | ▲ | ✳ | ☙ | ⇨ | ; | ✢ | ✚ | ⑩ | ⊃ |
| T | ▼ | ✴ | | → | ❾ | ⑨ | ③ |
| U | ◆ | ✵ | ① | , | ✌ | ✢ | ⑦ | ➾ |
| V | ❖ | ✶ | ④ | ↕ | . | ✑ | ✝ | ⑧ | ➹ |
| W | ◗ | ✷ | ➋ | ➣ | / | ✎ | ✝ | ↔ | ① |
| X | ❘ | ✸ | ⑥ | ⇒ | [spc] | | | | ❶ |

| | | a | A e | E i | I o | O u | U n | N |
|---|---|---|---|---|---|---|---|---|
| OPT | ` | ❨ | ➋ | ⇨ | ⇨ | ⇨ | ➘ | |
| OPT | e | ❩ | ◗ | ❩ | ⇨ | ⇨ | ⊃ | |
| OPT | i | ❩ | ➜ | ➡ | ☜ | ⇨ | ➥ | |
| OPT | u | ❴ | ❨ | ➡ | ☜ | ❵ | ❬ | |
| OPT | n | ❵ | ➌ | | | ❹ | | ❨ |

# A MAC ALMANAC CHART

## How to Mount a Disk That Won't

•••❯ Shut down and restart.

•••❯ Make sure you have the correct extension for mounting removable media.

•••❯ Check cables and connections.

•••❯ Correct any SCSI ID conflicts.

•••❯ Check SCSI termination.

•••❯ Rebuild the desktop.

•••❯ Zap the PRAM.

•••❯ Use a mounting utility.

•••❯ Reinstall system software if it's the system disk.

•••❯ Replace the drive's driver software.

•••❯ Use Disk First Aid.

•••❯ Use a disk recovery utility.

# A MAC ALMANAC CHART

## Keyboard Guide for the Basic Character Set

| Key | | SHIFT | OPT | SHIFT OPT | Key | | SHIFT | OPT | SHIFT OPT |
|---|---|---|---|---|---|---|---|---|---|
| A | a | A | å | Å | Y | y | Y | ¥ | Á |
| B | b | B | ∫ | ı | Z | z | Z | Ω | ¸ |
| C | c | C | ç | Ç | 1 | 1 | ! | ¡ | ⁄ |
| D | d | D | ∂ | Î | 2 | 2 | @ | ™ | ¤ |
| E | e | E |  | ´ | 3 | 3 | # | £ | ‹ |
| F | f | F | ƒ | Ï | 4 | 4 | $ | ¢ | › |
| G | g | G | © | ˝ | 5 | 5 | 5 | ∞ | fi |
| H | h | H | ˙ | Ó | 6 | 6 | ^ | § | fl |
| I | i | I |  | ˆ | 7 | 7 | & | ¶ | ‡ |
| J | j | J | Δ | Ô | 8 | 8 | * | • | ° |
| K | k | K | ˚ | | 9 | 9 | ( | ª | · |
| L | l | L | ¬ | Ò | 0 | 0 | ) | º | ‚ |
| M | m | M | µ | Â | ` | ` | ` | ~ | ` |
| N | n | N |  | ˜ | – | - | - | – | — |
| O | o | O | ø | Ø | = | = | = | + | ≠ | ± |
| P | p | P | π | ∏ | [ | [ | { | " | " |
| Q | q | Q | œ | Œ | ] | ] | } | ' | ' |
| R | r | R | ® | ‰ | \ | \ | \| | « | » |
| S | s | S | ß | Í | ; | ; | : | … | Ú |
| T | t | T |  | ˇ | ' | ' | " | æ | Æ |
| U | u | U |  | ¨ | , | , | < | ≤ | ¯ |
| V | v | V | √ | ◊ | . | . | > | ≥ | ˘ |
| W | w | W | Σ | „ | / | / | ? | ÷ | ¿ |
| X | x | X | ≈ | ˛ | [spc] | | | | |

| | | a | A | e | E | i | I | o | O | u | U | n | N |
|---|---|---|---|---|---|---|---|---|---|---|---|---|---|
| OPT | ` | à | À | è | È | ì | Ì | ò | Ò | ù | Ù | | |
| OPT | e | á | Á | é | É | í | Í | ó | Ó | ú | Ú | | |
| OPT | i | â | Â | ê | Ê | î | Î | ô | Ô | û | Û | | |
| OPT | u | ä | Ä | ë | Ë | ï | Ï | ö | Ö | ü | Ü | | |
| OPT | n | ã | Ã | | | | | õ | Õ | | | ñ | Ñ |

## ASCII Code Chart

| 32 | spc | 64 | @ | 96 | ` | 128 | Ä | 160 | † | 192 | ¿ | 224 | ‡ |
|----|-----|----|---|----|---|-----|---|-----|---|-----|---|-----|---|
| 33 | ! | 65 | A | 97 | a | 129 | Å | 161 | ° | 193 | ¡ | 225 | · |
| 34 | " | 66 | B | 98 | b | 130 | Ç | 162 | ¢ | 194 | ¬ | 226 | , |
| 35 | # | 67 | C | 99 | c | 131 | É | 163 | £ | 195 | √ | 227 | „ |
| 36 | $ | 68 | D | 100 | d | 132 | Ñ | 164 | § | 196 | ƒ | 228 | ‰ |
| 37 | % | 69 | E | 101 | e | 133 | Ö | 165 | • | 197 | ≈ | 229 | Â |
| 38 | & | 70 | F | 102 | f | 134 | Ü | 166 | ¶ | 198 | Δ | 230 | Ê |
| 39 | ' | 71 | G | 103 | g | 135 | á | 167 | ß | 199 | « | 231 | Á |
| 40 | ( | 72 | H | 104 | h | 136 | à | 168 | ® | 200 | » | 232 | Ë |
| 41 | ) | 73 | I | 105 | i | 137 | â | 169 | © | 201 | … | 233 | È |
| 42 | * | 74 | J | 106 | j | 138 | ä | 170 | ™ | 202 | | 234 | Í |
| 43 | + | 75 | K | 107 | k | 139 | ã | 171 | ´ | 203 | À | 235 | Î |
| 44 | , | 76 | L | 108 | l | 140 | å | 172 | ¨ | 204 | Ã | 236 | Ï |
| 45 | - | 77 | M | 109 | m | 141 | ç | 173 | ≠ | 205 | Õ | 237 | Ì |
| 46 | . | 78 | N | 110 | n | 142 | é | 174 | Æ | 206 | Œ | 238 | ó |
| 47 | / | 79 | O | 111 | o | 143 | è | 175 | Ø | 207 | œ | 239 | ô |
| 48 | 0 | 80 | P | 112 | p | 144 | ê | 176 | ∞ | 208 | – | 240 |  |
| 49 | 1 | 81 | Q | 113 | q | 145 | ë | 177 | ± | 209 | — | 241 | Ò |
| 50 | 2 | 82 | R | 114 | r | 146 | í | 178 | ≤ | 210 | " | 242 | Ò |
| 51 | 3 | 83 | S | 115 | s | 147 | ì | 179 | ≥ | 211 | " | 243 | Ú |
| 52 | 4 | 84 | T | 116 | t | 148 | î | 180 | ¥ | 212 | ' | 244 | Û |
| 53 | 5 | 85 | U | 117 | u | 149 | ï | 181 | µ | 213 | ' | 245 | ı |
| 54 | 6 | 86 | V | 118 | v | 150 | ñ | 182 | ∂ | 214 | ÷ | 246 | ^ |
| 55 | 7 | 87 | W | 119 | w | 151 | ó | 183 | Σ | 215 | ◊ | 247 | ~ |
| 56 | 8 | 88 | X | 120 | x | 152 | ò | 184 | Π | 216 | ÿ | 248 | ¯ |
| 57 | 9 | 89 | Y | 121 | y | 153 | ô | 185 | π | 217 | Ÿ | 249 | ˘ |
| 58 | : | 90 | Z | 122 | z | 154 | ö | 186 | ∫ | 218 | / | 250 | ˙ |
| 59 | ; | 91 | [ | 123 | { | 155 | õ | 187 | ª | 219 | ¤ | 251 | ° |
| 60 | < | 92 | \ | 124 | | | 156 | ú | 188 | º | 220 | ‹ | 252 | ¸ |
| 61 | = | 93 | ] | 125 | } | 157 | ù | 189 | Ω | 221 | › | 253 | ˝ |
| 62 | > | 94 | ^ | 126 | ~ | 158 | û | 190 | æ | 222 | fl | 254 | ˛ |
| 63 | ? | 95 | _ | 127 | none | 159 | ü | 191 | ø | 223 | fi | 255 | ˇ |

# A MAC ALMANAC CHART

## Hard Drive Setup & Maintenance

**Setup:**

- ▸ Update the driver software to the most current available.

- ▸ Format the drive to is fullest capacity.

**Daily:**

- ▸ Backup important files.

**Weekly:**

- ▸ Backup important files if you don't do it daily.

- ▸ Scan for viruses. (Daily or monthly for high- or low-use systems.)

**Monthly:**

- ▸ Rebuild the desktop.

- ▸ Run Disk First Aid.

- ▸ Run MacTools, Norton Utilities, or other disk diagnostic utility.

**Semi-Annually:**

- ▸ Defragment hard drive. (Or only annually, depending on level of use.)

# A MAC ALMANAC CHART

## Troubleshooting Procedures

**For general system problems:**

•••▶ Start up without extensions and see if the problem persists.

•••▶ Rebuild the desktop: Hold down Command and Option when you start up.

•••▶ Zap the PRAM: Hold Command-Option-P-R at startup.

•••▶ Check for viruses.

•••▶ Reinstall the system.

•••▶ Run Disk First Aid.

•••▶ Run disk diagnostic software.

•••▶ Back up the drive and reformat it.

**For general application problems:**

•••▶ Allocate more memory to the application.

•••▶ Trash the application's Prefs or Settings file.

# ❀ VENDOR LIST ❀

**Abaton** (CA) 800-821-0806 / 510-498-1111
**Abbott Systems** (NY) 800-552-9157 / 914-747-4171
**Addison-Wesley** (MA) 800-447-2226 / 617-944-3700
**Adobe** (CA) 800-833-6687 / 408-961-3769
**Affinity** (CO) 800-367-6771 / 303-442-4840
**Agfa** (MA) 800-227-2780 / 508-658-5600
**Aladdin Systems** (CA) 408-761-6200
**Aldus** (WA) 206-628-2320 / 206-622-5500
**AlSoft** (TX) 800-257-6381 / 713-353-4090
**Altsys** (TX) 214-680-2060 / 214-680-2060
**America Online** (VA) 800-827-6364 / 703-448-8700
**Amtex** (ONTARIO) 613-967-7900
**Apple Computer** (CA) 800-776-2333 / 408-996-1010
**APS Technologies** (MO) 800-233-7550 / 816-483-6100
**Ares Software** (CA) 800-783-2737 / 415-578-9090
**Articulate Systems** (MA) 800-443-7077 / 617-935-5656
**Attain Corporation** (MA) 800-925-5615 / 617-776-1110
**Barneyscan** (CA) 800-426-5674 / 610-562-2480
**Baseline** (TN) 800-926-9677 / 901-682-9676
**Berkeley Systems** (CA) 800-344-5541 / 510-540-5535
**Bit Jugglers** (CA) 415-968-3908
**BMUG** (CA) 510-849-9114 / 510-549-2684
**Broderbund** (CA) 800-521-6263 / 415-492-3200
**Cadlax Micro Distribution** (CA) 408-946-3004
**CalComp** (AZ) 800-458-5888 / 714-821-2000
**Casa Blanca Works** (CA) 415-461-2227 / 415-461-2227
**Casady & Greene** (CA) 800-359-4920 / 408-484-9228
**CE Software** (IA) 800-523-7638 / 515-221-1801
**Central Point** (OR) 800-964-6896 / 503-690-8090
**Checkfree** (OH) 800-882-5280 / 614-825-3000
**Chip Merchant** (CA) 800-426-6375 / 619-268-4774
**Chipsoft** (CA) 800-964-1040 / 619-453-8722
**CompuServe** (OH) 800-848-8199 / 614-457-8600
**Connectix** (CA) 800-950-5880 / 415-571-5100
**Costar** (CT) 800-426-7827 / 203-661-9700
**Custom Applications** (MA) 800-873-4367 / 508-667-8585
**Dantz Development** (CA) 800-225-4880 / 510-253-3000
**Davidson & Associates** (CA) 800-545-7677 / 310-793-0600
**DayStar** (GA) 800-962-2077 / 404-967-2077
**Delrina** (CN) 800-268-6082 / 416-441-3676
**Design Sciences** (CA) 800-827-0685 / 800-827-0685
**Digital Eclipse** (CA) 800-289-3374 / 510-547-6101
**DriveSavers** (CA) 800-440-1904 / 415-883-4232
**Dubl-Click** (CA) 800-226-9525 / 818-888-2068
**Easy Transfer Cartridges** (CA) 800-336-1599
**eWorld** (TX) 800-775-4556 / 408-996-1010
**Farallon** (CA) 800-344-7489 / 510-814-5000
**Fifth Generation Systems** (LA) 800-873-4384 / 503-334-6054

**Fractal Design** (CA) 800-297-2665 / 408-688-8800
**FreeSoft** (PA) 412-846-2700
**FWB** (CA) 415-474-8055 / 415-474-8055
**GDT Softworks** (BC Canada) 800-663-6222 / 604-291-9121
**Hayes** (GA) 800-254-2937 / 404-840-9200
**Hewlett-Packard** (CA) 800-752-0900 / 208-323-2551
**Inline Design** (CT) 800-453-7671 / 203-435-4995
**Intuit** (CA) 800-624-8742 / 415-858-6095
**Key Tronic** (WA) 800-262-6006 / 509-928-8000
**LaCie** (OR) 800-999-0143 / 503-520-9000
**Leader Technology** (CA) 800-922-1787 / 714-757-1787
**Leaf Systems** (MA) 800-685-9462 / 508-460-8300
**Learning Company** (CA) 800-852-2255 / 510-792-2101
**Logical Solutions** (MN) 612-659-2495 / 612-659-2495
**Logitech** (CA) 800-231-7717 / 510-795-8500
**MacConnection** (NH) 800-800-4444 / 603-446-4444
**Macromedia** (CA) 800-248-4477 / 415-442-0200
**MacWarehouse** (NJ) 800-255-6227 / 908-367-0440
**MacZone** (WA) 800-248-0800 / 206-883-3088
**Magic Software** (NE) 800-342-6243 / 402-291-0670
**Mainstay** (CA) 805-484-9400 / 805-484-9400
**Maxis** (CA) 800-336-2947 / 510-254-9700
**MBS Technologies** (PA) 800-860-8700 / 412-941-9067
**Microlytics** (NY) 800-828-6293 / 716-248-9150
**Microseeds** (VT) 802-879-3365 / 802-579-3365
**Microsoft** (WA) 800-426-9400 / 206-882-8080
**Microtech** (CT) 800-626-4276 / 203-468-6223
**Nova Development** (CA) 800-950-6682 / 818-992-3222
**Now Software** (OR) 800-237-3611 / 503-274-2800
**Olduvai** (FL) 800-822-0772 / 305-670-1112
**Paper Direct** (NJ) 800-277-7377 / 201-507-1996
**Pilot Technology** (MN) 800-682-4987 / 612-828-6806
**Portfolio Systems** (CA) 800-729-3966 / 408-252-0420
**PrairieSoft** (IA) 515-225-3720 / 515-225-3720
**Prodigy** (NY) 800-759-8000 / 914-993-8658
**Quark** (CO) 800-788-7835 / 303-894-8888
**Screenies** (CA) 707-939-6060
**Software Toolworks** (CA) 800-24-3088 / 415-883-3000
**Software Ventures** (CA) 510-644-3232
**Sophisticated Circuits** (WA) 800-827-4669 / 206-485-7979
**Sound Source Unlimited** (CA) 805-494-9996
**Symantec** (CA) 800-441-7234 / 408-253-9600
**TechWorks** (TX) 800-688-7466 / 512-794-8533
**Thought I Could** (NY) 212-673-9724
**ThunderWare** (CA) 800-445-3004
**Utilitron** (TX) 800-428-8766 / 214-727-2329
**Virgin Interactive** (CA ) 800-874-4607 / 714-833-8710
**Wacom Tablets** (WA) 800-922-6613 / 206-750-8882
**Working Software** (CA) 800-229-9675 / 408-423-5696
**Ziff-Davis Press** (CA) 800-688-0448 / 510-601-2000

# ❀ SEALS OF APPROVAL ❀

AboutFace
Drive7
FindPro
Guaranteed Undelete
MacTools
MenuFonts
Norton Utilities
PowerBalls

PowerMerge
QuicKeys
Reader Rabbit
Tempo
TypeStyler
Wallpaper
Where in the World is
Carmen Sandiego?

# ❀ BLUE RIBBON AWARDS FOR EXCELLENCE ❀

APS Technologies
BookEndz
Capture
ClickChange
ClickPaste
Disinfectant
Even More Incredible Machines
Flying Colors
Fontographer
Images with Impact!
Just Grandma and Me
Kaboom
MacPack

Navigator
PBTools
PowerPrint
Putt Putt
Safe & Sound
SCSI Boy
SCSI Doc
SCSI Sentry
SCSIProbe
ThinPack
Thunder
UnderWare
WetPaint

# SHAREWARE & FREEWARE AUTHORS

Mark Adams
Roger Bates
Ricardo Batista
Kevin A. Beers
Günther Blaschek
Kelly Burgess
Steve Christensen
Kerry Clendinning
Michael J. Conrad
Eric de la Musse
Charles Dunn
Riccardo Ettore
Jon Gary
Laurie Gill
Bill Goodman
Ben Haller
Michael Hecht
Naoti Horii
Bill Johnson
Scott A. Johnson
Rob Johnston
Peter Kaplan
Steve Kiene
Mayson G. Lancaster
Gregory D. Landweber
Jim Lewis
William Long
Robert S. Mah
Craig Marciniak
Robert Mathews
Bill Monk

Jim Moore
Don Munsil
Sean P. Nolan
John Norstad
Bruce Obervg
James Osborne
Brent Pease
Michael Pierce
Robert Polic
Alberto Ricci
Rick Kaseguma
Stepan Riha
Gregory M. Robbins
Melissa Rogers
John A. Schlack
Gordon Sheridan
Steve Snyder
Adam Stein
Christopher Suley
Victor Tan
Mike Throckmorton
Bruce Tomlin
Ross Tyler
Mark Valance
Dan Venolia
Maurice Volaski
Dan Walkowski
Ryoji Watanabe
Andrew Welch
Brian Westley
Joe Zobkiw

# ❄ SHAREWARE & FREEWARE INDEX ❄

# ❧ QUOTABLES ❧

*Just some of the people and publications quoted in this book:*

## Computer People & Publications

| | | |
|---|---|---|
| Adrian Coblentz | Chris Espinosa | MacUser |
| Adrian Mello | David Bunnell | MacWorld |
| Alan Cooper | David Ramsey | Michael Wesley |
| Andy Baird | Doug Clapp | Nat Aker |
| Arthur Naiman | Fred Davis | Neil Shapiro |
| Bill Atkinson | John Dvorak | Rich Wolfson |
| Bill Gates | Larry Tesler | Robert Wiggins |
| Bob Seaver | Louise Kohl | Steve Jobs |
| Bruce Horn | MACazine | |

## Books, Literature & Poetry

| | | |
|---|---|---|
| Anne Bodnoy | Lawrence J. Peter | Robert Benchley |
| Arthur C. Clarke | Lewis Carroll | Robert Frost |
| Ben Jonson | Mark Twain | Shakespeare |
| Fran Leibowitz | Old Farmers Almanac | Theodore Sturgeon |
| Franz Kafka | Oscar Wilde | Washington Irving |

## Music

| | | |
|---|---|---|
| Beatles | Fifth Dimension | Igor Stravinsky |
| Chicago | Grace Slick | Rolling Stones |
| Eubie Blake | Grateful Dead | |

## Politics

| | | |
|---|---|---|
| Edwin Meese | George Jacques Danton | Ronald Reagan |
| Eldridge Cleaver | Henry Kissinger | Rutherford B. Hayes |
| Everitt Dirksen | Lord Randolph Churchill | Walter Mondale |

## Art

| | |
|---|---|
| Frederic Goudy | Pablo Picasso |

## Entertainment

| | | |
|---|---|---|
| Bob Hope | Dragnet | Mr. Spock |
| Casey Stengel | George Lucas | Norma Desmond |
| Cinderella | Laurel & Hardy | Oscar the Grouch |
| Claude Rains | Monty Python | Snidely Whiplash |
| Clint Eastwood | | |

## Science

| | | |
|---|---|---|
| Albert Einstein | Thomas Edison | Blaise Pascal |

# ✦ ANSWERS TO POP QUIZZES ✦

Here are the answers to the Pop Quizzes sprinkled throughout the book. You expected some sort of key? What fun would that be? But these answers *are* in order: alphabetical order! Good luck!

- "God's wounds" (5 points)
- "To the unINITiated" (10 points)
- 8-2 (Et, tu?) Brutus (5 points)
- A milking machine (5 points)
- A single pixel at the extreme left of the window, between the lines of the window's header, means it's an HFS disk. (2 points; 10 points if you're new to the Mac)
- A Wang (10 points)
- Acme Bomb Company (5 points)
- Alarm Clock, Time & Date, General Controls (3 points each)
- Amy, Beth, and Little Jo (3 points each)
- AOL, CompuServe Information Manager, Freehand, SuperPaint, ClarisWorks, Illustrator, PageMaker, Word, Excel, HyperCard (3 points each; 10 point bonus for naming them all)
- Archie Bunker; meathead (2 points)
- Baby You Can Drive My Car (3 points)
- Batman and Robin (3 points); Bruce Wayne and Dick Grayson (5 points)
- Black hole, or singularity (20 points)
- c (2 points)
- Heavy metalist Yngwie Malmsteen (25 points)
- Heisenberg's uncertainty principle states you can know either a particle's position or its momentum but not both. (20 points)
- It's the top right row of letter keys read backwards (5 points)
- Laugh-In (5 points)
- Self-contained underwater breathing apparatus; situation normal all fouled (or better expletive) up (2 points each)
- Shoeless Joe Jackson; after he pleaded guilty to game-fixing; Black Sox Scandal; Field of Dreams. (10, 5, 15, 3 points, in that order)
- The early bird catches the worm; A stitch in time saves nine; A bird in the hand is worth two in the bush; Better safe than sorry; A penny saved is a penny earned; Look before you leap; Fools rush in where angels fear to tread; Don't look a gift horse in the mouth. (4 each)
- The loop at the back of a boot that you pull to get the boot on. (2 points)
- Nothing's wrong with it; the dots for the numbers are in the correct positions—unlike in many clip art packages. (2 points)
- The numbers have to go top to bottom so the letters on the keys remain in alphabetical order. (2 points)
- The Outer Limits (5 points)
- Wizard of Oz, Gone with the Wind (10 points each)
- Yellow Submarine (3 points)

A note from Joe Holmes: *If you answered twelve or more correctly, you are probably a genius, unappreciated, even resented, by those around you. Even more important, if you bothered to count up your score and read this evaluation, you are insecure, overly competitive, easily impressed by other people's hasty and dubious opinions of your worth as human being, and in desperate and pathetic need of positive feedback.*

And if these little puzzlers weren't enough for you, look for the secret phrase that's buried in the design of the book!

# ‑ INDEX OF DIALOG BOX MESSAGES ‑

# Ziff-Davis Press Survey of Readers

Please help us in our effort to produce the best books on personal computing.
For your assistance, we would be pleased to send you a FREE catalog
featuring the complete line of Ziff-Davis Press books.

## 1. How did you first learn about this book?

Recommended by a friend . . . . . . . . . . . . . . ☐  -1 (5)

Recommended by store personnel . . . . . . . .☐  -2

Saw in Ziff-Davis Press catalog . . . . . . . . . . .☐  -3

Received advertisement in the mail . . . . . . .☐  -4

Saw the book on bookshelf at store . . . . . . .☐  -5

Read book review in: _____ ☐  -6

Saw an advertisement in: _____ ☐  -7

Other (Please specify): _____ ☐  -8

## 2. Which THREE of the following factors most influenced your decision to purchase this book? (Please check up to THREE.)

Front or back cover information on book . . .☐  -1 (6)

Logo of magazine affiliated with book . . . . . .☐  -2

Special approach to the content . . . . . . . . . . .☐  -3

Completeness of content . . . . . . . . . . . . . . . .☐  -4

Author's reputation. . . . . . . . . . . . . . . . . . . . .☐  -5

Publisher's reputation . . . . . . . . . . . . . . . . . .☐  -6

Book cover design or layout . . . . . . . . . . . . . .☐  -7

Index or table of contents of book . . . . . . . . .☐  -8

Price of book . . . . . . . . . . . . . . . . . . . . . . . .☐  -9

Special effects, graphics, illustrations . . . . . . .☐  -0

Other (Please specify): _____ ☐  -x

## 3. How many computer books have you purchased in the last six months? _____  (7-10)

## 4. On a scale of 1 to 5, where 5 is excellent, 4 is above average, 3 is average, 2 is below average, and 1 is poor, please rate each of the following aspects of this book below. (Please circle your answer.)

| | | |
|---|---|---|
| Depth/completeness of coverage | 5  4  3  2  1 | (11) |
| Organization of material | 5  4  3  2  1 | (12) |
| Ease of finding topic | 5  4  3  2  1 | (13) |
| Special features/time saving tips | 5  4  3  2  1 | (14) |
| Appropriate level of writing | 5  4  3  2  1 | (15) |
| Usefulness of table of contents | 5  4  3  2  1 | (16) |
| Usefulness of index | 5  4  3  2  1 | (17) |
| Usefulness of accompanying disk | 5  4  3  2  1 | (18) |
| Usefulness of illustrations/graphics | 5  4  3  2  1 | (19) |
| Cover design and attractiveness | 5  4  3  2  1 | (20) |
| Overall design and layout of book | 5  4  3  2  1 | (21) |
| Overall satisfaction with book | 5  4  3  2  1 | (22) |

## 5. Which of the following computer publications do you read regularly; that is, 3 out of 4 issues?

Byte . . . . . . . . . . . . . . . . . . . . . . . . . . . . . . .☐  -1 (23)

Computer Shopper . . . . . . . . . . . . . . . . . . . . .☐  -2

Home Office Computing . . . . . . . . . . . . . . . .☐  -3

Dr. Dobb's Journal . . . . . . . . . . . . . . . . . . . . .☐  -4

LAN Magazine . . . . . . . . . . . . . . . . . . . . . . . .☐  -5

MacWEEK . . . . . . . . . . . . . . . . . . . . . . . . . . .☐  -6

MacUser . . . . . . . . . . . . . . . . . . . . . . . . . . . . .☐  -7

PC Computing . . . . . . . . . . . . . . . . . . . . . . . .☐  -8

PC Magazine . . . . . . . . . . . . . . . . . . . . . . . . .☐  -9

PC WEEK . . . . . . . . . . . . . . . . . . . . . . . . . . . .☐  -0

Windows Sources . . . . . . . . . . . . . . . . . . . . . .☐  -x

Other (Please specify): _____ ☐  -y

Please turn page.

6. What is your level of experience with personal computers? With the subject of this book?

| | With PCs | | With subject of book | |
|---|---|---|---|---|
| Beginner | ☐ | -1 (24) | ☐ | -1 (25) |
| Intermediate | ☐ | -2 | ☐ | -2 |
| Advanced | ☐ | -3 | ☐ | -3 |

7. Which of the following best describes your job title?

| | | |
|---|---|---|
| Officer (CEO/President/VP/owner) | ☐ | -1 (26) |
| Director/head | ☐ | -2 |
| Manager/supervisor | ☐ | -3 |
| Administration/staff | ☐ | -4 |
| Teacher/educator/trainer | ☐ | -5 |
| Lawyer/doctor/medical professional | ☐ | -6 |
| Engineer/technician | ☐ | -7 |
| Consultant | ☐ | -8 |
| Not employed/student/retired | ☐ | -9 |
| Other (Please specify): ________________ | ☐ | -0 |

8. What is your age?

| | | |
|---|---|---|
| Under 20 | ☐ | -1 (27) |
| 21-29 | ☐ | -2 |
| 30-39 | ☐ | -3 |
| 40-49 | ☐ | -4 |
| 50-59 | ☐ | -5 |
| 60 or over | ☐ | -6 |

9. Are you:

| | | |
|---|---|---|
| Male | ☐ | -1 (28) |
| Female | ☐ | -2 |

Thank you for your assistance with this important information! Please write your address below to receive our free catalog.

Name: ________________________________

Address: ______________________________

City/State/Zip: _________________________

Fold here to mail.

1439-11-17

NO POSTAGE NECESSARY IF MAILED IN THE UNITED STATES

**BUSINESS REPLY MAIL**

FIRST CLASS MAIL PERMIT NO. 1612 OAKLAND, CA

POSTAGE WILL BE PAID BY ADDRESSEE

**Ziff-Davis Press**
5903 Christie Avenue
Emeryville, CA 94608-1925
Attn: Marketing